John Feinberg reads theology with a philosopher's eye and writes it with a philosopher's sensitivity to illogic and incoherence. The special excellence of this long, learned, clear, and thorough exposition of historic Christian belief about God is its harvesting of the past half-century's brilliant philosophical work banishing muddles from the theological scene. This is the new landmark account of God that Bavinck might have produced had he been able to write his masterful *Reformed Dogmatics* a century later than he did. Feinberg makes the philosophical analyses as palatable as possible, and students who can handle them and lap up extended textual surveys as well will find this book a permanently fruitful and authoritative resource.

—J. I. PACKER
Professor of Theology
Regent College

This is a prodigious study biblically and philosophically of the doctrine of God set in the context of a probing analysis of the concept of God in contemporary thought. Feinberg judicially reconstructs aspects of the classical view of God in a way that proves more faithful than process and openness of God theisms. Arguably, this is the best study of theology proper in print.

—BRUCE DEMAREST
Professor of Theology and Spiritual Formation
Denver Seminary

This book contains some rare combinations: first, an author who is as concerned with conceptual clarification as he is with the absolute truthfulness of the biblical text; second, an argument that avoids the common "either-ors" and contends for the importance of both divine sovereignty and divine solicitude in equal measure; third, an approach that espouses divine determinism and divine temporality. *No One Like Him* takes on the most intractable intellectual challenges of contemporary evangelical theology.

—KEVIN VANHOOZER
Research Professor of Systematic Theology
Trinity Evangelical Divinity School

NO ONE
LIKE HIM

NO ONE LIKE HIM

THE DOCTRINE OF GOD

JOHN S. FEINBERG

WHEATON, ILLINOIS

ISBN-13: 978-1-58134-811-8
ISBN-10: 1-581-34811-8
PDF ISBN: 978-1-4335-1523-1
Mobipocket ISBN: 978-1-4335-0746-5
ePub ISBN: 978-1-4335-1956-7

Library of Congress Cataloging-in-Publication Data
Feinberg, John S., 1946–
   No one like Him : the doctrine of God / John S. Feinberg.
     p. cm.—(The foundations of evangelical theology)
   Includes bibliographical references and indexes.
   ISBN 1-58134-275-6 (alk. paper)
   1. God. I. Title. II. Series.
BT103.F45   2001
231—dc21   2001001912

Crossway is a publishing ministry of Good News Publishers.

SH		22	21	20	19	18	17	16	15	14		
15	14	13	12	11	10	9	8	7	6	5	4	3

In Memory of
My Wonderful Mother
Anne Priscilla Fraiman Feinberg
One of the First
To Teach Me about God

CONTENTS

PART ONE:
CONCEPTS OF GOD

Love

Grace

Mercy

Longsuffering

Goodness

Lovingkindness

Truth

History and the Doctrine of the Trinity

Tertullian
Dynamic and Modalistic Monarchianism
Origen
Arianism
Councils of Nicea and Constantinople
Clarification and Defense of Niceno-Constantinopolitan Creed
Filioque Controversy
Augustine

Formulation of the Doctrine of the Trinity
Logic and the Doctrine of the Trinity

PART THREE:
THE ACTS OF GOD

Classical Theism
Process Theism
Mediating Positions

Scripture and the Decree

Is There a Divine Decree?
What Is the Nature of God's Decree?
The Decree and Foreknowledge

Further Theological Formulation of the Doctrine of God's Decree
The Order of the Decrees

Dualistic Theories
Emanation Theories
Naturalistic Evolutionary Theories
Theistic Evolution
Creation Theories

Biblical Teaching on Creation

Creation Ex Nihilo
Other OT Themes
NT Themes

John Feinberg's *No One Like Him* is a magisterial work, one that truly deserves to be called a *magnum opus*. Formidable in size, it reveals its author as one of the only—perhaps the only—modern scholar whose work, like that of Carl F. H. Henry, can compare in size, detail, comprehensiveness, and intellectual acuity with the accomplishments of the late Karl Barth, who in turn is perhaps the only contemporary theologian whose work rivals that of the old masters—of Luther and Calvin—in scope. However, there is a serious difference between Henry and Feinberg on the one hand and Karl Barth on the other hand: Henry and Feinberg are firmly and deliberately in the tradition of what the late Francis A. Schaeffer called "historic Protestantism"; Barth, despite his genuine conservatism and his orthodoxy on many points, really is not. Karl Barth generated his theology in an atmosphere dominated by late nineteenth- and early twentieth-century liberalism. Henry and Feinberg work in an age when Protestant liberalism has been deemed passé, superseded by all manner of inventive theologies, and when evangelical theology itself sometimes stands on shaky legs on a slippery slope, willing to compromise with modernity and even with postmodernism as much as possible without falling into the abyss of what Georges Florovsky called "pious atheism," which is increasingly characteristic of modern and postmodern Protestantism.

Henry and Feinberg address the fundamental question of God and the world, time and eternity, incarnation and atonement, sin and salvation, on the basis of a sure and confident trust in the Holy Scriptures as God's inerrant and infallible Word, while for the Swiss master, the Bible is only the witness to God's revelation, the authoritative and essential witness, to be sure, but nevertheless a witness to the Word, not the Word itself. There is a difference between Henry's magisterial work (*God, Revelation and Authority*) and that of Feinberg in that Henry wrote in a time when evangelicalism was just emerging from the fundamentalist controversies, whereas Feinberg writes a generation later, when the players on the theological field have changed and to some extent the rules have changed; but the goal of the evangelical theologian is nevertheless to speak the truth—in love, be it understood—but plainly and clearly to speak the truth.

The fact that he rivals both Karl Barth and Carl F. H. Henry in completeness and erudition, while agreeing with the latter in his fidelity to Scripture as being divine revelation, not merely testifying to it, makes John Feinberg's work a reliable guide for the inquiring Christian reader to a degree that is not always the case with the author of the ponderous *Kirchliche Dogmatik.*

Feinberg's work is close to half as large as John Calvin's *Institutes of the Christian Religion,* but unlike the great Reformer's work, which covers the whole scope of Christian doctrine, John Feinberg limits himself to what is called special theology, i.e., the doctrine of God. Readers who find Calvin formidable and therefore might be put off by this comparison or by the sheer bulk of Feinberg's work should note that it is not at all necessary to read it from cover to cover to derive great benefit from it. Far from being merely another university or post-graduate level course in the doctrine of God, it is really a guide to several centuries of Christian thought. Consequently, it is able to serve as an immensely useful handbook providing accurate and readable information about scores of thinkers as diverse as the neo-Platonist Plotinus and the postmodernist feminist Nancey Murphy.

Feinberg offers a succinct and balanced treatment of speculative and esoteric approaches to understanding divine reality, from liberal Christian to modern pagan, and combines with it an insight into and critique of the efforts of contemporary thinkers within the evangelical tradition or close to it. He offers a thorough and nuanced discussion of specific points of controversy among orthodox Protestant Christians, such as whether God lives in timeless eternity or endless time. His treatment of God's eternity as well as of predestination, foreknowledge, and human freedom is fascinating, although—precisely because these are and remain *questiones disputatae*—his recommendations for their solution will not find universal agreement among all of his fellow evangelicals. Because of the massiveness and comprehensiveness of this work, it is sure to draw friendly as well as unfriendly fire from various quarters, but like that of Henry, it will doubtless emerge relatively unscarred.

If the dogma of materialistic, naturalistic evolution, of chance and necessity as the origin of all that is, as the late Nobel prizewinner Jacques Monod and scores of lesser authorities would have it, cannot be challenged, then Feinberg's work is irretrievably superfluous. In fact, however, it is not merely Christian theologians but scientists and scholars from other fields who are drawing increasing attention to the flaws in evolutionary dogma. To deal with the doctrine of God requires one to deal with the doctrine of his works, and in particular with creation, and here John Feinberg makes a distinct contribution to the discussion. His treatment of the various Christian efforts to relate the creation account in Genesis to the many secular theories that question or deny intelligent design and divine purpose is thorough and balanced. When he proceeds from criticism of errors to an attempt to present the truth, reasoning primarily on the basis of the scriptural witness and hermeneutical considerations, he reaches a conclusion that will be appreciated by advocates of a six twenty-four-hour day creation but which will not seem compelling to all upholders of biblical inerrancy.

The doctrines of creation and of the other acts of God, important as they are, are not Feinberg's primary interest in this volume. Instead, it is the doctrine of the nature and attributes of the infinite-personal God. Here we note a detailed interaction with alternatives to classical orthodoxy from within the Christian community, such as pantheism and process theology, and sometimes even from fellow evangelicals, such as the concept of the openness of God. With respect to the Trinity and the incarnation, Feinberg interacts extensively with interpretations and explanations offered by early church fathers, medieval scholastics, Reformation thinkers, and contemporary figures of various shades. Unwilling to leave the doctrines of the Trinity and of the incarnation entirely in the realm of transcendent mystery as many do, he seeks to go beyond traditional Nicene and Chalcedonian dogma and to make the mysteries as accessible to reverent analysis as can be done.

It is impossible in a few paragraphs or even in dozens of pages, to do justice to John Feinberg's work, but it is evident that even readers unprepared to follow each of his arguments and fully to endorse each of his conclusions must stand in admiration of his achievement. It is not risky to predict that his *No One Like Him* will come to be a milestone in evangelical theology.

Harold O. J. Brown

Why another series of works on evangelical systematic theology? This is an especially appropriate question in light of the fact that evangelicals are fully committed to an inspired and inerrant Bible as their final authority for faith and practice. But since neither God nor the Bible change, why is there a need to redo evangelical systematic theology?

Systematic theology is not divine revelation. Theologizing of any sort is a human conceptual enterprise. Thinking that it is equal to biblical revelation misunderstands the nature of both Scripture and theology! Insofar as our theology contains propositions that accurately reflect Scripture or match the world and are consistent with the Bible (in cases where the propositions do not come *per se* from Scripture), our theology is biblically based and correct. But even if all the propositions of a systematic theology are true, that theology would still not be equivalent to biblical revelation! It is still a human conceptualization of God and his relation to the world.

Although this may disturb some who see theology as nothing more than doing careful exegesis over a series of passages, and others who see it as nothing more than biblical theology, those methods of doing theology do not somehow produce a theology that is equivalent to biblical revelation either. Exegesis is a human conceptual enterprise, and so is biblical theology. All the theological disciplines involve human intellectual participation. But human intellect is finite, and hence there is always room for revision of systematic theology as knowledge increases. Though God and his Word do not change, human understanding of his revelation can grow, and our theologies should be reworked to reflect those advances in understanding.

Another reason for evangelicals to rework their theology is the nature of systematic theology as opposed to other theological disciplines. For example, whereas the task of biblical theology is more to describe biblical teaching on whatever topics Scripture addresses, systematics should make a special point to relate its conclusions to the issues of one's day. This does not mean that the systematician ignores the topics biblical writers address. Nor does it mean that theologians should warp Scripture to address issues it never intended to address. Rather, it suggests that in addition to expounding what biblical writers teach, the theologian should attempt to take those biblical teachings (along with the biblical mindset) and apply them to issues that are especially confronting the church in the theologian's own day. For example, 150 years ago, an evangelical theologian doing work on the doctrine of man would likely have discussed issues such as the creation of man and the constituent parts of man's being. Such a theology might even have included a discussion about human institutions such as marriage, noting in general the respective roles of husbands and wives in marriage. However, it is dubious that there would have been any lengthy discussion with various viewpoints about the respective roles of men and women in marriage, in society, and in the church. But at our point in history and in light of the feminist movement and the issues it has raised even among many conservative Christians, it would be foolish to write a theology of man (or, should we say, a "theology of humanity") without a thorough discussion of the issue of the roles of men and women in society, the home, and the church.

Because systematic theology attempts to address itself not only to the timeless issues presented in Scripture but also to the current issues of one's day and culture, each theology will to some extent need to be redone in each generation. Biblical truth does not change from generation to generation, but the issues that confront the church do. A theology that was adequate for a different era and different culture may simply not speak to key issues in a given culture at a given time. Hence, in this series we are reworking evangelical systematic theology, though we do so with the understanding that in future generations there will be room for a revision of theology again.

How, then, do the contributors to this series understand the nature of systematic theology? Systematic theology as done from an evangelical Christian perspective involves study of the person, works, and relationships of God. As evangelicals committed to the full inspiration, inerrancy, and final authority of Scripture, we demand that whatever appears in a systematic theology correspond to the way things are and must not contradict any claim taught in Scripture. Holy Writ is the touchstone of our theology, but we do not limit the source material for systematics to Scripture alone. Hence, whatever information from history, science, philosophy, and the like is relevant to our understanding of God and his relation to our world is fair game for systematics. Depending on the specific interests and expertise of the contributors to this series, their respective volumes will reflect interaction with one or more of these disciplines.

What is the rationale for appealing to other sources than Scripture and other disciplines than the biblical ones? Since God created the universe, there is revelation of God not only in Scripture but in the created order as well. There are many disciplines that study our world, just as does theology. But since the world studied by the non-theological disciplines is the world created by God, any data and conclusions in the so-called secular disciplines that accurately reflect the real world are also relevant to our understanding of the God who made that world. Hence, in a general sense, since all of creation is God's work, nothing is outside the realm of theology. The so-called secular disciplines need to be thought of in a theological context, because they are reflecting on the universe God created, just as is the theologian. And, of course, there are many claims in the non-theological disciplines that are generally accepted as true (although this does not mean that every claim in non-theological disciplines is true, or that we are in a position with respect to every proposition to know whether it is true or false). Since this is so, and since all disciplines are in one way or another reflecting on our universe, a universe made by God, any true statement in any discipline should in some way be informative for our understanding of God and his relation to our world. Hence, we have felt it appropriate to incorporate data from outside the Bible in our theological formulations.

As to the specific design of this series, our intention is to address all areas of evangelical theology with a special emphasis on key issues in each area. While other series may be more like a history of doctrine, this series purposes to incorporate insights from Scripture, historical theology, philosophy, etc., in order to produce an up-to-date work in systematic theology. Though all contributors to the series are thoroughly evangelical in their theology, embracing the historical orthodox doctrines of the church, the series as a whole is not meant to be slanted in the direction of one form of evangelical theology. Nonetheless, most of the writers come from a Reformed perspective. Alternate evangelical and non-evangelical options, however, are discussed.

As to style and intended audience, this series is meant to rest on the very best of scholarship while at the same time being understandable to the beginner in theology as well as to the academic theologian. With that in mind, contributors are writing in a clear style, taking care to define whatever technical terms they use.

Finally, we believe that systematic theology is not just for the understanding. It must apply to life, and it must be lived. As Paul wrote to Timothy, God has given divine revelation for many purposes, including ones that necessitate doing theology, but the ultimate reason for giving revelation and for theologians doing theology is that the people of God may be fitted for every good work (2 Tim 3:16-17). In light of the need for theology to connect to life, each of the contributors not only formulates doctrines but also explains how those doctrines practically apply to everyday living.

It is our sincerest hope that the work we have done in this series will first glorify and please God, and, secondly, instruct and edify the people of God. May God be pleased to use this series to those ends, and may he richly bless you as you read the fruits of our labors.

John S. Feinberg
General Editor

I must have been crazy to think that I could write a book on the doctrine of God. Still, like the moth drawn to a flame, I keep coming back to this topic. In one way or another, it has been the concern of much of my adult intellectual thought and publications. Of course, the subject is more than worthy of our attention, because nothing could be more important than coming to understand God better and hence worship him more.

But, even more so in the contemporary milieu, this topic has taken on enormously significant proportions. The movements in culture in general and theology in particular during the past century have been phenomenal. The advent and growing entrenchment of the postmodern mindset, not only in our universities but in culture more broadly, have had dramatic implications for our very understanding of who and what God is. Theologians and non-theologians alike are clamoring for a God who is engaged in our lives and responsive to our needs. The remote God of classical Christianity seems irrelevant to our contemporaries. Even Christians broadly in the evangelical community sense a need to replace or at least significantly alter the concept of the classical God.

Originally, I had planned a somewhat standard volume on the doctrine of God, but as I read and reflected on what is happening to God in contemporary thought, I saw that something else was needed. Most of the usual topics for a doctrine of God will be covered, but the whole discussion must now be framed in light of the issues of our times. In short, the question confronting the evangelical theologian is what to do about the classical conception of God that has been handed down through centuries of church history. Process theologians and openness of God advocates encourage us to abandon this God and replace him with their versions of a more responsive God. While I find their complaints about the traditional God very thought provoking, I cannot agree with them that their replacement "Gods" are the answer or that they more accurately reflect biblical revelation about God. Rather than totally abandoning the traditional concept of God, a substantial overhaul and reconstruction seems more appropriate. In the pages of this book you will see the results of such modifications.

One of the reasons for writing a volume exclusively on the doctrine of God is that it allows one to give more coverage of the doctrine than if one were writing a standard systematic theology. Even so, there are always decisions to make about what to cover and what to omit. Once I decided to address directly the contemporary situation in discussions about God, certain decisions were required. One of the early casualties was a section on angels, Satan, and demons as an extension of the doctrine of creation. Those doctrines will now be covered in another volume in this series along with the doctrine of man. Then, I had originally planned to include a chapter on the names of God, a most worthy topic; but as I saw how long the manuscript was becoming, I had to make another decision. Over at least the last half century there haven't been many developments with respect to understanding of the divine names, so that seemed a likely candidate for exclusion. Those interested in pursuing that topic can easily do so in various standard evangelical theologies. And, then, as I saw again the need to address in detail the issues surrounding the doctrine of providence, it became evident that I could not also cover every other divine action. Hence, though miraculous intervention in our world is certainly something God can and does do from time to time, I have not addressed that topic as such. In many ways, I feel it is better served in a more general work on apologetics.

In spite of these omissions, I soon realized that what I was doing in this book is not frequently done. There have been many books written solely on divine providence, or on creation, or on the divine attributes. There have not been many written which attempt to cover the whole doctrine of God in one single volume. Over the many years that it has taken to research and write this book, I have periodically thought about how crazy it is to try to do all of this in one book. And yet, by the goodness and grace of God, this work has been completed and it has given me a chance to look holistically at God. It is my hope and prayer that readers will find the structure and strategy of the book helpful and stimulating, regardless of whether they agree with my conclusions.

In doing a project of this sort, the help of others has been invaluable, and they should be acknowledged. First, various colleagues have read and commented on chapters of this book at one stage or another. These include Harold O. J. Brown, Paul Feinberg, Wayne Grudem, and Bruce Ware. Of special significance, however, has been the careful reading and detailed commenting on specific chapters of the manuscript by Kevin Vanhoozer, Willem VanGemeren, and Harold Netland. In particular, Harold Netland has read most of this manuscript in one stage of production or another. Because of suggestions and interaction especially by Harold, Kevin, and Willem, this work has greatly benefited. Whatever errors still remain are attributable to me.

There have also been countless student assistants over the years who have helped me by collecting bibliography for this project or by proofreading various portions of the manuscript. In several cases, these brothers have long since graduated and are themselves engaged in teaching and writing at various seminaries. Of specific note are Steve Wellum, Gregg Allison, and Adam Co. Other assistants have also helped, but these three were especially significant.

Then, a word of appreciation is in order for the board and administration of Trinity Evangelical Divinity School. Their gracious granting of sabbaticals during which I wrote most of this book was invaluable. Without their help this book could not have been written. Next, I must also express my gratitude to Crossway Books. Without their original approval of this series, let alone this volume, and their help and encouragement along the way, this work would not have been done. Of special note is the extraordinary competence and care in editing by Bill Deckard. Any academician would be eager to have such an editor. In addition, Crossway's gracious patience over the years as they have waited for this volume has been greatly appreciated. Finally, a word of thanks to my wife and children for their support and encouragement. There were many times when they gave up time with me so that I could work on this project, and for their sacrifice I am deeply grateful.

It is my hope and prayer that the pages that follow will not only inform but also stimulate you to love, worship, and serve our great God even more! I trust as well that they will help us all recapture a sense of the wonder and grandeur of God. Most of all, I pray that what I have written will be pleasing to God himself and will bring him glory. He is most deserving of all our worship and praise, for there is no one like him!

John S. Feinberg
July 2000

Amer Phil Quart	*American Philosophical Quarterly*
Austl J Phil	*Australasian Journal of Philosophy*
CSR	*Christian Scholar's Review*
Faith Phil	*Faith and Philosophy*
ICC	International Critical Commentary. Edinburgh: T. & T. Clark.
Int J Phil Relig	*International Journal for Philosophy of Religion*
J Relig	*The Journal of Religion*
JETS	*Journal of the Evangelical Theological Society*
J Phil	*The Journal of Philosophy*
JTS	*Journal of Theological Studies*
Mod Theol	*Modern Theology*
Perspect Rel S	*Perspectives in Religious Studies*
Phil Quart	*The Philosophical Quarterly*
Phil Rev	*The Philosophical Review*
Phil Stud	*Philosophical Studies*
Phil Phenomenol Res	*Philosophy and Phenomenological Research*
Phil Rel	*Philosophy of Religion*
Process Stud	*Process Studies*
Relig Hum	*Religious Humanism*
Relig Stud	*Religious Studies*
Relig Stud Rev	*Religious Studies Review*
SJT	*Scottish Journal of Theology*
Theol Stud	*Theological Studies*
TDNT	*Theological Dictionary of the New Testament.* G. Kittel and G. Friedrich, eds. G. W. Bromiley, trans. 10 vols. Grand Rapids, Mich.: Eerdmans, 1964–1976.
TWOT	*Theological Wordbook of the Old Testament.* R. Laird Harris, Gleason Archer, and Bruce K. Waltke, eds. 2 vols. Chicago: Moody, 1980.
Theol Today	*Theology Today*
Trin J	*Trinity Journal*
Tyndale Bul	*Tyndale Bulletin*
WTJ	*Westminster Theological Journal*

ONE

INTRODUCTION

In Isaiah 46 Israel's God compares himself to the gods of the Babylonians. They are mere idols, but not so the true and living God of Israel. In fact, no nation has a God like Israel's. In verse 9 God says, "I am God, and there is no other; I am God, and there is no one like Me." No one like the God of Abraham, Isaac, and Jacob! No one like the God and Father of our Lord Jesus Christ!

But if there is no one like this God, that still does not tell us what he is like.

Although it might not seem difficult to describe the God of the Bible, in our day there are various understandings of him. For many centuries of church history the predominant portrait of God has been the one painted by Augustine, Anselm, and Aquinas. In our time, many theologians are saying that this concept of God is both outmoded and unbiblical. The absolutely immutable, impassible, self-sufficient, sovereign, and omniscient God of the classical Christian tradition, we are told, is too domineering, too austere, and too remote to be at all religiously adequate. This God monopolizes all the power, and refuses to share it with anyone. If his human creatures don't like this, that is their problem.

Process theologians claim that this classical God is too infected with ancient Greek philosophy; the God of Anselm and Aquinas is not the God of Abraham, Isaac, and Jacob. Instead of the classical God, process thinkers propose a more relational and vulnerable God. He is a God who suffers with us and changes as we change. He increases in knowledge as he continually interacts with us and our world. The process God of Whitehead, Hartshorne, and Cobb is no divine monarch who rules with a rod of iron. Rather, he shares his power with his creatures. He won't force his creatures to do what he wants, but instead lovingly tries to persuade them to do what he deems best. Of course, they can refuse, and if they do, this God won't violate their freedom.

Process theologians don't claim to be evangelicals, but they think their depiction of God is more attuned to Scripture than that of classical Christian theism. Advocates of what is known as the open view of God agree that the biblical God is much kinder and gentler than the God of classical theism. However, proponents of the open view believe that process thinkers have strayed too far from biblical revelation. The open view of God purports to offer a mediating position between the classical and process views. Espousers of the open view believe they have captured the best insights from the classical and process traditions while formulating their concept of God in a way that more accurately reflects biblical revelation.

There is certainly much to fault in both the classical and process concepts of God. This does not mean, however, that the open view should be accepted as the best alternative. I agree that we need a mediating position between classical and process views of God, but the open view isn't that position. Hence, in this book I come not to bury God, but to reconstruct him—at least to refashion the idea of God from an evangelical perspective. I don't delude myself into thinking that all evangelicals will adopt my reconstruction. But, I intend to offer an account of God which is sensitive to process and open view concerns without altogether abandoning the best insights of the classical conception. And I intend to ground that conception in Scripture.

So, what does my model of God look like? Process and open view thinkers seem to believe that a commitment to the classical God's non-moral attributes (absolute immutability, impassibility, eternity, simplicity, omnipotence, etc.) requires a monarchical God who is distant from, unrelated to, and unconcerned about the world he made, and yet still exercises absolute control over everything that happens in it. Correspondingly, if one holds to God as a sovereign king, it is deemed inevitable that one will adopt the classical package of divine attributes.

Despite such assumptions, there is no entailment between the two. The God I shall describe is indeed a king, but he is the king who cares! I believe that process and open view critiques of the classical God are most persuasive in relation to the classical attributes, but my nuancing of those attributes even differs from their revisions. When it comes to how God relates to and rules over our world, in my judgment process and open view conceptions are least persuasive. The God I present is absolutely sovereign, but he is no tyrant, nor is he the remote and unrelated God of classical theism. He is instead the king who cares!

Indeed, there is no one like God, the king who cares. But though there is no one like him, there is no lack of competitors in our day, even as there were many false gods during biblical times. In order to understand more accurately the distinctness of the Christian God, we must place him alongside the pantheon of pretenders. Hence, the first section of this book is devoted to describing the various models and conceptions of God in the intellectual and spiritual milieu of our day. That will illustrate the issues that are on the minds of our contemporaries as they think about God, and it will help us to see why non-evangelicals and many evangelicals are clamoring for a revisioning of God.

Because the final two parts of the book will be devoted to articulating a specifically Christian conception of God, the first section will emphasize heavily non-Christian and non-evangelical notions of God. This doesn't mean nothing will be said relevant to the evangelical Christian concept, but only that we must first understand the whole range of views of God in contemporary thought and religion in order best to see that there truly is no one like the biblical God!

In the second section of the book, the discussion will turn directly to the Christian God. Here the focus will be the being and nature of God. In this portion of the book, I shall present my nuancing of the divine attributes. There will be some agreement with process and open view understandings of those attributes, but there will be significant differences as well.

After we have seen who and what the Christian God is, the third section of the book will turn to what God does—his acts. There are many things that God does which are covered in other volumes of this series. For example, God is in the business of saving humans from their lost and hopeless condition of sin, but his actions in redeeming lost humanity are covered in the volume on the cross and salvation.[1] God has also revealed himself in many ways, including Scripture, but the doctrines of revelation, inspiration, and inerrancy are treated in the volume on Scripture. The focus in this volume will be on God's acts of creation, his decree, and his providential control over our universe. It is on the last two matters that the greatest difference between my views and those of the open view will become apparent. The God I present relates to and cares about his creatures, but he is unquestionably king. He not only has sovereign power, but he uses it in our world—but not so as to eliminate human freedom and dignity. Impossible, you think, to wed divine control with human freedom? Perhaps so for some rigidly deterministic models of God, but not so on the soft deterministic model I shall offer.

Needless to say, the issues under consideration in this volume are both controversial and extremely important for Christian doctrine and practice. Though my intent is to offer a constructive piece of Christian theology, because of the controversy surrounding so much of the doctrine of God in our day, of necessity we cannot entirely escape polemics. My goal, however, is to engage in those debates for the sake of clarifying a biblically accurate and religiously adequate evangelical notion of God. This is no easy task, but we dare not allow the difficulty of the issues to deter us, for too much is at stake for Christian thought and life.

I

CONCEPTS

OF GOD

CHAPTER

T W O

GOD — THE VERY IDEA

Human beings are "incurably" religious. We sense that we are not alone in the universe. As we gaze upon the glory of creation, it is natural to think that someone or something with superior power, wisdom, and goodness made it all. The psalmist (Ps 19:1) tells us that this is so, and so does the apostle Paul (Rom 1:19-20). It is hard to imagine that it just "happened."

Humans also have a sense that there are rules of right and wrong to which we are accountable. But, rather than merely an obligation to some abstract notion like the moral law, we sense that there must be a moral lawgiver. That sense of accountability only increases when we disobey those moral rules and deem ourselves worthy of punishment. Though some people think there is no day of reckoning before an extra-mundane being, and hence, that we are free to make our own morality, there is still the nagging question of whether there is not a supreme lawgiver.

Belief in God, however, comes not merely from a perceived need to explain the existence of the cosmos, nor merely from a need to have a grounding of morality in an ultimate arbiter of what is right. It stems as well from a desire to understand who we are and why we are here. It arises from a need for a friend in times of trouble, a friend who not only sympathizes with our plight but is able to do something to change it. It arises from a need for someone with knowledge and wisdom beyond even the collective wisdom of all humanity to guide us as we face the changing circumstances of life. But most of all, belief in God issues from the fact that there is a God and he has revealed himself to mankind. He has done so through the natural world, through miracles, through the Bible, and most fully in his Son Jesus Christ. For the Christian committed to the inspiration and inerrancy of the Bible, God is the starting point for everything else we think and do. More than that, though, he must be our highest desire, joy, and delight!

It is not just Christians, however, who believe in God. People at all times and places have had some notion of God. That idea has not always been monotheistic, but it has been of something(s) that transcends mankind. There have, of course, been atheists, but even these people have some idea of what God would be like, if there were one. For others, even if only to have someone to blame or curse when things do not go to their liking, belief in some sort of God has seemed necessary. For these reasons and many more, one can certainly understand and to a degree concur with Voltaire's comment, "If God did not exist, it would be necessary to invent him." But even Voltaire added, "but all nature cries out that he must exist."[1]

With the entrenchment of the modern mindset over the last few centuries, many have increasingly thought it difficult to make a rational case for the existence of God and hence, for belief in God. However, with the advancement of a postmodern intellectual paradigm in the final decades of the twentieth century, it has again become acceptable, even if not entirely fashionable, to profess belief in some deity. Hence, in talking to many who do not know Christ as Savior, "making a case" first for the existence of any God is nowhere near as necessary as it was even thirty to forty years ago. This doesn't mean we should throw off all vestiges of modernity and warmly embrace everything postmodern. It only notes a cultural shift in attitudes about belief in God.

Lest Christians become unduly excited about these developments, however, we must see what sort of God it is in whom people are now believing. Here one is met with a myriad of models, conceptions, images, and motifs for understanding God. In many cultures where Christianity has been dominant, these different models claim to reflect the perspective of Scripture. But the notions of God one finds are so diverse that it is dubious that all of them are justifiable on scriptural grounds. Moreover, contemporary nations and cultures are so culturally diverse that along with various "Christian" conceptions of God come many visions of the religious ultimate from other world religions.

Because of this diversity in understanding of and commitment to God, we must begin by surveying the different conceptions of God in today's world. Still, this book intends to be a piece of evangelical Christian theology, not an apologetics text or a work in comparative religions. But because there is such difference of opinion on matters such as the meaning and reference of the term "God," the biblical conception of God, the most appropriate way to understand the Christian God's relation to our world, and how we should understand language about God, before we articulate distinctly evangelical Christian conceptions of God we must set such views within a larger framework of worldwide beliefs about God. This includes what might be called "secular," non-religious notions of God.

To illustrate the difference of opinion and, to some extent, confusion occasioned by these issues, consider for a moment the meaning of the term "God." When referring to a word's meaning, we can distinguish the term's sense from its reference. The sense of a word is its basic definition, a definition one might find in a dictionary. The sense tells us how the word is used in various contexts. On the other hand, a word's reference is the object, person, action, or event in our world to which the word points (if it points at all).

As an example, consider the phrase "the president of the United States." The phrase's sense is a certain political, governmental office and the person who holds that office in the country of the United States. The sense of this phrase has remained the same throughout the history of this nation. On the other hand, as I write this sentence, the person to whom the phrase refers is William Clinton. Prior to Clinton, George Bush held the office, prior to him Ronald Reagan was president, etc. Each referent is a different person, but each of those persons' position is correctly designated by the sense of "the president of the United States."

What should we say about the sense and reference of "God"? Here we find a great variety of ideas about both the sense and reference of that word. For example, Anselm claimed that the sense of "God" is "the being than which none greater can be conceived."[2] For Paul Tillich, "God" is "the name for that which concerns man ultimately."[3] For yet others "God" means "the One," "the Absolute," "the wholly Other," and so forth.

There is also great diversity of opinion about the referent of "God." For Tillich, what concerns us ultimately can only be something which determines our being or nonbeing. Consequently, Tillich's God is identified as the ground of all being or being-itself. For others, the referent of "God" is one, among many, finite beings who is in charge of one area of life or another (as in the Greco-Roman pantheon of gods). For Anselm, the referent is an immaterial being with all perfections. For pantheists, our universe is God. If they believe the universe is only material, then matter is somehow alive or divine in a way that no atheistic materialist would grant. Thus, the referent of "God" is the material universe. Other pantheists who think there are immaterial things as well as material identify the referent of "God" as the totality of all material and immaterial things in our universe. For John Hick, God is "the Real." What this exactly is in itself we cannot know. Still, "the Real" is the ultimate reality in the universe.[4]

So, how should we understand the meaning of "God"? As to its sense in Christian theology, one might initially be tempted to use Tillich's "that which concerns man ultimately," but I think this is too broad and ambiguous. Tillich notes that various cultures have had their gods, and these gods transcend the realm of ordinary experience in both power and meaning. Nonetheless, he claims that such gods are ultimately finite. "They are images of human nature or subhuman powers raised to a superhuman realm."[5] Since they are projections, they can't be what ultimately concerns us, since our ultimate concern is whatever determines our being or nonbeing. All other concerns are preliminary, regardless of how much emphasis we place on them.

Despite Tillich's claims, for many people "ultimate concern" conjures ideas of the ultimate passion of their life. In many cases, that ultimate passion is nothing like what the Christian tradition means by "God," nor does it correspond to what Tillich thinks is really of ultimate concern. For example, sometimes we say of someone, "He's making a god out of wealth (or pleasure)." By this we usually mean that this person is living as though wealth (or pleasure) is the most important thing in life; it is his ultimate concern. While few would say that things like wealth or pleasure qualify as superhuman beings, they might agree that such things are what most concerns them. Thus, if "God" means whatever concerns us ultimately, it seems too open to being understood in ways that move very far from what most religions and Tillich himself mean by God.

For our purposes, I prefer something like Anselm's sense for "God." "God" means the supreme being, even the greatest conceivable being (short-hand for Anselm's "being than which none greater can be conceived"). This doesn't mean that we must agree with everything Anselm thought made God the greatest conceivable being. It only means that this is an apt definition of what the term means at least for traditions like Judaism, Christianity, and Islam. Those traditions view God as infinite/unlimited and superior to any being that exists or could exist. Of course, it is debatable whether this would satisfy adherents of various forms of Hinduism, Buddhism, or Shintoism.[6]

What about the referent of "God"? If "God" means "the greatest conceivable being," what sort of being is that? To some this may seem an odd question. After all, there is only one God, and we should think of him as he has revealed himself. I agree that there is only one God, that he exists independent of any conception of him, and that he has in fact revealed himself. Still, that revelation doesn't tell us everything about him, nor is it entirely unambiguous. Moreover, even the parts of God's revelation about himself that are clear must still be understood.

So, we must think through what and whom we should understand the referent of God to be. The need to clarify our idea of God becomes even more apparent when reading the works of various theologians and philosophers. Even within conservative Christianity, the notion of God hasn't been uniform, and as we go beyond evangelical theology and even beyond Christianity, we encounter many different notions of God. Should we think of God as a being, or as a concept? As totally transcendent and unrelated to the universe he created, or as immanent and even interdependent with his creatures? Can God know when we are in pain and even feel the emotion of sympathy, or is he totally removed from our circumstances in both thought and emotion? Is ours a God we can go to in prayer for counsel and comfort, or are our prayers nothing more than talking into thin air—perhaps therapeutic for us after a fashion, but of no real value? How we answer these and other questions has significant implications not only for how we think about God but also for whether the God we envision is adequate to meet our religious needs.

Surveying the various conceptions of God can be confusing. Part of the problem, I believe, stems from terms such as "ineffable," "transcendent," "being-itself," "incomprehensible," and "immanent" used in various conceptions and category schemes for understanding God. My contention is that these terms and the ideas they denote do not all fit within one single category scheme. Rather, they are ways theists have answered distinct questions about God.

Specifically, we must distinguish three separate questions. In fact, it is around the answers to these three questions that I propose to organize our most fundamental thinking about God (as well as the rest of this chapter). First, many concepts of God intend to answer *what sort of reality God is,* or *what kind of reality God has.* This is, of course, an ontological question; it asks what the supreme being is. I have deliberately phrased this question in terms of God's reality rather than God's being, because while one answer to this question is that God is a being, as we shall soon see, there are other answers about the kind of reality God has.

The second question is *what sort of role(s) does God play in the universe?* In other words, how does God relate to our universe, if at all? The answer to this question has occasioned the most debate within all ranks of Christianity, including evangelicalism, within recent years. In answering it some have portrayed God as an absolute monarch ruling his domain from afar. Others prefer to depict God as a friend and confidant, immanently involved in everything that goes on in our world. And, of course, there are many other metaphors, models, and images[7] that have been used to conceptualize God's relations and functions in our world.

A third question asks *how we should understand language about God.* Some understand this question to ask whether in using religious and theological language we are making assertions about the world, simply expressing our emotional reaction to things, or stating our intentions to act in a certain way. This is an important issue for religious epistemology, but not the point I propose to discuss in this chapter. Put simply, assuming that our language intends to make descriptive assertions about God, should we understand it as literal or as figurative and metaphorical? In fact, can human language at all tell us what God is like?

It might seem that this third question should be handled even before addressing the other two. After all, how can we describe God's reality and how he relates to our world before we know how and whether our language about him works? Though I am sympathetic to this viewpoint, I believe that before we can ask whether our language about God should be understood literally, analogically, metaphorically, or not at all, we must know what sort of being we are trying to portray with our language. Once we understand the kind of reality God is, we may conclude that human language is incapable of describing literally the qualities he has and the actions he does. We may conclude something else, but in any case, we must have some idea of what God is before we decide whether and how further claims about him have meaning.

WHAT SORT OF REALITY IS GOD/DOES GOD HAVE?

D. Z. Phillips writes that "theology is the grammar of religious discourse."[8] By this he means that theology's task is to explain what sort of reality religious discourse speaks about. Each sentence has its basic structure (e.g., subject, verb, direct object), but that is its surface grammar. What we want to know is what some have called its depth grammar, i.e., what sort of thing it is actually talking about. "He organizes his room" and "he organizes his mind" have the same surface grammar, but organizing one's room significantly differs from organizing one's mind. Phillips's point, then, is to get to the depth grammar of religious discourse, to explain what it really is about and what reality or realities it refers to. That is also the purpose of this section.

Within various world religions, including Christianity, answers to this question have not been uniform. In fact, within some religions there have been several different answers to this question. This tends to make it hard to apply any specific taxonomy to all religions, especially since many religious believers may be somewhat imprecise in their conceptions of God. Still, we can offer a general category scheme as a way to begin to organize our thoughts about God's reality. I must add, however, that the taxonomy to be used is not a taxonomy of *religions* but a scheme for organizing various understandings of God's reality. The distinction is important for there are some religious traditions, such as Jainism, Zen or Theravada Buddhism, and some forms of Hinduism, that are actually atheistic and deny all deities. These are genuine religions, but fit nowhere in my taxonomy of answers about *God's reality*. Nonetheless, the basic answers to the ontological question are: God as a mental projection, as being-itself, as a being, and God without or beyond being, but there are variations in these broad categories.

God as Mental Projection

An initial answer to the metaphysical question is that God's reality is that of an idea or mental projection. God doesn't exist as anything external to our minds but is merely an idea (usually a projection) of some sort. Ludwig Feuerbach (1804–1872) is a well-known proponent of this view. In *The Essence of Christianity* Feuerbach explains that religion arises not from a transcendent God who reveals himself to us. Rather, religion arises from within us in that God is simply our self-consciousness projecting our own characteristics onto a God who is thought to have those attributes infinitely. Feuerbach writes:

> And here may be applied, without any limitation, the proposition: the object of any subject is nothing else than the subject's own nature taken objectively. Such as are a man's thoughts and dispositions, such is his God; so much worth as a man has, so much and no more has his God. Consciousness of God is self-consciousness, knowledge of God is self-knowledge. By his God thou knowest the man, and by the man his God; the two are identical. Whatever is God to a man, that is his heart and soul; and conversely, God is the manifested inward nature, the expressed self of a man,—religion the solemn unveiling of a man's hidden treasures, the revelation of his intimate thoughts, the open confession of his love-secrets.[9]

Feuerbach adds that people don't always realize that their God is a product of their own mental construction, but nonetheless, that is so. Of course, as one grows in life, one can come to see that what was worshiped at an earlier stage in life was just an objectifying of one's own characteristics. That is, one recognizes that she was actually worshiping an idol. This does not result in a person completely discarding religion. Rather, what typically happens is that an earlier form of religion is replaced by a later, more sophisticated notion of God, but even that more developed religion is a projection of one's own characteristics onto a supreme being.[10] As Feuerbach says,

> Now, when it is shown that what the subject is lies entirely in the attributes of the subject; that is, that the predicate is the true subject; it is also proved that if the divine predicates are attributes of the human nature, the subject of those predicates is also of the human nature.[11]

Sigmund Freud is a second example of this approach to God's reality. According to Freud, belief in God is simply wish fulfillment. Monotheistic religions in particular replace a fallible human father with an omnipotent and infallible father. Freud explains that such religious belief allows people to retain certain infantile behavior patterns even into adult life, in particular, infantile behavior in relation to guilt and forgiveness.[12] As others have noted, Freud also theorized that individuals would develop Oedipal conflicts which might be resolved by the person coming to belief in God.[13]

Since Freud saw religion as wish fulfillment, did that cause him to think it false? MacIntyre says no, because

> The falsity of religious beliefs is not, of course, entailed by their being the product of wish fulfillment. Freud believed in their falsity on independent grounds. But he thought of religion as a particularly damaging species of illusion, precisely because it militates against the scientific effort to distinguish between what reality in fact is and what we want it to be.[14]

God as Being-Itself

A second answer to the question about God's reality is that God is being-itself. Though some might think this is Martin Heidegger's notion of God because of his emphasis on Being, this is not so.[15] Instead, Paul Tillich's *Systematic Theology* is the best-known example of this view. Tillich refers to God as "being-itself," "the ground of being," "the power of being," "the structure of being." It is not entirely clear whether all of these terms are meant to be synonymous, though Tillich seems to use them interchangeably. Nonetheless, Tillich is clear about what he does *not* mean by being-itself.

For Tillich, God is being-itself, but this does not make God *a* being. To conceive of God as a being alongside other beings or as a being above others (even the highest being) is incorrect. As a being, God would still be subject to the categories of finitude, especially space and substance. The best way to avoid such confusion is to think of God as the ground of being, or being-itself.[16] Understood as the power of being, God is the power which resists nonbeing, a power inherent in everything.

Tillich distinguishes two kinds of nonbeing as opposed to being. The one is *ouk on,* and the other is *me on* (these terms come from the participle of the Greek verb *eimi,* "to be," and the Greek words for negation, "not"). *Oukontic* nonbeing is absolute nothingness. It has no relation to being at all other than being its absolute opposite. *Meontic* nonbeing, in contrast, is dialectical nonbeing. This sort of nonbeing is finiteness or finitude. All things in the universe other than God, including humans, are a mixture of being and *meontic* nonbeing. As being-itself, God is nonbeing in neither sense. Moreover, this conception of God means that Tillich thinks God has reality independent of minds that conceive him.[17]

Conceiving of God as being-itself has certain implications for Tillich. One is that it is equally atheistic to speak of God's existence as his nonexistence. This is so because such categories invoke distinctions between the existence and the essence of things, but such talk only makes sense of finite contingent beings. God is not finite, and he is not another being alongside others. He cannot be properly said to exist or not exist, because he transcends such categories. Whereas we might compare various beings as to their mixture of being and *meontic* nonbeing, all of these things are finite to one degree or another. God cannot be put into a grid where he is compared to other beings, for there is a radical and absolute cleavage between all beings (regardless of their finitude) and God.[18]

God is being-itself, but most things we say of God treat him as a being, and Tillich believes this is wrong. According to Tillich, once we understand that God is not a being but being-itself, we come to see that the only thing we can say of him non-symbolically is that he is being-itself; everything else we could say is symbolic. Hence, we can use language of God that we use for other beings, but such language can never be taken literally. It does point beyond itself to God, but does so symbolically.[19]

Another theologian who conceives of God's reality as being, or being-itself, is twentieth-century theologian John Macquarrie. Macquarrie is heavily influenced by Heidegger's analysis of being, but whereas Heidegger does not equate God and being, Macquarrie does. For Macquarrie, being is not *a* being, nor is it a property, class, genus, or substance. Nor is it the total compilation of all beings in our universe. Nor should it be understood as some invisible realm that lies behind the world of appearances.

Is being, then, really nothing? Not so for Macquarrie,[20] who offers two main points about being. He first notes that it transcends all beings, for without it nothing can or does exist. On the other hand, being is the letting-be of all beings in that it enables and empowers them to be and is that which brings things into being.[21] Hence, being is inclusive of everything that is, but it lies behind all beings and is more ultimate. This is clearly not a pantheistic view, which sees God's being as identical with the universe's being. Moreover, it isn't exactly a pantheistic view, according to which everything exists in God who interpenetrates all things without being identical to them (though occasionally one sees Macquarrie's views referred to as panentheistic). Bradshaw's comments on Macquarrie's notion of God as being are helpful:

> To regard Being as a Being entails putting a gap between the finite subjective being who thinks, and Being who is the object of this thought. Being cannot be in the order of objects, and beings are sustained by Being. The only relationship possible between Being and beings, therefore, is that akin to the relationship of life to the members of the body. Life transcends the members, but neither is conceivable without the other.[22]

In reflecting on Macquarrie's comments that being is the prior condition of anything there is, and is the letting-be that enables things to be, one wonders why being could not be a being. As O. C. Thomas explains, "Macquarrie's only response to this is that 'such a being would not be an ultimate because we could still ask about *his* being'."[23]

Though Macquarrie's presentation does not include all the details and distinctions one finds in Tillich, his main conception of God's reality squares with Tillich's portrait.[24] There will be more to say about this conception when discussing God's role in and relation to the world and in a later chapter on the being of God. For now, however, these two theologies are examples of conceiving of God's reality as being-itself.

God as a Being

A third reply to the question about God's reality is that God is a being. In fact, most conceptions of God perceive him as a being who exists independent of anyone's ability to conceptualize him. Though the views to be discussed have these elements in common, that is where their similarity ends. While most religions and theologians perceive God to be a being of some sort, there is little agreement about the nature of that being. Moreover, some conceptions are sketched with sufficient ambiguity to lead one to wonder whether they belong in this category or whether theologians who hold these views actually think of God as being-itself or even as a mere concept. So, there is room for varying interpretation of some of the views to be discussed.

Generally, positions that conceive God as a being portray him in one of three ways: an immaterial being, a material being, or a being with both immaterial and material parts. Let us examine each of these in turn. In what follows some views will be attached to a thinker who held it; in other cases, I'll simply describe the view as a possible variation someone might hold.

GOD AS AN IMMATERIAL BEING. An initial view in this category is animism. Animism is the term used for a theory offered by E. B. Tylor (1832–1917), one of the founders of modern anthropology, to explain the origin and development of religion. This theory was in harmony with the theory of evolution during his day. Following evolutionary theory, Tylor reasoned that in the early stages of evolution, humans developed more primitive religions. Animism was the name Tylor proposed for this more primitive religion, which associated a plurality of spirits and ghosts behind the natural world and the bodies of dead people. Tylor theorized that as humans evolved, so did their religions, going from animism to polytheism, and eventually to monotheism.

As various scholars note, however, Tylor's theory is unsupported by empirical and historical data. Even those who find evolution compelling as a theory of natural origins reject Tylor's application of it to religion.[25] Still, if we remove the idea of animism as associated with primitive cultures and connected with evolution, it does represent the beliefs of various people. Taken broadly, animism is the belief that there are immaterial, spirit beings that are either attached to bodies of which they are the real personality, or, in other cases, have no necessary connection to a specific body. In its various forms animism can refer to worship of spirits or spiritual beings associated with dead bodies or with various elements of the natural world (sun, moon, stars, etc.), or spirits existing distinct from any specific physical object. In our own day we find animism in some highly developed cultures. This is true of many Japanese, and it is arguable that there are elements of animism in contemporary New Age and neo-pagan thinking.[26]

A second form of belief in God as an immaterial being may be broadly labeled *polytheism*. Polytheism is the belief in more than one god (typically a belief in many gods). Depending on the religion, the gods may be material and immaterial (a combination of both matter and soul), or there may be some material gods and other immaterial ones. A few examples illustrate this kind of religion. In Western cultures the best-known brand of polytheism is probably the Greco-Roman pantheon. The Greeks and Romans believed in many different gods, which often were nothing more than a personification of some profession, object, or quality of human personality. Mars was the god of war, Ceres the goddess of grain, Zeus the king of gods, and so on. In Greco-Roman art and literature the gods are typically portrayed in very physical terms, but these are likely material representations of what were deemed fundamentally immaterial beings.

In Eastern cultures, there are also polytheistic religions. Though it is hard to characterize Hinduism as a whole because of the many different beliefs and practices that fall under that rubric—because of changes during its history, and because of its different forms—it is fair to say that some forms are polytheistic. As Netland explains, some Hindus believe in no supreme being, others believe in one God, yet others believe in several, and still others believe in many.[27] Among those gods are Shiva and Vishnu, and Vishnu is thought to have had various manifestations or appearances (known as *avataras*) on earth.[28] Whether all of these are immaterial is not entirely clear, because some are said to be manifested on earth presumably in a material way. Nonetheless, it is likely that some are thought to be immaterial.

In addition, for many Hindus ultimate reality is conceived as Brahman, the sustaining power of the cosmos. As Netland explains, in the Upanishads serious attention is given to the nature of Brahman and its relation to humans. Brahman is identified with the self (*atman*). Brahman pervades all of reality and underlies outward appearances. One way for humans to attain perfection is the way of higher knowledge or insight, which culminates in one's realization of one's identity with Brahman.[29] As to what can be said further about Brahman, Netland explains:

> Brahman was generally held to be utterly beyond characterization, incapable of being expressed in human concepts or linguistic symbols and without qualities—nonpersonal Being (*nirguna* Brahman). But the later Upanishads reveal a growing interest in the personal aspect of Brahman and give evidence of an emerging theistic emphasis. This shift is apparent in the Svetasvatara Upanishad (fifth or sixth century B.C.), which, while still concerned with release from *samsara*, suggests that such release comes not from knowledge of the nonpersonal *nirguna* Brahman, but rather from knowledge of the personal Lord identified as Rudra or Shiva, the personal manifestation of Brahman.[30]

In light of what is said about Brahman, it seems to be immaterial, and along with other Hindu gods it shows that some forms of Hinduism are polytheistic and many of their gods are immaterial.

Shintoism is a final example of a polytheistic religion with immaterial gods. Here the multitudinous *kami* function as gods. As Netland explains, the notion of *kami* is kept deliberately vague and imprecise, "but there is no question that the concept of *kami* is polytheistic."[31] In placing Shintoism in this category, however, this does not mean that all the *kami* are immaterial. Indeed, *kami* like the deities of heaven and earth that are referenced in the ancient records, plus the spirits of the shrines where these deities are worshiped, are immaterial. But there are other *kami*, such as sacred birds, animals, trees, mountains, and seas, that are surely material.[32] Any adherent to Shintoism may worship any combination of these *kami*.

Moving beyond polytheistic religions that portray God as an immaterial being(s), we come next to pantheism. Broadly speaking, pantheism is the belief that everything is God, but there are different versions of pantheism, and at least two conceive of God as an immaterial being. In both cases, the only thing or things that exist are entirely immaterial. In one version, there are many different immaterial beings, but each is a part of God or divine. This offers a somewhat "collective view" of God, in that many different beings make up God's being. However, everything that exists is immaterial, and so is God. The other form of pantheism might be labeled "psychic pantheistic monism." According to this view, there is only one being in the universe, an immaterial being. Everything that exists is simply a mode or expression of this one being. Students of Spinoza will recognize this as a variation of his pantheism. For Spinoza, the universe contains only one substance, and that substance is God. All individual things, whether material, immaterial, or a combination of both, are merely modes of that one all-encompassing substance. Psychic pantheistic monism says basically the same thing, except that every mode of the one being is immaterial, as is the substance of that God itself.

Another possible pantheistic view appears in the work of the great German philosopher G. W. F. Hegel (1770–1831). I say "possible," because Hegel's philosophy actually includes a number of different concepts of God, one of which is God as equal to Spirit, and it isn't entirely clear whether this God is pantheistic or monotheistic. What is clear is that this God is immaterial. Hegel's basic notion of "Spirit" or *Geist* refers to some sort of general consciousness, a single "mind" common to all people. For Hegel, Spirit is Absolute, but we must clarify what he means by Spirit. It is not the ordinary sense of spirit as opposed to matter, nor is it something entirely transcendent of our world. In addition, it is not a universal consciousness in the sense that all of us have the same thoughts, ideas, and feelings and are really just one universal mind. Hegel doesn't deny the individuality of minds or the privacy of thoughts. Moreover, Spirit is not universal consciousness in the sense of an abstract entity including the common properties of all individuals. For example, it is not like "the average middle-class suburban American." Spirit isn't for Hegel such an abstract entity or idea. Nor is it an immanent God-Soul discoverable by mystical insight. Spirit is immanent, but not in that sense.

For Hegel, Spirit is both a thing or phenomenon and also an activity. As a thing, it is the phenomenon or force of universal consciousness. Spirit is the underlying principle of consciousness and at the same time the underlying rational will behind all practical reason and action. This underlying principle is a doubling of self-consciousness whereby each individual self-consciousness recognizes the other and recognizes the unity of all self-consciousnesses. As Jean Hyppolite explains, "The universal self-consciousness which Hegel claims to reach, then, is not Kant's 'I think in general' but human reality as an *intersubjectivity*, a we which alone is concrete. Spirit is this we precisely insofar as it simultaneously brings about the unity and separation of the I's."[33]

With this view of Spirit it becomes clear why so many have thought it to be pantheism. On the other hand, it is also possible to see Spirit (as thing, rather than as activity) as *one* phenomenon, though present in all people. But that is not the end of the story, for Hegel sees Spirit not just as a thing but also as an activity of itself. That activity is Spirit's capacity of retaining over its preceding phases. Hence, rather than isolating one self-consciousness from another or one concept from another, Spirit is the activity of residing in and retaining each individual. Spirit moves from some split between things to unite them. An example would be the doubling of self-consciousness, i.e., associating them. It is easy to see how this activity relates to the Hegelian dialectic, for that dialectical movement synthesizes contradictories into increasingly complex and encompassing realities until it eventually engulfs all reality as the Absolute.[34]

For Hegel, then, God as Spirit is both a being and an activity. This "God" is immaterial and very immanent in our world, but not particularly personal. Our next example of God as an immaterial being is John Hick's notion of God as "the Real." However, I must immediately add that classifying this notion in this category (as opposed to, for example, God as being-itself) is not absolutely certain because of what Hick says about the Real. Hick draws upon Immanuel Kant's distinction between "things-in-themselves" and "things-as-they-appear-to us." The former Kant calls *noumena,* and the latter he labels *phenomena.* According to Kant, a noumenon is beyond human knowledge. For example, no one can see a thing as it is in itself. Because our understanding of things in the world is mediated through our sensory organs and our mind, all we can know is how things appear to us, the phenomena of our world.

Hick applies the notion of a noumenon to the ultimate reality, God, whom he calls "the Real." The Real does exist independent of our minds, but none of our concepts or attributes can be applied to the Real as it is in itself. Hence, it isn't entirely clear whether the Real is a being rather than being-itself or the ground of being. How does the Real relate, then, to the various gods of world religions? For Hick the gods of world religions are all products of the Real impinging on us and our culturally and historically conditioned responses to the Real which attempt, so to speak, to put a "face" on the Real. In fact, Hick claims that all of these gods which represent "God-for-us," the God we can experience, actually point to the same thing, namely, ultimate reality, the Real. Perceptions of the Real as personal Hick calls *personae;* perceptions of the real as impersonal are labeled *impersonae.* Though none of these masks is actually ultimate reality, all point to the same ultimate reality, the Real. Hence, all peoples actually worship the same supreme reality, even though they conceptualize that reality in a variety of different ways.[35] Hick explains:

> I want to say that the noumenal Real is experienced and thought by different human mentalities, forming and formed by different religious traditions, as the range of gods and absolutes which the phenomenology of religion reports. And these divine *personae* and metaphysical *impersonae,* as I shall call them, are not illusory but are empirically, that is experientially, real as authentic manifestations of the Real. . . . But for Kant God is postulated, not experienced. In partial agreement but also partial disagreement with him, I want to say that the Real *an sich* is postulated by us as a presupposition, not of the moral life, but of religious experience and the religious life, whilst the gods, as also the mystically known Brahman, Sunyata and so on, are phenomenal manifestations of the Real occurring within the realm of religious experience. Conflating these two theses one can say that the Real is experienced by human beings, but experienced in a manner analogous to that in which, according to Kant, we experience the world: namely by informational input from external reality being interpreted by the mind in terms of its own categorial scheme

and thus coming to consciousness as meaningful phenomenal experience. All that we are entitled to say about the noumenal source of this information is that it is the reality whose influence produces, in collaboration with the human mind, the phenomenal world of our experience.[36]

Though we have surveyed various conceptions of God's reality as an immaterial being, we must discuss one more before turning to the next set of conceptions. It is the concept of God found in Judaism, Christianity, and Islam. There are obvious differences among these religions in their notion of God, but all three share a commitment to one God who is an immaterial being. Moreover, this God is distinct from all other beings in the universe, and for these three religions the universe apart from God is populated by beings, some of which are material, others of which are immaterial, and yet others that are both material and immaterial. This conception of God in its Christian expression (one God in three persons) is the one I hold and shall elaborate in this book. As we shall see, in Christian theism there are different models for conceiving the divine attributes and the relation of divine power to our world. But the models I shall describe, including the one I espouse, conceive of God as an immaterial being.

GOD AS A MATERIAL BEING.   Our discussion can be briefer here in light of the positions already discussed. Anyone who believes that God is a being and also believes that everything in the universe is material holds beliefs that fall in this category. We begin with various forms of polytheism. As noted in discussing the Greco-Roman pantheon, it isn't clear whether these gods were deemed purely immaterial, or a combination of matter and spirit, or purely material. Nevertheless, they are depicted in Greek mythology and art in very physical ways. Of course, it is uncertain as to what the Roman and Greek people who believed in the gods understood their nature to be.

A clearer form of material polytheism is represented by many of Shintoism's *kami*. The notion of *kami* is so pervasive in Shinto thought that we would expect at least some to be physical. While many of the *kami* are purely immaterial, many others are physical. Trees, rivers, mountains, animals, and birds can be among the *kami*, but not just any are. Material things that are *kami* have become sacred because of some awe-inspiring quality they possess. What this means is that in the Shinto worldview, there is no clear ontological distinction between the supernatural (*kami* and spirits of ancestors) and the physical universe.

In addition, any form of idol worship that sees the material idols alone as gods (rather than understanding the idol as representing a spiritual god beyond the idol) falls into this category. Typically, idol worship is associated with more primitive cultures. Depending on the person and the religion, focus may be on many of these idols or on only one. Some of the pagan cultures mentioned in the OT would likely fit in this category.

Moving beyond polytheism, which believes in many gods but doesn't equate everything with God, we come to various forms of pantheism. One form we can label *materialistic monistic pantheism*. According to this view, there is only one substance in the universe and it is material. Every individual thing is but a mode of that one material substance; hence there are only material things in our world. Moreover, that one material substance is God.

The other main variation of pantheism that falls within this category can be called *materialistic pluralistic pantheism*. This view holds that the universe is composed of many distinct things, all of them are material only, and all of them are divine. Either each distinct thing is a separate God or all things taken collectively compose God's being. The difference between this view and the preceding is that whereas *materialistic monistic pantheism* claims that all things are modes of the one material substance that is the universe, this view grants that there are distinct material things. Nonetheless, all of them are divine and together comprise the material being of God.

Finally, there has recently been some talk of the universe (or at least planet earth) as God's body. It is not always clear whether such language is purely metaphorical or meant to be literal. Moreover, it isn't always clear whether God is identified as the body or is an immaterial thing that interpenetrates all things material. And there is a difference between saying that God just is a body (the identity thesis that makes God totally material) as opposed to saying he has one (thus he wouldn't likely be material, but would have access to matter in order to do things in our universe). Again, depending on the view in question, it might take the shape of pantheism or conversely it might claim that while God is material, there are other distinct material things in our universe (hence, pantheism would be ruled out). Several contemporary works pursue such lines of thought. Among them are Grace Jantzen's *God's World, God's Body* (Westminster, 1984); J. C. A. Gaskin, *The Quest for Eternity* (Penguin, 1984); and perhaps Sallie McFague's *Models of God: Theology for an Ecological, Nuclear Age* (Fortress, 1987). I say "perhaps," because it is not entirely clear that for McFague God just is identical to the world. Anyway, this metaphysical point (whatever her view is) isn't her main concern, as we shall see when discussing different conceptions of God's role in the universe.[37]

GOD AS AN IMMATERIAL AND MATERIAL BEING. This category contains several options. We have already placed various forms of polytheism in the previous two categories, and we should list polytheism here as well. In some cases, the gods are little more than glorified human beings. As such, they are a combination of both material and immaterial parts. As already noted, it is possible that this is the way the Greco-Roman gods and goddesses should be understood.

Second, we should include two forms of pantheism under this heading. According to one version, there is only one substance in the universe, though it has various modes of expression. Some modes are mental, others are physical, and yet others such as human beings are a combination of material and immaterial. An example of this form of pantheism is found in New Age thinking. As we shall see in chapter 3, New Age theology believes all things are god.

It also claims that all things are one, and this means that everything is inter-related, interdependent, and interpenetrating. Hence, perceived differences between a tree, an apple, a dog, and a person are just that—perceptions only. The differences are not real.[38]

Another version of pantheism holds that there are many distinct things in our universe, but all of them collectively make up the being of God. Some things are material only, and others (spirits) are only immaterial, but yet others are a combination of material and immaterial. This again is a "collective" concept of God according to which God exists in his totality nowhere. Each individual has its own place as part of the whole of God.[39]

Another form of the view that God is both material and immaterial is known as panentheism (all in God). This view is especially associated with process theology as originally set forth by Alfred N. Whitehead and developed by disciples, including Charles Hartshorne, Schubert Ogden, John Cobb, and David Griffin. Since there will be an extended discussion of process theology in chapter 4, I shall only briefly describe it here. According to process theism, God is an actual entity. All actual entities are dipolar or bipolar, so God is as well. God has a primordial, eternal, potential pole and a temporal, conse-quent, actual pole. According to process thinking, there exist certain eternal objects which may ingress into our world to become actual entities. Such eternal objects are pure potentials, and pure potentials cannot order and relate themselves; that must be done by an actual entity. Hence, there is a need for some nontemporal actual entity, and this is God in his primordial nature. In his primordial nature, God is like a backstage director who lines up the forms, getting them ready to ingress onto the stage of the temporal world. However, God's primordial nature shouldn't be seen as distinct from the order of eternal objects, i.e., the order is his primordial nature. The primordial, conceptual pole of God is clearly immaterial. On the other hand, as all other actual enti-ties, God has a physical, concrete pole to complete the "vision" of his poten-tial pole. In God's case, the consequent pole is the universe. This doesn't mean that God's actual pole is merely identical to the universe about us. Rather, process theists like to say that God's being interpenetrates everything without being identical to it. Hence, they prefer to label their view "panentheism" rather than "pantheism," for everything exists in God without being identical to him. God and the world are mutually interdependent, and what happens to one affects the other. So, God is a finite being with both material (consequent nature) and immaterial (primordial pole) elements.

Finally, there are views that see the world as God's body, but again do not give the impression that God is identical with the world in the strict sense of identity. Rather, these views seem to portray God as immaterial in some sense but as intertwined with the material world as his body. This sounds like process theology, but there are differences. While such views could be labeled panenthe-istic because God is in all things, these views differ from process theism in that they don't understand God to be dipolar. One example of this view is found in the Indian thinker Ramanuja, who lived in the eleventh century, far too long before Whitehead to be thought of as a process theist. Instead, Ramanuja saw the God-world relationship as analogous to the soul-body relationship.[40]

A second possible example of this view is Sallie McFague's conception. As noted already, she portrays the world as God's body. Though she claims that this is a metaphor (as are other descriptions of God such as Father, king, or shepherd), she clearly wants to affirm that all things are interconnected with one another. While it is not clear whether God for McFague is totally material, or immaterial in the material universe, one senses it is the latter when she says that we really are quite ignorant of who or what God is and how God is related to the world.[41] If the material universe or our planet alone were identical with God, it would be hard to imagine why we would be in deep ignorance of what God is and how he relates to the world. In a symposium on her book she explains her views a bit further. She says:

> The body of God, then, is creation, understood as God's self-expression; it is formed in God's own reality, bodied forth in the eons of evolutionary time, and supplied with the means to nurture and sustain billions of different forms of life. And what could that body be except God's own creation? . . . In a monotheistic, panentheistic theology, if one is to understand God in some sense as physical and not just spiritual, then the entire "body" of the universe is "in" God and is God's visible self-expression. This body, albeit a strange one if we take ours as the model, belongs to God.[42]

In light of the next to last sentence of the cited material, it seems that McFague thinks of God as a being who is both immaterial and material.

God Without or Beyond Being

A final answer to our metaphysical question invokes developments during the latter portion of the twentieth century. Here we cannot offer an exhaustive treatment, but I want at least to introduce this way of understanding God's reality.

During the final decades of the twentieth century, a postmodern mindset has emerged. That worldview will be described more fully in the next chapter, but some postmoderns have applied aspects of that mindset to a new kind of theological conception of God's reality. As many argue, "death of God" theologies didn't reject all gods but only a certain kind of God. What was rejected were theological and metaphysical systems that purport to offer a perspective of reality as a unified whole. Invariably, such systems ground reality in some ultimate thing that is the source of everything else and gives explanatory meaning to all other existing realities. Usually, that ultimate foundation is God, the supreme and absolute being.[43]

In contrast to this Being theology and metaphysics, philosophers such as Nietzsche, Heidegger, and many of their followers argued that there is no such unifying principle or being that is the source and explanation of all that is. According to these thinkers, systems that postulate such a foundation are invariably constructed to legitimize some social, political, or ecclesiastical structure that excludes from power all but a few. Instead, there are just individual beings with their different perspectives. No grand underlying narrative unifies and explains our world. Metaphysics and theology as traditionally done are no longer viable.

What does it mean for the reality of God, if Being theology (often called onto-theology) is denied? Postmodern theologians like Jean-Luc Marion contend that we must think of God as beyond or without being. This is not a rejection of God's existence, they claim, but rather a rejection of Being theology and metaphysics. According to onto-theology, God is just one being (albeit the supreme one) among others for whom he is the source and ground. If we imagine being as a great chain of existing things (a predominant picture in Western philosophy and theology for centuries) going from infinite being (God) to absolute finitude (total nonbeing), God is in one sense distinct from all else, but he is still part of an overall structure which he grounds. But this just repeats the same error made in Western thought that argues for a unified understanding of reality and for absolute truth rather than differing perspectives on truth (which allow room for that which is other, the excluded).

What we need, then, is a conception of a God who transcends the very categories of Being theology. Appealing back to Aquinas, Marion distinguishes *ens commune* from the divine being or *esse*. Traditional theology tends to unify all being, including God, but even Aquinas saw a difference between divine *esse* and creaturely *ens commune*. In all creatures, there is a distinction between their essence and their existence. That is, we can describe what they would be like if they existed, but for them to exist they must be brought into being or existence. In God's case, the essence/existence distinction collapses; he just is. If we grant what Aquinas is saying, then, argues Marion, clearly God should not be thought of along traditional lines we use for thinking of other beings. Marion explains,

> The divine *esse* immeasurably surpasses (and hardly maintains an *analogia* with) the *ens commune* of creatures, which are characterized by the real distinction between *esse* and their essence, . . . God is expressed as *esse*, but this *esse* is expressed only of God, not of the beings of metaphysics. In *this* sense Being does not erect an idol before God, but saves his distance.[44]

This type of postmodern theology, then, prefers to see God as beyond or without being, but this only means that it rejects the traditional categories theology and metaphysics have used for centuries for understanding God and our world. He is not just another being (even a supreme one) among many, but, as Marion says, immeasurably surpasses all else. At first reflection, this may seem equivalent to Tillich's God as the ground of being or being-itself, but it is not. For even Tillich's conception of God buys into and perpetuates the onto-theology wherein all beings are related to and grounded in some ultimate source.

Upon further reflection, God beyond Being may sound like theologies of the mystics and of those who have claimed that God is ineffable, not to be captured by categories of human reason and language. While such apophatic theologies may indeed be closest to what Marion, Derrida, Levinas, and others have in mind, even this is not clear in their work. If we ask of them what sort of reality God is or has, we find little answer. God is frequently spoken of as the gift or love, but what this means about the "thingness" or reality of God is unclear.[45] What is clear for these postmoderns is that we are not to think of God's reality in any way that invokes the old onto-theology or onto-metaphysics.

WHAT ROLE(S) DOES GOD PLAY IN OUR UNIVERSE?

In the previous portion of the chapter we discussed many different views about the nature of God's reality, but none of them explains God's role and relation to us and our universe. Is God aloof from creation and uninvolved in it, or is he intimately interactive with his creatures? Is it best to think of God as an absolutely sovereign monarch or as a friend and confidant? How does the Bible portray God's relationship to the world, and what does it allow us to say about his role in our individual lives and collective communities? There is a bewildering array of answers to these and other questions about God's relationship to our universe. And the plethora of views is not found only beyond the scope of evangelical theology. Within evangelicalism there is currently a great amount of discussion about all of these matters.

In handling this issue, I think it best to subdivide the discussion. Hence, I shall initially look at various biblical images, motifs, and metaphors used to describe God's relationship to us. Then, because a discussion of God's role in our world invariably invokes the categories of divine transcendence and immanence, we shall look at various portraits (within Christianity and beyond) of how we should understand these two notions. Finally, I shall describe several broad models within contemporary Christianity for understanding and explaining a large number of divine attributes and actions in relation to our world.

Biblical Images, Motifs, and Metaphors for God

Various images and metaphors used to describe God speak not only of different roles he plays and of how he acts in our world but also of the relationships he enters into with his creatures. Before turning to those motifs, I must explain what I mean by these terms. I do not use them to capture a whole metaphysical conception of all that God is and does in our universe. I reserve the term "model" for that notion, and intend to use "model" much as scientists do when they talk about a theoretical construct for organizing and explaining as much data as possible. My use of "image" and "motif" is much less pretentious. It designates only one kind of role or relationship God has to his universe, and makes no metaphysical comment about the ultimate nature and structure of all of reality. Further, I employ the term "metaphor" because many of the images and motifs to be mentioned cannot be literally true if God is conceived as immaterial as Christians and Jews traditionally have done. For God literally to function as these images suggest would require a body; hence, many of these images are metaphorical. That, however, does not mean they are untrue of God, but only that the biblical writers teach about God's roles using metaphorical language.

In Scripture, a wide assortment of images picture God's relationship to his creatures. Ian Ramsey is very helpful in dividing these motifs and metaphors into three broad categories.[46] An initial category of scriptural images is taken from family life and interpersonal relationships. It includes the image of God as a father. In the OT God's relation to Israel is likened on occasion to that of a father to a son. In Exod 4:22 God tells Moses to tell Pharaoh that Israel is his son, his firstborn; Pharaoh must let God's son go.

Probably the most tender example of a loving father's care and nurture of his child is seen in Hosea's comments about God's relation to Israel. In Hos 11:1 God says, "When Israel was a youth I loved him, and out of Egypt I called My son." Later (vv. 3-4) he adds, "Yet it is I who taught Ephraim to walk, I took them in My arms; but they did not know that I healed them. I led them with cords of a man, with bonds of love, and I became to them as one who lifts the yoke from their jaws; and I bent down and fed them." See also Isa 63:16; 64:8; Jer 31:9; Mal 3:17. But God is not merely a father to Israel, for he is portrayed as father to all who claim him as God. The psalmist writes (Ps 103:13) "Just as a father has compassion on his children, so the Lord has compassion on those who revere him." In the NT God is also portrayed as a father. Hence, Jesus tells his disciples that when they pray, they should say, "Our Father who art in heaven . . ." (Matt 6:9). Later in the same chapter Jesus tells his disciples not to worry about having food to eat, clothes to wear, or a place to sleep, because their heavenly father provides all these needs for the birds of the air, and surely his people are of greater concern to God (Matt 6:26). In fact, the Sermon on the Mount (Matthew 5-7) is filled with references to God as our Father. Moreover, throughout the Pauline epistles, Paul's typical opening salutation wishes his readers grace and/or peace from God our Father (Rom 1:7; 1 Cor 1:3; 2 Cor 1:2; Gal 1:3; Eph 1:2; Phil 1:2; Col 1:2; 1 Thess 1:1; 2 Thess 1:2; 1 Tim 1:2; 2 Tim 1:2; Tit 1:4; Phile 3).

God is also characterized metaphorically as mother. In Deut 32:18 the Jews are accused of neglecting the rock who begot them and forgetting the God who gave them birth. Isaiah speaks of a coming day and records God's word to Israel (Isa 66:13): "As one whom his mother comforts, so I will comfort you; and you shall be comforted in Jerusalem." In Isa 49:14-15 we see that though Israel thought God had forsaken her, God responds by asking, "Can a woman forget her nursing child, and have no compassion on the son of her womb?

Even these may forget, but I will not forget you." God's love for his people is likened to a mother's love for her child nursing at her breast. See also Isa 42:14, where the Lord says that things will change for Israel: "I have kept silent for a long time, I have kept still and restrained Myself. Now like a woman in labor I will groan, I will both gasp and pant." And Jesus likens his desire for communion with Israel to the way a mother hen gathers her chicks (Matt 23:37).

God is also portrayed in the OT as a husband. His covenant relationship to Israel is often presented under the image of a husband's relation to his wife. Unfortunately, as in Hosea's case, Israel was an unfaithful wife. God is portrayed as the wronged husband who continues to love his estranged wife and does whatever it takes to win her back (Hos 3:1-3). The NT similarly presents Christ as the church's husband and the church as his bride. In fact, Paul teaches that human husbands and wives should pattern their relationships after that of Christ to his church (Eph 5:22-32). Moreover, in one of the climactic scenes of the book of Revelation we find the marriage supper of the lamb as Christ, the bridegroom, celebrates his union with his wife, the church (Rev 19:7-9).

Two other images taken from family and interpersonal relationships are used of God. One is that of friend. God says to Israel, "Have you not just now called to Me, 'My Father, Thou art the friend of my youth?'" (Jer 3:4). In addition, several times Abraham is referred to as the friend of God, or simply "my friend" (2 Chron 20:7; Isa 41:8; Jas 2:23). The other image is one that McFague urges upon us, and it is that of a lover.[47] If, for example, the love poetry of Song of Solomon is taken to be a type of Christ and his relation to the church (or even of God's relation to his people), then the book is filled with powerful images of God as a lover. Beyond the Song of Solomon, God's relation to Israel as seen in Hosea is that of a husband who has a very warm and loving concern for his wife.

All of these images taken from family and interpersonal relationships show God to be very near, involved, and interactive with his creatures. The same is true of the second set of scriptural images and motifs Ramsey isolates. These metaphors depict God in terms of work, crafts, professions, and vocations. One of the best-known and loved metaphors is God as shepherd. In Ezek 34:31 he is a shepherd to his people Israel. He says, "As for you, My sheep, the sheep of My pasture, you are men, and I am your God" (see also Jer 23:1ff; Ps 78:52; 80:1). God is the shepherd not only of whole peoples but also of individuals. What student of God's Word does not love Psalm 23? Many of us in early childhood memorized this psalm by heart. The psalmist portrays God as our shepherd at every stage and through every experience of life. In the NT we find a similar relation between Christ and his people, God and his flock. Think of the parable of the lost sheep (Luke 15:3-7). Jesus' words depict not merely a tradesman doing his job, for Christ says he loves the sheep, and "lays down His life for the sheep" (John 10:11; see also vv. 12-16). Moreover, after his resurrection, Christ asked Peter three times if Peter loved him. Peter became a bit annoyed, but each time he answered affirmatively. Christ told him, then, to show that love by feeding and tending his sheep (John 21:15-17). Though Peter was disturbed by this repeated question, evidently he got the point, for in 1 Pet 5:1-2 he instructs those who would be elders in the church to "shepherd the flock of God among you." One can hear in these words of instruction about God's flock the voice of Jesus telling Peter to feed his lambs.

God is also portrayed as an artist. The heavens declare the glory of God, and the earth shows forth his handiwork, says the psalmist (Ps 19:1), just as the painter's easel demonstrates his artistry. But unlike other artists, God creates by the sheer power of his word (2 Pet 3:5). He is also likened to a potter molding and shaping clay (Isa 64:8; Jer 18:6; Rom 9:20-21). He is further described as a builder (Amos 7:7), a teacher and scribe (Isa 2:3; Jer 31:33); a warrior (Isa 42:13), and a tradesman (Isa 55:1). The messenger of the covenant, whom many think is the preincarnate Christ, is likened to a metal worker (Mal 3:2, 3). All of these show God very much involved in our world.

A final category of biblical images is taken from national settings. Undoubtedly the most frequent motif depicts God as ruling monarch. The universe is his domain, and someday he will actually rule and reign from Jerusalem (Jer 3:17; Isa 2:2-4). In Jer 10:7-10 he is described as "King of the nations" and "the everlasting King." One is also reminded of the majestic words from Rev 11:15, incorporated into the Hallelujah chorus of Handel's *Messiah*: "The kingdom of the world has become the kingdom of our Lord, and of His Christ; and He will reign forever and ever."

Another motif taken from national and even civic settings presents God as judge. Though this is not a particularly popular image of God, it is one that Scripture offers clearly. Here one thinks of passages such as Gen 18:25; Isa 2:4; Acts 10:42; and Heb 12:23. And there is the awesome picture of God on the throne at the Great White Throne Judgment (Rev 20:11-15).[48]

Finally, God is portrayed as savior, deliverer, redeemer of his people. Sometimes this is presented in terms of a family relative, the kinsman redeemer (cf. Ruth), but more often (especially in the NT) the picture is of someone not a family member who goes into the public square and pays the price to buy us out of the slavery of sin (Gal 3:13; 1 Cor 6:20; 1 Pet 1:18-19). Even the OT, however, offers this image of God—for example, in what Hosea does to win back his estranged wife, Gomer (Hos 3:2; cf. Isa 43:3, 11).

All of these images, motifs, and metaphors show God as very much involved in our world. Even more, they portray him as concerned for our well-being and desiring a relationship with us.

The Transcendence and Immanence of God

Another way to address questions about God's role and relationship in our world focuses on the concepts of transcendence and immanence. Theologians and philosophers frequently discuss whether conceptions of God portray him as distant or near to his creation. Although one might think that views stressing God's transcendence make him remote, while those emphasizing immanence make him near and involved, that is not necessarily so. In fact, some conceptions of God portray him as very distinct from his creation (hence, transcendent) while being very involved with it. Others understand him as spatio-temporally very close to the world yet without any particular interpersonal relationship with it.

The comment about interpersonal relationships raises a further point. It is often assumed that, as immanent, God is very personally involved with his creatures (a personal God), whereas as transcendent, he must be impersonal and devoid of involvement in his creatures' lives. While some concepts of God do follow this approach, we shall also see theologies in which God, though transcendent, engages in many personal relationships, and others in which he, though intertwined with the natural world, doesn't relate to his creatures in any personal way.

Turning now to divine immanence: immanence means that God is present to and in the natural order, human nature, and history. Depending on the conception of God, it may also mean that he is spatio-temporally close to his creation ("close" is deliberately ambiguous to allow my point to refer to views of God that are pantheistic, panentheistic, or that depict God as ontologically distinct from his creation but omnipresent in it). The closeness may also indicate that he interacts with and relates to his creatures, though in some cases God is metaphysically close to our world but relationally distant.[49]

A number of conceptions of God see him as immanent in our world. Various forms of polytheism, such as animistic religions and the Greco-Roman pantheon, tend to portray the gods as very close to our world. Moreover, the Greco-Roman gods are depicted at least in mythology as responding to and interacting with mortals. As well, those who believe in some form of animism often sense various spirits interacting with them and acting in the events of their lives. The same may be said of the many Shinto *kami*.

Moving beyond polytheism to pantheism, we find views according to which God is very immanent in our world. Depending on the version of pantheism, God may or may not be very interactive with the universe and personal. For example, in New Age pantheism, since everyone is divine, and since it is thought possible to contact spirits of departed friends and loved ones, the immanent God is very personal and quite involved in the lives of all living things. On the other hand, Hegel's immanent God as Spirit, the universal consciousness uniting all people, seems to depersonalize God. It is hard to imagine, for example, anyone praying to Spirit, nor is it clear how Spirit could answer such prayers.

Tillich's and Macquarrie's views of God as being-itself also make God in one sense very immanent. As the power of being which gives everything its being (or in Macquarrie's sense, lets all things be), God is very much involved in all things. But none of this means that God is personal. Since being-itself is not a being, it is hard to know whether it can reason, will, and feel—characteristics that seem necessary for personal relationships. So, God as being-itself is quite immanent, but not necessarily involved at all in any interactive way in creation.

Finally, one of the hallmarks of pantheistic views, whether in process theology or elsewhere, is that God interpenetrates everything that exists. Transcendence is downplayed dramatically. Pantheistic systems also maintain that their God is very personally involved with the universe. Process theists, for example, say that their God is affected by what happens to us; he changes with us, ever-increasing from moment to moment in his knowledge. Moreover, since his body is our world, he not only empathizes with us when we suffer but actually feels our pains and rejoices in our joys. This is no remote, unattached, disinterested God.

As opposed to immanence, divine transcendence means that God is separate from and independent of the natural order and human beings. It typically also means that he is superior to anything in our world.[50] As Erickson explains, within the biblical portrait of God, God's transcendence is often described in spatial terms. He is described as "high and lifted up," "one who dwells on high," and so forth. Though divine transcendence might suggest a remote God interpersonally, this is not always so. The transcendent God may in fact be very much involved in his creatures' lives.

There are many religions with a transcendent God. Allah, the God of Islam, is the only God, and all else is distinct from and inferior to him. Likewise, certain forms of orthodox Judaism and traditional Christianity portray God as a deity of great grandeur, thoroughly separate from humankind. There is nothing and no one like him. Depending on the particular theology, this totally other God may interrelate with his creatures or remain aloof and unaffected by what happens to them. As we shall see in the next section, a form of Christian theism associated with Anselm and Aquinas portrays God as an absolutely sovereign monarch who sits in the heavens unaffected by and unrelated to what goes on in our world.

There is also a sense in which Brahman of Hinduism is totally transcendent. And it goes without saying that the God of mysticism in its various forms is typically thoroughly transcendent and majestic. Depending on the form of mysticism, when a human actually reaches spiritual union with this God, the union may or may not obliterate the individual personality of the mystic.

In addition, we should also mention the views of the great Christian reformer Martin Luther. Luther distinguished what he called the *deus absconditus* (the hidden God) from the *deus revelatus* (the revealed God). The latter refers specifically to Jesus Christ, while the former speaks of God as an immaterial being about whom we know very little. Jesus, God's fullest revelation, somewhat shows us what the hidden God is like, but we can never get a precise picture of the hidden God.

Many neo-orthodox thinkers, such as Karl Barth,[51] and their predecessors, such as Søren Kierkegaard, incorporate Luther's distinction. Though they don't always use Luther's terminology, and though their teaching about both the hidden and the revealed God differs from Luther's, they do include this distinction in their work. God the Father is portrayed as high above us, totally other than we are. Thus, the God we can know much about is the God who reveals himself to us. For both Kierkegaard and the Barth of the *Church Dogmatics,* that revelation comes in Jesus Christ and is given to us in personal encounter. For Barth in particular, Jesus Christ, not Scripture or anything else, is the content of revelation. So, for these theologians God is the totally transcendent God who comes near to us in the person of Jesus Christ. Through Christ we establish a relationship to God. But, as Barth frequently reminds us, in Christ God both draws near to us but remains also hidden. God is veiled in his unveiling and unveiled in his hiddenness.[52]

Deistic views are far less concerned about matching the biblical account of God. Deism was especially popular during the seventeenth and eighteenth centuries. With advances in science, nature was thought to run like a machine whose laws could be ascertained by pure reason and scientific investigation. As a result, natural occurrences which previously had been unexplainable could now be explained in terms of the normal functioning of the natural order. No longer was there need to appeal to God as the ultimate cause of such events. The situation was ripe for the rise of deism. According to this view, God is distinct from everything in our world, and he does not interact with it. He initially created the universe, but then withdrew from it to let it run on its own. This was sometimes likened to winding a clock and leaving it to run. The deistic God does not act in the world or sustain it, but remains thoroughly aloof from it. From a practical standpoint this view is tantamount to atheism, but conceptually it is not, for it denies only God's interaction with our world, not his existence.

In these examples of divine immanence and transcendence, it may be difficult to recognize anything that matches the biblical God. In parts 2 and 3 of this book, I shall present a portrait of a God who is both immanent and transcendent. He is transcendent in that he is a distinct being who is infinite in his attributes, whereas every other existing thing is finite. None can compare with him, and all other gods pale in obscurity and puniness in contrast to him. Even as Job was overwhelmed by God's revelation of his awesome power and majesty, anyone who comes even remotely to understand this God recognizes that there is nothing in the universe that matches him or even comes close.

On the other hand, he is immanent as omnipresent. As David said (Ps 139:7-10), "Where can I go from Thy Spirit?" No one and nothing that ever happens can escape God's awareness. But this does not mean we should adopt either a pantheistic or a panentheistic conception of God. Scripture teaches that God is present with all that exists, but is distinct from everything. God is also immanent in that he is very much involved in our world (i.e., though transcendent ontologically, God can be very close to us relationally). Scripture shows us a God who cares about us deeply and is responsive to our needs. Language that speaks of him as answering prayers, going to war on our behalf, comforting us in times of sorrow should not be understood anthropomorphically. He is the king who cares.

Several Models of Christian Theism

In this section we turn to conceptions of God that correlate a series of ideas about God into an overall explanatory model for God's relation to the universe. Here I use the term "model" to represent a system of coherent ideas which intends to offer a well-rounded explanation of who God is and how he relates to the world. I am using it much as a scientist does when he speaks of different models or hypotheses for explaining a whole series of data. My concern in this section is models from the Christian tradition.[53]

For many centuries of church history there was a predominant way of envisioning God, his attributes, and his relationship to the world. That model is often referred to as the traditional or classical Christian conception of God. However, in recent centuries, especially the twentieth, there have been significant challenges to that model. Even among theologians committed to evangelical Christianity the classical model has been heavily critiqued and modified. On the other hand, theologians and philosophers outside the evangelical camp have abandoned the classical model in favor of entirely different ways of understanding God.

The result is that on the contemporary scene, there have been two major competing models of God: the classical model, and the model of process theism. Process theists portray these two options for Christians as an either/or, and since process thinkers believe the classical model is thoroughly outmoded, religiously inadequate, and less biblically supported than their own portrait of God, they believe the proper choice between the two is obvious. Many theologians agree and have to one degree or another adopted the process understanding of God.

Since these are the main competing models of God within Christianity, we must understand what each says. Moreover, because process theology is such a significant rival to traditional Christianity, I plan to give a more thorough analysis of it in chapter 4. Still, we can describe the basic contours of each model in this chapter. But many Christian thinkers find unpalatable the either/or of classical vs. process theism. Hence, within evangelicalism in recent years there has been significant rethinking of models of God with the intent of formulating a mediating position between the Scylla of classical theism and the Charybdis of process theology. Most notable among those attempts is the open view of God (sometimes called free-will theism). Our task in this section is to describe these three models of God. Critique will be saved for later chapters, but the position I shall espouse in this book is represented by none of the three. I shall offer a different mediating position, the model of the king who cares.

THE CLASSICAL MODEL. This model of God has dominated Christian thinking throughout most of church history. It is most closely associated with Thomas Aquinas and Anselm. Opponents often complain that it is also firmly rooted in ancient Greek philosophy. In fact, in literature about different conceptions of God one often finds a disjunction between "the God of the philosophers" and "the God of Abraham, Isaac, and Jacob, the God of the Bible." The former is the God of Aristotle and other Greek philosophers, and critics also believe it is too much like the God of classical theism. Thus, we are told that the classical God is not the God of the Bible.

As to the philosophical background of the classical model, ancient Greek philosophers were concerned to find some element of stability in a world where everything seemed to be changing and in the process of becoming. Heraclitus argued that all of reality is in a state of flux, but that thought was unsettling to the Greek mind. If everything is changing, and has been from all eternity, how could there have been a beginning, a bringing into being of anything that is? Must there not be some stability in a world of change to ground that world? Parmenides, Plato, Aristotle, and the Stoics didn't give exactly the same answer, but they all postulated some element of permanence in a world of flux.

Aristotle's answer is worth noting, since he had such a strong influence on Aquinas. Aristotle wanted to explain both the stability needed to ground the world, and motion or change itself. In order to ground the world, there must be a prime mover which is itself unmoved. Aristotle argued that this unmoved mover must be fully in being (perfect) without any potentiality unrealized. If there were potency in the unmoved mover, he would not necessarily be self-sufficient, for something else, fully in being, would be required to cause his motion toward act. Since Aristotle didn't hold to an infinite chain of movers, somewhere the chain had to end with a being that was fully in being with no reason to change, because it was already perfect and could not become better. This unmoved mover was sufficient for its own existence, and it did not and could not change in any way. Change would only be for better or for worse, but a perfect being could not get better, and there would no reason to become worse.

While Aristotle's unmoved mover grounded the changing universe in something permanent, it didn't explain motion within the universe. For, if an unmoved mover cannot change at all, how can he initiate motion and change in the universe? Aristotle replied that he doesn't do so by acting on the world, for that would require a change in him. Rather, he causes motion by being so beautiful and perfect that the universe desires to be like him, and so moves toward him.

Much more can be said about Aristotle and other Greek philosophers, but this is sufficient for our purposes. John Sanders argues that the bridge from Greek philosophy to Christian thinking was the Jewish thinker Philo of Alexandria (25 B.C.–A.D. 45) who tried to harmonize biblical teaching with Greek philosophy.[54] Regardless of exactly how these ideas found their way into Christian theology, scholars agree that the Greek influence is undeniable in the classical model of God. Aquinas's reliance on Aristotle is unquestionable. What concerns us now, however, are the details of the classical model.

The classical model fundamentally emphasizes two things. On the one hand, it refers to a cluster of attributes predicated of God. Central to the classical understanding of the divine attributes is that they are all perfections in God which he has to an infinite degree.[55] On the other hand, it is about how much power God has and how he chooses to use it in our world. Ronald Nash[56] and William Alston[57] are especially helpful in explaining the attributes that come with the classical model. Nash relies upon the portrait of process thinker David Ray Griffin (*God, Power and Evil*), whereas Alston appeals to process theologian Charles Hartshorne's comparison of the classical and process models (*Man's Vision of God* and *The Divine Relativity*).

As to the attributes of the classical God, Nash (via Griffin) isolates eight: pure actuality, immutability, impassibility, timelessness, simplicity, necessity, omniscience, and omnipotence. Following Hartshorne, Alston identifies nine: absoluteness, pure actuality, total necessity, absolute simplicity, creation *ex nihilo* by a free act of God, omnipotence, incorporeality, nontemporality, immutability, and absolute perfection. Hartshorne divides these attributes into two groups: the first contains the first four, and the second contains the remaining five. Obviously, there is overlap in Nash's and Alston's lists. Putting the lists together, we derive the following attributes of God: 1) absoluteness, 2) absolute perfection, 3) pure actuality, 4) necessity, 5) immutability, 6) impassibility, 7) timelessness, 8) simplicity, 9) omniscience, 10) omnipotence, 11) creation *ex nihilo*, and 12) incorporeality. Let me briefly define each, for in so doing a specific picture of God emerges.

First, God is absolute. By this Hartshorne means that the classical God is internally totally unrelated to the world. He bears no relation to it either by way of his knowledge of it or his actions.[58] Second, as absolutely perfect, the classical God cannot become better than he is, for he is already the best. No being surpasses him or even could, for he is the greatest conceivable being.[59]

Third, the notion of God as pure actuality harkens back to Aristotle. For Aristotle and his followers, every existing thing except God is a combination of actuality and potentiality. Hence, they can and do grow and change. However, Aristotle reasoned that potentiality is an imperfection, for whatever has potentiality is not fully the being it might be. Aristotle and Aquinas both concluded that since God is a perfect being, he must be totally actual with no potentiality to become anything more than he is. But, then, when one is perfect, what need is there for ability to change?[60]

Fourth, God is necessary, and this involves several things. It means that God exists necessarily rather than contingently. Unlike contingent things that can come into existence or go out of existence, God as necessary can do neither. It is impossible for him not to exist. In addition, necessity means that the various divine attributes are essential to his being; losing any of them, he could not be God. Finally, divine necessity means that every truth about God is necessarily true. There are no claims about him that happen to be true but did not need to be (i.e., they are contingent). Every truth about him is necessary.[61]

Fifth, the classical God is immutable in the strong sense of the term. This means he is devoid of any change, and in fact cannot change. He is change-less in his being, attributes, will, and purposes, but his knowledge also is unchangeable and he cannot change relationally. He cannot decide to forego some action he intended to do, and even if a sinner repents, God cannot change his relation to him from alienation and impending judgment to fel-lowship and blessing. Scriptural language suggesting otherwise must be understood anthropomorphically and, hence, not as literally true of God. Impassibility (sixth) comes along with immutability, for if God cannot change at all, he cannot change emotionally either, and classical theists agree that God cannot become angry, sad, or happy. As Anselm explains in an oft-quoted passage, God as compassionate means we experience things in times of need that suggest God's compassion, but God does not actually feel that emotion or any other.[62] Whether or not he is aware of our pain as we suffer, he certainly cannot feel it himself and suffer along with us. Impassibility also means that God cannot be acted upon. Hence, biblical accounts of Moses persuading God to relent from his decision to destroy Israel (Exod 32:1-14) are anthropomor-phic. No one's prayers or arguments can actually move God to do anything he had not already planned to do.[63]

Seventh, God is also timeless, and this follows in light of his immutability. All conservative Christians grant that God is eternal, but Christian thinkers have wrestled with how to understand that eternity. Does it mean that God exists forever within time, or that he exists outside of time? The classical notion of God opts for the latter, for if God is totally changeless, he cannot even undergo the change of temporal succession. Though he is outside of time, he sees all of it as an eternal "now."

A corollary to immutability, impassibility, and eternity is divine simplicity (the eighth classical attribute). This doctrine says God is devoid of all compo-sition; he is not made up of different parts. This means, among other things, that we cannot divide off God's essence from his attributes, nor ontologically is one attribute separate from another. God's attributes are identical with his essence, and this requires by logical implication that each of his attributes is identical with one another. Though we can distinguish analytically in thought the various divine attributes, in God those qualities are not ontologically distinct from one another. More will be said about divine simplicity when discussing divine attributes, but for now I note that though this doctrine seems very strange, it is part and parcel of the classical perception of God.

Next come divine omniscience and omnipotence. According to the for-mer, God exhaustively knows everything that can be known. He has no false beliefs, and there is nothing he could possibly learn. This also means that he has complete knowledge of the future, including the actions of all his created beings. How that can be so in light of human freedom has been debated across the centuries. Various answers have been offered, but one thing has remained stable: the classical view attributes to God knowledge of the future.

As to divine omnipotence, some have understood it to mean that God can do anything whatsoever, even actualize a contradiction, but the predominant view within classical theism places some limits on divine power. God cannot actualize a contradiction, but no one can, so this isn't deemed a significant limitation on God. He also cannot do anything contrary to his nature, such as sin, catch a cold, or fail a test. Since all of this means that he must be who he is, none of it is seen as a significant limit on God.

God has used his power to create our universe, and the most typical understanding within the classical tradition is (attribute number eleven) that God did this out of nothing (*ex nihilo*). Moreover, it is usually argued that creating a world is a fitting thing for God to do, but not the only fitting thing. Not creating would have been equally appropriate.[64] So, God is free to create or not to create, and he is free to choose whichever world he wants to create.

Finally, the classical God is an immaterial substance. As such, he is in no way composed of matter. This is one reason for holding divine simplicity (as incorporeal, he has no physical parts), but not the only reason. The portrait that emerges from this list of divine attributes is one of a self-sufficient God who needs nothing. He doesn't change at all, and seems aloof from our world. Though the classical tradition maintains that God somehow can and does act in our world (the classical view is not deism), for the most part the picture is of an unresponsive, remote God.

There is a second element to the classical picture, and it only strengthens the portrait of an impersonal, distant God. According to the classical view, God is the absolutely sovereign monarch over the world. He has his will and way in all things. Very little, if any, power is donated to his creation. Opponents decry this, claiming that it leaves no room for human freedom and moral responsibility. Nonetheless, the classical God holds humans morally accountable for their actions, even though they are merely following the divinely decreed course for their life.

Critics of the classical view believe it runs into insuperable problems over the problem of evil. If God ordains all things and carries out his desires in our world, how can he escape moral responsibility for the evil that occurs? Moreover, critics complain that this God is a cosmic bully who is boss and gets his way no matter what. Feminist critics in particular maintain that it is this domineering, tyrannical, unresponsive, isolated, and self-sufficient God who has been used to legitimize patriarchal, oppressive societies throughout history. The idea of a God who is a friend and confidant, sympathetic to our needs and concerned to help us develop our own potentialities, seems far from the God of classical theism.

Whether feminists are right, whether a God with this sort of sovereign control is actually a cosmic bully, and whether this view cannot possibly handle the problem of evil remains to be seen. Moreover, proponents of the open view of God (as process theists) seem to think that the list of attributes described above is inextricably tied to this notion of divine power and control in our world so that if God has these attributes, he inevitably exercises this kind of sovereignty over the world (and vice versa). I shall argue that there is no logical entailment between the two, but process theists (and open view espousers, I would argue) want us to believe there is, for then their alternative to the classical view seems the only viable one.

THE PROCESS MODEL. Process theologians love to use the classical model as their foil, and they delight in saying that their notion of God both corrects the excesses of the classical God and more accurately represents the God of Scripture. Since I intend to devote a separate chapter to this theology, let me here only present process views with respect to the two main items elaborated in the classical model: the list of divine attributes and the view of divine control in our world. As we proceed, we must remember that the process God is dipolar. God has an immaterial, primordial, conceptual pole, and a physical, consequent pole. The latter pole is our world, and that helps us to anticipate what process theists will say about the divine attributes.

In turning to the divine attributes we come first to absoluteness. Process theists deny this of God, for they view God as internally related to his creatures through his knowledge of them and his interaction with them.[65] He is not distant and aloof but vitally involved in his creation. He is a social God, engaged in all sorts of relationships with his creatures.

Second, as to absolute perfection, this is denied of the process God. Since God, as all actual entities, is constantly in the process of becoming, it is always possible to surpass his current greatness. His creatures continue to add value to him. The process God is more perfect at any moment than any other entity, but as he continues to grow and develop, he always surpasses his prior greatness.[66]

Third, pure actuality is denied of the process God. He is not as perfect as he could be and will be, but he has many possibilities for change and improvement. This is not to say that God will actualize all of the potential inherent in his primordial nature, but only that in contrast to the classical God, there are possibilities for him to actualize as he grows. As to necessity, process theists affirm that God's existence is necessary, but that does not mean that there is no contingency in God. For example, that he will change seems inherent to his being, but what he specifically will become is contingent, depending on how his creatures grow and develop.[67]

This brings us to immutability, impassibility, and timelessness, and process views are again quite predictable. Having a physical pole, God is clearly capable of changing, and does so. He changes not only in his relationships but also in his very being and attributes. His knowledge is constantly growing as he experiences new things along with his creatures. Charles Hartshorne says of the process God that he is immutably mutable (changeable). Likewise, this God is thoroughly passible. Rather than merely identifying with our joys and sorrows from afar, since we are intertwined with his being, he actually experiences our experiences as we have them. He suffers with us and also rejoices when we do. Moreover, he responds when we pray. Though the process God won't override human freedom, he cares about us very much and tries gently to lure us toward his best for us. Hence, seeking his aid and comfort through prayer does accomplish something. Biblical language about God changing his mind or emotional state is to be taken at face value, not treated as anthropomorphic. In addition, the process God is enmeshed in time, for his consequent pole is subject to temporal becoming just as we are. He knows what time it is and what is happening in our life when it happens.[68] Process thinkers argue that these characteristics (mutability, passibility, and temporality) make their God much more religiously adequate than the God of classical theism. And, of course, there is no room for divine simplicity in the process God. If nothing else, God's physical pole is filled with and composed of many different parts.

As to omniscience and omnipotence, the process God has limitations. Being mutable and involved in the process of becoming, his knowledge is finite and constantly grows and changes. Moreover, in light of human freedom, no one can know the future for certain. Having a primordial pole that is the repository of all possibilities gives him no help in knowing the future, for no one knows which possibilities will become actual until they do. If omniscience is defined as knowing everything there is to know, the process God's ignorance of the future is no limitation, for no one can know the future. As for omnipotence, God has all the power any agent can have, but that does not mean he is infinite in power, or that he can even do all things that are logically possible. His power is finite, and, of course, its operation in our world is always subject to the limitations put upon it by human freedom.

When it comes to God's creative activity in the world, process theism denies creation *ex nihilo*. The process God is a very creative God, but his creativity is exercised by continually offering new possibilities (via his conceptual pole) for becoming. According to process thinkers, matter is eternal, so God and the world of creatures are necessary, but specifically what either God or his creatures will become is contingent on the use of creaturely freedom.[69]

Finally, process theology denies the classical divine attribute of incorporeality. God's primordial pole is immaterial, but it is not a distinct being. His consequent pole, the world, is very much filled with corporeal things.

The process conception of divine attributes is quite different from the classical view, and deliberately so. But the story doesn't end there, for when it comes to how much power the process God has and uses in our world, there is again a stark contrast to the classical view. The process God is no absolute monarch nor an uninvolved, disinterested power monger who demands and gets his way no matter what. Though process theists don't use the imagery of a friend, their God is much more like a friend than a king. Of course, some friends can be very demanding and domineering, but not the process God. He does encourage us to follow his best for us, but he never forces us to do anything against our will. Rather he tries to lure us to his best by gentle persuasion.

As a corollary, process theists uniformly believe humans possess libertarian free will according to which actions are free only if not causally determined.

Hence, no matter how much God wants us to follow his aim for us, he cannot guarantee any outcome. We can always resist him and do whatever we choose. In light of this, God can't remove evil that we produce by abusing our freedom, but he can and does suffer along with us as we undergo trials and tribulations in this life. Process theists believe this is a more satisfactory answer than classical theism has for the problem of evil.

In reflecting on the process model, we must say that this God surely sounds like a very nice fellow. He is always with us and cares about us very deeply. He makes few, if any, demands of us, and always lets us do whatever we want. When we reject his attempts to persuade us to choose his goals and get ourselves into hot water, he does not say, "I told you so." Nor does he have the power to get us out of that trouble, but he does lovingly take his place alongside us and suffers with us.

If one were to construct a God to one's own liking, many would likely think this God fills the bill. As a result, the process model is a very powerful view of God in contemporary times, even among many who do not buy everything involved in Whitehead's metaphysics. One finds feminists and other liberation theologians quite attracted to this God who seems always to be on the side of the downtrodden without ever oppressing anyone himself. But, as we shall see in chapter 3, this view has many other supporters from a variety of contemporary quarters.[70]

THE OPENNESS MODEL.   Despite those attracted to the process view, others remain unconvinced. However, they don't advocate a return to the classical God. They contend that classical and process theism aren't the only options, for they propose a mediating corrective to both, which they call the open view of God.[71]

While the open view has affinities to both classical and process theology, there are also significant differences. Like the process view, the open view portrays God as deeply in love with his creation and most responsive to it. But open view proponents reject the process notion of a dipolar God. The incorporeal metaphysically distinct God of classical theism is sufficient for open theists, so long as he does not also include the remoteness and unrelatedness traditionally associated with the classical God. In addition, advocates of the open view don't want a God as impotent and finite as the process God, so they grant that God *has* all the power the traditional view attributes to him. It is just that he usually chooses not to exercise it so as to make room for human libertarian free will. All in all, open view proponents believe that their depiction of God is more true to the Bible at the same time that it offers a religiously adequate view of God. Moreover, they think their views actually square with the way most conservative Christians practice their religion, even though those Christians' practice seems inconsistent with the classical God they apparently espouse.[72]

Richard Rice offers biblical evidence for this view. He begins his description of the open God by saying that the book *The Openness of God* "expresses two basic convictions: love is the most important quality we attribute to God, and love is more than care and commitment; it involves being sensitive and responsive as well."[73] As a result, the open view offers a God whose relation to the world is dynamic rather than static.[74] Love becomes paramount and is the governing divine attribute in both Old and New Testaments.

What this means for the divine attributes associated with classical theism and attacked so heavily by process theists is that, for the most part, the open view sides with process thinkers, although in a few areas they agree with the classical view. For example, they agree with the classical view that God is incorporeal, they believe that God created the universe *ex nihilo,* and they hold that God has necessary existence and is absolutely perfect. However, they accept the process claim that certain things about God are contingent. As to pure actuality, they reject the process view of a "growing and developing God" who has metaphysical possibilities as yet unrealized. For the open view, God's nature and attributes are set, but because the notion of pure actuality is so attached in the traditional view to a static God who cannot change at all, they forego using such language of God.

The major defection of open theists from the classical view involves the other divine attributes. For example, open view defenders deny that God is internally unrelated to his creation (i.e., that he is absolute). In fact, a God who is dynamically related to and responsive to his creatures is one of the hallmarks of this perspective. In light of God's responsiveness, the traditional doctrines of strong immutability and impassibility are rejected. However, as to immutability, the open view's God is not quite so "under construction" as the process God. Proponents of the open view affirm that God's nature and attributes are immutable. He will not cease to be loving, just, benevolent, or holy, nor will he become more loving, just, and so forth; but God is not entirely immutable. For one thing, he changes his relationships. As an example, says Rice, the book of Hosea shows God casting off his people Israel for their unfaithfulness (Hos 2:2), and deciding to put them to public disgrace (2:10), but later portrays God as turning from revenge to reconciliation (2:14, 19-20).[75] In addition, Scripture often depicts God as changing his mind, and this language shouldn't be understood anthropomorphically; it signals real changes in God's thinking. Hence, the Lord was sorry that he created mankind, because they were so evil, and he decided to destroy them with the Noahic flood (Gen 6:6). He regretted that he had made Saul king of Israel (1 Sam 15:35) and decided to remove him. He was prepared to destroy Israel for worshiping the golden calf, but Moses interceded and persuaded God to change his mind (Exod 32:12-14). And of course, he promised through Jonah unconditionally to destroy Nineveh, only to change his mind when Nineveh repented.[76]

The NT also shows God changing relationships. The incarnation itself demonstrates God's desire to have a closer relationship with us. As for repairing relationships with himself that are damaged by sin, Rice says 2 Cor 5:18-20 "underscores the central New Testament truth that God is always the subject, and never the object, of reconciliation. He is the agent, not the recipient, of reconciliation."[77] This is not a God who remains aloof and unconnected to us.

Divine impassibility is also denied, because Scripture portrays God as having feelings and emotions. God is said to take delight or pleasure in many different things (e.g., Deut 30:9; Ps 149:4; Jer 9:24). He is a God of compassion and love (Jer 31:20; Hos 11:1, 3, 4, 8), but at times a God who also becomes angry and threatens judgment (Hos 2:2, 4, 9-10).[78] The life and ministry of Jesus are further examples of God's emotions of love and compassion for us. Rice finds especially telling the Luke 15 parables, for the parables of the lost sheep, lost coin, and prodigal son vividly illustrate God's attitude toward sinners. They show not only God's restoration of lost sinners but also his utter joy at recovering what was lost.[79] Moreover, this God not only sympathizes with us but also suffers with us in the person of Christ. And Christ's death shows God's commitment to establish a relationship with his creatures, for this was something God planned far in advance (1 Pet 1:20; Acts 2:23).[80]

Open theists also reject divine timelessness, for a God so intimately involved in our world must be both aware of the passage of time and subject to it. Moreover, since temporal changes (represented by God's different actions and reactions) give a sequence to his experience, we can no longer say that his experience is devoid of parts or indivisible into distinct experiences.

Next are omnipotence and omniscience, and the open view's understanding of these attributes is intertwined with its teaching on divine sovereign control over the world. Because open view defenders see the latter issue so closely tied to one's view of God's attributes, throughout their work they give the impression that if one buys one package (the classical understanding of the divine attributes or the classical view of God as absolute monarch), the other automatically comes with it. Central to the open view is a belief that humans have libertarian free will. This is the view that *"an agent is free with respect to a given action at a given time if at that time it is within the agent's power to perform the action and also in the agent's power to refrain from the action."*[81] That is, regardless of what the agent chooses, it was just as possible to choose and do something else. Actions are not causally determined, but free. David Basinger admits that sometimes God may override our freedom to accomplish his goals, but usually he doesn't.[82]

Does the commitment to libertarian freedom mean God is impotent rather than omnipotent? Not at all, says open theism. God is absolutely sovereign, but out of love for his creatures he has granted some power to them and refrains from exercising all his power. This again shows a God who is sensitive to our needs and desires, but he is still as sovereign as the classical view suggests; he just chooses not to use that power. God is also omnipotent in that he can do whatever is logically consistent and consistent with his nature. Of course, controlling the free actions of his creatures is not something he can do, nor can anyone else. All of this means that God takes risks with us. We

may use our freedom to love him and choose his way, but we may also use it
to reject and disappoint him as well. So, God is vulnerable, but as the caring,
loving God that he is, he decided to take the risks that free creatures pose.[83]

Such views have implications for God's knowledge. He is omniscient, so
long as omniscience means knowing everything that can be known. With
creatures who have libertarian free will, there is no iron-clad way to know for
certain what they will do. Hence, the open view rejects attempts to synthesize
divine foreknowledge and libertarian free will, and claims that God does not
know the future. He has a thorough knowledge of past and present, and he
knows us completely. This often enables him to have a good idea of what we
will do, but until we do it, there are no guarantees.[84] God's lack of knowledge
about the future also means that, though he has hopes and plans for what will
occur, he may need to scrap them and choose another course of action, once
he sees what we do.[85]

Some will wonder how this notion of divine omniscience can possibly
square with biblical prophecy. Proponents of the open view anticipate that
objection and answer by dividing biblical prophecies into three kinds. The first
set express God's intentions to do something in the future, regardless of what
his creatures do (e.g., Isa 46:10-11). Rice says of these prophecies, "If God's
will is the only condition required for something to happen, if human cooperation is not involved, then God can unilaterally guarantee its fulfillment, and
he can announce it ahead of time."[86]

A second set of prophecies indicate "God's knowledge that something will
happen because the necessary conditions for it have been fulfilled and nothing could conceivably prevent it."[87] God's prediction of Pharaoh's behavior
seems to fit this category, for his behavior was so rigid that God could predict
accurately what he would do.[88] The final category of prophecies tells us what
God intends to do *if* certain conditions obtain. Since these prophecies are conditioned on what we do, if we don't meet the conditions, God won't do what
he intended to do if we had met the conditions. None of this means God is
mistaken or has lied about the future, but only that these are not locksure predictions of what will happen. Jeremiah 18 is an example of this kind of prophecy, for it predicts destruction unless the people of Israel change their ways.[89]

It also follows with this model of God that God has not foreordained
whatever happens. To do so would be to act as a domineering monarch concerned only with what he wants. Since that is not the open God, history is not
the working out of his predetermined, irresistible, and sometimes inscrutable
decrees. Rather, history is open to whatever we make it. This makes the future
an unknown adventure, not only for us but also for God. Moreover, with such
a God our prayers and petitions really do matter, for by them we can move
God to do things he otherwise did not plan to do.[90]

Advocates of the open view also claim that their position provides the best
handling of the problem of evil. Unlike the process view, the open view doesn't
solve the problem of evil by making God so impotent and finite that he isn't

guilty for what happens in our world because he can't do anything about it. God does have the power to overturn evil, and on occasion he intervenes to do so. But the main reason God doesn't remove much evil, according to open theism, is that to do so would eliminate human freedom. Having decided to give us such freedom, God cannot make us freely do what is right. Hence, God is not the author of evil, and he has a morally sufficient reason for not preventing it.[91] Moreover, this handling of the problem of evil is deemed by the open view to be superior to the classical view. On the classical view, everything that happens results from God's eternal decrees and his outworking of them in history. But since God's plans for our world evidently included evil, the open view claims that the classical God must be guilty for making this world, both because he does not remove the evil in it and because through his eternal decrees he is the author of the evil. Defenders of the open view see the classical position as hopelessly flawed in this respect, whereas they think their view avoids such problems, satisfactorily answers the problem of evil, and does so without capitulating to the process view of God as impotent.[92]

The open view is a distinct alternative to both process and classical models of God.[93] It is a helpful reminder that those two options are not the only choices. However, in this book I shall argue that all three models should be rejected in favor of another alternative that attempts to mediate between classical and process views. The exact contours of that model await explication in upcoming chapters of this book.

Three Understandings of the Metaphysics of Christian Theology

There is a further general way to classify Christian theologies. The focus is God's obligations with respect to creating a world or not, and what sort of power God has and uses to create a world and set up its moral governance. These systems also address how human beings learn whatever rules God has established. Description of these theological systems is preparatory to considering the problem of evil, and since I shall discuss that topic in chapter 16, here I shall only sketch broad outlines of these systems.

The first system is known as theonomy. This world view should be distinguished from contemporary approaches to ethics which share the same label and are exemplified in the work of ethicist and apologist Greg Bahnsen. In the Middle Ages, theonomy as a metaphysical system was called voluntarism and was exemplified in the thinking of philosophers/theologians such as William of Ockham. According to this view, only God must exist, and he must have unlimited and unrestricted freedom to do whatever he pleases. In more radical forms of theonomy, God even has power to violate the law of noncontradiction. According to theonomy, whatever rules of ethics, epistemology, physics, etc., obtain in our universe are chosen by God, and he is free to choose any laws he wants. Moreover, if he wants to change those laws later, he has power to do so. As to morality, no action is intrinsically good or evil or better or worse, for each has its value only in terms of the value God places upon it. God is subject to those laws himself only if he decides so to obligate himself; otherwise, he is beyond the rules of good and evil that he ordains for us. Since God can choose and change the rules in any area of life (even arbitrarily, according to some forms of theonomy), the only way to know how the universe runs and what the rules are is through divine revelation of God's choices, and not at all through reason. Within the Christian tradition, theologies that stress God's absolute transcendence and unlimited power tend in the direction of theonomy. Hence, some forms of classical theism fit the theonomous approach, but a classical theist need not be a theonomist. We should also note that strongly orthodox Jewish and Islamic systems tend toward theonomy.

A second system appears in the work of the rationalist philosopher Gottfried Wilhelm Leibniz. As opposed to theonomy, where God's will rules, in Leibniz's universe reason rules. In his extreme rationalistic system, all laws of logic, ethics, etc., are necessary laws in the universe. Whatever is the case is so in virtue of the principle of sufficient reason, which stipulates that for anything that ever occurs there must be a sufficient reason why it occurred and not something else. Moreover, in Leibniz's system God must create a world, and it must be the best of all possible worlds (for Leibniz, the idea of a best world is intelligible). And whatever is true in this universe is discernible by the light of pure reason alone unaided by revelation. In theonomy God is prior to logic, but in Leibnizian rationalism, logic is prior to theology. Even God dare not violate the dictates of reason.

A final and mediating position is called modified rationalism. It is like theonomy in not claiming that everything is discernible by reason alone, nor does it maintain that everything about the world expresses some necessary law. Furthermore, modified rationalism doesn't demand that God create a world, but holds that creating a world is fitting for God to do (not creating would be equally fitting). For modified rationalism, there is no best possible world, but only good and evil possible worlds. If God decides to create a world, he must choose one of the good possible worlds lest he be guilty of doing something wrong in creating a world at all.

Modified rationalism also differs from theonomy in holding that there are things that are intrinsically good or evil apart from what God says about them. Moreover, whereas only some forms of theonomy require God's power to be subject to the law of noncontradiction, most modified rationalist systems define divine omnipotence so that God works within the rules of reason. Hence, in such a universe, things obtain according to reason, and one can often discern by reason why things are as they are. Some things, however, are knowable only by revelation.[94]

In relation to our previous discussion of three different models of Christian theism, many proponents of a classical model would also agree with modified rationalism. The open view also presupposes the modified rationalist metaphysic, and my own position does, too. In fact, many theologies fall under the umbrella of modified rationalism. However, the process model goes beyond the pale of historic evangelical Christianity (represented most by theonomy and modified rationalism) and fits under none of these three systems (though, of the three systems, process theism is most like modified rationalism).

How Should We Understand Language About God?

Various questions have arisen about the meaningfulness of theological and religious language. One issue asks to what the term "God" refers and what it even means.[95] Another asks what users of religious language intend to do by using such language. If they intend to assert facts (as one would in history and the sciences), it has been argued that this misunderstands the nature of religion and religious language.[96]

While both of these are important and interesting issues, we cannot cover all such philosophical issues here. There is, however, another problem (at least as old as medieval times) which is relevant to the rest of this book. In various chapters, I shall discuss the being of God, divine attributes, and divine actions. But how are we to understand these claims about God? Most claims we would make about God use language that is used of human beings, but God isn't a human being. In particular, he has no body, but many attributes and actions we would predicate of him seem to require that he have a body. Moreover, even when no reference to material parts is required to make a claim about God, how do we know that our words mean, when used of God, what they do when used of humans, since God is infinite and we are finite? In fact, how do we know that our words about God have any meaning?[97]

William Alston helps to explain the nature of the problem by distinguishing "extrinsic" and "negative" predicates, on the one hand, and "intrinsic" and "positive" ones, on the other. The former tell nothing about what the subject is like, whereas the latter attributes do.[98] Alston explains that the issue is not whether we can make any truth-claims about God, but whether any of our intrinsic and positive claims say anything literally true of God.[99]

What can we say, then, of God truly, and do we understand such claims as literally true or not? Throughout the history of this discussion, there have been various responses. A first answer denies that we can say anything about God, literally or figuratively, because God is incomprehensible and hence ineffable. Various mystics have adopted this view, but others have held it as well. Some theologians qualify the view by distinguishing between God as he is in himself and as he is in his relation to us. In himself, he is totally incomprehensible, so even though we can say something about his relations with us, none of that captures what he is in himself. Hence, we really do not know how much our language about God's relations with us tells us about God in himself.[100]

Harold Netland offers a most helpful survey of positions which claim God is incomprehensible and ineffable,[101] and raises significant objections to them. As he argues, there is something right with this view, in spite of significant problems. The element of truth is that we cannot know everything about God. There are undoubtedly mysteries about him which none of us understands. But we must recognize that this doesn't mean we know nothing about him whatsoever or that none of our claims, whether literal or figurative, are true.

As Netland shows, the major problem with the ineffability position is that it is difficult to formulate in a way that makes sense. Even more, it is hard to see how it avoids refuting itself. Netland offers four possible formulations and shows that each has such problems.[102] His first formulation illustrates the problems. It says, "No meaningful and informative statements about God can be made."[103] Netland rightly critiques this as follows:

> First, it rules out the possibility of any knowledge of God by implying that no true or false statements about God can be made. Not only is this theologically unacceptable, but we must also ask on what basis such a categorical denial of knowledge of God can be made. Second, this thesis is self-refuting. It does express a statement about God—namely, that the nature of God being what it is no meaningful statement about him can be made.[104]

A second response about how we can speak meaningfully of God is less pessimistic than the first. It agrees that God is ultimately incomprehensible but claims that we can make some truthful comments about him. However, central to this view is the notion that we can't make any positive predications of God, only negative ones. This approach is known as the *via negativa*, which holds that the only things we can say of God are things telling what he is not. Thus, attributing to him incorporeality, infinity, omnipotence, and omniscience simply means that he has no body, is not limited, is not powerless, and is not ignorant.[105] But none of this tells us positively what divine intelligence, power, etc., actually are. Given the difference between an infinite God and finite creatures, we can't with certainty know anything positively about how God exemplifies those attributes, even though we know how we do.

As Armstrong has shown, the *via negativa* has a long tradition in philosophy going back at least to the ancient Greek philosopher Plotinus. The Jewish philosopher Maimonides held this approach, and there have been others within the Christian tradition who did as well.[106] Despite its adherents, it has some significant problems. When we say God is omniscient, do we really mean no more than that he isn't ignorant? Most would say it means at least that God knows all things that are knowable and has no false beliefs. Isn't that something positive we can predicate of God? Undoubtedly, terms such as "incorporeal" and "infinite" fit the basic concept of the *via negativa* better, but that doesn't mean the same is true for all divine attributes. Moreover, we make positive claims about God when we predicate moral attributes of him such as love and justice. So while the *via negativa* is helpful to some extent and reminds us to specify as clearly as possible what claims about God mean, it does not seem the best way to handle the issue before us.

A third approach to this issue grants that God is ultimately incomprehensible and "totally other" from us. Nonetheless, it doesn't conclude that we can say nothing about God or only speak of what he isn't. Rather, all of these factors about God make us conclude that we must always judge speech of him to be metaphorical or symbolic. This has become a popular position in contemporary theology. Tillich says that everything we say about God is symbolic, except the claim that God is being-itself or the ground of being. Others have affirmed that because of God's difference from us, everything we say about him is metaphorical.[107]

This proposal has merit, but significant problems as well. On the plus side, it is true that various biblical claims must be seen as metaphors. To call God a rock, a shepherd, or a consuming fire, or to say that Jesus is the door, is using language not literally but metaphorically. Moreover, if we grant that God is pure spirit, when writers speak of the "hand of God," "the eyes of God," "the face of the Lord," their claims are anthropomorphic and, as such, metaphorical. So, there is an element of truth in what this position affirms.

However, there is also a major problem in holding that *all* language about God is metaphorical. This is so even if one grants Tillich's one literal claim that God is being-itself. Figures of speech (metaphors, similes, etc.) compare things, all of which are known. Because we know enough about what is literally true of each thing being compared, we understand the metaphor. If I say, "the trees shall clap their hands and sing," I am comparing humans and trees. Trees don't have hands, but they do have branches and leaves that rustle in the wind. I also know that when humans clap their hands and sing, that signifies approval or joy, or both. Because I know enough about what is literally true of trees and humans, I can understand the figure of speech contained in "the trees shall clap their hands and sing." But what if I were ignorant about the nature and activities of either trees or humans? How could I then understand the metaphor? It seems that I must know at least something to be literally true of both, if I am to do more than merely guess what the metaphor means. And if this is so for things on earth that have a material part to their being, how much more this must be so when one of the things being compared is immaterial and not subject to empirical observation! Hence, for metaphors about God to make sense, I must know some things about him that are both literal and true.[108]

If we must say something literal about God, does that mean language used of God must have the same sense as when used of humans? If not, does that mean it is used equivocally of God and us? St. Thomas Aquinas raised these issues long ago, and his answers are still very helpful. Predicating terms of God with the exact meaning they have when used of us is called univocal predication. Aquinas denied that our language of God works this way. "Univocal predication is impossible between God and creatures. The reason of [*sic*] this is that every effect which is not a proportioned result of the power of the efficient cause receives the similitude of the agent not in its full degree, but in a measure that falls short; so that what is divided and multiplied in the effects resides in the agent simply, and in an unvaried manner."[109] This answer appeals to Aquinas's doctrine that things true of an effect are so because they are derived from a cause with the same qualities. Hence, love in a human being comes from God the creator, who is also love. However, God and we are so different that we cannot be sure that the love that "resides in the agent simply" (i.e., in God) is the same thing his creatures possess in being loving.

If the difference between creator and creature means the same term cannot be predicated of both univocally, is it then used equivocally of them, i.e., in entirely different senses? Answering negatively, Aquinas explains that such language cannot be equivocal, "because if that were so, it follows that from creatures nothing at all could be known or demonstrated about God; for the reasoning would always be exposed to the fallacy of equivocation."[110] Some might think this only shows that we must get our ideas of God from revelation, not from reason. But that misses the point, for even if our idea of God comes, for example, only from Scripture, how would we know that when the Bible says God is love, love means what it does when used of us? Since God is so different from us, when Scripture says God is love, maybe we don't know what that means.

In light of these problems, Aquinas offers an answer followed by many. Aquinas claims that we predicate qualities of God analogically, i.e., as Aquinas explains, according to proportion. Both God and humans are loving, so both possess this attribute, but not to the same degree. Still, the difference is not so great that we must say one possesses the attribute and the other has it in no respect. They possess it analogically. Aquinas writes, "For in analogies the idea is not, as it is in univocals, one and the same; yet it is not totally diverse as in equivocals; but the name which is thus used in a multiple sense signifies various proportions to one thing."[111]

Though Aquinas's analogical predication has much merit, I find even more compelling William Alston's proposal in "Functionalism and Theological Language."[112] Alston begins by reminding us that no matter how hard we try to purge our language about God of language used for creatures, we cannot completely succeed. Even calling God being-itself doesn't avoid such language, for "being" is a term we use of creatures.[113] Alston's proposal focuses on psychological terms such as "know," "will," "intend," and "love," for it is the divine psychology that comes into our dealings with God as an essential background to divine action. That is, God impinges on our lives as an agent, doing various things such as guiding, enjoining, punishing, and redeeming, and such actions presuppose some antecedent psychological state in God.[114]

With divine and human psychology as the focus, Alston argues that though there are substantial differences between God and human beings, there is some univocity in predications of God and us. Specifically, it is possible to "identify a common core of meaning in terms for human and divine psychological states."[115] Hence, "the radical otherness of God might manifest itself in the *way* in which common abstract features are realized in the divine being, rather than in the absence of common features."[116] How can we make such a case? Alston proposes that we turn to functionalism, a movement in contemporary philosophy of mind. He defines it as follows:

> The basic idea, the source of the name, is that the concept of a belief, desire, or intention is the concept of a particular *function* in the psychological economy, a particular 'job' done by the psyche. A belief is a structure that performs that job, and what psychological state it is—that it is a belief and a belief with that particular content—is determined by what that job is.[117]

So, there is some thing that performs a certain function. Alston repeats the crucial claim that the internal nature of the thing that so performs is not specified. In his words, the crucial point is that "a functional concept of X is non-committal as to the intrinsic nature, character, composition or structure of X."[118] Hence, for example, it makes a certain amount of literal sense to say that a computer, a robot, and a human being "made a decision" even though the internal structure of each is quite different. Alston adds a further point before applying it all to theological predication. He notes that the fundamental function of the psyche, according to functionalism, is to regulate behavior. Whether behavior is carried out by a physical body, as usually happens in our case, or some other way, the regulation of that behavior is the psyche's role.[119]

How does this apply to theological language? Alston explains what he thinks by now is fairly obvious. The same functional concept of, for example, knowing something could be equally applicable to God and us, even though what it is to know something is true may differ radically between God and us. The function played by both the divine and human psyches is the same, even though how God goes about knowing may be a mystery to us. So also for God's intending or purposing to bring something about. While we don't know exactly what it is to purpose as God does, we know the result and we know what it means for us to purpose and bring something about. Both God's and our psyche can function in similar ways, even if we don't understand everything about what it is to be God or about knowing and purposing as he does.[120]

Alston applies his proposal to qualities like infinity and incorporeality that we predicate of God. His handling of incorporeality illustrates his views. Alston asks whether God can in fact perform some of the same psychological functions that embodied humans perform. He mentions several human actions, all of which require certain psychological functions, but also require a body to carry out. For God to do such things, he must be capable of behavior, but since he has no body, such behavior seems impossible. Alston explains,

> If God has no body to move, how can he *do* anything, in the same sense in which an embodied human being does things? But this is not an insuperable difficulty. The core concept of human action is not *movement of one's own body,* but rather *bringing about a change in the world—directly or indirectly—by an act of will, decision, or intention.* That concept can be intelligibly applied to a purely spiritual deity. It is just that we will have to think of God as bringing about changes in the 'external' world directly by an act of will—not indirectly through moving his body, as in our case.[121]

Analyses like this illustrate Alston's claims about the meaningfulness of theological language. He concludes that, despite differences between God and us, there is enough commonality in functional psychological states to say that our human psychological concepts of these functional states yield ideas that literally apply to God and hence generate "theological statements that unproblematically possess truth values."[122]

This approach seems the sanest to me. It avoids the self-defeating position that we can say nothing of God, but on the other hand, it resists the equally problematic positions that all talk of God is either literally true or equivocal, or that we can only say things about God which tell us what he is not. Moreover, it allows some of our language about God to be metaphorical and anthropomorphic. I do not even think Alston would reject the view that we often use language about God analogically. In fact, his point is that there are certain human psychological states, and functions they produce, that are so analogous to divine psychological states and functions that in God's case it makes sense to predicate language literally about these states and functions. Alston's proposal also allows us to avoid saying that everything we say of God is metaphorical, leaving us in the awkward position of explaining what the metaphor means since it refers to a God about whom we know nothing literally. And, Alston's view allows us to say that, when God reveals something in Scripture about his thoughts, feelings, and actions, these claims truly reveal something to us. We are not in a fog about what they mean.

Of course, none of this tells us whether any attribute or action predicated of God is metaphor, analogy, or literal (in Alston's sense). For example, some may wonder whether language about God repenting is literal or metaphorical and/or anthropomorphic, and may wonder also how we can tell. I shall address such issues more directly in chapters on God's being and his actions. For now suffice it to say that once we determine whether such language is metaphorical or not, and (if not literal) what the metaphor/anthropomorphism means, then given Alston's functional account of religious language, we can say that God performs the function designated by the language (literal or metaphorical) even as we do. So, Alston's proposal does offer a way, coupled with careful exegesis of the text of Scripture and thoughtful conceptual analysis of what exactly God is and does, to answer questions about what language about God means. It assures us that we can talk meaningfully of him.

THREE

WHAT HAPPENS TO GOD IN CONTEMPORARY THOUGHT?

In chapter 2, we discussed diverse understandings of God's reality and of his role(s) and relationships in our world. Many of those understandings are intended as alternatives to and even rejections of traditional evangelical Christian conceptions of God. However, much of our emphasis was on models of God within broadly evangelical theologies. The burden of this and the next chapter is to examine the major trends of our times in regard to perceptions of God. This should help to clarify where evangelical conceptions of God and the model I shall develop fit among rival conceptions.

This must not be misunderstood. I intend to present a model of God that is consistent both with Scripture and with the main views on God that conservative Christians have held throughout the centuries of Christianity. But I have read and taken seriously contemporary evangelical and non-evangelical conceptions of God and I am not insensitive to their concerns. Moreover, I don't reject everything models other than mine espouse. Hence, the reason for chapters 2–4 of this book is first to help readers better understand what I am reacting to and why, when I delineate my own understanding of God. My nuancing of divine attributes and actions, for example, might seem to be odd proposals at this time in history without an understanding of the intellectual context from which they stem and to which they respond. Moreover, it seems hard to speak to contemporary culture in terms it will understand if we have little idea of what it is thinking, especially of what it is thinking about the most important topic, God. I also hope that non-evangelicals will read this volume; without my showing awareness of what they are thinking on these subjects, they may be entirely disinterested in dialoguing with what I am writing.

Whole books have been written on contemporary theology, but we must place some limitations on our investigation since this is not *per se* a book on contemporary theology. First, our topic in this chapter is God in *contemporary thought*. In our day "modern" has a specific meaning as opposed to the postmodern. Since I intend to cover both movements, "contemporary" is more generic and allows me to cover a whole series of positions. Moreover, I speak of contemporary *thought* rather than *theology*, because modernity and postmodernity are broad movements that encompass much more than just theology. To understand contemporary *theologies*, we must understand contemporary philosophy, culture, etc., so this study requires more than a rehearsal of views of God in contemporary theologies.

Second, discussions about the charismatic movement, dispensational versus non-dispensational theology, or even Calvinistic versus Arminian conceptions of God are all theological and contemporary issues. However, this chapter's focus is not such intramural debates among Christians whose fundamental understanding of the nature, attributes, and actions of God are all evangelical. Instead, my concern is movements in non-evangelical thought. One of the hallmarks of those views is their interaction with the philosophies of their day. Of course, every theology interacts with and incorporates some philosophical position(s).[1] The difference on this matter between contemporary non-evangelical theologies and evangelical theologies stems from their perceptions about their ultimate authority and about the proper role of philosophy in theological formulation. While evangelical theologies incorporate some philosophy, one of their emphases is that Scripture is the final authority for faith and practice. Hence, evangelical theologians shouldn't include in their systems any philosophical notions that contradict biblical teaching. In contrast, non-evangelical theologies typically make reason or personal experience the final court of appeals. Moreover, for many of these systems philosophy is the guiding norm (as well as it is much of their substantive content).

Third, because of space limitations, I cannot discuss every contemporary thinker. Moreover, theologians who will be treated offer more than just a conception of God, but I must limit the discussion for the most part to their views on God. Hence, I offer a "taste" of contemporary thinkers without describing all that they say. There is another way to limit our topic, which I plan to resist. Our discussion could simply flit from one thinker to the next, noting with minimal explanation what they say about God, but to do so would treat the various thinkers and movements as isolated and unconnected to other thinkers and to intellectual and social trends of their day. That would not really explain what they are saying or why they say it. Hence, we need some background information, i.e., some understanding of the broad intellectual, cultural, and social movements and trends of the contemporary period, in order to have the framework for grasping how the various theologies understand God and our world.

With that in mind, I propose that the proper framework for understanding these various contemporary thinkers is a comprehension of *modernity* and *postmodernity* and how they relate to each other. That is, a major help in understanding contemporary notions of God is to see them against the backdrop of modernity and postmodernity. Of course, this means I must first clarify what modernity and postmodernity are.

Before turning to that descriptive task, I must mention several other themes that I believe are present in various contemporary theologies. One is the interplay between divine transcendence and immanence. Various theologies stress one or the other, and I believe that as we move through the contemporary period (and especially with postmodern theologies), the emphasis switches from divine transcendence (to the extent that it was emphasized in earlier theologies) to God as very immanent in our world.

Another trend we should note is how these theologies either deify man or humanize God. In both modern and postmodern theologies I maintain that there is a strong tendency to do just that, and this trend becomes especially prevalent among postmodern theologies. Moreover, the more a theology stresses differences between God and man (emphasizing God as a transcendent "wholly other"), the more that theology tends toward a view that such a God is dead. As we move into the postmodern period, contemporary theologies increasingly refuse to envision a remote God.

A corollary to both points just mentioned is that in the contemporary period non-evangelical Christian theologies increasingly place their emphasis on Jesus, especially, and on the Holy Spirit. Less and less is said of the hidden God, God the Father, of traditional theism. The reason in part is that Jesus especially (the Holy Spirit as well) makes God immanent, related to us, not remote and unapproachable. Of course, feminist theology says plenty about God as Father, but does so mainly to complain that theologies emphasizing God as Father are patriarchal and androcentric and should be rejected. Jesus, not in his maleness but in his nearness, relatedness, love, and compassion (as signified by his incarnation), plus the Holy Spirit get higher praise in feminist theology than God the Father.

Two other trends are worth noting as we study the contemporary period. First, as theology moves from modern to postmodern emphases, the focus increasingly shifts from theologies that reflect on God's being to those that emphasize his acting in our world. This should not be misunderstood, for neo-orthodox thinkers were certainly concerned, for example, about God's revelatory *acts*. My point is that while there was emphasis on such acts of God, there was also reflection on the hidden God, the wholly other, solely in terms of what he is like. In contrast, postmodern theologies, especially liberation theologies in various forms, speak only of a God of praxis, a God of action. This shift of emphasis can be described as a move from a metaphysic of substances to one of action and relationships.

The other point is that thinkers after Immanuel Kant take very seriously his emphasis on empiricism, his Copernican revolution in philosophy, and his claim to have put an end to metaphysics. All of these will be explained, and as we proceed, we shall see that not everyone reacts to Kant's doctrines in the same way. Nonetheless, the contemporary period takes Kant and his central insights in epistemology and metaphysics very seriously.

With these initial words of definition, limitation, and explanation, we can turn to modernity and postmodernity. My intention in this chapter is neither apologetic nor polemical, but rather descriptive. Undoubtedly, there will be points of critique of various thinkers, but my main objective is to acquaint the reader with the major trends in contemporary thinking about God.

What Is Modernity?

Modernity and postmodernity stand for a series of diverse items that conjointly offer a basic intellectual and cultural outlook on reality. My concern is to describe the elements of each that are significant for philosophy and theology. Though there is room for debate, broadly speaking, the modern era in a significant sense began with René Descartes (1596–1650) in philosophy and with Galileo and Isaac Newton in science. The period continued into the nineteenth-century rationalism and scientism that still influence our own times.[2] It is safe to say, however, that the modern project, often referred to as the Enlightenment, was at its apex during the eighteenth- and early nineteenth-century portion of the Enlightenment. About modernity, Jürgen Habermas writes:

> The project of modernity formulated in the 18th century by the philosophers of the Enlightenment consisted in their efforts to develop objective science, universal morality and law, and autonomous art according to their inner logic. At the same time, this project intended to release the cognitive potentials of each of these domains from their esoteric forms. The Enlightenment philosophers wanted to utilize this accumulation of specialized culture for the enrichment of everyday life—that is to say, for the rational organization of everyday social life.[3]

These comments get us started, but there is much more to say. Various authors emphasize one trend or another in describing modernity. For example, Langdon Gilkey, in speaking of the theological ferment in the late 1960s as Western cultures moved away from the modern mindset, characterizes the mood of the times (and hence, the general mood of modernity) as one of secularization. He identifies four general characteristics of the secular spirit: contingency (the world around us "is a result of causes that are neither necessary, rational, nor purposive"), relativism, the temporality or transience of all things (everything is changing and ultimately perishing), and the autonomy and freedom of man.[4] Though I think this is true of the modern era (and also the postmodern era), it is just part of a larger picture.

Nancey Murphy and James McClendon are helpful in capturing the mood of the times. They identify modern thought as describable along three separate axes, each of which focuses on a key characteristic issue for the modern era. One axis is epistemological and moves between foundationalism and skepticism as its two extremes. A second axis focuses on theories of meaning in philosophy of language. The two extremes here are what they label a representational (referential) theory of language and an expressivist (emotivist) theory of language. The third axis is more ontological in nature, for it focuses on whether reality should be understood in atomistic, individualistic terms or in relational, collective terms. The two extremes of this axis are individualism and collectivism.[5]

While I agree that the issues Murphy and McClendon raise are important for the modern mindset, I think there is more to it than that. For example, what they discuss under the first two axes is all part of the general area of modern epistemology, and their third axis is part of a larger emphasis on human freedom and individuality, but there is more to the modern spirit than this alone. Specifically, I propose to discuss modernity under the following six headings: human consciousness ("the subjective turn"), epistemology, naturalism, human freedom and individuality, science and progress, and the goodness of human nature.

Human Consciousness ("The Subjective Turn")

The modern period (at least philosophically) is thought to have begun with Descartes. The era prior to Descartes was one of tradition and authority. Various ideas were deemed correct, and working within the tradition of those ideas, one held them. Moreover, governmentally and ecclesiastically, it was also an age of authority. Descartes was born on the eve of the Reformation. The church fundamentally told people what was correct to believe, and if one was a Christian, one followed that. Philosophers working within the Western tradition were often also theologians. The point of philosophy was not primarily to prove God's existence (though we find a lot of that in thinkers such as Anselm and Aquinas), but to understand one's faith (*fides quaerens intellectum*, Anselm's motto). God was, so to speak, the starting point of philosophy, and if proofs were to be offered for his existence, that was one of the first things done in philosophical and theological writings (see, for example, Aquinas's *Summa Theologiae*).

With Descartes things changed, because Descartes wanted to know that what he believed about anything could be supported by evidence and argument. So he called into question everything he had believed, for the purpose of ascertaining whether there was anything he claimed to know that could not reasonably be doubted. If there was something of this sort, it would serve as the basis or foundation upon which to build everything else he knew. Descartes' search for certainty eventually led him to conclude that only one thing could not reasonably be doubted. It made no sense to doubt his own existence as a thinking thing, for in the moment he doubted it, he proved its truth. Nonexistent things do nothing at all, including doubting their own existence.

Descartes deemed the *cogito ergo sum* ("I think, therefore, I am") the one indubitable truth from which to build knowledge in any and every field. Of course, the *cogito* is only true for each person with reference to himself or herself. I cannot know for a certainty that you exist, nor you I. So, Descartes was still troubled about how to justify all other knowledge. He eventually came to a rationalistic conclusion that if he had a clear and distinct idea of something, this must be true of the world. But how could one be sure that when one thought he was having a clear and distinct idea of something, this was really so? This question led Descartes to formulate his version of the ontological argument for God's existence. If God exists, Descartes reasoned, he would ensure that whenever I think I am having a clear and distinct idea of something, I really am.

The details of Descartes' ontological argument needn't detain us, but the point should be clear. No longer is God the "starting point" of philosophy. Human consciousness is, and along with it comes epistemology as the center-piece of philosophy. It is up to human consciousness to structure and certify whatever is true. Perhaps Davis's comment is a bit strong when he says that "the fabrication of the modern subject was a divinication of man." But, he is surely right in maintaining that "Descartes' *cogito* to which we can trace the origin of the modern subject, transferred to man the function of God as the source of reality and intelligibility."[6]

For Descartes, one's knowledge of the world grew through clear and distinct ideas of things. For empiricists such as John Locke and David Hume, appeal to sense data from ordinary experience was the key. But in both cases attaining knowledge involves a subject-object relation, i.e., human conscious-ness is the subject, the knower, which attempts to ascertain what is true of the world (the object). Human consciousness takes the role of sitting in judgment of what is true in regard to reality.

This emphasis on human consciousness only became heightened with Immanuel Kant's "Copernican Revolution" in philosophy. Prior to Kant, the mind was deemed as fundamentally passive in the knowing process. Sense data from the external world came to it through the sensory organs. Those organs might distort the data, and that was thought to explain why, for example, two people looking at the same thing might report seeing things differently, but this account still portrayed the mind as basically passive. Kant disagreed, and argued that not only does the world act upon the mind (through the senses), but the mind in virtue of various concepts inherent in it (the Kantian categories) is also active. The mind structures the sense data and then makes a judgment about what is perceived. In light of this two-way pro-cess, Kant proposed his famous distinction between things-in-themselves and things-as-they-appear-to-us. He argued that while things really exist outside of our mind, no one can experience them as they are in themselves. Things which are not objects of our knowledge (including things-in-themselves) Kant labeled noumena. Things as they appear to us he called phenomena.[7]

With Kant the trend begun by Descartes of structuring the world from one's own consciousness continued. Human consciousness as active, not passive, becomes even more important. After Kant, it would be hard to find a phi-losopher who thinks the mind passive in the acquisition of knowledge. Instead, philosophers have increasingly emphasized the mind's action in an individual's understanding of reality. In addition, Kant, like other modern philosophers, was concerned to ground knowledge ultimately in certain foundational beliefs, but unlike Descartes the key was empirical data.[8] Throughout the rest of the modern era, the emphasis on empirical data as the key to knowledge remains. This is true for contemporary theology and in philosophical critiques of theology.

In sum, basing one's understanding of the world on the human consciousness's structuring of the world is crucial to the start of the modern era. Of course, with the role given to human consciousness, if either human reason or sensory organs malfunction, human beings are in serious trouble in respect to knowing and living in their world. During the modern era, many thinkers were quite optimistic about the mind's ability to "get things right" in its search for knowledge. As we shall see, postmoderns significantly disagree.

Knowledge, Truth, Objectivity, and Theory of Meaning

Because human minds can misinterpret and misrepresent data, we might think this emphasis on the subject's role in the acquisition of knowledge would only make it more difficult to secure a certain foundation for knowledge, but the modern mentality said otherwise. Reason was deemed capable of grasping and interacting correctly with the world, and it was held that this is true for all people. Just as Descartes wanted to find an indubitable foundation on which to base his knowledge, so others after him thought this was both necessary and possible. A universal perspective on reality was possible through reason, and belief in everyone's ability to find the truth made it possible in every discipline of study to know truth and error and to convince others, if one thought their views were wrong.

The picture of knowledge and rationality just described is often called the Enlightenment conception of rationality. That notion of rationality was most wedded to a theory of knowledge known as foundationalism. According to foundationalism, beliefs are justified in terms of other beliefs which ultimately are supported by beliefs that need no justification, because they are self-evidently true. Because of the belief in reason's ability to support beliefs, the Enlightenment or modern notion of rationality claimed that it is only rational to maintain a belief if one does so on the basis of sufficient evidence, arguments, or reasons for the belief.[9] Descartes' concern to believe only what cannot reasonably be doubted is clearly incorporated in this notion.

Of course, the next question is what counts as sufficient evidence, argument, or reasons for belief. How does one know that one has a right to hold a given belief? Foundationalism provides the answer. Classical foundationalism (which has been a predominant theory of knowledge within the modern era) claims that a belief has sufficient support if it is supported by evidences and arguments that are ultimately supported by (inferred from) beliefs that are properly basic. A properly basic belief is a belief that is either self-evident (like "all bachelors are unmarried men"), evident to the senses, or incorrigible (like the *cogito*).[10]

Whereas for Descartes the ultimate foundation was something rational, the empiricists emphasized sense impressions as the most basic beliefs that form the foundations of our knowledge. Kant combined both rational (the mind's categories that allow it to structure reality) and empirical (data from observation) as foundational. For Kant the only truths about the world that are deemed objects of knowledge are truths that can be known through the senses. Despite the mind's activity in interacting with the world, there was great optimism about an individual's ability to know rightly what is true or false. As David Griffin explains, the basic epistemological doctrine of the modern world is sensate empiricism, according to which knowledge of the world beyond ourselves comes exclusively through sense-perception.[11]

But what if a belief is not about a matter of pure reason (e.g., "round squares do not exist") nor open to sense perception? Kant said that things-in-themselves are not objects of sense perception, but neither are values and moral judgments, the world as a whole, nor God. All of these are noumena, not phenomena, and as such, they are not objects of knowledge. As a result, Kant claimed to put an end to metaphysics, for the subjects normally discussed in that discipline are beyond empirical investigation.[12] This didn't mean for Kant that there was no God, for example. Kant believed it necessary to posit the existence of God, but he did so as a grounding for morality. So God exists, according to Kant, but his existence is not a matter of knowledge; it is a postulate of practical reason.

If the only beliefs that qualify as knowledge are beliefs supported ultimately by foundational beliefs that are self-evident, evident to the senses, or incorrigible, it seemed to many moderns that the beliefs most capable of being justified are the beliefs of science. In fact, among the logical atomists and logical positivists of the late nineteenth and early twentieth centuries (and many others who followed their general empiricist emphasis), there was a desire to purify language, insofar as possible, of talk that is not empirically verifiable. If this were done, then our language would be basically the language of science, i.e., whatever is open to verification by empirical observation. The logical positivists, however, were even more negative than Kant toward things he called noumena. For the positivists, if a sentence isn't in principle verifiable by empirical means, the sentence is deemed nonsense, and that of which it speaks is considered nonexistent. This meant that talk of morals and of God are nonsense, and they do not exist.[13]

Ludwig Wittgenstein was a contemporary of the logical positivists. His early philosophy as set forth in his *Tractatus Logico-Philosophicus* presented a portrait of the world and language that was not unlike that of the logical positivists. Though the positivists appreciated Wittgenstein's work, he did not deem himself one of them. Nonetheless, he did hold that unless language pictures objects and states of affairs in the world, it is meaningless. If language is about something unobservable in the world, it should not be spoken. Unlike the positivists, however, Wittgenstein didn't conclude that things that were unsayable (because incapable of empirical verification) did not exist. Rather, he concluded, such things are not objects of knowledge, and so should not be spoken of at all.[14]

With these beliefs about knowledge, it follows that moderns believe there is truth, and for them the predominant theory of truth is the correspondence theory. According to this theory, propositional truth is a relation between language and our world. What we say about the world is said to correspond to or match what is true of the world. Moreover, moderns believe it is possible to know what is true by means of our rational and sensory faculties, and this is so for all people. Any human being can use his or her intellectual faculties to reach a correct conclusion about the world. Foundationalist criteria can be met for much of what we believe about the world.

This is a very optimistic view about the mind's ability to acquire knowledge, especially in light of Kant's claims about the mind as active in the knowing process. While moderns agreed that through our subjectivity we might misinterpret our empirical observations and err in our reasoning, they believed that none of that is inevitable. Objectivity is possible, and is most clearly seen in science. The fact that science works with data of the tangible world and uses an observational method that everyone can use to confirm or disconfirm scientific conclusions seemed to guarantee objectivity. Of course errors are still possible, and given the demand to justify beliefs ultimately by beliefs that are self-evident, evident to the senses, or incorrigible, it was granted that some might hold beliefs that are not justifiable by such criteria. But the predominant mood through much of the modern period has been that it is possible to be objective in our handling of data and to know what is true of our world.

Nancey Murphy and James McClendon argue that a further characteristic of modern epistemology is its emphasis on a representational or referential theory of language. According to such theories, words and sentences (or for some theories, the proposition a sentence is about[15]) refer to objects, actions, and events. Their meaning is what they refer to. Typically, the referential theory in question considers that meaning invariant. As Murphy and McClendon show, this fits very nicely with a theory of knowledge that says beliefs are to be justified in terms of more basic beliefs. Beliefs can be shown true by seeing that the things they refer to are true of the world.

But if a sentence doesn't name or picture something empirically observable, does it have any meaning? While theories such as the verification theory of meaning of the logical positivists concluded that such sentences are meaningless, not every theory agreed. Some philosophers of language argued that those sentences do have meaning, but not a meaning that refers to some object or state of affairs in the world. Rather, these sentences express either the speaker's emotional reaction or intentions to act in a certain way.[16] For example, "God is love" does not refer to anything that can be verified by empirical observation, but it is still meaningful. On an emotivist account of language it might mean nothing more than "I like God" or "I think God is nice." Another "expressivist" theory of language is what R. B. Braithwaite calls a conative theory. In this case, the sentence expresses the utterer's intention to act a certain way. Thus, "God is love" might mean that the speaker intends to act in a loving, agapeistic way.[17]

Naturalism

The two previous aspects of modernity focus on epistemology, but a third involves metaphysics or ontology. As David Griffin argues, the basic ontological doctrine of modernity is the mechanistic doctrine of nature. With the rise of Newtonian science coupled with rationalism and empiricism in epistemology, the world was thought of as a gigantic machine. This mechanistic view saw the physical world as composed of inanimate, insentient atoms which interact with one another by deterministic impact.[18] Natural laws govern whatever happens in our world, and by knowing the laws that apply to given objects, it is possible to predict what they will do.

As Griffin explains, two worldviews were possible with this metaphysical doctrine. On the one hand, following Descartes' mind-body dualism, one could opt for a dualistic understanding of things. This view posits the physical, natural universe plus immaterial human selves or souls distinct from the material order. Typically, the soul or self is deemed the only place where values reside in the world. Hence, morality and value judgments are not in the physical world but rather in minds that reflect upon that world. Moreover, this worldview fragments the human self from the natural world (as well as from other selves). One result of this fragmentation is a radical split between the physical sciences and the humanities.[19]

Ever since Descartes posited mind-body dualism, philosophers have wrestled with how two things so thoroughly different from each other could causally interact. As the modern period moved into the twentieth century, increasingly more philosophers concluded that there is no adequate explanation that views mind as immaterial. Hence, the other worldview of the modern era is materialism, which conceives of ultimate reality not in dualistic but in monistic terms. Mind becomes in some sense (depending on the theory of mind) an expression of matter, and immaterial substances of any sort are denied. Of course, if the universe is only matter, and it runs according to natural laws, then a materialistic worldview seems even more deterministic than one based on some sort of Cartesian dualism.

When we combine these metaphysical doctrines with the aforementioned epistemology, the only truths available about our world come through the natural sciences. Religion, theology, ethics, and metaphysics tell us nothing more about the world.[20] In light of such views, moderns claimed to explain everything that happens in our world in terms of natural processes. When some event occurs, there is no need to appeal to God to fill in the gaps of our knowledge. For many, these metaphysical and epistemological doctrines meant that there is no God. For others such as the deists, there is a God, but he does not act in our world. For yet others, there might be a God, but there is little we can know or say about him. None of this is deemed a significant loss, for there is always a naturalistic explanation for whatever happens.

This anti-supernaturalism has implications for one's understanding of the Bible. According to this view, there must be some naturalistic explanation for whatever the Bible says happened. Accounts of miracles come from a pre-scientific mindset and must be understood as myths. With the rise of biblical critical methodologies, even greater questions were raised about the Bible being anything but the product of human creativity. No divine intervention to reveal truth to the writers and inspire them to write was necessary to explain the Bible's origin. Moreover, with advances in science (especially the introduction of evolutionary theory to explain the ultimate origin and development of all things) even greater doubts were raised about the accuracy of Scripture.

A further result of this naturalistic worldview is the gradual secularization of society. Religion and theology could no longer be seen as serious intellectual disciplines (unless, of course, the point was to trace the history of a religion's development), and instead were marginalized and privatized. As Joe Holland explains, this was done so as to expand the autonomy of the secular, advanced by science and technology.[21]

Human Freedom and Individuality

Another hallmark of the modern era is its emphasis on the individual. As David Tracy writes, part of the "turn to the subject" involves emphasizing individual rights and freedom.[22] While premoderns relied on tradition and authorities like the church or the king for what they should think and do, the modern era involves a throwing off of all authorities in favor of the individual and what he or she deems appropriate. After all, the demand that one only has a right to believe that for which one has sufficient arguments, evidences, and reasons means that no one should have to follow another's views just because they said so. Each person is encouraged to decide on the basis of argument and evidence what is right to believe and do.

This emphasis on freedom and individuality did not stem solely from these epistemological doctrines, for it was also a logical implication of science's view of the nature of things. The world was seen as composed of discreet things that exist in isolation from other things. Those discreet bits of matter do causally interact with one another according to physical laws, but what they are in themselves doesn't depend on their relation to other things in the universe.[23] As applied to human beings, these doctrines encouraged individualism and concern for self-interest.

Politically, the emphasis on individual freedom gave rise to modern democracies. Societies are composed of individuals who have priority over the collective group. In fact, according to the social contract theory of government which had many followers during the modern era, individuals are equal with one another before they enter a society. People enter a society out of self-interest. They cede certain rights in order to gain other rights and privileges (e.g., protection by a society's military forces). All of this places emphasis on individuals, not the community as a whole. The most notable exceptions to these general social and political theories were found in Hegel and Marx. For Hegel, nothing exists in isolation, and to understand what something is, one must see it in its relation to others. Marxist collectivism follows these notions and applies them to both politics and economics, but the predominant mood in the modern era politically and economically has been to move to democracy and capitalism (or if socialism, at least a socialism that recognizes and rewards individual effort).

In the modern era human individuality and creativity are deemed virtues of the highest order, and their full and free expression must be a central feature of any society. As Joe Holland writes, "The modern world freed technology, politics, economics, and culture from nearly every restraint."[24] While this emphasis on individual rights and freedoms has encouraged and allowed many people to develop and use their abilities in ways unthinkable in premodern times, it has also fostered an attitude of self-sufficiency and self-reliance, isolation from community, and a belief that one may believe and do (in morals and religion) whatever one wants, so long as no one else's freedom and rights are abridged. We see repeated examples of such attitudes in our day. Rugged individualism and isolationism that go along with the privatization of religion destroy a sense of community. Coupled with a mechanistic view of the universe and the problems of modern industrial urban cities, modern life can be very bleak in spite of all the freedom. One thinks of T. S. Eliot's portrait of modern life as a wasteland, in his famous poem by that title. But even before Eliot and the twentieth century, the bleakness and desperation of modern life is portrayed in literature. In Charles Dickens's novels one gets such a picture, but perhaps the most depressing picture comes in the work of a Victorian writer, James Thomson. Thomson's poem "The City of Dreadful Night" is a portrait of modern life in an urban, industrial setting. It is written nearly a century before Eliot's "Wasteland," but its mood is far more somber and its message considerably more depressing and pessimistic than that of "The Wasteland." In the city of dreadful night there is no God, no hope, no meaning, and suicide is the only escape from this lonely, depressing condition.

The Goodness of Human Nature

One reason so many moderns have been willing to grant such individual liberty is their basic belief in the fundamental goodness of human nature. Once the rules for securing beliefs were explained and freedom was given to believe and do what people wanted, there was nothing to fear. There has been a prevalent belief that human beings, if left to themselves, will positively transform life for themselves and for others. Think of the inventions that spawned the industrial revolution and that have made life so much easier. These wonderful advances through scientific discovery are considered evidence of what human beings can and will do, if they are only allowed to develop freely their inherent abilities.

We frequently find this attitude in much public policy in the modern era, continuing even into our own day. As democracies began to arise, we often heard political thinkers argue that if you give people the right to vote and educate them, they will use the power to do what is in everyone's best interests. Even today, we often hear that problems of unemployment, crime, drugs, and the like are matters that can be corrected if we simply educate people and provide funds to create jobs so that they can work. The underlying assumption is that problems of modern culture do not stem from moral or spiritual inadequacies. Basic human nature is good, and people are rational enough to see what is in their best interests. If we just educate them so that they have the skills to work, then they will behave as positive, productive citizens. When was the last time we heard a politician say that the problems of our societies are at root spiritual and moral? No one denies that people can become corrupt, but basic human goodness remains and we can tap into that through education.

Through much of the modern period there has been this positive attitude toward human goodness, but in the twentieth century things have happened that give many second thoughts. Optimism about human nature was dealt a staggering blow by World Wars I and II and the atrocities associated with them. We have seen all too vividly the inhumanity of mankind, and we have seen it not only during the twentieth century's major wars but also in the repression of individual rights by totalitarian states. Still, we are assured that the answer is democracy, for if you give people freedom and educate them, they will do the right thing. Of course, we must be careful that the few "bad apples" don't gain power (political or otherwise), for we now understand that there is no absolute guarantee that everyone will treat others well. Nonetheless, many people still believe that while there is some bad in everyone, at rock bottom all people are basically good.

Science and Progress

David Tracy writes that "modernity includes all who still acknowledge the modern scientific revolution as not just one more important event in Western culture but as the watershed event that makes even the Reformation and Renaissance seem like family quarrels."[25] As Joe Holland explains, prior to the modern era there was a fatalistic acceptance of nature and history as reflecting God's immutable ordering of the world. In contrast, the modern spirit promised to liberate humanity from fate and all other restraints. "It promised a new vision, centered in secular science seeking freedom and progress for all the world."[26]

Throughout the modern era and even into our own day advances in science have been nothing short of staggering. This is true not only of the industrial revolution but also of ongoing advances in science in the twentieth century. Communication technology in the form of radio, television, and computer have developed dramatically in a relatively short time. Advances in transportation by automobiles and airplanes have brought the world much closer together. Advances in medical science are also astounding. In our day kidney, liver, and even heart transplants, though serious operations, are no longer science fiction. Even fifty years ago few would have imagined such advances, and we are now seeing revolutionary changes in the field of genetics. Once the human genome project is finished, changes in therapeutic medicine alone will be dramatic.

The modern world is clearly built on and relies heavily on science and technology. Moreover, the predominant attitude toward these developments is that they show human culture as continually progressing. Science and technology are seen by many as the saviors of society, having the capacity to lead us to a utopia.

A major scientific development during the modern period was the Darwinian theory of evolution. Among its other accomplishments, evolutionary theory has done much to undermine confidence in the truthfulness of Scripture. Moreover, this theory is so thoroughly entrenched that David Tracy says, "all moderns justly see the world of nature and ourselves within it in the context of some form of evolutionary scheme."[27] This does not mean that evolution is without its critics. There are ample reasons to reject it,[28] but scientists have no alternate naturalistic theory that explains better the origin and development of life, and their anti-supernaturalism makes it impossible for them seriously to consider a creationist account. Evolutionary theory persists, and with it comes a belief that life as evolving is constantly moving in an upward, progressive, positive direction. Some have also applied evolutionary theory to the social sciences. Such social Darwinism goes beyond optimism about progress of the human race biologically; it posits that socially, morally, etc., mankind is also advancing upwards.

Despite this great optimism about the future, in the twentieth century some of the most negative implications of science and technology have also become apparent. The advent of nuclear, biological, and chemical warfare has shown the evil to which scientific knowledge can be applied. Moreover, scientific advances in industry and the like have also fostered the increasing pollution of our environment. With the gradual depletion of natural resources, the hole in the ozone layer, and other results of the scientific encroachment upon life, many wonder how long our planet can continue to sustain life. Few would argue that we should or can scrap scientific advances and go back to premodern conditions, but there are serious questions about what sort of world we will leave for future generations.

This, then, is the basic picture of modernity. Many have subscribed to its program along the way and some still believe in its fundamental principles, but at the close of the twentieth century many are calling for a change of perspective. Describing their dissatisfaction with various elements and implications of the modern worldview, Joe Holland and David Griffin level the following charges against it:

> Thus, we see the negative climax of the modern scientific promise of freedom and progress: ever more destructive wars, threats of nuclear annihilation, genocide, totalitarianism, ecological poisoning, erosion of community, marginalization of the poor, and public suppression of religious Mystery. What emerged in the eighteenth century as a bold dream converts itself dialectically in the late twentieth century into a frightening nightmare. This is the cultural end of the modern world.[29]

> This worldview also promotes a technology devoted to perfecting instruments of coercion and death and an economic system in which profit is the only standard of excellence. Finally, this worldview relegates religion to illusion; of course, it can be an illusion that is useful (from the modern perspective), insofar as it promotes nationalism, militarism, and economically efficient behavior, and/or provides enough solace to individuals to keep them keeping on. But it is still an illusion.[30]

WHAT IS POSTMODERNITY?

Postmodernity refers to many different trends in various fields such as art and architecture,[31] literary criticism and interpretation, epistemology, and politics. Part of the challenge in describing postmodernity is that its developments are of such recent vintage that we need more time to pass in order to see exactly what will become of various trends. The themes to be discussed have been "brewing" for some time in the twentieth century, but not until the late 1960s and after have these themes become more conscious and explicit, and articulated as a whole vision of reality substantially different from the modern mindset. Despite some ambiguity over exactly what is involved in postmodernity, we can still trace some of its main themes. In general, we can also say that many of the main concerns of modernity are either rejected or significantly modified by postmodernism. We begin our description with David Griffin's general characterization of some major philosophical themes of the most negative forms of postmodernism:

> Philosophical postmodernism is inspired variously by pragmatism, physicalism, Lud Wittgenstein, Martin Heidegger, and Jacques Derrida and other recent French thinkers. By the use of terms that arise out of particular segments of this movement, it can be called *deconstructive* or *eliminative postmodernism*. It overcomes the modern worldview through an anti-worldview: it deconstructs or eliminates the ingredients necessary for a worldview, such as God, self, purpose, meaning, a real world, and truth as correspondence. While motivated in some

cases by the ethical concern to forestall totalitarian systems, this type
of postmodern thought issues in relativism, even nihilism. It could also
be called *ultramodernism,* in that its eliminations result from carrying
modern premises to their logical conclusions.[32]

This description is most apt for deconstructive postmodernism, but it hints
at several themes that are broadly true of the postmodern mood. Clive Marsh
offers another general explanation of postmodernism, presenting four main
themes: evolution, relativity, indeterminacy, and participation. Each of these
has certain epistemological implications. Evolution shows humanity to be
the result of random, natural processes. Hence, humans and everything else
are constantly changing and radically contingent. As a result of this radical
contingency, relativity becomes critical, for everything exists in its relations
to other things. Our beliefs and actions are products of our time and culture
in history. A further result of this contingency and relativity is that there is no
clue about the future. It is indeterminate, so mystery lies at the heart of reality.
Hence, each person must focus on the present moment and make the most of
it. Finally, because we participate in the evolutionary process and are related
in various ways to all that is, we must reject the notion of humans as isolated
observers who can watch disinterestedly what goes on. Instead, all knowers
participate in what is to be known.[33]

These summary statements by Griffin and Marsh are very helpful, but more
can be said.[34] In what follows, I shall offer a description of major emphases.

Postmodern Epistemology

The differences between modern and postmodern epistemology are substantial, and they create major differences of approach to topics such as knowledge, truth, and objectivity. Because it would be hard to imagine many of
postmodernity's emphases apart from its epistemology, I shall explain that
epistemology in some detail. With Descartes, philosophy took what is called
the "turn to the subject." Moreover, moderns characteristically adopt some
form of foundationalism as their theory of knowledge. In the postmodern
period, each human consciousness must still structure its understanding of the
world, but prospects of justifying one's beliefs by properly basic beliefs that
are self-evident, evident to the senses, or incorrigible are gone.

To begin to understand what is different about postmodern epistemology,
let me turn briefly to Michel Foucault, a leading postmodern figure. One of
Foucault's most notorious ideas is his proclamation of the death of man. In
The Order of Things he writes, "it is comforting, however, and a source of
profound relief to think that man is only a recent invention, a figure not yet
two centuries old, a new wrinkle in our knowledge, and that he will disappear
again as soon as that knowledge has discovered a new form."[35]

This sounds tremendously pessimistic and even nihilistic, but it needs explanation. Charles Davis explains that Foucault uses "man" to refer specifically to the modern subject (the knower whose consciousness structures its understanding of the world). He reserves "human being" for the wider sense of humans as subjects, a sense that goes beyond the notion of the subject fabricated by modernity. As Davis argues, Foucault's concern is with man as the subject of knowledge:

> In seeing man as a recent invention and one shortly to pass away, Foucault is drawing attention to man as an epistemological subject, namely to man as, not merely the difficult object of knowledge, but also the sovereign subject of knowledge. He is the being through whom that knowledge is attained which renders all knowledge possible. Foucault is attacking modern anthropocentrism, urging us to awaken from our anthropological sleep and pointing to the *aporias* into which our ego-centrism leads.[36]

In other words, Foucault does not wish for or anticipate the extinction of the human race, but rather rejects a certain notion of humans. The Cartesian, Enlightenment model of man as the disinterested knower who can objectively offer argument and evidence to prove his views true is what Foucault celebrates as passing away.

What has produced such pessimism about knowledge, objectivity, truth, and a story that puts together all reality in a way universally agreed upon by reason and sense experience? Several major developments in epistemology and philosophy of language have caused this dramatic shift in perspective. The first is a rejection of foundationalism, at least in its classical form, and at most in all its forms. Foundationalism has come under increasing attack over the last thirty to forty years for several reasons. A major complaint is that if classical foundationalism's criteria for proper basicality are accepted, then foundationalism should be rejected, for there is insufficient argument, evidence, and support for these criteria. Classical foundationalism held that beliefs must be supportable by ultimate beliefs that are either self-evident, evident to the senses, or incorrigible. But none of these three criteria is either self-evident, evident to the senses, or incorrigible, nor are they supported by other more basic beliefs that meet those requirements. Hence, no one should adopt foundationalism.

In place of foundationalism, postmoderns most typically adopt a coherentist theory of knowledge. Whereas foundationalism portrays knowledge as a building or a pyramid that ultimately rests on indubitable foundations, according to coherentism beliefs still must be justified by other beliefs, but no beliefs are more basic than any other. Nor are any beliefs directly in touch with experience outside the mind in a way that would confirm them as self-evident or indubitable. Instead of portraying knowledge as a building, it is now described as a web or net of interconnected beliefs. Such a view is often called a holistic theory of knowledge.[37]

But why this shift, and does it make a difference to the certainty of our knowledge? The answer begins to get to the heart of the matter. As noted when describing modernity, philosophers after Kant recognized that the mind is just as active in structuring knowledge as is the world that confronts the mind through the senses. But, if knowledge is a function of both mind and world, a nagging question remained about whether the mind could be totally objective in the knowing process. It was only a matter of time until skepticism about this rejected the ideal of pristine objectivity as an unattainable goal.

For a long time (especially in positivist thinking), it was believed that the world was just given to the mind as a set of brute facts for our inspection and objective understanding. As the twentieth century moved on, claims to objectivity have increasingly been rejected. Several developments were of crucial importance. In the late 1960s and early 1970s philosopher of science Thomas Kuhn published *The Structure of Scientific Revolutions*. Kuhn argued that despite the widely held belief that science (of all disciplines) operates with pristine objectivity and no bias in handling data, this is not so. According to Kuhn, there are no theory-neutral observations and no brute facts in our world that await our objective inspection. Instead, scientists' observations are colored by their conceptual framework, a framework that comes from their life situation, training as scientists, and knowledge of current scientific theory. No matter how hard a scientist tries to put presuppositions aside, it is impossible to do so. Inevitably, observations of data are shaped by the scientist's language, concepts, training, and experience.[38]

Kuhn distinguished what he called normal science and revolutionary science. Once a scientific paradigm like Newtonian physics is accepted, scientists work within that paradigm to explain the phenomena and data of the world. Their observations and conclusions are governed by the reigning theory. This sort of science is normal science. On the other hand, as scientists work within a paradigm, they notice certain data and problems that don't quite fit the prevailing theory. At some point, anomalies with the current paradigm become so hard to overcome that it is scrapped in favor of a new paradigm. The switch, Kuhn argued, does not come from a long, reasoned process that deductively or inductively yields the new view, but instead comes suddenly, almost like a conversion experience. This is revolutionary science, and once the revolution ends, normal science works within the new paradigm.[39]

In the early years after Kuhn's proposal appeared, there were many critics,[40] but in recent decades, despite lingering criticism, Kuhn's basic claim that all observation and reasoning is theory-laden has been widely accepted. The implications of such views are devastating to the notion of objective knowledge. If even science cannot know or be trusted to tell us the truth about the world, what hope is there of finding truth (let alone convincing anyone of it) in more abstract disciplines?

Another very influential work is Richard Rorty's *Philosophy and the Mirror of Nature*. Rorty argued that for several hundred years after Descartes, philosophy has been held captive by a certain picture of knowledge. It is the view that sees the mind as the mirror of nature. Various ideas are represented on that mirror, and then the individual compares those ideas with the world outside the mind. By these empirical and rational processes, one can ultimately support one's beliefs and so provide a foundation for knowledge. But Rorty argues that this is just not how the mind works. He explains the thesis of his work as follows:

> It is pictures rather than propositions, metaphors rather than statements, which determine most of our philosophical convictions. The picture which holds traditional philosophy captive is that of the mind as a great mirror, containing various representations—some accurate, some not—and capable of being studied by pure, nonempirical methods. Without the notion of the mind as mirror, the notion of knowledge as accuracy of representation would not have suggested itself. Without this latter notion, the strategy common to Descartes and Kant—getting more accurate representations by inspecting, repairing, and polishing the mirror, so to speak—would not have made sense.[41]

It is this picture—one that assumes the mind as a rational, objective observer (able to detect problems in representations of reality and correct them)—that must be rejected. We must recognize that this is a much more radical rejection of objectivity than the earlier philosophical complaint that sense perception is not always accurate because sense organs may malfunction or because people may view the same physical object from different vantage points. Instead, this view says that even if sense organs are functioning perfectly, and even if people have exactly the same vantage point, there is no guarantee that they will report seeing the same thing. Their conceptual framework, formed by their life experiences and by the linguistic and cultural community in which they were raised, is a major determining factor in how people view things and in what they actually perceive. If this is so for ordinary sense perception, our mindset must be even more of a factor in our understanding of abstract concepts and theories!

Prior to both Kuhn and Rorty, Willard Van Orman Quine had challenged both the foundationalist account of knowledge and the objectivity it presupposed. In his groundbreaking "Two Dogmas of Empiricism," Quine rejected the idea that all meaningful discourse can be translated or reduced into language about immediate experience. This could not be done with individual words or even with whole sentences. Instead, claimed Quine, the whole fabric of our knowledge confronts "the tribunal of experience." This does not mean we have the capacity to compare our beliefs objectively with experience to see if they match. Rather, Quine, incorporating the growing view that what we know and understand is a product of the communities in which we were raised, wrote the following:

> The totality of our so-called knowledge or beliefs, from the most casual matters of geography and history to the profoundest laws of atomic physics or even of pure mathematics and logic, *is a man-made fabric* which impinges on experience only along the edges. Or, to change the

figure, total science is like a field of force whose boundary conditions are experience. A conflict with experience at the periphery occasions readjustments in the interior of the field. Truth values have to be redistributed over some statements. Re-evaluation of some statements entails re-evaluation of others, because of their logical interconnec-tions—the logical laws being in turn simply certain further elements of the field. . . . But the total field is so underdetermined by its boundary conditions, experience, that there is much latitude of choice as to what statements to re-evaluate in the light of any single contrary experience. *No particular experiences are linked with any particular statements in the interior of the field,* except indirectly through considerations of equilibrium affecting the field as a whole (italics mine).42

These are remarkable claims! If all our language is man-made, then the world is not simply mirrored on our mind, allowing us objectively to read off the results. Nor do our observations and reasoning "see things as they are." What we claim to know is actually an interconnected web of beliefs that touch reality, experience, only at the borders of that web. But note that Quine says that the total field of our knowledge is underdetermined by experience. This means that experience and our contact with it are such that there simply is insufficient evidence from experience for us to know which beliefs are true or false or whether our whole perspective on the world is right or wrong. There is certainly no way to move back to indubitable foundations grounded in experience, especially when Quine says that no particular experiences are linked with *any particular statements* (beliefs) within the web of our beliefs. Hence, we are free to reevaluate any statement we like and make adjustments in other statements for the sake of logical consistency in the "overall story" we tell, but that does not mean we are in a position to know or prove that the whole story (or even individual statements within it) matches the world.

Quine clearly rejects the "myth of the given," the idea that the world is just there for us as a set of brute, theory-neutral facts which we can objectively know. Instead, what we see is our structuring of reality from the perspective of our own conceptual grid. As to truth, for most postmoderns the corre-spondence theory of truth is out. They wish they could say that their beliefs correspond to the world, but the human condition is such that we are in no position to know this through either our senses or reason. Our observations and reasoning are too theory-laden to allow that. Thus, postmoderns typically adopt some form of the coherence theory of truth, the pragmatic theory of truth, or a combination of both. According to the former, what is true is the set of sentences that fit together without contradicting one another (think here of Quine's picture of an interconnected web of beliefs that may require read-justing some of its components for the sake of logical consistency). According to the latter, what is true is what offers the most workable results when believed. Earlier pragmatists held that truth as correspondence was possible, but thought that for something to be true, it should do more than tell us that;

it should guide us to beliefs and actions that have the most desirable results.[43] Postmodern pragmatists disagree about the matter of correspondence. One cannot know what matches the world; the best one can do is choose beliefs that seem to work for him or her.[44]

In response, one might wonder if there isn't some way to validate one world-view as opposed to another. If every culture and person has their version of reality, isn't there still some grand, universal story that tells us which narratives are true and which are false? Postmoderns, drawing out the logical conclusions of their views, answer that there is no grand story, no "meta-narrative" that will somehow make sense of everything. A very influential work with this as one of its major themes is Jean-François Lyotard's *The Postmodern Condition: A Report on Knowledge*. In fact, many date the introduction of the term *postmodern* from its use in Lyotard's book. Lyotard argues that in premodern societies there were conventions about who would tell the story and who must listen. Of course, this allowed those in power to repeat the account of reality that kept them in power. In the modern era, there are still narratives, but they must be legitimized. For moderns, science legitimizes and verifies the account of reality offered. This seems to free people from the authoritarian oppression of the premodern, but what actually happens is that science depends on a narrative of its own, a certain story about how we attain, verify, and falsify beliefs. Lyotard argues that this meta-narrative, too, is authoritarian and must be rejected. What takes its place? Lyotard answers that there is no grand narrative, no big picture that makes sense of everything. There are only our individual narratives, our individual perceptions of reality as we see it.[45]

This repudiation of our mental and sensory faculties' abilities to know the world aright may seem perplexing since, as Diogenes Allen argues, Kant with his distinction between things-in-themselves and things-as-appearances fundamentally agreed that we do not have direct access to the world as it is but still believed that concepts of pure and practical reason were universal and that the mind and the senses can construct reality in a way agreed upon by all people.[46] Why are postmoderns so skeptical about this? In addition to items already mentioned, Diogenes Allen argues that cultural relativism is a key factor. Not only has epistemological foundationalism been rejected, but also denied are all claims of any viewpoint to be foundational in the sense that it has a privileged status of being assumed as true and exempt from critique. For someone to hold their perspective as exempt from objection and unquestionably true (in a correspondence sense) is to show one's bigotry and confusion about the status of knowledge. Whether or not we agree with Allen that cultural relativism is the key ingredient in postmodernism, it seems indubitable that cultural relativism is very important. Allen explains:

> When cultural relativism is added to the commonplaces we have mentioned, we then get the phenomenon of a postmodernist creed in philosophy and literature. It is only when the concepts we use in science,

literature, and philosophy are said to be wholly imbedded in culture, along with the obvious fact that cultures differ, that we get the heady mixture of postmodernism. We are plunged into its particular kind of relativism. We not only construct the world, so that all knowledge, value, and meaning are relative to human beings, as Idealists since Kant have argued, but now the radical conclusion is drawn that there is no reality that is *universally* constructed because people in different periods of history and in different societies construct it differently. There is no definitive procedure or universal basis to settle disputes in the natural sciences, in ethics, and in the interpretation of literature. Every domain of inquiry and every value is relative to a culture and even to subcultures.[47]

In short, according to postmodernism, there is no absolute truth, or if there is, no one is in a position to know what it is. Through all of this, I have hinted at another key element in this mix. Everyone is said to be a product of their cultural and linguistic community. It is this latter point, a point about a different understanding of what language is and how it works, to which we must now turn. In describing modernity, we noted that the prevailing theories of linguistic meaning were referential or representational. As a result of J. L. Austin's work and the later philosophy of Wittgenstein (as seen in his *Philosophical Investigations*), there has been a shift to a theory of meaning as *use*. Wittgenstein and Austin proposed and explained their theories from the 1930s through the 1950s. Let me focus on Wittgenstein, for his use theory has been most influential.

Wittgenstein's earlier philosophy (*Tractatus Logico-Philosophicus*) espoused a referential theory of language which he called the picture theory of language. A sentence is a picture of a state of affairs. In his later philosophy, Wittgenstein critiqued and rejected this earlier theory. He came to see words as having no fixed reference that is their invariable meaning, regardless of context. Rather, Wittgenstein viewed words and sentences as tools in a toolbox with which one could do a variety of things, depending on the context. There is no invariant referent for each word, but instead, the meaning of a word, phrase, or sentence depends on its use in a context.

Wittgenstein introduced the concept of language as a complex of language-games. He recognized that language, our verbal behavior, is embedded in a context broader than mere words. It is embedded in a whole matrix of non-verbal and verbal behavior appropriate to a given social situation and cultural milieu. Hence, a language-game is a form of life, a complete way of doing some activity, including verbal and nonverbal behavior. We do not first learn a language and then learn a culture with its particular social conventions. Nor do we learn the culture first and later the language. Rather in learning a language we learn a culture with its social conventions about nonverbal and verbal behavior, i.e., we learn a whole form of life.

How many language-games are there? According to Wittgenstein, countless numbers, for there are countless ways language may be used in various situations. And the number and nature of language-games is not set or fixed; it can change to meet new needs. Wittgenstein says, "for a *large* class of cases—though not for all—in which we employ the word 'meaning' it can be defined thus: the meaning of a word is its use in the language."[48] The same is true for sentences, for we should "look at the sentence as an instrument, and at its sense as its employment."[49]

To illustrate what Wittgenstein means by countless numbers of language-games, think of the act of raising a hand. Place that activity in a classroom of students interacting with a teacher. Now think of it occurring in a church service during a time of worship. Yet again, think of that hand raising as one stands on the street corner trying to hail a cab. In each case, the physical or nonverbal behavior is the same, but its use in each context gives the behavior its peculiar meaning, and the behavior in different contexts denotes distinct language-games.

Two more points about language-games are important for our purposes. One is that in learning a language-game, one learns a form of life, a way of doing things that is complete and distinct in itself. Each language-game has its own rules of procedure, and one plays the game by following the rules. For example, someone who moves a chess piece to capture an opponent's piece and says "Strike three, you're out" doesn't know the language-game. It is not that he has violated knowledge that is traceable to some indubitable foundational beliefs about the world. Rather, every language-game has rules and procedures for accomplishing one move or another. The person who says "Strike three" in the chess game simply doesn't understand how to play the game. What he needs is training and practice, just as does the person who thinks the answer to 2 + 2 in the language-game of mathematics is "false."

Wittgenstein's further point is that the language-games are logically independent of one another. Hence, the rules that govern the language-game of religion are independent of those that govern the language-games of science or history. Moreover, even if the language-games of history and science involve empirical investigation, that does not make them identical in how such investigation functions or what it proves. Nor does it mean that anything else in the two games is identical or even overlaps.

The notion of meaning as use and the identification of various language-games seems unobjectionable, especially since it does not rule out words referring to objects, persons, or events. Wittgenstein never ruled out words having reference, but only argued that a word's meaning and reference depend on its context (its use in a given language-game), and that decisions that words will be used in such ways in those contexts is a matter of social and linguistic convention. This in no way rules out a referential element to language, nor does it necessitate social or intellectual relativism. It merely recognizes how language works.

The specific idea postmoderns find so important and adapt for their own purposes is the notion that each person is a product of his or her linguistic and cultural community. Language is not learned apart from culture or culture apart from language; they come together. But then, in learning a language-game one learns a particular account of some aspect of reality, an account that is logically independent and distinct from other accounts and other language-games. As Wittgenstein explains, our perception of the world, "our seeing," is always "seeing as," i.e., it is guided and formed in light of the concepts, language, and culture in which we were raised. We cannot escape our conceptual grid, nor the language-games that we have learned to play. We may learn other language-games, but we are still products of those various language-games.

Is there not some grand language-game, an overarching game that tells us whether, for example, the language-game of Christianity or that of Buddhism is correct? In Wittgenstein's philosophy there is no such language-game. There is only a description of the many ways people use language in different contexts to perform various activities. All of this fits well with the other elements of postmodern epistemology already described. This emphasis on language as constitutive of cultures and persons is a large part of why postmodernity is called "the linguistic turn" (as opposed to the modern "subjective turn").[50]

Naturalism, But . . .

Previously, I noted that the predominant scientific paradigm for much of the modern era was Newtonian physics. In the twentieth century, before the dawn of the postmodern period, science switched paradigms to quantum physics and relativity theory. I shall discuss this in greater detail in chapter 4 on process theology, but I offer several points now. First, in contrast to Newtonian physics, which saw the universe as composed of static, changeless bits of matter that interact according to set natural laws, the new science claims that things in our world are interrelated in a continuous process of change and becoming. Even in the most solid bits of matter (at the atomic and subatomic levels) things are not static but in motion. Moreover, in virtue of these features of matter coupled with relativity theory, what a thing is and how it is to be understood can only be determined in terms of its relations with other things. Not only do individual things interact to make up wholes, but the opposite is true as well. As Murphy explains:

> Against the view that parts unilaterally determine the characteristics and behavior of wholes, these theorists maintain that *irreducible* features of the whole also help determine the characteristics of the parts. Biochemists were among the first to notice this; chemical reactions do not work the same in a petri dish as they do within a living organism. Thus, the higher-level system, including the entity and its environment, needs to be considered in giving a complete causal account. So a postmodern rejection of atomism involves recognition of two-way influences between part and whole.[51]

So the universe is not filled with discreet bits of isolated matter, but rather with "pockets" of energy/mass that are constantly changing and interacting with other such things. Moreover, as opposed to Newtonian physics which held that physical things interact according to set physical laws, quantum physics claims that there is a certain indeterminacy at least at the atomic and sub-atomic levels of existence. This means that rather than things functioning according to physically determining laws, there is genuine contingency even in otherwise inanimate things. Many have applied Heisenberg's indeterminacy principle to human freedom, and used it to argue for indeterministic free will.[52]

What does this mean for God acting in our world? Some argue that relativity theory suggests that we cannot be entirely sure that God couldn't act in our world in unexpected and unpredictable ways.[53] Nonetheless, most postmoderns still view the universe as a closed system that doesn't admit supernatural events. Postmoderns aren't ready to return to premodern conceptions that allow supernatural interventions in our world. Biblical accounts of miracles are still seen as myths.

But that is not the end of the story. Religious language is no longer deemed nonsense and meaningless, for religion and religious discourse occupy their own language-game. To be sure, it is not a language-game where statements can be empirically verified or falsified. But like other language-games, religious language has meaning and presents a given perspective on reality. Moreover, it has become more fashionable to speak of God and his action in our lives and world. Of course it is not always clear whether such speech should be taken as part of the language-game of religion (which many think makes no pretensions about making statements of fact) or whether the speaker really thinks she is talking of things that actually occur in our world.

Although some varieties of postmodernism include God, that does not mean the God envisioned has much in common with the God of the Judaeo-Christian tradition. Whether it is the God of theologians of hope, the process God, the New Age God (or gods), or the liberation and feminist notions of God, there are significant differences from the traditional God. Still, many postmoderns who believe in God claim to sense this God's presence in special, unusual ways. David Griffin's postmodern theology, which relies heavily on Whitehead's philosophy, appeals to presensory or non-sensory perception, called prehension, which differs from ordinary sense perception. As Griffin explains, ordinary sense perception cannot provide adequate evidence of a real world beyond ourselves (note the adoption of postmodern epistemology as opposed to modern notions). But there is a primitive form of perception shared by humans, dogs, insects, etc., which lets us "know" that there is a real world out there. Through this nonsensory perception we can sense any number of things beyond us, including God (of course, for Griffin it is Whitehead's process God).[54] Whether it is through such nonsensory perception, or ESP and channeling in New Age thinking, or some other means, many postmoderns conclude there is a God and they claim to experience him. As we saw in chapter 2, other postmodern theologies are also willing to believe in God so long as it is a God beyond Being.

While these metaphysical notions have a certain continuity with modern views, there are also significant differences. The predominant view is still naturalism and anti-supernaturalism, but at least postmoderns allow religious language to be meaningful and to be about something that somehow can be experienced. Quantum physics and relativity theory, with their doctrines of the interconnectedness and motion of all things, suggest that everything is striving together in a process of becoming. This is in stark contrast to Newton's doctrine of static, isolated, unconnected matter. This metaphysical doctrine is analogous *in ontology* to what Quine's and the coherentist's *epistemology* says about beliefs as an interconnected web of ideas, none more foundational than any others. So, postmodernism holds naturalism, but not the exact version told by modernity, nor with the same implications for belief, experience, and meaningfulness of God.

Human Freedom in Community

According to modernity, human freedom and individuality are supreme values, and should be given every opportunity for expression. Unfortunately, emphasis on the individual tends to isolate and fragment people and to encourage them to pursue only their own interests. In contrast, the postmodern spirit puts a high premium on relatedness and community. Human freedom is not to be squelched, but only used to further personal goals and development as part of a larger program for growth of the whole community. This emphasis on community means that the rugged individual, isolated from the rest of the community is no longer the ideal. Such individualism has led to modern ills such as erosion of family and community and pollution (even destruction) of the environment to further personal gain (usually economic) by exploitation.

In contrast, the postmodern notion of community includes not only human beings but also the natural world as part of a cosmic community. Ronald Allen writes of the significance of community in postmodern thinking:

> The postmodern vision regains emphasis on communality from pre-modernity. In the best communities, all realities live in relationship with other realities in mutuality, encouragement, support. Like their premodern counterparts, postmodern people think of nature as living. Humankind and nature live together in partnership. Even the tiniest forms of life and the most (seemingly) inanimate have their own integrity.
>
> Such community is the context in which entities achieve maximum fulfillment; the community itself is enhanced by the fulfillment of its members. Yet postmodernism treasures the sacredness of the individual. Communal decisions are judged, in part, by their effect on individuals. Individual welfare cannot be casually sacrificed in the name of community.[55]

This should resonate with those familiar with contemporary emphases such as building community through involvement of all members working together and protecting the environment. Note as well the emphasis on mutuality and partnership. As Allen says, emphasis on community in a sense returns to premodern thinking, but the community envisioned is much different. Rather than community glued together by the top-heavy authoritarian control of a king or the church, the community envisioned by postmoderns is one where all members are equals and partners, not only in sharing responsibilities but also in sharing power. These ideas have implications for relationships in the home, the church, the business office, and society at large. Individual development is critical, but always in the context of community rather than at the expense of others.

This facet of the postmodern spirit fits other postmodern themes well. The interconnectedness of communities and social relationships, so to speak, mirrors what science tells us about a proper understanding of the natural world. A universe of interconnected matter in the process of becoming together with all other developing things is analogous to postmodern social, economic, and political agendas. It is also worth noting that this communalism fits with many postmodern theologians' "rediscovery" of the doctrine of the Trinity. God is seen as communal at the most basic level of his being. Likewise, theologies that emphasize God's relatedness to the world are very attractive to the postmodern mind.

Notice also how this meshes with certain postmodern epistemological doctrines. The notion of people being shaped by their linguistic and cultural communities again stresses our interdependence on one another. As products of our culture and upbringing, the idea of the isolated individual looking out only for his or her own good makes little sense. We should desire to give back to the community that "made us." Moreover, the epistemological holism that sees our knowledge and belief structures as an interconnected web of beliefs, none more basic than others, is an apt parallel epistemologically to what postmoderns say about social and political realities.

Collectivism, but not totalitarianism, is the order of the day. Economically, this does not rule in socialism and rule out capitalism, but it does suggest that the kind of capitalism that makes a vast gulf between rich and poor, and that perpetuates the oppression and exploitation of the latter, must be rejected. If everyone in a capitalistic society can benefit and share the wealth, that is fine. Otherwise, some form of socialism guaranteeing sharing of wealth would be preferable. The whole community growing by virtue of each member developing as part of the whole is the key.

The Goodness of Human Nature!?

In the twentieth century, even prior to the advent of the postmodern ethos, there were mixed signals about the goodness of human nature. The assorted atrocities of that century have disillusioned many to the point of seeing human nature and the human condition as hopeless and meaningless. In spite of this despair, existentialists said that we are given radical freedom, which we must embrace and use to create our own meaning in an otherwise absurd and brutal world. But, if there are questions about the inherent goodness of human nature, shouldn't we be a bit fearful of what will happen if people embrace and use their freedom to make their own meaning?

Just as the late modern period witnessed this tension with regard to human nature, so postmoderns have, at times, held seemingly schizophrenic views on this issue. On the one hand, postmoderns are painfully aware of the human capacity for inhumanity to others and for destruction of the very world we live in. Moreover, since there is no universal method for knowing what is true and right, modernity's optimism that people will use reason to discern what is right and then do it is unwarranted. The more pessimistic postmoderns seem nihilistic about everything, including human beings.

On the other hand, there are signs of optimism about human nature in postmodern quarters. For one thing, emphasis on community and mutual development of the whole seems to presuppose that everyone and everything is worth "redeeming," if possible. Moreover, the modern attitude that if people are educated and given economic opportunity, they will be responsible citizens, is still heard today, and not just from politicians. And, as we shall see, some forms of postmodern religion amount to a deifying of everything, including humans. But, if those religions believe we are divine, must there not be great optimism about human nature and goodness? Isn't there reason to be optimistic about the future we will create for future generations? Of course, there are still some who deny the equality of all people and want to use power to exploit and oppress others, but the rest of us can keep an eye on such people and, hopefully, keep them under control.

Postmoderns, then, send mixed messages about human nature. However, with all the self-realization and self-help programs and all the hype about psychotherapy and the like helping us realize our potential, despite the horrible things that humans have done to one another in the twentieth century, there is, according to many postmoderns, room for optimism about the future.

Science and Progress

The postmodern perspective regarding science and progress is predictable in light of the other elements of the postmodern mood. Postmoderns know that in the twentieth century alone science has made dramatic advances in so many fields, and most of those advances have made life more enjoyable and better. Scientific discoveries in the fields of medicine and genetics hold out great hope for people with otherwise incurable diseases. Reproductive technologies now allow people to have children who could not do so previously. Similarly, developments in communications technology have been dramatic. All of these advances are welcome, and few postmoderns would decry them.

On the other hand, postmoderns are painfully aware (and frequently remind us) of the destructive capabilities of various advancements in science. Not only is nuclear annihilation a continuing threat, but other scientific inventions are poisoning our environment. Because the postmodern concern for community includes the natural world as part of that community, ecological concerns are very high on the agenda of postmoderns. Scientific and technological developments that threaten to deplete natural resources or harm the environment are denounced.

So, science and technology are viewed as both blessing and bane, and from the postmodern perspective not all scientific discoveries are progress. In some cases we must wait to see whether scientific advances are beneficial to life on this planet.

Finally, evolution remains very heavily entrenched. It is hard to know whether postmoderns refuse to reject it—in spite of so much counter-evidence—because of their view that no one really knows the truth and, anyway, evolution is still a useful theory, or whether evolution's stranglehold on contemporary science and culture stems from a belief that the only other alternative (creationism) cannot be accepted in virtue of its supernaturalism. Whatever the case, scientists continually revise evolutionary theory in attempts to plug one leak after another. With no other naturalistic theory on the horizon, evolution will not likely soon disappear.

Moreover, evolution fits nicely with some of the other postmodern doctrines. For example, concern for community and mutual respect for all living things fits hand in glove with the idea that everything that exists ultimately comes from evolutionary processes working with the same eternally existent matter. If we are already ontologically connected with everything else in our world through the process of evolution, the most reasonable response to other life-forms (and to other people) is mutual respect and preservation. Add to this quantum physics and relativity theory, which also stress relatedness and interconnectedness, and what postmoderns espouse in their social, political, and economic theory (as well as in theology) seems the natural conclusion.

GOD IN CONTEMPORARY THOUGHT

With the foregoing descriptions of modernity and postmodernity, we are now ready to examine views of God amid these changing milieu. I shall divide the discussion into two main sections, one dealing with theologies presented against the backdrop of modernity and the other describing theologies best seen as postmodern.

Contemporary Theologies in the Modern Mindset

KANT. Our discussion begins with Immanuel Kant, but we can be brief in light of what has already been said. As noted, Kant distinguished the noumenal from the phenomenal. The former contains things that are not objects of empirical investigation, and hence are not objects of knowledge. Among things that Kant put in the noumenal realm is God. Though God's existence cannot be proved, Kant believed that it must be a postulate of practical reason, necessary for moral governance of our world.

HEGEL. Next is Hegel (1770–1831) who is an extremely important figure for both philosophy and theology. Much of contemporary theology in non-evangelical perspective reacts in one way or another to Hegel. Hegel wanted to build an all-encompassing philosophy that covered all of reality. To do so, Hegel could not pit religion and philosophy against one another; rather, his philosophy had to incorporate religious entities. Moreover, his goal was a philosophy that unifies all things without destroying each item's distinctness by relating it to the whole. As a result, Hegel needed a religion for his final philosophy that would unify all of reality without destroying the uniqueness of each part.

Hegel concluded that Christianity was the right religion for this project. It already contained the proper content of his final philosophy; it only awaited speculative reason to transform it into the proper form. Christianity was deemed the appropriate religion for this final philosophy because within it there is a union of the infinite and the finite, and this union joins finite and infinite while allowing them to maintain their distinctness. This happens in Christianity, Hegel reasoned, in two important respects. The first is the person Jesus Christ. In him are united the infinite and the finite, but this union is such that it does not obliterate the difference and distinctness of each nature. The second way Christianity unites finite with infinite is in its teaching about God's relation to us through Jesus Christ. God in grace moves toward us and we in freedom move toward him to establish this relationship. Moreover, in believing in and worshiping Christ, we worship someone who is like us but like God as well. Hence, our relation to God joins the finite creature with an infinite God without destroying the distinctness of either.[56]

But what is Hegel's God like? In studying Hegel's philosophy one finds no single conception of God. Instead, one can identify at least five distinct notions of God. The first comes from Hegel's *Phenomenology of Spirit*. In the section on the unhappy consciousness, Hegel refers to a God.[57] However, since Hegel is talking about self-consciousness, many claim that this God is nothing more than a projection of the human mind in an attempt to unite itself with itself. So an initial notion of God for Hegel sees him as a psychological projection.

Second, Hegel also sees God as equal to Spirit, but not in the Judaeo-Christian sense of God as an immaterial being. In chapter 2, I described this view as portraying God as a force or general consciousness uniting all finite consciousnesses. This notion of God does not allow him to be a person who has personal dealings with us, but it does make him very immanent in our world.

A third notion of God in Hegel's work portrays him as equal to the infinite.

In various works, Hegel speaks of philosophy rising to infinity. Hegel calls this a rise to divinity or a divine viewpoint. Thus "God" or "Divinity" seem to be equivalent to transcending, all-encompassing thought. Hegel, of course, thought he had built a philosophy that did rise to this infinite, divine vantage point. In this conception of God, God is transcendent but is not necessarily a person.

A fourth concept of God comes from Hegel's understanding of the nature of religion. Hegel believed every genuine religion to be a relation of the human to the divine in which the divine is both other than the human and yet inwardly related to it. Hegel enumerated three basic traits of every genuine religion that are involved in relating the divine to the human: feeling, religious representation, and cult. As to the first, it involves being geared to the felt, but it cannot be a totally subjective feeling; there must be an object. Moreover, that object must be higher than a human being so that it can be worshiped as God, not as an idol. Hegel then says that representation is the human use of language and thought (which are limited) to point to an object which is infinite. This infinite object must be radically other than us or else the relation would not be genuinely religious, but it cannot be so totally other that it is entirely inaccessible and our representations of it point to nothing or to a something of which we know nothing. Hence, in order for us to make sense of the object of our feeling, we derive symbols which, while finite, point to an infinite about which we know something. That representation helps us think about and relate to the object of our feeling. Cult, the third element, is how we act out the relation between the divine and the human. It is a tangible way to keep our feelings and representations together. Hegel thought that the cultic life aspects which most unite divine and human in this way are baptism and holy communion.[58]

From this description of genuine religions we can say that the fourth concept of God in Hegel's thought sees God as the object toward which religious representation points symbolically. He is totally transcendent and does not seem to act in the world. He may be personal, but he is so totally other that it is impossible to know exactly how to describe him. Hegel's understanding of Judaism's God as a transcendent God with whom we cannot be united may well be an example of this conception of the divine.

A final notion of God sees God as Christ, but for Hegel it is not entirely clear whether he means this literally or whether he sees Christ as a symbol for what he means by the union of the transcendent and the immanent. In either case, Hegel sees Christ as uniting the infinite and finite in two ways. In Christ as incarnate, God and man are united, but beyond the incarnation, Christianity instructs its followers to believe in and follow Christ. This means that we should worship a person who is other than us (transcendent in that sense) and yet at the same time is the same as we (immanent in the sense that he is human as we are). So our relation to Christ further illustrates the union of the transcendent and immanent.[59]

This final conception is probably the closest to anything in the traditional Christian concept of God, but it isn't clear whether Hegel wants us to understand Jesus as literally God. Hegel seldom speaks of Christ as God; more often he is called the God-man to show his important function of uniting the immanent with the transcendent. Hence, it is dubious that this notion of God has much to do with traditional, evangelical theology.

In sum, Hegel's concepts of God incorporate many themes of modernity. The emphasis on the ability of consciousness to structure the world and the role of reason in building a coherent account of all reality are very modern. Hegel's stress on the relatedness of all things prefigures postmodern emphases, but his concern to unite distinct things without destroying their distinctness and individuality has affinities to both modern and postmodern concerns.

SCHLEIERMACHER AND LIBERAL THEOLOGY. After Hegel, we turn to classical liberal theologians. These theologians worked squarely within the modern mindset and took very seriously the implications of Kant's rejection of metaphysics, various developments in biblical criticism that undermined confidence in the veracity of Scripture, and the implications of evolution as well. Key classical liberal thinkers are Friedrich Schleiermacher (1768–1834), Albrecht Ritschl (1822–1889), Ernst Troeltsch (1865–1923), Adolf von Harnack (1851–1930), and in America Walter Rauschenbusch (1861–1918) and Shailer Mathews (1863–1941). Space does not allow handling all of them, but we should consider Schleiermacher as the father of the movement, and add some further comments about the general perspective of theological liberalism.

According to Enlightenment rationality, beliefs should be held only if supported by sufficient evidence. Humean objections to natural theology and Kant's critiques of traditional theistic arguments for God's existence made it difficult to find sufficient evidence for theistic belief. Whereas many grounded religion and especially belief in God on the foundation of Scripture, the results of biblical higher critics undermined Scripture as a support for religion. If God is unknowable through historical events and documents (the Bible), then what is the basis of religion? Liberal theologians shifted the basis of religion to religious experience.

Schleiermacher is considered the father of this liberal tradition in theology. His two best-known works are *On Religion, Speeches to its Cultured Despisers* (1799) and *The Christian Faith* (1821–1822). In the latter work Schleiermacher claimed that religion is based on a feeling of absolute dependence. This feeling is identical with the consciousness of being in relation with God. Richard Niebuhr argues that several ideas go into a proper understanding of what Schleiermacher meant. First, this feeling of absolute dependence is also a person's feeling of identity "through which the individual is conscious of his inner uniqueness."[60] According to Niebuhr, this means that the identity or life unity of a person is not taken from any intellectual or volitional relations that the self takes from other persons or forces. Second, Schleiermacher regarded this feeling of absolute dependence as identical with what he labeled "immediate self-consciousness" or "God-consciousness." We are able to discern this feeling, he said, because self-consciousness involves thinking and willing which allow us to relate rationally to our world. Through all of this we can distinguish our feeling of absolute dependence in relation to God from a feeling of relative dependence to things in the world. This happens because "in the latter a person stands in relations of community and reciprocity with nature and society, while in the feeling of absolute dependence there is no reciprocity present."[61] Hence, we can differentiate a feeling of dependence on God from one of dependence on relative things in our world. What does this mean for how Schleiermacher understands God? Niebuhr explains:

> The original meaning of the word "God" is not a concept of perfect being, or the like, but the felt relation of absolute dependence. Hence, religion arises not in ideas, nor—for that matter—in willing, but in the immediate consciousness of what Schleiermacher described to Lucke as "an immediate existence-relationship." . . . In fact, then, religion is more than a determination of feeling; it is the name Schleiermacher gives to the personal self-consciousness in which the feeling of absolute dependence and consciousness of the world coexist and must achieve or receive a living, stable order.[62]

According to Schleiermacher, every great religion arises in a particular social and historical form. Christianity is totally associated with its founder Jesus Christ. Our relationship to God in all its parts is also a relation in which our relation to Christ is actively present. Niebuhr concludes,

> Hence, Schleiermacher revived in his conception of the feeling of being absolutely dependent the Augustinian notion of the inseparability of the knowledge of the soul and the knowledge of God; at the same time he originated the distinctive form of modern Protestant theology—Christocentrism, or Christ as the center of the individual's inner religious consciousness.[63]

In assessing these views, it is hard to say whether Schleiermacher's God is a being distinct from us or merely a projection of human self-consciousness. In either case, it seems to be a view that makes God very immanent, even if not a distinct person with whom we can interact. As to the broader movement of liberal theology, Langdon Gilkey's description is especially helpful. After Schleiermacher, the next great member of this tradition is Albrecht Ritschl. Ritschl rejected appeals both to metaphysics and to religious experience as the basis for Christian doctrine. Instead, in concert with Kant's views, he emphasized the moral nature of man as the basis of religion. Ritschl held that religion provides the basic attitude toward reality and the basic values that make historical and personal development of humans as moral beings possible.[64] As Gilkey notes, the various liberal theologies that followed based religion on either religious experience, the moral nature of man, or some combination thereof. Rational inquiry, religious experience, or moral experience were the bases of these theologies.[65]

As Gilkey explains, these nineteenth-century liberal theologies reflected the spirit and guiding ideas of the age:

> To that scientific, immanentist, optimistic, and progressivist age, such traditional concepts as the supernatural and the transcendent, and the orthodox beliefs in miraculous intervention, in the fall of man into depravity, in the inability of man to know or to do the good, and in an ultimate condemnation of most men for eternity, seemed barbaric in the extreme, a function of the priestly gloom of earlier times, and by no means acceptable to a modern man.[66]

In place of such ideas, liberalism adopted beliefs more consistent with the secular attitudes of the age. In particular, the idea of reality as an immanent evolutionary process of development moving things over time from relative chaos to higher forms of life and culture was prevalent. "The divine force . . . whose immanent work in the process has brought about such progress toward higher, more coherent, more adaptive, and more moral goals, is what men have called God."[67]

Gilkey also notes that liberal theology was secular in that it accepted as normative criteria for theology the predominant philosophical, scientific, and moral ideas of the culture, and in that it saw Christian faith as relevant to modern man because of its creative potentialities for transforming lives of people in their historical and cultural situations.[68] Gilkey sees liberal theology as accommodating itself to modernity in four creative ways. First, in light of the advances, discoveries, and new theories in physical science, the notion of Christian truth as divinely given infallible propositions about whatever biblical writers discussed was rejected. Instead, doctrinal claims were seen as human constructs that tried to explain the mystery of reality. They are relative to time and place, but as mere human symbols intended to explain creatively the nature of reality, doctrines are not in conflict with accepted scientific or historical knowledge of the day.

A second and corollary accommodation is that doctrines themselves were no longer to be seen as eternal, unchanging truths, but as statements for a given age and time meant to reflect the cultural and historical situation of the theologian's own times.

Third, Christian life was no longer seen as directed by divine rules of holiness in preparation for achieving heaven upon death. Rather, the purpose of Christian living was to live a life devoted to making a difference in the present world. Promotion of worldly values such as justice, freedom, and welfare of all peoples (in a kind of social gospel) now became the point and emphasis of Christian lifestyle.

A final way that liberal theology accommodated itself to the modern world was to claim that a Christian's primary obligation is to love and tolerate all people, regardless of whether one shared their doctrinal commitments or not. Rather than separating over views deemed heretical, love and tolerance of those with whom one differed was the order of the day.[69] One is reminded often of the phrase "the fatherhood of God and the brotherhood of men" as descriptive of the central message of this movement. This stress on tolerance of personal freedom to hold one's own beliefs is very modern.[70]

SØREN KIERKEGAARD.   Søren Kierkegaard (1813–1855) was a contemporary of Schleiermacher and Ritschl, but his theology went in a decidedly different direction. Much of Kierkegaard's work is a deliberate reaction against the philosophy of Hegel and the Hegelianized brand of Christianity among his Danish countrymen.

Hegel wanted to produce the all-inclusive philosophical system that would rationally account for everything. As this was applied to Christianity as practiced in Denmark, it resulted in a dead orthodoxy in the church. Kierkegaard complained that Hegel's system, which treated truth as a set of objective propositions laid out side by side, actually left out the most important thing. What no conceptual scheme could ever capture is the existing individual in the act of becoming. Human beings are free and constantly changing; a set of ideas is a static object that cannot capture what it is to exist. Hence, life (Christian life especially) does not involve dispassionate reflection on a set of ideas, but rather passionate, personal involvement with the living God.

Much of Kierkegaard's concern was to articulate what it means to be a Christian, a disciple—and to become one himself. Being a Christian does not involve knowing a bunch of objective facts and performing a set of religious rituals. Rather, claimed Kierkegaard, it consists in becoming a spiritual contemporary with Christ. In all of this, Kierkegaard believed Hegel had led people astray from the true nature of Christianity.

Though it might seem that Kierkegaard's objective was to lead people away from philosophy and back to the Bible, that was not his point. The Bible, too, was a historical object, an objective set of propositions. Kierkegaard was well aware of the negative critique of Scripture at the hands of the higher critics, but even more, he was captivated by the German Gotthold Lessing and his comments about the nature of anything historical. Lessing argued that there is a tremendous ditch of time between our day and any past historical event. No matter how much information we have about that event, we are never in a position to go back and see if the accounts are accurate. Hence, there must always be a degree of uncertainty about anything historical. For someone living within the modern era with its concern for certain knowledge, this was a troubling proposal, indeed.

Kierkegaard applied the implications of the so-called Lessing's Ditch to theology and biblical studies. Even more, he applied it to our personal certainty of our relation to God and Christ. In his *Philosophical Fragments* and *Concluding Unscientific Postscript*, Kierkegaard addressed these matters among others. The overall issue of the *Fragments* is a comparison between idealism (Hegelian, in particular) and Christianity. Kierkegaard wanted to show that Hegel's system and its application to Christianity as practiced in Denmark had nothing to do with NT Christianity.

According to idealism, the truth is within each person and merely needs to be recollected. A teacher, if one has one, can at most serve as a catalyst to ask the right questions and point in the right direction. As a result of such probing, the individual will be led to the truth that is within him. All of this fits Hegel's notion of the development of the grand philosophical system. As thought reflects upon itself, it gradually unfolds the system that is immanent to it.[71]

In contrast, Kierkegaard argued that in genuine Christianity, truth is not in the individual but outside of him. No teacher by asking the right questions can ever help one to uncover the truth that is hidden within. How, then, does one come to the truth? Perhaps through historical research and historical documents like Scripture, but that was not Kierkegaard's answer. Higher critics had cast grave doubts on the veracity of Scripture, but beyond that, Lessing had taught Kierkegaard the contingency and uncertainty surrounding anything historical. In the *Postscript,* Kierkegaard clarifies beyond doubt his belief about whether we can come to the truth through something objective such as history and historical documents. He argues that, at most, what one finds from historical research is an approximation of the truth. This, Kierkegaard maintains, isn't enough, for who would be so foolish as to rest their eternal destiny on something contingent that is at best an approximation of the truth?[72]

How, then, can we be certain of God's existence and of our relation to him? How can we know the truth? Kierkegaard explains in the *Fragments* that truth is not latent in us, waiting to be recalled, but rather resides in God alone. For someone to receive the truth, God must bring the truth to the individual. This happens only when God in grace encounters the individual and gives him the truth and also the faith to grasp it.[73] Specifically, God gives us the truth in the person of Jesus Christ, who is given to us in personal encounter. Through repeated encounters and our response of faith, we become spiritually contemporary with Christ. We bridge Lessing's Ditch and gain certainty of God's existence and relation to us through this encounter in our current existence.

The faith God gives is not mere cold, intellectual agreement, but a passionate holding onto that which, rationally speaking, makes little or no sense. In fact, using Abraham's offering of Isaac as the paradigm case of true faith, Kierkegaard argues that faith requires a double movement. There is first a move to resignation, i.e., one resigns oneself to losing that which one hopes to gain or keep. The second move is a paradoxical leap of faith to believe that in spite of losing the object of one's hope, somehow one will still get it back.[74]

Through all of this, Kierkegaard contends that true Christianity is thoroughly different from the Hegelianized version of it present in the Denmark of his day. Moreover, he wants his readers to see that it is not easy to be a Christian. It involves faith, suffering, and becoming spiritually contemporary with Christ. Hence, one is always in the process of becoming a Christian.

From this theology we get a distinct picture of Kierkegaard's God.

One comes to know God by personal experience, but this is no God like Schleiermacher's. Schleiermacher's sense of absolute dependence proposes a very immanent God, perhaps part of our own self-consciousness. In contrast, Kierkegaard's God is the transcendent God from on high. But, we must not only speak of this God, but also of Jesus Christ. Kierkegaard refers to Christ as the Absolute Paradox. It is paradoxical and an offense to reason to think that the historical person Jesus is also God. This is a truth that can only be grasped by faith.

Kierkegaard's conception of God is reminiscent of Luther's distinction between the hidden God (*deus absconditus*) and the revealed God (*deus revelatus*). However, the way one comes to know this God according to Kierkegaard has significant differences from Luther's theology. One does not know God through something objective such as historical events, historical books like the Bible, or through rational arguments. One comes to know him in a way that is above reason and involves a personal encounter. This personal experience is not of some sense of the numinous or some feeling of absolute dependence, but rather it is a person-to-person encounter. In the *Fragments* Kierkegaard doesn't explicitly say the encounter is with Christ, but he says it indirectly by arguing that to be a real disciple of Christ we must become spiritually contemporary with him through the encounter. Joining this with his claims that God must bring us the truth in the moment of encounter, it seems clear that Kierkegaard believed the encounter is with Jesus Christ, the *deus revelatus.*

One final point about Kierkegaard on God has to do with reason's ability to discover God. Consistent with rejecting the Hegelian belief that reason can know and prove everything, and in keeping with his belief about the contingency of all things historical, Kierkegaard argues in the *Postscript* that one's eternal destiny should not rest on the dictates of reason. Hence, Kierkegaard rejects attempts to argue for God's existence (and thereby to offer assurance of it) and to establish a relation with him by using reason. Kierkegaard's point is not so much that there are good objections against the traditional arguments for God's existence, but that regardless of how compelling those arguments are intellectually, no one will be brought by them into the faith or out of it. For someone who has experienced God through the personal encounter with Christ, how could a rational argument possibly make them more certain of God's existence? Moreover, any rational arguments against God's existence would be meaningless for this person, since he knows there is a God by personally experiencing him. As for unbelievers, no argument or evidence could convince them, and given the contingency of our knowledge, why would they rest anything so important as their eternal destiny on such arguments?[75]

KARL BARTH.   Søren Kierkegaard is considered the father of Christian existentialism, while Nietzsche is the father of atheistic existentialism. Both lived in the nineteenth century, well in advance of the twentieth-century movement their thinking spawned. In Karl Barth (1886–1968), we see the outflowering of much of what we saw in Kierkegaard. Barth does not simply rehash Kierkegaard, but we know that Barth read Kierkegaard and was greatly influenced by his thought. Barth was also influenced by developments in higher criticism as well as liberal theology, but Barth and other neo-orthodox thinkers felt that liberalism was inadequate. Bernard Ramm explains some of what neo-orthodoxy found inadequate:

> Particular doctrines of liberalism were severely criticized. Its doctrine of revelation could not differentiate the voice of God from the voice of man. Its Christology made Jesus a nice, romantic Galilean fashioned in our image and not in God's. Sin was not seen in its terror and enmity against God nor for its sheer quality of rebellion against the divine will. Atonement had been reduced to psychological acceptance. Justification by faith had come to mean that there was no anger nor wrath in God. The gospel of liberalism was rejected as a gospel with no wrath, a cross with no judgment, and resurrection in which no Roman seals were broken.[76]

With such complaints, one might think the time ripe for a return to orthodoxy, but Barth and others like him lived in the modern world and could not countenance a complete return to what they viewed as a premodern understanding. In particular, Barth was concerned that revelation be seen again as a word from God, but neither Barth nor his colleagues could believe that Scripture is the Word of God. Higher criticism had undermined Scripture too much to equate it with the words of an absolutely perfect God. For Barth revelation does not come in propositions—in words—but in a person. The content of revelation is God himself given to man in a nonverbal, personal encounter with Jesus. The Bible is still valuable, but as a signpost pointing us to other times when God encountered people. And God might again use the reading or preaching of the Bible as an occasion to break through and encounter the reader or listener.[77]

Barth's concept of God is not surprising in light of his doctrine of the Word of God. However, his views do show development at various stages in his life. For the early Barth, most think of his *Church Dogmatics,* volume 1, part 1. There, God is depicted as wholly other, but this does not mean that he is so distant that we can ignore talking of him and speak only of Christ. God really does exist, but nothing can be known about him in his transcendence. We come to know about him only through the Word of God, Jesus Christ.

Barth says that the act of divine revelation is the self-unveiling of a God who according to his nature cannot be unveiled to us. Inscrutability and hiddenness belong to the nature of the God of the Bible. As creator, God is distinct from the world, and hence he does not belong to the realm of what humans as creatures can know directly about God. Moreover, Barth held that God cannot be unveiled even *indirectly* in the created world, because he is the Holy One whom we in our sin cannot see.

The God who has revealed himself, then, is the *deus absconditus*. This is the God to whom there is no way and no bridge, of whom we could not say or have to say one single word had he not, of his own initiative, met us as *deus revelatus*.[78] We must be careful not to misunderstand Barth, for none of this means that the God who is revealed is actually the *deus absconditus,* the transcendent God. Rather the hidden God has taken on a form in order to reveal himself to us. Barth says that God's doing this is his distinguishing himself from himself, a being of God in a mode of existence, not subordinate as compared with his first hidden mode of being as God, but just different.[79]

The fact that God takes on this mode of existence to reveal himself doesn't mean that this mode fully reveals God. Barth says, "It is not the form that reveals, speaks, comforts, works, helps, but *God in the form.*"[80] Further, this mode of revelation is not the *subject* of revelation, because that would mean that God could be unveiled to us after all and that there was no longer any need of God (the hidden God) for his revelation after all.[81] Notice what this means. For Barth, the transcendent God is still important, even though we cannot know him in his transcendence. Orthodoxy maintains that God can be known in his transcendent character. Theologians more radical than Barth will say that the only God we can know is the *deus revelatus* in the form of Christ. He is the subject of revelation and does unveil the transcendent; hence the transcendent God is no longer needed. Barth's earlier views, then, take a mediating position between orthodoxy and the more radical theologians.

Barth says that though the transcendent God has assumed various forms at various times, Christ is the form in which he is most revealed as well as most veiled. Christ is God's Word (God's revelation) to mankind, but in Christ God is unveiled in veiledness and veiled in unveiledness. The upshot of this is that our primary concern must be with Christ, God's Word to us. We cannot totally throw out the *deus absconditus* and never talk of him. We must speak of him as he acts in creation, revelation, and redemption, but we cannot know him in himself or talk about him in a way that corresponds to him in his transcendent self. In these views, the connections to Kierkegaard and to Kant's distinction between the thing-in-itself and the thing-for-us are discernible. Note also how this conforms with various aspects of modernity. On the one hand, there is still concern to find a certain foundation for knowledge, in this case religious knowledge. Of course, now the evidence is experiential, but those who have had this person-to-person encounter with God just know there is a God and know what he demands of them. Notice, as well, the individualistic nature of this theology. The encounter is not some mass experience the community shares and experiences together. Rather, one meets God as a solitary individual, and Barth emphatically denies that what God reveals in the encounter is transferable to anyone else. Attempts to verbalize God's revelation so as to share it with others of necessity distort it. Though this theology differs significantly from liberalism, both are filled with marks of modernity.

In his more mature thought, Barth was not so skeptical about speaking of God-in-himself, but that is because he believed that this is the God revealed in Jesus Christ. We see this as well in the further volumes of the *Church Dogmatics,* where Barth wrote substantial discussions on the divine attributes and the doctrine of creation. Still, in the more mature work all of this is deemed possible because of the focus on Christ as the center of God's revelation of himself to us.[82]

PAUL TILLICH. Since we have already discussed Paul Tillich (1886–1965) somewhat, we can be briefer. In his *Systematic Theology* Tillich proposes a method of correlation as the appropriate method for theology. This method requires the theologian first to analyze the human situation and then to go to Scripture to see how it answers questions raised by the human situation. The theologian correlates the biblical symbols to the analysis of the human condition. Tillich argues that such analysis in his day should be done in terms that are called existential. That is, they try to penetrate to the meaning of existence.[83]

Tillich applies this method in formulating his concept of God. He begins by explaining that the question of being is the question to which God is the answer. That question is an ontological one which, according to Tillich, arises in something like a "metaphysical shock"—the shock created when we realize our own possible nonbeing.[84]

If God is the answer to the question of being, what is that answer? Tillich distinguishes between the sense and reference of "God." The sense is that God is the name for what concerns us ultimately. What is of ultimate concern to humans must be that which is determinative of our being or nonbeing.[85] As to the reference of "God," Tillich says it is being-itself. Being-itself is not just a being alongside of other beings, for beings are still subject to finitude. Rather, God is the ground of being, the power of being, the structure of being (though not himself subject to it). This is all we can say about God without lapsing into symbolism and metaphor.[86]

This is a rather strange notion of God. On the one hand, it pictures him as very immanent to all things. One is reminded of Hegel's God as Spirit, that universal consciousness that penetrates and unites all things. But, despite the immanence of Tillich's God, there is no hint that he is personal, a God with whom we can establish any kind of relationship. Moreover, Tillich's claim that there is nothing we can literally say about God other than that he is being-itself gives his God a certain remoteness and distance. So, in a sense this God is both immanent and transcendent, but the overall description is of a very impersonal, remote, transcendent God.

As we might expect, Tillich places great emphasis on Jesus Christ. He is the bridge between us and God. Tillich speaks of the "new being" in Jesus as the Christ. New being is essential being under the conditions of existence, conquering the gap between essence and existence.[87] New being in Jesus as the Christ conquers all marks and kinds of estrangement between man's existential and essential being. However, this does not mean Tillich has an orthodox conception of Christ. Tillich believed Jesus was the bearer of the new being, but that is a contingent fact of history. If it hadn't been Jesus, it would have been some other human. Moreover, Jesus is not the God-man, a kind of third thing between God and man, for that would make Jesus just another god among many. Rather, we have in Jesus essential being under the conditions of existence. This is being-itself under the concrete conditions of finitude.[88]

LOGICAL POSITIVISM AND THE EARLY WITTGENSTEIN.   At the time many of these developments were occurring with liberal theology and neo-orthodoxy, in secular philosophy there were significant movements that impacted theology as well. In logical positivism, we see empiricism taken to a most rigorous conclusion. The logical positivists held what is known as the verification theory of meaning, which says that "the meaning of a proposition is its method of verification."[89]

According to the verification theory of meaning, unless one can specify verification procedures (a method of verification) for a proposition, the proposition is meaningless. This didn't mean someone actually had to verify or falsify the statement for it to be meaningful, but only that in principle it was verifiable. If it was impossible to state how to verify or falsify a claim, then the sentence was meaningless. Moreover, whatever the sentence spoke of was nonexistent.

For which kinds of sentences could one specify verification procedures? Fundamentally, only for sentences that are about empirically observable things in our world. Logical positivists concluded that while we can verify propositions of science, when it comes, for example, to ethical or value claims and claims about religious or theological entities, we cannot state verification procedures. Hence, such propositions are nonsense, and what they speak of doesn't exist.

The early philosophy of Wittgenstein as embodied in his *Tractatus Logico-Philosophicus* had various affinities to the philosophy of the logical positivists. Wittgenstein's theory of meaning was the picture theory of meaning. Words are the names of objects to which they refer, and sentences picture states of affairs in our world. If a sentence doesn't picture a state of affairs in our world, it has no sense. Though Wittgenstein's main point was not about how we verify or falsify a proposition, it was clear that "states of affairs in our world" meant empirically observable states of affairs. Hence, it was also clear how one would go about verifying or falsifying such propositions, but Wittgenstein's main point was that unless the proposition pictures a state of affairs in the world, it has no sense.

Wittgenstein concluded that propositions of ethics, theology, and philosophy (in its reflections about itself) are not about states of affairs in the world, and thus are meaningless. However, unlike the logical positivists, Wittgenstein didn't conclude that the things of which such propositions speak are nonexistent. They might in fact exist, but there just is nothing we can say about them. Only propositions about states of affairs in the world have sense.

With such attacks upon the very meaningfulness of language about God, coupled with notions of God that made him more and more transcendent and "out of this world," it was only a matter of time until theologians would read the signs and declare that God was dead. In the 1960s various theologians concluded just that.

DEATH OF GOD THEOLOGIES.   The "death of God" movement is associated with the 1960s in particular, but it was "brewing" for a long time. In the nineteenth century Nietzsche penned a famous passage found in his *The Gay Science*. Nietzsche writes of a madman running into a village square looking for God. When the villagers ask in amusement whether God was lost or on a sea voyage, the insane man replies that *"We have killed him,—you and I!"*[90] Nietzsche's point was that in the modern world there is no room for God. Science can explain our world without reference to God, and the traditional God is too otherworldly to be relevant to modern man. In addition, as we saw in chapter 2 in the discussion of God beyond Being, what Nietzsche was rejecting was ultimately the God of what is often called onto-theology. No longer could humans believe in an absolute God who grounded all of reality as its source and ultimate explanation.

Nietzsche didn't view this as something bad, but rather as necessary if humans are to be set free to make their own way in the world. While many people simply follow what Nietzsche called the "herd morality," this is not for everyone. There are special individuals, the "supermen" (*Übermenschen*), who take matters into their own hands, live by their own rules ("the trans-valuation of values," Nietzsche called it), and take society and culture to new heights. If God lives, there is an ultimate authority to which all are accountable; but if God is dead, then anything becomes allowable and possible.

William Hamilton says that the God Is Dead movement of the 1960s deliberately took its name and key theme from Nietzsche's *The Gay Science*.[91] These theologians wanted to invoke some of Nietzsche's main themes, but they add their own twists. Among this group of theologians are Paul van Buren (*The Secular Meaning of the Gospel*, 1963), Thomas J. J. Altizer (*The Gospel of Christian Atheism*, 1966), and William Hamilton (*The New Essence of Christianity*, 1966).

Each theologian has his particular nuance, but space does not allow us to cover them all. Our "taste" is Thomas J. J. Altizer's *The Gospel of Christian Atheism*. Altizer takes his cue from three nineteenth-century thinkers—Nietzsche, William Blake, and Hegel. In particular, it is traditional Christianity and its God that they find so offensive. Altizer believes their critique highlights the problem for the modern person who would be a Christian.

In his "Introduction," Altizer sounds the main themes of the book. He begins by asking if the Christian Word is forever inseparable from its historic ground in God's existence and power. Must Christians inevitably speak of God's glory and sovereignty? "These are questions which faith itself is now posing to the Christian and they are questions that must be met by the Christian who dares to accept the contemporary challenge of faith. It is the thesis of this book that the Christian, and the Christian alone, can speak of God in our time; but the message the Christian is now called to proclaim is the gospel, the good news or the glad tidings, of the death of God."[92]

Why must we speak of God's death? Altizer explains:

> For many years a conspiracy of silence removed theology from our contemporary human and historical situation. The modern theologian, while recognizing that God was no longer visible in the culture, the society, and the history of a dying christendom, was nevertheless persuaded that he was present, and present in his eternal form, in an autonomous Word of faith. Inevitably the price that had to be paid for such a choice was an isolation of faith from the concrete and present reality of human existence. . . . Under the impact of an increasingly profane history, this "answer" simply evaporated or lost all human meaning, and theology was reduced once more to establishing faith as a haven from the emptiness and the ravages of an indifferent or hostile world. Meanwhile, theology ceased to speak in any meaningful way about the Word of faith. The language of the theologian became largely the polemical language of attack, assaulting other theologians for either the sacrifice of faith or the complete abandonment of all clarity and coherence and even occasionally—and this much more timidly!—daring to attack the great outside world of unfaith or anti-faith.[93]

The answer to this problem, says Altizer, is rejection of the transcendent God and affirmation of a totally incarnate Word. This offers a faith that is totally engaged with the world, and rejects all forms that disengage from the world.[94] In coming to this stance, Altizer says the nineteenth-century vision helps us. Though this period was notorious for its atheism, it is very helpful to the Christian theologian. Altizer says that the nineteenth-century attack on Christianity was really aimed at theological forms and moral laws that are most opposed to the advent of a new man. On the other hand, atheistic prophets such as Nietzsche were positive to Jesus and even invoked his name or the Christian symbol of the incarnate Word to sanction their most radical proclamation.

Why were these nineteenth-century thinkers so anti-Christianity? Because they believed that traditional Christian faith is a flight from life, an evasion of suffering, a refusal to bear the burden and anguish of the human condition.[95] Altizer complains that all religions, including Christianity, are negative toward this world. What is truly unique, however, about Christianity is that

> The Christian Word appears in neither a primordial nor an eternal form: for it is an incarnate Word, a Word that is real only to the extent that it becomes one with human flesh. If we are to preserve the uniqueness of the Christian Word, we cannot understand the Incarnation as a final and once-and-for-all event of the past. On the contrary, the

Incarnation must be conceived as an active and forward-moving process, a process that even now is making all things new.[96]

Hence, Christianity must abandon the primordial Totality that negates the world. What is needed is a religionless Christianity, emphasizing the world and very much involved in it. Altizer explains:

> So long as the Christian God continues to be known as transcendent and impassive, or as a primordial deity who is unaffected by the processes of time and history, he cannot appear in his uniquely Christian form as the Incarnate Word and the kenotic Christ. Thus the radical Christian reverses the orthodox confession, affirming that "God is Jesus" . . . , rather than "Jesus is God." Before the Incarnation can be understood as a decisive and real event, it must be known as effecting a real change or movement in God himself: God becomes incarnate in the Word, and he becomes fully incarnate, thereby ceasing to exist or to be present in his primordial form. To say that "God is Jesus" is to say that God has become the Incarnate Word, he has abandoned or negated his transcendent form; or, rather, he remains present and real in his original form only where faith itself refuses to become incarnate.[97]

Altizer means that "God is dead" not only in the sense that the transcendent God is irrelevant to modern man but also in the sense that God in becoming incarnate literally died in his primordial form. Radical as this idea may seem, it appears elsewhere in the book.[98] This view of the incarnation makes Christ's kenosis very important, but it is not kenosis in the orthodox sense. According to evangelical Christology, Christ emptied himself by taking on full humanity while retaining full deity. He didn't get rid of deity, but laid aside for a time the exercise of the power and privileges that go with it in order to serve our needs. In contrast, kenosis for Altizer means a radical transformation of the primordial God into flesh. Here Altizer appeals to Hegel's notion of the Absolute and Spirit, and the idea of Spirit becoming immanent.[99]

One final word about Altizer's view of Jesus. What we have seen so far suggests that, for Altizer, Jesus as a person is important. What we find, however, is that Altizer later speaks of the concrete identity of the incarnate Word, and as he does, it becomes clear that ultimately "Jesus" functions as a symbol for human experience. Thus, there is more to thinking about Jesus than merely thinking of him as a concrete, distinct individual.[100] To those who wonder why we can't believe both in this incarnate Word and the transcendent God, Altizer says:

> Jesus cannot appear as the "Universal Humanity" until the transcendent realm has been emptied and darkened; with the eclipse of that realm no primordial archetype or paradigm remains present in consciousness, since humanity evolves to a fully universal and historical form only with the disappearance of its ground in a Being that is confined to a primordial or particular moment of time. . . . Indeed, the theologian must inevitably remain closed to the redemptive possibili-

ties of our history unless he is prepared to affirm the death of God as
an epiphany of Christ.[101]

Moreover, according to Altizer, this death of God must be an ongoing
process![102]

In God Is Dead theologies we find a mixture of modern and postmodern
themes. Science and reason have taught us that the traditional Christian God no
longer makes sense. A totally transcendent God may leave plenty of room for
human freedom, but such a God is remote and religiously inadequate. On the
other hand, God Is Dead theology's affirmation of this world and of a God who
relates to and becomes incarnate in it is quite consistent with the postmodern
mood. With God Is Dead theology, the table is set for postmodern theologies.

Contemporary Theologies in the Postmodern Mindset

Death of God theology appeared at roughly the time when the shift to a postmodern mindset was beginning. What arose in the latter part of the twentieth
century is a series of theologies that "resurrect" the notion of God. Lest we
become unduly excited about this, we must understand that the God of these
theologies is far from the traditional Judaeo-Christian God. As we shall see,
for most of these theologies, God is immanent to the exclusion of transcendence. Moreover, some theologians reintroduce metaphysics, but it is a very
empirically based metaphysic.

GEORGE LINDBECK'S THREEFOLD CATEGORIZATION OF THEOLOGIES. In a
much discussed book titled *The Nature of Doctrine: Religion and Theology
in a Postliberal Age* (1984), George Lindbeck proposed a threefold categorization of theologies. The first sort emphasizes cognitive aspects of religions
and treats doctrines as assertions of fact about objective realities. This kind of
theology is exemplified by Tridentine Catholicism and evangelical Protestant
theology. A second type of theology (linked with liberal theology since
Schleiermacher) stresses the experiential-expressive aspects of religion where
the focus of religion is the experiences of the human subject. This approach
interprets doctrines as "noninformative and nondiscursive symbols of inner
feelings, attitudes, or existential orientations."[103] The third kind (which
Lindbeck holds) he calls the cultural-linguistic. It differs from the first two as
Lindbeck explains:

> It has become customary in a considerable body of anthropological, soci-
> ological, and philosophical literature . . . to emphasize neither the cogni-
> tive nor the experiential-expressive aspects of religion; rather, emphasis
> is placed on those respects in which religions resemble languages together
> with their correlative forms of life and are thus similar to cultures (. . .
> that is, as idioms for the constructing of reality and the living of life).
> The function of church doctrines that becomes most prominent in this

perspective is their use, not as expressive symbols or as truth claims, but as communally authoritative rules of discourse, attitude, and action. This general way of conceptualizing religion will be called in what follows a "cultural-linguistic" approach, and the implied view of church doctrine will be referred to as a "regulative" or "rule" theory.[104]

The connections to the later Wittgenstein should be obvious, as is the implicit understanding that all our perceptions of reality are theory-laden. In fact, without such theories about reality we couldn't understand the world around us. Of course, those theories and concepts are taught to us and shaped by the culture where we were raised and live. As Lindbeck explains:

> Stated more technically, a religion can be viewed as a kind of cultural and/or linguistic framework or medium that shapes the entirety of life and thought. It functions somewhat like a Kantian *a priori*, although in this case the *a priori* is a set of acquired skills that could be different. It is not primarily an array of beliefs about the true and the good (though it may involve these), or a symbolism expressive of basic attitudes, feelings, or sentiments (though these will be generated). Rather, it is similar to an idiom that makes possible the description of realities, the formulation of beliefs, and the experiencing of inner attitudes, feelings, and sentiments. Like a culture or language, it is a communal phenomenon that shapes the subjectivities of individuals rather than being primarily a manifestation of those subjectivities. . . . Lastly, just as a language (or "language game," to use Wittgenstein's phrase) is correlated with a form of life, and just as a culture has both cognitive and behavioral dimensions, so it is also in the case of a religious tradition. Its doctrines, cosmic stories or myths, and ethical directives are integrally related to the rituals it practices, the sentiments or experiences it evokes, the actions it recommends, and the institutional forms it develops. All this is involved in comparing a religion to a cultural-linguistic system.[105]

What does this mean for the truth of a religion? The issue of truth arises in several respects. For a cultural-linguistic approach to religion, "religions are thought of as different idioms for construing reality, expressing experience, and ordering life."[106] To the extent that a religion succeeds in doing this, its categories are deemed adequate (the religion is "categorially" adequate). Second, the issue of truth also arises over whether the various parts of a system are logically consistent with one another. Truth in this sense is intra-systemic or "intra-textual."[107]

Of course, according to Lindbeck, none of this guarantees that realities of which the person speaks obtain in the world. According to the former invocation of truth, statements are adequate or inadequate because their categories do or don't help us express experience and construe reality, regardless of whether such realities actually exist. The second way Lindbeck speaks of religious truth is to speak of the religion's internal consistency or coherence, but a logically consistent story about reality is no guarantee that the story matches our world. Any good logician can construct a story that is internally consistent; that doesn't make it correspond to or match reality.

Lindbeck also speaks of truth in a sense he calls the "ontological" truth of religious utterances. Lest we think Lindbeck is reinstating traditional truth as correspondence, Lindbeck says of these utterances that "their correspondence to reality in the view we are expounding is not an attribute that they have when considered in and of themselves, but is only a function of their role in constituting a form of life, a way of being in the world, which itself corresponds to the Most Important, the Ultimately Real."[108] Presumably, these capitalized phrases are Lindbeck's terms for "God." He explains what he means by appealing to J. L. Austin's performative use of language (like Wittgenstein, Austin held a use theory of meaning and spoke of various actions we perform by uttering a sentence in a given context). "A religious utterance, one might say, acquires the propositional truth of ontological correspondence only insofar as it is a performance, an act or deed, which helps create that correspondence."[109] As an example, Lindbeck says that to say "Jesus is Lord" . . . "by the Holy Spirit" (1 Cor 12:3) simply means that one must do something about this, namely, commit oneself to a specific way of life. As another example, he says the claim that God is truly good in himself (though we don't know what this literally means, because God is so different from us) is very important, for it "authorizes responding as if he were good in the ways indicated by the stories of creation, providence, and redemption which shape believers' thoughts and actions."[110] Put differently, a religious statement corresponds to reality insofar as it serves to conform those who practice it "to the ultimate reality and goodness that lies at the heart of things."[111] Or, as Lindbeck argues, doctrinal statements are rules that regulate behavior. Insofar as we live our lives in conformity to those statements, they are true in a correspondence sense. This sounds a lot like Braithwaite's view that religious statements are used to state our intention to act in a certain way. The pragmatic character of this notion of truth should be obvious, though here the point is not so much that we find such propositions to be useful, but rather that in virtue of these claims we order our lives a certain way.

This is clearly a postmodern approach to religion and theology. What it means for the actual existence and attributes of God is unclear. But empirically we see people play various religious language-games. Moreover, these religious language-games are constitutive of how we live, even as our cultural and religious communities have made us the persons we are. Whether religion is more than wishful thinking and hoping for the existence of ultimate reality goes beyond our comprehension. For, if we knew, that would mean there must be some meta-narrative, some grand explanation that either tells us our religions are nothing more than helpful crutches or that they actually speak of a God to whom we are accountable. For someone committed to a postmodern epistemology, such a universal, all-explaining narrative is unavailable.[112]

THEOLOGY OF HOPE.   Theology of Hope arose in the 1960s, with a strongly
political emphasis. It never became as widespread as the various forms of
liberation theology, which also stress social and political themes, but many of
Theology of Hope's concerns are espoused in liberation theology.

The leading theologian of hope was Jürgen Moltmann. As Moltmann
explains, because neo-orthodoxy seemed to lock God out of history unless he
chooses to encounter us, and in light of Tillich's and others' depersonalizing of
God, the God Is Dead movement pronounced God dead. Theologians of hope
rejected this verdict, but because of what higher criticism and liberalism had done
to confidence in Scripture, there was no way to seek contact with God through
past history and historical documents. Moreover, contrary to neo-orthodoxy,
the likelihood of encountering God in the present and actually knowing that it is
God seemed remote. So where could mankind find God, if at all?

Since neither heaven nor earth could reveal God, theologians of hope
looked to the future. This means that questions about God's existence are
postponed for the future. Future, hope, and promise are the key words for this
movement. Past and present have value only in serving the future. It was also
agreed that preaching to twentieth-century people had to change to emphasize
the church as active in shaping society rather than shaping individual lives.
This emphasis on converting political and social structures to "bring in the
kingdom" made Theology of Hope a political theology.

Ernst Bloch is the philosopher most immediately behind this movement.
During the 1960s, he came to teach at Tübingen University, where he crossed
paths with Moltmann. Bloch's philosophy was really an adaptation of Marx's
dialectical materialism. Bloch saw historical processes moving toward the
future, but on this issue he was more like Hegel than Marx, for Bloch saw
history going toward no particular goal. Marx saw history moving toward a
communist, proletariat kingdom on earth. Traditional Christianity, of course,
sees history as culminating in the return of Christ and his kingdom. In keeping
with the Hegelian dialectic, which sees history continuously going onward,
Bloch saw the future as infinite and never-ending, and theologians of hope
view the future that way, too. Because of the possibilities of the "not yet,"
there is reason to hope about the future.

Moltmann adopted many of these themes. In line with the futuristic
emphasis, Moltmann argued that the proper way to do theology is to do it
as eschatology. This means that Christianity as eschatology is hope, forward
looking and forward moving. Hence, it also revolutionizes and transforms
the present. Hope must call us away from the rigidified utopia of realism.
Christian eschatology sees reality and mankind in the hand of him whose
voice calls into history from its end, saying, "Behold, I make all things new."
This gives Theology of Hope its marching orders.[113]

What does Theology of Hope say about God? Moltmann raises the question of God's existence, and argues that we must reject the idea that God's
existence can be proved either from the natural world (via natural theology)

or by existential encounter. The question of God's existence, like all questions, is open and will be solved in the future. Of course, we must remember that history is a directionless process. Moltmann and other theologians of hope use God in their system, but they do so without ever answering or allowing to be answered in the present the question of God's existence. In the eschatological future an answer will come, but it is never clear when we will get to that point, since history is going nowhere in particular.

Though Moltmann postpones answers to the question of God's existence, he does offer his thoughts about this God's nature. He sees no valid distinction between what God is in himself and what he does in the world. God's essence is confined to his history. Moreover, God is known and described in the OT and NT as a God of promise. This is the key to his nature. Moltmann explains:

> His essence is not his absoluteness as such, but the faithfulness with which he reveals and identifies himself in the history of his promise as 'the same'. His divinity consists in the constancy of his faithfulness, which becomes credible in the contradiction of judgment and grace.[114]

Of course, promises point to hope, and both hope and promise point to the future. Therefore, the God of the Bible is no intra-worldly or extra-worldly God, but the "God of Hope," a God with future as his essential nature. Carl Braaten, another theologian of hope, says that God is the power of the future pressing for a radical conversion of the present. God's being is his eschatological power; futurity is essential to his very being. This means that God is wrapped up in his promises which point to the future, but as Braaten says, "God is not other than his promises."[115] Braaten adds that God's nature as the power of the future is best revealed in Jesus Christ and especially in his resurrection. God's power over the future is revealed in Jesus' message of the coming of the kingdom of God, but also through his resurrection. Braaten writes that "Christian hope is grounded in the resurrection of Jesus of Nazareth because through it God defined himself as the power of the future beyond the finality of death."[116]

In light of God's promises for the future and his power to transform it, Moltmann and other theologians of hope call Christians to social activism. We cannot be satisfied with the social and political status quo, they say, but must proclaim a new order that is coming. As Moltmann says, "Those who hope in Christ can no longer put up with reality as it is, but begin to suffer under it and contradict it. Peace with God means conflict with the world, for the goad of the promised future stabs inexorably into the flesh of the unfulfilled present."[117] Our hope calls us to "creative discipleship." Moltmann writes:

> 'Creative discipleship' cannot consist in adaptation to, or preservation of, the existing social and judicial orders, still less can it supply religious backgrounds for a given or manufactured situation. It must consist in the theoretical and practical recognition of the structure of historic pro-

cess and development inherent in the situation requiring to be ordered, and thus of the potentialities and future of that situation.[118]

This is clearly a theology with many postmodern emphases. It believes in God, and demands that God's nature as hope and power over the future matter for us now. Moreover, there is a strong emphasis on people's life circumstances, and on a desire to change society so as to care for the needs of its members. This offers a caring God connected to us. He waits at the end of history and calls us to transform history now as we anticipate his coming kingdom.

LIBERATION THEOLOGY.   David Ray Griffin sees liberation theology as one of four main forms of postmodern theology. The liberation theologians he discusses most are Harvey Cox (*Religion and the Secular City: Toward a Postmodern Theology,* 1984) and Cornel West. Griffin argues that unlike modern theology's emphasis on totalitarian control which sometimes tended to legitimize oppressive, totalitarian governments and economic systems (capitalist and socialist), liberation theologies reject such systems and plead for freeing the oppressed. In addition, rather than separating theology from ethics, as is often done in modern theologies, liberation theologies opt for doing theology as praxis and thereby deliberately wed social ethics to theology.

Cox sees the modern worldview as that of the capitalists, the bourgeoisie. The function of modern religion has been to legitimize this worldview. In contrast, Cox holds that

> the postmodern age will be the age of the poor, the masses. Politics and religion will be reunited. Theology will not be academic, but liberationist, meaning political from the outset. It will not seek universality, but will focus on the particular concerns of the region, knowing that unity comes not through agreement on ideas but through social conflict. It will think in terms of the distinction between not believers and unbelievers but exploiters and exploited. Theology will try not to revise popular religion to make it credible to elites, but to strengthen it as a resource for the oppressed. Postmodern theology will be concerned less with the ideas themselves, and apologetic arguments for their truth, than with the social sources and the political uses of ideas. The sources for postmodern theology will come not from the top and the center, but from the bottom and the edges. This means, concretely, that the sources will be popular piety and contact with other religions. Postmodern theology will thereby involve a fusion of modern and premodern religious elements.[119]

This is a good introduction to liberation theology, but more can be said. In its early development, liberation theology took root in Latin America, but as it has grown, it has spread throughout the world in various forms. In North America (specifically, the United States) it has expressed itself in black theology. In Third World societies it is often referred to as People's Theology.[120] An Asian version, for example, is Korean Minjung theology. There are also

African versions, and even within Latin America this theology has a uniquely Central American nuance which differs from its South American version. In addition, North American feminist and worldwide womanist theologies are examples of this broad genre.

Several key themes are at the heart of liberation theology (here I refer to Gustavo Gutiérrez's *A Theology of Liberation*[121]). First, this theology has a particular method for theology in light of its understanding of theology's task. As opposed to earlier theologies, whose aim was to reflect on the being and attributes of God or to apply reason to natural and special revelation to discern what can be known about God, liberation theology is concerned with critical reflection on praxis. Gutiérrez writes that charity has been rediscovered as the center of the Christian faith, and this has led many to view faith as commitment to God and neighbor, a relationship with others. Hence, Christian spirituality involves not a contemplative, monastic life, but rather an attempt to mix contemplation with action, and the greater emphasis is on action. Theology must be critical reflection on our actions and our own basic principles.[122] This is no ivory tower theology with a remote and detached God.

Second, as liberation theology reflects on praxis it first analyzes the social and political conditions of the society, and it finds great oppression and exploitation of the poor. While many advocate a program of development for Third World societies to bring them to a higher standard of living, liberation theologians reject developmentalism in favor of liberation. Gutiérrez says that this liberation involves three interdependent levels. On the one hand, liberation expresses the hopes of oppressed peoples and social classes as they reflect on how the economic, social, and political processes put them at odds with wealthy nations and classes in society. This aspect of liberation is the socio-politico-economic aspect. On the other hand, liberation also applies to an understanding of history. This refers to liberating the human psyche in such a way that a new person is created, and with these new people a new society (this is the psychological or humanistic aspect of liberation). Finally, there is the theological facet of liberation based on biblical sources. In Scripture, Christ is presented as the liberator, the one who saves from sin, which is the ultimate root of all disruption of friendship and all injustice and oppression.[123]

As liberation theologians read Scripture, they find God on the side of the poor and oppressed. The exodus of Israel from Egyptian bondage by God's intervention is a major motif for this movement. God's indictment (through the prophets) of Israel's insensitivity to the poor and downtrodden (e.g., Isaiah 1) shows that God is on the side of the poor. Moreover, a favorite verse of many liberation theologians is Jesus' statement of his calling and mission (Luke 4:18-19), "The Spirit of the Lord is upon Me, because He anointed Me to preach the gospel to the poor. He has sent Me to proclaim release to the captives, and recovery of sight to the blind, to set free those who are downtrodden, to proclaim the favorable year of the Lord."

Even as God is on the side of the poor and Christ is the liberator, so we as Christians must work to overcome injustice and oppression. Gutiérrez says the OT is clear about the relationship between God and the neighbor. To exploit the humble and poor worker and to despise one's neighbor (Prov 14:21) offends God. On the other hand, to know Yahweh, which Gutiérrez says is equivalent to loving him, is to establish just relationships among men and to recognize the rights of the poor. The God of biblical revelation is known through inter-human justice, but when justice does not exist, God is unknown and absent.[124] For Gutiérrez we find a similar teaching in the NT in Matt 25:31ff. Gutiérrez asks, who are the nations judged by the Son of Man, and who are "the least of his brethren" (vv. 40, 45)? This is a judgment, he answers, of all people (Christians and non-Christians) according to their love of the neighbor, and particularly of the needy, "the least of the brethren."[125]

The liberation portrait of God is not an abstract metaphysical one focusing on what he is in himself. Nor is God depicted as impassive, unrelated, or uninvolved in human affairs. Rather, God is a God of action, a liberator, and a God who calls us to action. Our actions to liberate may in some cases require political revolution (much of early Latin American liberation theology bought into a Marxist analysis of class struggle and its call to overturn social, economic, and political structures), though that may not be necessary. With the demise of Marxist communism, liberation theology has lost none of its fervor, for there are still many oppressed people, and God is still in the business of liberating the poor. Moreover, the eschatological vision of and hope for the kingdom of God becomes operative when it comes in contact with the social realities of today's world and spawns what has been called political theology. In summarizing Ruben Alves's position, Ralph Moellering describes the God and program of liberation theology:

> What results is an adamant denial of "that which is"— a refusal to be limited to anachronistic precedents or to conform to conventional patterns. God is not the eternally Present One who renders superfluous the flow of history, but the Freedom which intervenes in the course of events to prevent the past from determining the future. To put it bluntly, he is the Subverter of the status quo.[126]

FEMINIST THEOLOGIES. Since the late 1960s there has been a veritable explosion of feminist theological thinking and literature. Rosemary Radford Ruether, Elisabeth Schüssler Fiorenza, and Mary Daly are some of the better known names, but many other women have taken up the banner of feminist theology. Their point is not merely that women want equal rights in the home, church, and society. Rather, they complain that traditional religions like Christianity are patriarchal and sexist. These religions, they say, portray God as an isolated, dominating, monarchical sovereign of the world who does what he wants; in short, a male. In Christianity, Jesus' maleness as incarnate is used to legitimize the notion that only men can properly represent God. Men are associated with the rational, soul part of man, which (according to vestiges of Platonism and Neo-Platonism) is the more spiritual and morally good part of human nature; and women are linked to the material, bodily, sexual aspects of human nature, and these features are deemed evil. Feminists contend that religions like Christianity not only put males in authority but are taken as models for the structuring of society, i.e., patriarchal religion legitimizes patriarchal control of society. Women are not only excluded from control of societal and cultural institutions; they are not even to participate in those institutions.

The feminist critique looks for a portrait of God using female metaphors and motifs. It seeks a God who is not remote and domineering but rather is relationally involved with humans as a friend and confidant. Some forms of feminism seek a religion that not only nurtures women and children but also is concerned about the environment in which we live. These "ecofeminist" approaches stress our connectedness not only to one another but also to the world around us, which bore all of us through the long processes of evolution.

As feminism has grown, it has also diversified. In fact, as Mary Catherine Hilkert notes, in the late 1990s even the term "feminist" is problematic, because it is typically associated with largely white, middle-class, well-educated women of North America; none of that speaks to the experience of American Black women and other groups. As Hilkert says, "In the U.S., the 'womanist' theology of African-American women and the 'mujerista' theology of Hispanic women now take their place at the table, along with the insights of Asian-American women."[127]

Within feminist theology, there is another major division between revolutionary or radical feminism and revisionist feminism. Revisionist feminists complain that, though Christianity is a sexist religion that legitimizes patriarchal structures in society, it still has some helpful insights; therefore, they advocate reforming or revising Christianity rather than rejecting it altogether, so as to encourage and affirm women and nurture their growth and equality in all societal institutions.[128]

Radical feminists disagree. They remind us that prior to the great monotheistic religions of Judaism, Islam, and Christianity, many societies had religions that worshiped a goddess or goddesses. When monotheistic religions won the day, they threw out worship of any feminine deity and instituted worship of the dominant, monarchical male. Societies were structured to fit this model, and the devastating results to women are a matter of history ever since. Radical feminists claim that sexism and patriarchy are so totally at the root of Christianity that no amount of revision could reform it to be positive to women and their concerns. The only answer is to jettison Christianity in favor of some pagan religion that visions God as female and hence empowers women. Radical feminists have turned to various "Goddess" religions and to witchcraft or feminist wicca. In all of these religions, women are portrayed as having supernatural powers. These religions, it is claimed, not only treat women as equal to men (in some cases as superior), but they also focus on feminist concerns about nurturing and relating to all people. They also stress our connectedness to all things, including the world in which we live.

Space does not allow for a description of the various versions of feminist theology, but we can catch the flavor of these theologies through an oft-reviewed and highly praised example, Roman Catholic feminist Elizabeth Johnson's *She Who Is*. Johnson's book touches many of the main feminist themes, and it does so in a work that is deliberately revisionist or reformist,[129] rather than radical or revolutionary. Johnson thinks Christianity is reform-able; *She Who Is* is her proposal for how to do so.[130]

Johnson poses what she believes is the crucial question: what is the right way to speak about God? This is a key question in part because God is the ultimate mystery that surrounds us and gives meaning to life, yet God is so beyond us that we don't know exactly how to speak of God. Human language about God is all symbolic, and we don't exactly know the nature of the reality the symbols depict. Still, how a community speaks of God is very important, for such speech and thought molds a community's corporate identity. In addition, says Johnson, the right way to speak of God is especially important because typically God has been spoken of in male symbols and metaphors. The question today is "whether the reality of women can provide suitable metaphor for speech about God."[131] Hence, the crucial issue for Johnson is "What is the right way to speak about God in the face of women's newly cherished human dignity and equality?"[132]

But why is this such a crucial issue? It is critical, Johnson claims, in that if God's reality is a mystery we can never fully understand,[133] we should realize that it is wrong to think that we must refer to God always and only in male images. Moreover, how we speak of God affects how we think of men and women and their relations in society. Since our culture is coming to recognize the full significance of women as *imago dei and imago Christi,* why can't we speak of God equally well using female metaphors as we do using male metaphors?

Johnson sees her project (and that of other feminists) as necessary because traditional speech about God is both "humanly oppressive and religiously idolatrous."[134] The primary culprit is classical theism with its male, dominat-ing God who is immutable, impassible, and disengaged from society. Johnson thinks this notion of God is really the idea of "man" in the patriarchal ideal.[135] Traditional Christianity is loaded with sexism, patriarchy, and androcen-trism,[136] and cultures where it has been present have reflected those attitudes in their social structures and attitudes toward women. As an example of this sort of thinking, Johnson cites Aquinas. According to her analysis of Aquinas, women are not subordinate just because men are inclined to be domineering; rather it must be that way because women are said to have a defective nature. Johnson cites a passage from Aquinas that amounts to saying that a woman is a defective male, i.e., the reason a woman was conceived rather than a male is that during the sexual relations that conceived her, her father wasn't quite up to his best capacity. If he had been, a male would have been conceived.[137] Such thinking is outrageous, of course, but Johnson believes it has been fairly well ingrained in the history of the Christian church:

> Christianity perpetuates these attitudes in the way it speaks of God. What is so bad about this is that to even the casual observer it is obvious that the Christian community ordinarily speaks about God on the model of the ruling male human being. Both the images that are used and the concepts accompanying them reflect the experience of men in charge within a patriarchal system. The difficulty does not lie in the fact that male metaphors are used, for men too are made in the image of God and may suitably serve as finite beginning points for reference to God. Rather, the problem consists in the fact that these male terms are used exclusively, literally, and patriarchally.[138]

How should we incorporate female images in our speech about God so as to uphold equality of males and females as both *imago dei* and as both saying something instructive about the divine mystery that is God? Johnson sees three basic ways to try to accommodate the issues she raises, but she thinks the first two are deficient in one respect or another. The first option *gives "feminine" qualities to a God* who is still imagined to be predominantly male. With this option, the typical traits attributed to God are gentle, nurturing ones traditionally associated with the mothering role of women. This results in softening the symbol of God as Father, which traditionally contains unlovely traits associated with ruling men in a male-oriented society, e.g., traits like aggressiveness, competitiveness, desire for absolute power and control, and demand for obedience. Adding feminine traits to God gives God qualities like gentleness and compassion, unconditional love, reverence and care for the weak, sensitivity, and a desire not to dominate but to be an intimate companion and friend, all traits that make God more "attractive."[139]

Despite these positive additions to the concept of God, Johnson says women theologians are virtually unanimous in noting the deficiencies of this approach. For one thing, the androcentric pattern still holds, for God is still envisioned in the image of the ruling man. God's "feminine traits" are subordinate to an overall symbol that remains masculine (evidence of this in part is the fact that God is still repeatedly referred to as "him").[140] This approach also "involves dubious stereotyping of certain human characteristics as predominantly masculine or feminine."[141]

The second option for speaking of God in female symbols *seeks a more ontological footing for the existence of the feminine in God.* Most frequently the inroad is found in the doctrine of the Holy Spirit who, in classical trinitarian theology, is coequal in nature with the Father and the Son. Though this may seem a better option, it still is problematic. An initial problem is that "the endemic difficulty of Spirit theology in the West insures that this 'person' remains rather unclear and invisible . . ."[142] Moreover, the overarching framework of this approach still remains androcentric, with the male principle still dominant and sovereign, since the Spirit is subordinate to the Son and Father. Stereotyping also plagues this option.

The third option for language about God "speaks about the divine in images taken equivalently from the experience of women, men, and the world of nature. This approach shares with the other two the fundamental assumption that language about God as personal has a special appropriateness. . . . God is not personal like anyone else we know, but the language of person points in a unique way to the mysterious depths and freedom of action long associated with the divine."[143] Johnson prefers this option, and in the rest of her book, she presents the contours of a theology that focuses on feminine imagery and symbols for a Christian feminist understanding of God.

Resources for this theology are three: women's interpreted experience, Scripture and its trajectories, and classical theology. Of course, Scripture contains much male imagery, but this is only problematic if one takes the imagery literally and considers the Bible as divinely inspired and inerrant.[144] Adopting the "hermeneutics of suspicion" that other postmoderns apply to Scripture and all other cultural texts, we must ask of each biblical text, *cui bono,* to whose benefit? With this question the text deconstructs before us as we realize that it was constructed by males in power who put it together to legitimize their continued control.[145]

On the other hand there are three major biblical symbols that have feminist overtones and implications. The first is Spirit/Shekinah. The second, the symbol of Wisdom/Sophia, becomes the main theme and symbol for the rest of the book. About this symbol, Johnson writes,

> This is the most developed personification of God's presence and activity in the Hebrew Scriptures, much more acutely limned than Spirit, torah, or word. The term itself is of feminine grammatical gender: *hokmah* in Hebrew, *sophia* in Greek, *sapientia* in Latin. While this does not in itself determine anything, the biblical depiction of Wisdom is itself consistently female, casting her as sister, mother, female beloved, chef and hostess, preacher, judge, liberator, establisher of justice, and a myriad of other female roles wherein she symbolizes transcendent power ordering and delighting in the world.[146]

Johnson notes the many texts in wisdom literature like Job and Proverbs where wisdom is personified. So, what happened to Sophia in Christian theology? Johnson sees Christianity's teaching about the Spirit as akin to this understanding of Sophia. Jesus as Logos is really the Christian adoption of Sophia theology, although it puts a male guise on it.[147] A third and final biblical female symbol for God is that of mother.[148]

The rest of Johnson's book offers her understanding of theology as viewed in a feminist mode, using feminine symbols to speak of God. All of it is cast in the model of God as Sophia. Johnson begins her discussion with Spirit-Sophia, because Spirit is the most immanent member of the Godhead, and Johnson thinks theology should begin "from below," not "from above." Johnson points to the Spirit's actions and notes the affinity of these with feminist values, highlighting as they do freely moving, life-giving, nonviolent power that connects, renews, and blesses. In particular, she cites several of the Spirit's activities: vivifying, renewing and empowering, gracing. Speaking of the Spirit in these ways leads to three insights important for feminist theology of God: the transcendent God's immanence; a divine passion for liberation; and the constitutive nature of relation.[149]

Johnson next discusses Jesus-Sophia. The basic idea of Christology, according to Johnson, is that

> God who is Spirit, at work in the tragic and beautiful world to vivify and renew all creatures through the gracious power of her indwelling, liberating love, is present yet again through the very particular history of one human being, Jesus of Nazareth. . . . Through his human history the Spirit who pervades the universe becomes concretely present in a small bit of it; Sophia pitches her tent in the midst of the world; the Shekinah dwells among the suffering people in a new way.[150]

If this is the essence of Christology, it is in no way negative to feminist issues, but Johnson says that feminist theology raises a most stringent critique, claiming that of all areas of doctrine, Christology is the most used to suppress and exclude women. This need not be so, says Johnson, for if we look at what Jesus did and said, we find an inclusiveness in his relations with other humans and with God, and this removes the male emphasis that so quickly turns to androcentrism. Specifically, Christ does the following: preaching, ingathering, confronting (all of which Johnson gives a feminist twist);[151] dying and rising (though Johnson doesn't believe Christ literally rose). Several other Christological themes are noteworthy: the whole Christ—males and females make up the body of Christ together; Christ is truly God and truly human, but the point of his humanity is not his gender, but that he is one with humanity, and that includes both men and women; and finally, Christ as the Wisdom of God (the Sophia theme is again invoked). Thinking of Christ in wisdom categories also emphasizes the following themes: relation to the whole cosmos; belief in a global, ecumenical perspective respectful of other religious paths; by becoming one with humanity in incarnation and suffering, Sophia, whose paths are justice and peace, shows that God's passion is aimed at lifting oppression and establishing right relations.[152]

Johnson discusses finally the third member of the Godhead, Mother-Sophia. The basic idea behind this member of the Godhead is unoriginate (beginningless) origin, and given this, women as mothers offer the most apt way to speak of Mother-Sophia. Johnson says we must think of God using the imagery of motherhood, but even here we must be careful. Patriarchy offers one idea of motherhood, and simply projecting that onto God will only perpetuate the enslaving stereotype. If these problems are avoided, the metaphor of God as mother can be both instructive and liberating.

Johnson also writes about Mother-Sophia's acts, and emphasizes two: mothering the universe, and establishing the mercy of justice wherein justice and compassion are juxtaposed.[153] In the final part of her book, the motif of God as Sophia remains, but Johnson tackles three specific doctrines. She offers her understanding of the Trinity, adopting a social communitarian view in which all members are coequal and mutually related. She also addresses the very being and nature of God and sees God's essence as relation—relation within the Godhead and with the world. Moreover, God is totally alive and the source of all living things. Because of this, says Johnson, the best way to speak of God, with feminist concerns in mind, is to call God "She Who Is" (patterned after "I am who I am" and the male version of this, "He Who Is"). A final doctrine focuses on God as suffering, portrayed as compassion poured out. Divine impassibility is thoroughly rejected.[154]

Feminist theology, including Johnson's, is clearly a theology stressing many postmodern themes. Johnson's version may seem rather startling, but she refuses to reject Christianity, and chooses instead to stay within the tradition, embrace it, and reform it. Hence, her theology is relatively tame in comparison to more revolutionary, radical feminist theologies.

NEW AGE THEOLOGY.   New Age Theology is another phenomenon of the late twentieth century. Douglas Groothuis has contributed several books that are exceptionally helpful in understanding this eclectic movement. In his *Unmasking the New Age, Confronting the New Age,* and *Revealing the New Age Jesus,* Groothuis chronicles the factors contributing to the rise of this movement, its basic tenets and themes, its handling of the person and work of Christ, the implications and agendas of New Age themes for science, politics, education, and the like, and he helps in combating this system, which is antithetical to evangelical Christianity. Space permits us only to cover New Age thinking about God.

As Groothuis notes, this is a very eclectic movement, so there are many variations in it. However, six main themes typify New Age thinking. First, New Agers believe that *all is one,* which means that there is a basic unity to everything. Another name for this foundational belief is monism, and it means that everything is interrelated, interdependent, and interpenetrating. Hence, whatever exists is part of a continuous reality that has no boundaries and no divisions. Perceived differences between a tree, an apple, a dog, and a person are only apparent, not real. Since all things are one, this also means that there is no difference between good and evil, for they are one and the same. Groothuis remarks,

> All is one; ultimate reality is beyond good and evil. This is the essential teaching of much of Eastern religion and occultism, and it is being

advocated by a host of New Age scientists. The physicist and philosopher Fritjof Capra says in his book *The Turning Point* that the ultimate state of consciousness is one "in which all boundaries and dualism have been transcended and all individuality dissolves into universal, undifferentiated oneness." There are not many selves but one Self, the One.[155]

Everything is one, but what is that one thing? New Agers answer that *all is God,* i.e., everything partakes of the one divine essence. This, of course, is nothing new, but just pantheism resurrected and recast in a different context. Since many parts of this unity have personality, one might think the New Age pantheistic God is personal, but, as Groothuis explains

> . . . it is argued that if everything is one and if all dualities in reality dissolve into the cosmic unity, then so does the idea of personality. A personality can only exist where it defines itself in relation to other beings or things. Even self-consciousness demands some form of a relationship. But if all is one, then there is only one being—the One. The One does not have a personality; it is beyond personality. God is more an "it" than a "he." The idea of a personal God is abandoned in favor of an impersonal energy, force or consciousness.[156]

Third, if everything is God, then *humans are God,* and this is precisely what New Agers claim. The New Age doctrine says:

> We are god in disguise. Only ignorance keeps us from realizing our divine reality. Our goal, according to New Age analyst Theodore Roszak, is "to awaken to the god who sleeps at the root of the human being." Swami Muktananda—a great influence on Werner Erhard, founder of est and Forum—pulls no pantheistic punches when he says: "Kneel to your own self. Honor and worship your own being. God dwells within you as You!"[157]

A fourth theme follows from the preceding: if everything is One and everything is God, why don't we know ourselves as God and see the unity among all things? The reason is ignorance, an ignorance engendered by Western culture that has shaped our consciousness. As a result, we are content with the everyday notions of human limitation and finitude. We need to be enlightened to our true identity. In other words, we need *a change in consciousness.* According to New Agers, this can happen in various ways, one being through sports. Enlightenment may also come in the scientist's laboratory. Alleged contact with a UFO or extraterrestrial may also do it. Change in consciousness may come spontaneously or through disciplined practice in meditation, yoga, or some other consciousness-raising technique. Others are "chanting, dancing or tripping their way into altered states of awareness. They may use self-hypnotism, internal visualization, biofeedback or even the sexual act."[158]

A fifth theme of New Age thinking is that *all religions are one.* If all is One and all are God, then all religions must really be about the same thing. Though the externals of religions differ, the essence of each religion is the same and is based on the same experience of the oneness of all things. Any claims that Christianity is distinct must be denied and dissolved into the cosmic unity. In fact, it is even claimed that Jesus' real teachings fit the central themes of the New Age. Moreover, Jesus is not who Christians think. As Groothuis explains,

> Jesus of Nazareth, then, is no longer said to be the only begotten Son of God, the God-man, the Lord and Savior of the cosmos. He is merely one of many appearances or manifestations of God throughout the millennia. His mission was to alert the sleeping masses to their innate divinity. Jesus is thus reverentially enshrined in the pantheistic pantheon where he echoes the chorus of the enlightened: all is one. The Christ of the Bible is redefined and made the ventriloquist's puppet for the New Age. Christ as the mediator between God and humanity is replaced with the idea of "Christ-consciousness," which is another word for cosmic consciousness. Likewise, the biblical teaching of eternal judgment (heaven or hell) is replaced by reincarnation in much New Age thought.[159]

A final New Age theme is *cosmic evolutionary optimism.* Julian Huxley was no New Ager, but he made a comment that typifies New Agers' optimism and hope for a better future. Huxley said, "Man is that part of reality in which and through which the cosmic process has become conscious and has begun to comprehend itself. His supreme task is to increase that conscious comprehension and to apply it as fully as possible to guide the course of events."[160] Groothuis explains, "As this philosophy gains ground and infiltrates all of life with the gospel of cosmic unity, it is predicted that humanity will be ready to take over the reins of evolution. Teilhard de Chardin, Jesuit philosopher and paleontologist, prophesied a progressive evolutionary harmonization and unification of world consciousness eventually reaching 'the Omega Point' where all consciousness is fused and all become one with the One."[161]

Much more can be said about the New Age movement, but let me close by describing New Age spirituality. It incorporates many ideas from classical Eastern religions such as Buddhism, Taoism, and Hinduism, but it is not simply reducible to those religions. It also incorporates items from the Judeo-Christian worldview and from paganism. The result is a hodge-podge of ideas and practices. And a lot of this is geared to the West's and North America's concern for efficiency and immediate results. It also includes many forms of occult practice. Another element is worship of the Great Goddess. The concern is to get away from patriarchal religion, i.e., religion that deified masculinity and demoralized femininity, establishing male exploitation of women and nature. And there is interest in various pre-Christian religions such as shamanism, an animist-pantheist emphasis, for instance in the Findhorn community of northern Scotland. Druidism, Celtic spirituality, and Egyptian religion are others. Even Jesus is recast as an Eastern thinker whose teachings echo the main thrusts of the New Agers.[162]

New Age thinking is clearly postmodern. God is very immanent, related, close to us, for we are God and everything around us is God. Thus, not only can we speak of God in our scientific world; we must do so, for once our consciousness is raised to see that we are God, then we are ready to transform all of life and society around us. Note as well how much of this depends on sense experience, though much of it goes beyond the normal five senses. New Age thinking can claim to satisfy many of the demands of an empirically based theology. And it also fits nicely with feminist and ecofeminist concerns.

PROCESS THEOLOGY. In 1929 Alfred North Whitehead published *Process and Reality*,[163] in which he presented the details of process metaphysics and the broad outlines of a theism based on that conception of reality. Though it took a while for this vision of God and reality to take hold, since the postmodern turn, process theology has become increasingly popular among academic theologians. Disciples like Charles Hartshorne and John Cobb have been extremely important in elaborating a theology based on Whitehead's process metaphysics. Because of the importance of this movement in contemporary theology, I shall devote the next chapter to process theology. Hence, at this point my remarks are limited.

One of the major motivating factors behind process theology is its critique of classical Christian theism. The totally transcendent, all-powerful monarch God who controls everything and never changes in any way nor feels any emotions, regardless of what happens in our world is deemed both religiously inadequate for contemporary times and inconsistent with the biblical God. In fact, the basic process critique of the classical Christian God is almost identical to that found in feminism.

In addition, process theists believe that Whitehead's metaphysics offers an empirically-based metaphysic and thus satisfies the demands of empiricism from Kant onward. Moreover, Whitehead's system incorporates the basic evolutionary mindset that sees all things as interconnected through the long processes of evolution, and as evolving and changing as biological organisms do.

The God of process theology, like all actual entities, is dipolar. He has a primordial, conceptual pole and a consequent, physical pole. The former is all the possibilities that actual entities can become, while the latter is the world, God's body, which is the progressive actualization of various of those possibilities.

Because God is so immanent and connected to the world, he grows and changes as we do. He feels our pains and joys, and not only identifies with our sorrows but actually suffers along with us. As intimately connected to us, his knowledge is also limited and it grows with every moment that passes. Process theists believe that their God, who lovingly grants us freedom to grow and become what we choose, and who is so responsive and interactive with his creatures, more accurately fits the biblical account of God than does the classical God.

This view of God sounds many familiar postmodern themes: a God who is immanent and relational; a God whose very being interpenetrates all things and hence underscores the connectedness of all things; a God who is not static but is constantly changing as he responds to our needs; and a God to whom we can contribute value as well as one who enhances our existence. Moreover, this notion of God allows one to take seriously modern developments in science, with its emphasis on the empirical and naturalism, while refusing, along with the basic postmodern mindset, to banish God altogether from our world and our lives.

It should be clear as to why some forms of feminism see process theism as an ally. Feminist theology tells what sort of personality God should have; process theism agrees, and process metaphysics offer an ontological grounding in the empirical world for this relational God.[164] Moreover, there is also an affinity with New Age thinking. Though that theology is avowedly pantheistic rather than panentheistic, many of the same themes about our relation to God and the rest of the universe appear in both theologies. Moreover, the political, social, and ecological agendas of New Agers (feminists and ecofeminists as well) fit hand in glove with the process God.

Process theology poses a formidable threat to traditional Christian understanding of God, and it also offers a way to synthesize various non-evangelical postmodern notions about God. It is not by accident that David Griffin, who edits a series of books meant to espouse and foster a postmodern vision of reality, structures his own theology (which he calls constructive postmodernism) with Whitehead's process metaphysics at its heart. Moreover, not only do many non-evangelicals find process thinking appealing; evangelicals positively inclined toward the "openness of God" camp also find much about it attractive. Process metaphysics is a highly technical conception of metaphysics, but it is not likely to pass from the scene quickly.

OTHER POSTMODERN THEOLOGIES. In *Varieties of Postmodern Theology*, David Griffin argues that postmodern theologies can be divided into four kinds. One type is the liberationist variety, discussed earlier. A second kind Griffin calls restorationist or conservative postmodernism, and he cites Pope John Paul II's theology as an example. Much in the pope's theology critiques modern society with its consumerism, technological threat to human existence on this planet, and fragmentation of community. The pope calls for a return to very traditional notions of God, but he also seeks a repudiation of the social and cultural aspects of the fragmenting modern mindset in favor of a more postmodern, communal vision of society.[165]

Griffin delineates two other types of postmodern theology. The most radical and negative form of postmodernity is deconstructionism, which stems from the work of Jacques Derrida and his followers. Derrida is thoroughly committed to the notion that we are all a product of our cultures and linguistic communities. Hence, we see things and present things from our own perspectives. One result of this perspectivalism is a recognition that there is no all-encompassing narrative that can decide for us once and for all what is true and what is false. Once we recognize this we also realize that throughout history cultures have been dominated by various visions of reality that claimed to be absolutist. A typical example, according to this line of thinking, is the Christian worldview, which says it is true because it is based on documents thought to be divinely inspired and inerrant.

In contrast, Derrida and his followers argue that we dare not absolutize any text, including Scripture, for each text reflects the culture and thinking of the times when it was written. Instead, we must use the "hermeneutics of suspicion" as we read. When we do this, we come to see that the text is usually the product of those in power, who used these texts to legitimize their continued control of power and suppression of those who didn't fit the ruling class. On the other hand, when we deconstruct these texts and learn when and why they were written, we de-absolutize their control over our lives. The other thing that happens is that we allow the "others," those at the boundaries of life, who have been marginalized in favor of the dominating traditional narratives that excluded them, to be heard and valued. In fact, David Tracy has argued that much of postmodern theology in general is a theological turn to the "other," an attempt in postmodern terms to include and celebrate the oppressed and marginalized.

Many critics claim that Derrida's deconstructing of texts and the institutions and power structures they support is an open invitation to anarchy, but Derrida and his supporters argue otherwise. John Caputo, a staunch supporter of Derrida, argues that deconstruction is neither negative nor destructive, but rather positive. Indeed, there is a deconstructing of texts and institutions, but not so as to destroy society. Rather, the deconstructing is done to "let in" the others who have been excluded. The intent is not simply to shift power from the "haves" to the "have nots," for this would substitute one form of repression for another. Instead, the goal of deconstructing so as to admit the coming or entrance of the other is to reconstruct society to be a new society that empowers all people and hears equally all different perspectives.[166]

This is an all-too-cryptic introduction to some of Derrida's ideas, but it suffices as an introduction to Mark Taylor's deconstructive postmodern theology as found in his *Erring: A Postmodern A/Theology*. Taylor's theology is based primarily on the deconstructionism of Jacques Derrida, whose thought is based in Hegel, Nietzsche, and Martin Heidegger. Taylor's postmodernism eliminates various ideas from premodern Western thought that modernity had retained even after the "death of God." Hence, Griffin calls it "eliminative postmodernism."

In discussing the basic mindset of modernity, we noted its rejection of a supernatural God, the God of traditional Christian theism. In its place was raised man and his importance and powers. Griffin says this effort to magnify the self by eliminating God is actually self-defeating, so there has really been a loss of the self as well as a loss of God. Many postmoderns, including Taylor, carry this process through to completion. The ultimate loss of the self is seen as a gain, because it is the modern notion of self that has brought us to the brink of total destruction.[167] The critique of the modern self as all-controlling, manipulative of nature, consuming all things for its own ends, and as focusing on the future rather than on the present, is a critique that many postmoderns, including Taylor, affirm.

Taylor essentially takes the modern death of the idea of the traditional God to its logical conclusions. "Taylor agrees with the death of the traditional God, but he does not replace Him with some less repressive notion of God. The idea of a unifying One or Center of existence is eliminated altogether. A central perspective, serving as the judge and criterion of truth, is denied. What remains is a multiplicity of perspectives, none of which is more normative than the others."[168]

Given these views, it also follows that there is no *truth*. This means more than that we cannot know the truth (though there is truth); it means that there really is no truth. The death of God means absolute relativism: there is no eternal truth, but only everlasting flux.[169] With the disappearance of God also comes the disappearance of the self. According to this view, the enclosed, centered, isolated self (typical of modernity) was actually created in the image of the enclosed, centered, isolated God of traditional theism. But once the notion of God is thrown out altogether, so is this notion of the self.[170] Instead of being completely independent of relations, the self is seen as *thoroughly* relational. Whereas the modern self was a substance in the Cartesian sense, requiring no relations to exist, the postmodern subject is primordially relational; it is *constituted* by its relations. This statement is intended radically, for the subject is not understood to be *causa sui* in any sense. Besides not being prior to its properties, it is not even distinct from them. It is "nothing other than the generative interplay of properties." Rather than in any way being responsible for its relationships, it is a mere function of the intersection of impersonal structures: "the subject is not self-centered but is a cipher for forces that play through it." No "inner transcendence" is to be affirmed. The self is thus not only desubstantialized but also completely deindividualized, which means that the self has really disappeared.[171]

Also eliminated is any translinguistic referent for linguistic signs. Signs refer only to other signs; they are not interpretations of some "real thing" beyond language. With God gone, there is no ultimate reference point for any of our language, for no one exists who guarantees the stability of anything. Hence, linguistic signs can refer to nothing more than other linguistic signs. This view also stems from skepticism about our ability to see the world as it is. Since all experience is interpreted through the grid of our cultural-linguistic framework, we cannot be sure that our language really points to anything other than more language.

Without God, there can be no notion of history as a directed process. The world is beginningless and has no end toward which it moves. History is a random sequence of meaningless occurrences. The postmodern person has no aim whatsoever, but is called to a life of erring, which means to wander "aimlessly and unprofitably."[172] Griffin writes:

> If history is meaningless, the present cannot be compared unfavorably with the past or future in terms of a distinction between reality and ideality. The present involves no fall from primal perfection, nor is it headed toward a perfect end, or even toward an increase in satisfaction. Because becoming need not be justified by reference to the past or future, it can be valued at every moment. Distractions from delight in the present due to feelings of guilt and yearnings for transcendence are silenced by rejecting the "opposition between what is and what ought to be."[173]

Removing the distinction between ought and is also means living beyond good and evil. "Taylor's postmodernist is called to follow Nietzsche in saying 'Yea' to everything on the basis of his (Nietzsche's) analysis of reality: 'In the actual world, in which everything is bound to and conditioned by everything else, to condemn and to think away anything means to condemn and to think away everything'."[174] Griffin argues that this position leads to absolute nihilism, which "also involves the denial of all meaning, all purpose, all moral and aesthetic norms. Nevertheless, this postmodern a/theology is said to be affirmative: rather than suffering these losses passively, it actively and willingly embraces nihilism and thereby overcomes it."[175]

Griffin is very critical of deconstructive postmodernism, but he favors a fourth type of postmodern theology, which he labels constructive or revisionary postmodernism. Griffin's version is not the only example, but he offers it in some detail. Many of his themes are familiar, so we can describe it briefly. Griffin contends that the way to overcome modernity is not to exclude all worldviews (as does deconstruction), but to construct a postmodern worldview through a revision of modern premises and traditional concepts. This will involve a new unity of science, ethics, aesthetics, and religion.

As noted above, two key dogmas of modernity are its epistemological belief in sensate empiricism and its ontological belief that the fundamental existents of the world are devoid of spontaneity or the power of self-movement (a mechanistic view of nature). Griffin calls this second view the nonanimistic view of nature, or nonanimism. He believes it was derived from supernaturalistic theism with its belief in divine omnipotence. As to sensate empiricism, it also arose in a supernaturalistic context: what could be known of the world comes from sense perception. Knowledge that is unavailable through sense perception would be provided by divine revelation of some sort. As modernity moved into its later period (eighteenth–twentieth century), God was omitted and people began adopting materialism with respect to the mind. As to knowledge about good and evil and God, it was deemed groundless and unconfirmable. The epistemological result was solipsism.[176]

As a corrective to the metaphysical doctrine, Griffin appeals to Whitehead's process metaphysics and writes:

In contrast with the nonanimism of modernity, Whiteheadian post-modernism develops a neoanimistic view in which all actual individuals embody a principle of spontaneity. The ultimate or absolute reality, which is embodied in all actual individuals, is *creativity*. Creativity eternally oscillates between two modes. In one mode, creativity is self-determination, final causation, or "concrescence," in which an individual becomes concrete by creating itself out of others. . . . As soon as this act of self-creation is completed, creativity swings over into its other mode, which is other-creation, efficient causation, or "transition." . . . The actual world is comprised entirely of creative events and the societies they form. . . . This perspective likewise contains no problem of how an experiencing mind can interact with non-experiencing physical atoms. It is part and parcel of this neoanimistic viewpoint to regard all creative events as "occasions of experience." . . . Because some level of experience is attributed to all actual individuals whatsoever, the avoidance of dualism does not require the assumption that the mind or soul is strictly identical with the body (or brain). The mind or soul can be thought of as a series of occasions of experience, each of which unifies the manifold experiences of the body (and the remainder of the past world) into a central experience of enjoyment and purpose. This doctrine avoids the substantial, isolated self of early modernity. . . . there is no underlying, enduring, unchanging subject of change for which relations to changing events are merely accidental. The things that endure, such as minds and molecules, "are not the completely real things." The completely real individuals do not *endure,* they *occur.* They are occasions of experience, which arise out of their relations to prior occasions of experience and include them in their own constitutions. This view is in fact so relational as to insist that the whole past is included in each occasion of experience.[177]

Griffin adds that this lack of an enduring substance does not mean there is no responsible, centered self altogether. Each actual entity has the power of self-causation and exercises self-creativity and freedom.

As to sensate empiricism, revisionary postmodernism based on Whiteheadian philosophy has a different answer. Griffin opts for a non-sensory perception, called prehension. This allows us to perceive things not ordinarily available through sense perception. Griffin explains:

Whitehead argues that sense-perception must be a high-level derivative form of perception. It is derivative from a primordial type of perception, called *prehension,* which we share with all other individuals whatsoever. This doctrine, that human beings share nonsensory perception with all other individuals, is simply the epistemological side of the ontological doctrine that all individuals are "occasions of experience" which arise out of their relations to (their prehensions of) previous individuals. Whitehead uses this doctrine of presensory perception to explain our knowledge that there is a real world beyond ourselves. Sensory perception by itself does not provide this knowledge. This knowledge also cannot be due to a high-level "judgment," because dogs and their fleas seem no less convinced of the reality of other things. This universal realism *can* be explained by a primitive form of perception shared by human, canine, and insect occasions of experience alike.[178]

Where is God in all of this? Griffin agrees with deconstructive postmodernism that we cannot believe in the supernatural God of premodern and early modern theology, but he does not remove God altogether. Instead, he opts for a naturalistic God, not a supernatural one. It comes as no surprise that Griffin adopts Whitehead's process God. According to Griffin, in supernatural theism, all power and creativity belong to God alone. In naturalistic theism, God and the world of finite existents share these things.[179]

JOHN HICK'S "THE REAL." Our discussion of what happens to God in contemporary thought concludes with John Hick's religious pluralism. Since it was already mentioned in chapter 2, we need not belabor it here. Hick, adapting Kant's distinction between the "thing-in-itself" and the "thing-for-us," argues that ultimate reality (the Real) is beyond comprehension and inspection. We have God only as we experience and understand him. Hick contends that the Real has been mediated through various means, including the natural world, to cultures at different times and places in history. Each society conceptualizes its own notion of ultimate reality in the form of the particular god or gods worshiped in that society. All of these conceptions in all religions are human attempts to articulate human experience and understanding of the ultimate reality.

According to Hick, the god or gods worshiped in various religions are all "masks" that different cultures have created in response to the Real's "presence" and "reality." The Real does exist, but there is little we can say about the Real in itself. Like other things-in-themselves, all we really can know is how the Real appears to us. Different religions' portraits of God point to the Real, but they are not identical to it.

The upshot of this is twofold. Hick presents God as both transcendent and immanent. The Real, which is the genuinely divine, is totally transcendent. The particular gods we conceptualize in response to our experience of the Real bring God nearer to us, and, depending on the religion and its conception of God, the "God-for-us" may be very immanent (as in pantheism and panentheism), or very remote (as in fundamentalist Islam and in the hidden God of neo-orthodoxy). We must understand, however, that neither the God of pantheism, panentheism, neo-orthodoxy, nor Islam is equal to the Real.

The other result of this view is that no religion is better or worse than any other. All point to the same thing, the Real. Which God you worship and which religion you follow is solely a function of your time and place in culture and history, but all roads lead to the same God. Hence, there is no reason to evangelize people from other religions, for all of us actually worship the same God, and all will be saved. Religious exclusivism is unnecessary.[180]

In concluding this chapter, I note how far the natural man strays from the truth of God, especially God's truth about himself. In addition, it is clear that many of the conceptions discussed are very appealing to contemporary people. While we cannot conform our notion of God to contemporary tastes and preferences, we do need to be sensitive to those themes. If the God of Scripture actually reflects themes like relatedness and responsiveness that are so dear to the hearts and minds of postmoderns, we should tell them so and show them the Scriptures that teach it. Moreover, amid the maze of conceptions of God, we must also be ready when needed to defend our understanding of the God of the Bible. In the face of complaints that the biblical God is premodern and antiquated, we must show otherwise! As we present our understanding of the biblical God, we must be sensitive to other views and concerns, and be careful to show that, where it does, the biblical portrait of God meets those concerns.

PROCESS THEOLOGY[1]

We have seen that process theology is a major contemporary alternative to traditional Christian theism. Moreover, its critique of classical theism is widely held to destroy anything like traditional Christian understandings of God. In fact, we have seen that a number of contemporary theologies, such as feminist theology, make the same fundamental criticisms of traditional theism as do process thinkers. In addition, we saw how various postmodern theologies find in process metaphysics an empirical understanding of reality that seems to follow logically from quantum physics, relativity theory, and evolution; hence, whatever the specific shape of the postmodern theology, Whiteheadian process metaphysics seems to fit it nicely.[2]

In light of the attractiveness of process theology and its powerful critique of traditional theism, many evangelicals are finding it harder to resist its call. We have seen this in describing the open view, but even evangelicals who don't favor the open view still find the process critique of the classical God's attributes very persuasive. Moreover, many evangelicals find themselves in substantial agreement with process theism's complaint that traditional theology is too immersed in and captivated by the philosophy of the ancient Greeks, especially Aristotle.[3]

A clear message in contemporary evangelical and non-evangelical literature is that process theism poses a significant alternative to traditional Christian theology. In light of these claims and the challenge process theology presents to evangelical theology, we must understand it and assess it accurately. That is the burden of this chapter.

In *Religion in the Making*, Alfred N. Whitehead wrote that "Christianity has always been a religion seeking a metaphysic."[4] He meant that, since the Bible records God's revelation and human responses, it mainly records religious experiences without clearly enunciating a general explanation of reality. While

Scripture surely presupposes a certain worldview, no metaphysic is explicitly stated in Scripture. Throughout the centuries theologians and philosophers have used various understandings of reality for communicating the Christian message to their own day. Whitehead purported to do the same for our day.

Had Whitehead never turned his attention to metaphysics, he would have been extremely important in twentieth-century philosophy. His monumental *Principia Mathematica,* coauthored with Bertrand Russell, and his work in physics make him an extremely important figure in philosophy of science. However, Whitehead wasn't content to work solely in philosophy of science. He applied his understanding of the new developments in science in the early twentieth century (as well as his understanding of philosophy and religion generally) to the construction of a new understanding of reality—process metaphysics. His system, most thoroughly expounded in *Process and Reality* (1929), was not merely an attempt to set forth a secular understanding of the nature of reality, for the principles of his system were intended to cover all of reality, including God. Hence, he concludes *Process and Reality* with a chapter on God and the world.[5]

Though Whitehead planted the seeds of process theology, it was up to his successors to develop it, and indeed, they have. The term "process thought" was first used by Bernard Loomer as a title of a seminar he taught at the University of Chicago Divinity School.[6] Other key figures in the development of process theology are Henry Nelson Wieman, Charles Hartshorne, John Cobb, Schubert Ogden, Bernard Meland, Daniel Day Williams, Norman Pittenger, Lewis Ford, and David Ray Griffin, to name a few. These names represent two distinct approaches within the process tradition: the rationalist approach (exemplified by Hartshorne), and the empiricist approach (exemplified by Henry N. Wieman). Hartshorne believed in the use of reason to probe *a priori* truth. He restructured the ontological argument for God's existence, which he thought successful. Of course, it is a Whiteheadian God that he has in mind. Those following in the rationalistic tradition have tended to be more concerned with the logical rectitude of the theology they were producing.[7] The empirical strain within process thought was less concerned with conceptual knowledge of God and rational proofs of him (let alone the rational consistency of beliefs). That is not to say they are anti-rational or irrational, but only that their emphasis was on what could be known through empirical data. This empirical approach went more in the direction of American pragmatism.[8]

In this chapter, my intention is two-fold. I intend initially to describe process theology, which is no small task because it isn't a monolithic structure. Though at points I shall speak of differences between process thinkers, my main concern is to present the major ideas of the movement as a whole. My second goal is to critique process theology (though some of its emphases are beneficial). I am especially concerned to evaluate process theology's claim that it makes the Christian message more intelligible than does evangelicalism.

Backgrounds of Process Theology

No conceptual system arises in a total intellectual vacuum, and process theology is no exception. In particular, four main influences help us understand the development and (to some extent) the appeal of process theology. They are 1) developments in science, 2) the perceived inadequacy of classical theism, 3) the philosophical influences behind the system, and 4) the theological and religious climate of the times.

Developments in Science

Some of the major influences that led Whitehead to his new metaphysic were developments in science. The breakdown of Newtonian mechanistic physics was especially important. According to the Newtonian conception, physical things are changeless, inert, "stuff-like."[9] Each thing has its own spatio-temporal location independent of everything else, so that bits of matter are essentially discrete and discontinuous with other bits of matter.[10] According to this view, the only kind of change possible is locomotion. In the seventeenth century, it was thought that God would occasionally intervene in the world to stimulate such motion, but by the end of the eighteenth century, scientists had discovered a way to render the intervention of God in the natural system unnecessary.[11] By the end of the nineteenth century, scientists had fully worked out the implications of this mechanistic conception, but anomalies had arisen. In the twentieth century Whitehead astutely saw some of the implications of new discoveries in science and began to apply those implications in constructing a new metaphysic.

Whitehead focused on several items. First, Whitehead saw that in James Clerk Maxwell's hands, electromagnetic theory had a shape which demanded that there be electromagnetic occurrences throughout all space. Hence, electromagnetic effects were conceived as arising from a continuous field.[12] This meant, of course, that the idea of discontinuous, discrete, and unrelated bits of matter could no longer be sustained. As to the concept of energy, the key issue was the doctrine of the conservation of energy, which entailed "a quantitative permanence underlying change."[13] All of this meant that matter was not the only kind of permanence, but also that there could not only be change in place (locomotive change), but change in energy. Since change in energy is not reducible to locomotive change, this meant that there could be other kinds of change than locomotive in the physical realm. Both the theory of energy and the theory of electromagnetism led Whitehead to reject the notion of the physical as changeless, inert matter. Instead, he claimed that the primary physical entities must be basically "event-like."[14] Leclerc explains what Whitehead meant by "event" when he writes,

> For "event" does not mean a mere or sheer "happening." Whitehead used the word "event" in its primary etymological sense of "to come out" (from the Latin *evenire*), which implies "something" which comes

out. This entails that the "something" must necessarily be *continuous* with that out of which it comes. And it also entails that the "something" must have an essential *discreteness* as itself different from that out of which it comes.[15]

As Whitehead notes, these scientific discoveries in the nineteenth century suggested that something was wrong with the old Newtonian mechanistic physics, but it wasn't until the twentieth century that a new physics emerged. The emergence of relativity theory and quantum mechanics proved to shape the scientific understanding of the twentieth century. To summarize the point on relativity, Whitehead explains that under mechanistic physics there is a unique meaning to time and space. Hence, whatever spatial relation means as measured on earth, the same meaning must be given when measured on a comet or by an instrument at rest in the ether. The same is true with respect to temporal relations. Relativity theory denies these assumptions.[16] Instead, what a thing is and how it is to be understood can never be determined in isolation from its relations to other things. The notion of simple location in space and time (devoid of relation to other things) could no longer be retained. Whatever is, is in part in virtue of its relation to other things.

As to quantum mechanics, Whitehead's key interest was that according to quantum theory, "some effects which appear essentially capable of gradual increase or gradual diminution are in reality to be increased or decreased only by certain definite jumps."[17] The net result is a revision of concepts of physical things. In particular, a theory of discontinuous existence is needed. "What is asked from such a theory, is that an orbit of an electron can be regarded as a series of detached positions, and not as a continuous line."[18] When coupled with the other items of scientific theory, this means the following: all things in the world are related to one another in a continuous process of change (atomic theory shows that at the atomic and sub-atomic level things are not static, but in motion, even in cases of the most solid bits of matter). What a thing is, must be understood in terms of its relation to other things also in process, but that is not to say that there is such continuity between individual entities that the entities blend together so as to be indistinguishable. Each entity, while bearing continuity with all other entities, is at the same time a distinct thing.

A final item of import from science is evolution. As Whitehead notes, one of the major scientific changes in the nineteenth century was the rise of evolutionary theory, the doctrine which "has to do with the emergence of novel organisms as the outcome of chance."[19] Though some have argued that neither specific evolutionary theories nor any overarching evolutionary cosmology played a significant role in Whitehead's metaphysics,[20] it is safe to say that his metaphysics presupposes this sort of theory and fits with it.[21] Moreover, within the development of process theology other thinkers do not hesitate to admit their acceptance of evolutionary notions of upward biological development.

Attack on Classical Theism

Process theists believe that classical Christian theism is inadequate, not just because its conceptions reflect outmoded Aristotelian and Newtonian physics, but also because some of its fundamental ideas portray God in ways that are both logically incoherent and morally repugnant. Invariably, process thinkers begin their theology with an attack on traditional theism. We have already described the process critique in chapter 2, so we can be brief here.

Process thinkers insist that in our modern scientific world, secular people simply cannot accept many of the ideas associated with traditional theism. For example, the notion of a created universe as portrayed in Genesis 1–2 is seen today as myth, not history. Moreover, biblical accounts of miracles, once held crucial to traditional Christian faith, are now seen as inessential, because many can be explained by naturalistic processes and others are just expressions of faith, not actual occurrences that produced faith. In addition, say these process thinkers, the eschatological perspective of Scripture must be rejected. The idea of a "last days," an end to the world, and Christ's return are clearly problematic. These events have gone unfulfilled for nearly 2,000 years, and there is no serious reason to think they will be fulfilled.[22]

As for the traditional Christian conception of God, process theists don't like the amount of power and control over our world that classical theism gives God. Whitehead claimed that Western theism consists of an amalgamation of three different images of God. Traditional theism's God is conceived in the likeness of an "imperial ruler (associated with the Roman Caesars), a hypostatization of moral energy (the Hebrew prophets), and an ultimate metaphysical principle (Aristotle)."[23] As Claude Stewart shows, under continued critique of classical theism, some of Whitehead's disciples (e.g., John Cobb and David Griffin) have claimed that the list of interwoven images actually includes five images: "God as cosmic moralist, as the unchanging and passionless absolute, as all-controlling power, as sanctioner of the status quo, and as male."[24]

In addition, traditional theism is said to rely on the metaphysics of ancient Greek philosophers, especially Plato and Aristotle. According to these Greeks, there are two types of reality. On the one hand, there is the present world of becoming, time, change, and real relations. On the other, there is another "world of timeless, changeless, and unrelated being, which is alone 'real' in the full sense of the word and so alone worthy of the epithet 'divine.'"[25] Especially repugnant is Aristotle's talk of substances. Process thinkers understand these to be static, unrelated, and isolated material things. Quantum physics, relativity theory, and evolution teach us, however, that nothing is unattached and unrelated to the rest of reality, nor are the ultimate realities static and unmovable. Process thinkers claim that when Aristotelian static substance was tied in traditional theism to God and the world, it meant that God is timeless, immutable, unrelated to the world, and unaffected by what happens in it (impassible). It also meant that God was the totally transcendent absolute with whom one could have no relation, and it meant that if the real is not in this world but in another world, then what goes on in this world is really insignificant.[26] Process thinkers, and contemporary philosophers and theologians more generally, reject the notion of persons as isolated, remote individuals (see critiques of modernity's isolated individualism in chapter 3). Hence, they detest speaking of God or anything else in substance language, which they believe incorporates the negative elements of Aristotle's metaphysics. As James Felt convincingly shows, it is dubious that this is what Aristotle actually said about substances, and it is equally clear that Whitehead misunderstood Aristotle.[27] Nonetheless, this conception of Aristotelian substances persists, and along with the Cartesian notion of individual things is roundly criticized in contemporary thinking, especially by process theologians.

None of this sits well with process thinkers. If God dare not enter into real relations with his creatures because that might cause him to change (as immutable, he can't change in any way), then, they say, the God of traditional theism is irrelevant to modern man.[28] Crucial to process critiques is rejection of the classical account of divine impassibility. If God cannot change, then surely he cannot feel emotions like compassion, because that would constitute a change in God. Hartshorne explains the problem by appealing to the parent-child relation. While we would not praise a parent whose actions were totally dependent on the whims of his child, or think it a sign of maturity if he were overly elated at his child's joys and totally depressed at the child's sorrows, on the other hand, we wouldn't praise a parent who was indifferent to his child's actions or was unmoved when the child was happy or sad. Nonetheless, Hartshorne complains, "Yet God, we are told, is impassive and immutable and without accidents, is just as he would be in his action and knowledge and being had we never existed, or had all our experiences been otherwise."[29] Hartshorne cites Anselm's statement that God is passionless and does not feel compassion toward man, though he can express compassion in terms of our experience. Hartshorne claims that this means we should love God, not because he can sympathize with us (if he could, that might mean his moods and feelings were in part dependent on us, and that dependence is unallowable in classical theism), but because he can do things for our benefit.

If God is unaffected by us, and if our world is not the real world, then, as Schubert Ogden says, nothing we ever do or suffer ultimately makes any difference to God, and nothing that happens in this world is of significance.[30] Moreover, it is useless to speak of our aim as glorifying God, for God is absolute, and it is beyond our power to contribute to his greatness.[31] Likewise, it is impossible to speak meaningfully of serving God, for, as Hartshorne claims, "if God can be indebted to no one, can receive value from no one, then to speak of serving him is to indulge in equivocation."[32]

The ultimate problem, according to process theists, is that this is so contrary to the biblical portrait of God and to common sense. Scripture shows God changing his mind (e.g., Gen 6:5-7), entering relationships with people (cf. his covenants with Abraham and David), and showing emotions like anger and compassion (all of which must be anthropomorphism at best and mythology at worst, if classical theism is correct). Likewise, if God cannot enter time because that would involve the potential for change and for entering relationships, then he is locked out of the world, but Scripture teaches otherwise. Finally, if what happens here really doesn't matter, why does Scripture record God's concern and his deeds to redeem us? Scripture and common sense show anyone that what happens in this world matters, not only to us but also to God.

One final belief of classical theism is especially upsetting to process thinkers: God as totally transcendent cannot be completely known by us. We may attribute our characteristics to God, but as Aquinas reminds us, we do so only analogically. As to divine qualities which we in no way possess, we must try to discover what they mean. This means that in traditional theism there are limits on knowing and naming God.[33] Of course, this means that God is transcendent and ultimately shrouded in mystery. Such a God, however, can easily be viewed as irrelevant to contemporary needs (as in God Is Dead theologies). Theists, when reaching the limits of knowledge about this God, like to say that he is shrouded in mystery and paradox. Hartshorne replies that this is just a typical theologian's ploy, for "A theological paradox, it appears, is what a contradiction becomes when it is about God rather than something else, or indulged in by a theologian or a church rather than an unbeliever or a heretic."[34] The answer offered by process theologians is to reconstruct our concept of God so that the ontological categories of process theology apply to every level of reality, including God.[35] Such a God, they believe, can be understood.

Philosophical Background

Many philosophical influences were important to Whitehead, but for our purposes, I note several significant items. First, there is the connection with Plato and Aristotle. In his metaphysics, Aristotle introduced the notion of Prime Mover. This was done not for religious reasons but for the sake of completing his own cosmology. Likewise, Whitehead's process metaphysics was incomplete without reference to God, but as with Aristotle, Whitehead's invoking God was not for religious or theological purposes but for metaphysical and cosmological purposes. In Aristotle, Whitehead saw a model not so much of how this could be done but of the need for it to be done and a model of the legitimacy of introducing God without thereby making religion foundational to metaphysics.[36] Moreover, in Whitehead's discussion of actual physical entities, he was concerned to relate the multiplicity of all such entities. Whitehead concluded that they are ultimately dependent upon what he called formative elements. Following Plato and Aristotle (who called these items *archai,* principles), he saw three such elements. In addition to the plurality of acting physical entities, he saw a general activity underlying all occasions of individual acting which was their ultimate source. This idea was analogous to (though not identical to) Aristotle's notion of substance. Whitehead's second formative principle is the eternal objects, and these are coordinate with Plato and Aristotle's notion of forms, though Whitehead's conception of the eternal objects is surely closer to Plato's conception than to Aristotle's. The third formative element in Plato and Aristotle upon which things depend is God, and Whitehead agreed, though his conception of God differs from Plato and Aristotle's.[37] He agreed with Plato that if there were to be any way to choose between the many possibilities (some good and some evil) which an entity could become, one of the formative elements (God) would have to be the source of the distinction between good and bad, better and worse. Otherwise, in choosing from the many possibilities, there would be no way to limit what might be chosen, so that one could actually decide. For both Plato and Whitehead God is (in Whitehead's terminology) that principle of limitation.[38]

Second, the influence of the British empiricists John Locke and George Berkeley on Whitehead has been traced by some.[39] Of special influence is Berkeley's theory of perception. Berkeley noted that there is a difference in the way an object such as a tower appears from a distance as opposed to nearby. The difference must not be in the tower itself but in the act of perception. Hence, what a person perceives depends more on the act of perception than on the thing perceived. As Whitehead noted, Berkeley said in his *Principles of Human Knowledge* that "what constitutes the realisation of natural entities is the being perceived within the unity of mind."[40] Adapting Berkeley's insight for his own uses, Whitehead wrote that "we can substitute the concept, that the realisation is a gathering of things into the unity of a prehension; and that what is thereby realised is the prehension, and not the things."[41] The relation of this concept of prehension to Berkeley's notion of perception becomes even clearer when one sees Whitehead's definition of prehension:

> The word *perceive* is, in our common usage, shot through and through with the notion of cognitive apprehension. So is the word *apprehension,* even with the adjective *cognitive* omitted. I will use the word *prehension* for *uncognitive apprehension:* by this I mean *apprehension* which may or may not be cognitive.[42]

Finally, to understand process theology one must understand contemporary epistemology. From the time of the empiricists (Locke, Berkeley, and Hume) the prevailing epistemology has been empiricism. Within that general tradition, Kant argued that all knowledge comes ultimately through experience, by which he meant interaction with the empirical world. Hence, Kant distinguished two levels of reality, which he called noumena and phenomena. As we have seen, in light of this distinction, Kant claimed to put an end to traditional or speculative metaphysics, which deals with things that belong to the noumenal realm, including God, the immortal soul, and things in themselves apart from our perception of them.

Epistemology following Kant kept his fundamental empiricist approach. By the twentieth century logical positivism with its empiricist foundations was very much in sway. When Whitehead was writing *Process and Reality*, logical positivism's influence was widely felt. To what extent Whitehead tried to accommodate himself to positivism and its verification theory of meaning is hard to say. What is clear is that Whitehead's metaphysics, in contrast to other metaphysical schemes, was built on empiricist foundations.

Whitehead sought to structure a new metaphysic, and his followers have in one form or another accepted his fundamental notions about reality. However, it is crucial to realize that process thinkers from Whitehead onward, though they may not speak much of the prevailing epistemology of our times, have all taken empiricism very seriously.[43] While some concluded that the findings of Kant and those after him really did destroy metaphysics altogether, Whitehead and his followers concluded that it only destroyed a certain type of metaphysics, a metaphysics that goes beyond the empirical. What is truly interesting is that while Whitehead's process metaphysics was written during the heyday of rigorous empiricism under logical positivism, his system, especially as developed by his followers, did not really begin to become popular until the twentieth century was moving into a more postmodern mindset.

Theological/Religious Climate of the Times

In the late nineteenth and early twentieth century, non-orthodox theology was in the grasp of old-line liberalism. Whitehead's *Process and Reality* with its comprehensive vision of reality was published in 1929, but it initially had little impact on theology and the church. Non-orthodox theology had turned from the bankruptcy of old liberalism to embrace Barthianism. Of course Barthianism, with its heavy dependency on existentialism, had little use for metaphysics. No metaphysical system could possibly capture the most important thing, a person in the act of existing and becoming. Moreover, for neo-orthodox thinkers, personal encounter with God (not reasoned argument or lengthy descriptions of God's nature as one might find in a metaphysic) confirmed his existence and revealed his nature.

Part of neo-orthodoxy's legacy is its belief in a transcendent, wholly other God. As existentialist theologians such as Tillich articulated this idea, it meant that God became more remote and impersonal. Some theologians, reading the signs in Tillich's work and sensing that the classical Christian God was equally remote and impersonal, declared shortly after mid-century that God was dead. If he was to be revived at all, he could no longer be an impersonal, remote God to whom our world makes no difference. If there was to be a gospel, it would be a secularized one. Classical theism was presumed incapable of filling the bill, but neo-orthodoxy seemed little better. Though one supposedly could encounter God in his Word Jesus Christ, such encounters still left God remote. While they might affect the individual, they had no effect on God, and since the private encounter was not available for public verification, no one could guarantee that *God* was encountered. As Schubert Ogden has argued, the time was clearly ripe for a new vision of reality and of God.[44]

Amid these theological trends, various cultural events had great influence on the tenor of the times. In particular, one cannot underestimate the significance of World Wars I and II on the mindset of the era. The old belief in the basic goodness and brotherhood of all people could hardly be upheld, especially after World War II. Moreover, many asked how there could be a God in view of the Holocaust. Those still inclined to believe in God found it difficult to believe in (let alone worship) a God who traditional theism claimed had foreordained the Holocaust and who was totally unmoved by all the suffering it wrought. If twentieth-century people could still believe in God, he must be deeply sympathetic to our suffering and must even suffer along with us. Moreover, he definitely could not be a God who predestined events like the Holocaust.

Process theology has risen to prominence since the late 1960s, but process thinkers have been at work through much of the twentieth century. Though process thought first gained acceptance in an Anglo-American context, its influence continues to grow worldwide. The emphasis on God's relation to the world and his concern for it is entirely compatible with the insights of political theologies such as liberation theology, feminist theology, and the social and political agenda of New Age thinking. Moreover, given its openness to world religions as evident in its understanding of Christ and redemption, it can be very attractive to peoples of other cultures and religions.[45] It seems more than coincidental, for example, that one of the greatest centers for process studies (with John Cobb), the Claremont School of Theology, is also a major center for the study of comparative religions (with John Hick).[46] It is also the location of David Griffin's project for promoting a postmodern worldview, and as noted in chapter 3, his own theology incorporates Whitehead's process theism.

MAJOR CONCEPTS IN PROCESS THOUGHT

Key Definitions

In explaining central process ideas, it is helpful to understand certain key terms.

ACTUAL ENTITIES.   For Whitehead, actual entities are the "final real things of which the world is made up."[47] There is nothing behind these entities or occasions, such as an underlying substance, which is more real. According to Whitehead, the world is a process, and that "process is the becoming of actual entities."[48] Moreover, he claims that *"how* an actual entity *becomes* constitutes *what* that actual entity *is*. . . . Its 'being' is constituted by its 'becoming'."[49] Actual entities are not static, for they are always in the process of changing and developing (becoming), nor are they isolated from other actual entities, for each actual entity can be incorporated into another entity and can incorporate other actual entities into itself, and actual entities are frequently a nexus, a set of actual entities united by their mutual grasping of one another.[50] Moreover, as Lowe explains, each actual entity, though in the process of becoming, is at each stage of development a unique individual entity.[51] Finally, actual entities are subjects.[52] They are centers of feeling, a feeling being "the appropriation of some elements in the universe to be components in the real internal constitution of its subject."[53] This means that all actual entities (humans, animals, trees, rocks, etc.) are attributed characteristics of the mental and of persons; they aren't mere objects.

PREHENSION.   "Prehension" is Whitehead's term for the acting of one actual entity upon another to relate it to itself. Each prehension (literally, grasping, though we have already seen the relation of this to perception and apprehension) or feeling is a taking of an item of the many into the arising unity of a new actual entity synthesized from the old.[54] In every prehension, Whitehead saw three elements: 1) the prehending subject (an actual entity); 2) the datum, whether a physical or eternal object, which is prehended; and 3) the "subjective form" of prehension, which is how the datum is prehended. There are various subjective forms, such as emotions, valuations, purposes, aversions, consciousness, etc.[55] Hence, if I prehend a new car, the subjective form of my prehension might mean that I cry over its beauty, I consider it a poor car and determine not to buy it, or I decide to raise money to purchase it.

ETERNAL OBJECTS.   Eternal objects are corollaries of Platonic forms or eternal ideas. Eternal objects are the pure potentials or possibilities which represent the range of possibilities that actual entities may become.[56] According to Whitehead, God doesn't create the eternal objects; they are just there.[57]

CONCRESCENCE.   A concrescence is the process of composition of prehensions.[58] As Whitehead defines it, "in the becoming of an actual entity, the *potential* unity of many entities—actual and non-actual—acquires the *real* unity of the one actual entity; so that the actual entity is the real concrescence of many potentials."[59]

SUBJECTIVE AIM.   "Subjective aim" refers to the goal of an actual entity in its becoming.[60] In Aristotelian terms it is the final cause of a thing. Whitehead refers to it as the "lure, whereby there is determinate concrescence."[61] He says, "the 'subjective aim,' which controls the becoming of a subject, is that subject feeling a proposition with the subjective form of purpose to realize it in that process of self-creation."[62] Not only is there an ultimate subjective aim for each actual entity, but there is a subjective aim for each stage in the emerging entity's becoming.

THE ONTOLOGICAL PRINCIPLE.   The ontological principle is the Whiteheadian principle that "every condition to which the process of becoming conforms in any particular instance, has its reason *either* in the character of some actual entity in the actual world of that concrescence, *or* in the character of the subject which is in process of concrescence. . . . it means that actual entities are the only *reasons;* so that to search for a *reason* is to search for one or more actual entities."[63]

Central Concepts

There are many key ideas in process thought, but my focus is those of import for theology.

REALITY AS PROCESS, BECOMING.   According to process thinkers, ours is a world of events (in the sense of a coming out of) and becoming. The ultimate real actualities are actual entities, but they are not static objects. Everything is in the process of becoming, and as such it is also in the process of perishing (i.e., its previous states slip from subjective immediacy). As events in process, all things have three elements. They are the objective results of the events out of which they arose, and they reflect the qualities of those prior events. Nonetheless, they are "subjects," i.e., distinct centers of feeling which are combinations of their constituent parts and data. And, as each actual entity at each stage perishes, it perishes from subjective immediacy and is swallowed up in the following events. As such, they become permanent givens in the data of history which influence new events which are coming to be.[64]

Process thinkers constantly remind us that theirs is a metaphysic of events and becoming, not of being and substance.[65] If this sounds strange to the Western mind with its predilection for substance philosophies, Hartshorne reminds us that Buddhism has espoused a philosophy of becoming. Buddhists rejected the notion of substances, including the notion of the soul as substance. They claimed that the fundamental realities are momentary experiences which are in a process of becoming or generating new experiences.[66] We must be careful not to misunderstand this. It would be easy to think that process thinkers mean that the most fundamental realities are events or happenings, but of course, one wonders what it is that becomes. That is, it appears that there must be specific entities in the world which are in the process of becoming. In arguing for a metaphysic of becoming rather than a metaphysic of being and substance, process thinkers are not rejecting being altogether. As we have seen, Whitehead believed the fundamental realities are actual entities. Moreover, process thinkers typically assert the eternality of matter. The point process thinkers are making is that one must not think of a world of beings which *qua* beings are static, unmovable, unchangeable. That kind of substance metaphysic is what they reject. Atomic theory, let alone common sense, shows us that everything is in a dynamic process of motion, even the most solid piece of matter. Hartshorne is especially helpful here:

> "Being" is here defined through becoming: That may be said to be which is available for memory or perception, for integration into ever new acts of synthesis, and in this sense is a potential for all future becoming. *To be is to be available for all future actualities.* It is to be noted that the foregoing doctrine literally defines "being," or permanent reality, in terms of becoming. Thus it is a misconception to suppose that process philosophy, siding with becoming, rejects being. Rather, it is a doctrine of being *in* becoming, permanence in the novel.[67]

Another significant point in understanding reality as a becoming is Whitehead's view that there are two kinds of processes. The first focuses on the movement from one occasion to the next (the change from an actual entity being at one stage, and hence one entity, to another stage, and thus being another entity). This may be called a process of transition, and it is a temporal process. The other kind of process is a process of the coming into being of an occasion itself, i.e., its subjective arising. This kind of process is called a genetic process.[68] It looks at becoming from the perspective of the actual entity subjectively experiencing that becoming. The former kind of process looks at the move from one stage to another without focus on the subjective experiencing of any stage. The transition involved in genetic process can only be directly experienced by the actual entity involved in the transition. A process of transition in a given actual entity may be observed by other actual entities, but what is going on "inside" the changing entity can only be experienced by the entity itself.

One of the obvious results of a metaphysic of becoming is that there is constant novelty. Though things which become arise in part from past prehensions and past history in general, each emergent stage involves the creation of a new, unique thing. As Tremmel explains, "Every occasion in time is a *new* occasion. It is an occasion that has just come into being. There is nothing like it anywhere else, or ever has been, or ever will be again."[69] This bespeaks both continuity and discontinuity.

A final point about reality as becoming is that it refers not only to animate beings, but to all actual entities, from the smallest "puff" of existence to the highest level of being. As to these entities, "though there are gradations of importance, and diversities of function, yet in the principles which actuality exemplifies all are on the same level."[70] Accordingly, process thinkers all subscribe to Whitehead's classic dictum that "God is not to be treated as an exception to all metaphysical principles, invoked to save their collapse. He is their chief exemplification."[71]

GOD AS BIPOLAR. So far, little has been said of God, but Whitehead included him in his system, and later process thinkers have developed quite extensively the concept of God. Process thinkers uniformly affirm that God, as all actual entities, is dipolar or bipolar. God has a primordial nature (his conceptual pole) and a consequent nature (his physical pole).

God's primordial nature is permanent and unchanging. It is the envisagement of the realm of possibilities, the eternal objects, but this has been understood in various ways even by Whitehead. Whitehead's main metaphysical assumptions demand that the principles relevant to God are the same as those for all other actual entities. Hence, just as God envisages eternal objects, so must all other actual entities. Each actual entity prehends its own possibilities plus the entire realm of all possibilities. In God's case, of course, the two are coterminous, whereas for other actual entities they are not. As John Cobb notes, this is the basic understanding of God's relation to the eternal objects we find in Whitehead's *Religion in the Making*.[72] Of course, God doesn't just know the possibilities (and know them more fully than other actual entities can), but he also organizes them with respect to their relative value and their possible joint actualization in any given occasion.[73] As some process thinkers portray God's primordial nature in line with this perception, it is nothing more than the ordering of the eternal objects, getting them ready for ingression into the world.[74]

In *Process and Reality,* Whitehead makes God's relation to the eternal objects significantly different from what we see in *Religion in the Making*. In *Process and Reality* he claims that since everything must be somewhere (i.e., it must be some actual entity), this must also be true of the general potentiality of the universe. The "somewhere" for eternal objects is the non-temporal actual entity (Whitehead's designation for God). That is, the primordial mind of God is the eternal objects. His relation to them is unmediated, whereas the relation of other actual entities to them is mediated. On this view, then, though God doesn't create the eternal objects but orders and evaluates them, they wind up being basically equivalent to his primordial nature.[75] Speaking of God, Whitehead says in *Process and Reality,* "Viewed as primordial, he is the unlimited conceptual realization of the absolute wealth of potentiality. In this aspect, he is not *before* all creation, but *with* all creation."[76] Though this distinction may seem a fine point in Whitehead, I raise it ultimately because I intend to argue that on either conception this notion of the primordial nature of God presents problems for process theology.

God's consequent nature, his physical pole, is changing and impermanent. Moreover, it is concrete. If God were nothing but primordial, he would be merely pure possibility apart from any reality. Thus, he must have a concrete, physical pole to complete the vision of the possibilities. That concrete pole is God's consequent nature, and in essence, the consequent nature is the world. In speaking about God's primordial and consequent natures, Whitehead says that "His 'consequent nature' results from his physical prehensions of the derivative actual entities."[77] According to the passage just cited, God's consequent nature results from physical prehensions of those actual entities.[78] How many? Obviously, all of them, but that means the world! Hence, process thinkers often refer to the world as God's body. From the process perspective, God's being and that of the world interpenetrate one another. Since the world is changing and developing, so is God, and changes in the world enrich his being.[79] Moreover, even as actual entities in the world are perishing, there is a sense in which God is also perishing. On the other hand, to perish means to pass from subjective immediacy to objectivity where the subject has no direct apprehension of the thing. For example, as I write this sentence, the ideas and words are immediate before my mind. As I move on, the previous sentence is objectively real in the world, but it has passed from being immediately before my thinking (and even from my visual field). Clearly, to perish isn't to be annihilated. Hence, process thinkers speak of God's consequent nature as "everlasting." "This means that it involves a creative advance, just as time does, but that the earlier elements are not lost as new ones are added."[80] In other words, the physical pole will always be there, but not necessarily in the same form as before.

God, then, is dipolar, a unity composed of a physical and a mental pole.[81] In so being, he is like all other actual entities; reality is bipolar. Whitehead had a habit in *Process and Reality* of abstracting the two divine poles from one another and speaking as though they function independent of each other. However, although God may do one thing in virtue of his physical pole and another in virtue of his mental pole, it is always God as a totality, the actual entity, who acts.[82]

A final point about the very being of God stems from a problem Whitehead left for his followers. According to Whitehead, God is an actual entity with a mental pole (the eternal objects) and a physical pole (the world). Since the world is always in the process of becoming (concrescing), the actual entity which is God is also always in the process of becoming. For Whitehead, in the case of every other actual entity, whatever is becoming (subject) cannot also be object, but only objects can be prehended. This means that when an actual occasion is in the process of concrescing, no one can grasp it in its subjective immediacy. It can only be prehended by other actual entities as they develop once it has reached its new stage of development and is some objective thing. The difficulty this creates for Whitehead is that God always provides the initial aim (in virtue of his primordial nature) for any actual entity, but if things that are becoming cannot be prehended, and God is eternally becoming, then he cannot serve in Whitehead's system the function he must serve for the rest of the world. That is, the world cannot prehend him, for it can only causally interact with something determinate and objectified, and God never fits that description.[83]

Charles Hartshorne (in *The Divine Relativity*) proposed a modification to Whitehead on this point, and many process thinkers have adopted it. His solution conceives of God as a personally ordered society of divine occasions. God as a society of occasions (God as social) could be both subject and object. Each new divine occasion achieves objective being as God moves on to the next occasion, and all objective occasions are available for prehension by the world. Nonetheless, since God is always becoming, there is some new occasion which is always subjectively immediate to him. Hence, God as a society of occasions can be both subject and object and thereby apparently solve the problem left by Whitehead. Moreover, Hartshorne says that his perception of God as a society of occasions is also true of all other actual entities.[84]

GOD AS PERSONAL, MUTABLE, AND PASSIBLE.   Process thinkers reject traditional theism's immutable and impassible God in favor of a God whom they believe is more personal. Hartshorne's treatment of these issues is representative.

In *The Divine Relativity* Hartshorne argues that the process God is a personal God, but what is crucial is his definition of "personal." For Hartshorne, to be personal means to be related.[85] Throughout *The Divine Relativity* Hartshorne's main thesis is that God, of all beings, is supremely related or "surrelative."[86] Of course, since God's being interpenetrates the being of all else so that his consequent nature is the world, he is definitely the supremely relative being. As Hartshorne writes, "a personal God is one who has social relations, really has them, and thus is constituted by relationships and hence is relative—in a sense not provided for by the traditional doctrine of a divine Substance wholly nonrelative toward the world, though allegedly containing loving relations between the 'persons' of the Trinity."[87]

As to immutability, from the description of God's consequent nature it is clear that the process God is mutable. Hartshorne claims that mutability has typically been rejected because it is assumed that if God changed, he would have to change for better or for worse. If for the worse, he would be unworthy of admiration, but if for the better, then in what sense could we speak of him as perfect, lacking nothing, as we typically do?[88] Hartshorne dismisses the idea that God could possibly change for the worse, because he doesn't believe it can be proved that there is ever more sorrow than joy in the world. Hence, there would always be a net increment of value accruing to God at any moment. As to apparent imperfection if he changes for the better, Hartshorne answers:

> My reply is that, as we are here using the term, perfect means completely worthy of admiration and respect, and so the question becomes, is such complete admirableness infringed by the possibility of enrichment in total value? I say it is not. We do not admire a man less because we know he would be a happier man if his son, who is wretched, became well and happy, or because we anticipate that when a child is born to him it will enrich his life with many new joys. Admiration is not directed to happiness, except so far as we feel that a person does or does not attain the happiness appropriate to the state of the world as known to him. We admire not the amount but the appropriateness of the joy.[89]

Though all process theologians argue that God is fundamentally mutable, there is one sense in which they believe he is immutable: whatever qualities God has, he has *immutably*. Hence, God is immutably mutable, immutably surrelative, immutably passible, and so on.

PROCESS THEOLOGY □ 165

It also follows, according to process theology, that God is not unaffected by the world. He experiences our sufferings and joys with us as we experience them.[90] As Whitehead says, God is "the great companion—the fellow-sufferer who understands."[91] Other process writers often cite this passage approvingly. What we think and do affects God, and that means, among other things, that we can enhance and enrich him, and add value to his being by our actions.[92] In describing John Cobb's process theology, Claude Stewart writes:

> Cobb's intent is to bring the notion of sympathetic responsiveness into our understanding of the divine character in general and divine love in particular. Both the content of the divine knowledge and "God's own emotional state" (!) are dependent upon his perception of and response to what is going on in the world. The divine love or agape, is not properly perceived as a contradictory state of "passionless compassion," but rather as compassion in the fully proper sense—that is, as inclusive of the element of sympathetic feeling, divine feeling of and with the feelings of worldly beings. God then is to be understood as *"responsive* love." But in Whiteheadian-Hartshornean-Cobbian perspective—that is, in process perspective—God is also to be understood as *"creative* love."[93]

Hartshorne adds that true religion is serving God, but serving God is not merely admiring or obeying him, but contributing and conferring benefit to God which he would otherwise lack.[94]

GOD'S ACTION. If God is as immanent in the world as process thinkers believe, it would seem that they would conceive him as being very active, but this is not the case. As we shall see, the idea of God as creator is denied, miracles in the sense of divine intervention to suspend natural laws are denied as vestiges of a mythological vision of reality, and God's action in Christ is seen as really quite passive.

What, then, can and does God do? Daniel Day Williams says that God exercises causality in the world, but always in relation to beings which have their own measure of causal self-determination as they interact with others.[95] This ultimately means that whatever the process God does, he won't infringe upon the freedom of other actual entities. In his *God, Power and Evil: A Process Theodicy,* David Griffin distinguishes two senses of omnipotence, "I" omnipotence and "C" omnipotence. "I" omnipotence is an omnipotent being's ability to affect unilaterally any logically possible state of affairs.[96] In contrast, "C" omnipotence means that it is not logically possible for God unilaterally to control the actions of self-determining beings, even if those actions are logically possible.[97] Griffin opts for "C" omnipotence, so God is omnipotent in that he can do anything that is doable, but controlling the acts of free, self-determining beings is not something that can be done. While this may sound equivalent to the classic free will defender's notion of free will, it is not entirely so. With respect to the proposition "Not all possible worlds contain self-determining beings other than God," the indeterminist Alvin Plantinga affirms it while Griffin denies it.[98]

How, then, does God act? Williams explains that in his primordial nature God acts "by presenting to the creatures the unity, the richness, and the limits of possibility as ordered by his vision."[99] In essence, God acts in his primordial nature not by acting but by being. Process thinkers are quick to note that this means God supplies for each actual occasion its initial subjective aim. Sometimes this idea is presented as though God merely lays out all possibilities without any instructions on what would be best to choose (like setting forth a smorgasbord of options), while on other occasions it is portrayed as though God consciously points out (while presenting all other possibilities) the ideal aim for each individual entity. In either case, God presents the possibilities for becoming, but even if God has a preference among them for the specific actual entity, process thinkers affirm that it is up to the individual entity to decide which of the possible aims to actualize. God will not limit the freedom of others. As to God's consequent nature, one might initially think that since God is constantly prehending the world to add to his being, he must be acting all the time. However, the world is God's body, which is composed of multitudes of actual entities which are themselves becoming (and God cannot limit their freedom), so in effect, God's action really is their action. Consequently, as Williams explains, God's consequent nature acts by being prehended, felt by the creatures.[100] That is, God's body (the world) is objectively present to each actual entity so that as it becomes, it prehends both from its particular past history (which is part of God's body) and from other actual entities (further parts of God's body) as well as from the eternal objects. Williams likens this to depth psychology's idea of one person absorbing another's feelings and reflecting them back with transformed meaning.[101]

If knowing is an action, then, process thinkers also agree that God acts in that way. In fact, they agree that God knows all things. Hence, all past events, persons, etc., are forever preserved in God's memory and never perish in that sense.[102] On the other hand, knowing all things means God knows whatever there is to know, but the future is unknowable. If it were knowable, then actual entities could not help but do what is known, and that would limit their freedom to do otherwise, so the future is unknowable.

Does God do anything unilaterally in the world? Williams replies that we must ultimately remain agnostic about that, for there is no way to separate God's acts from their involvement in the activities of the world. As Williams says,

> . . . to assign any particular historical event to God's specific action in the world is to risk ultimate judgment on our assertions. Faith leads us to take that risk. We say God sent his Holy Spirit at Pentecost. He spoke to Jeremiah, he heals diseases, he will send the Lord again. But all such assertions in so far as they conceivably refer to historical events require us to acknowledge the limits of our sight and our knowledge. In

specific assertions about what God is doing now, or precisely how he has acted, and how he will act, we surely can be mistaken.[103]

GOD AND CREATIVITY.   Given the process description of God, there must be a world, and process thinkers affirm this. However, while God needs some world, process thinkers claim that it didn't have to be this particular world. This world as a totality and each individual thing in it is contingent, even though there must be some world.[104]

Second, they hold that in virtue of how God acts, it is clear that God cannot create *ex nihilo*.[105] To create *ex nihilo* not only raises tremendous problems from a scientific standpoint but also lets God exert too much power over the world. Process thinkers insist that God's action is persuasive, not coercive.

Third, the process conception of God also requires that God is being created. In fact, he must be the prime case of creativity. As Whitehead explains, "Neither God, nor the World, reaches static completion. Both are in the grip of the ultimate metaphysical ground, the creative advance into novelty. Either of them, God and the World, is the instrument of novelty for the other."[106]

Fourth, from the preceding, God's specific creative activity should be clear. God creates by providing each actual occasion with its initial and ideal subjective aim. The occasion, of course, has its own subjective aim and may reject God's ideal, but nonetheless it prehends God. God's aim is realized not by force but insofar as he succeeds in persuading the actual entity to adopt his aim for itself.[107] And, as Cobb has said, "the only power capable of any worthwhile result is the power of persuasion."[108] This leads Whitehead to conclude:

> In this sense, God can be termed the creator of each temporal actual entity. But the phrase is apt to be misleading by its suggestion that the ultimate creativity of the universe is to be ascribed to God's volition. The true metaphysical position is that God is the aboriginal instance of this creativity, and is therefore the aboriginal condition which qualifies its action.[109]

As Cobb explains, Whitehead's doctrines entail a certain restriction on God even with respect to the provision of the initial aim. For example, the initial aim is not the ideal in some abstract sense, but God's ideal *given the situation*, i.e., God must adapt his purposes to the world as it is. Moreover, though the initial aim greatly influences the emerging occasion, it doesn't determine it, for the occasion makes its own decision. In that sense the occasion creates itself (*causa sui*). And, though the initial aim presents the eternal objects, as we have seen, God has no control over what they are, for he isn't their creator.[110]

While the preceding sets forth the process conception of God's relation to creativity, it leaves the impression that something other than God is the ultimate cause of creation, and that something is creativity itself. In Whitehead's metaphysical category scheme, there is one category he calls the ultimate. That category contains creativity, many, and one (Whitehead refers to them as notions) which are "presupposed in all the more special categories."[111] He defines creativity

as that "ultimate principle by which the many, which are the universe disjunc-
tively, become the one actual occasion, which is the universe conjunctively. . . .
'Creativity' is the principle of *novelty.*"112

Though this may sound like creativity is creator in the sense of efficient
cause, in Whitehead's system, as Cobb explains, only actual entities can be
efficient or final causes, and creativity isn't an actual entity. Hence, creativity
is for Whitehead what prime matter was for Aristotle, the material cause.113
As such, Cobb explains that creativity can never explain what things are, nor
why things are, nor why there is anything at all, i.e., it can never answer ultimate questions. In fact, creativity simply appears to be another word for the
change itself.114 Of course, if neither God nor creativity is the efficient cause of
creation, this appears to produce serious problems for process systems. Hence,
Cobb suggests that Whitehead's God must be given a more fundamental and
radical role in creation than Whitehead allowed.115

GOD AND EVIL. Process theologians believe that their handling of the traditional problem of evil is far superior to that of traditional theism. Of course,
as Michael Peterson shows, one must be willing to accept certain assumptions,
including the process notion of evil, in order to buy the process account. As
Whitehead explains, "The ultimate evil in the temporal world is deeper than any
specific evil. It lies in the fact that the past fades, that time is a 'perpetual perishing'."116 As Peterson explains, this tends to undercut the moral aspect of evil in
favor of evil as a mere metaphysical principle, namely, all things are perishing.117

Despite this emphasis on the metaphysical notion of evil, process thinkers
do address moral evil and God's culpability for it. The essential strategy of
process theodicies is to argue that God is finite in power. God does no evil
himself, but evil arises from the free choices of his creatures. The only way
God could avoid such choices is to limit the freedom of other actual entities,
and that he won't do. Hence, God's role is to present each actual occasion with
its ideal subjective aim and to lure it (persuade it) to choose in accord with the
ideal, but he cannot guarantee that the good will be chosen. Nonetheless, God
isn't guilty for the evil in the world (and hence the traditional problem of evil
is solved), because he is powerless to stop it.118

Though according to their view God is powerless to prevent or stop evil,
process thinkers remind us that, nonetheless, God is deeply sympathetic
toward our plight. In fact, he suffers with us, so it is clear that he deeply cares.
As Schubert Ogden says about evil and sufferings:

> . . . our sufferings also may be conceived as of a piece with a reality
> which is through-and-through temporal and social. They are the partly
> avoidable, partly unavoidable, products of finite-free choices and, like
> everything else, are redolent of eternal significance. Because they, too,
> occur only within the horizon of God's all-encompassing sympathy,
> they are the very opposite of the merely indifferent. When they can be
> prevented, the responsibility for their prevention may now be realized in

all its infinite importance; and, when they must be borne with, even that may be understood to have the consolation which alone enables any of us to bear them.[119]

Given this view, a paraphrase of 1 Pet 5:7 might be, "Cast all your cares upon him, for though he cannot do anything about them, he cares for you."[120]

PROCESS THEOLOGY AND PANTHEISM.   Though the description presented so far may sound like pantheism, process thinkers vehemently deny this. Two of the clearest explanations of why this is not pantheism come from Hartshorne and Ogden.

Ogden says that process conceptions differ from both pantheism and traditional theism in that process notions are dipolar while both other views are monopolar. As monopolar, both traditional theism and pantheism deny "that God can be in any way conceived as genuinely temporal and related to others."[121] He means that traditionally there have been only two apparent answers to God's relation to the world: either God is totally independent of it (traditional theism) or he is identical to it (pantheism). Of course, this means for traditional theists that God is neither related to the world nor in any sense temporal. For pantheists, it means that since God is the world, he cannot be related to anything outside it, and this particular world becomes necessary if God himself is a necessary being. But, that just means it had to be our world that was actualized (contingency is ruled out in that respect) and that whatever God does, the world does and vice versa, but in that case free action of individuals is an illusion.[122] Ogden contends that a dipolar view solves the problem, for it allows God to be really related to the world but independent of it in such a way as to ensure free action and contingency in the world.

At first blush one might respond that being dipolar merely means God has an eternal pole and not just a physical pole, and that is really the only difference between process views and pantheism. While the mental pole is one respect in which process views differ from pantheism, that isn't the whole story. On this point, however, Hartshorne seems more helpful than Ogden. Hartshorne prefers the term "panentheism" to describe process views, and he claims that the difference between pantheism and panentheism is that while the former identifies the being of God with the being of the world, panentheism is the view "that deity is in some real aspect distinguishable from and independent of any and all relative items, and yet, taken as an actual whole, includes all relative items."[123] This means more than just that God has a mental pole as well as a physical pole; it means that in both his mental and his physical poles, the being of God both encompasses all reality and remains distinct from it. In other words, God is present with everything and interpenetrates it all so that God and the world are mutually interdependent, but not present so as to be literally identical to the world. As Hartshorne explains, panentheism agrees with traditional theism that God must be logically independent of the world (and hence must not involve any particular world—contingency is maintained), but it also combines with it the insight from traditional pantheism that God cannot "in his full actuality be less or other than literally all-inclusive."[124]

In sum, panentheism is not pantheism in that the former is dipolar while the latter is monopolar. But, this means more than just having a physical pole plus a mental pole. It means that even in his physical pole God must be distinct from all else at the same time that he includes everything.[125]

IMMORTALITY.   Because of process thought's claims that everything is perishing, one might think it impossible to speak of immortality in a process system, but this is not so. However, we must distinguish subjective and objective immortality.

Subjective immortality, or the continuation of the present stream of consciousness after death, is usually denied by process thinkers, though not always. As Reeves and Brown show, Cobb in some of his works leaves open the logical possibility of such immortality.[126] Likewise Peter Hamilton, in *The Living God,* while not affirming it, at least thinks it is logically possible.[127] On the other hand, when discussing Christ's resurrection, he generalizes to all resurrections that "all I can do here is to suggest that there is a place today for a general concept of resurrection that sees permanent meaning and value in our lives without *depending upon* belief in individual life after death."[128]

On the other hand, process thinkers uniformly believe in objective immortality. As already noted, each occasion as it occurs has subjective immediacy to the actual entity. Once the occasion is complete and the entity moves on to the next occasion, the previous occasion perishes (leaves subjective immediacy), but in so doing it does not perish altogether; it has objectivity. To return to a previous example, the sentence I now write will perish from my immediate attention, but there will still be a remaining object (the words I have written) after I move on. The same is true of all actual entities. They are stored in God and remembered by him as part of his consequent nature. That is what objective immortality means, and this suggests its difference from subjective immortality (conscious life after death). As Tremmel explains:

> Because God prehends all the past, and thus preserves all past occasions (all actual entities and systems of actual entities), God embodies the past. Immortality is in God. Things in their perishing, as we observed, do not cease to be. They continue to exist as influences in the ongoing creative advance of the world, and they continue to exist in the prehensions of God. All is eternally preserved in the "rememberings" of God.[129]

ASSESSMENT OF PROCESS THEOLOGY

Process theology purportedly corrects classical theism's defects, better synthesizes philosophy and the Christian faith, and illuminates central elements of the Christian faith better than does classical theism. There are some positive contributions from process theology, but I believe its problems raise serious doubts about its claims of superiority.[130]

Contributions of Process Theology

There is little doubt that process theology has made significant contributions to contemporary theological discussion. For example, process theists are to be applauded for their attempt to do metaphysics and systematic theology at all. As already noted, in the twentieth century, many non-evangelical theologians concluded that it is a mistake to think one can form a system of thought which integrates all of reality. In fact, the twentieth century has seen few systematic theologies from non-evangelicals. Even if one disagrees with the process system, it is encouraging to see a school of theologians who think it is important to construct a system of metaphysics and do not think it is entirely impossible to do so.

Second, process theists insist that God relate to the world. He is not locked out of history, and he cares about what happens in it. Moreover, sometimes his relation to individuals does change. For example, repentant sinners are forgiven, and God's wrath is assuaged. All of this reflects biblical teaching, and should be part of our theology and preaching. As I shall argue, it is not true that evangelical theists must deny these truths or that evangelical theism automatically entails their denial. However, those theists who have denied these teachings do present an inaccurate account of God. The process critique of such teachings is a helpful reminder not to overlook or misrepresent these facets of biblical teaching. Moreover, there is little doubt that some evangelical Christians tend to focus so much on God's majesty, power, and transcendence that he is often portrayed only as an austere, omnipotent judge whom his creatures fear but find hard to love. It is helpful to be reminded that while God is transcendent and holy, and is the ruler of the world, he is also a compassionate comforter. To believers he is Father. To all he is the one who "so loved the world, that He gave His only begotten Son" (John 3:16) to redeem us from sin.

A related point is that process theists are in essence telling evangelicals that religion in general and God in particular must be conceived so as to be relevant to human beings. It is dubious that process theism meets these needs, but this emphasis is a helpful reminder to evangelicals that in their preaching and theologizing they need to show that God is relevant to contemporary needs. There is nothing wrong with being careful and detailed in our descriptions of God, but at some point the doctrines and principles must be applied to people's lives. Otherwise, they won't likely see God and Christ as having the answers to life's most significant questions.

Finally, implicit and explicit in process theology is the notion that our knowledge and understanding of the world grows and changes as time progresses. Every people is time-bounded and culture-bounded. As a result, we must always be reexamining and refining our theology. Process theists claim to have articulated biblical truth better at this time in history than any other system. If nothing else, this should challenge evangelicals to reexamine their own theological formulations in the light of Scripture and contemporary times. This is healthy for evangelicals. All theologians should remember that theology is a human conceptual enterprise. Scripture is inerrant, but there is no guarantee that our theologizing based on it is infallible. Hence, we must always hold our theology with humility and be open to reexamining and reformulating it when necessary. This may also necessitate reexamining the language of the historic creeds of Christianity to see if it adequately expresses both biblical revelation and contemporary understanding of the world. None of this means we should discard the cardinal doctrines of Christianity. It does, however, remind us not to become so rigid in our theologizing as to be incapable of critiquing and correcting our ideas when necessary.

Problems with Process Theology

FLAWED CONCEPTION OF GOD'S BEING.   Though process theism claims that its concept of God reflects contemporary understanding of science and philosophy and is superior to traditional theism, it is my contention that process theology offers us a God who is either nothing/nonexistent or is the God of pantheism after all, despite claims to the contrary. I can explain this by looking individually at the notions of God's primordial and consequent natures.

In discussing God's primordial nature I noted that there are differing conceptions of it in Whitehead, let alone in his followers. But, on either conception, it is hard to see that there is anything really there. On the first conception, God's primordial nature is merely the perceiving and ordering of the eternal ideas, but without some*one* to do the ordering it is hard to see how the ideas get ordered. The ordering isn't an actual entity, and on this interpretation of the primordial nature there is no actual entity that does the ordering. But, then, on this notion, God's primordial nature is a nothing. Even in Whitehead's system, the notion is inadequate, for he claims that the only real things are actual entities, but since the ordering of the eternal ideas is not an actual entity itself, it must be unreal, and since Whitehead offers us no one who does the ordering (other than just to say it is God, without defining what he is other than in terms of the primordial and consequent natures [and surely, the consequent nature doesn't do the ordering]), it is hard to see the primordial nature as anything other than an idea. On the alternate interpretation of God's primordial nature (that it is the eternal objects ordered by God), there is still a problem that is at least as old as Western philosophy; namely, are these eternal ideas anything other than abstract generalities from the concrete world (hence, in no way substances or, in Whiteheadian terms, actual entities) and where are they? Anyone who isn't convinced by Plato's doctrine of the forms can hardly find Whitehead's notion of the eternal objects compelling. Moreover, since the eternal objects represent only possibilities and not actualities, it is hard to see how on either a substance metaphysic or a Whiteheadian actual entity metaphysic, these eternal ideas are real things. Of course, if that is so, then the primordial nature of God is a something that is nothing.

In turning to God's consequent nature, the trick here is to avoid pantheism. Process thinkers claim that God as to his consequent nature interpenetrates and contains the world at the same time that this nature is distinct from the world. This doctrine avoids pantheism if true, but how does it hold up under analysis? Initially, we must remember that God's consequent nature is physical and is attached to the world, but we are also told that the world is physical and attached to God. Now the problem should become clear. Where does God's physicality end and the world's begin, and vice versa? If I must make that decision on the basis of empiricism (as Whiteheadian epistemology demands), I have no way to know what aspect of any physical thing is the entity itself, and what part is part of God's consequent nature. But, then, is it not just an unprovable theory that God's consequent nature in its physicality is distinct from the world's physicality? The net result is that if God's consequent nature really is distinct from the world (though tied up with it), there is no way of proving that, so for all we know, there really is no God after all distinct from the physical world. On the other hand, if God really is there, the only thing verifiably present is the physical world; but then the view lapses into pantheism, where God and world are identical. In sum, either God as to his consequent nature is just a concept but not a real thing (or if a real distinct thing not demonstrably so and thus, again, a something as good as a nothing); or he is real, but then only in the sense pantheism requires.

CAN GOD FEEL OR BE FELT? Robert Neville raises another serious problem for process thinking. As he shows, according to Whitehead's system no actual entity can be prehended while in the process of generating a new occasion. It must be entirely concrete to be prehended, but genetic processes don't allow this. *Per se* this doesn't seem problematic, but as Neville explains, the process conception of God's consequent nature shows that it is always in the process of becoming; it never completely concresces so as to be one determinate thing. But, if so, then how can God be prehended by any actual entity in its process of becoming?[131] This is a serious problem, since process thinkers claim that for an actual entity to become, it must prehend God in both his primordial and his consequent natures. However, since God's becoming is simultaneous with that of actual entities, and entities simultaneously becoming cannot prehend one another, there is a real problem. As Neville and others show, Hartshorne saw this problem and attempted to solve it by saying that God is a society of actual entities, but this doesn't solve the problem either. Since only those occasions in God (on this view) that are past can be prehended, then God (the totality of all occasions) still cannot be prehended. And, even if one grants that at least in part he can be prehanded (the past occasions), he cannot be prehended in those parts of his being that are most subjectively immediate to himself, the parts that are becoming.[132]

A further problem with this is that no one can prehend God in his subjective immediacy. But, the flip side of this is that God cannot prehend us in our subjective immediacy. If it is true that no actual entity can be prehended while in its genetic process, then it is true that no actual entity can experience another's experiences as the other is undergoing it. This means, however, that we really have no way of knowing what God is feeling nor can he experience what we are feeling and experiencing. However, one of process theology's complaints about traditional theism's God is that he is aloof, removed, and neither knows nor cares about what we undergo. On the contrary, it claims, the process God not only cares about how we feel—he suffers with us, for it is his experience, too. However, the problem just raised shows that process concepts make it impossible for God to enter into our subjective immediacy, so he really doesn't know what we feel like, nor does he suffer with us or rejoice as we do. Once our experience is over, God can experience the results of the event, but not before. The only way around this for process theism is to adopt pantheism, so that as we suffer, it is God who suffers, but process theists staunchly demand that God is distinct from the world while mutually interdependent. If so, the process God can no more suffer with us as we suffer and rejoice as we rejoice than can the classical God.

DIVINE FREEDOM AND POWER.   In analyzing the process account of God's action in the world, one concludes that the process God is entirely impotent. It isn't that God could act but refuses to do so in order to persuade rather than coerce. Rather, the process metaphysic will not let him act. Process metaphysics demand that humans have freedom (indeterministic) and that God not limit that freedom. But might not God act, anyway, when it doesn't affect the actions of his creatures? Given the process conception of God, this is impossible. In virtue of his primordial nature, God does nothing. As to his consequent nature, it is supposed to be distinct from the being of the world, but it is intertwined with the world in such a way that we are told by process thinkers that whatever is done in the world immediately affects God and vice versa. But then for God to act would also require the world to act (assuming that we can even distinguish God's physical being from the world's), but then whatever he would do would have to affect the freedom of his creatures. The only ways around this are to say that God just does only what his creatures do (hence there can never be conflict with their freedom) or to say what process thinkers say, namely, God acts by being felt, which, of course, is totally passive and hardly qualifies as action.

The results of this are truly problematic. Process thinkers claim that their view of God more accurately reflects the biblical God than does traditional theism. But Scripture portrays an active God, not a God who acts by being felt while remaining passive. Process thinkers say their God really cares about his creatures, but what good does that do when he cannot do anything to help them in their time of need to show he cares? Moreover, the most significant problem is that everyone and everything in the universe is free to make decisions and to act (actively, not passively), but not God! Not only does this contradict Whitehead's contention that God is not an exception to what is true of the rest of reality, it also offers an impotent God who for all intents and purposes appears no different than the deists' God. Both the process and the deistic conceptions of God keep him from acting in history, but the process God does it even more so. At least the deists allowed God to "wind up the clock." Process theology's view of creativity won't even allow that. Given this impotent God, the process God seems in practice irrelevant to this world.

INADEQUATE ACCOUNT OF DIVINE ATTRIBUTES.   Though the process account of many divine attributes is problematic, let me focus on three. First, consider divine omniscience. My objection is not just that process thought denies divine knowledge of future events,[133] but that its God cannot even know the present state of affairs, despite process claims that God is always aware of all that happens and genuinely cares about it. Of course, if God cannot know what is happening, it is hard for him to care, but two empirical facts that science tells us make it impossible for the process God to know everything simultaneously. Gruenler explains this significant point:

> The incontestable fact is that if God moves necessarily in time he is limited to some rate of velocity which is finite (say, the speed of light, if not the faster rate of some hypothetical tachyon). This means, unfortunately for Process theism, that it is impossible for such a finite deity to have a simultaneous God's-eye view of the whole universe at once, since it would take him millions of light years or more to receive requisite data from distant points and places. The other problem is peculiar to relativity theory. The doctrine is that no finite being (including God) could possibly embrace the whole universe simultaneously because there simply is no finite position that is not relative. Hence no possibility of simultaneity exists from any possible finite vantage point. Time does not advance along a well-defined front but processes in all sorts of relative patterns which cannot be correlated into any one finite system. That is what relativity means. There is simply no privileged position in the finite world.[134]

Second, there is reason to question the goodness and holiness of the process God, despite claims to the contrary. In our world there is much evil. However, the process God, according to his consequent nature, is tied to the world, so in some sense what happens there is his act as well. As Neville explains, Whitehead's views make actual occasions the cause of evil, but to the extent that those choices are hedged in by the divinely presented evaluations of the possibilities, won't God also be responsible? Even if choices are made totally independent of God, this does not prove that God is off the hook. Neville explains:

> Why should we want in the first place to exempt God from responsibil-
> ity for evil? Because of an antecedent commitment to God's goodness.
> But to deny God responsibility by denying divine causal agency is not
> to lend *support* to the doctrine of divine goodness; it only strikes down
> a counter argument. And the price of this move is to make the actual
> course of events *irrelevant* to God's moral character; this goes counter
> to the religious feeling that God's moral character is *revealed* in events,
> for better or worse.[135]

One becomes all the more suspicious of God's goodness, because on a
process account, God won't use force to curb even a Hitler! This becomes
very strange when process thinkers object to traditional theists who answer
the problem of evil by the free will defense because those free will defenders won't let God inhibit freedom occasionally to prevent horrendous evils.
The inconsistency is troublesome. If it is right to reject the free will defense
because you think God could coerce on occasion, then why turn around and
deny, as process thinkers do, that God can use coercion even when it would
mean stopping a Hitler?[136]

Moreover, process theology solves the problem of evil, but in a way that
is objectionable. It isn't that the process God could get rid of evil, but just
doesn't for some morally sufficient reason, as evangelicals argue.[137] The
process God literally is impotent to do anything, despite the fact that the evil
committed is harmful to his own being (via his consequent nature). Likewise,
having seen what process theists say about God's ability to act, one is hardly
optimistic about God's ability to harmonize every evil with good so as to
maximize good, as Hartshorne suggests he does.

Finally, what of divine immutability and impassibility? Here we really see
the process God's impotence. He is powerless to resist changes that would
be detrimental (Hartshorne's claim that change could not be for the worse
trivializes the evil in the world and is overly optimistic about the process
God's ability to ultimately turn evil into good, given the process deity's
impotence). Moreover, he increases in knowledge with each new event, but
such a God who needs to learn new things is hardly a God on whom one
can rely for the best solutions to problems even if he could act. What is
most troublesome is the reason process theology felt it necessary to posit a
mutable God. I don't believe process thinkers have shown that all evangelical theists interpret God's immutability and/or impassibility as they claim.[138]
Nor have they shown that it is impossible for evangelical theists to make
sense of immutability.[139]

In upcoming chapters on the divine attributes, I shall offer a nuanced
handling of divine attributes such as immutability. While I agree with process
theism that it is unwise and unnecessary to conceive those attributes as many
classical theists do, I shall argue that the process notion that everything about
God can change goes too far. There is a mediating position on these issues,
and it doesn't require the open view of God either.

CREATIVITY AND GOD. The process notion of creativity is seriously flawed, though it is consistent with the process view of God's action in general. As noted when creativity was discussed, God, according to process theology, is not the efficient cause of creation, nor is creativity (it is the material cause). Of course, this means that actual entities other than God are the creators. In fact, we are told that the world is even involved in creating God, which logically follows if his consequent nature is wrapped up in the world. Here again we see the inconsistency of process thinking. All reality is supposed to exemplify the same metaphysical principles, and yet God alone cannot create. We are told that he prehends the world and continues to develop, but this must be metaphor because of what we are told about how God acts in both primordial and consequent natures and because he cannot be the efficient cause in creation (to do so would limit the decisions of other entities about what they will become, and God isn't allowed to limit freedom). God turns out to be the exception, not the rule.

In addition, as Cobb points out, creativity as the driving force behind creation is inadequate; material causes effect nothing. Even Cobb argues that God must have a more active role. Likewise, Neville rightly explains that on the Whiteheadian conception of creation, the ontological principle explains why things are the specific determinate things they are, but it in no way explains why anything should become at all. That is, granting that the creative process is in operation, Whitehead's views explain why actual entities have the specific characteristics they do and also how the becoming process works; what his views don't explain is why the creative process goes on at all and doesn't simply stop. Appeal to creativity doesn't answer that question![140]

CONFUSION OF GOD'S REALITY AND GOD'S ROLE(S). In chapter 2 of this book, I noted that we must distinguish between the questions of what sort of reality God is or has, and what role(s) and relationships he has in our universe. It is at this point that I sense a confusion in process thinking. In general, one gets the impression that if one buys any of the process story, one must buy the whole thing.

William Alston has made a somewhat similar point, though he focuses on different aspects of the doctrine of God than I will. Alston evaluates Hartshorne's comparison of classical and process theism. As noted in my chapter 2, Alston considers ten attributes that Hartshorne discusses, and divides them into two groups.[141] Given the Hartshornean stance that the whole process notion of God hangs together with logical tightness, if one accepts one of the process attributes, the rest inevitably follow. In contrast, Alston argues that there is no such logical necessity. It is possible to hold a Hartshornean position on the first group of attributes together with a more Thomistic/traditional account of the attributes in the second group.[142]

Though I don't find the resultant conception of God as palatable as does Alston, a fundamental point he makes is correct: the choice is not all or nothing, as process theists have so frequently portrayed it (either the whole classical notion of God, as process theists understand it, or process theism).

My concern, however, is not with the two groups of attributes Alston delineates. Rather, it is with the confusion of God's reality with his roles. Just because one agrees that God can change in some respects and does have feelings (God's role(s) and relationships in our world), that doesn't mean that one must buy the concept of God as dipolar (God's reality). Similarly, just because one accepts one plank in the classical account of God's reality and roles, that does not mean one must inevitability swallow the whole thing. Specifically, I shall be arguing in later chapters that just because one holds that God is a substance, that does not mean he is isolated and immobile (further points about God's reality), nor does it mean that he is aloof, unrelated, and uninvolved in the world (items that relate to his relationship and role in the world). Moreover, because God is absolutely sovereign over the world (part of his role and relationship to the world), that doesn't mean that he is unattached, unrelated, uncaring about his creatures. Furthermore, if one grants that process thinkers make a valid point about God's roles and relations to our world, that doesn't automatically require him to yield all of his power whenever humans use their free will (an issue of God's role and relationship in the world), nor does it mean that we must buy Whitehead's process metaphysics or Hartshorne's dipolar view of God (an issue of the nature of God's reality).

In sum, it is my contention that the all-or-nothing approach of process theology is wrong, in part because it confuses answers to questions about God's reality with issues of his role and relationship. It further errs in thinking that if one agrees with one element in the process (or classical) conception of God's role/relationship to the world, one must buy the whole story of that view on God's role/relationship. And finally, it errs in thinking that if one adopts one element in the process (or classical) conception of what sort of reality God is/has, one must agree to the whole package of that view's account of God's reality.

RELIGIOUSLY INADEQUATE GOD. When you come to the end of all the theory, process theology does not in fact offer a God one can live with and worship. To be religiously adequate, shouldn't a God be at least as powerful, holy, and just as we are? Would he not have to be a God who not only cared about us but also could do something for us to express that concern? In order to ensure any kind of moral universe, wouldn't he have to be able to govern morally?

If you answer affirmatively, then you should agree that the process God is religiously inadequate. He isn't more powerful than humans, but less so, for he cannot act. Since his consequent nature is the whole world, he must be responsible in some way for the evil in it, but the evil of the whole is greater than that of any part. But, then, it seems that each of us individually must be more holy than God. We are told that God cares for us, but he can do nothing to help us. All he can do is show us the possibilities of a better way, but then, we could just as easily do that for ourselves and for one another. And how, on the process view, can we think of God as moral governor? If we sin (reject his initial aim), what will he do to us? How can he do anything to us? And what is our final destiny? God stores us in his memory bank, but there is no guarantee that physical death isn't the total end of any conscious existence. If the way God has stored up the billions who have gone before us so that none of us has any idea of who they are illustrates how God will objectively immortalize us, that isn't good enough![143]

In conclusion, though process theism attempts to be current in its understanding of the world, it is significantly flawed. It is also important to see how many process claims are postulated but never proved. For example, mind (or at least mental functions) is postulated of the inanimate, but unproved; and the consequent nature of God is supposedly independent of the world while encompassing it, but this is unproved. In fact, none of these claims (and many more as well) are provable empirically. That seems to be a serious defect for a theology and philosophy that is supposed to be empirically based and demonstrable! Indeed, that is the final irony (as well as an underlying deficiency) of this empirical theology.

11

THE BEING
AND NATURE
OF GOD

THE EXISTENCE AND BEING OF GOD

In part 1 we saw that regardless of background, culture, or historical situation, human beings will worship someone or something as God. Though belief in some God has been widespread, throughout the centuries people have wondered if God actually exists. Even Scripture grants that there are fools who have said in their heart that there is no God (Ps 14:1; 53:1).

Some people have wondered if there isn't a rational way to prove God's existence. During the modern era, the predominant concept of rationality has required that one have sufficient arguments and evidence before one is entitled to hold a belief. Many, adopting this maxim of rationality, have maintained that there isn't sufficient evidence to warrant belief in God.

Scripture, of course, doesn't try to prove God's existence but assumes it and then tells us about this God and his requirements of us. Though Scripture contains no formal proof of God's existence, in a few passages a kind of argument is implicit. Three passages illustrate my point. Ps 19:1 says that "the heavens declare the glory of God and the earth shows forth his handiwork" (author's translation). The psalm then extols the works and Word of God. While none of this *per se* argues for God's existence, we want to ask the psalmist, "How do the heavens declare God's glory?" "What does it mean to say that the earth shows forth his handiwork?" David's point seems to be that as we look at the heavens and the earth, we can easily see that someone with great power must have made them. Moreover, as we think of the nature of our planet in particular, we should realize that whoever made it must have great power and wisdom, and he must be a beneficent creator. It is just too hard to imagine that all of this fell into place by mere chance. Indeed, the world around us points to a creator and suggests something of his nature.

If this is David's point, it implicitly uses the fact and nature of creation to point to God as its creator. As we shall see, this is precisely what the cosmo-

184 □ No One Like Him

logical and teleological arguments do, so this passage suggests either (or both) of those traditional arguments for God's existence.

A second passage is Romans 1–2 (in fact, each chapter implies a separate argument). In these chapters Paul argues that everyone, regardless of cultural and historical background, has some revelation of God. In 1:20 Paul explains, "For since the creation of the world His invisible attributes, His eternal power and divine nature, have been clearly seen, being understood through what has been made, so that they are without excuse." No one can ever justly say they would have believed in God if only they had known there was one. Paul says that everyone knows, even if they never heard of the Bible or talked to a missionary. All they need to do is open their eyes and look at the world around them. Then they will understand that there is a God, and they will discern something of what he is like. The point is the same as David's in Ps 19:1, though Paul is even more explicit about the world as evidence for God than David was. This is again either an implicit cosmological or teleological argument, or both.[1]

In Romans 2, Paul continues his argument that everyone has revelation of God and is accountable for what they do with it. In that chapter, however, Paul turns from the world in general to human beings' consciences in particular. Paul says that even the Gentiles, who didn't receive the Mosaic Law from God as did the Jews, still have a sense of right and wrong, and they do the things contained in the Law anyway. This is so, because God has written his moral precepts on each person's heart (whether Jew or Gentile). As a result, everyone's conscience either excuses or accuses them for what they do. This, of course, is no formal proof, but it is very much akin to the moral argument for God's existence, which asks why among humans there is a universal sense of right and wrong, a universal sense of a moral law. The argument answers that this is best explained by the existence of a moral lawgiver. While this goes beyond the details of Rom 2:14-15, that passage contains the basic idea of the moral argument.

In addition to these implicit biblical arguments, within the Judaeo-Christian tradition philosophers and theologians have offered various rational arguments supporting belief in God. In fact, some have maintained that these arguments in one form or another are successful deductive proofs for God's existence. Though this book is not an apologetics text, we should at least understand the basic rational arguments and what they show.

Introduction to Theistic Proofs

Proofs for God's existence have been used in various ways, and evaluations of the worth of these arguments have also differed. Some philosophers have tried to prove God's existence because of the important role he plays in their philosophical system. For example, Descartes tried to prove God's existence to shore up his epistemology. He reasoned that if God exists, he would ensure that whenever people think they are having a clear and distinct idea of something, they are. No evil demon is tampering with their reason or sense perception.[2]

Other philosophers have thought it impossible to prove God's existence, but deemed belief in God necessary, anyway. Immanuel Kant believed that none of the traditional theistic proofs is sound, but we must postulate God's existence anyway. Without it, there seems to be no ultimate grounding for morality. Yet other philosophers claim that even though God's existence can't be proved by the traditional arguments, that doesn't destroy theism. For example, the contemporary atheist J. L. Mackie held that even though the traditional arguments for God's existence are unsuccessful, theists can claim to know God exists by some noncognitive means, such as personal experience.[3] Still other contemporary Christian philosophers have contended that for many theists belief in God does not rest on argument and evidence, nor need it do so in order for them to be within their epistemic rights in holding such a belief. Rather, for those believers, belief in God is properly basic and thoroughly rational, even if they haven't marshaled any evidence and argument for their belief.[4]

Theologians' opinions about these arguments vary as well. Some hold that the theistic arguments will convince no one who isn't already a believer, but for believers, these proofs offer grounds for thinking that their faith is not utterly irrational. Others make stronger claims, believing that one or more of the arguments is successful. While they agree that this forces no one to establish a relationship with God, they believe that any rational person must admit that there is a God, regardless of their relation to him. Finally, many theologians of a neo-orthodox bent argue that rational arguments for or against God's existence are irrelevant. For those who have experienced God in a revelatory encounter, what possible rational argument could wrest from them their belief in God? Moreover, what could a rational demonstration of God's existence add to their certainty that he exists? Besides, believers don't want the God who appears at the end of the philosopher's argument, anyway. The true and living God is not some static proposition that comes at the end of a demonstrative proof; he is the dynamic, living God of the universe! As for nonbelievers, it is equally dubious that a rational argument will convince them of God's existence or move them to establish a relation with him.

Traditional arguments for God's existence are either *a priori* or *a posteriori*. An *a posteriori* argument appeals to some feature about the universe as a basis for arguing to God, whereas an *a priori* argument does not. Instead, if one understands the concepts used in the argument, one can decide whether the argument is true or false apart from any empirical investigation. A true *a priori* argument is absolutely certain, whereas the premises and conclusion of an *a posteriori* argument are at best ninety-nine percent probable. The ontological argument is the only one of the traditional proofs that is an *a priori* argument.

One further feature of *a posteriori* arguments is noteworthy. Such arguments are of two basic kinds. Some, like the cosmological argument, move from some fact about the world to a conclusion that purportedly follows inevitably from the premises of the argument. While that fact about the world is at best highly probable (i.e., one could always be mistaken about an empirical matter, whereas the truths of math or logic couldn't possibly be wrong), nonetheless, if one grants it, some conclusion follows inevitably from it. For example, if there is an effect (the cosmos), there must be some cause adequate to explain the existence of that effect. If one grants the further assumption that the universe as a whole is ultimately intelligible, then, defenders of the cosmological argument claim, it follows that there must be an ultimate cause of the universe, and theists think God is that cause.

On the other hand, many *a posteriori* arguments are intentionally probabilistic in form. Appeal is made to some empirical fact, and various explanations of that fact are offered. One particular explanation is then deemed most probably true. Teleological and moral arguments typically follow this form. For example, the theist points to facts about the world, such as the instances of design in it. The theist doesn't claim that only God's existence could be the cause of the empirical fact, but only that God is the most probable cause.

THE ONTOLOGICAL ARGUMENT

St. Anselm of Canterbury was the first to formulate the ontological argument. It appears in his *Proslogion,* which he wrote in 1077–1078. Since that time the argument has been the cause of much debate. In some ways, it seems the least satisfying of all the theistic proofs, but it has proved, even to its critics, to be the most suggestive philosophically of all the proofs.

Anselm's argument appears in chapters 2 and 3 of the *Proslogion,* and there is every indication that Anselm thought he had written only one argument for God's existence. Today it is generally agreed that he actually produced two separate arguments. Though few hold out any hope for the success of the first argument, many think the second can be presented in a successful form.

In both of these arguments God is defined as a being than which none greater can be conceived (or the greatest conceivable being). The basic distinction between the two arguments is that the first compares existence to nonexistence (Anselm argues that the greatest conceivable being would not be the greatest if he didn't exist), whereas the second compares necessary existence to contingent existence, and contends that if God is the greatest conceivable being, he must have the former, not the latter. Of course, if he exists necessarily, it is impossible to conceive of him as not existing.

Anselm I

In chapter 2 of the *Proslogion,* Anselm presents the first formulation of the argument. He explains that everyone, even the fool who denies God's existence, has some concept of God. The idea of God as the greatest conceivable being (hereafter GCB) is in everyone's understanding, but that, of course, commits no one to belief in God's existence in reality. Anselm thinks it should, however, for if we really understand what it means to be the GCB, we should immediately see that a being which exists both in the understanding and in reality is greater than a being who exists only in the understanding. So God, the GCB, exists. If someone says they can think of a GCB as not existing, Anselm would answer that they don't understand the concept of the GCB and/ or they are not thinking of the being who is the greatest.

Though this may sound odd, a word of explanation clarifies Anselm's point. Imagine any number of potential candidates for the title "God," remember that God is the GCB, and write a list of all candidates' qualities. Suppose you narrow your candidates to two, A and B. You list all their attributes, and everything in both lists is identical except one thing. The final item in Candidate B's description is "exists," whereas that is omitted from Candidate A's list. Which of the two is God? Anselm's point is that though all else is equal, Candidate B is God, not Candidate A. Candidate B is superior to A, because B not only has all these attributes as part of its concept, but it exists in reality. That is, Candidate B really exists outside of the mind, whereas the description of Candidate A shows what A would be like if it existed outside the mind, but it doesn't. A is nothing more than a concept of the GCB, whereas B *is* the GCB, and a God who exists in reality is certainly greater than one who merely exists as a concept in the understanding. Anyone who denies this doesn't understand the meaning either of "greatest" or of "God" or of both.

Note that Anselm doesn't pose this argument in terms of the greatest being there is, but in terms of the greatest being there could be. It is tautological to say that the greatest being there is exists, and just because someone is the greatest being currently existing, that doesn't prove that this person is God. On the other hand, it isn't a tautology to hold that the greatest possible being is God and actually exists. Anselm's point is that God is the greatest conceivable being, and as such he exists.

The argument contains two further assumptions. First, it seems to require that existence is an attribute or quality. Consequently, Anselm contends that a God who has this quality is a greater being than one who doesn't. By claiming that existence belongs to the GCB's description, Anselm is suggesting that existence is an attribute.

Second, Anselm's argument requires existence also to be a perfection. If God is the GCB and that entails that he has all perfections, then to conclude that God exists in virtue of having all perfections is to conclude that existence is a perfection. We normally think of perfections as moral qualities, but existence is not a moral quality like justice or truth, so what does it mean to call it a perfection? The answer stems from Anselm's commitment to the common metaphysical tradition of his time. According to that tradition, being is good by its mere existence, and the more being there is, the more good there is. Lack of being, finitude, was considered evil. Thus, when terms like "good" and "evil" are used in this discussion, they are not used primarily in a moral sense, but in a metaphysical sense. That is, they relate to being and to the amount and quality of being. Thus, when Anselm defines God as the GCB, it is clear that the argument has no chance of succeeding if he is thinking only in terms of moral perfections. Metaphysical perfection is a crucial notion underlying the argument, and certainly, it is metaphysically better to exist than not to exist. Hence, the GCB cannot be metaphysically greatest and fail to exist.[5]

CRITICISMS OF ANSELM I.   A variety of criticisms against Anselm's first argument have appeared at various times in history. The first criticism was raised by Gaunilo, a monk of Marmoutiers. His fundamental point was that the conceivability of something doesn't guarantee its existence. Gaunilo tried to disprove Anselm's argument by a *reductio ad absurdum* argument. He constructed an argument about a perfect island, using the basic form of Anselm's ontological argument. Gaunilo argued that just because one can conceive of a perfect island, that does not mean it exists. If there are any doubts, try to find the island and you will see that it doesn't exist. So, conceivability alone does not guarantee existence.

This argument has been stated in more sophisticated ways by philosophers after Anselm and Gaunilo. Before turning to them, however, we should note Anselm's reply to Gaunilo. Anselm said that while Gaunilo's point is correct for everything in the finite, contingent world, it cannot be true of an infinite, necessary being. Thus, whether Gaunilo can conceive of perfect islands or anything else in this world, such things are not in the same category as God, for his existence is necessary and theirs is contingent. Anselm's reply contains the second form of the argument, as we shall see in more detail below.

Immanuel Kant raises this objection in a different way.[6] According to the ontological argument, the statement "the GCB exists" is analytic. An analytic statement is one whose predicate term is contained in the subject term. That is, if one understands the meaning of the subject term ("GCB" in this case) and the predicate term ("exists" in this case), one immediately sees whether what is said is true, for the meaning of the subject term either does or does not contain the meaning of the predicate. This can be known without ever investigating anything in the external world. The ontological argument maintains that if one understands the meaning of "God," one must immediately understand that God exists. This may sound promising, but Kant complained that all claims about something's existence are synthetic, not analytic. A synthetic statement is one whose predicate concept is not contained in its subject concept. By understanding the meaning of the subject term, one does not automatically know whether what is said about it (the predicate) is true; one must investigate. Since "the GCB exists" is synthetic, the ontological argument does not prove its truth.[7]

A second objection raised by both Pierre Gassendi and Kant is that existence is not a perfection. The ontological argument assumes that it is, but it isn't. The point is not just (as some have claimed) that it is moot whether it is preferable for something to exist rather than not exist (e.g., would an existing Hitler be greater than or more perfect than a nonexistent one?). The point is that when one describes two beings identically and then adds that one of them exists, one adds nothing to their basic description. It makes sense, contends Norman Malcolm, to argue from our perspective that an existing God is more perfect than a nonexistent one, but that doesn't mean that existence itself makes God more perfect. In fact, without existence God isn't perfect at all; he is a nonentity. So, by noting that he exists, we don't add a further perfection. Rather, we simply state a fact about him which allows all of his perfections to be instanciated.

This issue is still debatable. Surely, if one thinks only in terms of moral perfections, the point is well taken. On the other hand, the whole discussion takes on a different slant when viewed from the perspective of metaphysical perfections. And, of course, that is the notion that underlies the argument.

Claiming that existence is not a perfection that can be listed in a description of God suggests a final objection to the argument. Kant is most associated with this objection, which many consider the critical blow. Kant objected that existence is not a predicate. His point is that once one describes the nature of God (or anything else), to add that he exists adds nothing to the description of his nature. Instead, it merely asserts that the definition applies to something actual in the world. Put differently, by saying God exists, one adds no attribute to the description of the concept of God; one merely says that the concept is instanciated in our world.

Anselm II

This form of the argument plays upon the distinction between necessary existence and contingent existence. Anselm argues that we can think of a being who can be conceived not to exist, and we can also conceive of a being who *cannot* be conceived not to exist. In philosophical terminology, the former is a *contingent* being and the latter is a *necessary* being. Something contingent depends on something other than itself for existence and hence must be brought into existence. A necessary being depends on nothing but itself and cannot go out of existence. Anselm reasons that if God is the GCB, he cannot be contingent, since then he wouldn't be the GCB, for a necessary being is surely greater than a contingent one. So, a proper understanding of God as the GCB should convince us that God must exist and must do so as a necessary being. This is actually the key to Anselm's reply to Gaunilo that while contingent beings are not actual just because someone conceives of them, that is not so for God. In Anselm I, existence is considered a perfection, but in Anselm II *necessary existence* is the perfection.

INTERACTION WITH ANSELM II.   Most of the contemporary debate about the ontological argument centers around this second form. Some are certain it doesn't work, but others are just as convinced of its correctness.

John Hick believes that a major problem with Anselm II is that it tells us what kind of existence God must have if he exists, but offers no proof of his existence. That is, what Anselm actually proved is that a contingent being could not be God. Any being worthy of the title "God" must be a necessary being, for necessary existence is surely greater than contingent existence. But none of this establishes that in fact there is such a being.

Despite this complaint, Anselm II has had many defenders. Two of the most able are Charles Hartshorne and Alvin Plantinga.[8] Suffice it to say for our purposes that the jury is still out on whether Anselm II is successful. Whether it is or is not, it clarifies that only a being with necessary existence would qualify as God, the greatest conceivable being.

THE COSMOLOGICAL ARGUMENT

The cosmological argument is an *a posteriori* argument. As with the ontological argument, there is no such thing as *the* cosmological argument, but rather a series of arguments in various forms. In all forms it begins with some fact about the world (e.g., existence of the universe as a whole or existence of sets of objects) and argues to God as the cause.

The cosmological argument has a long history stemming from Plato and Aristotle. It especially flourished during the Middle Ages with Thomas Aquinas and, to a lesser degree, Duns Scotus. It was rejuvenated and given a forceful presentation in the eighteenth century by Samuel Clarke and Leibniz. In contemporary philosophy of religion it also has its defenders, Richard Taylor and Richard Swinburne being the most notable.[9] And there have always been critics. In recent centuries, it has been most severely criticized by philosophers like David Hume, Immanuel Kant, and Bertrand Russell.

William Rowe explains (in *The Cosmological Argument*) that the argument actually has two parts. The first, depending on the version, attempts to establish the existence of a first cause or necessary being which is a cause sufficient to produce the world (or some aspect of it). Typically, philosophers and non-philosophers treat this argument as if it were the whole of the cosmological argument. However, it cannot be, for even if it succeeds, it still does not show that the first cause or necessary being is also God with all the divine attributes. In fact, the being in question might be more akin to Aristotle's prime mover than to the Christian God. Thus, the second part of the argument tries to show that this necessary being has all the qualities of the Judaeo-Christian God. Our discussion focuses on the first part of the argument.

Cosmological arguments come in various forms, but we can divide them into three broad types. Some focus on a regress of causes; let us call them causal arguments. Others stress the contingency of the universe and offer a sufficient reason for the existence of the contingent universe; we can call these contingency arguments. Finally, Richard Swinburne presents an inductive cosmological argument that relies heavily on probability.

Causal Arguments

Two of the best-known examples of the causal form of the cosmological argument are the first two of Aquinas's five ways of proving God's existence, presented in his *Summa Theologiae*. The strategy of both is basically the same, but the details of each are distinctive. For our purposes Aquinas's first way is sufficient.

AQUINAS'S FIRST WAY. Aquinas begins with the empirical fact that some things in our world are in motion or changing. But if something is in the process of changing to another state, it is potentially in that state but not actually there. Aquinas argues that it is impossible for the same thing to be in the state of actuality and potentiality in the same respect. For example, water which is actually cold cannot be potentially cold at the same time, though it can be potentially hot. Aquinas then claims that whatever moves from the state of potentiality to actuality cannot move itself; it must be moved by something already in the state of actuality. However, whatever changes something else is itself changed, but there cannot be an infinite regress of movers or changers, for then there would be no first mover, and, consequently, no other mover, since subsequent movers move only inasmuch as they are moved by the first mover.[10] Thus, there must be a first mover, and he is God.

Various objections have been lodged against this argument, but two key ideas get the most attention. Objections are posed against the notion that if one thing causes another to change, the mover must actually be in the state toward which the changing object moves. In some cases, this is true. For example, a wet towel won't make anyone who is wet dry. Likewise, until the discovery of electricity it was believed that only something hot could make other things hot. However, there are many counterexamples to this principle. To bring about something's death, the mover need not be dead. There are such things as temperatureless currents of electricity that make wires hot, and someone who fattens up cattle for slaughter need not himself be fat.

Some might reply that Aquinas could revise the argument by claiming that while a mover needn't be in the state toward which it moves another, still, everything in motion must be moved by another. However, critics of the argument challenge precisely this assumption. As Rowe explains, Aquinas considers the possibility that things are the cause of their own change, and that they may be changed by something else. What he never entertains is the possibility that it is just a brute fact that some things are changing. Of course, if it is a brute fact that some things are changing, then the argument is in trouble. Assuming without proof that things in motion are caused to move by some agent begs the question. As Hick argues, the idea that things are as a brute fact in motion is not impossible, for it fits Newton's first law. Moreover, it is also possible that things in motion have been in motion eternally, so they never began to change.

The claim that there cannot be an infinite regress of changers has also been challenged. Hick explains that the infinite regress can be interpreted either temporally or causally. That is, Aquinas may mean that it is impossible to have a regress of causes that stretches back infinitely in time, or he may be saying that it is impossible for an infinite series of causes (perhaps all simultaneously occurring) to be causally related to one another. If we take the temporal interpretation, then the premise is objectionable to contemporary people, for they see no problem in an infinite temporal regression because of the belief that the universe is temporally as well as spatially unbounded. Hick believes that Aquinas was thinking of a causal regress. Thus, Aquinas's point is that it is impossible to have an infinite series of causally explanatory causes. If the series is infinite, we will never actually get an explanation of the phenomenon in question. But, why must there be an explanation? Hick and Rowe alike contend that the answer is the principle of sufficient reason, which seems to undergird many, if not all, versions of the cosmological argument. Later, we shall consider more directly the principle of sufficient reason, but we need now only note that Aquinas's argument ultimately rests on it. Critics who reject this principle see no reason why there cannot be an infinite regress of causes. If there can be, Aquinas's first way fails.

A final objection asks why God is the unchanged changer. If everything that moves is moved by something else, why is God exempt? This objection may be taken in one of two ways. According to the first, it means that granting that there is a first mover, why think that first cause qualifies as God? Of course, this objection reminds us that the cosmological argument has two parts: one to establish a first cause, prime mover, etc., and another to show that the first cause is the Judaeo-Christian God.

Understood by a second interpretation, this objection means that even if the first mover is God, why should we think he is unchanging? Granted, to stop the regress of causes something must have this quality, but how do we know God is the one with it? At this point, some might think that the cosmological argument appears to collapse into the ontological argument, for if we hadn't conceived of God as having all perfections, and hadn't judged being an uncaused cause a perfection, why would we think God would qualify as the uncaused cause? Of course, if God just is conceived to be the uncaused cause, do we really need the cosmological argument after all? Isn't the ontological argument enough?

Contingency Arguments

Examples of the contingency form of the cosmological argument appear both in Aquinas's Third Way and in the work of eighteenth-century philosophers Clarke and Leibniz. These arguments differ somewhat, but each rests on the principle of sufficient reason and the notions of contingency and necessity. Because of the similarity I shall present only one of the arguments.

Leibniz's formulation of the argument is the most typical. Leibniz held the principle of sufficient reason, according to which nothing ever happens without a sufficient reason why it occurs rather than something else. Hence, everything that happens is explainable, at least in principle. As we observe the world, we see contingent things, i.e., they were brought into existence and they can go out of existence. They didn't have to exist, but they do now exist. In our world, however, we see nothing but contingent beings. Of course, whatever is contingent owes its reason for existence to something else. The problem is that if everything is contingent, then everything owes its reason for existence to something else; we need a sufficient reason outside the series of contingent objects to explain why they exist. If everything in the explanation is contingent, we don't have a sufficient reason for the existence of the whole. What is required is a being which depends on nothing but itself, and thus needs no further explanation than itself to explain why it exists. That means there must be a necessary being (one who causes his own existence) if we are to find a sufficient reason and explanation as to why the world as a whole exists. That necessary being is God.

The contingency form of the cosmological argument has not escaped criticism. Several are noteworthy. Proponents of the contingency argument hold that the existence of an eternal God who causes his own existence is a sufficient explanation of the universe's existence, whereas the physical universe as eternal is not a sufficient explanation for its existence. However, many opponents of the argument ask why anything further needs to be said than that matter is eternal. If the options are that either we believe in divine creation (and then the universe is intelligible) or we believe that matter is eternal (and then the universe is not ultimately intelligible), that doesn't tell us why we should prefer the former over the latter.

Some who raise this objection add that appealing to God does not offer an adequate explanation because no one really understands what it means for a being to cause its own existence (or to be an uncaused cause, a necessary being). Consequently, God's existence appears ultimately to be a brute unexplainable fact, but, then, we have to choose between two brute facts: we either accept God's existence as a brute fact or accept an eternal universe as a brute fact. The cosmological argument offers these two options, but gives no grounds for preferring one over the other.[11]

Bertrand Russell also contended that the problem with the contingency argument is that it rests on a misconception of what it means to explain something or make it intelligible. Normally, we are satisfied that we have explained a phenomenon if we note the causal factors immediately surrounding it. We may look for some causes that are a bit more remote, but we needn't go back to "prehistoric" times to explain the thing. For example, in explaining the cause of an automobile accident, we refer to events immediately preceding the accident. We may also mention something that happened a bit earlier (e.g., perhaps one of the drivers had been drinking), but we don't begin our explanation by going back, for example, to the birth of the drivers. Russell further notes that what we include in our explanations are series of contingent facts. Consequently, the contingency argument's claim that something isn't really explained without an appeal to a necessary being and without a long historical analysis of causes simply goes beyond the normal notion of explanation. We do not reject lesser sorts of explanations as unintelligible when it comes to historical events, so why should we reject a similar kind of explanation for the cosmos as a whole? Why must our explanation end with a necessary being, since we never require that when explaining any other phenomena?

Much of the debate over the contingency argument centers around the principle of sufficient reason. Rowe explains that there is both a strong and a weak version of it. The strong version says that whatever exists must have an explanation of its existence. That explanation rests either in the necessity of its own nature or in the causal power of some other being. The weak version says that whatever comes into existence must have an explanation of its existence, one that rests in the causal efficacy of some other being. Some forms of the contingency argument rest on the strong version and others on the weak version.

Rowe notes that many who defend the contingency argument claim that if the principle of sufficient reason is wrong, the enterprise of science collapses. They claim that science proceeds on the assumption that everything has a cause which explains it. Rowe responds that even if scientists do work from this assumption, they deem it true for whatever happens, not in regard to whatever exists. It just isn't true that every existing thing must have a cause and an explanation, says Rowe. This is the same old point that some things are just brute facts. The problem arises, however, contends Rowe, in that some of the more forceful versions of the cosmological argument (e.g., Samuel Clarke's and Fredrick Copleston's) rest on the strong version of the principle of sufficient reason that claims that everything that exists has a cause. An appeal to science certainly won't support that idea, and consequently, it won't support contingency arguments that rest on the strong version of the principle.

Rowe thinks contingency arguments based on the weaker version fare no better. In fact, some philosophers believe that any form of the principle of sufficient reason is incorrect, for it demands that things be thoroughly intelligible in order to be intelligible at all, but as mentioned above, Russell considered this to be a misconception of what it means to explain something.[12]

If the principle of sufficient reason is false, does that mean that nothing in the universe is explainable or that science, for example, rests on a mistake? Philosophers who reject the principle of sufficient reason answer these questions negatively. As Russell claimed, one only runs into a problem if he has this strange notion of explanation that every explanation must end with a necessary being. Once we understand that some things are just brute facts and that others can be explained satisfactorily by listing a contingent set of factors, there is no great problem created by rejecting the principle of sufficient reason.

But if all of this is true, the principle of sufficient reason is to be rejected, and all forms of the cosmological argument based on it are defective. Advocates of the cosmological argument typically think otherwise.

Swinburne's Inductive Argument

Richard Swinburne (*The Existence of God*)[13] holds that cosmological arguments which deductively attempt to establish God's existence fail. There are no premises known with certainty, he says, that lead deductively to the conclusion that God exists. However, that does not mean the cosmological argument is bankrupt. It only shows that it should be structured in terms of probability.

As Swinburne shows, probabilistic, inductive arguments may show one of two things. To claim that a hypothesis is confirmed by evidence may mean either that 1) the evidence has raised the probability of the hypothesis as compared with what it was or would have been without the evidence, or that 2) the evidence makes the theory more likely than not to be true. Arguments of the first sort Swinburne calls C-inductive; arguments of the latter kind he labels P-inductive. Swinburne says that the argument from the existence of the complex physical universe to God is a good C-inductive argument.

Briefly, the argument goes as follows. Everybody agrees that there exists a complex physical universe. The question is how to explain it, and there are at least two hypotheses. One holds that there is no further cause or explanation of the universe beyond its mere existence. The other says that God created it. Swinburne argues that the probability that our universe should exist as a result of creation by God is greater than the probability that it should exist of itself. This doesn't mean that the probability that God created the world is high. In fact, Swinburne admits that it is low, for at first glance it seems more probable that there would be nothing than that the world would have been created. Even if there is a God, he isn't required to create anything, but we do have a world, and we must ask how it came to be. It is more probable that an uncaused God created it than that it just happened to be here. This isn't absolute proof, but it shows that the hypothesis that there is a God is reasonable, and even more reasonable than atheism.

Critics, of course, are unconvinced. Mackie, for example, sees no reason that the God-hypothesis is more probable than an atheistic one. He finds no problem in viewing the universe's existence as an inexplicable brute fact. Only an implicit acceptance of the questionable principle of sufficient reason, says Mackie, moves one to think the God-hypothesis more probable. But when you look at it more closely, the God-hypothesis is actually quite improbable. For example, the God-hypothesis necessitates that a non-embodied being has intentions about creating a world and accomplishes them, though he has no material parts to his being that would allow him to do anything in ways creatures normally do things. Given our lack of experience of non-embodied beings, it is highly improbable, argues Mackie, that any should exist, let alone create a world. So the probability of a creator isn't clearly higher than that of the world existing as a brute fact.

In essence, these objections amount to saying that, depending on our presuppositions, we are likely to disagree about the probability of the two hypotheses in question. And, that just means the inductive cosmological argument will appeal to those already inclined to theism and won't appeal to opponents.

TELEOLOGICAL ARGUMENTS

Historically, philosophers and theologians have maintained that more than just the mere existence of the universe points to God's existence. All the instances of design or purpose in our universe seem much easier to explain on the assumption that there is a God than on an atheistic assumption. The teleological argument or argument from design is one of the oldest arguments for God's existence. Philosophers have suggested its roots are even evident in Plato. Plato held that the physical universe cannot be understood apart from mind which moves and orders it. While this reflects somewhat the cosmological argument, it also has affinity to the central notions of the argument from design.

Though the argument apparently was introduced in ancient Greece, it has had much greater popularity in later centuries. Probably the most famous exposition of the argument is that by William Paley (1743–1805), a British theologian. Many claim, however, that the most sophisticated version of the argument is the one by F. R. Tennant (1866–1957), a professor at Cambridge University. More recent defenses have been offered by philosophers such as Richard Taylor (*Metaphysics*)[14] and Richard Swinburne (*The Existence of God*). The most current versions, however, emphasize the intricacy of various parts of the natural order, such as the human eye or the circulatory system, as opposed to emphasizing the design of the universe as a whole. Some of the newest versions also invoke the so-called anthropic principle, which points to how finely tuned this planet is for sustaining life in general and human life in particular.[15]

This argument has had both proponents and critics. Kant, who had little use for the ontological and cosmological arguments, felt that the teleological argument always deserved to be mentioned with respect. He considered it the argument most in accord with common sense. That doesn't mean Kant defended it, but only that he was nowhere near as negative to it as to the others. The most famous critique of the argument comes from the Scottish philosopher David Hume (1711–1776). His *Dialogues Concerning Natural Religion*[16] offers the most thorough and scathing objections to the argument ever produced. Defenders and opponents of the argument must interact with Hume's critique.

As with the ontological and cosmological arguments, the teleological argument is really a family of arguments. I shall present Paley's formulation, but first it would help to describe some of the argument's general characteristics in its various forms. The argument in all forms is an *a posteriori* argument, beginning with the fact that our world appears to exhibit purposive order or design. It then argues to God, an intelligent, purposive creator, as the most likely cause of that order and design. Teleological arguments are inductive in nature and often analogical as in Paley's formulation. As Plantinga (*God and Other Minds*) notes, these features make the argument much more difficult to assess than a strictly deductive argument. With a deductive proof, premises are either true or false and conclusions follow from premises or not. An inductive argument measures probabilities and often judges degrees of analogy or similarity, so it is more difficult to assess.

William Paley: The Watch and the Watchmaker

In the eighteenth century the argument from design was firmly entrenched in theistic thinking. David Hume's critique was written about the middle of the century, but was published posthumously. Consequently, the force of his critique was felt later. As it turned out, in 1802 Paley published his version of the teleological argument in his *Natural Theology, or Evidences of the Existence and Attributes of the Deity, Collected from the Appearances of Nature.* Though it postdated Hume's critique (appearing at the end of the eighteenth century), it captures the essence of the argument as held during that century.

Paley says that if he were walking and his foot struck a stone and he was asked how it came to be there, he might respond that it had been there forever. There is no absurdity in that answer. On the other hand, if he found a watch, and was asked how that came to be there, he couldn't give the same answer. In the case of the watch (as opposed to the stone) we can see that the various parts have been put together for a purpose. Its parts move so as to indicate the hour of the day. Having observed the various mechanisms in the watch, we must conclude that it had a maker who understood its construction and designed its use.

According to Paley, we would conclude this even if other potentially disconfirming facts were true. For example, even if we had never seen a watch made, this watch would convince us that it must have a designer. Moreover, even if the watch didn't always function properly, it still offers evidence of being designed rather than arising out of random chance. Third, even if we couldn't discover the function of some of the watch's parts, that would not weaken the inference that the watch as a whole was designed. Fourth, no one would think there was a principle of order inherent in things that automatically caused the pieces of the watch to come together. As Paley says, no one ever saw a watch made by the principle of order; nor can we conceive of a principle of order apart from the one who does the ordering. Finally, suppose we found that the watch had the ability to manufacture other watches so that the watch itself was probably produced by a previous watch. That still wouldn't cause us to question the design of the watch. Instead, we would marvel at the intelligence that produced the original watch in such a way as to allow the production of further watches. None of these facts would dissuade us from believing that the watch shows evidence of an intelligent purposive creator.

Paley applies this line of reasoning to the world. By analogy, we can see that nature gives evidences of design and purpose just as the watch does. Paley offers numerous examples of how various organisms and organs are fitted together so that creatures can survive. As evidences of design in the watch suggest an intelligent watchmaker, evidences of design in the natural order suggest an intelligent, purposive world maker. And that creator is God.

DAVID HUME'S CRITIQUE. In his *Dialogues Concerning Natural Religion,* David Hume offers the most comprehensive critique of the teleological argument ever given. Since his time, most critics of the argument begin with Hume, regardless of whatever else they say. In what follows I shall sketch some of the more significant objections with responses where appropriate.

First, the argument from design is an argument from analogy. However, Hume argues that the universe is not analogous enough to human artifacts like a house or clock to sustain the argument. If it were, we might be able to attribute design to it just as we can to human artifacts. Dissimilarity, though, destroys the foundation of the argument.

Alvin Plantinga (*God and Other Minds*) thinks Hume's objection is inconclusive. Granted that there are vast differences between the world and a house, and granted that one might think the world resembles a great floating vegetable or crustacean-like organism more than a machine; that still doesn't invalidate the argument. The key isn't that every feature of the world bears analogy to every feature of an artifact, but only that the world be a member of some classes to which an artifact also belongs. And this is so, for both the universe and human artifacts belong to the class of things which exhibit the curious adaptation of means to ends. Since we can't think of any artifact belonging to this class which isn't the product of intelligent and conscious design, we may rightly infer that the world, as part of that class, also exhibits adaptation of means to ends as a result of intelligent design. As Plantinga explains, Hume claims that the dissimilarity between the universe and an artifact makes it impossible to argue by analogy from the one to the other, but he doesn't tell us which items of dissimilarity would render this particular argument by analogy defective. Until he explains the areas in which the analogy must fail for it to be unusable, Hume's objection shows little. Moreover, it overlooks one area of similarity which is crucial to the argument.

Second, one of Hume's most important objections was that it proves little to point to various evidences of design in the universe. Any universe, regardless of origin, will *look* designed. If things in the universe were not adapted to one another (and thus apparently designed), how could there be a universe at all? So, the sheer fact of design isn't proof of God. It suggests that we should ask for the cause, but Hume maintained that nothing in the argument demands that God be that cause. It is always possible, for instance, that the universe contains an infinite number of atoms moving about randomly. Given infinite time, sooner or later they will fall into the combination we know as our universe. The teleological argument doesn't rule out the possibility that design resulted in that way.

Hume wrote well before Darwin's *Origin of Species,* but since Darwin's publication, critics of the design argument have said that Darwin's theory is just the naturalistic explanation of the design in the universe for which Hume was looking. The principles of natural selection and survival of the fittest, they say, offer all the explanation we need for instances of design in the universe. We needn't appeal to God. Of course, there are significant objections to evolution, and even if one accepts evolution, one must still show that instances of design are better explained by appeal to evolution than by appeal to creation by an intelligent designer.

Third, one of Hume's major complaints is that the argument from intelligent design at most establishes a finite God. The world (the effect) is finite and imperfect, so to produce this world all that is needed is a cause that is equal to or greater than the effect. But a cause that is even greater than the effect needn't be infinite. Thus, the God postulated by this argument may be very wise and very powerful, but need not be all-wise or all-powerful. Moreover, we need not even assume from evidences of design that there is only one God. Just as human artifacts like a house or ship are often built by a team of workers, why couldn't there be a team of gods who produced each instance of design? Or, perhaps each god was responsible for one instance of design in the world. Nothing in the standard teleological argument precludes these possibilities.

A final Humean objection says that it is illegitimate to make probability judgments in matters where the item under discussion is unique, and the origin of the universe is unique. Since we have only one instance, how can we judge that universes most probably are designed by God? If we had numerous experiences of the origin of worlds, then we could make a probability judgment, but given the uniqueness of the case, no such judgment should be made. This objection undercuts not only the teleological argument but also, apparently, any other argument for God's existence based on probability.

There are two ways to take this objection. On one account, it means that analogical reasoning on this matter is ruled out, given the uniqueness of the universe's origin. However, Plantinga has discredited such reasoning, for a thing's uniqueness (and in some sense everything is unique) does not entail that it has no quality in common with anything else. As Plantinga has shown, the world does share a quality with other artifacts, and that quality is crucial for the argument from design. On the other interpretation, Hume's complaint is about making probability judgments in cases where there is only one instance of the phenomenon.

In addition to Hume's critique, there have been other objections raised against the argument from design. One of the most significant is that if instances of design point to a divine intelligent creator, instances of evil and disorder suggest the opposite. This objection is actually the problem of evil, which will be discussed in a later chapter. Theists should grant that *prima facie* evil must count against theism's probability, and should explain why it doesn't actually defeat belief in God. But the facts of evil don't remove the critic's obligation to explain all the instances of design in our world. As Paley said about the watch, even if it didn't work, that wouldn't prove it had no evidence of design. Moreover, the critic must answer the following question: if there is no God, why does anything ever go right in our universe, and why is this so most of the time? Evolution and chance seem inadequate to explain why there isn't more evil than we already have.

MORAL ARGUMENTS

A third kind of *a posteriori* argument for God's existence is the moral argument. This kind of argument isn't as popular among philosophers (even Christian ones) as the others, but it is very appealing to ordinary people. There is a certain commonsense plausibility to it, as one can attest from C. S. Lewis's version in *Mere Christianity*.

As with the other classical arguments, "the moral argument" refers to a series of arguments. There seem to be two broad kinds of moral argument. One type is represented by Kant, who actually didn't try to offer any sort of demonstrative proof in either a deductive or an inductive form. His argument moves from the fact of moral obligation to the practical claim that anyone who takes such obligations seriously must believe in the reality of God.

The other, more prevalent form of the argument, infers from some facts about morality, such as the existence of objective moral laws or the fact of conscience, that God is their cause. This kind of argument is offered by philosophers such as Cardinal Newman, Hastings Rashdall, and C. S. Lewis. Unlike many teleological arguments, moral arguments are not arguments from analogy, but as with teleological arguments, they are probabilistic in nature. They don't claim that there is no other possible explanation for the empirical phenomena they cite; they only claim that God's existence is the most likely one.

C. S. Lewis's Moral Argument

In *Mere Christianity*, Lewis presents a powerful version of the moral argument. Lewis begins by noting that people make comments that presuppose some moral law. When promises are broken, they complain that the promise should have been kept. When someone picks on an innocent bystander, someone else may tell him to leave the victim alone since he isn't harming anyone. As Lewis says, these comments presuppose some accepted standard of behavior. Even the wrongdoer recognizes the standard by trying to explain away his actions. He doesn't simply reply "So what?" All of this suggests that there is some common standard of appropriate behavior, morality, or law of fair play. Without that standard, we couldn't even disagree about moral matters. It would make no sense to try to prove someone wrong on these matters if there were no accepted concept of what is right and wrong.

Some might deny that this notion of right and wrong is universal, but Lewis says it is. From one culture to another, there may be some difference in ethical norms, but there is more similarity in moralities than one might suspect. For example, it seems universally true that selfishness is frowned upon. The same is true for lying or promise-breaking. There exists a universal sense of moral law, but it is also universally true that people break that law.

Lewis knows that some will object that this moral law is only our herd instinct, and as an instinct it must have developed like any other instinct, but Lewis denies this. Indeed, we have various instincts, but none of them tells us whether we should follow it; it is just there. For example, we may have an instinct to help a drowning man but also an instinct to preserve our own life. Having these instincts doesn't tell us which to follow. Only a moral law tells us that; therefore, the moral law must be different than a mere instinct.

Others think the moral law is nothing more than a matter of mere convention taught by parents and friends. Lewis grants that morality is at least in part taught by parents, but he denies that it is a mere convention. He likens the moral law to mathematics. Mathematics must also be taught, but a convention is something that reflects the peculiar taste of a particular society. It need not be the same from one society to the next. Obviously, mathematics can't change from one society to the next. Likewise, Lewis argues, the moral law isn't a convention drawn up any which way a society wants. The moral law isn't mere convention, as is evidenced by the fact that from one culture to another there is great similarity in moral codes. Moreover, it makes sense to talk about some moralities as better than others and to speak of moral progress, but how could this be so if there were no constant standard of morality that doesn't change from time to time and place to place? The moral law must be more than mere convention.

Lewis then adds that the moral law isn't like the laws of nature. The term "laws of nature" actually refers to the regularities of nature. It reflects what happens in nature, but doesn't tell us what should happen. On the other hand, the moral law tells us how to behave. It does more than describe behavior; it prescribes it. From whence comes this sense of obligation or prescription that we feel? In fact, how do we generally explain any fact about the universe? Traditionally, there have been two main answers, a naturalistic one and a religious one. The former says that there is no particular reason why humans feel a sense of moral obligation or that anything is as it is. It just happened that way. The latter view is that there is something behind the universe which is more like a mind than anything else we know. That something is the source of the moral obligation we feel. Lewis says that each of us senses that there is something beyond the moral law; it didn't just happen that we have that sense of obligation. If what is true of us is true of others, we have reason to think that others feel there is something beyond us. When we examine the universe and the moral law, it is best to conclude that the something or someone beyond is God.

Objections

Moral arguments have been criticized on various grounds, but several objections are most prevalent and relate to most, if not all, of the arguments that infer God from some fact about the moral character of the universe. Most moral arguments assume the objectivity of moral values and the moral law. That is, they think there is an absolute morality independent of the mind, and they claim that conscience does not merely stem from some psychological trick of the mind. The first line of objection begins by asking whether moral laws and values really are objective. Many who reject moral arguments for God's existence answer that moral laws and values are subjective.

One popular form of moral subjectivism is cultural relativism, which interprets moral obligations in terms of social approval and disapproval. Every society has certain actions that it approves and others it disapproves. What makes an act right or wrong is what society thinks of it. Of course, societies may differ widely in their views about what is right and wrong. With this view no one should think ethical norms come from a God who reveals that certain things are right and others wrong. Moral objectivism is wrong and cannot serve as a basis for arguing to God.

All forms of moral subjectivism have been severely criticized by theists and atheists alike. Lewis's argument itself gives some telling responses to the view. Nonetheless, one way to reject moral arguments for God's existence is to believe in moral subjectivism. However, even if one holds moral objectivism, that does not automatically mean that moral arguments succeed. Many who believe that moral laws and values are objective still refuse to see this as pointing to God.

Most advocates of moral objectivism who reject God do so on the grounds that the objectivity of the moral law and the fact of conscience can be explained in a totally naturalistic way. Many claim that moral values and conscience arose as man evolved. The higher that life-forms became, the more people had to learn to live together in society by rules that protect everyone. Societies without such rules simply did not survive, whereas others that developed morality and lived by it found they were better able to survive. So, on this view, moral laws and conscience can be explained as the natural outcome of the evolutionary process. There is no need to appeal to God.

Those who reject evolution may opt for another naturalistic explanation of moral objectivism. They may think that ethical norms reflect the collective pressure of society rather than divine revelation of moral law. Societies follow these norms because they see that such behavior is in their collective and individual best interest. Conscience turns out to be nothing more than the pressure brought to bear upon an individual from what family, friends, and

THE EXISTENCE AND BEING OF GOD □ 203

society as a whole have told that individual to do. These phenomena need no further explanation.

Of course, all of these naturalistic explanations rest either on a belief that humans are essentially good and thus will know and do what is right, or on the view that morality is motivated totally by selfish interest to preserve well-being. Anyone committed to a biblical account of man must reject both notions. Scripture portrays human beings as too evil to do what is right even if they know what is right. Many people are motivated to do right solely because it pays to do right, but none of that guarantees that anyone will do right even if they know it pays to do so. Rom 1:31-32 is very explicit that even those who know that evildoers are punished do evil anyway, and encourage others to do the same. Obeying moral laws would preclude punishment, but despite knowing this, they are too perverse to turn from evil. In spite of these facts, those who prefer a naturalistic explanation of moral objectivism reject moral arguments for God's existence.

A final line of objection stems from the fact that moral arguments are proba-bilistic in nature. Theists hold that while there are naturalistic explanations of an objective moral law and conscience, the theistic explanation is more prob-able. Atheists disagree and maintain that the only reason theists think a theistic explanation is more probable is that they are already believers. Theists raise a similar complaint against atheists. Both objections amount to saying that the only reason each side accepts as more probable its own explanation is that each side begs the question. Each side is committed to its view before discussion begins, so the arguments become irrelevant for both sides. Arguments like the moral argument get us no closer to the truth about whether God exists.

Not even all theists think the weight of probability rests on the theist's side in favor of the moral argument. For example, Richard Swinburne, who sees probability on the side of the cosmological argument and the argument from design, thinks it is not at all clear that the theistic explanation of moral phenomena such as conscience is the most probable. Swinburne says that naturalistic explanations appear to be as plausible as theological ones. For example, is it abundantly clear that moral norms more likely come from God than from the collective pressures of family and society?

What this shows is that among philosophers (theists and atheists alike) the moral argument is generally the least popular of the theistic proofs. It does offer confirmation for the believer and some evidence for the nonbeliever open to argument, but for a confirmed atheist it is probably the least likely of the theistic arguments to be at all rationally compelling.

GENERAL VALUE OF THEISTIC ARGUMENTS

What should we conclude about the value of the major theistic arguments? Several points seem appropriate. First, the only argument that would establish the existence of the Judaeo-Christian God with all his attributes (if it worked) is the ontological argument. Unfortunately, it is the hardest to understand, and many think it least likely to be correct.

Second, all of the theistic arguments are valuable in showing that theistic belief is not thoroughly irrational. For theists, they offer rational confirmation of their belief. For atheists or agnostics, they provide rational grounds for belief in God. Arguments such as the cosmological and the teleological seem most compelling, but all offer some evidence for God's existence. None of the arguments alone provides a conclusive proof, but they are just the sort of evidences one would find helpful in making an overall cumulative case for God's existence.[17]

Finally, the arguments are valuable as sophisticated and interesting pieces of philosophical reasoning, regardless of their accuracy or inaccuracy. Even convinced atheistic philosophers, for example, agree that the ontological argument is extremely important philosophically because of what it teaches us about topics such as the nature of necessity. Consequently, the theistic arguments continue to engender much discussion, and interest in them is not likely to wane any time soon.

THE REALITY OF GOD

Once one settles the question of whether there is a God, the next issue is what kind of being this God has. In chapter 2, we distinguished this question from the question about God's role and relationships in our world. As we saw, some believe God to be merely a concept without reality outside of human minds. Moreover, Karl Marx claimed that "religion is the opiate of the people." He thought this not because there really is a God who satisfies the desires of human hearts for a supreme being, but because people have invented the idea of God to help them through the trials and tribulations of everyday life. God is deemed a crutch for those too weak to face the world on their own. Once they mature to the point of handling life's vicissitudes, they can recognize this crutch for what it is—a mere intellectual invention—and discard it. Life without God is for the intellectually and emotionally mature, those who have grown to where they can make their own meaning and find their own fulfillment in a world devoid of the crutch.[18]

God Is Real

In contrast to such skepticism, reason and Scripture both dictate that God is real, and that his reality is more than that of a concept. In the first portion of this chapter, we discussed rational arguments for God's existence. Though these arguments are not conclusive in themselves, they lend credence to belief in God. The cosmological and teleological arguments in particular offer evidence that matter in an organized form has not likely just been here eternally; it is likely that God created our universe, but of course, this God must be a real being, not a mere concept. As Thomas Morris has argued, if what he calls creation theology has any chance of being taken seriously, the creator of which it speaks must be a real being.[19] The *a posteriori* theistic arguments give us reason to believe this is so.

Throughout the history of Jewish and Christian thought, God's reality has been spoken of in various ways. For many centuries it was typical to say that God is a substance whose essence can be described in accord with a variety of attributes he possesses. By this, theologians and philosophers meant that God has reality outside of our minds. There is a "something" that underlies his characteristics and actions. In addition, God has attributes that inhere in his substance. Those attributes taken collectively can be called his essence.[20] In everything but God's case, we can describe its characteristics (its essence) without having to conclude that the thing described exists as anything more than a concept. God is different, for as some have said, his essence is existence, i.e., it is impossible to give an accurate description of God without including that he exists as an actual being external to our minds. Thus, the essence/existence distinction doesn't apply to God.

In contemporary discussions, talk of substances and essences has fallen on hard times. The most frequent objection is that such language invokes ancient Greek philosophy with its view of God as the static, unmoved mover. As we have seen, this view has affinities to the God of classical theism, and that God is deemed religiously, philosophically, and theologically inadequate. In contrast, critics claim that the biblical picture of God is of a relational being, involved intimately with the world, whereas the static God of substances and essences remains aloof and uninvolved in our world. Process and open view theists are especially disdainful of this God.

In light of these considerations, we must be careful in speaking of God's being. Whether or not we call God a substance with an essence, the basic point with which all sides concur is that God exists outside the mind. We can speak of his nature and existence not merely as concepts, but as descriptions of a real being.

In turning to Scripture we find ample support for the reality of God as a distinct being. Scripture portrays God as a being who acts. In the OT he creates (Gen 1:1ff.), he destroys the world by flood when mankind is exceedingly wicked (Genesis 6–9), he calls Abraham (Genesis 12) and later ratifies a covenant with him (Genesis 15 and 17), he brings the plagues upon Egypt (Exodus 7–11), parts the Red Sea as he leads the people of Israel out of bondage (Exodus 14), gives the Law to Moses on Mount Sinai (Exodus 19–20), delivers Daniel from the lions' den (Daniel 6) and so many other things. The NT also portrays God as a God of action. He sends his angel to announce the birth of Jesus to Mary (Luke 1:26-38), he becomes incarnate in Jesus Christ (John 1:14), he speaks his approval of Jesus at Christ's baptism (Matt 3:17), he raises Christ from the dead (Acts 2:24, 32; Rom 4:24; 1 Cor 6:14), and does many other things as revealed in the NT. Of course, nonentities do none of these things, so since Scripture teaches that God acts in our real world, it portrays him as a real being, not as a fabrication of fertile imaginations.

There are also passages that either directly state or clearly imply that God is a real being. Phil 2:6 is a prime example. Speaking of Christ, Paul says that he existed *en morphē theoû* ("being in very nature God"). The key word is *morphē,* translated "nature" (in many translations, it is rendered "form"). As Silva explains, in classical Greek *morphē* is not equivalent to *ousia* ("being," "essence"), but is used to speak "of essential or characteristic attributes and thus is to be distinguished from *schēma* (the changeable, external 'fashion')."[21] Silva further explains that the term is used in a number of different senses in Hellenistic literature and the Septuagint. Hence, we must rely on context, and two contextual factors greatly help us in this case. For one thing, *morphē theoû* corresponds to *isa theoû* ("equal with God"). Moreover, "*morphē theoû* is set in antithetical parallelism with . . . *morphēn doulou* ('form of a servant'), an expression further defined by the phrase . . . *en homoiōmati anthrōpōn* ('in the likeness of men')."[22] The point seems clear enough. Paul speaks of Christ's humiliation. Prior to becoming incarnate, i.e., "being in the likeness of men," Christ was "equal with God," i.e., "in the form of God." The phrases dealing with Christ's humanity show that he became a real man; he didn't merely appear to be human (hence the phrase "likeness of men"). Thus, he must have a human nature, but nonentities do not have any kind of nature and are not any kind of beings. As Silva notes, the phrases about Christ's humanity are in antithesis to the comments about Jesus' relation to God. Being "equal to God" in this context surely does not mean that being in the *morphē theoû* refers to the external appearance of God. God is immaterial, so he has no outward appearance anyway. Paul must be thinking of Christ's inner nature before the incarnation, but nonentities have neither an inner nature nor an outward appearance. To say that Christ existed in the "form of God" must mean that God has a nature and is a being.

In Gal 4:8 Paul speaks of the Galatians' condition before coming to Christ: " Formerly, when you did not know God, you were slaves to those who by nature are not gods" (NIV). The key phrase is "those who by nature are not gods" (*tois physei mē ousin theois*) and *physei* is the key word. When Paul speaks of those who by nature are not gods, we must be careful not to read *a priori* into *physei* Greek philosophy about being and essence. On the other hand, if Paul isn't referring to the essential nature or being, it is hard to imagine what he means. If Paul merely wanted to say that before the Galatians came to Christ, they worshiped other gods, gods about whose reality Paul did not wish to make any comment, he could have just said that they worshiped other gods. Evidently, he intended to say more than just that, but what could his point be if not that these gods don't exist (they have no nature)? By saying that these gods have no being, Paul seems to imply that, in contrast to these gods, there is a God who is a real entity. It makes abundant sense in this context to conclude that Paul believes that the God they now know, having turned to Christ, is that God who is a real being.

THE EXISTENCE AND BEING OF GOD ☐ 207

Rom 1:19-20 is also relevant to this point. In verse 19 Paul says that everyone has some revelation of God, and in verse 20 he clarifies this point by saying that "since the creation of the world God's invisible qualities—his eternal power and divine nature—have been clearly seen, being understood from what has been made, so that men are without excuse" (NIV). That is, by looking at the created order, anyone can reason that it must have been made by someone with significant power. In fact, Paul even says that everyone can see that this creator must be divine. The point for our purposes, however, is that nonentities create nothing. Hence, Paul can hardly be saying that as people look at our world they come to the *idea* of God and then conclude that a mere idea created what they see. Ideas don't have such power. Paul's point is that everyone can see that there must be a supreme being, namely, God who created this world.

Two other NT passages are noteworthy. In Hebrews 11 the author discusses faith and offers a list of heroes of faith. Verse 6 says, "And without faith it is impossible to please God, because anyone who comes to him must believe that he exists and that he rewards those who earnestly seek him" (NIV). More literally, the text says that the one who comes to God must believe that he is. By this the writer means that one must believe that there is a God, and that he exists as more than a concept. We cannot please God without believing first that he exists as a real being, and this clearly assumes that God is real.

The other NT passage is Col 2:9. Speaking of Christ, Paul says that in Christ "all the fullness of the Deity lives in bodily form" (NIV). If God is not a real being, then at most Paul is saying that Jesus had a very complete concept of what God is like. Of course, that does not mean that he personally was divine. However, Paul intends to teach the divinity of Christ at the same time that he teaches Christ's humanity. If in Jesus a divine nature and a human nature (not just concepts of either or both) combine to make the person Jesus Christ, this could not happen if there is no divine being external to our minds.

As for the OT, we already noted the many actions attributed to God, and he cannot do these things unless he is a real existent. In addition, in Exodus 3 God tells Moses to tell the Israelites that God has sent him. Moses asks what he should say if they ask who this God is. God answers (v. 14), "I AM WHO I AM. This is what you are to say to the Israelites: 'I AM has sent me to you'" (NIV). If God is nothing more than a concept, and if "I AM" is nothing more than a name or description of a concept, why would anyone follow its orders? Many note that the divine name shows God's consciousness of himself, but it also suggests his existence as a being. What is this "I"? Certainly more than an imaginary being or a concept, and anyway, concepts don't reveal anything, including their name, to anyone.

God Is a Being

Having established that the Christian God exists outside our minds, we must quickly add that he is *a* being, not being-itself, the ground of being, the power of being, or the structure of being. Moreover, he is distinct from the creation. Such claims are intended to safeguard the evangelical notion of God from several ideas prevalent among many contemporary non-evangelical theologians.[23]

In previous chapters, we saw that Paul Tillich espouses the view that God is being-itself. As O. C. Thomas notes, Tillich refers to God as being-itself, the power and ground of being, the structure of being and reality, existence itself, the basis of thought, and the presupposition of knowledge.[24] To understand being and God under so many different descriptions complicates matters, but in reading Tillich, what he means is clear enough. Tillich's main concern is that God not be thought of as *a* being, one among many, for then he, too, would be subject to ultimate being, being-itself. As Thomas explains:

> . . . Tillich asserts that God is being-itself and not *a* being, not even the highest or most perfect being, for if God were *a* being, he would be subordinate to being-itself and subject to the categories of finitude and thus not the answer to the existential question of human finitude. God as being-itself means that God is the ground of being or the power of being. Also, God is the ground of the structure of being. "He *is* the structure." God as being-itself is not the universal essence (pantheism) but rather beyond the contrast of essential and existential being.[25]

While this may sound like a pious attempt to keep God from being subject to anything beyond himself, on closer examination, one wonders what Tillich's God actually is. What sort of thing is being-itself, or the structure of being, or the power and ground of being? Are these entities themselves? If so, then they must be beings of some sort and God is, after all, a being. Tillich, of course, won't allow this, but then what sorts of things are these items? Are they concepts? If being-itself and the power of being are mere concepts, then they have no existence independent of the mind, and in fact are subordinate to the beings who think them as concepts. As we saw in previous chapters, it is hard to see Tillich's God as personal. In fact, it is hard to see him as anything real other than a concept or a being.

What about Tillich's major concern, though, that God not be just one being among many? This is definitely a problem if God is a human, angelic, animal, or inanimate being. However, once we understand what sort of being God is (our project in this chapter and the next ones on divine attributes) and what he does, we realize that though he is a being among other beings in the universe, he is no ordinary, run-of-the-mill being. So, it is hard to sympathize with Tillich's concerns about God being beyond specific beings. Moreover, Scripture is clear that God is a being distinct from others, not just being-itself. As creator, he is the source of all that exists, but that doesn't mean we should understand him as impersonal, abstract being-itself, rather than a personal creator.

There is another reason for affirming that God is a being distinct from his creation. We must safeguard the evangelical concept of God from pantheism and panentheism. God's being is not identical to the created universe. Hence, his being is not spread out across the universe bit by bit at each point in space. Omnipresence demands that God be somehow present *at* every point in space, but he isn't present *as* each point of space; otherwise, pantheism results. Likewise, Scripture never portrays the universe as God's body, the concrete pole of a dipolar being. Though panentheists claim that God is not identical with each point in space (they disavow a commitment to pantheism), they do believe that all things exist in God. Hence, the concrete universe is his body, but there is more to God than just his concrete pole.

In contrast to both pantheism and panentheism, Scripture teaches that there is no one like God. Isaiah writes (40:18), "To whom, then, will you compare God?" (NIV, see also Ps 35:10; 71:19; 86:8; 89:8). These verses compare Yahweh to anything else worshiped as God. There is no God like the God of the Bible, but we can and should go further. In the Decalogue (Exod 20:3-5), God commands Israel not to make any idols of him. Moses repeats the substance of this command and explains further why it should be followed (Deut 4:15-19). When the Lord spoke to the people of Israel on Mount Horeb (v. 15), they saw no form. Hence, they should not try to represent God by anything representing humans, animals, or anything else (vv. 16-18). Nor should they worship the sun, moon, and stars (v. 19). According to the apostle Paul (Rom 1:23), it is just this error that mankind made. Having revelation of the true God, they worshiped idols instead.

The point of appealing to these Scriptures is to show that the consensus of Scripture is not just that there is no God like the God of the Bible: even more, there is nothing at all in the universe that matches God. Hence, any attempt to represent him by some image or idol will not succeed. If this is true, however, neither pantheism nor panentheism can match the God of Scripture. Given pantheism, everything is God, so, of course, there are things that are like him, and we can represent him (or at least some aspect of him) by an idol of a human being or animal. As for panentheism, the same is true. Even if the universe is not all there is to God, the universe is identical to God's consequent pole. There is something like him and it should be possible to make images to represent various aspects of his physical pole. Since Scripture claims that no God and nothing else is identical to the true and living God (hence, it is impossible to represent him through any image), it is safe to say that the biblical God is neither the God of pantheism nor the God of panentheism. If so, then God must be a being distinct from the created universe.

GOD AS A PERFECT, NECESSARY, AND INFINITE BEING

The next task is to discover what sort of being God is. I begin by noting that God is the most perfect being and a necessary being. Each of these claims needs explanation and defense.

A Perfect Being

Thomas Morris's treatment of both matters in *Our Idea of God* is most helpful. As Morris explains, theologians must decide which method to use in forming the concept of God. One can rely solely on biblical revelation, but Scripture isn't written as a philosophy text. Thus, while evangelicals begin with Scripture and incorporate whatever it says about God, there will still be questions remaining when analysis of the Bible ends. Morris argues that one might instead use a method that starts with God as creator and plots out the implications of that. Such a method could incorporate Scripture, but using either creation theology or Scripture plus creation theology, some questions will remain. Morris suggests that we start with Anselm's insight (embodied in the ontological argument) that God is the "being than which none greater can be conceived," or more simply, "the greatest conceivable being" (the GCB).[26]

As Morris contends, Anselm's key insight was that no being could qualify as God if a greater being could be conceived. To say that God is the GCB means that "God is a being with the greatest possible array of compossible great-making properties."[27] Moreover, a great-making property is "any property, or attribute, or characteristic, or quality which it is intrinsically good to have, any property which endows its bearer with some measure of value, or greatness, or metaphysical stature, regardless of external circumstances."[28]

Though we might revise these definitions a bit, they catch Anselm's main thrust. As we saw when discussing the ontological argument, the key for Anselm is metaphysical greatness, for though God is morally perfect, the only hope for the argument to succeed is if God is the *metaphysically* most perfect being possible, for such a being would have necessary existence, and a being with necessary existence could not fail to exist. Moreover, we must narrow the range of greatness-making properties that can apply to God. For example, it is presumably greater for a rock to be hard than soft, because then it will be less likely to be destroyed. However, it makes little sense to say that since hardness in a rock is intrinsically valuable, God, as possessing all greatness-making properties, must be hard. We need to restrict our discussion to qualities that are intrinsically valuable for a personal divine being to have. For example, divine beings can have power, knowledge, and wisdom, and they exercise various moral virtues such as love, justice, and goodness. Anselm's definition of God teaches that if the God we conceive is truly the most perfect, he must have all of these qualities, and he must have them to the highest degree possible for a being of his sort. Furthermore, as Morris explains, whichever characteristics are greatness-making properties, it must be possible for them to exist jointly in an individual being. No single being could have both the properties of being married and being a bachelor. Similarly, if there are any greatness-making properties that one being cannot have along with other attributes, then God could not have them all.[29]

What I have said in the previous paragraphs is nowhere found in this form in Scripture, but that does not mean that Scripture or evangelical theology would disagree. Within Scripture there is a series of verses that teach that there is no God like the biblical God (Isa 46:9ff., for example). And in light of what biblical writers say about God in comparison to other gods, it is reasonable to think that biblical writers, if asked, would say that the biblical God surpasses anyone and everything in each of his attributes.

After making these claims about what he calls perfect being theology, Morris adds that in formulating our concept of God, relying only on the basic notions of perfect being theology will be too restrictive. Perfect being theology informs us that God must have all perfections a divine being can have (and each to the highest degree), but that does not tell us the list of characteristics God actually has. It is here, Morris explains, that we must supplement perfect being theology with creation theology and biblical teaching in order to get as full-orbed a concept of God's being as possible.[30]

A Necessary Being

In addition to God existing outside of our minds and being the greatest conceivable being, he is also a necessary being. I use the terms "necessity" and "necessary" in a philosophical sense, not in senses we use in ordinary language. Philosophers use these terms in a number of ways, but I am concerned specifically with two. One sense of "necessary" means true for all possible worlds. A possible world is the complete sequence of persons, objects, events, and actions throughout the whole history of that world from beginning to end. Philosophers often hold that there is an infinite number of possible worlds, though only one is actual.

Philosophers and theologians who speak of God as necessary in this sense typically mean two things. On the one hand, they mean that any attribute God has in a given possible world is part of his essential nature. He could not be the being he is without those attributes. In addition, to say that God is a necessary being means that he exists in every possible world. Remembering the logic of Anselm's view of God as most perfect being, we can see why the greatest conceivable being must exist in all possible worlds, not just a few. If he exists in some but not in all, there is a greater conceivable being, namely, one who exists in more possible worlds. In fact, the very greatest conceivable being would exist in every possible world. If so, then imagine any logically conceivable state of affairs you wish, and God would exist in it.

Philosophers also use "necessary" as opposed to the contingent. Something contingent doesn't have to exist, but it can. As contingent, it is brought into and maintained in existence by something else. Moreover, contingent things can cease to exist. In contrast, necessary beings depend on nothing for their existence; they neither come into nor go out of existence. In the contingency form of the cosmological argument, we saw that if everything that ever existed were contingent, there must have been some time in the past when nothing at all existed. But, from nothing comes nothing, and yet, we know by observation that something exists: our universe. The production of a universe, then, must depend on something which doesn't itself depend for its existence on anything else. That being is what philosophers and theologians committed to what Morris calls creation theology call God. The notion of God as a necessary being also harkens back to the second form of the ontological argument, which compares contingent existence with necessary existence and concludes that the latter is the greatest kind of existence there is. Hence, the greatest conceivable being must exist necessarily, not contingently.[31]

Does God as a necessary being square with the biblical portrait of God? Surely, biblical writers never use such philosophical language of God, but Scripture does say things that fit this notion. First, Scripture clearly affirms that God has always existed and always will exist (see my discussion of eternity in chapter 8). Moreover, Jesus says that the Father has life within himself, and has given to the Son to have life in himself as well (John 5:26). It is hard to know what this means other than that God depends on no one but himself for his life. Finally, Scripture emphatically proclaims God as the creator of all things (e.g., Gen 1:1; Exod 20:11), but it never speaks of God as created or as a creature.

These biblical ideas taken together lead me to conclude that God is a necessary being, not contingent. If God is not created, has life in himself so that he depends on no one for his existence, and has always and will always exist, then God qualifies as a necessary being in the philosophical sense of that term. God certainly could not be contingent and fit the biblical description set forth in the preceding paragraph.

As to God being necessary in the sense of existing in all possible worlds, Scripture never directly says this of him. However, it says that nothing was made without his agency, and it is reasonable to infer from such verses that the writers believe that God is not only the creator but also the only one with power to create anything. If so, he exists for this possible world, and it is hard to imagine how any other possible world could become actual without God creating it. So it is hard to imagine God as absent from any possible world, and that means that though the connection between Scripture and "necessity" in the sense of "true for all possible worlds" is not as clear as we might wish, what Scripture does say about God as the sole person with power to create suggests that it isn't inconsistent with Scripture to say that God is necessary in this sense.

An Infinite Being

In addition to holding that God is the GCB and a necessary being, Christian theologians and philosophers also maintain that God is unlimited or infinite. In the chapter on non-moral divine attributes I shall discuss this attribute in more detail, but a brief word now is in order. An initial point is that it is not clear that either perfection or necessary existence logically entails being infinite. For example, if it makes no sense to speak of an infinite quality or quantity of some attribute that is considered a greatness-making property, God could still be the GCB without being infinite or unlimited. Since God as the GCB does not necessarily include the idea of his infinity, it is proper to affirm separately that he is infinite or unlimited. This means that there are no limitations on God, except the laws of logic and his other attributes.

Second, because of the well-known difficulties surrounding the notion(s) of infinity (e.g., mathematical infinity is notoriously opaque—what is an infinite number, an infinite set, an infinite sequence?), some theologians prefer the term "unlimited." Of course, "unlimited" can be construed to mean the same thing as "infinite" with all its ambiguities. However, if "unlimited" simply means that there are no restraints on what God can do (apart from the limitations of logic and his character), that is the basic concept Christian thinkers espouse in holding divine infinity.

Finally, we must understand God's infinity or limitlessness in a qualitative sense, not a quantitative sense. Thus, to say that God is an unlimited being does not mean that he has a greater amount of being than anyone else, that his being incorporates all other beings, or that his being is equivalent to all things actual and possible. Such quantitative understandings of divine infinity lead to pantheism. Rather, the point is that the distinct being who is God is qualitatively unlimited. Such a being would be a necessary being, for as we have seen, this is the highest quality or type of being one could have. To be a necessary being, God need not possess more being than any other being; rather, he must be a different sort of being than anything contingent.

Similarly, to say that God is infinite or unlimited in love, justice, power, wisdom, or knowledge is not to say that he has an infinite amount of these qualities. Instead, it means that his attributes are qualitatively unlimited and thus make him a qualitatively different kind of being than anything else in the universe, a being who is unlimited in respect to those attributes. For example, God's power is not the sum total of all the power there is and could be (a quantitative notion). Instead, as omnipotent, he has the kind of power which allows him to do anything that is doable in conjunction with the laws of logic and the particulars of his character. To say that God is unlimited in knowledge and power to think does not mean that his mind is the sum total of all existing minds plus all possible minds (whatever that would mean). It means that there are no limitations to his cognitive powers. As a result, he knows all true propositions, though not because he has more mind quantitatively and hence has a big enough mind to store all that information. Rather, the mind he has functions so well that it is capable of knowing all things, and knowing them at once.

In summarizing this portion of the current chapter, we can say that God exists in the world outside our minds and is best understood as the greatest conceivable being and as a necessary, unlimited being.

214 □ No One Like Him

GOD AS SPIRIT

So far we have seen that God is a real being who is perfect, necessary, and unlimited, but nothing has been said about the fundamental nature of that being. Invoking the language of substances, we note that things that exist independent of mind are made of one of two types of substance (or of both). Some things are immaterial and others are material. Some beings are made of both, but the immaterial part isn't composed of matter and non-matter, and the material portion is not a mixture of matter and non-matter.

The difference between material and immaterial things is considerable. Material things are extended and bounded things. We can observe where one material object ends and another begins. In contrast, immaterial things are not made of matter, are not extended, and have no physical boundaries. The basic characteristic of immaterial objects is consciousness or cognition, i.e., immaterial things are thinking things. Material things don't think. Human nature has traditionally been understood as a combination of a material thing and an immaterial substance.[32] This mind-body substance dualism has been with us at least since the French philosopher René Descartes. Philosophers have tried to explain how thinking things that are not extended or bounded causally interact with material things that have those characteristics but do not think. To date no one has offered an entirely satisfactory explanation; hence especially within the twentieth century many have opted for a material-ist view of mind, denying altogether the existence of immaterial substances.

Regardless of whether one can adequately explain how immaterial minds interact with material bodies, Christian theists understand that more is at stake in this discussion than just a proper account of human nature. Traditionally, Jewish and Christian thinkers have maintained that the God of Scripture is an immaterial being, pure spirit. If one opts for an entirely materialist account of mind, the traditional Judaeo-Christian concept of God is in serious trouble.

Though we cannot here resolve the mind-body interaction question, we can answer whether Scripture depicts God's nature as material or immaterial. We begin with biblical evidence that God is pure spirit, but as we shall see, the issue is more complex than it initially appears.[33]

John 4 records Jesus' conversation with the Samaritan woman. By verse 20 the conversation turns to places of worship, and in verse 23 Jesus says that a time is coming when the place of worship (e.g., the temple in Jerusalem) will not matter, but the attitude and method of worship will. Jesus adds that his Father is looking for people who will worship him in spirit and truth. Then, in verse 24 Jesus says, "God is a spirit; and those who worship Him must worship in spirit and truth." The word "spirit" is the Greek *pneuma*. The sec-ond occurrence doesn't make an ontological claim about God's nature, but is used instead as part of the phrase prescribing the proper manner of worship. However, the first occurrence of *pneuma* asserts an ontological fact about

God: he is spirit.[34] Moreover, the Greek word order places *pneuma* as the first word in the sentence for emphasis.

Evangelicals usually cite this verse as teaching that God is pure spirit, and they think this settles the matter. However, it is not quite so simple, for while the verse affirms that God's nature is immaterial, by itself the verse shows only that God is *at least spirit, immaterial.* It does not say that he is *at most spirit.*

Throughout the centuries commentators have held that this verse does mean that God is only spirit, but there is reason to pause, for the Bible also portrays God as revealing his presence on various occasions in a physical or material way. Moreover, Scripture often speaks of God as if he has material parts. It talks about the "hand of God," the "eye of God," the "face of God." Theologians repeatedly call such language anthropomorphic. That is, biblical writers aren't really attributing physical matter to God but are instead referring to God's power ("hand of God") or knowledge and wisdom ("eye of God"). Since these parts of the human body play the roles in us attributed to God, and since human language is replete with references to physical things because humans have a body and live in a physical world, it is natural to speak of God in these physical terms. Everyone recognizes that the references to physical body parts is metaphorical, anthropomorphic, and that we use it because we have no other language to depict a nonmaterial thing acting in our world.

While it is assumed that such language is metaphorical, how do we know that language about God as spirit and invisible is not, instead, the metaphor? After all, doesn't Scripture say that the pure in spirit will eventually *see* God (Matt 5:8)? Job believed that his redeemer lives and that someday in his flesh he would *see* him (Job 19:26). This language also seems straightforward, so perhaps language about God as spirit and invisible should be taken metaphorically. John 4:24 says that God is spirit, but it doesn't say he is *at most* spirit. Perhaps he is a combination of immaterial and material.

Lest readers be unduly disturbed, I am not here arguing for God as material. My point is that we must be careful not to decide too quickly that physical language in regard to God is anthropomorphic. Rather, we need to make a case that it is so. We must offer evidence that shows both that God is *at least* spirit, and that he is *at most* spirit. If we cannot, it is really an open question as to whether physical language used of God is or is not anthropomorphic.

How do we make the case that God is *at most* spirit? John 4:24 is a good place to begin, but it is only a beginning. Jesus says that God is spirit, but what are the characteristics of spirit? Is spirit in any sense material? Such questions may sound odd, but they are not totally out of line, for there is evidence that in early church history some Christians, influenced by Stoic philosophy, held that God has a spiritual body. Stroumsa says of the Stoic view that "for them, there can be no incorporeal being, since existence is defined by the body. God, therefore, being a spirit, is only the purest of all bodies."[35] Hence, God has a nonmaterial body. As Stroumsa explains, it is in this context that Origen, committed to Platonism, argues against the idea of nonmaterial bodies and for a view of God as spirit as totally immaterial.[36]

Putting that controversy aside, what can we say of an immaterial thing? Here we have help from a comment by Jesus to his disciples after the resurrection. When he appeared to them in his glorified body, they could hardly believe their eyes. They thought he was a ghost, an immaterial spirit. Jesus showed them his hands and feet, and to reassure them that they were not seeing a spirit or imagining something, he said (Luke 24:39), "See My hands and My feet, that it is I Myself; touch Me and see, for a spirit does not have flesh and bones as you see that I have." A similar sort of disjunction between flesh (material) and spirit (immaterial) appears in Isa 31:3 as Isaiah pleads with his people not to fear the Egyptians but to trust in God. For after all, "the Egyptians are men and not God; their horses are flesh and not spirit" (NIV). These phrases set up parallel antitheses between men and God on the one hand, and flesh and spirit on the other. God is not man and spirit is not flesh. Men and horses are flesh, but God is spirit.

If God is spirit and not flesh, and if spirit has no flesh and bones, this language confirms what we said above about the basic characteristics of material and immaterial things. Moreover, if immaterial things contain no matter (hence, are neither flesh nor bones), they must be invisible. Only that which contains matter can be seen. In fact, Scripture repeatedly says that God is invisible, but before turning to passages that teach this, we must again confront the question of whether this language is metaphorical/anthropomorphic or whether the language about physical parts of God should be understood that way. How can we tell which is literal and which is anthropomorphic?

To answer these questions we must consult the immediate context of each claim to see if it offers any basis for judging one set of passages literal and the other metaphorical. If we deem either kind of passage metaphorical, we must explain the contextual grounds for this conclusion, and then we must explain what the metaphor means. For example, I have argued that Jesus' two references to "spirit" in John 4:24 do not mean exactly the same thing. The second indicates an appropriate attitude for worship, while the first literally refers to an ontological thing, an immaterial substance. If the first reference of "spirit" also refers to an attitude for worship, then the sentence is redundant. But if it does not speak of an attitude, what else could it mean, if it is not a reference to an immaterial substance? In that context, no other meaning seems to make sense. Similarly, when Jesus says in Luke 24:39 that a spirit has no flesh and bones as he does, if he is not talking about literal ontological things (immaterial and material substances), how would his comment satisfy their disbelief about whether it is really he? "Spirit" also can be used to refer to a spiritual relation, to the Holy Spirit, or to some attitude, but those meanings would be entirely irrelevant to the issue under discussion in Luke 24. Likewise, as we shall see shortly, attributions of invisibility to God do not appear to be metaphorical at all. If, for example, in 1 Tim 1:17 "invisible" is metaphorical, then as a member of a list of divine attributes ("eternal, immortal, invisible, the only God"), it would seem that the others in the list should also be considered metaphorical. But what would the metaphor for any of these attributes mean? Moreover, if "invisible" is metaphorical, but all the other attributes in the verse are literal, what is the hermeneutic that lets us draw such conclusions? None is forthcoming.

There is another side to the issue of anthropomorphisms, however. Just as we asked what the metaphor would mean in John 4, Luke 24, and 1 Timothy 1, we must ask the same thing of passages that speak of the hand of God, his face, and his eyes, and we must also explain what it means for the pure in heart to "see" God. Then, too, we must somehow explain the implications for the very being of God of the fact that at times he appeared in physical ways (a burning bush, the angel of the Lord, etc.). If we cannot explain what the metaphors mean and cannot correlate all of this with the physical appearances of God, then we must return to claims about God as spirit and invisible and look again for a metaphorical interpretation. Happily, it is possible to show that physical language about God can be explained anthropomorphically (i.e., the metaphors make sense), and we can make sense of physical appearances of God and of claims that God was seen or will be seen in a coming day. Therefore, because we can understand the physical language metaphorically and because it makes no sense to render passages such as John 4:24; Luke 24:39; and 1 Tim 1:17 as metaphorical at all, I conclude that it is most plausible to interpret the latter passages as literal claims that help us understand the ontological nature of God.

God is spirit, then, but we have noted that his spirit has no matter. Moreover, spirit as nonmaterial is invisible. First Timothy 1:17 is not the only passage that teaches God's invisibility. In John 1:18 we read that "no man has seen God at any time; the only begotten God, who is in the bosom of the Father, He has [declared] Him" (see also John 5:37; 6:46; and 1 John 4:12, 20). At first blush, this verse seems strange, since people did see Jesus, and he is God. The idea then must be that no one has seen God in his essential nature, and of course, the ultimate reason is not just that no one could see him directly and live (cf. Exod 33:20, 23) because his unveiled glory and majesty are too great for any human to behold. The further reason is that spirit is invisible, so there is nothing visual to see. Paul says of Jesus (Col 1:15) that he is the *eikon,* the image or exact representation of the invisible God. Moreover, in Rom 1:20 Paul says that from the created world God's "invisible attributes, His eternal power and divine nature, have been clearly seen." Since something invisible cannot literally be seen with the physical eye, Paul's point must be that people have understood from looking at things which are visible that there is a supreme being who made such things. Paul calls God's attributes invisible and then clarifies the ones he means, namely, God's power and divine nature. As Douglas Moo explains, the phrase "his eternal power and Godhead" (Rom 1:20, KJV) is in apposition to "his invisible attributes." That means that the phrase "eternal power and Godhead" spells out God's invisible attributes.[37]

Thus, God does not have invisible attributes *plus* power and Godhead. Rather power and Godhead are an elaboration of what Paul has in mind when he speaks of God's invisible attributes. But let us not get so enmeshed in the grammatical point that we miss the theological one. Paul is saying that God's divine nature ("Godhead") is invisible. This is exactly what we would expect of a God who is spirit.

Because God is invisible and unlike anything seen in our world, the OT forbids making any idols to represent him. This is Moses' point (Deut 4:15-19) as he reminds the people of Israel that on the day God spoke to them at Horeb, they did not see any form, i.e., he was invisible. Hence, they must not make idols in an attempt to represent God in any visible creaturely form. The injunction against worshiping idols (Exod 20:4 and Deut 5:8) is given not just because God is a jealous God who wants his people to worship him alone. It is enjoined because there is no physical likeness to him in anything in the universe.

Acts 17:28-29 and Heb 12:9 speak of humans as God's offspring and of God as the Father of spirits, and some think this teaches that God is spirit. They reason that the cause should be like the effect, and since the effect is spirit, the cause is also spirit (Heb 12:9). Moreover, since we are not made of wood and stone, we should not assume that our maker is either (again, the assumption of likeness between cause and effect). However, this line of reasoning is problematic, for God also created the whole universe. If the cause must be of the same nature as the effect, then God must also have characteristics of rocks, trees, mountains, stars, the sun, and the moon. Obviously, this is nonsensical, but that only underscores the error of reading into these verses the idea that the cause and effect must be similar or identical. Heb 12:9 says that God is the creator of spirits, but that merely shows that he has power to create spirits; it doesn't prove that he is spirit. Paul's point (Acts 17:28-29) is that the creature and the creator have similarities, so we should not try to represent God by things that are less than human creatures. But that in no way means that Paul is saying God is identical to us. That cannot be so, since we are finite and he is infinite. Moreover, we are physical and immaterial beings, but God is pure spirit.

What should we conclude from the preceding? Passages that say God is invisible and cannot be seen or pictured are hard to understand metaphorically. They seem to require a literal interpretation. Moreover, since matter is visible, the logical implication of God being invisible is that his being contains no matter. Hence, we began with John 4:24 teaching that God is *at least* spirit, but we have made a case that God is *at most* spirit.

This, of course, does not end the discussion, for we must now turn to passages that speak of God being seen or having various bodily parts. For sake of clarity, it is helpful to divide this material into several categories. The first group of passages reveal occasions when God appeared to someone or some group in a physical way. As we shall see, there seems to be no reason to understand these passages as metaphorical. Instead, in those instances people saw something physical, and Scripture shows that God was manifesting his presence. If it were not for the fact that these appearances are of different physical things (and some of those physical things contradict other physical manifestations, i.e., an angel is not fire [as in the burning bush]), and if it were not for the evidence already presented that God's nature is at most spirit, these passages would be reason to think of God as having a physical part to his being.

The OT is replete with times when some physical manifestation of God was seen. Jacob wrestles with a man at Peniel, but he realizes that it was God whom he had seen face to face (Gen 32:30). God appeared to Moses in the burning bush (Exod 3:1-6). One thinks as well of the pillar of cloud by day and of fire by night that led the people of Israel after their departure from Egypt (Exod 13:21-22). These were physical manifestations of the Lord's presence. In Exod 24:9-10 we are told that seventy Israelites saw God. Very little is described about what they saw, but verses 10 and 11 speak of his hands and feet, so it is reasonable to think that they saw either some human or some angelic form. If it were not for the commentary in the text that says they saw God, it would not be entirely clear as to who or what they saw. In addition, one is reminded of Isaiah's vision of the Lord (Isa 6:1) sitting on a throne in heaven. This is reminiscent of Micaiah's experience as recorded in 1 Kgs 22:19. In the NT (John 12:41), we learn that Isaiah actually saw Christ, but of course this was the preincarnate Christ, so whatever Isaiah exactly saw was not likely a permanent physical manifestation.

Daniel records the experience of his three friends Shadrach, Meshach, and Abed-nego in Nebuchadnezzar's fiery furnace. There was a fourth man in that furnace, whose appearance was like a son of the gods (Dan 3:25). Commentators and theologians have traditionally held that this was God himself (perhaps even the preincarnate Christ) protecting Shadrach, Meshach, and Abed-nego from the flames. In addition, at the outset of the book of Ezekiel, Ezekiel records a vision of the glory of the Lord. As described in Ezekiel 1, many physical things appeared, but all of it is said to be a vision of the Lord's glory. Finally, in various OT passages the writer records activities of the angel of the Lord. In many of these passages, the writer clarifies that this is no ordinary angel but rather God himself. Think of the incident recorded in Genesis 16 involving Hagar and the angel of the Lord. Though in verses 7-10 the figure is described as an angel, after he promises Hagar a son, Hagar's reaction is most informative. Verse 13 says, "Then she called the name of the LORD who spoke to her, 'Thou art a God who sees.'" We find the same kind of language in other passages where the writer records the angel of the Lord appearing to someone (see, for example, Judg 13:22). It is generally agreed that these visions of the angel of the Lord are visions of the preincarnate Christ. Once Christ becomes incarnate, we hear no more of the angel of the Lord.

In the NT God is present in the person of the God-man Jesus Christ, and we hear less of other physical manifestations of God. However, the NT is not totally devoid of them. For example, at Christ's baptism (Matt 3:16-17; John 1:32-33), the Holy Spirit descends like a dove, and we hear the Father voice his pleasure over his Son. On the Mount of Transfiguration (Matthew

17), we again hear the Father voice his delight with his Son Jesus Christ. Moreover, after his ascension Jesus confronts Saul of Tarsus on the road to Damascus (Acts 9). Finally, Paul is lifted into heaven and given a vision of God (2 Corinthians 12), and so is John (Revelation 4). Paul is not allowed to say what he saw, but John gives an account of his vision. Both of them probably saw various physical appearances.

Do these references to physical appearances mean that God is material after all? They might mean that, but it is unlikely that this is how we should understand them. Understanding them to predicate matter of God would contradict evidence that God is an invisible spirit. Moreover, if these physical manifestations intend to teach that God has a physical part to his being, the portrait one gets is rather strange. On some occasions, the physical part is flames of fire or clouds of smoke (not the same thing). On other occasions the physical thing is an angel (though it is not clear whether the intrinsic nature of angels is material), yet on other occasions it is a human being (Gen 32:30), and in still other instances it is a dove (Matt 3:16). If these passages refer to physical parts of God's intrinsic being, then God's material nature would be most strange to say the least. Moreover, we never see the angel of the Lord after the incarnation, and that raises questions about what happens to that physical "part" of God, if matter is part of God's internal nature.

All of these considerations lead us to look for a different and better way to understand physical language about God. What these passages show (together with those that teach God's incorporeality) is that although God's essential nature is spirit, that does not preclude him from making his presence known through some physical phenomenon that manifests his presence to those who see or hear it. This shouldn't be entirely surprising, for God, as creator of matter and spirit, certainly ought to be able to supply whatever matter he needs on any occasion to manifest his presence. Exactly how God does this, and how he produces such physical things without them permanently attaching to his being, we cannot say. However, Scripture records these physical appearances and yet suggests that the physical things do not become part of God's permanent essential nature, so we must affirm this. Of course, none of this is meant to suggest that the incarnate Christ's human nature is unreal and temporary. Once Christ becomes incarnate, the NT indicates that he stays that way forever. But, though he is fully human and his human nature is a permanent part of the person Jesus Christ, that does not mean Christ's divine nature is humanized or mixed with matter in any way. The church fathers at Chalcedon were very clear that the incarnation does not involve mixing or converting divine and human attributes in Christ. So, the incarnate Christ is a special case, for all other physical appearances and audible sounds demonstrating God's presence are not permanent and do not show that matter has become part of God's essential being. They show, however, that an incorporeal God can still make his presence known tangibly in our world.

A second set of passages is best understood as anthropomorphic language.

These are cases where the context makes it clear that the author is not making a metaphysical statement that God's being contains matter. Rather, the writer speaks of some divine attribute or action in terms that employ human body parts. Since we know how those physical parts function in the human body, we understand that the writer is drawing an analogy between what humans do in virtue of those parts of their physical body and what God is and does. Examples illustrate the point. Various passages speak of the "hand" of God (Exod 3:20; Deut 33:3; Ps 139:10; Isa 65:2; Heb 1:10; 10:31). A human hand can be used to point out directions, to hide something so others can't see, to protect things from someone's grasp or from physical harm or danger (as when one shields one's eyes with one's hands), to threaten other people, to hit others, and to control objects placed in it. In the passages listed above, many of these actions are attributed to God. The psalmist speaks of being led or directed by God's hand, and his point is that God has guided his life (Ps 139:10).

In several of the verses God's hand signifies judgment. In Exod 3:20 God says that he will stretch out his hand and strike the Egyptians with judgments intended to convince Pharaoh to let Israel go. This doesn't mean that there will be a literal boxing match between God and Pharaoh. The language is metaphorical to speak of God's judgment. Heb 10:31 says it is a fearful thing to fall into the hands of the living God. The metaphor speaks primarily of God's judgment but it also suggests God's sovereign control. Because God is sovereign, if we disobey him we cannot escape his reach, his judgment, for we are in his control (in his hands).

Other passages attribute other works to "God's hands." Heb 1:10 speaks of God's creative work in making our planet as the work of his hands. God doesn't have literal physical hands, so the writer is teaching that what we see about us is a product of God's creative doing. In Deuteronomy 33 Moses blesses the children of Israel. In verse 3 he says that God loves his ancient people Israel and that they are in his hand. This makes little sense if it asserts that human beings are physically located in a physical hand that God possesses. The verse means instead that God protects them. The metaphor also speaks of God's control and leading of his people. It is also possible to use our hands to comfort others. We hold out our hands in compassion to give help to those in need, we bid others to come to us, showing our desire to be near them, and then we use our arms and hands to touch them and hold them in sympathy. This seems to be the point in Isa 65:2. God says, "I have spread out My hands all day long to a rebellious people." In spite of their rebellion, God loved them and beckoned them back to himself.

From these examples, we can see that this sort of language is not intended to predicate literal hands of God, but instead metaphorically speaks of God's power, judgment, guidance, compassion, and the like. A careful study of references to other physical parts of a body in relation to God reveals a similar metaphorical/anthropomorphic use of such language. There are references to the "arm" of the Lord (e.g., Exod 6:6; Deut 4:34; 5:15; Isa 53:1). Such language invariably refers to God's power just as the human arm with its muscles symbolizes human power.

There are also references to the "eyes" of God (1 Kgs 8:29; 2 Chron 16:9; Prov 15:3; Amos 9:8; Zech 4:10; 12:4). They teach God's knowledge of what is happening and his sovereign, providential control over both the good and evil. Because he knows what is happening, when judgment falls, it is entirely deserved (Amos 9:8). Moreover, as in the case of Zech 12:4, sometimes God's eyes refer to his protection and concern for his people.

Biblical writers also refer to the "ears" of God (e.g., Neh 1:6; Isa 37:17; 59:1; Ps 34:15). Some of these passages teach that God knows what we are thinking and saying. Since he hears us, if we plan evil, God will notice (Isa 37:17; 59:1). Other passages show that he is attentive to the needs of his people, so that when they pray they won't simply be speaking to themselves (Neh 1:6; Ps 34:15). Not only does he hear prayers, but he listens in a way that gives reason for thinking he will answer our requests.

Certain Scriptures also speak of God's "face" (e.g., Gen 19:13; Ps 17:15; 34:16; 80:3; Exod 33:11; Num 12:8). In some of these passages the point is that someone or something is in God's presence and hence he is aware of it (Gen 19:13—the phrase translated "before the Lord" is in the Hebrew *et penê yhwh*, "in the face of the Lord"). In other cases the writer adds that God is also set to judge them (Ps 34:16), and sometimes God is asked to shine his face upon someone, and the idea is that God would bless them and grant them his favor (Ps 80:3). In the Exodus and Numbers passages cited, the point isn't that Moses literally sees God's face when the two of them converse. Rather, the intent is to differentiate God's relationship to Moses from his relationship to other prophets. God has a much more intimate relationship with Moses than with others; he communicates more directly with Moses. It is like a friend speaking with a friend (Exod 33:11). Hence, those who grumble against Moses should think twice because of God's special relationship with and high regard of him (Num 12:8).

There is a final set of passages we must address before leaving this topic of physical language used of God. A number of passages speak of someone eventually seeing God. Job expresses his belief that his redeemer lives and that someday he will see him (Job 19:25-27). Commentators see in this passage a suggestion of the resurrection of the body, but for our purposes the issue is how Job will actually see God. Jesus says that the pure in heart are blessed, for they shall see God (Matt 5:8). Paul says that we now know in part, but someday we shall know "face to face" (1 Cor 13:12). This speaks of knowing God, but it seems to teach that we will actually look upon God in a coming day. John also says that "when He appears, we shall be like Him, because we shall see Him just as He is" (1 John 3:2). Does this mean that in a coming day believers will see God? The writer of Hebrews enjoins believers to pursue peace and sanctification, because without these things we cannot see the Lord (Heb 12:14). Finally, speaking of the new heavens and new earth, John says we shall see the face of the Lamb (Rev 22:4).

How should we interpret such language? At the outset, we must recognize that all the passages cited are not identical. Some passages seem to refer to the resurrected, glorified Christ (1 John 3:2; Rev 22:4). Whether the event is his coming for the church (1 John 3:2) or his presence with us in the eternal state (Rev 22:4), as the God-man, he has a human nature which includes a body. Hence, it is certainly possible to understand these verses as teaching a literal viewing of the glorified Christ. As for the 1 Corinthians 13 passage, as Paul nears the end of that chapter he compares his knowledge now with his knowledge of spiritual truth later (presumably upon physical death, when he is in the Lord's presence). Much depends on how one interprets "the perfect" in verse 10. If one understands it to refer to Christ, then seeing "face to face" can again be understood as referring to a literal seeing of the glorified Christ. But if "the perfect" refers to something else, such as complete knowledge, then seeing "face to face" (as opposed to "in a mirror dimly") may mean nothing more than having firsthand knowledge of things we don't now fully understand. Such firsthand knowledge of spiritual truth may involve actually seeing the glorified Christ, or Paul may instead mean that once unfettered from the conditions of our non-glorified bodies, our knowledge will greatly increase.

Matt 5:8 and Heb 12:14 are a bit more difficult, but it is safe to say that whatever else they mean, these passages suggest that someday God's people will be in his presence and will receive the final and full measure of their salvation—eternal life in communion with God. We don't now know whether these verses also mean that, even though God is immaterial, in our glorified condition (or even in our disembodied state before resurrection) we will somehow see God's immaterial substance, or that he will manifest himself in some physical way so that we see him, or that we will "see" the glorified God-man. These verses may instead be nothing more than a metaphorical way of saying that we will have intimate contact and fellowship with God (the "mechanics" of how this happens is yet to be revealed). What we should not conclude, however, is that these verses really teach that God is somehow corporeal. That conclusion would require changing our understanding of all the verses studied earlier that seem literally to teach that God is incorporeal. Passages about him being only spirit would actually be metaphorical, but what could such metaphors mean? The proper response is that God is immaterial, and that it is not entirely clear what Matt 5:8 and Heb 12:14 exactly mean.

IMPLICATIONS OF GOD AS SPIRIT

God is a spirit, and several others things are true of him in virtue of that. First, as already noted, the basic characteristic of immaterial things is that they think, and this is certainly true of the God of the Bible. He reveals information about himself, he deliberates and chooses a plan of action, and he knows all things. This and much more make it abundantly clear not only that God thinks but also that his intellect is of the highest order.

Second, we also saw that God is pure spirit in light of his invisibility. Invisibility is exactly what we would expect of a being with no matter as part of his essential nature. Scriptures such as 1 Tim 1:17; John 1:18; 5:37; 6:46; and 1 John 4:12, 20 say or suggest that God is invisible.

Third, because God does not have a body or any matter in his being, he is also incorruptible and immortal. The former means that his being cannot at all decay or deteriorate. It doesn't wear out or need to be replaced. Matter is subject to such decay and destruction, but spirit is not. Likewise, Scripture gives the impression that immaterial things don't die. Of course they couldn't die physically, since they contain no physical matter, so if an immaterial thing were to "die," it is not entirely clear what that would mean. Perhaps that would involve annihilating it as an existing thing. In our day some have argued that nonbelievers will be annihilated, rather than be subjected to an eternity of conscious punishment, but this is contrary to Scripture. Whether the subject is our immaterial part or God's nature as pure spirit, Scripture teaches that immaterial substances are immortal.

Fourth, many have argued that because God is immaterial, he is also living. It is the immaterial part of human nature that brings it to life (cf. Gen 2:7); otherwise, there is only the form of life, but not real life. Only when the spirit enters our body do we come alive. Hence, it is argued, whatever is spirit is also alive.[38] Since God is pure spirit, he is entirely alive. Whether or not one entirely agrees, it is true that Scripture pictures God as living. Jer 10:10 calls him the true and living God. First Thessalonians 1:9 says that the Thessalonians turned from idol worship to worship the living and true God (see also Josh 3:10; 1 Sam 17:26; Ps 84:2; Matt 16:16; 1 Tim 3:15; and Rev 7:2). Moreover, Scripture speaks of spiritual death (relational separation from God) of non-believers, but not of ontological death or annihilation of the souls of either believers or nonbelievers. If this is true for us, how much more so for God! As pure spirit, he is alive eternally, which is another way of saying he is immortal.

Finally, some theologians have argued that God has the attribute of simplicity. Divine simplicity means that God is an uncompounded being and does not consist of parts. Gill links this to the fact that God is a spirit. Since spirits have no physical parts, God as pure spirit is not compounded from any physical parts.[39] If divine simplicity means only having no physical parts, we can surely agree that God is simple. However, divine simplicity means more than this, and it is with the "more" that the controversy begins. It is argued not only that God is devoid of physical parts, but also that there are no distinct parts of God's being at all. Hence, the divine attributes are not distinct from but identical to his essence, and it follows that if the attributes are each identical to God's essence, each divine attribute is identical to every other one. In chapter 6, we shall examine divine simplicity further to see if Scripture or reason teach it. At this point, we need only affirm that God is simple in the sense that as pure spirit, he is not composed of any physical parts. We cannot now affirm simplicity in any other sense.

GOD AS PERSON/PERSONAL

God, the spirit being who exists independent of our minds, is also a person and a personal being. Though it is important to attribute personhood to God, this is a very thorny issue. It is so for various reasons, not least of which is the matter of what it means to be a person.

The question of what it means to be a human person is a notoriously difficult philosophical issue.[40] In fact, it is so difficult that many believe it cannot be answered to the satisfaction of all. However, this issue has too many significant implications for us to ignore it altogether.[41] If it is hard to decide what it means to be a human person, the issue is not easier when raised about God. As we saw in chapter 2, there have been various conceptions of God as impersonal. In fact, it is hard to understand the ultimate being of some of the world's major religions as personal at all. Even religions that depict God as a person and personal do not always clarify what that means.

How, then, should we clarify what personhood is and whether God qualifies as a person? Lewis S. Chafer argues that our only recourse is to begin by defining what it means to be a human person. Humans are considered persons, and Scripture reveals that they are made in God's image. Hence, looking at our own personhood should help us define divine personhood and assess whether the God of Scripture is a person.[42]

While Chafer's proposal has merit, and while it seems inescapable that reasoning about God as a person will be to a certain extent analogical to our understanding of human personhood, we must proceed carefully. For one thing, if the point of departure is the fact that humans are the image of God, the first hurdle is to ascertain what that image is, and this, too, is a notoriously difficult and debated issue among Christian theologians. However, if we want to reason analogically but don't know which aspects of human nature are the image of God, it will be all the more difficult to determine what constitutes divine personhood.

Another problem with such analogical reasoning is that to be human involves having a body. In fact, theologians and philosophers debate whether a disembodied soul qualifies as a *human* person. Moreover, human beings are also divided by gender, and some have argued that, at least in part, gender determines the particular human person an individual is. Since gender seems to be essential to being a human, some have asked whether the very notion of human personhood involves gender. Regardless of answers to questions about bodies and gender, none of that is relevant to God, for he has neither a body nor is he male or female. But if these things are integrally wrapped up in what it means to be a human person, how can we be sure that analyzing human personhood will be very informative of what constitutes divine personhood?

In addition, the way some theologians and philosophers have discussed this issue serves only to muddy the waters more. For example, Keith Ward argues that we should deny that God is a person because Christians believe God is ineffable. Ward explains that "to say that God is ineffable is to say that the essential nature of God, that which is truly definitive of what God is, is beyond the range of any human concepts." Such a view "places God far beyond any limited conceptual categories, including, obviously, that of 'being a person'."[43] This, however, does not mean that Ward thinks God is impersonal. God has many properties that persons do; it is just that God is so much more than any being we would call a person. Hence, Ward thinks it best to say that God has some key person-properties, though he isn't a person, because he is so much more than a mere person.[44] This distinction does not clarify the meaning of human or divine personhood; it only confuses it more.

Stanley Grenz complicates the issue further. Whereas Ward says that God is not a person because he is ineffable or incomprehensible, Grenz argues that God *is* a person just because he is incomprehensible. This is not the only reason Grenz offers for ascribing personhood to God, but it is a rather peculiar claim as he argues it, nonetheless. Grenz explains that "we ascribe personhood to human beings on the basis of their relative incomprehensibility."[45] None of us completely understands the depths of existence of any other human, and surely God is more complex than we. Hence, because God is incomprehensible, he is a person.[46] This is surely a mystifying position. If we don't understand either ourselves or God, then are we sure that we even know what it means to be a person, let alone whether we or God are persons? Moreover, it is simply a *non sequitur* to claim that being incomprehensible qualifies someone as a person. Aren't there many things in our world whose existence no one ever fully fathoms? It certainly seems so, but then, on Grenz's account those creatures and objects would also qualify as persons. Being incomprehensible is neither a sufficient nor a necessary condition of being a person, nor does Grenz offer any argument for this view.

A further confusion makes some theologians dubious of attributing personhood to God at all. Their concern stems from the fact that the notion of "person" is applied to the members of the Trinity. But then it appears that we force Scripture and Christian theology to contradict themselves, for we say that the God of Scripture is a person, a personal being, but then we turn around and say that there are three distinct persons in the Godhead. That is confusing, and it causes some thinkers either to be wary of calling God a person at all,[47] or at least to demand that we note that the term "person" is used in two different senses when referring, on the one hand, to God as a person, and on the other, to the three persons in the Trinity.[48] Indeed, the term is used in different senses and each must be defined.

What, then, should we say about God as a person? Alister McGrath has a helpful discussion of this topic. He notes the etymology of the word "person," and speaks of some of its ancient uses in Roman culture. He then explains the development of the idea of personhood in early Christian theology. For example, Tertullian was important for the early Christian development of this concept. Tertullian defined a person as a being who speaks and acts. McGrath says that the final development in early Christian thought of the notion of a person comes from Boethius, who understood a person as an individual substance of a rational nature.[49]

All of this is somewhat helpful, but we must be careful not to confuse the meaning of a term ("person") with that of a concept.[50] Our concern is the conceptual study, not the word study. Nonetheless, McGrath does offer a helpful suggestion (though I intend to develop it differently than he does). McGrath argues that it would help us in this discussion to ask what we would mean by speaking of "an impersonal God."[51] This helps us to remember that often when doing conceptual studies we should go back to the very language we use in discussing the topic and ask what such language means. I do not intend to solve conclusively the meaning of human or divine personhood, for space doesn't permit that. However, we can articulate certain minimal things that should be true of anyone who qualifies as a person, and I suggest that we can begin to get help by attending to our language.

With that in mind, consider the following sentences: "That man on life-support machines is no longer a person." "She's a personal friend of mine." "I love my dog, but he's not a person." "At the moment of conception, there is a person in the mother's womb." "That university with all of its bureaucracy is very impersonal." "That teacher makes a point to be involved personally in each of her students' personal lives." "When making moral decisions, one must always treat other humans as persons, not as objects."

Upon reflection, it is clear that "person," "personal," and "impersonal" are not used identically in each sentence. In fact, a good place to begin is to distinguish the fundamental difference between "person" and "personal/impersonal." The distinction is not the difference between a noun and an adjective. Rather, when we use the term "person," we are normally thinking of a concept or set of concepts that differs from what we mean when we use the word "personal/impersonal." In fact, the ambiguity can even be seen by comparing two of the uses of "personal" in the sentences above. Most of the uses refer to having a relationship with others and being involved in their lives (or lacking a relation and being uninvolved and aloof—impersonal). But in speaking of a student's personal life, the point is the student's private affairs, not a point about being involved or uninvolved with others.

What, then, do we usually mean when we use the word "person"? As that term is typically used, it at least means that the individual can interact rationally with his or her environment. This suggests that a person is a conscious being, but it means more than that. Animals are also conscious, but they do not reason. Human beings are both conscious and capable of reasoning. This doesn't mean that one must be able to reason at a certain level to qualify as a person, but only that ability to interact rationally with one's environment and reason to some extent seems to be true of those we would label persons. Here as well my intent is not to exclude unborn babies and those in persistent vegetative states from qualifying as persons. As argued elsewhere, such individuals can and do qualify as human persons, though there is more to the matter than simply being able to reason or not at a given moment of one's life.[52] My concern is to differentiate things that can reason and interact with their environment from those things which are not now able, never were able, and never will be able to reason.

So, we can generally agree with Boethius's notion of a person as indicated above, but there is more to this than just being rational in general. As some theologians have argued, to qualify as a person, one's reasoning abilities must be of the sort that allow the individual to be self-conscious and self-determining.[53] Self-consciousness is awareness of oneself as a distinct thing (i.e., distinct from other beings—human, animal, or other—in our world). Animals are thoroughly capable of experiencing various sensations. If you step on a dog's foot, the dog will yelp in pain. However, animals don't seem capable of the second-order reflection that there is a self that is experiencing that sensation, and that they are that self. In contrast, humans not only experience pain but also know that they have a body distinct from other things and that their body is in pain, and they know which part of their body is in pain. Moreover, they can compare this sensation with other sensations they have had and understand that there is a continuous consciousness which possessed both the earlier and later sensations.

Self-determination refers to the ability to make decisions and carry them out. If someone is programmed to do whatever they do, that is determination by another. If one is forced to choose and act because of threats from someone else, they are not self-determined. Self-determination involves having the intellectual capacity to consider and weigh alternative courses of action, plus the use of one's mental faculties to make decisions in accord with one's desires, not as a result of being forced to act by another. As with self-consciousness, self-determination is true of humans but doesn't seem to be true of animals. Animals can be trained to respond to stimuli in a certain way, but that involves no weighing of alternatives. Though we sometimes attribute those abilities to animals when they pause at our commands and appear to be considering whether to obey or disobey, this seems to be a case of our attributing such abilities to them. The animal either responds to the stimulus given as a command or does not; there is no decision-making procedure going on "inside" the animal.

Rational thought, including self-consciousness and self-determination, seems to be a bare minimum quality we would expect of anyone deemed a person. I contend that this notion is not so infected with qualities wrapped up with other distinctively human characteristics that it couldn't apply to God as well. Hence, if God is a person, rational thought must be true of him.

But is this all we can say of someone who is a person? Many would say that this is not enough, for unless we include the notion of relatedness to others, we offer an empty notion of personhood. In fact, some seem intent on reducing personhood to relatedness and relationality alone.[54] On the surface, this appears too reductionistic, for there is certainly more to personhood than just being capable of and entering into relationships. On the other hand, those who point to relatedness that involves genuine interaction with others are surely correct in thinking that this is at least part of what we mean by "personal" as opposed to "impersonal."

Here the ambiguity of our language has again reared its head. We must again raise the distinction between our usage of "person" and of "personal." Though it can be argued that to be personal includes being rational, self-conscious, and self-determined, and though it can be argued that to be a person includes relatedness and involvement with others, the way we use the terms "person" and "personal" in ordinary language suggests that their meaning is not identical. The term "personal" is typically used in ordinary discourse to refer to the matter of relatedness as opposed to aloofness and isolation. We don't normally use it in ordinary language to refer to conscious rational thought, including self-consciousness and self-determination. In contrast, the term "person" is used usually in ordinary language to talk about personhood, and personhood is thought of in terms of the cognitive faculties mentioned. Hence, there is a difference between being a person and being personal, as we use those ideas in everyday language. Persons have the cognitive capacities mentioned, and normally those qualifying as persons can also enter relationships with others and do so.

With this distinction between the different senses of "person" and "personal," I believe that we want to say of God both that he is a person and that he is a personal being. Rather than reduce divine personhood to either concept, we should say both about God. We can debate whether relatedness is a part of what it means to be a person (divine or human), but we don't have to solve that problem in order to understand that, as I have defined the terms, there are several distinct things we are saying when we use this language, and all are true of God.

Does Scripture portray God as both a person and personal in the senses described? The answer is a resounding yes. Not only is God capable of conscious rational thought, but he is also thoroughly self-conscious. There are many indications of this in Scripture. For example, God reveals his name on a number of occasions (e.g., Exod 3:14; Gen 17:1; 31:13; 46:3; Isa 42:6; Rev 1:8). In Exod 6:3 God says that he appeared to Abraham, Isaac, and Jacob as ʾēl šadday, God almighty, but he did not reveal to them his name Yahweh. How could he reveal his name and claim what Exod 6:3 says without knowing who he is? God is entirely aware of who he is.

Second, God shows his self-awareness by telling his people that there is no God like him. This requires that he both know himself and other conceptions of so-called gods, and that he can judge who is better. Isa 43:10; 45:22; 46:9; Hos 11:9 are all passages in which God compares himself to other gods and shows that he knows that he alone is God.

Third, on various occasions God expresses his emotions or speaks of his intention to act in accord with those emotions. He says this of his anger (e.g., Job 42:7; Isa 13:3; Jer 15:14), his jealousy (e.g., Exod 20:5; Deut 5:9; Ezek 39:25; Zech 1:14; 8:2), his compassion and mercy (e.g., Jer 12:15; Isa 54:7, 8; Hos 1:7), and the like. Such passages indicate God's awareness either of his current mental state at the time of the utterance or of his intention to act in accord with his emotions, but that is impossible unless he is conscious of himself and his own character traits.

Fourth, Scripture teaches that all Scripture is the result of God's breath (2 Tim 3:16). That is, he has revealed it; he has spoken it all. As we read Scripture, we find much information about God's character and actions. How could God know this information if he were not conscious of himself as a distinct being?

Finally, divine self-consciousness is a logical corollary of divine omniscience. In knowing everything that is knowable, God must know himself and everything about himself. We have already seen evidence that this is so, but even without that data we must attribute self-consciousness to God in virtue of his omniscience.

In addition to God's self-consciousness, Scripture depicts him as self-determined. Not only can he choose as he pleases, but he also has power to do whatever he chooses. We read that if God decides to do something, no one can stop him (Job 42:2). Ps 115:3 says that God is in the heavens and does whatever he pleases. In the NT Paul says that God works all things according to the counsel of his will (Eph 1:11). As we shall see more fully in our discussion of divine providence, this means that God's decisions are based solely on his own purposes and desires, and his purposes and desires are based on no one and nothing other than himself. Among other things, this means that God has sovereignly chosen those who will be his people, and his decision was made from before the foundation of the world (Eph 1:4; 2:10; see also 2 Thess 2:13). God is no robot; he has the power of self-determination.

Not only does Scripture portray God as having these key ingredients of personhood, it also shows him to be personal in that he relates to his world and his creatures. He hears and answers prayer (Matt 7:7; 21:22; Jas 5:16), he comforts and gives strength and help to those who suffer and mourn (2 Cor 1:3-4; 7:6), he judges the wicked (2 Pet 2:4-9; Jude 15; Ps 75:10), and he blesses the righteous (Psalm 1; 1 Pet 3:14; Jas 5:11). Moreover, he loves us, and because of that love sent his Son into the world to die for us (John 3:16). As Paul teaches, God took on the form of a bondservant to serve the needs of sinful humanity (Phil 2:5-8; see also 1 Pet 3:18). Jesus himself said (Matt 20:28) that he came to serve, not to be served, and to give his life a ransom for many. He also says that he does always the will of the Father (John 4:34; 5:30; 6:38). Hence, in giving himself for us, he also expresses the Father's concern for us. Finally, God has chosen to reveal himself to us most fully by becoming incarnate (Heb 1:2) in his Son Jesus Christ.

This does not describe a deity who is aloof, uncaring, and uninvolved with his creation. What this means for divine attributes such as a strong sense of immutability and impassibility remains to be seen when we discuss them in chapter 6. But Scripture does portray God as described above, and if we take such language literally, God must be a relational God, and if so, then he is personal in the sense of being involved in our world and related to its inhabitants.

In this chapter we have advanced significantly in our understanding of God. We have gone from various concepts of God to a God who is a real being external to our minds. In addition, this God is immaterial, and he is at most such a being. We also have noted various implications of being an immaterial entity. In the final section, we have seen that God is both a person and a personal God. There is much more to say about the God of evangelical Christian theology. He is also a God of action, but before turning to his actions, we must speak of his attributes and then of the Trinity.

SIX

THE ATTRIBUTES OF GOD

The psalmist exhorts us, "Praise Him for His mighty deeds; praise Him according to His excellent greatness" (Ps 150:2). God has done many mighty acts, but even if he had done none of these wondrous deeds, he would still be worthy of praise because of the excellence of his person. As a contemporary Christian song says, "Lord, I praise you for who you are, not for all the mighty things that you have done." There is no one like our God, but what is he like? In answering this question we come to the divine attributes.

In chapter 5, we saw that God is pure spirit and we noted the implications of this truth, but there is much more that we can say about God. Biblical authors paint a rich and full picture of the grandeur of God. Their description of his attributes reveals not only who God is but also what we can expect from him and what he expects from us. We must not only examine how the biblical writers describe God but also see how they use the truth about God's person to comfort, exhort, warn, and encourage God's people. Seldom does a writer mention divine attributes as though he were writing a mere list of God's characteristics. Rather, he appeals to a divine attribute as a basis for addressing some need of God's people.

Earlier theologians included in a discussion of the divine attributes an exposition of the divine names. They did this in part because biblical names do not simply designate one person rather than another. Instead, a name was given to a person because it somehow described his or her nature or personality. More modern treatments of the divine attributes distinguish what we would call the proper names of God from a list of his qualities. Our focus is those characteristics ascribed to God in Scripture as well as qualities theologians have thought are implied by God's nature and attributes.

In speaking of someone's or something's attributes, we refer to the characteristics or qualities that express their nature. If entities had no attributes, it would be very difficult to conceptualize what they are. We might think that the world consisted of a series of real things, but beyond that we could say little about those things. Moreover, without appealing to attributes, it would be hard to differentiate one thing from another. All of this is also true of God; in fact, since God's being is pure spirit and hence invisible, without his attributes there would be little we could know about God, and it would be difficult to conceptualize him at all.

In discussing a thing's attributes, Aristotle introduced an important distinction between essential and accidental predicates. An essential attribute is one that belongs to the very essence or nature of a thing. It cannot be removed from the entity without destroying it, nor can it be added. For example, think of a line running from point A to point B. Midway between A and B is another point (call it point C). Now, point C is an essential attribute of line AB. If point C is removed, line AB no longer exists. That does not mean that nothing remains, but only that line AB no longer remains. Likewise, triangularity is an essential quality of a triangle. Remove one of the angles of the triangle, and the triangle no longer exists.

In contrast to essential attributes, accidental predicates are qualities which are not part of a thing's very essence. They may be lost or gained without destroying the thing in which they inhere. For example, human hair color is an accidental predicate, for one's hair color can and usually does change as one grows older. In addition, a particular height and weight are also accidental predicates of any individual. We can grow taller and lose weight or gain it without ceasing to be human. Moreover, characteristics of personality can change without destroying a person's humanity. At one point in a person's life, she has a pleasant disposition, but at another time she is basically cantankerous. These comments relate not to momentary mood swings, but to the basic qualities that describe a person's ongoing disposition.

How does the distinction between essential and accidental attributes relate to God? Theologians and philosophers within the Judaeo-Christian tradition have maintained that all of God's attributes are essential attributes. Unlike his creatures, God has no accidental predicates. Remove or change any of God's attributes and there would be no God.

Affirming that all of God's attributes are essential predicates must not be misunderstood. Some may think this is wrong, because there is a whole class of attributes that can be ascribed to God which in no way alter his very being. For example, as I write this chapter and as you read it, God has the quality of being-thought-about. In addition, on Sundays God has the quality of being-worshiped. On many occasions he is the-one-who-is-petitioned, as people pray to him. Moreover, he is the deliverer of Israel from Egyptian bondage, etc. The list of such qualities is seemingly endless, but none of them seems to be an essential property. That is, there would still be a God even if none of these things were true of him. If he had never created any world, it is hard to see how he could be Israel's deliverer or the lawgiver at Sinai, but failing to have those qualities would certainly not destroy his very being, nor did his very nature change when he acquired these qualities as a result of his actions. Moreover, when you and I stop thinking of God, that does not destroy him. So all these qualities seem to be accidental, and hence one wonders why theologians say that all of God's attributes are essential.

The answer usually offered both resolves the dilemma and delineates the exact subject of our discussion on the divine attributes. Many would say that the accidental qualities just mentioned should be called properties.[1] These properties are relational in nature and don't actually specify the constituents of God's very being. Instead, they reflect how we describe the various relations that creatures have with their creator and vice versa. Hence, while God is the lawgiver at Sinai, the deliverer of Israel from Egypt, the one who prophesies the end times, none of these properties is the subject matter of a discussion of the divine attributes. These properties that relate to various divine acts may stem from some divine attribute, but they are not what theologians mean when they speak of God's attributes. For example, in virtue of God's holiness, he is the lawgiver at Sinai; in virtue of his omnipotence, he is the deliverer of Israel; and in virtue of his omniscience and sovereign control, he predicts events of the end times. Holiness, omnipotence, omniscience, and sovereignty are the enduring characteristics of God's nature, not these other properties that may be ascribed to him. It is these permanent attributes of God's very being that are the subject of our discussion of the divine attributes.

CLASSIFYING THE DIVINE ATTRIBUTES

Throughout church history, theologians have used various schemes for classifying the divine attributes. Though we could debate which scheme is best, it is unnecessary to do so. A case can be made for and against each category scheme, but thankfully, no point of orthodoxy hinges on this issue. Since each division of the attributes is instructive in its own way, I shall only present the various classification schemes.

One scheme emphasizes how the divine attributes are known or how we form our idea of God. This scheme differentiates attributes known by way of negation, by way of causality, and by way of eminence. The first way refers to attributes known by denying of God limitations that apply to his creatures. Such attributes as infinity, immutability, and eternity fall in this category. The second way looks to God as the great first cause of every virtue seen in the effects he produces. Attributes known by the way of eminence are present in the creature but are lifted to a supreme degree in God. As some theologians have noted, this classification scheme actually involves only two broad categories, namely, those known by way of negation and those positive characteristics of God such as love, omniscience, holiness, justice, and truth.[2]

A second category scheme distinguishes absolute and relative attributes of God. Absolute attributes belong to the divine nature considered in itself, whereas relative predicates speak of the divine nature as it relates to the created universe. In the former category are qualities such as self-existence, eternity, unity, and immutability, whereas mercy, love, omnipresence, and truth fall in the latter category. This is not an easy distinction to maintain, however, since all of God's attributes belong to his very nature and would be true of him even if there were no created order. Moreover, theologians disagree over which attributes go into each category. For example, many would place love, holiness, and truth in the relative category and eternity and immensity in the absolute category. A. H. Strong does just the opposite, arguing that the latter two, for example, are relative in that they express God's relation to space and time.[3]

A third classification divides the divine attributes between natural or metaphysical predicates and moral characteristics. Natural attributes belong to God's very constitutional nature apart from his actions. These include infinity, aseity, unity, and eternity. Moral attributes include predicates that qualify God as a moral being and refer to qualities he displays as he acts in our universe. This group includes truth, goodness, mercy, and holiness. Though this classification scheme is helpful, it too has failings. Goodness, mercy, holiness, etc., belong to the very constitution of God just as the others do. We don't want to give the impression that these attributes somehow attach to the divine nature but are not part of it.

A fourth category scheme distinguishes attributes that are immanent or intransitive from those that are emanant or transitive. Strong links immanent attributes with absolute ones and emanant with relative ones. The basic distinction between the two groups is not unlike the difference between the metaphysical and moral. Immanent attributes are those perfections of God which do not go forth and operate outside the divine essence, but function within it. This group includes eternity, aseity, and infinity. Emanant attributes are those by which God produces effects external to his very being. These include omnipotence, benevolence, justice, and love.

As for the immanent attributes, Berkhof claims that if some divine attributes are purely immanent, it is hard to see how we would know of them.[4] In response, there is something to Berkhof's point, but there is also a problem with it. The problem is that we could still know of these purely immanent attributes by way of special revelation. On the other hand, the correct point is that these attributes are not known only by special revelation. But if that is so, one wonders if they are so totally immanent in God as the distinction suggests.

A fifth classification scheme appeals to the division of the constituent parts of human nature. In humans we can distinguish between the immaterial essence, the intellect, and the will, and the same is true of God. In the first group are infinity, aseity, and immutability; in the second are omniscience and wisdom; and the final category includes not only omnipotence and sovereignty but also justice and love, which speak of the qualities of the acts of his will.

Finally, a common category scheme differentiates incommunicable from communicable divine attributes. Incommunicable attributes are those which bear no resemblance or analogy to the creature. This group includes aseity, infinity, eternity, and immutability. Communicable attributes are those that do resemble or are analogous to qualities in the creature. To say that God has the attributes of love, truth, and justice does not mean that he has those attributes in exactly the same way that humans do. He has them to an infinite degree, whereas we have them only to a limited degree, but they still rightly fall in the communicable group because both creator and creature possess them.

As already noted, a case can be made for and against each classification scheme, but this is not a point worth arguing over. For myself, the simplest division of the attributes distinguishes those that reflect moral qualities of God and those that refer to non-moral qualities. I prefer this distinction over the natural vs. moral one, because I don't want to give the impression that God's moral attributes somehow don't belong to his very constitution or inner nature. All divine attributes are essential predicates and belong to the very nature of God. Some refer to qualities that designate God as a moral being whereas others do not relate to the moral nature of what God does. This doesn't mean that every divine attribute fits neatly into one group or the other. For example, it is not entirely clear where we should place attributes such as omnipotence or omniscience. Knowledge and power *per se* need not be moral notions, but God's use of his knowledge and power certainly has moral implications. So, to a certain extent, no matter what category scheme one chooses, the actual division of the various attributes into one class or another can be debated. Hence, my choice of a particular category scheme for the sake of logically arranging my discussion is not meant to convey some theological truth that is essential to evangelical theology.

NON-MORAL ATTRIBUTES

It takes minimal reading of theological and philosophical literature about the divine attributes to see that the non-moral attributes generate the most intellectual problems and hence get the most discussion. I want first to define these attributes as clearly as possible and to clarify biblical teaching about them. I shall also discuss the conceptual problems surrounding each attribute that generate philosophical and theological debate. However, there is one attribute, divine eternity, that raises such complex issues and has implications for so many theological doctrines that I shall devote a special chapter to it.

In using Scripture to define and elucidate the various divine attributes, we must remember two important points with significant methodological implications. First, biblical writers were not writing a systematic theology wherein they devoted special sections to God's attributes. Scripture is still usable for

238 □ No One Like Him

our discussion, but some of the nuanced definitions and debates in theological and philosophical literature about various attributes look far different from what we find in the pages of Scripture.

This might alarm some, but it need not do so. Biblical writers portray God as omnipotent, eternal, omnipresent, and the like, and usually do so to make some other theological or practical point. For example, God's eternity is sometimes used to reassure God's people that he will always exist, regardless of their need or circumstance. Or a writer mentions God's omnipresence not to discuss philosophically how an incorporeal being relates to points in a spatio-temporal continuum, but to remind the wayward that they cannot escape from God and to encourage the faithful that they can never go anywhere where God is unavailable.

Given this feature of the biblical portrayal of God, we can still use the biblical witness for theological formulation and philosophical reflection. The theologian must use whatever facts about God's nature the biblical writers offer, but frequently we must go beyond the biblical testimony about these attributes to formulate a definition or to resolve problems surrounding them. So long as the definition and/or the resolution to problems in no way contradict Scripture, there is nothing wrong with this methodology. Moreover, we must differentiate the traditional Christian understanding of an attribute from what Scripture actually teaches and warrants. If Scripture doesn't support a traditional understanding, we must side with Scripture and modify or reject the tradition.

Second, how do we use Scripture to determine the meaning of each attribute? A typical method defines a divine attribute by appealing to the meaning of the biblical term that names the attribute. Hence, if we understand the etymology and basic "dictionary meaning" of *terms* that speak of God as eternal, loving, wise, etc., we automatically know what the divine attribute is.

This strategy for defining the divine attributes is seductive (as well as very popular) but methodologically flawed. It confuses defining a term with defining a concept. To define a term, one does a word study, noting the various ways the term is used to mean one thing or another in various contexts. On the other hand, defining a concept tells us what sort of thing the concept designates. To illustrate the difference, we are not asking how the words "wise" and "wisdom" are used in Scripture (they are used both of God and of others as well). Nor are we seeking the etymology of the terms. Instead, we are asking what sort of thing wisdom (in this case, divine wisdom) is.

James Barr's *Biblical Words for Time* brilliantly reveals these methodological flaws when he discusses errors that have besieged studies of the biblical concepts of time and eternity, as well as many other conceptual studies based on the Bible.[5] Thinking, for example, that an etymological study of biblical words for time and eternity reveals the meaning of time and eternity in biblical or other thought patterns is wrong, because etymological study tells us the root meanings of words but does so apart from concrete linguistic contexts where the words actually appear. In order to understand the *concepts* a writer wants to communicate, we must understand his words as he uses them in a particular context.[6] That means that we are not likely to ascertain any thought pattern (concept) associated with the word by looking at it in isolation from a specific sentence, and certainly not by looking at the root words from which it is derived.[7]

It is also problematic to treat individual words for the attributes as though they communicate the concepts of the various attributes. As Barr explains, this type of error typically stems from the assumptions that

> the lexical structure of words must coincide with a mental structure of concepts, which latter is basic to biblical thought about time. It not only is natural, therefore, but from the dictates of the plan *must be* natural, that there should be a 'kairos concept'. It *must* be possible to conceptualize words.[8]

Though thinkers often err by treating a word like a concept, it is still an error. As Barr explains, one of the most obvious refutations of the idea that a term attaches to the concept it designates is the phenomenon of polysemy, i.e., one word has two or more senses. Which of the many senses represents "the concept" denoted by the term? None does, and that shows the error in thinking that we automatically designate a concept by defining a word. We can also convince ourselves of this point by reflecting on figures of speech and even slang. In such language terms take on very different meanings from their literal use. Do these figurative uses designate another concept for which the term stands? Clearly, to think so is to repeat the flawed methodology. As Barr says, "Surely one could not deal with modern English 'nice' by putting its main senses ('pleasant, attractive' and 'precise, exact') under the heading of 'the English nice-concept'."[9]

Does this mean that word studies are irrelevant to the topic of God's attributes? Not at all, but it does mean we must be careful about how we use them. Word studies are beneficial in two ways. An initial benefit is that this strategy often helps us identify verses that do teach something about a divine attribute. Moreover, an understanding of the meaning of those terms may offer some information about the meaning of the concepts associated with each divine attribute. So long as we remember that this is only a starting point in understanding the concept, and so long as we realize that there are other verses which don't use the term for a given attribute but teach something about the divine attribute in question, there is nothing wrong with starting with the word study. But our concern is a conceptual study, not a word study.

Aseity

Aseity (from the Latin *a se*, "from itself") is nuanced in a variety of ways, but the main idea of aseity is that God depends on nothing other than himself for his existence. This may be understood in one of two ways (or both). The first is that the ground of God's being is within himself; he is self-existent. Hence, no one brought him into existence nor does anyone or anything but himself sustain his existence. Some theologians express this idea by saying that God is his own cause, but many dislike such language, because they believe God is uncaused. To say that he is caused (even by himself) might somehow give the impression he had to be brought into being, and of course that is not so. Though God is uncaused, he is the cause of all other existing things.

The second interpretation of God depending on himself alone for existence means that there are not properties independent of God upon which he depends in order to have the constitutional attributes he possesses. Some theologians have thought that if God did depend on such universals, he would not control them and hence would lack aseity and sovereignty. In part to combat this possibility, they have argued for divine simplicity, according to which God just is identical to all of his properties, so there are no properties independent of him upon which he depends for his existence or for anything else.

As we shall see in chapter 7, there are other ways one might address this issue of properties independent of God, but I shall save that for our discussion of divine simplicity. For our purposes here, suffice it to say that Christian theologians fairly consistently maintain that God is self-reliant along the lines of the first interpretation above, whereas many reject this second interpretation of self-dependence (and the divine simplicity that accompanies it). In doing so, they believe they have given up nothing of significance for either divine aseity or divine sovereignty.

A second notion also attaches to aseity. It is the idea that God is independent of all things in that his choices and purposes are independent of influences from anyone and anything other than himself. As we shall see, this sense of aseity is very close to the notion of God's sovereign will according to which God has the faculty of absolute self-determination. Absolute self-determination means that God's choices depend on his own desires and purposes alone and that he has the power to actualize those choices.

It is this second aspect of aseity (independence in purposes, choices, etc.) over which many theologians (even evangelicals) disagree. Those of a Calvinistic stripe would concur, but beyond Calvinistic circles there is rejection of this aspect of aseity. We have already seen that this notion is inimical to process theology. Moreover, proponents of the open view of God staunchly protest that such a God is aloof from his creation, dominates it, and in no way is responsive to it or vulnerable before it. This God is the ruling monarch who always gets his way no matter what. Both process and open view proponents reject this notion, claiming that it cannot be borne out by Scripture.[10] In fact, process theology rejects aseity in any sense, and open view defenders are very suspicious of it.

It is by no means clear that more traditional Arminians would find this second aspect of aseity palatable. Undoubtedly, many would object that if God's purposes and choices are determined solely on the basis of his own desires without any consideration of his creatures' wishes and actions, and if God then accomplishes whatever he desires, there is little room for human or angelic freedom. Hence, God does not have aseity in this sense. Other Arminians might contend that God is independent in the sense mentioned, but in order to make room for creaturely freedom has chosen to limit the exercise of that power. Since God alone decided to do this, it is a self-limitation that in no way compromises his sovereign will. In later chapters on divine providence we shall deal with this debate more directly. For now, it is sufficient to note that not every theologian agrees with this aspect of aseity.

Some theologians have added a third concept to the idea of aseity. It is the notion that God as *a se* is totally immune to external influences so that nothing that happens in our world fazes him. What he thinks, feels, and does depends solely on himself.[11] This may sound like nothing more than saying that God is independent, but it is actually a stronger idea. Typically, it was linked by classical Christian theologians with a very strong notion of immutability according to which God as absolutely perfect is incapable of any change whatsoever, including change produced by influences from anything but himself.[12] According to this attribute, which is often called divine impassibility, what a creature thinks, says, or does cannot influence what God feels or does, for if it did, God would not be immutable (in this strong sense of immutability) nor would he be independent of his creatures in this respect. As Robert Brown has argued, and as we shall see in discussing human freedom and divine sovereignty, anyone who holds such views of aseity and immutability and adds to them human libertarian free will runs into problems in maintaining a consistent theology. Given libertarian freedom, human beings may do something unexpected, so in a certain sense God must wait for us to act before he decides what he will do. Brown appeals to the fall of Adam to illustrate his point. If Adam and Eve hadn't sinned, says Brown, there would have been no need for God to decide to redeem us. So, the free choices of human beings did effect how God relates to us, and that creates difficulties for the notions of immutability, impassibility, and aseity.[13]

We have already seen that neither process theists nor open view theists have any use for divine impassibility or this strong sense of immutability and aseity. Apart from the question of freedom and divine sovereignty, there is reason to think, regardless of whether one is a Calvinist or an Arminian, that aseity in this last sense is a stronger notion than we should affirm. It is not just that, as we shall see, these ideas don't reflect Scripture, but also that there seems to be no reason to think something is wrong with God if he doesn't have this kind of independence. Moreover, there are reasons to think that he doesn't have this sort of independence from us. If God hears and answers our prayers, and if he changes his attitudes toward us when we repent of sin, for example, it seems that his mental and emotional states at any given moment must to some extent be influenced by what we do. But, why is that a deficiency in God?

Holding that God's mental focus and emotional responses are determined in part by the actions of his creatures does not entail that his creatures either bring him into existence or maintain him in being. It doesn't even require that

God's purposes, desires, or choices depend on anything or anyone but himself. So the key concepts associated with aseity are retained even if one rejects this third item. Moreover, for Calvinists, God has already decided before the foundation of the world what he will think and do at the appropriate moment in response to us. For Arminians who think that God foresees the future free actions of his creatures, God has also already decided in advance what he will say and do. It would seem that the only way that the influencing of God's mental and emotional states (and even his actions) by his creatures could count as an imperfection in God would be for his creatures' thoughts and actions to force God to think, choose, or do things he does not want to think, choose, or do. But there is no reason for this to happen according to any Calvinistic theology nor for many Arminian theologies.

Aseity, then, is best understood as God's self-existence (in the sense explained) and independence in will, purposes, and desires. I believe that there are two lines of evidence that God is *a se:* biblical and rational. A major biblical passage that fits the notion that God is the ground of his own existence is John 5:26. Jesus says, "As the Father has life in Himself [*en heautō*], even so He gave to the Son also to have life in Himself [*en heautō*]." Jesus has been speaking first about the Father and himself physically resurrecting the dead (v. 21), and then he talks about giving spiritual eternal life to those who believe (vv. 24-25). In this context, the comment in verse 26 seems to be literal rather than metaphorical. It gives the reason that Father and Son can raise those who are physically dead and also give them spiritual life. They can do this because they have life in themselves and depend on no one else for their life. While it is dubious that Jesus intends to make a philosophical comment about aseity, it is hard to see what his comments mean if they don't relate to the notion theologians label aseity.

There are other biblical indications of God's self-existence, though they are to one degree or another more inferentially argued than in the case of John 5:26. One of the clearer passages is Acts 17:24-25, where Paul addresses the Athenians: "God that made the world and all things therein, seeing that he is Lord of heaven and earth, dwelleth not in temples made with hands; neither is worshipped with men's hands, as though he needed any thing, seeing he giveth to all life, and breath, and all things" (KJV). Paul first clarifies that God has made all things and that everything depends on him (see also verse 28, "In him we live, and move, and have our being"), but then he says that God needs nothing. If God needs nothing, but gives life, breath, and all things to everything else, the implication is clear: God does not need to be given life, breath, or anything else. This is so not because immaterial things don't breathe, nor because he already has life since someone else gave it to him. Rather, Paul wanted his listeners to understand that God does not need to be given life because he is self-existent and has life in himself.[14]

There is ample biblical testimony for aseity as divine independence in purposes, desires, and will. Since this touches ground we shall cover more thoroughly under God's sovereignty, I shall here only list the relevant verses.

Passages such as Dan 4:35; Rom 9:15-16; Eph 1:5, 9, 11; and Rev 4:11 speak of the independence of God's purposes, counsels, and will or choices. Ps 115:3 and Job 42:2 also teach that God is sovereign and independent in power. Whatever he wants to do, he does, and what he wants depends on himself alone, according to the Romans and Ephesians passages just mentioned. We can also infer from Rom 11:33, 34 (KJV) that God is independent in his thoughts, for he is so far above and beyond us that his judgments are "unsearchable" and "his ways past finding out" (see also Isa 55:8).

There is also rational support for aseity in the sense of self-existence. As we saw when discussing arguments for God's existence, most of them conclude that a necessary being must exist. This is especially true of the second form of Anselm's ontological argument and the causal and contingency forms of the cosmological argument. A necessary being, as opposed to a contingent one, never comes into existence or goes out of existence, and it depends on nothing to maintain it in being. It should be clear that this description of a necessary being fits the requirements for a self-existent being.

Though we granted that none of the naturalistic arguments conclusively proves God's existence, we also noted that they do offer some evidence for God's existence that is usable in a cumulative case defense of theism. Moreover, the naturalistic proofs do show that if God exists, he must be a necessary being, and if that is so, he must have the attribute of aseity. Scripture confirms that he does have it.

Infinity

The Judaeo-Christian God is also infinite, and the basic idea of God's infinity is that he is free from limitations. To say that God is unbounded or unlimited, however, only begins the discussion, for we need a clear understanding of what it means to be unlimited, for example, in power, love, and knowledge. Two recent discussions of God's unlimited character help to clarify this concept, so I begin with them.

Stephen T. Davis is concerned primarily with God's unlimited power (omnipotence), but he begins by explaining the phrase "unlimited being." Davis explains that there are two basic ways one might try to define the term "unlimited being." The first and simpler way says that an unlimited being is not bound by causal constraints. This being might be bound by logical constraints so that it cannot actualize contradictions (such as creating round squares), but no causal laws would keep it from doing things such as raising the dead, parting the waters of the Red Sea, or turning water into wine. The problem with defining "unlimited being" this way, however, is that the definition seems to relate only to power. It would not necessarily explain what it means to be infinitely wise, infinitely good, or infinitely holy. Hence, we need a definition that accommodates more of the divine attributes than just God's power.[15]

A second way to understand an unlimited being focuses on the notion of a "maximal degree" of something. As Davis says, some characteristics of beings are relevant to their greatness or likeness to God while others are not. Being red-headed is not a great-making property, but being all-powerful is. Davis calls great-making or Godlike-making properties G-properties. He also notes that some attributes admit of degrees while others do not. For example, being tall admits of degrees whereas being a prime number does not. Moreover, as to properties that admit of degrees, some possess an intrinsic or conceivable maximum while others do not. For example, the property of being tall has no intrinsic maximum, for something could presumably always become taller than it is. On the other hand, the property of having scored well in a golf match or bowling game does have an intrinsic maximum. The best possible score for eighteen holes of golf is eighteen, and the best possible score for a game of bowling is three hundred.[16]

In light of these preliminary qualifications, Davis offers a second definition of an infinite being. An unlimited being is

> (1) a being who possesses all the G-properties that it is possible for a being to possess; (2) a being all of whose G-properties that admit of an intrinsic maximum are possessed to the maximal degree (for example, being omnipotent); and (3) a being all of whose G-properties that admit of no intrinsic maximum are possessed to a degree unsurpassed by any other being that has ever existed or ever will exist (for instance, being more loving than any other actual being).[17]

As to item (3), I am inclined to add that an unlimited being with G-properties that have no intrinsic maximum must possesses those qualities to a degree unsurpassed also by any being that could but won't exist; hence, it is unsurpassed by any conceivable being.

Davis's second definition greatly clarifies what it means to be an unlimited being, but some ambiguities that still must be worked through surround the notion of an infinite being. In particular, there seems to be ambiguity surrounding the very idea of infinity, because one often thinks of mathematical infinity, and it is hard to square that concept with the idea of an infinite being. It is here that a recent article by Jill LeBlanc is helpful. LeBlanc's basic thesis is that we must differentiate between the potential infinite, the actual infinite, and the theological infinite. The first two concepts relate to mathematics but not to theology, whereas the third relates to theology but not necessarily to mathematics. Confusion arises when we impose mathematical infinity on theological concepts such as divine infinity.

LeBlanc defines the first two concepts of infinity as follows: "The potential infinite is an extension of the finite, constructible from the finite by some rule or process that is never in fact completed. The actual infinite, on the other hand, is conceived as an actually existing collection of an infinite number of parts. The actual infinite could be regarded as the completion of a process that builds the infinite from the finite. This is the actual infinite of set theory."[18]

These notions of mathematical infinity are clearly different from the concept of divine infinity. God's infinity is not constructed by a process that builds the infinite by adding to a finite set. Hence, God's infinite power is not just the sum total power of all humans who have ever lived and ever will live. His love is not the aggregate of all the love possessed by all creatures of all times. Moreover, we should note that LeBlanc's notions of mathematical infinity focus on adding to a finite set to extend it infinitely. There is also in mathematics the idea that between any two distinct points a line can be drawn, and that line is infinitely divisible. This mathematical notion is definitely not what theologians mean by divine infinity.

In contrast, there is the theological infinite. Unlike the mathematical infinite which (in LeBlanc's terms) can be conceived as a collection of parts, the theological infinite "is not conceived as an infinite collection, but rather as the unbounded or unlimited; it is not in any sense constructible from the finite because it is not a collection at all, not an extension of the finite."[19] This seems to be a correct and helpful clarification of the difference between mathematical and theological infinity. We must remove mathematical notions from divine infinity.

Divine infinity means, then, that God is unbounded or unlimited, but this is a fundamentally negative definition of the attribute ("not bounded," "not limited"). In positive terms, I believe Davis's second definition (with its three parts) defines positively what it means to be infinite. LeBlanc thinks the theological notion of infinity is ultimately shrouded in mystery so that we cannot define it in a positive way. She believes this because it is not clear what it means to say that God is unlimited in power or goodness. Descartes and Leibniz, for example, both held that an infinite God is unlimited or unbounded, but Descartes understood this to mean that a God of infinite power could actualize contradictions, whereas Leibniz thought otherwise.[20] Moreover, some theologians might claim that an infinitely good God would never allow any evil into the universe, whereas others might argue that God has some morally sufficient reason for doing so. Yet others might claim that God himself can do evil for the sake of ultimately producing some greater good. Such differences concerning what an unlimited being can do suggest for LeBlanc that theological infinity is too cloaked in mystery for us to define it clearly.

Although LeBlanc's concerns are clear enough, they rest on a confusion. My reason for even raising this point, however, is that it allows me to introduce further amplifications of divine infinity. LeBlanc's arguments don't actually mean that we can't define the theological concept of divine infinity. In fact, LeBlanc is very helpful in so doing by distinguishing divine infinity from mathematical concepts of infinity. All that LeBlanc's point shows is that when it comes to *applying* the notion of unlimitedness to each of God's attributes, we cannot say prior to reflection how it will apply and how we will understand resultant qualities such as unlimited power and knowledge. The fact that some thinkers believe an infinitely powerful God can actualize contradictions whereas others disagree does not mean that we don't understand what "unlimited," "G-property," and the like means. It only shows that as the concept of infinity attaches to each divine attribute we must ask further what it means to have unlimited power, knowledge, goodness, etc., because we are not immediately sure what is included in what a being with unlimited power can do or what a being with unlimited knowledge can know, for example. But we must decide those matters when we discuss omnipotence, omniscience, etc., in order to clarify those attributes. We don't need to discuss them to clarify what it means to be infinite!

This whole discussion underscores why some theologians and philosophers don't consider infinity a separate attribute of God, but say instead that it is a way of describing how God possesses his other attributes. That is, it functions as a qualifying adjective for other attributes. God is holy, true, just, good, powerful, and knowledgeable, and he has these qualities to an unlimited degree. Moreover, God's infinity guarantees that he has whatever characteristics are G-properties. I am unconvinced that the debate over whether or not infinity is a separate attribute is worth pursuing or is even decidable. For infinity conceived as a qualifying adjective for other attributes does not appear to be a separate attribute, whereas if infinity means that God has all G-properties, then it is itself a property. Of course, this latter element, which is part of Davis's definition, could be seen as equivalent to saying that God is the most perfect being, but then the debate would shift to whether "most perfect" and "infinite" are synonymous. Such debates may interest some, but given our purposes, they do not seem worth pursuing. I have chosen to discuss infinity separately from the other attributes, because even as a qualifier of other attributes we must conceptually distinguish divine infinity from the other attributes and understand what it means in itself and in relation to other aspects of God's being.

Before turning to the biblical data on infinity, several other points of clarification are in order. First, infinity as a qualifying characteristic of other divine attributes makes no sense in some cases. For example, it makes little sense to say that God infinitely possesses aseity, unity, or even immutability. That is, it makes no sense to say that God is unlimited in self-sufficiency (to be self-sufficient just means to depend only on yourself, so "infinitely" adds nothing to divine aseity, and tends toward redundancy) or unlimited because he is the only God (unity). God, of course, has these qualities, but they only relate to God's infinity in the sense that they are G-properties, not in that God has them in an unlimited sense.

A second point about infinity was made in chapter 5, so I need not belabor it here. It is that we must think of divine infinity in qualitative, not quantitative, terms. Thus, to call God an infinite being does not mean that he contains quantitatively an infinite amount of ontological material, for that would place us in the pantheist's camp, according to which God just is everything. Instead, to call God an infinite being means that the kind of being God has is qualitatively unlimited, i.e., he has (or is) the greatest kind of being there is, a necessary being. It also means, to use Davis's terms, that God's essential attributes are all G-properties, and for those attributes that admit of degrees, God's attributes have the highest degree possible.

The qualitative sense of divine infinity needs to be articulated for the various divine attributes as well. God's infinity in relation to time means that he is eternal. There are different ways to understand divine eternity, but the basic idea is that God never began to exist, nor will he ever stop existing. Moreover, to say that God is infinite in regard to space does not mean that his being takes up all of space or contains everything in space (that would be pantheism). Instead, it means that God relates to space in a qualitatively different way than his creatures do. God is omnipresent or at all places simultaneously in the totality of his being. When it comes to other non-moral and moral divine attributes, a similar sort of nuancing is required in terms of qualitative notions, not quantitative ones.

Third, because attributes such as power, wisdom, and the moral attributes are infinite in God, that does not obligate him to do everything he can. Infinite power does not obligate God to do every act he possibly can do. Infinite wisdom does not obligate him to do every wise thing possible. Infinite love does not require God to do every loving thing possible. Rather, being infinite in regard to these and other attributes means that he can perform such acts *and* that none of the actions he does displays impotence, or contradicts love, mercy, justice, truth, holiness, etc. It is easy, but wrong, to think that because God has these qualities infinitely he must do every loving, merciful, just act he is capable of doing. When God fails to do something he can do, we easily become angry and accuse him of wrongdoing. An example is thinking that because God is all-benevolent, he must remove all evil, regardless of any purpose it may serve and regardless of any goods that may be sacrificed in order to remove it.

In a later chapter I shall discuss the problem of evil, but I note here that the experience of evil often precipitates a religious crisis in the lives of believers and nonbelievers alike. This happens in some cases partly because the sufferer thinks that God's love, goodness, and mercy mandate that he do every loving, good, merciful thing possible. Removing affliction seems to be one of those possible things, so if God is infinitely loving, etc., God seems obligated to remove the affliction or never let it occur in the first place. When God does neither of these things, the sufferer becomes angry at God, accuses him of wrongdoing, and begins to doubt that God has the aforementioned attribute(s) after all. Recognizing that these divine attributes don't obligate God to do every loving, etc., thing possible but only obligate him never to act in an unloving, etc., way won't remove the pain of the affliction. But, it should help the sufferer see that God has not failed to do anything he is obliged to do.

A final point of clarification about divine infinity is that it should lead us to conclude that God is ultimately beyond our full comprehension. Even if God were finite, our finite intellects would not likely fully comprehend him, but when we couple human finitude with divine infinitude, we realize the folly of thinking that we can totally comprehend God. For one thing, some divine attributes have nothing in common with human capacities. Were it not for special revelation we might have no inkling that God has these attributes or know what they mean. Even with divine revelation, since we know of no one else with these qualities and since God is immaterial and incorporeal and we have so little experiential knowledge of such a being, it is hard to believe that we fully understand what an attribute such as aseity or even infinity entirely means. None of this means that we understand nothing about God or that biblical revelation about him is wrong, but only that there is much more to say and know about God than we can ever say and know in this life. His infinity should warn us against thinking that we have entirely figured out what can be known about God or have solved all mysteries surrounding his person and actions.

In turning to Scripture, we find many verses that teach the various divine attributes and suggest that God possesses them infinitely, but there aren't a lot that *per se* discuss divine infinity. Nevertheless, there is enough biblical revelation to assure us that we have a right to believe that God is infinite. In Job 11:7-9 we read, "Can you discover the depths of God? Can you discover the limits of the Almighty? They are high as the heavens, what can you do? Deeper than Sheol, what can you know? Its measure is longer than the earth, and broader than the sea." Though the word "infinite" does not appear in these verses, the concept is certainly there. In Job 5:9 (see also 9:10) we read that God does "great and unsearchable things, wonders without number." This speaks of God's power, and saying that he can do things beyond our comprehension (unsearchable) surely suggests that his power is infinite. In fact, the Hebrew word translated "number" is *mispār*. In some translations there are verses where this word is used in relation to God and the translators have rendered it "infinite." For example, Ps 147:5 uses *mispār* with respect to God's knowledge. The KJV and NASB translate the phrase "without number" as "infinite." In the KJV the verse reads: "Great is our Lord, and of great power: his understanding is infinite." The NIV translators did not use the word "infinite," but their rendering of the verse teaches that God is infinite in knowledge: "Great is our Lord and mighty in power; his understanding has no limit." To have no limit is to be infinite!

In Ps 145:3 the psalmist writes, "Great is the LORD, and greatly to be praised; and his greatness is unsearchable" (KJV). The English word "unsearchable" renders the Hebrew ʾên ḥeqer ("it is without searching"), and this phrase also appears in Job 5:9 and 9:10 in relation to God's greatness. The psalmist says of God's greatness that there is no searching it out. In other words, as Delitzsch explains, "it is so abysmally deep that no searching can reach its bottom."[21] If you can't reach the bottom of something, it must be unlimited, and that means infinite.

As we shall see in discussing other attributes, there is further evidence for God's infinity. To say that God's mercy, lovingkindness, and grace endure forever means that they never end and thus are infinite. To claim that God always was and always will be amounts to saying that he is infinite with respect to time, i.e., eternal. To assert that there is no place one can go where God is absent means that God is infinite in respect to space (omnipresent and immense). God doesn't possess his attributes in a limited way; he is infinite.

Immensity and Omnipresence

God's infinity in relation to space is omnipresence and/or immensity. Many theologians use these terms interchangeably, but others distinguish them. Those who distinguish them often use immensity to refer to the fact that God transcends all spatial limitations and is everywhere at once. As some theologians note, bodies are in space circumscriptively as bounded by it; spirits are in space definitively (they have a specific *where*), but God is in space repletively, i.e., he fills all of space.[22] Omnipresence, on the other hand, signifies that God is present in the totality of his being at each point in space.[23] Hence, there isn't one part of him at one place and another at a different place. Whether or not one differentiates omnipresence from immensity is not critical, so long as one recognizes that this attribute involves two ideas, namely, God transcends spatial limitations and so is present at all places at once in his total being.

These definitions are clear enough, and there is ample biblical support for this divine attribute, but it is also the source of some confusion. On the one hand, material things are the only things that take up space, but God doesn't have a body, so how can he fill *any* of space (let alone all of it at once) without a body? Moreover, God is present everywhere, but does that mean he is in hell? And if God is present everywhere, why does Scripture portray him as somehow absent from the wicked?

This doctrine generates other questions that also appear baffling. For example, Scripture says Christ and the Holy Spirit indwell believers, but if God is everywhere, doesn't he indwell nonbelievers as well? And if God indwells believers, is that presence any different than God's presence in the incarnate Christ? Finally, if God is everywhere, what does it mean to say that he is in heaven and comes down to earth on a particular occasion to do something? How can he come to a place where he is already present, and how can he be present in heaven in a different sense than he is present everywhere else?

Questions like these often move atheists and agnostics to question whether the very notion of omnipresence is logically coherent. These questions are not unanswerable, but they do show that a proper understanding of this divine attribute requires that God be both present in our universe in some senses and absent in other respects.[24] In delineating the respects in which God is absent and present in our universe, we can articulate a nuanced understanding of God's exact relation to space. Let me first discuss senses in which God is *not present* in our universe.

GOD'S ABSENCE FROM OUR UNIVERSE. Christian theologians have maintained that God is *absent* from our universe in several ways. First, he is not present *physically* anywhere in space. This is not so because God is present everywhere *physically*. Rather, because God as immaterial has no body, he is not *physically* present anywhere. Of course, we have seen that if God so desires, he can make his presence known in some physical way, but none of those physical manifestations are identical to his immaterial nature.

Second, we must distinguish *physical presence* from what I shall call *ontological presence*. Ontological presence means that some entity or being is actually present at a given place in space. If the being is physical in nature, the being that is really there (ontological presence) will also be physically present. However, if the being is immaterial, then it can still actually be somewhere (ontological presence), but as immaterial it cannot be present physically. With this distinction, we can affirm that God is not present *ontologically* in just one place. This is so not because as immaterial he is present nowhere physically, but rather because, as immense, he is not limited to being present in just one place at a time. He is simultaneously everywhere ontologically.

Next, in order to avoid pantheism, we must say that God is not present ontologically *as* each point in space. If he were present *as* each point, that would be pantheism, for his being would be identical with everything there is. To avoid pantheism Christian theists claim that God is present *with* (or *in addition to*) every point in space, but not *as* each point. In virtue of omnipresence, Christian theologians have also claimed that God is not present ontologically *in only part of his being at each point in space;* to be present that way would diffuse God's being throughout the universe, a point at each space. Rather, God is present ontologically at each point in space in his whole being.

Fourth, there is also a difference between *ontological* presence and *moral, spiritual,* or *ethical* presence. Ontological presence was defined above. To say that someone is morally, spiritually, or ethically present to someone else means that they have a relationship of fellowship with one another. As this relates to God and his people, it means that God has a spiritual relationship by saving faith with an individual and that no sin blocks fellowship and communion between God and that person. Given this distinction, we can see that two people could be ontologically present to one another (regardless of whether they are physical or non-physical beings) without being morally and spiritually present to one another. Moreover, two people could have a special relationship that we might label a moral or spiritual relationship even if they were not ontologically present with one another. In God's case, he is absent morally, ethically, or spiritually from the heathen and the wicked. Likewise, believers who have broken fellowship with God through sin and have not restored it by repentance don't experience God's spiritual presence in the same way as do believers in fellowship with him. Both kinds of believers are indwelt by the Holy Spirit according to the NT, but only those in fellowship experience God's moral presence in its fullest. Passages that show separation from God's presence and thus illustrate this point are Gen 4:16; Jon 1:3; Num 14:42-43; and Ps 10:1. The Genesis, Numbers, and Psalms passages seem to refer to separation from a special manifestation of God or lack of awareness of his presence because something is wrong in the person's relationship to God. Of course, God is still ontologically present. As for the Jonah passage, it states Jonah's intent about God's presence, but obviously the whole tenor of the book shows that he could not do what he intended to do (escape from God), nor was his thinking that he could do so correct. That he tried to do so indicated a problem in his spiritual relationship with God.

Finally, as just noted, God indwells NT believers in a special spiritual way that is not true in the case of nonbelievers. However, God is not present in believers *in the same way he is present in the incarnate Christ*. In Christ, the divine essence is united to a human nature to form the theanthropic person Jesus Christ. Though Christ and the Holy Spirit indwell believers, they do not do so in such a way that God's very being becomes a new entity added to our human nature so that believers become divine or literally God-men. In other words, Christ's special relationship with his people does not mean that the very constituents of their nature include another entity (the divine essence) so that they are deified.

SENSES IN WHICH GOD IS PRESENT.   There are various respects in which God is *present* in our universe. First, God is present *ontologically* (though not physically) everywhere at once *along with* and/or *at* each point in space. If we find this hard to grasp because of God's immaterial nature, we shouldn't. Anyone who believes that human minds are immaterial should have no problem with this notion. Just as a human immaterial mind takes up no space but is present with the person to whom it belongs, so that we can describe the general "spatial location" of that which is non-spatial, so God who is completely immaterial can also be present in our time-space continuum. Of course, God is ontologically present at all spaces, not just at one as in the case of our immaterial minds.

In addition, in virtue of omnipresence, God is simultaneously present ontologically at each point in the universe *in the totality of his being*. There is not one part of him at my house and another part at yours. Wherever he is (and that is everywhere), he is present in the fullness of his being. Moreover, God is present ontologically in all places and with all people, but he is not present *ethically* with nonbelievers. This means that God is ontologically present even in hell, but that does not mean hell's inhabitants have any awareness of God's presence or any moral or spiritual relation to him.

From the preceding point, we also affirm that God is present *morally* and *ethically, i.e., he has a spiritual relationship by faith, with his people.* Because of this relationship, God's people are often aware of or sense God's presence in ways that nonbelievers do not. Nonbelievers not only don't have an ethical relationship with God, but they may also be totally oblivious to God's ontological nearness.

As a corollary to the preceding point, the NT teaches that NT believers are indwelt by Christ and the Holy Spirit (see, e.g., Rom 8:9) and united to them in a way not available to OT believers. Such indwelling bespeaks a special spiritual presence, and the NT speaks of this as being united to Christ and having him abide in the believer. This does not mean that OT saints were not really saved or were less saved, but only that this special spiritual presence of Christ and the Holy Spirit in the life of the believer does not seem to have been available in the OT era. On special occasions, the Holy Spirit came upon a person for a special task but then left when the task was finished. Though the Holy Spirit's enablement was always available to those who asked for it, in the NT era such power seems even more accessible to believers because of the Holy Spirit's constant indwelling.[25] Of course, as already noted, this indwelling of Christ and the Holy Spirit in the NT believer in no way makes God's being part of our being so as to deify believers.

The last comment suggests another sense in which God is present in our universe. God is *present in Christ* in a way different than in any other being. The very nature of God is united to a human nature to form the theanthropic person Jesus Christ. Christ's divine nature is numerically identical with the divine essence possessed by the Father and the Spirit. Such a relationship to the divine nature is true of no created being.

Finally, there is a sense in which God is *manifested in a special way in one specific place or another*. For example, Jesus instructed us to pray to our Father "who is in heaven" (Matt 6:9). Along with Strong, we concur that language about God dwelling in heaven is best explained, for example, "either as a symbolic expression of exaltation above earthly things, or as a declaration that his most special and glorious self-manifestations are to the spirits of heaven."[26] There are also passages that speak of God coming down to earth from heaven. Gen 11:5-7 (God's coming down to the Tower of Babel), Gen 18:2 (his coming down to Sodom and Gomorrah), Exod 19:18, 20 (his coming on Mount Sinai), and John 17:21 (the Father sending the Son into the world) are examples. Such passages are probably best understood as referring to a special manifestation of God for a special purpose, although he is always present on earth. And then passages such as Job 1:12 and 2:7 speak of Satan departing from the Lord's presence. These verses don't mean that Satan could literally go to a place where God is absent. Rather, they mean that his conversation with God ended and he went about his efforts to afflict Job.

BIBLICAL TEACHING.   Scripture contains no words for our English terms "omnipresence" and "immensity," but the concepts are clearly and amply taught in Scripture. In fact, it affirms what I have said above about God's presence and absence in our universe. For example, many verses affirm that it is impossible to escape from what I have called the ontological presence of God, for God is present everywhere in our universe. In Jer 23:23-24 we read, "'Am I a God who is near,' declares the LORD, 'and not a God far off? Can a man hide himself in hiding places, so I do not see him?' declares the LORD. 'Do I not fill the heavens and the earth?' declares the LORD." One of the best-known passages teaching that there is no place without God is Ps 139:7-12. The psalmist asks, "Where can I go from Thy spirit? Or where can I flee from Thy presence?" (v. 7). He then lists the various places a person could be and affirms that God is at each of them (see also Acts 17:27-28; Rom 10:6-8; and Jon 1:3, 10, where Jonah tries unsuccessfully to flee from God's presence).

Many biblical passages teach that God cannot be limited to just one spatial location, for he transcends them all and is at all places at once. Hence, any who think it possible to contain him entirely at any one place are sadly mistaken. We see this in passages that speak about building an earthly temple for God in order to contain him there. In 1 Kgs 8:27 (see parallel in 2 Chron 2:6) we read, "But will God indeed dwell on the earth? Behold, heaven and the highest heaven cannot contain Thee, how much less this house which I have built!" In Isa 66:1 we read, "Thus says the LORD, 'Heaven is My throne, and the earth is My footstool. Where then is a house you could build for Me?'" In Acts 7:48-49 Stephen says that God does not dwell in temples made with hands.

In addition to these passages that speak about ontological presence, many passages speak of God's spiritual presence with his own people. Having God's presence as one goes forth to do a given task is a special blessing, but this is certainly more than ontological presence; it is spiritual presence, and it indicates God's hand of blessing on the one who has that presence. In Exod 33:14 the Lord promises his presence to Moses, and in verse 15 Moses responds that without God's presence, he doesn't want even to begin the task God has given. In regard to the oppression of Israel by Syria and its King Hazael in the days of King Jehoahaz, Scripture says (2 Kgs 13:23), "But the LORD was gracious to them and had compassion on them and turned to them because of His covenant with Abraham, Isaac, and Jacob, and would not destroy them or cast them from His presence until now" (see also 2 Chron 20:9).

Beyond these specific instances in Israel's history, the Psalms repeatedly refer to blessings coming to those in God's presence. Since everyone is onto-logically in God's presence, these passages must speak about the spiritual and moral presence of God in individuals' lives. The psalmist writes (Ps 16:11), "Thou wilt make known to me the path of life; in Thy presence is fulness of joy; in Thy right hand there are pleasures forever." And in Ps 51:11 the psalmist pleads, "Do not cast me away from Thy presence; and do not take Thy Holy Spirit from me" (see also Ps 31:20). Because of God's many bless-ings, his people are encouraged to worship him. Though they are always in his presence, the psalmist sometimes speaks of coming before God's presence with praise. This means, of course, coming before God in worship, that special expression of one's relation to God. Hence, the psalmist urges his readers (Ps 95:2), "Let us come before His presence with thanksgiving, let us shout joy-fully to Him with psalms" (see also Ps 100:2 and 140:13).

In the NT we also find that being in God's presence spiritually and morally brings blessings. Peter tells his listeners (Acts 3:19), "Repent therefore and return, that your sins may be wiped away, in order that times of refreshing may come from the presence of the Lord." In John 14:23; 17:21, 23 Jesus tells his disciples that he and the Father will indwell those who are his own. Though ontologically God is already with them, this indwelling is a special spiritual and moral presence. And in Matt 18:20 Jesus says that where two or three people are gathered together in his name, he is there in their midst. Of course, ontologically he is there, regardless of whether or not they gather in his name, so Jesus must mean that he will make his presence known in a special spiritual and moral way to his people when they meet in his name. In addition, believers are promised (Matt 28:19-20 and Acts 1:8) that as they witness for Christ, Christ and the Holy Spirit will be with them. This is true of everyone ontologically, so this must be the promise of a special spiritual presence and power as believers witness for Christ. Finally, one passage about Christ's ascension tells believers that Christ's ascension has special implications and blessings for them. In Heb 9:24 (KJV) the writer says, "For Christ is not entered into the holy places made with hands, which are the figures of the true; but into heaven itself, now to appear in the presence of God for us" (see also 1 John 2:1).

The Lord's moral and spiritual presence means blessing for his people, but his absence morally and spiritually means a broken spiritual relationship with God (as in Gen 3:8) and often signifies judgment. In fact, many passages speak of the Lord's presence as a special presence or coming in judgment, and in several passages, the absence of the Lord's presence in a moral and spiritual sense signifies judgment. For example, in Lev 22:3 removal from the Lord's presence is judgment. We read, "Say to them, 'If any man among all your descendants throughout your generations approaches the holy gifts which the sons of Israel dedicate to the LORD, while he has an uncleanness, that person shall be cut off from before Me. I am the LORD'" (see also 2 Kgs 24:20). We find a similar message in the prophets. In Jer 23:39 God says, "Therefore behold, I shall surely forget you and cast you away from My presence, along with the city which I gave you and your fathers" (see also 1 Chron 16:33; Ps 9:3; 68:2; Isa 19:1; 64:3; Jer 4:26; 52:3; Zeph 1:7; 2 Thess 1:9; and Rev 14:10).

Because God's presence often means a coming in judgment, the biblical writer may simply say that the earth trembles or the nations tremble in the presence of the Lord. For example, the psalmist writes (Ps 97:5), "The mountains melted like wax at the presence of the LORD, at the presence of the Lord of the whole earth" (see also Ps 68:8; 114:7; Nah 1:5). Moreover, sometimes the writer pleads for the Lord to come in judgment. Isaiah pleads (64:1-2), "Oh that Thou wouldst rend the heavens and come down, that the mountains might quake at Thy presence—as fire kindles the brushwood, as fire causes water to boil—to make Thy name known to Thine adversaries, that the nations may tremble at Thy presence!" (see also Jer 5:22; Ezek 38:20).

Indeed, God is an awesome, majestic God. In comparison to him, man is as nothing. Hence, even though Job knew of nothing wrong that he had done to warrant the affliction he had received, and even though he wanted to confront God and plead his case before him, he recognized that in his finitude he was no match for God. Job says (Job 23:15), "Therefore, I would be dismayed at His presence; when I consider, I am terrified of Him." Indeed, God's ways are not ours, and his grandeur is far above us. In fact, the apostle Paul says that God has deliberately chosen things that the world considers foolish to confound those who think themselves wise. He has done so (1 Cor 1:29, KJV) "That no flesh should glory in his presence." While these statements are far from the notion of omnipresence under discussion in this section, they are biblical uses of the notion of God's presence, and we need to see that biblical writers refer to God's presence in that way. Rather than try to escape from this God or contest him, we must commit ourselves, in the words of Jude 24, "to Him who is able to keep you from stumbling, and to make you stand in the presence of His glory blameless with great joy."

Eternity

God's infinity in relation to time is eternity. There is ample biblical evidence that God is eternal, but what isn't so clear biblically is how we should understand divine eternity. Historically, there have been two major understandings of divine eternity. The notion with the longest pedigree in the Christian tradition is timeless eternity: God's eternity means he exists endlessly outside of time. Paradigmatic of this view is Boethius's definition in *The Consolation of Philosophy*. In Book 5, Prose 6, Boethius writes that God's "eternity, then, is the complete possession all at once of illimitable life."[27] As Nelson Pike explains, this means that God has neither temporal location nor temporal extension.[28] We cannot say that God has lived for a certain number of years or will live a certain amount of time into the future. Nor can we say that it is now 2000 for God, because that would locate God in time. These ideas don't apply to God because he is totally outside of time. All of time is immediately before him, but he lives in no time at all.

The second notion of eternity views God as everlasting or sempiternal. The fundamental idea of sempiternity is existence at all times. God never had a beginning, nor will he die, but his existence extends endlessly backwards and forwards through every moment of time. As Thomas Morris explains, sempiternity is a *"temporal* notion, a conception of God's eternity in terms of time: God's existence is temporally infinite in duration, unbounded in the past and future. On this conception, there is in the life of God a past, present and future, as in the life of his creatures. But unlike any of his creatures, God is everlasting, and necessarily so."[29] When Morris says that God is necessarily everlasting, he means that God always has this attribute. It is an essential predicate of his nature, and it is necessary in that, since he will never die, he will always have it.[30]

Both conceptions of eternity agree that God's existence never ends. They disagree about whether that existence is in time or is outside of it. This issue is sufficiently complex and has implications for so many other theological issues within the doctrine of God that I shall devote chapter 9 to it. For our present discussion, we shall examine various biblical data to see what they teach about this eternal God and how the writers use God's never-ending existence to convey other truths about him. We can also ask whether any biblical passages require that eternity be either timeless or temporal.

Biblical revelation describes God as eternal, and uses certain words and phrases in both Testaments to do so. Sometimes, of course, the concept is taught without the use of any of these words or phrases. For example, a writer may say that God's years have no end. That sentence uses none of the typical words or phrases for eternity, but the concept is clearly there.

As for specific terms and phrases for eternity, the OT uses three terms in particular to refer to God's eternity: ʿôlām, ʿad, and qedem. ʿad is sometimes used not as a noun but as a preposition with the sense of "until." Of the three, ʿôlām is clearly the most prevalent, and qedem the least used with respect to God's eternity. ʿôlām is typically used with a preposition such as min, l, or ʿad (e.g., ʿad ʿôlĕmê ʿad in Isa 45:17, which might literally be translated "unto ages of duration," but is translated in the NIV as "to ages everlasting"). The fundamental idea in ʿôlām is perpetuity, but the prepositions min, l, and ʿad are used with it to indicate the direction of the perpetuity from the writer's perspective, i.e., past or future.[31] When ʿad is used as a noun, it has the same basic meaning as ʿôlām. In Hab 3:6 (harrê ʿad, "ancient mountains" or more literally, "mountains of perpetuity or antiquity"), it looks backward, and in Isa 9:6 (ʾăbî ʿad, "Eternal Father") and Isa 57:15 (šōkēn ʿad, "who lives forever") it can be understood as looking both backward and forward. However, the word, whether used of God or of other things, typically points toward the future (e.g., Ps 111:3; 112:3, 9 in re: God's righteousness enduring forever; Ps 45:17; 52:9 in re: God being praised forever; and Ps 10:16; 45:6; and 19:9 in re: God's throne and law enduring forever).[32] According to the *Theological Wordbook of the Old Testament*, in contrast to ʿôlām and ʿad, qedem denotes more the idea of antiquity or idyllic time.[33] Examples in regard to God are Isa 45:21 (NIV) ("Who declared it from the distant past?" [miqedem]) and Hab 1:12 (NIV) ("O Lord, are you not from everlasting?" [miqedem]). However, the reference to God as the "eternal God" (ʾĕlōhê qedem) in Deut 33:27, for example, does not exclude God's endless future existence.

In the NT, three terms denote eternity, especially in regard to God. The most frequent is aiōn, but aiōnios is also used with some frequency. The least frequent is aidios, with its main use in regard to God's being (Rom 1:20). All three convey the idea of eternity, but there has been some debate as to exactly what this means. Cullmann's basic thesis is that eternity in NT thinking differs from time only in that it refers to the unlimited entirety of time. If this is so, it would seem to make a case for God as sempiternal, not timelessly eternal. However, Barr argues forcefully and convincingly that the evidence does not support such claims. The problem again stems from flawed methodology.[34] As we will see in my study of the various passages about divine eternity, the NT data do not require that we view eternity as specifically either temporal or atemporal. They leave that matter open.

What we do find in the NT is that these terms are often used in phrases that help to elucidate the author's point. For example, it is not uncommon for a writer to say that something is true or has been done *pro tōn aiōnōn* ("before the ages" as in 1 Cor 2:7) or *apo tōn aiōnōn* ("from the age" or "from of old" as in Col 1:26 or Acts 15:18, where the definite article is missing). As these phrases apply to God, they look backward from the writer's perspective. They don't require unending existence, but they don't preclude it either. Someone who does something before the ages or from of old may have existed merely somewhat prior to creation, but he may also have existed forever prior to creation. As we shall see, nothing in the phrases or passages where they occur suggests that this person exists either temporally or atemporally.

Another typical NT phrase is *eis tous aiōnas*. Here the direction points to the future from the author's perspective. This phrase is frequently translated "forever," as in Luke 1:33; Heb 13:8; and Rev 4:9-10. While our English word "forever" can be used to designate all times (before, during, and after the writer's or speaker's comment), the context in these passages clarifies that the Greek phrase points to the future. Still, nothing in these passages necessitates that God's future (from our perspective) existence be either temporal or atemporal.

In addition to these typical words and phrases, the NT also refers to God's eternity in other ways. For example, Christ's kingdom has no end (Luke 1:33), and Melchizedek has no end of life and, like Christ, is a priest forever (Heb 7:3). In each case the English word "end" translates the Greek *telos*. Though *telos* may mean goal and purpose or even culmination, it may also mean termination,[35] and that is the point in these passages. Thus, the writers teach that something or someone has no end, and that just means it exists endlessly or eternally. First Timothy 6:16 illustrates another way to teach eternity without using any of the typical Greek words for eternity. Paul says that Christ possesses immortality. The word for immortality is *athanasia* (literally, "no death"). Though this need not mean that Christ existed forever prior to Paul's statement, it does teach that he will exist endlessly into the future from Paul's perspective, and that makes the same point Paul and other writers make with the phrase *eis tous aiōnas*.

These are the basic OT and NT terms and phrases used to teach God's eternity, but how does the Bible describe God's eternity? My usage study below fills in many details, but Charnock offers a helpful general description of biblical teaching. According to Scripture, God predates creation, and his existence extends endlessly backward. As Charnock says, this is the force of "from everlasting" in passages such as Ps 90:2.[36] Scripture also speaks of God enduring forever, and the biblical author means that from his perspective God will exist endlessly into the future.[37] Other passages teach God's eternal existence without reference to past or future. One passage (Job 36:26-27) makes this point rather poetically by saying that God's years cannot be numbered. This could be true because we do not know how long God has existed even though the number of years is finite; but in the context of the passage, the reason is that the number is infinite. Charnock also notes that God's eternity is not derived from anything else. Angels once created may continue to exist in perpetuity, but both their creation and their continued existence is due to God. The same is true of human beings. In contrast, God's eternity depends upon no one, for Scripture says he has life in himself (John 5:26).[38] Here we see the joining of two distinct divine attributes, aseity and eternity. That is, if God has aseity, he never began to exist, he cannot stop existing, and he depends on nothing but himself to exist. But then he must exist forever and hence is eternal.[39]

In turning to specific biblical passages, we find that Scripture has much to say about divine eternity. However, my contention is that the biblical writers make no comments explicitly or implicitly that help us decide whether God's eternity is temporal or atemporal.

It is possible to divide biblical teaching about God's eternity into many different categories. The first group of passages speaks about God's existence as endless, and the focus is his *endless existence in the past*. Consider, for example, Psalm 93, which speaks of God's majesty. Verse 2 says his throne is established from of old and that he is from everlasting. Hence, God always existed in the past; he has been ruler from of old (*mēʾān*). As a result, God is majestic, but the verse says nothing about whether his existence from of old was temporal or atemporal (see also Ps 102:24-27; Dan 7:9; Hab 1:11-12).

There is also Prov 8:23. In Proverbs 8, wisdom is personified and commends itself. It says the Lord possessed wisdom at the beginning of his way, before his works of old (v. 22). Wisdom says it was established from everlasting (*mēʾôlām*), from the beginning, from the earth's earliest times (v. 23). This means that from all eternity wisdom existed, and God had wisdom. The perspective is backwards endlessly, but the point is not a metaphysical point about the relation of wisdom to time and eternity. Moreover, the passage says nothing about whether God possessed wisdom temporally or atemporally, and we wouldn't expect it to do so since the passage's point is about wisdom.

A second set of passages also speaks of God's endless existence, but emphasizes God's *endless existence into the future*. OT passages such as Ps 9:7 teach this. Psalm 9 gives thanks for God's justice and judgment of the wicked. Verse 7 says the Lord abides (*yēšēb*) forever (*lēʾôlām*), and has established his throne for judgment. The psalmist's point is that there is no reason to fear that the wicked will escape judgment, for they cannot outlive God. He abides forever, and has decided to judge (set up a throne for judgment). Given the focus on judging the wicked, the verse looks to the future from the writer's perspective. However, it does not address whether God's endless existence will be temporal or atemporal (see also Ps 73:26 and the overall context of the certainty of God's future judgment of the wicked, though they currently prosper; and Ps 89:2 about God's continued lovingkindness to David through the Davidic Covenant).

Then there are psalms that speak of various divine attributes such as righteousness being everlasting (Ps 119:142, 144). Another psalm (48) extols the glory of Zion and her God. Verse 14 says this is God, our God forever and ever (*ʿôlām weʿed*). For that to be true, he could not go out of existence at some time in the future.

In Isa 60:19-20 the prophet portrays conditions in the millennial kingdom and on into the eternal state. Both verses say there will be no need in Jerusalem for sun or moon because the Lord will be Zion's everlasting light (*lĕʾôr ʿôlām*). The picture is reminiscent of Revelation 21–22 and the eternal state with the new heaven and new earth. In that dimension of existence, it is unclear if there will be time and how it will be measured, but Isaiah's point is certainly not a philosophical one about the nature of time in the kingdom and eternal state. Whether there will be time and whether God will be in it or outside it is not Isaiah's concern.

The NT also teaches God's endless future existence. Luke 1:33 is part of the annunciation to Mary of Jesus' birth. The angel says Jesus will reign over the house of Jacob forever (*eis tous aiônas*), and his kingdom will have no end or termination (*telos*). The verse does not tell us whether Christ's rule will be in time or outside of it, nor is that its point. Rather, the point is that Christ's rule will be perpetual; he will never lose authority.

First Timothy 1:17 is a doxology that wishes God honor and glory forever and ever (*eis tous aiônas tôn aiōnōn*). God is called the "king of the ages," i.e., eternal (*basilei tôn aiōnōn*). Though the passage seems to point to the future and implies God's continued endless existence, nothing in it helps us answer whether that endless existence is temporal or atemporal.

A favorite passage among Christians is Heb 13:8, which says that Jesus Christ is the same yesterday and today, and forever (*eis tous aiônas*). This is a somewhat poetic way of teaching the dependability of Christ. From the idea of dependability many have inferred immutability, but in the context of verses 5-7, dependability is the main point. Of course, to be dependable *always*, not just for awhile, Christ must remain the same in the future as he has been in the past. Thus, the verse implies that Christ's life is never-ending, and teaches the dependability of his character into the future. Of course, none of this says whether Christ's past, present, or future (from our perspective) existence is temporal or atemporal, nor is that the point of the passage. The pattern of yesterday, today, and forever suggests temporal location, but again, this is a poetic way of teaching dependability. We cannot affirm from this verse temporal eternity. See also 1 Tim 6:16; Rev 1:17-18 and 2:8, which speak of Christ as immortal, "the first and the last," and "alive forevermore." All of these passages teach Christ's eternity but make no statement about whether it is temporal or atemporal (see also Rev 4:9 in regard to God).

A third category of passages about God's eternity also claims that he exists endlessly, but in contrast to the previous two categories, the focus is neither exclusively backwards nor exclusively forwards. These passages teach that God *exists endlessly always*. OT passages that fit in this group are Gen 21:33; Deut 32:40-41; Job 36:26; Ps 41:13; 90:2; 92:8; 102:24-27; 100:5; 103:15-18; 106:48; Isa 9:6-7; 40:28; 57:15; Jer 10:10; and Dan 4:34. A sampling of these verses illustrates the theme. Gen 21:33 records the covenant between Abraham and Abimelech at Beersheba. Abraham plants a tree and calls on the name of the Lord, the everlasting God. He makes no metaphysical point by doing this. Instead, his point is that God is the God who always exists, unlike others. Hence, he is invoked to help maintain the covenant and protect Abraham, because he will always exist to do so. While this looks to the future from Abraham's perspective, his general point is that God exists always. Of course, nothing Abraham says tells whether God's existence is temporal or atemporal.

In Job 36:26 Elihu speaks of God's greatness. He says God is exalted and we do not know him. To illustrate this truth, he says the number of God's years is unsearchable. This might be so because he is atemporal, so that discovering the number of his years would be impossible; or it might be because he has lived and will live so long temporally that no one can count an infinite number of years. But such interpretations mistake the passage's purpose of extolling God's greatness. Unlike humans who live short lives and then are gone, God always exists. His years are incalculable, because no one lives long enough to know or discover how long he lives.

Psalm 100 is a great psalm exhorting everyone to praise the Lord. Verse 5 offers several reasons for doing so. God is good, his lovingkindness is ("to" or "for") everlasting (*lĕʿôlām*), and his faithfulness is to all generations. To say that lovingkindness is everlasting means at least that it will never run out, but it can also mean that it has always been there in the past. The phrase about faithfulness to all generations points backwards and forwards. For all of this to be true, God must exist at all these times, but nothing in the verse says whether he does so temporally or atemporally. See also Psalm 103, especially verses 15-18; Isa 40:28; and Dan 4:34.

Isa 9:6-7 describes the coming messianic ruler, Israel's future son. Verse 7 calls him, literally, a father of eternity (*ʾăbî ʿad*). This does not mean he originates eternity but that he is a father (to his people) who endures forever. Whether that duration is temporal or atemporal is not discussed in the passage.

Various NT passages also teach this theme. Rom 16:26 says "according to the commandment of the eternal God." This is part of Paul's concluding doxology. Paul speaks of the gospel and preaching of Jesus Christ, which is according to the revelation of the mystery that is now manifest and has been proclaimed by the Scriptures. Making the gospel known to all nations is done according to the commandment of the eternal God. In context, Paul's point seems to be that throughout the ages before the gospel was known, inscripturated, and proclaimed, God was there. God has existed through all the ages of time and before them, but this makes no comment about whether he existed temporally or atemporally (see also Heb 7:3; 9:14; Rev 1:8; and 4:8).

A fourth category of passages speaks of God's *existence before the author's time and even prior to creation.* Verses in this group are John 8:58; 17:5, 24; Acts 15:18; 1 Cor 2:7; Eph 3:9; Col 1:26; and Heb 1:10-12. In John 8:58, Jesus says, "Before Abraham was born, I am." In this passage, Jesus says Abraham saw his day and was glad. The Jews said this was crazy because Jesus was not yet fifty years old, yet he says Abraham had seen him. How could that be? Verse 58 records Jesus' answer, and then his hearers took up stones to stone him. They did this in part because he was calling himself God by calling himself "I am," the divine name. Claiming to exist even before Abraham *per se* necessitates neither atemporal nor temporal existence in the past, but only existence that predates Abraham. However, this does suggest that his existence extends back into the past indefinitely (see also Mic 5:2).

In John 17:5 Christ asks to be glorified with the glory he had with the Father before the world was. This suggests not only Christ's preexistence but also that his existence predates creation. Though this is a temporal sequence, it does not necessitate that God's or Christ's existence prior to creation was temporal rather than atemporal. If God can timelessly act and have it affect things at particular points in time, then this verse need not necessitate temporal eternal existence.

In 1 Cor 2:7 Paul says that he and the other apostles speak of God's wisdom (Christ) which he predestined before the ages (*pro tôn aiōnōn*) to our glory. As in other cases, this speaks of salvation being ordained prior to God's creating the world. It shows that God predated creation and acted prior to it, but it does not say he existed infinitely long before creating, and it does not say whether God's existence was temporal or atemporal.

A final passage is Heb 1:10-12. Verses 10-11a quote Ps 102:25-26. Verse 10 speaks of God laying the foundation of the earth, so he must predate creation. Verse 11a says these things will perish, but God remains. Verse 12 quotes Ps 102:26-27 and says God's years will not end. This does not require God to be a temporal being, but only means he will always exist in comparison with things of this world, which will pass away. All of this is said of Jesus Christ, the one introduced as the fullness of God's revelation in these last days of his revealing activity. Other passages that fit this category are Eph 3:9 and Col 1:26.

A fifth group of verses addresses God's decisions and purposes, and shows that those *decisions and purposes stem from before creation.* In most cases, the decisions and purposes relate to God's plan of salvation. For example, in 1 Cor 2:7 Paul says he and the apostles speak of God's wisdom (Christ), which he predestined before the ages (*pro tôn aiōnōn*) to our glory. This means that Christ was chosen as Savior prior to God's creation of the world (see also 1 Pet 1:20). Of course, it does not say he existed infinitely long before creating, nor does it say whether his existence was temporal or atemporal.

Eph 1:4 speaks of believers' election in Christ before the foundation of the world (*pro katabolês kosmou*). However, this says nothing about whether God's existence prior to creation was temporal or atemporal, nor does it state how long God existed prior to creation. See also Eph 3:11; 2 Tim 1:9; and Tit 1:2.

A sixth set of verses speaks of God or one of his attributes as eternal, but the point is to teach his *dependability*. Some verses teach that his protection is dependable, while others show that his love or some other quality is dependable. Many verses in this group also fit into other categories and have already been discussed, so we can handle them quickly. For example, God's promise of Canaan to Abraham and his descendents (Gen 17:8) for an everlasting (*ôlām*) possession shows that the promise is dependable; God will not revoke it. Abraham's calling the Lord the everlasting God (Gen 21:33) points to God's constant existence as a guarantee that one can depend on him to exist. Hence, he can be invoked to help maintain Abraham's covenant with Abimelech, because he can be counted on always to exist. Ps 103:17 points to God's reliable lovingkindness, and Isa 9:6 suggests that the coming Messiah can be counted on to function as a father to his people, because he will never cease to exist (he is *'ăbî 'ad*, "father of eternity"). Isa 40:28 shows that God is a dependable source of help, and Christ's constancy (Heb 13:8) means he is a reliable Savior and Lord. But, none of these passages intend to make a point about God's eternity as being either temporal or atemporal.

Other passages also fit into this category. Deut 33:27 emphasizes God as a refuge and protector. The writer says that the eternal (*qedem*) God is a refuge; underneath are the everlasting (*ôlām*) arms. Because God always exists, he can serve as a protector, and believers can depend on him to play this role in their lives (see also Isa 26:4; Jer 31:3 about Israel's future restoration; and Ps 119:142, 144).

A seventh group of passages about God's eternity uses it to teach the *authority and sovereignty of God*. Many of the verses teach divine eternity, but they appeal to it to underscore God's sovereignty as well. Consider, for example, Jer 10:10 and Dan 4:34. In Jer 10:10, the point of calling Jehovah the everlasting (*ôlām*) King is at least in part to attribute to him genuine authority over all things, as opposed to the idols heathen nations worship. Nebuchadnezzar's testimony that God lives forever (*ôlāma*) and that his dominion is everlasting (*ôlām*) is his way of acknowledging that God is sovereign over all kings and kingdoms. See also Lam 5:19-20; Dan 4:3; 7:14, 27; and Hab 1:12. In the NT, passages such as Luke 1:33; Rev 1:8, 17-18; 2:8; 21:6; and 22:13 all teach Christ's endless existence, but they also very vividly teach his sovereign position over all things. None of them, however, necessitates or even suggests that God's authority is exercised either temporally or atemporally, for they do not address that issue.

A final category is most interesting because verses in it appear to make a metaphysical comment about God's relation to time. The two verses in this category suggest that God has a different perspective on time than we have.

Though they do not say so explicitly, they seem to require implicitly that God has this different perspective on time because he exists endlessly. Hence, these verses seem to teach something about *the relation between possessing endless existence and one's perspective on time.*

Second Peter 3:8 says, "with the Lord one day is as a thousand years, and a thousand years as one day." This is part of Peter's answer to scoffers who doubt that the Lord will ever return and judge the world. Verse 4 offers their explicit argument that this will never happen because nothing catastrophic like a major judgment ever happens; everything remains the same. These scoffers also imply that (v. 4) God would have judged by now if he were going to, but since he has not and it has been so long, he won't. In verse 8 Peter answers this implicit argument. He says that what may seem like a long delay to us is not necessarily so to God, because God does not *perceive* time as we do. Peter does not say *why* God perceives time differently than we do. It could be because he is going to exist forever, so no amount of time seems the same to him as to us. Or it could be that he is in time, but in a different time than our physical, clock time, so that time measurement is different for him than for us. Or it could be that God is atemporal and is aware of all time at once, but does not experience time's passage. Hence, since everything is always present to him, one day is no different to him than a thousand years, because as atemporal he does not experience time's passage and can see all years or a few years at once. The text gives no clue as to which, if any, of these options is correct, and that is not Peter's point, anyway. The net result is that, while this passage initially seems to help with our philosophical questions about God, time, and eternity, it really doesn't. The verse is equally true regardless of whether God is temporal or atemporal.

Ps 90:4 is the other passage in this category. Psalm 90 contrasts our transitoriness to God's endless existence. Verse 4 says "a thousand years in Thy sight are like yesterday when it passes by, or as a watch in the night." The point is that what seems long to us is very short from God's perspective. This is so because God exists endlessly, and in comparison to that, a thousand years seems a small amount of time. Now, as was the case with 2 Pet 3:8, there might be several reasons why this is so. The psalmist does not clarify which is the case, but he probably means only that because God exists so long, a thousand years seems a small amount of time to him. It is hard to conclude much more from this passage, but if this is all we should conclude from this passage then it offers us little help with questions about divine eternity as temporal or atemporal. Nowhere does the verse tell us whether God experiences all these years successively (as temporal) or whether he always experiences all of them at once as present (as himself atemporal).

From this study of biblical teaching on God's eternity, several conclusions seem in order. First, no specific word or phrase in itself necessitates either atemporal or temporal eternity. Second, various assertions about God's eternity might at first glance seem to necessitate an everlasting or sempiternal God, rather than an atemporally eternal deity. However, no passage which

264 □ No One Like Him

discusses God's eternity addresses the metaphysical question of the nature of
that eternity, i.e., whether it is temporal or atemporal. In fact, many passages
about God's eternity actually intend to teach something other than God's
relation to time—such as God's sovereign authority or his dependability.
Consequently, I conclude that while Scripture affirms divine eternity and
teaches that this means unending existence always, we cannot answer from
the Bible alone whether God's eternity is temporal or atemporal in nature.

Immutability

In reflecting on all of God's wonderful perfections, it is reassuring to know
that our lives are entrusted to such a God. Still, we would be greatly troubled
if our magnificent king should lose or change some of those perfections. But
Christians can rest assured that this will not happen, because in addition to
all his other perfections, our God is unchanging.

Divine immutability is an encouragement to every believer, but in recent
years it has also become a matter of much theological and philosophical controversy. As we saw in chapters 2 and 4, process theists have led the attack
against this doctrine. In addition, the open view of God rejects the traditional
understanding of this divine attribute, and others within the bounds of evangelicalism have clamored that the immutable God of Anselm and Aquinas is
not the God of Scripture.

The strong conception of immutability associated with the classical theism
of Anselm and Aquinas says that God is utterly incapable of any change whatsoever. Theologians holding this view reason that if anything changes, including God, it must change either for better or for worse. Since God is already
perfect, he could not become more perfect, so any change in God would be
for the worse. Since that would mean that he would stop being perfect, there
would be no point in such change. So there is no reason for God to change and
plenty of reasons not to change. Hence, he must be absolutely changeless; and
if absolutely immutable, he must also be impassible, for change in emotions
and being affected by his creatures' thoughts and actions are changes.

It is this strong sense of immutability that process theists and open view
proponents find so objectionable.[40] They don't see how such a God matches
the biblical portrait of God. Scripture depicts a God who interacts with his
creation. On various occasions he changes his mind about judgment he threatened to bring. Moreover, he became incarnate in Jesus Christ, and suffered
and died as Christ went through his earthly pilgrimage. Process theists also
maintain that the God of classical theism is not a God who attracts worship-
ers. He is disengaged from his creation, appears unconcerned about what
happens in our world, and seems incapable of responding to our needs even
if he does care. The process solution is a God who is constantly changing. He
grows in knowledge and perfection, he shares our pains and sorrows, and he
is constantly in the process of becoming. Open view defenders reject the idea

that God grows in perfection and that his being is in the process of becoming, but otherwise repudiate divine immutability in this strong sense and the divine impassibility that goes with it.

Theists more conservative than process and open view thinkers also question whether the classical strong sense of immutability does justice to the biblical God.[41] Moreover, they argue that if God really is as static as portrayed, it is hard to see how he could act in the world. And there are problems for divine omniscience. For one thing, if God undergoes no changes whatsoever, he could not know from one of our days to the next that it is a different day for us. For him to know such a fact each day would mean a change in his knowledge, but if he is totally immutable, there cannot be any changes in his knowledge.

If the options on divine immutability are only the two mentioned, (i.e., either God is absolutely static or he is totally mutable), one can see why the process and open view approaches are so tempting. On the other hand, evangelical Christians may feel uncomfortable with the strong sense of immutability and its implications and yet are unenthusiastic about either the process or open view positions.

Is there a way out of this dilemma? I believe there is, and while it has affinities to each of the current views, it is identical to neither. What we need is a more nuanced notion of immutability, one that takes into account the criticisms of process and open view thinkers but still upholds the essential points taught in Scripture and demanded by the conservative tradition. Though some of the details of this nuanced view will be handled when I cover omniscience, there is still much to say about immutability now. I turn first to Scripture.

Scripture has no specific term for "divine immutability,"[42] but the concept is taught in one way or another. For example, a writer may say that God will endure, or that there is no change in God, or that God is the same from one day to the next. In comparing the heavens and the earth to God, the psalmist says (Ps 102:26—quoted in Heb 1:11-12), "They will perish, but Thou remainest; and they all will become old as a garment, and as a mantle Thou wilt roll them up; as a garment they will also be changed. But Thou art the same, and Thy years will not come to an end." In Mal 3:6 we read, "For I, the LORD, do not change; therefore you, O sons of Jacob, are not consumed." And in the NT, James writes (1:17), "Every good thing bestowed and every perfect gift is from above, coming down from the Father of lights, with whom there is no variation, or shifting shadow." What is true of God generally is true of Jesus Christ as well: "Jesus Christ is the same yesterday and today, yes and forever" (Heb 13:8). Such verses teach that God does not change.

Other verses specify a particular divine attribute and teach that this aspect of God's person does not change. Num 23:19 speaks of God's unwavering truthfulness. In Heb 6:17-18 we again see God's immutable honesty, and the writer also says that God's counsels (the plans—boulē—that spring forth from his deliberations about how to accomplish his purposes—cf. Eph 1:11) do not change. And the psalmist portrays God's mercy as never-ending, and hence, immutable (Ps 103:17).

In addition to constancy of being and character, Scripture also teaches that God's purposes do not change, and, having deliberated and chosen a course of action, he changes neither his counsels nor his will. Prov 19:21 says, "Many are the plans in a man's heart, but the counsel of the LORD, it will stand." The psalmist says of God's counsel (Ps 33:11) that it "stands forever." And Isaiah records the Lord's declaration about his purposes (Isa 14:24): "The LORD of hosts has sworn saying, 'Surely, just as I have intended so it has happened, and just as I have planned so it will stand'" (see also Isa 46:9-10 and Heb 6:17).

Finally, God is unchanging in his promises. This, of course, stems from his immutable truthfulness, but it is encouraging to read that God will keep whatever promises he has made. In 2 Cor 1:20 (KJV) Paul speaks of the promises God made to us in Christ: "For all the promises of God in him are yea, and in him Amen, unto the glory of God by us." By saying that the promises are yea and Amen, Paul means that God will keep his promises. The promises are not some yea and some nay, but all are yea.

These, then, are the basic biblical data concerning God as immutable. However, there are other passages and doctrines that relate more broadly to divine changelessness. For in spite of all the passages that say that God does not change, various biblical passages show that in one way or another God apparently does change. For example, passages such as Exod 32:10-14; Judg 2:18; Ps 18:26-27; 106:45; Jer 26:19; Amos 7:3, 6; Jon 3:10; Prov 11:20; 12:22, some of which even speak of God repenting of what he thought to do, seem to indicate changes in God. Moreover, we find a rather odd passage in 1 Sam 15:10-11, 28-29, for verses 10-11 say that God repents of what he was going to do, whereas verses 28-29 say he does not repent. In addition, the incarnation seems to be a rather dramatic change in the very being of God. Other passages speak of God changing in other ways. For example, Paul teaches that God's wrath is directed against those who are unrighteous (Rom 1:17), and yet when sin is repented, he forgives the sinner (1 John 1:9). Moreover, we see God reacting and interacting with various people. Think of God's interactions with Pharaoh at the time of the exodus. Through Moses and Aaron, he threatens a plague and brings it upon Egypt. Then Pharaoh relents for a time and God stops the plague. Pharaoh then hardens his heart, and God sends another plague.

DEFINING IMMUTABILITY. How should we understand this? On the one hand, it seems clear that we cannot hold the static view of God that so many within the classical Christian tradition have held. On the other hand, the passages teaching divine changelessness make it very difficult to swallow process theology's handling of divine immutability. I believe we need and can articulate from biblical teaching a more nuanced definition of divine constancy, according to which God is neither totally static nor totally in flux. But the proper starting point is an understanding of the different ways immutability can be understood. Here Richard Swinburne, William Mann, and Paul Helm help us tremendously.

Swinburne notes that immutability can be understood in a stronger and a weaker sense. In the stronger sense, divine immutability means that God "cannot change *at all.*" As Swinburne says, this notion of immutability is typically linked with divine timelessness. There is also a weaker sense of immutability, and though I would add more to it than Swinburne does, his definition covers the basic point theists want to safeguard about immutability. Swinburne says, "In the weak way to say of a person that he is immutable is simply to say that he cannot change in character. To say of a free and omniscient creator that he is immutable is simply to say that, while he continues to exist, necessarily he remains fixed in his character."[43]

The notion of immutability most frequently held by those committed to divine atemporal eternity is the stronger one. As Mann shows, this understanding of divine immutability was held by classical theists such as St. Augustine, St. Anselm, and St. Thomas Aquinas.[44] Paul Helm clarifies even further the sense of divine immutability involved:

> To say that God is immutable may refer to his essential character, or it may refer to any predicate that is true of God. And the immutability may be logical, or it may have some weaker force. This gives four possibilities:
>
> (a) God is immutable if in fact his character never changes;
> (b) God is immutable if his character could not change;
> (c) God is immutable if in fact nothing about him changes;
> (d) God is immutable if nothing about him could change.[45]

As Helm explains, immutability in sense (d) is the strongest and it seems equal to what Swinburne calls the stronger sense. It is the sense that Augustine, Anselm, and Aquinas apparently held.

My contention is that in order to choose a notion of divine immutability that best fits biblical data, we must delineate ways an individual might change and then see which of those ways could apply to God without destroying something essential to the biblical concept of divine immutability. First, there might be changes in the attributes of that individual's very constitution. In God's case, this would mean changing either his moral or his non-moral attributes, all of which have been deemed essential predicates. Second, a being might change her purposes or goals. Third, an individual might change his mind about what he chooses to do. As this relates to God, it would mean changing his decrees (for a Calvinist) or changing what he decides to do (a wording more palatable to those who prefer not to speak of God decreeing anything). Fourth, an individual, especially one with power over others, might change her ethical rules by which those under her authority are to live. Moreover, even if those norms did not change, the punishments for breaking the rules might change.

Fifth, someone with power over others might not change his basic goals and methods of operation, but he might change his way of administering programs he has implemented. Think, for example, of God's plan of salvation. As I have argued elsewhere[46], God's method of saving people from sin is always a grace method based on human faith in God in virtue of blood atonement being paid for sin. But how God administers that system changes from one era to another. Under the OT economy, sin was to be paid for by the sinner, in believing faith, bringing an animal sacrifice. Later on, Christ, the all-sufficient sacrifice, paid for all sins, and God in the NT era no longer requires repentant sinners to bring anything as a blood sacrifice in payment for sin. In fact, the book of Hebrews shows that the whole ceremonial law was cancelled as a result of Christ's sacrifice and the new order it implemented in God's dealings with us.

Sixth, individuals might change their relationships with others. Anger may change to forgiveness. Friendship may change to animosity but later change back to friendship. Indeed, someone might hold several relationships toward a given person at once. For example, as I write this, the president of the United States bears the relation of governmental leader of Chelsea Clinton, but he is also her father. Were she to join the military while her father is president, he would be her commander-in-chief. God also relates to us in various ways. He is our creator, and when we sin and don't repent, he is our judge. When we trust Christ for forgiveness of sins, God becomes our savior. When we are lonely and need comfort, he may function as our friend and comforter.

Seventh, another form of change a person might experience has been discussed in recent literature. It is also relational change, but not the sort mentioned above. In philosophical literature, it is called "Cambridge change." In fact, philosophers typically distinguish Cambridge changes from what they call real changes. The distinction seems to have come originally from Peter Geach's *God and the Soul*. Geach explains:

> The only sharp criterion for a thing's having changed is what we may call the Cambridge criterion (since it keeps on occurring in Cambridge philosophers of the great days, like Russell and McTaggart): the thing called 'x' has changed if we have '$F(x)$ at time t' true and '$F(x)$ at time t^1' false, for some interpretation of 'F', 't', and 't^1'. But this account is intuitively quite unsatisfactory. By this account, Socrates would after all change by coming to be shorter than Theaetetus; moreover, Socrates would change posthumously (even if he had no immortal soul) every time a fresh schoolboy came to admire him; and numbers would undergo change whenever e.g. five ceased to be the number of somebody's children.
>
> The changes I have mentioned, we wish to protest, are not 'real' changes; and Socrates, if he has perished, and numbers in any case, cannot undergo 'real' changes. I cannot dismiss from my mind the feeling that there is a difference here. . . . (Of course there *is* a 'Cambridge' change whenever there is a 'real' change; but the converse is not true.)[47]

In relation to God, an example of a Cambridge property is 'having his mercy thought about as I write this sentence'. Another Cambridge property is 'having his power thought about as I write this sentence'. At time t, I was thinking of the first property, and so God had the property of 'being thought about in that way at time t'. Then, at time t + 1, I thought about a different divine attribute, so God had the property of 'being thought about in that way'. The change in God's properties from time t to time t + 1 is an example of a Cambridge change. As Geach and others note, such changes are not real changes. This means that nothing internal to the being who undergoes Cambridge change actually changes.

Finally, someone might undergo a change in her knowledge of the truth of indexical propositions. What is an indexical proposition? Richard Swinburne explains that indexical expressions

> are words such as 'I', 'you', 'now', 'yesterday', 'tomorrow', 'here', 'five miles to the east of here'. When these words are used as indexical expressions they pick out places, times, people, etc. by their spatial or temporal relations to the speaker. 'Now' is the instant contemporaneous with the speaker's utterance, 'you' is the person to whom the speaker is speaking, and so on. When I say 'you are ill', I am predicating the property of being ill of an individual picked out as the individual to whom I am talking. When I say 'it is Tuesday today' I am predicating the property of being Tuesday of the day picked out as the day on which I am talking.[48]

Hector-Neri Castañeda concurs that indexical reference is "reference to times, places, events, objects, or persons by means of demonstrative or personal pronouns or adverbs."[49] The demonstratives in mind are words such as 'this' and 'that', 'here' and 'there', 'now' and 'later'. Adverbs in view are words such as 'currently', 'presently', 'previously'.

Consider now the indexical proposition 'It is *now* 2:56 P.M. as I write this sentence in single quotes'. It was true for me when I wrote the proposition in single quotes. But I can also write truly 'it is *now* 2:58 P.M. as I write this sentence in single quotes.' This represents a change in my knowledge, for it shows that at 2:56 I knew that one indexical proposition was true and at 2:58 I knew that another was true and the first was no longer true. This kind of knowledge involves change in one's knowledge, but such a change seems problematic for divine omniscience (and for immutability) if God is outside of time. It also poses a challenge to temporal eternity and omniscience, for if God is in time, there seems to be things he does not know, since at every moment he learns the truth of a new indexical proposition. If this changing knowledge means that God is not actually omniscient, that seems to be a major obstacle to adopting temporal eternity. On the other hand, atemporalists also have problems with indexicals, for if God is outside of time, he can know the exact sequence of everything that will occur but he cannot know *when* any indexical with the word "now" is true, because he cannot know when any event actually occurs for us. To know that, he would have to experience temporal succession and location, which is impossible for an atemporal being. Atemporal eternity would not undermine God's immutable knowledge, but it seems to compromise divine omniscience in that God could not know when any indexical proposition is true.

Which of these eight kinds of changes can we predicate of God while remaining true to biblical teaching and evangelical Christian theology? I contend that God must be immutable with respect to many of these kinds of change, whereas nothing biblical or theological is lost if he changes in regard to others. Let me explain.

At the heart of Christian theology is the belief that God does not change in his person (being and attributes), will (decree), or purposes. I think that none of the biblical passages that speak of God changing compromise immutability in any of these respects. There is no biblical evidence that any of his moral or non-moral attributes ever change. Some may object that the incarnation shows that God changes, but that misunderstands the incarnation. As I have shown elsewhere, what changes in the incarnation is not the divine nature; instead, the divine nature takes on a complete human nature. However, in the words of Chalcedon, this does not result in adding or subtracting any attributes to or from either nature, or in converting the attributes of one nature to the other. The natures remain distinct, so Christ's divine nature is exactly the same as it was in his preincarnate state.[50]

In addition, there is no evidence that God changes his will or purposes, as though he cannot make up his mind. I have already cited various verses which show that God does not change his will, counsel, or purposes. There are also verses that say that God foreordained one thing or another even before the foundation of the world (e.g., Eph 1:4; 1 Pet 1:20). Since the things foreordained have been accomplished without God changing his purposes or his plan, these instances offer further evidence that God changes neither his purposes nor his decrees. Because of verses such as these, Christian theologians have maintained that God is immutable in his purposes and will as well as in his person.

What about the fourth kind of change—change in ethical norms and punishments? Here a lot depends on one's ethical theory, and many could be consistent with the basic tenets of Christian theology. For example, someone holding a theonomous account of ethics, according to which things are right because God says so, would probably not find it problematic for their theology if God changed his ethical norms. On the other hand, if one holds a modified divine command theory of ethics such as I have outlined elsewhere[51], there will be a problem if God changes his ethical norms. I agree that God determines which actions are moral and which are immoral, but I disagree with forms of theonomy that say that his choices are arbitrary and could be anything else, for there is no act that is intrinsically right or wrong, better or worse. Rather, I believe that God's ethical norms in some way reflect his very being. Anyone who holds a view at all like mine will find it difficult to see how God's ethical norms are subject to change since his very nature is unchanging.

This must not be misunderstood. There is room for debate over which biblical rules are God's abiding ethical norms and which are not. For example, under Mosaic Law God commanded his people to keep a kosher kitchen. Those are surely rules, and they are not enjoined in the NT, but the key question is whether they are ethical rules or not. Theologians usually call them ceremonial rules and say that they are fulfilled in Christ and his work on Calvary, so that in the NT era we are not under these laws. But changes in ceremonial laws do not mean a change in God's basic nature or the basic *ethical* norms that stem from his character.[52] We might disagree about which rules are ethical norms and which are ceremonial rules, which are timelessly true ethical principles and which are applications of more fundamental ethical rules in a given historical setting, but the basic point remains: God's ethical rules had better not change.

Some will say that God's immutability, then, is jeopardized because it appears that God has changed his ethical norms. After all, under Mosaic Law adulterers and adulteresses were to be stoned to death. The same is true of homosexuals, those who commit incest, and those guilty of bestiality. In the NT, these practices are still immoral but the penalty has changed. Execution is no longer the punishment. In response, I would only say that punishments for breaking ethical rules are not themselves ethical obligations to live by. Hence, if God in mercy chooses to change the punishment for disobeying an ethical rule, that is within his province, and it in no way changes his ethical rules or his character. The only stipulation is that whatever penalties God ordains must be consistent with both his justice and his love. If God ordained a new punishment that was unjust, then we might conclude that he no longer had the attribute of justice. But there is no evidence that changes in any punishments prove God to be unjust or unloving.

So it appears that God must be immutable in his person, purposes, will (decree), and ethical rules, but he can change punishments for disobeying his commands without changing anything else about himself that must remain stable. What about the other kinds of changes? Must God be immutable in those respects? I don't think so. As to the fifth type of change (change in administering his programs), there is no reason why God cannot undergo that sort of change. The example I used was a change in administration of God's plan of salvation. In no way does this change God's purposes (he still intends to save people), decree (no more or less will be saved than before, and all will be saved by grace through faith on the basis of Christ's atoning sacrifice), his person (being and essential attributes), or his ethical rules. As the sovereign God who foreordained all things, he also foreordained a change in the administration of salvation. This in no way compromises any aspects of divine immutability deemed essential to evangelical theology.

What about changes in relationships? Is it somehow a defect in God to forgive a repentant sinner and no longer be angry at him? Does forgiving the sinner change any of God's moral or non-moral attributes or cause him to cease being pure spirit? Of course not. Nor does it change his purposes, decree, or ethics. In fact, in accord with God's ethical norms and the system of moral governance he has set up for the universe, God has no choice (if he is to remain consistent with his attributes and purposes and rules for moral governance) but to change from anger to forgiveness when a sinner repents.

As to "Cambridge" changes, I agree that these are not real changes, if what is meant is that they don't change the being and character of the one of whom they are predicated. Given the nature of Cambridge changes, it is hard to imagine how they could change God's being or attributes, his purposes, decree, or ethical norms. So, for God to have Cambridge properties and undergo Cambridge changes compromises nothing essential to biblical Christian theism.

Finally, what about changes in knowledge of the truth of indexical propositions? In a way, this is the hardest issue, because if we are not careful we can apparently compromise two of God's constitutional attributes—immutability and omniscience. I shall say more about this when discussing omniscience, but let me now say enough to show why I don't think a God who knows the truth of indexicals has ceased to be omniscient (clearly this sort of change would not compromise immutability of God's purposes, decree, or ethical norms—the potential rub is with his person, and in particular with omniscience).

In addressing this and other issues related to omniscience, how we define omniscience is crucial. I shall later define it in detail. For now I suggest that it means that God is the supremely rational being (i.e., his power of thinking is infinitely above that of anyone else, and he always knows and does what is best), and that God knows everything there is to know. But what can be known? It is possible to know everything true of the past, and I believe God can know everything true of the future. Moreover, I believe God has middle knowledge, so I believe he knows everything that could happen and what would follow upon anything that did occur. Another thing that is knowable is the configuration of all possible (logically possible) worlds, and God knows that. It is also possible to know the truth of indexical propositions such as 'it is not now yesterday', 'it is not now 1990 or 2005', 'it is later than 1994, but before 2005'. It is also possible to know the truth of indexicals such as 'it is now 4:31 P.M. on April 15, 1999', or, 'it is no longer 4:25 P.M. on April 15, 1999'. But, there are some indexicals that no one can know. As I write this sentence, it is 4:33 P.M. Therefore, I cannot know that 'it is now 5 P.M.' is true, because it is not now 5 P.M. But, if it is impossible right now to know that, there is no deficiency in my reasoning capacity or my knowledge; no one is deficient for not knowing the impossible.

Of course, for anyone to know the truth of indexical propositions, they must be in time, so the following discussion assumes that God is temporal. Having said that, what is true for *our* knowledge also applies to God. That is, being omniscient means he knows everything there is to know, and at 4:36

P.M. the indexical 'it is now 5 P.M.' is not something anyone can know. So God still qualifies as omniscient even if he cannot know that that indexical is true—because it is not true. Of course, if the indexical is false, God will know that. By putting God in time and letting him know the truth or falsity of all indexicals that can be known, we in no way compromise God's omniscience. And since we do not compromise his omniscience, we still have a right to say that he is immutable in his being. Neither immutability nor omniscience are compromised by allowing God to change his knowledge of indexical propositions.[53]

What I have said so far covers indexicals about the present or past, but what about future-tensed indexicals? Right now they cannot be known to be true, so it is no deficiency for anyone, including God, to fail to know them as true. In the future when they *are* true, a God within time will know they are true. Does this mean he will learn something he did not know? It is hard to speak of the scenario I'm sketching as a case of "learning," especially if we think that learning something presupposes some intellectual deficiency before one learned it. The fact that in the future God will know the truth of indexicals that are currently false does not mean his knowledge is deficient until the future.

I conclude, then, that by putting God in time so that he knows these indexicals, we in no way compromise divine omniscience.[54] Moreover, it allows God to know things that we would expect him to know and that he would need to know if he is to act and react at "the right time" in human history. I note also that allowing God's knowledge of indexicals to change in no way compromises divine immutability in any of the senses evangelicals want to maintain.

THE DEFINITION AND SCRIPTURE.   Having offered this nuanced definition of immutability, we must ask if it fits biblical teaching and evangelical theology. First, I think it is clear how biblical language about God as unchanging fits the concept of immutability I have defined. In fact, the preceding shows in what senses God must be immutable, and as we saw, many of the biblical comments about God as unchanging address respects in which I have claimed that God does not change. For example, we saw passages that speak of some attribute as unchanging and others that speak of no change in his purposes, counsels, or will. All of this is consistent with my definition.

The greatest test is how my understanding of immutability fits biblical language about God changing. First, some biblical passages about changes can be understood as anthropomorphisms. This is a view frequently voiced by evangelical theologians, and I think it is correct. However, some disagree, and I grant that sometimes it is difficult to know which passages do contain anthropomorphisms and which are examples of literal language. We need not solve that issue now, for my only point is that Scripture contains anthropomorphisms, and some of them, I believe, appear in passages that suggest that God has changed in some way.

Then some passages which appear to teach that God has changed do not compromise what evangelicals want to maintain about divine immutability because the only change is in God's relation to his people, whereas his being, purposes, decree, and moral rules have not changed. Consider Exod 32:14, a passage that open view proponents find very significant. God is angry with Israel because of her disobedience, and threatens to destroy her totally. Moses intervenes for his people, reminding God of his covenants with them, and in essence repents for the people. In light of Moses' advocacy, God repents of the evil he thought to do to Israel. It is important to remember that God's standards are such that he hates sin and must punish it. Hence, when Israel disobeys the Lord, there is no option for God, given his unchanging nature and moral rules, but to punish them. However, God has also stipulated that if a sinner repents, he will forgive and bless. So, when Moses pleads for the people and in effect repents, this effects a relational change between God and Israel, but this happens because God's holiness and standards of punishment and blessing are immutable. In this case as well, God must forego completely destroying Israel because of his covenant promises to Abraham (promises Moses reminds God of), promises that are unchanging. So God changes his relationship with Israel because of his unchanging covenants and unchanging moral governance of the world. The way the biblical writer reports this is to use the anthropomorphism that God "repented" of the evil he had planned to do. We should note as well that the impression that Moses "reminds" God of his covenant promises must also be an anthropomorphism. Though some views claim that God does not know the future, no proponent of omniscience can afford to claim that God has really forgotten promises he made in the past.

Two other cases of anthropomorphic language (Amos 7:3; Jon 3:10) seem even clearer, because in both cases the writer explicitly repents of sin or says that people repented of their sin. As a result, the Lord did not judge them. The biblical writer says God "repented" (KJV) in order to communicate the change in his relationship in light of his unchanging principles of moral governance. I also think that 1 Sam 15:10-11 speaks of this kind of relational change in virtue of God's unchanging moral rules, whereas the later verses in that chapter (vv. 28-29) that were mentioned, which say that God does not change, speak of his holy character, which is not subject to change.

So, some passages that speak about God changing are anthropomorphic and should be understood in the way explained. Second, some passages talk about changes God has made, but those changes are based on conditions being met. That is, God says, "If you do x, I will do y, but if you do p, I will do q." Sometimes the conditional language is more implicit than explicit, whereas at other times it is more explicit. In Deut 28:1-2, 15, for example, God tells Israel through Moses to obey the Law and they will be blessed, but if they disobey they will suffer his judgment. This language explicitly shows that what God will do is conditioned on what his people do. On the other hand, some have argued that Jonah's preaching at Nineveh is a case of implicit conditions. Jonah preaches doom and destruction on Nineveh apparently unconditionally; but then, in Jon 3:10, we learn that Nineveh repented as a result of

Jonah's preaching and God did not send judgment. Hence, Jonah's apparently unconditional message must have implicitly contained a condition.[55]

In accord with such explicit or implicit conditional language, we see God doing one thing or another that appears to be a change from what we expected him to do. However, since God's claims about what he would do in these cases were conditioned on what we would do, whatever God winds up doing does not entail changing any of his constitutional attributes, moral rules, purposes, or decree. In fact, for those who believe that God knows the future either because he has decreed all things or simply because he foresees it, there is no question about God changing his decree or purposes. Those who believe God foreknows because he foreordains also believe God has chosen not only what will happen but also the means to those ends. Even for those who believe that God foreknows because he foresees what we will do, there still need be no change in God's purposes or decree. God just sees that he will present people with various options contingent upon meeting or not meeting certain conditions, and he sees how they will respond and how he will react. So, in these cases, this conditional language and the changes that come in no way compromise divine immutability.[56]

A third type of change language in Scripture about God indicates literal changes, but invariably they are changes in God's relationships (and attitudes that go with changed relationships). As I have defined immutability, this sort of change in God is acceptable. Let me offer some examples. According to Acts 9, Jesus from heaven confronted Saul, who sought to persecute the fledgling Christian church. Jesus was angry about this and confronted Saul. As a result, Paul converted to Christianity and became a leading apostle of Christ and a great missionary. God's relation through Christ to Paul really changed, but none of that entailed a change in God's being, purposes, decrees, or ethical norms. Rather, the relational change was in accord with God's revealed method of salvation and moral governance of the world.

There are many instances of such relational change involving God, but I would also cite verses such as Gen 6:6 and 1 Sam 15:35 as illustrating this kind of change. When God saw the wickedness of the human race, he repented that he had made man (Gen 6:6). When God saw the wickedness of King Saul, it repented him that he had chosen Saul as king (1 Sam 15:35). This language simply means that God was sorry that he made man who had become so sinful and sorry that he had made Saul king of Israel. The change in attitude does not denote any change in God's being, decree, purposes, or ethical rules and moral governance of the world. It is a relational change in virtue of God's unchanging moral rules and governance.

Fourth, we have already seen that God sometimes changes his administrative orders for the world. This is so in regard to punishments for breaking ethical norms and in regard to changes in the administration of God's one method of salvation. Those points have already been made, so I need add only that such changes are consistent with immutability as I have nuanced it.

Finally, none of the verses cited earlier (or others that might be cited) about God changing necessitate at all a change in his constitution. That is, they in no way mean that he is no longer pure spirit or that he has lost any of his moral or non-moral attributes. This also means, as we saw in chapter 5, that biblical language about God appearing in the burning bush, etc., signal no changes in the divine essence but only show that God can manifest his presence in some physical way. And the incarnation in no way changed the divine being, purposes, decrees, or moral standards; it involved taking on a new nature and entering into new relationships, but all of that is consistent with my nuanced definition of immutability.

I conclude, then, that nothing about biblical language precludes the notion of immutability I am defending. When we move beyond Scripture to speak of other kinds of changes God might undergo, again I see no problem. Does God undergo "Cambridge" changes? Surely he does, but as explained, those changes don't compromise his immutable person, will, purposes, or ethical norms. What about change in God's knowledge of the truth of indexical propositions? The only possible conflict with this and immutability is that it might suggest that God is not omniscient, because his knowledge changes, but I have explained why this is not so. Hence, omniscience is not jeopardized as a result of change in God's knowledge of indexical propositions.

What about apparent changes in God's knowledge concerning the future course of events in our world and universe? Doesn't this show either that God cannot be omniscient, or that while God as omniscient knows everything that can be known, the future cannot be known by anyone? Most evangelical Christian theists have held that God in some way knows the future, so this is not a problem. On the other hand, some have claimed that God does not know the future, but see this as no problem for divine omniscience. My views fall into the former group, and that is enough for answering this objection to my notion of immutability. As for why I think God knows the future and as to other perspectives on this issue, I shall save that for my discussion of divine omniscience and my treatment of divine foreknowledge and human freedom.

In this section, I have argued that when one analyzes the relevant data, it is not necessary to understand divine immutability either as classical Christian theists like Aquinas and Anselm did or as process theists or open view proponents hold it in our day. While my position bears some affinities to the process and open views of divine immutability, there are significant differences. Moreover, nothing I have said requires process notions of a dipolar, finite God. Nor does it necessitate holding the open view's libertarian free will (and the view of divine sovereignty that accompanies it) or agreeing with its belief that God does not know the future.

SEVEN

THE NON-MORAL DIVINE ATTRIBUTES (II)

In chapter 6, we began our description of the non-moral attributes of God. We saw that various divine qualities such as omnipresence and immutability require a careful nuancing to reflect biblical revelation concerning God. In addition, I began to set forth the defining characteristics of the king who cares. In light of the nuanced understanding of divine immutability, it is necessary to reject divine impassibility. The king who cares experiences real emotions; he sympathizes with our pains and can rejoice over our joys. Though God cares about what happens to us, we want to know whether he can do anything to change our sometimes troubled plight and sustain us until he does change our circumstances. Such questions bring us to attributes such as divine omnipotence and sovereignty. These and the remaining non-moral divine attributes are the subject of this chapter. As with many attributes discussed in chapter 6, many of the predicates considered in this chapter also require careful nuancing.

OMNIPOTENCE

In Rom 1:20 the apostle Paul writes, "For since the creation of the world His invisible attributes, His eternal power and divine nature, have been clearly seen, being understood through what has been made." Of all the divine attributes revealed in creation, Paul names only power and then refers to the rest by the more general word *theiotēs*, "divine nature." Since God's power is so clearly revealed in creation, it is no wonder that when people think of God, they think of power!

Traditionally, Christian thinkers have held that God is omnipotent. Though no word in the OT is exactly equivalent to that English word, the OT does refer to God as *'ēl šadday*, "God almighty" (e.g., Gen 17:1), and when we see what the OT says about God, it is clear that it is right to conclude that Yahweh is omnipotent. In the NT, the term that is closest to our English word "omnipotent" is the Greek *pantokratōr*. *Panto* comes from *pas*, "all," and *kratōr* comes from *kratos*, "power" or "might." Hence, it is often translated "almighty," "all-powerful," or "omnipotent." *Pantokratōr* appears in the NT most frequently in the book of Revelation, where it is used only of God (Rev 1:8; 4:8; 11:17; 15:3; 16:7, 14; 19:6, 15; 21:22). Beyond these words, there are many biblical passages that teach divine omnipotence.

In spite of the biblical evidence that God is omnipotent, much controversy surrounds this divine attribute. The most specific problem is how to define and understand it. I can easily illustrate the problem of definition. Often discussions of divine omnipotence begin by defining it as God's ability to do all things. Immediately the question arises about whether this means God can do things like make round squares and married bachelors. Confronted with such challenges, theists usually retreat by saying that omnipotence is capacity to do whatever is logically possible. But this is not entirely satisfactory, for there is nothing contradictory in the very notions of committing a sin, scratching an ear, kicking a football, learning something that one never knew before, or forgetting something one did know. These are things that mere humans with limited power do all the time, so it seems that an omnipotent being should also be able to do them. But a morally perfect God cannot sin, an omniscient God cannot learn or forget anything, and an incorporeal being has no ear to scratch or foot for kicking.

So there seem to be many things that involve no contradiction but which God cannot do. And other questions arise over divine omnipotence. Can God, for example, make a stone so heavy that he cannot lift it? (This is sometimes called the paradox of the stone.) Does he have enough power to create another God? Could he commit suicide? Could he change the past? Could he, as many medievals queried, restore virginity to a woman who had lost it? If God creates humans with free will, has he made creatures he cannot control? Does evil's existence in our world mean that God is not powerful enough to stop it? Some have even asked whether an omnipotent and immutable being can forgive sin.

In recent decades theologians and especially philosophers have raised and discussed in some detail all of these questions. What one finds in reading the literature is that it is not easy to know how to answer some of these questions, and, regardless of how one answers, it can be even more difficult to explain how one's answers fit the notion of divine omnipotence. The most basic issue in light of these questions is whether we can define divine omnipotence in a way that makes sense. Some philosophers reply that it is impossible to explain omnipotence coherently, so we should jettison it altogether and opt for a God who is almighty, by which they mean that God's power is way beyond that of any other being, he is the source of all power, and he can do whatever he wills to do (Geach says that God can only will to do things that he can in fact do).[1]

Biblical Data on Omnipotence

In light of all these problems I suggest that we begin by seeing exactly what Scripture teaches about God's power. Then, with the biblical data in mind, we can attempt to define the concept of omnipotence (if Scripture teaches this of God), answering the questions raised above and explaining how things God cannot do fit with the notion of divine omnipotence.

As we turn to Scripture, we find many passages that speak generally of God's great power without specifying any particular action God can do. After his vision of God's power, majesty, and grandeur, Job says (Job 42:2), "I know that Thou canst do all things, and that no purpose of Thine can be thwarted" (see also Job 37:23). Various psalms also present this theme. In Ps 62:11 the psalmist says, "Once God has spoken; twice I have heard this: that power belongs to God" (see also Ps 21:13; 71:18; 145:11; 147:5). Nahum adds (1:3, KJV), "The LORD is slow to anger, and great in power, and will not at all acquit the wicked: the LORD hath his way in the whirlwind and in the storm, and the clouds are the dust of his feet."

The NT has similar general references to God's power. Jesus says (Matt 26:64), "nevertheless I tell you, hereafter you shall see the Son of Man sitting at the right hand of Power, and coming on the clouds of heaven." "Right hand of power" is best understood as referring to God the Father, but note that the divine attribute Jesus mentions is his power (see also Matt 6:13).

Jesus also claims to have this divine attribute. Jesus gives the Great Commission after saying (Matt 28:18, KJV), "All power is given unto me in heaven and in earth." Paul says of Christ that after God raised him from the dead, Christ was exalted (Eph 1:21) "far above all rule and authority and power and dominion, and every name that is named, not only in this age, but also in the one to come" (see also Col 2:10).

In addition to passages that speak generally of God's power, there are many references to God's might and to God as mighty. Moses tells the people of Israel to obey God and turn from their disobedience because (Deut 10:17) "the LORD your God is the God of gods, and the Lord of lords, the great, the mighty, and the awesome God who does not show partiality nor take a bribe." Job say's of God (Job 9:4, KJV), "He is wise in heart, and mighty in strength: who hath hardened himself against him, and hath prospered?" (See also Job 36:5.) Frequently in the Psalms we hear the same refrain. In Ps 89:6 and 13, the psalmist writes, "For who in the skies is comparable to the LORD? Who among the sons of the mighty is like the LORD? . . . Thou hast a strong arm; Thy hand is mighty, Thy right hand is exalted" (see also Ps 93:4 and 132:2, 5). And in Isaiah we see something similar. Often, as in Isa 1:24, Isaiah calls God "the Mighty One of Israel." Speaking of the Messiah, Isaiah prophesies (9:6) that he will be the mighty God (see also 10:21).

In addition, in both the OT and the NT many passages refer to God as "God Almighty" or "the Almighty." That designation typically functions as a proper name. That impression is given in part because no particular divine act is the focus of the verse. Instead, the writer just wants to emphasize God's great power. Passages where we find this use of "God Almighty" or "the Almighty" include Gen 17:1; 28:3; 35:11; 43:14; 48:3; 49:25; Exod 6:3; Num 24:4, 16; Ruth 1:20, 21; Job 8:5; 11:7; 13:3; 15:25; 21:15, 20; 22:3, 17, 23; 29:5; 31:2, 35; 40:2; Ezek 10:5; 2 Cor 6:18; and Rev 1:8; 4:8; 21:22.

Although Scripture contains general references to God's power, in many passages the writer speaks of God's power being displayed in one way or another. Many passages speak of God's power as displayed in his deeds. Ps 106:2 says, "Who can speak of the mighty deeds of the LORD, or can show forth all His praise?" (See also Deut 3:24; Ps 145:4, 12; and 150:2.)

Biblical writers mention God's power not only in terms of his deeds in general but also in specific examples of his deeds. For example, many writers speak of divine power in creating and controlling the universe. We find this in Job 26:12; Isa 40:26; and Jer 32:17. Frequently in Psalms we read of God's power in creating and sustaining the universe and in controlling the forces of nature (Ps 50:1). Even the winds are under his control, as we see in Ps 78:26 (see also Jer 10:11-12; 27:5; 51:15; Ps 19:1; 65:6; 68:33; 150:1).

In the NT we find the same theme. Rev 4:11 says, "Worthy art Thou, our Lord and our God, to receive glory and honor and power; for Thou didst create all things, and because of Thy will they existed, and were created" (see also Rom 1:20). NT writers also speak of God's sustaining power over creation (Acts 17:28). To Christ in particular is attributed the creating and sustaining of the universe (Col 1:16-17; Heb 1:3).

A frequent OT theme extols God's awesome display of power in the exodus of Israel from Egypt. We find this theme most frequently in the Pentateuch, as in Deut 4:37, "Because He loved your fathers, therefore He chose their descendants after them. And He personally brought you from Egypt by His great power" (see also Exod 32:11; Deut 4:34; 5:15; 6:21; 7:8, 19; 9:26, 29; 26:8). We also find this theme elsewhere in the OT (e.g., 2 Kgs 17:36; Dan 9:15).

Biblical authors also frequently speak of God's power in saving individuals from sin. After telling how difficult it is for a rich man to be saved, Jesus' disciples asked, "Then who can be saved?" to which Jesus replied, "With men this is impossible, but with God all things are possible" (Matt 19:25-26; see also 9:6). This theme is also evident in John's Gospel (1:12; 17:2). Because Christ has power to save repentant sinners, Paul says that the gospel message is a message of power. To the church at Corinth he writes (1 Cor 1:18), "For the word of the cross is to those who are perishing foolishness, but to us who are being saved it is the power of God" (see also Rom 1:16; 1 Cor 1:24; Col 1:13). In addition, Peter reminds us that God's power enables Christians to persevere in their faith (1 Pet 1:5), and both Peter and Paul affirm that God's power grants believers everything needed to live the Christian life and to develop the various Christian virtues (2 Pet 1:3; Col 1:11). Paul also writes that the power at work in believers is the same power that raised Christ from the dead (Eph 1:19-20).

Because believers have such resources, Paul exhorts the Ephesians (Eph 6:10) to "be strong in the Lord, and in the strength of His might."

Not only does Scripture teach God's great power in salvation, it also speaks of his ability to deliver people from physical danger and to protect them from harm. After being delivered from Saul's hand, David says (2 Sam 22:33, KJV), "God is my strength and power" (see also Gen 49:24 and Neh 1:10). Frequently the Psalms tell of God's power to deliver from physical danger and need (see Ps 59:16; 91:1; 106:8; 111:6). In Ps 59:16 (NIV) the psalmist writes, "I will sing of your strength, . . . for you are my fortress, my refuge in times of trouble." We also read of this expression of God's power in Isaiah (40:29): "He gives strength to the weary, and to him who lacks might He increases power." And God's power preserves Daniel in the lion's den (Dan 6:27). Moreover, the NT teaches that even when God does not remove physical infirmities and problems, his sustaining power is still there in the midst of affliction (e.g., 2 Cor 12:9). Because of God's power to deliver his people and sustain them in times of affliction, biblical writers or characters often plead for God's aid (e.g. 2 Chron 14:11; Ps 79:11).

Although God saves individuals spiritually and physically, his enemies experience his power in judgment and destruction. Hence he is portrayed as a God mighty in battle and in judgment. Many biblical passages make this point quite clear. Second Chronicles 25:8 says, "God will bring you down before the enemy, for God has power to help and to bring down" (see also Exod 15:6; Ezra 8:22; Job 12:19, 21; 24:22). This is also a common theme in the Psalms and prophets. In Ps 66:3, the psalmist advises, "Say to God, 'How awesome are Thy works! Because of the greatness of Thy power Thine enemies will give feigned obedience to Thee'" (see also Ps 24:8; 90:11). Isa 13:6 forecasts eschatological judgment: "Wail, for the day of the LORD is near! It will come as destruction from the Almighty" (see also Isa 11:15; 42:13; 49:25-26; Jer 20:11; 32:18; Joel 1:15).

The NT also speaks of God's judgment upon the wicked. In speaking about fearing other human beings, Jesus says (Luke 12:5), "But I will warn you whom to fear: fear the One who after He has killed has authority to cast into hell; yes, I tell you, fear Him!" Speaking of those who afflict believers, Paul says (2 Thess 1:9) they "will pay the penalty of eternal destruction, away from the presence of the Lord and from the glory of His power." The book of Revelation predicts many judgments upon the ungodly at the end time (see Revelation 16).

In addition to God's power in judgment, Scripture speaks of God's power to perform miracles and his power over demonic and satanic forces. The OT is filled with descriptions of various divine miracles, and so is the NT as it portrays the life and ministry of Christ and his apostles. Think of the OT promise of a son to Abraham and Sarah. This required a miracle because both were old and Sarah was past childbearing. They initially laughed at the thought of having a baby, but they knew that this was not impossible. As we see in Gen 18:10-14, the key issue is, "Is anything too difficult for the LORD?" The expected answer is that nothing is too hard for God.

The NT records many of Christ's miracles. On one occasion, Jesus heals a man sick with palsy and the crowd is amazed (Matt 9:6, 8—parallels in Mark 2:10-12; Luke 5:24, 26; see also Luke 5:17). Jesus also walks on water (Matt 14:22-33), and on another occasion calms the winds and sea (Mark 4:35-41). Because of his miracles, Jesus said the people should have believed in him, and he chastises them for not doing so (Matt 11:20-21, 23—parallel Luke 10:13ff.). Though many did not believe, many still marveled at his power when Christ did these miracles (see Luke 4:36; 9:43; 19:37; Matt 13:54; Mark 6:2). As a result, when the apostles referred to Jesus, they often spoke of him as a man with great power (see Luke 24:19 and Acts 10:38).

Not only did Jesus perform miracles; he gave this power to his disciples as well. Matt 10:1 (see also Mark 3:15 and Luke 9:1); Mark 6:7; and Luke 10:19 all record Jesus' words as he granted his disciples power to perform various miracles. Because they could perform miracles, many were amazed at the disciples' power and wondered how they did these deeds (e.g., Acts 4:7).

Not only did Christ perform miracles by God's power; Scripture also shows that his very life began with a miracle that displayed the great power of God. In Luke 1:35 the angel announces to Mary, "The Holy Spirit will come upon you, and the power of the Most High will overshadow you; and for that reason the holy offspring shall be called the Son of God." Of course, the greatest miracle involving Christ was his resurrection. Many passages speak of this as being done by the power of God. Jesus said of his forthcoming death and resurrection (John 10:18), "No one has taken it away from Me, but I lay it down on My own initiative. I have authority to lay it down, and I have authority to take it up again." This is also a very common theme in the Pauline corpus (1 Cor 6:14; 2 Cor 13:4; Eph 1:20). Consequently, Paul's desire is (Phil 3:10) to know "the power of his resurrection."

Not only was Christ raised from the dead by divine power; others were as well. According to John 11:43-44, Jesus raised Lazarus from the dead; and Mark 5:39ff. records the raising of Jairus's daughter. More generally Matt 3:9 and Rom 4:17 speak of God's power to raise the dead. And, speaking of God's power to raise the dead and the fact that someday Christ will return for his own and they will rise from the dead, Paul writes of the believer's body (1 Cor 15:43), "it is sown in dishonor, it is raised in glory; it is sown in weakness, it is raised in power."

Scripture also speaks of divine power in people's ministries. Before Christ left this earth, he promised his disciples divine power for the ministries to which he had called them (e.g., Luke 24:49; Acts 1:8). Moreover, Paul speaks of his commission as an apostle and relates it to God's power (Eph 3:7). In speaking of his ministry to the church at Corinth he writes (1 Cor 2:4), "And my message and my preaching were not in persuasive words of wisdom, but in demonstration of the Spirit and of power." And, in the book of Revelation the Lord promises to give power to his two witnesses to prophesy during the great tribulation (Rev 11:3).

Finally, various passages speak of a future eschatological return of the Lord, and teach that when he comes it will be with a great display of power and glory. In the Olivet Discourse, Jesus predicts (Matt 24:30—parallel Mark 13:26 and Luke 21:27), "and then the sign of the Son of Man will appear in the sky, and then all the tribes of the earth will mourn, and they will see the Son of Man coming on the clouds of the sky with power and great glory." In addition, at the end time there will be a great day of God's judgment upon the wicked. It will come with evident display of the power of God. Rev 19:15 says of Christ, "And from His mouth comes a sharp sword, so that with it He may smite the nations; and He will rule them with a rod of iron; and He treads the wine press of the fierce wrath of God, the Almighty" (see also Rev 16:14).

Indeed, our God is a God of great might and power, and he is inclined to use that power in behalf of his people. What he said to his people Israel in the days of Jeremiah is a promise and invitation that is available to all the people of God of all ages (Jer 33:3): "Call to Me, and I will answer you, and I will tell you great and mighty things, which you do not know."[2] Despite this great power, there are still some things that Scripture says God cannot do. He cannot lie (Heb 6:18); 2 Tim 2:13, and because of his absolute moral purity, he cannot commit any sin. In fact, according to Jas 1:13, God cannot even be tempted to sin.

Defining Omnipotence

Now that we have surveyed the biblical data about God's power, we can return to the task of defining omnipotence as precisely as we can. Theologians and philosophers have taken one of three approaches to this attribute. Some have held what may be called absolute omnipotence, a view that places no restrictions at all on God's power. At the other extreme are those who, when confronted by various logical and theological problems surrounding omnipotence, have opted for a God with finite power. A third group, the majority in evangelical Christianity, have chosen to specify various limitations to divine power and yet argue that God is still omnipotent in some meaningful sense. I take the third approach, but I shall first briefly explain the other two approaches.

Some theologians have placed no restrictions on God's power, and there are biblical passages that could be taken to make such a claim. Job's confession (Job 42:1-2) that God can do all things seems to place no limitations on God. Moreover, the question in Gen 18:14 about whether there is anything too hard for God anticipates a negative answer, and even Jesus' response about how anyone can be saved (Matt 19:26) may be taken as a broader comment than just a reference to what God can do in saving people. One might conclude that with God literally all things *are* possible.

A frequent objection to this view is that it apparently allows God to actualize contradictory states of affairs, and there have been Christian theologians and philosophers who have held such views.[3] Within the Christian tradition, there have been proponents of the position I described earlier as theonomy or voluntarism. This position was especially prevalent in the Middle Ages and up to the time of the Reformation. Theonomists were most concerned to protect God's absolute freedom and power of will. Hence, God's power was more significant than the laws of logic.

Theonomists often distinguished the *potentia absoluta* (absolute power) and the *potentia ordinata* (ordained or ordered power) of God. The latter power means that God can and has decided to do certain things according to the laws he has *freely* established, i.e., *de potentia ordinata*. On the other hand, God has absolute power (*potentia absoluta*) to do anything, regardless of what he decides to do *de potentia ordinata*.[4] Some theonomists placed no limitations on God's absolute power, whereas others thought that even his absolute power was restricted to things that don't involve a contradiction.

In attempting to safeguard God's power to do virtually anything, theonomists held that nothing in the universe except God and his will are a necessary law. That is, nothing about the universe must be as it is. There is no inherent rightness or wrongness, for example, about any action which cries out for God to require or forbid it. Rather, ethical rules are ordained solely by God's choice. Hence, God is free to mandate that we obey the opposite of the Ten Commandments. God could even require us to hate him, according to one theonomist.[5] As to the physical order, God could change matter into spirit or make a physical thing present in several places at once. As for human intellect, some held that God could give humans intuitive knowledge of nonexistent things, and could do so without our knowing that they don't exist.[6]

At the other extreme are those who limit God's power even (in some cases) to the point that his power is finite. I have already explained why process theologians hold to a God with limited power, but other theologians hold this view as well. There have been several reasons for doing so. First, some claim that the very act of creating a universe is an act of self-limitation on God's part.[7] Second, some Jewish and Christian theologians have thought that the only way to solve the problem of divine sovereignty and human freedom is to limit God's power. So long as the choice to limit his power is God's, God is still considered as sovereign as ever. Proponents of this view often see such a decision as analogous to Christ's decision to empty himself in the incarnation. Third, there are some who claim that God limits his power because he is loving, and this assumes an "understanding of love as making room for the beloved and as implying vulnerability in relation with the beloved."[8] Finally, some believe God is finite in power because they see that as the only way to resolve the problem of evil. If God's power is really unlimited, why would he allow atrocities like the Holocaust? If God's power is finite, however, he may not be able to prevent various evils but that is no sign that he doesn't care about what happens in our world. Hence, he could still be worthy of our worship and could be our ultimate moral governor.[9]

In my judgment, neither a theonomous approach nor a finite God is acceptable. Elsewhere I have explained my problems with theonomy, but my main objection is that I don't believe Scripture portrays God this way.[10] The same problem besets the notion of a finite God. Moreover, as we shall see in later chapters, there are ways to handle the free will/sovereignty issue and the problem of evil without surrendering divine omnipotence. So there is no inconsistency between love and power, especially when the one wielding both is morally perfect in thought and deed. For these reasons and many more, there is no need to espouse a God with finite power.

In light of the preceding, I follow those in the Christian tradition who have sought a nuanced definition of omnipotence according to which there are certain limitations on God's power without making him less than omnipotent in a meaningful sense of 'omnipotence'. What might this nuanced notion be? Anthony Kenny's discussion of divine omnipotence in *The God of the Philosophers* helps greatly in this matter. Kenny enumerates various definitions of omnipotence that have appeared over the centuries, and he explains the problems with each one. He then offers his own definition, which, with some modifications, seems to be a sound way to go.

The first definition Kenny entertains says God is omnipotent in that he can do everything. As Kenny notes, this definition was rejected by Aquinas, and with good reason. There are things that God cannot do, such as sin, die, cough, or forget.[11] A second option is one that Aquinas attributes to St. Augustine and rejects. According to this notion, divine omnipotence means God can do whatever he *wants* to do. Various problems beset this view. For example, the blessed in heaven and possibly even the happy on earth can do whatever they want to do, but that does not make them omnipotent. Likewise, wise people restrict wants to their power, but that does not mean that all wise people are omnipotent. Hence, this notion will not do.[12]

A third option is that God can do whatever is *possible*. However, as Kenny shows, Aquinas asked what "possible" means. It might refer to whatever is naturally possible or to whatever is supernaturally possible, i.e., possible to God. If the former, then God's power is no greater than the power of nature, and is, of course, severely limited. If the latter, then to say that God is omnipotent is to utter a tautology, for it means that God can do whatever God can do. If that's what omnipotence is, everyone is omnipotent, for everyone can do whatever they can do.[13]

Considerations such as these led Aquinas to hold that divine omnipotence is God's ability to do whatever is *logically* possible. God can do whatever does not involve actualizing a contradictory state of affairs. God can create a universe, but he cannot create a round square or a married bachelor.[14] Many theologians and philosophers have opted for this definition, but it alone seems inadequate, for there are many logically possible things that God cannot do. God cannot sin, forget, cough, or kick a football. All of these things are logically possible, and none engages us in a contradiction like believing in married bachelors. And Kenny complains that this notion of omnipotence does not resolve such problems as the paradox of the stone, i.e., can God make a stone so heavy that he cannot lift it? Nor does it tell us if God can make an immovable lamppost or irresistible cannonball.[15]

Kenny next turns to several formulations from Alvin Plantinga, all of which Plantinga rejects. The first says that "X is omnipotent iff ['if and only if'—my insertion] X is capable of performing any logically possible action."[16] This formulation is problematic, however, because there are logically possible actions which God cannot do. *Making a table that God did not make* is a logically possible action—I might have made it. Since *making a table that God did not make* is a logically possible action, but God cannot do it, on this definition of omnipotence, God is not omnipotent.[17]

In light of this problem, Plantinga suggests another definition of omnipotence: "X is omnipotent iff x is capable of performing any action A such that the proposition '*x performs A*' is logically possible."[18] But, as Plantinga explains, this definition is too liberal. The problem is that there is some man who is able only to scratch his ear. We could say of him that he can perform any action A such that the proposition 'the man who is capable only of scratching his ear performs A' is logically possible. However, on this construal, the only such action A is the act of scratching his ear, so the man who can only scratch his ear is omnipotent, whereas God, who has no ear, is not omnipotent.[19]

Perhaps the way around this dilemma is not to define omnipotence in general but in terms of *God's* omnipotence. In that case, the definition is "God is omnipotent iff God is capable of performing any action A such that the proposition *God performs A* is logically possible."[20] Though this might seem to solve the problem, Plantinga disagrees. Suppose that A is the act of 'doing what I am thinking of'. If so, it appears that 'God performs A' is logically possible, for it seems that God can do whatever I am thinking of. However, suppose I'm thinking of creating a square circle. In that case God cannot do what I am thinking of; no one can. But then we have the problem that 'God performs A' (where A stands for whatever I am thinking of) is logically possible, but in this case it cannot be logically possible.[21]

Having examined these three options, Plantinga abandons the attempt to define omnipotence. So far we have considered seven different formulations of omnipotence and found all of them wanting. Should we, too, abandon our attempt to define and hold divine omnipotence? At this point, Geach's suggestion may appear more attractive than it originally did, or perhaps we should accept Swinburne's suggestion. In response to the question of whether God is powerful enough to create a stone so heavy that he could not lift it, Swinburne says that, as omnipotent, God must have such power. But if he were to exercise that power, once he created the stone too heavy for him to lift, he would no longer be omnipotent. Of course, there is no reason to think God would use his power to create such a stone. Wanting to remain omnipotent forever, he would always retain the power to make an unliftable stone, but never exercise it.[22]

This handling of the paradox of the stone (as well as other like dilemmas) is certainly different than the way theologians and philosophers have usually resolved it, and it seems problematic. As noted at the outset of chapter 6, all of God's attributes are essential properties. That means (at least) that God cannot get rid of them without destroying himself; but God also has the attribute of aseity, which seems to preclude his destroying himself (committing suicide). But, then, if there is no way for God to get rid of an essential predicate (by killing himself or doing anything else), Swinburne's suggestion seems bankrupt, since, according to Swinburne, even if God never does anything to lose his omnipotence, he still could do so.

How, then, should we proceed? Kenny offers a suggestion, but it doesn't define omnipotence in terms of logically possible actions or states of affairs that actions bring about. Instead, he defines omnipotence in terms of logically possible *powers*. Kenny's definition is:

> A being is omnipotent if it has every power which it is logically possible to possess.[23]

Kenny adds that this definition must be supplemented by an explanation of when it is logically possible to possess a power. Kenny answers that "it is logically possible to posses a power, I suggest, if the exercise of the power does not as such involve any logical impossibility."[24] What he means in referring to the power as such is that the very idea and description of the power does not contain a contradiction. Of course, in some circumstances *exercising* the power may generate a contradiction, but the power is still logically possible if *some* use of it is logically consistent.

This may sound confusing, but Kenny's illustrations clarify his point. Consider again Plantinga's concern about God being able to do whatever I am thinking. That power as such contains no logical impossibility in its very description. Hence, this is a power an omnipotent being can have; but suppose that on one occasion I am thinking of creating a round square. In *that instance* God cannot exercise his power to do whatever I'm thinking of, for to do so would generate a contradiction, but that doesn't mean he does not possess in general the power to do whatever I am thinking of. All that Kenny's definitions require is that on some occasion the use of this power is logically consistent, and in most instances it would be. Kenny also argues that this definition and explanation of when a power is logically possible helps to solve dilemmas about whether God can make an irresistible cannonball or an immovable lamppost. Power to do either act is logically possible, i.e., there is no logical contradiction *per se* in the very idea of either of those activities, so an omnipotent being can have those powers. Of course, it is not logically possible for anyone, let alone God, to *exercise* both powers simultaneously, for that would generate a contradiction. However, God could exercise either one or the other alone. So the answer is that God has power to make an immoveable lamppost and an irresistible cannonball. There are instances when it is logically consistent for him to exercise one or the other of those powers, but it is logically impossible to use both powers conjointly.[25]

If omnipotence is defined in terms of logically possible powers, how should we understand any given divine power? As Kenny explains, "power to φ can only be defined and understood by someone who knows what φ-ing is."[26] Having heard this, however, we might still be troubled, for there seem to be many powers that are logically possible to have but that God does not have. God cannot sin, die, scratch his ear, or cough. Kenny is aware of these problems and answers that *divine* omnipotence must be differentiated from omnipotence *per se*. When we do this, we see that divine omnipotence is a narrower notion than omnipotence *per se*. Kenny explains the revised definition as follows:

> It must be a narrower omnipotence, consisting in the possession of all logically possible powers which it is logically possible for a being with the attributes of God to possess. (If the definition is not to be empty 'attributes' must here be taken to mean those properties of Godhead which are not themselves powers: properties such as immutability and goodness.) This conception of divine omnipotence is close to traditional accounts of the doctrine while avoiding some of the incoherences we have found in them.[27]

Once we define divine omnipotence this way, we can solve some of the other problems surrounding omnipotence. For example, the powers to weaken, sicken, or die are not powers that God as omnipotent can have, because other divine attributes such as aseity and immutability clash with it. Likewise, in response to the question of whether an omnipotent being can create a creature he cannot then control, given our definition, the answer is no. If an omnipotent being retains his omnipotence (and God does), power to create an uncontrollable being while remaining omnipotent is a logically impossible power for an omnipotent being to have. Since God is both omnipotent and immutable, he cannot give up his attribute of omnipotence. Hence, creating an uncontrollable being is not a power God as omnipotent possesses.[28]

Philip Devenish offers one addition which seems to help us handle questions about whether an omnipotent being should be able to commit one sin or another. Kenny defines divine omnipotence in terms of logically possible powers a being with God's attributes can have. Devenish suggests that we add the fact that God is perfect, by which he means morally perfect. So, when specifying God's powers, one must, as Kenny says, denote powers that fit his other attributes as God, and, as Devenish says, in enumerating God's attributes, one must remember that his moral perfection at least in part determines which attributes he possesses.[29]

With Devenish's proviso we can clearly handle questions about whether God has the power to sin. Since God is morally perfect (holy), he cannot also possess the power to lie, steal, commit murder, etc.[30] I shall return to this point later, but for now, if we accept Devenish's application of the point about God's moral perfection to the power to commit sin, we still might wonder if a being could be omnipotent and lack such a power. The answer seems to be twofold. Given Kenny's definition plus Devenish's addendum, the answer is no. God qualifies as omnipotent on that definition of 'divine omnipotence'. But this seems almost tautologous, so the question's point must be something else, and that something else is to wonder if a being with omnipotence as defined is really "omnipotent enough." That is, is Kenny's narrowed definition of divine omnipotence too narrow? I don't think so, but the reason needs explaining. If one could show that there is a being with divine omnipotence as defined by Kenny who can also do other things such as sin, etc., and if one could show that such a being is a greater and more omnipotent being than the being specified by Kenny's definition of divine omnipotence, then Kenny's definition is in trouble. But how could there be such a "greater" being of the sort imagined? If he has the power to sin, then presumably, following Devenish's analysis, he must not have moral attributes such as holiness, justice, love, truth—at least not to the infinite degree the Judaeo-Christian God does. Hence, the being we are imagining as "better" than Kenny's omnipotent God might have some powers Kenny's God does not have, but it isn't clear that he would be the greatest conceivable being (using Anselmian language), because he would lack many, if not all, of the moral attributes of Kenny's God. In other words, the only way to have a divine being with more power than the God required by Kenny's definition is to have a being who is not equivalent to the divine being. Thus, the God demanded by Kenny's definition plus Devenish's addendum has the most power that any being that would be divine could have. It is certainly proper to label such power omnipotence, and it is also clear that he has all the power we would want or expect a divine being to have. On this understanding of omnipotence, God is able to do everything Scripture shows him doing.[31]

Testing the Definition

Having defined divine omnipotence, we must next test our definition, and the way to do so is to assess it in terms of things that supposedly limit God's power. We have already seen how this definition handles logical contradictions such as the paradox of the stone, situations such as God creating what I am thinking of and creating immovable lampposts and irresistible cannonballs, and one way of handling God and sin. However, I want to look specifically at a set of things God allegedly cannot do and see if they compromise our notion of divine omnipotence. Yeager Hudson gets us started by considering five things that God allegedly cannot do. They are 1) the logically contradictory, 2) altering the past, 3) causing the free acts of other agents, 4) doing evil or sin, and 5) creating rather than merely exemplifying universals.[32] I suggest that most puzzles about omnipotence fall under one of these five items. I would add another item, namely, does God as immutable have the power to forgive sin?

First, if God cannot actualize a logical contradiction, is that a limit on divine omnipotence? Here I side with many in the Christian tradition in saying no. As I defined omnipotence, God has all the logically possible powers that a being with God's attributes can have, but power to actualize a contradiction is not a power any being can have. It isn't even clear that we know what it would mean to have power to create a round square or a married bachelor, or to make it the case that I am both typing and not typing this sentence now. As Kenny says, power to φ can only be explained by those who know what φ-ing is, and in these cases, it is not clear that anyone knows what such powers are.[33]

The second alleged limitation on God's power is the matter of changing the past. Some may argue via an appeal to backward causation or to time travel into the past that there is such a power, but it is dubious that this is so. The problem again seems to be one of logical contradiction. Take as an example the assassination of President Kennedy in 1963. For God (or anyone else) to have power to alter the past means that right *now,* even though Kennedy was assassinated, it is possible that he should not have been assassinated. This is a contradiction, and there is no such power, so God's failure to have power to change the past in no way disqualifies him as omnipotent.

The third alleged limitation to God's power is that he cannot cause the free actions of his creatures. This problem is especially acute for those committed to libertarian free will, which says that an action is free only if it is not causally determined. However, as we shall see when discussing divine providence and human freedom, this is not the only way to define freedom. According to a form of determinism known as compatibilism, an action is free so long as there are antecedent conditions which decisively incline the agent's will in one way or another without constraining it. To act without constraint means to act in accord with one's desires. If one adopts this notion of free will, then God can have power to causally determine the free (compatabilistically) actions of others. Hence, divine omnipotence is not compromised if one holds compatibilism.

If one holds libertarian free will instead, the way to handle this issue is to assert that the alleged inability of God is actually no inability at all, for it imagines something that is self-contradictory. It imagines an ability to causally determine actions that are not causally determined ("free" in that sense). Since this notion is clearly self-contradictory, there is no such power, and God's omnipotence is in no sense compromised.

The fourth area of concern is the compatibility of omnipotence and divine impeccability. Here there are two different avenues one might take. Invoking our definition of divine omnipotence and remembering that one of God's attributes is holiness or moral perfection, we may go Devenish's route and simply claim that God cannot sin. This is no limitation, however, because thinking that God can sin imagines the logically impossible. Thinking that God has power to sin means that he, as morally perfect, has power to act in a way that no morally perfect being can act. Clearly, the notion of 'having power as morally perfect to act in a way that no morally perfect being can act' is self-contradictory, and no one has power to actualize a contradiction.

This is an attractive resolution to the problem, and Thomas Morris suggests another. As Morris explains and I have argued elsewhere,[34] the idea of someone being able to do something may be understood in various ways. It may mean that someone has the opportunity to do the thing. It may also mean that one has the skill, practical knowledge (where required), or the power to perform the action. It may also mean that one has the moral character traits that lead him to obey moral rules.[35]

Given these distinctions, there are certain senses in which God has power to sin. There is opportunity for him to do so. Whatever skill and practical knowledge are needed to commit a sin, he would likely have it. But does he have power to sin? Here again I find Morris very helpful. Many might think God does not have such power, because they equate the following two propositions: 1) God cannot sin, and 2) God lacks power to sin. Though these two propositions may appear equivalent, they are not necessarily so. Morris argues that when one makes claim 1), one intends to say that it is impossible that God sin, but that is not the same thing as what proposition 2) says.[36] To illustrate the difference between propositions 1) and 2), Morris offers the following:

> Suppose Smith, a policeman, raises a 38 calibre hand gun in his right hand, aims it at Jones, whom he correctly believes to be an innocent person and for no good reason squeezes the trigger with the aim of killing Jones, which is thereby achieved. Surely Smith has thereby sinned, or done evil. Suppose now a parallel story that Smith, a policeman, raises the 38, aims it at Jones, whom he correctly believes to be a mass murderer about to commit his next heinous act which otherwise cannot be stopped, and squeezes the trigger with the aim of killing Jones, which is thereby achieved. In this second story we can suppose that what Smith does is, in the circumstances morally permissable [sic], however regrettable. Thus, in the first story he sins, in the second he does not. In the first story does Smith exercize a power which he does not exercize in the second story, a distinct power to sin? By supposition, he does not. The causal powers exercized remain, by hypothesis, invariant between the two stories.[37]

In light of this analysis, Morris thinks we must look more closely at the meaning of the phrase "the power to sin." Is it some distinct power to commit evil? In light of the examples just mentioned, evidently not. Now it seems to me that this is fundamentally correct. So-called power to sin is just power to act. In certain circumstances, performing that act is moral, whereas in other circumstances performing the act is immoral. Take, for example, the action of telling a lie. In order to tell a lie, one must have the power to communicate. Does God have such a power? Theologians of various religions have argued that he does. But it should be clear, then, that there is no power to lie that is separate from the power to tell the truth. In both cases, one simply uses the power to communicate a proposition. The difference is that in some circumstances the proposition will be true, whereas in others it might be false. And some propositions express a falsehood regardless of the circumstances, whereas others do not. The same abilities needed to communicate the lie, are, however, also required to communicate the truth. As to God, he has power to do what is necessary in order to communicate a truth or a lie. Because of his moral perfection, however, he never uses that power to communicate a falsehood.

If we follow this approach to the issue of divine omnipotence and impeccability, it means that for many sins, God does have the power to perform them, but because of his holiness, he cannot do so. Since power to sin is power to act in particular circumstances (and God can do those actions), God has the power to do these actions. However, it is impossible for him to use it because of his moral perfection. Because God is morally perfect, he does not have the power to do any act *as an act of sin,* i.e., in circumstances where doing the act would mean committing a sin.[38]

Regardless of which of these two answers one adopts, the problem of divine omnipotence and impeccability can be solved. Since that is so, divine omnipotence as we have defined it is in no way compromised. What about the fifth item over which God apparently has no control? Here the question is whether God creates according to "blueprints," "patterns," or "universals," and if so, whether he decides what these possibles are or whether he has no control over what they are or ability to change them. There are several ways one might answer this issue. For example, one might deny that there are such things as universals. If so, there can be no question about divine omnipotence in regard to ability to control or change universals.

A second approach to this problem claims that there are universals which express all the possible things God might create. However, what those universals are and whether they exist at all is subject to God's will. Moreover, God decides which universals he will actualize in our world. Theologians who want to maintain that God has control even over the creation of the possibles would likely handle the problem this way. Some forms of theonomy hold this sort of position.[39]

A third response to this problem says that universals exist, but God did not create them. Since they express whatever is logically possible, they must have always existed, i.e., they are coeternal with God. God as supremely rational would always know all concepts of whatever is thinkable, because as omniscient he knows whatever can be known. According to this metaphysic, however, God's inability to create the possibles or change them is insignificant. It only matters to someone holding a theonomous metaphysic, according to which there is some deficiency in God if the possibles are not subject to his will. Those holding a more rationalistic metaphysic would find no problem in any divine inability to create or change the possibles. Given the nature of the possibles and of thought, creating or changing them is not something anyone could do. Of course that would require God to have powers to do the logically impossible, and, as already shown, claiming that God lacks a power when there is no such power does not denigrate his omnipotence.

A final thing God allegedly cannot do is forgive sinners. Recently, some have argued that God cannot do this because his omniscience and moral perfection logically preclude conditions necessary for forgiveness. The argument is that forgiveness may be understood either noncognitively or cognitively. Noncognitively, forgiveness occurs within the context of healing broken relationships. In that context, the injured party will likely feel resentment and the injuring party (if repentant) will feel sorrow. God in this case would be the injured party, but, then, he could not forgive, for an omnipotent being cannot be vulnerable (as is someone who could be hurt by others' actions), a morally perfect being is incapable of resentment, and as immutable, God could not change his feelings toward the sinner if there is repentance.

A more cognitive account of forgiveness construes it as pardon, remitting of punishment. Here again, it is argued that God cannot forgive, for this notion of forgiveness involves reversal of judgment, and it is impossible for an omniscient and immutable being to reverse a judgment. So, God, though omnipotent, is incapable of forgiving sin.[40]

In response, these problems are not difficult to handle when we remember how immutability was defined. The change in relationship (from anger to blessing) required of noncognitive forgiveness is totally within the power of an omnipotent and immutable God. While it would be problematic if God harbored a grievance against a sinner, there is no indication that God does this. Scripture teaches that God hates sin, but it does not depict him as vengeful or as just looking for an opportunity to judge sinners and punish them beyond what their sin deserves. Nor does God delight in punishment at all. All the negative emotions that humans display do not apply to God, so there is no reason why God cannot forgive in this noncognitive sense of forgiveness.

As to forgiving in the more cognitive sense, God can do this as well. In virtue of his unchanging moral standards, when sinners repent, God has obligated himself to pardon them (cognitive sense of forgiveness). For theologians such as myself who believe that God has decreed all things according to his own purposes, the repentance is not unforeseen or unplanned. So his changed relationship does not change his knowledge or immutability.[41]

In closing this discussion of divine omnipotence, we would do well to recognize that this attribute does not obligate God to do everything he can do. For example, God has power to make me a millionaire, and though I might wish for him to do so, his ability to do this in no way obligates him to do it. God's moral attributes, including his wisdom, ensure that whatever he chooses in relation to this matter will be good, just, and loving, but those moral attributes do not obligate him to do this good and loving thing for me. Nor do they obligate him to do for me every loving, etc., thing he could do. Whatever God does expresses his omnipotence and his moral attributes, but omnipotence does not oblige him to do everything he can do.

In sum, the notion of divine omnipotence I am proposing adequately covers all the things that God can do, according to Scripture, and it also allows us to account for all the things he cannot do without denigrating divine omnipotence. The picture that emerges is of a being with unlimited power to do all the things a being with God's other perfections could possibly do. He cannot do everything whatsoever, nor is he required to do everything he can do, but anything we would want or expect a being of God's character to do, he has power to do. The king who cares has power to show tangibly that he does care for us!

SOVEREIGNTY

Divine sovereignty or God's sovereign will is closely related to divine omnipotence. Whereas omnipotence tells how much and which powers God has, sovereignty clarifies the extent to which God uses those powers. This is significant, because God could possess all the powers a being with his nature could have and yet never exercise them or do so only occasionally. Moreover, God might constantly use his powers over everything except human free will, or it could be that he created our universe and then decided not to intervene in it at all, not even in the natural events that occur. The attribute of divine sovereignty clarifies which of these suppositions, if any, is correct.

Divine sovereignty can be defined as God's power of absolute self-determination. This, of course, needs explanation and amplification. God has this power in virtue of his ability to deliberate and make choices, as opposed to others deciding for him. Moreover, self-determination means that God does his own actions, and that they are in accord with his choices.

What has been said so far is also true of humans and angels (assuming that they are free in some sense), but of course, they are not sovereign. What differentiates divine self-determination from human and angelic is that God's self-determination is absolute. This involves two main things. On the one hand, God's choices are determined only by his own nature and purposes. In contrast, human and angelic decisions are often decisively influenced by factors other than their own nature or purposes, by others' actions and by various events that happen. To say that God's sovereignty is absolute also means that his choices and control cover all things.

This notion of divine sovereignty means, of course, that God is the ultimate, final, and complete authority over everything and everyone. Whatever happens stems from his decisions and control. God's sovereign will is also free, for nobody forces him to do anything, and whatever he does is in accord with his own purposes and wishes. Theologians who have held these views about divine sovereignty have also claimed that all of God's decisions about what would occur were made at once, prior to his creating the universe. We also saw in our study of immutability that God's will and purposes are immutable.

Once God decided what would occur, he didn't change his mind. Finally, God's will is efficacious, i.e., whatever he decided about the course of events and actions in our world will occur.

This is a strong notion of divine sovereignty, one typically held by Calvinist theologians. I believe the biblical evidence about the areas of divine control support this understanding of sovereignty. However, some think it too strong, and in fairness to them, I must clarify how they understand this attribute. Many thinkers outside the evangelical camp deny that God has this attribute altogether. Proponents of process theism, for example, deny not only divine sovereignty but also divine omnipotence.

On the other hand, even within evangelicalism this strong notion has its critics. What typically leads them to object is their commitment to libertarian free will, the kind of free will espoused by traditional Arminians and the open view of God. As we shall see more clearly in our handling of divine sovereignty and human freedom, such freedom is incompatible with the strong view of divine sovereignty defined in this section. What proponents of libertarian free will do with God's sovereignty depends on the theologian in question. I shall develop this in more detail in the chapters on providence; for now I note two possible libertarian responses. Some hold that because God gave humans libertarian free will, he only maintains a general control over all things which normally does not interfere with our freedom, but he still maintains the right to intervene in our world in order to correct or overturn our mistakes and to ensure that his general goals and purposes are not frustrated. Proponents of this view usually deny that God has detailed purposes or goals for every-thing and everyone that cover even the minutia of life. Instead, he has general purposes that he wants to and will achieve, and within those general goals there are various possible avenues to their achievement. God, not wanting to abridge human freedom, is more than happy to leave open the exact route for accomplishing his purposes.[42]

Others in the Arminian tradition agree with Calvinists that biblical data on divine sovereignty do teach that in principle God has all the power and authority Calvinists claim he has. However, they believe that in order to make room for human free will, God decided not to exercise all of it. Since this was his own unforced decision, he is still fully sovereign.[43]

In turning to Scripture we find that it teaches that God controls everything. Some verses make this general point, and others speak of God's control over specific things. When we put these verses together, we conclude that divine sovereignty covers all things.[44] Though we will examine these passages in greater detail when discussing divine sovereignty and human freedom, in what follows I present a survey of the biblical material.

Various passages teach that God controls all things. In Eph 1:11 Paul writes of Christ, "In Him also we have obtained an inheritance, having been predes-tined according to His purpose who works all things after the counsel of His will." Though the specific subject is our salvation, Paul says that the one who predestines us to salvation also does all other things according to his will and purposes. In Ps 115:3 (NIV) the psalmist writes that "Our God is in heaven; he does whatever pleases him." After his "audience" with God, Job confesses (Job 42:2, NIV), "I know that you can do all things; no plan of yours can be thwarted" (see also Dan 4:35).

Scripture also portrays God's sovereign control in creating and preserving all things. He rules and controls the forces of nature as well as the activities of human beings. In Job 10:9 and 33:6 we see that God has made us. On several occasions, biblical writers teach mankind's total dependence on God by means of an analogy to the potter and the clay (Isa 29:16; 64:8). In Romans 9, in answer to those who think it unfair that the God who controls everything holds us accountable for the evil we do, Paul uses this image to show that God, as the potter, has the right to do as he pleases with the clay. In contrast, the clay has no right to complain and accuse God of wrongdoing (Rom 9:19-21). As to God's preservation of all things, Paul reminded the Athenians (Acts 17:28, NIV) that in God "we live and move and have our being." Moreover, as the psalmist says (Ps 135:5-7), God controls the forces of nature. Jonah's experience (Jonah 1) and Christ's power to calm the sea and the wind (Matt 8:23-26) illustrate this.

Ps 50:10 (KJV) sums up God's sovereign control over creation. As creator of everything, he also owns it all: "For every beast of the forest is mine, and the cattle upon a thousand hills."

In addition, biblical authors affirm that God is sovereign over government. This is true in two respects. It is true in that ultimately all rule belongs to God. He is the ultimate king, his kingdom lasts forever, and it includes all peoples of all times (1 Chron 29:11-12; Dan 7:13-14). Because God is the ultimate ruler whose kingdom is everlasting, Jesus concludes the Lord's prayer by saying (Matt 6:13), "For Thine is the kingdom, and the power, and the glory, forever. Amen." In comparison to God, we can say with Isaiah (40:15), "Behold, the nations are like a drop from a bucket, and are regarded as a speck of dust on the scales; behold, He lifts up the islands like fine dust."

God is also sovereign over governments in that during the years of human rule before God fully inaugurates his complete rule, kings and kingdoms are ultimately under God's control. Paul says this to believers living in the capital city of one of the most powerful human governments of all time (Rom 13:1). Rome had great power only because God gave it such might (see also Dan 4:32, 35 in regard to Nebuchadnezzar's rule; and Acts 17:26). Because he controls governments, God can use them to accomplish his purposes. In Isaiah 10 God predicts the judgment of Israel at the hand of Assyria. He then predicts that after Assyria has done his bidding, he will punish Assyria for its sins. For any who think this unfair, the answer is (Isa 10:15) "Is the axe to boast itself over the one who chops with it? Is the saw to exalt itself over the one who wields it? That would be like a club wielding those who lift it, or like a rod lifting him who is not wood." Human governments are the axe, the saw, the club, the rod, but they are all instruments in God's hands; he is the one who wields them (see also Jer 18:6). The writer of Proverbs (21:1) sums it up as follows: "The king's heart is like channels of water in the hand of the LORD; He turns it wherever He wishes."

God is also sovereign over all aspects of salvation. He chose Christ as Savior, and he was in control of Christ's sufferings in life and death. Speaking of the decision that Christ should die, Peter says (1 Pet 1:20, KJV; see also Acts 2:23) that he "verily was foreordained before the foundation of the world." Jesus recognized this as the Father's will, and submitted to it (Luke 22:42).

God also chose those who would be saved. In Eph 1:4, Paul says that God "chose us in Him before the foundation of the world." In verse 5, Paul tells the elect that God has "predestined us to adoption as sons through Jesus Christ to Himself, according to the kind intention of His will." That is, this did not happen because we deserved it or because God foresaw that we would believe anyway. It happened entirely at the kind intention of God's will (see Eph 1:11). Lest any think this choice depends on us, Paul is absolutely clear that it depends solely on God. As Paul says about election (Rom 9:15-16), "I will have mercy on whom I have mercy, and I will have compassion on whom I have compassion. So then it does not depend on the man who wills or the man who runs, but on God who has mercy."

God not only elects believers but also brings salvation to each person who believes. John clarifies that God is the giver of the new birth, and that he gives it according to his own will, not according to our efforts or our merit (John 1:12-13; see also 1 Pet 1:3 and Jas 1:18). Moreover, God sovereignly controls various aspects of the Christian's life and walk. Each believer has spiritual gifts that are to be used in serving the body of Christ, but which gift(s) one gets depends entirely on the Holy Spirit's decision (1 Cor 12:11). In addition, Paul shows that God controls the sanctification process. In Phil 2:12-13 he instructs his readers to move on in their walk with God, but then adds, "For it is God who is at work in you, both to will and to work for His good pleasure" (v. 13). It is also true that the afflictions that come into our lives as believers are under the sovereign control of God's will. In 1 Pet 3:17 Peter writes, "For it is better, if God should will it so, that you suffer for doing what is right rather than for doing what is wrong." The "if" clause is a first-class condition in the Greek. Such conditions are in accord with fact; that is, what is imagined is in fact what will occur.

Although many might grant God sovereign control over our salvation, they would deny that his control extends beyond that to the circumstances of our daily life and the manner and timing of our death. However, Scripture teaches otherwise. We must affirm, for example, what Hannah said of God (1 Sam 2:6-8), "The LORD kills and makes alive; He brings down to Sheol and raises up. The LORD makes poor and rich; He brings low, He also exalts. He raises the poor from the dust, He lifts the needy from the ash heap to make them sit with nobles, and inherit a seat of honor; for the pillars of the earth are the

Lord's, and He set the world on them." It is easy to forget God's sovereign control and to make our plans as though we control such matters, but James says (Jas 4:15), "you ought to say, 'If the Lord wills, we shall live and also do this or that'" (see the example of Paul on various occasions: Acts 18:21; Rom 15:32). Indeed, God controls our lives, and we would do well to recognize that (Prov 16:9, 33). As a result of God's sovereign control and his goodness, Paul says (Rom 8:28) that "we know that God causes all things to work together for good to those who love God, to those who are called according to His purpose." In the next verses Paul explains that this is so because God controls all aspects of our salvation. Without God's sovereign control over the details of our lives, Paul could not say what he does in verse 28.

If God controls all things, does he also control the evil deeds of angels and men? This seems to follow logically from God's control of all things, but it seems odd. Nonetheless, there are biblical indications that this is so. In addition to verses already cited that teach God's choice and control over all things, there are specific evil deeds that are said to be under God's control. The case of Job is an example (Job 1–2). Satan slanders both God and Job's love of God, but he must get God's permission before he can afflict Job. Even when God grants that permission, he sets up certain boundaries. In the first wave of affliction, Satan cannot touch Job's body, and in the second wave, Satan cannot take Job's life. What Satan does to Job is evil, and yet it is under God's control (Job affirms this in 2:10).

Scripture also teaches that God controls the evil deeds of human beings. This is true of what Joseph's brothers did to him (Gen 50:20): "you meant evil against me, but God meant it for good in order to bring about this present result, to preserve many people alive." Similarly, Paul suggests in Rom 11:11-14 that Israel's rejection of Christ was just part of God's overall strategy for winning both Gentiles and Jews to Christ. Israel's fall opened the door to the Gentiles, but God intended that giving salvation to the Gentiles would make the Jews jealous when they saw Gentiles enjoying the blessings of salvation. God planned to use their jealousy to turn them to Christ. Moreover, Peter says on the day of Pentecost (Acts 2:23) that wicked men killed Christ, but this was all according to "the predetermined plan and foreknowledge of God."

These passages raise significant theological and philosophical questions, but those questions cannot expunge the clear biblical statements that God as sovereign does foreordain and have control over these evil deeds without himself being evil. Process theists, open view proponents, and many more traditional Arminian theologians deem such views repugnant and think Calvinists cannot satisfactorily answer the problems they raise. The issue of God's relation to evil is a thorny one for all sides, but I believe it is resolvable even by a Calvinist. The place for that discussion, however, is the chapter on providence and evil. For now, I simply affirm that Scripture predicates a sovereign will (as defined in this section) of God.

OMNISCIENCE

Having unlimited control over the world would not amount to much if God's knowledge was finite. In fact, a relatively ignorant God with absolute power to do anything he wanted would be frightening, for his creatures might constantly fear that he would use that power in ignorance of the truth. He might not know who was truly guilty of sin, and hence might punish the righteous and bless the wicked, or without fully understanding the natural order, he might perform a miracle which, because of ignorance, produces something monstrous.

These and other like fears are unwarranted, however, for our God is infinite in knowledge. The Judaeo-Christian tradition, in accord with Scripture, has maintained that God is omniscient. As with omnipotence, omniscience is not easy to define, and even after settling on a definition, there are still questions about what exactly God can know. Moreover, there are biblical passages that appear to say that there are things which God does not know but later learns, and there are passages that suggest that God can and does forget certain things such as the sins of repentant sinners. How all of this can be true in light of divine omniscience has puzzled theologians throughout church history, and some of these debates continue in our own day.

The Bible and Divine Omniscience

Let us begin by seeing what Scripture says about God's knowledge, and then we can tackle the matter of definition and other questions that arise about omniscience. There are no biblical words in Hebrew or Greek for omniscience, nor is there some biblical word that translators have rendered as omniscience. Rather, biblical writers simply describe the various things God knows, and they also mention things he does not know. We turn first to verses that address God's knowledge in general, and the basic point they make is that God knows all things in general and that his understanding and knowledge are unlimited. In Job 36:4 we read that God is perfect in knowledge (see also Job 37:16). The writer of Hebrews concurs (4:13, NIV), "Nothing in all creation is hidden from God's sight. Everything is uncovered and laid bare before the eyes of him to whom we must give account" (see also Acts 15:18).

In light of this all-encompassing knowledge we read in Job 21:22, "Can anyone teach God knowledge, in that He judges those on high?" And Isaiah asks (40:14), "With whom did He consult and who gave Him understanding? And who taught Him in the path of justice and taught Him knowledge, and informed Him of the way of understanding?" The answers are obvious; no one teaches God anything, and he has sought counsel from no one (see also Job 12:13 and Prov 2:6). Because of the depths of divine understanding, Paul exults over God's plan for saving Jew and Gentile alike (Rom 11:33).

Biblical writers also mention specific things God knows. He even knows things that possibly could occur, even if they never do. For example, in Matt 11:21, Jesus says, "Woe to you, Chorazin! Woe to you, Bethsaida! For if the miracles had occurred in Tyre and Sidon which occurred in you, they would have repented long ago in sackcloth and ashes." In Jeremiah 38, Jeremiah speaks for the Lord and outlines for King Zedekiah two lines of actions and then he tells him what will happen if he chooses one option or the other (Jer 38:17-23; see also 1 Sam 23:11-12).

Turning from possible things to actual, we find that God's knowledge is indeed complete. He knows the details related to the material world in which we live. He made the physical universe, and did so in accord with his knowledge and wisdom (Jer 51:15; Ps 136:5). The psalmist writes (Ps 104:19), "He made the moon for the seasons; the sun knows the place of its setting." The sun "knows" what it is to do because God has made it to function appropriately, and he could not have done so if he did not know enough to make it function properly in our universe.

Not only did God create according to his knowledge, but after creating, God knows everything about the physical universe and its function. The psalmist writes (Ps 147:4-5), "He counts the number of the stars; He gives names to all of them. Great is our Lord, and abundant in strength; His understanding is infinite" (see also Job 28:23-24). God is also aware of what happens within the animal world (Ps 50:11 and Matt 10:29).

There are also ample verses that teach God's awareness of all humans in general and of the specifics of their lives in particular. In Ps 33:13-15 we learn that God is aware of all people even to the point of knowing what each of us is doing moment by moment. Because God is aware of all people, it is foolish to think that we could hide from him (Jer 23:24). Indeed, God knows about all of us. Hagar shows that she knows this (Gen 16:13), and when Israel was in Egyptian bondage, God knew what was happening (Exod 3:7). God knows not only what his own are doing but also what his enemies are doing and thinking (Gen 18:20-21; Isa 37:28; 66:18).

God's knowledge of us extends to the very details of our lives. What he says about Jeremiah (1:5) is surely true of all of us: "Before I formed you in the womb I knew you." Most likely, "I knew you" means more than just intellectual awareness of Jeremiah, though it surely means at least that. It means knowing by relationship, i.e., God knew Jeremiah in that he established a special relation with him to ordain a special task for him in life. Similarly, God knows each of us while we are in our mother's womb and already has plans for our lives. Ps 139:1-4 is a well-loved passage that teaches that God knows everything about us and that nothing can happen to us that will catch God by surprise: "O LORD, Thou hast searched me and known me. Thou dost know when I sit down and when I rise up; Thou dost understand my thought from afar. Thou dost scrutinize my path and my lying down, and art intimately acquainted with all my ways. Even before there is a word on my tongue, behold, O LORD, Thou dost know it all."

The Lord knows other details about our lives as well. The psalmist says (Ps 56:8), "Thou has taken account My wanderings; put my tears in Thy bottle; are they not in Thy book?" Jesus tells his disciples (Matt 10:30) that "the very hairs of your head are all numbered" (see also Job 14:16). God even knows our specific character traits and abilities, as we see in relation to Moses and Aaron (see Exod 4:14; 33:12, 17; Deut 29:16; and 2 Kgs 19:27).

God knows our hearts and innermost thoughts (Prov 24:12; Ps 139:2; Acts 15:8). Because God knows our innermost thoughts, it is foolish to think we can hide them from him (Isa 29:15; 40:27-28). In various passages as well, the writers record the Lord's word to an individual or to the nation of Israel. God says very clearly that he knows what they are thinking (Ezek 11:5; Deut 31:21; and Gen 20:6).

Not only does God know what we are thinking, but he also knows whether our thoughts and deeds are evil or good. This is so because he knows the difference between moral right and wrong. We see this in the various OT and NT passages wherein the Lord sets forth his moral law, but we also get a hint of this when we hear God's reaction to the sin of Adam and Eve (Gen 3:22, KJV): "And the LORD God said, Behold, the man is become as one of us, to know good and evil."

It is indeed a sobering thought that God knows our evil deeds. Even more, God judges those deeds, and of course he could not justly judge us for something he knew nothing about. Scripture shows that he knows; as the writer of Proverbs says (15:3, 11), "The eyes of the LORD are in every place, watching the evil and the good. . . . Sheol and Abaddon lie open before the LORD, how much more the hearts of men!" (see also Prov 22:12; Ps 94:9-10). Because God knows, on various occasions he presents his indictment of his people Israel and promises judgment (Amos 5:12; Jer 29:23 and Hos 5:3 cf. 2 Chron 16:9).

While it can be frightening to realize that God knows our evil deeds, it is encouraging to remember that he also knows our righteous deeds. Those who live according to God's precepts can echo Job's words (Job 23:10, KJV), "But he knoweth the way that I take: when he hath tried me, I shall come forth as gold." Further evidence that God knows the deeds of the righteous comes from the NT truth that someday believers will stand before the judgment seat of Christ and receive rewards for faithfulness in the Christian life (2 Cor 5; 1 Cor 3:11-14). How could God reward these deeds if he did not know what they are? Moreover, at the Judgment of the Nations (Matt 25:31-40) the sheep are told to inherit the kingdom. The Lord explains that this happens in part because of their good deeds toward him, by doing good to those he calls his brethren. The sheep are surprised to hear that they have done these good deeds, but the Lord shows that he knows.

If God's knowledge is all-comprehensive, it is only logical that he would know the future. In Scripture there are many predictive prophecies which show that he does. Beyond that, there are passages that state that God decided to do certain things, and those decisions were made before the foundations of the world. A few biblical examples illustrate the point. In Isa 46:9-10 the Lord makes the general point that he knows things that have not yet happened. The Lord says, "Remember the former things long past, for I am God, and there is no other; I am God, and there is no one like Me, declaring the end from the beginning and from ancient times things which have not been done, saying, 'My purpose will be established, and I will accomplish all My good pleasure.'" Christ's coming and his death were also foreknown and foreordained by God (1 Pet 1:20; Acts 2:23).

In addition, God predicted specific future events. For example, he knew what Cyrus would do (Isa 44:28). Christ's virgin birth is predicted in Isa 7:14, and Micah even predicts the exact place where the Messiah would be born (Mic 5:2). The succession of kings and kingdoms was predicted and recorded in Daniel 2, 7, and 8, even to the point that Daniel 8 names the second and third of the four kingdoms of Daniel 2 and 7 as Medo-Persia and Greece.

Because God has decided and knows what will occur, Daniel calls him the giver of knowledge. In Daniel 2, the point is about knowledge of the future events of nations. In Dan 2:21 we read, "And it is He who changes the times and the epochs; he removes kings and establishes kings; he gives wisdom to wise men, and knowledge to men of understanding."[45]

The biblical data presented thus far seem to warrant the conclusion that God knows all things. Nevertheless, there are other verses which suggest there is something that God does not know which he later comes to know. A few examples make the point. After the trial of Abraham's faith with respect to offering up Isaac on Mount Moriah, the Lord says to Abraham (Gen 22:12), "now I know that you fear God, since you have not withheld your son, your only son, from Me." On another occasion, God says that Israel's wilderness wanderings were in part for the Lord to determine whether the people of Israel would follow his command-ments (Deut 8:2). In addition, the Lord gave Israel various tests for determining whether a prophet was from God or was a false prophet. In Deuteronomy 13 the Lord offers a series of tests, and one of them was that even if a prophet's words come true, the people must see whether the prophet uses his prophecy to lead people to worship another God. In verse 3, God explains why he would allow such a false prophet in their midst: "you shall not listen to the words of that prophet or that dreamer of dreams; for the LORD your God is testing you to find out if you love the LORD your God with all your heart and with all your soul."

In addition, in Job and Psalms we read the following: "Let me be weighed in an even balance that God may know mine integrity" (Job 31:6, KJV); and, "Search me, O God, and know my heart; try me and know my anxious thoughts" (Ps 139:23). In both cases, the writers seem to think that God doesn't exactly know their spiritual condition but could learn the truth about them if he just examined them closely (see also 2 Chron 32:31).

Two other verses are worthy of mention. Matt 25:1ff. is the parable of the ten virgins. When the Lord returns, he says to those unprepared for his com-ing (v. 12), "Truly I say to you, I do not know you." This parable is meant to teach preparedness at any moment for the Lord's return, but it seems to suggest that when the Lord returns, there will be some that he will not know.

A final verse is Jer 31:34, which speaks of a future day when Israel will turn to God. The Lord says about that time, "'And they shall not teach again, each man his neighbor and each man his brother, saying, "Know the LORD," for they shall all know Me, from the least of them to the greatest of them,' declares the LORD, 'for I will forgive their iniquity, and their sin I will remember no more.'" The last phrase of this verse seems odd in light of omniscience. Ps 103:12 assures repentant sinners that "as far as the east is from the west, so far has He removed our transgressions from us." This shows that our sins will not be counted against us, but it does not say God will actually forget what we have done. The Jeremiah 31 passage says God will actually forget the sins of repentant Israel. There is no reason to think he will do that for them and not for the rest of us. But how can a God who knows everything ever forget anything?

This last point suggests another. If God forgets the sins of the repentant, it seems that he must remember the sins of the unrepentant. Since sin and evil cause him grief, does that mean that for eternity God will grieve over the sins of the unbelieving and grieve over their lost estate? If so, how can he be a happy and joyous God who will celebrate salvation and celebrate his own perfection with the redeemed forever? If God does not forget these sins and the plight of the lost, a mood of celebration hardly seems possible. But, as omniscient, how could he forget?

How should we respond to these concerns? Initially, I note that some of these passages will be handled in more detail in my discussion of divine providence, especially the chapter on freedom and foreknowledge. For now I note that they are not all of one piece but fall into several different groups. For example, the Genesis 22, Deuteronomy 8, and Deuteronomy 13 passages fall into one category. It is unlikely that the Lord really did not know the things mentioned in these passages. Instead, the Lord's point is to *demonstrate* especially for his people what he already knows to be true, and he wants these tests to strengthen the faith of those who experience them. Whether or not these verses are anthropomorphisms is unclear, but in light of other verses which show that God knows the thoughts and hearts of the evil and the righteous, it is hard to see these verses as offering information that God really did not know.

As to Job 31 and Psalm 139, these are the words of Job and the psalmist as they plead for divine justice and assert their own moral rectitude. In light of other passages which show that God knows our heart's condition and our deeds, it is unthinkable that God would learn something about a person's thoughts and actions that he did not already know. Nor do Job or the psalmist likely think that would happen. It is best to understand these verses as the person's assertion that they are righteous, and because of that, they ask God to act in their behalf. Again, it is unclear whether these verses are anthropomorphic or whether they are a poetic way of the writer expressing his own moral purity and asking for God's help. Likewise, Jer 15:15 cannot mean that God needs to learn something he does not already know. Rather, the prophet says that he has stood for God, and that he wants God to punish his persecutors and bless him.

What about the Matthew 25 passage? As already suggested, some passages speak about knowing someone where the idea is not simple intellectual knowledge but knowing by personal relationship. When Christ says he knows his sheep, it means that he has a special spiritual relationship with them. So, when in Matthew 25 there are some people God does not know, in light of clear passages already cited that say God knows all people, the verses most likely mean that God does not know these people in the sense of having a special spiritual relationship with them. But he knows intellectually who they are and everything about them that can be known.

As to Jeremiah 31, the simplest way to handle it is to see it as a poetic expression of the truth that God will forgive his people and not count their sins against them. If, instead, one thinks this should be interpreted more literally so that God removes something from his mind, the most likely explanation would be that God, in a way we cannot understand, blocks this information from his thoughts. Relatedly, what about God's knowledge of the sins of the unrepentant? We must return to this issue after discussing more fully the nature of omniscience, but even now we can say that though God knows about the plight of the lost, in a way beyond our comprehension God does not think about such things but focuses on things that bring him joy, instead.

Defining Divine Omniscience

Having examined biblical teaching about God's knowledge, we are in a better position to define omniscience. Since biblical data seem to suggest that God knows all things, the most natural place to begin is to say that divine omniscience is that perfection of God in virtue of which he knows everything. Others add that divine omniscience means that God knows all propositions, and he knows which ones are true and which are false. Another way that omniscience has been defined is that it means knowing everything there is to know. Often, proponents of this definition add a list of things that are unknowable. This definition is especially prevalent among those who believe that God knows all things and yet don't want to say that he knows the future for fear that such knowledge would rule out human free will. Hence, God knows everything there is to know; the future just is not something that can be known.

So far, then, we have the following proposals as a definition of divine omniscience:

(1) Divine omniscience means God knows all things.
(2) Divine omniscience means God knows all true propositions.
(3) Divine omniscience means God knows all propositions and knows which are true and which are false.
(4) Divine omniscience means God knows everything there is to know.

At first glance, it might appear that any of these four will do, for the matter of defining divine omniscience is not difficult. This is the opinion of Anthony Kenny, whose lead we followed on omnipotence. Kenny explains, "Omniscience appears to be analogous to omnipotence: just as omniscience is knowing everything, so omnipotence is being able to do everything. But *whereas it is easy to define what it is to be omniscient,* it is not so easy to define omnipotence."[46]

Though it may be easy to define omniscience *per se* (I am dubious about that), my contention is that it is by no means easy to define *divine* omniscience. In fact, I believe that none of the four options already offered is entirely adequate, though all contain helpful elements. I believe divine omniscience is hard to define, because a series of problems surround the notion. Those problems suggest either that 1) there is something that the Judaeo-Christian God does not or cannot know, or that 2) God's intellect does not function the way we might expect an omniscient being's intellect to operate. In what follows, I want first to raise those problems and to address them in ways consistent with biblical revelation and evangelical Christian theology. After addressing them, we can offer a more accurate definition of divine omniscience and better understand how the divine intellect functions.

In particular, I want to raise four problems about omniscience. I plan to address most of them in this section, but some will receive attention in another part of the book. The first and most frequently discussed issue is the question of how divine omniscience relates to freedom. This question usually arises over human freedom, but in contemporary discussions it is also raised in regard to divine freedom.

Those who hold what is called libertarian free will claim that an act is only genuinely free if it is not causally determined. Ethicists add that unless agents act freely, they cannot be held morally responsible for their actions. Now if God is omniscient, it seems that he must know all things, including the future actions of all agents, and our survey of biblical teaching shows why Christians have held that view. But if God knows what I will do on a given occasion, it appears that it is not within my power to do otherwise. God's knowledge does not cause my action, but if he really knows it, it will occur. But if it is certain to happen, then how am I free to do other than what God knows?

This a problem not only for human freedom but also for divine freedom. God has free will, even absolute freedom (self-determination), as we saw when discussing divine sovereignty. If God knows all future acts and events, he must know everything that he will do. But, if he knows what he will do before he does it, it appears that he is not free to change his mind and do other than what he *knows* he will do.

This is a very odd implication of divine foreknowledge, but the picture gets even worse. Remember that one is only morally accountable when acting freely. Otherwise one is neither praiseworthy when one does good nor blameworthy when one does wrong. As applied to God, this means that since he foreknows everything he will do, none of his actions are free, and in that case, God is not morally responsible for what he does. So it seems that if God foreknows his future acts, he can be neither moral nor immoral, but such consequences are inimical to evangelical Christian beliefs about God.

Theologians and philosophers have wrestled with the problem of freedom and foreknowledge for centuries. From what I have said about it, one can see why anyone who feels the force of this argument would be uncomfortable about defining divine omniscience along the lines of any of definitions (1)-(3) offered above. Even the fourth is unsatisfactory unless we add that the future is just not something that anyone can know.

Because this problem is so closely tied to the question of divine sovereignty and human freedom, and since I shall cover that topic plus the freedom/foreknowledge issue in later chapters, I won't address it here. However, in what follows, I shall try to define omniscience in a way that fits with either a compatibilistic or an incompatibilistic notion of free will.

A second issue related to divine omniscience must be addressed now. It is the general issue of divine omniscience and experiential knowledge. More narrowly, several questions arise under this more general question. Kenny raises an initial one about the traditional theistic belief that God is incorporeal. Since God has no body, it seems impossible for him to have the five human senses; but then there are many things that can be known which God cannot know. God cannot know anything that must be known by experiment and observation using physical sense organs. Thus, he doesn't know what it is like to feel cold or hot, wet or dry. He doesn't know what a sunset looks like, at least not as someone with physical eyes does. Since he has no ears, it also seems that he cannot hear the songs sung in his praise. Moreover, he cannot know what it is to taste food, and it is impossible for him to feel the sensation of physical pain. All of these experiences require a body and bodily senses, so these things that we know by experience are unknowable by God, even though he is omniscient.[47]

In addition, there are other things God cannot know, because he cannot experience them. God cannot know what it is like to fail or to feel like a failure, he cannot feel despair, fear, or frustration, for he is able to accomplish whatever goals he wants, and he can overpower anything that might pose a threat to his well-being. Moreover, God can't be embarrassed, worry, or be apprehensive, or be forlorn. All of these are things that humans know by experience, so it must be possible to have such knowledge, but God cannot know these things, despite being omniscient.[48]

In response, I begin with a distinction between propositional knowledge and relational or experiential knowledge. Propositional knowledge is knowledge of facts. It is knowledge that what a proposition asserts is true or false. When speaking of knowing some proposition, the locution typically used is 'I know that p', where 'p' stands for some proposition. Relational or experiential knowledge, on the other hand, involves knowing something or someone by personal acquaintance or experience. It is possible to have propositional knowledge about someone or something without having a relationship to them at all. Likewise, it is possible to describe accurately in propositions an experience that one has never personally had. One might simply repeat what others have said about the experience. And, of course, it is possible to experience some sensation, for example, without knowing (propositionally) what is happening until someone explains what happened.

With this distinction we are ready to address the first set of things that can be known only by experience. Anthony Kenny, who raises this issue, is very helpful in responding to it. Kenny borrows from the later philosophy of Wittgenstein to address the issue. As Wittgenstein's famous private language argument in the *Philosophical Investigations* shows, no one can construct a private language that allows him alone to name and identify private sensations. The only real language is language that is public. Thus, one person can *know* that another is in pain, even though it is impossible to feel the other person's sensation of pain. It is possible to know this about a person by their behavior (verbal and nonverbal—he moans, points to where it hurts, grimaces, etc.). The same is true of other sensations. We can know that something smells bad, tastes good, or feels wet by watching and listening to the behavior of someone who is having those experiences. But of course we cannot somehow "get inside" of that other person and have their experiences with them as they have them. As Kenny says,

> 'Only I can know my sensation' means either that others cannot *know* that I am (e.g.) in pain; or that others cannot *feel* my pain. If it means the former then it is obviously false; someone who sees me falling into flames and screaming as my body burns knows perfectly well that I am in pain. If it means the latter then it is true but trivial, and there is no question of knowledge here.[49]

What this means is that any of us, including God, can have propositional knowledge that someone is in pain, smells something malodorous, feels cold, etc. But, that doesn't mean that we can have the other person's private sensations as he or she has them. That sort of experiential knowledge is not open to any of us, so God's inability to feel my private sensations is no different than your inability to feel them. And it has nothing to do with whether one has a body or not. Since we don't count it a deficiency in our knowledge that we cannot experience someone else's sensations, there seems to be no reason that it should be counted against God's omniscience that he cannot do so either.

As Kenny rightly argues, having a sensation is different from acquiring knowledge about sensible objects. The blind man cannot have the sensation of seeing, but he can surely acquire all the information he wants about some sensory object, information he could gain himself if he could see. Likewise, God knows all the informational content of our perceptions and sensations. He just doesn't experience the very sensations themselves.[50] But no one experiences another person's sensations.

Although it is possible to have empirical knowledge of things such as sensations and the results of experiments (someone reports what was learned) without sense-experience, it is certainly not the case that God acquires this information by waiting on us to report it to him. Kenny appeals to Aquinas to explain how God learns these things. Aquinas distinguished between knowledge of understanding and knowledge of vision. The former deals with intellectual understanding of what is possible. The latter refers to awareness of reality. Kenny illustrates the distinction as follows:

> In these terms God's understanding of hypotheses will be part of his knowledge of simple understanding; his knowledge of their actualiza- tion will be his knowledge of vision. To put it in terms of essences: his knowledge that water is H_2O will be part of his knowledge of under- standing; his knowledge that there is such a thing as water, and how distributed, in what form, in what purity, and so on will be part of his knowledge of vision.[51]

But how does God have knowledge of vision, knowledge of what really is happening in our world? As Kenny explains, Aquinas says that God has this knowledge because God willed to create the world as it is.[52] This seems to me to be correct, and it is especially appealing for those like myself who are Calvinists and believe that God has decreed everything that occurs. Even though God as incorporeal cannot have various sensations and empirical knowledge through sensory means, that does not preclude him from know- ing the informational content of sensory experience. How does he know this information? Not by learning it from our reports but by decreeing everything that occurs and then creating the world in which those things happen.

There is something else that we must treat in regard to this complaint that God cannot know experientially and empirically. We noted that God cannot have our sensations, but no one can. Still, we can have our own sensations; we can know what seeing, tasting, feeling, and the like are by personal experience. God can know the informational content of these experiences, but as incorpo- real he cannot have the sensations himself. There is, then, a sense in which expe- riential knowledge is not available to God. Does that mean he is not omniscient?

The answer depends on how we define omniscience. If we define it solely in terms of propositional knowledge, then this alleged "deficiency" in God counts for nothing, for he can lack these experiences but still have complete propositional knowledge. Of course that would miss the point of knowing things by experience. Hence, defining omniscience solely in terms of propo- sitional knowledge seems inadequate. Likewise, if omniscience means that one knows everything that can be known, then God is not omniscient, for knowing sensations by experience is something that can be known, but as incorporeal, God cannot know such things.

In light of these considerations, whatever else we may want to say about divine omniscience, we should take our cue from the way Kenny nuanced his definition of omnipotence. Kenny defined divine omnipotence as having the power to do anything that a being with God's attributes could do. Devenish added that lest we think this keeps God from doing something worth doing, we must remember that all of God's attributes are perfections. Hence, what God can do in accord with his attributes probably will not omit something we would expect or want him to do.

Similarly, I propose that our definition of omniscience should include the notion of God's attributes and the fact that they are perfections. Hence, we can say that divine omniscience means at least knowing everything that a being with attributes such as God's can know. When we add that all of God's attributes are perfections, we see that though some of his attributes (such as being incorporeal) preclude him from knowing things such as what various sensations are like, that doesn't mean he lacks knowledge of something that he should know.

With this proviso to our notion of omniscience, we can also handle the second experiential complaint against divine omniscience. Some address this objection by claiming that God really can be frustrated, feel physical pain, etc., and others argue that the incarnation answers it, but neither approach seems correct. The first ultimately depends on the idea that God is in some way finite. The latter is problematic because it rules out omniscience as traditionally understood, for it entails that prior to Christ's incarnation, God was not omniscient. It also means that divine omniscience is contingent or dependent upon the incarnation, which seems odd, and it also means that the incarnation was not just for our sake but for God's as well.[53]

But with our proviso about omniscience covering things that a being with God's attributes can know, we have a way to handle this concern. Since one of God's attributes is omnipotence and another is sovereignty, it is indeed impossible for him to know what it is like to fail, be discouraged, be frustrated, be afraid, etc. Is God's inability to have these experiences an indication that he is deficient of some knowledge that we should expect a most perfect being to have? I don't see how it is, nor do I see that God's inability to experience such things in any way means that he lacks knowledge he should have. Hence, so long as we do not define omniscience as knowing everything there is to know, but define it in the way I have, there is no reason to think our conception of the divine attributes is inadequate. God can be both omnipotent and omniscient, as long as we understand that a being with God's attributes, one of which is omniscience, cannot have certain sorts of experiences. And we must add in accord with Kenny's points about empirical knowledge, that even though God cannot experience frustration, fear, etc., he can still have the informational content about those experiences and can know who is having such experiences and who is not.

Lest the reader think that this is all there is to defining omniscience, a caution is in order. With what we have said so far, by transference it might seem that anyone could be omniscient. That is, if omniscience means knowing everything that a being with a certain set of attributes can know, then some human might claim to be omniscient, despite deficiencies in their propositional knowledge. When challenged, they might simply reply that as a finite creature (one of their attributes) it is possible to know a lot of things (and they do), but not everything; hence, they qualify as omniscient. We should feel uncomfortable with this, and we should see that we must add more to our definition of divine omniscience. What is needed in part is a statement about the extent of the propositional knowledge possessed by a being with divine omniscience. Before we specify the extent of that knowledge, however, we must address other issues surrounding divine omniscience.

A third issue about omniscience is very significant and requires a good deal of our attention. It involves knowledge of what philosophers call indexical propositions. The issue isn't just about omniscience, however, for it also impacts divine immutability and our understanding of divine eternity.

In chapter 6, I offered Richard Swinburne's definition of indexical propositions. Swinburne's comments distinguish three kinds of indexical propositions: spatial indexicals, temporal indexicals, and indexicals about people. Temporal indexicals most concern us in relation to omniscience, immutability, and eternity, and I shall address them more fully in the chapter on divine eternity. For now, I shall handle the other two kinds of indexical propositions and then say a few things about temporal indexicals. Let us first consider indexicals about persons.

The truth value of indexicals about persons (sentences usually including personal pronouns) can change, depending on who utters the sentence; and, of course, the referent of the pronoun changes when different people utter it. Take, for example, the proposition 'I am ill'. When I utter that sentence, it refers to me, but when you utter the same sentence it refers to you. If I utter that sentence now, it would be false, for I am not ill as I write this sentence. If you speak the same proposition and you are ill, it would be true. If God's omniscience means simply that he knows all propositions that are true, these indexicals apparently give him trouble, for God can never utter truly 'I am ill', so he can never know that proposition to be true. But, obviously, there are many occasions when someone utters such propositions and they are true. So does this mean that God never knows those propositions to be true—since whenever he says one of them, it is false?

Actually, this question contains some confusions. It is true that God can never say truly 'I am ill', for he never is, but why should that be problematic for omniscience? God cannot know false propositions as true, so when 'I' in 'I am ill' refers to himself, God never knows that the proposition is true. If omniscience means at least that God knows all true propositions, in this case there simply is no true proposition for him to know. But what if someone who is ill utters the proposition? Can God know the truth of that proposition? Absolutely. Nothing keeps God from knowing that the referent of 'I' in this case is some other person, and if that person is ill, God can know that. What God knows is that when person x utters the proposition 'I am ill', the proposition is true. If person x is not ill but utters the proposition, God knows the proposition is false.

What about spatial indexicals? Given the doctrine of omnipresence, I think these indexicals are even less problematic than the preceding sort. Consider the following propositions as examples: (1) 'Chicago is forty-five miles from here'; (2) 'My computer is on top of my desk'; (3) 'New York is east of me'; (4) 'As one travels eastward through Illinois, Canada will be to one's left'. Can God know the truth or falsity of these spatial indexicals? I see no reason why he can't, especially since there is no reason that he cannot know the referent of words such as 'here', 'my', 'me', and the like. If I say (1) and do so while I am spatially in a suburb forty-five miles away from Chicago, God will know the geographical point designated by 'here' since he knows where I am, and he will know how far it is from where I am to Chicago. Hence, God will know whether the proposition is true or false from my perspective when I utter it. As for God saying it, the situation is different because of omnipresence. If by 'here' God means wherever he is, then since he is at all locations, 'here' will mean locations that are forty-five miles away and he will know that the proposition is true of those locations. On the other hand, if he intends to designate locations not forty-five miles away, he will know the proposition is false of those locations. If God should utter a sentence like (1), he likely would have already named a geographical location in a way that alerts us that when he says (1) we know that 'here' refers to that location. If that location is forty-five miles from Chicago, then God would say that proposition; otherwise, he would not say it.

As for proposition (2), God knows that 'my' refers to me, and since God knows about everything I own, he knows which computer is mine and where it is located. Thus he knows whether that proposition when spoken by me is true or false. Likewise, he knows the same information about everyone else, so he knows whether the proposition, when said by anyone, would be true or false. I doubt that God would ever use this proposition of himself, but if he should, he would know that he owns a computer and a desk and that the computer is on the desk.

Proposition (3) can be handled just as (1) was. In this case, however, God will only need to know the referent of 'me' rather than 'here'. As to proposition (4), again there is no problem. As long as the referent of 'one's' is someone who is not omnipresent, and as long as God knows the meaning of words like 'eastward' and 'left' (and he does), God can know that this proposition is true. It is dubious that God would use this proposition about himself (here he would be the referent of 'one'), for it isn't clear what it would mean to say that God was traveling eastward through Illinois. However, if some sense could be made of that idea, God could use that sentence truly of himself.

In sum, there appear to be no major problems for omniscience from indexicals about persons or spatial indexicals. What should we say about temporal indexicals? 'It is *now* 2:56 P.M. as I write this sentence in single quotes' is a temporal indexical and a true one at the time I wrote the proposition in single quotes. But I can also write truly 'it is *now* 2:58 P.M. as I write *this* sentence in single quotes'. This shows that at 2:56 I knew that one indexical proposition was true and at 2:58 I knew that another was true and the first was no longer true.

In addressing this issue, I note initially that this problem was handled already in relation to my definition of immutability, so I can be brief. The concern now is with omniscience, and it is important to define omniscience very carefully. I have already suggested several items that should be included in the definition, but let me add a further nuance. I suggest that we add that omniscience includes knowing only things that can be known. Contradictions are false, so they cannot be known as true. False propositions cannot be known as true, for they are not true. Some also claim that propositions about the future free actions of human agents cannot be known until they occur. We shall also see if there are temporal indexical propositions that are impossible to know.

What kind of trues, then, can be known? It is possible to know everything true of the past. Moreover, as a determinist committed to absolute divine sovereignty, I believe it is possible for God to know all future actions and events. In addition, I believe God has middle knowledge (knowledge of counterfactual conditionals), so I think God knows everything that could happen and what he could and would do depending on which of the possibilities becomes actual. The configuration of all possible (logically possible) worlds can be known, and God knows it. It is also possible to know the truth of temporal indexicals such as 'it is not now tomorrow' and 'it is not now 1990 or 1995'. It is also possible to know the truth of indexicals such as 'it is now 4:31 P.M. on April 15, 1995' if it is that time when one says, writes, or thinks that sentence. Of course, if God is outside of time, it is hard to see how God can know these temporal indexicals, but that does not mean they are unknowable for everyone. On the other hand, if God is in time, then it is also possible for him to know them.

There are some temporal indexicals that no one can know. As I write this sentence, it is 4:33 P.M. Therefore, it is impossible for me to know the truth of the proposition 'it is now 5 P.M.', because it is not now 5 P.M. If it is impossible right now to know that it is now 5 P.M., then there is no deficiency in reasoning capacity or knowledge if one does not know it. God is not deficient for failing to know the impossible and the unknowable.

I conclude, then, that by putting God in time and allowing him to know temporal, spatial, and personal indexical propositions, we in no way compromise divine omniscience. We have earlier also seen that this does not compromise our nuanced definition of immutability either. Moreover, this account of indexical propositions allows God to know things we would expect him to know and that he would need to know to act and react at "the right time" in human history.

The next issues surrounding omniscience deal more with how God knows and how his mind functions, rather than with the extent of his knowledge. An initial issue concerns divine omniscience, deliberation, and intentional action. According to Bruce Reichenbach, to deliberate means to try to "make up one's mind about one's own, future, possible actions, given certain beliefs, wants, and intentions one has."[54] If so, it is hard to see that God deliberates about any of his future actions, since as omniscient he already knows everything about the future, including what he will do. But if God cannot deliberate, can he act intentionally, i.e., in a rational, purposive way to achieve a goal?[55]

Reichenbach answers that not all intentional acts are deliberative. For example, his acts of going to school and teaching a class or giving his son water when asked are intentional, but they require no deliberation whatsoever. Since humans act intentionally without deliberating, there is no reason to think God is any different.[56] This seems fundamentally correct, so, even if God cannot deliberate, that does not rule out divine intentional actions.

This issue of divine deliberation suggests another question. Suppose we conclude that, as omniscient, God does not deliberate. Suppose we add that God has always known everything, so he has always known exactly what he and anyone else would do. If so, then it seems that neither now nor ever in God's life has he deliberated or even decided what he would do. He hasn't needed to do so, because he has always known what would happen. But if this is so, are we not faced with two significant problems? On the one hand, this appears to necessitate fatalism. On the other, how can we square the idea that God has never deliberated and made a decision with biblical passages that speak of God doing all things according to the counsel of his will (e.g., Eph 1:11)? That is, Scripture portrays God as making decisions. He decided to create a world rather than not create, and he chose to create this possible world rather than others. But how can this be so if, as omniscient, God has always known everything? Is biblical and theological talk about God choosing just anthropomorphic?

In response, let me address the second item first. Here we must remember what we have said so far in defining omniscience. We have said that it is no stain on divine omniscience if God fails to know what cannot be known, and we have already seen things that God cannot know. Now, it seems that what God has always known throughout the endless ages of his existence is the shape of all possible worlds, so that if he should decide to create a world, he would not have to fumble around mentally to construct one or more possible worlds before deciding on which one to actualize. Because Scripture does portray God as deciding to create a world and also says that all things are done in accord with the counsel of his will, at some point in God's existence a decision to create a world must have been made. Given God's intelligence, there is no reason to think the decision about which world to create took him very long.

But, wouldn't God foreknow that he would create and foreknow which world it would be? As already stated, divine omniscience means, among other things, that God only knows what can be known. Until God decided to create and chose to actualize a particular possible world, there was nothing to know about whether and what he would create. Does this mean that once God made the decision, he came to know something he hadn't known before? Yes, but this is only damaging to omniscience and immutability if what he came to know was information available before he came to know it. God could be aware of all the possibilities open to him in advance of choosing any of them, but until he decided to create a world and which one to create, he could not know whether he would create, and if he would, which possible world he would create.

Although this response may seem strange, I think that it is the most plausible way to understand biblical language that says God decided to do one thing or another before the foundation of the world, and that he makes decisions not arbitrarily but based on the counsel of his will. If God never actually made any decisions or deliberated about anything, then such language must be anthropomorphic, but if it is purely anthropomorphic, it is hard to know what the anthropomorphisms could possibly mean. Moreover, I believe that my answer to this issue shows the way to handle the concern about fatalism. Fatalism is only ruled in if no one, including God, ever has any choice about whether there will be a world and what events and actions will be in it. My contention that God always knew all possible worlds, but made at some point in his life a decision to create one of them, forestalls fatalism.

One further point should be made about this matter. Once God decided to create and chose our particular world, was it ever again possible for him to deliberate and decide? The answer partly depends on whether one is a determinist or an indeterminist. For determinists (other than fatalists), once God decides to create and picks a particular world, he forever after knows everything that will happen, including what he will do in every circumstance and situation.[57] But, since he will know this, it does seem that deliberation and decision are thereafter ruled out. As we shall see, however, human and divine freedom are not thereby ruled out, if one defines freedom as does a compatibilist.

In contrast, indeterminists who don't think God can foreknow the future will likely respond that, though God can know some things about our world once he decides to create it, he cannot know many things about it, such as what his free creatures will do and how he will respond. Indeterminists who believe God can know many things about the future, but not the indeterministically free choices of his human creatures, would give the same answer. Of course, for indeterminists who think God does know the details of the future (despite humans and God somehow still remaining incompatibilistically free), it is dubious that they would see God as deciding or deliberating on anything. Having once decided to create our world, there is no further need to choose or deliberate about anything in it. Remember, however, that this does not mean that God does not need to act or cannot act in our world. As Reichenbach shows, intentional action is possible without deliberation. This only means that God no longer needs to deliberate about what he will do in our world.

Having surveyed a series of problems about divine omniscience,[58] we are ready to collate our conclusions and propose a definition of omniscience. Throughout this discussion, I have insisted that we follow Kenny's strategy in defining divine omnipotence. If we do so, we derive as a start the following definition of divine omniscience:

> Divine omniscience is ability to know everything that a being with
> God's attributes can know. Since his attributes are all perfections, they
> do not likely preclude his knowing something he should know as the
> maximally-great being.

Though this is a start, it doesn't incorporate everything we have learned
through our discussion of the various problems of omniscience. The issue
of experiential knowledge suggests that we should add something about the
distinction between propositional and experiential knowing. Moreover, our
discussion of indexical propositions led us to conclude that certain things
are impossible for anyone to know, regardless of whether they are divine or
human. Our definition should not require God to know such things. Given
these additions, I suggest the following definition of divine omniscience:

> An *omniscient* being can only be capable of knowing what can be
> known by anyone—contradictions cannot be known, nor can false
> propositions be known as true, nor can what others' internal sensations
> feel like to them be known by anyone else, nor can future indexical
> propositions be known before the future occurs. A *divine* being who is
> *omniscient* knows the informational content of every proposition and
> every experience that a being *with God's attributes* can know. Since
> his attributes are all perfections, they do not likely preclude him from
> knowing something he should know as the maximally-great being.

The first sentence of this definition limits what anyone can know, including an omniscient being. The second sentence adds further limits in light of
God's other attributes, but given that God's attributes are all perfections, and
given God's intellectual abilities to think and store knowledge, even with the
limitations suggested, God knows infinitely more than any other being in the
universe. Moreover, by speaking of knowing the informational content of
propositions and experiences, I make room for God to know that I am in pain,
for example, without him having to experience my sensation of pain. Finally, I
suggest that this definition is sufficiently nuanced to allow either atemporalists
or temporalists with respect to divine eternity to adopt and use it.[59]

Although I believe this definition to be accurate, I also think there are
other things we should say about the divine intellect and its functioning. In
the words of Charles Taliaferro, nothing in the definition *per se* identifies
adequately the cognitive power of an omniscient being. Taliaferro believes
that something about divine cognitive power should be included in a definition of omniscience. While I disagree that such is needed to specify the concept
of omniscience, I agree that we must say more if we want a fuller account of
what an omniscient mind can do. Taliaferro helps us to understand divine
cognitive power when he writes:

> The notion of cognitive power can be readily illustrated. When I know
> certain things to be the case, say that I now see something green or I

am hearing music, I am exercising cognitive power or ability. I have certain cognitive powers with respect to my sensory states so that I can grasp truths about the world, or at least truths about my sensory and perceptual states themselves. When I know 2 + 2 = 4 I am exercising my cognitive power to grasp the truth value of a necessary proposition. I believe that the traditional theistic understanding of God's omniscience includes attributing to God unsurpassable cognitive power.[60]

So far, there seems to be no reason for disagreement, but why make this point about cognitive power? Taliaferro suggests a thought experiment which allows us to see that there is something more to say about God's intellect than what my definition of omniscience captures. Imagine two beings, Christopher and Dennis. Christopher is omniscient in virtue of using his own cognitive powers. He knows the truth of true propositions incorrigibly and infallibly. Moreover, what he knows about the world doesn't come from consulting any sort of evidence, but rather the mere occurrence of an event is sufficient for him to know it. Dennis, on the other hand, knows everything Christopher knows, but knows because Christopher tells him this information. It doesn't matter whether Christopher creates Dennis with this knowledge or whether Dennis is so linked to Christopher that whatever Christopher knows Dennis also knows by being linked to Christopher. Now, reasons Taliaferro, both Christopher and Dennis are omniscient (in the sense of knowing the truth or falsity of all propositions), but Christopher clearly has maximal cognitive power (and exercises it), whereas Dennis does not. Taliaferro argues that this notion should be included in the concept of omniscience, and if it is, then Christopher is omniscient whereas Dennis is not. Hence, omniscience should be understood not only in terms of *what* one knows, but also *how* one knows. According to Taliaferro, we would not consider a being omniscient if he had maximal cognitive power but used it only for trivial purposes, so that there were multitudes of knowable things he did not know. Likewise, knowing a certain amount of information without knowing it by means of maximal cognitive power wouldn't be omniscience either (think of Dennis). An adequate account of omniscience must combine both how and what is known.[61]

Because I believe the notion of omniscience is about what one knows, I think my definition is sufficient. However, in light of divine omniscience, natural questions arise about how powerful God's mind is and how he knows what he knows, and it is here that we must take Taliaferro's concerns seriously. God's mind is not just a mind with an IQ of, say, 300, that is stuffed with endless amounts of knowledge. To think that of God is probably still to think of his mind as finite, though surely one that functions better than any human mind. What we need, instead, is to think of God's intellectual capacities as infinite. He is a better knower than we are, not just because he knows more than we do but also because his cognitive capacities are infinitely above ours. His mind functions in ways and at speeds to know amounts of information that are way beyond anything of which we are capable. Taliaferro's concern to include a comment about divine cognitive abilities is correct in describing God's intellectual capacities. I do not think, however, that we need to add it to a definition of omniscience.

Another item about God's intellect deals with how God knows whatever he knows. In his excellent article "Does God Have Beliefs?" William Alston discusses whether God has beliefs or instead should be understood only as possessing knowledge. That is an interesting issue, but my main concern is what he says about how God acquires knowledge.[62] Alston claims that the construal of divine knowledge which is superior to any kind of true-justified-belief construal of knowledge is the intuitive conception of knowledge. He explains it as follows:

> This is the view that knowledge of a fact is simply the immediate awareness of that fact. In H. H. Price's felicitous formulation, knowledge "is simply the situation in which some entity or some fact is directly present to consciousness." Despite the curious conviction of many contemporary Anglo-American epistemologists that the true-justified-belief conception of knowledge is "the traditional conception," the intuitive conception has been much more prominent historically. . . . On this view, knowledge is quite a different psychological state from belief. Obviously, I can believe that p without its being the case that p. But I cannot be in the state of knowledge that p, so construed, without its being the case that p; for that state just consists of the presence of that fact to my consciousness; without that fact there could be no such state. . . . Thus knowledge, on this construal, is infallible in a strong sense; its inherent nature guarantees the reality of the object.[63]

As Alston explains, intuitive knowledge is not the right way to think of human knowledge (we don't have the mental ability it requires), but it is the best way to conceive of God's knowledge.[64]

I believe this is correct, and I note that my definition of omniscience doesn't preclude this understanding of how God knows. I would, however, make some slight modifications to Alston's account of intuitive knowledge of propositions. For one thing, it seems to be stated in terms of matters that are empirical in nature. Hence, it is hard to see how God would know intuitively that "2 + 2 = 4" or that "all bachelors are unmarried men," if knowing intuitively (as Alston states it) requires being presented with the objects that are known. In the case of the analytic truths just mentioned, what sorts of objects would be immediately present to God's awareness? I think this is a minor issue which can be rectified by adding that, in the case of analytic truths, to say that God knows them intuitively means he does not need to attain knowledge of them by inferential or discursive reason. He simply knows all such facts.

One final question remains with respect to God's knowledge and intellectual capacities. Is God always consciously aware of everything he knows, or could God know something without it being immediately before his mind?

These questions may seem odd, especially since many evangelical Christians would probably say that God is always consciously aware of whatever he knows. They might be inclined to say this for fear that denying it would suggest that God forgot something he knows, and of course it seems that God's cognitive power and omniscience forestall his forgetting anything.

Here, however, I think the fear is unfounded. In regard to humans, we know many things that we are not thinking about consciously at any given moment. Our intellectual capacities don't allow us to be aware of everything we know all at once, but just because we can't have before our consciousness everything we know does not mean that we have forgotten things that aren't immediately before our mind. For example, most (if not all of us) know our own name, we know who our parents are, where we live, and what our telephone number is. But much of the time we don't consciously think of any of these things that we know. Does that mean we don't really know them or that we have forgotten them? Of course not. Our ability to recall various pieces of information that we normally don't have before our minds is confirmation that we do know those things. Now, if humans are not required to be conscious of everything we know in order rightly to claim that we know those things, why must God have everything he knows always before his conscious mind to be omniscient?

Some may object that the nature of God's maximal cognitive powers requires that he always have everything before his conscious mind. But do we know that having maximal cognitive powers requires this? Maybe it does, but that does not seem self-evident. So long as we agree that someone really knows something even if that item of knowledge is not consciously before his mind, there seems to be no reason to think that in order to qualify as omniscient (in the sense I have defined it) or to have maximal cognitive powers, one must at every moment of one's life consciously be aware of everything one knows.

This must not be misunderstood. I believe that God, if he wants, can consciously be aware of everything he knows. My concern is that we not require this in order for God to be omniscient. Why, however, might we deny that God always is consciously aware of everything he knows? The reason is that there are some theological issues and puzzles that may be resolvable if God is not consciously aware every moment of all he knows. I am not saying that these resolutions prove that God sometimes is not consciously aware of things he knows. I am only proposing that someone who adopts this view may find it useful in solving certain theological problems.

Specifically, there are three places where this notion might be helpful. Consider first the matter of fellowship within the Godhead. Scripture depicts the members of the Godhead in conversation with one another. Theologians have typically also held that members of the Trinity eternally enjoy fellowship with one another. But if God is always consciously aware of everything he knows, since all three members of the Trinity have this characteristic, how is fellowship within the Godhead possible? One member cannot draw the attention of another to one particular thing they know, because their attention is always fully on everything. Moreover, there is no reason to suspect that one member might be thinking of something that another is not thinking of, for all of them are always thinking of everything. So if God is always consciously aware of everything he knows, then talk of fellowship within the Godhead must be anthropomorphic, and it is very difficult to know what such an anthropomorphism means. On the other hand, if the members of the Godhead are not always consciously thinking of everything they know, then conversation, drawing of attention to one particular truth they know, and fellowship are possibilities.[65]

Second, not only can we ask about fellowship within the Godhead, but one also wonders how God can fellowship with *us,* if everything he knows is always before his mind. If fellowship is a relational concept involving more than one party, then there seems to be a problem. We can talk to God, and he can communicate things to us that we don't know or need to be reminded of, but we can never say anything to God that isn't consciously before his mind. Our prayers intend to draw his attention to our specific needs, but his attention is already fully on those needs, so what exactly do our prayers accomplish in relation to God? Likewise, there seems to be no need to inform God that we love him, nor to praise him, for he always is consciously aware of our thoughts. On the other hand, if God is not always thinking of everything he knows, talk of fellowship with him makes more sense.

Finally, there is the matter of forgetting our sins. As suggested earlier, the best way to handle this may be to say that this is just the biblical writers' way of saying that God does not count these sins against us. On the other hand, there may be another way to handle it. If God is always thinking of everything he knows, then he must always be thinking of my sins. In fact, even before I was born and after I die, he must always be thinking of them. On the other hand, if God is not always consciously aware of everything he knows, then perhaps what happens when God "forgets" our sins is not just that he doesn't count them against us but also that they are not consciously before his mind. Of course, he hasn't literally forgotten them, for that would compromise omniscience, but perhaps he has "forgotten" them in the sense mentioned.

As I close this section, I must make several comments about this matter of God "forgetting" our sins. First, it seems hard to square it with an atemporal notion of eternity, for on that view all of history is "present" to God timelessly and endlessly. If that is so, it may never be possible for God to escape thinking of everything he knows. On the other hand, with temporal eternity, this notion that not everything is always consciously before God's mind would help to explain why the present (which God experiences moment by moment) has greater immediacy before God than does the past or future.

Second, I should qualify this view in at least one respect. In light of what Scripture says about God's awareness of everyone's needs at once, it is probably right to hold (if one holds that God is a temporal being) that God is consciously aware of everything presently happening in our world. There may be matters about the past and future that are not immediately before his mind at any given moment, but at any given moment his attention would be focused on everything happening in our world.

Finally, the preceding discussion on what God is consciously aware of is not meant as an endorsement of the view that he need not always be consciously aware of everything he knows. Certain aspects of this view are attractive, but Scripture does not appear to contain enough information for us to decide whether it is true or false. Moreover, before a decision can be made on this issue, we must decide whether God is temporal or atemporal, for, as suggested, that matter has implications for this. But even if one decides that God is in time, that in itself cannot confirm this notion as correct. I raise the issue, then, because I believe it to have a certain degree of plausibility, and because I can see how it would help to handle the issues I have mentioned in regard to divine fellowship and divine "forgetting" of sins. Beyond that, I hope this discussion will cause readers to reflect further on the various issues that go into an understanding of the divine intellect and its knowledge.

WISDOM

Not only is God omniscient, he is also omnisapient, or all-wise. Divine wisdom is an aspect of divine omniscience, but it is not identical with it. Wisdom involves more than merely having all facts at one's disposal. It also involves knowing how to use those facts to accomplish ends in the best way. While knowledge, at least human knowledge, tends to be more theoretical, wisdom is more practical. For humans, knowledge is usually attained through books whereas wisdom is more often attained through experience. Whereas humans can be very knowledgeable but not very wise, or wise without being very knowledgeable, God is both all-knowing and all-wise. He knows everything there is to know, and beyond that, he knows what to do with that information.

In light of these features of wisdom, Berkhof defines divine wisdom as "that perfection of God whereby He applies His knowledge to the attainment of His ends in a way which glorifies Him most."[66] While I agree, I think the definition is incomplete in that we should add that God's wisdom is exercised in decision making along with his other attributes of holiness, love, justice, goodness, etc. Without this addition, it is possible to think of God merely as the great tactician who knows how most efficiently to get the results he wants, regardless of what his decisions mean to his creatures. However, when we factor into the exercise of divine wisdom the moral attributes of God, we can be sure that decisions that will accomplish ends that bring him the most glory are also decisions that are in his creatures' best interests. Of course, omnisapience would not amount to much if God knew the best thing to do in any situation but was powerless to do it. Hence, in virtue of God's omnipotence and sovereign will, his wisdom can become functional in our universe to do what he knows is best.

In turning to Scripture, we find no passage that says God is all-wise. However, Scripture predicates wisdom of God, and in light of his infinity and the fact that all of his attributes are perfections, it is safe to say that omnisapience applies to God. We should also add that biblical authors use various words for wisdom, but two are the most basic: *ḥokmāh* in the OT and *sophia* in the NT.

While occasionally biblical references to wisdom seem to refer more to worldly erudition than to practical know-how, most references to wisdom, especially divine wisdom, speak more about applying knowledge in concrete situations. One instance where wisdom does seem to refer to intellectual knowledge is 1 Cor 1:21 where Paul says, "For since in the wisdom of God the world through its wisdom did not come to know God, God was well-pleased through the foolishness of the message preached to save those who believe." With all its erudition and brilliance, the world didn't find its way to a relationship with God. Paul adds that God was pleased through the "foolishness of preaching" (foolish in human terms) to save men and women.

As we look at biblical testimony, we find various passages that directly attribute wisdom to God. We see it typically in doxologies like the ones in Jude 25; Rom 16:27; and 1 Tim 1:17. In addition, Elihu says of God (Job 36:5, KJV), "Behold, God is mighty, and despiseth not any: he is mighty in strength and wisdom" (see also Job 9:4).

In addition to passages that speak generally about wisdom, biblical writers relate divine wisdom to one activity or another. A frequent theme is that God's wisdom is wonderfully displayed in creation. In Ps 104:1-34 the psalmist speaks with great detail about God's works of creation, and in the midst of this psalm (v. 24) he pauses to say, "O LORD, how many are Thy works! In wisdom Thou hast made them all; the earth is full of Thy possessions" (see also Ps 136:5; Prov 3:19; Jer 10:12; and 51:15).

Scripture also teaches that God's wisdom is marvelously displayed in his work of salvation. Speaking of the difference a saving relationship to Christ can make, Paul says (1 Cor 1:24), "But to those who are the called, both Jews and Greeks, Christ the power of God and the wisdom of God" (see also v. 30). Speaking of his preaching of the gospel message while ministering among them, Paul tells the Christians at Corinth (1 Cor 2:7), "but we speak God's wisdom in a mystery, the hidden wisdom, which God predestined before the ages to our glory." In Ephesians 1 Paul speaks of the believer's redemption and forgiveness of sins as a result of Christ's sacrifice. He then adds that God has "lavished" these things upon us "in all wisdom and insight" (Eph 1:8; see also Eph 3:10; and Rom 11:33).[67]

Not only does Scripture speak of God as wise, it also says he gives wisdom to humans for handling one task or another. Of course, if his wisdom gives them ability to handle these situations successfully, it is unthinkable that he personally is not wise enough to do the same. The writer of Proverbs says that God's wisdom is sufficient for living life successfully in general (Prov 2:6-7):

"For the LORD gives wisdom; from His mouth come knowledge and understanding. He stores up sound wisdom for the upright; He is a shield to those who walk in integrity."

In addition, many passages speak of God giving someone wisdom to accomplish a practical task, and it is safe to say that he could not grant wisdom if he didn't have it himself (see, for example, Exod 31:3; 35:31; 36:1-2; Ezra 7:25; 1 Kgs 3:12 cf. 1 Kgs 5:12). A well-known example is God granting wisdom to Solomon in handling interpersonal disputes (1 Kgs 3:9-12). The famous dispute between the two women over the baby came early in Solomon's reign. The reaction of the people was (1 Kgs 3:28), "they feared the king; for they saw that the wisdom of God was in him to administer justice." Later in Solomon's life, his reputation as a wise man continued to grow. As we read in 1 Kgs 10:24 (see also 2 Chron 9:23), "All the earth was seeking the presence of Solomon, to hear his wisdom which God had put in his heart." In addition, Daniel and his friends gained favor while in Babylon because God granted to them special wisdom (Dan 1:17; 2:20-21, 23). Of course none of this would be possible if God himself were not all-wise.

Finally, we learn that divine wisdom is both available and sufficient for handling another practical matter, temptation to sin. Jas 1:5 says, "But if any of you lacks wisdom, let him ask of God, who gives to all men generously and without reproach, and it will be given to him." This verse is often taken out of context and generalized to mean that God will grant wisdom for any practical endeavor, but a closer look at context shows that the topic under discussion is temptation to sin. James's point is that when we are confronted with temptation, if we don't know how to handle it so as not to fall into sin, God will grant such wisdom. We may also seek divine wisdom for other tasks, but the specific focus of this verse is temptation to sin. Paul tells us (1 Cor 10:13) that no one will be tempted by something that has never confronted anyone else. Moreover, God will grant us a way of escape, and it seems reasonable to believe that on certain occasions the way God helps us escape is to grant wisdom to see how to avoid the temptation altogether or to resist it when it comes.

Indeed, as the writer of Proverbs says (Prov 2:6-7), God lays up wisdom for the righteous. He does so for handling temptation and for all other matters of life and godliness. What an encouragement to know that our heavenly Father not only knows everything there is to know, but also knows what to do with it. And, he is more than willing to share that information with us!

UNITY

In light of all the wonderful divine attributes and the wonderful things God has done and continues to do for us, we might wish for many gods, but Scripture teaches clearly that there is only one. Theologians make this point by speaking of the unity of God. Moreover, they have distinguished between the *unitas singularitatis* and the *unitas simplicitatis*. The latter is the doctrine of divine simplicity, which I shall address in the next section. The former is our focus now—the doctrine of unity.

God's unity refers to two specific things. The first is that there is numerically only one God. All forms of polytheism are excluded by divine unity. In addition, when theologians predicate unity of God, they mean that he is unique. All of this bears amplification.

To say that there is only one God does not mean that all people recognize only one or that those who worship God worship the Judaeo-Christian God. In chapter 2, we saw many different conceptions of God, and some religions postulate many gods. What Christians mean when they speak of God's unity is that the Judaeo-Christian God, the God of the Bible, is the only true God. All other gods are idols, false gods, products of the imagination and wishful thinking. People may treat these gods as real, but they are not real. Moreover, not only is the biblical God the only true and living God; he is numerically one. And he is unique, not just because he alone truly exists, but because the biblical description of this God differs from conceptions of other so-called gods.

Some might think that the God of Scripture is not really so unique, for there are other monotheistic religions, such as Judaism and Islam, whose God seems similar, if not identical, to the God of Christianity. Indeed, there are similarities, but differences as well. One of the most significant differences is that the Christian God is triune, and neither Judaism nor Islam make such a claim. Of course, some think the doctrine of the Trinity refutes the Christian claim that there is only one God, but as we shall see when discussing the Trinity, Christians don't believe in three Gods (tritheism), but only one God manifest in three persons.

Scripture in both the OT and NT teaches that there is only one God. Undoubtedly, one of the best-known verses in Judaism is Deut 6:4, the *šĕmaʿ*: "Hear, O Israel! The LORD is our God, the LORD is one." The Hebrew word for one (*ʾeḥod*) occurs some 960 times in the Bible as a noun, adjective, or adverb. Some suggest that it is best rendered in an adverbial sense, so that the verse says, "The LORD is our God, the LORD alone." If so, the point would be that of all the gods Israel might worship, Yahweh is the God with a special relation to Israel.[68] Of course, this understanding of the verse does not require that there be only one God. It only mandates that Israel worship Yahweh alone. While this interpretation is possible grammatically, so is the more traditional understanding that the verse asserts that there is only one God.

Lest there be any doubts, however, about whether OT writers think there is more than one God, there is ample evidence to the contrary. In Deut 4:35, 39 (KJV) we read, "Unto thee it was shewed, that thou mightest know that the LORD he is God; there is none else beside him. . . . Know therefore this day, and consider it in thine heart, that the LORD he is God in heaven above, and upon the earth beneath: there is none else" (see also Deut 32:39; Ps 18:31; 83:17-18; Isa 43:10; 44:6, 8; 45:5-6).

In the NT we find the same thing: there is numerically only one God. In Mark 12:32 (NIV) we read, "'Well said, teacher,' the man replied. 'You are right in saying that God is one and there is no other but him.'" In John 10:30 Jesus says, "I and the Father are one." His Jewish listeners took up stones to stone him, because Christ, being a mere man in their opinion, made himself equal to God. This was problematic for them not only because they thought he was just a man, but also because they believed there was only one God. Jesus says nothing to disabuse them of that idea (see also John 5:44; 17:3).

Paul's letters include repeated claims that there is only one God. In 1 Cor 8:4 (KJV) Paul says, "As concerning therefore the eating of those things that are offered in sacrifice unto idols, we know that an idol is nothing in the world, and that there is none other God but one." In Eph 4:5-6 (KJV) he writes, "One Lord, one faith, one baptism, One God and Father of all, who is above all, and through all, and in you all" (see also 1 Tim 1:17; 2:5; 6:15; and Rom 3:30).

Not only is there only one God, but he is also unique among those things worshiped as God. Many theologians point to many of the verses cited above as proving not only numerical oneness but also uniqueness. However, there are other indications of God's uniqueness. In Exod 8:10 (KJV) we read, "And he said, Be it according to thy word: that thou mayest know that there is none like unto the LORD our God" (see also Isa 46:9). In addition, there are two explicit ways in which God is unique. For one thing, no God performs miracles that can match his. This is not true just because all other gods are nonexistent, but because even if we treat other gods as real, when we look at the miracles attributed to them by their followers, they don't compare to the miraculous deeds ascribed to the God of Scripture. This point is made specifically in Deut 4:32-39, as God refers to the miracles he performed in Israel's behalf at the time of the exodus and asks what God performs miracles like these. Indeed, think of other miracles God performed, such as during Elijah's contest with the prophets of Baal. Not only did God send fire to consume the offering, but it also burned up everything even though it was all drenched with water. What god can match that miracle? Certainly not Baal, nor any other! Likewise, what god raises people from the dead? The miracles attributed to the God of Scripture are without parallel.

In addition to his unique miracles, the true and living God is also unique in that he alone can predict the future without error. Soothsayers and lucky guessers may occasionally foretell an event, but they can't match the God of Scripture. Isa 44:6-8 makes this point, but we see this truth throughout Scripture. One need only think of the fulfillment of Daniel's prophecies with all their specific details to recognize that there is no parallel. In fact, Daniel's prophecies are so detailed and accurate that anti-supernaturalists have tried to discredit them by giving the book so late a date that it could not be prophecy but rather history. That move in itself suggests how accurate Daniel's predictions are, for if the prophecies were vague or inaccurate, there would be no reason to adjust the book's date in order to discredit its supernatural nature.

Indeed, our God is unique. One thinks of Job 38–41, where God answers Job. The majestic description of God in those chapters not only shows Job and us that God is way beyond the majesty, power, and grandeur of mere mortals. In comparing those chapters with descriptions of the gods of other religions, it is clear that the Christian God is without parallel!

SIMPLICITY

In addition to God's uniqueness, many theologians believe that God is one in the sense of being simple. By simplicity, they mean that God is free from any division into parts; he is free from compositeness. We might expect this, because as immaterial, it is impossible to divide God's being into physical parts, but proponents of divine simplicity mean more than this. They mean that it is impossible altogether to divide God into constituent parts. Thus, we cannot differentiate God's substantiality from his attributes. Nor can we say that God's nature is composed of various attributes. Rather, God's essence *is* his attributes, and those attributes must be identical with one another and with him; otherwise, we could distinguish various parts of God's nature.[69]

Stump and Kretzmann note that the doctrine of divine simplicity also maintains that, internal to God's nature, there cannot be any accidental properties. In fact, all of God's attributes must be essential properties. If some were essential and some accidental, that would mean division and composition within God's being. But even saying that all of God's attributes are essential is not enough, for if we could distinguish one of those attributes from another, it would mean that there is division in God. Hence, there cannot be any real distinction in God between one of his essential attributes and another. Moreover, this also means that, unlike God's creatures, there is no distinction between God's essence and his existence. For created things, it is possible to describe what they would be like if they existed, apart from them actually existing. In order to bring something into existence, God must add existence to its essence (nature). However, if God is simple, distinguishing his essence from his existence would imply not only division in God's being but also composition (joining existence with essence), so God's essence is not distinct from his existence.[70]

William Mann summarizes the concept of divine simplicity as follows:

> The Doctrine of Divine Simplicity (DDS) maintains that God has no 'parts' or components whatsoever. He has no properties, neither essential nor accidental. He has no spatial extension. Nor does he have any temporal extension: there is no division of his life into past or future stages, for that would imply temporal compositeness. The DDS in turn

is motivated by the consideration that God is a perfect being, and that *qua* perfect, he must be independent from all other things for his being the being he is, and he must be sovereign over all other things. If God himself were composite, then he would be dependent upon his components for his being what he is, whereas they would not be dependent upon him for their being what they are.[71]

The last part of this quote adds an important element to the discussion of simplicity. It explains part of the motivation behind this doctrine. That motivation is what Alvin Plantinga and others have labeled the aseity-simplicity intuition. As we saw when discussing aseity, God depends on nothing for his own existence. However, if attributes such as love, justice, eternity, etc., are conceived as universals independent of any being, and *God's* love, justice, etc., as just instances of those universals, then God apparently depends on these attributes (universals) for his own nature. If that is so, however, it seems that divine aseity must be rejected. In order to safeguard divine aseity, many theologians have opted for divine simplicity. In that case, God just is (in the strict sense of identity) identical with justice, love, and eternity, and each of those properties is identical with one another. By opting for divine simplicity, theologians saw a way to maintain the basic intuition behind aseity that God depends on nothing but himself for his own existence.

The doctrine of divine simplicity was much more prevalent during medieval times than today, but there are still theologians and philosophers who currently hold and defend it.[72] One reason for doing so is the belief just mentioned that without divine simplicity, it is impossible to hold divine aseity. Another reason, as we shall see in the chapter on God, time, and eternity, is the apparent logical connection between simplicity and atemporal eternity. A temporal being would undergo temporal succession, so there would be different temporal parts to its existence. An atemporal being would have no temporal parts, which fits the idea of divine simplicity, which says God has no parts at all, temporal or otherwise.

The arguments just suggested are typical of how divine simplicity is defended, and there is another argument that many proponents find quite compelling. It is the relationship between God as the most perfect being, divine aseity as self-dependence, and simplicity. Aseity is said to be a logical implication from the notion of God as the most perfect being. St. Anselm makes this argument in a long line of argument that moves from divine perfection to divine simplicity, and then on from simplicity to immutability and eternity. We need not examine all of this, but can focus on the parts most relevant to aseity and simplicity.

Anselm begins his *Monologium* by arguing that things which have their goodness through something else (i.e., they are contingent) are not supremely good. Only that which has its qualities through itself is supremely good.[73] This certainly fits what we have said about aseity as self-existence. By the end of chapter 4, Anselm has argued that there can be only one such being, and that it is what it is through itself. In chapters 5–14, Anselm argues that everything else exists through creation by this supreme being, but it depends only on itself. In chapter 15, Anselm concludes that this being must be whatever in general it is better to be than not to be. In chapter 16, the argument moves to establish simplicity. Anselm asks whether God's attributes are or are not properties independent of God's nature. He answers that God's attributes are not independent of his nature (he is simple), for then his nature would depend on them for existence, and that would contradict the point Anselm already made that God depends on nothing for his existence.[74]

Anselm predicates simplicity of God, but note the reason why! To say that an attribute is separate from God's nature as an abstract entity means that God depends on it in some way for his existence. But Anselm has already argued that the supremely perfect being exists through itself, not through anything other. To depend for its existence on something else, even an abstract entity such as a property, is to deny that it depends for its existence only on itself, and to deny that is to deny that it is the most supreme being. The most perfect being is supreme in virtue of depending on nothing but itself for its existence.

This notion of depending for one's existence only upon oneself is the attribute of aseity. Anselm's argument that eventually derives divine eternity from divine perfection is now clear. It moves from perfection to aseity, from aseity to simplicity, and then from simplicity to eternity.[75] So this argument for divine simplicity argues that a most perfect being could not depend on anything else for its existence, i.e., it must be *a se*. But for God to be self-dependent, he cannot rely on abstract properties in order to have a nature. The way to ensure that this does not happen is to argue that God is simple. If so, he just is identical to his nature and properties, and hence depends on nothing but himself for his existence.

Some theologians have found such arguments quite compelling. However, it is important to see whether Scripture teaches divine simplicity. In consulting various systematic theologies, one is hard pressed to find one that offers biblical support for the notion. There is no verse that explicitly teaches that God is simple. Nonetheless, theologians such as Louis Berkhof argue for it inferentially by appealing to other attributes that Scripture does teach. Berkhof's admission about its biblical backing is most revealing. He writes:

> The simplicity of God follows from some of His other perfections; from His self-existence, which excludes the idea that something preceded Him, as in the case of compounds; and from His immutability, which could not be predicated of His nature, if it were made up of parts. This perfection was disputed during the Middle Ages, and was denied by the Socinians and Arminians. *Scripture does not explicitly assert it, but implies it where it speaks of God as righteousness, truth, wisdom, light, life, love, and so on, and thus indicates that each of these properties, because of their absolute perfection, is identical with His being.*[76](italics mine)

While Berkhof admits that we must infer the doctrine from passages that speak of God's other attributes, Bavinck is more positive about its biblical

329 □ No One Like Him

support. Bavinck says that God's oneness is more than just the fact that there is only one God. It also means he is simple. Bavinck offers the following biblical support for this:

> This becomes clear when one considers the fact that Scripture in giving us a description of the fulness of God's being uses not only adjectives but also nouns: it tells us not only that God is faithful, righteous, living, omniscient, loving, wise, etc., but also that he is the truth, righteousness, life, light, love, wisdom, etc., Jer. 10:10; 23:6; John 1:4, 5, 9; 14:6; 1 Cor. 1:30; 1 John 1:5; 4:8; and that every attribute is identical with God's being by reason of the fact that every one of his virtues is absolutely perfect.[77]

What about this line of argument from Berkhof and Bavinck? As to simplicity logically following from immutability, I refer the reader to our discussion of immutability. If immutability means that God cannot change in any way, including relationally, then simplicity probably does follow from immutability. On the other hand, if one defines immutability as I have, so that God can change his relationships, then it isn't clear that an immutable being must also be simple.

As for the biblical passages Berkhof and especially Bavinck propose, such arguments beg the question and wrongly use surface grammar as indicating that these verses teach the doctrine. Bavinck and Berkhof assume that because there are biblical passages that speak of God as righteousness and truth, the writer is making the metaphysical point that God's being *is* these attributes. However, as even Bavinck admits, there are also biblical passages that refer to God as righteous (rather than righteousness) and true and faithful (rather than as truth). So, if we only look at the surface grammar of these passages, we can make a case against and for simplicity using Bavinck's and Berkhof's line of argument. Since there are two types of passages, it is question begging to appeal only to the one kind and argue that they tell us that the Bible teaches simplicity.

There are other problems with this line of argument. As noted, Berkhof and Bavinck assume that the surface grammar of certain passages tells us their depth grammar, and that the depth grammar makes a metaphysical point about the relation of the attribute named to God's being. That is, they assume that the biblical author is teaching us by the surface grammar of what he writes something about the way the attribute named relates to God's very being. This is question begging in several respects. It is dubious that the writer is trying to say anything more than that God has the attribute named. There needs to be further evidence in the text before we can conclude that the author intends to say either that the attribute named is equal to God's being or that it is only a part of God's being. Put differently, when John says that God is love, is the "is" the "is" of identity or the "is" of predication? If the former, then what John says allows us to infer simplicity. If the latter, then simplicity is not implied. From the context alone, we cannot tell which "is" it is, but given the general nature of the contexts in which such statements appear, it is dubious that the writer wants to teach some metaphysical doctrine about the relation of God to his attributes. Of course it is possible that the writer is making that point, but if so, he needs to make that clearer. As it stands, biblical data do not offer convincing support for the doctrine of divine simplicity. The data underdetermine the issue.

Perhaps Berkhof would reply that I have focused on only part of what he said. His point is not just that Scripture portrays God in the way he mentions, but that each of God's attributes is an absolute perfection and because of that God must have them in the way a simple being would have them. In response, I don't find this very illuminating. Why must an absolutely perfect being be simple? That is, why do perfect righteousness, love, and justice require that God be simple? Defenders of simplicity will likely say that these perfect attributes require simplicity because otherwise God depends on them for his very existence and then aseity is compromised. How could a perfect being not be *a se*? I shall address this matter momentarily, but I only note that it is an issue that goes well beyond what Scripture itself teaches.

The upshot of this discussion about the Bible and simplicity is that the Bible does not explicitly teach it. One must infer it in one of the ways Bavinck and Berkhof suggest. However, some of those inferences are clearly question begging, and others are not necessarily the only inferences possible from the biblical data about God's attributes. For anyone committed to a biblically based notion of God, the lack of biblical evidence for divine simplicity should be disconcerting at the least, and a good argument against it at most.

Apart from lacking biblical support, what is so wrong with divine simplicity? Why have philosophers and theologians found the doctrine so objectionable? Thomas Morris is very helpful by noting that divine simplicity may refer to any or all of three different claims. Those claims are:

(1) God is without any spatial parts (the thesis of spatial simplicity),
(2) God is without any temporal parts (the thesis of temporal simplicity), and
(3) God is without the sort of metaphysical complexity which would be involved in his exemplifying numerous different properties ontologically distinct from himself (the thesis of property simplicity).[78]

From these three theses, we can see where the debate lies. Since the Judaeo-Christian God is pure spirit, there is no debate over spatial simplicity. All sides agree that God is simple in this sense. The real points of contention are theses (2) and (3). Morris raises objections to both, whereas Alvin Plantinga critiques primarily thesis (3). Because I plan to discuss God, time, and eternity in chapter 9, I shall save objections to proposition (2) until then. My focus now is proposition (3).

In contemporary discussions, there have been two forms in which property simplicity has been held. The first has a much longer history and is called the "property view of divine simplicity." According to this view, there exist various properties as universals. To say that God is simple is just to say that there is no distinction between God's nature and these properties. He just is identical to properties such as wisdom, love, and power. Of course, if God's essence is identical to these properties, then each of these properties (either in God or independent of God as universals) is identical to the other properties. Thomas Morris explains the property view of divine simplicity as follows:

> We customarily, and permissibly ascribe numerous predicates to God—We say, for example, that God is wise, good and powerful. However, we are not thereby properly attributing a multiplicity of different properties to him. That is, we are not to be understood as holding that God stands in relations of exemplification or participation to a diversity of properties existing distinct from, and independent of, him. In the case of God, and of God alone, there is no multiplicity of properties instantiated. He is rather numerically identical with any property truly attributed to him. Thus, God = Wisdom, God = Goodness, God = Power, God = Justice, and so on. And of course, from this it follows by the principles governing identity that each divine property is identical with every other divine property, which means that in reality there is only one property that God has—a property with which he himself is identical.[79]

It is this notion of divine simplicity that Plantinga criticizes. He offers various compelling objections, and we should note the main ones. First, if God is identical with each of his properties (as is required with the property view of simplicity), then each of his properties is identical with each of his properties. But, then, God only has one property, and that does not square with the traditional Christian claim that he has a series of properties (justice, love, omnipotence, etc.), none of which is identical to any other.[80]

Second, and Plantinga thinks this is a monumental problem, if God is identical with each of his properties, then since those properties are each properties, God must be nothing more than a property. But, of course, "no property could have created the world; no property could be omniscient, or indeed, know anything at all. If God is a property, then he isn't a person but a mere abstract object; he has no knowledge, awareness, power, love or life."[81]

Perhaps, then, Plantinga reasons, we shouldn't speak of God as identical to a property but rather should speak of states of affairs consisting in God's being wise, powerful, etc. Though this may help with the first problem about God being identical with properties and all properties being identical with one another, it still has serious problems. For one thing, Plantinga notes that it does not resolve the problem for which simplicity was invoked. He explains:

> The underlying motivation for that doctrine was to provide a way out of the dilemma whose horns were: either God has no nature or else God isn't genuinely sovereign. The simplicity doctrine aims to escape

between the horns by holding that God has a nature and properties, all right, but they aren't distinct from him, so that he cannot rightly be said to be limited by something distinct from himself. But on the present suggestion, he does have a nature and properties distinct from him. On this view, God is identical with a certain state of affairs; even so, on the view in question, he has essentially such properties as goodness and knowledge and is distinct from them. Since they are essential to him, furthermore, they exist in every world he does. But Aquinas holds that God is a necessary being; he exists in every possible world. If so, the same must be said for these properties. But then how can they be dependent on him? That they exist and have the characteristics they have is not up to him. And won't he be dependent upon them for his nature and character? The dilemma remains untouched.[82]

Another problem with this view is that now God is no longer a property but a state of affairs, and that is just as troublesome as being a property. States of affairs are mere abstract objects which do not create, love, know, etc., anything.[83] So this modification won't help the property identity thesis at all.

Plantinga raises yet another problem with the simplicity doctrine. So far, we have only talked of typical divine properties such as omnipotence, love, and justice. God has these properties essentially, so without them there is no God. On the other hand, God also has accidental properties that do not refer to his very being but which are true of him.[84] For example, God has the property of having created Adam, the property of knowing that Adam sinned, and the property of being thought of by me as I write this sentence. God has many other similar properties, and none are essential to his very being. There are possible worlds in which Adam doesn't sin and I don't write these sentences, and there are other possible worlds in which Adam and I don't even exist. But the problem is deeper than whether all of God's properties are essential or some are accidental. The problem is that simplicity's property identity thesis makes God not only identical with his mercy, love, power, but also identical with these other properties, and they are identical with one another. It is hard to see how such properties can be identical to one another, and why one would hold a view that makes God *identical with* properties that are purely accidental.[85]

In light of such critiques, a second formulation of divine simplicity has arisen. William Mann, one of the ablest contemporary defenders of divine simplicity, proposes that instead of holding that God is identical to various attributes, we should say instead that he is identical with *his own instances* of these attributes.[86] This version of divine simplicity is called the "property instance view" of divine simplicity.

What does this mean? We can think of a *property* as an abstract object capable of being instantiated in various things. On the other hand, a *property instance* is a particular instantiation of a given property. As such, it is concrete rather than abstract. Even on this understanding, God's attributes as property instances seem distinct from one another, but with the notion of simplicity, each of those instances is identical with God's instanciations of his other attributes. This form of simplicity doesn't mean that wisdom, power, and love are identical with one another, but that God's wisdom, God's power, and God's love are identical with one another.[87] Since no property instance could be a person, this seems problematic. To counter this objection, Mann introduces the notion of a "rich property." A rich property is just a conjunctive property "whose conjuncts are all and only the essential and accidental properties of that person."[88] Every person, then, is just an instance of a rich property. This should meet the objection that no property instance could be a person, for if each individual is an instance of her own rich property, and if a rich property contains everything true of the person, it appears that a property instance can be a person. Mann explains the property instance view as follows:

> It identifies God with his own omniscience, his own omnipotence, and the like, where, for example, 'the omniscience of God' is construed as referring to an instance of the property *being omniscient*. The property instance view maintains that 'God', 'the omniscience of God', and 'the omnipotence of God' all refer to the same property instance, namely, God. Against the possible objection that no property instance could be a person, I have argued on behalf of the property instance view that on the contrary, every person is an instance of a *rich property*, a conjunctive property whose conjuncts are all and only the essential and accidental properties of that person.[89]

Various objections have been raised against the property instance view of simplicity. Thankfully, Mann has responded to some of the most significant, so we can see what he would say and assess its cogency. An initial complaint comes from Brian Leftow. He writes:

> Mann then argues that some attribute-instances are concreta: for example, we ourselves are instances of certain attributes. If this is so, Mann contends, one can maintain that a simple deity is identical with attribute-instances and yet concrete. But Mann's proposal either reduces to a version of the claim that God is identical with attributes *simpliciter* or is not really a doctrine of divine simplicity at all. For either there is or there is not some entity involved in an attribute-instance which is distinct from the attribute being instanced. If there is nothing in an attribute-instance which is distinct from the attribute instanced, what Mann proposes is only a shift in terminology, and in fact on his doctrine as on Aquinas', God is identical with attributes. If there is something in an attribute-instance which is distinct from the attribute involved, then an attribute-instance is a metaphysically complex thing, and so is a God who is identical with an attribute-instance.[90]

This objection might lead to another complaint. If God is identical to his attribute instances, then since there is more than one divine attribute, God appears to be a composite of various attribute-instances, in which case he is not simple. Now, Mann might respond that his notion of a rich property solves this problem. God is identical with only one property instance, namely, his rich property. However, Mann defines a rich property as a conjunctive property made up of all of an individual's properties. If this is so, however, then the rich property seems to be a composite, and if God is identical to his rich property, then he cannot be simple.

Perhaps Mann would reply that this problem does not arise, since it turns out with this view of divine simplicity that property instances are identical to one another. Thus, in saying that God's rich property is a conjunctive one, we don't predicate multiplicity in God, since each of the conjuncts is identical with each of the other conjuncts of this rich property. However, this doesn't seem to solve the problem any more than saying that properties are identical (on the property view of simplicity). For just as it makes little sense to say that power just is love, and that those two attributes are the same properties as eternity, likewise it makes little sense to say that God's property instance of power just is identical with his property instance of grace. Are not instances of two distinct attributes distinct instances as well?

So, according to this line of argument, Mann's proposal faces a dilemma. Either God's rich property really is a composite of distinct property instances and then God is composite rather than simple, or God's rich property, though a conjunct of all his property instances, is still not composite, because each property instance is identical to every other one of his property instances. But in the latter case, all property instances are identical, and that seems problematic.

Mann might respond that the answer to this dilemma is to hold that God's rich property is a conjunctive property, but that does not necessitate composite-ness, because God's instance of omniscience, for example, just is identical with omniscience, his instance of love just is identical with love, etc. In that case, since God's property instances are all identical with the properties they instanciate, the instances and the properties must genuinely be identical with one another, so there really would be no complexity in God's nature after all. I shall return to this proposal, for Mann does use it to answer other objections, but let me say now that this still seems to have the problem of making properties identical that are quite disparate (this was a problem that Plantinga raised with the property view of simplicity), and it doesn't explain any better how a property instance of one attribute can be identical to a property instance of another.

Thomas Morris offers another significant objection to the property instance view. One of the reasons proponents of divine simplicity hold it is an appeal to the simplicity-aseity intuition. However, as Morris argues, the property instance view of simplicity runs into just as much of a problem on this matter of aseity as does the property view. For now we need not say that God depends on his properties to be who he is, but instead he depends on other abstract objects (property instances) to be what he is. If we say that God has only one rich property, God is still an instance of that property, so he still depends on something independent of himself.[91]

Mann recognizes that this is a problem for his view. If one holds the property instance view of simplicity, then one contradicts divine aseity. If one opts instead for the property view of simplicity, then one runs aground on Plantinga's complaints about transforming God into a property.[92] Mann proposes to handle this dilemma by grasping both of its horns. He explains:

> The property instance view identifies God with, for example, his own omniscience. The property view identifies God with omniscience itself. What I propose is to identify God's omniscience with omniscience itself. The proposed identity has the following immediate consequences. First, it obviates Morris's objection. If God and his omniscience just are omniscience itself, then there is no property distinct from God of which he is an instance. Second, since the property of omniscience is identified with its instance, God, it follows that if we are monotheists we will be committed to holding that omniscience either is not or cannot be replicated, depending on the modal strength of our monotheism. Analogous remarks will hold for omnipotence and the other standard divine attributes.[93]

This is the view I raised above about *God's* instance of an attribute being identical with the attribute itself. As already noted, this doesn't explain how attributes that are clearly different are identical. Mann might say that this only seems problematic because these qualities in humans are so distinct, but divine omniscience, divine love, divine justice, and the like, are attributes that really are identical. Here one is inclined to invoke Wolterstorff's reply to the proposal that God's instance of omniscience just is omniscience, etc. He says that this proposal appears to be ad hoc. As he explains:

> One looks for a general discussion of properties and property instances in which it is shown that certain properties are self-instantiating (n.b., not self-exemplifying but self-*instantiating*), in which the general conditions under which that is the case are laid out, and in which it is shown that these conditions are satisfied in the case of omniscience, omnipotence, omnibenevolence, and the rest of God's properties. But Mann offers no such general ontological discussion.[94]

Here I agree with Wolterstorff and would add that if Mann were to say that the *divine* attributes really are identical with one another (though in humans the attributes differ), and that this is so because they are divine rather than human, such claims would also be ad hoc. I am not saying that there is no difference between divine and human attributes whatsoever, but only that I have seen nothing from Mann or anyone else which shows that they are different in that, while power and love in us, for example, are separate qualities, in God they are identical. Hence, the resolution seems ad hoc.

But there is a second problem with Mann's equation of God's omniscience with omniscience, etc. As Wolterstorff explains, "if God is identical with the property instance, God's omniscience, and if that property instance is identical with the property, omniscience, then it follows that God is a property."[95] Of course, we have already seen the problems with saying that God is a property. So if we adopt Mann's move, the property instance view of simplicity reduces to the property view of simplicity, and it is subject to all of Plantinga's criticisms.

Mann is aware of this potential problem, and even though he thinks his proposal solves the aseity issue, he admits that it doesn't necessarily address Plantinga's complaint against the property view that if God is a property, he must be an abstract object, incapable of having the personal attributes which belong to God. Mann replies by rejecting Plantinga's assumption that properties are abstract objects. Instead, he holds that properties are causal powers. Mann explains:

> P is a property of an object, x, only if P's presence in x confers some causal power(s) on x. P and Q are the same property if and only if (1) P and Q confer the same causal powers on their objects and (2) whatever is sufficient to bring about an instance of P in an object, x, is sufficient to bring about an instance of Q in x, and vice versa. . . . Much more work needs to be done to elaborate and defend a causal theory of properties, but this is not the occasion to carry out that task. All I need to note presently is that if properties are causal powers and if God is a property, then he is a causal power. Moreover, if the property that God is is variously identified as omniscience, omnipotence, moral perfection, and the like, then the property *cum* causal power that God *is* looks more and more analogous to the causal powers that ordinary persons *have*.[96]

This is certainly a strange view of properties, and as many note, Mann develops it so little that there is little we can make of it. He offers no argument for it other than the implicit assumption that if one adopts it, it appears to handle the objection that properties are abstract objects. But that in itself is not reason enough to agree that properties really are just causal powers.[97]

So, there appear to be problems with both the property view of simplicity and the property instance view. These philosophical problems plus the biblical considerations raised earlier lead me to conclude that simplicity is not one of the divine attributes. This doesn't mean that God has physical parts, but that the implications of the doctrine of metaphysical simplicity are too problematic to maintain the doctrine.

Before closing this discussion I must return to the matter of aseity. One of the reasons for adopting simplicity is to safeguard divine aseity. In chapter 6, I noted that aseity as self-reliance or dependence can be understood in two different ways. It is the second way that is now under consideration. If we reject simplicity, must we also abandon aseity as self-dependence? Of course, if simplicity is objectionable on grounds independent of the aseity question, we cannot hold it, regardless of what we think this means to God's aseity. And we have already seen that there is ample reason to reject simplicity. Still, for several reasons, I don't believe that rejecting simplicity significantly endangers divine sovereignty or aseity. First, as Thomas Morris shows, it isn't clear that simplicity safeguards aseity as the simplicity holder believes. So that motivation behind holding simplicity does not succeed. Morris explains:

> What the simplicity theorist is concerned about is that, given the necessary goodness of God, for example, if goodness is thought of as a property distinct from God, then it is true that
>
> (1) If the property of goodness did not exist, then God would not exist.
>
> But this is just an expression of the idea that God's goodness is essential to him—that God is good in every circumstance in which he exists. But since, on the view we have been developing, it is also true that God exists necessarily, in every possible world, it can also be said of the property of goodness that it is essentially such that it is possessed by God. And this can be seen to support the truth of
>
> (2) If God did not exist, then the property of goodness would not exist.
>
> The simplicity theorist thinks that (1) expresses the dependence of God on the property of goodness. But if it did, (2) would express the dependence of the property of goodness on God. But, presumably, ontological dependence, dependence for being or existence, can only go in one direction—if my parents brought me into existence it cannot also be the case that I brought them into existence. Thus, the mere existence and truth of propositions like (1) and (2) cannot alone be taken to show ontological dependence. Their truth merely reflects the logical relation which holds between propositions about necessarily existent entities, and alone implies nothing about the ontological dependence or independence of those entities.[98]

Thus it isn't clear that even if God has a nature, i.e., one made of properties that are independent of him, he cannot have aseity, especially since he is a necessary being.

Plantinga offers a second line of argument relevant to the simplicity/aseity issue. Having rejected the idea that God is identical to his nature (i.e., divine simplicity is incorrect), and the idea that God has no nature (nominalism which denies that there are abstract entities like properties that exist independent of specific things in our world), Plantinga concludes that God does have a nature and that there are properties independent of him over which he has no control. Does this mean God is no longer sovereign and no longer has aseity? As Plantinga shows, if one holds a view like Descartes' (Plantinga labels it universal possibilism), then probably God's having a nature and there being properties over which he has no control would mean that God is not sovereign and is not *a se*. But, of course, this is so because universal possibilism postulates that God has power to the extent that everything is possible, even the logically contradictory. If this sounds familiar, it should, for it is just the position we have labeled theonomy and medievals called voluntarism. So, if one is a theonomist, indeed, it will compromise aseity as self-dependence (in the sense under consideration) and sovereignty to say that God has a nature and that there are properties over which he has no control.[99] But why should one be a theonomist?

On the other hand, if one rejects theonomy of the variety that Descartes seemed to hold, then God can have a nature and there can be properties over which he doesn't have control, but this is a limitation that is not significant.[100] We might need to revise slightly our notion of sovereignty and to interpret aseity as self-reliance only in the first sense articulated in chapter 6, so that sovereignty and aseity do not include God's control over the properties that make up his nature but God still remains sovereign and *a se* in senses already articulated.

What I am saying is that there is no need to hold simplicity to safeguard aseity, unless one holds a metaphysic such as theonomy and defines aseity and sovereignty as a theonomist would. But if you hold a more rationalistic metaphysic such as modified rationalism, then God's aseity does not require him to control things such as properties in general, or the specific properties that make up his nature. Hence, we need not hold simplicity to safeguard aseity. In addition, on a rationalistic metaphysic, aseity and sovereignty do not require God to be capable of doing the logically impossible, but no Leibnizian rationalist and few, if any, modified rationalists would deem this limitation significant to whether God is sovereign and *a se*. So, unless one holds a theonomous metaphysic, there is nothing about aseity and sovereignty that simplicity protects that should really concern one, and simplicity can be discarded without damaging aseity, sovereignty, or a rationalistic metaphysic.

This discussion yields two conclusions. First, there are ample grounds for rejecting the doctrine of divine simplicity (Morris's proposition [3]) apart from anything relevant to aseity. Second, there is no need to hold simplicity in order to protect aseity and sovereignty. For one thing, if Morris's argument is right, it doesn't protect it anyway. Moreover, there is no need to hold simplicity to protect aseity unless one is a theonomist and interprets aseity along theonomous lines; otherwise God can still be sovereign and *a se* in meaningful senses even without simplicity.

THE MORAL ATTRIBUTES OF GOD

If the non-moral attributes cause us to stand in awe of the grandeur, power, and majesty of God, his moral attributes evoke no less wonder. It is God's moral attributes that offer us the best picture of how God treats his creatures. In reflecting on how he handles us, we are led to rejoice over his gracious and loving treatment. It is so wonderful to know that our lives and destinies are in the hands of one who is not a malignant being but a good God! To be subject to an omnipotent but evil God would terrorize us moment by moment. What a blessing to know that we are in the hands of a loving, just, and compassionate deity!

As we reflect on the moral excellencies of God, we must remember a point raised in previous chapters. Divine attributes such as love, goodness, truth, and justice do not obligate God to do every loving, just, good, and true thing he possibly can do. Instead, these attributes guarantee that everything God *does* exhibits these qualities. At times we may not understand how his actions are loving, gracious, and merciful, but at any moment our perspectives are so limited to the details of the immediate. It is at points like these that the only assurance we may have beyond the Holy Spirit's witness to our minds and hearts is the truth of biblical revelation that God does possess these attributes and always acts in character.

HOLINESS

In Hebrew a series of terms are used to refer to divine holiness. The main verb is *qādaš,* which means to be holy or sanctified and to consecrate or sanctify. In the Qal it designates the state of things that belong to the sphere of the sacred. They are set apart or consecrated to sacred use rather than profane.

This concept, of course, is amply exemplified in the cultic rituals and restrictions in the Mosaic Law. In the Piel and Hiphil the verb connotes the action by which the distinction between sacred and profane is effected. In other words, it often indicates the act of consecration, as in Exod 19:23. In the Niphal the verb can mean the proving of one's holiness. For example, God proves or demonstrates his holiness by judging sin (Lev 10:1-3) or by keeping his promises (Ezek 20:41; 28:25; 39:27).[1]

In addition to the verb for holiness, there are several nouns that seem to stem from the verb *qādaš*. For example, *qōdeš* (translated "apartness," "holiness," "sacredness") designates the concept of holiness. It indicates "the essential nature of that which belongs to the sphere of the sacred and which is thus distinct from the common or profane."[2] Moreover, the adjective *qādoš* (translated "holy," "holy one," and "saint") is used to refer to someone or something that is intrinsically sacred or that has been admitted to the sphere of the sacred by a divine rite or cultic act. Of course, God is intrinsically holy. Finally, there are several instances where the Hebrew adjective *ḥasîd* is used of God (Ps 16:10; 89:20[Heb]; 145:17). Though this term seems to come from the root *ḥsd*, a root from which come such words as *ḥesed* (often translated "steadfast love," "lovingkindness," or "loyal love"), it is often used of God's people. Whether the writers use it this way because God's people were recipients of his *ḥesed* or were themselves characterized by this *ḥesed* or both is not entirely certain. However, the term is used of God and is translated "holy."[3]

In the Greek, a cluster of terms is used to designate holiness. The main verb is *hagiazō* and the adjective is *hagios*, "holy." In the NT God, Christ, and the Holy Spirit are spoken of as holy, but the church and the life of the Christian are also described as holy.

As these Hebrew and Greek terms are used of God, Scripture offers a twofold picture of divine holiness. On the one hand, God is holy in that he is distinct or separate from everything else. Some call this aspect of divine holiness majesty-holiness. This aspect of God's holiness is the one less thought of, and it actually bears greater affinity to infinity, aseity, and unity—non-moral divine attributes. As the majestic God whose qualities know no boundary, God's being is infinitely above his creatures. Moreover, as distinct from creation, he does not depend on anyone or anything to bring him into existence or to sustain him in being. And, of course, there is only one being with such majesty and perfection. He is the unique (unity) God.

Many biblical passages portray God as the majestic and powerful one. In 1 Sam 2:2 we read, "There is no one holy like the Lord, indeed, there is no one besides Thee, nor is there any rock like our God." This speaks both of his majesty and of his uniqueness. Similarly, we find in Exod 15:11, "Who is like Thee among the gods, O Lord? Who is like Thee, majestic in holiness, awesome in praises, working wonders?" In Ps 99:3, 5, 9, the psalmist encourages readers to exalt the Lord for his holiness. This again speaks of his majesty (see also 2 Chron 20:21; Ps 22:3; 30:4; 33:21; 68:17, 35; 98:1).

We find this theme in the prophets as well. Isaiah's vision of the Lord includes angels surrounding God's throne and saying, "Holy, Holy, Holy, is the LORD of hosts, the whole earth is full of His glory" (Isa 6:3). Isaiah responds by repenting of his sin, but he was impressed with more than God's moral purity. The portrait is one of the great power and grandeur of God. In Isa 52:10, we find a linkage between God's power and holiness (see also Ezek 39:25).

This theme of majesty-holiness also appears in the NT. After Mary learned that she would give birth to the Messiah, she said (Luke 1:49), "For the Mighty One has done great things for me; and holy is His name." In Revelation 4 we find a scene reminiscent of Isaiah 6. John describes what he saw as he was lifted into heaven before God's presence (Rev 4:8; see also Rev 3:7).

In addition to these passages that speak so directly of God's majesty-holiness, other passages that speak of his holiness may be seen as referring to his majesty. In specific verses it is hard to tell whether the focus is on God's grandeur or his moral purity, but the contexts where these verses are found clarify that the focus is God's majesty. For example, in many passages the writers extol the virtues and greatness of God and also speak of God's holiness. In such contexts, the focus is most likely primarily on God's majesty-holiness. First Chronicles 16:10, 35; 29:16 all offer praise to God for his many excellencies (see also Ps 68:5 and Prov 9:10).

Likewise, the psalmists often praise the Lord for his many-faceted greatness. In so doing, they speak of God's holiness. In Ps 105:3 we read, "Glory in His holy name; let the heart of those who seek the LORD be glad" (see also Ps 106:47; 108:7). In one passage (Ps 47:8), the psalmist praises God for his sovereign control: "God reigns over the nations, God sits on His holy throne." In another, the psalmist extols God's mighty deeds (Ps 111:9).

Because of God's majesty and grandeur, even the places where he dwells and is worshiped are considered holy, and the thought is primarily of his majesty-holiness. We read, for example, in Ps 46:4, "There is a river whose streams make glad the city of God, the holy dwelling places of the Most High." In Isa 57:15 we read, "For thus says the high and exalted One who lives forever, whose name is Holy, 'I dwell on a high and holy place'" (see also Deut 26:15; Ps 3:4; 11:4; 20:6; 28:2; 48:1; 65:4; 68:5, 17, 35; 87:1; Isa 57:13; Jer 25:30; Ezek 28:14; Joel 2:1; Zech 2:13).

Likewise, the Lord's very name is holy, not just the places and things associated with him. "Bless the LORD, O my soul; and all that is within me, bless His holy name" (Ps 103:1). See also, for example, 1 Chron 16:10, 35; 29:16; Ps 105:3; 106:47; 145:21. In their respective contexts, these verses emphasize God's majesty and grandeur.

Moreover, various writers, when speaking of God, refer to him by a descriptive phrase that includes the word "holy," and the contexts in which many of these phrases appear relate to God's majesty-holiness. For example, the writer of Kings says (2 Kgs 19:22), "Whom have you reproached and blasphemed? And against whom have you raised your voice, and haughtily lifted up your eyes? Against the Holy One of Israel!" By far, the author who most often uses such a descriptive phrase to designate God is Isaiah. Repeatedly, he speaks of the "Holy One of Israel." Passages where the emphasis is primarily the grandeur of God are plentiful. In Isa 31:1 we find, "Woe to those who go down to Egypt for help, and rely on horses, and trust in chariots because they are many, and in horsemen because they are very strong, but they do not look to the Holy One of Israel, nor seek the LORD!" (see also Isa 10:17; 12:6; 17:7; 37:23; 40:25; 41:14, 16, 20; 43:3, 14, 15; 45:11; 47:4; 48:17; 54:5; 55:5; 60:9, 14). Though this descriptive phrase is most frequently found in Isaiah, other OT writers also use it to speak of God's majesty-holiness (see Ps 71:22; 89:18; Jer 50:29; Hab 1:12; 3:3).

The second sense in which God is separate or set apart from everything is in his moral purity and perfection, the concept we most often associate with divine holiness. God is free from the pollution of sin, for he cannot sin. In fact, he is so pure and perfect that Scripture says he cannot even be tempted to sin (Jas 1:13). Though God could have decided not to obligate himself to obey any moral rules, the description of God's actions in Scripture shows that he abides by the same standards he has set for us. In fact, God's moral norms are expressions of his moral attributes, so in obeying those norms God is just being consistent with who he is.

Many are the biblical passages that speak of God's moral purity and uprightness. The psalmist says of God (Ps 145:17, KJV), "The LORD is righteous in all his ways, and holy in all his works" (see also 1 Sam 6:20). In some cases (e.g., Ps 105:42) God is shown to be holy in virtue of his actions: "For He remembered His holy word with Abraham His servant." In fact, in virtue of his holiness, on some occasions God swears that he will do something. Being morally pure, which involves truthfulness, he cannot fail to keep his promises. The psalmist writes (Ps 89:35), "Once I have sworn by My holiness; I will not lie to David" (see also Amos 4:2). In the NT, Peter, citing Leviticus, writes (1 Pet 1:15-16), "But like the Holy One who called you, be holy yourselves also in all your behavior; because it is written, 'You shall be holy, for I am holy.'" As to Jesus, the author of Hebrews writes (7:26), "For it was fitting that we should have such a high priest, holy, innocent, undefiled, separated from sinners and exalted above the heavens."

In addition, we find in Hos 11:9 a clear picture of the difference between God and man. Though the focus is not explicitly moral holiness, the context suggests that to be the point. Despite Israel's unfaithfulness to God and his right to judge them, he says, "I will not execute My fierce anger; I will not destroy Ephraim again. For I am God and not man, the Holy One in your midst, and I will not come in wrath." A human, as morally impure and finite, would seek revenge, but not God. Other passages that speak of God's moral purity are Josh 24:19; Ps 60:6; Isa 5:16; Jer 23:9; Mal 2:11; Heb 12:10.

Another way that biblical writers speak of God's moral holiness is to refer to his purity. Because of his holiness, his word (whether part of Scripture or not) is pure and true (Ps 12:6; see also Ps 119:140; Prov 30:5). Thus, God's commands must be morally right also. The psalmist agrees (Ps 19:8): "The precepts of the LORD are right, rejoicing the heart; the commandment of the LORD is pure, enlightening the eyes." Not only are God's words and commands pure; his very person is morally pure, and God's purity far exceeds ours. That is the implication of Eliphaz's question to Job (Job 4:17): "Can mankind be just before God? Can a man be pure before his Maker?"

In the OT Holiness Code, we find that God wanted his people to be separate from other peoples and to worship him in purity alone. Repeatedly in the Holiness Code, the Lord reminds Israel that these regulations are given because of his holiness and his desire for them to be holy (Lev 19:2; 20:3, 26) In the NT as well, God demands of his people moral purity, and the standard for that purity is God himself (1 Pet 1:15-16). In 1 John 3:3 John says that believers who shall someday be like the Lord when he returns need even now to lead holy lives.

As in the case of majesty-holiness, some passages that speak of God's holiness do not clarify whether majesty-holiness or moral purity is in view, but the context makes it clear that moral purity is the most likely focus. In Ps 24:3, the psalmist asks, "Who may ascend into the hill of the LORD? And who may stand in His holy place?" In light of the answer that only those with clean hands and a pure heart can do so, moral purity is likely the point (see also Ps 97:12).

There are also passages about God's holiness where the focus seems to be moral purity but separation from the profane and ceremonially unclean is also the point. Consider Lev 11:44-45; 21:8. Consider also Isa 29:23, which carries the note of consecrating or separating God apart as special to be worshiped as opposed to pagan gods: "But when he sees his children, the work of My hands, in his midst, they will sanctify My name; indeed, they will sanctify the Holy One of Jacob, and will stand in awe of the God of Israel." Moreover, in Ezek 22:8, 26 we hear God's complaint against Israel that she has violated his moral and ceremonial cleanness.

In some passages that speak of God's holiness, the context seems to require a reference both to God's moral purity and to his majesty. For example, Ezekiel, speaking of God's eschatological deliverance of Israel, says (Ezek 36:22), "Thus says the LORD GOD, 'It is not for your sake, O house of Israel, that I am about to act, but for My holy name, which you have profaned among the nations where you went'" (see also Ezek 39:7 and Rev 15:4).

Just as God's majesty-holiness is associated with places where he dwells and is worshiped, the same is true of his moral purity. The psalmist asks (Ps 15:1), "O LORD, who may abide in Thy tent? Who may dwell on Thy holy hill?" In another psalm (Ps 138:2), the writer expresses his intention to worship in God's holy temple. Once he had tried to run away from God, Jonah recognized his moral separation from God (Jon 2:4, 7; see also Exod 15:13; Ps 43:3; Ezek 44:13; Dan 9:16, 20; Mic 1:2; Hab 2:20). In addition, many passages that associate a place with God's moral holiness are eschatological in nature. For example, Isa 11:9 says, "They will not hurt or destroy in all My holy mountain, for the earth will be full of the knowledge of the LORD as the waters cover the sea" (see also Zech 8:3; Isa 27:13; 56:7; 65:11, 25; 66:20; Joel 3:17; Zeph 3:11).

The Lord's name is frequently referred to as holy, and in many contexts the point is his moral purity. Quite frequently this is so in the book of Ezekiel. For example, in 20:39 we read, "'As for you, O house of Israel,' thus says the LORD GOD, 'Go, serve everyone his idols; but later, you will surely listen to Me, and My holy name you will profane no longer with your gifts and with your idols'" (see also Ezek 36:20-21; 43:7-8; Amos 2:7). As in the case of majesty-holiness, the descriptive name "the Holy One of Israel" is also used in contexts where the primary thought is moral purity (see Isa 1:4; 5:24; 30:11; Jer 51:5). In the NT our Lord Jesus Christ is referred to in this way. On one occasion he is called the "Holy One of God" by demons he casts out (Mark 1:24; parallel Luke 4:34). In several instances this term is ascribed to Jesus, but it isn't clear whether the focus is moral purity or majesty-holiness. For example, in Acts 2:27 (quote of Ps 16:10) we read, "Because Thou wilt not abandon my soul to Hades, nor allow Thy Holy One to undergo decay." Peter says (Acts 3:14; see also 13:35), "But you disowned the Holy and Righteous One, and asked for a murderer to be granted to you."

God as morally pure cannot stand sin, and Scripture shows that he hates it. The writer of Proverbs is very specific about sinful behavior that God hates. He writes (Prov 6:16-19), "There are six things which the LORD hates, yes, seven which are an abomination to Him: haughty eyes, a lying tongue, and hands that shed innocent blood, a heart that devises wicked plans, feet that run rapidly to evil, a false witness who utters lies, and one who spreads strife among brothers" (see also Zech 8:17). Consequently, the psalmist pleads (Ps 97:10), "Hate evil, you who love the LORD."

Not only does God hate sin, but Scripture shows that he must and will judge it, for a morally perfect God cannot allow sin to go unpunished. We see this theme repeatedly in the Pauline epistles (e.g., Rom 1:18; Eph 5:6; Col 3:6; see also an instance of such punishment in the OT in Ps 78:31). Not only does God punish individuals for their sins, but the book of Revelation shows repeatedly the outpouring of eschatological wrath against the corporate wickedness of the nations (see Rev 14:10, 19; 15:1, 7; and chapter 16).

Because of God's hatred of sin and the awesome power of his judgments, his people are warned to worship only him, for (Deut 4:24) "the LORD your God is a consuming fire, a jealous God." Likewise, in the NT believers are encouraged to worship and serve God unswervingly, "For our God is a consuming fire" (Heb 12:29). In the face of such awesome majesty and moral purity, regardless of how close one is walking to the Lord, the only appropriate response when confronted with God's majesty and purity is that of Isaiah (6:5), "Woe is me, for I am ruined! Because I am a man of unclean lips" (see also 42:5-6).

Finally, there are passages that in one way or another designate a particular member of the Godhead. The psalmist seems to refer to the Holy Spirit when he says (Ps 51:11), "Do not cast me away from Thy presence; and do not take Thy Holy Spirit from me" (see also Isa 63:11). The apostle John says of the Father (1 John 2:20), "But you have an anointing from the Holy One, and you all know." The anointing seems best understood as a reference to the Holy Spirit himself. In the following verses, John says that because of this anointing which is the Holy Spirit, his readers don't need the false teachers who claim to lead them into the depths of truth. Having the Holy Spirit, they have all the access they need to the deep truths of God (see also 2 Tim 1:14).

In addition, in Jesus' prayer (John 17:11) he refers to God as the "Holy Father," and various NT passages refer to Jesus as holy (e.g., Acts 4:27, 30).

RIGHTEOUSNESS

In addition to God's other moral perfections, we can see his moral purity through his righteousness. As righteous, he has established a moral order for the universe, and he treats all creatures fairly.

In the OT, the basic words denoting righteousness and justice cluster into one word group. Whether we are looking at the verb *ṣādaq* ("to be righteous"), the various nouns in this group—*ṣedeq* ("rightness," "justice," "righteousness"—masculine) and *ṣĕdāqāh* ("rightness," "justice," "righteousness"—feminine)—or the adjective *ṣaddîq*, the basic meaning is the same. The root word basically speaks of conformity to an ethical or moral standard. In the OT that standard is the character and nature of God. Hence God is called just and righteous in himself, and in a forensic sense, his judgments and dealings with mankind are just.[4]

In the NT as well, we find a rich set of words that connote the righteousness and justice of God. The main terms are the adjective *dikaios* ("righteous") and the noun *dikaiosunē* ("righteousness"). These terms are used in a variety of senses in classical Greek and in the NT as well. They speak of right conduct before God, but also of just judgments and rule. In the NT, especially the Pauline literature, *diakaosunē theoû* ("the righteousness of God") is often used to speak of the forensic transaction whereby the sinner is pardoned and justified by God.[5]

There is a wealth of biblical material on the righteousness and justice of God. In many instances God is referred to as righteous, and the point is that he is morally pure. He does what is right, and thus is characterized by moral rectitude. In Isaiah 45 we read (verses 19, 23-24), "I, the LORD, speak righteousness declaring things that are upright. . . . I have sworn by Myself, the word has gone forth from My mouth in righteousness and will not turn back, . . . They will say of Me, 'Only in the LORD are righteousness and strength'" (see also Exod 9:27; 2 Chron 12:6; Ezra 9:15; Neh 9:8; Job 4:17; 35:2; 36:3; Ps 5:8; 31:1; 33:5; 40:10; 45:4, 7; 69:27; 71:2, 19; 89:16; 111:3; 116:5; 119:123;

143:1; 145:7, 17; Prov 2:9; 15:9; Isa 46:13; 51:6, 8; 53:11; 54:17; 59:16, 17; Jer 23:5; Lam 1:18; Dan 9:7, 16; Hos 2:19; Zeph 3:5; Zech 8:8; 9:9).

In the NT we find similar references to God's righteousness. Jesus said in the Sermon on the Mount (Matt 6:33): "But seek first His kingdom and His righteousness; and all these things shall be added to you." In the great passage on the imputation of Adam's sin and of Christ's righteousness Paul writes (Rom 5:18, 21): "So then as through one transgression there resulted condemnation to all men, even so through one act of righteousness there resulted justification of life to all men. . . . that, as sin reigned in death, even so grace might reign through righteousness to eternal life through Jesus Christ our Lord." Of Christ, Peter says (1 Pet 3:18): "For Christ also died for sins once for all, the just for the unjust." And John writes (1 John 2:1): "if anyone sins, we have an Advocate with the Father, Jesus Christ the righteous" (see also Heb 1:9; 1 John 2:29; 3:7).

Though there is massive biblical material on God's righteousness as his moral purity, this isn't all that Scripture says about the righteousness of God. There is a biblical theme that theologians refer to as the *rectoral justice* of God. This refers to God's instituting moral governance in our universe. As a result, there are rules that define good and evil acts and stipulate rewards and punishment for those who obey or disobey, and God enforces those rules as judge over all. Are the rules arbitrary, immoral, or unfair? Not at all, for God's rectoral justice means that he has ordained rules that are morally right, and they are fair because they are not impossible to obey, even though we are inclined to disobey. God's moral governance is also fair in that God's punishments are appropriate to our crimes. As we read in Job 34:23 (KJV), "He will not lay upon man more than right." Again Job 37:23 says: "The Almighty— we cannot find Him; He is exalted in power; and He will not do violence to justice and abundant righteousness" (see also Gen 18:25).

Numerous other passages speak of God's rectoral justice. Many teach that he has implemented morally right rules to govern his creatures. We see this repeatedly in Psalm 119 (vv. 62, 106, 137-138, 160, 164, 172). We find the same point in Hos 14:9: "For the ways of the LORD are right, and the righteous will walk in them, but transgressors will stumble in them."

God is also a righteous moral governor in his handling of our salvation. We see various evidences of this especially in the book of Romans. Though God loves the sinner, he hates sin and must punish it. But he sent Christ as our substitute, and this act showed his great love to us. Moreover, by requiring his Son's death to pay for our sin, God also demonstrated that the demands of his righteous law must be met. Paul says of Christ (Rom 3:25-26), "whom God displayed publicly as a propitiation in His blood through faith. This was to demonstrate His righteousness, because in the forbearance of God He passed over the sins previously committed; for the demonstration, I say, of His righteousness at the present time, that He might be just and the justifier of the one who has faith in Jesus." Not just any righteousness will satisfy God. Those who try to please him by keeping the law will fail. Only the righteousness which is by faith is sufficient to give anyone right standing before God. In Romans 10 Paul speaks of the error of his Jewish brethren in this matter (10:3): "For not knowing about God's righteousness, and seeking to establish their own, they did not subject themselves to the righteousness of God." God as a righteous moral governor has ordained a specific way for handling salvation, and no other way will do. Hence, Paul's desire (Phil 3:9) is to "be found in him, not having a righteousness of my own derived from the Law, but that which is through faith in Christ, the righteousness which comes from God on the basis of faith."

Many other passages speak of Christ's coming reign on earth in what is known as the millennial kingdom. Regardless of whether the passage is in the OT or the NT, it is clear that when Christ establishes his kingdom on earth he will be ruler over all, and he will rule in righteousness. Fair laws will be implemented and enforced, sin will be punished, and obedience to the King will be rewarded (Isa 11:4-5; Jer 33:15; Heb 1:8).

A final indication of God's rectoral justice is the fact that he is judge of all the earth. Many passages show that he has the authority to judge, and that he judges with fairness. We see this especially in the Psalms (9:8; 36:6; 50:6; 51:14; 72:1-2; 96:13; 97:2; 99:4).

In addition to God's rectoral justice, he is fair in his treatment of individuals. It would not be very comforting to know that there is a moral order, with a judge to enforce moral rule, if we also knew that the judge was not inclined to enforce that law or enforced it unfairly. Philosophers typically talk of two kinds of social and political justice. On the one hand, there is *egalitarian justice,* and on the other, there is *distributive justice.*

Egalitarian justice distributes exactly the same thing to everyone. No one gets more or less than anyone else. Distributive justice, on the other hand, renders to each person exactly what is due; no more and no less. Though everyone might deserve the same thing, that rarely happens; and even if everyone merited and received the same thing, that would still be distributive justice, not egalitarian. When egalitarian justice is the norm, possibly no one would merit anything, and yet everyone would get the same. On the other hand, distributive justice specifically aims to give each person what they have earned.

It is significant that nowhere does Scripture even vaguely suggest that God operates on principles of egalitarian justice. Nor do any of his attributes obligate him to do so. The fact that God is all-loving doesn't obligate him to do the same loving things for everyone. It only means that regardless of what God does, it must be an act of love. Moreover, that God is all just means that all of his actions are just, but it certainly doesn't obligate him to use egalitarian justice in his handling of our world.

Some might think God does operate on principles of egalitarian justice, because Scripture teaches that all sinners are headed for an eternity of separation from God. Though all of us face this fate apart from Christ, this is so because on principles of distributive justice all of us deserve that punishment.

In fact, the uniform biblical portrait shows God functioning in accord with distributive justice. Theologians distinguish distributive justice from rectoral justice in that the latter indicates that God has set up a just, moral universe, whereas the former teaches that God actually administers justice fairly to each individual. Within the broad category of distributive justice, theologians also make another distinction. They differentiate the granting of reward that is due (remunerative, compensative, or recompensive justice) from the meeting out of punishment that is deserved (retributive justice). As we turn to Scripture, we see many passages that show that God gives each person what they deserve. Though Job complains about his circumstances, Bildad asks (Job 8:3), "Does God pervert justice or does the Almighty pervert what is right?" Of course not, even though neither Job nor his friends knew the exact reasons for Job's calamities. Nonetheless, we can say with Moses (Deut 32:4), "The Rock! His work is perfect, for all His ways are just; a God of faithfulness and without injustice, righteous and upright is He."

This means that those who deserve punishment receive it. In fact, in some passages we even see people who were punished admit that God's punishment was just. The psalmist pleads for the Lord to judge the wicked and acknowledges that God knows what they deserve (Ps 7:9). In another Psalm, the writer praises God for judging the wicked and giving them just recompense for their deeds (Ps 129:4): "The LORD is righteous; He has cut in two the cords of the wicked" (see also Rom 2:5; 2 Thess 1:6). And, Micah admits in regard to God's judgment upon Israel (Mic 7:9), "I will bear the indignation of the LORD because I have sinned against Him, until He pleads my case and executes justice for me. He will bring me out to the light, and I will see His righteousness" (see also Dan 9:14). In the book of Revelation we read of many judgments at the end time. Revelation 16 predicts the pouring out of the bowls of God's wrath. In verses 5 and 7, angels say that the judgments being poured out are deserved; they are just! (See also Rev 19:2.)

Scripture also teaches that God rewards those who do good. Paul speaks of rewards God will give believers, and he is confident that God will do this, because the Lord is a righteous judge (2 Tim 4:8). There are also passages whose broader context shows that God rewards righteous deeds (Job 33:26; Ps 11:7; 24:5; 36:10; 103:6). Other verses that mention God's distributive justice are 1 Sam 26:23; Neh 9:33; Ps 48:10; 71:15-16; Isa 26:9; 45:21; Mal 4:2.

Indeed, Scripture is clear that God distributes reward and punishment as it is deserved. Moreover, someday there will be a full-scale judgment with Jesus as the righteous Judge. We read in Acts 17:31, "Because he has fixed a day in which He will judge the world in righteousness through a Man whom He has appointed, having furnished proof to all men by raising Him from the dead." Will Jesus be just in his judgments? Certainly, for Jesus says of himself as a Judge (John 5:30), "I can do nothing on My own initiative. As I hear, I judge; and My judgment is just, because I do not seek My own will, but the will of Him who sent Me."

LOVE

Because God is so holy and righteous, we might stand in fear of him, feeling that it is impossible to please him and that a positive relationship with him is unthinkable. However, God's holiness and justice are counterbalanced by the fact that he is also a God of love. God's love is one of the grandest themes in all of Scripture. In fact, the Bible in many ways is a love story, a story of God's love for all creatures. In the OT the basic Hebrew words for love are ʾāhēb (verb) and ʾahăbāh (noun). Though the verb ʾāhēb frequently describes the love of human beings for one another, it is also used in relation to God. God commands us to love him (Deut 6:5), but he also affirms his love for mankind. He has, of course, a special love for his covenant people Israel (Deut 4:37; Isa 43:4; Mal 1:2). In addition to his love for people, God is also said to love things such as the gates of Zion (Ps 87:2), righteousness and judgment (Ps 33:5), and the holy temple (Mal 2:11). The noun ʾahăbāh has a similar breadth in meaning.[6]

As for the verb ḥābab (Deut 33:3), it is translated "to love," but it also has the connotation of "having in the bosom." Thus it speaks of a tenderness and closeness of feeling toward the object of love. The verb ḥāšaq appears more frequently in relation to divine love than does ḥābab. This word emphasizes that which attaches to something or someone. When used in regard to emotions (and biblical usage is limited to this), it speaks of a love which is already bound to its object. Such inward attachment is true of God's love for Israel (Deut 10:15), and yet that happened because of his own free will, not because Israel did anything to deserve it (Deut 7:7). This is the love that won't let go of the object of love.[7]

The NT's terms for divine love have a very special meaning as well. Greek has three terms for love, each with its own meaning. *Eros* is the term for sensual love, and *philē* refers to the love of friends. The love which God extends to us is represented by the verb *agapaō* and the noun *agapē*. This kind of love is love that loves even the unlovely and unlovable. It is a self-sacrificing, self-giving love. It is given not because of the desert of the recipient but because of the giver's choice. It is love that seeks the benefit of the recipient, not the giver.

God loves us very deeply, and as a result he has paid for our sins himself through the sacrifice of Christ so that we need not pay the penalty demanded by his holy and just law. When people refuse to repent of sin and accept Christ's provision for sin, God hates to judge, and so he is longsuffering with sinners. But when sinners continue in sin, God, as morally pure and as a righteous moral governor, eventually must punish their sin. Still, God takes no delight in punishing them, for though he hates sin, he never stops loving the sinner.

One of the most striking love stories ever is God's unchanging love for his ancient people Israel. God didn't make Israel a special object of love because they deserved or earned it. Instead, Deut 7:7-8 explains: "The LORD did not set His love on you . . . because you were more in number than any of the peoples, for you were the fewest of all peoples, but because the LORD loved you and kept the oath which He swore to your forefathers, the LORD brought you out by a mighty hand, and redeemed you from the house of slavery, from the hand of Pharaoh king of Egypt." God chose Israel because he is a God of self-giving love and a God who keeps his promises (see also Deut 10:15; 33:3; and cf. Ps 78:68, which speaks of God's choice of Judah and Mount Zion because he loved them, even though the nation as a whole had disobeyed on that occasion).

According to many OT passages, God's love for Israel was the motivation behind the exodus from Egyptian bondage. Few passages portray the tenderness of divine love toward Israel at this early stage in her history as does Hosea 11. In Hos 11:1, 4 we read, "When Israel was a youth I loved him, and out of Egypt I called My son. . . . I led them with cords of a man, with bonds of love, and I became to them as one who lifts the yoke from their jaws; and I bent down and fed them." We find the same theme in Deut 4:37 and 7:8.

Because of his love, the Lord did other things for Israel. He turned Balaam's curse into a blessing upon Israel (Deut 23:5). After a visit with Solomon during which she saw his greatness, the Queen of Sheba says that God gave Solomon to Israel as king because God loved Israel (1 Kgs 10:9—parallel 2 Chron 9:8), and the king of Tyre concluded the same thing (2 Chron 2:11).

In the prophets' writings, we find frequently that in a coming day the Lord will restore, save spiritually, and bless his people Israel, and the reason is because he loves them so much. In Jer 31:3, we find a similar prophecy: "The LORD appeared to him from afar, saying, 'I have loved you with an everlasting love; therefore I have drawn with lovingkindness'" (see also Isa 48:14; 63:9; Hos 14:4; cf. Ps 47:4). As a result, when God does restore his people Israel, we read (Zeph 3:17, KJV), "The LORD thy God in the midst of thee is mighty; he will save, he will rejoice over thee with joy; he will rest in his love, he will joy over thee with singing." The picture the phrase "he will rest in his love" gives is that of a proud parent whose child has just taken first place. That parent sits back in pride, joy, and love, and savors the moment. Similarly, when Israel is restored to her God, in his love and joy God will savor the change of Israel.

God's love toward Israel is a wonderful story, but in a certain respect it is also amazing. It is amazing not only because they didn't deserve to be chosen in the first place but also because of their repeated unfaithfulness to God. Yet God continues to love. We see this beautifully portrayed through the life of the prophet Hosea. Hosea's wife Gomer was an unfaithful wife, giving herself over to harlotry. God used the situation in Hosea's own home as an object lesson to Israel of his relation to her. Hence, in Hos 3:1 God commands Hosea: "Go again, love a woman who is loved by her husband, yet an adulteress, even as the LORD loves the sons of Israel, though they turn to other gods and love raisin cakes." God knew what Gomer had done, and he knew that she had done it in spite of Hosea's love for her. Though Hosea might have thought he had every right to cast her off, God told him to love her, anyway. Hosea's love was to be patterned after God's love for Israel. Israel, too, was an unfaithful wife. She had looked to other gods. The reference to flagons of wine is God's "exhibit A" to prove his case. These flagons of wine were used by Israel in her worship of the pagan Goddess, the Queen of Heaven (Jer 7:18; 44:19). Despite Israel's unfaithfulness, God never stopped loving her. The pattern of that love for Israel was the pattern God wanted Hosea to follow in relation to his estranged wife Gomer (see also Mal 1:2, where God expresses his love to Israel, but she pretends not to know that he loves her).

The OT also teaches that God loves individuals. For example, in Isaiah 38, Isaiah announces that King Hezekiah will die soon. Hezekiah pleads with the Lord to spare his life, and the Lord heals him. Hezekiah then says (Isa 38:17, KJV), "Thou hast in love to my soul delivered it from the pit of corruption: for thou hast cast all my sins behind thy back." Moreover, many see the Song of Solomon as symbolizing Christ's relation to his church. In one passage, the Shulamite woman (she would represent the church) says of her loved one (Song 2:4), "He has brought me to his banquet hall, and his banner over me is love."

In the NT we repeatedly see references to the unbounded love of God. In 1 John, John blatantly states that God is love, i.e., he has that attribute. John tells his readers that if they do not love one another, then they do not have a personal relationship with God (1 John 4:8). Those who know God as Savior will evidence his character in their lives. Those who do not love cannot be saved, for God's character is love, and if they knew him, they would love as well (see also 1 John 4:16). Because God loves us, we should naturally love him (v. 19).

The NT teaches that God's love extends to all people, not just to those who trust him. In fact, we find that God not only loves the world, but he showed that love by sending his Son to die for our sins. John 3:16 makes that point in a well-known and much-loved verse. As Jesus said (John 15:13), "Greater love has no one than this, that one lay down his life for his friends." But Christ died even for those who are not his friends. As Paul says (Rom 5:8): "But God demonstrates His own love toward us, in that while we were yet sinners, Christ died for us." The sacrifice of Christ is for all people, believers and nonbelievers alike, as 1 John 2:2 says.

What greater love could there be than to sacrifice one's life for the sake of others? That is precisely what Christ did. John contends that Christ's death is the supreme expression of God's love toward us. In his life and death for us we see most clearly that God loves us. In 1 John 3:16 John says, "We know love by this, that He laid down His life for us; and we ought to lay down our lives for the brethren" (see also 1 John 4:9-10; 2 Cor 5:14; Gal 2:20; Eph 2:4; Tit 3:4; Rev 1:5).

Not only does God love the whole world (as shown by Christ's sacrifice), but the NT clearly shows that he has a special love for those who trust Christ and follow him. Because of that special love, many blessings and benefits come to believers. As John revels in God's love to his own, he writes (1 John 3:1, KJV), "Behold, what manner of love the Father hath bestowed upon us, that we should be called the sons of God." What a great privilege to be a member of the family of God! Moreover, because we are God's children there is a great future in store for us. As John says (1 John 3:2), "Beloved, now we are children of God, and it has not appeared as yet what we shall be. We know that, when He appears, we shall be like Him, because we shall see Him just as He is." Peter says that because of God's love and mercy to us, he gave us a new birth into his family. As a result, we have an inheritance waiting for us that is incorruptible, undefiled, and does not fade away (1 Pet 1:3-4). This means that when we were born into God's family, we were born rich!

Not only do believers have the great privilege of being God's children, they also have the assurance of God's love and his indwelling them (John 17:23, 26). Wonderful as are the believer's position and possessions in Christ, these blessings would be muted if they could be lost either in time or for eternity. In fact, believers might think those blessings could be lost amid affliction, but Paul explains that God can use afflictions to bring about positive benefits in the believer's life (Rom 5:3-4). Moreover, amid afflictions believers have hope for release from the problems now and for an eternity with the Lord. The ground of the believer's assurance is the love of God (Rom 5:5). Later in this epistle Paul sounds the triumphant note that nothing can ever separate the believer from the love of Christ. Even more, no matter what happens in life, believers can be conquerors through Christ (Rom 8:35, 37-39).

Being a member of God's family is a great privilege, but it also carries with it great responsibilities. The primary responsibility for the believer is to obey the commands and demands of Christ. This is stated repeatedly in the NT, and especially frequent is the command that believers love one another. Invariably, the rationale for obeying the command is that God or Christ loves us, so we also ought to love others or obey other commands he has given. For example, Jesus says (John 13:34), "A new commandment I give to you, that you love one another, even as I have loved you" (see also John 14:21, 23; 15:9, 10, 12; Eph 5:2). Moreover, Paul uses Christ's love for his church as the example of how husbands should love their wives (Eph 5:25).

Indeed, since God's love is shed abroad in the hearts of his followers, the mark of the Christian is that we obey God's command to love one another. As Jesus said (John 13:35), "By this all men will know that you are My disciples, if you have love for one another" (see also 1 John 2:5; 4:7, 11). That love is not merely to be an abstract feeling, for it must be accompanied by concrete deeds of love (1 John 3:17). If the Spirit of God is truly working in our lives to conform us to Christ, it will be evident, for Gal 5:22 says that the fruit of the Spirit is love. Without such love in our lives, there is reason to think we are quenching the Spirit's work in us.

If we disobey his commands, Christ lovingly will attempt to correct our ways and will likely say what he said to the church at Laodicea (Rev 3:19), "Those whom I love, I reprove and discipline; be zealous therefore, and repent." On the other hand, if we obey his commands, we are promised

THE MORAL ATTRIBUTES OF GOD □ 353

(2 Cor 13:11): "Finally, brethren, rejoice, be made complete, be comforted, be like-minded, live in peace; and the God of love and peace shall be with you."

The NT also shows us something of the love between the members of the Godhead. In John 10:17 we read of the Father's love of Christ: "For this reason the Father loves Me, because I lay down My life that I may take it again." In John 14:31, Jesus explains, "but that the world may know that I love the Father, and as the Father gave Me commandment, even so I do."

Finally, God's love is so wonderful and so characteristic of him that biblical authors frequently refer to it in opening or closing salutations to their letters or in benedictions that they wish upon their readers. We see this in Paul's letters: "The grace of the Lord Jesus Christ, and the love of God, and the fellowship of the Holy Spirit, be with you all" (2 Cor 13:14; see also Eph 6:23; 2 Thess 2:16; 3:5). We find it also from John's pen (2 John 3) and from Jude (21): "Keep yourselves in the love of God, waiting anxiously for the mercy of our Lord Jesus Christ to eternal life." From Genesis to Revelation the Bible is the story of God's love for all people!

GRACE

Scripture depicts God as a God of grace. The Hebrew words for grace come from the same basic word group. The verb is *ḥānan* ("to be gracious," "to deal graciously") and the noun is *ḥēn* ("grace" or "favor"). As for *ḥānan*, it depicts a heartfelt response by someone who has something to give to someone in need. The majority of occurrences of this term in the OT (some forty-one) are used in relation to God. For example, the plea *ḥonnēnî* ("be gracious [or merciful] to me") occurs some nineteen times in the Psalms.[8] The noun *ḥēn* ("favor," "grace," "charm") occurs some sixty-nine times in the OT, including forty-three as part of the phrase "to find favor in the eyes of." Most occurrences are secular and not theological, but in theological passages it is typically God's grace that is spoken of as given or poured out upon someone. "In contrast with the verb *ḥānan*, the focus of attention is not on the giver, but on the recipient, of what is given," according to one writer.[9]

The NT is replete with references to grace, and to God's grace in particular. The most common term for grace in the NT is *charis*, though on one occasion (1 Pet 2:3) the adjective *chrstos* is used of God. As to *charis*, it has the basic meaning of "good," "favor," and "fortune" in secular Greek. In the NT it still maintains this basic meaning, although it is most frequently used in relation to salvation that God provides. Pauline usage is most frequent, but Paul uses the term in a variety of ways. It often appears in opening and closing salutations of his letters (e.g., Rom 1:7; 1 Thess 5:28). Paul also speaks of God's gift to him of his apostolic office as grace (Rom 1:5). But most frequently he uses the term in relation to the gift of salvation (Eph 2:8).[10] As *chrēstos*, when used of God it means that he is "mild," "kind," or "helpful" in his attitudes and actions toward us.[11]

As for the concept of grace, it is best understood as unmerited favor. That means that something good happens to you even though you have done nothing to merit or earn it. Scripture portrays God as a God of abounding grace. It is important to understand that God owes no one any grace. This is so not just because God is not *prima facie* obligated to any of us, and not just because none of us have done anything that merits such favor. It is so as well by the very nature of grace as *unmerited* favor. If God or anyone else were obligated to give grace, it would no longer be grace—blessing would simply be a matter of justice. The very nature of grace, however, is that it is never owed or earned.

When we understand this fact about grace, we see how good and loving our God is to grant us grace. We should also recognize that when God extends grace to others in need but not to us, God is not treating us unjustly. Withholding grace could only be unjust if God owed us grace, but grace is unmerited, so it is never owed. If God chooses to be gracious to some and to withhold grace from others, he has done nothing wrong, for there is no obligation he failed to fulfill. Hence, those who don't receive a particular expression of grace have no right to be angry at God for passing them by. Their anger shows that they are expecting God to do something he has never obligated himself to do, for to do it would be grace, and grace is never owed. So, even though it is human nature to complain and be angry at God when others receive a blessing that we do not receive, such attitudes are totally inappropriate.

Theologians often divide God's gracious activities into two broad categories. On the one hand, there is common grace, and on the other, there is saving or salvatory grace. Common grace refers to God's gracious activity in sustaining all creation, in restraining evil and wickedness so that societies don't collapse altogether, and in allowing mankind to develop and function in societies. This grace is called common because it falls on all members of the human race (and more generally on all creatures in the universe) regardless of whether they are God's children by faith. Moreover, these expressions of grace don't bring people to a saving knowledge of Jesus Christ, although these blessings, when rightly seen as coming from a gracious God, may move nonbelievers closer to God.

These blessings are often taken for granted, but God owes us none of them. Even as God had no obligation to create a world, he is not required to sustain it in being. But as a gracious God, he provides for all creatures. In Col 1:17 Paul says of Jesus Christ that "He is before all things, and in Him all things hold together." The fact that our planet retains its orbit and does not collide with other planets and is not otherwise destroyed results from God's grace. Moreover, we have air to breathe, food to eat, water to drink, and strength to work. The psalmist says (Ps 145:9), "The LORD is good to all, and His mercies are over all His works." As we read in Acts 17:28, "For in Him we live and move and exist" (see also Acts 14:17; and Jesus' words in Matt 6:28-30). In Luke 6:35, Jesus says that God is even "kind to ungrateful and evil men." As to restraining the evil in our hearts, God does so in many ways. Societies often seem on the verge of turmoil and collapse. That this does not happen more frequently is due to the grace of God. We are even told in Rom 13:1ff. that God instituted government to restrain the evil that men do and to reward them for good. We may not always like our government or its leaders, but Paul clearly says that governments serve as ministers of God in keeping order and distributing justice. That they perform these functions is due to God's marvelous grace.

In contrast to common grace, there is saving grace, God's grace extended to us to establish a spiritual relationship with God and to grow believers in that relationship. The NT in particular details the various expressions of divine salvatory grace. However, saving grace is not absent from the OT. We find repeatedly that OT saints believed in God, and God graciously counted their faith as righteousness. Moreover, rather than make believers pay for their own sins, God implemented the Mosaic sacrificial system. Those sacrifices didn't have the sufficiency of the once-for-all sacrifice of Christ (Heb 10:4), but when God saw the blood of the sacrifice brought in repentant faith, he forgave the sinner and restored fellowship. All of this was an expression of God's gracious provision of a substitute for sin even during the OT era, for "the soul who sins will die" (Ezek 18:4, 20). Without God's graciously allowing the animal sacrifice to pay for sin, all men and women would have had to pay.

Verses that speak of God's grace fall into several categories. First, some verses simply speak of God as having the attribute of grace. For example, in Exod 34:6 we read of God revealing himself to Moses: "Then the LORD passed by in front of him and proclaimed, 'The LORD, The LORD God, compassionate and gracious, slow to anger, and abounding in lovingkindness and truth.'" The psalmist says (Ps 145:8), "The LORD is gracious and merciful; slow to anger and great in lovingkindness" (see also Ps 111:4; Jon 4:2). In the NT as well, grace is predicated of God. When encouraging those undergoing affliction, Peter appeals to the work of the gracious God as their source of comfort and encouragement (1 Pet 5:10). As John introduces his Gospel, he speaks of the incarnate Christ as full of grace and truth (John 1:14).

In addition, many passages speak of God as gracious in that he will give blessing or does give some blessing to someone. This divine action is called gracious because none of it is owed to the recipient. The nature of the blessing varies from passage to passage. In some cases it is physical deliverance. Gen 6:8 (KJV) says, "But Noah found grace in the eyes of the LORD." He and his family alone escaped the universal catastrophe of the flood. Likewise, it was because of God's grace that Lot was delivered when God destroyed Sodom and Gomorrah (Gen 19:19). We see God's gracious hand of protection and deliverance at other times in Israel's history. We see it in the days of Ezra (9:8), in the time of Nehemiah (Neh 9:31; see also 2 Kgs 13:23; 2 Chron 30:9), and in Jeremiah's day (31:2). In the Psalms, we find expressions of gratitude for God's gracious deliverance from danger or from enemies. Ps 86:15 and 116:5 are examples, and both passages are in contexts that speak of a need for deliverance from danger and enemies. Moreover, Isaiah speaks of a future day when the gracious Lord will deliver his people from their enemies (Isa 30:19). Finally, 1 Pet 1:13 refers to the final deliverance from all problems and struggles which awaits believers at Christ's return: "Therefore, gird your minds for action, keep sober in spirit, fix your hope completely on the grace to be brought to you at the revelation of Jesus Christ."

In other cases, the blessing is forgiveness of sin upon repentance. For example, Neh 9:17 says, "but Thou art a God of forgiveness, gracious and compassionate, slow to anger, and abounding in lovingkindness." Joel (2:13) pleads with his people to return to the Lord, "for He is gracious and compassionate, slow to anger, abounding in lovingkindness, and relenting of evil" (see also Amos 5:15).

In other cases, the writer refers to the ministry God has given him as a gracious gift of God's blessing. Paul speaks this way not only of his salvation but also of his apostolic office (Rom 1:5): "through whom we have received grace and apostleship to bring about the obedience of faith among all the Gentiles, for His name's sake." Moreover, he also speaks this way of his specific commission to preach the gospel to the Gentiles (Eph 3:2): "If indeed you have heard of the stewardship of God's grace which was given to me for you" (see also Eph 3:7-8; 1 Cor 3:10; 15:10; 2 Cor 1:12; and also Rom 12:3 and 15:15, where Paul instructs the Romans in virtue of the grace God has given to him, and he is likely appealing to his apostolic office as the ground for what he writes).

There are also instances when God's blessing is material. We find this in 2 Cor 8:1, where Paul speaks of the material blessing which God gave the churches in Macedonia so that they were able to give liberally to the work of the ministry. Likewise, Paul encourages the Corinthians to give by reminding them that God is able to provide them with the financial means so that they will have this ministry of giving as well (2 Cor 9:8).

In some cases the gracious blessing in view is God's sustaining grace. That grace may be given amid affliction to help the believer withstand it. This is so in Paul's case as the Lord revealed that he wouldn't remove Paul's physical infirmity (2 Cor 12:9). In other cases, God promises to give his sustaining power to those who submit to his will and to the will of those in authority over them. This may be very difficult, but God will enable us to do it. As Jas 4:6 says, "But he gives a greater grace. Therefore it says, 'God is opposed to the proud, but gives grace to the humble'" (see also Prov 3:34; 1 Pet 5:5).

Finally, many passages speak of God's grace toward someone meaning that he will bless them or that he has chosen them for blessing, but the specific nature of the blessing is not detailed. We find this in Exod 33:13, 16, and 17 (KJV): "Now therefore, I pray thee, if I have found grace in thy sight, shew me now thy way, that I may know thee, that I may find grace in thy sight: and consider that this nation is thy people. . . . For wherein shall it be known here that I and thy people have found grace in thy sight? . . . And the LORD said unto Moses, I will do this thing also that thou hast spoken: for thou hast found grace in my sight, and I know thee by name" (see also Exod 34:9; Judg 6:17). In Ps 45:2 we read, "Thou art fairer than the sons of men; grace is poured upon Thy lips; therefore God has blessed Thee forever" (see also Ps 84:11; 103:8; Gen 43:29; Exod 22:27; 33:19; Ps 77:9; Isa 30:18; Mal 1:9).

In the NT, we read of Jesus (Luke 2:40): "And the Child continued to grow and become strong, increasing in wisdom; and the grace of God was upon Him." John (1:16) reminds believers that they have received multiplied grace through Jesus Christ. In the book of Acts we read of God's grace resting upon someone and the apostles being commended to God's grace as they set forth to minister (see, e.g., Acts 4:33; 14:26; 15:40). Moreover, believers are exhorted to bring their petitions to God in prayer to the throne of grace (Heb 4:16). And then, because believers have already experienced the grace of the Lord, they should desire all the more to grow in their salvation (1 Pet 2:3, KJV): "If so be ye have tasted that the Lord is gracious."

Because of the wondrous nature of God's gracious blessing on his people, NT writers frequently begin or end a letter with a benediction, wishing grace or asking God to pour out his grace upon their readers. As an example, consider Paul's letter to the Romans. Early in the epistle, he writes (Rom 1:7): "To all who are beloved of God in Rome, called as saints: Grace to you and peace from God our Father and the Lord Jesus Christ." At the end (16:20), he says, "And the God of peace will soon crush Satan under your feet. The grace of our Lord Jesus be with you" (see also Rom 16:24; 1 Cor 1:3; 16:23; 2 Cor 1:2; 13:14; Gal 1:3; 6:18; Eph 1:2; 6:24; Phil 1:2; 4:23; Col 1:2; 4:18; 1 Thess 1:1; 5:28; 2 Thess 1:2; 3:18; 1 Tim 1:2; 6:21; 2 Tim 1:2; 4:22; Tit 1:4; 3:15; Phile 3, 25; Heb 13:25; 1 Pet 1:2; 2 Pet 1:2; 2 John 3; Rev 1:4; 22:21).

There are also many biblical references to God's saving grace. Grace is a work of God on our behalf (Tit 2:11). It is God's gift bestowed on us (Eph 2:8). Moreover, it is divine power working in us (1 Cor 15:10), and Paul refers to it as a method of God saving people (Rom 3:24) as opposed to any works method. Saving grace is also a realm of God into which people may enter by faith and in which they may abide and experience all the blessings brought by God to them (Rom 5:2).

Many are the works of divine grace in the provision and application of salvation. It was by God's gracious provision that Christ tasted death for everyone (Heb 2:9). It is through Christ's gracious sacrifice that we have been redeemed and have forgiveness of sins (Eph 1:7). Moreover, our election is by grace (Rom 11:5), as is our calling to salvation (Gal 1:15; 2 Tim 1:9). Faith is by grace (Acts 18:27), and so are justification (Rom 3:24; Tit 3:7) and sanctification (Phil 2:12-13; Heb 10:14). Hence, we are exhorted to grow in grace and knowledge of Christ (2 Pet 3:18).

In addition, believers have consolation and hope by grace (2 Thess 2:16), strength in grace (2 Tim 2:1), and eternal life by grace (Rom 5:21). Consequently, their standing as believers is in grace (Rom 5:2). In fact, the whole salvatory process from beginning to end is by grace (Eph 2:8). God has done everything necessary for us to find eternal life and abundant life even now while on earth. When we do what pleases God, it is through his grace as well. In fact, NT writers even speak of the spiritual gifts given to believers for serving the Lord and one another as a provision of God's grace (Rom 12:6; Eph 4:7; 1 Pet 4:10). Clearly, all that we are in Christ is due to God's grace (1 Cor 15:10). Other passages that relate grace to some aspect of salvation are John 1:17; Acts 11:23; 13:43; 14:3; 15:11; 20:24, 32; Rom 4:4, 16; 5:15, 17, 20; 6:1, 14, 15; 11:6; 12:6; 1 Cor 1:4, 30; 2 Cor 4:15; 6:1; 8:9; Gal 1:6; 2:9, 21; 5:4; Eph 1:6; 2:5, 7; 4:29; Col 1:6; 2 Thess 1:12; 1 Tim 1:14; Tit 2:11; Heb 12:15; 13:9; 1 Pet 1:10; 3:7; 5:12; Jude 4.

Finally, on at least two occasions (one in the OT and one in the NT) the Holy Spirit is referred to as the spirit of grace (Zech 12:10 and Heb 10:29). All three members of the Godhead, Father, Son, and Holy Spirit, are characterized as gracious. Our God is a God of grace!

Mercy

A series of Hebrew terms are used in Scripture for mercy. One group stems from the verb *rāḥam* ("to love," "pity," "be merciful"). This term speaks of deep love often rooted in some natural bond. In the Piel, the verb refers to the deep inward feeling that is compassion, mercy, or pity. This term is used frequently of God, and it tends to be used in one of two ways. The first refers to the strong tie that God has toward those who are his children. Just as a father has pity on his children, so God relates to those who are his own (Ps 103:13). The second relates to God's unconditional choice. Based solely on his sovereign will, he has mercy on whomever he chooses (Exod 33:19).[12] Closely related to the verb are the nouns *raḥămîn* ("bowels," "mercies") and *raḥămîm* ("bowels," "mercies"), and the adjective *raḥûm* ("pitiful," "merciful"). For example, the noun *raḥămîm* suggests that God's tender mercies are rooted in his free love and grace. Often, as well, this word is combined with *ḥesed* ("steadfast love," "kindness") in speaking about God. The adjective *raḥûm* has the same idea and is almost exclusively (Ps 112:4 being the one possible exception) used in regard to God.[13]

In several instances (Deut 21:8; 32:43), we find the verb *kāphar* used to refer to God's mercy. This is the typical Hebrew term (meaning "to cover, pardon") for making atonement for sin by covering. Of course, since the one bringing the sacrifice is guilty of sin and since God does not owe anyone a pardon from sin, the fact that God covers and pardons the sin is a sign of his great mercy. Hence, though *kāphar* is not the usual word for mercy, it is surely appropriate.

In addition, there is another Hebrew word group stemming from the verb *ḥāsad* ("show self kind"). The noun is *ḥesed* ("kindness"), and the adjective is *ḥasîd* ("kind"). All of these terms speak of God's steadfast love, but in various contexts translators have rendered them as mercy. In his tender love, God is merciful to those who need mercy.

Finally, two other Hebrew words are used in respect to God's mercy. The first is the verb *ḥānan* ("be merciful to"), and the second is the noun *ḥemlāh* ("pity"). As for *ḥānan*, it depicts a heartfelt response by someone who has something to give the one in need. The majority of instances of this term in the OT (some forty-one) are used in relation to God. For example, the plea *ḥonnēnî* ("be gracious or merciful to me") occurs some nineteen times in the Psalms.[14] As for *ḥemlāh*, the term seems to stem from the verb *ḥāmal*. Basically, this root connotes the emotional response that results (or may result) in action to remove its object (and/or its subject) from impending difficulty. As to the noun *ḥemlāh* ("mercy"), it appears twice (Gen 19:16; Isa 63:9) to describe God's mercy in rescuing and protecting from danger.

The Greek word used to speak of God's mercy is *eleos*. In Greek usage, it is an emotion that is stirred when one sees someone who is undeservedly afflicted. In the NT it often is used to speak of the attitude that God requires of us in our relations with others (see Matt 9:13; 12:7; Luke 10:37). When used of God, it often refers to his faithfulness, i.e., he is graciously faithful to us. In Eph 2:4 and 1 Pet 1:3 the element of graciousness predominates. Often the word is used of God's acts in salvation history, especially in relation to Christ (Tit 3:5; Rom 9:15).[15]

The concept of mercy is closely related to grace, and of course it is an expression of God's love and goodness. However, there is a significant difference between grace and mercy. Both involve unmerited favor, but the difference is that whereas grace may be given to those who are miserable and desperately in need of help, it may also be given to those who have no particular need. On the other hand, mercy is given specifically to those whose condition is miserable and one of great need.

Perhaps the distinction between mercy and grace can be illustrated as follows. If I am in an altruistic mood, I might find someone and write him or her a check for one thousand dollars. Suppose that the recipient is very wealthy and doesn't need what I give. Still, the recipient has done nothing to merit my generosity, so my gift is an act of grace. On the other hand, suppose I am in a generous mood and I go to a part of town where the homeless often live on the streets. I find someone whose clothes are tattered and torn, and who has had little to eat for several days. In this case, if I write him a check for a thousand dollars, it is still a good act that he doesn't deserve, but I do it because I take pity on his miserable situation. My generosity to the man of means is an act of grace. My generosity to the homeless person is an act of mercy.

According to Scripture, God is a God of both grace and mercy. With respect to our need to pay for sins and be forgiven, the human race is in great need. What God did for us in Christ on Calvary is an act of great mercy. If one is accused of a crime and the case is about to come to trial, one needs a good defense lawyer. On the other hand, if the trial is over and you have been convicted and sentenced to death, you don't need a defense lawyer. You need a pardon. The human race without Christ needs a pardon from sin. A defense lawyer will not do, because we have no defense; we are guilty. We need a pardon, lest we spend eternity in torment and separation from God. God recognized our pitiful situation, and he could have responded by telling us that it is our problem and we should work it out ourselves. But our compassionate God saw our need and took it upon himself to provide the solution.

As with God's grace, there are some biblical passages that refer to God as a God of mercy. For example, in 1 Chron 16:34 (KJV, see also 16:41; Exod 34:6; Ps 103:8) we read, "O give thanks unto the LORD; for he is good; for his mercy endureth for ever." And Mary, after learning that she would be the mother of the Messiah, says (Luke 1:50): "His mercy is upon generation after generation toward those who fear Him."

In addition, many passages in the OT and NT speak of God extending physical deliverance from difficult and even disastrous circumstances. Such deliverance comes to Israel as a whole and to particular individuals as well. As a result, we often hear in Scripture a plea to God for mercy in time of trouble. Examples of individuals in need are plentiful. Consider, for example, 2 Sam 24:14 (parallel 1 Chron 21:13): "Then David said to Gad, 'I am in great distress. Let us now fall into the hand of the LORD for his mercies are great but do not let me fall into the hand of man.'" We also hear such talk of a need for God's mercy quite frequently in the Psalms. Ps 86:3, 6, 15-16 is representative: "Have mercy on me, O Lord, for I call to you all day long." . . . "Hear my prayer, O LORD; listen to my cry for mercy". (NIV) . . . "But thou, O Lord, art a God full of compassion, and gracious, longsuffering, and plenteous in mercy and truth. O turn unto me, and have mercy upon me" (KJV) (see also Ps 6:9; 9:13; 28:2, 6; 30:8; 31:22; 57:1; 116:1; 119:132; 130:2; 140:6; 142:1; 143:1). And in Phil 2:27, Paul says about Epaphroditus, "For indeed he was sick to the point of death, but God had mercy on him, and not on him only but also on me, lest I should have sorrow upon sorrow."

Passages where the nation of Israel as a whole pleads for mercy include Deut 4:31; 21:8; Neh 9:31; and 13:22. We find this theme as well in the prophets. Isa 49:13 (KJV) says, "Sing, O heavens; and be joyful, O earth; and break forth into singing, O mountains: for the LORD hath comforted his people, and will have mercy upon his afflicted" (see also Isa 54:8). Speaking of a coming eschatological deliverance, we read (Isa 60:10, KJV): "And the sons of strangers shall build up thy walls, and their kings shall minister unto thee: for in my wrath I smote thee, but in my favour have I had mercy on thee" (see also Jer 33:26; Hos 1:7; Zech 1:16).

Not only does Scripture portray God as merciful to the needy, but we also see Christ in particular as one to whom the blind, the infirm, and the demon-possessed appealed for mercy to combat their circumstances. In Matt 9:27

two blind men plead, "Have mercy on us, Son of David!" See also Matt 15:22; 17:15; 20:30, 31; Mark 5:19; 10:47-48; Luke 18:38-39.

Not only does Scripture speak of God's mercy in helping those in need of physical deliverance, but there are also many passages that speak of God's great mercy in salvation. In both the OT and NT, sinners are encouraged to repent and turn to God. He will forgive, because he is a God of mercy. This message comes both to Israel as a whole and to individuals within the nation. Num 14:18 (KJV) says that "the LORD is longsuffering, and of great mercy, forgiving iniquity and transgression." On a different occasion, the children of Israel are told to repent (2 Chron 30:9, KJV), "For if ye turn again unto the LORD, your brethren and your children shall find compassion before them that lead them captive, . . . for the LORD your God is gracious and merciful, and will not turn away his face from you, if ye return unto him" (see also Jer 3:12; Joel 2:13; Deut 13:17).

As a result of God's mercy in forgiving sinners, David pleads for mercy in forgiving his sins (Ps 41:4, NIV): "I said, 'O LORD, have mercy on me; heal me, for I have sinned against you'" (see also Ps 51:1; 79:8; Luke 18:13). Because of God's great mercy shown by his willingness to forgive sin, the writer of Proverbs says (28:13, NIV): "He who conceals his sins does not prosper, but whoever confesses and renounces them finds mercy" (see also Isa 55:7; Mic 7:18).

Not only does God extend mercy in forgiving sin, but Paul shows also that God's mercy is the ultimate ground of his electing individuals to salvation. In Romans 9 Paul argues that God's choice of the elect does not depend on their merits but rather on God's mercy. Though the general focus of the chapter is on God's choice of Israel to be his special people, Paul distinguishes between election to privilege and election to salvation. What he says about God's choice of individual Jews to salvation is true of Gentiles as well (Rom 9:15-16, 18, 23).

In Romans 11 Paul argues that Israel's rejection of her Messiah did not surprise God. Rather, God planned it as a means for extending mercy to the Gentiles as well (11:30), and the ultimate goal was that Gentile belief would stir the Jews to jealousy so that they would turn back to God (11:11, 14). All of this is so that God can shower his merciful salvation on Jew and Gentile alike (see Rom 11:30-31). In fact, Paul shows that the ultimate reason God allowed the human race to fall into sin was so that he could extend it mercy in providing salvation (Rom 11:32).

Indeed, it was while we were steeped in our sin, that (Eph 2:4, NIV) "because of his great love for us, God, who is rich in mercy" stepped in to save us. Regeneration, the new spiritual birth, comes to believers as a result of the mercy of God (1 Pet 1:3). As a result, those who had no relation to God are now his people (1 Pet 2:10). None of this happened because of us, but because of God's great mercy! As Paul says (Tit 3:5, NIV): "He saved us, not because of righteous things we had done, but because of his mercy." Consequently, regardless of a person's former manner of life, God extends mercy to save that person and, by doing so, he shows himself to be the merciful God (see Paul's comments about himself, 1 Tim 1:13, 16). The ultimate result of God's mercy to those he saves is eternal life! Hence, Jude exhorts believers (Jude 21, NIV): "Keep yourselves in God's love as you wait for the mercy of our Lord Jesus Christ to bring you to eternal life."

The mercy of God toward those with physical needs and God's mercy in salvation are such wonderful themes that many NT writers wish mercy upon their readers. We find this often in opening and closing salutations of letters, and in benedictions (see Gal 6:16; 1 Tim 1:2; 2 Tim 1:2; 2 John 3; Jude 2).

Indeed, God has been merciful to all of us in many ways. As a result, we can say with the psalmist (Ps 89:1, KJV), "I will sing of the mercies of the LORD for ever: with my mouth will I make known thy faithfulness to all generations."

LONGSUFFERING

Another aspect of God's love and goodness is his patience toward us. Both OT and NT portray God as a longsuffering and patient God. The Hebrew phrase for longsuffering is *'erek 'ap*. The term *'erek* comes from the verb *'ārak* ("to be long"). The form *'ārek* ("long") appears only in the construct form *'erek*. It is used ten times in the OT with respect to God, and most frequently it is used of God in construct to the word *'appāyim*. It is typically translated "longsuffering," "slow to anger or wrath." "Literally, when the Bible says God is 'longsuffering' (Ex 34:6; Num 14:18; Ps 86:15; etc.) it reads 'God is long of nose.' When he is angry, his nose becomes red and burns. It may be questioned whether in the living language the idioms had not already dropped their etymological associations and did not merely mean to be longsuffering and to be angry. When he is compassionate his nose becomes long, so long in fact that it would take forever to burn completely."[16]

All OT passages that refer to God's longsuffering or patience use the phrase *'erek 'ap*. In the NT, writers refer both to God's longsuffering and his patience. The Greek term is *makrothumia*. This family of terms is used in the LXX to translate the Hebrew *'erek 'ap*. In the Gospels, *makrothumia* is shown (in the parable of the unmerciful servant) by the king to the wicked servant (Matt 18:23-35) who is then expected to show the same to his debtor, but doesn't. In Pauline literature, God's longsuffering is frequently related to his wrath (e.g., Rom 2:4; 9:22).[17]

Several passages refer to God's longsuffering in a list of descriptions about his character even though the writer's point is not simply to list various qualities of God. Rather, he intends to fit this attribute with the theme of God's patience with sinners in forestalling judgment upon their sin. For example, after God gave the Decalogue at Mount Sinai, Moses came down from the mount and found the people already breaking the first commandment. In his anger, Moses broke the two tablets on which God had written the Law. In Exodus 34, the Lord commissioned Moses to take two new tablets so that he could write the Decalogue on them again. Moses went up to Mount Sinai again for the Lord to write the Decalogue. Before the Lord did so, however, verse 6 (KJV) says, "And the LORD passed by before him, and proclaimed, The LORD, The LORD God, merciful and gracious, longsuffering, and abundant in goodness and truth." Verse 7 speaks of God's mercy and willingness to forgive sin. Though the reference in verse 6 is just to this divine attribute (among others), in the context of what had happened, it was appropriate for God to underscore his longsuffering character. If he were not patient, he would not be merciful and forgiving to his people Israel, who had broken the first commandment at the very time it was being given. That there even is a second giving of the Decalogue, rather than destruction of the people, shows how longsuffering God is.

Numbers 14 is a second example. The scene is the rebellion of the people of Israel after the spies return from spying in the Promised Land. All of them except Joshua and Caleb say that there are giants in the land and that the Israelites will be destroyed if they try to conquer the land. But God had brought the Israelites from Egypt through the wilderness to this land, and he had promised to give it to them. Still, when the people heard the report of the spies, they murmured against God and Moses and asked to return to Egypt. God was infuriated and threatened to destroy them, but Moses interceded for his people. Moses appealed to the fact that God is a longsuffering God. Moses said (Num 14:18, KJV), "The LORD is longsuffering, and of great mercy, forgiving iniquity and transgression." Confronted with this plea for pardon, God spared the people, though those who murmured against God were condemned to wander in the wilderness for some forty years, and they didn't possess the land.

A rather interesting passage is Jer 15:15. In the first part of the chapter, the Lord pronounced doom and judgment as inevitable upon sinful Judah. Because of Jeremiah's stand for the Lord amid a wicked people, he wasn't a very popular man and he received much persecution. In verse 15 (KJV), though, he pleads with the Lord to take vengeance on the ungodly who were persecuting Jeremiah as well. He then says, "O LORD, thou knowest: remember me, and visit me, and revenge me of my persecutors; take me not away in thy longsuffering: know that for thy sake I have suffered rebuke." Jeremiah in effect is saying, "Lord, I need release from my persecutors. These people are worthy of judgment and I plead with you to judge them. But I know that you are a longsuffering God, and because of that you don't always judge immediately. But if you are longsuffering now, the result will likely be that your enemies and mine will succeed in taking me away." This is indeed an unusual passage, for many passages appeal to God's mercy and patience and ask him to be patient with the sinner. In this passage Jeremiah fears that because God is longsuffering, Jeremiah will suffer because his afflicters won't be punished.

In the NT, God's longsuffering toward sinners is evident again, and in some cases the reason is to give sinners a chance to repent and turn to God. For example, in Romans 1 Paul catalogs sins into which the heathen have fallen. He begins chapter 2 by saying that those who do such things are guilty of pun-

364 □ No One Like Him

ishment. Those who think they will escape judgment when they do the same thing are fooling themselves. God may have withheld punishment, but they must be careful not to mistake the delay. Rom 2:4 (KJV) clarifies the reason: "Or despisest thou the riches of his goodness and forbearance and longsuffering; not knowing that the goodness of God leadeth thee to repentance?" God is slow to judge sinners, but not because he doesn't care about their sin or because he isn't powerful enough to judge. He is patient in order to give them a chance to repent.

Not only does God forbear judgment on sinners to give them time to repent, he also sometimes withholds judgment so that when it does fall, it will be abundantly clear that it is deserved. This seems to be Paul's point in Rom 9:22, but this isn't the only point, for in verse 23, it becomes clear that God's purpose in withholding judgment upon the unrepentant is also to show those he saves (who equally deserve such judgment when judged on their *own* merits alone) how incredibly merciful he is to them. In doing so, he shows himself to be patient with the elect (cf. 1 Pet 3:20).

In addition, God was patient with the apostle Paul not merely to give him an opportunity to repent and turn to Christ. Doing this and then using Paul as a mighty spokesman for the gospel allowed God to offer Paul as a prime example of divine patience (1 Tim 1:16). Any who think they have remained in sin too long and strayed from God too far for God ever to save them need only reflect on the example of Paul!

Two other NT passages contain the theme of God's patience with sinners in order to allow them time to repent, but there is a slight twist to one. In 2 Peter 3, Peter addresses the error of those who say that one can live as one pleases because the Lord will never return in judgment. Peter says the Lord will return and judge the ungodly, and in verses 5-9 he offers reasons why the Lord's return and judgment are certain. In verses 8-9 in particular, Peter addresses why God has delayed judgment so long. Verse 9 (KJV) says, "The Lord is not slack concerning his promise, as some men count slackness; but is longsuffering to us-ward, not willing that any should perish, but that all should come to repentance." How do men count slowness or delay in judgment? Undoubtedly, they think it means either that there is no God or that if there is one, he is too powerless or even too disinterested to punish the wicked. But this is mistaken. God is longsuffering for a specific reason. There are textual problems in this verse, and one is noteworthy. Some manuscripts read "longsuffering to us," but the better manuscript tradition reads "to you." Who are the "you"? They are the readers of Peter's letter, who were believers. Why would God be patient with them because he doesn't want any to perish? They won't perish, because they are already saved. The reason for God's patience is that believers are the messengers to the lost. Now Peter's point becomes clear. Believers enticed by the idea that it is all right to live as one pleases because God will never judge sin, have totally misunderstood the forbearance of divine judgment. God forbears so that believers will get busy in bringing the gospel to those who don't believe. God waits patiently for believers to do this because their witness is the appointed means for bringing the lost to Christ, and God wants to save them, for he does not desire that they should perish (see also 2 Pet 3:15 for the same idea).

Though most biblical data on divine longsuffering and patience focus in one way or another on God's patience with sinners, one other passage has a different sense. Psalm 86 contains David's plea for divine help, but the point does not seem so much to be help for David as a sinner. In verse 2 (KJV) David says, "Preserve my soul; for I am holy: O thou my God . . ." Throughout the psalm David emphasizes God's excellencies as a basis for him to intervene for David. In verse 14 David recounts the fact that the proud and violent who care not for God have set themselves against David as well. In verse 15 (KJV) David then says, "But thou, O Lord, art a God full of compassion, and gracious, longsuffering, and plenteous in mercy and truth." In light of these qualities, David pleads for God's help in combating his enemies (v. 16). How does the idea of divine longsuffering fit here? Probably David had asked for divine intervention before and received God's help. Because of God's mercy and compassion, surely he would help David again. And, because he is patient, he would not likely be put off by yet another request by David for divine help. As Delitzsch also notes, in verse 15 David supports his petition by appealing to God's testimony about himself in Exod 34:6.[18]

Finally, the more Christlike believers become, the more their lives will exhibit patience. The more we walk in the Spirit, the more our lives will be characterized by longsuffering. Hence, in Gal 5:22 Paul includes longsuffering as a fruit of the Spirit. We become more patient even as is our God, and to the extent that our lives do not exhibit longsuffering, to that extent we show our further need to be remade into Christ's image through the Spirit's ministry.

GOODNESS

One of the most familiar themes of Scripture is the goodness of the Lord. He is good in so many different ways to all creatures. He is a merciful, gracious, lovingkind, and longsuffering God. This doesn't mean that each of these terms is identical, but only that a God who is fundamentally good expresses that goodness in so many different ways.

The basic Hebrew words for divine goodness are *ṭôb* and *ṭûb*. However, on a number of occasions (e.g., Exod 34:6; Ps 33:5; 52:3[Heb]; 107:8, 15, 21, 31) we find the word *ḥesed* rendered "goodness," "compassion," or "loving-kindness" in various translations. In addition, on one occasion (Ps 51:18) the term *rāṣôn* is used to speak of the good pleasure or will of God toward Zion. Finally, in a number of passages we find the verb *yāṭab* ("to do good") used of God. As for *ṭôb* and *ṭûb*, there are many senses in which these words are used in the OT, even as this is true in English or any other language. As one author notes, five general areas of meaning can be differentiated in the OT. They are: "1) practical, economic, or material good, 2) abstract goodness such as desirability, pleasantness, and beauty, 3) quality or expense, 4) moral goodness, and 5) technical philosophical goodness."[19] In this last sense, it refers to the highest good, and appears in Eccl 2:24 in a discussion of the highest good a person could pursue in life (cf. also Eccl 3:22; 8:15). As for God, he is morally good, but he also gives his creatures material good to meet their everyday needs.

The verb *yāṭab* not only means "to do good" but is also used in the senses "to be good," "be pleasing." In relation to God, it refers to God's beneficent attitude toward and dealings with his people. Clearly, though, when people ask God to do good to them or when Scripture says he will do good to someone, it is because they know God has the attribute of goodness. From his goodness stems his beneficence to his people and to all creatures.

As for *rāṣôn* ("pleasure," "delight," "favor"), it has three major shades of meaning in the OT. The main sense is God's "favor" or "good will" (Deut 33:16; Isa 60:10; Ps 5:12; 30:6[Heb], 8[Heb]; 51:18). The second sense focuses on the "delight" or "acceptance" of an individual. The third is "desire" or "pleasure" in the specific sense of God's will (Ezra 10:11; Ps 40:9[Heb]).[20]

The NT term for goodness is *chrēstotēs*. This particular word is used of a human attribute in Rom 3:12. It is used of God only in the Pauline corpus and conveys the idea of being kind and helpful. Most typically in Paul, it designates God's goodness and kindness in salvation through Christ (Rom 2:4; 11:22; Tit 3:4ff.). Applying this word to God's saving work in Christ "implies that this work is appropriate to God. In Christ God acts as the One He is by nature, or, conversely, by His work in and through Christ God is manifested according to His true nature."[21]

When we look at the biblical concept of divine goodness, one major idea stands out. It is that God is concerned about the well-being of his creatures and does things to promote it. Of course, God is interested in doing what is morally good and right, but biblical writers capture that idea by referring to his righteousness and holiness. Moreover, because he does what is righteous and holy in his dealings with all, the result is promotion of their well-being. This is so regardless of whether the issue is their physical and material well-being or their spiritual benefit. In sum, Scripture says (Jas 1:17): "Every good thing bestowed and every perfect gift is from above, coming down from the Father of lights, with whom there is no variation, or shifting shadow." Moreover, if humans who are evil give good things to their children, we can expect no different from a heavenly Father who is only good (Matt 7:11).

Many biblical passages refer to God's goodness without relating it to any particular deed he has done for any person or group. In Exodus 34 Moses requests a new vision of the Lord, and the Lord gives it to him. Verse 6 (KJV) says, "And the LORD passed by before him, and proclaimed, The LORD, The LORD God, merciful and gracious, longsuffering, and abundant in goodness and truth" (see also Exod 33:19; 1 Chron 16:34; 2 Chron 5:13; 7:3). The

Psalms are replete with praises for the goodness of the Lord. We read in Ps 107:8 (KJV), "Oh that men would praise the LORD for his goodness, and for his wonderful works to the children of men!" The psalmist repeats this refrain in verses 15, 21, and 31. In Ps 135:3, we read again of the goodness of the Lord and of the need to praise him for it (see also Ps 136:1). Hence, the psalmist encourages his readers to experience God, for if they do, they will see that he is good (Ps 34:8): "O taste and see that the LORD is good" (see further references in Psalms to God's goodness at 25:8; 33:5; 52:1; 100:5; 106:1; 107:1, 9; 118:1, 29; 145:7, 9).

The NT also speaks of God's goodness. When a man came to Jesus asking how to attain eternal life, he called Jesus "Good Master." Jesus answered (Matt 19:16-17, KJV; parallel Mark 10:17-18; Luke 18:18-19) that "there is none good but one, that is, God." In addition, Jesus likened his relation to his own to that between a shepherd and his sheep. But Jesus is not just any sort of shepherd. He is the good shepherd who gives his life for the sheep (John 10:11; see also v. 14).

Throughout Scripture there is ample evidence of God's concern for the physical and material well-being of all. As evidence of his goodness in providing the basic necessities of life, we find passages such as Acts 14:17, "And yet He did not leave Himself without witness, in that He did good and gave you rains from heaven and fruitful seasons, satisfying your hearts with food and gladness" (see also Jesus' words in Matt 6:28-30). The psalmist also, after speaking of the Lord's goodness in bringing water so that the natural order will flourish, says (Ps 65:11), "Thou hast crowned the year with Thy bounty, and Thy paths drip with fatness" (see also Ps 104:28).

Indeed, God is good to all, even to those who disobey him and walk far from him. As Eliphaz said to Job about the wicked (Job 22:18), "Yet He filled their houses with good things; but the counsel of the wicked is far from me." Jesus says: "For He causes His sun to rise on the evil and the good, and sends rain on the righteous and the unrighteous" (Matt 5:45); and Luke 6:35 (KJV) says God "is kind unto the unthankful and to the evil."

In addition to God's general care and concern for the basic necessities of life, Scripture points to many instances of God acting for the benefit and welfare of individuals and groups. Moreover, he does so regardless of whether we have a glaring need or are experiencing bounty and blessing. As to corporate good, Jethro rejoices over the Lord's goodness in delivering Israel from Egypt (Exod 18:9), and in Deuteronomy we find repeated references to the good land which the Lord gave Israel for a possession (Deut 1:25; 4:21, 22; 6:18; 8:7, 10, 16; 9:6; 11:17). That Promised Land was a token to Israel of the Lord's goodness. Speaking later in Israel's history, Nehemiah rehearses what the good Lord did for Israel when the people went to conquer the Promised Land (Neh 9:25). As Joshua says (Josh 21:45): "Not one of the good promises which the LORD had made to the house of Israel failed; all came to pass" (see also Josh 23:14). Other OT passages that speak of God's manifold goodnesses to his people Israel are Num 10:29; Deut 26:11; 28:12, 63; 30:5, 9; 1 Kgs 8:56; Ezra 3:11; 8:18; Neh 9:20; Ps 128:5.

Not only did God do good to Israel in the past, but he also promised her good for the future. Through the prophet Jeremiah, God promised his people return and restoration from Babylonian captivity (Jer 24:6; see also Jer 29:10). Moreover, God promised through the prophets a final eschatological restoration of Israel which is future even to our own day. In chapter 32, Jeremiah speaks of a new covenant that God will make with Israel to bless her (32:39-42): "and I will give them one heart and one way, that they may fear Me always, for their own good, and for the good of their children after them. And I will make an everlasting covenant with them that I will not turn away from them, to do them good. . . . And I will rejoice over them to do them good. . . . 'Just as I brought all this great disaster on this people, so I am going to bring on them all the good that I am promising them'" (see also Jer 31:12, 14; 33:9, 11, 14; Hos 3:5).

God is not only good to his ancient people Israel, but he also cares for the poor and the needy. As we read in Ps 68:10, "Thou didst provide in Thy goodness for the poor, O God." And he is good to individuals. Leah speaks of the good that God has done to her in giving her children (Gen 30:20). Jacob speaks of God's good promises of a manifold seed. Though Joseph's brothers sought to do him evil by selling him into Egypt, Joseph says (Gen 50:20) "but God meant it for good in order to bring about this present result, to preserve many people alive." After receiving news that God would establish his throne forever, King David says (2 Sam 7:28—parallel 1 Chron 17:26), "And now, O Lord GOD, Thou art God, and Thy words are truth, and Thou hast promised this good thing to Thy servant." For other examples of divine goodness to individuals see Judg 17:13; 1 Sam 25:30; 1 Kgs 8:66; 2 Chron 7:10; Neh 2:8, 18; 5:19. As a result of God's blessing upon individual lives, the psalmist says with assurance (Ps 23:6, KJV), "Surely goodness and mercy shall follow me all the days of my life" (see also Ps 21:3; 144:2).

Because of God's well-known goodness, individuals often plead for God to do good to them. The psalmist pleads for forgiveness of sin (Ps 25:7). Nehemiah asks for God's good (Neh 13:31). Many psalms are filled with petitions for the Lord's goodness (Ps 51:18; 69:16; 109:21; 119:39; 125:4). Because of God's goodness, at times people are content to let the Lord do whatever seems good to him (1 Sam 3:18; 2 Sam 10:12). And the psalmist desires to know God's statutes (Ps 119:68), for "Thou art good and doest good; teach me Thy statutes."

God's goodness extends beyond caring for personal and corporate physical and material needs to people's spiritual needs. Paul says that God's elect were chosen because of God's good purposes (Eph 1:5, 9), and because of the results, we can see that God's good purposes and pleasure are beneficial to the elect. Moreover, we see the results of God's salvation to those who believe (whether Jew or Gentile), and it is all an evidence of God's goodness (Rom 11:22).

Moreover, once saved, we know that because of what Christ has done for us, we have an "eternal comfort and good hope by grace" (2 Thess 2:16). And the sanctification process continues in us, not because we have the power to become more like Christ on our own but because of God's continued working within us. As Paul says (Phil 2:13): God "is at work in you, both to will and to work for His good pleasure." Likewise, it is encouraging to know that, because he is good, God stands ready to forgive our sins when we repent. Both the OT and NT affirm this great truth about God's goodness. Not only does he forgive sins, but his goodness leads people to repent. The psalmist writes (Ps 86:5): "For Thou, Lord, art good, and ready to forgive, and abundant in lovingkindness to all who call upon Thee" (see also Rom 2:4).

God is also good in that he showers special blessings on his own people who follow his will and way. The psalmists say: "How great is Thy goodness, which Thou hast stored up for those who fear Thee, which Thou hast wrought for those who take refuge in Thee, before the sons of men!" (Ps 31:19). "The young lions do lack and suffer hunger; but they who seek the LORD shall not be in want of any good thing" (Ps 34:10; see also Ps 65:4; Lam 3:25). As Paul says (Rom 8:28): "And we know that God causes all things to work together for good to those who love God, to those who are called according to His purpose" (see also Job 22:21; Nah 1:7; Ps 84:11). Truly God is good to us, and because of his goodness and concern for us Peter tells us (1 Pet 5:7) to cast "all your anxiety upon Him, because He cares for you."

Because of God's goodness to believers, our lives should exemplify that goodness to others. If we don't do good to others, there is reason to wonder if we are letting our good God rule and reign in our lives. As John says (3 John 11), "Beloved, do not imitate what is evil, but what is good. The one who does good is of God; the one who does evil has not seen God." And Paul reminds us in Gal 5:22 that the fruit of the Spirit is goodness. Even as God is good to all people, we must also be good.

LOVINGKINDNESS

Closely related to God's love, goodness, mercy, and grace is his lovingkindness. While the NT does not have a separate term for this word, the OT term that is translated "lovingkindness" in the KJV and the NASB is ḥesed. Most of the references appear in Psalms, but some are in Jeremiah and one is in Hosea.

Many references to God's lovingkindness simply extol him for having this quality. Ps 36:7 says, "How precious is Thy lovingkindness, O God!" Ps 63:3 says, "Because Thy lovingkindness is better than life, my lips will praise Thee" (see also Ps 103:4 and 138:2).

Most references to God's lovingkindness, however, ask God to demonstrate it. In Ps 40:11 (KJV) we hear the plea, "Withhold not thou thy tender mercies from me, O LORD: let thy lovingkindness and thy truth continually preserve me" (see also Ps 17:7; 36:10; 51:1; 69:16; 119:88, 149, 159; 143:8). In some instances as well, the writer records God expressing his desire to be lovingkind or to continue showing forth his lovingkindness. We see such a tender expression of his love for Israel in Jer 31:3: "The LORD appeared to him from afar, saying 'I have loved you with an everlasting love; therefore I have drawn you with lovingkindness'" (see also Hos 2:19). What an encouragement to God's people, especially those in need, to know that God remains steady in his loyal love! Other passages that speak of God's lovingkindness are Ps 26:3; 40:10; 42:8; 48:9; 88:11; 89:33; 92:2; 107:43; Jer 9:24; 16:5; 32:18.

TRUTH

Our God is also a God of truth. He knows the truth and only speaks the truth. Hence, his promises are reliable and he is dependable and faithful. In the OT there are two basic word groups that refer to God's truthfulness and faithfulness. The first stems from the verb ʾāman ("to confirm," "support," "uphold" in the Qal; "to be faithful," "be established" in the Niphal; and "to be certain," "to believe in" in the Hiphil). The root idea of the word is firmness or certainty. In the Qal its main idea is that of support, and it is used in the sense of a parent supporting a helpless infant. In the Niphal, the meaning is "to be established," and the Niphal participle which means "to be faithful, sure, dependable" is used to describe God upon whom all certainty rests. In the same word group are the noun ʾĕmûnāh which, when applied to God, speaks of his dependability, and the nouns ʾōmēn and ʾāmēn. As to the former, it carries the idea of truth (when used as an adjective, it means "true"). As to the latter, it typically is translated as "truly," but is used in Isa 65:16 as a noun to describe the Lord as the God of truth. Finally, in this word group we have the noun ʾĕmet. The basic idea in this word is certainty and dependability. The term is used to describe God's character (e.g., Gen 24:27; Exod 34:6; Ps 25:5; 31:5) and his words (Ps 119:42, 151, 160; Dan 10:21), and as one of the divine attributes, it becomes the means by which humans know and serve God as Savior (e.g., Josh 24:14; 1 Kgs 2:4; Ps 26:3; 86:11; 91:4; Isa 38:3).[22]

A second set of Hebrew nouns, qĕšôṭ (Dan 4:37) and qōšeṭ (Ps 60:4), occur much less frequently than the terms in the ʾāman word group. These words come from a root which means the right or truth. In the two passages cited, they speak of God as true.

In the NT, there are two main terms for truth. The first is alēthēs, which refers to the reality of a thing, i.e., that something actually is the case. It is used of God in Rom 3:4 (NIV), where Paul says, "Let God be true, and every man a liar." In this passage Paul is responding to the idea that what God has promised might not be fulfilled; he affirms that even if all others fail, God will do what he has said. His nature is true, and reality matches what he promises. The second NT term is alēthinos, and it carries the idea of being genuine or conforming to the ideal. Paul uses it in 1 Thess 1:9 to note that the Thessalonians turned from worshiping idols to the true and living God. Though there were other gods to worship, the God of Scripture is the only one who matches the ideal of what God should be (see also John 17:3).

In addition, the NT also teaches that God is faithful, and the term used to describe that quality is *pistos*. Here the thought is that God is ever mindful of his promises and fulfills them; he is dependable. It is used of God in passages such as 1 Cor 1:9; 2 Tim 2:13; and Heb 10:23.

Scripture portrays God as true in several respects. However, we must initially distinguish between two primary senses of God as true. Both senses (in fact, all uses of truth in regard to God) depend on a more fundamental theory of truth. A theory of truth explains what sort of thing truth is. As I have argued elsewhere,[23] there are several main theories of truth, but the one that underlies ordinary language is the correspondence theory of truth. According to this theory, sentences are true if what they assert about the world matches what we find in the world. While Scripture doesn't teach any one theory of truth as the correct theory, when the biblical writers wrote, they presupposed some form of correspondence theory of truth.

With this introduction, we can now explain what Scripture says about God's truthfulness. As with many of the divine attributes, many biblical passages simply ascribe truth to God without clarifying the sense in which he is truth. Examples of such passages are plentiful. As we might expect, many passages that speak of God's truth are in psalms that extol God's virtues. The psalmist says (Ps 40:10-11): "I have not concealed Thy lovingkindness and Thy truth from the great congregation. . . . Thy lovingkindness and Thy truth will continually preserve me." Moreover, this truth of God is everywhere and it never ends, so the psalmist can say (Ps 108:4), "For Thy lovingkindness is great above the heavens; and Thy truth reaches to the skies" (see also Ps 117:2). In the presence of such a God of truth, the only appropriate response is (Ps 138:2): "I will bow down toward Thy holy temple, and give thanks to Thy name for Thy lovingkindness and Thy truth" (see also Exod 34:6; Ps 31:5; 57:10; 71:22; 86:15; 89:14; 91:4; 96:13; 98:3; 100:5; Isa 65:16; Jer 4:2).

In the NT many passages speak of God as a God of truth. In fact, each member of the Godhead is said to have this attribute. John says of Jesus (John 1:14), "We beheld his glory, glory as of the only begotten from the Father, full of grace and truth." Jesus referred to himself as the truth (John 14:6), and the NT speaks of the Holy Spirit as the Spirit of truth. Jesus promised to send him, and promised that he would lead the disciples into truth and help them remember the deeds and words of Jesus (presumably, so they would know and speak the truth when they preached and wrote about Christ). We see this in John 14:17; 15:26; and 16:13. And in 1 John 2:27 John speaks of the anointing the believer has received. Commentators attest that the anointing is the Holy Spirit himself.

Scripture attributes truth to God, and it tells us in what sense he is true. The first primary sense in which God is true is that he alone is genuinely God. While many peoples have worshiped one thing or another as God, none of these things matches the genuine concept of deity. On the other hand, the God of Scripture is the real thing. He is everything a God should be; he fully matches the ideal.

There are passages in the OT and NT that speak of God as truth in this sense. In 2 Chron 15:3 we read, "And for many days Israel was without the true God." And in Jer 10:10 we find, "But the Lord is the true God." Speaking of Jesus, John writes (John 1:9), "There was the true light which, coming into the world, enlightens every man" (see also John 15:1; 17:3; 1 Thess 1:9). In a similar vein John writes (1 John 5:20), "And we know that the Son of God has come, and has given us understanding, in order that we might know Him who is true, and we are in Him who is true, in His Son Jesus Christ. This is the true God and eternal life." Believers have a relation with the one who is truly God, and with his Son who is truly God.

Second, God is truth because he always tells the truth. Of course, in order to tell the truth he must know it, and as omniscient, he does. But one could know what is true and deliberately hide it or lie. God cannot lie (Num 23:19; Tit 1:2; Heb 6:18), and as omniscient, he cannot be mistaken about what the truth is. None of this means that God tells us all the truth he knows, or that he is obligated to do so. It only means that whatever God says matches the way things are.

Scripture is replete with verses that say God tells the truth. Scripture, which is God's Word, is true (Ps 119:142, 160). Jesus, knowing full well that the Bible is the Word of God, says (John 17:17), "Sanctify them in the truth: Thy word is truth."

Beyond these assertions that Scripture (God's Word in written form) is true, biblical figures claim that God tells the truth whenever he speaks. Here a few verses will suffice, because so many say this about God. We read (2 Sam 7:28), "And now, O Lord God, Thou art God, and Thy words are truth, and Thou hast promised this good thing to Thy servant." The psalmist says (Ps 132:11), "The Lord has sworn to David, a truth from which He will not turn back." And Isaiah writes (25:1, kjv): "O Lord, thou art my God . . . thy counsels of old are faithfulness and truth" (see also Gen 24:27; Ps 86:11; Jer 42:5).

In the NT all members of the Godhead speak the truth. In Matt 22:16 (parallel Mark 12:14) we read, "And they sent their disciples to Him, along with the Herodians, saying, 'Teacher, we know that You are truthful and teach the way of God in truth.'" In regard to the Father (John 3:33), "He who has received His witness has set his seal to this, that God is true." And in regard to the Spirit (John 5:32), "There is another who bears witness of Me, and I know that the testimony which He bears of Me is true." Because God is true, the gospel that his apostles proclaim is true. It does not lie about man's lost condition, nor does it offer some false remedy. It tells the exact way to come to God (Gal 2:5, 14; Eph 1:13). Other NT passages that speak of God as the one who tells the truth are Mark 12:32; John 7:18; 8:14, 26; Eph 4:21; Rev 3:7, 14; 6:10; 21:5; 22:6.

There is another noteworthy strain of biblical teaching about God's truth. God not only knows and tells the truth, but also does the truth, and his commandments and laws are often spoken of as the truth. What does this exactly mean? To say that God's laws and statutes are true means that they correspond to the way things should be. The writers who make such claims are assuming that there is such a thing as an objective moral standard of right and wrong, and they contend that God's laws correspond to that objective standard. Of course, that is precisely what we should expect if, as I have argued elsewhere, God's moral laws ultimately express his own moral perfection.[24] In saying that God's rules match what he knows to be the objective standards of right and wrong (rules based on his own moral perfection), the biblical writers simply say his commandments are true. Not only do God's moral rules conform to objective moral law, but Scripture also tells us that God's actions are what they should be; they correspond to the moral law he has revealed.

With this explanation, we can understand various biblical passages that speak about God's statutes and actions as true. Neh 9:13 says, "Then Thou didst come down on Mount Sinai, and didst speak with them from heaven; Thou didst give to them just ordinances and true laws, good statutes and commandments." The psalmist says (Ps 119:151), "Thou art near, O LORD; and all Thy commandments are truth" (see also Ps 19:9). As to God's works, he does what is true. As the psalmist writes (Ps 33:4, KJV): "For the word of the LORD is right; and all his works are done in truth." And we see these themes again in the book of Revelation (Rev 15:3): "Great and marvelous are Thy works, O Lord God, the Almighty; righteous and true are Thy ways, Thou King of the nations" (see also Rev 16:7; 19:2). Other passages that show that God's rules and judgments correspond to what is right and show that he does the truth are Deut 32:4; Ps 25:5, 10; 111:8; Isa 16:5; 42:3; Dan 4:37; 9:13; Mic 7:20; Zech 8:8; John 1:17; Rom 2:2. Because God is truth and tells and does the truth, his people in whom the Holy Spirit is working exhibit the fruit of the spirit. Those fruits, according to Eph 5:9, are "all goodness and righteousness and truth."

Moreover, because God knows, tells, and does the truth, all of his teaching is corporately labeled the truth. Those who follow God and his ways are said to follow "the truth." For example, Ps 26:3 speaks of keeping God's commands as follows: "For Thy lovingkindness is before my eyes, and I have walked in Thy truth." More generally, in Isaiah we hear a promise to teach divine truth to one's children (Isa 38:19). Knowledge of the truth must precede doing the truth, and in the NT the salvation message is referred to as the word of truth (Col 1:5).

Closely related to God's truthfulness is his faithfulness. The biblical concept is that God is dependable and reliable. Many passages teach that God is dependable in that he keeps his promises. For example, Num 23:19 says, "God is not a man, that He should lie, nor a son of man, that He should repent; has He said, and will He not do it? Or has He spoken, and will He not make it good?" (See also Isa 11:5; 25:1.) It is also the point of Deut 7:9: "Know therefore that the LORD your God, He is God, the faithful God, who keeps His covenant and His lovingkindness to a thousandth generation with those who love Him and keep His commandments." And I believe it is the point in 1 Cor 10:13: "No temptation has overtaken you but such as is common to man; and God is faithful, who will not allow you to be tempted beyond what you are able, but with the temptation will provide the way of escape also, that you may be able to endure it." God has promised not to allow a temptation beyond what we can bear, and he keeps that promise. Heb 10:23 and 11:11 also show that God keeps his promises. Finally, 1 John 1:9 teaches that God has implemented a means for cleansing of sin, and has promised to forgive repentant sinners. He keeps his word in doing that when we confess.

In addition, there are some passages that speak of God or Christ as faithful, and the idea is that they tell the truth. In Revelation we find several references of this sort to Jesus (Rev 1:5; 3:14; 19:11). It is he who is faithful and true.

The vast majority of verses that speak of God's faithfulness, however, simply teach that he is dependable. When we need him in time of trouble, he is there. As we reflect on the events of our lives, we can see God's hand upon us, for he has been a dependable help, guardian, and friend all along the way. He has never let us down, never lied to us, and has always done what is in our best interests even when it was hard to understand what he was doing or how what he did was really for our betterment. Many passages speak of this faithful God, and a few examples will suffice. Ps 89:1-2, 5, 8 says: "I will sing of the lovingkindness of the LORD forever; to all generations I will make known Thy faithfulness with my mouth. For I have said, 'Lovingkindness will be built up forever; in the heavens Thou wilt establish Thy faithfulness.' . . . And the heavens will praise Thy wonders, O LORD; Thy faithfulness also in the assembly of the holy ones. . . . O LORD God of hosts, who is like Thee, O mighty LORD? Thy faithfulness also surrounds Thee." (See also Ps 36:5.) As Jeremiah says of God's mercies and compassions, they do not fail. "They are new every morning; great is Thy faithfulness" (Lam 3:23). The NT heralds God's faithfulness as well: "God is faithful, through whom you were called into fellowship with His Son, Jesus Christ our Lord" (1 Cor 1:9). "Faithful is He who calls you, and He also will bring it to pass" (1 Thess 5:24; see also 2 Tim 2:13). Other passages that speak in one way or another of God's faithfulness are Ps 40:10; 89:24, 33; 92:2; 119:75, 90; 143:1; Isa 49:7; Jer 42:5; 2 Thess 3:3; Heb 2:17; 1 Pet 4:19. Though we sometimes fail to meet our obligations and are not always dependable, what a comfort and encouragement to know that the God with all the power to meet our needs cares about us and is dependable at all times!

NINE

GOD, TIME, AND ETERNITY

In Ps 90:2, the psalmist says, "Before the mountains were born, or Thou didst give birth to the earth and the world, even from everlasting to everlasting, Thou art God." These sublime words speak of God's eternity, and the psalmist later contrasts God's eternal existence with our temporary life span. Theists in various religious traditions agree that God is eternal. Believers often find comfort and solace in knowing that their God is not limited by time. In times of trouble, it is comforting to know that whatever happens, God will be there. He will be there not only because he cares for us but also because he will always exist.

While the doctrine of divine eternity is a comfort religiously, and an essential theological doctrine of Christianity, it is also important in that it has significant implications for many other doctrines. Unfortunately, it is also a doctrine fraught with problems. In chapter 6, we saw that the most fundamental question about divine eternity is what it means. Is eternity timelessness, or is it never-ending existence within time? The doctrine raises other key issues as well. If God is timelessly eternal, can he act within time? If he is timelessly eternal, must he also be totally immutable? If so, how can he act and react to his creatures who are in time, since responding to them seems to involve change on God's part? On the other hand, if God's eternity is temporal, isn't God's life as fleeting as ours? In fact, if God is in time, doesn't he become so enmeshed in time and change that our concept of God becomes that of process theology?

Unfortunately, there are no simple answers to these questions. However, the implications of this doctrine are far-reaching. Hence, in this chapter I intend to examine the main arguments for the two conceptions of divine eternity. Before turning to the issues and arguments surrounding God's eternity, we must clarify the two ways of understanding this notion. Stephen Charnock helps us get started with his claim that "eternity is a perpetual duration, which hath neither beginning nor end."[1] Something eternal, then, always exists. It never comes into being or goes out of being. This may appear to be adequate, but it isn't. The crucial issue is whether something eternal exists within time or outside of time.

The notion of atemporal or timeless eternity has a long tradition in Christian thought. It was held by such theologians as Augustine, Boethius, Anselm, and Aquinas. It is clearly the more complex of the two concepts of eternity. Nelson Pike's handling of timeless eternity is extremely helpful in unpacking the concept. According to Pike, something timelessly eternal has two closely related characteristics: it lacks temporal extension, and it lacks temporal location.[2]

Something that lacks temporal extension lacks temporal duration. World history extends through time both backwards and forwards, and we can speak of successive moments in history. Something timeless, however, has no temporal spread or succession whatsoever. As Pike says of God's timeless eternity, "it is not just that the life of God lacks temporal limits: the point is that it has no temporal spread at all."[3] Thus, it makes no sense to talk of "how old" God is, for age is measured by temporal duration but God does not endure temporally. It isn't only we who cannot know how old God is; he cannot know either, for a person's age implies temporal duration, but according to the notion of timeless eternity God lives for no amount of time nor through any period of time.

Temporal location refers to a particular time when something exists, but it involves more than giving a date for events and more than being able to identify "now" by some reading on the clock and calendar. It also means saying of something or someone that it existed or happened "before" or "after" something else. That is, it involves locating one's position at a specific point on the continuum of time. However, someone or something that is timelessly eternal lacks temporal location. It doesn't exist now or later, before or after. This is so, not because it is nonexistent or because it exists simultaneously to all times. It is so because it is outside of time. Even existing simultaneously with all time is to have contact with time and to have innumerable temporal locations. As for God's timeless eternity, he may perceive all times at once, but that does not mean he is temporally located at all or any of those times. In summing up these two elements of timelessness, Pike explains, "The point seems to be that God is not to be qualified by temporal predicates of any kind—neither time-extension predicates (such as, e.g., 'six years old') nor time-location predicates (such as, e.g., 'before Columbus')."[4]

All of this suggests Boethius's classic definition of divine eternity. In his *The Consolation of Philosophy*, Book 5, Prose 6, Boethius writes that "eternity, then, is the complete possession all at once of illimitable life."[5] Stump and Kretzmann claim that there are four essential ingredients in this definition. The first is that anything eternal in this sense has life. Obviously, in God's case, this cannot be biological life, but at minimum it is a life of consciousness.

The second ingredient in the definition is illimitability. This means that an eternal being's life cannot be limited, for it can have neither a beginning nor an end. The third element in the definition is duration. Something with unending life must endure, but if it is timeless it cannot endure through time. Hence, timeless eternity incorporates the concept of atemporal duration. In fact, atemporality is the fourth element in the definition. It is required by the phrase "possession all at once." Whatever exists temporally, exists sequentially. Some events that happen to it are past, some future, and some present, but a temporal being does not nor can it possess all actions and events involving it at once, since these actions and events occur sequentially. The only way for a living being to possess all of its life at once is for it to be atemporal. Hence, timeless eternity involves not only duration, but atemporal duration.[6]

But what is atemporal duration? If timeless eternity is to make sense at all, we must clarify this concept. Stump and Kretzmann are as helpful as any in explaining this notion, but at some point in this discussion we must ask whether it really makes sense. They claim that the "existing of an eternal entity is a duration without succession, and, because eternity excludes succession, no eternal entity has existed or will exist; it *only* exists."[7] They begin to explain this notion in terms of the idea of a moment: "The temporal present is a durationless instant, a present that cannot be extended conceptually without falling apart entirely into past and future intervals. The eternal present, on the other hand, is by definition an infinitely extended, pastless, futureless duration."[8] In other words, take that *temporally* durationless moment and extend it indefinitely, and you have the idea of atemporal duration.

Despite this explanation, atemporal duration may still seem odd. As Stump and Kretzmann explain, part of what led philosophers to this idea was a desire for permanence amid the flux of ongoing life. Things that last through time appear genuinely to endure, but with temporal succession there is change. Hence, the apparent permanence is only apparent. But in order to ground the world of flux there must be something that really endures, i.e., it must exist and simply be there without change. For this to be so, it must be timeless.[9] According to Stump and Kretzmann, some of the oddness of the concept of atemporal duration passes once we go beyond the idea that the very concept of duration can only be thought of as persistence *through* time. Atemporal duration postulates persistence outside of time.[10] Moreover, the notion loses some of its strangeness when we remove from it any thought of succession. Temporal duration, of course, involves successive states; atemporal duration removes all succession.

But, what exactly does this mean and how should we explain it? About the closest we get comes in Stump and Kretzmann's explanation of atemporal duration in their reply to Paul Fitzgerald, as follows:

> The existence of a typical existent creature is spread over years of the past, through the present, and into years of the future. But neither its past nor its future is extant for any creature—the child you were, who appears in family snapshots, no longer exists—and any creature's present must be understood as a durationless instant at which its past is continuous with its future. Such radically evanescent existence

could not be the existence of an absolutely perfect being. The mode of existence for such a being, the permanent, utterly immutable actuality on which the evanescent realm of becoming depends, must be characterized by genuine, paradigmatic duration. And such duration must be fully realized duration, none of which is already lost or not yet gained—an atemporal infinite duration, in short. So the classic ancient and medieval expositions of the concept of eternity are attempts to frame the notion of a mode of existence consisting wholly in a present that is limitless rather than instantaneous. Such a present is indivisible, like the temporal present, but it is atemporal in virtue of being limitless rather than instantaneous, and it is in that way infinitely enduring. . . . atemporal duration, conceived as a beginningless and endless present, cannot admit of succession. . . . neither successiveness nor plurality of intervals can be features of the atemporal duration that characterizes the mode of existence of the absolute perfect being.[11]

Clearly, as Stump and Kretzmann understand atemporal duration, it includes divine simplicity. Moreover, for an atemporal being, the four elements in the definition have certain implications. In particular, an atemporal being cannot properly be said to do anything that involves time. An atemporal mind like God's "cannot deliberate, anticipate, remember, or plan ahead, for instance; all these mental activities essentially involve time, either in taking time to be performed (like deliberation) or in requiring a temporal viewpoint as a prerequisite to performance (like remembering)."[12] In contrast, mental activities such as knowing and willing require neither a temporal interval nor a temporal viewpoint, so an atemporal being can do such things.

Having defined timeless eternity, I turn now to *temporal eternity*, which some philosophers label *sempiternity* while others refer to it by saying that God is *everlasting* rather than eternal. This is clearly a much simpler concept. The fundamental notion of sempiternity is existence at all times. God's existence extends endlessly backwards and forwards from our point in time. He never had a beginning, nor will he cease to exist. As Morris explains, sempiternity is a "*temporal* notion, a conception of God's eternity in terms of time: God's existence is temporally infinite in duration, unbounded in the past and future. On this conception, there is in the life of God a past, present and future, as in the life of his creatures. But unlike any of his creatures, God is everlasting, and necessarily so."[13]

Just as there are implications from atemporal eternity, there are implications of temporal eternity. If God is a temporal being, then he is temporally extended and temporally located (in Pike's terms) at any moment. Moreover, this means that God's life is divisible into different temporal parts which follow one another successively, and this rules out divine simplicity. In addition, it rules out the strong sense of divine immutability associated with classical theism. Moreover, if God is temporal, what time is he in? Granting that his time is some measured time, which measured time is it? Our clock time? Cosmic time?

Or, what? And was time created when God created the universe, or was there time before creation?

From these clarifications, we can see that there is a certain sense to both atemporal and temporal eternity, but there are also questions that arise about the meaning of both. To what extent they are resolvable will become apparent as we consider arguments for and against each concept. Before turning to that argumentation, we should address two other preliminary matters. The first is what Scripture teaches about atemporal and temporal eternity, and here we can be brief because of our handling of the biblical data in chapter 6. The second issue is a historical one: in light of the oddness of atemporal eternity, how did the concept get into Christian theology?

THE BIBLE AND DIVINE ETERNITY

Can the Bible help us answer our question about atemporal or temporal eternity? It can if the biblical writers engage in what Paul Helm and James Barr call a "reflective context," which involves a second-order reflection on what sort of thing time and eternity are.[14] In other words, if there are passages where biblical authors offer metaphysical and philosophical reflections on the nature of time and eternity, those passages may help answer our question. If this is the requirement, however, we are in serious trouble, for our investigation of the biblical data in chapter 6 showed that there are no such passages.[15]

Paul Helm mentions a second way the Bible might help us answer our question. Helm explains:

> The second is that it does not teach it, but that it teaches many things which make the idea of timelessness a reasonable theological concept to employ, given these data, when certain controversial questions which the biblical writers did not themselves raise have arisen over the question.[16]

Since we have already seen in chapter 6 that the first strategy for using the Bible doesn't answer our question, if we are to employ Scripture at all we must do so according to Helm's second strategy. As we shall see when we turn to arguments for both positions, many of the arguments follow this second strategy. It remains to be seen, of course, how cogent such arguments are.

HISTORICAL INTERLUDE

How did the idea of atemporal duration become part of Christian theology? My intent in this section is not to give a detailed historical analysis of everyone who has held this doctrine. Rather, my concern is to discover who brought the idea into Christian theology, and why they deemed it necessary.

As to the origin of the idea of atemporal eternity altogether, William Kneale's "Time and Eternity in Theology" is very helpful. Kneale traces the origin of the idea to Parmenides and the Pythagorians, and he also finds it in Plato. Stump and Kretzmann agree on Parmenides and Plato, but they also trace the idea to Plotinus.[17]

The idea, then, clearly predates Christian theology, but who brought it into Christian thinking? Various theologians in church history have held the doctrine, but the key theologians are Augustine, Boethius, Anselm, and Aquinas. A brief survey of their thinking will show that they held this view and will explain why they held it.

In light of Augustine's (354–430) knowledge of Plato, it is not surprising that he was familiar with this idea of timeless eternity. In fact, as Kneale shows, in Augustine's *De Civitate Dei,* he refers explicitly to a passage from Plato's *Timaeus* in his comments on the sentence from Genesis 1 and 2, "God saw that it was good."[18] However, Augustine's most famous statement of divine atemporal eternity appeared in his earlier *Confessions.*

In Book XI of the *Confessions* Augustine notes that some ask what God was doing before he created the heavens and the earth. They reason that if he was at rest, there was no reason for him not to continue resting. If from all eternity he had planned to create, then why isn't creation itself eternal, and why didn't he create before he did? On the other hand, if the decision to create was not there from all eternity, then it came after God had existed for a period of time; but then it seems that God himself is not eternal. This is so because God's will is taken to be part of his substance or being. But, then, if the will is something new (i.e., it wasn't there for all eternity), then God's substance must not be eternal.[19]

Augustine's main reply amounts to saying that the question is ill-founded. It is ill-founded because it doesn't recognize a difference between time and eternity and that God is eternal. Thus, the idea that God might not intend to create, and then later decides to create, is based on thinking that God's existence involves temporal succession. Once one recognizes that God is eternal and that there is no past or future in eternity, one sees that it makes no sense to talk of God not willing something "for a certain amount of time" and then "beginning to will it" at a later "time." Hence, Augustine claims, the question rests on a mistake.[20]

A bit further in his discussion Augustine offers his answer, which contains his famous statement about God as timelessly eternal. Augustine affirms that God creates all things, so if there was time before creation of the heaven and earth, then God was not idle then, for he created that time. On the other hand, if there was no time before the creation of the heaven and the earth, it makes no sense to ask what God was doing "then," because "if there was no time, there was no 'then'."[21] Augustine further explains,

> Furthermore, although you are before time, it is not in time that you pre-
> cede it. If this were so, you would not be before all time. It is in eternity,

which is supreme over time because it is a never-ending present, that you are at once before all past time and after all future time. For what is now the future, once it comes, will become the past, whereas *you are unchanging, your years can never fail*. Your years neither go nor come, but our years pass and others come after them, so that they all may come in their turn. Your years are completely present to you all at once, because they are at a permanent standstill. They do not move on, forced to give way before the advance of others, because they never pass at all. But our years will all be complete only when they have all moved into the past. Your years are one day, yet your day does not come daily but is always today, because your today does not give place to any tomorrow nor does it take the place of any yesterday. Your today is eternity. And this is how the Son, to whom you said *I have begotten you this day*, was begotten co-eternal with yourself. You made all time; you are before all time; and the 'time', if such we may call it, when there was no time was not time at all.[22]

This is clearly the notion of timeless eternity, and as Pike says, it especially illustrates the view that things that are timelessly eternal lack temporal duration or extension.[23] Augustine says God lacks temporal duration because he is beyond time.

Boethius (480–524) seems to be the next great Christian thinker to adopt this notion, but his reason was considerably different from Augustine's. Boethius's most lengthy discussion of eternity appears in the last chapter of *The Consolation of Philosophy*. Boethius invokes atemporal eternity to resolve the dilemma of human free will and God's foreknowledge of future contingent actions. I shall discuss this issue at length in a later chapter, but I can summarize it now. If God really knows what we will do in the future, how can we escape doing what he foresees? Boethius saw the question of human freedom and divine foreknowledge as a genuine problem, and he seems to have been the first to think it could be resolved by applying the notion of timeless eternity to it. Boethius defines eternity and explains its relation to the freedom/foreknowledge problem as follows:

Eternity is the complete possession of eternal life all at once. This will appear more clearly if we compare it with things temporal. All that lives under the conditions of time moves through the present from the past to the future; there is nothing set in time which can at one moment grasp the whole space of its lifetime. It cannot yet comprehend tomorrow; yesterday it has already lost. And in this life of today your life is no more than a changing, passing moment. . . . What we should rightly call eternal is that which grasps and possesses wholly and simultaneously the fullness of unending life, which lacks naught of the future, and has lost naught of the fleeting past; and such an existence must be ever present in itself to control and aid itself, and also must keep present with itself the infinity of changing time. . . . Since then all judgment apprehends the subjects of its thought according to its own nature, and God has a condition of ever-present eternity, His knowledge, which passes over every change of time, embracing infinite lengths of past and future, views in its own direct comprehension everything as though it were taking place in the present. If you would weigh the foreknowledge by which God distinguishes all things, you will more rightly hold it to be a knowledge of a never-failing constancy in the present, than a foreknowledge of the future. Whence Providence is more rightly to be understood as a looking forth than a looking forward, because it is set far from low matters and looks forth upon all things as from a lofty mountain-top above all. Why then do you demand that all things occur by necessity, if divine light rests upon them, while men do not render necessary such things as they can see? Because you can see things of the present, does your sight therefore put upon them any necessity? Surely not. If one may not unworthily compare this present time with the divine, just as you can see things in this your temporal present, so God sees all things in His eternal present. Wherefore this divine foreknowledge does not change the nature or individual qualities of things: it sees things present in its understanding just as they will result some time in the future. . . . And God looks in His present upon those future things which come to pass through free will. Therefore if these things be looked at from the point of view of God's insight, they come to pass of necessity under the condition of divine knowledge; if, on the other hand, they are viewed in themselves, they do not lose the perfect freedom of their nature.[24]

A third major figure in the Christian tradition who held to God as time-lessly eternal is St. Anselm, but his reason for holding it was different from Augustine's and Boethius's. Anselm's comments on this topic appear in both his *Proslogium* and his *Monologium*. In chapter 19 of the *Proslogium*, Anselm writes about God:

Thou wast not, then, yesterday, nor wilt thou be to-morrow; but yesterday and to-day and to-morrow thou art; or, rather, neither yesterday nor to-day nor to-morrow thou art; but simply, thou art, outside all time. For yesterday and to-day and to-morrow have no existence, except in time; but thou, although nothing exists without thee, nevertheless dost not exist in space or time, but all things exist in thee. For nothing contains thee, but thou containest all.[25]

This is clearly the notion of eternity, and as Pike suggests, it denies that God has temporal location.[26] But why specifically did Anselm hold this view of divine atemporal eternity? Anselm is clear about this in both the *Proslogium* and the *Monologium*. Both works portray God as the greatest conceivable being. Anselm does more than just argue that the greatest conceivable being must exist. He adds that such a being must have qualities or attributes that make him the greatest. As Anselm suggests in the *Proslogium*, the supreme being lacks no good. As a result, he is "just, truthful, blessed, and what ever it is better to be than not to be."[27] Anselm elaborates qualities that are better to have than not have and says of God, "So then, thou are truly sensible (*sen-*

sibilis), omnipotent, compassionate, and passionless, as thou are living, wise, good, blessed, eternal: and whatever is better to be than not to be."[28] Clearly, then, God is eternal, because God has every perfection or greatness-making attribute, and Anselm considers eternity to be a perfection. He doesn't explain why eternity is a perfection, but merely affirms that it is, and therefore God, as the most perfect being imaginable, must have it.

In the *Monologium,* Anselm makes the same point but in a more round-about way. Anselm again argues that there is only one being that is the greatest and exists in the highest degree of all.[29] Anselm later says of this supreme being that to be it is better than to be anything else.[30] Having established that God is better than any other being, and is the greatest conceivable being, Anselm then explains that a greatest being would be simple, not composed of parts. But it follows, Anselm argues, that if God is simple, he must be eternal, for to exist at various times would mean he is composite, not simple. If God could exist as a whole at individual times in the past, present, and future, since eternity (all times) is part of God's essence, his essence would be divided into parts, and herein lies the problem.[31]

Anselm's logic is clear enough in the *Monologium.* God is the greatest conceivable being. That being's attributes are perfections. To be simple is a perfection, so God must be simple. But simplicity logically entails atemporal eternity, so it must also be a perfection, and God must possess it. In both the *Proslogium* and *Monologium,* Anselm's rationale for divine atemporal eternity is clear.

Finally, we come to Aquinas. Aquinas held divine atemporal eternity as Boethius defined it, but his reason for doing so is more like Anselm's than Boethius's or Augustine's. Still, Aquinas doesn't simply repeat Anselm. In his *Summa Theologiae,* Part I, Question X, Aquinas takes up the eternity of God, and he first discusses what eternity is. From this section, two comments tell us how he understood eternity and how it differed from time:

> So two things characterize eternity. First, anything existing in eternity is *unending,* that is to say, lacks both beginning and end (for both may be regarded as ends). Secondly, eternity itself exists as an *instantaneous whole* lacking successiveness. . . . There are two things to be noted about time, namely, that time itself is successive, and that an instant of time is imperfect. To deny that eternity is time Boethius uses 'instantaneously whole'; to deny temporal instantaneity the word 'perfect'.[32]

Clearly, Aquinas accepted Boethius's definition of eternity. A given moment of time is imperfect because it is not all of time and because it has a particular temporal location. As Pike explains, to deny that eternity involves existing at a particular moment (an instant of time), Aquinas says eternity is perfect rather than imperfect.[33] This, of course, is Aquinas's explanation relying on the term "perfect" in Boethius's definition of eternity.

Not only does Aquinas adopt Boethius's definition of eternity, but he also agrees that God is eternal. In Question 10, Article 2, Aquinas asserts that God is eternal and explains why he thinks so:

> We have shown already that the notion of eternity derives from unchangeableness in the same way that the notion of time derives from change. Eternity therefore principally belongs to God, who is utterly unchangeable. Not only that, but God is his own eternity, whereas other things, not being their own existence, are not their own duration. God, however, is his own invariable existence, and so is identical with his own eternity just as he is identical with his own nature.[34]

From this passage we see very clearly why Thomas felt it necessary to affirm eternity of God. The last two sentences of the passage teach not only divine eternity and immutability but also incorporate divine simplicity. Thomas's *Summa* has three parts. The first part is about God and begins with the question of God's existence. Having established by argument that God exists, Thomas then turns to "the way in which it exists, that we may come to understand what it is that exists."[35] Aquinas then explains that we cannot know how God is but only how he is not, i.e., we can only predicate of him attributes that explain qualities he does not have. Aquinas turns first to God's simplicity, which he affirms. Since in the material world simplicity is a sign of imperfection and incompleteness, Aquinas turns next to God's perfection.[36] This leads him later to discuss God's limitlessness, and then he turns to God's immutability. Moreover, as he says in the portion quoted above, immutability requires timeless eternity.

Aquinas's derivation of atemporal eternity and his reason for holding it are clear. As in Anselm's case, it is a logical outgrowth of other claims about God's nature. However, whereas Anselm moves from God's perfection to his eternity in the *Proslogium* and from God's simplicity directly to his eternity in the *Monologium*, Aquinas's basic line of thought moves from simplicity to immutability and from immutability to timeless eternity.

ARGUMENTS FOR TIMELESS ETERNITY

Timelessness a Logical Derivation from Other Doctrines

Invariably, proponents of atemporal eternity claim that it is logically required by other doctrines the theist must hold. If this is so, then divine atemporal eternity is an essential Christian doctrine. I shall present Anselm's derivation of the doctrine, for it is as clear as any.

In his *Proslogium,* the derivation is rather simple. Anselm says God is the greatest conceivable being and as such he has every greatness-making attribute. Anselm then lists the attributes he thinks fall into this category, and eternity is one of them. He doesn't explain, however, why a most perfect being must also be eternal. He just says that eternity flows from God's perfection. Unless we can explain why atemporal eternity is a greatness-making attribute, this attempt at logical derivation seems doomed.

In Anselm's *Monologium* we find a clearer argument. As already shown, in his *Monologium* Anselm argued that a perfect being (greatest conceivable being) could not be perfect unless he is simple.[37] From simplicity, Anselm moves to God as unlimited and eventually to God's timelessness. Here we might simply move directly from simplicity to eternity, as many have. If so, the logical derivation goes from perfection to simplicity to timelessness.

We already suggested in chapter 7 that there is a logical entailment between simplicity and timelessness, regardless of whether one thinks either notion is correctly predicated of God. The nub of the issue now is whether perfection entails simplicity. *Prima facie,* there seems to be no apparent reason why a perfect being could not be perfect and composite at the same time. However, Anselm explains why a perfect being must be simple. In my discussion of simplicity in chapter 8, I explained the basic structure of Anselm's argument. Let me now fill in more of the details of the entailment step by step.

Anselm begins the *Monologium* by arguing that things which have their goodness through something else (i.e., they are contingent) are not supremely good. Only that which has its qualities through itself is supremely good.[38] By the end of chapter 4, Anselm has reasoned that there can only be one such being and it is what it is through itself. In the following chapters (5–14) Anselm argues that everything else exists by being created by this supreme being. In chapter 15, Anselm concludes that this being must be whatever in general it is better to be than not to be, and in chapter 16 the argument takes a crucial turn. Anselm discusses what it is for God to be just. Any attribute would make Anselm's point, but he happens to pick justice. At issue is whether justice or justness is or is not a property independent of God's nature. Anselm opts for the latter position, and his reasoning is most instructive for our topic. He writes:

> It seems, then, that by *participation* in this quality, that is, justness, the supremely good Substance is called just. But, if this is so, it is just through another, and not through itself. But this is contrary to the truth already established, that it is good, or great, or whatever it is at all, through itself and not through another. So, if it is not just, except through justness, and cannot be just, except through itself, what can be more clear than that this Nature is itself justness? And, when it is said to be just through justness, it is the same as saying that it is just through itself.[39]

This introduces the crucial concept, simplicity, and explains why it is necessary. To say that justness or any other attribute is separate from God's nature makes him participate in each separate attribute. But if this is so, there must be parts to God's nature. On the other hand, to say that God's nature is justness, etc., means his nature is identical to each of these attributes, and if his nature is identical to each of them, they are identical to each other. This is clearly the doctrine of divine simplicity, but note why Anselm predicates it of God! To say that justness or any other attribute is separate from God's nature as an abstract entity is to say that God depends on them in some way for his existence. However, Anselm has already argued that the supremely perfect being exists through itself, not through anything other.

What is this notion of depending for one's existence only upon oneself? As we saw in chapters 6 and 7, this is aseity! But now the logical derivation becomes clear. It is not from perfection *per se* to simplicity and then to eternity. Rather, it is from perfection to aseity, from aseity to simplicity,[40] and then from simplicity to eternity.[41] In more modern terminology, the logical derivation we find in Anselm moves from God as a necessary being (he is perfect in that he cannot fail to exist and depends on nothing for his existence) to his aseity, from his aseity to his simplicity, and from his simplicity to his eternity.

So, initially, the entailment to eternity moves from aseity to simplicity. From that point, the entailment may go one of two ways. Simplicity may be seen to imply eternity, and eternity to imply immutability, or simplicity may be taken to imply immutability and immutability to imply eternity.[42] The former way is more typical and in many respects the clearer.

Taking the route from simplicity to timeless eternity and then to immutability, why must a simple being be timeless? William Mann is most helpful in explaining the connection between these concepts. In his definition of simplicity we begin to see its connection with timelessness:

> The Doctrine of Divine Simplicity (DDS) maintains that God has no 'parts' or components whatsoever. He has no properties, neither essential nor accidental. He has no spatial extension. Nor does he have any temporal extension: there is no division of his life into past or future stages, for that would imply temporal compositeness. The DDS in turn is motivated by the consideration that God is a perfect being, and that *qua* perfect, he must be independent from all other things for his being the being he is, and he must be sovereign over all other things. If God himself were composite, then he would be dependent upon his components for his being what he is, whereas they would not be dependent upon him for their being what they are.[43]

Here we have a clear statement of the relation between aseity and simplicity and between simplicity and timelessness. Mann later explains very clearly the move from simplicity to timelessness and from timelessness to immutability as follows:

> The DDS implies that there are no temporally successive stages to God's existence. It is thus incompatible with God's being sempiternal. In fact, the DDS implies that God is eternal in Boethius' sense, i.e., that God enjoys 'the complete possession all at once of illimitable life'. 'Complete possession all at once', because there are no past or future

stages in a simple being's life; 'illimitable life', because a simple being, *qua* perfect, must be supremely active, and activity presupposes life. Now it is clear that if God is eternal, he is immutable: if there are not even two stages in his life, then *a fortiori* there are no two stages in his life such that something in the one stage is different from something in the other. Thus the DDS implies that God is eternal, which in turn implies the DDI.[44]

The rationale is clear. To be simple is to have no parts; to be temporal is to have successive stages in one's life, but that is parts. A timeless being has no temporal stages in his existence, so a simple being must be timeless. Moreover, if there are no stages, temporally or otherwise, in God, then he must always be identical with what he is at any moment of his existence. That is, he never changes what he is, and that means he is immutable.

In sum, if one holds divine simplicity, immutability, etc., it seems that one is logically required to hold atemporal eternity, and of course, that is a strong argument for atemporalism. Of course, it may seem to be such a strong argument that it forestalls any further discussion or debate, but that is not so. There are at least three possible ways one might reject it. The first is to deny that God has one or more of the attributes aseity, simplicity, and immutability. If a case can be marshaled against one or more of these attributes, then even if they do entail one another, the overall argument loses its force. A second way to refute the argument is to grant that God has all of these attributes but claim that there are other ways to understand aseity, simplicity, and immutability which are more acceptable biblically, theologically, and rationally, and then claim that on those other interpretations of these attributes, the entailment to timelessness does not succeed. A final strategy grants that God has the attributes mentioned and that they are to be understood as typically defined, but then argues that one or more of the entailments does not work.

From reading my chapters 6 and 7, it is clear which strategy I would follow. Nonetheless, for anyone convinced of these divine attributes, the argument that very atemporalism is entailed by the other attributes is a powerful one.

Immutability Necessitates Timeless Eternity

Someone might not know the logical connections between aseity, simplicity, and all the rest, but agree that Scripture teaches that God is unchangeable. If one accepts God's immutability, that in itself might be used to argue for divine atemporal eternity.

We have already seen that atemporal eternity logically entails a strong sense of immutability. This argument says the entailment runs in the opposite direction as well. If God is totally unchangeable, nothing at all about him changes. If God always existed, but did so in successive stages so that what he was or knew differed from one point in his life to the next, he would not be immutable. Even if his knowledge and his being never underwent change, if there were succession in God so that one could speak of his being at point t and then at point t +1, etc., that would involve change.

Now, the proponent of atemporal eternity argues that the kinds of change envisioned are ruled out by immutability. Moreover, it should also be clear that the kind of succession involved must be temporal succession; otherwise, what is the difference between state of affairs t and t + 1? But if succession in God rules out immutability, and if the only kind of succession that makes sense (it is hard to imagine what atemporal succession would be) is temporal succession, then for God to be immutable, he must also be timeless.[45]

Of course, traditional theism based on Scripture holds that God is immutable. Whether my nuanced understanding of immutability entails timelessness remains to be seen, but clearly, absolute immutability (which allows no change at all) does.

Nature of Time Necessitates a Timeless God

Time as we know it is physical or clock time, but that time is a function of the relation and movement of our planet to the sun. Any other time in the universe would also seem to be a measure of the relation of physical objects to one another. In addition, modern relativity theory tells us that there is no absolute time across the universe, so it is hard to speak of a given moment as simultaneous across the whole universe.

If this is the nature of time, then it is argued that God cannot be in time. He is not a physical object, nor can he be physically present at any point in the universe. Typically, theologians and philosophers say that God transcends all spatial locations. Moreover, God does not depend upon his relation to physical objects and their relation to one another for what he knows. Hence, it really does not make sense to speak of God as in time.[46]

Thomas Morris notes that temporalists usually are unimpressed by this line of argument. They concur with atemporalists about the nature of physical time and about God's nature. But they maintain that at most this means that "his existence and experience are not confined by any of the restrictions due only to the limitations of a particular physical time-frame."[47] As omnipresent and omniscient, God is in touch with each physical time-frame, and he knows how all time-frames relate to one another without his actually being rooted in any of them. Moreover, to say that God is in time doesn't mean that he exists within a particular time zone, but only that he is a being whose life encompasses successive states. He knows when one thing happens on earth and then when another does, and he responds to certain of those events. If this involves sequence and succession *within* God's life, then God qualifies as a temporal being. So the nature of physical time does not require God to be timeless but only mandates that he cannot be temporal in the same way physical objects are.[48]

This may convince some, but many atemporalists will be unimpressed. For one thing, because God is omniscient, he knows everything that will occur, and knows the exact sequence of actions and events. He need not be in time to know that. This is especially so if he knows because he decreed it, but even with a more indeterministic approach to human freedom, as long as one believes God foreknows the future (many indeterminists believe this), God can know what will happen and in what sequence. But none of this necessitates sequence and succession *within* God's life, nor does it require that he comes to know successively what occurs successively. He can know all at once the whole sequence of temporal events, rather than learning them sequentially and successively.

There is another angle to this nature of time argument. If God is temporal, it seems that he must always have been and always will be, but then, there seems to be a problem for the temporalist. It is one thing to claim that God operates within our physical time without being subject to it. But if God is a temporal being, he must have been temporal before the creation of anything, but what could that temporality amount to? It couldn't be temporality in the sense of physical, clock time, for no physical objects existed before God created; but then, what is the reference point for measuring time for God before creation?

Infinity and God as Everlasting

This argument for God's timeless eternity rests on a fundamental principle embodied in what is known as the *kalaam* cosmological argument for God's existence. That principle is that it is impossible to have an actual infinite. If so, the world must be finite and contingent and, hence, caused by a being who is necessary. In regard to the divine eternity issue, that principle is applied to God himself.

The divine atemporalist asks what it would mean for a temporal God to have never-ending existence. To exist forever means to exist infinitely, and if that existence is temporal, that means God has already existed at an infinite number of moments in the past. If so, however, how is it that we have come to the present? As Paul Helm explains, this makes God's existence an instance of an actual infinite, and that has the following problem:

> For such a prospect requires that an infinite number of events must have elapsed before the present moment could arrive. And since it is impossible for an infinite number of events to have elapsed, and yet the present moment has arrived, the series of events cannot be infinite. Therefore, either there was a time when God began to exist which is impossible, or God exists timelessly. Therefore, God exists timelessly.[49]

Two objections to this argument have been raised, but neither seems tremendously compelling. Morris notes that some temporalists will reply that the argument only shows that "there cannot ever be a realization of an additive, infinite succession *which has a beginning*. But God's existence from all eternity past is not the sort of series or succession which has a beginning."[50] Since the temporalist's God has no beginning, the atemporalist's argument does not apply.

In response, it is true that this argument shows that there can never be an actual infinite formed by an additive, infinite succession which has a beginning. However, it is not clear why the argument does not also apply to a temporal being with no beginning. As already noted, if the being has no beginning and exists infinitely temporally, it must have already existed an infinite number of successive moments in time, but given the meaning of infinity, this infinitely existing being will not have arrived at the present, but we are at the present. So, the atemporalist's argument, if it works at all, seems to apply to any temporally infinite being, regardless of whether or not it has a beginning.

A second temporalist response maintains that God's existence before creation was undifferentiated. There is a difference between saying that infinite time existed before the creation and saying that an infinite series of events existed before creation. Only the latter produces problems about an actual infinite, but if God's existence was undifferentiated before creation, there was no infinite series of events prior to creation.[51]

Helm is skeptical about this, because he denies that time could be undifferentiated before the existence of the world. According to temporalists, a timeless God would be rather lifeless, but Helm argues that a temporal God existing in undifferentiated time, i.e., time without events, would also be rather lifeless. However, Helm explains why prior to the universe's existence the being we know as God could not have existed in undifferentiated time, even if he were temporal:

> The full implications of what such divine life in undifferentiated time means are not clear, but presumably one thing that it must mean is that there is a succession of thoughts in the divine mind, a mental life. But if this is so then time could not be undifferentiated before the creation but would be marked by a series of mental events in the divine mind. But then if so either God exists in a timeless eternity or he exists in time with a 'life' which is differentiated by events. But this latter idea is ruled out by the arguments for the impossibility of an actual infinite. Therefore God exists in a timeless eternity.[52]

Of course, if God never had a beginning, never ends, and endures infinitely, though atemporally, the same problem still seems to remain, namely, God's atemporal infinite existence is itself an example of an actual infinite. If God is atemporal, the infinite is not derived by totaling up an infinite number of temporal moments of God's life, but it is still infinite atemporal duration, and since God actually exists, it seems that we again have an instance of an actual infinite.

The upshot of the preceding is as follows. If an actual infinite is impossible and God exists temporally, then since he also exists infinitely, the idea that God is temporal seems to be in trouble. On the other hand, the atemporal view of eternity seems to face the same problem, because the atemporalist's views about God's unending existence apparently require an actual atemporal infinite, and if actual infinites are absurd, this one must be, too. Perhaps an atemporal actual infinite can escape the force of this argument, but until atemporalists can clarify what it means to be an atemporal actual infinite and can offer a non-question-begging example of one, their atemporalist position also seems to be gored on the horns of this argument. In sum, if the argument against an actual infinite is cogent, both temporalists and atemporalists have a problem.

Creation and a Sempiternal God

In my discussion of Augustine, I noted that he adopted divine timelessness to resolve a problem about the creation of the universe. It is that problem that concerns us now. If God is sempiternal, he must have existed an infinitely long time before creating our universe. But creating this universe was certainly a good thing to do, so why did he wait to create until he did? What was he doing before he created? On a temporal view of eternity, there seems to be no adequate answer to these questions.[53]

In Augustine's day, there was a joke that what God was doing before he created our world was "preparing Hell for people who pry into mysteries."[54] Augustine says that this frivolous reply misses the question's point. His answer is that God was doing nothing *before* he created the world, because God is outside of time. As such, there was no "before" and "after" for God's actions. Put simply, this problem only confronts a sempiternal notion of God's eternity, because if God is atemporal, there is no "before" and "after" for him. Moreover, atemporalists believe that God eternally wills (timelessly) this act and all other acts, so it cannot be said that God delayed willing any action until some specific time.[55]

Timelessness and Divine Freedom

Not only does divine foreknowledge raise questions about *human* freedom, it also raises a dilemma about *divine* freedom. Of all beings in the universe, one would think that God would be free, but if God knows all things, including whatever he will do in the future, then there seems to be no way for him to avoid doing those things. And if this is so, how can he be free?

Regardless of whether one is a temporalist or an atemporalist on divine eternity, this is a legitimate question. As Brian Leftow explains, many are inclined to argue as follows:

i. any agent A can choose freely to do only what appears to A to be one alternative among a field of open alternatives,
ii. an alternative cannot appear open to A unless it appears open relative to what A believes,
iii. an alternative appears open relative to what A believes only if A does not already believe that he or she will do it or refrain from doing it, and
iv. if God is omniscient, then for any action and time t, God knows prior to t whether He will or will not do that action at t.[56]

Leftow isn't certain that all four premises are true, and he offers various criticisms. However, he isn't sure that his objections are decisive, or that it would be impossible to construct a compelling argument of this sort about divine freedom.[57]

Leftow's basic argument, however, is that even if an acceptable argument can be made about divine freedom and divine foreknowledge, appeal to God as timeless handles the argument. The argument about divine freedom and foreknowledge says that since God *fore*knows what he will do, in accord with (i) above, he cannot do it freely. Of course, if God is outside of time, then he never knows anything beforehand, for there is no before or after in timeless eternity. He can never know any action prior to his doing it. As atemporalists say, God acts timelessly and all at once. Hence, given his mode of acting as a timeless being and the impossibility of his knowing anything "sooner" than he does it, it is simply impossible for God's freedom to be limited by his foreknowledge in the way the four-step argument above suggests.[58]

Of course, if one is an atemporalist and believes that God acts timelessly, Leftow's response to the argument seems to handle the problem, but the whole discussion is significant only for those who hold libertarian free will and divine foreknowledge. Those who should most feel the force of this argument are libertarians who hold temporal eternity, but even here there is an answer. The libertarian temporalist might reply that God's knowledge of what he will do does not *cause* his actions, and since what he will do is what he wants to do anyway, it is hard to see how this argument eliminates divine freedom after all. There are, of course, other ways for a libertarian temporalist to respond to this argument, but that will become clearer when I discuss libertarian freedom as it relates to divine providence. For now my point is that, for those committed to libertarian free will, atemporalism may serve as a way to solve the divine freedom and foreknowledge problem, and if so, that is a positive point in atemporalism's favor. However, those who do not hold libertarian free will or who do but are temporalists have adequate ways to respond to this issue.

Temporal Duration Inadequate for the Ground of All Being

In my historical section, I noted that the concept of timeless eternity seems to have arisen with Parmenides, Plato, and Plotinus. I offered a lengthy quote from Stump and Kretzmann's "Eternity" which tries to clarify the meaning of atemporal duration and explain the thinking behind it. William Hasker rightly notes that the passage from Stump and Kretzmann not only explains the concept but also includes an implicit argument.[59] In this section, I want to clarify that argument.

In constructing an argument for atemporal duration, perhaps the key point of Stump and Kretzmann's explanation is the following:

> Being, the persistent, permanent, utterly immutable actuality that seems required as the bedrock underlying the evanescence of becoming, must be characterized by genuine duration, of which temporal duration is only the flickering image.[60]

Temporal duration is only the flickering image of genuine duration (which Stump and Kretzmann think is atemporal duration) because the past is gone and the future has not come. When past becomes present, it won't last but a moment, so things caught in time may appear to have permanence, but temporal flux shows that there is no genuine permanence. Temporal things are changing every moment, but, the argument goes, something must be genuinely enduring, lest there be no ontological basis for all that has being but constantly changes. Hence, not only the Greeks perceived a need for genuine permanence; we, too, should see that there must be some permanent actuality "as the bedrock underlying the evanescence of becoming." As Stump and Kretzmann show, the candidate for permanence is being itself, and permanence comes by predicating timelessness and immutability of it.

There are two possible objections temporalists may raise. First, they may complain that the argument says that temporal duration is not genuine or real duration. However, if there is no identity whatsoever between an object at one moment and at the next, then there is no genuine duration, because the object would go out of existence. With each new moment it would either become a totally different object or cease to exist altogether. But, none of this can be true of God, even if his duration is only temporal duration. Yes, there is change from moment to moment, but it is not an all-or-nothing change.

Hasker raises a second objection. As he rightly observes, this argument has force only for someone who has made the value judgment that permanence is better than change. Among contemporary thinkers, aversion to change as change is not very appealing. As for Hasker, he writes, "I do not find permanence to be inherently preferable to change; a workable universe, it seems to me, needs both in full measure."[61]

Convinced atemporalists will probably find the former argument more cogent than the latter. As to the latter, even Hasker says there needs to be both permanence and change in the universe, but if something must be permanent, why not God? And, if the only real permanence is atemporal duration, then God must be atemporal.

Analogy of God as Spaceless

Theologians have often held that time and space are analogous enough that whatever one says about God's relation to space will be parallel to what one says about his relation to time. Schleiermacher, for example, in *The Christian Faith* claimed that space and time are directly parallel concepts.[62] Schleiermacher says God's spacelessness consists of two things. On the one hand, God lacks spatial extension; he has no height, and hence, does not fill space. On the other, God bears no "spatial contrasts" to other things. As Pike explains, this means we can't locate God in relation to other things; he isn't three feet to the left of or above a particular object.[63] Using the analogy between space and time, Pike argues that timelessness consists in lack of temporal extension and temporal location.

There is an obvious implicit assumption in this, namely, that space and time are analogous enough so that whatever is true of God's relation to one is likely true of his relation to the other. Paul Helm sees in this analogy a strategy for constructing an argument for divine timelessness. He admits that the argument and its strategy are oblique and indirect, but he believes it is valid.[64] Here I can only summarize the strategy.

Helm argues first that the issue of timelessness is indeed analogous to that of spacelessness. He attempts to show this by offering several arguments raised against divine timelessness and arguing that parallel arguments can be constructed against divine spacelessness. If the one set of arguments proves that God is in time, then the parallel set shows that he must be in space. Helm lays out the implications of God being in space and shows that they are objectionable to traditional theism, but then, if God being in space is objectionable and being in space is analogous to God being in time, then a temporal God must also be objectionable.

Temporal God Leads to Process Theism

One final argument for timeless eternity is noteworthy. According to this argument, the notion of a timeless God safeguards against adopting other views about God that are objectionable. This alone doesn't prove that God is timeless, but it does clarify potential negative implications of believing in a temporal God.

What specifically is lost if timelessness is rejected? If God is temporal, then in some sense he is mutable, and if he is mutable, he is probably not impassible. He can really experience emotions, and perhaps even suffers with us as we suffer. Moreover, if he is temporal and mutable, divine simplicity must be abandoned. We have already seen the logical interconnections among these doctrines, so the reasons for rejecting these other beliefs if timelessness is denied should be clear enough.

In addition, if God is in time, it can be argued that he cannot know all of time at once, but must know it successively as it occurs. Of course, one could hold that God is temporal but just foreknows the future. This wouldn't be a problem for a determinist but would be for an indeterminist. And indeterminists who hold that God is temporal cannot solve this problem by appeal to the Boethian strategy. Some other reply is required, and many indeterminists think that this problem can be solved only by denying divine foreknowledge of the future altogether.

All of these divine attributes as understood by traditional theism seem in jeopardy if divine timelessness goes. But if divine timelessness goes, toward what notion of God is one moving? The picture of God that begins to emerge if God is temporal (with all that it entails for other divine attributes) is the process concept. If, however, the process God is objectionable, we shouldn't hold it and shouldn't hold views that seem to lead inevitably to it. So this argument for divine timelessness encourages us to adopt that notion as a safeguard against slipping into process theology.

Those who reject process views in favor of a more traditional view of God should find this argument significant. Of course, before we conclude our discussion of divine eternity we must consider whether it is logically possible to hold that God is temporal and avoid adopting process theism. If not, then that would be a major argument for atemporalism for anyone wanting to hold anything like traditional theism.

ARGUMENTS AGAINST TIMELESS ETERNITY

Though many arguments favor timeless eternity, it has many problems as well. In this portion of the chapter I shall present some of the most frequently voiced complaints against it.

Timelessness and God as a Person

Some have complained that a timeless being could not be a person, because there are various activities that are typical of a person which a timeless being could not do. Richard Coburn makes the point forcefully when he argues:

> Surely it is a necessary condition of anything's being a person that it should be capable (logically) of, among other things, doing at least some of the following: remembering, anticipating, reflecting, deliberating, deciding, intending, and acting intentionally. To see that this is so, one need only ask oneself whether anything which necessarily lacked all of the capabilities noted would, under any conceivable circumstances, count as a person. But now an eternal being would necessarily lack all of these capacities inasmuch as their exercise by a being clearly requires that the being exist in time. After all, reflection and deliberation takes time; deciding typically occurs at some time—and in any case it always makes sense to ask, 'When did you (he, they, etc,). decide?'; remember-

ing is impossible unless the being doing the remembering has a past; and so on. Hence, an eternal being, it would seem, could not be a person.[65]

To these activities Sturch adds that a timeless being couldn't speak, write a letter, smile, grimace or weep, be affected by any other being (since being affected is a change and as immutable, it couldn't change), or respond to anything since responses come after their stimuli, and a timeless God has no before or after.[66]

Many philosophers note that this list of actions is a mixed bag, so to speak. Many who hold atemporal eternity agree that a timeless being could not perform *some* of the activities mentioned. Sturch, for example, agrees that a timeless being could not (logically) deliberate, anticipate, or remember.[67] Still, he isn't sure that a timeless being could not do any of the other activities.[68]

Though it is generally agreed that a timeless being could not do these activities of personhood, some atemporalists think such a being could do the other activities. Consider several examples, such as intending and purposing. When someone intends to do X, she wishes to do X, so to say that God intends the salvation of mankind means he wishes all to be saved. One can surely be timeless and have such a wish.[69] But there is another sense of "intend" in which it means to intend to achieve X by doing Y, and Sturch claims that one need not be temporal to intend in this sense. He explains that intending in this sense means "at least, to do X in the belief that Y will follow, where one would not have done X without that belief. And in such a case, though the action X must be temporally related to Y, the *agent* need not be so related (provided, of course, that a timeless agent can act on the temporal at all . . .).[70]

Sturch's parenthetical proviso is an important one, and he thinks it can be met. Still, even if an atemporal being could act in the world, to do so he would have to know what time it is in our world, and, as we shall see, it is dubious that an atemporal being can know that. Some atemporalists say this doesn't matter, since God acts timelessly from all eternity and then has the affects of his actions occur at just the right time for us. Of course, we must ask whether this notion even makes sense.

Sturch also addresses being affected by other things [71] and responding to them. He thinks "affecting God" can be handled by the atemporalist, but admits that "response" by God is more difficult. Sturch appeals to the story of Ahab and Naboth's vineyard (1 Kings 21). God responded to Ahab's treachery by telling Elijah to prophesy disaster against Ahab. In response, Ahab repented, and God postponed the disaster. How can we make sense of this if God is outside of time? Sturch explains:

> In order to do so, I think we must conceive of God's decrees as being normally conditional. (So Moses took them; cf. Deuteronomy 30:15-20.) God must be thought of as, in the very act of creation, laying down what his actions (to us, *reactions*) would be in every possible set of circumstances that his creatures might bring about. This would include the intention to threaten destruction on the house of Ahab if

he seized Naboth's vineyard and the intention not to do so if he didn't; the intention to postpone the disaster if Ahab humbled himself, and the intention to bring it on quickly if he remained obdurate; and indeed intentions which we cannot guess, to allow for (let us say) the possibility that Ahab might never have been born.

It is arguable that something like this is required by any Christian who takes seriously the saying that 'God is not a man, that he should repent'. If this is so, then whether God be timeless or not, his plans must be thought of somewhat in the way I have been describing. He does not then change; but we do.[72]

This handling of response is fraught with problems. First, Sturch's last point about thinking of God's plans this way is problematic, for it fails to recognize that the language is anthropomorphic (as we saw when discussing immutability). On the other hand, not all language about God is anthropomorphic. For example, the Num 23:19 passage that Sturch cites compares God to human beings. The point is that while human beings really do lie and change their minds, God does not. This is so because God's intentions and his standards are unchangeable. However, when we change our attitudes and actions toward God, in light of his unchanging purposes and standards God must respond differently than it first appeared he would (e.g., impending judgment changes to blessing when we repent of our sin, but it is we who change, not God's being, will, or purposes). This does not seem, however, to be a case of anthropomorphic language. In addition, it is worth noting that the point of the verse Sturch cites is God's immutability, not his reacting. Hence, it is hard to see how this verse handles the way an atemporal God would react to our actions.

Apart from Sturch's handling of this passage and this language, however, I don't see that his account of responding will work. For one thing, if God must plan responses for all of our *possible* reactions, then he must not really know what we will do or he knows it but only by middle knowledge. If he knew exactly what we would do, he would only need to plan a response for that course of action. So, to accept Sturch's proposal, we would have to limit God's omniscience to include only those things which can be known, adding that our future actions cannot be known at all or can only be known in terms of possible things we might do. This is surely not a position consistent with biblical theism, though it has gained much popularity in our time.[73] On the other hand, if we grant that God really does know what we will do, then he can plan and perform all at once his responses to our actions. In that case, the credibility of the atemporalist's God being able to react to us reduces to the plausibility of the atemporalist's claim that God does all things timelessly. If that claim doesn't make sense, we cannot make sense of God reacting to us even if he knows exactly what we will do.

There is a second problem beyond that of God's knowledge. Atemporalists tell us that whatever God does, he would do it timelessly all at once from eternity. Let us grant for the sake of argument that this makes sense. According to Sturch's resolution to the issue of God responding, God must then not only perform all actions that will affect actual states of affairs, but he must also perform timelessly all at once all possible actions that might be needed, depending on our actions. But why should we think there is only one possible divine reaction to each of our actions? There may be many reactions for each of our actions, and that just means that if God reacts to our actions in the way Sturch suggests, he must plan potentially myriads of reactions to cover all of our actions over even a short period of time, let alone a lifetime. Proponents of middle knowledge won't find this particularly troublesome, but holding an account like Sturch's, holding middle knowledge, or simply denying that God knows our future, and coupling those views with atemporal eternity creates horrendous problems for the atemporalist. Let me explain.

Atemporalists tell us that all at once God *does* all of his actions timelessly and plans the effects to occur at the appropriate time. But given the numerous possible responses *God* might have to any of our actions and the numerous possible things *we* might do which would engender one of those divine responses, and given that God has middle knowledge, he must all at once perform an incredible number of actions with their effects just to cover all the possibilities for just one person for one moment of that person's life. If God performs all such actions timelessly as atemporality demands, there are some strange consequences. For one thing, God winds up actually doing myriads of actions that turn out to be unnecessary and never wind up actually occurring in our world. Once having done an action and having planned its effect, how can God undo it? How can he cancel all the reactions that become unnecessary? This problem is especially acute if God is timeless, because canceling all unnecessary reactions seems to require that God act anew each moment in response to each of our actual actions, but that is impossible for a timeless God. Moreover, for God to eliminate his unnecessary reactions for each moment, he must know exactly what time it is in human history, but it is dubious that an atemporal God can know that.

The problems raised in the preceding paragraph are especially acute for someone holding libertarian free will. For a theological determinist, God needs only to plan and do one action in reaction to our action, for he has chosen both our actions and his reactions. This still leaves open the question of how a timeless God can act timelessly and have his actions accomplish effects in our history at the right time, but at least it resolves the problem that confronts the libertarian of having God perform all sorts of needless acts and then somehow at the appropriate moment cancel them.[74]

There is a final reply that atemporalists may offer to this argument about God as a person. Atemporalists may reply that the persuasiveness of this line of reasoning rests heavily on the assumption that we know the criteria for personhood, but personhood is such a debated concept that it is unlikely that we can agree enough on what constitutes personhood to do anything with this argument. Or one might answer as does William Mann. Mann offers what he thinks are necessary criteria of personhood, and then argues that on these criteria, an atemporal being qualifies as a person. Mann appeals to Daniel Dennett's work which shows that "there have been at least six different notions of personhood put forth in the philosophical tradition, each offered as an individually necessary if not sufficient condition of personhood."[75] The criteria for someone (call her A) to be a person are as follows:

(1) A is a rational being.
(2) A is a being to which states of consciousness can be attributed.
(3) Others regard or can regard A as a being to which states of consciousness can be attributed.
(4) A is capable of regarding others as beings to which states of consciousness can be attributed.
(5) A is capable of verbal communication.
(6) A is self-conscious; i.e., A is capable of regarding him/her/itself as subject of states of consciousness.[76]

Does an immutable (hence, timelessly eternal) being qualify as a person on these criteria? Mann thinks so. Even if all six criteria must be true for a being to be a person, a timeless being seems to qualify. In regard to (5), for example, God can bring it about that Moses heard certain statements when God is said to have spoken to him. Just because hearing the statement takes time, that doesn't mean that God's bringing it about that Moses heard is a temporal process nor that it must happen at a certain time.[77] As to being rational (item [1]), certain elements of rational conduct are impossible for a timeless being, but others are not. For example, an eternal, immutable being cannot make inductive inferences based on past experiences, but "such a being could *understand* that 'B' is a consequence of '(A→B)' and 'A' and understand that evidence *e* is good evidence for hypothesis *h*."[78] These things show that a timeless being is rational. What about (2), (3), (4), and (6)? Mann says these require states some of which are impossible for a timeless being, but many of which are possible.[79]

How should we respond to this? It seems that, on one hand, neither side can make much capital debating what constitutes personhood. Even people on the same side of the temporal/atemporal eternity issue may not agree on what counts as a person. Hence, if the temporalist presents this argument solely in terms of what constitutes personhood, that kind of argument may lead down a blind alley.

On the other hand, there is a significant argument here against atemporal eternity. It isn't that a timeless being cannot do things like anticipate, calculate, or fall in love. Since the Bible hardly portrays God as doing such things, it is dubious that the traditional concept of God loses much if God can't do those things because he is atemporal. However, there are some things that an atemporal being cannot do, and Scripture does portray God as doing those things. Activities such as intending or purposing, remembering or forgetting, responding to prayers and petitions, becoming angry, rejoicing, and being affected by the actions of others are all things that Scripture attributes to God, yet none of these seem possible for an atemporal being. Whether that makes a timeless God non-personal doesn't seem worth debating. Whether it makes him inconsistent with the biblical portrait of God is worth noting, and is a significant argument against divine atemporality.

Divine Eternity and Divine Action

Whether God can do the various things mentioned in the previous section depends in part on whether God can act in our world. Scripture, of course, depicts him as doing any number of things in our world. He creates the universe, parts the Red Sea, leads the children of Israel out of Egypt, sends fire to consume Elijah's sacrifice, becomes incarnate, raises Christ from the dead, answers prayers of his people and, according to Nebuchadnezzar (Daniel 4) is involved in the rise and fall of empires and kingdoms. The difficulty for atemporal eternity in this is at least three-fold. It takes time to do such actions, so for God to do them seems to involve him in acts that have a beginning, middle, and end. Of course, this is impossible for an atemporal God, for he has no successive stages (Stump and Kretzmann explain, "the nature of a temporal action is such that the agent itself must be temporal"[80]). Moreover, such actions occur at specific points in time and doing them at the right time seems to require God (when he acts) to have temporal location.[81] Finally, for God to act at certain times in our history, he must know exactly what time it is in our history, and yet as atemporal, all events are present to him. He knows the successive order of events in human history, but he cannot know that it is now time in our world for event p, and then at time t+1 know that it is t+1 in our world. For him to know such things would mean that his knowledge changes as time moves on, but that is impossible for an atemporal being.

In a later argument, I shall address the matter of whether an atemporal being can know exactly what time it is in our world, but I raise it now because it is one of the problems involved in the broader issue of whether God can act in our world. If this argument about divine action is correct, an atemporal God seems locked out of the world, but that is contrary to Scripture and an unwelcome position for traditional Christian theism. As Pike shows, in essence Schleiermacher, in holding atemporal eternity, did lock God out of the world. God could not create anything, though he could sustain it. However, as Pike notes, the same problems that arise for an atemporal being creating a world confront the idea of such a being sustaining it. It seems that the preserver would have to have temporal duration.

Pike invokes Schleiermacher and an illustration to clarify the problem, and it is worth seeing how he argues the point:

> Let us suppose that yesterday a mountain, 17,000 feet high, came into existence on the flatlands of Illinois. One of the local theists explains

this occurrence by reference to divine creative action. He claims that God produced (created, brought about) the mountain. Of course, if God is timeless, He could not have produced the mountain *yesterday*. This would require that God's creative-activity and thus the individual whose activity it is have position in time. The theist's claim is that God *timelessly* brought it about that yesterday, a 17,000 feet high mountain came into existence on the flatlands of Illinois. . . . The point seems to be that if God were to create or produce an object having position in time, God's creative activity would then have to have occurred at some specific time. The claim that God *timelessly* produced a temporal object (such as the mountain) is absurd.[82]

This is a significant argument, and atemporalists have proposed several ways of handling it. In the rest of this section, I want to sketch and assess their responses. I begin with Stump and Kretzmann. Stump and Kretzmann reply that this argument is wrong, because it fails to recognize an important distinction. It is one thing to act (a) "in such a way that the action itself can be located in time" and another to act (b) "in such a way that the effect of the action can be located in time."[83] For temporal creatures like us, the distinction makes no difference, but it does matter for an atemporal being, since (a) is impossible for an atemporal being. There can be no temporal events in the life of an atemporal being. However, none of this argues against (b) in regard to an atemporal being. Stump and Kretzmann's answer (and that of many atemporalists), then, is that God acts outside of time, and yet, given his omnipotence, is able to have his actions have effects in time (we should add, at just the right time).[84]

This account of divine action raises several questions, and atemporalists have replies. Is there temporal succession in God's atemporal acts since there is temporal succession in the effects? That is, since each event in time is separate, must God outside of time perform a separate act for each individual effect in time? If so, there still seems to be sequence and change in God's atemporal acting.[85] The answer to this dilemma is that God does not atemporally do each act as a separate exercise of his power. Instead, he does everything he plans to do at once. All his actions and responses to all of our actions are done in one timeless act.

Though this may sound odd, it is less so for Calvinists who believe in God's unconditional decree. In their thinking, God chooses his plan for all of history all at once.[86] What about Arminians who hold atemporal eternity? Typically, they reply that God does one act timelessly that includes everything he does and results in all the effects that occur. This answer is just as consistent with Arminianism as with Calvinism, so long as the Arminian theologian believes God knows all things, including our future. On the other hand, if an Arminian believes that, given human libertarian free will, God cannot know our future actions, then it will be very hard for God to plan and execute in one timeless act all responses to our actions. Perhaps the best he can do is plan and execute all possible reactions to all possible actions we could do. So, regardless of whether the atemporalist is an indeterminist or a determinist, the typical answer to whether God effects separate results in our world by separate exercises of his power is that he does not. He does everything in one timeless act.

If this sounds strange, it gets even stranger. Given that God is atemporal and immutable, he dare not at one timeless point of his existence do these acts and then stop doing them. If he stops doing them, that would not only involve some sort of temporal sequence but would also destroy immutability in the strong sense the atemporalist uses. The way to avoid this problem is to hold that God is always doing his one timeless act. It never begins or ends.

Though he considers this view strange, Nicholas Wolterstorff helps to clarify it. He differentiates between an *everlasting* event and a *temporal* event. An everlasting event neither begins nor ends, while a temporal event either begins or ends. The best way to keep God's actions outside of time and from being infected with temporal elements is to say that all his actions are everlasting. Wolterstorff explains:

> All God's actions are everlasting. None has either beginning or ending. Of these everlasting acts, the structure of some consists in God's performing some action with respect to some event. And at least some of the events that God acts with respect to are temporal events. However, in no case does the temporality of the event that God acts with respect to infect the event of his acting. On the contrary, his acting with respect to some temporal event is itself invariably an everlasting event. So whenever the biblical writers use temporal-event language to describe God's actions, they are to be interpreted as thereby claiming that God acts with respect to some temporal event. They are not to be interpreted as claiming that God's acting is itself a temporal event. God as described by the biblical writers is to be interpreted as acting, and as acting with respect to temporal events. But he is not to be interpreted as changing. All his acts are everlasting.[87]

This idea, when coupled with the notion that God acts all at once, means that whatever God does (timelessly) relative to the state of affairs prior to creation, relative to the history of the universe, and relative to the post-universe period (if the temporal universe as we know it ceases), he does all at once (i.e., together, not sequentially), and he does it forever (i.e., none of his acts begin or end).

A second major issue regarding divine action is whether causes must either precede or be simultaneous (temporally) with their effects. Some may think this question isn't worth asking, for it requires of an atemporal God that temporal categories (like precede and simultaneity) apply to him. However, atemporalists recognize that the question really suggests a much deeper difficulty they must address. If atemporal and temporal existence are different modes of existence and have no contact with one another, how can they causally interact? Unless there is a way for what happens in an atemporal time frame to intersect with a temporal time frame without one frame becoming the other or taking on its characteristics, all talk of acting timelessly and having the effects occur in time is meaningless.

Atemporalists are aware of this problem, and have responded to it. The best-known answer is Stump and Kretzmann's view called ET-simultaneity. I shall discuss their proposal in a section on the problem of the simultaneity of time and eternity. Suffice it to say here that atemporalists agree that they must answer this objection lest atemporality be rejected.

A final problem for divine action by an atemporal God centers around knowing what time it is in our world. God can decree and do at once the whole sequence of events and actions (including our actions and his reactions) for all of world history, but for his reactions to occur at the right time in our history, God must know what time it is from our perspective in order to guarantee that his action done timelessly will affect us at the time in our world when it is supposed to do so. But how can a God outside of time know exactly what time it is in our world? For him to know this means that at one moment in our time he would know that on earth it is now time t, and at the next moment on earth he would know that it is not time t on earth but time t + 1. But for this to happen, there would be changes in God's knowledge that occur with the passage of our time, and that would establish a temporal sequence for him. It would, of course, also rule out immutability, for God's knowledge would change. So the atemporalist's dilemma is clear: 1) either God knows what time it is for us in the way outlined, but then he is temporal and mutable; or 2) God remains atemporal and immutable, but doesn't know what time it is in our world. If one opts for the first horn of the dilemma, atemporalism is lost. If one opts for the second horn (as atemporalists usually do), then God doesn't know what time it is in our world and he seems incapable of getting his reactions to our actions to occur at the right time.[88] This argument also raises the problem of how an atemporal God can know temporal indexicals, but more on that in a later section.

In sum, we have discussed several items in this section, and temporalists hold that they are very damaging to atemporalism. In later sections we will see how atemporalists have responded, but those unconvinced by the responses will find these difficulties about atemporalism and God's action a major objection to atemporal eternity.

Divine Eternity and Divine Simplicity

Atemporalists argue that atemporal eternity is logically derived from other divine perfections. The argument runs through divine simplicity directly to atemporal eternity, or from simplicity to immutability and on to eternity. So simplicity is said to entail atemporal eternity. As I noted when discussing this argument, temporalists may respond using any of several strategies.

Temporalists have frequently argued that even if simplicity entails atemporal eternity, there are good reasons to reject the doctrine of divine simplicity. Hence, simplicity cannot be used against temporal eternity. Of course, if God is not simple, that would not prove that he is temporal, but it would fit with a temporal God.

In chapter 7, I presented a case against simplicity, and I need not repeat it. Suffice it to say that anyone finding that attack compelling will reject divine simplicity. Once simplicity is discarded, any arguments for atemporalism incorporating divine simplicity lose their force.

Divine Eternity and Divine Immutability

Atemporalists also argue that divine immutability and atemporal eternity logically entail one another. There are at least three ways temporalists could respond. First, they might deny that God is immutable. Process theologians often take this approach, but it would be unacceptable to traditional theists, especially those who base their theology on Scripture. A second strategy maintains that God is immutable in the atemporalist's sense and then claims that atemporal eternity and the strong sense of immutability don't logically entail one another. This strategy seems to be of limited value, for if one defines the doctrines as atemporalists do, it will be very hard to break the entailment. Moreover, even if one can break the entailment, the strong sense of immutability involved (God undergoes no changes of any kind) doesn't fit the notion of a temporal God, for such a God would change even if only in that he would know each day that it is no longer the previous day.

The third strategy argues that the traditional strong sense of immutability is not the only way to define it and remain true to Scripture. Immutability needs a more nuanced definition, and once that is given, temporalists can show that it is consistent with God being in time and that it also maintains the aspects of divine immutability Christians have been most concerned to preserve. In light of my nuanced definition of immutability (chapter 6), this third strategy seems the most promising. I argued that God must be immutable in his being, attributes, purposes, will, and ethical norms. He could change relationally, and his knowledge of indexical propositions could change without any damage to evangelical conceptions of God. Upon minimal reflection, however, it should be clear that a God who is immutable in this sense can be in time and cannot be atemporal. If Scripture supports this conception of immutability as I have argued, so much the worse for atemporalism.

Biblical Portrait of God Sanctions Sempiternity

Some proponents of divine temporal eternity claim that only their view makes sense of biblical descriptions of God. The God of the Bible acts in history. He calls Abraham from Ur of the Chaldees, sends the ten plagues upon Egypt, leads the people of Israel across the Red Sea, and most significantly, becomes incarnate to redeem lost sinners. These divine acts involve knowing what time it is in human history and acting in history, and such knowledge and action is inconsistent with an eternal being who is immutable. In addition, God grieves over the suffering of a saint, becomes angry at sinners, and sends judgment on the wicked. All of these things require change, but a timeless God is immutable. Thus, the biblical picture of God requires us to conclude that God is sempiternal, not atemporal.[89]

Thomas Morris says that many atemporalists will respond that such biblical language is anthropomorphic. Biblical authors were not trying to make a metaphysical statement about God as temporal. Rather, they wrote for average people, and wanted to share with them what God has done for them and what he expects in response. Reading metaphysical conclusions into these descriptions turns the Bible into a piece of philosophical theology and God never intended that. Atemporalists also reply that if citing Scripture proves one's position, then 2 Pet 3:8 favors atemporalism, for it says that "with the Lord one day is as a thousand years, and a thousand years as one day." How could this be true, we are asked, unless God is atemporally eternal? Moreover, Mal 3:6 teaches that God does not change. How can that be true of a temporal God?[90]

Though he doesn't espouse the view, Wolterstorff says there is another way atemporalists might respond. In discussing Aquinas, he says that atemporalists may choose to speak of God's actions as everlasting. By "everlasting" Wolterstorff means "an event which neither begins nor ends." In contrast, "an event which either begins or ends" is temporal.[91] Given this distinction, even though an event like the exodus happened at a particular time in history, that doesn't mean Aquinas would say that God acted temporally in that event. God's bringing about the exodus may be an everlasting event, even though the effects of his action only occurred at a specific point in history.[92] Wolterstorff summarizes:

> So the best way of extrapolating from Aquinas' hint would probably be along the lines of the following theory concerning God's actions and the biblical speech about them. All God's actions are everlasting. None has either beginning or ending. Of these everlasting acts, the structure of some consists in God's performing some action with respect to some event. And at least some of the events that God acts with respect to are temporal events. However, in no case does the temporality of the event that God acts with respect to infect the event of his acting. . . . So whenever the biblical writers use temporal-event language to describe God's actions, they are to be interpreted as thereby claiming that God acts with respect to some temporal event. They are not to be interpreted as claiming that God's acting is itself a temporal event.[93]

Wolterstorff then notes that even if this way of handling biblical language about God's acts is correct, it necessitates that God is not atemporally eternal. As he explains:

> For consider God's acts of bringing about Abraham's leaving of Chaldea and of bringing about Israel's passage through the Red Sea. These would both be, on the theory, *everlasting* acts. Both are always occurring. Hence they occur simultaneously. They stand to each other in the temporal order-relation of simultaneity. And since both are aspects of God, God accordingly has a time-strand on which these acts are to be found. Hence God is not eternal. Further, these are surely change-relevant aspects of God. Hence God is fundamentally noneternal.[94]

What shall we say about this? The answer may appear simple, but I think it is not. The simple answer is that biblical writers show God acting in time and undergoing various changes; therefore, they must be teaching a temporal and mutable God. But this is far too facile a solution. Let me respond first to issues raised by Morris and then to those raised by Wolterstorff.

First, I agree with atemporalists that Scripture is written for ordinary people and is not intended primarily as a book in metaphysics or philosophical theology. However, that doesn't mean none of its claims are usable in metaphysics. Theologians frequently cite Scripture to explain the biblical perspective on God and his relation to our world. Though the primary intent of the passages cited may not be some metaphysical point, that does not mean the verses quoted don't have metaphysical implications, nor that theologians have incorrectly deduced a metaphysical point from the passage. Hence, I don't think this sort of argument helps either side. As Morris shows, atemporalists, having argued that Scripture is not philosophical theology, often turn around and cite passages such as 2 Pet 3:8 and Mal 3:6 to make their *metaphysical* point. So this line of argument achieves little, and if pushed too far could be understood to suggest the impossibility of forming a systematic theology on the basis of Scripture (if systematic theology is at all about metaphysics and Scripture contains no metaphysics, then it should be off limits for systematic theologians). Such a reaction is unwarranted and unnecessary.

Second, as Morris notes, many atemporalists would answer this argument by saying that the passages cited are simply anthropomorphisms. This raises some significant issues. What is the evidence that these passages are anthropomorphic? Moreover, what are the criteria for determining that we are dealing with anthropomorphisms? We need answers that admit that some language about God is anthropomorphic and some is not. What atemporalists must do to discredit the temporalist's biblical evidence is explain what criteria tell them the language is anthropomorphic. No doubt some will reply that if God is an immaterial being, he doesn't have a literal voice box with which to speak, nor can he lead Israel out of Egypt with a literal hand, because he has none. Both temporalists and atemporalists would agree that such language is anthropomorphic or metaphorical, but the temporalist should add, don't be confused by the "surface grammar" of these sentences. God cannot lead Israel out of Egypt with a literal hand, but don't think that means God can't do the act at all. God is acting, and temporalists want to know how God can know when to act, and can act at that right time, if God is atemporal.

This suggests a further point about these alleged anthropomorphisms. Even if the temporalist grants that the language is anthropomorphic, still, what does it mean? To say that a sentence is an anthropomorphism does not mean it can mean *anything*. The writer is saying something specific, and whatever it is, it must be tied to the details of the text. Temporalists will demand that we look below the text's surface grammar to see that the writer is asserting that God is somehow acting at a particular time in history. Temporalists will ask how that can be so, if God is atemporal. Atemporalists will answer that God is acting timelessly in an everlasting act whose effects will occur at the right moment in human history. But then the debate has shifted to the coherence of such notions, and as already argued, it is not easy to make sense of them.

Divine Eternity and Simultaneity with Events in Time

Throughout the discussion of how an atemporal God can act in a temporal world, an issue has been lurking in the background. It is the same issue suggested by atemporalists' belief that timeless eternity means all of time is a timeless "now" for God. That issue is how an atemporal being relates and causally interacts with temporal things. The way temporalists and atemporalists have addressed this issue has both a positive and a negative result. Atemporalists need to remove the negative and show how they can make sense of the positive point.

I begin with the negative point about eternity's relation to time. The point was stated rather pointedly some years ago by Anthony Kenny. If for an atemporal God every temporal moment is "simultaneously" (to use Boethius's terminology) present to him, then by logical extension, every temporal moment must be simultaneous with every other temporal moment. Of course, that is absurd, but since the absurdity stems from the atemporalist's notion of eternity, that notion should be rejected. Kenny explains:

> The whole concept of a timeless eternity, the whole of which is simultaneous with every part of time, seems to be radically incoherent. For simultaneity as ordinarily understood is a transitive relation. If A happens at the same time as B, and B happens at the same time as C, then A happens at the same time as C. If the BBC programme and the ITV programme both start when Big Ben strikes ten, then they both start at the same time. But, on St. Thomas' view, my typing of this paper is simultaneous with the whole of eternity. Again, on this view, the great fire of Rome is simultaneous with the whole of eternity. Therefore, while I type these very words, Nero fiddles heartlessly on.[95]

In light of this problem, atemporalists must explain how God can be simultaneous with events in time so as not to make them all simultaneous with one another. Some may think the problem evaporates when we realize that a timeless being cannot be simultaneous with anything. Hence, the transitive relation Kenny sets forth doesn't infect temporal events with the aforementioned problem, because there is no transitive relationship between anything in time and eternity. Simultaneity is a temporal concept, but temporal ideas do not apply to atemporal beings.

This may satisfy some, but it is a resolution with a price. Atemporalists need a way for an atemporal God to be simultaneous with events in time. This must be resolved, because it is hard to see how two beings in separate reference frames (one temporal and the other atemporal) could causally interact with one another. If they can't, the idea of an atemporal God acting in our world is in trouble. Atemporalists face a dilemma. They would like to solve Kenny's problem by saying it is a pseudo-problem since temporal concepts like simultaneity don't apply to an atemporal God, but that answer only seems to push an atemporal God further away from a temporal world and makes it harder to explain how the two can causally interact.

Atemporalists are painfully aware of the problem, and have offered several answers. In what follows, I want to discuss the resolution that has received the most attention in the literature.[96] It is an elaborate theory proposed and later revised by Stump and Kretzmann. They first offered their proposal in their important article "Eternity." They begin by noting that if something eternal and something temporal are to interact, they must somehow be simultaneous. This poses a challenge because "the temporal present is a durationless instant, a present that cannot be extended conceptually without falling apart entirely into past and future intervals. The eternal present, on the other hand, is by definition an infinitely extended, pastless, futureless duration."[97] This is also challenging, because we need an account of simultaneity between the eternal and the temporal that doesn't turn the eternal into the temporal.

Stump and Kretzmann believe they can solve the problem with a series of concepts leading up to what they call ET-simultaneity. They offer definitions of the general notion of simultaneity, temporal simultaneity (what it is for two temporal things to be simultaneous), eternal simultaneity (what it is for two eternal things to be simultaneous), and finally simultaneity between an eternal and a temporal thing—ET-simultaneity. I begin with the first three definitions:

(G)   Simultaneity = existence or occurrence at once (i.e., together).

(T)   T-simultaneity = existence or occurrence at one and the same time.

(E)   E-simultaneity = existence or occurrence at one and the same eternal present.[98]

So far so good. It seems that a definition of the same form dealing with simultaneity of something eternal and something temporal would complete the picture, but Stump and Kretzmann say that this will not do for ET-simultaneity, for two reasons. The definitions of temporal and eternal simultaneity include the phrase 'at one and the same_____'. To construct a definition of ET-simultaneity along those lines would treat the two relata as though they were in the same time frame. Something eternal would be made temporal or vice versa, but this would actually destroy the relation between temporal and eternal things. As Stump and Kretzmann explain, "what is temporal and what is eternal can coexist, on the view we are adopting and defending, but not within the same mode of existence; and there is no single mode of existence that can be referred to in filling in the blank in such a definition of ET-simultaneity."[99] If there is to be simultaneity, it must be between the truly temporal and the truly eternal.

The second reason ET-simultaneity cannot follow the same pattern as (T) or (E) simultaneity, according to Stump and Kretzmann, stems from Einsteinian physics. Einstein's special theory of relativity showed that even with temporal simultaneity the simultaneity is relative to the observer's frame of reference. Events in time may appear simultaneous from the vantage point of one observer, and not simultaneous from the vantage point of another. Stump and Kretzmann illustrate the point:

> Imagine a train travelling *very* fast, at six-tenths the speed of light. One observer (the 'ground observer') is stationed on the embankment beside the track; another observer (the 'train observer') is stationed on the train. Suppose that two lightning bolts strike the train, one at each end, and suppose that the ground observer sees those two lightning bolts simultaneously. The train observer also sees the two lightning bolts, but, since he is travelling toward the light ray emanating from the bolt that strikes the front of the train and away from the bolt that strikes the rear of the train, he will see the lightning bolt strike the front of the train before he sees the other strike the rear of the train. 'This, then, is the fundamental result: events occurring at different places which are simultaneous in one frame of reference will not be simultaneous in another frame of reference which is moving with respect to the first. This is known as *the relativity of simultaneity*'.[100]

Were the two events temporally simultaneous or not? Given the special theory of relativity, the question bespeaks a confusion. Within time, all time frames are relative to the observer's perspective. But which one was right after all? Again, this is a confused question, according to Einsteinian thinking, because there is no privileged position from which to observe exact time at any point in the universe, nor to observe simultaneity between two items within time. For many, this rules out Newtonian absolute temporal simultaneity across the universe. Stump and Kretzmann propose that we revise our notion of temporal simultaneity with another definition:

(RT)   RT-simultaneity = existence or occurrence at the same time within the reference frame of a given observer.[101]

In light of the nature of eternity and the issue of relativity with respect to time, it won't be easy to specify a simultaneity relationship between the two. Still, from the preceding, we learn that

> Because one of the *relata* for ET-simultaneity is eternal, the definition for this relationship, like that for E-simultaneity, must refer to one and the same present rather than to one and the same time. And because in ET-simultaneity we are dealing with two equally real modes of existence, neither of which is reducible to any other mode of existence, the definition must be constructed in terms of *two* reference frames and *two* observers.[102]

How, then, should we define ET-simultaneity? As follows:

(ET) for every x and for every y, x and y are ET-simultaneous iff
    (i)   either x is eternal and y is temporal or vice versa; and
    (ii) for some observer, A, in the unique eternal reference frame, x and y are both present—i.e., either x is eternally present and y is observed as temporally present, or vice versa; and
    (iii) for some observer, B, in one of the infinitely many temporal reference frames, x and y are both present—i.e., either x is observed as eternally present and y is temporally present, or vice versa.[103]

In light of condition (ii), a given temporal event, when observed by an eternal observer, is ET-simultaneous with every eternal entity or event. Condition (iii) means that when an eternal event is observed as eternally present by some temporal observer, that eternal entity or event is ET-simultaneous with every temporal event or entity.

In a later article Stump and Kretzmann respond to various critics and offer an illustration of how to conceptualize ET-simultaneity. They write:

> Imagine two parallel horizontal lines, the upper one representing eternity and the lower, time; and let presentness be represented by light. Then from a temporal viewpoint the temporal present is represented by a dot of light moving steadily along the lower line, which is in this way lighted successively, while the eternal present is represented by the upper line's being entirely lighted at once. So from a temporal viewpoint the temporal present is ET-simultaneous with the infinite present of an eternal being's life. On the other hand, from the viewpoint of a being existing in the persisting eternal present, each temporal instant is ET-simultaneous with the eternal present, but only insofar as that instant is temporally present, so that from the eternal being's point of view the entire time line is lighted at once. From an eternal viewpoint, every present time is present, co-occurrent with the infinite whole of the eternal present.[104]

One advantage of ET-simultaneity is that it handles the problem raised by Kenny. Things in the temporal realm do not become simultaneous with one another just because they are ET-simultaneous with eternity. Since each event and entity stays in its own mode of existence, we don't have the absurd result that the temporal becomes eternal so that all temporal events become simultaneous with one another.[105]

There are other advantages with this theory. For example, from his eternal viewpoint God knows all events within our temporal time frame. Hence, he already knows when in time President Clinton will die, and from his eternal perspective sees Clinton dead. But, seeing all things at once, he also sees Clinton alive. Since God sees both Clinton's life and his death as present, does he know which is occurring on earth? Of course, because he is ET-simultaneous with time. Clinton's death from our perspective is future. God, being ET-simultaneous with 1999, knows that Clinton as a temporal being isn't dead yet. Hence, God doesn't see him via ET-simultaneity as a dead *temporal* being. From his eternal perspective, of course, he sees as present both Clinton's life and Clinton's death. At some point in our future, Clinton will die, and the time and manner of his death will not surprise God, since in God's eternal perspective, he knows about it already. When that actual day comes within time, God will know that Clinton's death is happening in our "now," because as ET-simultaneous with us, God will know exactly what time it is for us, and thus will know that an event which, from his eternal perspective, has always been, has now happened within time.[106]

Stump and Kretzmann believe that the concepts of atemporal duration and of God timelessly acting, when joined with ET-simultaneity, solve the problem of how an atemporal God can act timelessly and have the effects occur at the right time in our history. Since God is eternal, he must do timelessly all that he does, but since he is ET-simultaneous, he can plan the effects of his action to occur at specific points in our history and can actually know what time it is in human history, so that his responses occur at just the right time relative to us.[107]

To say the least, this is a very creative way to solve a series of problems for atemporalism. As expected, however, it has its critics. Let me offer what seem the most significant objections (plus Stump and Kretzmann's answers where available), and then assess the view.[108]

Delmas Lewis raises a series of objections to Stump and Kretzmann's proposal, and several are worth noting. Lewis turns to the definition of ET-simultaneity and asks what condition (ii), which speaks of a temporal y being observed as temporally present by an eternal x, could mean. He raises possible meanings and finds them all deficient. Lewis writes:

> Perhaps something like this: an eternal x eternally observes that a temporal y exists, and knows that y stands in certain temporal relations, not to x, but to other temporal entities or events. For on the view Stump and Kretzmann are defending, it cannot be said that an eternal x observes a temporal y *now* because, in that case, there would be succession in the observations of x. Whether or not this interpretation is correct, (ii) clearly involves the idea that an eternal x eternally observes

a *y* which does not itself exist eternally. This raises the further question of what is is [*sic*] that *x* observes. It cannot be something which comes to be, for then *x*'s observation would come to be, with the result that *x* could not be eternal. But a great many things do come to be; thus, so must the observations of them. So it just is not clear how an eternally observed object (or, alternatively: an object observed in eternity) can be observed as *temporally present.* In fact, on the view under consideration, it turns out that *all* temporal events and entities are observed as temporally present to an eternal observer, so the phrase "as temporally present" cannot be taken to refer to what is presently going on [*sic*] the world. This suggests an important deficiency in the knowledge of any eternal being . . . [109]

This is a significant objection, for it shows that Stump and Kretzmann have not solved the problem their proposal intended to solve. Stump and Kretzmann remind us that time and eternity are two modes of existence. They need to be related, but they must be so related that what is eternal doesn't become temporal and vice versa. Lewis's point about God observing our temporal now is that in many cases for that really to happen, God's observation must become temporal, which would make him temporal. The other option is also problematic. If God were to observe a temporal object eternally, that would turn the object into an eternal object. But, then, God would not observe it in time as it is occurring. Moreover, since God already observes the object or event as eternal, he need not raise the temporal event to an eternal one by observing it eternally.[110]

Lewis's second objection centers on condition (iii). Whereas Lewis noted problems with an eternal entity trying to observe a temporal entity as temporal, his second objection raises problems with a temporal observer observing what is eternal. Lewis argues:

According to (iii), some *x* is "observed as eternally present" to a temporal *y*. The "as" here is misleading, for it suggests that eternality may be an observable property of an eternal entity in the way that squareness is an observable property of baseball diamonds; but this is wrongheaded, because the eternality of an entity can no more be observed than its (say) omniscience or perfect goodness. So the claim that some *x* is observed as eternally present to a temporal *y* can only mean that, at some *t*, *y* observes *x* (that is, *x* is observationally present to *y*) and *y* knows that *x* is eternal. The problem is that these two putative facts are incompatible: how can a *temporal* observer *observe* anything without bringing that thing into the temporal series?[111]

The only other way a temporal being could observe an eternal being would be for the temporal being to become eternal and observe it eternally, or for the temporal being to observe the eternal entity in a mode that is neither temporal nor eternal but a hybrid of both. As to the former option, it is impossible, for how can a temporal being become eternal while temporal, and even if it did, in what sense would it then be ET-simultaneous? At most it would be E-simultaneous. As to the latter option, what and where is this hybrid mixture of time and eternity?

Lewis raises a further point about divine causality and the Stump and Kretzmann proposal, and I think it is crucial. Stump and Kretzmann's proposal in essence makes God and temporal beings epistemically present to one another, i.e., they can know what is "presently" occurring in each other's mode of existence. But even if that is true (we've seen reasons to doubt it), how does it prove that they can causally interact with one another? Epistemic presence and causal presence are not the same thing, nor do they necessarily entail one another. I can be epistemically present by way of television to President Clinton in Washington, D.C., as he gives a speech, but that doesn't mean that as I watch I can causally affect him. For me to do that he must be present to me in a mode of existence (physical temporal presence) that allows me to interact with him causally. Seeing him on television won't do, for what is present to me are images of him, not him. If his speech is taped and delayed, as I view the tape, I'm not even temporally present to the time he gave the speech. And, of course, I am in no way present to him so that he is epistemically aware of me.

Though my illustration may not be absolutely analogous to Lewis's point, it catches the main thrust. In order to causally interact, two things must exist in the same mode of existence. This doesn't happen with ET-simultaneity, because Stump and Kretzmann demand that the temporal observer remain temporal while observing eternity, and vice versa. If that is so, even granting epistemic awareness of one another, how does that allow temporal and eternal to connect causally to one another?[112]

Brian Leftow raised a series of objections to ET-simultaneity,[113] and in response to one, Stump and Kretzmann reformulated their definition of ET-simultaneity. Leftow notes that conditions (ii) and (iii) require that two observers exist and make certain observations. But that is a strange and problematic requirement, for the following reason:

> One wants to say that whatever ET-simultaneity might be, an eternal being could bear this relation even to temporal reference-frames entirely without observers: God, for instance, would still be ET-simultaneous with any Earthly reference-frame even after some calamity emptied it of observers. One also wants to say that an eternal reference-frame might be ET-simultaneous with a temporal reference-frame even if both were devoid of observers, provided that if these frames did contain observers, these observers *could* note the appropriate relations.[114]

In an article meant to reply to various critics, Stump and Kretzmann offer a revised definition of ET-simultaneity as follows:

(ET') For every x and every y, x and y are ET-simultaneous if and only if

(i) either x is eternal and y is temporal, or vice versa (for convenience, let x be eternal and y temporal); and

(ii) with respect to some A in the unique eternal reference frame, x and y are both present—i.e., (a) x is in the eternal present with respect to A, (b) y is in the temporal present, and (c) both x and y are situated with respect to A in such a way that A can enter into direct and immediate causal relations with each of them and (if capable of awareness) can be directly aware of each of them; and

(iii) with respect to some B in one of the infinitely many temporal reference frames, x and y are both present—i.e., (a) x is in the eternal present, (b) y is at the same time as B, and (c) both x and y are situated with respect to B in such a way that B can enter into direct immediate causal relations with each of them and (if capable of awareness) can be directly aware of each of them.[115]

This revised definition seems to help with the problem raised by Leftow, but Stump and Kretzmann believe it also answers adequately Lewis's objection about epistemic awareness not guaranteeing the ability to causally interact. I don't believe this solves a thing. Let me explain. Stump and Kretzmann say that the new definition includes clauses that demand that direct and immediate causal relations and direct awareness between the temporal and the eternal exist. They then say this implies that

> an eternal God could have temporal entities as the immediate objects of his awareness, even though he is eternal and they are not. Those clauses also imply that temporal entities and events are *metaphysically present to God and not just epistemically present. If being metaphysically present is not entirely captured by these specifications, it is not clear to us what else is necessary* (italics mine).[116]

In certain respects this seems incredible. What does it mean to be metaphysically present to something? Stump and Kretzmann don't say, but must it not at least mean existing in the same mode of being? If so, that means God must either exist as temporal when causally interacting with the temporal, or the temporal must exist as atemporal when causally interacting with the atemporal. This, however, is precisely what Stump and Kretzmann have said all along cannot happen. God must remain eternal and temporal things must remain temporal while bearing the relation of simultaneity to one another (ET-simultaneity). On this understanding of metaphysical presence, that stipulation is contravened.

Perhaps Stump and Kretzmann mean something else by metaphysical presence. Still, if God and the world are to interact causally, they must have direct contact with one another, and that contact must be more than merely epistemic. Stump and Kretzmann's revised definition says there is that contact, but it still doesn't explain how. In failing to do so, they still have not solved how a being outside of time can act timelessly and have the effects of the action occur in time.

This is not the end of the matter, for earlier in their paper, Stump and Kretzmann offer a reply to Lewis and Hasker[117] which they think solves the problem. The argument about epistemic awareness seems to rest on the following principle, according to Stump and Kretzman:

> (H)   To be directly aware of temporal beings requires being temporal oneself.

They also think that Lewis's argument about causation rests on the following principle:

> (L)   To be metaphysically present to an eternal being, a thing must be eternal itself.

Stump and Kretzmann think both (H) and (L) are false.[118] Their reason, though, is most intriguing. They begin by claiming that (H) rests on a more general principle as follows: "(GP) x can be directly aware of or epistemically present to y only if x and y share the same mode of existence," and they admit that (GP) is incompatible with ET-simultaneity.[119] How, then, do they escape the objection's force? They write:

> But surely neither Hasker nor any traditional theist would be willing to accept (GP) as applied to *space*. Since God is traditionally described as non-spatial, it would follow from (GP) that God cannot be directly aware of spatial beings. And if traditional theists cannot accept (GP) as applied to space, they cannot reasonably apply it to time. If God can be directly aware of his creatures without sharing their *spatial* mode of existence, why should we suppose that he cannot be directly aware of them without sharing their *temporal* mode of existence? (H), therefore, seems false.
> 　　And similar considerations weigh against (L). God is traditionally described as omnipresent—i.e., every spatial location is present to him. But according to (L) the attribute of omnipresence would require either that spatial locations be non-spatial or that a non-spatial God be spatial. If, then, (L) is false as regards space, why should we accept it as regards time.[120]

In response, I note first that the whole line of argument appeals to an analogy between space and time without showing that they are analogous. Second, why should Stump and Kretzmann think that it is possible for a metaphysically eternal being to be either spatially or temporally present to another metaphysical being unless they have already accepted the idea of ET-simultaneity? But that is question begging!

Third, Stump and Kretzmann repeatedly talk about direct awareness of x and y. They think (GP) is wrong, because one can be directly aware of something that doesn't share one's mode of existence. But what does "direct" awareness mean? Here I return to my illustration of watching Clinton on television. Why should we believe that ET-simultaneity gives things in time direct awareness of an eternal being or an eternal being direct awareness of things in time? Saying that it does seems to mean that the one directly perceives the other, but then, for example, God's perceiving me eat breakfast at 8 A.M. must occur at 8 A.M. when I am actually eating; at 10 A.M. I won't be eating breakfast, so God cannot perceive me at that time doing so. Upon minimal reflection, one should see that this just puts God in time! If Stump and Kretzmann mean instead that God's direct perceiving of the temporal happens by God directly perceiving all things in the eternal present, then what he perceives is the eternal mode, not the temporal mode *directly!* This was Lewis's point about conditions (ii) and (iii) in the definition of ET-simultaneity. Stump and Kretzmann's answer doesn't solve those problems.

Finally, appealing to the spatial analogy is problematic in another way. The problem stems from mixing two dimensions of the space-time continuum (space and time) as though that tells us something about two modes of one dimension of the space-time continuum (time). Let me explain. When we discuss time and timelessness, we are considering two modes of being as relates to time. Now it should be clear that one could be spatial and exist in time, but one could also be spatial and exist in eternity (atemporally understood). At least Christian theism has always maintained this about resurrected, glorified human bodies in the eternal state (eternal understood here as atemporal). That is, having a body (even a glorified one) doesn't make it impossible from the standpoint of time either to function in time (think of Jesus' glorified body after the resurrection and of his interaction then with his time-bounded disciples) or outside of time (think of glorified saints in the eternal state, which atemporalists would agree is timeless). My point is that atemporalists who believe in eternal life of resurrected, glorified believers agree that being spatial does not inhibit one from existing timelessly.

So far I have been considering a spatial being in relation to time and timelessness. Let me turn to a non-spatial thing. Surely, atemporalists will grant that a non-spatial being can exist atemporally; that is what they believe in holding that the Christian God is pure spirit and timeless. Could a spaceless being exist in time? Anyone who believes that mind is immaterial would have to answer affirmatively. My immaterial mind is associated with my material body and causally interacts with it. Surely, we would not say that because it is spaceless, my mind must be atemporal and yet it causally influences and is influenced by my physical, time-bounded body. The most natural conclusion is that, though my mind is spaceless, at this stage of my life it is within time.

The point of the previous two paragraphs is that a spaceless being could be temporal or atemporal and that a spatial being could exist in a temporal or atemporal dimension. But if one grants my point, one should also see that Stump and Kretzmann's argument rests on confusing two dimensions of the space-time continuum in order to solve a problem about two modes of one of those dimensions (i.e., a problem about time). Hence, by appealing to spacelessness, I don't see that they have proved anything about (H) and (L), which are not about space but about relations of beings in two different *temporal* dimensions. Likewise, I don't see that they have shown that Lewis and Hasker are wrong in holding a proposition such as (H) and demanding that there be existence within the same temporal mode in order for there to be *direct epistemic awareness* (remember here my point about the meaning of "direct"). Nor does their appeal to spacelessness necessarily prove that (L) is wrong or that things in two different metaphysical time frames can causally interact with one another.

I conclude, then, that despite its creativeness, ET-simultaneity does not solve the problem of simultaneity between time and eternity.[121] Moreover, the question of how a timeless God can act in time remains.

Divine Omniscience and Timeless Eternity

The issue of divine omniscience actually raises several questions about divine atemporal eternity. They are 1) the problem of human freedom, foreknowledge, and eternity; 2) the question of whether God knows what time it is now in human history, i.e., does God know the truth of temporal indexical propositions; and 3) the problem of whether God knows events as successive (and if so, in what sense).

The first issue has received the most attention throughout history.[122] Since I plan to cover this issue in the chapter on freedom and foreknowledge, and since a decision on this issue is not conclusive for the temporal/atemporal eternity debate, I shall not pursue it in this chapter. Moreover, the third argument seems to be of lesser significance, and due to space constraints I won't handle it here.[123]

The second problem involving divine omniscience and atemporal eternity asks whether a timeless God can know what time it is in human history from our perspective. This is the problem of temporal indexical propositions. I raised it in chapter 7, but now I want to address it specifically as it relates to the debate over divine eternity.

There is no question as to whether a timeless being can know the whole plan of history and know the relation of one event to another (e.g., that one is before or after the other). Those who believe God has decreed all things would, of course, expect him to know every event of history and in the right order. Those who do not believe God decreed all things solely on the basis of his purposes but do believe he somehow knows everything throughout our history would also agree that a timeless being knows all history and knows it in its right sequence. Moreover, in knowing the plan of history, God knows that I would write this sentence at 11:14 A.M. CDT on October 30, 1999.

If God knows all of this, there seems to be no problem for divine omniscience if God is atemporal. However, there are many things an atemporal God cannot know about our world. He can know the date and time when I am writing this sentence, but he cannot know that this very moment is that date and time. In other words, a timeless God doesn't know exactly what time it is in our history, even though he knows exactly what is going to happen at any moment of history. This sounds paradoxical, but various philosophers have clarified the problem. The argument was first offered by Arthur Prior in an article titled "The Formalities of Omniscience," but Robert Coburn's statement of the argument is exceptionally clear. Coburn writes:

> If a being is omniscient, then presumably it follows that this being knows everything which (logically) can be known. But it is easy to see that an eternal being could not know everything which (logically) can be known, and this is because some of the facts which (logically) can be known, are knowable only by temporal beings, by beings who occupy some position (or some positions) in time. Consider, for example, the fact that the day which is now elapsing (I write this on May 12, 1962) is May 12, 1962; or more simply, that today is May 12, 1962. Clearly to know this fact is tantamount to knowing one's temporal position, and being oriented in time. But if this is true, then a necessary condition of knowing this fact, it would seem, is having some position in time concerning which there are truths of the type indicated to be known. To see the matter in another light, assume that the idea of a non-temporal knower makes sense. Then ask, could such a knower know, e. g., that today is May 12, 1962? The obvious answer, I submit, is that, it could only if it could use temporal indicator words. For otherwise, it could not express and *a fortiori* could not entertain a truth such as the above. But a necessary condition of being able to use temporal indicator words is being an occupant of time. Hence, God's alleged eternity is logically incompatible with his alleged omniscience.[124]

This is the problem of indexicals I raised when discussing immutability and omniscience. Hence, it isn't just about atemporal eternity and omniscience, but about atemporal eternity, omniscience, and immutability.

Norman Kretzmann summarizes this point: "Thus the familiar account of omniscience regarding contingent events is drastically incomplete. An omniscient being must know not only the entire scheme of contingent events from beginning to end at once, but also *at what stage of realization that scheme now is.*"[125] It appears, then, that if God is timeless, there are certain things he cannot know. Moreover, a strong sense of immutability goes with atemporal eternity, but Kretzmann argues that when immutability and atemporality are joined to omniscience, there is a further problem. Kretzmann states the argument in seven propositions:

(1) A perfect being is not subject to change.
(2) A perfect being knows everything.
(3) A being that knows everything always knows what time it is.
(4) A being that always knows what time it is is subject to change.
(5) Therefore, a perfect being is subject to change.
(6) Therefore, a perfect being is not a perfect being.
(7) Therefore, there is no perfect being.[126]

Here a brief word of explanation is in order. Premise (1) assumes a strong sense of immutability and premise (2) is, of course, about omniscience. Premise (3) lists something that an omniscient being can be expected to know. Of course, a being who always knows what time it is must pass through the moments of temporal succession in order to know exactly what time it is. But to undergo temporal succession is to undergo change; hence, premise (4). However, if a perfect being (assumed here to be immutable, omniscient, and atemporally eternal) undergoes change, it is not immutable, and that contradicts premise (1). Hence, the problem stated in premises (6) and (7). As a result, either God is outside of time, and this dilemma arises, or God is temporal and not immutable in the strong sense, and then this dilemma does not arise, but then too much has been compromised for God to qualify as a perfect being.[127]

This is a major problem for atemporalists who want to maintain divine omniscience, and they have responded to it in various ways. In what follows, I want to offer a "taste" of those responses, and show how a temporalist might counterrespond.

I turn first to Brian Leftow's handling of this issue. Leftow basically follows a two-fold strategy. His first approach argues that there are just some things humans know that God does not know, but God need not know those things to be omniscient or supremely perfect. Leftow then grants that in God's eternal reference frame, he doesn't know events in the way we know them in our temporal reference frame. But this is not something we should expect God to know for him to be the supreme being or even omniscient. To be factually omniscient, a being must know every fact knowable within its reference frame, but since facts indicated by indexical propositions are not genuinely facts in God's frame of reference, he doesn't have to know them to be omniscient, the most perfect being, or worthy of worship.[128]

This is Leftow's basic strategy, but let me fill in a few details. As to things we know that God does not know or need to know, Leftow suggests that the situation is parallel to omnipotence. God is omnipotent, but he can't breathe, run, or sin. He can't do these things, not because they are logically impossible, but because they cannot be done by a being of his nature. However, nobody denies divine omnipotence on these grounds, so evidently, omnipotence doesn't require God to have every ability we have, and he can still be omnipotent without being able to do these things.[129]

If God can be omnipotent without being able to do some doable things, perhaps he can be omniscient without knowing everything knowable, and so Leftow argues. For example, if we rig a test so that someone who seldom fails can know experientially what it means to fail, we may succeed in tricking the intended victim, and the victim may experience what it feels like to fail. But God cannot fail and he cannot be tricked into failing, so it is impossible for him to experience what it feels like to be a failure. Leftow summarizes, "So it seems that God's very perfection, by entailing that he cannot fail, entails that he cannot be propositionally omniscient—that there are knowable truths God cannot know."[130]

There are other propositions which only one person could know. The kind of proposition Leftow has in mind is one like 'I am John' said by myself, 'I am Herman' said by Herman, etc. As Leftow explains, "If such privately knowable truths as 'I am Herman' exist, this is because each of us is one person rather than another. God's not knowing these truths, then, might reveal no more than that he is one person rather than another, as are we all."[131] Still, Leftow maintains that even though God lacks such knowledge and hence, is not propositionally omniscient, that need not compromise his omniscience.

Even granting Leftow's point that there are things an omniscient being cannot know, so far he hasn't shown that the truth of temporal indexical propositions is in that category. Leftow has an argument, however, to show that God doesn't need to know such things to be omniscient, and it brings us to the second stage of Leftow's argument. Leftow argues that we must distinguish the eternal reference frame from various temporal reference frames. Within the eternal reference frame, Leftow says, there is no motion, so propositions such as 'It is now 3 P.M. on October 30, 1999' and 'It is now 3:05 P.M. on October 30, 1999' cannot be genuine facts within that reference frame. The truth of those propositions requires temporal succession, and knowing the truth of those propositions requires one to undergo temporal succession, but neither of those things can be true of an atemporal being or of his timeless reference frame.

So, according to Leftow, does God know the truth of temporal indexicals? Does he know what time it is in history for us right now? The answer is yes and no. He knows these truths in his eternal reference frame, but in that reference frame he doesn't know them temporally, so the most he can know about any temporal fact is how it relates to any other temporal fact. He cannot know when it is true as it is true in our temporal reference frame. The temporalist charges that an atemporal God doesn't know what time it is in history and cannot know the truth of indexical propositions when they are true, and Leftow agrees. Does that mean that Leftow's God is somehow less than omniscient? According to Leftow, not at all, because the truth of propositions about what time it is in history are not the sort of propositions that can be known in an eternal reference frame. God still knows everything knowable in that frame, so he qualifies as omniscient.[132]

In response to Leftow's handling of this issue, several things need to be said. First, his basic point about God not knowing and not needing to know everything we know in order to be omniscient is correct. However, there are indexicals that are knowable by more than one person at a time, and God should know them. Specifically, there are indexicals about what time it is in our history at any given moment. Leftow's examples show that there are things God need not know to be omniscient, but his examples don't prove that among them are indexicals about what time it is in history. All of this amounts to the following: temporal indexicals are knowable by any person who is temporal. If God is temporal, he can know them, but if he is atemporal, it is not within his nature to know them. So, depending on how the debate over atemporal and temporal eternity comes out, God can be omniscient and know temporal indexicals or not know them.

What all of this further shows is that the first part of Leftow's argumentation shows at most that God need not know temporal indexicals *if he is atemporal.* It doesn't show that he is atemporal, or that he need not know temporal indexicals. Moreover, it shows that God can know them *if he is temporal.* But neither of these statements proves that God either is or is not temporal or atemporal. Thinking this argument solves the debate only begs the question.[133]

Temporalists want to say more, however. Atemporalists such as Leftow have shown that atemporalism is consistent with not knowing temporal indexicals, but they haven't shown that it is acceptable for God not to know such indexicals. Temporalists think it is unacceptable for God to be ignorant of the truth of those indexicals for a very important reason. Scripture shows God acting and reacting in our world, but if God doesn't know the truth of such indexicals, it is hard to see that he can act and react at the right time in our world. It is also hard to see how he can arrange for the results of his timeless actions to occur at just the right time for us, if he never knows exactly what time it is for us. Atemporalist responses are well known, but as already seen, they are problematic.

Atemporalists are concerned about this problem, and the greatest amount of effort to solve it has been invested in a strategy by Castañeda. First, Castañeda invokes the distinction between an A-theory and a B-theory of time (and between an A-proposition and a B-proposition). According to the A-theory of time, time is real, and propositions are tensed, i.e., past, present, and future tenses are about real specific times, not timeless so as to transcend specific times. Time references in an A-proposition refer to specific points in time, not time in general or all time transcendently.

According to the B-theory of time, propositions indicate whether one event is earlier than, later than, or simultaneous with another event, but the proposition isn't about saying that the event is present, past, or future with respect to the time when the proposition is expressed. In addition, many B-theorists believe that time is not real, but rather is in our minds. That is, time is our analysis of what is happening in the world outside our mind when we see various events and actions occur in sequences, but in the actual world outside our mind there is no such thing as time or the passage of time. In addition, many B-theorists hold that propositions are tenseless. That is, even though verbs in these sentences have some grammatical tense, the proposition isn't meant to refer to that specific time. Consider the proposition 'Joe knows the alphabet'. The verb is in the present tense, but the idea of the sentence is not that the only time Joe knows the alphabet is the present, whereas he didn't know it in the past and won't in the future. The proposition expressed is about Joe's knowing, but it doesn't intend to specify a particular time when Joe knows.

From these definitions we can see that the problem of temporal indexicals is about God's knowledge of indexicals that are A-propositions, especially A-propositions including some designation of a particular time. Finally, I must define "tokening a sentence" and "tokening rule." Tokening a sentence typically refers to A-sentences. To token an A-sentence is for someone to intend a particular A-sentence including demonstratives, personal pronouns, or adverbs to refer to himself (if personal pronouns are used) at a particular time (if words like 'now' or 'later' are in it) and/or place (if words like 'here' or 'there' are in it) and to say of himself that conditions are such in the world that the sentence intentionally tokened in the way(s) mentioned expresses a true proposition. As Gale explains, "The meaning of an A-sentence is given by its 'Tokening Rule,' which specifies the conditions under which an intentional tokening or use of it expresses a true proposition, e.g. the intentional tokening of 'Event E is now present (past, future)' expresses a true proposition if and only if it is simultaneous with (later than, earlier than) event E."[134]

With these definitions, we can now turn to Castañeda's handling of temporal indexicals. Castañeda responds to Kretzmann's argument in his "Omniscience and Immutability." As Castañeda sees it, Kretzmann argued for two theses: (A) the incompatibility of divine omniscience and immutability and (B) the incompatibility of omniscience and theism. Kretzmann's case for (A) and (B) depends on certain features of indexical reference. Castañeda explains:

> The argument for (A) relies essentially on the fact that a person's indexical references to time, e.g., by means of the word 'now', are ephemeral: at different times of utterance 'now' refers to different times. The argument for (B) depends essentially on the fact that a person's indexical references to himself, e.g., by means of the first-person pronoun 'I', are intransferable: nobody can refer to another man by means of a genuine first-person reference. [135]

As Castañeda then explains, the issue is broader than whether an omniscient being can know the truth of indexicals tokened by someone else or even know the truth of temporal indexicals if he is outside of time. The issue is whether and how anyone can formulate for and by himself an indexical proposition which contains indexical reference by some other person. Kretzmann's argument assumes that the answer to this general question is that it cannot be done. Castañeda, however, wants to show that it is possible to formulate another person's indexical statements qua indexical by means of using what Castañeda calls "quasi-indicators." If this works for us in using indexicals to refer to other people, there is no reason why God cannot formulate indexicals about other people and about time, even if he is atemporal.[136]

Castañeda begins by returning to Kretzmann's seven-step argument, and notes that the key premise is premise (4) "A being that always knows what time it is is subject to change." Combining (4) with Kretzmann's argumentation about various times and the use of 'now' in regard to those times, Castañeda says Kretzmann's crucial premise is:

(4a) First X knows that it is now t_1 and not t_2, and then X knows that it is now t_2, and not t_1.[137]

From this premise, Kretzmann concludes that X knew something different at t_1 than he knew at t_2, and hence, there was a change in him.

Castañeda replies that, in ordinary usage, indicators such as 'now', 'I', and 'here' are used even in indirect discourse (and [4a] is an instance of *oratio obliqua*, indirect discourse) to make indexical references by the *speaker* of the sentence, not to make indexical references by the person spoken about. This means that normally we would think 'now' in (4a) refers to now for Kretzmann, but of course, Kretzmann means it to refer to 'now' for X. Since there are two occurrences of 'now' in (4a), that sentence is meant to designate two separate times and what X knows at those separate times. And Kretzmann assumes that what X knew at the first time differs from what X knew at the second time mentioned. But is it possible that X may have known all four propositions involved in (4a) at both t_1 and t_2 (two propositions about X, and two about the speaker of the sentence)? The key to this question lies in the indexical reference of 'now'.[138] Castañeda answers this question and what he says is significant, so I quote him at length:

> Obviously, if the indexical reference of Kretzmann's statement at t_2 'it is now t_2' cannot be captured intact at time t_1, then at t_1 this statement cannot even be formulated, let alone be known by X or by Kretzmann himself. Hence, if this is the case, it would seem that Kretzmann is after all justified in deriving (4) from (4a). . . . There is, however, a serious but subtle difficulty with Kretzmann's argument. As the preceding analysis shows, the argument relies heavily on the fact that the clause 'it is now t_2' in (4a) expresses an indexical proposition. But it is Kretzmann's own indexical proposition, *since indicators in oratio obliqua express indexical references by the speaker, and leave it open whether the person spoken about refers to the same objects indexically or not.* Thus, when I say 'Privatus believes that I (you, this) weigh (weighs) 150 pounds,' I do not imply that Privatus has made an indexical reference to me (you, or this). Indeed, my sentences of the form 'Privatus believes that I . . .' have a certain misleadingness, since Privatus cannot refer to me in the first person! More strikingly, when Gaskon says "Yesterday Privatus thought (guessed, predicted, etc.) that it would be raining now (today)," Gaskon's statement both contains his own indexical uses of 'now' ('today') and fails to imply that Privatus referred indexically to the time at which Gaskon makes his statement. Likewise, Kretzmann's statement (4a) above both formulates Kretzmann's *own* indexical references to t_1 and t_2, and does *not* imply that X referred to t_1 or t_2 indexically. . . . We must, then, reformulate Kretzmann's argument without the word 'now'. Furthermore, Kretzmann means to be making a general point that has nothing to do with him or his indexical references. His point is both that, to know what time it is at a given time, a person has to make some indexical references of *his own* that will put him into the stream of changes in the world, and that, thus, that person

cannot be immutable. Hence, the very effectiveness of Kretzmann's argument requires that we be able to reformulate it without mentioning or alluding to Kretzmann's own indexical references, i.e., without using the word 'now'.[139]

But, can this be done? Castañeda answers affirmatively and offers a reformulation of (4a) as (4b) with the appropriate changes made:

(4b) At t_1 X knows [tenselessly] *then* t_1, but not t_2, and at t_2, later than t_1, X knows that it is *then* t_2, but not t_1.

The semantic difference between (4a) and (4b) is enormous. Castañeda explains:

(a) 'now' does, while 'then' does not, express an indexical reference by the speaker; (b) 'then' does, while 'now' does not, attribute to X an indexical reference to time t_1 in the first and to time t_2 in the second conjunct; (c) whereas sentence (4a) cannot be used by Kretzmann or anybody else to make exactly the same statement at times other than t_1 and t_2, sentence (4b) can be used repeatedly at any time by anybody to make exactly the same statement on each occasion of its utterance. Thus, 'then' as used in (4b) is not an indicator: it is, in my terminology, a *quasi-indicator*. Among its syntacticosemantical characteristics are: (i) its appearing in *oratio obliqua*, i.e., in a clause subordinated to a verb expressing a propositional attitude; (ii) its having an antecedent not in the same oratio obliqua, which in (4b) is 't_1' for the first occurrence of 'then' and 't_2' for the second occurrence; (iii) its not being replaceable by its antecedent with preservation of the proposition or statement formulated with the whole sentence; in our example, sentence (4b) clearly formulates a different statement from that formulated by

(4c) At t_1 X knew that it was t_1 at t_1, but not t_2, and at t_2, he knew that it was t_2 at t_2, but not t_1.

The statement expressed by (4c) is true if X knows that t_1 is different from t_2, even if at t_1 or at t_2 he does not know what time it is then.[140]

The key issue here, then, is that according to (4b), X knows four propositions to be true, but can he know all four to be true at both times mentioned in (4b)? If he can, then Kretzmann's argument for (4) is wrong. Castañeda thinks so, but says that in order to see that, we need to add another principle, which he calls (P):

(P) If a sentence of the form 'X knows that a person Y knows that . . .' formulates a true statement, then the person X knows the statement formulated by the clause filling the blank ' . . .'.[141]

Putting all of this together, Castañeda draws the following conclusion:

Thus, (4b) is compatible with

(4d) Time t_2 is later than t_1, and at t_1 X knows both (1) that it is then$_{t1}$ t_1, but not t_2, and (2) that somebody knows (or would know) at t_2 that it is (would be) then$_{t2}$ t_2 but not t_1.

By (P), (4d) entails that at t_1 X knew not only the two propositions that according to (4b) he knew at t_1, but also the other two propositions that by (4b) he knew at t_2. Hence, it does not follow from (4b) and (4d), or from (4b) alone, that at t_2 X underwent a change in knowledge. Therefore, Kretzmann's argument for his premise (4) is really invalid.[142]

From all of this, we can see what Castañeda's answer would be to the argument against atemporal eternity. Castañeda would say that Kretzmann can know at time t_1 what someone else knows at that time and at a later time, so the same is true for God. Of course, time t_1 for an atemporal God is no *time* other than the *timeless eternal present*. But, using Castañeda's strategy, the atemporalist can say that at any moment of our time God can know (timelessly) what we know at that moment and what we know at a later moment.[143]

Does this answer to the problem of temporal indexicals and omniscience work? If it did, it would bring together time and eternity in that an atemporal God would know what we know about a particular time in history when we claim to know it. But I don't think Castañeda's answer solves the atemporalist's problem. I appeal here to Richard Gale's line of argument.

Gale appeals to an argument found in Peter Geach's *Providence and Evil*. Geach claims that God can timelessly know an A-proposition in *oratio recta*, even though no A-proposition is identical with any B-proposition. This is an interesting claim in that Castañeda made his point via *oratio obliqua*. Geach follows the rule that "'God knows that p' is true if and only if the plain 'p' is true."[144] Geach then writes:

> We need not lose our heads in dealing with tensed propositions; we need only stick to the simple rule I have just given. In 1939 it was true to say 'Hitler is alive'; it was therefore true to say in 1939 'God knows that Hitler is alive'. In 1970 it was true to say 'Hitler is dead'; it was therefore true to say in 1970 'God knows that Hitler is dead'.[145]

As Gale notes, no temporal qualification is stated as to when God knows, for on an atemporal view of eternity, God knows timelessly. "Whatever is temporally qualified is the proposition He knows and when we time-bound creatures can truly say that God timelessly knows this proposition."[146]

Gale also notes that there is an ambiguity in Geach's presentation which stems from how we are to understand indexicals such as 'now' in indirect discourse. As Castañeda showed, the indexical term in indirect discourse expresses the speaker's indexical reference, not necessarily the indexical reference of the one spoken about. In fact, Castañeda claimed that it expressed only the speaker's indexical reference. Quasi-indicators were necessary to express the indexical reference of the person spoken about. Gale is not so sure that this is true with respect to 'now'. He thinks there can be cases of indirect discourse where 'now' expresses the indexical reference of both the speaker and the person spoken about. Now, if we agree with Castañeda that an occurrence of 'now' in indirect discourse expresses only the speaker's indexical reference, then "Geach would have failed to show that God can know an A-proposition; for it could be true that God knows that Hitler is now dead without God making a present tense indexical reference to the present moment and thus without God knowing any A-proposition. In this case we underdetermine the proposition known by God."[147] To understand this, we must remember that the God who is using the 'now' is a timeless God. Hence the problem Gale raises.

From the preceding, Gale concludes that the only way to save Geach's argument is to construe an indirect discourse occurrence of 'now' as expressing both the speaker's and the believer's indexical reference. Gale writes:

> and we could adopt the convention that when and only when an *oratio obliqua* construction is represented in the explicit paratactic manner are we so to construe it. If I say "God knows that (this): Hitler is now dead," the *oratio obliqua* occurrence of "now" expresses both my and God's indexical reference; and thereby, I do attribute to God knowledge of the very same A-proposition as I express by my use of "Hitler is now dead." This is how we must construe Geach's example. Thus, Geach winds up with the seemingly bizarre position that God is able to make a present tense indexical reference to the present moment *without doing so at any time.*[148]

Though this sounds bizarre, as Gale says, sometimes the bizarre is true, so we need an argument against it. What Gale offers is the argument I quoted from Robert Coburn's article. Gale not only quotes it but also recasts it into the following argument, which explains why an omniscient being who is atemporal cannot know the truth of temporal indexicals. The argument elaborates a premise Gale stated earlier in introducing the argument against an atemporal being knowing temporal indexicals. He labels that proposition (4). Gale's proposition (4) says "It is conceptually impossible for a timeless being to know an A-proposition."[149] Now we can state the argument against Geach's view that Gale recasts from Coburn:

(4b) A person can know a proposition only if she can truly express it.
(4c) A person can truly express a proposition only if she can truly token a sentence which expresses this proposition.
(4d) A person can truly express an A-proposition only if she can truly token a sentence which expresses this proposition. (From (4c) by universal instantiation.)
(4e) An A-proposition is expressible only by the tokening of an A-sentence.
(4f) A person can truly express an A-proposition only if she can truly token an A-sentence. (From (4d) and (4e).)

(4g) A person can truly token an A-sentence only at a time.

(4h) A person who can truly token an A-sentence exists in time (From (4g).)

Therefore:

(4) It is conceptually impossible for a timeless being to know an A-proposition. (From (4b), (4f) and (4h).)[150]

Gale claims that this argument which is valid is also sound, because its premises are true. This means that the most Castañeda's approach can do is guarantee that God knows the *content* of any proposition we know or will ever know, including our temporal indexical propositions. But, being outside of time, he cannot know when a proposition we would utter or think that includes a 'now' would be true, for nothing Castañeda has said shows that God has a way of knowing precisely what time it is in human history. Thus, God knows whatever the content of our knowledge is whenever we know a proposition, with the exception that when we utter or think a proposition including 'now', God doesn't know when it is *now* in human history, because, being outside of time, he doesn't know what time it is. Thus, he cannot truly token an A-proposition that includes the indexical 'now'.[151]

What should we say, then, about this matter of immutability, omniscience, and eternity? Temporalists will claim that with atemporalism God's omniscience is compromised because of the problem of temporal indexicals. In contrast, temporalists can hold without problem that God knows all temporal indexicals about the present and the past. Which indexicals are about the present and which about the past is constantly changing because of time's passage, but this does not mean God is mutable in his person, purposes, will, or ethical rules. As to temporal indexicals about the future, no one can know their truth, so it is no deficiency that God doesn't know them. The inability of an atemporal God to know these temporal indexicals is problematic because even if we grant that he is still omniscient, he still cannot act and react in our world at the "right time," because he never knows exactly what time it is for us.

ATEMPORAL GOD OR A TEMPORAL GOD?

In the preceding sections of this chapter we have seen the evidence in favor of an atemporal and a temporal notion of eternity. It is now time to make a decision on which of the views is more likely correct. With an issue as complex as this, there are good arguments on both sides. Hence, it is unlikely that we can make a decision that approximates 99 percent objective certainty. This doesn't mean we can't decide at all, but only that our decision is a probability judgment and we should be open to further evidence and argument.

Despite these disclaimers, for a number of reasons, I believe that the best way to understand God's relation to time is to see God as temporal. In what follows I shall explain why I am inclined to that view. Of course, if an evangelical theologian in our day opts for a temporal God, he may be accused of taking a first step down a slope that eventually leads to process theology. Hence, I must explain why I think one can hold to a temporal view of God while remaining thoroughly within the bounds of evangelical theology.

Why a Temporal God?

The first reason for opting for temporal divine eternity is that it is hard to make sense of the notion of atemporal eternity. The problem is not that atemporalists have offered no explanation of this notion, but rather that at the end of the explanation one still wonders what all the verbiage amounts to. Let me suggest what I find troublesome about this very idea.

As noted in discussing Stump and Kretzmann's understanding of Boethius, they claim that timelessness is atemporal duration. They agree that duration normally incorporates temporal ideas, but they tell us to remove all temporal concepts from atemporal duration. We are to think of the non-durational extent of a point in time, and just expand that idea indefinitely. However, this is very hard to do since no instantaneous point lasts longer than an instant, and anything that endures seems to do so through time. It is hard to imagine what it means for something to endure without thinking of its endurance temporally. Of course, if we think of endurance in temporal terms, we shouldn't think of it solely in terms of physical clock time, especially if we are thinking of God, who is not confined just to our planet where we are most familiar with one kind of physical clock time (time measured by the earth's rotation on its axis and revolution around the sun).

But if God is not confined to any one place in our universe, and if before creation there were no physical objects by which to measure time, atemporalists may say that these facts make it impossible to speak sensibly of God in time. How could you measure the time of such a God? Some temporalists have claimed that before creation God existed in undifferentiated time, by which they mean, I take it, that there was some sort of time, but no way to differentiate one moment of it from another because there was no way to measure it (as one might with some sort of physical clock time). Atemporalists might well respond that undifferentiated time is just as difficult to understand as atemporal duration, so when it comes down to it, one is simply making a decision between two concepts, neither of which is entirely clear. If this is the atemporalist's reply, it commits the logical fallacy known as *tu quoque* (you too). That is, neither side will win this debate by answering an argument against their position by saying that the other side has a similar problem. Hence, while temporalists have some explaining to do, that doesn't make atemporal duration a clear idea. Atemporalists must still make sense of this idea.

A second reason that it is hard to understand what atemporal duration is and how it could be true of anyone stems from the fact that atemporalists also say that there is no temporal sequence in God's thoughts. This doesn't mean that there is no temporal or logical sequence in things within time, but only that it takes God no time to know what that sequence is. It is hard to imagine how humans could come to understand the logical sequence of ideas without their doing so taking time, but God's intellect is far above ours. What we must reason out over a period of time, God knows intuitively all at once. Hence, whether a sequence of events is temporally ordered or simultaneous with a logical order among them, God would know the sequence without taking any time to learn or know it.

Granting that an omniscient, supremely rational being could know everything there is to know, using no time at all to know it, are we ready for the implications of this? This is the point that troubles me about claiming that there is no temporal sequence whatsoever in God's thought life. If the content of God's conscious mind is always everything he knows, and if he knows everything an atemporal being can know, wouldn't this mean that God always has the same thought, namely, he is always thinking everything, and that there is never any variation in what he thinks? If God is in time, one might still argue that omniscience means that he must always think everything he knows, but at least each moment there would be new things to know (e.g., the truth of all temporal indexical propositions) in addition to all the other things he knows. And, if he can somehow block from his conscious mind things that he knows and focus on one part of his knowledge and then another, such a sequence in his thought life is no problem if he is temporal.

I raise this issue for several reasons. For one thing, the picture atemporalism suggests is that God always thinks the exact same thing. Perhaps that wouldn't bore him, but remember that if he is atemporal, he cannot think anything new or in a new way, because that would be a change, and change is ruled out for an atemporal God. Always thinking the same thought (everything he knows) is surely not the way Scripture depicts God. Now, someone might argue that omniscience means only that God knows everything there is to know; it doesn't mean he must be consciously aware of all of it. As suggested in chapter 7, this scenario would maintain omniscience, and could apply to a temporal God, but it cannot apply to an atemporal God. For some things to be in God's unconscious mind and then be brought to his conscious mind requires a change and sequence (even if only a change in the sequence of God's thoughts), and as atemporalists so rightly tell us, change and sequence require time. But time, change, and sequence are impossible for an atemporal God. Hence, an omniscient atemporal God has no choice but to think everything always, and that is problematic, as suggested.

In addition, with atemporalism how can we speak of fellowship[152] within the Godhead, as theists traditionally do. If all members of the Trinity are equally omniscient (and they are), and there is no possibility of sequence in what any of them consciously thinks, then all three always have the same thought they have always been thinking and always think exactly what the other two members are thinking. But, then, how is fellowship possible? With atemporalism, they cannot at one time focus on one aspect of what they know and then on another at another time. They can't at one point feel no emotion toward what they know and then at another moment rejoice with one another. Anticipating anything new is impossible. In such circumstances, it is hard to make sense of how the members of the Godhead could fellowship with one another, if fellowship means what we normally take it to mean.

Scripture also portrays God as having fellowship with and interacting with human beings at various times in their lives. How is this possible for a God who has no sequence in his mental life? It isn't just that God doesn't know what time it is in human history. Even if he did, as atemporal, he cannot think or do anything different than he ever has. But, then, either God has always had that interaction with someone for every moment of his life, or God has never had and will never have such interaction. Of course, atemporalists believe that their account of God's acts and their effects solves this kind of problem, but as we have seen and as I shall mention shortly, there are problems with that resolution.

The upshot of my point about no temporal sequence in God's thought life is that it is just hard to understand how it could be so. And yet it must be so if we hold that God endures without time and that while he knows the logical and temporal relations of all things in time, there is no sequence in his coming to know that order or in knowing it. In fact, the locution "coming to know" is imbued with temporal overtones, and cannot even make sense in relation to a timeless God.[153]

Not only is it hard to understand the notion of atemporal duration, but atemporalist claims about God acting timelessly and having the effects occur at the right time are hard to understand. The point is not that we don't know how God could do this because we don't know how an immaterial being acts; the point is that, however an immaterial being acts, it is hard to see how he could act before anything is created and have those actions occur at just the right time in history. This is so in part because an atemporal God cannot know what time it is in history as that moment occurs in history. Moreover, it is just very difficult to understand what happens to that action between the moment God does it and the time its effects occur in the world. Presumably, with atemporalism, whatever God decided to do was decided all at once and long before he created ("long before" strictly cannot relate to an atemporal being, but we don't want to say that prior to creation God existed only the equivalent of one timeless instant). But, then, what happens to the action as it "waits for" the world to be created and the right moment in history to arrive? This doesn't make sense, and it won't do for atemporalists to claim mystery as the answer. Indeed, it is mysterious as to how an immaterial being can act, but if it can act, there is no mystery as to how it would act at one moment and bring about a result at another time shortly after. What compounds the mystery needlessly is saying that an immaterial being acts, but nothing happens to that act for ages, and then somehow, though the act was done outside of time, the effects of the act occur just at the right time within time. This indeed is a hard saying.

There is another problem with the atemporalist's account of divine action. Given the notion of immutability that goes with atemporality, we have seen that an atemporal God must do whatever he does all at once. Moreover, he must be doing it for all eternity, because to stop or start doing it would be to change, and that is ruled out by divine immutability. Think of the implications of such a view. It means that God must still be doing things, the effects of which have already occurred hundreds and even thousands of years ago. As I now write this sentence, God must still be doing the actions that brought the ten plagues on Egypt. Likewise, he must still be doing whatever he did to resurrect Jesus Christ from the dead, even though Christ ascended into heaven and has been present with the Father for nearly two thousand years. In fact, even after God creates the new heavens and new earth, he will still be doing all the actions he ever did in relation to the current heavens and earth. If this sounds strange, one can see why temporalists find it so hard to make sense of the notion of atemporal eternity.

Not only is it preferable to adopt a temporal notion of divine eternity because it is hard to make sense of atemporal eternity, but many of the arguments used against atemporalism are also quite compelling. In particular, arguments about God as a person, God's action, the biblical portrait of God's interactions with the world, the problem of divine simultaneity with events in time, and some of the issues raised about divine omniscience are difficult to handle with atemporalism. I need not rehearse the substance of these and other objections already raised against atemporal eternity, but only refer readers to those arguments.

Despite these objections, some may still believe it is necessary to hold atemporal eternity because if one does not, one must give up divine simplicity and immutability. Of course, the major reason for holding simplicity is that it seems logically necessitated by God as a perfect being and as *a se*. However, there are compelling arguments against divine simplicity, and rejecting simplicity need not necessitate giving up aseity, unless one holds a theonomous metaphysic which demands that God control absolutely everything. But to cede simplicity in no way means that God is brought into being, maintained in being, or *caused* to have the qualities he does by anyone or anything else. Nor does it mean he is no longer the creator of all things other than himself, or that creation *ex nihilo* is impossible. So it is difficult to see why one would have to give up aseity in the sense defined in chapter 6 if simplicity goes.

As to immutability, I have argued that we should not discard it, but should nuance it differently. The heart of the evangelical conception of immutability is that God is unchanging in his being and attributes, will, purposes, and ethical norms. Both atemporalists and temporalists who wish to remain evangelical in theology would have to hold that God is immutable in these respects. On the other hand, the ways God could change seem consistent with Scripture and reason, but many of them (if not all) would be inconsistent with the absolutely static notion of immutability demanded by atemporal eternity. Of course, if atemporalists are determined to hold the strongest sense of immutability possible, so much the worse for atemporalism, because there is too much biblical and rational evidence to show that God does undergo these kinds of changes to adopt the idea that God undergoes absolutely no kind of change whatsoever.

So, a nuanced notion of immutability is needed to accommodate biblical theism, but such a nuanced notion won't fit atemporal eternity. For example, a God who changes his relationship with a repentant sinner incorporates a sequence in his handling of that person, but that sequence necessitates time and so rules out atemporalism. On the other hand, the nuanced notion of immutability I have presented fits quite well a temporal God, as well as biblical theism. Hence, evangelical theists shouldn't worry that giving up atemporalism will undermine their commitment to evangelical theology on the matter of immutability.

Finally, it is helpful to remember why the notion of atemporal eternity was invoked in Christian theology at all. Boethius, Augustine, Anselm, and Aquinas all did so to solve a theological puzzle or to fit other doctrines. However, if atemporalism doesn't solve the problems for which it was invoked, or if it isn't required by other doctrines one holds, one has just removed a good bit of the rationale for holding the view. Is it true that atemporal eternity doesn't solve the problems it was intended to solve and isn't necessitated by other doctrines the theist holds? I believe so.

First, we turn to Augustine, and I need not belabor the point. Augustine invoked atemporal eternity to solve the problem of why God waited to create until he did. But that question confronts both temporalists and atemporalists, and there is an answer apart from adopting atemporalism.[154] What about Boethius? He incorporated this notion to address the freedom/foreknowledge issue. I shall handle this in a later chapter, but I can make some initial comments. For determinists of some form, there is no problem of freedom and foreknowledge, so invoking atemporal eternity is unnecessary on that account. Of course, determinists must make sense of how their determinism fits with human freedom and moral responsibility and how it allows us to solve the problem of evil, but I have shown elsewhere (and will do so again in later chapters) how a determinist theist can solve such problems.[155]

As for indeterminists, they must address this issue, but there are various answers indeterminists have given. As I have argued elsewhere and will argue again when dealing with freedom and foreknowledge,[156] there is reason to think the Boethian resolution doesn't actually solve this problem. Moreover, none of the other indeterminist answers require an atemporal notion of divine eternity. Hence, if the reason for holding atemporalism is to solve this problem, that is not an adequate justification of atemporalism.

As to Anselm and Aquinas, they held atemporalism because they saw it as a logically necessary concomitant of doctrines such as aseity, simplicity, immutability, and absolute perfection. However, as we saw in chapter 7 and in this chapter as well, there is no reason to think it impossible to believe that God is the most perfect being, immutable, and *a se,* if one holds a temporal view of God. As to simplicity, I have argued that we should abandon it altogether.

Therefore, if one holds atemporalism to address any of the issues Augustine and Boethius thought it addressed, or if one holds it for fear of otherwise rejecting divine attributes that are essential to the evangelical Christian conception of God, one should give up atemporalism. The reasons why Augustine, Boethius, Anselm, and Aquinas adopted the view are understandable, but flawed to one extent or another.

In light of atemporalism's inadequacy to address the issues for which it was originally invoked, and in light of the other problems it creates for Christian theism, I conclude that it is neither a necessary doctrine nor particularly helpful for theists to hold.

Temporalism and Process Theology

Atemporalists may reply that there is still a valuable reason for holding atemporality: it is a safeguard against traveling all the way down the slippery slope to process theology. Whether or not this is so is debatable, but I need to explain why it is not. I need to show that it is possible to hold temporalism, avoid process theism, and be consistent with evangelical Christian theology.

First, process theism commits one to dipolar theism. In addition, it requires an essentially impotent God, for it claims that God acts on the world persuasively, rather than coercively. God presents to us the lure of his highest subjective aim for us, but he doesn't force us to act in accord with that lure. Moreover, the process God is (in Whiteheadian terms) an actual entity. As such, God must have a physical body. Since this is so, and since the world is considered God's body by process theism, God wasn't free to decide to create nothing. There must be a world, but God cannot create it *ex nihilo,* for that would give God, according to process thinkers, too much power over the world. In addition, since God's consequent nature is the world and it is constantly in the process of concrescing, God is constantly being created. In fact, he is the prime case of creativity. As Whitehead explains, "Neither God, nor the World, reaches static completion. Both are in the grip of the ultimate metaphysical ground, the creative advance into novelty. Either of them, God and the World, is the instrument of novelty for the other."[157]

As to divine attributes, a dipolar God whose consequent nature is the world must be finite. He is also personal, mutable, and passible, but we must understand what this means for process thinkers. As to mutability, God is mutable in virtue of his consequent nature, which is always in the process of becoming. This means that the process God undergoes changes to his very being and attributes. As to his will, that also can change as he leaves room for creaturely freedom. God wants us to follow his highest subjective aim for us, but he won't coerce us to do so. Thus, when we choose other than what God wishes, God may need to change his intentions in regard to us. As to divine omniscience, all past events, persons, etc., are forever preserved in God's memory, and in that sense, never perish.[158] Of course, according to this view, the future is unknowable, so God doesn't know it. And given the new experiences he has according to his consequent nature, he learns and experiences new things. Finally, since the process God is not omnipotent, process thinkers see a way to solve the problem of evil. God doesn't remove it, because he doesn't have the power to do so.[159] However, those who suffer under the world's evil should be encouraged by the fact that God suffers with them.[160]

Given this brief rehearsal of process notions, must we hold such doctrines if we accept God as temporal? For the most part, I think not. I begin with God's action, and here a lot depends on one's view of free will. For those who hold libertarian free will, the process notion of God's actions, omnipotence, and knowledge of the future may seem attractive. However, as we have already noted, libertarians need not claim that God doesn't know the future. Moreover, libertarians who are evangelical typically limit God's exercise of his power in our world to some extent, but they don't have to limit it to the extent that process theists do, essentially making God impotent. Evangelical Arminians would hardly claim, for example, that the only divine actions in our world are those that are persuasive in an attempt to get us to do what he wants. God does perform miracles (process theists deny that such events happen—in our modern world such things aren't believable), and he acts in history. In addition, Arminian libertarians wouldn't solve the problem of evil as do process theists, for they appeal to the free will defense to handle it. We should add that even proponents of the open view disagree with process views about divine action and power. They hold that God has absolute power and reserves the right to interfere with human freedom, but most of the time he doesn't do so. Hence, while there is a certain attractiveness of process ideas for those who hold libertarian free will, there is no logical necessity for a libertarian to adopt the process account of divine action, omnipotence, knowledge of the future, or the process answer to the problem of evil.

Process ideas about these doctrines are even less attractive to a determinist like myself. As I shall show when discussing providence and freedom, the soft determinism I hold allows God full control of the world while leaving room for human freedom and moral responsibility. For a Calvinist like myself, it would be impossible to hold that God doesn't know the future, doesn't act in our world, or doesn't have control over events in our world. Not only does

God know the future; he decrees it, and for a Calvinist like myself who also is a temporalist, God knows what time it is in human history and so knows when to act. So the process account of divine action, omnipotence, and omniscience is not required for a determinist who adopts the view that God is temporal. As to the problem of evil, elsewhere I have shown how a compatibilist like myself can solve the problem of evil, and it has nothing to do with the process answer to that problem.[161]

What about the other aspects of process theism? I see no reason why temporalists would in any way be logically constrained by temporalism to hold a dipolar view of God. God is pure spirit without any matter (hence, God has no material consequent nature); making him temporal doesn't require him to be material. Moreover, nothing about temporalism demands that God be understood as an actual entity in the Whiteheadean sense. Moreover, temporalism doesn't rule out God as a creator *ex nihilo,* nor does it mandate that there be a world in order for God to have a body. And there is no reason why an evangelical temporalist would claim that God himself is undergoing creation! Furthermore, I argued in chapter 4 that, despite denials, process theism amounts either to pantheism, or if not, it portrays God as a something that is nothing. There is no reason why putting God in time would force one to hold either pantheism or that God is nonexistent after all.

As to the divine attributes, why does being in time mean that God must be finite and limited to only one place at a time? Temporalist theists need not jettison omnipresence and immensity. It is no less or more difficult to understand how a temporal God can be everywhere in his total being at once than it is to understand how an atemporal God can do those things. Moreover, temporalist evangelicals agree that God is personal, mutable (in the senses defined) and passible, but there is no need to understand mutability in the process theist's sense. Moreover, neither Calvinists nor Arminians perceive God to be impotent and unwilling to act in the world. Hence, there is no reason to hold that God changes his purposes or will in order to accommodate creaturely freedom. While some Arminian libertarians might be very sympathetic to such notions, they usually feel no necessity to hold such views. Even if they felt a necessity, that would be based on their notion of free will, not on the question of temporalism vs. atemporalism. As for Calvinists, they have no reason to say that God changes his will or purposes. Putting God in time does not make such changes necessary. But there are some respects in which God can change, and all of them are compatible with temporalism, and only some are compatible with atemporalism. It may be that God is mutable in some of those senses for process theism as well, but nowhere is it written that in order to be evangelical one must disagree with process thinking about every theological concept. Is God passible, as process theists suggest? Evangelicals who hold temporalism could agree that he is, even if they didn't think so for the same reasons as do process thinkers. More importantly, however, divine passibility seems most consistent with biblical revelation about God's relations with his human creatures. Such passibility is dubious on an atemporal view of eternity but is thoroughly consistent with a temporal view.

In sum, there is no inevitability of slipping into process theism if one abandons atemporal eternity. Indeed, I think process ideas are more attractive to proponents of libertarian free will, but even so there are plenty of safeguards for the libertarian. As to determinist temporalists, there should be even less attraction for process notions of divine power, action, and the like. But regardless of whether the evangelical theist is a determinist or an indeterminist, there is absolutely no reason to adopt the process dipolar view of God, see God as less than the creator, see God as under construction, understand his very being to be a Whiteheadean actual entity, slip into pantheism, or see God as mutable in his person, purposes, will, or ethical rules just because one holds divine temporal eternity. When one understands fully what process theism says about God, one sees that temporal eternity does not lead inevitably to it, nor need it even be a good excuse for evangelicals to adopt process theology.

TEN

THE DOCTRINE OF THE TRINITY

Many things said about God in previous chapters could also be said of the God of other religions, especially monotheistic ones such as Judaism and Islam. The doctrine of the Trinity, however, is a uniquely Christian doctrine. Some may think this doctrine is not so special after all, for many religions worship multiple gods, and this doctrine makes Christianity a form of polytheism. However, that clearly misunderstands what Christians mean in asserting that God is triune. Christianity insists that only one God exists, but it is just as emphatic in maintaining that the Father, the Son, and the Holy Spirit all are God.

When critics complain that it is a blatant contradiction to say that there is one God and yet call three divine, many Christians answer that this doctrine is a paradox, a mystery, but not a contradiction. For many, however, it is hard to understand how this doctrine makes sense (and what its sense is), and it is difficult to explain away the apparent contradiction. Thus, though this is Christianity's unique doctrine (and in that sense should be a "showcase" for Christianity's distinctiveness), many see it as an embarrassment, a case of "creative mathematics" intended to assert something, though exactly what is uncertain.

Despite protests that this doctrine is engulfed with various intellectual subtleties that seem incredibly esoteric, Christians feel compelled to uphold it, for they believe that biblical revelation demands it. Briefly stated, the doctrine claims that God is one as to essence and three as to persons. Nowhere does Scripture make this statement. In fact, as we saw in discussing God's being, it is difficult to find biblical language that talks about the "divine essence" (perhaps the closest is Paul's claim about the "form of God" in Phil 2:6, though Paul's intent is not to teach the Trinity). Moreover, the sense in which "person" is used in the trinitarian formula is hard to find in Scripture. Still, Christians for centuries have maintained that while the doctrine is nowhere stated as such in Scripture, it is a logically warranted inference from what Scripture does say about God.

This doctrine also has a long and rather contentious history behind it. It has been the subject of various church councils and has resulted in various creedal expressions. Specifically, it was the councils of Nicea (A.D. 325) and Constantinople (381) that officially settled the formulation of the doctrine. However, the wording of the creeds of those councils as well as the so-called Athanasian Creed seems rather technical and remote to our way of thinking. We sense the church fathers were reacting to something, but exactly what is not clear. Moreover, history tells us that not everyone agreed with the decisions of the councils, and the implications of the creedal formulations for what Christians say about the Son's and the Holy Spirit's relations to one another and to the Father continued to be a bone of contention for many centuries among Christians. In fact, one difference of opinion about the Trinity (the *filioque* issue) still divides the Western (Latin) and Eastern (Greek) churches to this day.

The issue is not just whether Scripture teaches or warrants the doctrine, for most Christians grant that it does. Rather, the debate is over how we are to understand what we are saying when we teach that God is triune. This suggests that this doctrine is really quite complex, and we can begin to see some of that complexity by clarifying what the doctrine asserts. In recent philosophical and theological discussions of the doctrine, various thinkers have argued that the Athanasian Creed amounts to at least the following claims:

(1) The Father is God.
(2) The Son is God.
(3) The Holy Spirit is God.
(4) The Father is not the Son.
(5) The Father is not the Holy Spirit.
(6) The Son is not the Holy Spirit.
(7) There is exactly one God.

Even a brief perusal of these propositions raises the specter of a logically contradictory set,[1] and as we shall see, these seven claims are only part of what Christian theology says about the Trinity.

In the several centuries prior to the twentieth century, the doctrine of the Trinity didn't receive much attention beyond evangelical theology. Much of the Western church was captivated by classical liberal theology, and that theology tends to be Unitarian. Schleiermacher, often considered the father of liberal theology, devotes very little attention to the doctrine. In his massive *The Christian Faith,* he relegates it to the end of the book and treats it in about fifteen pages. Since Schleiermacher saw religion as generated from our consciousness of absolute dependence on something greater than us, and since he thought everything ultimately depends on our own consciousness, it is predictable that he gave the Trinity short shrift. As Schleiermacher said, this is not an immediate utterance concerning the Christian self-consciousness, so we should not expect to hear much about it from him.

Despite neglect of the doctrine for several centuries, in the twentieth century it has come again to the forefront of theological reflection. Undoubtedly, this is due in no small measure to the work of Karl Barth. Barth begins his massive *Church Dogmatics* with a lengthy discussion of the Trinity, for Barth argues that humanity only knows about God through divine revelation of himself. However, the presupposition of such revelatory acts is God as triune, so the doctrine of the Trinity cannot be a "footnote" to Christian theology; it must be at its heart. What one finds in studying twentieth-century non-evangelical theology is that, especially in neo-orthodox thinkers and the post-God-is-dead theologians, the Trinity becomes very important. As to the latter, I noted in chapter 3 that the latter part of the twentieth century has seen the emergence of a postmodern mindset along with theologies that mirror postmodern themes. A key postmodern theme is the relatedness of all things (as opposed to modernity's isolation and individualism). Of course, if one wants to emphasize the interconnectedness and relatedness of all of reality, what better place to begin than with a God who is tri-personal, all of whom mutually relate to, love, and work with each other in perfect harmony! Many argue that this relational God should be mirrored in human institutions and interpersonal relations.

Though my concern is the evangelical doctrine of the Trinity, there is ample contemporary non-evangelical handling of the doctrine from any number of different perspectives, such as process theology and feminism. The reader may consult some of that literature to get a taste of how this doctrine is handled in current discussions.[2] For our purposes, however, suffice it to say that a loud and clear message comes from these contemporary discussions (including some evangelicals) that if one wants to wade through all the niceties of Greek and Latin terminology that surround this doctrine and the long history of the seemingly esoteric controversies that have surrounded it, one had better by the end of the discussion show its practical relevance to everyday living. If the theologian can't explain either the theological significance or especially the practical relevance of this doctrine, many are simply unwilling to devote the time needed to comprehend all the details. As some have suggested, when it comes to the typical Christian in the pew (even very conservative ones), though they assent to this doctrine, few really understand what it says, and many actually live as practical tritheists. That is, in the minds of many, God, Jesus, and the Holy Spirit are divine, but they often think of them and relate to them as though they were three separate Gods.

Since I believe this is an important doctrine both intellectually and practically, I must explain something of the doctrine's significance. For one thing, any Christians who think it important to understand who and what their God is must recognize that the Christian God is triune. As Wolfhart Pannenberg replies to those who think this doctrine is unimportant:

It is not a doctrine of only secondary importance in addition to some other basic concept of the one God: if the issue is considered in terms like that, the case for trinitarian theology is lost. It can be defended only on the condition that there is no other appropriate conception of the God of Christian faith than the trinity. In that case we cannot have first a doctrine on the one God and, afterwards, in terms of some additional supernatural mystery, the trinitarian doctrine. Rather, if the trinitarian doctrine is sound, Christian monotheism can only mean that the three persons of the trinity are not three gods, but one God only. Everything that is said in Christian theology on the one God has to be predicated, then, of the three persons of the trinity in their communion.

If a case can be made out for trinitarian theology, the decisive argument must be that the trinitarian doctrine simply states explicitly what is implicit already in God's revelation in Jesus Christ and basically in Jesus' historical relationship to the Father whom he proclaimed to be the one God. If Jesus' relationship to the Father could be adequately described and accounted for in other terms than those of trinitarian doctrine, the case for that doctrine would be lost. It can only be defended if the trinitarian concept of God can be shown to be the only adequate and fully explicit expression of the reality of God revealed in Jesus Christ.[3]

Indeed, this is a most significant doctrine theologically. If Father, Son, and Holy Spirit are not coequally God and not of the same essence, there are serious problems, for example, for the doctrine of salvation. It is generally agreed in evangelical theology that because of human sin and guilt before God, a radical remedy is required. Someone must die to pay the penalty, but who? Evangelical theology contends that it must be a human being, for humans have incurred the guilt and penalty. But no mere human could atone even for their own sins, let alone those of the whole world, so the Savior must be God. But if Jesus is less than God (above humans and even above angels, but still not equal to the Father and the Spirit), how can he serve as the atoning sacrifice for all? Redemption is in jeopardy. Moreover, if there is not equality of being and purpose, then perhaps Christ's desire to offer a sacrifice is contrary to the Father's thinking about how to atone for human sin. Perhaps, as some earlier in church history have supposed, the Son's propitiation of the Father attempts to win over a Father who is not inclined to handle sin in this way. And what if the Father decided to reject the Son's sacrifice?

As to the Holy Spirit, if he is not fully God, the implications for salvation are again serious. Scripture teaches that the Holy Spirit regenerates believers and indwells and fills them, but if the Holy Spirit is a lesser God or no God at all, how can we be sure that he can do any of these things? Moreover, unless he is coequal in being and purpose with the Father and the Son, what guarantees that even if he tried to do such things, the Father and Son would recognize his actions as appropriate and relate to us accordingly?

The doctrine of the Trinity is also significant in terms of the truth of revelation. In 1 Corinthians 2, Paul tells us that the hidden things of God have been revealed to us by God's Spirit, the Holy Spirit. In verse 11 Paul writes, "For who among men knows the thoughts of a man except the spirit of the man, which is in him? Even so the thoughts of God no one knows except the Spirit of God." Paul's logic is hard to fault. Who would better know what you are thinking than you? Similarly, who would better know the truths of God than God's own Spirit? But what if the Holy Spirit does not share the divine essence but is a lesser being (even a non-divine one)? Then, according to Paul's logic, the Holy Spirit would not necessarily be in a position to know the truths of God, and if that is so, we are in deep trouble in relation to Scripture. Scripture clearly teaches that revelation of God's truth comes through the Spirit and that the Spirit inspired Scripture (1 Cor 2:9-13). Believing this to be so and believing the Spirit to be coequally God so that he really knows the truth of God, evangelicals take the Bible to be God's Word and understand it as a true revelation from God about himself, ourselves, etc. As Paul says, who would better know what someone is thinking than that person himself? If the Holy Spirit doesn't share the divine essence with the Father and Son, he is not in a position to know. The implications for our knowledge of God are staggering!

Think as well of the implications for revelation if Jesus is not coequally God. Scripture says that Jesus is the exact image of God (Heb 1:3) and that in him dwells all the fulness of the Godhead in bodily form (Col 2:9). Jesus adds that those who have seen him have seen the Father (John 14:9). John says that while no one has ever seen God, the Son knows him and has revealed him to us (John 1:18). But if Jesus is a lesser God or only a mere man, there are no such guarantees. In his very person he cannot reveal God, for he is not coequal with him. Moreover, we cannot even be sure that his teaching about God reveals the truth, for if he is not coequal with God how can we know that he really knows what he's talking about when he speaks of God? Perhaps he is just a very religious human being, a genius at religious things, but not really one who knows (let alone reveals) the truth about God. If so, then in knowing about Christ and knowing him personally by faith, we cannot be sure our knowledge of God increases at all.

The doctrine of the Trinity safeguards against all of these devastating possibilities. The one who dies on the cross is fully God as well as fully human. Salvation is not merely his idea, an idea of whose merit he must convince the Father; it is the plan and work of the whole Godhead. The Holy Spirit does have the power to regenerate, and in indwelling believers he brings the very presence of God (Father, Son, and Holy Spirit) into our lives. Moreover, the Spirit as God knows accurately the things of God, so we can be sure that the Scriptures he inspired are both the truth of God and truth about God. And Jesus is, as Scripture says, the highest revelation of God that we have. Yes, he is a genius in religious matters (and all other matters), but he is more; he is God!

The Trinity has other important practical implications worthy of mention. For one thing, the doctrine of the Trinity offers an example for interpersonal relationships, not the least of which is family relations. Even as Father, Son, and

Holy Spirit deeply love one another, work together to accomplish their goals in our universe, and when needed, submit their individual will to the wishes and plans of the other members of the Godhead (e.g., Matt 26:39, where Jesus says not his will but the Father's), we find our model for interpersonal relations.

Another practical implication of this doctrine is that we can expect the same reactions and relations from all members of the Godhead. Think of divine attributes such as God's love. In knowing that God is all-loving, we can expect this from each member of the Godhead. There is no reason to fear that one will want to shower his love upon us while other members of the Trinity will not be loving. Moreover, since all members are truthful and faithful, we can be certain that the Holy Spirit will not tell us something that contradicts what the Father or Son know to be true and best for us. If God makes promises in his Word, we need not worry that one or more of the members of the Godhead will default on those promises, even if one of the three wants to remain faithful. All three are reliable, dependable, and truthful.

Amid trial and tribulation, the whole Godhead says that they will never leave us nor forsake us! Think of what that means. The Father (who out of love and mercy sent his Son to die) indwells us along with Christ and the Holy Spirit. The Father who raised Christ from the dead dwells in every believer, and can use that same power in our lives. As Paul writes (Rom 8:32), "He who did not spare His own Son, but delivered Him up for us all, how will He not also with Him freely give us all things?" In addition, the Son who emptied himself and submitted to death on a cross also indwells us. Scripture says that it was through his power that the worlds were created (John 1:3, 10). Isn't it encouraging to know that the one who has power to bring the world into being out of nothing dwells within you? Scripture also tells us that Christ is our advocate with the Father (1 John 2:1). When Satan accuses us, Christ defends us.

It is also a great blessing to have the Holy Spirit indwell us. He is not only the revealer of truth about God, but his ministry illumines the Word of God so that we can see how it applies to us. He is there to guide us through the difficult circumstances of life, but he is also the comforter in times of afflictions (2 Cor 1:3-4). Moreover, he helps us when we don't know what to pray, by bringing the proper petitions before the Father's throne (Rom 8:26). It is the Holy Spirit who also gives us spiritual gifts for ministry, and it is he who uses us and our ministry to accomplish things in people's lives that could not happen otherwise. He convinces and convicts of sin, and then he helps us change behavior we want to abandon but are helpless to relinquish through our own power. What a blessing to know that the Holy Spirit indwells us, wants to fellowship with us, and will never leave those who know Christ as Savior!

Of course none of these practical benefits are guaranteed if Father, Son, and Holy Spirit are three separate Gods, or if only one is God and the others are lesser created beings. But because of the truth of the Trinity, we know that in Christ all the fullness of the Godhead dwells in bodily form (Col 2:9). Christ dwelling in us is the hope of glory (Col 1:27). Christ as fully God dwells in us by the Holy Spirit's power, and hence, Father, Son, and Holy Spirit are present within believers' lives. If God seems remote from us, the fault is clearly ours. The truth of the Trinity guarantees that the whole Godhead is there within us. Isn't it wonderful to know that they are not at odds among themselves about us or anyone or anything else? They are ready to fellowship with us and to work out their will in lives that are yielded to their leading and power.

Given the great theological and practical import of this doctrine, we must understand it. We shall first investigate its biblical basis, and then explain the debate that arose over the Trinity and how the early church fathers resolved that debate. We must also ask about the logical coherence of this doctrine. The rest of this chapter is devoted to those tasks.

THE BIBLE AND THE DOCTRINE OF THE TRINITY

Does Scripture teach the doctrine of the Trinity? A lot depends on what "teach" means. If it means that Scripture explicitly states this doctrine, then the answer is negative. The formula "God is one as to essence, three as to persons" is nowhere found in Scripture. Some will reply that 1 John 5:7 (KJV) comes as close to a formulaic statement as we can get, for it reads "For there are three that bear record in heaven, the Father, the Word, and the Holy Ghost: and these three are one."

Unfortunately, this reading is supported by a weak textual tradition, and hence, is likely spurious. The preferred reading (supported by א, A, B, K, P) says, (v. 7) "Because there are three who bear witness, (v. 8) the spirit, and the water, and the blood, and the three are one." On this reading, the verse doesn't state the doctrine of the Trinity in any form.

While no passage states the doctrine *per se,* there are other ways Scripture can teach something. If Scripture makes various claims which, when taken together, necessitate or even warrant a doctrine, then the Bible teaches the doctrine by implication. It is easy to show that Scripture teaches that there is only one God. Moreover, Scripture applies terms such as 'God' and 'Yahweh' and predicates various divine attributes and actions to more than one individual. Of course, this might be a case of using various ways to refer to one and only one thing, but there is also evidence that the individuals designated by these names and descriptions are distinct and exist simultaneously with one another.

If Scripture does teach all of this, it doesn't "say" that God is one in essence and three as to persons, but it requires the theologian and exegete to do a lot of explaining. For how can there only be one God and yet several distinct, simultaneously existing individuals are attributed divine qualities, called by divine names, and portrayed as doing things that, according to Scripture and reason, only a divine being could do? If the theologian and exegete are to avoid a contradiction, the traditional formulation of the doctrine of the Trinity seems required.

All of this means that the doctrine of the Trinity is inferred from things that Scripture teaches without actually being stated anywhere in Scripture. Inferential reasoning is notoriously slippery, for from one set of data it may be possible to generate several distinct inferences, each of which mutually excludes the others. For example, from the data mentioned it is possible to infer tritheism, the belief in three distinct Gods who are one in that they wholly agree as to their purposes and decisions. It is also possible to infer that biblical writers, taken as a whole, have contradicted one another on this issue so that the truth is either that God is really one or that tritheism is true. In that case, some biblical authors are wrong in asserting the contrary alternative. And yet again, it is also possible to conclude from the biblical data that God is somehow one and three at the same time without those claims generating a contradiction.

These three possible inferences from the biblical data (others may also be possible from the same data) *prima facie* appear to have equal plausibility. If we move beyond *prima facie* evidence and add the doctrines of biblical inspiration and inerrancy, plus the belief that contradictions are errors, then the second inference mentioned doesn't look plausible. But between the first and third options, initially there isn't a lot to commend one over the other. To demonstrate one as more probable than the other, further exegetical and theological work are required.

None of this means that we should despair of understanding correctly what Scripture teaches on this matter, but it does underscore the need to be very careful in our exegetical, theological, and philosophical reasoning about this issue. Formulating doctrines by inference from other truths Scripture teaches can be difficult, but it is not an illegitimate way to formulate doctrine. If the data warrant the inference, there is no reason to be apologetic about the doctrine.

Beyond these cautions about inferential reasoning, two other "ground rules" for this discussion are worth noting. First, we do know what early church fathers and church councils concluded about this doctrine. We also know from the writings of church fathers who attempted to expound and defend the decisions of the church councils that rather sophisticated metaphysical distinctions were used to explain and defend this doctrine. They introduced Greek and Latin terms (such as *ousia, hypostasis, substantia, subsistantia, persona*) to elucidate this doctrine, terms that were never used in this way in Scripture to speak of the Trinity. This should caution us to be careful not to impose these terms and concepts on Scripture so as to force biblical writers to make sophisticated metaphysical points that they never intended to make and possibly knew little about. It is disturbing to read various theological treatments of this doctrine in which theologians essentially "read back" into Scripture conclusions of the church councils that biblical authors never intended. That doesn't mean biblical writers would disagree with these claims and sophistications, but only that while we want to say whatever Scripture says about this topic, we should not make the biblical authors say more than they did. Similarly, I would caution contemporary readers against reading current notions of "person" back into Scripture and into the formulations and writings of the church fathers who grappled with these ideas. As we saw in chapters 2 and 3 of this book, some dramatic changes occurred with Immanuel Kant in our understanding of how the mind functions in the knowing process, and all of that has implications for our notions of consciousness and self-consciousness, and those concepts have significant implications for what we mean by a person. Don't assume that fourth- and fifth-century thinkers, living more than a millennium prior to Kant and Descartes, understood consciousness, knowledge, or personhood as Descartes or Kant did, let alone as we do.

A second "ground rule" deals with the relation of the NT to the OT. Progress of revelation means that God has not said everything he wants to say about a topic in just one passage. It also means that as salvation-history progresses, earlier revelation is amplified and clarified by later revelation. This is especially true with the doctrine of the Trinity. The truths that form the foundation of the doctrine are most clearly presented in the NT. Parts of the doctrine are at best only vaguely hinted at in the OT. It is tempting to read NT truth into OT passages, but we must, insofar as possible, resist that temptation. The reason is not that the NT contradicts the OT or doesn't flow from it, but rather that the OT does not say entirely what we claim on the basis of NT teaching. It is one thing to say, for example, that we can see how an OT passage that says the coming Messiah would also be God (Isa 9:6-7) fits NT teaching that Jesus of Nazareth is the long-awaited Messiah, and is the Son of God. It is another thing to say that *Isaiah* is teaching that Jesus is God. Or again, it is one thing to say that a passage such as Isa 63:7-14 teaches that God, the angel of his presence, and God's Holy Spirit were all involved in Israel's exodus from Egypt and through the wilderness pilgrimage, and that if the second member of that trio is the preincarnate Christ, then though this passage doesn't teach three distinct members of the Godhead, it can be made to cohere with such a doctrine. On the other hand, it is another to say that this OT passage teaches not only plurality in the Godhead but also that each of the three individuals mentioned are distinct persons of the Godhead and coequal with one another.

By being careful with OT texts, I don't think we lose anything of significance to the doctrine of the Trinity. On the other hand, we can clearly see intimations of a triune God, "outlines" which, if not completely understood by the OT person, are still understandable in the NT era as seeds from which the fuller and clearer teaching would grow. Moreover, for the observant OT saint, those OT passages could have been a clue that there is more to say about God than just that there is one God and Yahweh is his name.

With these methodological caveats in view, let us turn to Scripture to see what it says about God. Having investigated biblical data, we will be in a better position to see what the early church was trying to explain, and to judge how true to the biblical text their explanations and doctrinal formulations were.

There Is Only One God

Our discussion of biblical teaching begins with the claim that there is only one God. This rules out all forms of polytheism. Moreover, Scripture makes it clear that this one God is Yahweh, the God of Abraham, Isaac, and Jacob. He is not Baal, Molech, or any of the other pagan deities. Both OT and NT are very clear about this.

In the OT there are many indications that there is only one God. Perhaps the best-known verse is the *šĕmaʿ* of Deut 6:4, "Hear, O Israel! The LORD our God, the LORD is one!" Though the syntax is a bit difficult in the original, the meaning of the verse is quite clear. The word translated "one" is *ʾeḥod*. It occurs some 960 times in many contexts throughout the OT,[4] and its predominant use is to designate something that is numerically one, and that seems to be its sense here. There is only one Yahweh; no one else qualifies as God. Other peoples have their own gods, but Israel's God is Yahweh alone. For Jews and Christians, the God of the Bible is the true and living God, so no other god is real. In light of Yahweh alone being God, verse 5 instructs Israel to "love the LORD your God with all your heart and with all your soul and with all your might." Exod 20:3 and Deut 5:7 command Israel to "have no other gods before Me."

When Moses asks God what to tell Israel if they ask the name of this God (Exod 3:13-14, NIV), God replies that Moses should answer, "I AM WHO I AM. This is what you are to say to the Israelites: 'I AM has sent me to you.'" "This is my name forever, the name by which I am to be remembered from generation to generation" (v. 15, NIV). At various places in the OT God emphatically reiterates that he is the only God and there is no other. Deuteronomy repeatedly makes this point. Deut 4:35, 39 (NIV) reads, "You were shown these things so that you might know that the LORD is God; besides him there is no other. . . . Acknowledge and take to heart this day that the LORD is God in heaven above and on the earth below. There is no other." See also Deut 32:39.

In 1 Kings and Psalms we read the same thing (1 Kgs 8:59-60; Ps 86:10), but by far it is Isaiah who makes this point most frequently. Isa 43:10 (NIV) says, "'You are my witnesses,' declares the LORD, 'and my servant whom I have chosen, so that you may know and believe me and understand that I am he. Before me no god was formed, nor will there be one after me.'" And in Isa 45:5-6 (NIV) we find, "I am the LORD, and there is no other; apart from me there is no God. . . . there is none besides me. I am the LORD, and there is no other" (see also 44:6; 45:14, 18). Several verses later (Isa 45:21-22, NIV) the Lord says, "There is no God apart from me, a righteous God and a Savior; there is none but me. Turn to me and be saved, all you ends of the earth; for I am God, and there is no other." And finally, in Isa 46:9 (NIV), God says, "I am God, and there is no other; I am God, and there is none like me."

The last line of Isa 46:9 says more than that there is only one God. It also says that there is no one, even including the highest of all beings beside God, to compare with him. In Exod 15:11 (NIV), Moses makes a further point that when Yahweh is compared with other nations' god or gods, there is no comparison. Moses asks, "Who among the gods is like you, O LORD? Who is like you—majestic in holiness, awesome in glory, working wonders?"

The NT repeats this message in various ways. On one occasion (Mark 12:29-30) Jesus was asked which of the Ten Commandments he thought most important. In reply he quoted from Deut 6:4 and then repeated the first commandment. In verse 31 Jesus adds the command to love our neighbor as ourselves, and then his interlocutor agrees (v. 32, NIV) that "God is one and there is no other but him." On another occasion, as Jesus prays to the Father, he says (John 17:3, NIV), "Now this is eternal life: that they may know you, the only true God, and Jesus Christ, whom you have sent."

In the Pauline epistles, several passages claim that there is only one God. This is exactly what we would expect from a man who was raised in orthodox Judaism and refers to himself as a Hebrew of the Hebrews and Pharisee according to the law (Phil 3:5). At the end of Romans 3 Paul concludes that all people are guilty before God and can only be justified through faith in Christ. Lest one think that these rules apply only to Jews and not to Gentiles, Paul adds (Rom 3:29-30, NIV), "Is God the God of Jews only? Is he not the God of Gentiles too? Yes, of Gentiles too, since there is only one God, who will justify the circumcised by faith and the uncircumcised through that same faith." The logic is clear: there is only one God, so whatever rules apply to one group of people, apply to all.

In 1 Corinthians 8 Paul discusses issues of Christian liberty (matters morally indifferent in themselves). The particular practice in question is eating food sacrificed to idols. In 1 Cor 8:4ff. Paul explains that idols are not real gods, and eating or not eating food sacrificed to them is morally indifferent. However, because some have scruples about such things, believers should be careful not to offend. As he makes this point, Paul affirms the traditional Jewish and Christian belief in only one God. In verses 4-6 (NIV) he writes, "So then, about eating food sacrificed to idols: We know that an idol is nothing at all in the world and that there is no God but one. For even if there are so-called gods, whether in heaven or on earth (as indeed there are many 'gods' and many 'lords'), yet for us there is but one God, the Father, from whom all things came and for whom we live; and there is but one Lord, Jesus Christ, through whom all things came and through whom we live" (see also Eph 4:3-6).

Then, as Paul writes Timothy, he encourages all believers to pray for those in authority. The hope is that God will give them wisdom in their rule so that there may be peace and tranquility for all under their authority. In 1 Tim 2:4 Paul explains that this is important because God wants all people to be saved. The thought is that in times of peace it is easier for the gospel to have free reign. Having shared God's desire for all to be saved, Paul adds the following about the salvation God provides (vv. 5-6, NIV), "For there is one God and one mediator between God and men, the man Christ Jesus, who gave himself as a ransom for all men—the testimony given in its proper time." There is only one God to whom we are accountable, and he has given one means by which we must be saved, namely, through Jesus, the only mediator between God and man.

A final NT passage is Jas 2:19. In chapter 2, verses 14ff., James treats the relation of faith to works. Those who say they believe but do not have a life of works pleasing to God offer no evidence that they really believe. They may hold intellectually that there is a God, but that amounts to little since their works show that they live as though God doesn't exist and makes no difference to them. In Jas 2:19 (NIV) James speaks about the person who only has an intellectual belief that there is a God: "You believe that there is one God. Good! Even the demons believe that—and shudder." James agrees that there is one God, but his point is that if one only has an intellectual belief in God, that isn't worth much. Even the demons who are resolute in fighting God know intellectually that he exists. The message is clear: while works save no one, they show that a person truly believes in a way that goes beyond mere intellectual agreement to a commitment to live in accord with this one true God.

In these passages, then, the NT affirms that there is only one God, and this agrees with the OT. Progress of revelation does not make this point clearer in the NT.

Evidences of Plurality in the Godhead

Scripture teaches in various ways that deity is true of more than one individual. This is abundantly clear in the NT, but even the OT hints at this truth. Because the NT evidence is so much clearer than OT evidence, and because we want to be careful not to read the NT back into the OT without warrant, I want to examine each testament independently. Indeed, some NT passages clarify that a person mentioned in an OT passage was God the Son or the Holy Spirit, but that evidence will be discussed under my handling of the NT.

OT INTIMATIONS OF PLURALITY IN THE GODHEAD. Though the OT is nowhere near as clear as the NT in teaching plurality in the Godhead, the idea is not entirely absent from the OT. It is dubious that anyone living during OT times and reading the OT would conclude that three persons—Father, Son and Holy Spirit—are divine, and would understand what that means. On the other hand, a careful student of the OT could have suspected that it teaches something more about God than just monotheism. In this section, I want to present OT evidence which suggests plurality in the Godhead. Of course, without NT teaching about Father, Son, and Holy Spirit as divine, we might not think the OT teaches anything more than that there is only one God.

We begin with the fact that the typical OT word for Israel's God is 'ĕlōhîm, and it is plural. There has been much ink spilled over the significance of this. Some say that the plural form was used typically by polytheistic religions, so its use in the Bible (in spite of the OT's clear teaching that there is only one

God) is significant. Specifically, some say that this plural form serves as evidence for the careful observer that there is plurality in the Godhead.[5] Perhaps even more significant is that there are biblical passages where Israel's God is referred to as *ʾĕlôah*, the singular of *ʾĕlōhîm* (e.g., Deut 32:15; Ps 18:32[Heb]; 114:7; Hab 3:3; and most frequently in Job). Since this singular form is available and was used on various occasions, the fact that the plural is also used most often to refer to Israel's God is considered significant. Unless the intent is to make a point about plurality, why not just use the singular *ĕlôah*?

In contrast, however, many argue that we should see the plural form as nothing other than a plural of majesty. As such, it designates the majesty of Israel's God but says nothing about how many members there are in the Godhead or about multiple gods.[6] Between these two views it is hard to decide, and if the whole case for divine plurality in the OT rested on this one item, it would be a weak case. Happily, there are other more substantial OT indications of plurality in the Godhead. As to the plural form of *ʾĕlōhîm*, it occurs so frequently in the OT that it is likely no more than a matter of style. To assume that writers use it to make a metaphysical point about God's nature probably concludes more than we should. What seems to require more explanation are the infrequent uses of the singular form *ʾĕlôah* in books that typically use the plural. On the other hand, the singular is so frequent in Job that it is probably there only a matter of style. Whatever the reason for the singular in other books, that is not likely to teach much of anything about plurality in the Godhead, since *ʾĕlôah* is singular.

I believe we are on safer ground when we focus on two other aspects of word usage in the OT. As noted, the more typical word for God is the plural *ʾĕlōhîm*. Though this word is plural, it is so commonly used to refer to Israel's one God, Yahweh, that it is most often used with a singular verb. Normally, nouns and verbs agree in number, so this is grammatically unusual, though stylistically normal in the OT. In fact, it is so typical to use this plural noun with a singular verb that it becomes significant when a *plural* verb is used with *ʾĕlōhîm* to refer to Israel's God. Several instances will make the point. In Gen 20:13 *ʾĕlōhîm* is used with a plural verb for "caused to wander," and in Gen 35:7 God is spoken of as having "revealed" (plural in the Hebrew) himself to Jacob. In 2 Sam 7:23 we are told that Israel's God (*ʾĕlōhîm*) went (*hālĕkû*—third person plural) to redeem Israel. Though it is hard to build a lot on such instances, since the singular verb with *ʾĕlōhîm* was so much more common, the reader of these other passages should have at least wondered why the writer used plural verbs in these cases.

A third linguistic phenomenon is the use of plural pronouns to refer to God in various passages. Since pronouns are supposed to agree with their noun in number, case, and gender, we would expect to see plural pronouns referring to *ʾĕlōhîm*. However, since that noun was understood in biblical Hebrew (when used of Israel's God) to refer to one God, it was most typical to use singular pronouns to refer to *ʾĕlōhîm*. Hence, in instances where plural pronouns appear (grammatically correct but contrary to typical usage), those cases seem to suggest plurality of some sort in the Godhead. Four passages are noteworthy. In Gen 1:26 (NIV) God says, "Let us make man in our image"; the verb "make" (*na‛ăśeh*) is plural, and so is "our." Some have tried to discount this passage by arguing that the Lord may be making this comment to the angelic hosts of heaven. However, that is unlikely since humans are made in the image of God, not of angels, so it would be hard to explain why God would make such a comment to the angelic hosts. Others might see the comment as an example of an editorial "we." In fact, sometimes people in authority when making commands say "we would like this or that." Though this is true in general, it is not the most frequent way the OT portrays God as referring to himself and his actions. Though one might note that we have similar instances in Gen 3:22 and 11:7, that still does not prove that this is Moses' most usual way of recounting God's pronouncements about his intentions. Hence, it is highly unlikely that this is happening in any of these three instances.

Two other passages using plural pronouns for God are Gen 3:22 and 11:7. After Adam and Eve sinned, God laments (Gen 3:22, NIV) that "man has now become as one of us (*mimmennû*), knowing good and evil." Then, the verb "go down" in Gen 11:7 is plural, and since the subject of the sentence is contained in the verb, the subject is "us"—hence, "let us go down." Again, it may be objected that the Lord is speaking to the angelic hosts, and that is possible. However, in the contexts of Genesis 3 and Genesis 11 there is no mention of angels, so one must "read" them into the passage. One might reply that there is no reference to other members of the Godhead either. Indeed, this is so, and that is why such evidence is not a certain proof of Trinity. However, in both passages the main characters in the narrative are God and Adam and Eve (Genesis 3), and God and the humans at Babel (Genesis 11). Hence, the most natural way to read these verses is as a reference to God. Of course, this seems strange in light of clear teaching that there is only one God, but that just shows that this line of evidence in itself cannot be conclusive. Still, such references should have made ancient Jews wonder what was being said.

A final instance of plural pronouns used to refer to God occurs in Isa 6:8. In Isaiah 6, Isaiah has a vision of God's throne room in heaven. In the midst of that vision (v. 8, NIV), he hears the Lord ask, "Whom shall I send? And who will go for us?" Since angels have just been mentioned in the preceding verse and throughout the context, skeptics will undoubtedly reply that God is asking this question of the angels, and in this passage such an interpretation seems easier to support than in the other instances. Commentators, however, disagree on this issue. Delitzsch and Gray, for example, argue that the reference is to the heavenly company.[7] On the other hand, Calvin sees in it a reference to the Trinity, though he offers little explanation why.[8] Geoffrey Grogan concurs that it likely refers to God. He grants that "there are, of course, many biblical passages that picture God surrounded by the heavenly host. Not one of these, however (unless, of course, the present passage is an exception), suggests that he, the omniscient and all-wise God, called on them for advice or even identified them with him in some way in his utterance."[9]

THE DOCTRINE OF THE TRINITY □ 451

Though this passage is admittedly more difficult than the others, I am inclined to agree that it does hint at plurality in the Godhead. In addition to Grogan's argument, I think it is important to note the point of the question and the purpose of this whole incident. Isaiah 6 recounts Isaiah's call to the ministry, a call to preach to an Israel that would be stubborn and refuse to obey. The questions of verse 8 are not instances of God asking for information he doesn't know or for advice for a decision he hasn't made. They are a rhetorical device used to alert Isaiah to a need for his services. Even more, these questions constitute a call of Isaiah to this ministry. But who is it who calls Isaiah to this ministry? Certainly not the cherubim and/or seraphim, but rather God! God could just as easily have said "Who will go for me?" and the questions would have functioned to call Isaiah to the ministry. But God put the question differently, and I think that is significant. Moreover, the fact that this is God's call (no one else's) to ministry makes it much less likely that "us" refers to the angelic hosts.

Beyond these linguistic and grammatical points that hint at plurality in the Godhead, there are other OT teachings that support the idea. For one thing, there are OT passages that seem to attribute a son to Yahweh. At the outset of Proverbs 30, Agur speaks of the Holy One (v. 3) and asks a series of questions about this God (v. 4). One question asks what the Holy One's name is and what his Son's name is. In addition, Psalm 2 (understood to be a messianic psalm) asks why the nations rage and conspire against the Lord and his anointed (his messiah). In verses 4-6 the Lord answers the nations, and then in verse 7, the anointed one recounts God's words to him: "Thou art My Son, today I have begotten Thee."

Both of these OT passages seem to ascribe a son to Yahweh, despite the fact that Israel knows that Yahweh is the only God. We must be careful, however, not to see too much in these verses in their OT context. It would be easy to read NT teaching about the Trinity or even a precise formulation of the doctrine back into these passages. What helps in handling these passages more conservatively is the realization that there are other instances in the OT where others are referred to as sons of God, and it is clear that deity is not being ascribed to them. For example, angels are referred to as sons of God (e.g., Job 2:1), Israel is called on various occasions God's son (Exod 4:22; Hos 11:1), and in 2 Sam 7:14 God promises David that after he dies, God will raise up David's son as king (this was fulfilled through Solomon). God says that he will be a father to Solomon, and Solomon will be a son to him, and it was not unusual in that culture to think of kings as a kind of son of God. But, clearly, neither the king nor Israel are divine, and angels are not divine either. So, speaking about a son for Yahweh may suggest a divine person (as I believe it does in Proverbs 30 and Psalm 2), but the reference is not entirely clear from the OT perspective because of these other instances of mere humans or angels being called sons of God. Moreover, even if the son in Proverbs 30 and Psalm 2 is divine, that is a far cry from identifying that son as Jesus, and a far cry from trinitarian language about sharing the divine essence.

A further intimation of plurality in the Godhead comes from the various references to the angel of the Lord (mal'ak yhwh). Obviously, many angels are mentioned in the OT, but one appears on various occasions and seems to be more than just one of God's angels. In fact, in his case, "angel of the Lord" seems to be as much a title or name as a description of his function or nature. What is significant about this angel of the Lord is that various passages refer to him as God, and yet he seems to be distinct from Yahweh. Genesis 16 records the story of Abraham, Sarah, and Hagar. Hagar fled from Sarah into the wilderness, and the angel of the Lord found her (v. 7). In the next verses the angel tells her about the son she will bear. Then, in verse 13, Hagar "called the name of the LORD who spoke to her, 'Thou art a God who sees.'" But she was speaking to the angel of the Lord, so this passage identifies the angel as God and Yahweh.

Genesis 22 recounts Abraham's offering of Isaac on Mount Moriah. During this incident, the angel of the Lord (v. 11) intervenes to stop Abraham. Abraham finds a ram and sacrifices it instead, and in verses 15-16 an angel speaks of his pleasure with Abraham's faith. But, as he speaks (v. 16) he is called the Lord: "By Myself I have sworn, declares the LORD, because you have done this thing . . ." Here again we see that this is no mere angel; rather it is identified as God. Similarly, in Gen 31:11, Jacob wrestles with the angel of the Lord who then (v. 13) identifies himself as God. And in Judg 13:6ff. the angel of the Lord visits Manoah and his wife. After he departs (vv. 20-22), Manoah refers to the angel and says that he and his wife will surely die, for they have seen God. Perhaps the clearest designation of the angel of the Lord as God is found in Exod 3:2-6, the incident of Moses and the burning bush. Verse 2 says the angel of the Lord appears to Moses in the burning bush, and by verse 4, it is clear that this angel is God. In verse 6 he tells Moses that he is "the God of your father, the God of Abraham, the God of Isaac, and the God of Jacob." Moses hides his face, because he was afraid to look at God. Of course, he saw the angel of the Lord in the burning bush, so the identity of the angel with God is clear.

In other passages the angel of the Lord is clearly distinguished from God. Think of Num 22:22-35, the account of Balaam and his donkey, and Judg 6:11-23, the account of Gideon at the battle of Midian. There is also evidence of this distinction even in Judges 13, for in verse 8 Manoah asks God that "the man of God" whom God has sent might come to them again. It would be hard to argue that the angel of the Lord in Numbers 22 and Judges 6 is any other than the one we have seen in the other passages, especially with what we see in Judges 13, where there is both identity and distinction between the angel and God. Still, whereas in some passages examined the angel is referred to as God, in Numbers 22 and Judges 6 he is mentioned along with the Lord as a distinct individual. One further point is noteworthy about the angel of the Lord. In Judg 13:17 Manoah expresses his desire to honor and worship the angel, and later offers a sacrifice to God. Moreover, in Exodus 3 Moses is told to take off his shoes as a sign of respect, because he is on holy ground, but of course he has seen the burning bush in which the angel of the Lord appears. Exod 34:14 is very clear that only God is to be worshiped, not mere humans or even angels, but in neither Exodus 3 nor Judges 13 does the angel of the Lord refuse the various acts of reverence and worship. This suggests, when joined with Exod 34:14, his divine nature.

What should we conclude about this angel? Many argue that he is the preincarnate Christ, and it is true that after the incarnation there is no reference to the angel of the Lord. Nonetheless, for someone living during OT times it would be extremely hard to identify the angel with Christ, but the data do show something. Specifically, they show that an individual known as the angel of the Lord is identified as God and yet in various passages is also distinguished from God. From this we can hardly deduce the doctrine of the Trinity, but these data warrant saying that while there is only one God, in some sense there is plurality in the Godhead, for the angel of the Lord is called God and yet is distinguished from God.

Further OT evidence of plurality in the Godhead comes in teaching about the Messiah, God's anointed. Some passages identify the coming Messiah as God. Think, for example, of Isa 9:6-7, which prophesies the birth of a son to Israel. This is no mere human child, however, for the passage clarifies that he will sit upon David's throne and his kingdom will last forever. This can be no other than the long-awaited Messiah, but note the description of this child. Among other things, verse 6 reveals that he is the mighty God, so this passage connects Messiahship with deity. We find something similar in Jer 23:5-6, where God says that he will raise up for David a righteous branch who will reign as king over Israel and Judah. Commentators uniformly understand this as a prophecy about the Messiah, but beyond that, verse 6 says that his name will be called "The LORD our righteousness," or "Yahweh our righteousness." This is more than a mere prophecy that people in Messiah's day will think positively of him. Rather, he will be called this because they will recognize him as God and will be thrilled with the justice and righteousness that he does in the land (v. 5). So this passage also identifies the Messiah as divine.

Another well-known passage makes a similar identification. Mic 5:2 predicts the birthplace of the Messiah as Bethlehem Ephrathah. It also says that his goings forth are "from long ago, from the days of eternity." What could this mean other than that he existed prior to his going forth from Bethlehem? In fact, he has gone forth (existed) from eternity, according to the verse, but this cannot be true of any mere human being, nor can it be true of an angel (the prophecy is not about an angel being born, whatever that would mean). What is said of this king could only be true of God. Here again the OT links the Messiah with deity.

Perhaps Messiah is just another term for Yahweh, i.e., maybe this evidence just means that there is only one person in the Godhead, who can be called any number of different names, including Yahweh and Messiah. This is possible but implausible, for there are passages that distinguish the Messiah from God. For example, Psalm 2 is typically understood as a messianic psalm, but the anointed king whom God has set on his holy hill is clearly not himself but his Son, and hence distinct from him. Moreover, in Psalm 45, also considered by many a messianic psalm, verse 6 says that God's throne is established forever, and then the king is told (v. 7) that "God, Thy God, has anointed Thee with the oil of joy above Thy fellows." Clearly, the one anointed is distinguished from his God, and if the anointed one is the Messiah, then we see the Messiah distinguished from God. Not infrequently, commentators also see the promised, coming "messenger of the covenant" in whom Israel delights as a prophecy of the Messiah (Mal 3:1). However, this verse is spoken by the Lord. The terms of the verse clearly distinguish the Lord from the coming messenger of the covenant. So, if this is a messianic prophecy, it is another verse that distinguishes the Messiah from God. There are also the many servant songs in Isaiah, which are often understood as prophecies of the coming Messiah. There is no question, however, that the suffering servant in these passages is distinguished from Yahweh himself.

How should we evaluate this evidence about the Messiah? As with the data about the angel of the Lord, deity is attributed to someone (the Messiah) who is not absolutely identical to Yahweh in all respects. Of course, in light of OT monotheism, he must somehow be identical to Yahweh, or he would not be called God. This identity plus plurality is not explained in the OT, but it is hard not to conclude that these passages teach some kind of plurality in the Godhead.

The OT also frequently refers to the Spirit of God. Though in some passages such as Gen 6:3 ("My Spirit shall not strive") and Ps 139:7 (the psalmist asks God, "Where can I go from Thy Spirit?") it is not entirely clear whether the Spirit is a distinct personage or rather a reference to God the Father's Spirit, there are many passages in which the Spirit is distinct. We see the Spirit of God hovering over the formless earth and its waters (Gen 1:1-2), God says he has filled Bezalel with the Spirit of God (Exod 31:2-3), and Moses says the same of Bezalel (Exod 35:31). In Num 24:2 the Spirit of God comes upon Balaam, and in Num 27:18 the Lord tells Moses to lay his hands on Joshua, "a man in whom is the Spirit." Job says that the Spirit of God has created him (Job 33:4), and the psalmist pleads with God (Ps 51:11), "do not take Thy Holy Spirit from me." In Isa 48:16; 61:1; and 63:7, 10 we not only find references to the Spirit of the Lord and the Holy Spirit, but each passage distinguishes the Spirit from the Lord himself. In 48:16 the speaker says "the LORD God . . . and His Spirit" has sent him. In 61:1 the speaker says the Spirit of the Lord God is upon him, because the Lord has anointed him, and in chapter 63, we read that despite the Lord's lovingkindness to his people Israel, they have rebelled and grieved his Holy Spirit. As a result, God has turned against them and has become their enemy. Finally, in Hag 2:4ff. the Lord of hosts tells his people that his Spirit is abiding among them.

In light of this evidence, it is hard to think that the Spirit of God or Holy Spirit is less than divine. Moreover, several passages cited distinguish him from Yahweh, so the Holy Spirit is somehow both identical and distinct from the Lord. The respects in which he is identical and different are not explained in the OT, but a fairly straightforward reading of the OT about the Spirit of God suggests that there is plurality in the Godhead. Moreover, attributes and actions that could only be true of God are attributed to the Holy Spirit. Ps 139:7-10 suggests his omnipresence, and Gen 1:2 and Job 33:4 show his involvement in creation (something only God can do).

Three final OT items are relevant to our study. There are several passages where the name of God or the notion of deity is applied to more than one person. Three of these passages appear in Isaiah. In Isa 48:16 the speaker says "the LORD God has sent Me, and His Spirit." Many interpreters judge the spokesman of the verse to be the second member of the Godhead. If one agrees, then all three persons are linked together in this verse. On the other hand, if one rejects that identification, the verse still speaks of the Lord God and his Spirit. Isa 61:1 is a second passage, and again the Lord God and the Spirit of the Lord are said to be upon the one who speaks. From the context of chapter 61, this one who is anointed by the Lord and his Spirit does things (vv. 1-9) that could only happen in messianic times, so one might on the basis of this chapter alone conclude that the Messiah is speaking. What seals the issue for many, however, is the fact that in Luke 4:18ff., Jesus turns to this passage, reads it, and says that he fulfils it. Christ's statement linking himself to Isaiah 61 is for many conclusive evidence that Isaiah 61 mentions all three members of the Godhead.

Isa 63:7-14 is another passage where multiple persons appear to be divine. The subject is God's love for Israel, especially what he did to deliver them from Egyptian bondage and care for them during their wilderness journey to the Promised Land. In this passage, we clearly see the Lord God and the Spirit of the Lord involved in these activities, but beyond that, verse 9 refers to "the angel of His presence" as their Savior amid troubles. Many see this angel as the angel of the Lord, and as we have seen, that angel is called God at the same time that he is distinguished from the Spirit and God the Father. A final passage where multiple persons are linked together and with the notion of deity is Hag 2:4, 5, and 7. This passage refers to the Lord of hosts (v. 4), God's Spirit (v. 5), and another figure called "the desire of all nations" (v. 7, KJV). Many commentators think this third person is the second member of the Godhead. Even if one disagrees, the passage at least refers to the Lord of hosts and his Spirit.

A second piece of evidence centers on four OT passages that speak of God as creator or maker of our universe (Job 35:10; Ps 149:2; Eccl 12:1; Isa 54:5). The Job and Ecclesiastes passages speak of God as the creator of human life, whereas the other passages emphasize God's special relationship to his ancient people Israel. In each passage, the English speaks of God as maker or creator, but what is most interesting is the Hebrew words translated "maker" or "creator." In each case the Hebrew word is in the plural. The Septuagint of these passages translates the term into Greek in the singular, but the Hebrew forms are plural. What we should make of this is hard to know, since the comments are cryptic and don't appear to be making any metaphysical point about plurality in the Godhead.

Finally, we have seen that the OT refers many times to the Spirit of God or the Holy Spirit. In addition, we have identified the angel of the Lord as divine and have seen the teaching about the Messiah as divine. Other references to the Lord God, Yahweh, and the Lord of Hosts are typically understood to refer to the one whom the NT clearly designates as God the Father. What is interesting is how infrequently the OT speaks of God as Father. In fact, the name (or, we might say, title) God the Father, so common in the NT, is absent from the OT.

This must not be misunderstood. Many OT passages speak of the God of our fathers, but of course, the fathers in view are the patriarchs. Moreover, various OT passages liken God to a father or portray him in a fatherly role. For example, in a whole series of passages God promises David (or simply promises) that he will be father to David's son Solomon (2 Sam 7:14; 1 Chron 17:13; 22:10; 28:6). In a doxology, God is blessed as the Lord God of Israel, our father (1 Chron 29:10). In one psalm, the psalmist calls God his Father, his God (Ps 89:26), and in two other psalms, God is likened to a father who has compassion on his children or who serves as a father to the fatherless (Ps 103:13; 68:5). In several places in Isaiah and Jeremiah, God is called or calls himself a father to Israel (Jer 31:9) and is told "Thou art our Father" (Isa 63:16; 64:8). And in Jer 3:19 God tells Israel, "You shall call Me, My Father." Finally, in Malachi God asks why there is no honor for him if he is a father, since others who are fathers receive honor (Mal 1:6). The writer later (Mal 2:10) asks his people, "Do we not all have one father?" There is only one creator, isn't there?

From these passages, it is abundantly clear that God plays a fatherly role to many individuals and to peoples as a whole. My point, however, is that the phrase "God the Father," which in the NT often functions as a proper name, is absent from the OT.[10]

NT TEACHING ON PLURALITY IN THE GODHEAD.   In light of the progress of revelation, we would expect more evidence for the doctrine of the Trinity in the NT, and there is ample NT evidence of plurality in the Godhead. Moreover, the NT clearly agrees with the OT that there is only one God. None of this means that we find talk of "essences" and "persons" in the NT, but only that in the NT, OT intimations of the Trinity become much clearer, and one can see why the church felt compelled to formulate a doctrinal claim to represent NT data.

Indeed, the NT data on plurality in the Godhead are so plentiful that one hardly knows where to begin. However, I shall organize NT teaching around a series of points that elucidate what the NT says about God as plural.

God the Father is presented as God.   God the Father is portrayed as divine in many NT passages. In the Gospels, we see Jesus having rich and intimate fellowship with his heavenly Father, and Jesus clearly thinks of him as God. In Matt 6:25-34 Jesus instructs his disciples not to worry about where they will get their food and clothing. Jesus reminds them that the heavenly Father feeds the birds of the air, and he cares about our needs as well (v. 26). As to clothing, Jesus reminds them that God arrays the lilies and grass of the field in great beauty, and he will see that his disciples' needs are also met (vv. 28-30). Throughout this passage Jesus uses the terms "God" and "heavenly Father" interchangeably, sometimes attributing the sustaining of us and our needs to God, and sometimes to the heavenly Father. For Jesus these are not two distinct persons; God is our heavenly Father. Hence, the Father is divine.

Later Matthew records Jesus' last words from the cross. In Matt 27:46 (NIV) Jesus addresses his Father, but he addresses him as God: "My God, my God, why have you forsaken me?" Despite what is happening, Jesus continues to claim his Father as God; even more he acknowledges the Father as *his* God. On a different occasion (John 6:27), Jesus told his listeners to work for the food that endures to eternal life. That is food which Jesus promises to give them himself, but then he adds that he is the one on whom the Father, God, has set his seal. This again clearly indicates that the Father is God.

The Pauline epistles contain further affirmation of the Father as divine. As is typical of his style in opening his letters, Paul invokes God's blessings on his readers. In Rom 1:7 he prays for the blessing of God the Father upon his readers. In Gal 1:1 Paul says that he is an apostle sent by God the Father, and in verse 3 he wishes his readers grace and peace from God our Father and the Lord Jesus Christ. But beyond these opening salutations, Paul affirms that the Father is God. In 1 Corinthians 8 he speaks about food sacrificed to idols. He says (v. 4) that though food has been sacrificed to idols, there is only one God, and in verse 6, he repeats this point with special reference to the Father. He says, "yet for us there is but one God, the Father, from whom are all things, and we exist for Him."

In 1 Timothy, Paul writes about salvation and says (2:5-6) that there is one God and one mediator between God and man, namely, Christ Jesus. From this we can see that the mediator between God and man is a distinct person, but Paul makes it clear that the mediator is Christ. So the reference to God must be to another member of the Godhead (since it would make little sense to say that Jesus, as mediator, mediates between himself [God] and man). It is more natural to think that he mediates between the human race and God the Father (though, of course, his sacrifice also reconciles himself and the Holy Spirit to us).

Then, there is 1 Pet 1:2. As Peter begins this letter, he reminds his readers that though they are scattered throughout what we call Asia Minor, they are the chosen ones of God. In verse 2, Peter calls the Father God, and notes his work (along with that of the Spirit and Jesus Christ) in saving the chosen ones.

Before leaving our discussion of the Father as God, we should note that the NT presents God as Father in several different respects. First, he is the Father of Jesus Christ in a very special sense (Matt 3:16-17; John 5:26; Matt 11:27; John 1:18; 3:16, 18; 5:26; 1 John 4:9). We must clarify that sense when we formulate the theological doctrine, but the language about Christ as only begotten Son suggests that God's fatherhood of Jesus is unique. It is also true, however, that God is Father in a special sense to those who know Christ as personal Savior. He becomes the Father of believers by giving them spiritual birth. John speaks of believers being born of God, and hence, being unable to engage in a continual pattern of sin (1 John 3:9). Peter speaks of the God who has begotten us (believers in Christ) to a living hope (1 Pet 1:3). Finally, God is called father of all in that he is the creator and sustainer of the universe (Acts 14:15; 17:28; 1 Cor 8:6; Heb 12:9).

Jesus Christ is God. The NT clearly teaches that Jesus Christ is God. In various ways, NT writers show that he is as fully God as is the Father. Of course, in light of such clarity about Christ's nature, it appears that the NT contradicts itself when it says that there is only one God but then designates the Father and Jesus as both God. These phenomena are what the early church fathers wrestled with as they tried to make sense of what Scripture says about God and Christ.

In many different ways the NT teaches that Jesus is God. First, many passages, though not calling Jesus God, amount to saying that he is divine. In two passages in John, for example, Jesus in effect claims to be deity. In John 5 we find Jesus healing a man on the Sabbath, which infuriated the Jews. When they challenged Jesus, he replied (v. 17), "My Father is working until now, and I Myself am working." This made the situation worse, for his accusers understood Jesus to be calling himself God's son and making himself equal with God (v. 18). If Jesus meant that he was God's son in the sense that angels or humans were called sons of God (see discussion of OT data on plurality of God), that would not have merited the charge of blasphemy. But as his accusers complained, Jesus was making himself equal to God, and he never denied their charge, for that was exactly what he meant.

John 10 records a similar incident. Jesus calls himself the good shepherd who gives eternal life to his sheep. In verse 29 Jesus says the Father has given him the sheep, and no one can take them from his hand. Jesus adds (v. 30), "I and the Father are one." Now Jesus might have meant that he agreed with God's will as set forth in Scripture, but, if that was his point, no one would have accused him of blasphemy. When the Jews heard this, however, they took up stones to stone him. When asked why they were doing this, they answered that they did this because he, a mere man, was making himself out to be God. Jesus answered the charge of blasphemy, but not by denying that he is God. His listeners understood him only too well. Rather, Jesus' defense was that in the OT Scriptures mere men (even evil men) who served as judges in Israel were called gods without blasphemy, so why should they object when he did good works and called himself God? His accusers couldn't answer him, but don't be mistaken: Jesus wasn't suggesting that they misunderstood him; he meant that he is God.

The Pauline epistles also contain very strong affirmations that Jesus is divine. In chapter 5, I discussed Phil 2:6, and it is relevant again here. Paul says of Jesus that before the incarnation, he existed in the form of God. As we noted, the phrase *morphē theoû* is best understood as referring to the divine nature; Paul is saying that Jesus is God. Paul adds that Jesus did not think that equality with God was something to be grasped and held onto, no matter what. How could Christ possibly have this attitude if he was not divine himself? Paul says that because Christ had this attitude, he emptied himself, but one cannot empty oneself of something one does not already possess. The point seems quite clear: Jesus is God, but he didn't consider it necessary to hold onto everything that goes with that position. He didn't get rid of his divine nature, but he set aside some of the privileges that come with it by taking on the form of a bondservant and by being made in the likeness of men (v. 7).

In Colossians, Paul makes two very powerful statements about Christ as divine. In Colossians 1, Paul says that in Christ we have redemption and forgiveness of sins. He then says (v. 15) that Jesus is the "image of the invisible God." The word for "image" is *eikōn,* which means "representation" or "likeness." Of this term in this passage Kittel writes:

> Image is not to be understood as a magnitude which is alien to the reality and present only in the consciousness. It has a share in the reality. Indeed, it is the reality. Thus εἰκών does not imply a weakening or a feeble copy of something. It implies the illumination of its inner core and essence.[11]

With this sense, we might even say that Jesus is a "carbon copy" of God. How this could be true and he not be divine is hard to see. In the other passage (Col 2:9), Paul says that in Christ "all the fullness of Deity dwells in bodily form." The Greek is *to plērōma tês theotētos* ("fullness of the Godhead"), and *theotētos* means "Godhead" or "divinity"; it occurs only here in the NT. In this passage, Paul warns the Colossians to beware of philosophies and deceptions that would capture their minds. Rather than following a false belief that claims to initiate one into the depths of spiritual truth, they should follow Christ. Everything they need and all the depths of truth they could desire are to be found in Christ, for "in him dwells the fullness of the Godhead in bodily form." It is hard to imagine that Paul thinks of Jesus as anything but divine.

We should also note Heb 1:3. The writer begins this book by saying that though God revealed himself in many ways during past times (the OT era), in these final days of revelation he has revealed himself in his Son. Verse 3 says that the Son is the radiance of God's glory (*apaugasma tēs doxēs*) and the "exact representation of His nature" (*charaktēr tēs hypostaseōs autoû*). In regard to the former phrase, F. F. Bruce says that *apaugma* appears in both Philo and the Book of Wisdom, but it doesn't mean the same thing there as here. He explains:

> For them the Logos or Wisdom is the personification of a divine attribute; for him the language is descriptive of a man who had lived and died in Palestine a few decades previously, but who nonetheless was the eternal Son and supreme revelation of God. Just as the radiance of

the sun reaches this earth, so in Christ the glorious light of God shines into the hearts of men.[12]

How can this be so? It is so because Christ is the exact representation of God's nature. Bruce's explanation is most illuminating:

> Just as the image and superscription on a coin exactly correspond to the device on the die, so the Son of God "bears the very stamp of his nature" (RSV). The Greek word *charaktēr*, occurring here only in the New Testament, expresses this truth even more emphatically than *eikōn*, which is used elsewhere to denote Christ as the "image" of God (II Cor. 4:4; Col. 1:15). Just as the glory is really in the effulgence, so the substance (Gk. *hypostasis*) of God is really in Christ, who is its impress, its exact representation and embodiment. What God essentially is, is made manifest in Christ. To see Christ is to see what the Father is like.[13]

It would be hard to say it more clearly than this. Jesus Christ is God.

In addition to these general statements that attribute deity to Christ, there is further evidence of his divinity. For example, divine names and titles are applied to Jesus by various NT authors. In a number of passages, he is directly called "God" (*theos*). In John 1:1 John says *theos ēn ho logos* ("the Word was God"). In verse 14, we read that the Word became flesh and dwelt among us. This speaks of Christ's incarnation; hence, John is calling Jesus the Word. But in verse 1 John says the Word was God. Jehovah's Witnesses like to claim that the absence of the definite article with *theos* means that John is saying Jesus is a god (a lesser deity), but not equal to God. However, grammatical studies have shown that in this passage the anarthrous noun before the verb (ēn) focuses on the quality of the thing designated by the noun. So in this case John is saying that the Word was of the quality of God, or qualitatively God. John is saying, then, that the Word is God.[14]

In John 1:18, John calls Jesus the only begotten God (*monogenēs theos*). Later we will discuss what "only begotten" means, but the verse does call Jesus God. Similarly, John refers to Jesus as God in 1 John 5:20. There he calls Jesus the "true God" (*alēthinos theos*), and *alēthinos* means true in the sense of genuine. In other words, Jesus conforms to the ideal Godhead; he is the "real thing" (see also John 20:28).

In Tit 2:13, Paul calls Jesus "our great God and our Savior, Jesus Christ" (author's translation). At first glance, it might seem that Paul is speaking about two separate individuals, one who is the great God and the other who is Jesus Christ. However, grammatically, when two singular nouns are connected by "and" (*kai*), and the second has no article, the article governing the first noun governs the second. Hence, "God" and "Savior" form a conjunct that refers to the same person. Paul says Jesus is both God and Savior (see also Rom 9:5).

A final passage where Jesus is called God is Heb 1:8. The writer depicts God the Father saying various things to angels, but then (v. 8) he says something to the Son. The writer quotes from Ps 45:6 as what the Father says to the Son: "But of the Son He says, 'Thy throne, O God, is forever and ever.'" Jesus is called God, and it isn't the writer but God himself who says this.

In addition to Christ being called "God," there are NT passages where he is called the Son of God, and it means that he has the divine nature. We already noted John 5:18, where Christ's Jewish listeners were upset that he made himself equal to God. The verse also says that he was calling God his own Father; the phrase, "making himself equal with God," is then offered as an explanation of what it meant for Christ to call God his Father. Though the wording doesn't say that Jesus is God's Son, the phrase in question clearly means just that. Moreover, from the phrase "making himself equal . . ." we see that Jesus' hearers understood him to mean that he was divine.

We have also discussed John 10:30ff. As Jesus defended himself, in verse 36 he asks why his accusers are disturbed when he calls himself the Son of God, since Scripture uses that language in regard to wicked judges (vv. 34-35 quoting Ps 82:6). After his betrayal, when Jesus is brought before the high priest, the high priest asks him if he is the Son of God (Matt 26:63). Jesus' reply (v. 64) affirms that he believes himself to be the Son of God, and that is exactly what the high priest understood (v. 65). Christ is accused of blasphemy, and blasphemers are to be put to death (v. 66). This is the specific charge brought against Jesus to put him to death. Later, when the Roman magistrate Pilate asks what wrong Jesus has done, the Jews' complaint (John 19:7) is that he claimed to be the Son of God.

Frequently in the NT Jesus is also called Lord. The Greek word is *kyrios*, the word the Septuagint uses to render the OT יהוה, the name of Israel's God. To apply this name to Jesus clearly asserts his full deity. Many NT passages call Christ Lord, so the following list is only selective. Matthew 3 begins with John the Baptist calling people to repentance. Matthew says John fulfills Isaiah's prophecy in Isa 40:3, but that prophecy predicted a forerunner who would make ready the way of the Lord (*kyrios*). Since John announces Jesus' coming, Matthew is in effect calling Christ Lord by applying Isa 40:3 to him. In Luke 2:11, the angel announces the birth of Jesus who is Christ the Lord. After Jesus washes his disciples' feet, he notes that they call him teacher and Lord, and says that they are right, for he is. In the great kenosis passage, Paul writes that because of Jesus' willing humiliation to the point of death to meet our needs, God raised Christ from the dead and gave him a name that is above every name. Paul then adds that someday every knee will bow and every tongue confess that Jesus Christ is Lord (*kyrios*). Though many rejected him, they will have to admit that he is the one true living God (Phil 2:10-11). See also Rom 10:9; Eph 1:2; Gal 1:3; 1 Cor 1:3-4.

Another title of deity applied to Jesus is "The Lord of Glory." In 1 Cor 2:8 Paul says that if the worldly wise were truly wise, they would have recognized who Jesus is and would not have crucified him. In crucifying him, they put to death the Lord of Glory. This designation for Christ becomes even more signifi-

462 □ No One Like Him

cant in light of Ps 24:8-10. The psalmist speaks of the King of Glory and asks who that is. He replies that it is the Lord. From such an OT passage the linking of Yahweh with the King of Glory would have been well-known to Paul. In 1 Corinthians 2 Paul applies this title to Jesus, clearly attributing deity to him.

In Acts 3:14 Peter tells his listeners that they disowned the Holy and Righteous One, when given a choice between Jesus and a murderer, Barabbas. This is significant in light of OT designations of God as the Holy One. In Hos 11:9 God refers to himself as the Holy One, in contrast to a mere mortal, and it clearly signifies his deity. Isaiah is especially fond of referring to God this way (e.g., Isa 1:4; 5:19, 24; 10:20; 12:6; 17:7; 29:19; 30:11, 12, 15; 41:14, 16; 43:14; 45:11; 48:17; 49:7; 54:5; 55:5; 60:9, 14; see also Jer 50:29; 51:5; Ezek 39:7). With so many of these references to Yahweh, it is hard to miss the point of calling Jesus the Holy One.

In Rev 1:17-18 Jesus is called "the first and the last" (v. 13 clarifies that it is Christ of whom John speaks). Applying this title to Jesus is again significant because of what we find in the OT. In Isa 44:6, Yahweh, the King of Israel says, "I am the first and I am the last, and there is no God besides Me" (see also Isa 48:12). Hence, in Revelation 1 a title clearly applied to Yahweh is now applied to Christ, and the intent to attribute deity by doing so is hard to mistake.

The result of applying these names and titles to Jesus is significant. Most NT authors were Jews who had been raised in Judaism. They knew the OT well enough, and as Jews they would have been intensely monotheistic. Despite all of this, they deliberately applied these titles to Christ, thereby indicating their conviction that he is God. Likewise, Jesus fully knew the OT import of these names, and he also knew what the Mosaic Law said about blasphemy. Nevertheless, he not only permitted these terms to be used of him but at times even encouraged his followers to do so, and on various occasions he used some of these titles in regard to himself.

Further evidence of Christ's deity stems from the fact that NT writers predicated attributes of Christ that belong only to God. By saying that Christ possesses those qualities, they were attributing deity to him. We find, for example, that he is eternal and fully living (John 1:4; 1 John 5:11, 12). He is immutable (Heb 1:10-12; 13:8); omnipotent (Phil 3:20-21; John 5:19; Rev 1:8); omniscient (John 2:24-25 [cf. Jer 17:9-10]; 6:64; 21:17); omnipresent, despite his limitations in space and time during his earthly pilgrimage (Matt 18:20; 28:20; John 14:23); loving (John 13:1, 34; 1 John 3:16); truth (John 14:6); holy (Luke 1:35); and possessing life in and of himself, i.e., having the attribute of aseity (John 5:26). Mere humans might possess some of these attributes, such as love and truth, in a limited sense, but the large spectrum of attributes mentioned could only be true of one who is God. NT writers were fully aware of this, and yet did not hesitate to attribute these characteristics to Jesus. These attributes underscore the truth of Paul's claim (Col 2:9) that in Christ all the fulness of the Godhead dwells.

Another line of evidence for Christ's deity is the various works he does. While a mere human could do some things he did, other things only God could do. For example, through Christ all things were created (John 1:3, 10; Col 1:16), and by his power the whole universe is sustained (Col 1:17; Heb 1:3). To paraphrase Paul (Col 1:17), it is because of Christ that our universe does not come unglued. Then on occasion Christ forgives sins (Mark 2:5-12). Human beings can say that they forgive others' sins, but only God can do so in a way that clears the records before God. Hence, Paul urges believers in their interpersonal relations to forgive others for wrongdoing, even as Christ has forgiven our sins (Col 3:13). Then, even as no one but God can create and give physical life, only God can give eternal life. In speaking of his relation to his sheep, Jesus says that he gives them eternal life so that they won't perish, and no one can take them out of his hand (John 10:28). In addition, only supernatural power can resurrect the dead, and Jesus claimed that he was the resurrection and the life (John 11:24-25). But he did even more than that: he raised Lazarus from the dead (John 11:43-44; see also John 5:21, 28-29). And finally, only God has the right to judge humankind and determine their ultimate destiny, but the NT teaches that judgment of all people is given to Christ (Acts 10:42; 17:31; John 5:22, 27). If Jesus Christ is not divine, then claiming that he can do these works that only God could do is blasphemy. NT writers would know that, but they attributed those works to him, anyway. They clearly understood him to be God.

Two other lines of evidence show that Christ is divine. One is the NT habit of taking OT passages about God or God's Son and applying them to Jesus. For example, in Isaiah 6 Isaiah is lifted into heaven and catches a vision of God seated on the throne, but John 12:41 says it was actually Jesus whom Isaiah saw. In Ps 2:7 God says, "Thou art My Son, today I have begotten Thee." However, as Paul preaches in Pisidian Antioch (Acts 13:33), he applies this verse to Christ, claiming that he is God's Son. Similarly, in Hebrews 1, the author introduces Jesus as the fullness of revelation of God. He is above the angels, for, as the writer says, to which one of the angels did God ever say, "Thou art My Son, today I have begotten Thee"? (v. 5) The answer is none, but God did say this to Christ. Furthermore, Ps 110:1 is applied on several occasions to Christ. On the day of Pentecost (Acts 2) Peter says that God raised Christ from the dead and exalted him to the right hand of God. To further make his point, in verses 34-35 Peter quotes Ps 110:1 and notes that it was not David, the psalm's author, who ascended into heaven and whom the Lord told to sit at his right hand. Peter says this passage refers to Christ, and the writer of Hebrews similarly applies Ps 110:1 to Jesus (Heb 1:13; 10:12-13). Certainly these writers knew that Psalm 2 and 110 were considered messianic psalms and that in effect they were predicating deity and sonship to the Messiah. Yet none of them hesitated to apply these passages to Christ (see also Paul's application of Ps 68:18 to Christ in Eph 4:7, 8; and Peter's allusion to Isa 8:13 as he commands believers in 1 Pet 3:15 to sanctify Christ as Lord in their hearts).

This is consistent with what we saw about OT teaching concerning the

Messiah. In various places the OT identifies him as God. We saw the same thing about the angel of the Lord. In the NT, Jesus is repeatedly presented as the long-awaited Messiah of Israel (e.g., Matt 1:16; 16:16, 20; John 11:27). Moreover, we have also seen that he is repeatedly called God. Hence, exactly what we expected from OT teaching—that there is plurality in the Godhead because of a Messiah who is divine—is confirmed in the NT. What the NT adds, of course, is that Jesus of Nazareth is that person who is both Messiah and God.

The final line of NT evidence teaching Christ's deity is the worship given to him. In the NT on various occasions apostles refused to let people worship them (e.g., Acts 10:25-26; 14:11-15). Moreover, mere angels refuse worship (Rev 22:8-9). Jesus himself explicitly taught that only God deserves worship. In light of these facts, it is most instructive to see that Christ did accept and even encourage worship of himself (Matt 15:25-28; 28:9-10; John 9:35-39). In fact, Jesus even said (John 5:23) that those who do not honor the Son do not honor the Father who sent him, so those who think it is appropriate to worship the Father and ignore the Son are severely mistaken. Beyond that, the Father commands worship of Christ (Heb 1:6), and Paul writes that someday worship of Christ will be universal (Phil 2:10-11). If Jesus is not God, all of this is blasphemy.

The conclusion from all these data rings loud and clear: Jesus Christ is God! How that is so in light of biblical teaching that there is only one God is nowhere resolved in Scripture. It is, however, a major reason why early church fathers felt compelled to work out a synthesis of these seemingly incompatible data. Those living during Christ's life on earth and who even saw him after the resurrection experienced him as divine. The NT affirms the same thing. There is no question that some sort of discussion (even controversy) about how these things all could be true was inevitable.

The Holy Spirit is God. Further NT evidence of plurality in the Godhead comes from NT teaching about the Holy Spirit. Uniformly, he is affirmed as God. Let us consider some of the NT evidence for his deity.

First, various passages call the Holy Spirit God. For example, Acts 5 records the incident of Ananias and Sapphira lying to the Holy Spirit (v. 3). Peter is clear that they have lied to God (v. 4). In 1 Cor 3:16-17 and 6:19-20, Paul speaks about believers being the temple of the Holy Spirit. These passages clearly show that to be indwelt by the Holy Spirit is to be indwelt by God. Moreover, in 2 Cor 3:17-18, Paul writes that the Lord (*kyrios*) is the Spirit. It would be hard to say more directly than this that the Holy Spirit is God. Furthermore, Stephen (Acts 7) accuses his Jewish listeners of resisting the Holy Spirit as their fathers did. But whom did their fathers resist? The OT shows that they resisted God.

Some NT writers cite OT passages and attribute then to the Holy Spirit, even though the OT passages are uttered by God. A few examples illustrate the point. In Acts 28:25-27 Paul says that the Holy Spirit spoke through Isaiah to their fathers. He then quotes from Isa 6:1-13 (esp. vv. 9-10), but in Isaiah 6, it is the Lord God who says these words. This deliberately links the Holy Spirit with God. Implicitly, Paul is saying that the Holy Spirit is God.

Two other examples appear in the book of Hebrews. The writer introduces Heb 3:7-11 with the words, "just as the Holy Spirit says," and then he quotes from Ps 95:7-11. However, in Psalm 95 it is the psalmist telling the people to listen to God's voice (vv. 7-11 capture the basic content of Heb 3:7-11). This is an example of the habit of many NT writers to equate the words of Scripture (whether spoken by God or the human writer) with those of the Holy Spirit. Since Scripture was deemed revelation from God and inspired by the Holy Spirit (see 1 Cor 2:9-13), by quoting OT Scripture and attributing it to the Holy Spirit, the writer of Hebrews attributes it to God. But that means he must think the Holy Spirit is God. An even clearer case of calling the Holy Spirit God is found in Heb 10:15-17. The author says that "the Holy Spirit also bears witness to us, . . . saying . . ." and then he quotes from Jer 31:31-34. But, in Jeremiah 31, the Lord utters the words quoted in Heb 10:16-17. Granting biblical inerrancy, the most natural conclusion is that the writer of Hebrews assumes that the Holy Spirit is divine.

In addition to instances where the Holy Spirit is declared to be God, we also find that he has attributes only God could have. He is eternal (Heb 9:14); omniscient (1 Cor 2:10-11; John 14:26; 16:12f.); powerful (Rom 8:2; 15:19); and truth (1 John 5:7). Moreover, various works that only God could do are ascribed to the Holy Spirit. He regenerates those who turn to Christ in faith (John 3:5-8); he sanctifies believers as they grow in Christ (1 Pet 1:2); and he reveals God's truth to biblical writers and inspires what they write (2 Pet 1:21; 1 Cor 2:12-13). Moreover, it is the Holy Spirit who convicts the world of sin, righteousness, and judgment (John 16:8-11), and we even learn in Rom 8:11 that he was involved in resurrecting Christ from the dead. Only God could do these deeds. NT writers would know that, and yet they said that the Holy Spirit did those things. They thought of him as God.

There are also passages that describe the Holy Spirit exercising the prerogatives of deity. For example, Acts 8:29 shows that he can issue a direct order, and when he does, it must be obeyed. He exercises a sovereign will in distributing spiritual gifts as he chooses to believers (1 Cor 12:4, 7-8, 11). Moreover, even as the Father and Son are to be worshiped and reverenced, so also the Holy Spirit. In fact, Jesus is very clear that rejecting the Holy Spirit's testimony is blasphemy, and those who do so will be punished (Matt 12:31-32). In fact, Christ says in this passage, rejecting the Holy Spirit's testimony, and thereby not taking him seriously, is the one sin that is unpardonable.

NT writers clearly consider the Holy Spirit deity. But this only heightens the impression of logical inconsistency, for the NT not only claims that there is only one God, but also that the Father, Son, and Holy Spirit are all divine. Before turning to the historical controversies over these ideas, we must present further NT teaching about the plurality of God.

Father, Son, and Holy Spirit are distinct persons. One way to resolve the apparent inconsistency of God being one and yet three is to claim that Father, Son, and Holy Spirit are not really distinct individuals. Rather, these are three different names given to the one God, names that bespeak various roles God plays in relation to the world. Though this would remove the alleged contradiction, this option is foreclosed by biblical teaching that the three are distinct. Several passages make this point.

Matt 3:16-17 records the baptism of Jesus. Jesus is God, so we might think that on this occasion God is functioning solely in his "Son role." However, as Jesus is baptized the Spirit descends upon him as a dove, and out of heaven the Father says, "This is My beloved Son, in whom I am well-pleased." If Father, Son, and Holy Spirit are not distinct persons, this is quite a feat of ventriloquism and optical illusion! And, it isn't clear, then, whether it is the voice from heaven, the dove, or Jesus performing these feats. The most sensible way to understand this incident is that the three are distinct persons.

In John 14 and 15 Jesus tells his disciples of his nearing departure, but he explains that they won't be left alone, because he and the Father will send the Holy Spirit as "another Helper" (John 14:16, 26; 15:26). If Father, Son, and Holy Spirit are not distinct persons, this promise makes no sense. It is the Son alone who would do the sending, and he would send himself. Or, if the Son is only a mirage (i.e., he is really the Father or the Spirit in disguise), we have a similar problem with either the Father sending himself or the Spirit sending himself. Moreover, it makes no sense to promise *another* Helper, for unless Jesus, the Father, and Spirit are distinct, there is no *other* Helper. The sanest way to understand these promises is that Father, Son, and Holy Spirit are distinct individuals.

Other instances of distinct persons are recorded in John 12:27-30 (the Father is invoked, and then the multitude hears the voice from heaven) and at the Mount of Transfiguration (Matt 17:5; Mark 9:7; Luke 9:35; 2 Pet 1:17). There are also passages that speak of various members of the Godhead involved in the salvation process but with distinct roles; if they are not distinct, such language is misleading and inappropriate—e.g., 1 Pet 1:1-2; 2 Thess 2:13-14. Beyond that, if Father, Son, and Holy Spirit are not distinct persons, think of what that does to Jesus' prayers to his Father. When he asks that the cup of agony that awaits him be removed (Matt 26:42), he is really only talking to himself; and when he asks to be glorified with the glory he had before the world was (John 17:1, 5), he is only speaking to himself. In fact, his whole high priestly prayer (John 17) is no prayer after all. On the contrary, these things indicate the distinctness of the three persons of the Godhead.

Yet Father, Son, and Holy Spirit are one. If Father, Son, and Holy Spirit are distinct individuals, then perhaps they are three separate Gods. Obviously, this will not exactly resolve the tension between biblical teaching about God as one and yet three, but it is one possible conclusion from the data already presented that call Father, Son, and Spirit God.

Though this is a possible conclusion, further NT teaching forestalls it. There is evidence that the Father, Son, and Spirit are considered as one. Various passages show that the writers and speakers mean more than just that the three happen to think alike. Rather, ontological (though that word is never used in Scripture) unity is the point. Christ's listeners understood this to be his point, and they accused him of blasphemy. That charge could easily have been refuted by Jesus saying that his point was that he agrees with God's way of thinking. While Jesus and the Father do agree, Jesus never used that defense. Instead, his response to the accusation shows that he was saying exactly what they thought.

John 10:30 is perhaps the clearest assertion to that effect, but Jesus also says that having seen him, his disciples have seen the Father (John 14:9), so they need not further ask him to show them the Father. The language of Christ's high priestly prayer (John 17:21, 22, 23) about Christ being in the Father and the Father in him suggests the same thing. Moreover, passages such as Col 1:15 and Heb 1:8 not only clarify that Christ is God, but the language (eikōn, charaktēr) speaks of unity between the two.

There are also passages that teach that the Son and the Spirit are one. In Rom 8:9-10 Paul speaks of the indwelling of the Holy Spirit, but he says that anyone who does not have the Holy Spirit does not belong to Christ. Thus, in having Christ, one also has the Holy Spirit and vice versa. All of this suggests their unity. Moreover, consider 2 Cor 3:17. As we have already seen, this verse says that the Lord is the Spirit, and the word for Lord is kyrios, the Greek for the Hebrew yhwh. Many see kyrios here as a reference to Jesus who, of course, is often called by this name. In that case, the verse asserts unity between the Son and the Spirit.

Finally, there is unity between the Father and the Spirit. First Corinthians 3:16 is often adduced for this point. Paul tells believers that their bodies are the temple of the Holy Spirit, for in them God dwells. Apparently, then, in having the Spirit in us, we also have the Father (Col 1:27 speaks of Christ also indwelling the believer). The unity between Father and Spirit is also evident in 1 Cor 2:10-11, for their unity enables the Spirit (as no mere human could) to reveal the things of God.

From these data, we see that the way to resolve the tension between one and three is not to deny the unity of God in favor of polytheistic tritheism. The unity of Father, Son, and Holy Spirit requires us to look elsewhere for a resolution.

Various NT phenomena suggest equality of the three. From biblical teaching surveyed so far, the most natural conclusion is that if there is only one God and yet Father, Son, and Holy Spirit are God, the three most likely are equals. Indeed, if there is any metaphysical difference among them in terms of their essence, we are on the road to polytheism. Hence, the most natural conclusion is that they are ontologically equal. Scripture uses neither the term "ontological" nor "metaphysical," and outside of the data presented to the effect that the three are one, there is no direct biblical claim that the three are equal. Still, certain elements of NT teaching fit this notion of equality, even if they don't directly teach it.

An initial point is how NT authors list the members of the Godhead when speaking of all three together. If the three were inherently unequal, we might expect a consistent order in listing them whenever they are mentioned together. This might even seem like a formulaic prioritizing of the three. However, the NT refers to the three together in a variety of orders. In Matt 28:19 Christ tells his disciples to baptize new disciples in the name of the Father, Son, and Holy Spirit. In 1 Cor 12:4-6, the order is Spirit, Lord (Jesus), and God. Yet again in Eph 4:4-6 Paul speaks of one Spirit, one Lord, and one God and Father of all; but in 2 Cor 13:14 his order is Lord Jesus Christ, God, and the Holy Spirit. When Peter speaks of each one's part in salvation (1 Pet 1:2), his order is the "foreknowledge of God the Father, by the sanctifying work of the Spirit, that you may obey Jesus Christ and be sprinkled with His blood."

We must not conclude too much from these facts. NT writers are not saying that they use various orders in listing the three *in order to* make the further point that the three are equal. To conclude that would be more than the data warrant. On the other hand, if the three did form an ontological hierarchy and were always listed in a certain order, we might suspect that there was a reason for such a consistent formula. Of course, to confirm that this is what the writers meant to communicate, they would need to tell us that this consistent order is intended to make an ontological point. However, any ontological point that might be made to that effect is totally undercut because NT writers seem to associate the three as equals and refer to them in no particular order. That this is so suggests to some that in fact the three must be equal.

Others have noted that Jesus commands that new disciples be baptized in the name of all three (Matt 28:19). The verse's grammatical construction links the three (Father, Son, Holy Spirit) together as three coordinate nouns by using the word *kai* ("and") between each of the three nouns. The argument is essentially that converts are to be baptized in the name of each because each is fully and equally God. If one or more were of lesser worth or dignity, we might expect the baptismal formula to refer only to the greatest.

Here again this line of argument cannot be conclusive. The grammatical point is well taken, but we need arguments other than general rules to prove that the author intends this construction to say that the three are equal in being. It is dubious that grammar alone can make that conceptual point. Moreover, it could be argued that all three are listed because all three participate in the salvatory process, but that participation does not itself prove ontological equality. Human beings also participate in that process by exercising faith, but that doesn't make us divine. It seems that the most we can say is that the baptismal formula is consistent with equality of the three, but it doesn't teach it directly, nor can it prove that point.

Some have also argued that equality is suggested by the formula of the Pauline benediction in 2 Cor 13:14. Each member of the Godhead is invoked along with a particular activity or attribute, and the three are linked together grammatically with *kai* between each phrase. Though this may suggest to some equality among the three, my initial responses are the same as those made about the baptismal formula. In addition, I think it is risky business to make too much over the form and content of opening or closing salutations of NT epistles. If we force them to make ontological points, we are in serious trouble at least in regard to many of the Pauline letters. Paul begins many of his letters by wishing his readers grace and peace from God the Father and the Lord Jesus Christ, with no mention of the Holy Spirit. If we are to draw ontological conclusions from such salutations, should we conclude that the Holy Spirit isn't divine at all, since he is not invoked? Obviously, such a conclusion would be unwarranted, but then we should see that the same applies with respect to this closing benediction. It is even more critical not to conclude too much about such formulas, because although 2 Cor 13:14 ends the book by invoking the blessing of all three, 2 Corinthians begins with wishing the readers grace and peace from the Father and Son, but doesn't mention the Holy Spirit at all (2 Cor 1:2).

Perhaps more suggestive of equality are passages in John's Gospel that speak specifically of the Son's relation to the Holy Spirit. In John 14:16 Jesus promises to send another Helper (the Holy Spirit) when he leaves. The word translated "another" is *allos*, which typically means "another of the same kind." Some would like to understand this as affirming ontological equality between Son and Spirit. That is possible, but it is equally possible that Jesus is only saying that the Holy Spirit will be the same kind of Helper that he is. That need not be an ontological point at all, but may simply recommend the Spirit as a very capable Helper. What makes this latter point all the more probable is that *allos* modifies the noun *paraklētos*, "Helper." So, it is not particularly clear that Jesus is saying that the Holy Spirit is a divine being of the same kind or essence that he is. The least we can say is that Jesus believes that in getting the Holy Spirit, they will lose none of the help he would give them. His ability to help and that of the Holy Spirit are of equal kind.

Later in chapter 14 (v. 26) Jesus says that the Father will send the Holy Spirit in Jesus' name. To some this suggests equality among the three. That may be part of what Jesus is thinking, but the fundamental point is that the sending of the Holy Spirit after Christ's departure is an event in which Father, Son, and Holy Spirit will all participate. To conclude something about ontological equality of the three on this basis seems to conclude more than the verse warrants.

Perhaps the best passage in John's Gospel from which to argue the equality of the three is John 16:13-15. Jesus speaks of the Holy Spirit guiding the apostles into all truth. He says that the Spirit will take of his things and disclose them to the disciples. He then adds that all things that the Father has belong to him as well. But then, if the Holy Spirit takes of the things of the Lord, he also takes of the things of the Father. Since the subject of these verses is revealing truth, the likely point is that the three members of the Godhead each know what the others know (a point further confirmed in 1 Cor 2:11ff.

about the Father and the Spirit). From this we may conclude that if one of the three is omniscient, then the other two must be as well. Of course, while this may be a warranted inference from John 16, it is an inference several steps removed from the specific teaching of the passage.

These, then, are the kinds of data that some thinkers find suggestive of equality of Father, Son, and Holy Spirit. The last item is most helpful, but all of these data are inferential, and the inference to equality of being is not the only possible inference. Still, these teachings are part of the data one finds in the NT with respect to Father, Son, and Holy Spirit.

NT clarification of member of Godhead involved in a divine act. Here the point is about the relation of OT and NT texts. In the OT various actions are attributed simply to God, in particular to Yahweh. On the other hand, the NT more specifically attributes those divine acts either to the Son or to the Holy Spirit. Hence, while all members of the Godhead are involved in every divine action, a certain member is more particularly designated in the NT as the one doing it.

The point is easy enough to illustrate. In the OT Yahweh is depicted as the redeemer and savior, whereas in the NT it is the Son of God who clearly stands out in that capacity. See such OT passages as Job 19:25; Ps 19:14; 78:35; 106:21; Isa 41:14; 43:3, 11, 14; 47:4; 49:7, 26; 60:16; and Hos 13:4. In contrast, the NT depicts Christ as Savior in passages like Matt 1:21; Luke 1:76-79; 2:11; John 4:42; Gal 3:13; 4:5; Phil 3:20; and Tit 2:13-14.

This same narrowing of focus also occurs with respect to the Holy Spirit's ministry. In the OT, Yahweh is said to dwell among Israel and in the hearts of those who fear him (see, for example, Ps 74:2; 135:21; Isa 8:18; 57:15; Ezek 43:7-9; Joel 3:17, 21; and Zech 2:10, 11). In the NT, the Holy Spirit indwells the members of the church (see Acts 2:4; Rom 8:9, 11; 1 Cor 3:16; Gal 4:6; Eph 2:22; and Jas 4:5).

None of this means that either the Son or the Spirit were idle in the OT, or that the Father is idle in the NT. It just shows that in the progress of revelation things become clearer as to how the divine persons participate in various divine acts.

NT language of begetting of the Son and sending/proceeding of the Spirit. There is another set of phenomena we must mention before leaving the biblical data. I raise it now but will postpone explanation of it until later in the chapter. The reason for mentioning it now is that these passages figure in some of the controversies over the Trinity in early church history. We need to understand them in light of those controversies.

Though the Son is clearly divine and cannot be created, a number of NT passages speak of him as though he did begin to exist. In Johannine literature, Jesus is repeatedly called the only begotten Son of the Father. The Greek word is *monogenēs*, and the phrase "only begotten Son" (or in John 1:18, "only begotten God") appears in John 1:14, 18; 3:16, 18; 1 John 4:9. Outside of these references, the phrase isn't used again of Jesus. We should add, however, Ps 2:7, if we consider it a reference to the Messiah (the LXX reads *sēmeron gegennēka se*, "this day I have begotten you"). In addition, we should include Paul's claim (Col 1:15) that Jesus is the "firstborn of all creation." The word for "firstborn" is *prōtotokos*, and the whole phrase is used only here in regard to Jesus Christ. What we should make of such language isn't clear, nor does Scripture itself explain it. That doesn't make it impossible to understand these verses, but only means that no other passage explains what these verses mean. From these verses various early church fathers felt compelled to hold the doctrine of the eternal generation of the Son, but more on what that means in the historical section of this chapter.

As to the Holy Spirit, Jesus says that he will send the Holy Spirit when he leaves (John 16:7). Jesus also promises in John 14:26 that the Father will send the Spirit after Jesus' departure. Moreover, in John 15:26 Jesus promises to send the Spirit from the Father. But he also says that the Spirit "proceeds from the Father." On the surface, these passages seem only to be about the coming of the Holy Spirit, which occurred in a special way at Pentecost. However, theologians have seen in these phrases (especially the claim that the Spirit proceeds from the Father) much more. They have concluded that these verses teach the eternal procession of the Spirit, parallel to the eternal generation of the Son.

This concludes our survey of biblical data relevant to the doctrine of the Trinity.[15] While Scripture says much about this, there are things it does not say. Nowhere does Scripture use the term "Trinity," nor does it state the doctrine as it has been passed down through church history. Nor is there explanation of how there can be only one God, and yet Father, Son, Holy Spirit, Messiah, and Angel of the Lord are called God. Moreover, there is no talk of one *essence* or of three *persons*. Biblical writers don't talk about subsistences, substances, or modes of being (the first and third terms are nowhere used in any sense in Scripture). But such language and more is used in doctrinal formulations of the Trinity, and evangelical theology in our own day articulates the doctrine in these very terms. What does this language mean, how did it get introduced into the discussion, and why? The answers are the subject of our historical study in the next section.

HISTORY AND THE DOCTRINE OF THE TRINITY

As we have seen, the doctrine of the Trinity is nowhere in Scripture stated as such, but biblical teaching implies it. It is always difficult to construct historical explanations of why certain events or movements of thought arise. Still, we can offer some idea of what motivated the development of this doctrine.

Roger Haight argues that the question about the Trinity initially arose out of early Christians' experience of salvation in or through Jesus and in the Holy

Spirit.[16] Jesus' disciples during his life on earth came to view him as Messiah and Lord. Moreover, as the gospel spread in the decades after the life of Christ, more people came to experience the salvation and lordship of Christ. It was natural that Christians would begin to ask about Christ's exact relation to God.

Questions about Christ raised problems from two perspectives. On the one hand, most of the very first Christians converted from Judaism. With their intensely monotheistic background, there must have been some cognitive dissonance between their belief in one God and their belief that Jesus is divine. The monotheism of these Jewish-Christians plus the NT guarded Christianity from moving too far in the direction of a tritheistic view of three divine beings.

On the other hand, as the gospel began to spread throughout the Greco-Roman world so that significant numbers of Gentiles turned to Christ, there were several tensions upon Christian thinking from the Greco-Roman milieu. Gnostic thinking was one of them. Gnostics held that there were a series of emanations from the primal reality, and each emanation was of a different order or rank. Some joined this idea with Christian belief about Christ and viewed him as one of those emanations. Of course, this could not match biblical teaching, for Scripture does not suggest that Christ is just one of a series of emanations. Nor does biblical language about Jesus as God and equal with the Father fit the Gnostic idea of a being dependent on a higher being.[17]

In addition to Gnostic pressures, there were also influences from Platonism and Stoicism. According to various forms of Platonism, God's mind contains the forms or archetypal ideas for all things. He created specific things in the world after the pattern of their perfect archetype. Divine reason that contains such ideas and created according to them was the Logos. In Philo's philosophy, the Logos in creating all things is born or projected into the world. As Hodge explains, Philo called the Logos as manifested in the world in this way "not only λόγος, but also υἱός, εἰκών, υἱὸς μονογενές, πρωτόγονος, σκία, παράδειγμα, δόξα, ἐπιστήμη, θεοῦ, and δεύτερος θεός."[18] The concept of the Logos was easily connected to Christianity by transferring it to Christ. Of course, this makes Christ's deity subordinate and his generation less than eternal.

There was also a third pressure from Greco-Roman thinking that is not often noted. William Schoedel argues persuasively that in confronting the Greco-Roman world, Christianity, on the one hand, had to answer the charge of atheism, and on the other, had to make itself palatable to people who believed in the Greco-Roman pantheon of gods. So prevalent was the belief in multiple gods in the Greco-Roman world that Christianity was accused of atheism because of its belief in only one God. As many historians have shown, a major part of the burden of early church apologists was to show that Christianity is not atheistic. Schoedel argues persuasively that part of the impetus for the church to flesh out the doctrine of the Trinity was to offer it as an alternative to polytheism without being exclusively unitarian. For people inclined to believe in various gods a Trinity in unity offered a more attractive option than strict unitarianism.[19]

Tertullian

Though we cannot discuss every turn in the historical development of the doctrine, some of the more important events are worthy of mention. Initially, we turn to Tertullian's (A.D. 160–225) contribution.[20] It was Tertullian who first coined the term "Trinity" (*trinitas*) and used the concept of persons. Both Tertullian and Hippolytus are credited with introducing the idea of the "economic" Trinity, which emphasizes how the persons in the Godhead relate to one another in their work of creation and redemption. According to Tertullian, at the point of creating the universe, the Son was generated, though prior to that time God could not be said to have a Son in the strictest understanding of the doctrine of God. But, being generated to accomplish this task, the Son was a person (*persona* in Latin).

This must not be misunderstood. As Kelly explains, Tertullian basically adopted the view of God held by the Apologists and articulated by Irenaeus. For Irenaeus, in himself God is the Father of everything, but he contains in himself his Word and his Wisdom. Hence, Son and Spirit are eternal, as is God, but it is only in the process of God's self-disclosure in creating (and later, in redemption) that God extrapolates or manifests the Son and Spirit.[21] The comprehensive term that Irenaeus used for these activities was *oikonomia* (Greek) or *dispensatio* (Latin).[22] The English translation is "economy," but connotations of that English word mask its meaning in this discussion. An economy or dispensation is a particular ordering of things. Since the "ordering of things" that we know of in regard to God is his work in the world, the notion of the "economic Trinity" is often used to refer to the actions or works of God in our world and to how the three persons of the Godhead relate to one another in accomplishing that work. Strictly speaking, however, the notion of the economy of the Trinity meant in Irenaeus, Tertullian, and Hippolytus the manifesting of God in the persons of the Son and Spirit in creation and redemption.

In holding this view, Tertullian argued that God was alone before creation in that there was nothing external to him, but of course, there was always with him his own Reason or Word as a distinct individual. In addition, there is the Spirit, who is the Son's representative. He comes forth from the Father by way of the Son, just as a "shoot is third from the root, and as the channel drawn off from the river is third from the spring, and as the light-point in the beam is third from the sun."[23] Tertullian also refers to the Spirit as a person, so there are three persons, or a Trinity, in the Godhead. Tertullian writes:

> We believe in one only God, yet subject to this dispensation, which is our word for economy, that the one only God has also a Son, His Word, Who has issued out of Himself . . . which Son then sent, according to His promise, the Holy Spirit, the Paraclete, out of the Father.[24]

Hence, Tertullian claimed that there is divine unity, despite the three distinct persons. But Tertullian was most concerned to maintain that there was unity in the Godhead. The three persons were a distribution (*distinctio* or *dispositio*) of the divine nature, but not a division or separation (*separatio*) of it. As Kelly explains, Tertullian typically expressed this unity by saying that the three are one in "substance" (*substantia*). Father, Son, and Spirit have the same substance, which has been extended or distributed into three persons but is not separated into distinct substances.[25]

So the term "substance" for Tertullian meant what we have described as the being or essence of the divine nature. However, Tertullian spoke of the diversity in the Godhead in terms of persons. The Greek for this is *prosōpon* and the Latin is *persona*. The Greek term originally meant "face" and thus, "expression" and later "role," but it eventually came to signify "individual," with the emphasis on the external or objective presentation of a thing. The Latin term comes from two Latin words *per* ("through") and *sonō* ("to sound"). So a *persona* was something one could make a sound through. Quickly, this term came to mean a "mask" that actors used in a play to portray a character. The actor would literally speak his part through the mask ("sound through") in portraying the character. From this meaning, it wasn't far to apply it to the actor or actress who wore the mask and to the character portrayed. In a legal sense, it came to refer to the holder of a title of a property. For Tertullian, its use in relation to the Trinity denoted the concrete presentation of an individual as that individual. To understand this, we must remember what Tertullian says about the Word and Spirit always being with the Father, but then later being distributed and extrapolated in the economy of creation and redemption; i.e., in creation and redemption, Son and Spirit become distinctly manifested as specific agents in these divine actions. The idea of presenting objectively as an individual what is inherent and internal to a thing seems clear. As Kelly and others note, this sense of person is rather removed from modern conceptions of person as distinct centers of consciousness possessing self-consciousness.[26]

Though Tertullian mentions Father, Son, and Spirit as distinct persons, his main concern is to affirm the unity of the divine nature against any who would think Christians are polytheistic in any way. After Tertullian, we find two developments in the late second and third centuries that underscored the church's need to reach some agreement on its understanding of the Trinity. Those two developments are dynamic monarchianism and modalistic monarchianism.

Dynamic and Modalistic Monarchianism

The term "monarchianism" comes from two Greek words, *monos* and *archē*. The former means "one" or "sole," and the latter can mean "beginning," "origin," "first cause," "authority," or "ruler." As monarchianism is applied to God, in its two forms (dynamic and modalistic), it means that the Godhead is limited to a single origin or first cause. While this might sound fine since

Christianity is monotheistic, monarchianism did not allow ontologically for more than one possessor of the divine essence.

The originator of dynamic monarchianism is thought to have been a Byzantine leather merchant named Theodotus, who brought the idea to Rome in 190 A.D. The basic idea of this form of monarchianism is that Jesus was not of the same nature as the Father, but rather was a mere man who was adopted to be God's Son. According to Theodotus, Jesus lived as an ordinary man (except that he was supremely virtuous) until his baptism. At that time, the Spirit or Christ descended upon him, and he began to work various miracles. Nonetheless, Jesus never became divine according to Theodotus, though others of his persuasion claimed that Christ was deified upon resurrection. Perhaps the best-known dynamic monarchian was Paul of Samosota in the Eastern church, who was eventually condemned at the synod of Antioch in 268. According to Paul of Samosota, Jesus was not the Word of God, but only a mere man. "The Word" referred to God's commandment and ordinance, so that in calling Jesus the Word, the meaning is that God ordered and accomplished his will through Jesus. But none of that means Jesus was divine; only the Father who created all things was God. As to the Spirit, Paul of Samosota saw "Spirit" as nothing more than a term for the grace that God poured out on the apostles.[27] As Erickson explains, what links Theodotus and Paul together as dynamic monarchians (despite differences in their views) "is that God was dynamically present in the life of the man Jesus. There was a working or force of God upon or in or through the man Jesus, but there was no real substantive presence of God within him."[28]

While dynamic monarchianism was not widely held and did not represent the thinking of Gentile Christians, modalistic monarchianism was more prevalent. As with dynamic monarchianism, this view underscored the unity and oneness of God. However, the modalistic position seemed to allow Father, Son, and Spirit all to qualify as God. Among of the thinkers associated with this view are Noetus of Smyrna and, most notably, Sabellius in the Western church, after whom this view is often named.

The main foundation of this view was the insistence that there is only one God who is the Father. As to Son and Spirit, if they were fully God as Scripture taught and Christians believed, they must, then, be identical with the Father. Otherwise, there would be multiple gods. But then, what do the designations "Son" and "Spirit" mean? Modalists answered that they don't stand for real distinctions within the Godhead, but instead are names applicable to God at different times. The picture one gets is of one God, who is able to play different roles at different times. For example, at one point, he functions as the Father as he creates our world, whereas at another he enters the virgin's womb as Jesus, and then later suffers on the cross. What is crucial is that modalists held that at no time do all three members of the Godhead act distinctly and simultaneously. Hence, biblical passages like the one recounting Christ's baptism (when all three members of the Godhead do different things simultaneously) are extremely difficult, if not impossible, to explain.

Modalism, if adopted, has the further consequence that the Father literally suffered on the cross with Christ. This notion is called "patripassianism," and initially it may seem innocuous, for all Christians would say that the Father's heart broke and he empathized and sympathized with Jesus while he was on the cross. But that is not what patripassianism means. It means that the Father, in playing the "Son role" while Christ was on earth, actually suffered and died on the cross. This conclusion seemed inescapably to follow from belief in only one divine nature and in the three "persons" as nothing more than different names that designate different roles or activities played at one time and another. But patripassianism met with strong resistance for a very simple reason. Typically, early Christians believed that God is atemporally eternal. As such, he is absolutely immutable, for change comes with time but is absent from an atemporal being. Moreover, if God is absolutely immutable, he cannot experience changes of any sort, including changes in his emotional and physical state (if he is at all physical). Therefore, patripassianism was clearly objectionable. It destroyed atemporal eternity and divine immutability and impassibility. God could suffer, he could undergo change; and if the divine nature was thoroughly resident in Jesus, then God was subject to time, or so it seemed.[29]

While modalism offers a way to resolve the apparent paradox between God's oneness and threeness, it does so at the expense of Father, Son, and Holy Spirit being coequal, simultaneously existing persons. While the view was held more widely than dynamic monarchianism, the church eventually concluded that it was heterodox and rejected it.

Origen

While many of the things described so far were occurring in the Western church, there were interesting developments in the Eastern church. Of special import was the view of Origen of Alexandria (A.D. 185–254). Origen was committed to middle Platonism, and it is reflected in his view of the Trinity. God the Father is at the top of Origen's system, and he transcends all being. However, since God is perfectly good and powerful, there must always have been objects on which he could display those attributes. As a result, he brought into existence a set of spiritual beings or souls that are coeternal with himself. To mediate between himself and these souls and to mediate between himself as atemporal and the world as temporal, the Father begets the Son in an eternal act. In addition, there is the Holy Spirit, whom Origen referred to as "the most honourable of all the beings brought into existence through the Word, the chief in rank of all the beings originated by the Father through Christ."[30]

All of this meant for Origen that Father, Son, and Holy Spirit are three persons, and they were so eternally. Thus, rather than postulating distinct persons for the purpose of divine manifestation in the "economy," as Hippolytus and Tertullian had done, Origen maintained that there were three such persons eternally, apart from any activity they did in the world. These three "persons" he referred to as *hypostaseis*. *Hypostasis* and *ousia* had been used synonomously to refer to the real existence or essence of a thing. Origen kept that meaning for *hypostasis,* but he frequently preferred to use it to mean an individual subsistence and thus individual existent.[31]

So far this may sound rather orthodox. The distinction between the Trinity in itself (often called the ontological or immanent Trinity) and the economic Trinity is a valid distinction. Moreover, Origen's emphasis on distinct *hypostaseis,* separate persons, surely seems to combat the error of modalism. But in order to guard against modalism, Origen paid too high a price, for he reasoned that Jesus Christ, though distinct from the Father, was an inferior being, a "secondary God," since his deity was derived from the Father. The Spirit was also a deity to a lesser degree, deriving his divinity from the Father through the Son. This ontological subordination meant that in one sense there was only one hypostasis (the Father) who was fully divine—in that respect it seemed to follow the lead of dynamic monarchianism. On the other hand, this was a different kind of subordination than that found in the dynamic position, for Origen believed the Son and Spirit truly to be divine, even if of a lesser deity than the Father. Moreover, Origen's view could answer modalism by demanding three distinct, simultaneously existing persons.

So, on balance, Origen's basic intuitions seemed correct. He wanted to safeguard monotheism without capitulating to either dynamic or modalistic monarchianism. But he still fell into error, and it isn't entirely clear that he escaped a form of tritheism. The oneness of the three persons he located in the unanimity, harmony, and identity of their wills.[32] As Jevtich explains:

> The fundamental weakness and fallacy of Origen was that he spoke also of the *substantial* subordination of the Son to the Father, and of the Spirit to the Father and the Son; that the Son of God by *nature, power* and *honor* is subordinated to the Father and is lower than the Father, and the Holy Spirit is lower than both of them.[33]

Amid such views and debates over various forms of monarchianism, it was becoming evident that a meeting of the minds on the issue of the Trinity was necessary. One of the things that complicated this issue was the difference in approach between the Eastern and Western churches. Western theologians invariably tended to begin by emphasizing the unity of the divine nature, i.e., God is one as to essence, and only secondarily dealt with the three persons as persons. Hence, there was a certain tendency as evidenced in monarchianism (especially the Sabellian form) to fuse the persons into the one essence entirely. On the other hand, the Eastern church emphasized and started its trinitarian reflection with the real existence of the three unconfused divine persons or hypostases and then stressed the oneness of the divine nature secondarily.[34] This difference resulted in the Western tendency to fuse the persons of the

Godhead and thus open the door to some sort of monarchianism, while the Eastern church tended to divide the persons of the Godhead and hence moved in the direction of tritheism of some sort (cf., e.g., Origen and Arius).

Arianism

Into this whole mix entered the Arian controversy. Arius, a bishop of Alexandria in the east, was greatly influenced by Origen's views, but he saw an inconsistency in them. Christians agreed that Jesus is divine, but the question was how divine Jesus is and exactly what "divinity" means in his case. Arius simply pushed Origen's answer to its logical conclusion. If Jesus is really a distinct *hypostasis* (person), doesn't that require a difference of being? Arius reasoned that it did, and thus argued that Jesus is not coeternal with the Father. Though the Son existed before any other creature, and the Father created the world through him, still he was himself a created being. Moreover, he was not created from the Father's essence but was of a similar, though not identical, substance. This means, of course, that Jesus is not divine in the same sense, if at all, as the Father. Arians relied heavily on Scriptures that talk about the Son as only begotten of the Father. Moreover, a key passage for them seems to have been Prov 8:22, in which Wisdom is personified and states (on one reading of the text) "The Lord created me at the beginning of his way." Arians understood the personified Wisdom to be an OT representation of Christ, and argued that the verse teaches that God created Christ. Though Arianism was about Christ's relation to the divine nature, another controversy developed concerning the Holy Spirit. Pneumatomachianism said of the Holy Spirit what Arianism said of Christ, i.e., that the Holy Spirit is a created being of a different essence than the Father. Hence, he is a lesser "God," if divine at all.

While it is easy to criticize Arius as deliberately heretical, a more charitable and accurate evaluation is that he was trying to avoid problems he saw in Origen and his followers' theology. One of Origen's followers was Alexander, bishop of Alexandria 313–328. R. D. Williams argues that Alexander tolerated language about the substantial unity of God the Father and Son in an effort to underscore the Son's unique dignity and special role as God's primary image.[35] As Williams explains, this prompted Arius to pose the following logical dilemma:

> Alexander's language is either (nonsensically) ditheistic, or else it is Sabellian—in which case it is *completely* subversive of the Son's dignity, since it altogether denies his independent existence. If this is a correct reading of the evidence, Arius' polemic, especially his catalogue of unacceptable views about the Son in his credal letter, can be understood as taking all possible senses of the terminology of substantial union and showing that they are all heretical or illogical.[36]

This rather clearly sums up the problem the church faced in trying to make sense of the Trinity. On the one hand, if one emphasizes the unity of the divine nature, there is always a tendency toward Sabellianism. On the other hand, if one stresses the distinction of the three persons, this can tend toward tritheism. Origen's resolution moved away from Sabellianism but didn't entirely seem to escape tritheism; Arius simply pushed Origen's thinking to its logical extreme. On Arius's views, Christianity is clearly monotheistic, though the emphasis on one divine being doesn't lead to Sabellianism. Sabellianism is avoided by holding that Jesus and the Holy Spirit are created beings who have a similar nature to the Father, but not identical. Their nature is neither the identical *kind* of divine nature the Father has (e.g., they differ in attributes from the Father at least in that he is eternal and they are not), nor is it *numerically* identical with his.

Councils of Nicea and Constantinople

Sabellianism and tritheism are forestalled by Arian logic, but the price is too high. To accept Arianism, one must reject NT affirmations about the Son and the Spirit as divine and equal with the Father. Clearly, something had to be done to resolve disputes over various conceptions of the Trinity. Emperor Constantine called a church council to decide the issue. It met in 325 at Nicea, and Athanasius championed Christ as of the same essence as the Father. But Nicea by no means settled the dispute. The Nicene Creed agreed that Christ was begotten, but denied that he was made—that he was a created being. The decree of the Council reads:

> We believe in one God, the Father Almighty, Maker of all things visible and invisible. And in one Lord Jesus Christ, the Son of God, the only-begotten of his Father, of the substance of the Father, God of God, Light of Light, very God of very God, begotten, not made, being of one substance (*homoousion, consubstantialem*) with the Father. By whom all things were made, both which be in heaven and in earth. Who for us men and for our salvation came down from heaven and was incarnate and was made man. He suffered and the third day he rose again, and ascended into heaven. And he shall come again to judge both the quick and the dead. And we believe in the Holy Ghost. And whosoever shall say that there was a time when the Son of God was not, or that before he was begotten he was not, or that he was made of things that were not, or that he is of a different substance or essence from the Father, or that he is a creature, or subject to change or conversion—all that so say, the Catholic and Apostolic Church anathematizes them.[37]

The crucial word or phrase is "being of one substance," the translation of the Greek word *homoousios*. In contrast, Arius's position is represented by the word *homoiousios* ("being of similar substance"). At first glance this may appear to be much ado about very little, a tempest over the Greek letter iota.

But it is far more, and the debate over these terms was actually far more complex than is often appreciated. It is easy, for example, to read of some Eastern fathers who overtly accepted the *homoousios* wording but continued to push a *homoiousian* position, and to conclude that those Eastern fathers were either confused or dishonest about their views. However, to conclude this would be to foster and perpetuate a serious misunderstanding.

The simple truth is that *these terms are ambiguous in meaning and actually reflect two separate sets of issues*. Remember that in the Eastern church, trinitarian discussion typically began with the three hypostases, the distinct persons, whereas in the West, the unity of the divine nature was the focus. This underscores the fact that, upon careful analysis, we can distinguish two different though interrelated questions that were under discussion. The first is a question about the divine nature itself: is there one divine essence, two, or three? The second is about the nature of the deity of each member of the Godhead: do the Son and Spirit have the same deity as the Father, or is theirs a lesser deity?

As to the former question, answer that there is more than one divine essence and you are headed in the direction of polytheism. Hence, the church fathers (the Westerners in particular) argued that *homoousios* must be inserted into the creed. If Christ is of the same essence as the Father, they reasoned, there could only be one God, and Jesus must have equal dignity to the Father. On the other hand, if *homoiousios* was used, then polytheism seems inevitable, and the dignity of Christ is lowered. Of course, even with *homoousios,* modalism is possible, unless one argues that God's oneness as to essence is not all there is to say—that one must posit three distinct persons along with the one divine essence. But, to repeat, if the topic is how many divine essences there are and whether Jesus equally shares the divine essence, *homoousios* is the preferred term.

But there was also the second question about the nature of the divinity of each of the three persons, and we have already noted the Eastern preference for beginning trinitarian reflections with discussion of the persons. On this point some in the East were especially concerned about the term *homoousios*. If one takes this term too far and applies it not only to the divine essence but also to the divine persons (hypostases), Sabellianism seems inevitable. After all, hadn't Marcellus of Ancyra, while agreeing to Nicene consubstantiality of Son and Spirit with the Father (thus agreeing to *homoousios*) actually espoused Sabellianism? As Jevtich explains, St. Basil, one of the great Eastern Cappadocian theologians, complained to Athanasius:

> even until now those from the West in all their letters to us never cease mercilessly to anathematize and excommunicate the notorious Arius, while at the same time they never criticize Marcellus of Ancyra who spreads an opposite heresy and impiously denies even the existence of the divinity of the Only-begotten, wrongly interpreting the name 'Logos'.[38]

Because of concern to emphasize distinct persons in the Godhead, in the East there arose a movement around Basil of Ancyra (St. Basil, the Cappadocian, was aware of Basil of Ancyra and his followers) emphasizing homoiousian theology. However, these theologians were not offering *homoiousios* as the answer to how many divine essences there are. Rather, in an effort to avoid Sabellian modalism, they were using it to say that there are three distinct persons in that essence. For if one asks about the number of persons in the Godhead, and the answer is that Father, Son, and Holy Spirit are *homoousios,* that can be taken to mean that there is only one person in the Godhead, one who at times manifests himself as Father, or Son, or Holy Spirit, but never as more than one person at any given time. On the other hand, by saying that the three are of like (*homoi*), but not *identical* (*homo*) nature, and by focusing on the issue of *persons* in the Godhead, (rather than on how many, numerically speaking, divine *essences* there are), one can avoid the error of Sabellianism. Moreover, these homoiousians, if charged with the heresy of tritheism, could deny it, because they were talking about persons, not essences, when they used the term *homoiousia.*[39]

Perhaps part of the ambiguity stems from the fact that even though the Eastern fathers spoke of hypostases when referring to the three members of the Godhead, *hypostasis* was, as we noted above, understood by many as synonymous with *ousia.* Hence, talk of the same *ousia* might well mean to an Eastern Christian only one *person* (*hypostasis*) in the Godhead, thereby suggesting some form of monarchianism. Whatever the reason for the ambiguity, it is critical to understand that two distinct (though related) issues were under consideration, and it is equally important to see why and how the Nicene formula using *homoousios* continued the ambiguity rather than resolving it. The net result was in part that the council of Nicea did not end the trinitarian debate, and the Nicene Creed had to be supplemented and reworked.

One of the Nicene Creed's shortcomings was that it said very little about the Holy Spirit. The Nicene fathers, however, believed him to be consubstantial with the Father, and at the Council of Constantinople in 381 (called by Emperor Theodosius) the teaching of Nicea was extended to the Holy Spirit. In place of the Nicene statement "And we believe in the Holy Ghost," the Council of Constantinople added:

> And we believe in the Holy Ghost, the Lord and Giver-of-Life, who proceedeth from the Father, who with the Father and the Son together is worshipped and glorified, who spake by the prophets. And we believe in one, holy, Catholic and Apostolic Church. We acknowledge one Baptism for the remission of sins, and we look for the resurrection of the dead and the life of the world to come. Amen.[40]

As Stramara notes, this meant that the council issued a decidedly trinitarian declaration of faith, namely, "there is one Godhead, Power and Substance of the Father and of the Son and of the Holy Ghost; the dignity being equal, and the majesty being equal in three perfect hypostases, i.e., three perfect persons (προσωποις)."[41]

This, then, was the doctrine as embodied in the Niceno-Constantinopolitan Creed. As J. N. D. Kelly argues, this creed was a turning point, for no longer was it acceptable to hold that the Son and Holy Spirit are inferior in essence to the Father. Not only is their essence of equal majesty, it is also numerically identical to the Father's essence. Trinitarianism, as opposed to Sabellianism on the one hand and tritheism on the other, was made the official doctrine of the church.[42] But that does not mean it was immediately adopted by all or even understood by those who did hold it. It fell to the Cappadocian Fathers St. Basil the Great, Gregory of Nyssa, and Gregory of Nazianzus to elaborate and defend this doctrine. In fact, at the Council of Constantinople, the Council Fathers and Emperor Theodosius commissioned Gregory of Nyssa to be the official ambassador to present the church's doctrine. It is to that elaboration and clarification that we now turn.

Clarification and Defense of Niceno-Constantinopolitan Creed

One of the key elements in Eastern theology retained by the Cappadocian Fathers is the idea of the monarchy of the Father. This does not mean that either Son or Spirit are not God, but rather that the Father is seen as the fount, source, or cause of the deity. Hence, Christian theology believes in one God the Father who has an only begotten Son born from him and a Divine Spirit proceeding from him.[43] In citing St. Cyril of Jerusalem and relating his comment to St. Basil the Great, Jevtich shows the pervasiveness of this notion:

> In the words of St. Cyril of Jerusalem . . . the "reality of the monarchy" of the Christian God consists precisely in the identifying of the monarchy with the dignity of the Father: "For it is necessary not only to believe in the one God, but also that He is the Father of the Only-begotten Son," "the timeless beginning (*archē*) and the fountain-head (*pēgē*)" of the divinity of the Son and the Holy Spirit. These words of St. Cyril concerning the monarchy of the Father will be almost literally repeated by St. Basil the Great many times in his works: *Against Eunomius* (I: 20, 24, 25; II: 12; III: 6); *On the Holy Spirit*, c. 18, which is dedicated to the theme "how to preserve in the confession of the three hypostases the precious dogma of the monarchy"; and in sermon 24, "Against the [*sic*] Sabellius and Arius and the Eunomians." . . . The famous and very important words of St. Basil from his aforementioned sermon 24: "*Eis theos hoti kai patēr*," "God is one because He is the Father," will be frequently repeated by St. Gregory the Theologian and St. Gregory of Nyssa.[44]

From this it is clear that the Cappadocians took very seriously biblical language about the Son being begotten of the Father and the Spirit proceeding from the Father. In fact, for Gregory of Nyssa such causal relations indicated the unique characteristic of each member of the Godhead in their relations to one another within the Godhead (the immanent or ontological Trinity). Though there is only one God, each of the three persons has his mode of existence which can be distinguished from that of the others in terms of their identifying properties. The Father's property is unbegottenness or the property of being ungenerate (*agennēsia*). The Son's characteristic is begottenness (*gennasia*), and the Spirit's is mission or procession (*ekpempsis*, *ekporeusis*).[45] From this we can see that the Cappadocians held, as did many others at that time, the doctrines of the eternal generation of the Son and the eternal procession of the Spirit. We have seen some of the biblical bases for these doctrines, but they are hard to grasp. Proponents of these views emphasize that any notion of natural generation must be removed from these concepts. Moreover, the word "eternal" is crucial, for espousers of these doctrines stress that whatever this generation and procession consist in, they cannot mean that there was a time when neither Son nor Spirit existed, and then at a later time they came into being. Rather, this generation and procession have been occurring for as long as God has existed (forever). Typically, advocates of these doctrines explain that they mean that the Father makes in common the divine essence with the Son and Spirit. We shall return to this shortly and discuss its plausibility. For now, it is enough to note that these doctrines are closely tied into early church trinitarian thinking.

There is more to Cappadocian thinking than just the monarchy of the Father. As noted, Eastern thinkers were most concerned to maintain three distinct persons as divine. But how could that be done without slipping into tritheism? Gregory of Nyssa addressed this issue in his treatise *Ad Graecos*. Gregory considers how we can call Father, Son, and Holy Spirit all God without winding up with three Gods. His fundamental answer (and the basic approach the Cappadocians took) likened this to the relation of a universal to its particulars. Think of the following two universals: God and man. Each refers to a kind or species of thing. While there is only one universal (one general term), there are a number of particular instances of the universal. Hence, "man" refers to human nature in general, while Peter, James, and John are particular instances of the common human nature. Now if this is how it works, then by analogy, divinity is the universal, and Father, Son, and Holy Spirit are particular instances of that common divine nature. However, that would mean that Father, Son, and Holy Spirit are three distinct Gods, each with a distinct divine nature, though one which is related to that of the others because all are particular instances of the universal. This was the issue Gregory addressed in his treatise.

What becomes clear again is a certain ambiguity in terms. Specifically, we have seen that *ousia* or *homoousia* is ambiguous, and have explained part of the ambiguity surrounding these terms, but now we can clarify it even further. When talking about an *ousia* (a nature, or essence), one may be referring to a *general kind* of thing such as humanity, which could be possessed by various things that are *numerically* distinct. On the other hand, when using the term *ousia* in this discussion, one may also refer to that nature or essence which is itself *numerically* one. So, in approaching this problem, we must remember that a nature or essence (*ousia*) may refer to a class or kind of things, or it may designate a numerically distinct thing. Moreover, we must also remember the difference between an *ousia* (essence) and a *hypostasis* or *prosōpon* (person, the second term is Gregory's preferred term for person).

Gregory explains that if the term "God" denotes the person, then to speak of three persons would be to speak of three Gods. However, "God" refers to the essence (*ousia*), and in that case there is only one. But now, if that essence is like "man," i.e., if it is a universal that has particulars, then even if there is one essence to which "God" refers, it would still seem that since there are three particulars (persons), we have three Gods, just as Peter, James, and John are three men who share a common nature "man." But it is here that the ambiguity in the term *ousia* shows itself. It may refer to a kind of thing or to a numerically individual thing. When we say of "man" that it is a universal essence, we make a point about a certain kind of thing, but we are not saying that there is, numerically speaking, only one human being who has ever had that essence. Rather, the universal is an abstract category (a concept of a kind of thing that has many specific instances) that may have many different particular concrete instances. Hence, each human shares a common essence in the sense of a general kind of thing, while at the same time each is a numerically distinct individual.

If we apply the same description to God, there would be three Gods— Father, Son and Holy Spirit. Of course we cannot, but why not? The reason is that the divine essence or nature (*ousia*) does not simply refer to a kind of thing which may then have a number of discrete individual instances (many gods). Rather, what Christian theology holds is that the divine nature not only refers to a certain kind of being, but in addition, there is numerically only one instance of that kind of thing. Hence, both senses of *ousia* (as designating a species of things and as a numerically distinct thing) apply in God's case, whereas with human nature in general, we are designating a kind of thing, but a thing that may be possessed by a number of numerically distinct individuals. This means that the analogy between universal and particular in God and man breaks down in the first place with respect to what we would call the universal term, the essence or nature. For in the case of "man," the universal is only considered as it designates a certain kind of thing which may be possessed by many distinct individuals, whereas with "God," this universal designates a kind of being and affirms that there is numerically only one instance of it.

The analogy also breaks down in regard to the particular. In the case of "man," since it refers to a general and abstract conception of human nature, there can be many numerically distinct particular human beings. Of course, each has its numerically distinct human nature, though it fits the pattern of what others have. When we call each of these humans *persons*, we refer to individuated essences, not to the general human nature (the universal). When it comes to God, however, we talk about three particular persons—Father, Son, and Holy Spirit—but in light of what we have said about the universal referring both to the kind of being God is and to a numerically exclusive instance of that kind of being, the three persons cannot necessitate three distinct essences. They must share the divine essence which is numerically one. What, then, are the three persons, if they are not distinct essences (three separate Gods)? The Cappadocians answered that they are distinct modes of existence or subsistences of the numerically single divine nature. One of the terms frequently used to express this idea is "coinherence" or "perichoresis." The three are distinguishable by the identifying property each has in his internal relations with the others: the Father is ungenerate, the Son is begotten, and the Spirit's characteristic is procession. Exactly how three distinct persons can be modes or subsistences of one essence is a mystery, but to deny this is to lapse either into tritheism on the one hand or modalism on the other.[46]

Filioque Controversy

Two other developments are noteworthy before ending this historical section. One has to do with the *Filioque* controversy. As noted, the Council of Constantinople (381) affirmed the full deity of the Holy Spirit. However, upon examining the resultant creed, we see that the church fathers claimed that the Holy Spirit proceeds from the Father. The Latin word *filioque* means "and from the Son," but this word was not part of the sentence that speaks of the Spirit's procession from the Father. Theologians in the Western church reasoned that if the divine nature was equally shared by all members of the Godhead, and if the Son was truly related to the Spirit, it made no sense to say that the Spirit proceeded from the Father alone. Theologians in the Eastern church strongly disagreed. Their concern was upholding the Father as the sole origin and source of divinity (see above on the Father's monarchy). Moreover, there had to be a way to distinguish the respects in which the Son and Spirit derived from the Father, or it would be more difficult to explain how the Son was distinct from the Spirit. Alister McGrath explains:

> Within this context, it is unthinkable that the Holy Spirit should proceed from the Father and Son. Why? Because it would totally compromise the principle of the Father as the sole origin and source of all divinity. It would amount to affirming that there were *two* sources of divinity within the one Godhead, with all the internal contradictions and tensions that this would generate. If the Son were to share in the exclusive ability of the Father to be the source of all divinity, this ability would no longer be exclusive. For this reason, the Greek church regarded the western idea of a "double procession" of the Spirit with something approaching stark disbelief.[47]

Gerald Bray details this lengthy and divisive controversy. At the Council of Chalcedon in 451 Pope Leo I's reply against Eutyches was read. Four years earlier Leo had included the *filioque* clause as part of orthodox teaching on the Trinity when he wrote a letter to Turibius, the bishop of Asturica in Spain. But Leo's *Tome* against Eutyches read at Chalcedon didn't contain it.

Moreover, in addition to handling the Christological controversies that had arisen, Chalcedon set forth the Niceno-Constantinopolitan Creed in its final form, and the clause didn't appear in it.

On the other hand, in the Western church the *filioque* clause was used by Augustine, and it also appeared in the so-called Athanasian Creed that was likely written around 500 (hence, it wasn't written by Athanasius, but was in concert with his understanding of the Trinity). Moreover, by the Council of Toledo in 589 in the Western church there was general commitment to the *filioque* clause, and that council officially added it to the Niceno-Constantinopolitan Creed. This debate continued to develop for centuries, and many historians think this disagreement was at least part of the reason for the split between the Eastern and Western churches in 1054.[48]

Augustine

Before leaving this discussion of the early development of the doctrine of the Trinity, we should say something about Augustine. His work on the Trinity follows the typical Western approach of emphasizing the unity of the Godhead. Hence, Son and Spirit are in no sense inferior to the Father, and the action of all three can be seen behind the work of any of them.

One distinctive of Augustine's work on the Trinity is his use of "psychological analogies" of the Trinity. He reasoned that it is likely that God has left vestiges of his own being in creation. Since humans are the crown of creation and are made in the *imago dei,* we should especially expect to find vestiges there. Relying on his neo-Platonic presuppositions, Augustine reasoned further that since the human mind is the highest part of human nature, we should most likely find in it reflections of God. Augustine believed that the structure of human thought can be seen as triadic, and thereby reflects the Trinity. McGrath explains, "He himself argues that the most important such triad is that of mind, knowledge, and love (*mens, notitia,* and *amor*), although the related triad of memory, understanding, and will (*memoria, intelligentia,* and *voluntas*) is also given considerable prominence."[49]

Perhaps the most distinctive element in Augustine's thinking about the Trinity is his understanding of the Holy Spirit. He believed that the Holy Spirit must have proceeded from both the Father and the Son. Proof of procession from the Son is John 20:22, according to Augustine, which says that Christ breathed on his disciples and said, "Receive the Holy Spirit." But even more distinctive is his understanding of the Holy Spirit as the bond of love between the Father and the Son. He argued that the members of the Godhead are defined by their relations to one another, and hence, the Holy Spirit is to be seen as the relation of love and fellowship between Father and Son. It is also the Spirit who unites believers to God, allowing God to dwell in us and us in him. He is God's love gift to us in this respect.[50]

THE DOCTRINE OF THE TRINITY □ 487

Though there are others figures of interest in the early development of the doctrine of the Trinity, the preceding suffices to set forth the main understanding of the church on this doctrine as it developed over the first few centuries of church history. Other interesting developments occurred later in church history, but the main contours of the doctrine were set during these early centuries of controversy. We must now put together the biblical data with these historical considerations to formulate our doctrine of the Trinity.

Formulation of the Doctrine of the Trinity

The results of what we have learned in the previous sections can be stated in six main ideas, though each major point needs explanation and amplification. In what follows I shall use the term *ousia* to refer to a nature or essence. Hence, when talking of the divine essence, I shall refer to the divine *ousia*. On the other hand, when speaking of persons or subsistences within the divine nature, I shall use either *hypostasis* or *prosōpon*.

First, *there is only one God*. This means that there is only one divine essence or nature (*ousia*). Biblical support is found uniformly in the OT and NT, and need not be repeated. In light of this point, we can say that any view of God that postulates more than one distinct divine nature (*ousia*) embraces polytheism and has nothing to do with the God of Christianity.

Second, *the one divine essence (ousia) is distributed or manifested in three distinct persons (hypostaseis or prosōpoi)*. Calling the persons distinct means that the Father is not the Son, the Son is not the Spirit, and the Father is not the Spirit. This does not, however, mean that each subsistence (*hypostasis/prosōpon*) has its own distinct essence or nature (*ousia*). Rather, each divine person shares the numerically one divine essence (*ousia*); they are all ontologically God. *Ousia* as a universal term referring to a kind of being applies to all three persons of the Godhead, but numerically speaking, there is only one divine *ousia*, and all three persons coinhere in that one nature. Making the point about the three persons and their relation to the divine essence guards against a series of heretical, non-biblical views. On the one hand, it guards against tritheism and any other polytheistic position that unduly splits or separates the divine essence. On the other hand, it also guards against heresies that retain monotheism only by claiming that the Son and Spirit are either lesser gods or not God at all. Hence, it rules out views such as Arianism and Origen's position that make Christ a lesser God, and dynamic monarchian or adoptionist views that deny Christ's deity altogether. Similarly, it excludes any form of pneumatomachian doctrine which makes the Holy Spirit ontologically inferior to the Father and Son.

The biblical warrant for this second point is twofold: 1) all verses taken conjointly that predicate deity of Father, Son, and Holy Spirit; plus 2) the clear teaching that, nonetheless, there is only one God. If there are both one and three in respect to essences, that is a contradiction. If there are both one and three in respect to persons, that is also a contradiction. To avoid such contradictions, God must be one in a different sense than he is three; hence the claim that God is three as to persons, all of whom manifest the one and only divine nature.

Third, *the three persons (hypostaseis/prosōpoi) coinhering in the one divine nature (ousia) exist simultaneously with one another as distinct subsistences or persons.* This means that the divine essence is not at one time entirely manifest as the Father (but not in or as the Son or Spirit), and then at another moment manifest exclusively as the Son, and yet again at another time solely as the Spirit. Rather, all three persons (*hypostaseis/prosōpoi*) exist simultaneously. Scriptures that show more than one member of the Godhead acting at the same time require this. It is also a logical implication of there really being three persons, not just one masquerading at different times as one or another of the other two. This plank in our formulation of the doctrine of the Trinity eliminates all forms of modalism or Sabellianism.

Fourth, *from the preceding points we can also say that Father, Son, and Holy Spirit are equal ontologically.* That is, they all share the divine essence, and thus are coequally God in being or nature. There is no ontological subordination within the Godhead; each divine person is as fully God as are the others. This guards against positions such as Arianism, pneumatomachianism, and Origen's views that make Christ and/or the Holy Spirit a lesser God. It also protects against adoptionist views that deny Christ's deity altogether.

Fifth, *there is a distinction between the "ontological" or "immanent" Trinity, on the one hand, and the "economic" Trinity on the other.* The "ontological" or "immanent" Trinity refers to God in himself, and concerns the internal relations members of the Godhead have with one another. The "economic" Trinity deals with the self-disclosure of the Godhead in the members' work in the world. As to the economic Trinity, we can say several things. On the one hand, while each member of the Trinity is active in each divine action, Scripture (the NT in particular) frequently associates a given activity with one member of the Godhead more than with the others. The Son is most specifically the Savior and the Spirit the inspirer of Scripture, but all three members of the Godhead are working in each of these actions. Moreover, in their economic roles, certain members of the Godhead are functionally subordinate to other persons in the Godhead. For example, the Son submits to the Father's will in going to the cross, and the Spirit's main ministry is to testify of Christ and point people toward him. This functional subordination, however, in no way indicates any ontological inferiority among the three members of the Trinity.

Sixth, *in regard to relations within the ontological or immanent Trinity, the church historically has affirmed that the Son is eternally generated and the Spirit eternally proceeds. Despite their firm entrenchment in both Western and Eastern traditions, the doctrines of eternal generation and eternal pro-*

cession are unclear and are not required by Scripture. In saying this I part company with a host of theologians throughout church history. As noted, the Cappadocian Fathers in particular liked to speak of the characteristic of each member of the Trinity in their internal relations with one another. The Father is ungenerate (nowhere does Scripture say he is generated by or proceeds from anyone or anything), the Son is generated by the Father (biblical language about Christ as only begotten and firstborn are said to prove this point), and the Spirit proceeds from the Father (Eastern church) or Father and Son (Western church). Despite the firm hold of these doctrines within the Christian tradition, we must see what they mean and whether Scripture warrants them.

As to the meaning of these doctrines, we begin to see problems. Eternal generation of the Son is said to mean that the Father communicates the divine essence to the Son. To communicate the essence means to share it in common. But proponents of this view quickly add that we must remove all thought of human generation from this idea; this is not a begetting at all like human begetting. Moreover, since Christ is eternal and has always existed, we must say that this generating has been happening as long as God has existed, which is forever, and it never began to happen. But think of what is being proposed, and one can see that this makes little sense. If Christ does not begin to receive the divine essence because as divine he always exists as God, i.e., he has always had the divine essence, how does it make sense to speak of the Father making in common with him something he has always had anyway? Moreover, this generating has been happening for as long as God has existed, but we are not to think of it as at all akin to human generating. How can this make sense? If anything is true of human generation it is that something that has no being at one moment receives being or existence later. Moreover, human generating is not eternal but happens at some particular time. Now, if eternal generation of the Son must be different from human generation, then how can we make sense of it? Christ cannot get something he already has, nor does it make sense to say this receiving has been happening for all eternity. If we are told that this is a mystery, the proper response seems to be that this is not mystery, but nonsense and confusion.

The same line of explanation is given for the Holy Spirit's eternal procession, and it is just as problematic as eternal generation of the Son for the same sort of reasons. The Holy Spirit cannot be given what he already possesses, nor does it help to say he has been receiving it for all eternity. Why would the church feel obliged to hold such doctrines? In fairness to proponents of these doctrines, they are trying to explain biblical language about the Son as only begotten or firstborn and the Holy Spirit as proceeding from the Father. However, I contend that closer analysis shows that the biblical data do not demand these views.

Consider the support for eternal generation. Some point to Prov 8:22-25 where personified Wisdom reputedly claims that the Lord created it at the beginning of his work. This line of argument says that Wisdom is actually Jesus Christ, and that he is saying that God the Father created him. But, of course, proponents of eternal generation remind us that this cannot be a literal creating, for Christ is not a creature. This should suggest that something is amiss. Grudem offers an alternate interpretation of verse 22 as follows:

> The Hebrew word that commonly means "create" (*bārā'*) is not used in verse 22; rather the word is *qānah*, which occurs eighty-four times in the Old Testament and almost always means "to get, acquire." The NASB is most clear here: "The Lord possessed me at the beginning of his way" (similarly KJV). . . . This is a legitimate sense and, if wisdom is understood as a real person, would mean only that God the Father began to direct and make use of the powerful creative work of God the Son at the time creation began: the expression "brought forth" in verses 24 and 25 is a different term but could carry a similar meaning: the Father began to direct and make use of the powerful creative work of the Son in the creation of the universe.[51]

What about Ps 2:7? As Buswell explains, this passage is a messianic psalm, so it is likely that the point is that the Lord declares the Son to be the Messiah, the King.[52] Moreover, when we see what the NT does with this verse (Acts 13:32-33; Heb 1:5; 5:4-6), it is even more dubious that it refers to eternal generation. In the Acts passage, as Paul preaches he associates the declaration "Thou art My Son; today I have begotten Thee" with the resurrection of Christ. Hence, the point is that, by resurrecting Christ, God has declared him to be the Messiah. As to the Hebrews passages, they are not connected to any specific event, but as Buswell argues, they may be understood as declaring Christ's eternal exalted Sonship. They need not be seen as teaching eternal generation of the Son.[53]

But don't all the Johannine passages that call Christ the only begotten Son or even the only begotten God require the doctrine of eternal generation? The answer is that they do not. The reason these verses for so long were thought to require that view is that the word for "only begotten," *monogenēs,* was thought to have at its root *monos* and *gennaō*. The latter word means to "beget" or "generate," and if this is the meaning of *monogenēs*, there is reason for thinking eternal generation is required. However, through linguistic studies in the twentieth century it has been discovered that the word doesn't come from *gennaō* but from *genos*, which means "class" or "kind."[54] Hence, *monogenēs* doesn't mean "only begotten," but rather "one of a kind," and the phrase means "one of a kind" or "unique Son." Wayne Grudem explains the word as follows:

> Linguistic study in the twentieth century has shown that the second half of the word is not closely related to the verb *gennaō*, "beget, bear," but rather to the term *genos*, "class, kind." Thus the word means rather the "one-of-a-kind" Son or the "unique" Son. (See BAGD, p. 527; D. Moody, "The Translation of John 3:16 in the Revised Standard Version," *JBL* 72 [1953: 213-219]. The idea of "only-begotten" in Greek would have been not *monogenēs* but *monogennētos*.[55]

In light of this evidence, it is clear that a major biblical support for the eternal generation doctrine evaporates. As Grudem further notes, confirmation of the corrected meaning of *monogenēs* comes in Heb 11:17, where the writer uses it to speak of Isaac as Abraham's *monogenēs*. If in fact *monogenēs* means "only begotten," then the biblical text is in error, for Isaac was not Abraham's only begotten son. Ishmael was also his son, though by Hagar. While Isaac was the only son of Abraham by Sarah, the text makes no comment about the mother. If, instead, the point is that Isaac was Abraham's unique son, that makes sense. Though Abraham had another son, Isaac was unique in that he, and he alone, was the child of promise.[56]

What about Col 1:15, where Paul calls Jesus the firstborn of creation? Doesn't this necessitate eternal generation? Here the word translated "firstborn" is the Greek word *prōtotokos*. While this word may mean "first-begotten," it may also mean "preeminent," referring to the one who has the rights of the firstborn. In Luke 2:7 the word appears, but there refers to the incarnation, when Mary gave birth to Jesus; but surely that is not the point of the eternal generation doctrine at all, and it is not the point of Col 1:15. In Rev 1:5 Jesus is called the "firstborn of the dead," but this clearly refers to his resurrection and has nothing to do with the notion of eternal generation. Paul also uses the term in Rom 8:29 to speak of Christ as the "firstborn among many brethren," but the point is soteriological, as the context speaks of predestination and then moves on to other elements in the application of salvation. The point is not about the relationship of Father and Son within the Godhead. In Col 1:15, it is not necessary to see this term as referring to the doctrine of eternal generation. Rather, the point can be simply that Christ is preeminent over all that exists.[57]

What about the eternal procession of the Spirit? This doctrine seems to fare even worse than the eternal generation of the Son. The biblical support seems limited primarily (if not exclusively) to John 15:26. Jesus says, "When the Helper comes, whom I will send to you from the Father, that is the Spirit of truth, who proceeds from the Father, He will bear witness of Me." The main point of the verse is not what has been happening in eternity past but rather what is going to happen once Jesus is gone. He promises his disciples that he will send the Holy Spirit. The verse says very clearly that not only will Jesus send the Spirit, but so will the Father. While it is possible that the phrase "who proceeds from the Father" may make a separate point about eternal relations within the Godhead, that seems unlikely. Why, in making a promise to send the Spirit, would it be relevant to say anything about the relationship that has held between the Father and Spirit for all eternity? Some will undoubtedly reply that if this phrase doesn't say what they claim, then it is redundant of the first relative clause in the sentence. However, that is not so, because the whole clause also includes the comment about the Spirit being the Spirit of truth who proceeds from the Father. The Spirit as the Spirit of truth has not already been mentioned in the verse. Moreover, the first relative clause says the Son sends the Spirit "from the Father." This second clause specifies more clearly how it is that the Spirit comes from the Father.

Perhaps the strongest objection to this verse as teaching eternal procession is that to adopt that interpretation means that we think the apostle John intended to make this subtle metaphysical point about the internal relations of the members of the Godhead. That is rather hard to believe, especially since John wrote this far before Nicea, Constantinople, and the *filioque* controversy. This seems to be a case of forcing metaphysical distinctions and doctrines into the text of Scripture where they don't belong.

In sum, it seems wisest to abandon the doctrines of eternal generation and eternal procession. They are shrouded in obscurity as to their meaning, and biblical support for them is nowhere near as strong as supposed. Indeed, Scripture speaks of Christ as the Son, but everyone grants that he must be Son in some metaphorical sense. Even the doctrine of eternal generation doesn't allow him to be Son in the literal sense that we use that term. So, if the term is used metaphorically, why must we demand that the metaphor means the doctrine of eternal generation?

Rejecting these doctrines must not be misunderstood. It doesn't mean that there is nothing to the distinction between the ontological or immanent Trinity and the economic Trinity. The former speaks of the Trinity in their internal relations, but since those relations are internal to their own being, and since Scripture reveals so little about those relations to us, there isn't a lot we can say about them. Surely, it is worthwhile to distinguish the Trinity in itself from the Trinity in its actions in the world, and there is much to say about how the three work together in our universe.

A final point about this is how sad the history of the *filioque* controversy is. If my rejection of the doctrines of eternal generation and eternal procession are correct, then there are really no grounds for a controversy over whether the Spirit proceeds just from the Father or from Father and Son. To the extent that the split between the Eastern and Western churches resulted from this dispute, the split was totally unnecessary.

These six points (with their elaboration and explanation) complete our formulation of the doctrine of the Trinity. Throughout church history there have been attempts to offer analogies to the Trinity. One of the more popular appeals to water (H_2O) as capable of occurring in a liquid, solid, or gaseous state. The problem, however, with this analogy is that one and the same molecule of water, numerically speaking, cannot occur simultaneously as a gas, solid, and liquid. Other analogies have been suggested, but all fail in one respect or another. That should not surprise us, however, for nothing in the world as we know and understand it can be characterized in this way, i.e., one essence manifest in three distinct, simultaneously existing subsistences. The doctrine of the Trinity is a unique claim that Christians make about their God.

LOGIC AND THE DOCTRINE OF THE TRINITY

Over the last half century, philosophers have rather vigorously discussed whether this doctrine is logically coherent. Much of the discussion has tried to show in one way or another how it is logically consistent. In this section, I shall present what seems the most satisfactory of those explanations. Before doing so, however, I must clarify what it means to say that a set of ideas contains a contradiction, and about the requirements for rebutting the charge. A contradiction is the affirmation and denial of one and the same thing at the same time in the same way. If a set of ideas is genuinely contradictory, there is no possible way to explain the ideas so as to remove the contradiction. This is not because we don't know how to remove the contradiction now but will someday, nor is it that God knows how the ideas fit together consistently but we don't. Rather, it is because no one, including God, knows now or will ever know how the ideas can all be true at once.

This is, of course, an extremely strong accusation to level against a set of ideas, but we must also see that answering the charge of contradiction isn't as difficult as it first seems. Since the complaint is that there is no possible way that the ideas can all be true, the defender of their consistency need only show a possible way for all to be true. Of course we should seek the most plausible explanation, but strictly speaking, the requirement is only a *possible* way.

With these "ground rules" in place, I now turn to the explanation. The solution that I find most acceptable is what some label relative trinitarianism, for it stems from the notion of relative identity. I do not claim that this is *the* explanation which correctly shows how God can be three and yet one (there may be a better one), but only that this proposal is a possible way for the doctrine of the Trinity to be logically consistent. Some may think this an unnecessary exercise, for we should just admit mystery and say either that the law of noncontradiction doesn't apply or that it does but it is a mystery as to how to satisfy it in regard to the Trinity. In reply, Bartel rightly argues that if we exempt this doctrine from the law of noncontradiction, then there is no reason not to do the same with any other apparent contradiction about God. He writes,

> Why not affirm that, for all we know, God the Father is both almighty and impotent, the Word became and did not become flesh, the Holy Spirit did and did not speak through the prophets? For it is unbearably arbitrary and counterintuitive to imagine that some theological contradictions are true whilst others are false. No: logical inconsistency is a sure sign of falsehood.[58]

Clearly, we should seek a resolution to the apparent contradiction, and I believe the place to begin is with some brief comments about the logic of identity. Bartel raises the distinction between *polygamous* and *monogamous* predication. An example of the former is "x is better than y," but of course, this

won't help until we know the answer to the question "x is a better *what* than y."
As Bartel explains, the answer to this question is a *sortal,* and a sortal is a general noun which denotes objects of one particular kind. Examples of sortals are
"woman," "bird," "star," "dog," "color." Polygamous predication is neither
true nor false unless it can be "expanded" by some sortal. On the other hand,
monogamous predication needs no expansion to be true or false. An example
is "x is an aunt of y." This is either true or false without any modification.[59]

The relevance of this to identity predication is that such predications are polygamous, not monogamous. Hence, we cannot just say that "x is the same as y," but
rather we must specify with respect to what x and y are the same, and the answer
will be some sortal. Bartel adds that "identity predications are *sortal-relative:* that
is, for at least one substitution-instance of '*x* is the same as *y*', one of its sortal
expansions is true while another is false. This is the thesis of relative identity."[60]

How this applies to the Trinity should be rather clear. Consider the following identity claims: (1) "Jesus is the same *God* as the Holy Spirit"; and
(2) "Jesus is the same *person* as the Holy Spirit." The sortal noun in (1) is
"God" and the sortal in (2) is "person." In both sentences "Jesus" and "the
Holy Spirit" have the same referent. Still sentence (1) is true and (2) is false.
Relative to the sortal "God," Jesus and the Holy Spirit are the same. Relative
to the sortal "person" (and here we must think of the sense of "person"
articulated in our historical study), Jesus and the Holy Spirit are not the same.
This is really just a more philosophical way of making the point made in the
previous sections about the difference between a nature (*ousia*) and a person
or subsistence (*hypostasis/prōsopon*) of that nature.

Appeal to relative identity seems to satisfy the logical demands of the doctrine of the Trinity, but Bartel is not so sure, for two main reasons. The first
appeals to each member of the Godhead's non-incarnational property. The
church, as we noted, said that the Father is ungenerate and that he begets the
Son. The Son's property is being eternally begotten by the Father, and the
Holy Spirit's property is his procession from the Father (or Father and Son).
Given these respective properties, if we are speaking about the sortal noun
"deity" or the adjective "divine," we seem to have a problem, according to
Bartel, for we can now write an argument like the following:

> God the Son is eternally begotten of the Father *qua* divine.
> God the Father is not eternally begotten of the Father *qua* divine;
> Therefore, God the Son is not the same deity as God the Father.[61]

If Jesus and the Father are numerically the same God, this argument underscores the problem. As Bartel explains, "just as absolute identity will not
tolerate divergence in properties exemplified *simpliciter,* so *being numerically
the same f as* will not tolerate divergence in properties exemplified *qua f.*"[62]

This may seem to be an insuperable dilemma, but Bartel thinks not, and I
agree. The way to avoid this problem is to reject the doctrines of the eternal

THE DOCTRINE OF THE TRINITY □ 495

generation of the Son and eternal procession of the Spirit. Bartel complains that this departs significantly from the orthodox tradition about the Trinity, but as I have argued, it is a departure we should make. Moreover, I fail to see that doing so cedes anything genuinely significant in the doctrine—it doesn't undermine the notion that there is one God in three persons. However, even if one holds such doctrines, one can still escape Bartel's objection. The reason is that being eternally begotten and eternally proceeding are not properties the Son and Spirit have in virtue of being divine, but in virtue of being distinct subsistences of that divine essence. Hence, the premises of the above should read "*qua* subsistence or person," and the conclusion should say, "Therefore, God the Son is not the same person or subsistence as God the Father."

Bartel, however, thinks there is a second and even more serious problem with relative trinitarianism. Traditional Christology affirms that in the incarnate Christ there are two complete but distinct natures, one divine and one human. Incarnational properties of Christ are typically attributed to his human nature, so those properties do not apply to Jesus as divine, nor do they apply to the Father or the Spirit. On the other hand, Christ's divine mind has the property of being co-personal with his human mind. But since his divine mind is numerically the same essence as that shared by the other two persons, it seems that the Father and the Spirit must also possess the property of being co-personal with Jesus' human nature. The net result, argues Bartel, is that all three members of the Godhead become incarnate in Christ, and of course, that contradicts evangelical theology; it smacks of Sabellianism. One way around this is to grant that each member of the Godhead has his own essence, but that runs aground as tritheism. Thus, Bartel proposes that we abandon relative trinitarianism in favor of what he calls a "social theory" of the Trinity. This theory proposes that each member of the Trinity is absolutely distinct from the others. While this ultimately yields some form of tritheism, Bartel thinks it can be defended as consistent with orthodoxy anyway.[63]

Though this seems to be a devastating objection, I don't believe it is. I think, however, that it contains a mixture of truth and error. The element of truth is that, since there is only one divine essence shared equally by all three persons, there is a sense in which all three persons "do" whatever any of them does. On the other hand, insofar as it makes any sense to speak of distinct persons, i.e., distinct ways in which that divine essence is manifest, it also makes sense to attribute specific actions to only one of the three members. Hence, it is the second member of the Godhead (not the others) who becomes incarnate as Jesus of Nazareth, the Christ. If it was the divine essence alone (and we didn't designate that essence as subsisting in a particular person of the Godhead) that became incarnate as Jesus Christ, then we would have to say that all three members of the Godhead became incarnate in Christ. Christians maintain, however, that it is the second person of the Godhead who became incarnate, just as they say that the third person of the Trinity inspired the Bible. Granted, it is hard to see how all three members can have the numerically identical essence while only one of them becomes incarnate (which involved keeping the divine nature, while adding a human nature), but that is the mystery that we can't understand. Anyone who grants, for example, that the voice praising Jesus at his baptism is the Father's and not a case of ventriloquism, and that the dove that descended is not just a dove nor a hallucination but the Holy Spirit, must also grant that somehow each divine person can act distinctly from the other two, even though all three in some sense do every deed of each member of the Godhead.

The response to Bartel, then, is that in considering the incarnation (that divine action), we are focusing on the sortal "person," not the sortal "God." Hence, the second member becomes incarnate, not all three, whereas if we were looking at this event from the perspective of the sortal "God," since there is only one divine essence, we would say that God becomes incarnate.

There is another way to make this point. Bartel's complaint seems cogent because, in effect, it is a challenge to explain the "mechanism" (the "how") by which only one person can become incarnate, though that person shares the one essence with two other divine persons. However, our ignorance of how God does this does not mean that the logical coherence of the doctrine of the Trinity is jeopardized by invoking relative identity. God is one relative to the sortal "deity," and three relative to the sortal "person," and such claims are logically consistent. This shows how it is *possible* for God to be one and three at the same time without contradiction; and remember, all we need to meet the charge of contradiction is a possible way the various claims can all be true. Our inability to specify how one of those persons does any act by himself alone (despite sharing the same essence with the other two) doesn't prove that our *formulation* of the doctrine of the Trinity in terms of relative identity fails to remove the logical contradiction.

Macnamara, Reyes, and Reyes have recently proposed a different model for understanding relative trinitarianism, but what they defend is fundamentally what Bartel and so many others, like Peter van Inwagen and Peter Geach, have offered (and in some cases defended).[64] According to Macnamara, Reyes, and Reyes, the apparent problem with the Trinity stems from thinking that it follows the logic of normal set theory. If we understand the set of Divine Persons to be a subset of the set of Gods, then a problem arises. As they note, the inclusion relation among sets is one to one. That is, if "A is included in B, then for each member of A there is a member of B identical with it, and identity being a symmetric relation, there are as many B's identical with A's as there are A's with B's. The identity implicated in set inclusion implies that the B's cannot be less numerous than the A's."[65]

In this case the A's would be divine persons and the B's would be Gods, so if there are three divine persons, there must also be three Gods. Of course, that is contrary to the evangelical doctrine of the Trinity. What this shows is that the relation of Divine Persons to Gods cannot be understood along the lines of set-theoretic inclusion; some other interpretation is needed. What is required is an interpretation under which all A's are B's but there are still fewer B's than A's. At first blush this may sound impossible, but Macnamara and company offer examples where this actually happens. Imagine an airline passenger Smith who takes three trips on the same airline to the same place in three separate months. Smith counts as three separate *passengers,* but of course, in each case it is the same *person.* So there are three if we count *passengers,* but only one if we tally *persons.* Everyone who counts as a passenger is also a person, but we don't add another person each time we count a passenger. Otherwise we would say that three separate people made the three trips when in fact it was Smith each time.

Someone may reply that since it was Smith each time, we can only add one to the passenger list as we count the number of passengers for the three trips. But this is certainly wrong, as is evident from a simple illustration. Suppose this flight is long enough to require meal service. Can the airline tell Smith, "We know you're making three flights, but since it's you and not three separate people, we'll only order one meal, and it'll have to serve you for all three flights; perhaps you'll want to eat just one-third of the meal on each flight, so that you'll have something for each flight"? The airline may tell Smith this, but they aren't likely to get away with it. If the rule is that every *person* gets one meal, then poor Smith, regardless of how many times he takes this trip using the same airline, will be served the total of only one meal ever. On the other hand, if the airline company counts the number of *passengers* on each flight, and if each passenger gets a meal, Smith need not worry about going hungry.[66]

Lest we think this is the only example of all members in one group being included in another, while the second group has fewer members than the first, Macnamara, Reyes, and Reyes offer the following series of examples:

> Other examples of the same phenomenon are patients admitted to a hospital, diners in a restaurant and customers in a shop. The counts of patients, diners and customers need not equal the corresponding counts of persons. Particularly interesting for us is the case of majors in a university. A single person can at one and the same time major in philosophy and mathematics. The Department of Philosophy and Mathematics will separately include the student in their lists of majors and the university will add the lists and count two majors although only one person is involved. Other such examples are patients and professors. A single person can simultaneously be the patient of a urologist and of a heart specialist: that is be two patients. A person can be a professor in two separate universities. There are many such examples. They are particularly relevant because the Divine Persons, being eternal, are simultaneously a single God.[67]

The relation of this to the Trinity is easy enough to map. The key point is that we have two separate categories indicated by the nouns "Divine Person" and "God." That is, each label designates a kind. This is significant, because proper names denote an individual in a kind. Our typical use of "Father," "Son," and "Holy Spirit" treats them as proper names. Hence, the only question is to which *kind* do the individuals designated by the names "Father," "Son," and "Holy Spirit" belong. The answer is that they are individuals in the kind "Divine Person," not individuals of the kind "God." If the kind

"Divine Person" is category A, and the kind "God" is category B, then all A's are B, but there are more members in category A than B. In the case of the airline traveler, every passenger on each flight is a person, but when the same person takes several flights, the number of *persons* doesn't increase but the *passenger* count does. Similarly, Father, Son, and Holy Spirit (all Divine Persons) are God, but that doesn't mean there are as many gods as divine persons. It is the same God manifested in three distinct persons, just as it is the same person "manifested" on three separate passenger lists and flights.[68]

In light of these principles, Macnamara, et al. explain that the three propositions "the Father is God," "the Son is God," and "the Holy Spirit is God" should be understood as saying the following: "underlying the Divine Person that is the Father is a God," "underlying the Divine Person that is the Son is a God," and "underlying the Divine Person that is the Holy Spirit is a God."[69] Of course, Scripture says, and the doctrine of the Trinity agrees, that there is only one God, so the God spoken of as underlying each divine person is one and the same God, numerically speaking. If this is hard to grasp, think of the relation of persons to passengers in the airline illustration.

If the three persons are the same God, how can we distinguish one from the other? Macnamara, Reyes, and Reyes suggest that we use predicates applicable only to each individual member of the Trinity. They offer the standard predicates associated with the immanent Trinity, i.e., the Father is ungenerate, the Son is generated by the Father, and the Spirit proceeds from the Father and Son.[70] I have argued that such doctrines should be abandoned, so how else can we distinguish the three persons? Here we must focus on predicates that are true of each alone in their economic roles. For example, the Son alone became incarnate, and he alone was baptized. The Father alone spoke words praising Jesus at Christ's baptism, and the Holy Spirit alone descended as a dove at that event. We could multiply other unique predicates that would distinguish the three, but the point is already served. Even if we deny predicates usually applied to members of the Trinity according to their internal relations, we can still distinguish each from the others.

These two proposals by Bartel and by Macnamara, Reyes, and Reyes, and the various illustrations offered show that the doctrine of the Trinity is not logically contradictory. There are possible ways to explain how one being could at the same time be one and three. Moreover, I believe that the doctrine as formulated earlier in the chapter accurately reflects biblical teaching. I grant that it goes beyond what Scripture explicitly says, but in light of biblical teaching, the parts of the formulation that go beyond biblical statements seem warranted, even necessary. Are the Niceno-Constantinopolitan and the Athanasian Creeds adequate to express this doctrine? With the exception of claims about eternal generation and the like, I believe they are. However, as we have seen, it requires careful historical analysis to understand exactly what the fathers meant when they said that God is one as to essence and three as to persons or subsistences. But once we understand the language, we see that it does convey the concepts Scripture and reason require.

III

THE ACTS

OF GOD

THE DECREE OF GOD

What a magnificent, majestic God we have! Who or what is like the God described in the preceding pages? Even if he never did anything, he would be eminently worthy of our adoration and praise in virtue of who and what he is! Creating a world, redeeming lost sinners, establishing his kingdom of righteousness and peace add absolutely nothing to God's infinite worth. But all of those acts demonstrate the grandeur of God, and he has in fact decided to show his glorious nature by acting in the universe.

While God has done many things in our world, only some are the subject of this volume. Separate areas of theology deal with God's revelation of himself, salvation, and his ultimate victory over evil as he establishes his kingdom through his church and through a future inception of the kingdom here on earth. Those theological doctrines and the actions they bespeak are the subjects for other volumes in this series. Still, several divine acts are traditionally the subject matter for a volume on the doctrine of God, and our discussion focuses on them.

God decided to act beyond the immanent bounds of fellowship within the Godhead. This involved a decision to create our universe. Once God created that universe he did not withdraw from his creation. Instead, he exercises providential control over what he created. Exactly what that involves is debated. However, divine action in creation and providence presuppose two issues, one already addressed and a second that we must address in this chapter.

Because ours is a temporal universe, if God acts in it, he must do so within space and time. As already seen, there is a major question about how an eternal God relates to time. Whether one believes that God is timelessly eternal or that he is temporal, one must show that he can act in our space-time world. If he can't, there is no use in discussing any of the topics in this section of the book, for it is impossible for God to do such acts. In fact, the question of God's relation to time and how he acts in it is even logically prior to handling the problem of God's relation to evil. If God cannot act in our world, then he cannot rid the world of evil, nor can we hold him accountable for failing to do so.

Scripture and Christian theology, however, uniformly affirm that God is a God of action. I have already argued that a better case can be made for God's acting in our world if he is temporal, rather than atemporal. Granting that God can and does act in our world, specifically what has he done, and how are we to understand it? Even more fundamentally, does God act according to a plan he has already worked out, or does he decide what to do as he sees the history of our universe unfold? It is my contention that God would not create a universe he had not planned to make in the first place. He would not send a Savior and call a people to himself without previously deciding to do so.

To what extent has God planned human history, and to what extent does he control it? These are the issues I shall introduce in this chapter and complete in chapters 13–16. Theologians who talk about a divine plan typically do so under the rubric of the divine decree. What this means, however, needs explanation. In common parlance, the term "decree" conjures visions of a potentate issuing statements of his wishes, his laws, his rules for his subjects. This is not, however, the basic point theologians make when speaking of the divine decree.

The Westminster Shorter Catechism says that the decree of God is "His eternal purpose according to the counsel of His will, whereby, for His own glory, He hath foreordained whatsoever comes to pass."[1] This definition contains a great deal of theology which we must clarify, but the basic notion is clear enough. God's decree is his decision concerning whatever will happen in our universe. His decision made actions and events certain. Millard Erickson argues that this amounts to saying that God has a plan which he has thought out, a plan that covers whatever happens.[2] In my discussion, I shall use the terms "decree(s)" and "plan" interchangeably unless otherwise indicated.

Various biblical terms speak of God's plan and purpose. The OT uses a number of terms. The term 'āṣah, from yā'aṣ, means "to counsel or give advice," and it suggests the intellectual element in the decree, i.e., the decree was not arbitrary, without forethought and reason. This term appears in Job 38:2; 42:3; Ps 33:11; 106:13; 107:11; Prov 19:21; Isa 5:19; 14:26; 19:17; 46:10, 11; Jer 32:19; 49:20; 50:45; and Mic 4:12. Another Hebrew term that stresses the intellectual element in the decree is sôd, from yāsad. In the Niphal stem it means "to sit together in deliberation," and it occurs in Jer 23:18, 22. Then there is mĕzimmāh, from zāmam, which means "to meditate," "to have in mind," or "to purpose" (Jer 4:28; 51:12; Prov 30:32). Moreover, yāṣar carries the idea of purpose and prior determination. It appears in Ps 139:16; Isa 22:11; 37:26; and 46:11. Two other OT terms are noteworthy. One is ḥaphēṣ, which refers to inclination, will, or good pleasure (Isa 53:10), and raṣôn (Ps 51:19; Isa 49:8), which means "to please" or "to be delighted," and hence refers to delight, good pleasure, or sovereign will.[3]

In the NT various terms also relate to the divine plan. *Boulē* (and various forms of the verb *boulomai*) is used of the decree in general, but especially emphasizes that God's plan is based on counsel and deliberation. This term appears in passages such as Acts 2:23; 4:28; Eph 1:11; and Heb 6:17. A second term is *thelēma* (from *thelō*—also *thelēsis*). The major focus of this term is God's will or volition. Rather than stressing the deliberative element in God's plan, it emphasizes more the actual willing of his plan. We see this sense, for example, in Eph 1:11. A third major term is *eudokia* which, in the context of God's plan, refers to the purpose(s) God sought to achieve by his plan. It also speaks of God's freedom in making his plan, in that his choices are determined by his good pleasure or purpose alone. Moreover, in some passages it also speaks of God's delight in what he has decided to do. Passages that use this term are Matt 11:26; Luke 2:14; and Eph 1:5, 9. Several other terms are also noteworthy, for they speak of God's predestining or foreordaining of events, his purposing and planning of various events. Those terms are *prooorizō* ("predestine"), which occurs in Acts 4:28; Rom 8:29, 30; 1 Cor 2:7; and Eph 1:5, 11; *protassō* ("to order or prescribe") in Acts 17:26; *proetoimazō* ("prepare beforehand") in Rom 9:23 and Eph 2:10; and *protithēmi* and its noun *prothesis* ("plan, purpose, intend"), which appear in Rom 8:28; 9:11; Eph 1:11; 3:11; and 2 Tim 1:9.[4] Other terms such as *proginōskō* and *prognōsis* speak of God's knowledge of future events and actions, and they come up more specifically in discussing the divine decrees, foreknowledge, and free will.

In light of this biblical terminology, one might think there is agreement about the decree of God, but that is not so. The idea of an eternal divine plan covering everything that occurs raises significant questions. If God plans everything that happens, including humans' actions, how can those actions be free? And what about God himself? If he has already planned everything that will occur, is he free to change his mind and interrupt the fulfillment of that plan in favor of a new plan? Moreover, if everything is pre-programmed so that God's creatures do exactly what he has chosen, how can they be held morally accountable for their acts? Conversely, since God foreordained our sin, how can he escape moral responsibility?

These are some of the many questions raised by the issue of the divine decree, and theologians disagree on how to answer them. Because this is such a contentious issue, I shall handle it in several chapters. This chapter will be devoted to the different opinions about whether there even is a divine decree or set of decrees. Having described the various viewpoints, I shall then turn to the biblical data and ask whether Scripture teaches that God has such an all-encompassing plan, and if so, what its nature is. A final section of this chapter treats the issue of the order of the divine decrees.

In this chapter, I shall argue that Scripture warrants belief in a divine, all-encompassing plan. That still leaves unanswered a host of questions mentioned above. These issues will be addressed in this and subsequent chapters.

Is There A Divine Decree? Positions Described

At several points in this book we have seen the interplay between various theological models of God. That is true of this issue as well, though there is even more variation on the issue of the decree than on some other aspects of the doctrine of God. As we proceed, we must note not only what various models say about the divine decree, but also their rationale.

Classical Theism

Classical theism sees God as a reigning monarch who controls everything. Critics of this model contend that divine attributes such as absolute immutability, impassibility, simplicity, and atemporal eternity—attributes that are part of the classical conception of God—only make God more remote, uninvolved, and unrelated to our world. Hence, they underscore the portrait of a solitary, domineering monarch who has little to do with his subjects.

The classical model of God is the one most closely associated with the doctrine of the divine decree, although there are variations within the classical view. Proponents of this model affirm that there is a divine decree and that it covers everything that will ever occur. God made the decree according to his purposes, many known only to him, and whatever God has willed comes to pass. God's plan for history was made in eternity past, and it is immutable.

This understanding of the divine decree fits very well the classical set of divine attributes. Because God is timelessly eternal, according to this model, he could not will part of his plan at one point and then later will another part. Moreover, once having willed his plan, he could not change it. Doing either of these things is impossible, for both require a sequence in God's actions, and that introduces a basis for temporal measurement, but an atemporal God is not subject to such measurement. Moreover, we have seen the connection between strict immutability and atemporal eternity. Any change in God's decree undercuts atemporality, but it also destroys the absolute immutability that atemporality seems to entail. In addition, the classical God knows all things, including the future. If God, however, doesn't have an all-encompassing plan, a plan chosen all at once, then as our time passes, it seems that he learns things he didn't previously know. To postulate such changes contradicts immutability, atemporality, and omniscience, so whatever God knows, he must know forever. The classical tradition believes that Scripture teaches that the future can be known, and God knows it.

Within the classical tradition, there has been variation in understanding of the decree. For example, Calvinists who hold the classical conception uniformly affirm that God's decree covers and controls all things. Though some speak of God's permitting sin and evil in our world, Calvin was uncomfortable with this language, for it suggests that at times God steps back and lets us control the course of things. Calvin denied that God does any evil or is morally responsible for it, but the idea that any action or event falls outside of the divine decree was foreign to his thinking.[5] Moreover, within strongly Calvinistic thinking one finds supralapsarianism, the view that logically before God decreed the creation of mankind, he decreed its fall and a savior for its sin. Such views are found in Beza and among many modern Dutch Reformed thinkers. Demarest and Lewis add that it is present in Luther and in medieval thinkers such as Gottschalk.[6]

On the other hand, other theologians in the classical tradition have held somewhat different views of the decree. They agree that there is a divine decree and that it covers everything. They also grant that it was made in eternity past and is immutable. Still, they understand the logical order of the decrees along an infra- or sublapsarian scheme, according to which the decree of the human race's fall into sin and the decree of salvation logically come after God's decision to create the world and the human race. Moreover, theologians in this category such as Augustine and Aquinas distinguish between God's unconditional will and his permissive will. The former covers God's decision to create a universe and his election of some people to salvation. The latter covers matters such as the evil humans do and the ultimate reprobation of those who reject Christ throughout their life without turning to him. God simply passes over them and leaves them in the sin they have freely chosen. Augustine explains the point as follows: "Nothing comes about unless God wills it so, either by permitting it to happen or himself performing it."[7] Similarly, Aquinas distinguished God's unconditional will from his permissive will. As to evil, it is the free act of human beings or Satan, but God did grant the freedom to commit such evil. "Since the very act of the free will is traced to God as a cause, it necessarily follows that everything happening from the exercise of the free will must be subject to divine providence. For human providence is included under the providence of God, as a particular under a universal cause."[8]

The preceding description of classical theism must not be misunderstood. One might think it means that anyone in this camp also holds some form of Calvinism, but this is surely incorrect. For example, a theist committed to the classical package of divine attributes might be a deist. In that case, God planned to create the universe and did, but God had no other plans, so what happens in our world is completely up to us. Given divine omniscience and immutability, deists might also say that God foresaw the future (otherwise his knowledge would grow, contrary to divine immutability), but that doesn't mean he controls or chooses anything that occurs.

A deistic conception of the classical God is not the only alternative to a Calvinistic understanding of the decree. Any Arminian theologian holding the classical conception of the divine attributes might also believe in a divine decree. Of course, to make room for the creaturely freedom that goes with Arminian theology, such Arminians would say that God's decree is based on his foreseeing what we will do if created. Here foreknowledge means God's intellectual awareness of our freely performed actions in advance of their occurring. God, of course, can choose and do certain things unilaterally (e.g., various miracles he performs), and those divine actions would be part of the decree. But most things that occur in our world do not involve God's exclusive action but rather involve the acts of God's creatures. So God cannot predetermine what free creatures will do, but he can, on this view, foresee their deeds and then choose to create the world containing those creatures and actions, rather than not creating at all or creating some other world.

On this wedding of Arminian theology with classical theism, God is still absolutely immutable and atemporally eternal. His knowledge of what will happen and his decision to create the world must be timeless, and whatever God does in our world must be done timelessly in the way atemporalists describe God acting. The only potential hitch for the Arminian classical theist is that with the Arminian notion of free will, there are no guarantees about what free creatures will do with their freedom, and hence it is hard to understand how God could actually know ahead of time what they will do. But the problem of free will and foreknowledge confronts all defenders of libertarian free will, not just classical theists who would hold this notion of freedom. In a later chapter, we shall look in detail at this issue. For now let us grant that God knows what free creatures will do. If so, there is no reason to fear that God will have to alter his plan or actions, so Arminians could espouse the classical model of God and its basic teaching about the decree.

In sum, setting aside deism, two broad theological traditions can and do subscribe to some form of classical theism. One is the more Reformed tradition associated with Calvinism, and the other is more Arminian. The more Reformed group invariably argues that the decree covers everything and is based solely on God's purposes and desires. The more Arminian wing of classical theism holds that the decree is based on what God foresaw his creatures would freely do, if created. God has general plans and purposes, and he may decide to do certain things unilaterally in our world, but since most things are done by the free actions of his creatures, his general plans and purposes must be accomplished in light of what he foresees about their actions. With this theology, God isn't quite so totally in control of things as he is in a more Calvinistic understanding, but there is a decree which covers everything that occurs.

Though there have been Arminian theologians who believed in a divine decree and also held classical theism's views about divine attributes and actions, most classical theists who believe in the decree have been more Calvinistic. The net result for the Calvinistically oriented is that God has very strong control of everything that happens, even if he is not the sufficient or efficient cause of all (e.g., he doesn't do or cause evil, but controls it). It is just this view of a God who monopolizes all power that is so offensive to process theologians. If classical theism of the more Calvinistic vintage represents one extreme on the decree, process theology is the other.

Process Theism

Process theists reject the classical description of an isolated, unfeeling, all-knowing, all-powerful, domineering monarch God. The process God is mutable, passible, temporal, and limited in power and knowledge. Though he acts in our world, he does so in a noncoercive way. In light of these views, there can be no talk of divine decrees or divine control. As a caring and responsive God who is sensitive to our needs at any moment, God cannot have a predetermined plan for history. Instead, he must wait and see what happens before deciding what he will do. A preset plan would undoubtedly override human freedom and reassert the power monopoly of the classical God. This the process God will not do.

In addition, even if the process God wanted to plan a future, his limited knowledge would not let him. In virtue of his primordial pole, he knows the possibilities for becoming, and can present any of them to his creatures for prehension, but who knows what his creatures will do? Process theology also rejects the idea that God just foresees what we will freely do and plans accordingly, because libertarian freedom makes it impossible for anyone to know the future.

So, a divine decree is impossible both because of God's limited knowledge and because our future free actions cannot be foreseen. A divine decree is also impossible because of the process account of divine power and action. The process God is not omnipotent, and what power he has must be exercised so as not to abridge creaturely freedom. Given these strictures, it makes no sense to talk of an all-comprehensive divine plan that God wills and inevitably accomplishes. Some might think the process God could still plan to do certain things and accomplish certain goals in our world while letting us decide the exact course events will take leading to those goals. However, this won't fit with the process God. What happens if God's planned actions and goals disrupt and even cancel human freedom? In advance, there is no guarantee that they won't do so, and since the process God will not abridge our freedom, it is senseless for him to make specific plans or have particular goals for the future. At any given moment, God knows the ideal subjective aim for any of us, but he will not force us to do it. His attempts to persuade us are totally resistible. So, if God makes plans, he must be ready for some or even all of them to be frustrated.

Mediating Positions

Between classical and process theism, there are several theologies whose views on the divine decree are noteworthy. We saw that there is an Arminian form of classical theism that holds to the decrees, but there are also Arminians who reject some of the classical tradition's account of the divine attributes and also believe that there is a decree of God. For example, some Arminians reject the strong sense of divine immutability and impassibility in favor of a modified notion. Those thinkers might also claim that God is temporal rather than atemporal. Still, they believe in God's general providential control over the world and even believe that the divine decree gives a blueprint for history. Of course, Arminians who hold to a decree typically argue that it is based on what God foreknows about the free actions of his creatures. Hence, God has general goals and plans, but the specific path he might use to reach them is constructed in light of his foreknowledge of his creatures' free actions. This allows God to accomplish his goals without nullifying human freedom.

Of course, this form of Arminianism must explain how, given libertarian freedom, God can foresee the free actions of his human creatures, but theologians in this tradition are not without answers. Two answers are not open to the sort of Arminian I am describing, however. Some proponents of libertarian free will hold that God doesn't know the future, so there is no sense in speaking of a decree, for a decree presupposes that God knows the future. Others committed to libertarian freedom opt for the Boethian resolution to the freedom/foreknowledge issue, but this option isn't open to the sort of Arminian now in view, for Boethius's resolution puts God outside of time, whereas the Arminian position now under discussion puts him in time. Still, the position under consideration has answers. Someone holding this view might handle the freedom/foreknowledge problem by appealing to middle knowledge,[9] or they might appeal to the Ockhamist strategy or to simple foreknowledge. What these strategies involve and how successful they are will be handled in a later chapter. I mention them now to show that there is an Arminian position that is a mediating view between classical and process theism, and to say that this system has several ways it can respond to the problem of freedom and foreknowledge raised by its commitment to libertarian free will and a divine decree.

The open view or the risk view of divine providence (part of what John Sanders labels relational theism[10]) presents itself as a mediating position between classical and process theism. On the one hand, it concurs with process theism in rejecting absolute divine immutability and impassibility, simplicity, and atemporal eternity. On the other hand, it grants God omnipotence and sovereignty like classical theism, but nuances those attributes so that they are much closer to the process account of God than to the classical account. Moreover, the open view rejects the process notion of God as dipolar. As to divine providence, the decree of God, and divine omniscience in relation to divine foreknowledge, the open view is far closer to process views than to classical systems that affirm a decree.

According to the open view, "God's will is not the ultimate explanation for everything that happens; human decisions and actions make an important contribution too. Thus history is the combined result of what God and his creatures decide to do."[11] Since God gave his creatures *libertarian* free will, he cannot guarantee ahead of time how they will use it. God must simply wait and see what happens and then respond. Clearly, this system has no room for an eternal decree setting forth a blueprint for all of history.

Despite rejecting a decree, open view defenders still believe that God exercises providential control over our world. Sanders distinguishes between specific sovereignty, according to which God foreordains everything that happens, and general sovereignty. According to general sovereignty, God sets up the general structures of our world and he has general purposes he wants to accomplish. Those purposes stem from his desire to establish a loving relation with his creatures who will freely respond in love. However, "general sovereignty denies that each and every event has a specific divine intention."[12] Within the general structures of the world God has established, he allows certain things to occur, good and bad, which he does not specifically intend. Thus, specific sovereignty (sometimes called meticulous providence) does not obtain in our universe. Clark Pinnock believes he has the conclusive answer for those who insist that God plans everything and has total control:

> Just the fact of our rebellion as sinners against God's will testifies it is not so. The fall into sin was against the will of God and proves by itself that God does not exercise total control over all events in this world. Evils happen that are not supposed to happen, that grieve and anger God. Free will theism is the best way to account for this fact. To say that God hates sin while secretly willing it, to say that God warns us not to fall away though it is impossible, to say that God loves the world while excluding most people from an opportunity of salvation, to say that God warmly invites sinners to come knowing all the while that they cannot possibly do so—such things do not deserve to be called mysteries when that is just a euphemism for nonsense.[13]

Still, in light of these commitments, we might wonder how the open God can accomplish even his general purposes and goals for our world. Sanders quickly replies that the God who takes risks is supremely wise and creative. Regardless of what we do, God is creative and perceptive enough to see how to respond so that he will still ultimately accomplish his main goals. As Sanders says, "if one of God's plans fails, he has others ready at hand and finds other ways of accomplishing his objectives."[14] Though some proponents of libertarian free will believe that God will ultimately get the future in all its details that he wants, Sanders disagrees, for this overlooks the pervasive and irrational nature of human sin. God can accomplish his general goals, but exactly what happens ultimately depends in part on his creatures' responses, so there can be no guarantees about details.[15] In answering whether God's will can be thwarted, Sanders writes:

> In terms of the boundaries, structures and goals of the project that God has sovereignly established, there is no question whatsoever that God gets what he wants. God can create the world, provide for it and

grant it his love without anyone or anything being able to thwart his overarching desires. If God decides to create a world with persons capable of reciprocating the divine love and if God establishes genuine give-and-take relations with them, then it is proper to say that nothing can stymie God's intentions. If God does not force the creatures to reciprocate his love, then the possibility is introduced that at least some of them may fail to enter into the divine love, and thus certain of God's specific desires might be thwarted. It is important to note that if in some cases God does not get what he wants, it is ultimately because of the decision *God* made to create the sort of world in which God does not get everything he wants.[16]

Sanders makes it very clear that he believes God doesn't always get what he wants. His creatures can and do sometimes thwart his will. Moreover, Sanders thinks Scripture supports such views.[17]

Given these views, the open view's account of divine knowledge is predictable. Open view proponents uniformly agree that God's knowledge is less extensive than Calvinists hold. For one thing, God cannot know what free creatures will do before they do it, for to know that would mean that they could not do otherwise, and that contradicts libertarian free will. Still, God is omniscient, for as William Hasker explains, God's omniscience means that *"at any time God knows all propositions such that God's knowing them at that time is logically possible."*[18] Hasker then explains that, consistent with libertarian free will, it is impossible to know what creatures with such freedom will do; hence, it is logically impossible for God to know the future free actions of his creatures. Still, God knows everything knowable, so he is omniscient.

But don't biblical prophecies show that God exhaustively foreknows whatever will come to pass? In response, open view defenders adopt what they call *presentism*. According to presentism, God has exhaustive knowledge of the past and the present. As a result, he has various beliefs about what people will likely do in a given situation. If God predicts what they will do, given his exhaustive knowledge of their character and all the events past and present that have shaped them, it is a fairly good bet that God's prediction will be correct. But with libertarian free will, there are no guarantees, so God cannot infallibly predict what his creatures will freely do.[19]

As to biblical prophecies, we saw in chapter 2 that advocates of the open view repeatedly divide prophecies into three categories, none of which requires exhaustive foreknowledge or meticulous providential control of all things. The open view raises issues that will be addressed in later chapters, but here we can say that it rejects the idea that there is such a thing as a divine decree. It arrives at that position on different grounds than do process thinkers and Arminians who reject a decree, but it agrees that no divine plan covers and controls whatever happens.

The view of the divine decrees that I shall be arguing in this and later chapters is also a mediating position between classical and process theism. My

THE DECREE OF GOD □ 511

position on whether there is a divine decree and about how much control God has over our lives is a form of the Calvinism described under the classical view, but it is not identical to it. I have already shown my divergence from the classical understanding of the divine attributes, and my understanding is neither that of the process or open view, nor does it require those views or any form of Arminian theology. I hold that there is a divine decree and that God foreordains all that comes to pass. This doesn't mean he personally and exclusively does everything that occurs, but it does mean he decided what will occur and he has control over all that happens. Just what that control is and how it relates to freedom and moral responsibility will be explained in later chapters. As to the order of the decrees, I shall argue that neither supra- nor sublapsarianism is preferable, because the discussion itself rests ultimately on conceptual errors that I shall explain. So my position mediates between classical and process views, but it is neither a traditional Arminian nor an open view position.

SCRIPTURE AND THE DECREE

Does Scripture teach or warrant the doctrine of the divine decree? In this section, we investigate that matter with two main questions in mind. The first is whether Scripture teaches that there is a divine decree or plan for our world. If so, then we must ask secondly about the decree's nature. In addressing the first question the key is not whether Scripture uses the term "decree," but whether it teaches the concept.

Is There a Divine Decree?

The OT contains many passages that teach God's control over this world's affairs. Moreover, some passages say he made a plan long ago and will carry it out. Several passages in Psalms are a good place to begin. In Ps 103:19 David claims that God has established his throne in heaven and rules over all. In Ps 115:3 the psalmist contrasts pagan gods with Israel's God. He says, "Our God is in the heavens; He does whatever He pleases." Again in Psalm 135 Israel's God is compared to idols. The psalmist says, "Whatever the LORD pleases, He does, in heaven and in earth, in the seas and in all deeps" (v. 6). Likewise, after his trials and confrontation with God, Job says (Job 42:2) "I know that Thou canst do all things, and that no purpose of Thine can be thwarted." Job received such a vision of God's majesty and grandeur that he realized that it is foolish amid trials to wonder if God is in control or if he can help us. God can do whatever he wants, and if he decides to do something, nothing can stop him.

These passages are in stark contrast to claims that God's purposes can be thwarted by our choices. Moreover, biblical writers say that even when we think we control what happens, God is in charge, and he has a plan that will be accomplished. In Prov 19:21 the writer says that there are many plans in a man's heart, but "the counsel of the Lord, it will stand." The point is rather clear. Though we may plan our course and even choose a path, we cannot always guarantee that we can go that way. In contrast, whatever God decides will be accomplished. Similarly, we may think that apparently chance occurrences such as the roll of dice are left entirely open, but the writer of Proverbs says that the outcome is in the Lord's hands and comes from him (16:33).

Isaiah vividly shows that God's plan will be accomplished, despite our intentions to the contrary. In chapter 10, we learn that Assyria was God's chosen instrument to punish Israel. However, Assyria was not intent merely to capture booty and seize plunder but also wanted to destroy and cut off many nations (vv. 5-7). In verses 10-12 God says that after he has used Assyria to punish Israel, he will punish Assyria himself. After all, God is in charge, not Assyria. In verse 15 God asks, "Is the axe to boast itself over the one who chops with it? Is the saw to exalt itself over the one who wields it? That would be like a club wielding those who lift it, or like a rod lifting him who is not wood." Obviously, such things are folly, and it is also folly to think that God (the wielder of the axe) will be subject to the whims of Assyria (the axe). Again in chapter 14 Isaiah records the Lord's warning of judgment to Assyria; God has planned it, and no one can stop it. As the Lord says (v. 27), "The LORD of hosts has planned, and who can frustrate it? And as for His stretched-out hand, who can turn it back?" Some may claim that this only refers to the incident of punishing Assyria, but we must realize that this instance is an example of the more general principle we saw in Ps 135:5-6; Job 42:2; and Prov 19:21. Whatever God wants to do, he will do, and no one will successfully stand in his way.

In Isaiah 46 God compares himself to the idols of Babylon. God asks to whom Israel would liken him. Though some plead for help from an idol, the idol cannot answer (vv. 5-7). Verses 10-11 say that God is the one "declaring the end from the beginning and from ancient times things which have not been done, saying 'My purpose will be established, and I will accomplish all my good pleasure'; calling a bird of prey from the east, the man of My purpose from a far country. Truly I have spoken; truly I will bring it to pass. I have planned it, surely I will do it." This is surely more than a comment about God's supremacy over Babylonian idols. God says he has purposes and plans and he will bring them to pass. What idol can say and do that? No wonder God says in verse 9 that there is no one like him. See also Isa 22:11; 37:22-29; and 45:1-9.

A good summary of this point comes from the lips of Nebuchadnezzar. Nebuchadnezzar was overwhelmed by a sense of self-importance, so God humbled him and drove him out to live with the wild beasts. Eventually, he came to his senses and the Lord restored his sanity. Nebuchadnezzar was a great king, but he came to see that there is no king like God, and no kingdom like God's (Dan 4:34). Nebuchadnezzar says (v. 35), "All the inhabitants of the earth are accounted as nothing, but He does according to His will in the host of heaven and among the inhabitants of earth; and no one can ward off His hand or say to Him, 'What hast Thou done?'" God is in control and will get his way in heaven and on earth. This doesn't mean that God does not care about us, for in studying the divine attributes, we saw that he does. God cares for us, but don't think that means we can manipulate him or that we are somehow his equals. Nebuchadnezzar thought less of God and more of himself than he should; he learned the hard way that doing so is a losing proposition (see also 1 Chron 29:11; Ps 66:7; Jer 23:20).

OT passages already mentioned speak of God's rule over all and of his plans being carried out. As the writer of Proverbs says (16:4), "The LORD has made everything for its own purpose, even the wicked for the day of evil." In light of these Scriptures, it is hard to maintain that the OT doesn't teach that God has a plan and doesn't warrant holding specific sovereignty.

This is confirmed and clarified by the NT. Many passages speak of God's plan and purposes, and they often add that the plan was predetermined, predestined, or foreordained. Consider, for example, Christ's death. Contrary to what some suggest, God was not counting on Christ gaining such acceptance that the cross would be unnecessary, only to learn later that Christ was rejected and it was necessary to change plans.[20] On the day of Pentecost, Peter told his audience (Acts 2:23) that Christ was delivered up by the predetermined plan and foreknowledge of God. Indeed, humans gladly put him to death, but none of this was unplanned or unforeseen. Similarly, after the release of Peter and John (Acts 4:17-23), they relate what happened, and their friends lift their voices to praise God. They say, "For truly in this city there were gathered together against Thy holy servant Jesus, whom Thou didst anoint, both Herod and Pontius Pilate, along with the Gentiles and the peoples of Israel, to do whatever Thy hand and Thy purpose predestined to occur" (vv. 27-28). In 1 Pet 1:18-19, Peter reminds his readers that they are redeemed by Christ's blood. He explains in verse 20 that this was "foreknown before the foundation of the world." As we shall see later, this foreknowing is foreordination. Christ's death was clearly planned from all eternity.

Not only did God plan Christ's death, he also planned its purpose. Scripture teaches that Christ's death is the price to win redemption for lost sinners, but God didn't send Christ into the world to die in hope that someone might receive the payment made for them but without any guarantee that this would happen. Rather, God elected some to salvation in Christ before the foundation of the world (Eph 1:4). In verse 5 Paul explains that, through Jesus Christ, God predestined us to adoption as sons of God; and he adds that this was done "according to the kind intention of His will." It wasn't foreseen deeds or merit that moved God to elect us, but the kind intention of his will. In verse 9 Paul repeats that God revealed the mystery of his will according to the kind intention which he purposed in him, that purpose being the summing up of all things in Christ (v. 10). In verse 11 Paul repeats that believers have been predestined to salvation. As Paul begins 2 Timothy, he returns to this theme in chapter 1, verses 8-9. Paul speaks of the power of God who has saved us. In verse 9 he says that this wasn't done on the basis of our works, but "according to His own purpose and grace which was granted us in Christ Jesus from all eternity." Grace is a free, unmerited gift, not wages that are earned. Paul says salvation is an unmerited gift given for God's purposes, and God made that decision from all eternity.

To further underscore the point that salvation depends on God's gracious choice, we need only turn to Romans 9. I shall say more about this passage in a later chapter on the decree and freedom, but I must now comment especially on verses 15-18. In the preceding verses, Paul notes that God chose Jacob over Esau even before they were born (v. 11) "in order that God's purpose according to His choice might stand, not because of works, but because of Him who calls." Paul then imagines the objection that this seems unfair, and replies that it is not. God was totally within his rights (vv. 14-15), for it is his right to have mercy and compassion on whom he wills; none of this depends on man's works or merit, but on God's mercy alone. To illustrate this point, Paul turns to God's dealings with Pharaoh (v. 17). God says in the Scriptures to Pharaoh, "For this very purpose I raised you up, to demonstrate My power in you, and that My name might be proclaimed throughout the whole earth." Paul repeats (v. 18) that God has mercy on whom he desires and hardens whomever he wishes. These examples in Romans 9 are used to teach that God elected Israel to be his special people. He also chose beforehand to save many Gentiles (vv. 22-26).

In Eph 3:8-11 Paul says that God made him a minister of the gospel to the Gentiles so that God's manifold wisdom might be made known through the church. This was done, according to verse 11, "in accordance with the eternal purpose which He carried out in Christ Jesus our Lord." Having heard this, we might wonder if this divine plan covers anything more than foreordaining Christ's death and electing believers to salvation in Christ. The answer is affirmative, as Eph 1:11 shows. There will be more to say about this passage when discussing the decree and freedom, but a word is now appropriate. Paul says that believers have been predestined to salvation, but then broadens the scope of his teaching by saying that predestination was done in accord with the purpose of the one who works all things after the counsel of his will. That one is none other than God. Paul's point is that predestination is but an instance or example of a more general activity—God's choice of all things. Moreover, the choice is based solely on the counsel of God's will.

Other verses in both OT and NT teach God's control over all things. The NT more explicitly than the OT speaks about an overarching divine plan from eternity, but both Testaments teach the same thought. Moreover, whereas an OT author says that God does whatever he pleases, the NT clarifies that this depends solely on his purposes, his mercy, and the counsel of his will. Verses like those presented above allow us to answer affirmatively our first question about whether Scripture teaches that there is a divine decree or plan.

What Is the Nature of God's Decree?

In the next section there will be a theological summary of the doctrine of the decree. In this section, I focus solely on what we can conclude from Scripture alone. The theological section will elaborate the discussion beyond specific scriptural teaching.

From Scripture we can say first that the decree is founded in God's wisdom. This is taught in part by passages that use the term 'counsel' of God's decree and suggest that God's choice came from careful thought and deliberation (Eph 1:11). Creation is one of God's actions, and Scripture says he created in wisdom (Prov 3:19). The psalmist says (Ps 104:24) of God's many works that in wisdom he made them all. In light of God's wisdom, there is no reason to think that what is true of his creating is any different from the rest of his decree and works.

Scripture also teaches that God's decree is eternal. Many passages speak of God ordaining or planning something before the foundation of the world. This is true of God's choice of Christ as Redeemer and of his election of people to salvation (1 Pet 1:20; Eph 1:4). Other passages speak of God's eternal purposes carried out in Christ Jesus (Eph 3:11), and yet others speak of our salvation resulting from God's purpose and grace granted in Christ from all eternity (2 Tim 1:9). In Revelation 13 John records a vision of the future rule of the beast, and says that many will follow him. He adds (v. 8) that these are those whose names have not been written in the book of life from the foundation of the world. Here again we see that God's decision to save or not save someone was made before the foundation of the world. Moreover, the OT says that God planned various deeds "long ago" (Isa 22:11; 37:26).

God's plans were made in eternity past, but can they be frustrated at some future time? The psalmist (Psalm 33) instructs us as he praises God for his attributes and his act of creation. He says (vv. 10-11), "The LORD nullifies the counsel of the nations; He frustrates the plans of the peoples. The counsel of the LORD stands forever, the plans of His heart from generation to generation." From this we see not only God's control over world affairs but also that his plans are eternal in that they will continue indefinitely into the future without annulment.

Third, Scripture also speaks of the ultimate purpose of God's plan. Though God has many purposes, the ultimate reason for all of it is to bring him glory. Of course, it wouldn't be done if it were not first planned, so things done for God's glory were also planned for that purpose. In Eph 1:4-6 Paul says that believers are predestined to adoption as sons according to the kind intention of God's will, and he adds that this is all to the praise of the glory of God's grace. In the same chapter (vv. 11-12) Paul speaks again of God's working all things according to the counsel of his will, and doing so for the purpose that those saved should be to the praise of his glory. Moreover, the Holy Spirit is given to believers as a pledge of their inheritance and ultimate redemption to the praise of God's glory (vv. 13-14). Speaking of salvation as a work of God's grace, Paul says that those who boast about their redemption and sanctification should do so in the Lord (1 Cor 1:26-31). God clearly deserves the praise, and we often read that what God has done is for his name's sake (Isa 48:11; Ezek 20:9). As Paul summarizes his teaching about God's relation to Israel and marvels at the wonders of God's ways, he writes (Rom 11:36), "For from Him and through Him and to Him are all things. To Him be the glory forever. Amen."[21]

Fourth, God's decree is efficacious. What he has planned will most assuredly be accomplished. As Job learned, no purpose of God's can be thwarted (Job 42:2). As the psalmist says, "Whatever the LORD pleases, He does, in heaven and in earth, in the seas and in all deeps" (Ps 135:6). Isa 14:24-27 says that God will execute his plan against the Assyrians, for, as verse 27 says, who can frustrate God's plans? This is true whether the plan covers the destiny of nations or God's redemptive plan. If God has decided something will happen, it will, for it is he who works all things according to the counsel of his will (Eph 1:11).

Fifth, as one reads the OT and NT, it is clear that God's decree is all-comprehensive; it covers everything. It isn't just passages like Ps 135:6 and Eph 1:11 that say God does whatever he wants and that his plan covers all things. Throughout Scripture these general comments are particularized as writers teach God's control over one thing and another. For example, the rise and fall of kings and kingdoms and the boundaries and times set for nations all fall within his control. A sampling of verses illustrates these points. In the song of Moses (Deut 32:8) we read that the Most High gave the nations their inheritance and set the boundaries of the peoples. In Job 12:23, Job says of God that "He makes the nations great, then destroys them; He enlarges the nations, then leads them away." This is also a recurrent theme in Daniel. In Dan 2:21, as Daniel begins to explain Nebuchadnezzar's dream, he says that God "changes the times and the epochs; He removes kings and establishes kings." Eventually, Nebuchadnezzar came to agree that God is king of an everlasting dominion, does whatever he wishes in heaven and in earth, and no one can stop him (Dan 4:34-35; see also v. 25). As the psalmist writes (Ps 22:28), someday all peoples will turn to God, for the kingdom is his and he rules over nations. Can God really control the king's heart to do his bidding? The writer of Proverbs says (21:1), "The king's heart is like channels of water in the hand of the LORD; He turns it wherever He wishes."

The NT agrees. As Paul addressed the Athenians on Mars Hill, he said (Acts 17:26) that God "made from one, every nation of mankind to live on all the face of the earth, having determined their appointed times and the boundaries of their habitation." The same apostle told Christians in Rome to submit to civil authorities, for "there is no authority except from God, and those which exist are established by God" (Rom 13:1). Revelation 17 prophesies that at the end time the great political leader of the day, the beast, with his legions will destroy the great harlot. They will do this (v. 17), "For God has put it in their hearts to execute His purpose by having a common purpose, and by giving their kingdom to the beast, until the words of God should be fulfilled."

Scripture also teaches that the various aspects of salvation are under God's control and plan. Christ's sacrifice was according to God's preordained plan (Acts 2:23; 1 Pet 1:20), and election of believers is also part of God's plan, for he predestined us according to his plan (Eph 1:11). As we have seen, election depends not on our will or merit, but on God's choice (Rom 9:15, 16). Regeneration is also according to God's plan (Jas 1:18), and sanctification is accomplished in the believer in accord with God's plan, but not so as to allow us to be passive in the process. Paul strikes the right balance as he encourages Philippian believers (Phil 2:12-13) to "work out your salvation with fear and trembling; for it is God who is at work in you, both to will and to work for His good pleasure" (see also 2 Thess 2:13).

From the preceding one might think God controls major things like the rise and fall of nations and salvation, but not the lesser, mundane things of life. However, Scripture teaches otherwise. Apparently chance occurrences like the outcome of the roll of the dice are under God's plan and control (Prov 16:33). Moreover, God controls the details of our life. Job 14:5 says that he controls and determines the length of our life. The psalmist says (Ps 139:16) that God not only knows us in the early stages of development in our mother's womb but also knows how long we will live: "in Thy book they were all written, the days that were ordained for me, when as yet there was not one of them." In Ps 31:15 the psalmist says, "My times are in Thy hand." God is also in charge of the very circumstances of our lives. Hence, James warns those who make plans without considering what God wants (4:14-15): "Yet you do not know what your life will be like tomorrow. You are just a vapor that appears for a little while and then vanishes away. Instead, you ought to say, 'If the Lord wills, we shall live and also do this or that.'"

The decree also includes the suffering of believers. Think of Job's experiences. After the first round of affliction, Job says (Job 1:21), "Naked I came from my mother's womb, and naked I shall return there. The LORD gave and the LORD has taken away. Blessed be the name of the LORD." We might paraphrase this as follows: "I didn't come into this world with anything, and I won't take anything out of it. All that I have was given by God, so if he wants to take it or give it, that is up to him. He is in control." After the second wave of affliction, Job's wife counsels him to curse God and die. Neither of them knew why this was happening, but even Job's wife's counsel shows that she believed it was under God's hand. Job answered his wife (Job 2:10), "Shall we indeed accept good from God and not accept adversity?" As time passed and the afflictions continued and the questions got louder, Job still maintained that this happened according to God's plan and control. In Job 12:7-10 he says, "But now ask the beasts, and let them teach you; and the birds of the heavens, and let them tell you. Or speak to the earth, and let it teach you; and let the fish of the sea declare to you. Who among all these does not know that the hand of the LORD has done this, in whose hand is the life of every living thing, and the breath of all mankind?"

Job and his friends said many incorrect things, but nothing suggests that this view of suffering was wrong. In fact, it matches exactly what we learn in chapters 1 and 2 as we "eavesdrop" on God's conversation with Satan. The NT also teaches this truth. First Peter addresses at length suffering for Christ's sake. In 1 Pet 3:17, Peter writes, "For it is better, if God should will it so, that you suffer for doing what is right rather than for doing what is wrong." The conditional clause "if God should will it so" in the Greek is a first-class condition, a grammatical construction that bespeaks a condition according to fact. Hence, we could just as easily translate the phrase "since God wills it so." Though we don't understand at times why God sends afflictions or how he escapes culpability for evil that befalls us, Scripture maintains that even affliction is within God's plan for the believer.

God's plan includes not only the sufferings of the righteous but also the evil deeds of men and angels. In Job 1–2 we see God's control over Satan's actions. God notes Job's fidelity, but Satan complains that this is only because God has set a hedge around Job. God does not deny that there is a hedge around Job; he only denies that this is why Job serves him. Though God grants Satan permission to afflict Job, it is permission within limits. In the first set of afflictions, there is a hedge; Satan may not touch Job's body (1:12). When Job refuses to reject God, Satan then complains that God won't let him afflict Job's body. God again grants permission, but still within limits; Satan may not take Job's life. It is hard not to conclude that God controls what happens.

Other Scriptures also teach that evil acts of human beings are under God's plan and that God can bring good even out of a horrible situation. When Joseph finally reveals himself to his brothers and they apologize for what they did to him, Joseph says (Gen 50:20) "You meant evil against me, but God meant it for good in order to bring about this present result, to preserve many people alive." We have also seen that Christ's death, the most evil act of murder of a righteous man, was governed by God's preordained plan (Acts 2:23; 4:27-28; see also Luke 22:22). Moreover, Paul clearly contends that Pharaoh's hardening and stubbornness of heart, though acts in which Pharaoh willingly participated, were according to God's plan in order to demonstrate his power (Rom 9:17-18).[22] Of course, it is natural to wonder how we can be morally responsible for doing the evil that God ordains us to do (Rom 9:19). We also wonder how God escapes censure for such acts, since he decreed them. In later chapters on the decree and freedom and the problem of evil I shall address such issues. Troublesome as they are, they do not negate the fact that Scripture clearly teaches that such evil acts are planned and controlled by God.

Sixth, God's decree is based on his desires and purposes, and so it is free, i.e., nobody and nothing other than God caused him to put into his plan what he has put there. As already noted, Ps 115:3 and 135:6 teach that God does whatever he pleases in heaven and in earth. Isa 46:10-11 shows that God accomplishes his good pleasure, and in Eph 1:5, 6, 9, and 11 Paul says that the various aspects of our salvation were accomplished according to God's good pleasure, kind intention, and purpose. The picture is clearly that of choices that were made in freedom. Moreover, many passages affirm that the various aspects of salvation are accomplished on the basis of God's grace. Since grace is unmerited favor, it cannot be something forced upon the giver; it must be freely given, for if it is given to reward something in the recipient, it is no longer grace but justice. Eph 2:8-9 makes this point clearly, and so does Rom 9:15-18. God has mercy on whom he desires and hardens whom he wants. As verse 16 says, it doesn't depend on man who runs or wills, but on God who has mercy (see also John 1:11-13).

There are other indications that God's plans are made freely. Isa 40:12ff. speaks of God's greatness. Through a series of rhetorical questions whose answer is "no one," Isaiah teaches that nothing can compare with God. He writes (vv. 13-14), "Who has directed the Spirit of the LORD, or as His counselor has informed Him? With whom did He consult and who gave Him understanding? And who taught Him in the path of justice and taught Him knowledge, and informed Him of the way of understanding?" As the apostle Paul reflects on God's unsearchable ways in bringing both Jews and Gentiles to himself (Rom 11:33-35), he quotes from this very passage. He quotes it again in 1 Cor 2:16 after writing of God's wisdom which was revealed through the Holy Spirit, transferred to Scripture (2:13), and illumined by the Holy Spirit (2:14-15). But if no one has counseled the Lord, if he has consulted no one, and if no one has taught him anything, then whatever he thinks and whatever he chooses must stem from his own desires and purposes. In other words, he chose his plans freely, and as we have seen, his plans cover everything.[23]

The Decree and Foreknowledge

How can God's decree be freely made when Scripture says he made his decisions on the basis of his foreknowledge? Rom 8:29 says God predestined to salvation those whom he foreknew. Peter says (1 Pet 1:1-2) that believers are elect according to God's foreknowledge, and in the same chapter he adds that Christ, God's sacrificial lamb, was foreknown as the Redeemer before the foundation of the world (see also Acts 2:23). Doesn't this mean the decree was based on what God foresaw would occur? If so, how can we say it was free, unaffected by his creatures and what they would do?

These are significant questions, but the apparent contradiction is just that, apparent, for *foreknowledge does not mean what the objection suggests*. The confusion arises from our English word "foreknowledge," which masks the fact that in the Greek and Hebrew there are several uses of the words for "know" and "foreknowledge."

The simplest way to make this point is to survey biblical uses of "know" and "foreknow." In Hebrew, the word is *yāda*, whereas Greek has three separate words. The first is *epistamai*, which refers to reasoned out knowledge.

This is the knowledge one has at the end of an argument whose premises lead to a conclusion. A second Greek verb for "know" is *oida*, and it typically refers to intuitive knowledge, that which is known without a process of reasoning. The third term is *ginōskō*, which refers more to experiential and/or relational knowledge. In speaking of our personal acquaintance with someone, we might use *ginōskō* when we say that we know them. The NT uses *oida* and *ginōskō* in most instances of knowing something intellectually. The Hebrew has no particular word for "foreknowledge," but the Greek does have words for "foreknowing" and "foreknowledge." The former is *proginōskō* and the latter is *prognōsin*.

While these lexical items are helpful, they are not the exact point. Many instances of the Hebrew *yāda'* refer to nothing other than intellectual awareness or knowledge. Likewise, the same is true for biblical usage of the Greek terms. However, both in the OT and NT there are various contexts where these terms cannot mean mere intellectual knowledge. A few examples illustrate the point. In the OT the Lord says to Israel (Amos 3:2), "You only have I known among all the families of the earth" (author's translation). If this is mere intellectual awareness, it makes no sense, since God is cognizant of all peoples and nations. It cannot even quite mean that only with Israel is God personally acquainted, for God interacted with other peoples as well. In Hos 13:4 the Lord again tells Israel that she was "not to know any god" except him, but what does this mean if it refers only to intellectual knowledge? Was God saying that they were to be totally ignorant intellectually of the gods of other peoples? How could that be possible, since Israel interacted with neighbors who worshiped other gods? Surely, something else is the point.

Another example of this different sense of knowing appears in Psalm 101. In verse 4 David says, "I will know no evil." His point certainly cannot be that he will be ignorant of evil deeds, for he knew too well that he was a sinner, and he also saw the sins of others. Actually, we begin to sense what he means from the first part of the verse which says, "A perverse heart shall depart from me." Then, he adds, "I will know no evil." One further passage illustrates the point. The prophet Nahum says of God (1:7) that "the LORD is good, a stronghold in the day of trouble, and He knows those who take refuge in Him." If the point is mere intellectual knowledge, then there is no point in saying this, for God is also intellectually aware of those who do not take refuge in him. Being omniscient, he knows everything; the meaning must be something else.

What do these verses have in common? Their point is relational knowledge. Amos 3, Hosea 13, and Nahum 1 mean that God has a special relationship with his people. The Hosea 13 command to know no other god is a command to have no relationship with other gods, neither to worship them nor have anything else to do with them. The psalmist's point is that with the departure of a perverse heart, he will have nothing to do with evil; he wants no relation to it. Thus, there are instances in the OT where knowing someone or something means to make it a matter of personal concern and relation. In passages such as Gen 4:1, the same term speaks of intimate sexual relations between a husband and wife.

In the NT we also find various instances of "know" where the point also must be relational knowledge. Jesus speaks of the coming kingdom (Matthew 7) and says that not everyone will enter the kingdom of heaven. Some will cry to him (v. 22), "Lord, didn't we prophesy in your name?" Jesus says (v. 23) that he will reply, "I never knew you." For an omniscient, risen, reigning king, this is an odd thing to say if his point is intellectual ignorance of their existence. Likewise, it can hardly be Jesus' point that he hasn't yet been introduced to them. Something else must be the point. In John 10:27, Jesus says of his people that he knows his sheep. If he means mere intellectual awareness of their existence, there is no reason to say this, since he also knows intellectually those who are not his sheep.

In Paul's letters we find a similar usage of "know." In Gal 4:9 he says, "But now that you have come to know God, or rather to be known by God . . ." How could an omniscient God come to be intellectually aware of the existence of various people? While Paul may be saying that the Galatians have become intellectually aware of the true God, that isn't likely because of the rest of the verse. If the Galatians have only an intellectual awareness of God but no personal relationship through Christ, why ask why they are turning back to the weak and worthless elemental things, rather than moving on in their relationship with God? Those with only an intellectual knowledge of God have no relation with him and hence cannot be expected to grow in their current state. The sense of knowing must be something other than mere intellectual knowledge. In 1 Cor 8:3 Paul writes that "if anyone loves God, he is known by Him." This is again odd if the point is mere mental awareness, for God also intellectually knows those who don't love him. Instead, the passage means that God's knowledge of us fits with our loving him, but then this can be no mere intellectual knowledge (see also 2 Tim 2:19).

A final NT passage has an interplay between the two senses of "knowing" that we have been examining. In 1 John 2:3, John says, "By this we know that we have come to know Him, if we keep His commandments." If the two instances of "know" in this verse are identical and refer merely to intellectual awareness, the first use of "know" is redundant. John could have written instead, "By this we know him, if we keep his commandments." Knowing in the first case is intellectual awareness, intellectual certainty, but knowing in the second case is knowing by relation. If someone replies that this is not John's point, because he is saying that whoever keeps God's commandments shows thereby that he is intellectually aware that there is a God, I would answer that the context does not allow such a reading. Verses 3 and 4 alone might warrant that understanding (apart from the redundancy this would create in verse 3), but in verse 5 John explains further what this means. He says that "whoever keeps His word, in him the love of God has truly been perfected." If the sole point of the passage is that people are intellectually aware of God and his commandments, then keeping those commandments wouldn't prove anything more than that one knew them. By saying that obeying the commands shows that God's love is perfected in the obedient person, the passage shows that the knowledge involved is more than intellectual.

As in the OT, these instances of knowing refer to knowing by personal relationship and experience. To know someone in this sense (in both OT and NT) is to make that person an object of concern and acknowledgement and to regard that person favorably. It means having a relationship with that person. When we add to this the notion of foreknowing, or knowing beforehand, all that is added is that at some time prior to the present, there was a decision to establish such a relationship. Hence, foreknowledge in this sense can be defined as uniting oneself beforehand to someone in an act constituting a relationship and making that person an object of care and concern for the one uniting with him. In some instances, as we shall see, it means foreordination.

None of this means that "knowing" and "foreknowing" cannot and do not ever refer to intellectual knowledge. Rather, that is not the only possible biblical meaning of these terms. But then, now we are ready to look more closely at passages that speak of foreknowing and foreknowledge. As noted, the Greek term for "foreknow" is *proginōskō*, and for "foreknowledge" is *prognōsis*. Only seven passages in the NT use either the verb or the noun, so that helps to limit our investigation to determine the most likely meaning of God's foreknowing something. Those passages are Acts 2:23; 26:5; Rom 8:29; 11:2; 1 Pet 1:2, 20; 2 Pet 3:17.

Two of the seven passages clearly can only mean knowing something intellectually in advance. Acts 26 records Paul's defense before Agrippa. Paul says that if Agrippa has any questions about his character and lifestyle, he should check with Paul's Jewish acquaintances from Jerusalem and environs, for Paul says (v. 5), "they have known about me for a long time previously." "Known previously" translates *proginōskō*. Paul says that in light of what they know, they can confirm his point about his manner of life. It is hard to understand this as anything but personal acquaintance that gives intellectual knowledge of something. Similarly, 2 Pet 3:17 must mean awareness of information, for Peter, having instructed his readers about the Lord's return and judgment, tells them that since they know beforehand what will happen, they should be alert so as not to be fooled by those who deny that these things will happen.

Both of these instances refer to prescience, knowing something in advance or prior to its happening. Hence, any who think *proginōskō* can never mean prescience in Scripture are mistaken. However, it is crucial to note that these passages speak of humans knowing something in advance; neither refers to divine foreknowledge. The other five passages do refer to God's foreknowledge, and a good case can be made that none of them means prior knowledge, but foreordination instead. I shall begin with the clearer passages and then move to the more debatable ones. First Peter 1:20 is as clear as any of the passages. Peter writes about Christ's sacrifice for our redemption (vv. 18-19). In verse 20 he adds that Christ was foreknown before the foundation of the world, but has appeared in these last times for our sake. Now what would it mean to say that God was mentally aware from before the world's foundation that Christ would be the sacrificial lamb? How could God foresee Christ being the Redeemer without having chosen it to be so? If the point is simply prescience, we must ask the basis of this prescience. In the case of foreknown *human* actions, one could argue that God chose them not because he sovereignly willed them to occur but because he foresaw that we would do them, anyway. But how could that be the case with God foreseeing his own actions? Are we to imagine that God and Christ had not decided to send Christ as Redeemer, but then saw that Christ would become incarnate and die anyway, so they decided to place these actions in the decree? It is beyond reason to imagine that God first consults what he foresees himself doing before he ordains himself to do it. The point is rather that even before the world's foundation, God foreordained Christ as Redeemer. The meaning of *proginōskō* here differs from its meaning in Acts 26 and 2 Peter 3.

Next is Rom 11:2. In Romans 9 Paul teaches that what happened to Israel resulted from God's choice. However, Israel is not freed from guilt, for chapter 10 shows that Israel only too willingly rejected Jesus as her Messiah and hence is morally culpable. What, then, is yet in store for Israel? Has she so fallen into God's disfavor that there is no hope for future restoration? Has God "rejected His people?" (v. 1). If so, then God has failed to keep his promises. As Cranfield so ably explains, what is ultimately at stake in Romans 9–11 is the veracity of God. Does he make promises and then take back what he has given, or does he fulfill his promises?[24] Paul's resounding answer is the strongest form of negation there is in the Greek. *Mē genoito*, Paul writes. "If only it were not so, and it isn't!" He then adds (v. 2), "God has not rejected His people whom He foreknew." It is certainly possible that this instance of foreknowing refers only to seeing something in advance, but that is highly unlikely. If the point is mere intellectual knowledge, then God intellectually knows all people beforehand; why is God's prescience of Israel relevant as proof that she is not totally cast off? Critics may reply that this means that Paul knows God won't cast off Israel, because this verse means he foresees that she will believe, return to Christ, or whatever. But there are problems with this interpretation. Those who adopt it want to avoid any idea of foreordination, because foreordained actions preclude libertarian free will. But if we grant libertarian free will to those merely foreseen, how can there be any guarantees that they will respond to God in the future? With this sort of freedom, the agent can always do otherwise, so there can't be any certain *mē genoito*. If there cannot be certainty because of libertarian free will, there is no guarantee that God will deliver on his promises to Israel; Paul has no right to be dogmatic that God has not cast off his people.

In contrast, if the point is that God previously decided to make Israel his special object of love, i.e., he established a relationship with them beforehand and covenanted that they should realize the fulfillment of his promises to Abraham, Isaac, and Jacob, then to say that Israel is foreknown does guarantee that they won't be cast off. At the end of Romans 11 Paul invokes again the promises made to the fathers (v. 28), and then adds that God's gifts and calling are irrevocable. If people have libertarian free will and thereby can reject God, there can be no irrevocability about it, unless God decides to bless people just because they are ethnically Jewish, something contrary to the whole tenor of Romans 4 and 9–10 in particular, and the rest of the NT. The most likely meaning of 11:2 is relational knowledge based on God's prior decision to covenant with Israel as his people. Prescience is not the point here.

In Acts 2:23 Peter—the same Peter who wrote 1 Pet 1:20—speaks of Christ's death. Peter tells his Jewish listeners, "this Man, delivered up by the predetermined plan and foreknowledge of God, you nailed to a cross by the hands of godless men and put Him to death." It is certainly possible that Peter means that God foresaw what they did. The proponent of such a view would most likely hold libertarian free will, and hence would argue that the predetermined plan was based on God's foreseeing what would happen. But then, the verse does not—contrary to what most commentators contend—note the respective parts of God and man in Christ's death, for the focus really becomes the human part. God's foreseeing and predetermining are in relation only to what human beings would do. God's decree merely "rubber stamps" what will happen anyway, and hence is redundant. On this interpretation, Peter says nothing more than that they put Christ to death, and God foresaw that they would. What does the comment about God foreseeing it add to Peter's overall argument? Moreover, if one holds libertarian free will, there can be no guarantee that God would foresee anyone putting Christ to death. All could chose to do otherwise, and might in fact do so. But, then, there was really nothing for God to foresee.

Another problem with thinking that foreknowledge here is mere prescience is that the verse says Christ was "delivered up" by God's predetermined plan and foreknowledge. Who delivered him up? Peter's point seems to be that God did so in accord with a predetermined plan and foreknowledge. If God delivered up Christ in accord with what he foresaw would happen, then God foresaw himself delivering up Christ and then decided to ratify what he would do. The problem is the same as that explained in regard to 1 Pet 1:20. How can God foresee himself certainly doing something before he has decided to do it? In light of these considerations, the most likely understanding of "foreknowledge" in Acts 2:23 is not prescience but foreordination.

We turn next to the harder verses, and come first to Rom 8:29. This verse says about salvation that "whom He foreknew, He also predestined to become conformed to the image of His Son." Many would contend that the passage says that predestination is based on God's foreseeing that we would believe; it isn't based on God's foreordination apart from whatever we might do. To be sure, it is possible that the verse means this; foreordination is also possible. Neither grammar nor lexicography settles the matter, so the case for either view must be made on grounds of context. I believe a stronger case can be made for foreordination.

Verse 29 begins with an explanatory *hoti*, "because." What it explains is verse 28, a frequently quoted reassurance to troubled Christians. Paul writes that we "know that God causes all things to work together for good to those who love God, to those who are called according to His purpose." How does Paul know this, and is he talking about all matters of comfort and convenience in our life? The answer to the second question is negative, for Paul refers specifically to things that promote our ultimate salvation. Still, how does Paul know that God will work all things together for the benefit of our salvation? Verses 29-30 explain: there is an irreversible process into which God has placed his children that runs all the way through glorification. Paul uses these facts stated in verses 29-30 to argue in verses 31-39 that absolutely nothing shall separate us from God's love in Christ Jesus. No one will be able to bring a charge that will stick against God's elect; no one can condemn us (vv. 33-34).

In this context, what is Paul most likely saying in verse 29? Is he saying you can be sure your salvation will be completed because God foresaw that you would believe and then put his stamp of approval on what would happen anyway, i.e., he predestined you because of your foreseen faith? You will be saved because it all ultimately stems from your decision, a decision God foresaw you making. Or is Paul more likely saying you can be sure you will make it to final salvation because God originally decided to enter a loving relationship with you (foreknew you), and on the basis of that decision, he decreed to save you, and then called, justified, and will eventually glorify you? Salvation is all guaranteed because of God's work on your behalf each step of the way. With the first view, the guarantee comes because of what we will do; but if it ultimately depends on us, that is nowhere near as certain as when it relies entirely on God. On these grounds alone, it is more likely that Paul uses "foreknew" in the sense of relational knowledge, not intellectual foresight. This conclusion becomes even more certain when we remember that the prescience view invariably holds that humans possess libertarian free will. If the human actions foreseen are done with libertarian free will, there cannot be any guarantees about what we will do. As we shall see in the chapters on freedom and foreknowledge, many proponents of libertarian free will even argue that there is nothing for God to foresee if libertarian free will obtains, for nobody knows until decisions are made what a person will do.

In the seventh passage (1 Pet 1:2), Peter tells his readers that they are elect according to the foreknowledge of God the Father. Peter is either saying election is based on God's foreordination to save them, or that it is based on what God foresaw them doing. Either option is possible, and neither grammar nor lexicography is decisive; context must decide. Remember first the context of 1 Peter. Peter writes to encourage suffering saints scattered over various parts of the Greco-Roman world. What would be the more encouraging thing to say? Would it be that amid trials they should remember that God chose them because he foresaw that they would believe anyway? If that is the point, then if the choice were left entirely to God, he might not have chosen them, but since it was up to them, he saw that they would believe and so chose them. Hearing that God might not have chosen them if it were up to him is not exactly the most comforting thing to hear. Moreover, if what God does depends on what he foresees them doing, then in the future God may not be able to do what he would like to do to sustain them. He may have to allow the free actions of their enemies to continue afflicting them, because stopping those acts would curtail libertarian freedom.

Or would it be that despite their afflictions Peter's listeners should take heart, for though they are disenfranchised in this world, they have clout with God. He chose them, not because he had to or because they were going to believe anyway. He chose them to be his people because he decided beforehand to enter a relation with them to save them. Hence, they are God's people because of God, and surely the same God who chose them and saved them is able to intervene in their circumstances and even overturn the problems that beset them. Moreover, since proponents of this view probably would not say that humans have libertarian free will, God's decisions need not be based on leaving room for libertarian freedom. If God wants to stop the afflicters, he doesn't have to forego doing so to maintain their libertarian freedom.

Either option is possible. To some it may be more comforting that God chose them on the basis of their foreseen decisions, and more comforting in difficult circumstances that God is available to help so long as libertarian freedom isn't abridged. But in my judgment it is far more comforting to know that I am a child of God entirely because of him, not at all because of me. The God who chose me is the same God who is ready to act on my behalf amid difficult circumstances. In addition, there is another argument already heard several times over. A major motivation behind the alternate view is to leave room for human libertarian free will. But if so, then it is hard to see how God's decision can be based on a foreseen use of that freedom to choose him. I need not belabor this point, since I have made it several times already.

In light of the preceding, I conclude that when Scripture says God's decisions and actions are based on his foreknowledge, it means that God acts according to a prior decision to enter into a covenant relationship with someone to save them. God's decree is based on his foreknowledge, and that means that it was made in accord with his good pleasure, purposes, and will. There is no contradiction in saying that God's decree is based on his purposes and good pleasure and also based on his foreknowledge. Once we understand the biblical concept of foreknowledge, we see that God's doing things in accord with his foreknowledge means that he does them according to what he desires, wants, purposes, wills.

FURTHER THEOLOGICAL FORMULATION OF THE
DOCTRINE OF GOD'S DECREE

In addition to scriptural data about the decree, there are other things that round off our understanding of it. An initial point is that the decree is unconditional, but this needs explanation, for many have misunderstood the point and rejected the notion of the decree altogether. There are three respects in which the decree might be conditional or unconditional. The first deals with *God's reason for making the decree.* A view committed to a conditional decree holds that God's decision of what to decree was based on some factor or condition external to God. Depending on the view, that factor might be the foreseen actions of people who would live, or their foreseen merit. For example, conditional election of someone to salvation could be based either on that person's merit which warranted election or their foreseen belief in Christ as Savior. The former view fits a Pelagian perspective, whereas the latter reflects an Arminian understanding of election. In contrast, an unconditional decree is based on nothing outside of God that moved him to choose one thing or another. Thus, an unconditional decree to elect someone to salvation would be based solely on God's grace and desire to save that person, not on anything they would do or any merit they might have. So this first sense of unconditional/conditional refers to whether God's decree is based on something external to his will or solely on his purposes and desires, things all internal to God.

A second way the decree might be conditional or unconditional has to do with *how items in the decree relate to one another.* A decree would be conditional in this sense, if certain actions or events were contingent upon (depended upon) the occurrence of other actions and events. Someone's believing in Christ as Savior might be conditioned on hearing a gospel message by a preacher. Saying that decreed events and actions are conditional in this sense just means that God has ordained means to ends, i.e., outcomes depend upon other things happening. To say that a decree is unconditional means that nothing that ever happens results from or is contingent upon anything else that occurs. Hence, there would be no means to produce ends, no situations where an event or action might have another event or action as its cause. It is hard to imagine what a world of this sort would be, since no events and/or actions would be connected to anything else that ever occurs.

It is just at this point that many mistakenly reject a Calvinist account of God's decree because the Calvinist says the decree is unconditional. Some hearing this claim erroneously assume that it means that the decree is unconditional in this second sense, and since such an unconditional decree would be absurd, the Calvinist position is deemed absurd. However, when Calvinists call the decree unconditional, they mean it in the first sense, not the second. In the second sense, Calvinists grant that the decree is conditional. To say that God's decisions are based on nothing other than his own desires and purposes in no way means that the contents of the decree must exclude acts and events that depend for their occurrence on other events and actions.

There is a third possible sense of conditional and unconditional in regard to the decree. Sometimes theologians say that parts of the decree and some of God's actions are conditional in that *he works through the agency of his creatures, whereas other parts of the decree and other divine actions are unconditional in that God does them entirely on his own without using his creatures' actions.* This sense of conditional and unconditional clearly differs from the previous two. To say that God's actions are conditional in this sense could mean that God first acts through another agent and then in response to his actions another of his agents does something. For example, through an angel God warned Joseph to take Mary and Jesus and flee from Herod. Joseph's departure was conditioned or contingent upon the dream in which God through the angel warned him. In this case, the sequence of actions was conditional in the third sense and also in the second sense. In another instance, God's actions might be conditional in this third sense but not conditional in the second sense. Through one of the apostles he might heal a person with a disease, or through Balaam's donkey he might speak to Balaam. The end in the first case is healing and in the second case instruction to Balaam. Since both goals were accomplished by one act in each case, the action was unconditional in the second sense described above, but since God did it through one of his creatures, it was conditional in this third sense.

From the preceding, we can see that the second and third senses of a conditional or unconditional decree are not equivalent, nor do they logically require one another. Moreover, the third sense is not equivalent to the first. Here again some misguidedly have assumed that Calvinists, in claiming that the decree is unconditional, mean that God is the only actor. Whatever he chooses will be done entirely by him alone, so we may remain entirely passive. This would mean that if God chose someone to be saved, we need not witness to that person, because God will save that person himself. This is a gross misunderstanding of the Calvinist position. In saying that God has unconditionally elected someone to salvation, Calvinists do not mean that our witness or other secondary means are unnecessary because God will do it all himself. Rather, Calvinists mean that God's decision to save was based on nothing outside of his gracious will. Of course, God ordains means to ends (second sense of conditional), and he uses various agents to carry out and accomplish his goals (third sense of conditional), so just because God unconditionally elects someone to salvation, that doesn't mean that everyone else can be passive and watch while God saves this person.

Now that these three senses of a conditional and unconditional decree are clarified, I can apply them to what Scripture says about the decree. On the one hand, salvation, for example, is based solely on God's grace and purposes; hence, it is unconditional in the first sense. On the other hand, God also commands us to witness to nonbelievers, and he suggests in passages such as

Rom 10:14-15 that many people will respond upon hearing the gospel from a human witness. Hence, our salvation is conditional in the second sense in that our belief is contingent upon hearing the message, and it is conditional in the third sense in that we hear the message not from God directly but through the witness of one of God's people. But since the decree of our salvation is unconditional in the first sense, God's decisions to give us the gospel through one of his people, and that our belief would result from hearing the gospel, was based on nothing but the good pleasure and purposes of his gracious will. This is precisely what Calvinists mean, and I contend that this understanding is sanctioned by Scripture. I add that what I have said about God's decree of salvation as unconditional in one sense and conditional in others also applies to other things God decrees. That is, all things are decreed unconditionally in the first sense. Whether they are conditional or unconditional in the second and third sense depends on the act or event in question.

The next two points about the decree stem from the biblical concept of foreknowledge. Often theologians ask whether God knows the future because he decrees it or decrees it because he foresees it. Theologians and philosophers who hold the latter typically also hold libertarian free will. Proponents of the former claim that God foreknows what will happen because he has foreordained it, and his decision was based on his own purposes, not on what he foresees us do. From our study of the biblical meaning of foreknowledge and the biblical teaching that God's choices are based on his grace, desires, and purposes, the view that God knows the future because he decrees it is preferable.

A second implication of God's foreknowledge and its relation to the decree is that God decreed all at once the whole set of actions, events, persons, and things (that is, a whole possible world). Rather than deciding some things at one time and others later, God decreed all of history at once. Of course, not all theologians agree with this. Both process theologians and advocates of the open view deny that God decrees anything in advance, for he doesn't know what will happen before it occurs. If proponents of these views were inclined to speak of a decree at all, they would speak of it being made incrementally. That is, God would have goals for his creatures, and he might even decide to do certain things himself at various times, but not knowing what people with libertarian freedom will do in any given situation, God must wait until they act before he decides what he will do.

When we move from these views to more traditional Arminian perspectives, we find one of two options. On the one hand, some Arminians are dubious about anyone knowing what free creatures will do in advance. These Arminians either reject the idea of a decree altogether or hold that God decrees as he sees what his creatures do. On the other hand, many Arminians believe that God somehow foresees the future, including the free actions of his creatures, so they might speak of a divine decree. Moreover, if God does foresee everything that will happen, there is no reason to make the decree in several stages. God would will everything at once in virtue of what he foresees.

In contrast, Calvinists are most comfortable talking of a decree. For Calvinists, since the decree is based on what God decides, not on what he foresees, and since an omniscient God envisions myriads of complete possible worlds all at once, there is no reason to will a partial possible world at one time and another part at another. He chooses it all at once.

A further point about the decree stems from God's decree being founded in his desires and foreknowledge, and from divine omniscience and immutability as defined in earlier chapters: God's decree is immutable. The decree is grounded in God's good purposes and pleasure and his foreknowledge (in the sense of deciding to enter a relationship with people). We also saw in discussing divine immutability that God does not change his will and purposes. Since God envisions a whole possible world at once, since his choice of a particular world is based solely on his own purposes and desires, and since it is impossible for an omniscient God to be mistaken about what he really desires or about whether a possible world actually accomplishes his goals, there is no reason for him to change his decree once he makes it.

Of course, positions that deny a decree altogether would disagree. Those who think God's knowledge of the future is limited would hold that if God decrees anything, he must be open to revising it in light of what actually happens. Arminians who believe God accurately foresees the future and decrees on that basis might agree that the decree is immutable, but of course, their reasoning would differ from that of the Calvinistic positions described.

A final point in our theological elaboration of the doctrine of the decree is especially noteworthy, because it is so often a source of misunderstanding, especially among opponents of anything like a Calvinistic understanding of the decree. It is about the role the decree plays in our world. Some theologians speak of the decree as if it were an agent operating in our world to accomplish various ends. As such, it is sometimes portrayed much like an agent nipping at the heels of humans to push them to do what it foreordains. The truth of the matter, however, is that the decree is not an agent at all. Rather, it is a blueprint for all that happens, but it doesn't do anything itself, nor does it exert causal influence. While one person's actions might cause another to act, or a storm might cause a flood, the decree isn't something that acts or happens in our world, but rather the blueprint for whatever occurs.

Another way to make this point involves the distinction between ultimate or remote causes of an action or event and proximate or near causes. When asking what caused an event or action, one is asking for the sufficient condition(s) that brought it about. That condition may be simple (it involves only one cause), or it may be complex (many factors together bring about the action or event). To illustrate the difference between remote and near causes, think of an automobile accident. The proximate cause of the accident might include the movement of one car into the path of another, one driver's running a red light instead of stopping, and/or his turning the steering wheel in a direction so that his car hits the other one. A more remote cause might be the argument he had with his wife before going to work, an argument that preoccupied his attention so that he didn't notice the red light. All of these factors (and perhaps others) compose the sufficient condition that caused the accident, but we can easily distinguish causes or conditions that occurred in the immediate context of the accident and those that were more removed from it.

As for God's decree, it is never the proximate cause of an event or action, for to think it is treats it as if it were an agent of some sort operating in the situation, and the decree is not an agent of any kind. God, angels, human beings, and animals do things, but God's blueprint for history is not an agent that does anything. On the other hand, we can see the decree as the ultimate cause of any event or action, but not because it is an agent or has causative power over anything. Rather, it is God and other agents who exercise causal power in our world. But since they do so in accord with what God has decreed, we can say that there is a sense in which the decree is the remote or ultimate cause of all things.

A very important implication stems from the fact that the decree is not an agent functioning in history. Some have supposed that if everything that happens is already set forth in the decree, there is no point to history. But this is a major confusion of the difference between a plan and the working out of the plan. If the decree were itself the very "doing" of history, then, of course, there would be no point to anyone trying to live out in history whatever is decreed, for things decreed already would have happened. But God's plan for history is no more history than the plan is itself an agent in history. Nor is every divine action set forth in the decree the same as the actual divine doing of it in history—God's work in our world is not finished just because he planned everything he will do. Having planned it, he must then execute the plan. The decree no more makes the "doing" of history irrelevant than the architect's blueprint makes the building of the building unnecessary. One is the plan, the other executes the plan.

The points about the decree made in this and the biblical sections offer a full-orbed understanding of it. Of course, nothing said so far explains how the divine decree leaves any room for human freedom, or how we can make sense of divine and human moral responsibility for evil. Those issues will be handled in later chapters, but the biblical evidence presented in this chapter establishes that there is a decree, and that we should understand it along the lines explained in this and the preceding sections of this chapter.

THE ORDER OF THE DECREES

The debate over the order of the decrees has occasioned a substantial amount of heat in certain circles, though not always a lot of light. As Demarest and Lewis note, some of the views involved in this debate go back at least to the Middle Ages, though it was with the Reformers and their followers that the debate really began to heat up.[25] Louis Berkhof writes that this debate was

originally about whether God predestined humans' fall into sin or merely foresaw it. As the debate developed, however, the major adversaries in the debate
(supralapsarians and infra- or sublapsarians) came to agree that the decree
included the fall, and the debate shifted to a different issue.[26]

What, then, is this debate about? First, it is not about whether God first
decreed one thing and then later another, and yet something else at a later
time, and so on. Those who hold divine atemporal eternity would reject such
an idea, but even temporalists who believe in a decree believe that all of history
was decreed at once. Second, this is not a debate over whether man's fall and
the decree of some to everlasting punishment were foreordained on the basis
of God's purposes alone or whether they were decreed as a result of being
merely foreseen. And finally, this isn't about whether the decree of everyone's
sin and the reprobation of some was permissive as opposed to positive.[27]

The debate about the order of the decrees focuses most precisely on the
logical order of the decrees. Although it makes little sense (at least from a
Calvinistic perspective) to ask about the temporal order of the divine decrees,
one can still ask what God logically decreed first, second, and so on to happen.
This question isn't about everything in the decree but only about the creation
of humans, their fall into sin, the election of some to salvation, and the decision to send Christ as a Redeemer. Did God first (logically) decide to save
certain individuals and damn others and then decree to create humans and
ordain their fall as means to the end of saving some and condemning others?
Or did God first, logically speaking, decide to create humans, then permit their
fall, then elect some to salvation, etc.?

As this debate developed especially during and after the Reformation, two
main positions came to the forefront. However, two others were also proposed, one roughly within Calvinism and the other more Arminian in nature.
The two main positions are held by various forms of Calvinism. The first is
supralapsarian, and was so designated because it claims that the decree to
elect some to salvation and reprobate others was made (logically) prior to the
decree either to create humans or to permit their fall (the lapse referred to in
the label). This view is deemed by many the most repugnant of all, because it
apparently postulates that creation was a means to the end of damning certain people to eternal perdition. Moreover, it says that the decision to save or
condemn was made even prior to God's decision that these people would fall
into sin. For some, this sounds too fatalistic and unfair.

The second position, known as sub- or infralapsarianism, proposes that
God decreed first (logically) to create humans, second to permit their fall
into sin, and only then to choose some to be saved while others would be
lost. Depending on the form of infralapsarianism in question, the decree of
damnation might be construed as a positive choice, but more frequently it is
viewed as a permissive decree according to which God simply passed over
some sinners, choosing not to extend them saving grace, but to give them the
just reward for their sin. While this position is deemed a "softer" position by

many, it is typically still unpalatable to non-Calvinists, for the decree of the fall and election to both salvation and perdition are conditioned on nothing other than God's good pleasure, and opponents think this unfair.

A third variation appears in the writings of a French Protestant from the seventeenth century, Moise Amyraut. Amyrauldianism on the order of the decrees is really a variation of infralapsarianism. The standard infralapsarian position places the decrees of election and reprobation prior to the decree of Christ's atonement, and typically, infralapsarians think Christ's atonement paid only for the sins of the elect. In contrast, Amyrauldians see the decree of Christ's atonement as making salvation possible for all (unlimited atonement), and claim that it followed (logically) the decree to permit the fall into sin and preceded (logically) the decree to elect some.

Finally, while some Arminians prefer not to talk about this issue at all, others do. Those who do hold various views, but the greatest difference in Arminian understandings is distinction from anything that smacks of Calvinism. For example, an Arminian scheme might begin with the creation of humans, then claim that God, foreseeing his creatures' fall into sin, decreed to send Christ to provide redemption for all and decreed that faith would be the basis of attaining salvation. Third, God, foreseeing that some would cooperate with the prevenient grace he would offer, turn to Christ from their sin, and per-severe in godly living, purposed to save them. Others he foresaw would neglect prevenient grace and reject Christ, or after accepting Christ would later turn from him, and these he decided to leave in their guilt and condemnation. Most of what God decrees on an Arminian scheme of the sort suggested is based on what he foresees about the free actions of the creatures he decides to create.

The chart on the following page shows an example of the order of decrees for each of these four positions.

Various arguments have been offered pro and con for the different positions. One is free to investigate them if one wants,[28] but I won't present them, because I believe the whole discussion is misguided. This question should not have been asked and possibly would not have been if certain facts about divine omniscience and the nature of the decree were understood. Let me explain.

I begin with the notion of a possible world. A possible world is a complete set of all persons, places, things, actions, and events that will ever occur in the history of that possible world. This world is possible in that all of these things fit into one world without contradicting anything else in that world. It is also possible in that God can actualize it, but he need never do so. There is an infinite number of possible worlds; each contains a finite number of things and lasts a finite length of time. In any given possible world not only do the items mentioned above exist, but they do so interconnectedly with one another. Hence, if in a given possible world I am working on this chapter at this moment, I cannot also be at the grocery store, sleeping, or doing some other contradictory activity at the same time. Moreover, if my wife or family need me, their requests for help would be interconnected with my working on this chapter.

Order of the Decrees
(Four Views)

Supralapsarian Scheme	Infralapsarian Scheme	Amyrauldian Scheme	Arminian Scheme
1) Decree to elect some to eternal life and others to eternal punishment	1) Creation of humans in God's image	1) Creation of humans in God's image	1) Creation of humans in God's image
2) Creation of humans in God's image	2) Fall of humans into sin	2) Fall of humans into sin	2) Foreseeing human sin, God decreed to send Christ to make atonement for all
3) Fall of humans into sin	3) Election of some to eternal life and others to eternal punishment	3) Atonement of Christ to make salvation possible (unlimited)	
4) Atonement of Christ (limited)	4) Atonement of Christ (limited)	4) Election of some to moral ability	4) Foreseeing that some would co-operate with prevenient grace, accept Christ and persevere in holiness, he purposed to save them
5) Gift of Holy Spirit to convict the world	5) Gift of Holy Spirit to convict the world	5) Gift of Holy Spirit to convict the world	5) Foreseeing that others would neglect grace and reject Christ, or having turned to him, would turn away, he decided to leave them in their guilt and condemnation
6) Regeneration of the elect	6) Regeneration of the elect	6) Regeneration of the elect who believe	
7) Sanctification of the regenerate	7) Sanctification of the regenerate	7) Sanctification of the regenerate	

Since events and actions, people, places, and things are interconnected with one another, it makes little sense to abstract one action or event, for example, from the context of a whole possible world. We must see an act or event as part of the whole matrix of a possible world. A different act or event at a given moment may have significant implications for other things that occur. For example, in one world, person A fires a gun and kills person B by doing so. In another possible world, at the same moment everything else is the same but person A has no gun, and hence doesn't fire it or kill person B. In this second possible world, there is a further history for person B (perhaps another thirty years of life), and his actions after this point affect other lives and actions.

The reason for discussing possible worlds is to uncover the error in the basic assumptions behind the order of the decrees issue. The fundamental assumptions are that in deciding what the decree would contain, God picked and chose isolated persons, places, things, actions, and events, and then coupled them together with other persons, places, actions, etc. Hence, the idea of Adam as existing is abstracted from the idea of Adam sinning. God can either decide to create Adam and couple that choice with his sinning, or leave that part out. Similarly, God picks and chooses step by step which items to put together to construct the whole decree.

The problem is that this understanding tends to ignore the interconnectedness of any action, event, etc., with other things in a given possible world. Hence, it is dubious that God made the decree in the way just suggested. Rather, God as omniscient would see a whole interconnected possible world at once; in fact, he would see all possible worlds at once, and then choose to create none of them or to actualize one of them. Hence, God doesn't choose to create Adam, and then decide that Adam will sin; nor does God choose first to save Adam, and then decide to create him, and yet in a further (logically speaking) choice decide that he will sin. Rather, God sees Adam as part of a whole interconnected possible world. Of course, there are possible worlds in which Adam commits no sin, but philosophers remind us that this is not the Adam of our world but a counterpart to that Adam. Everything about Adam before he is tempted to sin may be identical in many possible worlds, but once he sins in a given possible world, he becomes a counterpart to the Adam of worlds where Adam does not sin.

This explanation of possible worlds and God's relation via his omniscience to all possible worlds shows that the order of the decrees debate is fundamentally wrongheaded. It is so because it treats God's decree as sequential—granted, it contains a logical rather than a temporal sequence, but it is sequential nonetheless. However, individual actions are not disjoined from one another so that God can pick and choose specific items as he constructs the decree for our world. Instead, as God deliberated, he was confronted with an infinite set of possible worlds. He first (logically) decided whether to create at all, and then, having chosen to do so, he chose which of the many worlds he would actualize. But in choosing to actualize any given possible world he would already see Adam and everyone else as sinners or not, and either as saved or not. In worlds with sin which is paid for by Christ's atonement, God would see at once all the sinners, saved and unsaved, along with Christ's sacrifice. There simply is no logical sequence of choices to construct when what God chooses is a whole world, not individual events, actions, etc. Hence, it is wrong to ask whether God decreed first (logically) to create human beings, to save the elect, or whatever.

As a result, if there is a significant question about the logical order of God's choices, it is not about the things supra- and infralapsarians and Amyrauldians debate. Rather, the logical order (though not chronological order) of God's choices is as follows: initially, God decides whether to create a world or create nothing. If he decides to create, he must then decide whether to make a world that contains humans in unglorified bodies with the basic capacities we have, or a world without such creatures. Then, he must decide whether to choose a world with such creatures that includes them sinning, or one without sin. If he chooses one with sinners, then he must select the possible world that deals with sin as he wishes (presumably there are various ways God could handle payment for human sin, and various possible worlds would instanciate those divine methods). And finally, if he decides to actualize a possible world in which not all are saved, he must choose the one with just the saved people he wants, not another world with a different mix of saved and unsaved. But even this is misleading as to how God makes the choice, for God sees all possible worlds at once (presumably, given his omniscience, he sees them intuitively without a reasoning process of any length), and chooses one of them with all it contains, lock, stock, and barrel. Hence, even the logical order of choices suggested in this paragraph is misleading, for it tends to adopt the same picture of fragmented choices and fragmented, isolated bits of possible choices which, when chosen together, construct a whole world. Since the traditional order of the decrees debate is confused, the proper thing to do with it is not to try to reform it but to jettison it.

In this chapter, we have discussed many things about God's decree, and have left others for later chapters. At the outset of this chapter I suggested we begin discussing God's acts with the decree, for God would not do something he had not planned. The decree or plan of God is the "presupposition" of the other divine acts. As we investigate the working out of the decree, our first topic will be creation, for that was God's next act after making his plan.

TWELVE

THE DOCTRINE OF CREATION

It is more than 140 years since the publication of Charles Darwin's *Origin of the Species* (1859). Darwin's work offered a comprehensive theory to explain in a totally naturalistic way the origin of our universe and life in it. Those who doubted the biblical account of beginnings now had in the theory of evolution a weapon of immense power for the escalating war between science and Scripture.

Scientists and non-scientists alike realized that what was at stake was not merely how life began nor how the natural processes of life work. The ultimate question was the place and significance of life, especially human life, in our universe. Is mankind the result of a divine plan and action to make creatures in God's own image? Are humans the crown of creation with a God-ordained destiny? Does history have a rationale and purpose so that it is heading toward some divinely appointed goal? Or are humans the result of a long process of biological development from lower forms of life, a process not run by an intelligent designer but goaded onward by random chance and subject to the mindless lottery of natural selection?

As advancing scientific knowledge increasingly explained our universe without reference to God, it precipitated for many a major crisis of faith. In a poem by the great Victorian writer Matthew Arnold (*"In Utrumque Paratus"*—"ready or prepared for either") printed ten years before publication of Darwin's *Origin of the Species* we see vividly the implications for faith of the discoveries and theories of science. Arnold details the differences between man's origin according to the biblical account of creation and man as a fortuitous product of natural processes:

> If, in the silent mind of One all-pure,
>> At first imagined lay
> The sacred world; and by procession sure
> From those still deeps, in form and color drest,

Seasons alternating, and night and day,
The long-mused thought to north, south, east, and west,
Took then its all-seen way;

O waking on a world which thus-wise springs!
        Whether it needs thee count
Betwixt thy waking and the birth of things
Ages or hours—O waking on life's stream!
By lonely pureness to the all-pure fount
(Only by this thou canst) the colored dream
        Of life remount!

. . . .

But, if the wild unfathered mass no birth
        In divine seats hath known;
In the blank, echoing solitude if Earth,
Rocking her obscure body to and fro,
Ceases not from all time to heave and groan,
Unfruitful oft, and at her happiest throe
        Forms, what she forms, alone;

O seeming sole to awake, thy sun-bathed head
        Piercing the solemn cloud
Round thy still dreaming brother-world out-spread!
O man, whom Earth, thy long-vexed mother, bare
Not without joy—so radiant, so endowed
(Such happy issue crowned her painful care)—
        Be not too proud![1]

Though this poem presents the possibility that humans are not related to the "brother-world" by natural biological development but rather come from the mind and plan of an omnipotent creator, some eight years after the publication of Darwin's *Origin of the Species* Matthew Arnold's "Dover Beach" appeared. In this poem Arnold wrote of the sea of faith as receding. Clearly, the theory of evolution was taking its toll. By the last stanza of "Dover Beach" there is no longer the possibility that everything came from a beneficent creator. The war between science and faith continues, and it is pretty clear which side is winning. Stripped of any cosmic significance, what meaning and purpose is left for a creature who is nothing more than a rung on the ongoing, meandering ladder of evolution? Arnold doesn't advise us just to believe in divine creation, anyway, but he isn't entirely ready either to capitulate to the emerging scientific worldview. His answer comes in the last stanza of "Dover Beach:"

Ah, love, let us be true
To one another! for the world, which seems
To lie before us like a land of dreams,
So various, so beautiful, so new,
Hath really neither joy, nor love, nor light,

Nor certitude, nor peace, nor help for pain;
And we are here as on a darkling plain
Swept with confused alarms of struggle and flight,
Where ignorant armies clash by night.[2]

The only answer to questions about the meaning and significance of life, says Arnold, is love; that is all there is. Meanwhile, the *ignorant* armies of science and biblical creationism clash in the darkness. What minimal hope one might find in Arnold's poems, that perhaps the creation story is right after all, dwindled as the nineteenth century went on.[3]

Anyone who thinks the question of origins is merely an esoteric topic for scientists and perhaps theologians and philosophers to squabble over, with very little relevance for the rest of us, should see that these issues matter very much. During the nearly century and a half since Darwin introduced his ideas, evolution has become the dominant scientific paradigm. It has implications not only for understanding the origin and development of life but also for astronomy, physics, paleontology, and geology. That speaks of its influence in the natural sciences, but some sort of evolutionary model is also generally predominant in the social sciences.

None of these scientific disciplines has remained static. Darwin's theory and its implications have been elaborated and refined in many of the sciences. There has been, however, in recent years a very interesting scientific development concerning the origin of the universe. For many years many scientists assumed that matter is eternal and so is our universe. We can't explain how it got here; its existence is a brute fact that we must deal with. But recent developments in physics and astronomy have convinced many scientists that our universe had a specific beginning. That beginning, typically referred to as the Big Bang, offers no explanation of where matter came from in the first place, but it does postulate that our universe, though exceedingly old, has not existed in its current form forever. If our universe did have a beginning, then also, perhaps someone started it. The thought that the universe had a beginning greatly troubled Einstein, for he recognized that it meant it would be possible to invoke God as the originator of the process. Still, Einstein finally agreed that the universe must have had a beginning at a particular point, regardless of whatever that means about God's existence.[4]

So even though science prided itself on its ability to explain origins and the data of our world without referring to God, it now appears that some sort of specific beginning to the universe is likely, and that opens the door for God as the cause. Robert Jastrow, noted astronomer, notes the irony in this when he writes:

> For the scientist who has lived by his faith in the power of reason, the story ends like a bad dream. He has scaled the mountains of ignorance; he is about to conquer the highest peak; as he pulls himself over the final rock, he is greeted by a band of theologians who have been sitting there for centuries.[5]

Indeed, theologians have spoken about origins for centuries, but they are not unified in what they have said. That is even more so in our time, when many are trying to accommodate evolutionary thinking to the biblical accounts of creation while at the same time others are working just as hard to prove "scientifically" that six-day creation *ex nihilo* is correct. Christians affirm the Apostle's Creed, which says "I believe in God Almighty, the creator of the heavens and earth." But what do we mean by calling God the creator, and what exactly do we think he did? These questions will occupy our attention in this chapter.

VARIOUS THEORIES OF ORIGINS

Throughout history there have been various theories about the origin of the universe and the development of life. As Colin Gunton traces the historical development of the doctrine of creation, he shows its relation to other theories held at various times. He isolates two specific issues that help us to categorize theories of origins and understand better their basic approaches.

The first question deals with whether the universe is in some sense divine or is other than divine. Theories that opt for the former are typically pantheistic, whereas those that choose the latter are not.[6] Those that are not pantheistic need not deny God's existence altogether. The Christian notion of origins clearly distinguishes the universe from the one who made it, but that does not at all mean Christians think there is no God or that blind naturalistic forces produced our universe.

While the first issue deals with the "status" of the universe (is it divine or not?), the second deals more specifically with its manner of origin. Specifically, has the universe somehow produced itself out of itself, or has it resulted from the action of an agent independent of it? Gunton vividly describes the difference between these two options when he writes:

> How easily it happens that where God is no longer understood as the overall creator and upholder of the universe there is a reversion to the pagan attribution of agency to the impersonal worlds of molecules, evolution and chaos. The choice is inescapable: either God or the world itself provides the reason why things are as they are. To 'personalize' the universe or parts of it, particularly inert substances like molecules, is to succumb to crude forms of superstition.[7]

Despite this warning about superstitious personifying of impersonal forces, in our day we still hear that sort of talk from those who offer a purely naturalistic explanation of origins. Appeal to "mother nature," "chance," or "natural selection" as the grand former of all of life are examples of what Gunton mentions. As he notes, the two options (either God or the world produced the world) have been present from ancient history, and the history of the debate over origins ultimately is a history of positions that offer one or the other of these answers to how the universe came to be.

It is also worth noting that one's answer to the first question (is the universe divine or not?) does not entail either answer to the second question or vice versa. One might, for example, believe that the universe was formed by itself from forces and materials inherent in it, and the fact that the universe is all there is means it must also be divine. On the other hand, one could claim that the universe is not divine and also believe either that God created it or that it somehow produced itself. And of course, one could hold both that God made the universe and that it partakes of his being and hence is also divine. In describing various theories of origins, we shall find all of these combinations in answer to Gunton's two questions.

Dualistic Theories

Dualism as a theory of origins takes various forms, but the fundamental idea of dualism is that there exist two distinct, coeternal, self-existent principles. In one form of dualism, the two principles are God and matter. Matter is imperfect and inferior in being, but it is not necessarily inherently evil. It is, however, subordinate to God's will, and God forms it into the world about us. One of the basic maxims of this sort of theory is *ex nihilo nihil fit* ("from nothing comes nothing"). If one grants this principle, then God cannot create the universe out of nothing, for from nothing comes nothing. Rather, God must be coeternal with matter so there is something for him to work with as he frames the world. Moreover, many proponents of such a dualistic view saw in the inferior matter a way to account for the problem of evil. Evil stems from matter, but God is not responsible, for matter is eternal. Moreover, by forming matter into our world God has done what he could to make the most of matter. The dualism described in this paragraph is represented in some of the writings of Plato and Aristotle, but it also appears in some forms of Gnosticism (Basilides and Valentinus, living in the second century A.D., are representatives).[8]

The other major form of dualism holds that there are two eternally existing spirits, one good and the other evil. According to the Zoroastrian variation of this view, matter is not necessarily negative and imperfect, for it is the creation of the good being. On the other hand, Manichaeanism claimed that matter is the work of a personal malevolent being who wages war against all good. In either form, however, the good and evil spirits are at war with one another. This general form of dualism also explains evil in a way that doesn't attribute it to God or the good spirit.[9]

In both of these broad forms of dualism there is a fundamental distinction between the world and God. In both, matter is self-existent and eternal, but it doesn't mold itself into our universe. God, the good spirit, or the evil spirit does that, but the "organizer" of our universe doesn't create its material out of nothing; he works instead as an artisan fashioning something out of preexisting matter.

Emanation Theories

Emanation theories hold that the universe and its constituents are products of successive emanations from God's being. Depending on the theory, such emanation is either a necessary or a free act of God. In either case, however, emanation theories are invariably pantheistic.[10] One of the more significant emanation theories is that of the ancient Greek philosopher Plotinus. His views were highly influential on later thinkers, including Christians such as Origen, Augustine, and Pseudo-Dionysius.

Plotinus held a hierarchical view of the universe. At the bottom of all that exists is matter, but not as we experience it in our world. Rather, if material things were stripped of all qualities, what would be left is pure, formless, and quality-less matter. Plotinus called this nothingness (*to mē on* in Greek), but it isn't the absolute nothingness or nonexistence that is total lack of being (represented by the Greek phrase *to ouk on*). Though such matter may seem to be incorporeal, Plotinus held that a particular thing's qualities give it corporeality and make it a specific thing.[11]

At the other end of the hierarchy of being is the One. It has no name or form, but is the source of everything that exists. All things flow from it "and it remains completely unaffected and undiminished by their outflowing."[12] Since matter and the One are at opposite ends of the chain of being, what lies between, and how does the One give rise to existing things that fall between the two extremes? Just below the One is Thought or Mind (*nous*). As Gunton explains, "this is eternal and beyond time, but contains within it an element of plurality or multiplicity. It contains the whole multitude of ideas or forms though it contains them indivisibly."[13] Below Mind is *psychē* or soul, which seems for Plotinus to connect the higher world and the world of sense. The higher aspect of *psychē* connects with Mind, while the lower element (nature or *physis*) connects with the soul of the material world.[14] Human souls take part in both elements and hence are a link between the intellectual and sensory world. Moreover, for Plotinus human souls are preexistent, so their becoming incarnate in a body is a "fall," because the soul links with a lower level of being.[15]

To this hierarchy of being Plotinus added the idea of emanation from the One. The actual material world receives from the higher levels of reality as much reality as can be mediated to it. Just as light naturally flows from its ultimate source, similarly being flows from the One. Moreover, just as the light shines more dimly as one goes further from the source, the same is true with lower forms of matter that are a greater distance from the One. Gunton explains how the lower realms of being are derived from the One:

The answer Plotinus gives is by emanation, which is a metaphor derived
from the flowing of a river. Creation flows from the One, which is like
a spring which has no source outside itself (3. 8. 10). Commentators
differ on whether the One can be conceded to be free in creating, and in
what sense. Copleston claims that the system is necessitarian: the world
has to flow from the One by an automatic process, although that is not
necessarily to say that it is pantheistic. It is certainly to be distinguished
from free creation out of nothing. Rist on the other hand argues that
although there is no willing or choice in what happens, emanation is
spontaneous, in the sense that there is no external constraint.[16]

Emanation theories, as one would suspect, are often pantheistic in some
way. Hence, though they may make a distinction between the source from
which being emanates and the resultant realities, these theories posit a close
connection between the two, because that which is formed by emanation
is an expression of the source's reality. Moreover, there is a sense in which
emanation theories propose that the universe is formed out of itself, given the
interconnectedness of all being. Hence, the One or "God" is part of all that is.
On the other hand, emanation theories typically distinguish between the being
of the One and that of the many. Hence, there is a sense in which emanation
theories say that the universe is produced by what is "other." Demarest and
Lewis claim that in the Christian tradition John Scotus Erigina and the mystic
Meister Eckhart held a form of emanation theory.[17]

Naturalistic Evolutionary Theories

Charles Darwin is associated with evolution, but since Darwin's time, the
theory has undergone many changes and refinements. Though some in the
secular scientific community doubt its validity, evolution is clearly the reigning
paradigmatic explanation of origins. While Darwinian evolution was specifically concerned with the origin and development of all living things, including
human beings, "evolution" is an umbrella term that covers not only theories
about biotic evolution but also beliefs about the universe's origin and age. It
has implications for sciences like geology, astronomy, physics, and paleontology as well as biology.

Naturalistic evolutionists claim that the origin and development of the universe can be explained in entirely natural terms in virtue of purely natural laws
operating over natural phenomena. As Richard Dawkins has said, "Darwin
made it possible to be an intellectually fulfilled atheist."[18] This is not to say
that all evolutionists are atheists, but only that according to evolution, a full
explanation of our universe is possible without including God.

We must distinguish two different kinds of evolution, micro-evolution and
macro-evolution. Micro-evolution is change within species. Mere observation
of changes in the natural world, including human beings, from one generation to the next shows that such change takes place. There is no reason for

Christian creationists to reject micro-evolution. On the other hand, macro-evolution claims that the processes described also resulted in changes from one species to another, ultimately culminating in human beings. It is macro-evolution that is most distasteful to creationists who believe that the variety and complexity of life-forms is attributable to an intelligent designer, God, not to the blind, random processes of nature.

As to the origin and development of life, evolution says that from non-living matter there ultimately resulted a living cell capable of reproducing itself. Gradually over eons of time, ever-more complex life-forms continued to develop. Those that were least fit died, whereas the fittest reproduced. Through this process genetic characteristics that were most beneficial to survival persisted, and traits that were not helpful gradually left the gene pool as life-forms with those traits died off.

The mechanism of biological evolution is natural selection, a totally random process that works through natural reproduction. Life-forms that are the fittest will be the most successful in reproducing themselves, so the genetic makeup of the fittest will dominate the gene population. But natural selection means also that over time genetic tendencies that represent advantageous characteristics (i.e., qualities that help a life-form survive better than other members of its species) will accumulate so that eventually there will be large-scale characteristic changes in life-forms. The result is evolution to new species that are better adapted to their environment and thus more likely to survive and reproduce.

How can new genetic options arise which eventually lead to new species? Evolutionists answer that genetic mutations are the source of this material. So natural selection, given enough time, by chance and mutations resulted in the multiplicity of life-forms in our world today.

Biological evolution postulates enormous amounts of time for developing the various life-forms that have existed and now exist in our world, and this has implications for one's cosmology. According to various calculations in astronomy, physics, etc., scientists committed to evolution typically postulate that the universe is some 10 to 15 billion years old. This doesn't mean that matter had an ultimate beginning, for evolutionists answer questions about ultimate origins by claiming that matter in general and the universe in particular are just brute, unexplainable facts. Still, matter is eternal, and somehow the universe began around 10 to 15 billion years ago. As to planet earth, estimates vary, but current scientific thinking postulates its origin somewhere around 4.5 billion years ago. As for humans, their ancestors probably first appeared around 1.5 billion years ago.

How does science get these dates, and how does it think our current universe began? As to the dates, they are set in a variety of ways. During this century discoveries in astronomy indicated that ours is an expanding universe. Calculating backward using the speed of expansion, scientists arrive at such dates. Moreover, scientists believe that various radiometric dating procedures tell us the age of various layers of the earth, along with the age of fossils found

THE DOCTRINE OF CREATION □ 545

in those layers, and thus confirm an old universe. Scientists also believe that other data gleaned from rocks, etc., taken from the moon further confirm the age of our solar system.[19]

Scientific evidence (discovered in the twentieth century) for an expanding universe has brought changes in scientific explanations of how our universe began. During part of that century, it was thought that our universe is an eternal but oscillating universe. That is, it expanded to a point and then contracted, only to expand again in a new cycle. However, scientific evidence that suggests continuous expansion and gradual movement toward disorder of the universe has led scientists to propose a different theory. If the universe is expanding at a fairly constant rate, we should be able to extrapolate backwards to a time when it was "totally" compacted. If there was such a point in the universe's history, how did it then begin to expand? Scientists answer that the expansion began with a gigantic explosion known as the Big Bang from this singularity when the basic matter of the universe was compacted together.

Though some who invoke God hold that he created the material of the universe at the outset and then somehow caused the Big Bang, evolutionists typically demur. For example, Stephen Hawking (*A Brief History of Time*) argues that questions about how long things existed before the Big Bang, and about who produced the material from which this explosion came, are simply non-issues. Hawking thinks the problem stems from Einstein's general theory of relativity. When dealing with the universe's expansion after the Big Bang, the general theory of relativity works well, but its problem is that it doesn't incorporate the small-scale effects described by quantum mechanics. "At the scale of ordinary bodies, planets and galaxies, quantum effects are negligible for the most part; but at the scale of the very early universe, if a Big-Bang model of cosmic evolution is essentially correct, they should become hugely significant."[20]

The net result is that Hawking believes that the general theory of relativity breaks down in the universe's earliest seconds and stages. However, he thinks that by combining the general theory of relativity with quantum mechanics to form a quantum theory of gravity, it is possible to eliminate the singularity predicted by general relativity alone. And, if there is no singularity, then there is no boundary to space-time and the universe. Hence, we need not invoke God as the start of the cosmos, nor can we talk of what happened or how long it was before the Big Bang.[21] None of this necessarily means Hawking thinks there is no God. Rather, his point is that even if there is a God, we need not invoke him in explanations of the universe's origin. Of course, while Hawking has proposed this theory, that doesn't mean it has been shown to be correct.[22] Still, if one accepts his proposal, there is no need to appeal to God for an ultimate explanation of things. Naturalistic evolutionary cosmological accounts offer all the explanation needed.

Theistic Evolution

While most evolutionists think everything is explainable without God, a substantial number of Christians, especially within the scientific community, wed evolution with creation. They believe that science tells what happened and how it occurred, whereas the Bible explains who was behind it and why. There are variations of theistic evolution, but all say that science has established evolution as the means by which the universe and life-forms, including humans, began and developed. Although evolution was the mechanism, the whole process was ultimately guided by God, who ensured that things developed as he wanted.

Exactly what did God do, according to theistic evolutionists? Some say that God's direct intervention occurred at several distinct points where naturalistic processes alone would not suffice, but otherwise he left nature to evolve by its own processes. Others postulate God's intervention at points like the move from non-living things to the first living organism or the change from ape-like creatures to man. As to the origin of humans, some hold that evolutionary processes provided the material constituents of human nature but God gave the soul, which when joined with the physical created the first human. For others, the whole of human nature arose by evolution.

Theistic evolutionists also believe that the process is not so random and so ruled by chance as atheistic evolutionists claim. Still, even with God guiding the process and occasionally intervening, scientists are right about how long it took to produce the universe and life as we know them. Moreover, some theistic evolutionists adopt and others reject belief in a first human being Adam.

Strict creationists often hold that theistic evolution pits science against Scripture, but many theistic evolutionists disagree. Scripture is not written as a science textbook, they say, nor did the biblical authors intend that. Rather, Genesis 1–2 makes the theological points that God is the ultimate cause of creation and has guided it through its development. As to the exact details of how that happened, we rely on science for the answer.[23]

A noteworthy contemporary version of theistic evolution is Howard Van Till's. He decries the label "theistic evolution," but his position is surely closer to it than to a strict creationist position. Van Till prefers to call his view "the fully gifted creation" view. According to Van Till, one reason so many Christians find evolution in any form unpalatable is that it is so naturalistic; it seems to leave no place for God in the process. Though this is true for many evolutionists, Van Till argues that we must distinguish evolutionary naturalism as a worldview from the biological theory of evolution. The former is a worldview that says everything in our universe, including the origin and development of life-forms, is explainable in purely naturalistic terms without reference to God. This naturalistic worldview pervades not only science but all disciplines. On the other hand, the theory of biological evolution is only a picture of how life-forms developed on this planet. It need not indicate at all that God isn't working in our world. For Van Till, God originally created the material universe and he has also intervened in history to redeem people and to raise Christ from the dead. Unfortunately, Van Till claims, many Christians and non-Christians alike think biological evolution is a strong argument and evidence for a purely naturalistic worldview, but there is no reason to think this. Still, many Christians, believing that evolution and naturalism go hand in hand, throw the baby ("evolution") out with the bath water ("naturalism"). This creates an incorrect either/or dichotomy: one either buys biological evolution *and* naturalism, or one is a creationist and hence has a theistic worldview.[24]

Van Till argues that scientific data make it clear that ours is an old universe and earth. Moreover, he thinks evidence shows that life-forms developed from a common ancestor through biological evolution. As for God, Van Till says that the origin of the material universe occurred when God created it *ex nihilo*. But God didn't merely produce the "stuff" of the universe with little or no inherent capacities for survival and development. Rather, he greatly gifted the creation with resources and abilities that constitute its being and endue it with the capacity to transform itself into a world such as ours. Van Till calls these capacities "creation's formational economy."[25]

Given the concept of creation's formational economy, Van Till believes we can now pose the problem of origins in a new way:

> Is the creation's formational economy sufficiently robust (that is to say, is it equipped with all the necessary capabilities) to make it possible for the creation to organize and transform itself from elementary forms of matter into the full array of physical structures and life-forms that have existed in the course of time?[26]

Van Till answers a resounding "yes." He explains:

> Drawing from a number of biblical and theological considerations, I envision a creation brought into being in a relatively formless state, but brimming with awesome potentialities for achieving a rich diversity of forms in the course of time. Drawing also from the vocabulary of the natural sciences, I envision a creation brought into being by God and gifted not only with a rich "potentiality space" of possible structures and forms, but also with the capacities for actualizing these potentialities by means of self-organization into nucleons, atoms, molecules, galaxies, nebulae, stars, planets, and the life-forms that inhabit at least one planet, perhaps more.[27]

Some theistic evolutionists believe that at various points in the evolutionary process there are gaps, both in our knowledge of how the processes took the next step and in the natural world's ability to make that next jump. Van Till disagrees. Others invoke God to fill the gap and move the process on to the next stage, but Van Till sees no need for a "God-of-the-gaps," because God has sufficiently gifted creation with the inherent capacities to form itself, using purely naturalistic processes. Rather than granting naturalism (the worldview) too much by postulating totally naturalistic development after creation, Van Till argues just the opposite. Here is a way, Van Till thinks, to avoid alienating naturalists: by granting them that their story about evolutionary development is right, while still maintaining that God is the ultimate source of all things via initial creation. And we can see God working all along the way through evolutionary development so long as we understand that he is working mediately through the wonderfully rich capacities for development with which he gifted creation. With this view, there is no capitulation to a naturalistic worldview, and there is much reason to marvel at the wisdom and power of a God who could so richly gift creation that it has inherent abilities to develop the wonderfully diverse life-forms we find in our world.[28]

In terms of Gunton's two issues concerning origin theories, theistic evolutionary theories distinguish God's being and the universe's being. On the other hand, they hold that the universe came to be in its present form from the combined efforts of the universe itself and of God. Atheistic evolution sees the universe as fundamentally self-formative, but this isn't true of theistic evolution. To hold, however, that God is entirely responsible lapses into some form of creationism.

Creation Theories

Biblical theists have invariably held that God created the universe and all its contents. But that doesn't mean they have all agreed about God's creative activity. For example, Van Till prefers to be thought of as a creationist, but there have been other creationist alternatives to divine *fiat* creation. In this section, I shall describe the broad variations.

CREATION FROM ETERNITY. Eternal creationism has been held in different forms and for various reasons. One of its earliest and main Christian proponents was Origen. He held that God's attributes not only required him to create but also to do so from all eternity. Origen reasoned that divine attributes like omnipotence and love must be expressed in specific acts that demonstrate them. As a result, he concluded that God has always been creating, though not necessarily just one world. In fact, God has created a succession of worlds, ours the most recent, and after he is finished with ours, others will follow.[29]

In my discussion of the divine attributes, I remarked that a proper understanding of characteristics like omnipotence and love does not require God to do every loving or powerful thing possible. In fact, it doesn't even require him to do anything loving or powerful. It only mandates that whatever he does exhibits those characteristics. So there would be no problem if he had chosen not to create. Origen, reasoning otherwise, deemed it necessary that God create.

Another variation of eternal creationism stems from a belief that divine atemporal eternity and absolute immutability require creation from eternity. This line of argument was explained in the chapter 9. In order to remove temporal sequence in God's acts, if God creates a world he must do so from all eternity. This doesn't mean that the world must have existed forever but only that God's action has gone on eternally. Atemporalists explain that the results of God's acts can occur at specific times, but not the action itself.[30]

A final eternal creation view is that of process theology. The process God is dipolar, and his consequent or physical pole is our world. Since Whitehead maintained that all actual entities have both a primordial and a consequent pole, God cannot be an actual entity if he has only a primordial pole. Hence, for the process God to exist, there must be a universe, and it must have existed for as long as God has existed. Process theists accept evolution, and like many evolutionists are agnostic about whether the universe had a beginning and how it was brought into being. Since God and the world are tied together in process theology, this also means that God somehow has been creating from all eternity and has himself been "under construction" for as long as he has existed. Of course, God creates by presenting the world novel possibilities to actualize and then by luring them toward those he thinks are best. The process God refuses to coerce our choices, so he can't guarantee the results. Given such views, the universe is in a sense divine, but it is formed out of itself with help from God's primordial pole.

GNOSTIC VIEW. Various forms of Gnosticism held a creation theory of origins, but their beliefs were significantly different from the traditional Christian doctrine of creation. Colin Gunton is extremely helpful in isolating four main features of Gnostic views about creation. First, Gnostics typically believed that the God of the OT and the God of the NT are two different Gods. The OT God is an inferior deity, but he created the world. His work of creation had to be corrected by the God made known in the immaterial Jesus Christ (Gnostics believed that Jesus wasn't really human but only seemed to have a real human body).[31]

Second, Gnostics held that creation was mediated by lower beings arranged in a hierarchy of being. Since creation was the work of a lesser god, it could not be the achievement of the highest god. The lower beings who actually did the creating ranged somewhere between the divine and the material. Third, as Gunton explains, there is an absolute dualism between creation and salvation in Gnosticism. The OT God is concerned with matter, whereas the NT God is concerned with spiritual things. Thus, what the OT God did in creating the material world must be "tidied up" by the NT Savior God. This bifurcation of spirit and matter not only correlates with the difference between the Gods of the two Testaments but also makes the works of creation and salvation antithetical to one another.[32]

Finally, the traditional Christian account proclaims the world as created good. In contrast, the creation of Gnosticism's lesser God contains evil because the world contains matter. Of course, Gnosticism proposed a method of salvation from this evil, but the material world by simply existing is still evil. As Gunton explains, this view differentiates Gnosticism not only from traditional Christian teaching but also from emanation theories such as that of Plotinus:

> It is here that we see the gulf between Gnosticism and Plotinus, even though they share some assumptions. Both believe that the source of evil is to be found in matter, yet Plotinus rejects the Gnostic view of the unutterable evil and ugliness of the world as we experience it. Because the world flows from the One, and not from the clumsy efforts of a lower divinity, it is, as a whole, to be affirmed as beautiful and good. 'No one should reproach this world as if it were not beautiful or the most perfect of corporeal beings'.[33]

For Gnosticism there is a definite distinction between God and the world, the latter being much lower in the hierarchy of being. Moreover, the world is formed by beings other than itself. Still, the other elements of Gnostic thinking decisively mark it as a Christian heresy.

CREATION *EX NIHILO* WITH A SPECIFIC TEMPORAL BEGINNING. A final set of creation theories are held in Judaism and Christianity and understand Scripture to teach divine *fiat* creation. The initial creation of matter was accomplished *ex nihilo* by God's very word (he spoke and it was done), but the universe was not created in a finished form. Over time through further commands God fashioned matter into the universe around us. This fashioning included making the sun, moon and stars, the planets, and all life-forms on them, including human beings. While creationists grant that God could have created everything *ex nihilo* in a finished form, in light of passages such as Gen 2:7, they hold that it was the original creation of matter that happened *ex nihilo*.

Regardless of whether these theories deem Gen 1:1 to refer to the original creation of matter or to the beginning of God's fashioning the universe from the matter he had created, creation theories typically claim that when God created our universe, he also created time. As Augustine said, God did not create the universe *in* time, but *with* time.[34] Time as we know it can be called physical clock time. This means that time is measured by the movement and relative positioning of various physical bodies to one another. Time on earth is measured by the earth's rotation on its own axis and by its orbit around the sun. Prior to the creation of matter there could be no physical clock time.

Many scholars of Ancient Near Eastern cultures note how different the biblical account of creation is from the tales in other Ancient Near Eastern religions. Invariably those stories are mythological accounts of wars between various gods. At the end of these battles, one of the gods is slain and the victors use its body to create the universe. This is precisely the pattern followed in the ancient Babylonian story. The gods Marduk and Tiamat war against each other. Marduk eventually wins and then slays Tiamat, cuts her in half, and uses one half of her body to make the earth and the other half to create the heavens. Clearly, this is not creation *ex nihilo*. Moreover, Scripture presents one God who is sovereign over all. There is no battle with other gods; the universe is not born in violence. Rather, God creates as an opportunity to express his love toward other beings. Neither in part nor in toto is the universe made from gods, defeated or otherwise. Matter is created out of nothing and then fashioned into our world. Creator and creature are radically distinct, though prior to the fall (Genesis 1–2) we see intimate fellowship between God and his human creatures.

Though Christian creationism widely differs from theories of ancient cultures and even from theories prevalent in the Greco-Roman world, that doesn't mean that all biblical creationists understand creation exactly alike. For much of church history there was widespread agreement about the manner and timing of creation. It was widely held that creation resulted when God spoke and brought things into existence. This took six days, as recorded in Genesis 1 and 2, and those days were deemed literal twenty-four-hour days by most Christians. Of course, some Christians like Augustine were uncertain about how to understand the days of Genesis 1 and 2. In fact, he states that he actually believed that God produced the whole creation instantaneously in a finished form, so the days of Genesis 1 need not be taken literally. Despite some who were uncertain about the timing of things, the predominant view even through the Reformation and beyond was six literal twenty-four-hour days.[35]

In accord with this interpretation, the Irish Archbishop Ussher, understanding the genealogies of the early chapters of Genesis to be complete, calculated backward and concluded that original creation (chronicled in Gen 1:1) must have occurred in 4004 B.C. Many of us can remember receiving a copy of the old *Scofield Reference Bible* with all of its explanatory notes. That Bible also listed dates atop the text of Scripture or in the margins. At the beginning of Genesis, one could find Ussher's 4004 B.C. date.

Despite these settled opinions, science continued to advance. Well before Darwin, discoveries in geology and other sciences pointed to an earth that was much older than previously thought. The date of 4004 B.C. wasn't just a little off but seemingly erred by billions of years. Over the last few centuries various creation theories have been proposed to explain the days of creation so as to harmonize Genesis with science. When we look closer at Genesis 1–2, I shall detail the different theories. Suffice it to say for now, that most of those theories understand the days of Genesis 1–2 as allowing for science's dates for the age of the universe, earth, and mankind.

BIBLICAL TEACHING ON CREATION

Scripture teaches a rich variety of themes concerning creation. In this section, we shall survey the main ideas found in both the OT and NT. Because of the significance of creation *ex nihilo* in the Christian tradition, I begin with that theme.

Creation Ex Nihilo

Creation *ex nihilo* is one of the trademarks of the Christian doctrine of creation. When Christianity began, the predominant Greco-Roman view was belief in the eternity of matter. The Greek maxim *ex nihilo nihil fit* means that you can't get something from nothing. When Christian thinkers say that God created *ex nihilo,* we must understand what that means. As already noted, Plotinus believed in a hierarchy of being. However, Plotinus held to two kinds of nonbeing. One kind is the total absence of any being, whereas the other is relative nonbeing. As to the latter, Plotinus and his followers saw matter without qualities as the lowest type of being, but it still is something. However, it was often referred to as nonbeing, since only by adding qualities to this formless matter is there a specific something. When Christian thinkers speak of creation out of nothing, they are not talking of nothing as though it is a something out of which God made things. Creation out of nothing means creation despite the absolute absence of anything.[36]

Accepting creation *ex nihilo* commits one to believing that God's creative activity involved a miracle. If creating something out of nothing somehow happens by naturalistic processes, we have no clue that this is so, or what those processes are or how they function. We must add, however, that most of God's creative activity, though it fashioned various things from matter God originally created *ex nihilo,* also consisted in many miracles. For example, making a human being from the dust of the ground doesn't involve any naturalistic processes we know of, nor could we possibly repeat this feat if we tried. It is a divine miracle.

Creation *ex nihilo* seems to be the predominant position in Christianity, but it raises some questions. One will occupy our discussion: does Scripture anywhere teach the doctrine or even warrant it?[37] We might quickly affirm that it does, but the biblical case is not quite so clear as it first appears.

Though we might want to begin an exegetical study of this topic with the basic Hebrew and Greek words for create and creation, that offers only limited help. Three basic Hebrew roots/lexemes are used for creation. The first is *bārā',* and in its original meaning, it means "to split," "to cut," or "to divide." It also means, however, "to fashion," "to create," and in a more derivative sense, "to produce," "to generate," and "to regenerate."[38] This word is extremely significant in that it is used in Gen 1:1, the verse thought to refer to God's initial creation *ex nihilo.* Etymological studies of cognates in languages such as Akkadian, Arabic, Phoenician, Aramaic, and Ugaritic suggest that the basic idea of this word is that of "shaping," "fashioning," or "building."[39] While such meanings certainly don't exclude creation *ex nihilo,* they don't demand it.

A second Hebrew word for "create" is *'āśāh.* This word's meaning is more general than *bārā'* and can be rendered "to do" or "to make." Frequently, *'āśāh* is used to refer to making something from existing materials, but again that doesn't mean it is impossible for it to designate creation *ex nihilo.* Context must decide. Finally, there is *yāṣar*. This word seems to suggest most distinctly fashioning out of preexisting material, but that is not its only meaning. None of this requires creation *ex nihilo,* but it fits that idea if context requires it.[40]

NT Greek uses various words for "create," but there are two main terms, *ktizō* and *poieō.* The former means "to create" (Mark 13:19), while the latter means "to do" or "to make" (Matt 19:4). In addition, there is *themelioō* (Heb 1:10) which means "to lay the foundation of something," and *katartizō* (Heb 11:3) which means "to put in order," "to restore to its former conditions," "to make complete," "to prepare," "to make," and "to create." Finally, *kataskeuazō* (Heb 3:4) and *plassō* (Rom 9:20; 1 Tim 2:13) also appear. The former means "to make ready," "to prepare something," "to build," "to construct," and "to create." The latter means "to form" or "to mold."[41] As with the Hebrew terms, these Greek terms *per se* do not require creation *ex nihilo,* though they don't preclude it either.

In moving beyond etymology to usage, we again find that none of these terms requires creation *ex nihilo.* For example, *bārā'* is used in a number of ways. In Gen 1:27 and 2:7 it refers to the creation of man, and that was not done *ex nihilo.* It is used of the sea creatures in Gen 1:21, but nothing in the text indicates that they were made out of nothing. Beyond that, the term is used in soteriological contexts such as Ps 51:10 and to speak of the works of providence in passages such as Isa 45:7; Jer 31:22; and Amos 4:13. In Isa 43:15 the term speaks of God's relation to Israel. Surely none of these uses requires creation *ex nihilo.*

In addition, many note that *bārā'* is sometimes used interchangeably with *'āśāh,* and that term is not thought to require creation out of nothing. For example, in Genesis 1 the two terms are used interchangeably, and in Gen 2:3 both are used in close association. In addition, Gen 1:1 uses *bārā'* to speak of creating the heavens and the earth, but Gen 2:4 uses *'āśāh* to refer to creation of the same universe. Then, in Gen 5:1 and 6:6, 7 both terms are used for the creation of man, but we know from Genesis 2 that this was done out of pre-existing matter. Moreover, some passages use a wide variety of terms to speak of God's creative activity. Isa 45:12 uses *'āśāh* and *bārā'.* A few verses later (v. 18) we find forms of *bārā', yāṣar, 'āśāh,* and *kôn* or *kônen.*[42]

Having said this about *bārā',* there is a further point to note. The word is used some thirty-eight times in the Qal stem and ten times in the Niphal in the OT. It is significant that the word in these two stems is used only of God. Passages that speak of men making or fashioning something typically use *'āśāh.* While this alone does not require creation *ex nihilo,* it does suggest that *bārā'* is a special word biblical writers reserve for God's creative activities.[43]

In the NT, *poieō* appears in many places where it does not mean creating out of nothing. Matt 3:3; 4:19; Mark 10:6; Luke 19:46; John 9:11; 1 Cor 10:13; Eph 2:15; and 2 Pet 1:10 are just a few of many such instances. Interestingly, the Septuagint translates *bārā'* with *poieō* in Gen 1:1 where one most likely thinks of creation *ex nihilo,* but *poieō* is also used in Gen 1:27 for the creation of human beings. In fact, *poieō* is the LXX rendering for all three instances of "create" in that verse. We might, then, expect to find *poieō* in the LXX of Gen 2:7, but instead the LXX used *plassō.* Such usage suggests that we must be careful about imbuing either *bārā'* or *poieō* with the notion of creation *ex nihilo.* Context must determine whether it has that meaning.

The same point applies to *ktizō.* Though it can be argued from context that *ktizō* in Col 1:16; Rev 4:11; and 10:6 means creation *ex nihilo,* this is certainly not the case in other Scriptures. For example, 1 Cor 11:9 says that woman was created for man, not man for woman. Genesis 1 and 2, however, say that both Adam and Eve were created from existing material. Moreover, Eph 2:10 and 4:24 speak of believers being created for good works and, thus (4:24), they should put on the new self which as believers has been created by Christ in righteousness and holiness of the truth. Both Ephesians passages refer to spiritual recreation, not creation *ex nihilo.*

The basic biblical terms for creating, then, do not etymologically require creation *ex nihilo,* and in many contexts they aren't used in that sense. Still, a number of passages warrant the idea. This doesn't mean that Scripture anywhere uses the phrase "creation *ex nihilo.*"[44] Rather, contextual considerations demand it in various passages.

Gen 1:1 is a case in point. Some commentators interpret "in the beginning" as a construct so that verses 1-2 are one sentence which reads, "In the beginning of God's creating of the heavens and the earth when the earth was without form and void." However, the preferred reading sees "In the beginning" not as a construct but as used in the absolute sense. Still, some have wondered if the verse refers to the absolute beginning of all of God's creative activity, or whether it only speaks of the absolute beginning of his creative work on our universe, allowing the possibility that he may have made other things before making our universe. If the writer's point is only that this began God's work on this universe, but wasn't the very first thing he created, the passage appears otherwise. Moreover, nothing else in Scripture suggests any creating prior to Gen 1:1. In Exod 20:11 Moses again speaks about the creation, and he explains that during the six days of creation (Genesis 1), God created the heavens, the earth, the seas, and all that is in them. Whatever was created was made during that sequence of activity recorded in Genesis 1–2.

While it is not absolutely impossible that God created prior to Genesis 1, there is no evidence that this is so. Thus, if Gen 1:1 is the start of God's creative activity, it seems that this initial creative act was done *ex nihilo.* The verse says he created the heavens and the earth, a typical Hebrew way to refer to all there is. But if in the beginning God created everything, nothing could have existed before Gen 1:1 from which to make the heavens and the earth.[45]

Jon Levenson has argued that in recent years it has become the consensus among many biblical scholars (non-evangelical at least) that the point of Genesis 1 and 2 is not to teach creation *ex nihilo.* Rather, the point of this and other creation passages in the OT is that, as supreme, God has defeated and controls chaos and its forces that periodically erupt in our world. Creation itself is connected to God's subduing of chaos, and throughout Israel's history at various points we see chaos of one sort or another raise its ugly head. God must then quash it to reassert his enthronement as supreme ruler. Levenson argues that this theme is prevalent in Ancient Near Eastern literature and that we see traces of it in Scripture as well.[46]

Levenson's analysis is steeped in biblical critical presuppositions and methodology, and we need not agree with everything he proposes about the connection of Genesis 1–2 and the OT in general with other cosmogonies. However, one can detect the motif of taming the chaos at various points in the OT (e.g., Genesis 1; Job 38:8-11; Ps 74:10-20; 104:6-9; Isa 51:9-11). Still, this doesn't mean that it is impossible to conclude from Genesis 1–2 or other Scriptures that God created *ex nihilo*. For example, in Ps 33:6-9 the psalmist says that the heavens were created by the very word of God. That echoes the divine *fiats* of Genesis 1. Acts 4:24 says that God created the heaven, the earth, and the sea, and everything in them. This hardly sounds like anything is omitted. Moreover, passages such as Eph 3:9; John 1:3; Col 1:16; and Rev 4:11 say that all things were created by God through Christ and that they exist by God's will. The language of John 1:1-3 is especially reminiscent of Gen 1:1. These passages teach that God created all things, and if these NT passages include things made before the creation of the current universe (i.e., pre-Gen 1:1), none of them evidences that.

Millard Erickson offers a second line of evidence which is a bit more inferential but still to the point. He notes that a host of NT passages refer to the beginning of the world or creation. Since their major point is not to inform us about the nature of creation, they are all the more significant, for whatever their point, it could have been made without mentioning the foundation of the world or the beginning of creation. The fact that these passages speak of a beginning of creation leads one to ask what preceded that beginning. From the biblical authors' viewpoint it seems that nothing did, except God. Hence, implicit in comments about the foundation of the world or the beginning of creation is the idea that the "beginnings" of our world were made without preexisting matter. Erickson offers a series of examples: 1) passages about the foundation of the world are Matt 13:35; 25:34; Luke 11:50; John 17:24; Eph 1:4; Heb 4:3; 9:26; 1 Pet 1:20; etc.; 2) verses that say "from the beginning" are Matt 19:4, 8; John 8:44; 2 Thess 2:13; 1 John 1:1; 2:13, 14; 3:8; and 3) Scriptures that speak of the beginning of the world or creation include Matt 24:21; 2 Pet 3:4; Mark 13:19; Rom 1:20; Heb 1:10; Rev 3:14.[47] A careful reading of these passages confirms Erickson's claim that their main point is not to comment on creation, so including such language was unnecessary. Its inclusion, however, should lead us to ask why it was included. Erickson's inference seems the most likely answer.

Similarly, various OT passages speak of God's eternity in comparison to mankind and the universe. They say that God existed long before those other things. While this doesn't absolutely rule out the possibility of unformed matter preexisting the creation of our world, no biblical passages teach such a thing. The point is uniformly God's eternity in comparison to creation's finitude, but the writers never suggest that eternally existing matter (from which he made our universe) accompanied God prior to creation. For example, Ps 90:2 says, "Before the mountains were born, or Thou didst give birth to the earth and the world, even from everlasting to everlasting, Thou art God." See also passages such as Ps 102:25-27.[48]

A final set of passages are noteworthy, for in them we come closest to a direct statement of creation *ex nihilo*. The first is Rom 4:17. In Romans 4 Paul teaches that justification before God comes only through faith. He appeals to Abraham as a prime example of this truth. In verses 16-17 Paul speaks of the promise that Abraham would be the father of many nations, and God fulfilled that promise in accord with Abraham's faith. Paul says it was done this way to show that God's provision of a child was an act of grace.

As we reflect on the story of God giving a child to Abraham and Sarah, we are reminded of how unthinkable that seemed. Sarah was barren, and Scripture says that both Abraham and Sarah were old and past childbearing (Gen 17:17; 18:11). In fact, *'ōraḥ kannāšîm* suggests that Sarah was already past menopause. So, when Abraham and Sarah heard the promise of Isaac, Sarah laughed. How could this be possible? But Abraham believed God, anyway, and Paul (Rom 4:17) explains that it made sense to believe God even for this promise because God is the one "who gives life to the dead and calls into being that which does not exist." Not only can God resurrect the dead and give a child to those whose bodies are as good as dead for childbearing, but he also calls into being things that don't exist. "Calls" is reminiscent of the Genesis 1 account, according to which God spoke and things came into existence. If these things don't exist prior to God creating them, and if that is so of all things, then the thought seems to be creation *ex nihilo*. While it is possible that God calls things into existence out of preexisting matter, that doesn't seem to be Paul's point. Even humans can make things from preexisting materials, but that isn't reason to think we could perform a miracle like God did when he gave Abraham and Sarah a son.

A final passage seems clearest for creation out of nothing. Hebrews 11 chronicles various heroes of faith, but before recounting their exploits, the writer says that it is by faith that we believe God created the universe. This is the gist of Heb 11:3, but the actual wording is quite instructive: "By faith we understand that the worlds were prepared by the word of God, so that what is seen was not made out of things which are visible." Three key points stand out in this verse. First, all things clearly stem from God. Creation is not done through intermediaries like angels, but by God's direct work. Second, consistent with Genesis 1–2, all of this was done by God's very word. How it was done is beyond our knowledge, but the verse shows that God spoke and the worlds resulted. The final point, and the one most decisively favoring creation *ex nihilo,* is that the verse says that things seen (the material universe) were not made from things that are seen, i.e., not made from matter, since matter can be seen. This excludes creation from preexistent matter.

Some might respond that the universe may not be made from visible matter, but this verse would allow it to be produced from invisible material. Here one thinks of the Greek idea of formless, quality-less matter, the relative non-being of Plotinus. Let us evaluate this notion in light of Hebrews 11. The purpose of the chapter is not to make a metaphysical point about different kinds of matter (visible vs. invisible), nor is the point that God created things out of invisible matter rather than visible. This is a chapter about the necessity of faith; it shows us various people who triumphed over difficult circumstances by trusting God. In that context, it is most reasonable to think that the writer is only saying that by faith we come to understand and accept that God created this universe and that he did so by his powerful word, calling things into existence out of nothing. The most natural understanding of the claim that visible things were not made from other visible things interprets the writer as teaching creation *ex nihilo,* not some technical metaphysical point about two different types of matter (one visible and the other formless and invisible).

In light of these evidences, we are warranted in concluding that Scripture teaches creation *ex nihilo.* Though the very phrase never appears in Scripture, biblical revelation sanctions it, and Rom 4:17 and especially Heb 11:3 are very close to an explicit statement of the idea.

Other OT Themes

GOD THE CREATOR.   The predominant OT creation theme is that *God* made all things. From Genesis 1–2 we see that he created the heavenly bodies, the earth, and everything in heaven and earth, including mankind. He also created the seas and all that is in them (Neh 9:6). God made the pillars of the earth and set the earth upon them (1 Sam 2:6-8). As God began to answer Job, he reminded Job with rhetorical questions that it was God who laid the earth's foundations, set its boundaries, laid its cornerstone, and bounded the seas (Job 38:4-11). In Ps 148:1-6 the angels, sun, moon, stars, the heavens and the waters above the heavens are commanded to praise God, for he made them. God is also the maker of clouds, rain and lightning (Jer 10:13); he controls the forces of nature, and he made everything (Jer 10:16). Other passages that say God is creator of all are Ps 96:5; 115:15; Isa 42:5; 45:7-8, 18-19; 48:13; Prov 8:22-30; Jer 51:15; Zech 12:1. Hence, Moses says (Exod 20:11), "For in six days the LORD made the heavens and the earth, the sea and all that is in them, and rested on the seventh day."

Because God made all things, certain other truths follow. The psalmist says that as their creator, God owns all things (Ps 89:11). He is above everything (Isa 37:16), and as their owner should rightly be praised by the creature (Ps 95:4-6). Another Psalm reveals that God made all these things (sun, moon, earth, and heavens) with skill (Ps 136:4-9). Anyone who understands the complexity of life-forms and how finely tuned our planet is to sustain life recognizes this truth. After listing the various things God created, Isaiah concludes that surely nothing compares to God, the creator (Isa 40:12-14, 25-26, 28-31). The psalmist makes the same point when he writes, "For all the gods of the peoples are idols, but the LORD made the heavens" (Ps 96:5). In other words, other so-called gods are nothing but idols, fabrications of human imagination. But what can an idol do? Nothing, and this is in stark contrast to Yahweh, who not only can do something; he created the heavens! Psalm 102, however, reminds us that even though God's creation is marvelous, eventually it will wear out and cease to exist. In contrast, God will never pass away; he endures forever (Ps 102:24-27). Still, all these things have a purpose in God's plan: "The LORD has made everything for its own purpose, even the wicked for the day of evil" (Prov 16:4).

Since God created everything in heaven and earth, it follows that humans are also his creation. Genesis 1 and 2 clearly teach God's special creation of both Adam and Eve. Elihu also reminds us of this truth when he tells Job (Job 33:4), "The Spirit of God has made me, and the breath of the Almighty gives me life." This echoes Gen 2:7, which teaches that God formed Adam out of the dust of the ground, breathed into him the breath of life, and Adam came alive. But Scripture says even more. Not only is God involved in creating the newborn baby, the adolescent, the adult, but he is even involved during the various stages of pregnancy. God wove us in our mother's womb, and saw us during those days of development. Before we were born, God already knew how long and what sort of life each of us would have (Ps 139:13-16). God reminds Jeremiah that even as Jeremiah was being formed in his mother's womb, God had already appointed him to be God's prophet to the nations (Jer 1:5).

CREATION BY GOD'S WORD. When we make something, we gather various materials and put forth great effort with our hands, arms, and other body parts to make the new thing. Sometimes the task is very tiresome, requiring much sweat and energy. In contrast, Scripture shows that God created by the mere power of his word. Who can forget that the six days of creation (Genesis 1–2) all begin with God's spoken word ("Let there be . . .")? Whether it was creation *ex nihilo* or fashioning out of matter already made from nothing, God's powerful word did it. The psalmist (Ps 33:6-9) puts it beautifully when he writes, "By the word of the LORD the heavens were made, and by the breath of His mouth all their host. He gathers the waters of the sea together as a heap; He lays up the deeps in storehouses. Let all the earth fear the LORD; let all the inhabitants of the world stand in awe of Him. For He spoke, and it was done; He commanded, and it stood fast." Creation required enormous skill and effort, but God did it all by the power of his word with such ease and grandeur!

CREATION DISPLAYS GOD'S POWER AND GLORY. Not only did God create *with* great power (Jer 27:5), but the created universe *displays* his power, splendor, and glory. Jeremiah writes that God "made the earth by His power" (Jer 10:12). In Job 9, Job speaks of God's powerful hand in creation (vv. 5-10): "It is God who removes the mountains, . . . who shakes the earth out of its place, and its pillars tremble; who commands the sun not to shine, and sets a seal upon the stars; who alone stretches out the heavens, and tramples down the waves of the sea; who makes the Bear, Orion, and the Pleiades, and the chambers of the south; who does great things, unfathomable, and wondrous works without number" (see also Psalm 104). From God's power displayed in creation, Job concludes that no one could argue with God and expect to win (Job 9:2-4). A similar theme comes from God's answer to Job in Job 38–41. God overwhelms Job with a description of his majesty and power as displayed in creating and controlling the world. In light of such power and transcendence, who are we to question whether God controls what happens to us or whether he knows what he is doing and has power to accomplish it? The psalmist, upon reflecting on creation, exults, "O LORD, our Lord, how majestic is Thy name in all the earth, who hast displayed Thy splendor above the heavens!" (Ps 8:1). In Ps 19:1 we read that "the heavens are telling of the glory of God; and their expanse is declaring the work of His hands." If so, then by simply opening our eyes and paying attention to the creation around us, we should conclude that a powerful, majestic God made it all.

CREATION TEACHES GOD'S SOVEREIGNTY. A major OT theme about creation is that the power displayed therein shows that God is absolutely sovereign over all. He made everything and controls it as well. In 1 Sam 2:6-8 we hear Hannah's prayer. Verse 8 ends with her affirmation that the pillars of the earth are the Lord's, and he set the world on them. All of this is used to explain what she said in verses 6-8a: "The LORD kills and makes alive; He brings down to Sheol and raises up. The LORD makes poor and rich; He brings low, He also exalts. He raises the poor from the dust, He lifts the needy from the ash heap to make them sit with nobles, and inherit a seat of honor." God's power in creation demonstrates his sovereign control over all things. A similar note is sounded by Job and his friends in several passages (Job 26:7-13; 28:25-27; 36:26-33). In these passages we see that God controls the rain, thunder and lightning, the earth and the heavens, the seas and the luminaries in the sky. Not only did he make them but he also controls their continual operation. This clear note of the creator's sovereignty over all things is also sounded by Isaiah (44:24-28), Amos (4:12-13; 5:8-9), and the psalmist (Psalm 104).

To underscore this point, Isaiah and Jeremiah invoke the imagery of a potter and clay. Even as the potter molds the clay as he wishes and has a right to do whatever he wants with any lump of clay or anything formed from clay, so God has a right to do what he wants with his creation. Exemplary of this motif is Isa 29:15-16: "Woe to those who deeply hide their plans from the

LORD, and whose deeds are done in a dark place, and they say, 'Who sees us?' or 'Who know us?' You turn things around! Shall the potter be considered as equal with the clay, that what is made would say to its maker, 'He did not make me'; or what is formed say to him who formed it, 'He has no understanding'?" Of course, the potter can do whatever he wants with the clay (see also Isa 45:8-9; 64:8). In Jer 18:1-6 God says that as Israel's maker, their potter, he has a right to do what he wants with them. Though God's sovereignty over creation is not conclusive "proof" for the model of God espoused in this book, it is consistent with it and far from the depiction of both process and open view accounts of God's control over his creatures.

In light of God's sovereign control as creator, several things follow. For one thing, Job recognizes that no mere human could win an argument with God (Job 9:1-12). Moreover, even though Job doesn't know why things have happened to him as they have, he is sure that it is God who has done this to him (Job 12:7-9).

On a more encouraging note, the psalmist explains that because God is sovereign over creation, he is able to defeat our enemies, if he so chooses. In Ps 74:12-17 the clear note of God's control over all creation rings loud, but in this psalm the psalmist speaks about devastation and defeat by the enemy and pleads for God to intervene. Levenson relates this passage to the struggle-with-chaos theme. Though the OT portrays God as sovereign ruler over creation, his is not an uncontested control. The forces of evil are ever-present to disrupt that rule, and in this case it appears that they have won a temporary victory. Hence, the sovereign ruler is entreated to resume his rightful mastery of chaos so as to rescue his people. God has power to defeat the enemy. If only now he would do so! Levenson argues that we only rightly understand God's mastery over creation if we see it in dialectical relation to the forces of chaos that war against divine control.[49] Levenson's analysis is grounded in his understanding of comparative Ancient Near Eastern cosmogony literature; his affirmation that there are times when Yahweh has failed to master chaos which instead has won seems to rely too heavily on his understanding of that extra-biblical literature. However, it is unquestionable that both OT and NT speak of spiritual warfare in which God, angels, and humans are engaged. Given God's sovereignty, ultimate victory is assured, and even defeats along the way serve God's ultimate purposes; but none of this means that there is no genuine warfare.

Because of God's sovereignty as displayed over creation, various biblical writers point to God's creative activities, and then affirm him as their helper. Presumably, the point is that any God who could do what our God did in creating the world around us surely has power to help us in time of need. In Ps 121:2 the psalmist writes, "My help comes from the LORD, who made heaven and earth." David writes (Ps 124:8) that "Our help is in the name of the LORD, who made heaven and earth." Amos 9 is a wonderful passage promising God's deliverance from Israel's enemies and a great day of restoration and blessing. The picture is millennial, and in the midst of his description Amos pauses to reflect on God and his power. In verses 5-6 he writes: "And the Lord GOD of hosts, the One who touches the land so that it melts, and all those who dwell in it mourn, and all of it rises up like the Nile and subsides like the Nile of Egypt; the One who builds His upper chambers in the heavens, and has founded His vaulted dome over the earth, He who calls for the waters of the sea and pours them out on the face of the earth, the LORD is His name" (see also Amos 5:8-9). Can Israel's God fulfill the promises of restoration? How silly a question in light of his being the one who touches the land so that it melts! We should also note Isa 51:12-13, where the specific help promised Israel is God's comfort. There is no reason to fear the enemy when your God is the one who "stretched out the heavens and laid the foundations of the earth."

GOD A WISE AND GOOD CREATOR. OT writers also affirm that creation was made by a wise creator. "The LORD by wisdom founded the earth; by understanding He established the heavens" (Prov 3:19). Jeremiah writes that God "established the world by His wisdom" (Jer 10:12; 51:15). Indeed, as we consider creation, it is clear that nothing escaped God's attention in creating. Every creature is molded so that its various parts function to sustain life. Moreover, God ordered the environment on earth so that it can support life. All of this shows a very wise creator, but it also reveals that he is good. It is one thing to know how to make things correctly, another to have power to do so, and yet another to have the goodness of heart and will to do it. The wise, powerful, and benevolent creator made a masterpiece in creating our world!

CREATION IS GOOD. As opposed to ancient theories that say matter is inferior at best and evil at worst, God pronounces good everything he created. In fact, at the end of the sixth and final day of creating, God saw that everything he had made was very good (Gen 1:31). By pronouncing everything good, the point is not so much that everything is morally good, for things like the sun, moon, stars, and planets are morally neutral. While humans as created had not yet sinned and so were morally good in that sense, the basic point is more of a functional one. That is, saying that the sun and moon are good means they are what they should be and they perform their appointed function. The further point is that God did what he intended to do, and did it exceedingly well. God's assessment and approval of the created order leaves no room for thinking that the material world as created is evil or somehow morally inferior to the immaterial. This has profound implications philosophically and theologically, but it also has practical consequences. We should value and protect creation. Exploiting the environment, especially in ways destructive to it, is ruled out.

GOD AND HUMANS. In some passages God is compared to mankind or mankind is compared to the rest of creation. For example, Ps 90:2, 4 tells us that though the earth had a beginning in time, God existed long before that, for he is eternal. We are transitory creatures and very much notice time's passage, but for a God who lives forever a thousand years "are like yesterday when it passes by." In Psalm 8 David marvels at the wonders of creation, but he adds that in light of all that God has made and its grandeur, man seems so insignificant. It is truly amazing that God cares about us, and yet he does. He has even crowned the human race with glory and majesty (8:3-5).

GOD'S WORK OF PRESERVATION.   Various OT passages also show that God's relation to creation did not end with the six days of creation. God continues to be involved in our world, sustaining and preserving it in being. This is no deistic god who "wound up the clock" and left it to run on its own. The OT picture is that without God's sustaining power the world could not go on, and God has graciously and faithfully continued to preserve it. The psalmist says (Ps 119:90), "Thy faithfulness continues throughout all generations; Thou didst establish the earth, and it stands." In Ps 65:9-13 David offers more details. Not only does God preserve the earth, but he also causes rain so that things can grow and flourish. He brings forth grain for food. Surely, he has greatly blessed the earth and its inhabitants!

FUTURE CREATION.   Though God created all things in the past and preserves them through the present, the OT shows that God's creative activity is not entirely finished. Isa 65:17-18 speaks of God's future creation of a new heavens and a new earth. The rest of the chapter speaks of conditions on that new heaven and earth. There will be great peace, prosperity, and blessing. The NT more fully tells us what God will do, but even in the OT God sends this message to encourage Israel.[50]

In light of God's great power, wisdom, and majesty so marvelously displayed in creating and preserving the universe, there is only one appropriate response from his creature: praise. Psalms 97–99 are an almost uninterrupted extolling of God's attributes and of his works in creation and salvation of his people. Along with the litany of divine virtues and accomplishments is a constant call to praise God. We could hardly do better in closing this discussion of OT themes than to quote the psalmist as he encourages all of creation to praise the Lord (Ps 148:1-6): "Praise the LORD! Praise the LORD from the heavens; praise Him in the heights! Praise Him, all His angels; praise Him, all His hosts! Praise Him, sun and moon; praise Him, all stars of light! Praise Him, highest heavens, and the waters that are above the heavens! Let them praise the name of the LORD, for He commanded and they were created. He has also established them forever and ever; He has made a decree which will not pass away."

NT Themes

GOD THE CREATOR. The NT presents most of the themes found in the OT. Many passages affirm God as creator of all things. Acts 4:24 says that God created the heaven, earth, and sea and all that is within them. Stephen quotes from Isa 66:2, which offers God's rhetorical question "Was it not My hand which made all these things?" (Acts 7:50). At Lystra, Paul, Barnabas, and the other apostles tell the listeners to turn to the living God "who made the heaven and the earth and the sea, and all that is in them" (Acts 14:15). In his sermon on Mars Hill in Athens, Paul speaks of God as the one who gave life and breath to all things, including humans in all nations (Acts 17:24-26). As a result, he calls humans God's offspring (v. 28, NIV), for in God we live and move and have our being.

The Pauline epistles teach the same thing. Paul says that all things are from God, through him, and to him (Rom 11:36). Paul offers final instructions to Timothy and charges him in the presence of God "who gives life to all things" to keep those instructions (1 Tim 6:13). In 1 Cor 11:12 Paul teaches about the relation of women to men, and he says that all things originate from God (see also 2 Cor 4:6; Eph 3:9).

Beyond the Pauline epistles we find the same truth. In Rev 10:6 John sees in a vision an angel who swears by the one "who created heaven and the things in it, and the earth and the things in it, and the sea and the things in it." Clearly, God is creator of all, and certain things follow from this truth. Because the true and living God created all things, he doesn't dwell in temples made with hands, nor is he served with human hands as though he needs anything (Acts 17:24-25). Moreover, because he created all things, he deserves all the glory (Rev 4:11); since he is creator of all, we should worship him! (Rev 14:7).

While the OT speaks of God as creator and portrays the Holy Spirit brooding over creation (Gen 1:2), the NT most clearly shows the Son's role and clarifies that of the Father. Both Testaments together teach that creation is a work of the whole Godhead. First Corinthians 8:6 states that God is the source of all, but it is through Christ's agency that all things have been created. John's Gospel begins with words that echo Gen 1:1 as he tells us that Christ, the Word, was always with God. Moreover, through Christ all things were made (John 1:3), and lest there be any doubts about what this means, John adds that nothing created was made through any agency other than Christ's. In verse 10, John repeats that the incarnate ("in the world") Christ made the world, even though the world didn't recognize him as creator or understand why he came.

A very clear passage affirming Christ as creator of all things is Col 1:16. If we wonder how inclusive "all things" is, Paul enumerates them. Christ made all things "in the heavens and on earth, visible and invisible, whether thrones or dominions or rulers or authorities." Paul then repeats the summary statement that "all things have been created through Him and for Him." Invisible thrones, dominions, and authorities undoubtedly refer to angelic and demonic powers—even these were created by Christ, and like all other things, they were created for him. Moreover, Christ didn't just leave them to run on their own, for verse 17 teaches that in Christ all things hold together. The verb has the idea of gluing something together. Hence, Christ's preserving power keeps our universe from coming unglued. Elsewhere (Acts 17:28) this creative and preserving power are attributed more generally to God, but Colossians 1 specifically says that Christ is the preserver.

CREATION BY GOD'S WORD. In 2 Peter 3, Peter says that the Lord will certainly return and judge the wicked. Some doubt this because they think nothing catastrophic ever happens, but Peter replies that catastrophic changes have already occurred. God made the heavens and the earth, he also brought the flood in the days of Noah; likewise he will someday destroy the current heavens and earth in judgment (vv. 5-7). Peter relates that all of this happens as a result of God's word. God spoke and the heavens and earth were formed. He spoke again and the flood came. And in a future day, by the mere power of his word, judgment will fall again. The ungodly who believe they will never face a day of accountability delude themselves.

CREATION IS GOOD. The NT also asserts the goodness of creation, although the context significantly differs from that of such OT affirmations. In 1 Timothy 4 Paul predicts that in the end time some will fall away from the faith as a result of following various heresies. Some will even forbid marriage and advocate abstaining from eating certain foods God created and intends for us to eat. Paul adds (v. 4) that "everything created by God is good, and nothing is to be rejected, if it is received with gratitude."

CREATION DISPLAYS GOD'S POWER AND GLORY. The NT also repeats the OT teaching that creation displays God's attributes. The difference in the way NT writers use this point is significant. Paul claims (Rom 1:19-20) that since the creation of the world, it has been possible to see the world around us and understand that there is a God. Creation evidences God's attributes, especially his power. As a result, everyone knows there is a God, and they are guilty if they reject him. Unfortunately, rather than worshiping the God revealed in creation, mankind worshiped the creature (1:25). The point not mentioned as such in the OT is that because creation reveals God, all know there is a God and are accountable for what they do with that revelation.

CREATION TEACHES GOD'S SOVEREIGNTY. 1 Cor 8:6 affirms that there is only one God and one Lord, Jesus Christ. All things come from God and we exist for him; we are under his sovereign control. Heb 2:10 speaks of Christ's preparation by God to be the Savior who would bring many sons to glory. Of this God we are told that all things are for him and through him. Westcott explains that this means God is the final cause and the efficient cause of all things.[51] That is, all things have God as their goal and purpose, and he brought them into being in the first place. He is sovereign over all.

In accord with God's sovereignty, the potter/clay motif appears in Romans 9, where Paul uses it to teach divine sovereignty and specifically to affirm predestination. Throughout chapter 9 Paul speaks of God's decision concerning who will be blessed and who will be damned. All things stem from God's desires and will (v. 18). Paul then imagines an objection that, if God determines everything that happens, including evil, he cannot justly condemn people for doing the evil he foreordained them to do (v. 19). Anyway, who could contravene God's will? Such questions raise significant intellectual issues, but Paul senses that they betray a serious attitudinal problem; the objection accuses God of being unfair, and it purports to put him on trial. In verses 20-21 Paul addresses the attitudinal problem. He reminds those who would accuse God that, as creatures, they have no right to put God on trial and demand an explanation. God is the creator and can do whatever he wants with his creatures. Just as clay has no right to complain about what the potter does with it, so we, as God's creation, have no right to object to the lot in life he ordains for us. Creators have certain rights over their creation!

GOD AND HUMANS. Though this theme occurs less frequently than in the OT, there is an NT passage that compares God with his creation. In Heb 1:10-12, the writer quotes from various OT passages and says that God made the heavens and the earth. His point is about God's eternity and constancy. Though the heavens and the earth will perish, God will not. He lives forever, and he does not change. The created universe is a wonderful thing, but it is transient; it cannot compare with God.

The NT also shows God as the source of spiritual life and the sovereign Lord over all believers. Paul makes this point in Eph 4:6 about Christ's church when he writes that there is "one God and Father of all who is over all and through all and in all." This speaks of God's sovereign lordship over the church and his immanence in it, presumably by indwelling each member. In addition, Paul says that those who accept Christ as personal Savior are new creatures or creations (2 Cor 5:17). He further adds in Col 3:10 that believers are being renewed according to the image of the one who created them. In both of these passages the point is spiritual creation, the establishing of a spiritual relation with God. The imagery of birth and begetting is elsewhere attributed to God, especially the Holy Spirit (e.g., John 3:5-8; 1 Pet 1:3, 23).

AFFIRMATION OF OT CREATION ACCOUNTS. At various points I have mentioned that NT writers quote OT passages about creation, but I should add something more. Various NT passages also assert as historically true different aspects of the stories of the creation and fall. For example, in his discourse on divorce and remarriage (Matt 19:4, 8; Mark 10:6), when the Pharisees ask if it is permissible to divorce one's wife for any reason, Jesus points them back to God's original design for marriage instituted with Adam and Eve (Gen 2:24). Clearly, Jesus takes the creation of Adam and Eve and the story of their marriage as historically true. Paul likewise affirms the creation narratives. In his instructions about head coverings (1 Corinthians 11), the rationale for his teaching is that man did not originate from woman, nor does he exist for her sake; rather, woman comes from man and was made for his sake (vv. 8-9). This is precisely what the Genesis 2 account of Eve's creation says. Likewise, in 1 Tim 2:12-14, when Paul commands that women not take leadership roles in the church, his reasons are twofold: Adam was created first; and Eve was deceived. Regardless of how one understands these verses' prohibitions, there can be little question that Paul thinks the story of Eve's creation and the account of the fall are historically accurate.[52]

FUTURE CREATION.   A final NT theme echoes another OT theme, but the NT gives more details. God's creative work is not done. He sustains the world, but there is more than that. In a coming day, God will destroy the current heavens and earth and create a new heaven and earth. Peter speaks of this in 2 Peter 3. In verses 10-12 he writes of the coming destruction of the current world order—this time by fire, not by flood. He says (vv. 10 and 12) that the elements will be destroyed with intense heat. The Greek text doesn't indicate the annihilation of matter but rather the collapse of all existing structures—a gigantic meltdown. Afterward God will create a new heaven and a new earth (v. 13). Will it be refashioned from the former elements? We are not told, but that is certainly possible, or God may create the new heavens and earth *ex nihilo*. As to when this will happen, Peter doesn't say, but we can piece together some idea from other passages. All OT and NT indications are that Christ's millennial rule will be upon the current earth. After his vision of that thousand-year reign, John saw a vision of the Great White Throne Judgment (Rev 20:11-15), and then Revelation 21 and 22 describe the new heavens and earth and the new Jerusalem. John tells us at the outset of his description of the Great White Throne Judgment that (Rev 20:11) heaven and earth had fled away from the presence of him who sat on the throne; no place was found for them. If we take this literally, it means that sometime after the millennial kingdom but before the Great White Throne Judgment God will destroy the current heavens and earth as Peter predicts in 2 Peter 3. After John describes this Judgment, he then tells us about the new heavens and new earth (Revelation 21–22). If these chapters in Revelation present a chronological order, then they seem to tell us something of the timing of the events Peter predicts. Scholars agree that Revelation 21–22 speaks of conditions in the eternal state. God's creative work is not yet finished!

GENESIS 1–2 AND THE DAYS OF CREATION

Genesis 1–2 is the most extended biblical discourse about creation. These chapters are also the source of much contention, for it is here that biblical teaching seems most in conflict with science. Thus, we must look more closely at these chapters and the issues surrounding them.

Though many items in these chapters are points of contention, I shall begin with things that are less troublesome. An initial point is the obvious one that these two chapters contain two distinct accounts of the creation story. Higher critics like to attribute these stories to two separate writers and two distinct narratives (P, the priestly author is said to have written 1:1–2:4a, and J, the Yahwist, is deemed author of 2:4b–3:24).[53] Many agree that, in their present form, these two accounts are woven together to give different but complementary accounts of the creation events. Blocher explains:

> In any case, in their differences the two tablets complete each other. Far from standing as a rival of the first, the second, as Renckens recognizes, 'is not in fact a second creation narrative at all'. It is interested above all in the emergence of evil, and the prominent Jerusalem scholar, U. Cassuto, stresses that the Torah's answer on this fundamental point 'flows from the continuity of the two sections'; we receive the answer only 'when we study the two sections as a single sequence'. The great critic von Rad has rightly seen 'that the two creation stories are in many respects open to each other' and that exegesis must be carried out on both together. As for what the two have in common, the formation of the man and the woman, their agreement is substantial, as we shall have occasion to point out, and the differences concern the viewpoint and the method of exposition.[54]

Actually, the construction of these two chapters is not unusual for Hebrew style at all. Frequently in Hebrew literature, the author gives an opening general statement of the whole topic and then spells out the details. Many see Gen 1:1 as the general topic statement about what God did, and the rest of chapter 1 and the first four verses of chapter 2 as offering specific details of the major steps in God's creation of all things. After giving the basic framework of the seven days, in chapter 2 the author focuses specifically on the events of the sixth day. All of that prepares for the account of the temptation and fall recorded in chapter 3. Viewed this way, Genesis 1–3 is a carefully crafted piece of literature.

Despite the continuity of themes, there are differences of perspective in the two accounts recorded in chapters 1 and 2. Rosemary Nixon observes that in these two chapters we have two different perspectives on the creator and his method of creating and relating to the creation. Chapter 1 portrays the creator as an absolute ruler, a king who gets his way and does all things well. Just as an absolute monarch speaks and his commands are obeyed, so the creator merely speaks and his orders are accomplished. The most recurrent formula in the first account is "and God said, Let . . . and it was so." The creator also *sees* that what results from his commands is good. We don't get a description of the mechanics of fulfilling the commands, nor do we glimpse the artisans at work. Rather, the supreme ruler speaks and it is done.[55]

In contrast, chapter 2 portrays the creator more as a craftsman or artisan who works patiently with his materials to form them as he wants. The artisan responds and reacts to situations. One of the clearest instances of this appears in verses 18ff. when the creator notices that man is alone and concludes that this is not good for him. The creator forms the animals and brings them to Adam to name, but in the process he notes that none is a fitting helpmate for Adam. The creator goes back to work and forms woman from man. Though I cannot agree with Nixon's judgment that the creator is not working from a pre-planned strategy, I do agree that the second account of creation depicts God as molding things himself, a creator very much involved with his creation.[56]

Though these two portraits (king and artisan) differ, Nixon is surely correct[57] that the writer wants us to think of the creator in both terms. Either picture alone gives only part of the story. Moreover, we must note the significant differences between the two accounts. In particular, there is a difference in emphasis in each account. Genesis 2 focuses on events that culminate in the creation of humans as male and female and the institution of marriage between them. None of God's other creatures have such dignity, nor do they receive such extended attention in the Genesis creation accounts. In chapter 1, there is also a special emphasis on the creation of man after the divine council (1:26-28), but the focus is on all six days of creation and God's sovereign, omnipotent, orderly creation of all things, not just human beings.

What is somewhat disputed is exactly where the first account ends and the second begins (2:4 or 2:5). Thankfully, this issue is not determinative of overall theological positions, so we may be brief. Some see 2:4 as a summary statement of 1:1–2:3 which rounds off the first narrative, and then verse 5 begins the next. Buswell is an adamant proponent of this view, for to see 2:4 as introducing the second account "does violence to the whole meaning of the passage. There isn't the slightest suggestion that the human race was even metaphorically begotten by the heavens and the earth or in any way construed as descendants thereof."[58] But this argument is hardly convincing, for even if the verse refers to the preceding, the previous account talks about the creation of man as male and female (1:27), so if 2:4 says the heavens and earth generated man, the same problem is there, regardless of whether 2:4 refers to what follows or what precedes.

While many scholars see 2:4 as introducing the second account,[59] not all agree. Of course, we should avoid any strategy that fractures the verse as a composite (4a and 4b) put together by a redactor from the documents by J and P.[60] Perhaps Cassuto's approach is wisest. He notes that the formula *'êlleh tôlĕdŏt* ("these are the generations") appears in some passages where it refers to what was said earlier (e.g., Gen 36:13, 17, 18) and in other cases it refers to what comes after (e.g., Gen 5:1; 10:1). Given the possibility of both options and the phrase's use in this context, Cassuto argues that it is a bridge between the two narratives, tying them together:

> Our verse is, therefore, an organic whole and belongs entirely to the section of the garden of Eden. It serves to connect the narrative of the first section to that of the second; and its meaning is: *These*—the events described in the previous portion—constituted *the history of the heavens and the earth,* when they were created, that is, when the Lord God made them; and now I shall tell you in detail what happened at the conclusion of this Divine work.[61]

Cassuto's suggestion of seeing the verse as a link between the two accounts makes much sense.

Creation and Ancient Near Eastern Literature

In the late nineteenth century the Babylonian accounts of creation (*Enuma Elish*) and the flood (a portion of the *Epic of Gilgamesh*) were published. Since then creation stories from other Ancient Near Eastern peoples have also been unearthed. The initial tendency was to note the similarities alone so as to downplay the biblical account's uniqueness, and in response conservative biblical scholars felt a need to defend the idea that the biblical accounts are distinct from those other religions. While one might have thought that similarities with other accounts would give credibility to the biblical accounts (i.e., if all cultures have similar stories, a likely reason is that they all reflect events that actually occurred), the similarities were often used instead to explain away the biblical accounts as nothing unusual, and probably just examples of a prevalent mythological genre of creation stories. In more recent years, however, there has been more willingness to notice both similarities and significant differences.[62] Cassuto helps to distinguish the various creation stories. Beginning with non-biblical accounts, he writes:

> They began, as a rule, with a theogony, that is, with the origin of the gods, the genealogy of the deities who preceded the birth of the world and mankind; and they told of the antagonism between this god and that god, of frictions that arose from these clashes of will, and of mighty wars that were waged by the gods. They connected the genesis of the world with the genesis of the gods and with the hostilities and wars between them; and they identified the different parts of the universe with given deities or with certain parts of their bodies. Even the elect few among the nations, the thinkers who for a time attained to loftier concepts than those normally held in their environment, men like Amenhotep IV—the Egyptian king who attributed the entire creation to one of the gods, the sun-god Aten—and his predecessors . . . , even they pictured this god to themselves as but one of the gods, be he the very greatest, as a deity linked to nature and identifiable with one of its component parts. Then came the Torah and soared aloft, as on eagles' wings, above all these notions. Not many gods but One God; not theogony, for a god has no family

tree; not wars nor strife nor the clash of wills, but only One Will, which rules over everything, without the slightest let or hindrance; not a deity associated with nature and identified with it wholly or in part, but a God who stands absolutely above nature, and outside of it, and nature and all its constituent elements, even the sun and all the other entities, be they never so exalted, are only His creatures, made according to His will.[63]

Clearly, the Genesis 1–2 account is no mere repetition of current stories among neighboring peoples. The distinctions are equally as significant as the similarities.

Structure of the Accounts

Waltke helpfully notes that the first account falls into five parts. The first is a summary statement of the whole teaching (Gen 1:1), followed by a negative comment about the state of the earth at the time of creation (1:2). The account of the six days of creation (1:3-31) takes up most of the chapter, and this is followed by a summary and conclusion (2:1). After this is an epilogue about the Sabbath day (2:2-3).[64] The second chapter fills in details about the creation of humans as male and female, and then speaks of the planting of the Garden which Adam and Eve are commissioned to till. In the midst of this, the writer records the divine prohibition against eating of the tree of the knowledge of good and evil. All of this prepares for the events of chapter 3.

Various writers point out that the six days of creation are arranged in two triads.[65] The first three days involve forming the basic structures of the universe, whereas the final three are used to fill the various spheres created during the first three days. Moreover, there is a one-to-one correlation between each day of the first triad and each day of the second respectively. On day one, light is created, and on day four the luminaries (sun, moon, and stars) are put in their place and assigned their function. On day two, the sky or atmosphere ("firmament" in many translations) and the water are separated, and this corresponds to day five when fish and birds are formed to fill these two places. Finally, day three sees the formation of land distinct from the seas and the production of vegetation on the land. Correspondingly, on day six God creates the beasts and mankind to populate the land.[66]

Theological Themes

Regardless of whether one sees chapters 1–2 as straightforward history, or as a parable meant to teach theological truths about the creation, or as some other genre, there is little question that the author wanted to teach some key things about God, man, and the creation. It is important to note when this was written. Granting Mosaic authorship, it is likely that this was written between 1400 and 1500 B.C., and it is not unlikely that it was written after the exodus from Egypt. Israel had been in Egypt for more than four hundred years, and the Egyptians worshiped many gods. This polytheism must have been somewhat of a temptation to the people, but that would not be the only challenge to belief in Yahweh. One might expect that once Israel reached the Promised Land and conquered it, Israel would uniformly praise and worship Yahweh, but God knew there would be great temptation to idolatry from Israel's neighbors. As a people oppressed for many centuries and then released to wander in search of a new homeland, Israel might have thought that, given their plight, their God was not as powerful as the gods of other peoples. In this context, we can see the creation accounts performing some very specific functions at the outset of the Torah, the formative document for Israel's life as a nation.

YAHWEH IS SUPREME. With this in mind, it seems safe to say that one of the purposes and themes of the creation accounts in Genesis 1–2 is to teach that there is only one God, the God of Israel, who has unlimited power. He released Israel from Egyptian bondage, and he also created all things out of nothing by the power of his word (see also Psalm 104, where Yahweh is portrayed as sovereignly taming the forces of nature and forming them into our world, and doing so without opposition). In contrast to Israel's pagan slave masters (Egypt) and pagan neighbors in the Promised Land, there is no deification of the forces of nature. Moreover, there is no struggle among the gods of nature or between these gods and a supreme God, Yahweh. Rather, nothing in nature is divine, for all things are mere creatures made by the one true living God and are subservient to him. It is important to note in this respect that the specific things created in the six days of creation were all worshiped by one or another of Israel's Near Eastern neighbors. As Conrad Hyers explains:

> In the light of this historical context it becomes clearer what Genesis 1 is undertaking and accomplishing: a radical and sweeping affirmation of monotheism *vis-a-vis* polytheism, syncretism and idolatry. Each day of creation takes on two principal categories of divinity in the pantheons of the day, and declares that these are not gods at all, but creatures— creations of the one true God who is the only one, without a second or third. Each day dismisses an additional cluster of deities, arranged in a cosmological and symmetrical order.
> On the first day the gods of light and darkness are dismissed. On the second day, the gods of sky and sea. On the third day, earth gods and gods of vegetation. On the fourth day, sun, moon and star gods. The fifth and sixth days take away any associations with divinity from the animal kingdom. And finally human existence, too, is emptied of any intrinsic divinity—while at the same time all human beings, from the greatest to the least, and not just pharaohs, kings and heroes, are granted a divine likeness and mediation.[67]

This theme of Yahweh's supremacy over everything and his uniqueness is also at the heart of the major formative event in Israel's history, the exodus, which Moses also records. God removed his people from bondage by bringing a series of ten plagues on Egypt. Each plague was a stroke of judgment against something worshiped as God in Egypt. Before this episode in Israel's history was over, she would see very vividly who was the supreme God, and if the Egyptians had any doubts, they should get the message as well. Think of the ten plagues and how each of them relates in some way to one of the major things God created according to Genesis 1–2. The first plague turned the Nile and all of Egypt's waters to blood (Exod 7:17-21); on day three of creation God formed the seas. The second plague was a plague of frogs that came up from the rivers and streams (Exod 8:1-4); on day five God made all the water animals and on day six the land animals. The third plague was a plague of lice from the dust (Exod 8:16-18); on day three God distinguished the land from the sea and on day six created things that creep on the ground. The fourth plague was a swarm of insects (Exod 8:21-24); on day five, God created things that fly through the air. The fifth plague was upon the livestock (Exod 9:3-7); God formed livestock on day six. Plague six was a plague of boils on man and beast (Exod 9:8-12), and of course, on day six, God made both man and beast. The seventh plague was hail with thunder and lightning, and it fell on many beasts and plants (Exod 9:18-26); on day two of creation God showed his control over the firmament and the clouds above earth, clouds that would later bring rain. On day three he formed vegetation, and on day six the beasts of the earth. The eighth plague was a plague of locusts that ate up all the plants and fruit of the trees (Exod 10:4-15); on day three God formed the vegetation that filled the land, and on days five and six formed the birds and other creatures of the air and the beasts of the land. The ninth plague was a plague of darkness, blotting out the sun (Egypt, like many other ancient peoples, worshiped the sun); on day one God created light, and on day four put the sun, moon, and stars in their place and appointed their proper functions. Finally, the crown of creation is man (day six), and in Egyptian thinking the king was a god and so was his son. The killing of the firstborn was a final stroke of judgment against a god of Egypt, even as the creation of man was a final act showing God's control over all things.

From this description it should be clear that the plagues upon Egypt are God's statement of his supremacy and control over things worshiped as god in that land. But every one of the plagues also correlates with something God created on one of the six days of creation—again showing his supremacy over them. Of course, there is a major difference between the two sequences. In the case of the ten plagues, God shows his supremacy by bringing judgments on Egypt that show he is greater than their gods. In Genesis 1–2 we see God's supremacy not through judgment but through creation and control of his creatures.

While we shouldn't stretch the parallels between these two accounts too far, it is interesting that when a part of the creation rebels against God, he shows his supremacy over it by judging it with the flood (Genesis 6). In the exodus story, the full and final removal of God's people from Egypt is not complete until God makes one final statement of his power over the Egyptians by drowning them in the waters of the Red Sea. Those who worship other gods or who choose to contest the God of Israel will lose. That message is loud and clear, and was likely meant to encourage the fledgling nation of Israel.

GOD AND CREATION DISTINCT.   According to Genesis 1–2, God is distinct from his creation, and the creation depends on him. Unlike views of that day which deified things in the natural order, and unlike later views that would be pantheistic, Genesis makes a radical distinction between the being and power of the creator and the creature. Moreover, while things in the created order have value and, in some cases, a certain dignity, nothing emanates from God's being or anything else. God is immanent in his creation not because the creature is divine but because the creator God longs to commune and fellowship with his creatures (Genesis 2 and 3), but ontologically, he thoroughly transcends all that is.

DIGNITY OF HUMANS.   These creation narratives show something of the status of the human race. Though we are not gods, we are the apex of creation. Moreover, we are created in God's image and likeness (1:26-27), and this is said of no other creature, not even of angels. Humans are given dominion over the earth and its creatures, not to exploit them for our own selfish purposes but to rule and tend them for God their maker. That seems to be the point of 1:28 and 2:15. Moreover, as Clements notes, the portrait of mankind in the Genesis accounts greatly differs from accounts in pagan cultures. For example, in the Babylonian story, human beings are created to perform work for the gods.[68] While humans should live in submission and obedience to God's will, the biblical account of creation portrays humans as valuable in themselves, not just valuable instrumentally to serve and cater to the wishes of the gods. Contrary to either ancient or contemporary portraits of humanity that grant it little meaning and purpose and consider humans mere outcomes of mindless biological processes, the Bible portrays humans as having great dignity, value, and purpose.

SABBATH REST.   Many authors note that a major theme Moses intended to teach is that of Sabbath rest. Great emphasis is made of God's resting on the seventh day after ending his creative work. Moreover, Moses, as he records the Ten Commandments, links the Sabbath commandment to the creation narrative of Genesis 1–2 (Exod 20:10-11) and uses the creation account as the rationale for the Sabbath legislation. Though it is dubious that we should see the whole point of the creation narratives as ultimately leading to the Sabbath legislation,[69] this is undeniably a significant theme of these chapters. And, we must not miss the point of the Sabbath. God wants us to take time away from work for relaxation, but that is only part of the point. What should we do with that day of rest? The rest of the Pentateuch makes it quite clear that a major purpose of that day is to worship the great God who made all things. God finished creation and called it very good. God's human creatures are to govern the creation for God most of the week, and then devote a part of each week to resting and to worshiping the wonderful God who made this marvelous world in which we live.

Literary Genre of Genesis 1 and 2

Is the author teaching these theological truths with a historical account of exactly what occurred, a scientific statement, a poem, a cultic liturgy, or a myth? None of these may accurately represent the literary genre of these two chapters, but our decision on this matter has significant implications for how we understand this passage and whether we think it necessary to correlate it with the findings of natural science.

The literary genre of Genesis 1–2 is a hotly debated issue among exegetes and theologians. What further complicates it is that the accounts in Genesis 1 and 2 do not seem to have the same genre. The first is highly calculated and structured. Various exegetes note the repetition of certain motifs and phrases in groups of seven, three, and ten. Moreover, as already noted, there seems to be a deliberate division of the acts of creation into two triads, each day of the first triad correlated to a respective day of the second.[70] On the other hand, the second account which focuses on the creation of Adam and Eve, reads more like a narrative story. Are we to understand this (along with chapter 3) as history, is it a parable, or just what? And does the story in chapter 2 mesh with the account in chapter 1?[71] In what follows, I shall describe the various options and then try to reach a conclusion.

Noting the balanced structure of the first account with its recurring phrases, Buswell argues that the style is mnemonic. This means that it has been "arranged in convenient symmetrical patterns for memorizing."[72] The second account is quite different, taking on the style of simple narrative. There is no evidence of artificial and deliberate arranging of materials for ease in memorizing.[73] We can agree with Buswell that the styles of the two chapters differ, and we might even conclude that the author's intention in chapter 1 was to write something easy to memorize. But whether or not the style is mnemonic tells us little about the literary genre *per se*. One could arrange a list of scientific elements in a form that would be easy to memorize, or one could do the same thing with a poem or prose. That the writer wanted to help readers memorize the contents doesn't tell us whether he intended to recount what actually occurred, or wished to tell a story meant to teach spiritual and moral truths, or something else entirely.

Perhaps the genre is myth, as some have argued. The problem is how one defines myth. John Rogerson has shown that there are at least twelve definitions of myth, and they are not necessarily mutually exclusive. Brooke summarizes them into four main notions. First, a myth may be something that lacks rationality, postulating causes for things that show a defective understanding of scientific causes. Second, "myth" can refer to stories that describe profound truths about human experience which require symbolic interpretation. Such myths assume that the truths they are meant to teach have objective validity apart from the myth itself. Third, a myth may embody a society's common values and ideals and then expresses them in acts of worship. And finally, myth can be so defined as to harmonize with history, even if some details of the myth don't match exactly what happened in history. Thus, if one sees God at work in history, one might express that through the genre of myth in this fourth sense.[74]

Of these four senses of myth, probably the last comes closest to what we find in Genesis. Likewise, Genesis 1 and 2 are intended to describe profound truths (sense 2). However, it is dubious that we can agree that what is contained therein has only a general relation to what actually happened historically. As already shown, various NT writers and figures, including our Lord, understand various aspects of these texts as historically accurate, so to say that they may not be entirely accurate not only raises major questions about how much of Genesis 1–2 is historically accurate but also undermines some significant NT doctrinal teaching. Moreover, in light of contemporary attitudes that link myth with fairy tales and the imaginary, we should demur on labeling Genesis 1–2 myth. Moreover, since it is hard within the context of Genesis 1–3 to make a case for any of the characters or events as symbolic, to claim that these chapters are not entirely historically accurate would then require one to specify which things are literally true and which are symbols, and that would be no easy task. Moreover, one would have to be careful not to beg the question by deciding *a priori* that anything that involved a miracle could not be historically true.

Claus Westermann is hesitant to call the chapters myth, but won't say they are straightforward history either. He suggests that one finds four types of creation stories in ancient literature. The first is creation by birth or by a succession of births, and Westermann thinks that Genesis 1 implies this in the formula in 2:4a ("these are the generations"). A second kind of creation story sees creation resulting from a struggle or victory typically between the gods (as in the Babylonian *Enuma Elish* which details the struggle between Marduk and Tiamat). A third type of creation story portrays creation by an action or activity that usually involves an act of separating or dividing and then creating people by forming them from clay. A final kind of creation story involves creation through word.[75] Brooke sums up Westermann's own position from among these four options as follows:

> For Westermann Genesis 1:1–2:4a is a narrative whose content shows almost nothing of struggle-type creation (except the faintest echo in Gen 1:2), very little of generative creation (especially since there is no mention of the birth of the gods), something of creating by making, effecting by division, and most of creation by word. If that describes its content, its form is a clear adjustment of eight acts into six days, two sets of three parallel days, days five and six also having climactic blessings. The six days are followed by a seventh whose concern is God's rest; God is thus included in the created order and shown to be active in time and place as he is in the rest of Israel's history. For Westermann myth is not an apt classification of Genesis 1, although he might agree with something of Rogerson's fourth category.[76]

George Coats offers another suggestion. He doesn't consider Genesis 1 a myth, nor does he think it is a tale with a plot and resolution of a crisis. Instead, enumerating the different days makes our text seem more like a genealogy and like wisdom literature. Coats concludes that 1:1–2:4a is a report, and explains that this genre presents events for the sake of communication, not for the sake of the events. "As a report, the unit can communicate its teaching (about the Sabbath) in terms of event (the first Sabbath) and relate all subsequent events to the power of its position. All orders of creation derive from God. All events of creation derive from this primary event."[77] As Brett says, Coats differentiates a report from history in that "a report is 'basically brief, with a single event the subject of its record.' He is stretching this definition slightly if he construes creation as a single event, but one can at least agree that Gen. 1 is briefer than, say, the Deuteronomistic History."[78]

Gordon Wenham's commentary on Genesis 1–15 proposes that the genre of the early chapters of Genesis is "proto-historical" stories. This is so for two main reasons. First, the chapters would likely have been understood as factual reports by the original audiences that read and heard them, but that doesn't mean they are history in the precise sense we think of today. Though this makes a certain amount of sense, Brett makes the good point that it is unlikely that the author intended these chapters as "proto-history." In fact, such a category makes much sense only in light of what we understand by history; hence, the classification is anachronistic, for it presumes the kind of historical writing we know of today.[79]

What should we say, then, about the genre of these chapters? Waltke is surely right that we cannot read them as a science textbook, for that was hardly the author's intent.[80] Moreover, he is also correct in saying that the substance of the chapters makes significant theological points, but that doesn't mean it is written as one might write a theology.[81] Likewise, Waltke agrees that the chapters have a historical air to them, but we wouldn't understand them as straightforward history. To understand these chapters as straightforward history creates certain tensions (we might even say contradictions) between the two accounts and even within each account.[82]

Waltke agrees with Henri Blocher's identification of the genre as a literary-artistic representation of creation. In the next section we shall see exactly what that means, but for now I note that Blocher claims that the genre is composite. There is narrative, but "the mode of writing is that of Wisdom writing; the Wisdom theologian who draws up his thoughts gives us 'knowledge in a most concentrated form', matured in meditation on the finished works of God."[83] Blocher details very carefully the literary structure of the passage, noting the system of numerical harmony set forth by Cassuto. Surely, Blocher concludes, this cannot be straightforward history. It is a literary-artistic way of making some very significant historical points. How much of it should we understand literally? Blocher cites Augustine's options of taking it either entirely materially, entirely spiritually, or as a combination of the two. Blocher prefers the third, which means that some things must be taken as occurring just as recorded, while others should not be.[84]

From my perspective, Genesis 1–2 is the work of a first-rate literary artist. The symmetrical presentation of events in the first account in particular can hardly have occurred by chance. Moreover, we can agree that the author did not intend to write a science textbook, and from what I have said about themes, he definitely selected and reported events in a way that makes some very specific and important points. I agree also that this is not history in the sense of modern history or chronicling wherein a historian tries to be absolutely precise in reporting or to give us a veritable unedited snapshot of all details. And, as many defenders of biblical inerrancy argue, biblical authors often use approximations in reporting numbers and give us the gist of what happened or was said, rather than giving us a verbatim quote or an exact counting of numbers and recounting of events. However, even understanding their conventions in reporting history, we don't think they have stated falsehoods about the events.

Still, I am concerned with Blocher's conclusion about Adam and Eve—a result of his seeing this as a literary-artistic presentation of creation. Blocher explains that we cannot be certain that the story about Eve being created from Adam's rib should be taken literally.[85] The problem with this claim is that once one begins to question such things, how does one know where to stop? What hermeneutic will tell us? Moreover, if we question the historical character of these elements of the story, what does that mean for the doctrine of the imputation of Adam's sin (perhaps there never was an Adam, or if there was a first man and woman, the events of Genesis 3 didn't happen, because this is a parable that teaches some moral or spiritual truth); Jesus' teaching about marriage, divorce, and remarriage; and NT teaching on the role of men and women in marriage and in the church? All of these teachings presuppose the historical accuracy of various elements in Genesis 1–3. What is also troublesome is that one could make the same kind of claims about Moses' account of the ten plagues and Israel's exodus from Egypt. That is a much longer narrative, but it teaches the theological truth that God is supreme over all that is worshiped as God, and it repeats various phrases like "let my people go," "God hardened Pharaoh's heart," "Pharaoh's heart was hardened." Do these facts about that narrative mean that the ten plagues are merely a literary-artistic device the author uses to teach that Israel was delivered from Egypt and that Israel's God was victorious even though it is dubious that these ten plagues ever happened? If we say that this and other narratives of the Pentateuch, produced by a first-rate literary craftsman, are historically accurate, how can we then say that the creation accounts are mere literary devices for making important theological points about creation? What are the criteria for making such a distinction?

In sum, I believe we must affirm that what these chapters record did happen historically. But like any historian, Moses didn't record every single event that occurred, nor did he give us all the details of how the events happened. He selected events which did happen and crafted them into the basic statement of the events of creation (chapter 1) and the narrative that reads more like a story (chapter 2) of the creation of Adam and Eve and the preparation of the Garden. But, by using various literary devices to present the content, that does not mean he falsified the facts. This is not precise, blow-by-blow history, a snapshot capturing everything at once, as a historian writing it today might try to write. Moreover, it unquestionably is crafted to teach us truths about God's relation to the creation, about mankind's place in creation, about the instituting of human marriage, and about the entrance of sin with its consequences into the human race; but that in no way means the events described did not occur. If the author did not intend to tell us things that are historically accurate, then why, for example, all the details about creating trees that have their own seed within them, and why all the details about the four rivers that nourished the Garden of Eden? What is the theological or even literary point of such information? If none is evident, then it is hard to explain why they are included in so carefully crafted a document unless they tell us things that actually occurred. So, I can agree that a combination of genres is likely used, and I would not say that this is nothing but a straightforward historical account, much like a grocery-list of events, a snapshot of whatever there was to see.[86] But that in no way means that these chapters are fiction or unhistorical. Rather, it records history in the way OT writers compose it, and it uses these historical facts to teach significant truths about God, mankind, the world, and their relations.

The Days of Creation and the Age of the Universe, Earth, and Mankind

Apart from the overall debate between atheistic evolution and creationism, questions about the days of creation and the age of the universe constitute probably the most contentious issue even among those who hold a biblical account of origins. They agree that God is the creator and that creation is entirely dependent on him, but when we ask how God did it and how long it took, disagreements quickly surface. The rest of this chapter is devoted to discussing various proposals for harmonizing Scripture with the findings of science.

Though some might see this issue as a test of orthodoxy, so long as one's views do not clearly contradict biblical teaching on origins one could hold them without compromising evangelicalism. There is room for charity toward many who hold views that differ with ours. Having said this, I note that many theories that will be discussed seem to have originated in an attempt to fit Scripture with science. Those who hold such theories think God has the power to create all things in six consecutive, literal, twenty-four-hour days, but they believe that evidence, especially from science, suggests that he did it a different way. We should not ignore the data of disciplines such as science, but as evangelicals we must determine our views insofar as possible on the basis of biblical teaching. Hence, appeals to science to support either an old earth or a young earth cannot be determinative if the biblical and exegetical data do not warrant the view.

Having read this, some may sense an inconsistency in my position. Throughout this book I have appealed to various secular disciplines, especially philosophy, to help with doctrinal formulation. In the next chapters, I shall rely heavily on philosophy in attempting to harmonize human freedom with divine sovereignty. But in this chapter I rely very little on the findings of science in coming to my position. I want to explain why I don't see this as inconsistent, and to suggest how I use the secular disciplines in theology.

As an evangelical, Scripture is my final authority. Moreover, it is the source from which theological reflection must begin, though it is not the only source. I begin with Scripture and try to do my exegetical work apart from any philosophical reflections so as to let biblical authors say whatever they intended to say without distorting it by imposing the findings of philosophy, science, or any other extra-biblical discipline. What I find particularly troublesome in too many presentations on the doctrine of creation is that a primary goal (if not *the* primary goal) in interpreting the biblical text is to harmonize it with the prevailing scientific understanding of our world. For me, that is not the way to do evangelical systematic theology. I would no more determine what Genesis 1–2 means by attempting to make it square with the current findings of science than I would settle on an understanding of end time events by reading the newspaper or listening to newscasts and trying to correlate current events with the details of prophetic passages. Scripture must be allowed to speak for itself on its own terms, and then we turn to the secular disciplines to see if their teaching is consistent or inconsistent with biblical truth and what they can add to it.

None of this mandates only one possible interpretation of a given text, for in cases like Genesis 1–2, even apart from what science says about origins, there are elements within the text that are consistent with more than just one interpretation. The findings of science, philosophy, history, etc., may help us to see that there are other possible interpretations of a biblical text than we previously thought, but the data from those disciplines need not be determinative for which interpretation we choose, especially if the scientific viewpoint actually contradicts what Scripture clearly teaches. Unfortunately, some issues are sufficiently complex and some texts offer so little information on a topic that the textual data underdetermine all possible interpretations. That is, the evidence is not strong enough to conclude that one particular interpretation is unequivocally correct. In such cases, appeal to secular disciplines for further evidence is entirely appropriate and may in the final analysis be decisive for which position we adopt. Such a procedure is not problematic, for it still allows Scripture to be the final authority and the touchstone for what we believe. It is just that some questions have answers that go beyond what Scripture actually says.

Having said the preceding, I must add that I don't think biblical data allow either an atheistic or a theistic evolutionary account. This judgment is based both on exegetical and theological reasons, but also on a judgment of the scientific case in favor of any form of evolution. This goes against the findings of the contemporary scientific community, but that doesn't bother me unduly, for I would prefer my views to be consistent with Scripture even if that means they are inconsistent with science. All of this has certain implications, however, for how I approach this topic. For example, the fact that current scientific theory and data generally support an old universe and old earth does not move me to conclude that the days in Genesis 1–2 are ages or eons of time. Though I may conclude that such is the best understanding of the text, that conclusion for me must be reached insofar as possible on the basis of exegetical data from the text, not on the basis of the deliverances of science. None of this means that I am "doomed" to espouse a woodenly literal interpretation of Genesis 1–2 or any other biblical passage. It only clarifies my methodology and is intended to encourage others to use the same methodology.

So what is the difference between appealing to science on this topic and appealing to philosophy on the providence issue? As we shall see, Scripture clearly teaches both free will and divine sovereignty. Of course, to teach both that God ordains all things and controls all things and that humans are free and morally responsible seems contradictory. While Scripture creates this tension, it doesn't resolve it. That is why I go beyond Scripture to philosophy to see what it tells us about different notions of free will, and different concepts of how events and actions occur. Philosophy shows me that there are two broad perspectives on these issues, determinism and indeterminism, and it helps me grasp the difference between them. So I appeal to philosophy because scriptural teaching creates a tension without resolving it, and I sense that philosophy may help me see how to do so. This does not mean I can choose any philosophical position I want on these matters. My evangelical commitment to Scripture automatically rules out any philosophical answer that contradicts biblical teaching. On the other hand, if more than one philosophical position fits Scripture without contradiction, then I could choose any of those answers, but I still look for the position that allows me to understand biblical passages in their most natural sense.

The situation regarding biblical teaching on origins and scientific theory is different. As with free will and determinism, there is also a tension in this discussion. However—and this is the crucial difference—the tension in this case does *not* arise *within* Scripture, as it does in the free will/sovereignty issue. Scriptural teachings about the origin of the universe and of all life are consistent with one another. The tension arises when we try to match the teachings of Scripture with science. Since evangelical theology must give greatest weight to Scripture, if science contradicts what Scripture clearly teaches, the conclusions of science must be rejected. Of course, the way I have stated this requires us to be sure about what Scripture really teaches, and we must also make a judgment about what the scientific data really require. Hence, my methodology doesn't automatically make it impossible to find any help from science in formulating the doctrine of creation, but it does warn us to exercise healthy skepticism about what science says and to test it very carefully before we use it in reaching a doctrinal conclusion.

In sum, the difference between my use of secular disciplines in the case of creation as opposed to the case of the free will/sovereignty issue is as follows: in the latter case, Scripture creates the tension without resolving it, and philosophy can help us remove that tension; in the former case, however, the tension arises not within Scripture but between Scripture and science, and in such a case, evangelical theology requires opting for Scripture. I also use this procedure in handling other doctrinal issues. If Scripture creates the tension, or if it simply does not address certain issues at all, then we may consult the secular disciplines to help us resolve the tension or fill in the missing details, *so long as the material adopted from the secular discipline does not contradict the clear teaching of Scripture*. On the other hand, if the teaching of a secular discipline contradicts Scripture, the theologian shouldn't use it, even if Scripture leaves various ideas in tension or simply leaves unanswered questions we want to answer.

With these words of introduction, we may now turn to the various explanations of the days in Genesis 1–2 and their relation to the age of our universe and everything in it.

PICTORIAL-REVELATORY DAY THEORY. This theory, proposed by scholars such as J. H. Kurtz, P. J. Wiseman, and James M. Houston, clearly attempts to accommodate the findings of science with the Genesis account of creation. According to the most typical form of this view, the days of Genesis 1 are six consecutive twenty-four-hour days, but they are days of God's revelation to Moses, not days of creation. That is, during a six-day period God revealed to Moses what he had done. It may in fact have taken millions and billions of years for God to create the universe, our solar system, and life on this planet, but that is a matter for science to determine. What we know from Genesis 1 and 2 is that God was the creator and in six consecutive days he revealed to Moses what he had done. As for arranging the materials into the six days, it is a topical arrangement rather than a chronological sequence. Thus, we don't really know the order of events; the apportioning of the data into the six days of creation was either the way God organized the material he revealed or the pattern Moses used to present the account.

In support of this view, some note the fairly obvious grouping of materials into two corresponding triads of events. This is deemed evidence that the account is not a strict chronology or chronicle of what happened but rather a way of organizing the story of God's creative activity. Moreover, we are reminded that the purpose of Genesis 1 and 2 is not to teach science but to present God as creator as an introduction to Genesis and to the Pentateuch more broadly. And Wiseman further argues that the Hebrew word *'āśāh* ("to make"), used widely in Genesis 1–2, actually means "to show."[87]

This is an ingenious way to have your Bible and science, too, but there is little to commend it textually. There is no hint in Genesis 1–2 that the days are days of revelation. To be sure, the account *reveals* what God did, but that does not mean this is an account of six days of revelation to Moses rather than six days of creation. The record of each day of creation begins with the formula "then God said," but in no case does Moses write that God said, for example, "On this first day of showing you what happened, I'm revealing that I created light." Nor does Moses end any of the days by saying, "and it was evening and it was morning on the first day of revelation." If Moses wanted to say that these are days of revelatory dreams, visions, or the like, he surely knew how to do that, for elsewhere in Genesis he recounts various dreams and visions that people had. Moreover, to adopt this view, one would have to hold that after reading the first two chapters of Genesis, we are fundamentally ignorant about the order and even the nature of the events that happened—that we can't be sure that any of this is historical fact. But as noted when discussing literary genre, if this is so, there are some serious implications for various doctrinal claims. Finally, Wiseman's suggestion about the meaning of *ʿāśāh* is problematic. It is dubious that "show" is the typical OT meaning, but there are even problems with this suggestion in Genesis 1 and 2. For example, in Gen 1:26 God says "Let Us make man in Our image," and the verb translated "make" is *ʿāśāh*. Is it really true that all God is saying is that he should *show* Moses that man is God's image? How could we sustain such a reading? Moreover, in 1:27 we have the account of God creating man as male and female. The verb "create" occurs three times in the verse, but none is an occurrence of *ʿāśāh;* the verb in all three instances is *bārāʾ*. Does Wiseman mean to argue that the basic meaning of *bārāʾ* is also "to show?" That would be extremely hard to prove. Clearly, *ʿāśāh* and *bārāʾ* are used interchangeably here, so whatever one means, the other must also mean. But then the most likely reading is that God speaks of creating, not of showing.

PRE-GENESIS 1 CREATION THEORY.   Another attempt to fit science with Scripture proposes that, prior to Genesis 1:1, God created a different world and a pre-Adamic race of men. Supporters of this view might cite Isa 45:18 and Job 38:7 as evidence of creation *ex nihilo*, and note that the Isaiah passage says God didn't form the heavens and the earth as a waste place but to be inhabited. Hence, there must have been all sorts of life-forms on the original earth. Why didn't God just stick with that original creation? According to this theory, something must have provoked God's judgment. We can't be sure what the problem was, but perhaps it had to do with Satan's fall, and in response, God judged the world. Gen 1:1 is a summary of what follows in chapter 1, but then 1:2 shows us an earth that is formless and void at the time God began to refashion it into our present heavens and earth. The rest of chapters 1 and 2 give the details of that recreative work. Since the state of the earth as described in Gen 1:2 differs from that recorded in Isa 45:18, Genesis 1–2 must present events that happened chronologically after the initial creation and the judgment upon that creation.[88]

This is not the famous gap theory, for with that theory God creates (Gen

1:1) and then there is a gap between verses 1 and 2 during which God judged the creation he made. The pre-Genesis 1 creation theory posits a gap between an initial creation (Isa 45:18; Job 38:7) and Gen 1:1. In adopting this view, one can add eons of time to the age of the earth and universe. Moreover, one can claim that ancient fossils from dinosaurs and the like represent life-forms that inhabited the originally created world that was judged prior to Gen 1:1.

Despite this theory's apparent ability to harmonize biblical teaching about creation with science, it has little biblically to commend it. There is no evidence that Job 38:7 speaks of a temporally prior heaven and earth. God asks Job where he was when God laid the foundations of all that is. The description of God's work is meant to show Job God's power and majesty and to assure Job that in spite of all of his questions, there are still many things he doesn't know. Of course, Job could easily see that God has great power by looking at the created world around him. If, however, God's point is about a pre-Genesis 1:1 world, what is the point for Job? Job wasn't present then, nor could he see the results of that creative activity, if it actually occurred. The only world Job could see is the present heavens and earth, not some pre-Adamic world; but it is critical to God's point about his majesty and power that what God speaks about is something Job can to some extent experience. A pre-Genesis 1:1 world is beyond all of our sensory abilities.

As to Isa 45:18, it is a general statement that God created all things, and it affirms that he didn't create the universe to be empty, but that in no way presupposes that there must have been a pre-Adamic race of people. Genesis 1 and 2 show us various stages of God's creative activity, and it is clear that God did not create the present heavens and earth to be uninhabited, for these two chapters show him filling it with plant life, fish, birds, animals, and human beings. Moreover, the earth's condition described in Gen 1:2 does not necessitate that it got that way as a result of judgment. Nothing in the text says so, and since the author relates the gradual creation of all things in various stages—since God didn't create everything fully formed with his first "Let there be . . ."—it is not at all surprising that 1:2 depicts the world in an incomplete stage of development. These verses teach that after God created matter *ex nihilo,* he shaped that material into the universe around us in a series of stages. No judgment need be read into Genesis 1.

Beyond the Job and Isaiah passages there is little justification for this theory. There is ample evidence of Satan's fall; but that it occurred prior to Gen 1:1 and resulted in the destruction of a first world is pure speculation. Moreover, if there was a pre-Adamic race of humans on earth, what does that mean for biblical teaching that death entered the human race as a result of Adam's sin? Remember that this theory says that the earlier world isn't totally discontinuous with this one, but then there are significant problems for biblical teaching about sin and death. The pre-Gen 1:1 theory says that death and destruction came to the world either as a result of Satan's fall or perhaps because of the sin of that earlier race of humans. Neither of these options fits biblical teaching that death came to the human race through Adam's sin and that, prior to Adam, no one died.

THE GAP THEORY.   Scientific discoveries in geology, astronomy, and paleontology during the eighteenth and nineteenth centuries seemed to offer substantial evidence for an old earth. But how could that be harmonized with the six literal days of creation recorded in Genesis 1 and 2? What is known variously as the gap, reconstructionist, restitution, or divine judgment theory proposed a way to leave the Genesis account fairly well intact while allowing science's dates to have their due. The Scottish preacher and theologian Thomas Chalmers (1780–1847) seems to have been the first major proponent of this view,[89] but it has had a number of advocates even into the twentieth century. The noted OT scholar Franz Delitzsch held it, and the old *Scofield Reference Bible* offered this explanation as to why the earth was without form and void (Gen 1:2); no other explanation was offered. The new *Scofield Reference Bible* gives two options. The first, called the original chaos view, says 1:2 portrays the condition of the unformed earth after the original creation of matter *ex nihilo* (1:1). The second option is the gap theory (labeled the divine judgment view). In both editions of the *Scofield Reference Bible* the fall of Satan is given as the reason for judgment and destruction, although this is much clearer in the earlier edition.

The gap theory claims that Gen 1:1 speaks of God's original creation of a perfect universe. However, verse 2 shows things in a state of disorder and destruction. Evidently, between original creation (1:1) and the situation in verse 2 there must have been a tremendous gap of time. Moreover, during that time period sin must have entered the world (typically this is attributed to Satan's fall), and it evoked God's wrath and judgment which was poured out on the original creation. All of this happened millions and even billions of years ago (no one knows for sure), and creation remained in this judged and wasted condition for eons. In Gen 1:2 we see the universe in that condition, and then God decided to reconstruct and restore it. The events depicted in verse 2 and following are of much more recent origin (some would say they began around 4000 B.C., and others speculate that the reconstruction began somewhere between 10,000 and 20,000 years ago). In fact, the six days recorded in chapter 1 may have been six successive twenty-four-hour days. Still, scientific discoveries can be accommodated when we realize that the original creation and then destruction happened eons ago. In addition, gap theorists typically postulate a pre-Adamic race of humans that populated the original earth. If not, it would be hard to harmonize fossils of early humans with the Genesis account.[90]

In support of this view various arguments are proposed. First, it is argued that the verb *hāyĕtāh* in verse 2 should be translated "became" rather than "was." The reason is that verse 1 speaks of the original condition of creation, whereas verse 2 shows us conditions following judgment. Since God would not have created things disordered at the outset, the world must have become that way after judgment.

Second, it is argued that *tōhû wābōhû* ("without form and void") refers to a state of confusion, chaos, and disorder. Since God wouldn't create things that way, this must have resulted from God's judgment. Moreover, the same phrase appears in Jer 4:23 and the same terms in Isa 34:11, and in both cases emptiness and void are mentioned in contexts about divine judgment. In addition, Isa 45:18 says God didn't create the earth to be a waste place (*lōʾ tōhû*), but to be inhabited. However, Gen 1:2 says the earth was a waste and formless place, so something must have happened between original creation (1:1) and the situation in 1:2. If anyone thinks that God does not judge in this way, consider Isa 24:1: "Behold, the LORD lays the earth waste, devastates it, distorts its surface, and scatters its inhabitants." Isa 24:1 doesn't refer to Gen 1:2, but it shows that the judgment suggested by the gap theory is something God might do.

Third, after creating Adam and Eve, God tells them to be fruitful, to multiply, and to fill the earth (Gen 1:28). The verb translated "fill" is *mālēʾ*, but it really means "to fill again." Hence, the earth must have been filled already (Gen 1:1), and now God, after reconstructing the world, tells its new inhabitants to fill it again.

Fourth, some defenders of this view also distinguish *bārāʾ* and *ʿāśāh*. They claim that the former is a strong verb meaning "to create," and it appears in Gen 1:1 to speak of original creation. On the other hand, *ʿāśāh* is a weaker verb that can mean "remake," and it appears in Gen 1:7, 16, 25, 26, 31; 2:2, the segment of the account that gap theorists believe deals with restoration and reconstruction of the created order.[91]

Finally, gap theorists see passages such as Isa 14:3-23; Ezek 28:11-19; and Rev 12:7-9 as teaching Satan's revolt and fall. We know that Satan was created and that by the events of Genesis 3 he had revolted against God. The six days of creation in Genesis 1 mention nothing of Satan's creation or fall, despite giving a fairly complete general account of the categories of things God created during the six days. Hence, Satan was probably created prior to the six days of creation, and since we hear nothing about his fall in Genesis 1 or 2, it must have happened between Gen 1:1 and 1:2. If so, that helps us understand why the earth was in the condition described in verse 2.

In spite of these arguments and the potential advantage of the theory's fit with science, it has serious problems. An initial concern deals with the meaning of *hāyĕtāh*. It is certainly possible that the word means "became," but there is a preponderance of evidence against that meaning. The word occurs many times in the Pentateuch and in the whole Bible.[92] The exact form *hāyĕtāh* appears in the Pentateuch some forty-nine times. Of all the occurrences in the Pentateuch only six (all in the Qal) are clearly in contexts that require the rendering "became." Those six instances are Gen 3:22; 19:26; 21:20; Exod 7:19; 8:13(Heb) (8:17 in the English text); and 9:10. One instance in the Niphal also requires the meaning "become" (Deut 27:9). None of the six instances in the Qal is in the form *hāyĕtāh*. Two of the six (Gen 3:22 and Exod 8:13[Heb]) are the form *hāyāh*, two more instances (Gen 21:20

and Exod 9:10) are *wayĕhî*, a fifth instance (Gen 19:26) is *watĕhî*, and the final instance (Exod 7:19) is the form *wĕyihĕyû*. Of course, in each of these, context clearly demands "became." *Hāyĕtāh* may also mean "became" in Gen 1:2, but judging just from usage of this verb in the Pentateuch, such a rendering is highly unusual and unlikely. What ultimately determines the meaning of a given word, however, is context, and this is where the gap theory reading of this verb is in serious trouble, for nothing *in the immediate context* of this verse demands the rendering "became." What could demand it in this verse other than the presupposition of the gap theory? But of course, reading that translation into the text on the basis of holding the gap theory is question begging.

Some will reply that "without form and void" requires the reading of "became" for *hāyĕtāh*. However, this does not follow, for "without form and void" does not necessarily connote a state of affairs that resulted from something negative, such as evil or a judgment. There is no question that in Isa 34:11 and Jer 4:23 the phrase appears in contexts of judgment, but neither of those passages refers to Genesis 1. In fact, gap theorists don't say that these passages talk about Genesis 1; their only point is that a phrase that appears in Gen 1:2 also appears in these two verses. In the latter two verses it speaks of a condition after judgment, they say, so we should see it as meaning the same thing in Gen 1:2. But this is surely improper reasoning, for admitting that Isaiah and Jeremiah aren't talking of the same event as Genesis 1 means that the most those passages can tell us is that "without form and void" *possibly* is used in Gen 1:2 to describe the results of judgment. If something in Genesis 1 indicated a context of judgment, then we might be inclined to think that 1:2 speaks of a judged earth, but nothing in this chapter suggests a scene of judgment unless one begs the question and imposes that idea on the text. "Without form and void" in Gen 1:2 need mean nothing more than that at that stage of God's creative work, earth wasn't ready for habitation. This was also true probably until day four after sun, moon, and stars were in place, but surely the divine activities on days one through three were not judgments just because the earth wasn't quite yet ready for habitation on those days.[93] So it isn't clear that "without form and void" means there has been a judgment.

I already dealt with Isa 45:18 in relation to the pre-Gen 1:1 creation theory, and need not repeat the response. As to Isa 24:1, God indeed has such power, but nothing in Isaiah 24 suggests that the particular devastation in view in that verse has anything to do with Gen 1:1-2 and creation. What about Gen 1:28 and the meaning of *mālē'*? Can this Hebrew word mean "refill?" Possibly so, because at least one other instance can be read that way. The same verb is used in Gen 9:1 when God tells Noah after the flood to fill the earth. Since the earth was filled with people and animals prior to the flood, and since the flood killed most of them, it is true that if Noah and his family obeyed the command, they would "refill" the earth.

But granting this reading as possible does not make it likely. We must also note that the verb may simply mean "fill." Two instances show this possibility. One is Gen 1:22, day five, when God tells the sea creatures to fill the seas. Since the seas are the ones God just formed on day three, the order to fill them must refer to a first filling, not a refill. Note as well Exod 10:6, where the verb occurs again and speaks of filling the Egyptians' houses with hail. Since this is predicted as one of the ten plagues, and God had not brought a plague of hail before in this sequence, when the text speaks of filling the Egyptians' houses from this plague, it can't mean refilling them.

From this brief word study of *mālē²* it is clear that it *could* mean in Gen 1:28 either "fill" or "refill," though further word study shows that preponderance of usage favors the former. Still, context must be determinative, and the context of Genesis 1 requires the reading "fill." The only possible way it would require "refill" is if the chapter taught that there had been a previous created order that was destroyed. Nowhere does this passage say this, however, and assuming that the word must mean "refill" here so as to fit the gap theory is just question begging.

A final point concerns Satan's fall. It is beyond our purpose to decide whether Isaiah 14 and Ezekiel 28 refer to Satan's fall, but even if not, that doesn't mean Satan did not fall. The problem for the gap theory, however, is that no passage in Scripture speaks of Satan's fall happening after an initial creation and before a second creation. Hence, the proposal that the earth is judged and thus empty and void as a result of Satan's fall is mere speculation. Moreover, Gen 2:1 is a summary of the six days of creation, and it says that the heavens and the earth and all their hosts were created as detailed in the previous chapter. If the hosts of heaven include both the sun, moon, and stars, and also angelic beings, and if all that was created to fill heaven and earth was made in the six days of creation (this seems also part of the point of Exod 20:11), then the gap theory proposal that Satan and his legions were created prior to the six days of creation is in serious trouble.

Naturalistic Evolutionary Theories

Naturalistic evolution, often joined to atheism, offers a major alternative to creationism. Many who hold it would likely say that Genesis 1–2 is theology, not science. It is a mythological way to teach that God made the universe. Of course, many other ancient cultures had creation stories, so it is not unusual that the Bible contains the same. Still, none of this is science, and if we want an explanation of what actually occurred, we must turn to science. When we do, we find that the best scientific explanation is that the universe is some 15 to 20 billion years old. The best current explanation is that all of it was formed as a result of the Big Bang. The earth is somewhere around 4.5 billion years old, and human ancestors (*homo habilis*) began to appear on earth somewhere between 2 and 3.5 billion years ago.[94] Hence, if the days of Genesis 1–2 are taken at all seriously, they are not literal twenty-four-hour days. The whole evolutionary process took much more time than this.

This is not an apologetics text, so I won't offer as full a case against evolution as I would in such a work, but I must mention some considerations that argue against an evolutionary account of origins. This is significant for many reasons, not least of which is that theistic evolutionists believe they can harmonize science and Genesis by invoking God. However, if there is significant evidence against the occurrence of evolution at all, it is hard to see why someone would try to rescue it by invoking God, and thus it is dubious to think that including God would save the theory.

There are many objections to evolution, but several will suffice for our purposes. The first concerns evolution's mechanism, which is the random process of natural selection. Evolutionists hold that by natural selection, a totally random process, life-forms that are the fittest will be the most successful in reproducing themselves. Hence, the genetic makeup of the fittest will dominate the gene population, because only survivors can reproduce. But natural selection is also supposed to function so that over time genetic tendencies that are advantageous (i.e., qualities that will help the life-form survive better than others of its species) will accumulate so that eventually there will be large-scale characteristic changes in life-forms. The result is evolution to new species that are better adapted to their environment and thus are more likely to survive and reproduce. But within species as they are, there are only so many possible genetic variations. Genetic mutations provide genetic options that eventually yield change into a new species.

In reply, Phillip Johnson (*Darwin on Trial*) shows how difficult it is for scientists even to formulate the idea of natural selection in a non-vacuous, non-tautologous way.[95] But the major question is whether there is any evidence of such massive shifts. Evolutionists have no evidence that natural selection alone has accomplished such feats. Some appeal to what can happen with artificial selection when breeders breed for certain characteristics and thereby dramatically change the traits of certain life-forms. The problem, however, is that artificial selection is choice by intelligent design, that of the breeder. In contrast, natural selection rules out any intelligent design.[96] It asks us to believe that reproductive forces left solely to themselves will select qualities that yield more fit organisms and ultimately new species. Evidence suggests no such inherent capability in a non-animate, non-intelligent process, and there simply is no evidence that the sort of thing evolution postulates has happened.

In addition, there are major problems in thinking that genetic mutations can provide the necessary grist for the evolutionary mill. First, there simply is no evidence that an organism could have mutations so great that, for example, a mutant gene in a fish would produce a wing like a bird. Genetic mutations don't open the door for the mutant gene to be just anything. Moreover, even if a fish could have a mutant set of genes that produce a wing (or wings), this wouldn't give a more fit fish unless there was another massive mutation that gave the fish lungs so that it could breathe out of water while flying. What is the evidence that a non-intelligent, random process ever has produced or ever could produce such a combination of mutant characteristics?

Second, if macro-mutations are unlikely, perhaps the major changes could occur through the compilation of a host of micro-mutations that eventually equal a macro-mutation. Of course, this seems to require an intelligence guiding the process so that just the right combination of micro-mutations occurs and does so in a timely enough way so that the "big change" doesn't fail to occur because it takes "forever" to happen and the process in the meantime breaks down. If chance is left to make all the right mutations in combination and to see that at every stage the intermediate organism is truly the fittest and does survive, it is passing credibility that this should all occur. Darwin himself said that, "If it could be demonstrated that any complex organ existed which could not possibly have been formed by numerous, successive, slight modifications, my theory would break down." Richard Goldschmidt (UC Berkeley) around mid-twentieth century concluded that any number of things, from mammalian hair to hemoglobin, could not have been produced by the accumulation of micro-mutations.[97] The final and perhaps greatest problem with the proposal about mutations is that scientists agree that most mutations are not beneficial but harmful, even lethal. So how likely is it that random mutations would make a given life-form more fit and more likely to survive?

A second major area of problems with evolution involves the fossil record. Despite the improbability that evolution would occur, scientists think the fossil record shows that it did. This is supposed to be empirical evidence that supports the dates scientists postulate about the history of life on our planet and also shows that macro-evolution happened and did so repeatedly. However, the fossil record actually is strong evidence against macro-evolution.

In order for the fossil record to confirm evolution, it needs to show the following: 1) slow, gradual change from one species to another; 2) transitional forms "between" species (the result would be no clear line between distinct species. Hence, any boundary-drawing would essentially be arbitrary to suit the perceptions of the one reviewing the evidence); 3) evidence of slow, gradual extinction of species that were less fit.

What do the fossils actually show? First, there are significant gaps in the fossil record, i.e., fossils are missing all along the supposed ascent of life-forms. What is especially troublesome is the lack of transitional fossils throughout the fossil record. If evolution moved gradually from species to species, we ought to find evidence of transitional life-forms which were partly one species and partly another. Of course, part of the problem is that one rarely if ever sees a clear set of criteria for judging whether a given life-form is transitional or entirely in one species or another. Still, there are too many gaps in the fossil record in terms of any life-form that could reasonably be considered a transitional form between two species. It is not surprising that when Darwin first proposed his theory there were many gaps in the fossil records, but in the 140 years since, one would have expected many of the gaps to have been filled as scientists searched, guided by Darwinian theory. However, the missing fossils are still missing.

Second, the fossil record gives evidence not of gradual extinction but of catastrophic extinctions of certain species that might have resulted from something such as a comet colliding with the earth.[98] In addition, the fossil record shows stasis of species, i.e., fixed boundaries between species (largely because it's so hard to find fossils of alleged transitional forms). Moreover, Johnson documents cases of fossils thought to be ancestors alongside of fossils thought to be their descendents. In other words, the two fixed, distinct species lived at the same time, even though the one was supposed to have gradually given way to the other over time.[99]

Perhaps the biggest embarrassment for evolution's fossil record is the sudden explosion of all sorts of life-forms in the Cambrian period while no fossils appear in pre-Cambrian rocks. This doesn't square with evolutionists' typically held principle of uniformitarianism. Johnson explains the significance of the Cambrian explosion:

> Nearly all the animal phyla appear in the rocks of this period without a trace of the evolutionary ancestors that Darwinists require. As Richard Dawkins puts it, "It is as though they were just planted there, without any evolutionary history." In Darwin's time there was no evidence for the existence of pre-Cambrian life, and he conceded in *The Origin of Species* that "The case at present must remain inexplicable, and may be truly urged as a valid argument against the views here entertained." If his theory was true, Darwin wrote, the pre-Cambrian world must have "swarmed with living creatures."[100]

Very little evidence of any life-forms existing in the pre-Cambrian era (with the possible exception of some bacteria and algae) has ever shown up, yet Darwin's theory persists. Surely it is risky to build an empirically based theory on lack of empirical data!

A further point about fossils is that scientists often sketch pictures, on the basis of fossils, of what life-forms must have looked like. The sketches are drawn so as to portray a gradual ascent in life-forms from, for example, ape-like creatures to humans. Seeing the sketches and being told that the fossils exist to prove such creatures existed, it is natural to think this is established fact. However, this is quite deceptive when one realizes that the fossils in many cases are not whole skeletons, and not even a whole skull. Rather, from bone fragments from a jaw or an arm or leg, scientists reconstruct an artistic conception of what the whole life-form must have looked like. But when you only have fragments, how can you be sure? Moreover, from the same fragment an artist can construct a picture that looks very much like an ape or like a human being. All of this leaves one wary about the supposed conclusiveness of the fossil record.

What becomes even more troublesome is admissions about the fossil record by some evolutionists when they tell us the truth. Of special note is the statement by renowned evolutionist George Gaylord Simpson in his book *The Meaning of Evolution*. Simpson is a committed evolutionist, but he makes a very revealing admission as he discusses the work of paleontologists and others who deal with fossils. His comments are somewhat extensive, but they are worth quoting:

> Some paleontologists have been so impressed by the frequent trend for animals to become larger as time goes on that they have tried to work it the other way around. If they find, say, a Pleistocene bison that is somewhat larger than a Recent bison (so-called *Bison taylori*, associate and prey of early man in America, is a good example), then they conclude that it is not ancestral to later bison *because* it is larger. You can establish any "rule" you like if you start with the rule and then interpret the evidence accordingly.
>
> This suggests some brief digressive but pertinent remarks on certain psychological factors in the interpretation of the necessarily imperfect evolutionary record. A really complete evolutionary lineage is never preserved; this would mean fossilization and recovery of all the animals that ever lived as parts of that lineage, an absurdly impossible chance. Museum curators know that even if the miracle of fossilization occurred, recovery and study would be impossible if only on grounds of expense. The actual data, then, normally consist of relatively small samples of the lineage, scattered more or less at random in space and time. The process of interpretation consists of connecting these samples in a way necessarily more or less subjective, and students may use the same data to "prove" diametrically opposed theories.[101]

The honesty is refreshing, but at the same time it is unbelievable that such a convinced advocate of evolution would still be convinced and expect others to agree in light of such revelations. Claims like these from the "experts" who should best know how their science works and what data are available make many of us highly skeptical of evolution.

There are many other significant objections to evolution both from evangelical Christians and from nonbelievers such as Michael Denton (*Evolution: A Theory in Crisis*), but one further item will suffice. As J. P. Moreland and colleagues have written, there is a very significant movement among scientists and philosophers in support of a new design argument. This isn't the older version along the lines of Paley's watch and watchmaker argument, an argument from analogy. The new design arguments differ considerably, for they focus on various existing life-forms and the complexity of their make-up. As scientists have made advances in molecular biology and the like, they have come to see that at the most fundamental levels of matter, systems occur in our world in ways more complex structurally and biochemically than previously realized. The likelihood that these systems arose by the random processes of natural selection and mutation is so staggeringly small that it isn't even worth considering. The most reasonable and plausible explanation for the existence of such things is intelligent design, and since purely naturalistic evolution omits intelligent design, naturalistic evolution is highly improbable.[102]

Day-Age Theories

Various Christian thinkers contend that the days of Genesis 1–2 represent lengthy geological ages during which God did the creative work Genesis records. Since this theory and the ones discussed in the next two sections are the most frequently held among evangelicals, I shall just describe the theories and the arguments that favor them. Evaluation will come in a final section of this chapter.

Day-age theories come in many varieties. Not only have late-nineteenth- and twentieth-century theologians held them, but there is also evidence that much earlier in church history some were uncertain that Moses intended the days of Genesis 1 and 2 as twenty-four-hour days. Early church fathers such as Irenaeus and Origen and later Aquinas questioned whether the days of Genesis 1 don't refer to long periods of time.[103] In recent times, the theory has been held by systematic theologians and biblical scholars such as W. G. T. Shedd, Charles Hodge, J. O. Buswell, Bernard Ramm, Bruce Demarest, Gordon Lewis, Gleason Archer, Robert C. Newman, and Herman Eckelmann.

This theory makes it is much easier to harmonize the findings of science with Scripture, so this general position is often called the concordist position. It is also called progressive creation, in which case Genesis 1–2 is understood as relating distinct divine creative acts at various times in the history of the universe. After each creative act, God used natural processes working over eons of time to develop the various life-forms in our universe. So God is still the creator, but he works by both miraculous and natural means. Some proponents of the day-age theory see the various eras as distinct, whereas others such as Buswell suggest that the days (and hence eras) to a certain extent overlap. Such an understanding allows for micro-evolution but does not require macro-evolution. God is still responsible for the major creative changes.[104]

Age-day theories have the obvious advantage of correlating to some extent Scripture and the findings of science, but proponents of this view typically argue it on biblical grounds. The most frequent argument is that Scripture uses the word "day" (Heb. *yôm*) in various ways, not just to refer to a literal twenty-four-hour day. The term is used to designate daylight as opposed to darkness (Gen 1:5, 16, 18) and light and darkness together (Gen 1:5, 8, 13). It also refers to indefinite periods of time in phrases such as "the day of His anger" (Job 20:28); "the day of trouble" (Ps 20:1); "the day of battle" (Prov 21:31); "the day of distress" (Prov 24:10); "the day of prosperity" (Eccl 7:14); and "the time [day] of harvest (Prov 25:13). It is also used of "the day of LORD," which in most cases is an eschatological day whose length only God knows (Isa 13:6, 9; Joel 1:15; 2:1; Amos 5:18; Zeph 1:14). Most revealing, claim age-day theorists, is its use in Gen 2:4 as a summary of the preceding chapter: "This is the account of the heavens and the earth when they were created, in the day that the LORD God made earth and heaven." Since "day" in this verse refers to all six days of creation, plus the events of Gen 1:1 (creation *ex nihilo*), it cannot in 2:4 mean one twenty-four-hour solar day. The different uses of *yôm* show that the days of Gen 1 could be literal twenty-four-hour days, but they could just as easily be much longer.[105]

Second, it is often argued that we should be hesitant about demanding that the six days of creation be twenty-four-hour days because it is unlikely that this could be true of all six. If the events of day four, for example, mean that the sun, moon, and stars were not actually created and put in place until the fourth day, how could the first three days be solar days like we experience now? On the first day God created light, but if that light was not the sun, there is no way to think of the first three days as solar days. Moreover, the purpose of creating sun, moon, and stars (Gen 1:14) was to separate day and night and to serve as signs for days and years. What kind of days and nights, days and years could these be if not the days, nights, and years we experience in the present created order? But if so, and if these luminaries didn't begin to function until day four, how can we be sure that the distinction between light and dark during the first three days was anything like what we mean by days and nights. It seems that only days four through six could be literal twenty-four-hour solar days as we know them, but then we should reconsider whether it is mandatory that any of the days be twenty-four-hour days.

Some suggest that the luminaries actually were created on the first day, but during the first stages of creation there was such a cloud cover around the nascent earth that the sun, moon, and stars could not be seen. Hence, from anyone's perspective on earth (had there been anyone), these heavenly bodies could not perform their appointed function of marking the difference between day and night and the counting of days and years. It wasn't until the fourth day that the Lord parted the clouds enough so that these lights became visible and could serve their appointed duties for those on earth. This would mean that the Hebrew word *wayya'aś* in 1:16 should not be translated "made" but rather "had made," referring to what had been done on day one. Since these heavenly lights existed before day three, but only became visible on day four, there is no way of telling how long (from earth's perspective) the first three days actually lasted. It could have been ages.[106] Moreover, those who think a day-age theory doesn't fit with vegetation being created on day three and lasting for eons without photosynthesis capacity from the sun can be answered. The sun was present from the first day, and though it was not visible on earth, that doesn't mean none of its rays penetrated the cloud cover at all. As long as there was some penetration, photosynthesis would likely be possible. Moreover, no matter how long the first three days were, since the luminaries became visible on the fourth day, the cloud cover was probably gradually lifting during at least the third day, so we can't be sure that there wasn't enough light for the vegetation.

Third, though Moses wrote Genesis 1 and 2, he didn't observe what happened. These two chapters are God's revelation, and thus the story is told from God's perspective, not ours. But if so, then it is significant that Scripture says that a day is to the Lord as a thousand years, and a thousand years as a day (see Ps 90:4; 2 Pet 3:8). An eternal God has all the time in the world and doesn't need to work as quickly as we must in our short life-span. Since the creation story is told from God's perspective, how can we be sure that the days in Genesis 1–2 lasted only twenty-four hours each?[107]

Fourth, if we demand that each day of creation was a twenty-four-hour solar day, there are problems because the events listed for some days would seem to take more than twenty-four hours. The sixth day as elaborated in Genesis 2 is a case in point. On the sixth day Adam is created first (2:7) and then God plants the Garden of Eden and puts Adam in it (2:8ff.). God sees that Adam is alone and decides to do something about this (2:18). He creates the beasts and birds and brings them to Adam for naming. Adam does this (2:19-20), and who can guess how long this must have taken? Still, he finishes the task, and God says that none of the animals is a suitable mate for Adam. God puts Adam into a deep sleep, takes one of his ribs, and makes Eve. Adam awakens and recognizes that Eve is the proper mate (2:21-25). How could all of this have been accomplished in a mere twenty-four hours? Gleason Archer replies:

> It has become very apparent that Genesis 1 was never intended to teach that the sixth creative day, when Adam and Eve were both created, lasted a mere twenty-four hours. In view of the long interval of time between these two, it would seem to border on sheer irrationality to insist that all of Adam's experiences in Genesis 2:15-22 could have been crowded into the last hour or two of a literal twenty-four-hour day.[108]

Even if God started the process early in the day, many agree that this is just too much to pack into one solar day.[109] If it is dubious that the sixth day took only twenty-four hours, we shouldn't force the other days into a twenty-four-hour mold.

Further evidence that we shouldn't see the days of creation as literal twenty-four-hour days stems from the seventh day, on which God rested. That day continues to this very hour, so it is much longer than twenty-four hours. If the days of creation are parallel, then it hardly makes sense to say that the seventh day has lasted all these years (perhaps billions of years) but the first six days were only twenty-four hours each. If the days are not parallel, then the point of the Sabbath legislation (one day of rest to six days of labor—Exod 20:9-11) seems lost. Since the seventh day is much longer than twenty-four hours, the first six must have been much longer than twenty-four hours as well. Even the writer of Hebrews, we are told, refers to the seventh day as the beginning of God's Sabbath rest (Heb 4:4, 10). In fact, all of Heb 4:1-11 implies that God's Sabbath rest continues until now.[110]

In addition to arguments about the meaning of the days, day-age theorists offer other evidence for an old universe and earth. What generates a young earth position isn't just the belief that the days of creation are twenty-four-hour days, but also the belief that the genealogies in Genesis (chapters 4–5, 10, and 11) offer a strict chronological list. In fact, assuming that there are no gaps in the genealogies, exegetes such as Bishop Ussher started from the end of the list and worked back to the beginning, concluding that original creation must have occurred in 4004 B.C. However, for a long time all parties in the debate have acknowledged that genealogies throughout Scripture, including these in Genesis, are not intended to be a complete list of everyone who lived. There is always a certain logic to the names chosen, but the lists don't follow a strict chronology. In some cases, a person listed as father may actually be a great-great grandfather of the person named as a descendent. Once we recognize this, we also should see that we really don't know how many years we should count in order to go all the way back to Adam. If that is so, however, the notions of an old earth and days of creation that took considerably longer than required for a young earth become more plausible than the alternative.[111]

Sometimes proponents of twenty-four-hour-day creation ask why, if the six days of creation are not literal solar days, the writer uses the formula "it was evening and it was morning" at the end of each day? This normally designates a literal day. Age-day theorists Demarest and Lewis reply:

> Although references to the "evening" and the "morning" on each of the creation days (Gen. 1) has seemed to many to indicate twenty-four-hour days, the literal meaning is not invariable even after the fourth day. Sometimes the beginning of the day is evening (Est. 4:16; Dan. 8:14) and sometimes morning (Deut. 28:66-67). And clearly figurative uses for longer periods of time do, in fact, occur. The brevity of human life is like that of grass, for "in the morning it springs up new, by evening it is dry and withered" (Ps. 90:5-6). As the original *Scofield Bible* note on Genesis 1:5 explained, "The use of 'evening' and 'morning' may be held to limit 'day' to the solar day; but the frequent parabolic use of natural phenomena may warrant the conclusion that each creative 'day' was a period of time marked off by a beginning and ending."[112]

Hence, this formula may be nothing more than a literary device to mark the start and end of God's various creative activities. It need not require literal solar days.

Age-day theorists also respond to solar day proponents' use of Exod 20:9-11. This passage is taken to teach that all of God's creating was done in the six days of Genesis 1, and then he rested on the seventh day. The Mosaic legislation demands that Israelites work six days and rest on the seventh, and it justifies this command in terms of God's parallel actions in creation. If the days of creation are not solar days, it is hard to see how God's actions recorded in Genesis 1 serve as a basis for the Sabbath legislation that clearly refers to a literal week of twenty-four-hour days. In response, age-day theorists remind us that there cannot be a one-to-one correspondence between God's "work week" and ours, since God's seventh day continues indefinitely. Our Sabbath cannot go on forever or we would never get any work done. If there isn't an exact correspondence between our work week and God's, there still is a point in Moses' justifying this legislation in terms of Genesis 1. The basic formula of six to one for our pattern of work to rest is exemplified by God's actions and shows how we should order our weeks of twenty-four-hour days. But that is Moses' only parallel point, and he can still make it as long as God's pattern was six to one, even if it was six ages to one period of rest.

Another argument deals with the relation of sin to death. In Genesis, Adam and Eve disobey God, and God pronounces various curses. Part of the curse is that they will die, just as God had warned (Gen 2:17). Paul picks up this theme in Rom 5:12 and explains that sin entered the world through Adam and death spread to the whole human race. Sometimes, twenty-four-hour-day creationists say that this means that before Adam and Eve's sin, there was no death in the world. This fits with the fall coming not long after God finished creating. Prior to the fall, there would not have been ages of time for animals, for example, to be born and die. However, if creation took ages of time to accomplish, as age-day theorists claim, it is dubious that no animal or plant-life would have died prior to the fall of Adam and Eve. Some age-day proponents anticipate this argument and have a response. They say that the teaching about death resulting from sin applies only to the human race. Paul teaches in Romans 5 that death spreads to all men, but he says nothing about other life-forms. Hence, nothing in Scripture forbids the death of plants and animals prior to Adam's fall.[113]

So far the arguments for the age-day view have been exegetical in nature, but proponents of this view add that their view can accommodate the findings of science. Moreover, those data can correlate and corroborate the age-day understanding of Genesis 1–2. For various examples of how one might do this, the reader should consult such works as Newman and Eckelmann's *Genesis One and the Origin of the Earth;* Hugh Ross's *Genesis One: A Scientific Perspective;* and Davis Young's *Creation and the Flood.*[114] While we shouldn't absolutize science and declare it infallible, it is dubious that science is wrong about all that it says about origins. Moreover, those who think science is usually accurate in its understanding of our world, but refuse to accept it on this one set of issues, seem somewhat inconsistent.

In line with this argument from science, age-day theorists believe there is a major problem with the twenty-four-hour-day position. When confronted with the fact that the various parts of our planet and our universe seem to be millions and billions of years old, young earth proponents often argue that this is so because God created things with apparent age. Adam was not created as a baby, nor was Eve; but then, moments after they were created they appeared to be adults. Similarly, if God created trees, flowers, etc., rather than just the seeds for such things, the moment they were created they would look rather mature. To have created life-forms on the earth as babies or seeds (in the case of plants, trees, and flowers) would have meant that creation was in its nascent stage.

Land where there would be grass, flowers, and trees would be barren. Adam and Eve would be newborn infants likely unable to care for themselves. Hence, God had to create things in a rather "finished" form. Similarly, science claims that it takes millions of years for light to travel from distant stars, considerably more time than is possible for a young earth and universe view. This again means that God would have created the universe with light already reaching earth, seeming to have traveled millions of light years when in fact it hadn't.

Age-day theorists reply that if this is right, God has deceived us. When we test phenomena around us by scientific means, our universe looks very old. To say that it isn't because God created it with apparent age means that God is a deceiver, and that is impossible, because God cannot and does not lie. As one writer says about light from distant stars, "As most of the universe is more than ten thousand light-years away, most of the events revealed by light coming from space would be fictional. Since the Bible tells us that God cannot lie, I prefer to interpret nature so as to avoid having God give us fictitious information."[115]

Twenty-four-hour-day Theories

Though at various times in church history some questioned whether the days of creation were literal solar days, the predominant view at least until the 1700s was that the days of creation were six twenty-four-hour days. Both Luther and Calvin held this position.[116] Archbishop James Ussher, as we have noted, believed that the genealogies in Genesis 1–11 held the key to the date of the start of all things. He put the origin at 4004 B.C. John Lightfoot, the great Bible exegete and commentator, went even further. He calculated that creation occurred during the week of October 18-24, 4004 B.C. Moreover, God created Adam on October 23 at 9 A.M., fourth-fifth meridian time![117]

On the contemporary scene, the twenty-four-hour-day theory is held in two major forms. The first says that creation was finished in six twenty-four-hour days but it began longer ago than 4004 B.C. Proponents grant that the genealogies in Genesis 1–11 are not complete and have gaps, but that doesn't warrant interpolating into them such huge gaps of time that the incredibly old dates proposed by science can be harmonized. The universe didn't start in 4004 B.C., but it didn't start 15 to 20 billion years ago. Human life probably began somewhere between 10000 and 20000 B.C., and of course, the other days of creation preceded that, but still ours is a young earth, not an exceptionally old one.

How do defenders of this view explain scientific evidence for the age of the earth and the various life-forms on it? In general, two or three tacks are taken, and sometimes proponents combine several of these. One approach explains the geological data (the age of the earth's rocks, their configuration in layers, and the fossils in them) in terms of the Noahic flood of Genesis 9. In addition, some add that God created things with apparent age by making a fully formed and functioning universe, not a world with everything in "seed" form. Hence, things look much older than they actually are. Proponents of this brand of solar day creationism have also argued that what science measures is processes that occur by natural means. However, with creation we aren't talking about natural processes but supernatural miracles. So who is to say that God couldn't miraculously do all that Genesis 1–2 says he did within six twenty-four-hour days? We would agree with science's dates if what was done to produce our universe were not miracles; miracles nullify attempts to make naturalistic sense of things.

The other contemporary form of twenty-four-hour-day creationism fundamentally agrees with everything described, but adds that there is bountiful scientific evidence to support the young earth, six-solar-day creation position. Over the last thirty to forty years at least, conservative Christians and scientists under the auspices of the Creation Research Society (or at least in concert with its approach) have written a series of works on various aspects of origins. Their intent is to be biblically and exegetically sound and at the same time to marshal empirical evidence in support of their biblical conclusions. Their writings include scientific evidence to refute evolution, but they also include treatises that offer evidence for intelligent design and for a young earth. As to a young earth, this so-called scientific creationism appeals heavily to the Noahic flood as the cause of what geology finds in the earth's rocks. The difference from the previous approach is that rather than merely proposing the flood as a possible way to harmonize a young earth with science, scientific creationists offer scientific evidence for both the flood and a young earth. Creation scientists also appeal to apparent age, and they agree that creation involved miracles, but they still believe that there is plenty of scientifically credible evidence to support the Genesis story. One of the first works espousing this viewpoint was Whitcomb and Morris's *The Genesis Flood,* but much more has been produced through the Creation Research Society.[118]

Proponents of the twenty-four-hour-day theory offer various biblical and theological arguments for it. An initial set of arguments deals with the meaning of *yôm* ("day") in Genesis 1–2. While the term has various uses throughout the OT, the most frequent one refers to a twenty-four-hour solar day. It is agreed that *yôm* in Gen 2:4 must refer to the whole creative sequence, but the verse's point clarifies that. Moreover, when other passages speak of "the day of adversity," "day of battle," "day of wrath," or "the day of the LORD," context shows it must refer to more time than twenty-four hours. However, when one reads Genesis 1 in its most natural sense, the context seems to refer to literal twenty-four-hour days. What in Genesis 1 would lead us to think the days are actually ages? It seems that only our awareness of scientific findings leads us to think this, but this just means we don't find the evidence for age-days in the text, but outside of it. Moreover, proponents of this view stress that we must think of what Moses would likely have intended to say and what his readers would have understood. We cannot impose on them our modern scientific knowledge to make Moses teach what modern science claims to have discovered only in the last few centuries.[119]

A further point should be made about the various uses of "day" that sup-posedly show it can mean more than a twenty-four-hour period. As several scholars have noted, those other instances of "day"—in passages such as Gen 2:4; Job 20:28; Ps 20:1; Prov 21:31; 24:10; 25:13; and Eccl 7:14—are all uses of "day" in compounds or bound expressions. As such, they are part of a larger expression that may tell us little or nothing about what the word means apart from such expressions, some of which may even be idiomatic. Bruce Waltke, though not espousing the twenty-four-hour-day approach, makes the linguistic point as follows:

> The appeal to "day" in compounds such as "in the day" (Gen 2:4) and "the day of the Lord" to validate the "Day-Age Theory," the theory that "day" in Genesis 1 does not necessarily denote the twenty-four hour diurnal day but may designate a geologic age or stage, is linguisti-cally flawed. The use of "day" in syntagms, "the ordered and unified arrangement of words in a distinctive way," such as these is clearly different from its use with numerals: "first day," "second day." The argument is as fallacious as saying that "apple" does not necessarily indicate the round edible fruit of the rosaceous tree because this is not its meaning in "pineapple."[120]

Waltke's comment about *yôm* with numerals raises another point. Twenty-four-hour-day creationists note that when *yôm* is used with a specific number, it seems invariably to mean a twenty-four-hour day (cf. Gen 8:14; 17:12). Zech 14:7 appears to be an exception, but the whole verse shows that *yôm 'eḥod* isn't meant to number a day in some list, for it has a different meaning altogether. The passage speaks about eschatological events when God pours out his judg-ment. The preceding verse tells us that this will occur in a day when there will be no light, for the luminaries will dwindle. Verse 7 says, "For it will be a unique day which is known to the LORD, neither day nor night, but it will come about that at evening time there will be light." This is the NASB rendering of the verse, and it captures the point. Since there will be light at evening, despite the dwindling of the luminaries (v. 6), the most the prophet can say is that this will be a unique day. Surely, this is a different use of *yôm* than those instances where numbers are used with "day" to list a sequence. And part of the confusion over Zech 14:7 arises only because the word "one" in many languages can serve as a numeral but can also mean "sole," "solitary," and "unique." This latter meaning is in view in Zechariah 14. In cases where it means "one" or "first" and is used with "day," it refers to twenty-four-hour days.[121]

The belief that the days of Genesis 1 are literal solar days is also bolstered by repeating the phrase "it was evening and it was morning, the ___ day." The phrase occurs after each of the first six days, and seems to clarify the length of each day as a literal day. As Berkhof writes, "Each one of the days mentioned has just one evening and morning, something that would hardly apply to a period of thousands of years."[122] Some might answer that we shouldn't take this too seriously, because no such formula follows the seventh day on which God rested, but solar day creationists can reply that the phrase is the author's way of rounding off his description of God's creative activities for that day, but on the seventh day God didn't create, he rested. Hence, the absence of the formula makes sense. Moreover, in the sequence of six days, the phrase marks off one day's creative activities from the next, but since the Lord rested from the seventh day onward, why would Moses need to distinguish the first day of rest from a second, third, or hundredth day of rest? Hence, including the formulaic phrase at the end of each creative day makes sense, whereas it makes little sense after the seventh day.

Next, twenty-four-hour-day creationists point to Exod 20:9-11 and 31:17 and the Sabbath regulation. Israel is commanded to labor six days and rest a seventh, because the Lord made heaven and earth in six days and then rested on the seventh. "Sound exegesis would seem to require that the word 'day' be taken in the same sense in both instances. Moreover the Sabbath set aside for rest certainly was a literal day; and the presumption is that the other days were of the same kind."[123] To those who respond that the point of the legislation is that our work week should be analogous, but not identical, to God's creation week, Fretheim replies:

> It should be noted that the references to creation in Exodus are not used as an analogy—that is, your rest on the seventh day ought to be like God's rest in creation. It is, rather, stated in terms of the imitation of God or a divine precedent that is to be followed: God worked for six days and rested on the seventh, and therefore your should do the same. Unless there is an exactitude of reference, the argument of Exodus does not work.[124]

A final point about *yôm* in Genesis 1–2 is that what the age-day theory, for example, proposes is that the term is used figuratively, not literally, in these chapters. Even Buswell admits that his day-age proposal means that the Genesis 1 days are figurative to represent geological ages.[125] Many twenty-four-hour-day theorists would reply that if the days are not literal (despite a straightforward reading suggesting that they are), how do we know that other elements of the account are not also figurative? Perhaps none of it is literally about the true and living God Yahweh, but just another creation myth that suggests something about origins. Moreover, if the days are not literal, perhaps the part of the story about Adam and Eve is imaginary or symbolic; but if so, there are serious problems for Christology, since Christ treated Adam and Eve as historical characters, and serious problems for the doctrine of imputation of sin, which is based on the events in the Garden literally occurring (Rom 5:12, 14-19). The days may be figurative, but only context can confirm that, and we need some hermeneutical principles to help us know what is literal history and what is a figure of speech.

What about arguments that question whether details of the Genesis 1–2 accounts fit twenty-four-hour days? For example, how can there be solar days before day four, and how could everything recorded for day six have happened in just twenty-four hours? As to the first three days, solar day creationists most frequently reply that even if there is no sun, God still has the earth revolving on its axis, and he knows how long his activities took. Hence, even if sun, moon, and stars are not in place until day four, the events of the first three days still could have lasted twenty-four hours apiece. God would know how long (from our perspective) his actions took, so when Genesis 1 tells us that the first three days were equal to the next three, that is enough reason to think all six days equal in length. A miracle-working omniscient God who could create the whole universe surely knows how to calculate time in that universe at any stage of its existence.

The response is slightly different for those who think the sun, moon, and stars were created on day one but only became visible on day four. Even if the luminaries aren't visible from earth until day four, they are still present and time can be measured by the earth's rotation around the sun. As to all the activities of day six, this sounds like a day that was incredibly full, but given God's power, why should we think it impossible? How long (in our time) does it take for a miracle to occur? Perhaps if the work of day six gets started late in the day things begin to get cramped, but why think God didn't start his work early in that day? For those who think it would take an incredibly long time to parade all the animals before Adam and have him name them, the answer might be that Adam named them quickly without observing them very long, or that he only named representative animals from various groups.[126]

As to creating vegetation on day three before creating the sun on day four, twenty-four-hour-day proponents have both an answer and an objection to the age-day theory. The answer is that on the twenty-four-hour-day theory, vegetation created on day three would not have to wait very long before the sun was in place. Moreover, on day one light was created, and even if this isn't light from the sun, moon, or stars, God was surely able to use that light, whatever it was, to keep plant life alive until day four. On the other hand, the fact that vegetation was created a day before the sun was in place creates a problem for the age-day theory. If the days are really long geological eras, it is hard to imagine that vegetation could go without sunlight for that long and still live. True, God created some light on day one, but to use that light for possibly billions of years to keep plant life alive before the sun's creation seems hard to accept. In reply to those who hold that the sun was created on day one but only appeared on day four to things on earth, how likely is it that the sun's rays could penetrate sufficiently through the cloud coverage still present on day three to sustain plant life on earth? Any of this may be possible, but it makes greater sense to understand the whole issue of vegetation and its need for light in the framework of a short creation week.

In addition to these arguments, solar day theorists have answers to various objections. For example, the objection that six days wouldn't be enough time for Satan to be created, be in God's presence, and then lead a revolt, all tend to assume that the events of Genesis 3 occur immediately after the events of Genesis 1 and 2. However, there could easily have been sufficient time between the end of creation and the events of Genesis 3. This doesn't mean that the events of Genesis 3 occurred ages after the completion of creation. The only point is that chapter 3 surely could and probably did happen more than six or seven days after the beginning of creation. Moreover, there may not appear to be enough time for these events to happen, because we are conditioned to think in terms of the time various activities take humans on earth. But who can say that angelic time or time in heaven mirrors what we experience on earth. What may seem like a very short time to us on earth may have been ample time for Satan to lead his revolt.

What about the complaint that God acted deceptively if he created things with apparent age? Of course, one could hold the six-solar-day theory and not appeal to apparent age. However, in an attempt to explain the vast inconsistency of scientific dates with the proposed dates of biblical creation, many twenty-four-hour-day proponents make this appeal. Their answer to this objection is that there is no deception since God told us what he did. He revealed that he created Adam and Eve as adults, rather than babies. Moreover, the basic narrative of Genesis 1–2 seems to say that things were not created as babies (in the case of animals and birds) or seeds (in the case of plants, trees, and other vegetation). Factors like these in the Genesis account tell us enough to know what God is doing; there is no deception.[127]

In addition, proponents of this view grant that there are gaps in the genealogies of Genesis 1–11, and thus it is wrong to postulate 4004 B.C. as the start of creation. Moreover, they can and should grant that names in biblical genealogies are normally chosen for a purpose, so the main point of the genealogy isn't likely to teach chronology. But having granted this, it is dubious that gaps in the genealogies allow for Adam's creation as early as 1.5 billion years ago or for the earth's origin at approximately 4.5 billion years ago, as science proposes. Many who hold this view of creation think that, at earliest, Adam was created between 10000 and 20000 B.C., and some also note that this basically fits dates scientists propose for the appearance of *homo sapiens*—human beings as we know them. This is a far cry from the dates science offers for life on this planet.

What about animal death and Rom 5:12? Though Adam and Eve alone are told that they will die, and Paul appeals to Genesis 3 to explain how sin and its penalty transferred to the human race, this is only part of the story. For one thing, we already see from Genesis 3 that the fall caused various changes in nature (Gen 3:17-19). Moreover, the same apostle Paul who wrote Rom 5:12 also wrote Rom 8:18-22 about creation being subjected to futility, groaning, and corruption. Certainly, Paul is referring to results of the fall. Moreover, eschatological passages such as Isa 11:6-9 seem to show that, when the Messiah rules on earth in his kingdom and spreads abroad his righteousness, there will be a change in animals' behavior toward one another. In light of these considerations, it seems that there is reason to think there was no animal or human death prior to the fall; but of course, if that is so, that doesn't mesh with the age-day understanding of things.

Finally, there is the Noahic flood. One need not go so far as "scientific creationism" in claiming that the flood entirely or even predominantly explains the various geological facts of our world. One only needs to see that this was no ordinary flood. The text tells us that it rained for forty days and nights (Gen 7:12, 17) and that there was so much water that it covered the tops of the mountains (Gen 7:19). Verse 11 says that water came not only from the sky but from the fountains of the deep, and according to verse 24 it took some 150 days before the water drained off. Though some think this is myth and others see it as a flood local to Palestine, this hardly seems possible. The data already mentioned are hard to fit with only a local flood. Moreover, if this is not historical, why all the minute details about the number of days it took for this to occur, and detailed information about when it started and ended (Gen 7:11; 8:4-6, 13)? Such details are contrary to mythology and give the tale a historical ring. But having said this about the flood, is it likely that such a catastrophe would not have had major consequences for the topography of the earth and would not also have affected layers of earth below the crust? While it is dubious that the Genesis flood explains all geological data, let alone "proves" a creationist position overall, it is also quite dubious that the flood is responsible for none of the geological features of our world.

Literary Framework Theory

Having considered arguments for the age-day and twenty-four-hour-day theories, one might be in a quandary over which to choose. On the contemporary scene, however, a growing number of scholars have concluded that one need not decide between these two theories, for a third option avoids the dilemma of whether the days were twenty-four hours or lengthy eras. Moreover, it also eludes the problem of how to fit Scripture with science. This option is the literary framework theory, defended by N. H. Ridderbos, Ronald Youngblood, Meredith G. Kline, Willem VanGemeren, and Henri Blocher, to name a few.

As already noted, the author of Genesis is a literary artist of first rank. We saw, following Cassuto, the apparently deliberate arranging and sequencing of phrases in chapter 1 to produce sequences of sevens, threes, and tens.[128] The literary framework view says that the structuring goes even further. Put simply, the whole sequence of seven days of creation is not a chronological account of the sequence of historical events when God created our universe. Rather, it is a literary device the writer uses to tell a story that conveys great theological truth. In other words, the "days of creation" happen to be the mold in which the writer chose to tell the story of God's creation and sovereign rule of the universe. They should not be understood as teaching that God created in six literal days.

If one thinks this proposal is odd, it isn't, for writers use literary forms and motifs to convey messages all the time. For example, a parable is a story with a moral or practical lesson, but everyone understands that the details of the parable need not be and usually are not historical events. The message of the parable is still clear and true. This is not to say that Genesis 1–2 is a parable, but rather to illustrate what is meant by a literary device.

As to the particular themes the author presented in this way, depending on the proponent of this view, the answer may vary slightly. Moreover, if one wonders whether the actual events of creation at all followed the order in the Genesis days, some would say this might be possible, but it really isn't the point of the narrative. In explaining the basic idea of the literary framework theory, Blocher answers such questions as follows:

> The literary interpretation takes the form of the week attributed to the work of creation to be an artistic arrangement, a modest example of anthropomorphism that is not to be taken literally. The author's intention is not to supply us with a chronology of origins. It is possible that the logical order he has chosen coincides broadly with the actual sequence of the facts of cosmogony; but that does not interest him. He wishes to bring out certain themes and provide a theology of the sabbath. The text is composed as the author meditates on the finished work, so that we may understand how the creation is related to God and what is its significance for mankind.[129]

If we take this interpretation of Genesis 1 and 2, the literary framework view claims that the only historical points to be made are that God did it, and that somewhere in the mix of whatever he did, he created a first man and woman (Adam and Eve) who fell into sin and implicated the whole race by so doing. Once we remove the idea that the days teach a historical sequence, the age-day vs. twenty-four-hour-day debate ends. The most natural thing to say about the days is that they are ordinary days like ours. That does the least violence to the normal meaning of "day" and of our text. However—and this is the crucial proviso—all this means on the literary framework theory is that the author chose the literary device or motif of seven days to make his theological points. It doesn't mean that the days are actual historical days of any sort. Think again about a parable—for example, the story of the good Samaritan in Luke 10, which isn't called a parable but clearly functions as one in that Jesus uses it to teach a lesson about who qualifies as our neighbor. In that story there is no reason to think that the thieves who rob and harm the traveler, the traveler himself, the good Samaritan, or the inn where he takes the injured man are symbols of some abstract ideas. Rather, *in the story* they are not symbols at all, but the story as a whole makes a very important spiritual and moral point. However, the events in that parable never likely occurred in actual history. Similarly, this is how we should think of Genesis 1–2. We can say some things historically from these chapters, but the length of days or how many days God used to create are not among them.

What are the implications of this view for correlating science and Scripture? Defenders of the view think they are quite good, for one understands that Moses' intent was to write neither science nor chronologically ordered history. The literary framework position leaves to science questions about how creation was done, when it was done, or how long it took. There cannot be a conflict between science and Scripture on this point, for they address two different sets of questions.

In support of this view, proponents offer various arguments, many of which are intended to show that Genesis 1 and 2 do not offer a chronological sequence; the ordering is logical to make certain theological points.[130] The most obvious argument for a logical order is the arrangement of the six days into two triads with each member of the first triad corresponding to a coordinate member of the second (days one and four are the first in each triad, and they correspond to one another; days two and five correspond to one another; and days three and six correspond to one another). The first triad deals with forming the structures that the second triad populates.[131]

In a recent article articulating and elaborating the literary approach, Meredith Kline argues that we need to see in these chapters a cosmogony that he calls a two register cosmology. The upper register contains God and everything in heaven, while the lower concerns man on earth. Scripture constantly shows the interplay between events and agents in the two registers.[132] What happens in the upper register is intended as an archetype of what goes on in the lower register. Kline argues that the two-register cosmology applies to both spatial and temporal phenomena. He explains what this means for the days of creation (temporal notions from the lower register):

> We naturally expect then that in the case of time, as of space, the upper register will draw upon the lower register for its figurative depiction. Therefore, when we find that God's upper level activity of issuing creative fiats from his heavenly throne is pictured as transpiring in a week of earthly days, we readily recognize that, in keeping with the pervasive contextual pattern, this is a literary figure, an earthly, lower register time metaphor for an upper register, heavenly reality.[133]

In other words, the days of God's creative activity recount what he does from his register. They are not literal days like ours here on earth, for God is not subject to that. However, the reason the writer speaks of "days" in regard to God is that he takes something that makes literal sense in the lower register and projects it onto the upper register to give us something to help us understand what God did. Both day-age and twenty-four-hour-day views invoke the lower register, but God functions from the upper register.

In addition, there are other problems with seeing Genesis 1 and 2 as having a chronological sequence. Kline raises a problem with the relation of days one and four. On the first day, light is created and God separates light from darkness. On the fourth day, sun, moon, and stars are created and put in place to separate night and day and to mark seasons, years, and days. Both days, then, involve setting up lights and instituting time for the lower register. Kline argues that what we actually have is a recapitulation on day four of the events of day one. Chronologically, days one and four are the same. Day one gives God's *fiat* order and day four shows its fulfillment. The results of setting the luminaries in place on day four are "the same effects that are already attributed to the creative activity of day one (Gen. 1:3-5). There too daylight is produced on the earth and the cycle of light/day and darkness/night is established."[134] Since day four returns us to day one, the literary sequence of the days is not the same as the temporal sequence of events. That is, the ordering of the days cannot be chronological as regards days one and four, but must be logical instead. The logic is likely that of balancing the two triads of forming and filling.

Kline is aware of various attempts to avoid this conclusion. To the proposal that the luminaries were created on day one but only appeared on earth on day four Kline replies that the phrases "Let there be" and "God made" and "God set" (Gen 1:14-18) are clearly the language of actual production. The same kind of language is used for the other days of creation, and everyone grants that it involves bringing into existence something new. In none of the other cases does it mean "revealing" something already present. Why, then, should we think it means that in this case? Others claim that the main point of day four is that previously existing luminaries began on this day to perform the functions of separating days from nights and allowing to calculate days, years, and seasons. Kline thinks this won't work since the primary point about day four is the creation of sun, moon, and stars, which takes us back to day one. Others try to avoid this problem by claiming that the verbs in verses 16 and 17 should be read as pluperfect. Hence, they would say, "And God had made," and would refer to what happened on day one; then day four could involve nothing more than the luminaries becoming visible. However, Kline argues cogently that this won't work, for the consistent pattern in Genesis 1 is a divine *fiat* followed by the phrase "and it was so." After this the writer details what occurred on that day. Verses 14-17 follow this pattern, so if the verbs in verses 16-17 are pluperfect, then they occur prior to the *fiat* of verses 14 and 15a, and of course that is impossible. The only way around that problem would be to make all the verbs in 14-17 pluperfect and cast the whole day four in the pluperfect as referring to what God had done earlier. This, however, would ironically push the creation and the placing of the luminaries earlier than day four (perhaps even back to day one), and that would just show that the sequence of days here is not chronological, a conclusion meant to be avoided by introducing the pluperfect.[135] It can also be added that if one introduces the pluperfect into the verbs of verses 16-17, why not do the same for verbs dealing with activities on the other days of creation, since they are all in the same basic tense? Of course, that would require the absurdity that none of the events listed for any of the days happened on those days, but occurred previously. If that is what Moses means, however, why bother detailing specific events for each day, if the events don't happen on that day?

A final argument for this view and against seeing any sort of chronology (especially one of twenty-four-hour days) in the passage is considered utterly conclusive by some. It deals with Gen 2:5, the start of the second creation narrative. That verse says, "Now no shrub of the field was yet in the earth, and no plant of the field had yet sprouted, for the LORD God had not sent rain upon the earth, and there was no man to cultivate the ground." An initial point is that as we read further in chapter 2 we learn of Adam's creation (v. 7) and then of the planting of vegetation and rivers (vv. 8ff.). So the second account puts the creation of man prior to the creation of vegetation, but this contradicts the account in chapter 1, which says vegetation appeared on day three and on day six God created human beings. One way to avoid the apparent contradiction is to adopt the literary view, which says that the point is not strict chronology, so apparent conflicts between the two accounts over timing don't matter.

There are more significant points to be made about Gen 2:5. The first is that the explanation of why there was no vegetation on earth has nothing to do with a lack of supernatural action. Rather, the explanation presupposes naturalistic conditions. As Kline says, "Gen 2:5, however, takes it for granted that providential operations were not of a supernatural kind, but that God ordered the sequence of creation acts so that the continuance and development of the earth and its creatures could proceed by natural means."[136] What is the point? Is it that we should believe the days are ages, because this verse teaches that nature was allowed to develop by natural means, means which make little sense in a sequence of rapid supernatural acts as the solar day position proposes? Not at all. The initial point is that this does not fit six solar days of supernatural intervention, but that doesn't mean the age-day theory wins by default. Indeed, age-day theorists grant that much went on during the ages of creation by God's providential working through natural means, but there is still a major problem for age-day theorists. Gen 2:5 seems to introduce us to day six, on which Adam, Eve, and the animals are created, but can it really be true that there was no rain on earth from days one through five (remember, for age-day theorists, days one through five are long geological ages)? If so, how would life-forms created on day five have sustained themselves without rain and vegetation? Perhaps some will reply that the reference to vegetation in 2:5 actually takes us back to day three, and then 2:7 moves us to day six. But if that is the answer, the literary framework proponent should reply that this quick movement from one day to three days later just shows that the author is not minding strict chronological sequence.

Gen 2:5 raises yet a further problem for a chronological understanding of events, especially for the solar day position. On the solar day approach, each of the six days of creation is only twenty-four hours. Remember also that on day three dry land appears and vegetation appears on it. The scene in 2:5 seems to take us to the sixth day, but then that means that the time differential between the planting of vegetation and the sixth day is three days. It would be, for example, like the difference between Tuesday and Friday of a given week. But now the problem should become clear. Granting that 2:5 speaks of natural processes, between Tuesday and Friday of the same week is not long enough to make absence of rain result in land devoid of vegetation. Plants and trees can go far longer than three days without rain and not even begin to die. Doesn't this problem show that we cannot understand the six days of creation as teaching anything about the chronological order of God's creative work? Demanding a chronological order only creates contradictions like these. In regard to the explanation of why there were no plants according to Gen 2:5, Blocher writes:

> That explanation presupposes the normal activity of the laws of nature for the growth of plants (an operation of divine providence), and a sufficient length of time for the absence of rain to be able to constitute the cause of the absence of plants. That does not fit the hypothesis of a literal week for the creation of the whole cosmos. If the dry land did not emerge until Tuesday and if vegetation has existed only from that day, an explanation is not going to be given the following Friday that there is no vegetation because there is no rain! Such reasoning would be against reason. Now the inspired author of Genesis, who revised the tol*dot and constructed the prologue, the wise man (whom we are bold enough to name as Moses) would not have preserved a contradiction in 2:5. If he repeated the explanation given, it is because he did not understand the days of the first chapter literally. It is a necessary implication that in Genesis 2:5 Scripture supplies the proof that the week of the Genesis prologue is not literal; this proof has not been refuted.[137]

Assessment and Evaluation

To say that this is an enormously complicated issue puts it mildly. Despite the number of years since Darwin and all the advances in a host of fields, one senses, to paraphrase and adapt Matthew Arnold's words, that the plain is about as dark as it was in Arnold's day and the armies are still quite ignorant as they fight on.

Initially, I note that when there are so many different data to correlate, there are usually several different theoretical models that can explain to one degree or another the whole complex of data. This is so for competing world-views, competing scientific theories, and different theological systems meant to explain a large and complex array of data. In such cases, theoreticians understand that it is unlikely that any conceptual scheme can so explain the data as to leave no anomalies whatsoever. Hence, as one evaluates the various options, one should not expect to find a perfect fit with all the data. What is wrong, however, is to adopt a model whose foundational claims are refuted by the evidence that all theories must explain.

What, then, should we conclude about the various options? I think we can reject a number of positions in light of evidence that disconfirms major planks in those positions. For example, though I offered only a small portion of the evidence against naturalistic evolution, those arguments raise sufficient questions about central tenets of evolution to reject it.

Some think theistic evolution adequately answers the key objections to atheistic evolution, but I disagree. Considering only the three areas of evidence presented against evolution, it is true that the evidence for intelligent design could be handled by invoking God's participation, as theistic evolutionists do. But the other two areas of evidence, problems with the mechanism of evolution and problems in the fossil record, are not solved by theistic evolution. As to fossils, there are still all the gaps where transitional forms should be. To say that God intervened at those points to make the jump to new species departs from a theistic evolutionary approach and essentially adopts the position of progressive creationism, which in no way requires macro-evolution. As to natural selection, even with theistic evolution the problems remain. Mutations serve as the source of new genetic material, but mutations are normally deleterious. Moreover, as we saw, to develop certain organs a whole set of these mutations must occur at just the right time and they must all be beneficial. One can say that God sees to it that this happens, or one can say that God just intervenes at the right moment to make the new species, but all of this sounds suspiciously like an admission that God did it after all and we need not appeal to evolutionary processes to account for it.

Perhaps, then, we should follow Howard Van Till and argue that God pre-programmed things so that the creation would have intrinsic capacities to accomplish not only micro-evolution but also macro-evolutionary changes. I find this quite unconvincing. Van Till repeatedly states that scientists who are biologists whom he knows tell him that such capacities exist. But, exist in what? One of the problems is that Van Till doesn't tell us the exact nature of the creation he is talking about. What is it that God created originally and endowed with these capacities? Is it formless matter, formed but inorganic matter, organic matter, actual life-forms like primitive creatures such as trilobites, etc., more complex life-forms, or what? Van Till doesn't say, but the question is significant, for until we know what originally received these capacities, it will be hard to judge whether that could be so or whether from such things it really is possible to develop naturally a world populated as is ours. Even if the claim were that God created various animals, birds, and fish with such capacities, it is hard to see how such life-forms would have inherent capacities that could someday result in producing human beings. But that option is hardly worth considering, since Van Till would likely claim that original creation *ex nihilo* resulted in rather primitive, unformed material. When you hold that evolutionary forces can take such elements and produce (eventually) our world, there is no need to start with complex life-forms or even simple ones. Moreover, despite evidence to the contrary, Van Till thinks the fossil record supports macro-evolutionary claims, and this also raises an interesting point. Among the contributors to the Moreland and Reynolds volume, there is disagreement over what the fossils show, and it isn't just the theologians and biblical exegetes in that volume who question the fossil record. This sounds like what we might expect in light of comments (quoted earlier from G. G. Simpson) that subjectivity enters into one's interpretation of the fossils.[138]

Arguments already presented against the pre-Gen 1:1 and gap theories make it safe to discard those views as unlikely. That leaves the age-day, twenty-four-hour-day, and literary framework theories. Which should we adopt? I believe one could hold any of the three in some form and be consistent with evangelical theology, so one's decision need not be a test of orthodoxy or a basis for evangelicals to break fellowship if they choose different options.

Having said this, it is still hard to choose. I find problems in all three of them, but remembering that these are alternative models of explanation that will leave some unanswered questions, I am most comfortable with a combination of the twenty-four-hour-day and the literary framework position. In what follows I shall explain what I mean and my reasons for it.

I begin by noting that if one accepts a creationist account of origins and concludes that God did it at all like Genesis says, then one holds that creation *ex nihilo* and the forming of created matter into our universe are divine miraculous acts. But these are not "ordinary" miracles, if any miracle is ordinary. With most miracles someone is or was in a position to observe conditions before the miracle was performed and afterward. In fact, it is the ability to do so that helps assure us that a miracle has indeed occurred. Think, for example, of the resurrection of Christ. People saw Christ alive before the crucifixion, others saw him die, and there were those who certified that the body put in the tomb was indeed dead (he hadn't just swooned or passed out, later to be revived). After these events there were many people who claimed to see Jesus alive again. Some touched him, others talked with him, and yet others ate with him. When we put these facts together, the best conclusion is that someone physically dead miraculously came back to life. We say this happened miraculously, because in the normal course of things, dead things do not through any natural process we know of come back to life. Now, no one was present to observe the miracle as it was occurring, nor do we have instruments to measure or explain how God did this miracle. Still, the evidence we have about states of affairs before Christ's death and after his burial make a very strong case for believing in the resurrection.

With the various miracles performed in creating matter and fashioning the world, no human being was in a position to observe conditions before the miracles happened and then to compare them with conditions afterward. Moreover, Scripture says the fall of Adam and Eve had a dramatic impact upon creation itself. Hence, our world is not the pre-fallen world. Even if we had been present during these events of creation, we still would have no way of explaining the naturalistic means (if there were any) by which God performed these miracles, but at least we might have eyewitness reports of the "before" and "after" conditions so that we would better know what facts about our world confirm that a miracle or miracles had occurred. But no such information is available to us from any humans, for none were in a position to observe.

One may agree but wonder about its point. The point is that, given the fact that we are talking about miracles, miracles that no human could have observed, nor could they have observed conditions before the miracles so as to compare them with the "after," it shouldn't be surprising that there is little natural, empirical evidence in our world today to which we can point as conclusive support of these miracles. There may actually be any number of things in the natural order which evidence the miracles of creation, but we simply are not in a position (as were some people with respect to Christ's resurrection, for example) to know that these facts about our current world are proof of the miracle of creation. The only eyewitnesses to creation were God and any angelic beings that may have been around during some days of creation. The angels didn't write about what happened, but evangelicals believe that God did testify in Scripture to what happened. Still, the biblical accounts that God revealed and inspired omit many details. We know more than we would without Scripture, but an analysis of my current chapter shows that we were not given enough to rule out conclusively all positions except one. Hence, we must observe the postfallen world and study Scripture. Shouldn't this forewarn us about how much empirical support for the various miracles of creation we are likely to find from scientific observations of the current world?

If this is correct, I believe it has significant implications. One is that we should be wary of attempts to scientifically "prove" creationism. Though I greatly appreciate the intent of scientific creationists, I don't think a young earth/ universe position hinges on whether they are successful in their project. Much of what they offer at most shows a possible fit with Scripture. Undoubtedly, their work has been very helpful in providing evidence against evolution, but arguments against evolution are not positive proof of six-solar-day creationism. Evidences of intelligent design point to a creator, but they don't tell us whether he created in lengthy geological ages or in six twenty-four-hour days.

Another implication of my point about miracles is that we should not be unduly disturbed about complaints from those who reject creationism altogether or attempt to wed it with scientific data that they don't find empirical evidence for short days of creation and a young earth. If the creative acts are miracles, and no one was around to observe conditions before and after the miracles except God (and he gave us few details), what empirical evidence would you expect to find that this has occurred? It seems that there can't be a lot, and the type of empirical evidence we will find will likely at most show that twenty-four-hour-day creationism could fit many of the facts about our world, but that doesn't conclusively prove such creationism. The fact that it doesn't is only crucial if the critic can specify the kind of empirical evidence that should be present in our world to prove a miracle if it had occurred. I can't see that there is anything critics would reasonably require as proof that seems to be lacking.

Any creationist should take seriously these points about creation being a miracle, but that alone won't determine which of the three positions we are now considering should be chosen. As to the day-age theory, there are significant objections to it. For one thing, I don't find the word study data on *yôm* convincing. It shows that the word can mean lengthy periods of time, but possibility is not proof. We need evidence within the immediate context of Genesis

1–2, and it doesn't seem forthcoming. Moreover, the formula "it was evening and it was morning" seems to be counterevidence. If not, age-day theorists need a cogent explanation as to why not. Appeals to the seventh day as omitting the phrase won't do, for reasons set forth above when discussing this issue in relation to the solar day approach. Moreover, I take very seriously Waltke's and Collins's comments that the typical examples of "day" used to prove that it need not mean twenty-four-hour days are inconclusive, if not irrelevant, since they aren't cases of *yôm* with numerals, but instances in bound expressions. As Collins notes, in bound expressions a term may be used in an idiomatic way, and hence have a quite different meaning than it does outside the idiomatic expression.[139] Even if we think none of the uses of *yôm* in expressions that were cited is an idiom, we must still be careful about how we use these word studies.

A further troublesome aspect of the day-age approach is that it often seems motivated by a concordist mentality which I believe grants too much weight to the so-called "facts" of science. Even as we need careful study of the text of the biblical creation accounts, we also need careful study of the data of science to be certain that the "facts" are really facts. However, there is another concern here, and in a perceptive article Paul Seely raises it. Seely argues that in interpreting the Genesis creation accounts we must understand them in terms of what they would likely have meant for someone living in an Ancient Near Eastern culture. This requirement applies to both the author of the document and its readers. The problem is that concordists tend to read the text in terms of their scientific understanding, which inevitably puts on the text information and a worldview that differs from that of the writer and his readers. Though it isn't clear that concordists take as many liberties with the text as Seely claims, his general point and many of his specific points with respect to various individual days of creation as presented in the text seem very sound.[140] All of this should caution us about embracing too quickly age-day theorists' attempts to harmonize science with Genesis 1 and 2. I think this should also be a warning to those who try scientifically to prove or support creationism, i.e., be sure you provide evidence for what the text *in its own context* would have meant, not for a creationism based on a twentieth-century understanding of the world.

I also find unconvincing day-age theorists' handling of day four. For those who interpret it as the day on which the heavenly luminaries are first created, there seems to be a problem with vegetation being present from the third age and only primordial light (whatever that was) for the first three ages of the earth's creation. Many age-day theorists take this objection seriously, and opt for the view that on day four the luminaries created on day one become visible. Thus, the verbs that speak about creating the sun, moon, and stars must be pluperfects. I believe Kline's arguments against such a reading are not only cogent but also decisive. Moreover, we need an explanation of why the *fiat* command on this day means existing things are to be revealed when it has no such meaning on the other days, despite the fact that the verb, its force, and form are the same for each day.

As to age-day theorists' objection to solar day creationism that the seventh day is indefinitely extended and the text doesn't conclude with the formulaic "it was evening and it was morning," several things can be said. The first has to do with the omission of the concluding phrase, but I have already made that point and refer the reader to those comments. Still, something must be said about the length of the seventh day. Many say that it has lasted until now, and will possibly go on endlessly, so there is no reason to think the other days lasted only twenty-four hours. If they are parallel with the seventh day, they will be much longer. But if we are looking for parallelism, God's rest from original creation goes on forever, so should these other days also be eternal? Obviously, if that were the case, we would never finish even the first day; for-ever never ends. Moreover, and more directly to the point, God has not been resting altogether ever since day six. Day seven was God's rest from creative work, however long that rest lasts. But none of this means God waited ages of time before doing anything else. God's rest from creating was over long ago; though he hasn't done more creating since the sixth day, he hasn't been idle either. The point about the Sabbath legislation is not six days of creating to one day of rest for us, but rather that we follow God's initial pattern in creation of six days of work to one day of rest. None of that means the seventh day goes on indefinitely or that God does nothing of any sort.

This leaves either the twenty-four-hour-day position or the literary frame-work view, and from what I have said so far, I might appear to be heading in the direction of the latter view. However, several considerations keep me from adopting it altogether. An initial question that troubles me is that, if the days of creation are just a literary device that is figurative, how do we know where to stop with figures of speech in Genesis 1–3? The days seem no more figurative or literal than Adam and Eve, the serpent, vegetation, animals, and all the rest. Moreover, if these things are figures of speech, literary devices, all of them could be symbols of something else quite different (anyone who under-stands how a symbol works in a novel, for example, understands my point[141]). Blocher seems to grasp this point when he explains that age-day theorists claim that "day" is used figuratively in the Genesis 1 and 2 days of creation, but then they treat them as though they aren't figurative by trying to correlate the dates and events science proposes with the days of creation. As Blocher says, age-day theorists haven't fully appreciated what it means to say that the days are figurative.[142] But my point is that I am not sure that even Blocher has fully understood the implications of this subtle point that he raises. Blocher wants us to see the days of Genesis 1 and 2 as a literary device, a framework on which to hang the creation story without really meaning that it occurred in days of any particular sort. But remember that if this is a literary-artistic presentation, it not only includes reference to days but to God, Adam and Eve, the serpent, etc. And if the days may be figurative, then why not God, etc., as figures to represent something else? What is the hermeneutic that tells us that some ele-ments in this story are figures of speech and literary devices and others are not?

No explanation is forthcoming! Once you claim that an apparently historical story is figurative, a literary way of relating the creation story, it becomes difficult to interpret the story, since it all may point to something other than what it appears to teach at face value, including whatever it says about God.

All of this is especially troubling, because if we cannot be certain about the historicity of the events recounted in Genesis 1–3, there are problems for other theological points. I have already noted the Christological implications of these passages and the implications for the imputation of Adam's sin. But there is even more. When Blocher discusses Eve's creation from Adam's rib, he asks whether we should take this literally, and replies that it is most likely a figurative description of what happened.[143] While such an interpretation fits entirely a belief that the story is a literary framework for making some theological points about creation and thus need not be taken entirely literally, it still creates significant problems for NT teaching. In 1 Cor 11:8-9 Paul refers to Eve's creation as justification for his teaching about women's use of head coverings while praying or prophesying in church. In 1 Tim 2:12-15 he refers to the Genesis account of Eve's creation as historical and uses it to justify his rules about women teaching and holding authority over men. Regardless of what one thinks these *regulations* mean and how they apply today, their *justification* assumes as historical the account of Eve's creation. That is, we must distinguish the rule from its justification, and regardless of what we think the rule means, that in no way warrants saying the justification doesn't include a reference to a historical event when it seems to do so. But Blocher's handling of Eve's creation makes it unclear as to exactly what we should think is the historical truth about her creation.

These are just some of the problems that stem from seeing the creation story as a literary way of presenting things that shouldn't be taken literally, but there is another problem. If this story and these days are only a literary device, then granting that the author can make his theological points by using any number of literary devices (if what he says is in no way historical, it matters little which literary device he chooses), why choose this one (the six days)? Whatever theological points the author wants to make can be made in other literary formats. In fact, biblical writers tell us various things about creation in many different passages (see the earlier section of this chapter), and they do so without ever referring to the different days of creation. We still get the point that God is the creator, is sovereign over creation, created *ex nihilo*, etc., from passages that don't mention the days of creation. In fact, we could still know those truths even if Genesis 1–3 were removed from the Bible, or we had never read them. So, if biblical authors want to make some theological points about creation, why do it with this literary device (the six days), a device that for all the world looks like an account of actual happenings on real days of some sort? Moreover, if this account is just a literary device, what does that tell us about other stories Moses recounts? Are the ten plagues at the time of the exodus another literary device, not to be taken literally? Are the genealogies just a literary device meant to teach us something besides information about various people who lived at one time or another? Once you treat a piece whose literary genre seems to involve history as though it does not, that also raises serious questions about other texts that appear to be history of some sort.

For all these reasons, I am uncomfortable with adopting the literary framework view in its entirety. How, then, do I answer the objection to a chronological account that Kline raises concerning Gen 2:5? Moreover, does this mean I think Genesis 1 and 2 are a straightforward account of seven successive twenty-four-hour days? As to Gen 2:5, I shall come back to it after explaining my view more fully. In response to whether I am opting for a strict chronological account of twenty-four-hour days, the answer is not exactly. At one time, I did hold something like that view, but the concerns of both age-day theorists and literary framework proponents have convinced me that a modified twenty-four-hour-day view is preferable. Let me explain.

As noted when discussing literary genre, these chapters do tell us things that are true in a historical sense. However, this is not historical writing as moderns write history, so it shouldn't surprise us if it is not absolutely precise. Moreover, sometimes biblical writers use approximations in writing history, but their work is still understood to be historically accurate. What this means is that the actual number of days it took to create may be more than six days, but I doubt that we are talking about vastly longer periods than the days so numbered. At some point, if the time extends too far beyond a literal day, it would be hard, even if the writer uses approximations, to call it a day. But numbers in Scripture are not always precise, nor is the counting of days or years.[144]

What in Genesis 1–2, however, makes me think this is not precise history in our modern sense of history? Here I find compelling some arguments offered especially by literary framework theorists. For example, it is hard to miss the symmetrical two-triadic structure of the six creation days. Even if some days actually took more than twenty-four hours, so long as they didn't last extended amounts of time (for example, ten years while other days lasted twenty-four hours each), we need not demand just twenty-four hours per day, nor should we think slight differences in the days of creation ruin the artistic symmetry. However, the fact that the writer structured the events symmetrically doesn't prove that there is no chronology in the first chapter or that we aren't at all getting an accurate historical account. I agree that the form of chapter 1 contributes in communicating that God is a sovereign king who does things in an orderly way without battles, conflicts, and missteps, but that in no way means the events recorded are not historical or chronological at all. When historians write, they must be selective; they cannot record every minute detail as a photograph might. Since they must be selective, if they happen to see patterns in the details presented, why is it illegitimate to write the account in accord with those perceived patterns, so long as doing so doesn't distort the truth of what occurred?

My point is twofold. On the one hand, it recognizes that chapter 1 especially is highly crafted literarily. The kinds of patterns Cassuto notes are just too pervasive to think they just happened to fall together by coincidence. However—and this is the other point—just because the author sees a broad pattern of two triads of days, for example, in the events he records, and writes his account accordingly, that doesn't make his account ahistorical or entirely figurative. In order to fit the pattern of six days and two triads, he may have to say a given day's events lasted a day, an approximation if the events actually took several days, but his account is still history. Approximations to fit the literary symmetry would not exclude this litera- ture from being historical or turn it into a figurative piece meant solely to teach some theological truths.

Several things suggest that the author uses some approximations, and here I take seriously what opponents of the solar day theory have said. For example, if the sun isn't created and positioned so as to perform its functions until the fourth day, I can agree that we can't be sure that the first three days are solar days of the length we experience. Of course, even if no sun is in place, God would know when an amount of time equal to three solar days had passed. Hence, his revelation to Moses about the first three days could actually match what happens in three of our solar days. Of course, the amount of time could also have been longer or shorter than three of our solar days. Only God knows the precise length of these days and how they relate to our solar days, and in Genesis 1 he probably hasn't told us; but he need not do so, since the purpose of Genesis 1 is not to give a scientific account of how time was measured on earth before the sun was in place. As long as the difference from our three days is not so great that inspiring Moses to call the first three periods of creation "days" would communicate something false (i.e., it isn't just an approxima- tion, but is far from the truth), there seems nothing wrong with God revealing these events as happening in three days, even if they couldn't have been solar days in our sense.

Arguments about the sixth day taking more than twenty-four hours also have a certain degree of plausibility. Though no one knows how fast God works or when on that day he began to work, tasks such as naming the ani- mals would have been enormous. Considerations like these make it reasonable to think that the events of the sixth day lasted more than twenty-four hours, but that doesn't mean they must have taken eons to finish. Only God knows for sure how long it took, but claiming that it all happened on the sixth day can be an approximation that isn't false, so long as the actual amount of time did not extend months or years.

Some proponents of a stricter twenty-four-hour-day position might say I am being too loose with the text because whenever a cardinal or ordinal number is used with *yôm* it means a literal twenty-four-hour day. In response, I generally agree with the point about numbers coupled with *yôm*, but the issue is more complex than at first appears. As some commentators explain, this is the only place in the OT where we have a list of days with numbers attached, so it is hard to say for sure exactly what the number plus *yôm* means. This must not be misunderstood. It doesn't mean there are no other OT passages where a number is used with *yôm*; that happens in various passages. What does not occur is an ordered, numbered list of days all in the same passage as we have here. Hence, who can say that it is impossible to have an ordered list of numbered days that are not twenty-four hours apiece? It is hard to make universal generalizations from a sampling of one case.

Suppose, however, we grant, as I do, that *yôm* with numbers usually refers to solar days. Still, numbered days can appear in Genesis 1 and 2 and not be absolutely precise; they may be approximations of the sort I have been describing. So, even this line of argument need not undermine the position I am espousing.

A further point also leads me to think that the days are each approximately twenty-four hours. We should ask whether the seven days of creation are strictly successive. That is, does day four end at the stroke of midnight and day five start immediately thereafter? Those who hold a very strict chronology in these chapters seem to think so. But if there can be some gap between the end of one creative day and the start of a new one, I think this further accommodates some of the concerns about whether the first three days were solar days, and concerns about getting everything done on the sixth day. I am not suggesting large gaps, because that would counteract the claim that this took a week. All I am saying is that the claim that it took a week may also be an approximation. If there can be small time gaps between the days, the whole process still took approximately a week, and some concerns raised by a rigid succession of twenty-four-hour days are addressed.

Undoubtedly, some strict solar day proponents will reply that this would ruin Moses' reasoning behind the Sabbath legislation. That legislation says that God did it all in six days and then rested; hence we should work six days and rest on the seventh. Here I am inclined to agree with those who argue that, while there is an analogy between God's work week and ours, it doesn't require absolute identity. The main point is a pattern of six days of work to one day of rest; nothing about that pattern and the Sabbath legislation regarding it seems endangered by understanding the twenty-four-hour days as I am proposing. Moreover, we must be careful not to push the details of the Sabbath regulation too far or we wind up with absurdities. For example, on some of the days of creation, the work God did may have taken only a few moments. Does that mean that on the corresponding day of our week we only have to work a few minutes? Or, pushing the passage too hard in a different direction, it says that we are to work six days and rest the seventh. Does that mean that on the six days we must work all twenty-four hours? No doubt some will say no, because God didn't work twenty-four hours on those days; but if our work time must be identical to God's, we return to the absurdity that on some days we need only work a few minutes. So, we should be careful not to push the argument about the Sabbath too hard.

Let me turn now to considerations which, though not proof of my view, are details which any model of explanation must handle, and I think my position handles them well. An initial item is the absence of the sun until day four, even though vegetation appears on day three. Even if the light God created on day one would not support this plant life, within approximately twenty-four hours after vegetation appeared, the sun would be in place. If God needed to perform a miracle to sustain the vegetation in the meantime, that would be no problem since creation involved a series of miracles, anyway. So, the text can be historically accurate when it says vegetation preceded creation of the sun.

Second, I must reiterate that the preponderance of biblical evidence favors the Genesis flood in the days of Noah as historical. I need not repeat arguments presented previously, but only add a further point: various NT authors consider the flood to be a historical event. Second Peter 3:6 is an example, but we must understand the context of this statement. In 2 Peter 3, Peter predicts that in the last days people will scoff at the idea of Christ's return and a final judgment (v. 3). Even more, they will believe they can prove that such things could never happen. Verse 4 records their argument: nothing catastrophic ever happens; so there is no reason to fear something cataclysmic such as Christ's return and final judgment. Nature just flows on, uninterrupted by catastrophes. Peter answers this argument specifically in verses 5-7. He says that those claims willingly ignore the facts. The facts are that catastrophic events have happened. Creation is a major change (v. 5); God created the heavens and earth by his word. Beyond that, the earth he created (clearly this means the whole earth, not just Palestine) was later destroyed by a flood which came upon the earth by the power of his word (v. 6). That is no ordinary event either. Likewise, by fire God someday will destroy the current heavens and earth by the power of his word. So don't think that the course of nature is uniform and that, thus, you need not worry about a cataclysmic judgment. There is a day of accountability.

Peter not only considered the Noahic flood a historical event, but he did so to the point that he appealed to it to prove his doctrinal point. If, in fact, the flood did not occur, Peter's theological point is in trouble. But if a flood of the magnitude described in Genesis happened, it is hard to believe that it didn't make some radical changes in the topography, etc., of our earth. I am not ready to make claims and draw the conclusions about it that some creation scientists have proposed. Rather, my points are that Scripture teaches the flood as a historical event, and that its magnitude likely made a significant difference to our planet. Hence, any position on origins and on the earth's age that takes Scripture seriously must somehow incorporate the flood into its explanation of origins.

Next, a further comment is in order concerning the genealogies in Genesis and time in relation to Genesis 1–2. I entirely agree that the genealogies have gaps in them. Hence, Archbishop Ussher's dates are significantly skewed to the point that we can in no way say the universe began in approximately 4004 B.C. Moreover, Gen 1:1 requires, as argued above, creation *ex nihilo* of the

THE DOCTRINE OF CREATION □ 619

material God used to form and fashion the universe. When the writer picks up the story at verse 2, he shows us that the earth was not in a habitable form. How long of a time was there between creation *ex nihilo* and the first *fiat?* Put differently, how long was the earth in existence but "without form and void" before God began to fashion it into a habitable planet? Nobody other than God knows; Moses surely doesn't tell us. But isn't it possible that some of the supposed ages of layers of rock could be accounted for during that time between creation *ex nihilo* and day one? Some may object that this still does not explain ancient dates of other constituents in our universe, nor does it explain why those dates seem to coincide with dates of rock layers on earth. But nothing in Scripture says that when God originally created the earth, he didn't also produce the other planets. It is possible that all of them were created at once in completed or uncompleted form, and that could be partly why scientific dates of things elsewhere in our universe tend to coincide with dates of layers of rock on earth. Surely this is speculative, but so is much of what science proposes about origins. My point is that Scripture tells us many things about creation but it also leaves some gaps into which we may be able to fit more time. Hence, there is no need to hold the twenty-four-hour-day view with an unusually rigid chronology that mandates the earth's creation in 4004 B.C. or even in 10000 B.C. None of this means, of course, that we are warranted in postulating the lengthy dates proposed by science and the age-day position, but there is more room in the Genesis account for adding time than some strict solar day theorists have proposed.

What about God creating things with apparent age? Here I am torn in two directions. On the one hand, I agree that this is not deception, since God told us enough in Genesis 1–2 to expect apparent age. That is, Adam and Eve seem to be created as adults, and plants and trees apparently were not created as seeds but in a more mature state. These things fit the notion of apparent age. Moreover, I agree that if light from distant stars, etc., is to be seen on earth at its creation, apparent age is involved there as well. So the proposal makes sense, but I can't see this as conclusive. The reason is that this is a claim that we are capable of neither verifying or falsifying. It makes sense, but no one can go back and verify whether things were created mature with apparent age. So the point about apparent age cannot be conclusive.

Next, we must address Kline's argument about Gen 2:5. This has been conclusive for some, for the details of that verse seem so blatantly to contradict the chapter 1 account that the only way to avoid the contradictions seems to require the literary framework view. However, there is good reason to think Genesis 2 can be harmonized with Genesis 1. In fact, Cassuto has proposed explanations for the items apparently in conflict, and I think they meet the charge of contradiction. This doesn't mean Cassuto holds my position, but only that he shows how one can make the accounts in Genesis 1 and 2 consistent. Let me turn to his explanations.

Cassuto specifically addresses the apparent inconsistency of saying in

chapter 1 that vegetation was created before man and saying in chapter
2 that vegetation appeared after Adam was created. I believe Cassuto's
answers satisfy concerns raised by Kline, Blocher, and others about Gen
2:5. As to the absence of vegetation (2:5), Cassuto explains that a key is the
meaning of the words translated in the NASB "shrub" and "plant." English
rendering may give the impression that these words designate all plants,
trees, etc., in general, and hence, that the writer is saying there was no vegetation at all. But as Cassuto explains, this reads into the text something
that isn't there. The text doesn't teach absence of the vegetable kingdom as
a whole, but says rather that two kinds of vegetation were lacking, the kinds
designated by the words "shrub" and "plant." Hence, there is no inconsistency with the account of day three, once we see that the text doesn't deny
all vegetation but only a certain type.[145]

This may seem counterintuitive, but that is because the English translation
is misleading. The two terms in question are *sîaḥ* and *ʿēseb*, and Cassuto says
that to understand what they mean, we must turn to the end of the story in
chapter 3. The answer appears in 3:17-18. As a result of Adam's sin, God
cursed the ground, and verse 18 explains that this meant that thorns and
thistles would grow and make tilling the ground difficult. Moreover, God
told Adam and Eve that they would eat the plants of the field. The word for
"plants" in 3:18 is *ʿēseb*, the same word as the second term in 2:5. Moreover,
"thorns and thistles" are synonymous with the *sîaḥ* of the field in 2:5, being a
particularization of the general concept conveyed by *sîaḥ*. So, the point about
the *sîaḥ* is that they did not exist until after Adam sinned; hence, they were
not present on the earth in 2:5, prior to Adam's creation.[146]

As to *ʿēseb*, we are told that, as a result of the fall, Adam had to till or cultivate the ground in order to get his food. Gen 3:23 says God expelled Adam
from the Garden to cultivate the ground. The phrase "cultivate the ground"
in 3:23 is the exact same phrase as "to cultivate the ground" in 2:5. But what
is the point? The point is simply that 2:5 is talking about plants that must be
sown and cultivated, as opposed to trees and plants that reproduce themselves
by seed alone (the kind Scripture meticulously points out were created on
day three). So Gen 2:5 does not mean there was no vegetation on earth of
any sort, but rather that the one kind of vegetation, thorns and thistles, was
absent because it hadn't rained, and there was no need for their presence since
Adam hadn't sinned. Moreover, as to the other kind of vegetation (the *ʿēseb* of
the field), it wasn't present, and there was no need for it, because there were
plenty of trees and plants that reproduced themselves from which Adam and
Eve could eat. None of this means that no vegetation at all was present, only
that these two types were absent. Cassuto is well worth quoting at length:

> Thus the term עֵשֶׂב *ʿēsebh of the field* comprises wheat and barley and the
> other kinds of grain from which *bread* is made; and it is obvious that
> the fields of wheat and barley and the like did not exist in the world

until man began *to till the ground*. In the areas, however, that were not tilled, the earth brought forth of its own accord, as a punishment to man, *thorns and thistles*—that שִׂיחַ *śîaḥ of the field* that we see growing profusely to this day in the Land of Israel *after the rains*. How the rain was related to man's punishment and how the ground was irrigated by the waters of the deep before he sinned, we shall see immediately below. Here we must point out that the two reasons given in our verse [for the absence of thorns and grain] follow the same order as the two preceding clauses that they come to explain: no thorns of the field were yet in the earth, because the Lord God *had not caused it to rain* upon the earth, and the grain of the field had not yet sprung up, because *there was no man to till the ground*.

Now we are able to understand why the Torah emphasized in the previous section *the seed* and the *yielding of seed* in connection with the plants. The purpose was to remove the discrepancy that might have been felt to exist between the account of creation given by the ancient poetic tradition and the story of the garden of Eden as recorded by the same tradition. To this end Scripture stressed again and again that the world of vegetation, as it was formed on the third day, was composed of those trees and herbs that naturally reproduce themselves by *seed* alone. Those plants that needed something else, in addition to seed, were excluded: to this category belonged, on the one hand, all species of corn, which, even though isolated specimens might have existed here and there from the very beginning, were not found in the form of fields of grain until man began to till the ground; and on the other hand, thorns and thistles, or שִׂיחַ *śîaḥ of the field*, whose seeds are unable to propagate and grow fresh plants until it rains. After man's fall and expulsion from the garden of Eden, when he was compelled to till the ground and the rains began to come down, there spread through the earth thorns and thistles and fields of wheat.[147]

We can see from this explanation that Gen 2:5 does speak about natural processes. However, the conclusion literary framework proponents draw is erroneous. It does not signify a lengthy time for day three (rather than twenty-four hours), nor does it show us that the account is not chronological because of an alleged conflict between day three in Genesis 1 and this account. Rather, it talks about things that were not yet the case, but would be after the fall. No one denies that after the fall and Adam and Eve's expulsion from the Garden, natural processes take over entirely. Moreover, as Cassuto has shown, the verse doesn't mean absence of all vegetation prior to Adam's creation, but only absence of certain kinds. Some may object that still verse 9 talks of God planting vegetation after Adam is created, but this misses the point, for verses 8 and 9 speak about God's preparation of the Garden of Eden after Adam's creation. It says nothing about vegetation elsewhere in the world.

All of this means that the supposed contradictions between the Genesis 1 and 2 accounts of vegetation are only apparent, not real. Even if one doesn't like this resolution, one must remember that the charge of contradiction means there is no *possible* way for the various claims all to be true. To meet the charge of contradiction, the defender need only show a possible way to fit things together. Cassuto's explanation is a possible way, and it isn't far-fetched, but is grounded in the text.

Several final considerations lead me to think that all of God's creative activities do not require an ancient earth or universe. The first has to do with death as a result of sin. We have already rehearsed the basic argument surrounding Rom 5:12 and Gen 3:19. As noted, many claim that this refers only to the entrance of death into the human race, so animals could live and die on earth for many thousands of years prior to our creation. I find this problematic and have already suggested my concerns, but let me amplify. What seems crucial is Rom 8:18-22. This says that the creation was subjected to futility, but not of its own will (v. 20). Moreover, it was subjected in hope of a removal of that futile state when the sons of God are revealed (v. 21). As Moo, Cranfield, and other able commentators explain, this must refer back to the results of the fall in Genesis 3 and the anticipation of the lifting of the curse when believers are glorified and creation is restored in a coming day. But note also what verse 21 says about creation's subjection. It says that the creation is enslaved to corruption or decay, a corruption that will lift with the revelation of the glory of the sons of God. To what does this decay and corruption refer? Certainly not moral corruption, because animals and plants are not moral agents capable of moral decline. It must refer to physical decay, but doesn't that ultimately involve physical death? If not, then what? Certainly whatever it is, it must be rather painful, since Paul talks about the creation groaning and suffering the pains of childbirth as it awaits its restoration. What can such language mean if not that there is pain and suffering within the natural order? And the most natural understanding of this is that such decay includes death.[148] Hence, it seem that Adam's sin brought death into the whole world, not just into the human race.

In light of these considerations, I conclude that death entered not only the human race but also the animal kingdom through Adam's sin. This is a problem for any view that postulates long periods of time for animals to have been on earth and die prior to Adam. But there is another problem, which relates to the problem of evil. As I have argued elsewhere and will note again in a later chapter of this book, there are many different problems of evil. One that gets little attention is the problem of animal pain and suffering. It isn't my purpose to solve that problem here, but rather to make a point about creation theories. It is difficult enough as is to answer the problem of animal pain and suffering. Postulating vast stretches of time with animals present on earth and preying upon one another (even before the creation of human beings) only exacerbates the problem. If it is hard to know why an all-loving God would allow morally innocent animals to suffer when human beings are around, the problem becomes even worse when one multiplies the animal suffering and death by postulating long epochs of time with only plants and animals on earth. To theistic evolutionists who believe life-forms came from a common ancestor, we can say that the evolutionary process is a tortuously slow one that would involve suffering and death of many animals just to get to human beings. Given God's power to avoid such suffering by creating species by divine *fiat* (theistic evolutionists don't deny God such power, though they believe he didn't exercise it), it becomes almost impossible to imagine how one can solve the problem of animal suffering when it is posed against a scenario of slow evolutionary development. This doesn't mean the problem evaporates if one buys a twenty-four-hour-day version of creationism, but only that the problem is much worse for any position that postulates lengthy periods of time prior to creation of humans when animals are on earth and die.

There is a final reason why I am skeptical about views that postulate eons of time for the creative process, and it relates to divine revelation to the human race. Theologians agree that God has revealed himself through natural revelation and through various forms of special revelation, including Scripture. A critical difference between the two broad categories of revelation, however, is that while natural revelation through our conscience (Rom 2:14-15) gives us the sense that we are guilty of wrongdoing and worthy of punishment, natural revelation does not reveal a means of salvation from the human predicament. Special revelation, especially Scripture, offers God's answer to our problem of sin and our need for salvation. Suppose, however, that the oldest book of the Bible was not written until somewhere between 1500 B.C. (the time of Moses) and 2000 B.C. (the time of Abraham). The final books of the Bible were completed by the end of the first century A.D. But, now, how long were people on earth before getting written revelation from God in any form? At least from Adam to Moses or thereabouts. The OT shows us that God revealed himself to people like Noah, Enoch, and Abraham in special ways, but these people seem to have been unusual cases. We don't sense that most people had such a special revelation from God, and we know they didn't have a Bible. Yet Scripture tells us clearly that, since Adam, human beings have been guilty of sin before God. This means that between Adam and the writing of the first OT book there is a long time, and relatively few people seem to have had any special revelation from God, revelation which could offer them a message of salvation.

This means, among other things, that many people lived between Adam and the writing of Scripture who never would have heard any message of salvation. Some may say that Paul tells us (Rom 5:13) that sin is not imputed when there is no law, and between the time of Adam and Moses there was no formally stated law revealed from God. But this doesn't excuse people from Adam to Moses, for Paul says people still died between Adam and Moses, and they did so because in Adam they had sinned. So these people were guilty of at least one sin (Adam's), but God apparently revealed no remedy, no word of salvation, to most of them. It is already hard enough to uphold God as just in condemning such people, who never heard and never read a Bible because there was none. But if it is hard to defend God for waiting that long to reveal a written message of how to be saved, the problem only intensifies when we start postulating thousands or even millions of years between Adam and the first writing of Scripture. Why would a loving God, knowing their need of salvation, give so many people over such a long time no message explaining the remedy for their problem? While this cannot be a conclusive proof of recent creation and a young earth, it is a significant issue that must be faced by those who postulate that humans have been present on earth for eons of time.

Considerations of the sort mentioned throughout this evaluative section lead me to adopt a modified twenty-four-hour-day proposal of the kind presented. Upon reflection, one can see that the primary arguments for it have been biblical and theological and the primary concern has been to understand fairly what Scripture says about origins. To those who think my case weak because it doesn't appeal to "scientific" data, I only repeat my dictum that the way to determine the meaning of a text is by exegesis of that text, and that theological formulation is to be based on fit with God's Word, not on compatibility with the claims of science or any other extra-biblical discipline. I don't claim that my model of explanation answers all questions and solves all problems. There is surely much that none of us knows. But when we take seriously the fact that these are miracles of the sort mentioned, and when we let Scripture say what the author in his day and culture would have meant, I believe the proposal defended in this section explains best how God created our world and its life-forms.

THIRTEEN

DIVINE PROVIDENCE:
THE DECREE AND HUMAN FREEDOM

God created everything, and by his omnipotent power he lovingly sustains the universe in being. But does God's control over people, events, and actions in our world end there? In discussing the divine attributes, we saw that God is omnipotent and absolutely sovereign, but sometimes sovereigns don't exercise their power so that their subjects may have freedom to do what they want. Is this so in our universe, or is God's hand somehow present (even if not evident) in everything that happens?

These are difficult and controversial issues. In chapter 11, on the divine decree, I argued that there is a divine plan according to which God controls our world and moves all things to his appointed end. Though the biblical evidence for this seems clear, some conservative theologians disagree. It isn't that they deny the biblical evidence already presented, but they contend either that the data cited can be interpreted differently or that this is only part of the story; when all evidence is considered, it isn't clear that the interpretation I have given is the most plausible understanding. To be sure, if a doctrine taught in one set of passages is correct, it can't contradict other clear biblical teaching. Hence, when the idea of the decree conflicts with other things Scripture teaches, there is reason to question the traditional Calvinistic understanding of the decree.

Though issues surrounding the divine decree are contentious, they are too important for both doctrine and practice to bypass. If someone wants to know God's will for his or her life and how to find it, there are several approaches to these questions, depending on how one handles the issues of this and the next chapters. In addition, we are often burdened to give unbelievers the gospel, but does it even matter if we do? Some think that if God determines who will be saved, he will save them regardless of what we do, so we need not witness. Others contend that we must witness, for our witness is the decreed means to the end of their salvation. Yet others say that since no one, including God, knows exactly who will be saved until they freely turn to Christ, we must give the gospel to all people.

In addition to the practical issues, there are other issues that theologians and philosophers have debated for many centuries. For example, if God controls all things and, as Eph 1:11 says, works all things according to the counsel of his will, how can humans have free will in any meaningful sense? Moreover, if God has already decided what will happen, including his own actions, is he no longer free to do otherwise? And if humans are free to choose or reject God's wishes, how can God foreknow their actions? On the other hand, if he does not foreknow our deeds, how can he plan his response before we act?

With so many different issues, how should we proceed? My response stems from a fundamental contention that the watershed issue that broadly divides positions into two main camps is the meaning of human freedom, and whether there is such freedom in our world. Not every theologian and philosopher agrees that we have free will, but many do. Those who do believe that we have free will divide into two camps, one that holds the general thesis of indeterminism and the other that holds determinism. Whatever one believes about free will correlates with some understanding of God's sovereign control in our world.

Because free will is so important and yet the concept of freedom is ambiguous, I propose to begin by describing and defining indeterminism and determinism in their various forms. After clarifying these concepts and stipulating which forms of these views allow human freedom, I will then describe how these notions of freedom fit various concepts of divine control over our world. The models of providence that result from such correlation can be divided into two general categories, general sovereignty and specific sovereignty.

BASIC DEFINITIONS

A complicating factor in defining terms is that the terms and concepts are used in the physical sciences as well as in the sciences that deal with human actions. Nevertheless, we can start with some general definitions, and then narrow our focus to issues that relate to human actions.

Indeterminism

The basic idea of indeterminism is that the state of the world up to a given point plus all existing natural laws are *not* sufficient to guarantee only one possible future. For example, even if one could specify all actions and events that precede a particular decision, all causal influences playing upon the agent's will, plus all laws of nature governing the decision, it would still be just as possible for the person to choose one option as opposed to any other.[1]

Indeterminism can be applied not only to human actions but also to events in the natural world. Because nature is so orderly and appears to run according to physical laws, many assume that indeterminism could not apply to physical occurrences. Moreover, anyone who believes that mind is material and subject to the general laws that govern physical objects might also hold that mind and will as material must also function deterministically whenever choosing. However, indeterminists, regardless of whether they are materialists with respect to the mind, deny that human choices and actions are causally determined. As Edward Sankowski explains:

> "Causal determinism" often means "universal causal determinism," i.e., a determinism applicable to all natural phenomena. And philosophers may discuss the implications for human freedom of determinism on this level. But "causal determinism" may function in a much more modest way in other philosophical discussions of free will. The modesty, which I emulate, is sometimes an expression of agnosticism about whether universal causal determinism is true. On this more modest level of discussion, philosophers inquire into the implications for freedom of causal determinism . . . of particular events or states of affairs. Usually "free will" amounts to "free action" in such discussions.[2]

While some suppose that the Heisenberg indeterminacy principle in physics means that indeterminism is correct in the physical universe, this is not necessarily so. The Heisenberg principle claims that "certain pairs of the variables of motion as defined in fundamental physics are related to each other in a peculiar way: the more accurately one member of the pair is known, the less precisely is the other member specified."[3] This suggests that at the atomic and sub-atomic levels of reality we cannot entirely predict what particles will do. Some conclude that this must mean that larger objects in the material world must also be indeterminate, and others want to transfer this principle about physical reality to the operations of the mind and will.

However, such conclusions seem unwarranted. Although there may be indeterminacy at the atomic and sub-atomic levels of reality, the larger bodies of which those atoms are a part seem to function in a rule-governed way. That is, whatever indeterminacy there is at a micro-level of physical reality does not guarantee indeterminacy at macro-levels. The bulk of scientific evidence, for example, seems to "predispose us toward the deterministic view of macro-physical events."[4] In addition, others wonder whether our ascription of indeterminacy actually reflects the nature of things in the physical world or whether it bespeaks our ignorance of exactly how atomic and sub-atomic particles function. Regardless of the answers to such questions, it is indeed dubious that one should draw any conclusions about whether human actions are free on the basis of principles that relate to how physical reality functions. This is so for both those who believe mind is immaterial and those who think it is material. Mental functioning, including willing, is too complicated for us to reduce human choosing to the level of physical processes. As Francis Gangemi argues, we have no right to conclude anything about human freedom on the basis of whether physical reality is determined or indeterminate. Hence, even if determinism operates at the physical level of our universe, that would not remove the possibility of free human action.[5]

The moral of this story is that determinism and indeterminism can be discussed from a number of different perspectives, and whatever we say about one perspective (for example, the physical sciences) doesn't tell us what to think about a different perspective. My concern in this chapter is not determinism and indeterminism in the physical or natural sciences, but in regard to human action. Hence, let us turn to what indeterminism means in respect to human action.

Indeterminists believe that humans have free will, but that must be clarified. The fundamental idea of indeterministic free will is that genuine free human action is incompatible with (or rules out) causal determinism. Because an agent is not causally determined to choose or do a particular act, regardless of which option the agent chooses, it was possible to choose and do otherwise. This kind of freedom is clearly defined by Alvin Plantinga as follows:

> A person is free with respect to an action A at a time t only if no causal laws and antecedent conditions determine either that he performs A at t or that he refrains from so doing. . . . The freedom of such creatures will no doubt be *limited* by causal laws and antecedent conditions. They will not be free to do just anything; even if I am free, I am not free to run a mile in two minutes. Of course my freedom is also *enhanced* by causal laws; it is only by virtue of such laws that I am free to build a house or walk on the surface of the earth. But if I am free with respect to an action A, then causal laws and antecedent conditions determine neither that I take A nor that I refrain.[6]

This sort of freedom is often called incompatibilism, for it holds that genuine freedom is incompatible with determinism. Others label it contra-causal free will, which means that despite the direction in which the causes, antecedent conditions, and causal laws push an individual at the time of decision making, the person can still choose an option contrary to the direction the causes suggest.[7] Others call this freedom libertarian free will. Whenever I use any of these terms, I am referring to the same thing, unless I specify that I am using a term differently.[8]

Defining the basic notion of libertarian free will, however, does not sufficiently clarify it. Initially, I note that libertarians are not saying that every human action is free in this sense. They agree that sometimes we act under forces that causally determine our act so that it is not free. Still, many acts are free, and libertarians contend that they are free because they are not causally determined; hence, the person could do otherwise.

A second point follows from the first. Some think libertarians are saying that acts are free only if they are uncaused, but this is mistaken. As Peter van

Inwagen explains, the thesis that every action and every event is caused by something or other may well be true, but in no way does it rule out the possibility that many of our actions are free in a libertarian sense.[9] But how can this be so, since it seems that if an act is caused it cannot be free?

Though this sounds confusing, it need not be. To make headway, however, we must distinguish two separate issues. The first is the question of whether an act is or is not caused, and derivatively, what causes a particular action. Causal determinists, of course, hold that every act is caused, perhaps even by a physical event or events that are its causal antecedents. On the other hand, indeterminists deny that actions are causally *determined* or *necessitated* by any physical or mental state, action, or event that precedes them. There are few indeterminists, however, who would claim that a person's actions are totally uncaused, not even caused by the agent who does them.[10] Most hold that the agent causes his or her actions.[11]

So the answer to what causes an action is that the agent does, but this need not mean causal determinism is true; it may mean nothing more than that agents control their own acts. Many determinists agree, i.e., they grant that agents control and cause their own actions. Since both libertarians and their opponents can agree that a person's actions are self-determined, i.e., the agent causes the act, some incorrectly assume that this resolves the debate that has raged for many centuries between indeterminists and determinists over human freedom.[12] Those who think so, however, fail to see a second issue that is different from the question of what causes an act. That second matter asks what causes the agent to act. Granted that everyone causes their own acts, in any instance what caused the agent to choose one action over another? Libertarians and their deterministic counterparts disagree about this. The usual libertarian answer is that when someone acts freely (in the libertarian sense) no causal antecedent nor set of antecedents, laws of nature, or other factors is sufficient to incline the will decisively to choose one option over another. No matter how strong the forces upon the will, the agent could choose another option, even if he doesn't.

To sum up this point, to say that an act was done with libertarian free will doesn't mean it was uncaused, nor does it mean that no factors in any way influenced the agent as he or she chose and acted. The agent caused her own acts, but did not do so because of any causal conditions that decisively inclined her will in one direction rather than another.[13]

Third, some think that if a free act is not causally determined, it must be done for no reason in particular and, hence, is arbitrary or random. This objection assumes that reasons are or at least often function as causes. Of course philosophers debate that, but apart from that debate, the objection to libertarianism is clear enough. If free actions are not causally determined, and if reasons do function as causes, then actions that are free in the libertarian sense must be done for no reason(s) (otherwise they would be causally determined) and thus are random.

Libertarians heartily disagree. They grant that people usually deliberate on a course of action before choosing, and they agree that various reasons enter into the person's thinking. What libertarians typically deny (especially if they hold that reasons can function as causes) is that there is any reason or group of reasons that are strong enough to move the agent decisively to choose one thing over another. Even if a person agrees in light of various reasons and arguments presented that one course of action is preferable, that in no way guarantees that it must be followed. The agent can still refrain and choose another course of action.[14]

Though this point is true of libertarianism in general, in recent years some indeterminists have said that an agent's mental state does in fact cause him or her to do a particular deed. That is, the agent controls her actions through her prior reasons, which may be part of her overall belief-desire mental complex. However, this is not a case of causal *determinism*, for the belief-desire complex doesn't necessitate a particular action. The agent has control over his own mental states, and even if an act is chosen in light of a particular portion of one's beliefs, nothing made it inevitable that he would focus on those reasons and arguments as he did or weigh them as more significant than others. As Timothy O'Connor explains, the ultimate motivation behind these theories represented in the work of thinkers such as Robert Nozick and Robert Kane[15] is two-fold, as it is with libertarianism in general. On the one hand, they believe that for an act to be genuinely free, it cannot be random; it must be under the control of the agent who does it. On the other hand, such theorists believe that agent control must be exercised in a way that allows for alternate possible choices to be made in any given situation. These two requirements, then—agent control and alternative possibilities—are key requirements for freedom from the libertarian perspective.[16] And as just noted, some have argued that an agent's acts are both caused and controlled by the agent and his or her mental states, and yet the actions are indeterminate in the sense mentioned.

Some of the theories just mentioned come extremely close to forms of determinism that hold that humans are free (though not in the libertarian sense). To avoid unnecessary technicalities and confusion and to focus on the view that runs through the theological positions we shall discuss, my primary focus will be on the more standard libertarian theories, which hold that the agent controls and causes his own actions but does so without the will being decisively inclined one way or another by antecedents of the action.

Finally, some correctly note that even if one holds that agents cause their own acts and act in virtue of their own wishes and desires, causal determinism may still creep in unless wishes and desires are formed freely. If events, actions, genetic factors, etc., causally determine what a given person's disposition, preferences, desires, and wishes are, and if choices flow out of that disposition and those preferences, the person in question does not seem to have libertarian free will.

These considerations suggest a distinction between one's wishes and desires, what one actually wills or chooses to do, and the carrying out of those choices.[17] If a person's wishes and choices are indeterminate, but she cannot carry out her choices, she is not free. Someone might freely wish to go shopping and choose to do so, but not be free to do so because of being in jail. Or the hindrance which makes it impossible to do what one wishes and chooses to do might be a factor internal to the person. For example, I might wish and choose to climb Mount Everest, but my overall physical conditioning makes it unlikely that I could. Even if I were physically fit enough to do this, my fear of heights would probably keep me from climbing very far. Thus, in one sense I am free to climb Mount Everest, but in other significant ways I am not.

In accord with these considerations, we can say that to be absolutely free in the indeterministic sense of "free," one must be able to use one's faculties both to choose whatever one wishes to do and to translate those choices into actions without any external hindrances (such as a governmental opposition) or any internal hindrances (such as psychological or physiological problems) that make it impossible to choose and do what one chooses. Moreover, to be absolutely free, one must not only be able to choose what one wishes to do, but the very forming of the wishes or desires must also be totally undetermined by any external or internal factors. If this is freedom in the most absolute sense, then it is dubious that anyone, even God, has such freedom. In God's case, it is likely that even his desires stem from his nature. But none of this should trouble indeterminists unduly, for even if one's desires result from one's nature and experiences, so long as neither those wishes nor any other internal or external factor of the sort mentioned decisively incline the person's *will* in one direction or another, the agent can still choose from among alternate possibilities, and what the libertarian holds seems safeguarded sufficiently. Of course, one must be able to carry out choices in order to be free, but again, the will may still function as libertarians say.

In this section, we have set aside determinism and indeterminism in the physical world (and the natural sciences), and have focused on human action. I haven't factored in matters such as the effects of sin on human ability to choose what pleases God, but such matters will be raised later. For most libertarians, an action is free if it is not causally determined. Moreover, it must be in the agent's control, and lack of causal determination means that there will be alternate actions the agent could just as easily do, regardless of the choice actually made and the act performed.

Determinism

The general thesis of determinism is that for everything that happens, there are conditions such that, given them, nothing else could occur.[18] Many definitions of determinism seem fairly clearly to refer to processes in the natural universe. Sometimes determinism that pertains to the physical world and natural sciences is called LaPlaceian or Russellian determinism. "LaPlaceian determinism is the thesis that given the state of the world at any time, and the laws of nature, the state of the world at any future time is logically determined."[19] The physical world at state one plus relevant causal laws logically necessitate what will be the case at state two.

The reference to Russell is to Bertrand Russell and his concept of causation. In setting forth what Russell called the law of universal causation, we see the sort of causation required by the determinism of which Pierre-Simon, Marquis de LaPlace spoke. Russell explains:

> The law of universal causation . . . may be enunciated as follows: There are such invariable relations between different events at the same or different times that, given the state of the whole universe throughout any finite time, however short, every previous and subsequent event can theoretically be determined as a function of the given events during that time.[20]

This means that a given event A is "*causally determined* if and only if there is some set of actual antecedent events (usually any one of many alternative sets will do), and some set of (actual) causal laws, which together make it *causally necessary* that A occurs. Such a set of antecedent events constitutes a *causally sufficient condition* for the occurrence of A."[21] An implication seems to be that if this determinism actually functions in our universe, then any event (and any action, if this sort of determinism applies to human actions) is traceable to other occurrences that extend backwards in time, perhaps indefinitely.

The kind of determinism described so far relates to the physical or natural sciences, but does it also apply to the social sciences and to human action in particular? For those who hold that all existing things are material, it is likely that determinism must apply to human actions. Some materialists with respect to the mind have thought otherwise, and those who believe mind is immaterial are even less likely to hold that the kind of determinism operative in the physical sciences adequately accounts for human action. Moreover, as already suggested, at the level of physical reality, some cite the Heisenberg principle as evidence that even in the natural world determinism isn't so pervasive as many think. Even among scientists there are some who claim that scientific evidence supports indeterminism in the physical world.[22]

Though some think determinism in the physical world also applies to human action, it is dubious that it does. Moreover, it is critical to understand that Calvinistic determinists with respect to human actions do not mean by determinism the sort which operates in the natural world. Because Calvinist determinists are not postulating that physical determinism governs human actions, objections to Calvinist determinism that misconstrue it as physical determinism are simply misguided and in no way refute Calvinism.

Just because the determinism operative in physical processes doesn't govern human actions according to most Calvinists, that doesn't mean that all determinism is absent from human actions. Many claim that human actions are causally determined in some sense, and among them are many who think that in some sense human actions are free. Moreover, some philosophers distinguish causal determinism from statistical or probabilistic determinism. In the latter case, given past occurrences of an event in circumstances of a certain sort, it is statistically probable that in similar circumstances, the same thing will happen again.[23] My concern is causal determinism (not statistical determinism), because that is the position in view in theological discussions of divine control and human freedom.

FATALISM. There are various forms of determinism, and the most extreme is fatalism. Typically, those who hold it in its most rigorous forms apply it to all natural phenomena as well as to human actions. In philosophical literature one finds several different senses of fatalism. Though we need not describe them all, several are worth noting.

Fatalism is frequently associated with inevitability, but even this needs clarification, for something may be inevitable in one of several respects. One form of fatalism claims that in "every situation, regardless of what we do, the outcome will be unaffected by our efforts."[24] If there were some giant astronomical body headed on a collision course for the earth, regardless of what we would do, it is hard to imagine how we might stop it. But the fatalism and inevitability envisioned goes even deeper. Suppose that a diabetic goes into a glucose shock or that someone has a heart attack and is gasping for breath. We would think it would make a difference in the first case whether we gave the diabetic a shot of insulin or of sugar, and we would believe it mattered dramatically whether we placed an oxygen mask on the heart attack victim or put a pillow over his face, but the fatalism under discussion says that none of these acts would make any difference to the outcome. If it is time for these people to die, they will die no matter what we do, and if it isn't, they will live.[25]

This sort of fatalism is often what people think of when they hear the term. It suggests that everything that ever happens is set in advance, and no one can stop it. In a sense everyone is a victim of fate. Systems of this sort which include God hold that even God is helpless to change a thing. In fact, some proponents of this form of fatalism may hold that God was not free to choose whether to create a world or not; he had to create, and there was only one possible world to create. He wasn't even free to change some items in it before actualizing it.

Some believe that this sort of inevitability is required by determinism and that this fatalism is the only kind there is. Adolf Grünbaum helpfully explains how and why this kind of fatalism relates to the determinist thesis more generally:

> The mere fact that both fatalism and determinism affirm the fixity or determinedness of future outcomes has led some indeterminists to infer fallaciously that determinism is committed to the futility of *all* human effort. The determinist maintains that existing causes determine or fix whether certain efforts will in fact be made at certain times, while allowing that future outcomes are indeed dependent on our efforts in

particular contexts. By contrast, the fatalist holds falsely that such outcomes are always independent of all human efforts. But the determinist's claim of the fixity of the outcome does not entail that the outcome
is independent of our efforts. Hence determinism does not allow the
deduction that human intervention or exertion is futile in every case.[26]

These are very important points, as we shall see when evaluating certain arguments against Calvinistic conceptions of divine sovereign control. For many
opponents seem to think that Calvinism is fatalistic because it is deterministic,
and they conclude that because of this fatalistic inevitability, it makes no difference whether we pray or witness to those who don't know Christ. If God
has already decided what happens and who will be saved, and if whatever
God plans will happen regardless of our efforts, prayer and witnessing become
irrelevant. When we see, however, that determinism does not entail this sort
of fatalism, we also realize that Calvinism doesn't either, and so prayer and
witnessing are not irrelevant. But more on this later.

A second form of fatalism says that there are things I could do in a given situation to change the outcome, but I am ignorant of them. Hence, I might try to do
something to change the outcome, but I would do the wrong thing and would
not escape after all. Van Inwagen says that in such cases, it is weakly inevitable
that something will occur. He offers the example of someone in a burning building. At first he doesn't realize that the building is burning, but he soon will. Van
Inwagen asks that we suppose the following as true of this situation:

> "(i) if I do not try to leave the building, I shall be burned to death; (ii)
> if I try to leave by the nearer exit, I shall be burned to death; (iii) if I
> try to leave by the more remote exit, I shall succeed and save my life;
> (iv) I have no reason to think that either exit is more likely to lead to
> safety than the other, and have no way of finding out if either exit is
> preferable; (v) if I believed I were in danger and saw two routes of pos-
> sible escape, I should always choose the nearer unless I had some good
> reason to regard the more distant as preferable. If (i)-(v) are true, then
> my death by burning is now weakly inevitable for me."[27]

With a final form of fatalism no inevitability attaches to what happens,
but if someone does a particular thing, it is the only thing they could do. If
they fail to do it, they could not have done it anyway. Right now I am writing
this portion of this chapter. According to the fatalism now being considered,
a thousand years ago it was true that I would be doing this at this moment;
in fact, it was true forever that this would be so. Of course, if I were doing
something else now, it would have always been true that I would be doing that
other thing at this moment. From all of this, the fatalist of this sort concludes
that *"irrespective of the antecedent circumstances,* 'nothing that does occur
could have been helped and nothing that has not actually been done could
possibly have been done'."[28] The only option open is the one taken.

It is proper to note that someone might believe in causal determinism and still reject this form of fatalism. Even if I believe that, for example, I act as a result of causes that decisively incline me to choose the act, that doesn't mean I could do nothing else. I had the ability to will and do an alternate act, and if I had done so, a determinist would still say the act was causally determined. So determinism does not necessitate this kind of fatalism. Of course, a key question is what "the person could not have done [could have done] otherwise" means, and we shall discuss that in some detail. However, even at this point it isn't clear that, even if someone does a particular act that is causally determined, there was never anything else he or she could have done.

HARD DETERMINISM. Hard determinism removes the idea of inevitability more than does fatalism. A hard determinist believes that all that happens is causally determined. As a result, there is no human free will of any sort. That is, some hard determinists agree with libertarians that the only notion of genuine freedom is libertarian free will, but they add that since everything is causally determined, no one has such freedom. Other hard determinists might understand free will as soft determinists (described below) do, but still hold that causal conditions are sufficiently strong that no one can actually exercise such freedom.

While hard determinists agree with fatalists about freedom, hard determinism is not fatalism. As to stronger forms of fatalism, a hard determinist would deny that everything is inevitable in that God could not have chosen to forego creating or that once having decided to create, there was only one possible world he could create. Rather, a hard determinist theist would likely grant that God could choose to actualize any possible world he wanted, but then every act and event in that world is causally determined. Moreover, it isn't clear that all hard determinists would say that in any given instance, there is only one thing the agent could do. Some hard determinists might hold such a position, but a hard determinist would not have to do so. Still, even though in any situation the agent has several options and has power to choose and do more than one of them, whatever he chooses is causally determined in such a way as to eliminate any kind of freedom.

Consider, for example, a bank teller confronted by a bank robber who threatens the teller with a gun. The thief orders the teller to give him the bank's money or lose her life. Now this situation certainly doesn't stem from physically determined events in nature in conjunction with laws of nature. Moreover, the bank teller has more than one option; she can hand over the money, refuse and be shot, or try another tactic to escape the situation. Whichever option she chooses, however, hard determinists would say her act was causally determined, and the causes were strong enough to remove her freedom in any sense of the term.

SOFT DETERMINISM. Soft determinists agree that everything that happens is causally determined, but they also believe that some actions are free. The freedom in view, however, is not libertarian free will, so we must clarify what soft determinists mean by freedom. Soft determinism is also called compatibilism, and in order to understand it, we must first define necessity and constraint.

In philosophy, necessity is used in various ways. For example, something necessary is true under all circumstances, i.e., true for all possible worlds. In a related sense, something necessary cannot *not* be. Hence, to say that God exists as a necessary being means he cannot go out of existence, and that he never began to exist. He always existed and is himself the reason and cause for his own existence. Contingent things exist as a result of being brought into being by something else. A further sense of necessity refers to things that cannot be changed. The past is necessary, for nothing can alter it.

Two other senses of necessity are important for our discussion. According to the first—call it necessity$_1$—an act or event is necessary if it must occur. There is no way to avoid or change it. Whatever events and actions God has decreed are necessary in this sense. A second sense of necessity—call it necessity$_2$—refers to acting according to one's internal nature, i.e., spontaneously in light of what a thing is. For example, if I want to move under my own power from one point in a room to another, given my nature as a human being I may do so in various ways (walking, running, crawling, etc.), but I cannot move my arms and legs so as to fly from one point to another. Such abilities are not inherent to my nature. I will probably walk to the new spot, and do so voluntarily, spontaneously, in accord with my nature. I act as I can, given my nature.[29] Acting with necessity$_2$ in a given instance doesn't mean I also act under necessity$_1$. Though I act according to my nature, if I am an indeterminist, I would deny that I act according to necessity$_1$.

As for constraint, in general it is a force that is not part of a person's nature, a force which moves them to act against their wishes. Often, the constraining force is external to the person, though a psychological neurosis might also constrain someone to act against his will. Two specific senses of constraint are relevant for our purposes. The first—call it constraint$_1$—involves a force that doesn't entirely remove willing by the person constrained, although what is chosen is contrary to what they wish to choose. Think again of the bank robbery. The bank teller must exercise her will. She doesn't like either option (Your money or your life!), but she must choose one. She will likely hand over the money, but she does so under constraint.

A second kind of constraint (constraint$_2$) removes willing altogether. The force exerted on the constrained person produces bodily motion, but not movement that their will in any sense brought about. For example, suppose I am standing by the side of the road. A careless driver comes along, and his car veers off the road and strikes me. The force of this jolt propels me twenty feet from the spot where I was standing. I have moved from one point to another, but not of my own choosing. I was constrained even more than in a case of constraint$_1$, for I don't will this moving at all. I am a total victim, a projectile or missile hurled by a force outside of me.

Neither form of constraint leaves room for freedom in any sense. Neither indeterminists nor determinists consider actions done under constraint free. Of course, determinists hold that all actions are causally determined, and at first blush this seems to mean that all acts are constrained and thus unfree. Soft determinists say otherwise, and we can now define their position.

Soft determinism says that genuine free human action is compatible with causal conditions that decisively incline the will without constraining it. The causal conditions are sufficient to move the agent to choose one option over another, but the choice and resultant action are free as long as the person acts without constraint. Acting under constraint means that one is forced to act contrary to one's wishes or desires. Acting without constraint means acting in accord with one's wishes or desires. So, an act is free, though causally determined, if it is what the agent wanted to do. Various factors, including the agent's character and experiences as well as the circumstances surrounding the choice, may have produced the desires she has, but as long as the choice is made in accord with those desires, it is considered free. The agent has mental and volitional ability to choose another option, but given the prevailing circumstances and causes, she will choose the option she does. Adolf Grünbaum speaks about constraint (he uses the term "compulsion") and determinism, and makes this point in regard to physical constraint as follows:

> We act under *compulsion,* in the literal sense relevant here, *when we are literally being physically restrained from without in implementing the desires which we have upon reacting to the total stimulus situation in our environment and are physically made to perform a different act instead.* . . . But *causal determination of voluntary behavior is not identical with what we have called literal compulsion*! For voluntary behavior does not cease to be voluntary and become "compelled" in our literal sense just because there are causes for that behavior.[30]

Several words of explanation are in order. First, compatibilists are not claiming that every action is free in the compatibilist sense. Just as libertarians grant that some acts are causally determined and thus not free, so compatibilists grant that some actions are constrained and unfree. Compatibilists contend that there are free actions and that those actions, though causally determined, are free because they are done in accord with the agent's wishes.

Second, it should be clear that libertarian free will and compatibilism not only are two contrary notions of freedom but they are logically contradictory. The former says that an act is free if it isn't causally determined, while the latter says that an act is free, though causally determined, if the causes are non-constraining. The former says that regardless of what the agent does, it was possible to do otherwise, for the factors playing on the agent's will left the decision indeterminate. The latter says that given the causal factors prevailing at the time of decision, some condition (or set of conditions) was strong enough to guarantee a particular outcome so that there is a sense in which the agent could not have done otherwise. These two positions clearly contradict each other, and thus any viewpoint that incorporates one cannot at the same time incorporate the other without generating a contradiction in the overall system. This is especially important when we recognize that theological Arminianism in its various forms is committed to libertarian free will and that compatibilism is a position many Calvinists would hold. Hence, even though it may be possible to blend some elements of Calvinism and Arminianism, on the central issue of human freedom, the two theological positions contradict each other.

Third, compatibilists agree that it is very difficult to determine in certain cases whether an act was compatibilistically free or constrained. Still, though we may conclude that particular acts were constrained and not free, that doesn't prove that compatibilism is wrong or that there are no free (compatibilistically speaking) acts after all. Similarly, disagreements over which actions are incompatibilistically free do not prove that there are not any such actions at all. Sometimes it is very hard to decide whether an act was free in any sense or unfree. Think, for example, of Paul's conversion on the Damascus Road. A compatibilist could argue that Christ's confrontation of Paul was just what Paul needed to convince him to desire to follow Christ, and that once he had that desire he chose Christ as Savior. Hence, he accepted Christ freely (compatibilistically). Others might say that Paul chose Christ as a result of that experience, but being confronted that way made it clear what Paul had to do, and so out of fear of disobeying, he accepted Christ. He did so under constraint, and thus was not free. I have also heard incompatibilists argue that Paul's decision was free in the libertarian sense. Paul's confrontation by Christ was a major factor in his thinking, but Paul could just as easily have rejected Christ, and his encounter with Christ did not decisively incline his will toward Christ. He just decided to accept him. We need not quibble over instances like these, for regardless of how one understands Paul's conversion, compatibilists and incompatibilists would still hold that there are free actions in their sense, and hard determinists and fatalists would say that no actions are free.

Finally, some may wonder how a compatibilistically free act might occur. The problem doesn't arise when causes move us to do what we want to do, anyway. Nor need there be a problem when we are ambivalent to the various options. In either case, we can easily imagine how causes could move us to act without forcing us to act against our wishes. The real problem arises, however, over actions that we don't want to do. This is especially significant for our theological discussion, for if God has foreordained all things that occur, surely he has decreed that we will do some actions which we don't initially wish to do. An example is salvation of the elect, for if we agree with Scripture that no one on their own is righteous or seeks God, how can God, if he elects us to salvation, bring us to accept Christ without constraining us to choose him?

More will be said below about God bringing about actions that we don't initially wish to do, but I can explain the basic idea behind compatibilistic free will by an illustration. Suppose I am teaching a class, and for some reason I decide that a given student will leave the room before the class ends. There are at least three ways I can bring to pass what I have decided. If I were strong enough (and perhaps ornery enough), I might just walk over to the student, physically pick him up and carry him outside of the classroom. His removal would be an instance of constraint$_2$. No position would say he left the room freely.

Alternately, I could threaten the student. I might say that unless he leaves the room I will give him an *F* for the course. If this doesn't work, I could threaten bodily harm, perhaps even blandishing a gun that I brought to school. In this case, my student really doesn't want to leave because the lecture is so captivating, but on the other hand, he doesn't want to destroy his grade (who would want to take this course again!), and he surely isn't ready to sacrifice his life. So, he makes a decision and reluctantly leaves the room. He did so under constraint$_1$, and neither the libertarian nor the compatibilist would say he left freely.

But there is another way to get the student to leave. I could point out various factors that make it advantageous for him to leave the room, though nothing I say in any way threatens him. He might be so determined to hear the rest of the lecture that it will be hard to convince him to leave. Eventually, I convince him by reason and argument (without threats or warnings of danger if he refuses to go) to leave. Perhaps I know that there will be a wealthy philanthropist outside the door just waiting to give free financial aid to the first five students who ask for help, and I share this information with the student. Hearing this, many others may also leave, but nevertheless I accomplish what I decided would happen. Though my student didn't originally want to leave, considering all the pros and cons of staying or leaving, his desire to stay changed to a desire to leave, and he then acted on that new desire. In this instance, the libertarian would likely say the act was causally determined and thus unfree. The soft determinist would say that though the act was causally determined, the student was not constrained to leave but did so voluntarily (in accord with his nature—necessity$_2$), according to his wishes and thus freely.

Other Definitions

I have defined the two major senses of free will, but those definitions come from philosophy of action, apart from any theological concepts. There are some other definitions which include theological concepts.

CALVIN ON "FREE WILL." Commentators on John Calvin note that he used "free will" in three basic senses. First, he used it of Adam's freedom before the fall. That freedom was having the power or ability to choose equally between good and evil. Prior to the fall it was just as easy for Adam to choose good as to choose evil, for not having sinned, he wasn't weighed down by a sin nature that inclined him toward evil. Of course, once Adam and Eve sinned, this freedom was lost.

Calvin also used "free will" to refer to choosing only good. Here theological and biblical teaching about the devastating effects of evil in one's life is invoked. Calvin thought that the will that chooses only good is the truly free will. This can happen in this life, of course, only through the assistance of divine grace. Though that grace is available, we don't always use it to choose good. In light of this sense of free will, in our glorified state we will be the most free, for then it will be impossible to choose or do evil. An indeterminist, looking at the matter solely from the perspective of philosophy of action, would not agree, for someone in a glorified state has only one alternative at any time: choosing good. Even soft determinists might say that since glorified people cannot sin, something must constrain them from doing so. Calvin's point, however, is about the bondage and enslavement of sin of which Scripture speaks so clearly. To be free of the ability to sin, and to be rid of its consequences in one's life, from a theological perspective, is far greater freedom than merely having the ability to do either good or evil—even better than being free to do both equally, as Adam was before the fall.

Calvin also uses "free will" in a third sense, which accords more with secular action theory. He speaks of a voluntary will, which means that a person's decisions are based on their internal nature, not on some external force. Hence, the person acts spontaneously, in accord with what their nature causes them to do. This sort of free will incorporates necessity$_2$, and it is also most consistent with compatibilism, for it grants that a person's actions may stem from his nature and, hence, be causally determined. Moreover, because Calvin held that God decrees and controls all things, this third kind of freedom cannot be libertarian freedom, for divine control involves determinism, which libertarianism rejects. So Calvin believed that our acts are governed by God, but he called them free in that they stem from our nature and are not forced upon us against our will. This is the basic idea of compatibilism.

BOUND WILL.   Calvin also speaks of a bound will. This blends both theological and action theory ideas. Calvin says that our wills are bound as a slave to sin, and hence we cannot do anything in our natural state but sin. However, this doesn't mean we sin against our will, for we sin spontaneously and voluntarily in accord with our desires. As unregenerate, we only desire what displeases God. So the unregenerate condition is that we have voluntary free will, i.e., we act spontaneously according to our nature, but since the spontaneous thing for us is to sin, our will is in bondage to sin. For Calvin, the unregenerate can never do good spontaneously, and hence the highest freedom (in his opinion), doing only good, is not something they can attain on their own. Only when someone turns to Christ is the will's bondage broken. A new nature is implanted, even though the old sin nature also remains, and through God's grace and enablement, the regenerate person can will the good. Unfortunately, believers often choose to act in line with their old nature and commit sin, but the good news is that we no longer need to be enslaved to sin (Rom 6:14-18).

Nonbelievers have bound wills, but they exercise them in accord with their wishes, and hence freely (voluntarily without constraint) commit sin.[31]

Proponents of libertarian free will and indeterminism would not necessarily agree with these definitions from Calvin. For one thing, voluntary free will need not be libertarian free will and is not as Calvin and Calvinists use it, so indeterminists would be dubious about it. As to Adam's freedom before the fall, libertarians would likely say that Adam had a greater inclination to good than he did after the fall. However, if humans have libertarian free will after Adam's fall, then even a sin nature cannot causally determine them to sin. As to true freedom involving only choosing good, philosophical indeterminism would not count this as any freedom, especially if people cannot do evil because they are glorified. Divine enablement to do good and glorification which makes it impossible to do evil would both count as causal determinism, and hence there would be no freedom in the libertarian sense. Still, the libertarian could grant on theological grounds that it is truly liberating to be rid of the effects of sin in one's life. Hence, they might also agree that someone who sins repeatedly is in bondage to sin, though libertarian free will makes it possible to avoid sin at any time. If someone is so steeped in sin that they cannot choose good and are always moved to do evil, libertarians would deny that those sinful acts are free (in the libertarian sense).

CAUSE. A final concept worth clarifying is what it means to cause something. In a very helpful discussion, Lionel Kenner distinguishes six senses in which we might use the word "cause." In the first, we might say that someone's comment caused us to doubt his sanity. What he said was so strange that only an insane person would make such claims.

A second use of "cause" involves cases when a police officer says that he caused a criminal to be arrested. This means that in his capacity as a law officer, he gave an order which was carried out by his subordinates. A third use of "cause" appears in analyses of the causes of the decline of the Roman Empire, or the causes of the rise of communism. In each of these cases, giving the causes gives the course of what is to be explained. Then, there is the use of "cause" in the social sciences. Here we might talk about the causes of teen-age pregnancy, or what causes someone to become a drug addict. These cases refer not only to events that led to such states of affairs, but also to the motives and reasonings that produced them.

There is a fifth sense in which we use "cause." Here we might say that the chance of seeing the Mona Lisa caused me to visit the Louvre in Paris, or the possibility of seeing Michelangelo's Last Judgment caused me to go to the Sistine Chapel in the Vatican in Rome. What causes us to do either of these things is the purpose we had in mind when we decided to visit those places. A final sense of causality is natural causality or causality as it occurs in nature. Here we might say that a bolt of lightning caused a forest fire or a certain substance rubbing against our skin caused a rash.[32]

As Kenner rightly states, the concept of causation typically associated with determinism is natural causality. This causation is said to stem from the state of affairs prior to an event plus the laws of nature. As Kenner shows, if this is the kind of causality and determinism in view, the first five senses of "cause" are not relevant to it. Moreover, we already noted that determinism in the natural sciences must not be confused with determinism in the social sciences. But, then, this sixth sort of causation is not likely what we mean when we say someone's act is causally determined.

Kenner later quotes A. J. Ayer's explanation of why something being caused doesn't necessarily mean that it is compelled (or to use our word, constrained). Ayer says in "Freedom and Necessity,"

> A correct analysis of 'cause' will show that causes do not compel. For
> . . . all that is needed for one event to be the cause of another event is
> that, in the given circumstances, the event which is said to be the effect
> would not have occurred if it had not been for the occurrence of the
> event which is said to be the cause, or *vice versa,* according as causes
> are interpreted as necessary or sufficient conditions. . . . In short, there
> is an invariable concomitance between two classes of events, but there
> is no compulsion in any but a metaphorical sense.[33]

From this we may say that for something to cause an act or event means that it is sufficient to bring it about. When someone, for example, acts compatibilistically freely, she does so in virtue of the various factors (events, reasons, arguments, etc.) that play upon her will and move her to do a particular deed. If the causes that bring about an action are of the sort involved in natural causality, we might say that the act is not only determined but is determined in a way that disallows any freedom, for forces outside the agent's will guaranteed the action's occurrence apart from the agent's wishes. On the other hand, none of the other five senses of cause require such compulsion and hence could fit soft deterministic free will.[34]

In sum, to cause an event or action is to be the condition(s) sufficient to bring about its occurrence. However, we must look closely to see what kind of causality is involved in a given case before we conclude that the event or action being caused removes the possibility of it being free in any sense of that term.

MODELS OF PROVIDENCE

The English word "providence" comes from the Latin *providentia,* and that term corresponds to the Greek *pronoia.* Literally, it means foresight or pre-science, but it is used to convey other theological truths. Foresight refers to God's plans for the future, but also to the realization of those plans. Hence, in theological discussions providence "has come to signify the provision which God makes for the ends of His government, and the preservation and government of all His creatures."[35] As Paul Helm reminds us, God's providence most fundamentally refers to the fact that God provides, and does so continually. The key is for whom he provides, what he provides, and how he does it.[36]

Though God provides sometimes by miraculous intervention in our world, Brian Hebblethwaite reminds us that typically theologians distinguish direct miraculous intervention from divine providence. As to the latter, it normally refers to God's action "in and through natural agencies to bring about his purposes."[37] Suppose Joe plans to leave work at a certain time, but is delayed by a phone call and leaves five minutes later than planned. Along his route home, he comes to an intersection where there has been a horrible automobile accident. Those involved are severely injured, and ambulances have already started taking them to the hospital. Joe asks how long ago this happened, and is told that it occurred about five minutes ago. Joe realizes that had he left work when he had planned, he likely would have been involved in the accident. He might see the phone call as a lucky break, but being a religious sort, he reasons that the phone call was providential. He sees God's hand in the ordinary course of events, keeping him from serious harm and injury. Those involved in the accident may ask where God's protecting hand was, but Joe will still view his late departure from work as providential.

Examples like this raise questions about the extent to which God governs our world and how he does so. Throughout church history there have been debates over such matters. Few Christians deny God's sovereignty over creation, but they don't all agree as to how he exercises it. A major reason for such debates has to do with the topic already discussed in this chapter—free will. If humans have free will in some sense, how can it operate in a world governed by an omnipotent, sovereign God? Does it matter whether humans are free incompatibilistically as opposed to compatibilistically as to the kind of control God exercises in our world?

Answers to such questions have generated what I shall call different models of providence. A model of providence is an explanatory attempt to correlate divine sovereign control and governance of the world with the actions of God's creatures, especially humans. All models of providence in evangelical Christianity agree that God preserves the created universe in being. Likewise, they agree that God established a system of moral governance for this world. Where they disagree is over how and how much God intervenes in our world to achieve his goals, and what that intervention does to human freedom.

General Sovereignty vs. Specific Sovereignty

Broadly speaking, Christian models of providence divide into two categories: models that postulate God's *general sovereign control* and models that espouse his *specific sovereign control* over our world. Let me describe each.

General sovereignty models hold that in creating our world God decided to give humans free will, i.e., libertarian free will. If humans have such freedom, God cannot control their free actions. Therefore, "to the degree to which God gives us freedom, he does not control earthly affairs."[38] This doesn't mean that God does not get any of his goals accomplished, but only that he sovereignly chose to create a world in which he "sets up general structures or an overall framework for meaning and allows the creatures significant input into exactly how things will turn out."[39] The key with general sovereignty models is that God does not have specific purposes for everything that occurs, for how could he actualize such purposes without often overriding free will? Instead, God has general purposes that he accomplishes within the overall framework of the room that our freedom leaves him to maneuver. As David and Randall Basinger explain, some who hold general sovereignty see God frequently overriding freedom by directly intervening to accomplish his goals. Others see God doing this much less frequently, and some, such as process theists, see God's action as only persuasive, so that he never overrides human freedom. Within more traditional Christianity, most proponents of general sovereignty fall somewhere between process theism and the view that God frequently contravenes our freedom to accomplish his ends.[40]

Clearly, according to general sovereignty models of providence, God has significantly limited what he can do and control. In deciding so to limit himself, God took a risk. In fact, those who hold that God does not or cannot know how humans will use their freedom see every moment of history as somewhat risky for God.

Advocates of general sovereignty see none of this as detrimental to their theology. In fact, they see these things as recommendations for their views. If one holds libertarian free will and limits God's control of what happens, one removes the need to explain how even the most horrible tragedy somehow happens according to God's will and fulfills his ends. Moreover, God's willingness to take risks with his creation shows how much he loves us and wants to maintain the integrity of our freedom. Coordinately, he knows that when we do follow him, we do so because we want to, not because we were decreed to do so. Proponents of such models of providence see this situation as a win-win situation for both God and us. John Sanders, an advocate of the open view of God (which limits God's control to accomplishing only his general purposes) explains general sovereignty as follows:

> Since God macromanages the overall project (while remaining free to micromanage some things), God takes risks in governing the world. In contrast to specific sovereignty, this model does not claim that God has a specific purpose for each and every event which happens. Instead, God has general purposes in connection with the achievement of the divine project. Within these general structures God permits things to happen, both good and bad, that he does not specifically intend. Yet God may act to bring about a specific event in order to bring the divine

project to fruition. The incarnation and the exodus are examples of God's electing to bring about particular events. . . .

God's normal way of operating is to allow the creatures significant freedom and, consequently, not to control everything. Even when God wants humans to perform some particular task, God works to persuade free creatures to love God and serve him instead of forcing them to do so. Take Moses, for example. He was chosen by God for a specific purpose . . . yet God did not force his cooperation. . . . But most of the Israelites (and most of us) are not chosen for specific roles. Take the case of Susan. That Susan has a job with excellent benefits is part of the general structure of the world in which God gives humans the freedom to create and staff jobs. Whether her work helps fulfill God's project depends on her and her relationship with God. If she is raped and dismembered, it is not the case that God specifically chose her to experience that horror. General sovereignty allows for things to happen that are not part of God's plan for our lives; it allows for pointless evil.[41]

The other kind of model of providence is specific sovereignty. Sometimes specific sovereignty is called meticulous providence. In contrast to general sovereignty, specific sovereignty claims that God does have a plan for all things. Moreover, advocates of this view typically believe that God has foreordained and controls everything that happens so as always to accomplish his ends. Even if he doesn't want us to sin on a given occasion, it still in some way is part of God's overall plan and contributes to his purposes (though we may not know what those purposes are in a case of tragedy). Hence, God exhaustively controls whatever occurs, even if he does not exercise causal power to bring about certain things and even though he is not the proximate cause and/or doer of much that happens.

Typically, those who describe specific sovereignty are its critics, so they speak of micromanaging actions and events, bringing about sin and evil, and choosing or electing someone to be raped and dismembered.[42] Such language is, of course, highly emotive and unfortunate in that regard, but in addition, much of it tends to misrepresent what advocates of specific sovereignty actually hold. Fundamentally, specific sovereignty is a logical outgrowth of belief in the divine decree which is based solely on the counsel of God's will (unconditional in the first sense explained in chapter 11). God knows everything that will happen, because he decided in eternity past what would happen. Though espousers of specific sovereignty deny that God unilaterally and directly does all things, nonetheless, they typically agree that God somehow works out everything he has decreed. Exactly how he does this will be explained as we proceed, but this model of providence raises other questions as well. If God has decreed and controls everything, using it to accomplish his ends, how can there be any meaningful human free will? God's power seems unlimited, and accordingly, no power seems to be left for human beings. Some proponents of specific sovereignty conclude just that, but others disagree. Those who hold that humans still have free will, despite divine control, understand freedom as compatibilistic free will.

Specific sovereignty also raises problems about human and divine moral responsibility for what happens. If God decreed that we will sin and we do what God decreed, why should we be morally guilty for following God's plan? Moreover, since God decreed evil, why isn't he guilty to some extent? And if God totally controls our world, why doesn't he stop much of the evil that is all around us? That he doesn't seems a major strike against this model of divine sovereign control.

Some of these questions will be addressed in this chapter, but others relate to the problem of evil, a subject for chapter 16. From the preceding, one might think there are no advantages to a specific sovereignty model, only problems, but that is not necessarily so. For example, from a practical standpoint it is tremendously encouraging to know that the all-powerful, all-wise God has already planned everything that will happen to us. Nothing will catch him unprepared or off guard. Though we may not know how to escape difficult circumstances, and though we may not see how God will bring good out of evil situations, it can be very reassuring to know that God has already figured this out. Moreover, he has chosen only things that will contribute to his ulti-mate goals for our universe and specific goals for our lives. This may be dif-ficult to swallow at a time of crisis, but no less troublesome than those general sovereignty models which hold that God won't likely contravene someone's freedom even if doing so would save the person from horrific evil. And if the general sovereignty model denies that God foreknows the future, then perhaps we will wind up dealing with some terrible problem that would not have been part of any possible world God would have chosen if he exercised specific sovereignty and decreed a world before creating it.

In sum, there are varieties of both specific and general sovereignty models of providence. General sovereignty proponents are invariably indeterminists of some sort, holding libertarian free will. Advocates of specific sovereignty usually hold some form of determinism. Those who believe that despite divine control, humans have and exercise free will mean compatibilistic free will, not incompatibilism. Throughout church history many have thought it impos-sible to synthesize divine sovereignty and human freedom, but this is not so. In what follows, I shall present a series of ways to relate those two concepts.

GENERAL SOVEREIGNTY MODELS OF PROVIDENCE.   I shall describe three gen-eral sovereignty models of providence. Each is a free will theism, which means that each incorporates libertarian free will. I will focus on a more traditional Arminian approach, and on a model I shall label paradox indeterminism, and on the open view of God.

Traditional Arminian theologies hold that humans have libertarian free will. They contend that God deemed it better to create people with such freedom than to create robots or automata. If God had created us without freedom, he could guarantee our love and obedience, but it would be forced love and obedience. On the other hand, if God gave us libertarian free will, he could not guarantee that we would love him, but those who do would love him because we want to, not because we are forced. God concluded that love from such creatures was worth the risk that we might go our own way.

If humans have such freedom, how can God exercise sovereign control over our world? Arminian systems answer in various ways, but usually say that God has basic plans and goals he wants accomplished, but must leave the rest of what occurs up to his creatures. For some Arminians this means that God exercises only very limited power, perhaps even because he only *has* a limited amount of power. God can perform a miracle to achieve his goals, but he does not usually do so. A more typical Arminian perspective is that God is just as absolutely sovereign as strong Calvinism claims, but to make room for libertarian free will, God foregoes exercising his power and control much of the time. Since that decision is God's own and is not forced on him, it in no way limits his sovereignty. In reply to those who think God would not cede use of his power, Arminians have two basic answers. They first point to the incarnation as a prime example of God doing just that. Phil 2:5-7 teaches that Christ took on a full human nature. In so doing, he emptied himself, and as argued elsewhere,[43] the best understanding of the emptying is not that he gave up his divine nature but that he set aside the *use* of his power and privileges to serve our needs.

The second factor that leads Arminians to conclude that God limited use of his power is biblical teaching on human free will. If humans can fall into sin and even apostatize once saved (2 Pet 2:20-21; Heb 6:4-6), God must limit his ability to impose his will on us. Since Scripture portrays humans as free (Arminians conclude that this is libertarian freedom), something must give somewhere. They conclude that God lovingly yields the exercise of some of his power to make room for our freedom. Of course, God still works in our world. For example, Arminians believe that God gives each person prevenient grace, with which they can cooperate to turn to Christ. So God is not idle, but we are always free to use grace to choose Christ and free to reject it and turn our own way.

Some may still wonder how God can guarantee that any of his goals are achieved, given libertarian freedom. Most traditional Arminians answer that God knows the future, so he can plan in advance how he will respond to our actions so as to accomplish his goals. As to how divine foreknowledge can be reconciled with libertarian free will, Arminians have offered several responses, which we shall discuss in detail in chapter 15.

A second general sovereignty model of divine providence can be called *paradox indeterminism.* According to this model, God is absolutely sovereign over everything; Scripture requires it. In addition, humans have libertarian free will; Scripture portrays humans as free, and this must mean libertarian freedom. Often, advocates of this view are either unaware of compatibilistic free will or they know of it but believe it isn't genuine free will.

The strong view of divine sovereignty espoused by this position doesn't fit with libertarian freedom. Defenders of this approach recognize the inconsistency but feel that Scripture requires both concepts. As to how divine sovereignty avoids contradicting libertarian free will, proponents answer that the resolution is a paradox. God knows how these concepts fit together, but we don't. Still, paradox indeterminists believe they must hold both views in tension, because Scripture teaches both.

A third general sovereignty model of providence is proposed by the *open view* of God. The open view sees God as a risk taker. While this model has much in common with traditional Arminian positions, there are also significant differences. The greatest point of agreement is on the matter of libertarian free will and its implications for divine sovereign control. John Sanders explains that general sovereignty positions do not require God to have a plan for everything that happens, and Sanders's open view adopts that position. Sanders and other open view advocates claim that God has general goals that he hopes to accomplish, but usually he does so within the limits of circumstances his free creatures give him to work with. Hence, God may expect to accomplish a goal in one way, only to learn once his free creatures act that he must choose another way to meet his ends, since his creatures' acts remove God's first option.[44] Of course, God's only way to reach a given goal may be to override our freedom. God always retains the right to do so, though this is not his typical way of achieving his purposes.[45]

The open view sees room for human libertarian freedom, because it, too, claims that God decided to forego use of his sovereign power in many cases. Since this was God's decision and no one forced it upon him, it is totally consistent with the contention that God is absolutely sovereign. As evidence that God decided to limit use of his power, open view proponents again point to Christ, but they add that Scripture shows various instances when God planned to do one thing but changed his mind when one of his creatures presented a case against his plans. For example, Exodus 32–34 records the breaking and renewing of the covenant between God and Israel. God was furious with Israel for worshiping the golden calf, and intended to destroy her, but Moses persuaded God to change his mind and forego punishment.[46] This and other instances, open view proponents claim, show that God does not demand that he always get his way.

In response, some may complain that if this interpretation of these incidents is correct, God must be mutable, contrary to traditional Christian theism. Defenders of the open view agree, but that is part of their point. They reject the classic Christian view of an absolutely immutable, impassible, simple, and atemporally eternal God. Doing so, they argue, results in a God who is much more sensitive to his creatures' needs and more interactive with them. Scriptures that show God changing his mind, grieving, or responding to the needs of his people must be taken literally. They are part of an overall case that God is not a power-mongering monarch, but a responsive, sensitive, caring God. Though many current theologians are rejecting some of these traditional divine attributes, many traditional Arminians still hold them. So, one difference between the open view and many traditional Arminians is their perception of these divine attributes.[47]

Perhaps the greatest difference between the open view and more traditional Arminian forms of free will theism is their account of divine knowledge. Most Arminians hold that God exhaustively knows future events and actions. On the other hand, many secular philosophers holding libertarian free will, and open view defenders, say that God does not have exhaustive knowledge of the future. Rather, he possesses what open view advocates call present knowledge. Present knowledge is complete knowledge of the past and the present. From that knowledge, God may be able to predict with fairly good accuracy what some people will do in the not-too-distant future, but there are no guarantees. God has little, if any, knowledge of what people will do in the more distant future. He must wait to see what happens, and then decide how to respond. As a result, some of his plans may have to be scrapped, and other goals may need to be accomplished in other ways than he intended.

SPECIFIC SOVEREIGNTY MODELS OF PROVIDENCE.   There are many possible variations of the specific sovereignty model, but I shall focus on three. Specific sovereignty models of providence are deterministic in nature, and usually reflect some form of Calvinism.

According to an initial specific sovereignty approach, everything that happens is decreed in advance by God. His decree is unconditional, based solely on his will and desires. Of course, if God has such control over all things, there is really no room for human free will. Proponents of this model usually think that free will, if there were such a thing, would be libertarian, but the divine control they propose eliminates libertarian free will. Theologies of this sort incorporate what was described earlier as hard determinism. Hence, God chose the possible world he wanted and decided whatever happens in it. This doesn't mean that God does everything, for he is never the proximate cause of evil nor does he tempt anyone to do it. Nor does he perform our morally neutral and morally good deeds. We do these actions, but not freely in any sense.

Such hard determinist theologies tend to emphasize the absolute transcendence and sovereign power of God in contrast to the puniness of his creatures. Depending on the theology involved, God's control removes not only human free will but also our moral responsibility. More typically, however, within strong Calvinist forms of hard determinism, humans are still held morally responsible. Rejecting human freedom doesn't mean that we are robots, but only that since our acts are causally determined, they cannot be free. To those who think that holding humans morally responsible in such a world is unfair, the answer is typically that God as sovereign has the right to set up any scheme of moral governance he wants, and there is no room for us to debate him about that or to accuse him of wrongdoing. Defenders of this view often add that sinners, though their acts are causally determined, sin very willingly; no one forces them to commit sin against their will. Hence, they are justly guilty before God. Those who still think this is unfair are wrong, because Scripture says God is just, so whatever he does must be fair.[48]

Since God foreordains everything, he also decrees evil. Some theologies, attempting to maintain God's control over what happens in our world without implicating him in evil, claim that God permits evil deeds, but he doesn't positively will them. In contrast, the hard determinist model of specific sovereignty usually says that God does not just permit evil but specifically wills it to occur. We may not understand how, but even evil serves God's purposes. As Paul said about Pharaoh's hardening, God did it so as to use Pharaoh as an object lesson of God's power and superiority (Rom 9:17). Proponents of such views often believe that God doesn't merely pass over the non-elect and leave them in their unregenerate state, but he actively decrees their reprobation. Hence, this kind of theology frequently teaches a double decree, that is, some are elected to salvation while the rest are chosen for damnation.

As to divine omniscience, these theologies believe that God has exhaustive and infallible knowledge of the future. This is so in part because he foreordained everything that will happen. Hence, biblical prophecies about the future are not educated guesses or hunches; they are instances when God shares with us beforehand portions of his decree. Nothing can surprise God, for he knows everything and has planned whatever happens.

The God described is often also thought to have the traditional attributes predicated of the classical Christian God (strong immutability, impassibility, atemporal eternity, simplicity, aseity). Though it is logically possible to hold this hard determinist approach and reject one or more of these attributes, that is not usually the case. Moreover, the God described in the last few paragraphs is often thought to be the quintessence of Calvinist thinking. This view is caricatured as teaching that because God controls everything, we need not witness or pray, for whatever will be, will be; God has already decided it. Though the caricature isn't true of many who hold this form of Calvinism, in light of the basic commitments this view espouses, the caricature is understandable even though it is wrong. Sadly, open view advocates at times give the impression that in refuting this form of specific sovereignty they have made a good case against all forms of specific sovereignty. Attacking one's opponents' views in their most radical expression often ensures that one wins the debate, but it usually presents a false dichotomy of options (either "my" view or this outrageous position I'm attacking), and it doesn't engage the most significant ideas of all forms of the view which are portrayed most sanely in moderate forms of the position.

A second specific sovereignty position can be called paradox determinism. As with paradox indeterminism, this view requires several concepts to be held in tension. Proponents of paradox determinism believe that God is absolutely sovereign over everything; he has foreordained whatever happens, and whatever he decreed will happen. Paradox determinists agree that if God has such control over our world, there is no room for libertarian free will. Believing that the only possible free will is libertarian freedom, paradox determinists conclude that humans are not free. In addition, philosophers and theologians maintain that no one is morally responsible for doing what they could not fail to do, or for failing to do what they could not do; that is, no one is morally accountable for an act unless they do it freely. In light of this ethical principle, we would expect paradox determinists to hold that humans are not morally responsible for their actions, since they don't do them freely. Instead, paradox determinists say that humans are morally culpable for their actions because Scripture clearly teaches this. How this strong divine sovereignty fits with human moral responsibility when it removes free will is a paradox we cannot explain. Still, since Scripture demands a strong sense of both divine sovereignty and human moral responsibility, we must hold these ideas in tension.[49]

A final form of specific sovereignty is the position I am defending in this book. The God espoused in this view is definitely king, but he is a king who cares. My model incorporates compatibilistic free will, which claims that even though actions are causally determined, they are still free as long as the agents act according to their wishes, i.e., without constraint. According to this model of sovereignty, God did not have to create anything, but having decided to create, he chose our world from among a number of possible worlds. His decision to create this world was unconditional, i.e., it was based on nothing other than his sovereign purposes and the counsel of his will. Because the decree is efficacious (as we saw in chapter 11), whatever God decrees comes to pass, and Scripture teaches that the decree covers all things. Hence, God is absolutely sovereign and has not limited that sovereignty to make room for libertarian free will.

Still, humans have free will. Those who think libertarian freedom is the only possible kind of freedom are mistaken. Compatibilistic/soft deterministic freedom is not self-contradictory, and it offers a way to harmonize human freedom with a strong sense of divine sovereignty. How it does so needs some explaining, and I turn to that now.

To say that God decrees all things and works them out according to the counsel of his will means that he decrees every action and event, and the means to those actions and events. These actions and events are part of a whole interconnected world, so God can will means to ends and can see how his plans for one person affect his plans for others. Divine omniscience lets God see all the interconnections of everything in any possible world, and divine power allows him to bring about whatever possible world he chooses.[50]

Scripture says that God not only wills all things but also works them out according to his foreordained plan (Eph 1:11). This doesn't mean that God does every action that ever occurs, but to explain this, we must introduce further distinctions. The first is between God's immediate and mediate agency. To say that God acts immediately means that he doesn't use any intermediary agents to perform a given deed, but does it entirely himself. Scripture portrays God as acting this way on various occasions, but he never acts this way (or mediately) to do evil.

While God does some things immediately, he does most things mediately through his creatures' (humans, angels, animals) actions. God has decreed our acts, and some may think this makes him the ultimate cause of our deeds. I hesitate to say this, because it tends to treat the decree as an agent with causal efficacy, whereas I argued in chapter 11 that the decree is not an agent of any sort, but rather a blueprint for what happens. The doing of that blueprint, of course, involves various agents exerting causal power, but the decree is not such an agent.

As to the doing of actions, several years ago a symposium appeared in *Christian Scholar's Review,* sparked by an article by George Mavrodes titled "Is There Anything Which God Does Not Do?" Mavrodes cites Amos 3:6, which asks, "If a calamity occurs in a city has not the LORD done it?" Mavrodes replies, "His question seems to expect the answer, 'No, no evil befalls a city unless the Lord has done it.' And that rhetorical question, along with its expected answer, suggests the following generalization: *Whatever is done, God is the doer of it.*"[51] Mavrodes takes as a paradigm case the hardening of Pharaoh's heart, a deed attributed to both God and Pharaoh. Mavrodes searches for an explanation of how God can be the doer of all things, even evil. He offers four options, rejects them all, and then writes, "if it is a truth that God hardened Pharaoh's heart, then I do not know what truth that is."[52]

It was my privilege to participate in that symposium, and in explaining how God can be involved mediately in doing things like hardening Pharaoh's heart, I introduced and illustrated a distinction. It helps to explain my soft determinist model of specific sovereignty, so I introduce it here. I suggested that when God does something mediately, he can do it in at least one of two ways. In the first, the creature is the proximate cause of the act, his efforts being the sufficient condition that produces the deed. On the other hand, God's action in such instances is more remote. As to the second kind of divine mediate action, God may be the remote cause in some sense, but along with the creature, he is also the proximate cause of the act. What God does as part of the proximate cause differs from what his creature does, but their joint efforts produce the intended end.

As an example of the former kind of divine mediate action, I cited God's use of Assyria to judge the Northern Kingdom of Israel. Of course, God decreed this beforehand, but Isa 7:18-20; 8:6-8; and 10:5-6 also clarify that in some way God incited the Assyrians to attack Israel. He used Assyria's action to punish Israel, but the proximate cause of the destruction was clearly the Assyrian army. A further example is God's part in Job's afflictions. Satan brought those trials on Job and his family, but Job 1–2 shows God also involved in granting permission to do this.

As to the second type of divine mediate action, an example is the inspiration of Scripture. God decided to reveal himself to us and he moved the biblical writers to write his Word (he was the remote cause of their writing in that sense). But God did more than give the writers a general order or assignment to write. Second Peter 1:21 says that as the writers wrote, the Holy Spirit bore them along (the Greek is *pheromenoi,* a present participle indicating God's continual action). Hence, they wrote at the Holy Spirit's promptings and under his supervision; he was involved at all times of their writing, but they actually wrote the words; they were not just taking dictation. So, both the Holy Spirit and the human writer were the proximate cause of Scripture's writing.

In sum, God does some things immediately, but most things mediately in one of the two ways just explained. Critics of a soft determinist model of specific sovereignty wonder how God can accomplish his decree without removing our compatibilistic free will, especially if he wants us to do something we don't want to do. Moreover, they also wonder how we can be accountable morally for doing the evil God decrees, and how he escapes culpability as the one who decrees everything that happens.

In reply, we must first remember that God creates none of us in isolation from our environment and from other people alive at the time. Hence, by coming into this world and living from day to day we find ourselves in various circumstances interacting with many different people. Many things we do each day are morally neutral and are part of our daily routine. It is unlikely that God needs to rearrange circumstances much at all to put us in a position to do these morally neutral acts; and our doing of them, while causally determined by various factors, need not be constrained in the least, nor is it. As for morally neutral decisions that do not arise in our daily routine, in order to get us to make such decisions God must first arrange for us to be surrounded by circumstances that even raise the issues involved in such decisions. Moreover, God, knowing us thoroughly, knows exactly what factors would convince us to do a given deed in a given situation, so God can work to bring about those actions, events, etc., that would lead us to conclude that we should do the action God has ordained. Of course, bringing about circumstances to move us (but not constrain us) to act will undoubtedly involve actions of other people, and God will have to arrange things so as to move them to do things and be places that will coincide with the details of our life. Being omniscient and able to see a whole interconnected world at once, God can do such things. In some cases, it may mean that one agent or another does act under constraint (and hence, unfreely) in order for him or her to do something involved in getting someone else to act freely. But compatibilists never claim that every act ever done is free in their sense.

When it comes to doing morally neutral deeds, God need not be the proximate cause. Even if one holds that fallen creatures on their own are totally unable to do what pleases God, those humans need no divine aid to do these acts, since the deeds are morally neutral.

As to morally good actions, the story is much the same as to how God gets us to do them. If we are inclined to do them, God will need only to place us in circumstances where such actions can and need to be done. He will have little trouble, if any, persuading us to do them according to our wishes. Still, for those who believe that apart from divine enablement humans cannot do what pleases God, when it comes to doing these deeds, God is not only remotely involved (by bringing circumstances into our life, convicting us of sin and of the need to do right, etc.), but is also involved as part of the proximate cause (along with us) in actually doing the deed. This would be an instance of the second type of divine mediate action mentioned above. Is this biblically possible? Not only do passages like 2 Pet 1:21 suggest so, but so does Phil 2:11-12, which says that God works in us both to will and *to do* of his good pleasure. His working in us involves both convincing us to do what is right, and also empowering us to do it as we obey. Moreover, it is correct to say that both God and we did the act in question.

What if God has decreed that we will do something good, but we don't want to do it? If so, God will have to convince us without constraining us, and God knows exactly what circumstances must occur in our life to do so. Having known from eternity all possible worlds, God knows which include his bringing about those circumstances that will convince us to do what is right, even though at first we don't want to do it. Of course, this doesn't mean we know ahead of time whether the world God chose is one in which he will get us to do something right freely (without constraint) or unfreely, but as events unfold, we can make that judgment in retrospect. As with morally neutral actions, so also in these cases God has planned the interaction of various of his creatures so as to bring about in each life what he has decreed. When it comes to doing the morally good action, God is involved mediately in the second sense mentioned above, enabling us and working through us to do the good deed that we now want to do. Hence, it is not inappropriate to attribute the good deed both to God and to the human who does it.[53]

As to morally evil actions, Scripture is very clear about God's overall role. He never does evil himself, and cannot even be tempted to do evil. Moreover, he tempts no one to sin (Jas 1:13). James explains that our temptations originate with our own desires. Those desires in themselves may not be evil, but when they move us to want things that God has forbidden, trouble comes. But God does not tempt us. Now any of us can be tempted in any circumstance. Even while sitting in church I can let my mind wander to think about someone I envy and I can become even more envious. Or something in the sermon may move me to think about someone who treated me poorly, and I can become very angry as I think about that deed. Or I can entertain impure, lustful thoughts about someone I see a few rows away from me.

For God to remove even the possibility of anyone ever being tempted, he would literally have to isolate us from everyone and everything else. But even that might not work, for in such a circumstance we might become frustrated and tempted to curse God for placing us in that situation. As for our temptations, they arise in the course of events of each day. The usual circumstances in which we find ourselves each day (going to work, being at school, shopping, etc.) are themselves morally neutral, so if God orders our lives to be in those situations, no culpability for our temptation and sin attaches to God.

Of course, once we are in any circumstance, temptation can arise. It doesn't come from God, nor need he be involved. Given our normal desires and the situations that surround us, we turn these morally neutral situations into occasions for temptation and sin. God participates as proximate cause in none of this. Even as a remote cause, his only involvement is ordaining and bringing about the circumstances in which we are tempted, but as argued, since those scenarios are the everyday routines of life, to remove the possibility of temptation, God would have to take us out of this world. In other words, he would have to forego creating a world altogether, and surely he is not obligated to do that. But then neither is he guilty for creating a world and a history in which people in various circumstances are tempted and fall into sin. Moreover, those who are tempted are not tempted against their own desires, since it was they who let their desire start and advance the temptation process. Since the evil deed, if done, stems from what they desired at the time, it would be hard to say that they didn't do the evil (compatibilistically) freely. Of course, sometimes we are forced to do evil against our will, and in those cases we would not act freely, but when evil stems from our temptations which arise from our desires, the resultant acts qualify as unconstrained and thus free.

When we sin, God neither does the act nor enables it (as with righteous deeds) by doing it through the sinner. He doesn't need to do any of this, for we are thoroughly able and willing to do it on our own. So God is neither the proximate cause nor the remote cause of such acts in the sense of being the ultimate mover of the act.

At this point, we are very close to what I shall say about the problem of evil, so I need not pursue this further now. Anyway, enough has already been said to understand how God can control all actions, including evil, without participating in them or being morally responsible for them, and without removing compatibilistic human freedom. Some may complain that sometimes when people are tempted to sin, God provides grace to help them avoid falling, and thus God has done something wrong in *not* giving us all grace to avoid sin at other times. However, this complaint is misguided, for grace is never obligated. That's why it is grace and not justice. But then, if grace is unmerited, undeserved favor which God owes no one, God has done nothing wrong by failing to grant grace to someone on a particular occasion. Nor did God's grace obligate him, before he chose any world, to choose a world in which nothing ever goes wrong and everyone is overloaded with blessings. Grace is never owed, so if it isn't given, the one who doesn't give it has done nothing wrong.

One further comment is in order about the decree and evil deeds. What about the case of God using Assyria to punish Israel? Isn't this a case of God doing an evil deed mediately? Surely God was very angry with Assyria once the deed was done. We first note that God as moral governor of the universe has the right to judge wickedness. Moreover, as creator and sovereign of all, he has a right to use whatever he chooses as his instrument of judgment. So what God did through Assyria to Israel is morally right for God to do. On the other hand, being chosen as the attacking army to mete out God's judgment, the Assyrians could use the occasion as an opportunity to be tempted to ravage Israel in ways that went beyond mere punishment. God didn't tempt the Assyrian army to do this; they did it themselves. Though God was the remote cause of the Assyrian army attacking Israel, he wasn't the proximate cause, nor was he either the remote or the proximate cause of their doing it in a way that went far beyond mere punishment through military defeat. By granting the soldiers the opportunity to attack, by not intervening on behalf of Israel to stop it, and by sustaining these soldiers in being so that they could do what they did, God was "involved." But none of that warrants moral culpability on God's part, even though it is right to say that God punished Israel. In doing this deed as they did, the Assyrians accomplished both God's purposes and their own, but that doesn't mean God's purposes coincided with all that they purposed to do and carried out.

From the preceding account of morally neutral, good, and evil actions, we can see that God can foreordain everything that happens, bring it to pass, and yet do so in such a variety of ways that humans act with compatibilistic free will. Moreover, God can have purposes not only for larger events in our lives and world but also for everything. It should also be clear that, on this model of providence, God exhaustively knows the future, because he decreed it.

A CASE FOR GENERAL SOVEREIGNTY THEOLOGIES

Earlier I noted that a key issue for all models of providence is whether they think humans have free will, and what they mean by freedom. General sovereignty models incorporate libertarian free will. This means for some that God cannot constantly interrupt and overturn our freedom. Since we are sinners and all too often do what God has forbidden, how things fit God's overall plans must remain somewhat in doubt. By creating free creatures, God decided to live with a certain amount of risk. Depending on the free will theology in view, God's risks will be greater or lesser, but with any of these theologies there will be risk.

Having heard this story, why should we be inclined to believe it? In the rest of this chapter, I want to present arguments in support of one or more general sovereignty models. I shall divide the arguments into two categories: biblical and theological arguments, and then philosophical arguments. I shall first present arguments that all forms of free will theism could hold, and then move to arguments specifically relevant to the open view.

Biblical/Theological Arguments for General Sovereignty

A central point (if not the starting point) for general sovereignty models is their commitment to libertarian freedom. Hence, we should begin with arguments for this notion of free will. General sovereignty advocates see ample biblical evidence of free will, and they conclude that the freedom in view must be libertarian.

Proponents of libertarian freedom contend that there are many Scriptures that require people to choose between various options. But if everything is determined so as to rule out free will, such requirements make no sense. Moreover, if God can so order things to produce in us desires for what he wants, it seems that even compatibilistic freedom rules out real choices. However, Scripture seems to teach that people are offered choices between options, and what they do is up to them. God commanded Adam and Eve to obey him, but gave them a choice.[54] Joshua (24:15) told Israel to choose whom they would serve. On another occasion Elijah asked Israel why she wavered between two opinions (1 Kgs 18:21). In the Sermon on the Mount Jesus speaks of a narrow or a wide road that people may choose to travel (Matt 7:13-14).[55]

Not only were people asked to choose between options, but Scripture commands us to respond to the gospel and accept Christ. The gospel call assumes that people have free will, for if not, why invite them to receive Christ?[56] If people do not have free will, they cannot do what God wants unless he makes them do it. If he has foreordained their salvation, he can bring it about without their freedom, so asking them to accept Christ as if they could legitimately refuse makes little sense. Moreover, if God has not predestined them to salvation, it makes no sense to invite them to Christ. In fact, it is a cruel joke if they can't do what they are commanded to do. All of this assumes that we are free.

In addition, though Calvinists say that God always gets what he wants, Scripture seems to teach otherwise. People resist and ignore God and the truth, and Scripture says God holds them accountable; but it would be unfair to do so, if they didn't make these decisions freely. The basic moral rule is that agents are morally accountable only if they act freely. Of course, if God doesn't always get his way, that is further evidence that God rules the world in a general way and accomplishes his general purposes in spite of many specific things happening that he doesn't want.

Is there biblical evidence that God's plans are sometimes foiled? Defenders of general sovereignty answer affirmatively. God was so exasperated with mankind prior to the flood that he decided to destroy it and "begin again." King Saul was God's choice for Israel's king, but eventually he disobeyed God, and God removed him and chose another (1 Samuel 15 and 16; see also Isa 5:7). Human sin in general isn't what God wants, but it happens. Peter speaks of people in the end time who will doubt their accountability to God because they willfully ignore the truth (2 Pet 3:3-5).

What about God's plans for our salvation? Scripture affirms that God "is not willing that any should perish" (2 Pet 3:9, KJV), and that he "desires all men to be saved and come to the knowledge of the truth" (1 Tim 2:4). But these plans are thwarted by our unbelief and resistance to God's attempts to draw us to himself.[57] One of the most blatant cases of humans rejecting God's will is mentioned in Matt 23:37, Christ's lament over Jerusalem. Jesus says,

"How often I wanted to gather your children together, the way a hen gathers her chicks under her wings, and you were unwilling." There it is; what Christ willed, Jerusalem rejected. How can this be so unless people are free?[58] Clark Pinnock sums up this line of evidence for libertarian freedom as follows:

> According to the Bible, human beings are creatures who have rejected God's will for them and turned aside from his plan. This is another strong piece of evidence that God made them truly free. Humans are evidently not puppets on a string. They are free even to pit their wills against God's. We have actually deviated from the plan of God in creating us and set ourselves at cross-purposes to God. Obviously we are free because we are acting as a race in a way disruptive of God's will and destructive of the values God holds dear for us. It is surely not possible to believe that God secretly planned our rebelling against him. Certainly our rebellion is proof that our actions are not determined but significantly free. . . . We may not be able to thwart God's ultimate plan for the world, but we certainly can ruin his plan for us personally and, like the scribes, reject God's purpose for ourselves (Lk 7:30).[59]

This evidence means not only that we are free in some sense but also that we are free in the libertarian sense. That is clearly what Pinnock and others mean by "significant freedom." Pinnock adds that "the biblical evidence leads me then to a strong definition of freedom. It is not enough to say that a free choice is one which, while not externally compelled, is nonetheless determined by the psychological state of the agent's brain or the nature of the agent's desiring. . . . The sin God condemns us for is a sin we did not have to commit. They are actions for which there are not prior conditions which render them certain."[60] This is libertarian free will!

John Sanders agrees. After espousing libertarian free will, he offers arguments for it. Two of his biblical arguments are very much to the point made above. Sanders says that if God did not intend for there to be sin, then libertarian free will must be true. For if compatibilism is true, then God could have changed Adam's desires to want to obey, and then he would not have fallen into sin. Only if libertarian freedom obtains, so that God didn't intervene to stop Adam because he couldn't and maintain libertarian free will, can we make sense of what happened. Second, unless humans have libertarian freedom, it makes no sense for God to grieve over sin, for why would God grieve over what he had foreordained? Moreover, our prayers make no sense if everything is already predetermined, for they can't change what God has decided. The fact that we can grieve God and can move him to respond to our prayers shows that we must have libertarian free will. It also affirms James's claim (Jas 4:2) that we don't have because we don't ask.[61]

Jack Cottrell agrees. He discusses positions which say that God determines everything unconditionally and also that humans act freely by doing what they desire. Cottrell says that acting according to one's desire is not an appropriate criterion for claiming that an act is free.[62] The problem, says Cottrell, is that advocates of such views believe that God has determined everything (and has done so unconditionally), and believe that what he has decreed must occur. Cottrell says that this decree "logically entails determinism, which logically excludes free will."[63] Hence, soft determinist claims that their freedom is genuine freedom are misguided. This is not free will at all![64] Cottrell, as others committed to general sovereignty, believes that Scripture teaches that we are free, but since compatibilism isn't meaningful freedom, biblical teaching that we are free supports the only kind of freedom left, libertarian freedom.

Since God's plans are sometimes foiled, however, how can we say God gets even his general purposes and goals accomplished? Advocates of general sovereignty offer several assurances. For one thing, God can achieve general goals because he can anticipate whatever obstructions his free creatures may put in his way and then respond effectively so as to achieve his general goals. Some individuals may, for example, reject Christ, but this doesn't mean God cannot or will not persuade others, nor does it forestall his kingdom from coming. God is incredibly intelligent and creative, so he will anticipate obstacles and will know a way around whatever we put in his way.[65]

But how does God do this? Richard Rice explains that God's plans are goals that he pursues in different ways. Some things he does unilaterally; creation is an example. In other cases, he interacts with his creatures in moving toward his goals. His creatures aren't always receptive to his leading, but God can still work in and through the various situations that arise. Think of God's use of Joseph's brothers' hatred of him. They intended to destroy Joseph, but God used their hateful actions ultimately to save Israel from famine (Gen 45:4-7). Later, he used Pharaoh's hard heart to heighten the drama of Israel's deliverance. As Rice summarizes:

> at times God simply does things, acting on his own initiative and relying solely on his own power. Sometimes he accomplishes things through the cooperation of human agents, sometimes he overcomes creaturely opposition to accomplish things, sometimes he providentially uses opposition to accomplish something, and sometimes his intentions to do something are thwarted by human opposition.[66]

All of this means, as John Sanders explains, that God's general goals will be met, and we get some inkling of what God ultimately wants when we look at Christ and what he did. But that doesn't mean God's way of achieving his goals is predictable. God is open to taking any number of different routes to meet his ends, depending on what options we leave him. Some proponents of general sovereignty believe that God will achieve the kind of future he desires in all of its details, but Sanders disagrees, for sin is irrational and mysterious, and our sin may preclude God from getting what he wants in every detail. Still there is no question that his general goals will be achieved:[67]

Will God win in the end? Is it simply unwarranted posturing for proponents of relational theology to claim that God will achieve victory? The prophets envisioned a time when God would reign victorious over all and shalom (peace and well-being) would be pervasive. The most significant step in achieving this vision was taken when God, through Jesus, achieved victory over the opposing powers (Col 2:15). Yet God is still working to bring the effects of this victory to greater realization. Jesus has inaugurated the reign of the God of powerful love, but clearly it has not yet been consummated. God is still working to make his de jure rule a de facto one.

We should not underestimate God's ability or overestimate our own in this enterprise. God is omnicompetent, resourceful and wise enough to take our moves into account, mighty enough to act and faithful enough to persist. If one of God's plans fails, he has others ready at hand and finds other ways of accomplishing his objectives.[68]

God is tremendously resourceful in achieving his basic goals, regardless of whether we cooperate or not, but the fact that we don't always cooperate is reason to reject the idea that God plans everything that happens, decreed it all, and never has his plans thwarted by what we do.

If all of this is true, what does it mean to say that God is sovereign? Can God really be sovereign in light of human libertarian freedom? General sovereignty advocates claim that these doctrines mean that God must limit the use of his power, but since he has freely chosen to do so, he is still as sovereign as ever. They also believe that there is biblical and theological evidence that God has done this. The clearest example of God's self-limitation is the life of Christ. During his earthy pilgrimage Jesus didn't exercise all the power at his disposal. What we see in Christ's life is that "when God sent his own Son, he lived out the role of a servant and did not try to push people around."[69]

There are other evidences as well that God limits his power. For one thing, creating a world at all limits God, since God is no longer the only thing that exists.[70] Moreover, theologians typically agree that there are certain things God cannot do because of his nature or because those things are not doable. He can't actualize contradictions, he can't sin, etc. Limitations on God's power are even part and parcel of many specific sovereignty theologies, let alone those that espouse general sovereignty.[71]

Then, in contemporary theological discussions, a major reason for holding to limited divine power stems from belief in a loving God. It isn't just that God loves us, but that love makes room for the beloved and implies vulnerability toward the beloved. "Anyone who loves, by his love makes himself dependent on the good-will and the response of his beloved."[72] To exercise dominating power over others doesn't show them love. Scripture depicts God as loving and longsuffering with the human race, and that suggests a willingness to limit his use of power.

Supposedly, the clinching evidence for divine self-limitation is the sort of world God created, namely, one with incompatibilistically free creatures. God chose this world freely, but it is impossible to create such creatures and then control everything they do, so creating free creatures implicitly commits God to limiting his own power. Jack Cottrell explains:

> God limits himself not only by creating a world as such, but also and even further by the *kind* of world he chose to create. That is, he chose to make a world that is *relatively independent* of him. On the one hand, this applies to nature and natural laws. In the very beginning God endowed his creatures with built-in forces or animal instincts enabling them to function without his having to determine their every move. On the other hand, the concept of relative independence applies to the free-will creatures God made to inhabit his universe. . . . man is free to act without his acts having been predetermined by God and without the simultaneous and efficacious coaction of God. . . . By not intervening in their decisions *unless* his special purposes require it, God respects both the integrity of the freedom he gave to human beings and the integrity of his own sovereign choice to make free creatures in the first place.
>
> This creation of free beings is indeed a true form of self-limitation for God, especially in the fact that this God-given freedom includes human freedom to rebel and to sin against the Creator himself. By creating a world in which sin was possible, God thereby bound himself to *react* in certain specific ways should sin become a reality. To be specific, should sin occur, God's love was bound to express itself in *grace*, involving a plan of redemption centered around his own incarnation and the offer of forgiveness for all who would accept it.[73]

A third argument for general sovereignty relates to whether God's decrees are conditional or unconditional. Calvinists opt for the latter, whereas Arminians and general sovereignty proponents who believe in a decree opt for the former. Cottrell says that God has a specific purpose for all creation in general, and that is unconditional. That purpose is to glorify himself and share his goodness. However, God has no specific unconditional purpose for each person, event, and object in the created order. The reason is that most of God's dealings with specific aspects of the universe are conditioned. Cottrell explains:

> his foreknowledge is conditioned on the actual occurrence of events themselves (as foreknown); the entire plan of redemption, with all its many elements from Genesis to Revelation, is conditioned on (is a response to) man's sin; answers to prayer are conditioned by the prayers themselves (as foreknown). But in all of this God is *no less sovereign* than if he had unconditionally predetermined each specific component of the whole.[74]

A fourth argument appeals to the salvation of believers. Jerry Walls agrees that if Calvinism with its unconditional election is true, then compatibilistic free will must also be the case, as many proponents of specific sovereignty maintain. However, Walls argues, there is a major problem for such views, because with compatibilism God can bring it about that everyone is saved. He can effectually call everyone to salvation and cause them to want to accept Christ. If so, why hasn't God done so? Calvinists usually reply that the answer is hidden in God's unsearchable will (the decree) and is a mystery. However, this is entirely unsatisfactory for a number of reasons. For one thing, it means that God both foreordained Adam's fall and decided that all would be guilty as a result. Then, God decreed that only some would be saved, and the rest would be left to eternal damnation. Since God is the ultimate cause of all of this via his decree, and since, given compatibilism, God could have foregone it all, that he did not do so suggests that he is morally guilty for the evil that occurs and for the many who go to a Christless eternity. Calvinists disagree, but it is hard to see how they can escape such problems.

Even if one answers that by decreeing the fall, God made a reason for the incarnation, and the incarnation shows the wonderfully merciful character of God in sending his Son to live among us and die for us, there still is a problem. None of it justifies God deciding only to save some, when he could save all and arrange for them freely (compatibilistically) to choose to love and serve him. The Calvinist explanation of God's decision to save only some is also unsatisfactory, because there is a better explanation that makes sense and doesn't require compatibilism and specific sovereignty at all. The explanation agrees that a good God would save everyone if he could, but having given his creatures libertarian freedom, he cannot then decree that they will all be saved and bring it about that they freely (incompatibilistically) accept Christ. If he brings it about that they do anything, then they don't do it freely. Of course, now we see why, despite God's power and sovereignty, so many reject Christ, and we also understand why they, not God, are guilty for doing so. Moreover, God sent Christ to pay for their sins, so that everything needed to satisfy God's justice is in place. All they need do is freely accept God's free gift in Christ. When they refuse, God cannot be morally accountable for what they decide, but with specific sovereignty, there is a sense in which God is responsible for everything, since he decreed it. Clearly, general sovereignty has a better explanation than specific sovereignty on these issues, and hence is preferable.[75]

Relatedly, general sovereignty advocates extend this argument to the issue of evil in general. All Christian theologies must answer why an all-loving and all-powerful God would create a world where there is both moral and physical evil. For the sake of this argument, let us stick to moral evil alone. Given determinism in any form, God can bring it about that no one ever does anything morally evil. Given compatibilism, God should be able to do so in such a way that we freely do only moral good. God has not done so, and we must wonder why. Some may justify God in the face of such evil by saying that God allows it because it serves a purpose in our world. It either results from greater goods or prevents greater evils, and hence, in philosophical jargon, is non-gratuitous, i.e., it serves a purpose. But if so, how could any human who sins be held morally guilty for doing so? And yet, it is standard evangelical belief that humans freely sin, and God punishes them for it. If that is true, then the evil must serve no purpose (must be gratuitous), and then is worthy of punishment.

In short, the determinist faces a major dilemma. On the one hand, he says there is gratuitous evil in the world and those who do it are worthy of punishment; but given compatibilism, this evil was both decreed by God and avoidable if God had exerted the requisite influences to keep us from it. So it seems that God must be guilty and should not have allowed it. On the other hand, the compatibilist says that moral evil is non-gratuitous, but then when it occurs God shouldn't disapprove of it, and he certainly shouldn't punish those who do it, since it serves his further purposes.[76]

If all of this seems intractably difficult, the problem is determinism in general, and compatibilism in particular. Beyond that, proponents of libertarian free will believe there is a better way to explain the existence of moral evil in our world. No one sins because God desires it or ordained it; rather it happens because we sin in disobedience to God's precepts. Moreover, we shouldn't be surprised that some instances of moral evil seem to serve no purposes whatsoever, i.e., are truly gratuitous. God is more than justified in punishing us for that evil, because we do it freely. Moreover, he bears no culpability, for he did not foreordain it, cause it to occur, or do it himself, nor could he stop us from doing it without removing our free will. God is entirely sovereign, omnipotent, and all-loving, but even an omnipotent creator cannot actualize a contradiction, and it would be a contradiction to expect God to *cause* us to do anything (incompatibilistically) freely.[77]

A related argument stems from God's goodness. God is all-loving and good, but then what would he wish for his creatures? Would he want them to be saved and to obey his precepts, or would he choose for some to disobey him? The answer is obvious, according to general sovereignty advocates like Jerry Walls, for a good God would not want, let alone decree, that his creatures do evil, especially when doing so results in their punishment. Walls argues that free will theologies ultimately stem not from libertarian free will but from reflections on God's goodness. By asking what a good God would do if he had the power, and by seeing that he hasn't done it, the indeterminist concludes that the only reasonable explanation is that his creatures possess libertarian free will which limits what God can do. Walls states this argument in seven steps:

1. A good God desires happiness for all his free creatures.
2. Happiness for free creatures is found only in a relationship of willing obedience to God.
3. God desires the willing obedience of all his free creatures.
4. Some of God's free creatures disobey his will and reject his offer of salvation.
5. Since God does not desire any of his free creatures to reject his will and his offer of salvation, he must be unable to cause them to do otherwise.

6. If God is unable to cause his free creatures to obey his will and receive salvation, it must be that he has made them free in such a way that they are actually able to obey or disobey, to receive or reject salvation (i.e., incompatibilism).
7. Such freedom must be a good which outweighs the evil it entails.[78]

As Norman Geisler says, "Irresistible force used by God on his free creatures would be a violation of both the charity of God and the dignity of humans. God is love. True love never forces itself on anyone. Forced love is rape, and God is not a divine rapist!"[79]

Another line of biblical evidence is presented by the openness of God perspective in particular. Advocates of the open view believe their story about God's interaction with the world could only be true on their understanding of the divine attributes. Put briefly, if God is the relational God that openness proponents propose, he cannot be absolutely immutable, impassible, simple, and outside of time. He cannot be so transcendent that he is unaffected by us and unreachable. Rather, he must be vulnerable, interactive, and sensitive to our needs. Numerous passages suggest that this is so. God changes his mind, repents or regrets what he had planned to do, reacts to the plight of his people, and answers prayer. Passages like the conversation between God and Abraham about Sodom (Genesis 18) and between God and Moses over Israel's fate (Exodus 32–34), show that God can be bargained with. Sometimes the deliberative process changes his mind (as with Moses), and sometimes not (Abraham and Sodom). This fits a picture of a God who doesn't demand absolute control, but has ceded some power to his creatures. Hence, God's very nature and actions as portrayed in Scripture are further evidence that he governs the world according to only a general sovereignty approach.[80]

Still, some may wonder how this picture can be true in light of passages that say that God controls and ordains all things. General sovereignty proponents are aware of those passages, and in some cases have addressed them. Some responses will be saved for my discussion of those passages from the specific sovereignty standpoint, but for now I note some of those passages. John Sanders has offered the most extensive response, so I turn to his handling of several OT and NT texts.

Sanders understands that various OT passages seem to mean that God causes and controls all things. He believes that a fundamental problem with the handling of those passages is the hermeneutic used to interpret them. All too often, the text in question refers to a single event, but it is taken out of context and generalized to become a universal statement of how God always operates. Isa 45:7 and Amos 3:6 are cases in point. The former says, "I am the LORD who does all these [things]." This is taken by some to teach a general principle that God is responsible for every good and evil act in the entire universe, but the verse only refers to Yahweh's dealings with Israel, and more specifically, with a particular historical event, Israel's experience in exile. As for Amos 3:6, this doesn't teach that every calamity that befalls a city is due to God. In 3:7 Amos states that God reveals his judgments on Israel through his prophets. Hence, 3:6 is about a specific instance of God's judgment of Israel. Indeed, God has the right to bring judgment on the wicked, but this certainly does not mean that whenever something untoward happens in any city (a terrorist attack, an earthquake, etc.), God will announce it by his prophets and do it himself. The verse cannot be generalized beyond the situation in Amos's day.[81]

What about passages like Prov 16:9 and 21:1? The former says man plans his way, but God directs the steps. The latter says that the king's heart is in the Lord's hand, and the Lord turns it whichever way he wills. Surely these are universal claims, but Sanders is not impressed. He says that these sayings must be seen, as with all proverbs, as guidelines for godly living, not universal principles that always hold true. As to the meaning of 16:9 and 21:1, Sanders explains:

> The proverbs about human plans and the Lord's purposes should be seen in terms of the book's call for seeking the covenant God's wisdom in our planning. The God of Israel desires that his people seek his input instead of doing what they (on their own) think is best. Just as with Adam in the garden, so for the people of Israel. No one can chart a wise course through life without trusting in divine wisdom (20:24). God directs his people's steps (16:9) and guides the king of Israel (21:1) *when they seek God's wisdom* [italics mine]. When they do not, God stands against them.[82]

Sanders adds that if God controls all kings, it is hard to explain why God was angry, for example, when Israel's kings broke the covenant, for they only did what God ordained them to do.

One other set of OT passages is noteworthy: Isa 29:15-16; 45:9-13; and Jer 18:1-10, about the potter and the clay. While many interpret these passages as showing that God controls all things and has a right to do with them as he pleases, Sanders demurs. As to the Isaiah verses, Sanders says there were some people in Isaiah's day who said God had no right to do what he was doing. Isaiah responded that God as the sovereign potter has a right to do what he was doing in that instance. If he decides to bring judgment on the wicked, he is fully within his rights. As to Jeremiah 18, it is again a question of God's rights and privileges. Doesn't God have a right to change his plans for Israel? Can't he forego fulfilling a prophecy if his people's behavior changes? That is all these passages say. They don't assert God's universal control over everything and the right to do whatever he wants to do. Rather, they underscore his prerogative to judge the wicked and change his actions if people change their behavior.[83]

Sanders handles many NT passages, but several show his strategy. Sanders raises passages such as 1 Pet 1:20 and Eph 1:4 that speak of God foreknowing something. As to the former, all that is required is that Christ's incarnation was chosen from the beginning as part of God's overall plan for our world. The key with Eph 1:4 is that it speaks of our corporate election in Christ, but even here we must not misunderstand the verse. Corporate election means "God elects a course of action and certain conditions by which people will be counted as 'in Christ.' According to corporate election it is the group—the body of Christ—that is foreordained from the foundation of the world, not specific individuals selected by God for salvation."[84]

Acts 2:23 is another key passage that speaks of human involvement in Christ's death, but also says this happened by the predeterminate plan and foreknowledge of God. Being able generally to foresee that not everyone would react positively to Christ, God foresaw that some would put him to death. And also seeing the need of paying for sin for anyone to be saved, God planned to send Christ as Savior. That is all this verse requires. Sanders writes:

> It was God's definite purpose (*hōrismenē boulē*, a boundary-setting will) to deliver the Son into the hands of those who had a long track record of resisting God's work. Their rejection did not catch God off guard, however, for he anticipated their response and so walked onto the scene with an excellent prognosis (foreknowledge, *prognōsei*) of what would happen. The crucifixion could not have occurred to Jesus unless somehow it fit into the boundaries of what God willed (*boulē*, Acts 2:23; 4:28). But this does not mean that humans cannot resist the divine will. Luke says that the Jewish leaders "rejected God's purpose *[boulēn]* for themselves" (Luke 7:30). God sovereignly established limits within which humans decide how they will respond to God. In this sense God determined that the Son would suffer and die and sent him into a setting in which that result, given the history and character of the covenant people, was quite assured.[85]

Finally, there is Romans 9–11, especially chapter 9, which is frequently taken to teach unconditional election to salvation and reprobation. Sanders rightly notes that what is at stake is God's relation to Israel in light of her rejection of her Messiah. The ultimate question is whether God's intentions for his covenant people have failed. Paul's major theme in these chapters is that God's plans and purposes for Israel have not failed. In 9:6-16, Sanders says that Paul has a twofold message. The first is that ethnic standing in Israel doesn't assure proper standing before God. The second is that God intends to bring into covenant with him those who are Gentiles. And God has a right to extend mercy to whomever he pleases, even if they do not have the typical badges of covenant membership (Jewish descent, circumcision, etc.). Sanders claims that the key is God's merciful will, even in regard to God's actions with respect to Pharaoh. God strengthened Pharaoh's heart in rebellion because he hoped by doing so to bring him to his senses so that he would repent. Similarly, God is now hardening Israel, hoping to drive her to repent and be redeemed (Rom 11:7, 25). As to the potter/clay imagery in Rom 9:20-22, Paul uses it as Isaiah and Jeremiah did to speak of God's judgment upon his people in order ultimately to restore them. It does not teach God's control and pan-causality of everything. Finally, in 9:23-33 Paul speaks again of God's desire to save the Gentiles. God didn't foreordain Israel's rebellion (v. 22), but he is resourceful enough to use the situation to further his general goal of bringing Gentiles to Christ. Rom 11:11-27 shows that God similarly intends Gentile salvation to provoke Israel to jealousy of the Gentiles, to the end that the Jews will turn to Christ. So the passage shows God's mercy, God's resourcefulness when things don't go as he wants, and God's ability to bring about his general plans (salvation of Gentiles) even if he has to take alternate routes from the ones he first planned. The passage also shows that while God's general plans are fulfilled, God doesn't get everything he wants, for God wanted the Gentiles to perform a certain role in his plans for Israel, but that has not happened. God had hoped that the union of Jew and Gentile in the church would vis-ibly show his wisdom in the plan he implemented through Christ. That may still happen, but so far, it hasn't been very successful. So, some of what God desired has happened, but not everything. This passage hardly teaches what specific sovereignty proponents claim.[86]

Jack Cottrell interprets Romans 9–11 differently, but still denies that chapter 9 speaks of an unconditional decree of salvation. Cottrell grants that the chapters teach God's unconditional choice of some things, but "the best understanding of this, however, is that God unconditionally chooses indi-viduals and nations for temporal roles in his plan of redemption. That is, he chooses whom he pleases for service, not salvation."[87]

Cottrell adds that Paul's main point is to defend God's right to reject Israel as his chosen people, those intended to perform special service for him. Romans 1–8 teaches that not all who are of Abraham are true Jews (4:9-16) and that anyone who trusts Christ is a true Jew (2:25-29). Doesn't this sug-gest that God is breaking faith with Israel? Cottrell replies that Paul answers that the sovereign God has a right to choose whomever he wishes to serve him and help him work out his purposes of making grace available through Christ. Lest we be disturbed by this, Cottrell reminds us that "it is not as if he were rejecting them individually for salvation; he is simply setting them aside col-lectively—as a nation—as far as their service of preparation is concerned."[88] Cottrell then asks and answers a question his readers may be entertaining:

> But even if it be granted that Paul is talking about an unconditional choice for service, would this not indicate that God is a God whose decrees are unconditional with regard to everything? Certainly not, as Paul clearly shows in this very section. In fact, Paul affirms the *conditionality* of the main thing Calvinists want to view *uncondition-ally*, namely, salvation! This is clear from his discussion of the eternal destiny of individual Jews. Any who are rejected as far as salvation is concerned are rejected because of personal unbelief (Rom 9:32; 11:20). Likewise, any Jew can be saved by accepting Jesus as Messiah (10:13-

17; 11:23-24). In fact God is pictured as constantly pleading with Israel to come to him, but they remain disobedient and obstinate (10:21).

In summary, Romans 9–11 shows that God's election and rejection of the Jews as a nation with regard to their role of service was a matter of God's sovereign choice, while his acceptance or rejection of individual Jews with regard to their salvation is conditioned on their belief or unbelief.[89]

Readers can choose which of the two interpretations (Sanders's or Cottrell's) of Romans 9–11 they prefer. With either interpretation, however, the text doesn't teach what specific sovereignty says.

Philosophical Arguments for General Sovereignty

There are many philosophical arguments for general sovereignty. They mainly stress the nature of human action, what it means to be free and morally responsible, and how causal determinism removes free will and moral responsibility. General sovereignty proponents, given their commitment to libertarian free will, find many of these arguments quite compelling.

The starting point of many philosophical discussions on free will is the meaning of freedom. Invariably, defenders of this viewpoint offer a definition of libertarian or incompatibilistic free will—an act is free only if it is not causally determined. Many who espouse this notion of freedom not only present it to define freedom but also, it seems, as an argument for the position. Though this sounds question begging, it need not be. Their point is that we must analyze what determinists of any stripe say about actions, and when we do so and compare it to our basic intuitions about freedom, we find that the two notions (determinism and freedom) conflict with one another.

The point can be illustrated by reflecting on what we mean when we say humans are free. The key, many libertarians argue, is their interpretation of choice. It is natural for all of us to think that most of our choices are undetermined, especially when we sense no one and nothing pushing us to do one thing rather than another.[90] As Alvin Plantinga explains in defining libertarian freedom of action, "no antecedent conditions and/or causal laws determine that he will perform the action, or that he won't. It is within his power, at the time in question, to take or perform the action and within his power to refrain from it."[91] If either the state of the world before the agent acts (antecedent conditions) or causal laws (such as the laws of nature), or we might even add, some other agent, determine the agent to do a given action, those conditions and laws, not the agent, seem to control what the agent does. But, if agents don't control their actions, i.e., they may have power to do them, but which acts they do are controlled by factors such as antecedent conditions and/ or causal laws, how can we meaningfully attribute freedom to them? Isn't it intuitively clear that unless we control our desires and the intentions and actions that stem from them, something (or someone) other than we ourselves is in control, and thus we are not free? Libertarians not only believe this is so, but that it is a strong argument for incompatibilism.[92]

Patrick Francken extends this point beyond a particular action or two to the thesis of universal determinism. What he says is significant, because though it refers to natural factors and laws that causally determine whatever occurs, one could very easily substitute God or the divine decree as the factor that accomplishes universal determinism. Francken argues that universal determinism is just incompatible with free will, and again the key issue is the matter of controlling one's actions. Francken writes:

> Let us say that an event á *determines* an event ß only if (i) á occurs, (ii) ß occurs, and (iii) it was never up to anybody whether if á occurs, then ß occurs. Universal Determinism, then, we understand to be the doctrine that every event (and *a fortiori*, every action) is determined to occur by previous events. . . . When one event determines another, therefore, it can at some time be up to an agent whether the latter event occurs, only if it was at some time up to him whether the former occurs. But if *universal* determinism is true, every event in the agent's lifetime will have been determined, ultimately, by some event that occurred in the remote past, before the agent was born. Hence every event in the agent's lifetime will have been determined by antecedent events over which the agent *had no control* [italics mine]—events whose occurrence was never up to the agent. . . . So none of the events in the agent's lifetime is such that it will ever have been up to the agent whether they occur. Since the events in the agent's lifetime include all of his actions, it follows that none of the agent's actions is such that it will ever have been up to the agent whether to perform them. None of the agent's actions are up to him, or therefore, free, if universal determinism is true.[93]

Here again we see the critical import of who controls one's actions. The argument is that if causal determinism is true, the agent isn't ultimately in control, but how could anyone ascribe freedom to someone who didn't control their own actions? Of course, if humans have libertarian free will, God can't rule with specific sovereignty, but only general control.

A second argument follows, if being free means having control over one's actions. Truly having power to choose and do what you want means that you could just as easily choose and do a different act from the one you do. In fact, it is argued, unless the agent has power to do other than what he does in any circumstance, he is not truly in control of his act. If antecedent conditions, causal laws, etc., forestall every alternative but one (even if it is the one the agent most wants), the person does not have genuine freedom. To be genuinely free, one must be able to do otherwise.

It is important to add that those who hold this say that the agent's being able to do otherwise assumes that all circumstances remain the same, for if situations change, that might preclude taking an option that otherwise would be open if things stayed the same. Hence, libertarians argue that without the situation changing, an individual must be able to choose and do other than she does in that very situation.[94] In fact, as some have noted, even compatibilists generally agree that to be free a person must be able to do other than what he does.[95] Libertarians add that while a person is only free if he could do otherwise, this can only be so in a real situation if determinism is false.[96] To see why this is so, we need to note that whether or not a person is free (and to what degree they are free, if it makes sense to speak in such terms) is a function of three things: possession of skills or abilities relevant to doing certain actions, lack of external constraints imposed by other rational agents, and freedom from the kinds of internal factors that psychologists point out as limiting action (e.g., a compulsive character make-up). Some think that even this is not enough to hold that someone is free in doing an action, for it could refer only to the doing of the action, not the choosing or the forming of desires from which choices flow. In order to be free, the person must have ability and freedom from external and internal constraints when it comes to explaining why they have the desires they do, why they choose one option rather than another, and why they do one thing as opposed to another.[97] Libertarians contend that it is really possible in a given situation for agents to do otherwise only if they both have the abilities needed to choose and do otherwise and are free from constraints. However, if determinism is true, there are factors that either serve as internal or external constraints or limit the agent's abilities so that she doesn't entirely control either her desires, choices, or actions.[98]

Libertarians note that some determinists try to escape this argument by interpreting "could have done otherwise" conditionally. They claim that "the agent could have done otherwise" simply means, for example, "he would have done otherwise, if he had tried." But of course the libertarian will respond, "but what if he couldn't have tried?" Surely, the conditional interpretation doesn't guarantee that the agent could try; some factors might inhibit him from trying. In response, the determinist might offer another conditional interpretation, namely, "the agent could have tried" just means "he would have tried to do otherwise, if he had chosen." Of course, this solves little, the libertarian responds, because it isn't clear that the agent could have chosen.[99] Others have suggested that "he could have done otherwise" just means that "if he had chosen otherwise, he wouldn't have been frustrated by lack of ability or by circumstance." But this again runs into problems in that we can still ask if the agent could have chosen.[100]

The net result is that libertarians believe it is incorrect to interpret "could have done otherwise" as a disguised conditional of the sorts described, a conditional that would leave the door open to say, for example, that compatibilistic freedom is genuine freedom, because the agent could have done otherwise in one of these conditional senses. How should we understand the meaning of "could?" It means that it is up to the agent and within her power to do the act in question. It is also within her power to do some other action. This is not what we mean when we say "a hot stove can fry an egg" or "a roulette wheel can pick an even number or an odd one." It makes no sense to say it is up to the stove to fry an egg or within the power of the roulette wheel to pick a certain number, because these things are not animate and are not agents. But a human being is an agent with such power or capacity.[101]

In recent years, this line of argument has been presented as the Consequence Argument, and Peter van Inwagen is its best-known and ablest defender. The argument stated briefly is:

> If determinism is true, then our acts are the consequences of the laws of nature and events in the remote past. But it is not up to us what went on before we were born, and neither is it up to us what the laws of nature are. Therefore, the consequences of these things (including our present acts) are not up to us.[102]

This results if determinism is true, but it certainly seems false that our actions are beyond our control and are traceable to events and deeds that happened long before we were born.

Van Inwagen believes this is a good argument and presents it in a longer form. He asks us to imagine a judge who presides over a case involving a capital offense. At a certain time, T, in the proceedings, all the judge has to do is raise his hand to prevent the execution of a death sentence. In the judge's country, raising the hand is the conventional way of granting special clemency. Suppose also that on the said occasion, the judge refrained from raising his hand, and the criminal was executed. The judge's inaction didn't stem from his being bound, injured, or paralyzed in his arms. Nor did it result from any pressure to decide one way or another or from the judge being under the influence of drugs, hypnosis, or anything of the sort. He made the decision after a period of calm, rational, relevant deliberation, and if a psychologist were to analyze him, he would find no evidence of anything psychology would call abnormal. Van Inwagen says that even if all of this is so, if determinism is true, the judge still could not have raised his hand at T.

What is the substance of the argument and how does it show determinism to be problematic? Van Inwagen notes that determinism says that what anyone does on any occasion results from the laws of nature in conjunction with the complete state of the world prior to and up to the time of acting. If so, what would it take to do other than what the complete world-state and the laws of nature dictate? Given determinism, either of two things would grant such power: 1) doing something that would change the past so that the current action could be different, or 2) doing something that would change the laws of nature. Clearly, no human is in a position to do either. Hence, the judge could not have raised his hand, despite there being no physical or psychological hindrances to keep him from doing so. But if the judge is unencumbered by such restraints, it certainly seems counterintuitive that he could not have raised his hand if he had wanted to. Something, then, is wrong, and that something is determinism, for it produces the absurd consequence that one can only do otherwise if one can change the past or change a law of nature (both impossible).[103]

The next line of argument underscores why freedom and the power or ability to do otherwise are so important. It is critical, libertarians argue, because it is fundamental to moral responsibility. Suppose that only one course of action is open to someone and it is an immoral one. How can this person be morally responsible for doing the only thing possible in the situation? Someone can be held morally accountable only if he has more than one option, and makes his choice apart from being determined to do so. Only then do we know that the act was really *his* choice, and only then is it right to hold him morally accountable.

Though freedom is necessary for ascription of moral responsibility, soft determinists believe in freedom, so compatibilistically free actions must be morally responsible. Libertarians disagree, because causal determinism says that because of causal conditions surrounding an agent's choice, there really is only one thing the agent can do. This is a problem, the libertarian reasons, for moral responsibility can only meaningfully be ascribed when someone chooses from several options, all of which are genuine possibilities. If I have only one option in a situation, then even if I want to do it, it is hard to see that I am morally accountable when I choose it, for it isn't clear that if there were alternatives I would still have chosen the same option.[104] Even if we have no sense of being compelled or controlled against our will, if our acts are actually causally determined, the libertarian would say that the agent is not morally responsible for them.[105]

The indeterminists' argument can be stated more formally by two premises that lead to a conclusion:

> If a man could not have done otherwise than he in fact did, then he is not responsible for his action. (That is, "He could not have done otherwise" is a recognised excuse).

> If determinism is true, it is true of every action that the agent could not have done otherwise.

> If determinism is true, no one is ever responsible for his actions.[106]

This argument seems cogent enough. The conclusion seems to follow from the premises, seems valid, and has a certain plausibility, but its conclusion should trouble us, for if it is correct, how could we ever hold anyone accountable for what they do? Moreover, the argument removes grounds not only for punishment but also for praise of good deeds. For if one is not responsible for the good things one does, why praise her for doing well? Something is amiss in this line of reasoning, and, the libertarian argues, it is determinism.

In light of such considerations, philosophers hold that if agents are to be held morally responsible for their actions and those actions are at all determined, then the deeds must be causally determined by the agent himself. [107]

The next line of argument addresses an objection that determinists frequently raise against indeterminism. Determinists frequently complain that if actions are indeterministically free, then they are not causally determined, but if not, they must be random, arbitrary or chance events. Such acts are not done for a purpose, are not under the agent's control, and hence are not morally praiseworthy or blameworthy. Hence, libertarian free will seems to remove moral accountability from the world.

Libertarians are very sensitive to this dilemma, for it appears that an act is either causally determined or entirely capricious. For libertarians, either alternative removes moral accountability, because in either case the agent doesn't control his or her actions. Libertarians offer several replies, and many of the answers focus on whether an undetermined act is necessarily also an uncaused act. If it is, then even the agent could not cause it; it must be random. If, on the other hand, an act can be caused without being determined, then actions are caused by the agent who does them, but there was no inevitability about what the agent would do, for the act wasn't determined by antecedent conditions, laws of nature, or anything else. All of this needs explaining, and several indeterminist philosophers do try to explain it.

Thomas Talbott argues that we must clarify what a chance or random occurrence is. Talbott says that indeterminate actions are not uncaused or random, but no condition or set of conditions is sufficient to guarantee that a given act will be done rather than another (i.e., the deed is not determined).[108] There is more to the story than this, Talbott argues. We must clarify what it might mean to call an act random or chance, for it could be a chance occurrence in one of two senses of "chance." According to the first sense, a chance occurrence is unexpected, unplanned, and even unintended; this is the more ordinary sense of "chance occurrence." But if this is what chance means, it doesn't rule out the event being caused. For example, if two cars accidentally collide at a certain intersection, it is dubious that this was expected, intended, or planned, but that doesn't mean the accident was uncaused. In fact, legal authorities and insurance companies have great interest in determining the cause in order to determine liability. Talbott argues that if this is the meaning of "chance" action or event, the indeterminist could agree that an incompatibilistically free action might be a chance action in this sense and yet still be caused by an agent. Hence, libertarian free will doesn't require actions to be out of the agent's control and thus arbitrary.[109]

There is a second sense of "chance occurrence," though Talbott says it is not the ordinary sense. It is, however, the critical sense for the determinist's argument against incompatibilism. According to this second sense, an event or action is chance if it is uncaused: chance is identical with the lack of cause. With this definition of chance occurrence, surely the determinist is right that indeterminism, in believing in chance occurrences, holds that acts are uncaused and thus cannot be within the agent's control. Unfortunately for the determinist, Talbott explains that the second sense of "chance" and "uncaused" begs the question. That is, determinists and indeterminists debate whether an incompatibilistically free chance (undetermined) action is also uncaused. Determinists can't win that debate by assuming without proof that a chance act is uncaused. Indeterminists hold that the act is undetermined, not that it is uncaused, and they further claim that an act can be a chance act and still a caused one (hence, a free act for which there is moral responsibility). If we use the first and ordinary sense of "chance event," no questions are begged in favor of either determinism or indeterminism, and certainly, an unexpected act or event can still be a caused one. Hence, it isn't random, arbitrary, or totally out of the agent's control.[110]

This may be confusing, for how can an act be caused and yet undetermined? It is at this point that several other philosophers are most helpful. We must first remember what it means for an act to be determined. It means that in advance of the deed, the state of affairs in the world plus laws of nature are such that they can produce only one result. That is what determinism in the physical sciences means. Granted, it may be very hard to state laws that cover human behavior and make certain outcomes inevitable, but when it comes to determinism of human action, a set of conditions at the time of decision making is sufficient to incline the agent decisively to choose and do one act rather than another.[111]

If this is what determinism means, however, the causes of all future events already exist and are even now determined and perfectly predictable. In fact, Calvinistic determinists seem to hold such a view in believing in the divine decree. In contrast, however, Axel Steuer, citing the work of the logician Lukasiewicz, argues that we must be sensitive to the temporal element in causal chains. As Lukasiewicz has shown, there are causal chains of certain acts and events that commence only in the future, and hence at the present time those actions and events are not set, so we can still choose the better and avoid the worse future actions. Thus, Steuer explains, we are not left with the option of saying that an action is either causally determined or purely random. We need not adopt the view that actions are predetermined, but can grant that they are currently open. At some time in the future an agent will be confronted with a decision, will make a choice, and will act. The agent will cause the action, so it won't be random, and yet it will be incompatibilistically free, because nothing in advance determined what the choice would be.[112]

This may still seem counterintuitive, but it hinges on a distinction between being determined and being caused.[113] The two are not necessarily the same. In recent literature there have been examples of acts or events that are definitely caused but could not rightly be called determined. Patrick Francken offers an example from philosophers Fred Dretske and Aaron Snyder, and then comments on it. We are asked to consider the following:

Box R contains a randomizing device; once activated it proceeds, in a perfectly random manner, to one of its one hundred different terminal states. Each of the terminal states may be supposed to be equally probable so that the probability of the box ending in state number 17 is 0.01. . . . Attached to Box R is a loaded revolver which fires when (and only when) the terminal state happens to be number 17. We take this device and place it next to a cat, point the revolver at the cat and activate the box. Things go badly for the cat; the improbable occurs and the cat is killed. The cat's master, if informed of our doings, would almost certainly insist that we had killed his cat, that we caused the cat's death, or at the kindliest, that his cat's death resulted in part from what we did.

Dretske and Snyder think this a case in which it is correct to say that our activating of R caused the cat's death, despite the fact that it is consistent with the laws of nature, the occurrence of the cause (and any other relevant background conditions), that the revolver should not go off, and the cat not die. Thus if, in this case, it is correct to say that our activating of R caused the cat's death, it is correct to say that an event need not determine another to be its cause.[114]

This shows that a particular event or action can be caused without being determined in advance. In fact, as in the example, it need not even be probable that it will occur, and yet whoever set up the box with the revolver is responsible and caused the cat's death. This just shows that the objection that says an act is either determined or uncaused (and hence not really free in any sense, since it is random) is just wrong. Libertarian free will should not be rejected on that ground.[115]

A final philosophical argument focuses on deliberating about what is determined and is in a sense inevitable. Peter van Inwagen argues that if an act is causally determined, it makes no sense to think one can deliberate about whether to choose and do it or not. In the first place, philosophers agree that "one cannot deliberate about whether to perform a certain act unless one believes it is possible to perform it."[116] Van Inwagen says that if you think this isn't so, then imagine that you are in room with two doors, one unlocked and the other locked and impassable (though you don't know which door is which), and try to imagine yourself deliberating about which door to leave by. Deliberating about this makes no sense, and similarly, unless one believes it is possible to do a deed, one can't deliberate about it. Of course, being able to do an act, according to van Inwagen, means that one decides between or among various options which cannot be jointly chosen and put into practice. Moreover, van Inwagen rejects the idea that the possibility of doing an act should be understood conditionally, i.e., that "the agent could have done otherwise" just means that an agent could have done something else *if* they wanted to, had different desires, or had chosen differently.[117]

Van Inwagen adds that anyone committed to determinism must believe that their future actions are inevitable and that no other actions are possible.

Still, human beings, including determinists, deliberate about whether to do certain acts. But if it makes no sense to deliberate unless alternate courses of action are possible, and if no alternate choice is possible, then deliberating either makes no sense or it does, because determinism must be false. Hence, libertarian freedom must be true, and any system espousing determinism and claiming that we can meaningfully deliberate about future choices is self-contradictory and thus false.[118]

The preceding biblical/theological and philosophical arguments for general sovereignty are substantial. In the next chapter, we turn to the case for the other side. We not only need to see whether specific sovereignty positions can answer indeterminist objections, but also what kind of positive evidence they offer for their model of providence.

FOURTEEN

A CASE FOR A COMPATIBILIST SPECIFIC SOVEREIGNTY MODEL

The arguments for general sovereignty models of providence are impressive, but there is also a substantial case for specific sovereignty. Because my theology is a specific sovereignty approach that incorporates compatibilistic free will, I shall argue for that model in particular. This means that there will be some arguments against hard deterministic understandings such as fatalism and hard determinism. Other arguments will explain why I hold specific sovereignty instead of general sovereignty.

BIBLICAL/THEOLOGICAL ARGUMENTS FOR COMPATIBILISTIC SPECIFIC SOVEREIGNTY

In shorter publications, I have defended a moderate Calvinism incorporating compatibilistic free will.[1] In those cases, I started my defense where Calvinists typically begin, divine sovereignty. On the other hand, Arminians and other free will theologians invariably begin with biblical teaching on human freedom and moral responsibility. Sometimes it is said that one's starting point is crucial, because it shows what one deems most important, and one tends to wind up where one started. This can and does happen on both sides of this issue. However, as one committed to Scripture's full inspiration and inerrancy, I am obliged to take seriously everything it teaches. Thus, regardless of the starting point, the outcome should be the same, since all biblical revelation must be given its due. In that spirit, I shall begin this defense with human freedom.

The Bible says much about human beings. Various passages discuss human nature, and we also see humans in various situations. Scripture also clarifies what God requires of us. Moreover, the OT and NT tell us what human beings must do to have right standing with God. The message of both Testaments is that trust, faith in God, is required both for salvation and for living our lives in proper relation to God. The NT commands us to accept Christ and to follow the precepts of God's Word. Those who have a personal relationship with Christ through faith are also instructed to tell others the same message. As Paul told the Corinthians (2 Cor 5:20), "Therefore, we are ambassadors for Christ, as though God were entreating through us; we beg you on behalf of Christ, be reconciled to God!"

Commands addressed to believers and nonbelievers seem inappropriate if humans do not have freedom to respond positively or negatively to them. Considerations like these, plus the biblical passages marshaled in favor of free will when I presented the case for general sovereignty, lead me to conclude that human beings are free. In addition, I agree fully that Scripture teaches that each person individually is morally accountable before God for his or her own actions. We are neither saved nor damned because of what our friends, relatives, or acquaintances do. The evidence for this was already presented in support of general sovereignty, and I need not repeat it. I also agree with the commonly held moral principle that no one is morally accountable for their deeds unless they act freely. Being held responsible for acts that are unfree is considered unjust in both ethics and law. Scripture clearly affirms that God is just, and if such claims are to mean anything, they must invoke concepts of justice we can understand. Otherwise, we have little idea of what it means to say that God is just. But if God is just, and if it is unjust to hold someone morally accountable who does not act freely, then God could not justly hold us accountable for our actions unless we are free.

In light of these considerations, I conclude that any theology that rules out human freedom and/or moral responsibility is deficient biblically. This doesn't mean all our acts are free, but only that humans have the capacity for free action and that they use that capacity much of the time. Adopting a theology that grants human beings free will has certain intellectual and theological implications. Most immediately, it means that any theology and model of providence that excludes human freedom completely must be rejected. Hence, several models of providence described earlier are unacceptable. All models that include fatalism are excluded; not only do they remove human freedom, but frequently they deny freedom to God. Moreover, all models incorporating hard determinism which also rule out any human freedom must be rejected, and paradox determinism cannot be adopted, for it explicitly denies that humans are free.

This affirmation of biblical teaching on human freedom and moral responsibility may seem to require general sovereignty, but that is not so. As we already saw, there is an indeterministic notion of freedom and a deterministic one; neither concept is impossible, i.e., neither is self-contradictory as is the idea of a married bachelor or a round square. Since both notions are possible, at this stage of the discussion we can say that any theology with either notion of freedom is *possibly* correct. Hence, all forms of general sovereignty are possibilities, and the soft deterministic form of specific sovereignty is also possibly correct.

Advocates of general sovereignty see the evidence that humans are free and morally responsible, and many contend that this proves that incompatibilism is true. They conclude this because they think this is the only kind of freedom there is or could be. One frequently sees in their writings phrases such as "genuine freedom" and "real freedom," by which they mean libertarian free will. Any other notion is only a pretender to the "real thing." However, since both libertarian and compatibilistic free will are possible types of freedom, it begs the question to claim that only libertarian freedom is "real," "genuine," or "meaningful" free will. Such question begging maneuvers are not arguments or evidence for one's views; they merely reassert one's definition of free will and illegitimately refuse to consider other possible alternatives. Suffice it to say that neither side can win this debate by defining its opponent out of existence as "unreal," "not genuine," or "not meaningful." We need an actual argument that the sort of freedom described is correct.

What I have just said about question begging is entirely beside the point if Scripture teaches not only that humans are free but also that our freedom is incompatibilistic. The truth of the matter, however, is that Scripture does not say what sort of freedom we have; it only teaches that we are free. This should not surprise us, however, since Scripture is not a philosophy text which intends to offer a precise (metaphysically speaking) definition of human freedom.[2] Moreover, this point has some significant implications. One is that we cannot prove either libertarian or compatibilistic free will just by citing passages that teach human freedom and/or moral responsibility. If we want to choose one or the other concept of freedom on biblical and theological grounds, we must support our views in a more indirect way. That is, we must argue the case for a particular kind of free will inferentially from other truths taught by Scripture which best fit our notion of freedom. Inferring our conclusions about the kind of free will we possess doesn't mean we can't justify those views. Rather, it reminds us of the kind of issue this is, and reminds us that no biblical passage directly and explicitly defines freedom.

The Basic Argument

How, then, should we proceed? Since the issue is a relational one, i.e., since we must decide how human freedom relates to divine power and sovereignty, we must turn to the other half of the question, divine sovereignty. Depending on our understanding of God's sovereignty and the degree to which he exercises it, we should be able to say something more about the type of freedom humans possess.

As to divine sovereignty, recall our discussion of the decree in chapter 11. I won't repeat the evidence, but from passages that speak about the decree, we concluded that it is unconditional in that it stems from and depends on nothing but God's own desires and purposes. Our study of foreknowledge also confirmed that things decreed in accord with God's foreknowledge are based solely on his own purposes and desires. Moreover, we noted the many passages that show conjointly that everything (our salvation, the length of our life, the time of our death, or the minute details of our lives) is decreed by God. We also saw that the decree is efficacious and that the decree is not itself an agent but rather a blueprint for all of history.

While many verses teach these things about the divine plan (see especially Ps 115:3; Job 42:2; and Dan 4:35 for the all-inclusiveness of God's plan), I suggested that one verse, Eph 1:11, is especially compelling. Paul writes, "also we have obtained an inheritance, having been predestined according to His purpose who works all things after the counsel of His will." This is part of Paul's description of the blessings we have in Christ because of our salvation. It speaks of our inheritance as believers, an inheritance that is ours because God predestined us to salvation. So, the general theme of the section and of the verse in particular is our salvation. The phrase "who works . . . His will" is a relative clause which modifies "His." The relative clause is part of a participial clause ("having been predestined . . . His will") that modifies the main verb "obtained." So the initial focus of the verse is that in Christ, believers have received an inheritance. The rest of the verse amplifies and explains how this has happened. It has happened because we were predestined according to God's purpose. Moreover, the one who predestined us also works all things after the counsel of his will.

Unless there is a distinction in this verse between the purpose, counsel, and will of God, it is tremendously redundant. Commentators suggest that the different terms are not identical in this passage. "Purpose" (*prothesin*) refers to the goal God intends to accomplish; it is his ultimate design. Paul says that our predestination to salvation was done according to that design or aim. This means that our election wasn't based on what God foresaw about how we would respond when told the gospel. If Paul had meant that, he could have easily said that. Saying that we were predestined according to God's purpose suggests that his decision was based solely on his desires, i.e., it was unconditional.

The next phrase (the relative clause) confirms that election was based on God's design alone. Again Paul could have said that God works all things or even some things (or at least salvation) according to what he foresees about us. Instead, he writes that election fits the purposes of the one who works everything after the counsel of his will. Election is a particular instance of God's general *modus operandi*. As to the distinction between "counsel" (*boulē*) and "will" (*thelēma*), "counsel" indicates purpose and deliberation. It can even refer to the plan that springs from such deliberation. On the other hand, "will" simply denotes choosing. The whole participial phrase then teaches that our predestination to salvation was done according to a divine pattern. That pattern is: God has a purpose or goal he wants to accomplish. He deliberates about the best way to reach his goal, and from that deliberative process springs forth a plan (*boulē*) that he deems best. God wills (*thelēma*) that plan, and then brings it to pass (*energountos*). Nothing in this verse suggests that the purpose, the deliberating, or the choosing of the plan is based on anything other than God. Hence, the verse seems to teach God's unconditional decision.[3]

The verse also says that God works out or accomplishes all things. This needs explanation, and it relates to my discussion in chapter 13. I noted there that God does some things immediately (by himself without using any intermediary agents), but most things mediately (through the agency of his creatures). I also introduced a further distinction concerning God's mediate action that I raised in a symposium with George Mavrodes. I need not repeat those points, but only refer readers to chapter 13.

Two further points about this verse are noteworthy. One is that the focus of the main verb is clearly salvation. Moreover, the participle that begins the participial phrase ("having been predestined") refers to matters of salvation. As a result, some think that the rest of the verse, including the relative clause, must only be about God's activities in relation to salvation. This is certainly a possible understanding of "all things," but not the only one. There is no reason that a writer speaking about one topic cannot make a point about that topic and then generalize the point (by means of a relative clause) to cover a number of things that go beyond the immediate topic under discussion. Thus, Paul could be extending his point about predestination according to God's purpose to explain that God handles everything this way. In fact, there is good reason to think this is exactly what he is doing. If the relative clause means only that God works all things concerning our salvation after the counsel of his will, rather than that God works everything whatsoever according to the counsel of his will, then the relative clause seems redundant. The redundancy isn't just that Paul has already said in verse 11 that we were predestined according to his purpose, but also that verses 3-10 already speak about our election according to the kind intention of God's will (vv. 4-5), our adoption, Christ's redemption, and the like. Having reminded readers of all the things God has done to save them because of his good purposes and the kindness of his will, and having already repeated in verse 11 that we are predestined according to his purpose, for Paul then to repeat that predestination was done in the way God does everything else *in relation to salvation* would seem redundant. On the other hand, if the point of the relative clause is that what God has done in saving us matches the procedure he uses for everything that happens, that is not redundant or repetitious.

The other point about this verse is that Paul does not say that God has authority and power to predestine us according to his purposes alone, but never exercises it. Nor does Paul say that God as sovereign has the power to work all things according to the counsel of his will, but he chooses to forego using that power. Rather, Eph 1:3-14 speaks of things that God not only has the right and power to do but also actually does. If the libertarian proposal about God limiting his power is true, there is no hint of it in this passage. Instead, Paul revels in the thought that God has such power and in beneficent mercy has used it to save us.

How does Eph 1:11 square with biblical teaching that humans are free and morally responsible? As already noted, biblical passages about our freedom don't say whether it is libertarian or compatibilistic freedom. However, whatever the nature of our freedom, it must be exercised in relation to God's sovereignty. While Eph 1:11's robust notion of divine sovereignty would fit many hard deterministic systems, we cannot adopt them, because Scripture also teaches human freedom, and hard determinism rules out all senses of freedom. Can such a strong notion of sovereignty as taught by the decree and by passages such as Eph 1:11 fit libertarian free will? Not if that sovereignty is exercised consistently in the way Eph 1:11 suggests. The fact that general sovereignty advocates who grant God such power in the first place add that he restricts use of it to make room for libertarian freedom shows that they understand that such sovereignty, not only possessed but exercised, doesn't mesh with libertarian free will. For God to guarantee that his decree will be accomplished means that on at least some occasions libertarian free will must be overridden. If not, there is no guarantee with libertarian freedom that God's ends will be achieved.

If libertarian free will contradicts this kind of sovereignty when it is exercised, then on biblical grounds, no model of providence incorporating libertarian free will should be adopted. Other arguments may support general sovereignty, but on the biblical grounds presented so far, it is in serious trouble. On the other hand, is there some model of providence that incorporates some notion of freedom along with this strong sense of divine sovereignty? If not, then we should reconsider whether God has such sovereignty or whether he has it but chooses not to exercise it. But there *is* a model of providence that incorporates this strong sense of sovereignty *and* free will. Through this process of inferential reasoning we find that the best fit with biblical teaching about both divine sovereignty and human freedom is a model of specific sovereignty that incorporates compatibilistic free will. Scripture does not explicitly say that humans have compatibilistic free will, but compatibilism is chosen because it is the only notion that fits a model of providence that incorporates freedom (and reflects Scripture in that respect) and a strong notion of divine sovereign control (and squares with biblical teaching in that regard).

As to how this model understands human freedom operating alongside of divine control, I refer readers to my description of a soft deterministic model of providence in chapter 13. General sovereignty advocates, of course, object to what I am proposing, so I turn to their objections. In the process of answering those objections, I can explain more fully how this model of providence works, and offer further biblical and theological evidence for it.

Objections to My Handling of Eph 1:11, and My Responses

Advocates of general sovereignty will likely respond to my handling of Eph 1:11 with one of two objections: 1) my interpretation is incorrect; a reinterpretation of the passage is in order; or 2) I have properly interpreted the passage, but there is biblical evidence that God decided to limit his use of his power to make room for libertarian free will. Let me address each objection separately.

Suppose that one rejects my interpretation of Eph 1:11. What reinterpretation might one propose? Let me suggest three possibilities, and evaluate each. A first reinterpretation says that my understanding of the verse makes it apply to everything that ever occurs. However, a closer look at the passage shows that it is only about salvation. Taking the relative clause in verse 11 to refer to everything broadens the scope of the verse too much. The verse does teach that whatever God does in regard to salvation is done according to the counsel of his will, but it does not say that everything that ever happens was decreed by God.

As previously noted, this is a possible way to understand the relative clause. However, I explained my reasons for thinking that the relative clause does broaden the verse's teaching to everything that happens, and I need not repeat those arguments. In addition, if the proponent of general sovereignty interprets the verse this way, he harms his own position. On this interpretation, the verse teaches exactly what advocates of specific sovereignty say about God's control in our world; the only difference is that it limits the verse to God's control of salvation alone. Such an interpretation is detrimental to the general sovereignty view. Defenders of general sovereignty maintain that God gave us libertarian free will because he thought it preferable to have creatures love and follow him freely, not because they were causally determined to do so. Of all the choices human beings make, decisions about our relationship to God and Christ are the most significant, and God surely wants those decisions to be made freely (in the libertarian sense), according to general sovereignty advocates. However, the proposed reinterpretation of Eph 1:11 still makes the decision to accept Christ causally determined by God's electing decree. Hence, precisely the decision libertarians most want free is now, on this interpretation of Eph 1:11, causally determined and hence not (incompatibilistically) free.

There is even a further problem with this reinterpretation. Anyone committed to a strong view of divine sovereignty and to some form of determinism will wonder why, if God can causally determine beforehand what will happen with respect to this choice by humans, he cannot also decree everything else that ever occurs. Having allowed divine foreordination and causal determinism into the universe to cover this decision, why remove the same divine control from everything else that happens? So, all of these problems with this first reinterpretation remove it from serious contention.

Bruce Reichenbach offers a second reinterpretation of Eph 1:11. In his response to my essay in *Predestination and Free Will,* he says that the relative clause in question is ambiguous. It can be understood in one of two ways.

According to the first, the phrase says that God works everything according to the counsel of his will. A second reading understands it as saying that God works *everything that he works* according to the counsel of his will. With the first understanding, God controls everything. But the second reading says instead that whatever God does, he does according to the counsel of his will. Of course, that doesn't require God to decree or do everything. It suggests only that God does some things that happen in our world, and that he does them in accordance with the counsel of his will. Of these two possible understandings of the relative clause, which is preferable? Reichenbach says that the grammar of the sentence doesn't help us decide between the two interpretations.[4] Though Reichenbach doesn't say the second understanding is definitely correct, he seems to prefer that reading. At any rate, the mere possibility of this alternate interpretation shows that my argument based on this verse is far from conclusive, in Reichenbach's opinion.

If Eph 1:11 says what Reichenbach suggests, that would surely blunt the force of my argument. But how likely is Reichenbach's proposal? Upon examining the original text of the verse, there is no such ambiguity as Reichenbach claims. The Greek reads *prooristhentes kata prothesin tou ta panta energountos kata tēn boulēn tou thelēmatos autou* ("having been predestined according to the purpose of the one who works all things according to the counsel of his will"). The word for "works" is the participle *energountos*. For the verse to say what Reichenbach proposes, there would have to be another relative pronoun for "which," and another occurrence of the verb *energeō* in the third person singular. And all of this would likely precede the final *kata* clause. Clearly, the words needed in the Greek text to support Reichenbach's second reading are not there, nor are they present in English translations either. If the verse were ambiguous in the way Reichenbach proposes, we might expect to see the second reading in some Greek texts or English translations. The absence of such readings, plus the absence of the needed words in the original text, suggest that the verse is not ambiguous in the way Reichenbach proposes. So, although this reinterpretation of Eph 1:11 would avoid the implications of the verse that I suggest, it has little to commend it.

Jack Cottrell offers a third proposal. He agrees that the passage offers considerable support to Calvinism if the scope of "all things" is universal or absolute. However, he believes this is unlikely, because there are limitations put upon it by the context. Rather than explaining what those limitations are, Cottrell points to other Scriptures where "all things" is used in a limited sense. He cites John 19:28; Acts 17:25; Rom 8:32; 1 Cor 6:12; 12:6; and Eph 6:21. Cottrell thinks 1 Cor 12:6 is especially significant because the language is exactly parallel to Eph 1:11. The Corinthians passage says that God works all things in all people, but clearly in context, the topic is the gifts of the Spirit. In a similar way, Cottrell argues that there is a limiting factor in the context of Eph 1:11. That factor is in verse 9, which speaks about "the mystery of [God's] will." What is that mystery? Cottrell answers that 3:6 tells us; it is the uniting of Jews and Gentiles together in the church under the one head Jesus Christ (1:10). Hence, the "all things" of 1:11 refers to everything required for uniting Jews and Gentiles under Jesus Christ in one body.[5]

Previously, I granted that the relative clause could function more narrowly than I interpreted it. However, I have offered reasons to think otherwise. Are Cottrell's arguments convincing reasons for thinking that we should restrict the scope of "all things?" I think not for several reasons. Cottrell cites a number of passages wherein he thinks "all things" is not universal. Even if we grant this for all the passages cited, his argument is an example of "in principle" argumentation. That is, the most it shows is that something has happened once, so the principle is established that this sort of thing *can* occur on other occasions. If it happened once, there is no principle that precludes its occurrence a second time. Unfortunately, far too many biblical exegetes and theologians think this sort of argument is conclusive. This is a logical error of the first order, for it moves from the principle that something has occurred once to the conclusion that it is occurring again. Word studies like Cottrell's at most show that it is *possible* that "all things" in Eph 1:11 is used in a restrictive sense. It doesn't prove that this actually is the case in that passage. We need an argument from Eph 1:11 that this is happening again, and we don't get it by appealing to 1 Cor 12:6, even if the structure of the sentence resembles that in Eph 1:11. A similar grammatical structure and word choice in both passages doesn't prove that they mean the same thing. One need not be a philosopher of language to know that the exact same words uttered in separate contexts have different meanings! The phrase "look out" has various meanings depending on context. This point is especially significant in our case since Cottrell admits that 1 Cor 12:6 appears in a context about spiritual gifts. That is surely not the same context or topic we have in Ephesians 1, as even Cottrell explains. So why should we think this line of argument proves anything more than that "all things" *could* have a limited scope in Eph 1:11 because in other passages, it does?

Still, we must acknowledge that Cottrell does find something in Ephesians 1 which leads him to think we should restrict the scope of "all things" in verse 11. That factor appears in verse 9, which speaks of "the mystery of his will." Unfortunately, rather than sticking with the immediate context of chapter 1 to find out what that mystery is and how verse 11 relates to it, Cottrell jumps to Eph 3:6 where he thinks he finds the meaning of "the mystery of His will." Eph 3:4 mentions the mystery of Christ, and verse 6 does speak of uniting Gentiles and Jews as fellow-heirs in the body of Christ, but that doesn't prove that the context of chapter 3 is talking about the specific point under discussion in chapter 1. However, Cottrell thinks it does because 3:6 is reminiscent of 1:10, which says "with a view to an administration suitable to the fulness of the times, that is, the summing up of all things in Christ, things in the heavens and things upon the earth." Cottrell links the implicit headship of Christ (1:10) with the more explicit headship of Christ in 3:6, and thinks he has shown that chapter 1 and chapter 3 are talking about the same thing. Since chapter 3 speaks of a mystery that only involves bringing together Jew and Gentile in the church, "all things" in chapter 1 must refer only to all things concerning that program for the church.

Here again is another case of linking two passages' meaning on the initial ground of the same word ("mystery") appearing in both. That is inadequate grounds for thinking the two passages are speaking about the exact same thing; but beyond that, even if both passages are generally about some divine mystery, how does that tell us the scope of "all things" in Eph 1:11? Linking passages that generally speak about a divine mystery is not enough to tell us the meaning of a very specific phrase in a relative clause of a sentence that doesn't mention the mystery. But Cottrell thinks there is more reason to link the passages than just the word "mystery." Both talk about Christ's headship, and chapter 3 clearly shows his headship of the church, a body incorporating both Jews and Gentiles. But this is a second problem with Cottrell's invoking chapter 3 into chapter 1, for chapter 1 makes no comment about Jews and Gentiles; its point of reference is the salvation of all believers. In fact, it isn't until chapter 2 that Paul begins to talk about Jew-Gentile relations and the bringing of them together in one body, the church. So why should we think we should read chapter 3 back into chapter 1, let alone allow it to be decisive for the meaning of a specific phrase in 1:11?

Cottrell would likely point to 1:10, but this also doesn't make his case, for several reasons. The phrase "the summing up of all things in Christ" can reasonably be taken to refer to the lordship and headship of Christ. This undoubtedly refers to his headship over the church, but the verse refers to more, because Paul then says that "all things" includes "things in heaven and things upon the earth." That is surely much more inclusive than the bringing of living Jews and Gentiles together into the church. What do all things in heaven and on earth have to do with that? This must not be misunderstood. I am not saying that Christ's headship over the church is not included, but only that it is a subset of everything that Paul speaks about as summed up under Christ. By the end of the first chapter Paul makes the point explicit by returning to Christ's lordship over all rule, power, and dominion (vv. 20-21), *and* over the church (vv. 22-23)—but note that he doesn't distinguish Jew from Gentile in the church in those verses! So the mystery of God's will which he purposed in Christ (1:8-9) is the universal headship of Christ over all things in heaven and earth (v. 10).

This is ample reason to reject the idea that the mystery of his will (1:9) refers only to bringing Jew and Gentile together in the church, and to reject imposing that notion on the meaning of a phrase in a relative clause in verse 1:11. But there is further reason to avoid this mistake, namely, verse 11 itself. The sentence begins at the end of verse 10, and the main clause says literally "In Him, in whom also we have obtained an inheritance." A key word here is "also" (*kai*). The reason I say this is that its use here shows that Paul intends in verse 11 to make a further point beyond the point(s) he has been making.

Since that is so, the further point need not be about exactly the same thing Paul has just said. Hence, even if we grant what Cottrell claims about the mystery and grant the treatment of verses 9-10 that he proposes, the fact that Paul make a further point (*kai* in v. 11) shows that Paul is not necessarily carrying over his point from the previous verses, i.e., there is no guarantee that everything said in verse 11 relates only to things dealing with bringing together Jews and Gentiles in the church (an interpretation of vv. 9-10 that I have suggested is suspect, anyway). In verse 11, the general theme is salvation, but Paul makes a point (at least one) about salvation that he hasn't previously made in this passage. That point is that our election was accomplished according to the purpose of the one who works all things according to the counsel of his will. While Paul has already talked about election in this passage, the new element is the claim that God controls everything and does so in the same way that he handles predestination to salvation.

For these reasons, I find Cottrell's interpretation wanting. He should be commended for seeing that the verse needs response from general sovereignty proponents, and his suggestion, like the other two mentioned, does grapple with the text. But in the final analysis it is deficient. There may be other possible reinterpretations of Eph 1:11, but I am not aware of them. Unfortunately, this verse doesn't often get handled by either side in the debate. Until a more convincing interpretation is offered, I see little reason to abandon the understanding I offered as part of the case for specific sovereignty.

General sovereignty advocates might take another tack. They might grant that the verse teaches that God has absolute sovereign power, but argue that he has chosen to restrict its use to allow room for our libertarian free will. In an earlier publication,[6] I said that if I could find even one verse that says God limited his sovereign power as proposed, I would grant the Arminian case. Arminians often respond by citing verses that show humans are free and morally responsible. Of course, none of those verses define free will as libertarian, so they don't prove the free will theist's case. However, general sovereignty advocates could grant that those verses alone don't make the case, but those verses plus the evidence presented earlier that God limits himself do require that God has limited the use of his power, so the freedom we have is libertarian freedom.

This line of argument is very helpful, for it clarifies the point that needs response. Since both soft determinists and incompatibilists agree that Scripture teaches that humans are free, we need a way to decide what kind of freedom that is. I argued that biblical teaching on freedom and divine sovereignty fits compatibilistic freedom best. The general sovereignty proponent may reply that Eph 1:11 does teach a strong notion of sovereign control, but more evidence must be considered before we draw a final conclusion about the kind of freedom humans have. The further evidence is all the evidence that God chose to limit the use of his power. If this is correct, my understanding of Eph 1:11 can be right but it won't really matter, because evidence that God restricts his power favors the conclusion that our freedom must be libertarian. So we must examine the evidence for God's limiting his power.

Advocates of general sovereignty first point to Christ's incarnation as compelling evidence that God limits his power to serve our needs. Indeed, during the years of Jesus' earthly life and death we saw the extent to which God humbled himself for our sakes, but some thirty-three years of humiliation doesn't prove that the whole Godhead has decided to limit use of their power throughout all of human history. It doesn't even show that God exercised none of his sovereign power during Christ's lifetime. On the contrary, many Scriptures (e.g., Acts 2:23; 1 Pet 1:20) show that what happened to Christ while he was on earth was entirely within God's sovereign plan and control. Moreover, Scripture also teaches that Christ is Lord and ruler over all and that God has subjected all things to Christ's sovereign rule (Eph 1:19-23).

Another problem with this argument is that it is another example of in principle argumentation. Because Jesus in his earthly life greatly humbled himself, that establishes the principle that God can lay aside the use of his divine prerogatives to serve our needs. Specific sovereignty advocates agree that God did this and that it is *possible* for him to do it again. What specific sovereignty defenders like myself want to know is what evidence there is that what God could do is what he has *actually* done in regard to his control of human history. Showing that God can again restrict his power because he has done so in Christ's earthly life and death, doesn't prove that he has done so for the rest of human history!

The second and third arguments for divine self-limitation are especially unconvincing. Claiming that creating a world limits God since now others inhabit the universe is no argument at all. This could only matter to God's exercise of sovereign power if, by creating other beings, either God's power and control or his exercise thereof is automatically restricted. Obviously, the fact of creation proves no such thing, so this argument amounts to nothing. It is no more compelling than saying God had to create, because if he didn't, he would be limited by being the solitary existent in the universe and thereby having nothing over which to exercise his control.

As to the claim that God cannot do the logically impossible or things that contradict his nature, this is true but irrelevant to the point in question. God's inability to do the logically impossible in no way proves that he cannot decree all things and exercise sovereign control over his universe. Indeed, God cannot control human action if it is incompatibilistically free, but it hasn't been shown that humans have such freedom. In fact, this line of argument was constructed to prove that libertarian free will does obtain in our world; assuming that it does at this stage of the argument is question begging. Moreover, God's inability to do the logically impossible or to contradict his nature is no evidence that he has decided to limit his sovereign control over our world. It is a *non sequitur* to think the former logically requires or is even evidence for the latter.

The fourth evidence for self-limitation of divine power is the fact of God's love. We are told that love makes room for the beloved and implies vulnerability toward the beloved. Those who love make themselves dependent on the good-will and response of their beloved. To exercise dominating power over others doesn't show them love. Now there is no question that God loves us, and whether he has a positive relation to us or not depends in part on our response to him. But how does that alone prove either that God must forego the use of his power in order for us to love him, or that he has in fact decided to cede the use of his power and control over history? Loving someone definitely means that you take them into account, and that you are vulnerable to the possibility that they may reject you, but again, none of that means that it is impossible to exercise authority over them. If it did, then parental love for and exercise of parental authority over one's children are mutually exclusive, and that is clearly false. So the fundamental assumption behind this argument is flawed. Love and exercise of power and authority are not contradictory. There are many times when we use our authority and power to forestall untoward consequences for others because we do love and care about them.

The final evidence that God has limited his power is that creating a world with the sort of creatures present in our world limits God's exercise of his power. This is so because, we are told, those creatures have libertarian free will. Indeed, if humans have libertarian free will and are allowed to use it, God cannot exercise the kind of control that determinism allows. But what is at issue *is* whether human freedom is libertarian. Saying that *if* humans have such freedom, God must have limited his control, is true, but it proves nothing about whether humans in fact have this sort of freedom or whether God has restricted his power *in this way*. Thinking that the *if* sentence (the conditional) proves libertarian free will or divine self-limitation is question begging.

Where does this leave us? Remember that the question is whether we should take Eph 1:11 as I have interpreted it, or whether we should grant that God has the power of which this verse speaks but argue that he has chosen to limit his use of it. The general sovereignty case for God limiting his power is found wanting. It is filled with in principle arguments, *non sequiturs,* and question begging. Hence, neither attempts to reinterpret Eph 1:11 nor attempts to show that God has chosen to limit his power are convincing. I conclude, then, that the best way to understand what Eph 1:11 and other passages about the divine decree say, along with biblical teaching on human freedom and moral responsibility, is along the lines of the compatibilist model of specific sovereignty I have proposed.

This doesn't end the debate, however, for the general sovereignty proponent has a further counter argument. This objection is especially prevalent among defenders of the open view. Since various Scriptures seem to portray God as having less than full control over situations and as not getting exactly what he wants, we are faced with a major question. Are such passages the key ones for understanding God's sovereign control in our world, or are passages such as Eph 1:11 about God's decree the normative passages? The passages that are normative for a given subject determine Scripture's teaching about that subject. Of course we can't ignore passages that seem to teach something contrary to the "normative" passages. All Scripture is inspired, but which passages are normative and which are secondary for a given doctrine?

This is no small issue, and it relates not only to Scriptures about God's control of our world, but also, as open view proponents remind us, to many passages about the divine attributes. Some passages say that God is immutable, but others show him changing his mind, repenting of actions he originally thought to do. If God is immutable, then he is also apparently impassible, but many Scriptures depict him expressing emotions. God is said to be omniscient, but some passages seem to show him learning something he didn't know, and there are other passages where he seems to be caught off guard, all of which seems impossible if, as omniscient, he knows and anticipates everything. As openness of God advocates are quick to note, their opponents usually assert that such passages are anthropomorphisms or anthropopathisms and should not be taken literally; passages that assert immutability, omniscience, and absolute sovereignty are deemed normative and literally true, whereas passages open view defenders cite are considered secondary, in need of modification as metaphorical in light of the other passages which are to be taken more literally. Open view proponents loudly protest that such a decision is at best a mistaken handling of the text, and at worst gross indulgence of question begging. Hence, when specific sovereignty advocates cite passages that Sanders calls pancausality passages, open view proponents see no reason why these are not the nonliteral passages that must be nuanced to fit the more literal passages that teach that God doesn't control everything.[7] In discussing the open view's notion of limited divine omniscience, Basinger answers those who claim that passages used to support limited omniscience are anthropomorphisc. His hermeneutical point (and logical point) is the same one open view proponents make about which passages are normative and literal in regard to divine control of our world, and which are secondary and metaphorical. Basinger writes:

> Of course, there are many passages in which God is described anthropomorphically or anthropopathically. However, none of the passages on which we base our position requires that God possess "literal body parts" or a literal human personality. They require only that God *literally* be a being who observes that which is occurring, is affected by it and decides how to act in response. And we find no nonquestion-begging basis for assuming that the passages we believe portray God in this fashion are simply figures of speech.[8]

Is there a way out of this impasse, or are we simply left to consult our presuppositions and then choose the passages as normative and literal that agree with those assumptions? If so, there is little hope that citing verses and offering one's interpretation of them will convince anyone who doesn't already agree that the verses we mention are the "key" verses. Thankfully, there is a way to break the impasse, and I contend that it depends on a critical point of theological method that is too frequently overlooked or missed altogether in theological discussions. Let me explain.

If you wanted to formulate the biblical/theological doctrines of justification, inspiration of Scripture, or the second coming of Christ, for example, to which passages would you turn? Which would be the determinative passages for those doctrines? Wouldn't the passages that address those subjects be the key passages? It seems hard to contest this, for if we should not form doctrines using passages that speak about the doctrine, how can we claim to reflect scriptural teaching on that topic?

What are the passages that address the topics in question? Richard Rice in *The Openness of God* offers a biblical case for the open view. John Sanders in *The God Who Risks* offers a lengthy chapter of biblical evidence from the OT and another with NT evidence in support of the open view. Both authors cite many passages that relate to human freedom and divine control over our world. But what sort of passages do they choose for painting their portraits of God? Repeatedly, they select narrative passages that record one incident or another of God's dealings with various people. These passages that describe God's interactions with his world are taken to be the key for determining our conceptual understanding of the divine attributes and divine action and control in our world. In contrast, passages such as Eph 1:11 and the passages cited in my chapter on the decree that state that God decreed one thing or another are not narratives of incidents involving God and some person or group of people. Rather, they are didactic passages that explain the concept of divine action and control in our world.

Which kind of passage has precedence and should be seen as normative? This doesn't mean that the other passages don't matter and can be ignored. Since both sets of passages are Scripture, we must treat them all. But are passages that offer didactic information about the concept in question the central passages, or are passages that show us God and man interacting the key? What is the proper way to do theology? The answer should be clear. One should go first to passages that directly address the concept in question, for they are the basis for our fundamental understanding of the concept. We must also address the other passages, but they should be understood in light of the passages that didactively set forth the concept. If I am working on the doctrine of justification, for example, I go first to passages in Romans and James that cover the concept of justification and discuss how it relates to works and faith. I don't turn to passages that describe someone witnessing and the hearer accepting Christ. The latter passages offer examples of people who were justified by faith, but they don't explain what justification is or what it means to say that justification is by faith. Similarly, the passages (such as Eph 1:11; Ps 115:3) that tell whether God has decreed all things and controls them are passages that directly address the kind of control God has and uses in the world, not passages that tell a story about what God did on one occasion, how some human responded, and then how God reacted to that response. A major problem with the open view's biblical case is that it relies heavily on passages of the latter sort, rather than grappling with passages of the former kind. For all his lengthy treatment of biblical passages, Sanders never touches Eph 1:11. Some passages that are didactic do get coverage (I shall say more shortly about Sanders's treatment of passages from Proverbs and Romans 9, for example), but those are not the passages he thinks normative. Rather, his views about God's attributes and God's exercise of power come from the many biblical stories he recounts.

Rice doesn't treat Eph 1:11 either, but he does cite passages that speak of predestination and divine foreknowledge. However, they are raised in a sub-section of a larger section titled "problem passages." A problem for what? For the open view, which he believes he has already shown to be true by recounting (for most of his chapter) various narrative passages (stories) from which he believes it appropriate to infer one thing or another about divine attributes and actions. As with Sanders, didactic passages that present concepts are secondary to the narrative stories. Rice lists many didactic passages but interacts with none of them. Instead, in a summary response, he points first to passages, many of which he already examined (many of them narrative passages), which seem to disagree with predestination passages. He then points to further passages he thinks somehow teach doctrines that defeat the other predestination passages (without ever giving a thorough exegesis of either set of predestination passages), and then he returns to the narrative passages which support his own perspective. Note his response to the predestination passages:

> Are these accounts of foreknowledge and predestination compatible with the open view of God? Or do they require us to conclude that the future is entirely foreseen by him and to a significant extent, if not entirely, determined by him? The first thing to bear in mind is the wide range of biblical testimony. In addition to the sort of passages just noticed, which speak of God's plans being fulfilled, numerous passages (including a number already examined) indicate that this is not always the case. To cite a general example, the Bible asserts that God does not want "anyone to perish, but everyone to come to repentance" (2 Pet 3:9); he "wants all men to be saved and to come to a knowledge of the truth" (1 Tim 2:4; cf. Tit 2:11). Yet it appears that not all will be saved. According to Jesus' statement, all of the dead will come back to life—"those who have done good, to the resurrection of life, and those who have done evil, to the resurrection of condemnation" (Jn 5:29 NRSV). Other passages indicate that some human beings set themselves against God for eternity (Mt 21:41-46; Rev 20:14-15; cf. Mt 7:12-14). In this important respect, then, God's will does not guarantee the outcome that he desires.[9]

The next paragraphs of Rice's essay return to the narratives that he cites as evidence that God doesn't always get his way. Rice's comments above about God's will not guaranteeing the outcome he desires (supported by appeal to 2 Pet 3:9; 1 Tim 2:4; John 5:29; Mt 21:41-46; Rev 20:14-15; and the like) rest on a confusion I will address in dealing with the next objection to be raised against specific sovereignty. For now, I only ask the reader to note that none of this interacts with verses such as 1 Pet 1:20; Acts 2:23; 4:27-28; 1 Pet 1:2; Eph 1:4-5; Rom 8:28-30; Rom 9:10-11; etc., all of which Rice cites (he even quotes some) but never addresses directly. Instead of grappling with these passages, he shifts the ground of the discussion to previously discussed passages—2 Pet 3:9; 1 Tim 2:4; and the like—and more narratives.

This mere quoting of Scriptures that fit one's own position in response to those that don't, rather than grappling with the hard passages, isn't the way to win this debate. Just because you believe you have good evidence for your view, that doesn't turn the good evidence for your opponent's view into no evidence at all. But my major point is about proper theological method, and that point is that doctrines are to be based first on passages that directly address the concepts in question. Narrative stories that we deem relevant to the topic cannot be ignored, but they must be interpreted in light of passages that directly raise and address the topic.

From the preceding I conclude that objections that dismiss as non-normative and secondary passages such as Eph 1:11, which speak directly about what God has decreed, are wrongheaded and should themselves be rejected.

Other Objections

A major support for the general sovereignty model is biblical evidence that things happen that God doesn't want. For example, I cited Richard Rice's claim that evidently God does not control everything, since he isn't willing that any should perish (2 Pet 3:9) but many do perish. All of this supposedly shows that, if there is a decree, it is conditional.

THWARTING GOD'S WILL. This objection raises a fundamental question about whether God's creatures can thwart his will. Job concluded that no one can (Job 42:2), but the evidence seems to suggest otherwise. In response, let me begin with 2 Pet 3:9 and 1 Tim 2:4. Peter says that God "is patient toward you, not willing for any to perish but for all to come to repentance" (author's translation). Paul tells Timothy (1 Tim 2:4) that God is a Savior who "wills all men to be saved and to come to the knowledge of the truth" (author's translation). The word for "willing" in 2 Pet 3:9 comes from *boulomai*, and the word in 1 Tim 2:4 is from the verb *thelō*. Both words correlate to words we find in Eph 1:11: *boulē* ("counsel") and *thelēmatos* ("will"). Since I argued that those words in Eph 1:11 refer to God's decree, it is natural to think that the same terms in 2 Peter 3 and 1 Timothy 2 also refer to the decree.

As hinted above, however, this objection to specific sovereignty confuses two distinct concepts. According to Rice's understanding, "willing" in 2 Pet 3:9 means "decreeing." If so, the verse means that "God is patient toward you, not decreeing that any should perish." Now, if God decrees everything that happens, and if the verse is about God's decree, then if God decrees that none will perish, he must decree everyone to be saved. On this reading, however, Peter is teaching universalism, and that contradicts biblical teaching that not everyone will be saved. Clearly, something is amiss if we adopt this interpretation.

Some might reply that the verse only teaches that God doesn't decree anyone's damnation. That is, there is no double decree, so people are lost because they reject Christ, not because they are predestined to damnation. Even if we grant this for the sake of argument, I can make the same point in regard to 1 Tim 2:4 about willing equaling decreeing. Anyway, commentators, including Rice, seem to think the two passages teach the same truth. What happens, then, if we read "wills" in 1 Tim 2:4 as "decrees?" Then the verse says God is a Savior who decrees all men to be saved. That is universalism, but throughout the Pauline corpus, he teaches that not everyone will be saved. So, if the passage is about God's decree, there is a major problem for any evangelical who rejects soteriological universalism.

To be sure, something is wrong with reading "willing" as "decreeing" in these two passages, but what? The problem is that we need to distinguish between God's will and his wish or desire. Some may think this improper, because the same Greek words are used in other passages that clearly speak of God's will/decree. However, usage shows that in some cases these terms refer to God's will (even his decree), whereas in others they refer to his wish or desire. I contend that in 2 Pet 3:9 and 1 Tim 2:4 the terms refer to God's wish or desire, not his will or decree. With this understanding, neither verse teaches universalism, nor does 2 Pet 3:9 make any comment about a double decree. Both verses speak of God's desire that everyone be saved, even though he has not decreed this to be so.

So, do these verses teach that one can thwart God's decree? Not at all. When properly understood, they show that one can do something contrary to God's desires, but that doesn't prove that one can thwart his decree. But there is more to the story than this, and it involves further distinctions. I am proposing that the notion of God's will is ambiguous, and this ambiguity fosters a great deal of confusion theologically and practically when people ask if they are in God's will or how they can find his will. Beyond the fundamental distinction between God's will and his wish, several further distinctions pertain to God's will itself.

The first distinction is between God's *preceptive will* and his *decretive will*. God's preceptive will refers to the moral norms for governing life that God set forth in his Word. It includes the Ten Commandments, but it involves any commands God orders us to obey. It includes commands to present our bodies as a living sacrifice (Rom 12:1), to be kind, tender-hearted, and forgiving toward one another (Eph 4:32), and commands not to grieve the Holy Spirit (Eph 4:30), but to be filled with the Holy Spirit (Eph 5:18). These precepts detail what God wants us to do with respect to the moral conduct of our life. Thus, frequently someone can know God's will for their life, if "God's will" means his preceptive will. Moreover, many theologians often refer to God's preceptive will as his *revealed* will. This idea stems from Deut 29:29, which distinguishes God's revealed and secret will. Of the revealed will Moses says, "But the things revealed belong to us and to our sons forever, that we may observe all the words of this law." The connection of the revealed will to the words of the Mosaic Law (the referrent of "this law") is the basis for calling God's preceptive will his revealed will.

In contrast to God's preceptive will is his *decretive will*. The decretive will of God refers to God's sovereign choice by which he decides whatever happens. The divine decree is God's blueprint for the history of our universe. God's decretive will contains everything he and his creatures will do throughout all of history. As previously explained (chapter 11), God's decree doesn't make history irrelevant, for it is not history, but its blueprint, and there is an obvious difference between a plan and its accomplishment. As also argued, God's decree is based on nothing but his own purposes, and his purposes are determined by nothing but God's own nature and his intentions to achieve certain goals; it is unconditional in that sense.

Most things in God's decree are known only to God before they occur. Hence, theologians, appealing to Deut 29:29, which also speaks of "the secret things," often refer to the decree as God's *secret will*. The only parts of God's decree that we know before they occur are the parts of God's Word that are predictive prophecy. Prophecy is nothing other than God sharing with us beforehand what he has decreed.

Since God's decree covers everything that ever occurs, whatever someone does is within God's will, i.e., the decretive will. Of course, not everything we do obeys God's precepts. Since the decree covers everything, it includes our sinful acts, but those sinful acts are contrary to God's preceptive will. So, an act may be in God's will (part of his decree), but outside of his will (preceptive will) at the same time, because it is sin.

More must be said about God's decretive will. Within the all-comprehensive decree we can distinguish two separate portions. The first can be called God's *perfect will*. I use this phrase as follows: the part of the decree which is God's decree of all morally good actions is his *perfect will*. In addition, there are various actions decreed which are in accord with God's best for us, even though no moral precept covers them. Here I am thinking of matters such as whom we should marry, what career we should pursue, where we should live. God's decree contains our decisions about those matters, and when God decrees that our decisions about such matters agree with his best for us, those choices are also part of God's perfect will. God's perfect will, then, refers to that part of the decree which contains all actions that obey God's moral rules and all actions that are in accord with God's best for us.

The second part of God's decree is his decree of all morally evil deeds. Those acts are contrary to God's moral law, and God doesn't want us to do these things, but he has decreed that we will do them, anyway. In addition, this part of the decree contains all our choices and acts which, though not covered by a moral precept, are still contrary to God's best for us (again, this covers matters such as whom we should marry, etc.). This portion of the decree is typically called God's *permissive will.* Theologians use this locution to safeguard against the idea that God is somehow morally responsible for evil, since he has decreed it. Though I understand why this label is used, I am hesitant to use it, because it gives the impression that God somehow surrenders control of things when we sin, for example, by letting us do what we want without foreordaining our actions.

On this matter I am influenced by Calvin. Calvin rejects the idea that God does not decree evil but only permits it. He affirms that God must be completely in control of all things, regardless of the consequences:

> From other passages, where God is said to bend or draw Satan himself and all the wicked to do his will, there emerges a more difficult question. For carnal sense can hardly comprehend how in acting through them he does not contract some defilement from their transgression, and even in a common undertaking can be free of all blame, and indeed can justly condemn his ministers. Hence the distinction was devised between doing and permitting because to many this difficulty seemed inexplicable, that Satan and all the impious are so under God's hand and power that he directs their malice to whatever end seems good to him, and uses their wicked deeds, to carry out his judgments. And perhaps the moderation of those whom the appearance of absurdity alarms would be excusable, except that they wrongly try to clear God's justice of every sinister mark by upholding a falsehood. It seems absurd to them for man, who will soon be punished for his blindness, to be blinded by God's will and command. Therefore, they escape by the shift that this is done only with God's permission, not also by his will; but he, openly declaring that he is the doer repudiates that evasion.[10]

Now, we don't have to agree with Calvin that God actually does the evil. Still, I am very sympathetic to his disdain for the word "permissive" because it does suggest that somehow God relinquishes control. Of course, God's decree of all things, including evil, does not mean that he is pleased with such acts or that he really wants or desires us to do them. In light of all these considerations, I prefer to call this portion of the decree God's *undesired will.* This is not the usual way to refer to the decree of evil, but I think it helps to avoid both the idea that God has no control over such acts *and* the idea that he is somehow pleased with them since he decreed them. If some insist on retaining the term *permissive will,* I don't think it is a point worth quibbling over. My only concern is that if we use that term, we remove from it any notion that God lacks control of these deeds, and we explain that we invoke it instead to underscore the point that God, though he decrees evil, does not do these deeds and is in no way morally responsible for them.[11]

Everything I have been saying about God's *will* (in its various senses) is in distinction to what I said about God's *wish*. Hence, we must distinguish God's wish from his decree. By God's wish, I mean God's desires about what he really wants us to do and his wishes about what he wants to happen. God's wish coincides in part with his *preceptive will*, for God really wishes us to obey his laws. God also has wishes or desires about things he knows are best for us, even if they aren't covered by some moral rule.

With this understanding of the different senses of God's will and with the distinction between God's will/decree and his wish, several questions arise. First, why must we distinguish God's wish from his decree? If God wants something to happen, doesn't he just decree it? Can't we just assume that if something is not in the decree, God didn't want it to happen, and if it is in the decree, God did want it? Is there a genuine difference between what God wishes and what he decrees? Indeed there is, and the distinction is necessary for at least two reasons.

The first reason for the distinction begins with Scriptures that teach God's decree and control of all things. The Bible also reveals God's precepts, and God definitely wants us to obey those laws. But if God decrees everything and some things that happen are evil and yet God doesn't want us to do evil, then strange as it may seem, logic demands that God must have decreed things which are contrary to divine laws that he wants us to obey. And Scripture confirms that God has decreed things that are contrary to his precepts. For example, God has revealed that he wants no one to commit murder. It is also clear that Christ's death was the murder of an innocent man. But Acts 2:23 affirms that this murder was decreed and controlled by God. *From the standpoint of God's redemptive purposes,* God wanted the crucifixion to occur. But in analyzing the crucifixion *in terms of its conformity to God's moral norms about murder,* we must say that God did not want it to happen. Hence, we can say that God decrees acts that are contrary to his wishes, i.e., they disobey his moral norms and/or his best for us, even though they are in accord with his ultimate plans and purposes for our world. So there is a sense in which God did and a sense in which he did not want Christ to die. Granted, this sounds ambiguous, but with careful attention to the distinction between the decretive and preceptive will (and with an understanding of how God's wish relates to his precepts and his decree), we can understand what seems otherwise hopelessly confused and unclear.

Given the two different standpoints just mentioned, we can also see why it is just too simplistic to claim that if some horrible evil occurs and Calvinists are right about the divine decree, God must really want that evil to occur. General sovereignty proponents frequently raise that objection, but it fails to understand that what God decrees can be in one respect what he wants, and in another not what he wants.

A second reason for this distinction between God's will (decree) and his wish relates to our discussion about 2 Pet 3:9 and 1 Tim 2:4. Without this distinction, these verses teach universalism, and that contradicts clear biblical teaching to the contrary. There are definite reasons, then, for distinguishing between God's will (decree) and his wish. The idea that God sometimes decrees things he really wishes would not occur, however, immediately suggests another question: if God sometimes chooses evil acts and events as means to his ends, and in those cases omits good actions and events as means to his ends, why would he do that? Isn't there a possible world God could have created in which only good events and deeds serve as means to his ends? This question is especially acute for compatibilists, who hold that God can decisively incline someone's will without constraining it to do a given act. Moreover, hard determinists who aren't worried about whether our actions are free should recognize even more that the kind of divine control their systems propose means God can put whatever he wants in the decree and make it happen. Even incompatibilists, however, face this challenge. Though they say that God cannot remove moral evil and guarantee human freedom at the same time, many wonder whether God should not have foregone giving us freedom in favor of removing evil. In light of divine power, it seems that all evangelicals grant God the ability to avoid all evil, so why hasn't he?

The questions posed in the preceding paragraph amount to the problem of evil. In chapter 16, I will address that issue, and however one handles that problem is how one should answer why God would allow (even decree) things that he doesn't really want to happen.

To sum up our discussion on God's will, the various senses of "will" and the distinction between God's will and wish are necessary for understanding biblical teaching about God's will.[12] These comments also rebut the objection that specific sovereignty cannot be a correct model of providence because it suggests that God's will is always done, whereas sometimes people seem to thwart God's will. A proper understanding of the distinctions I have made shows the confusions in this objection.

DECREE AS CONDITIONAL.   Jack Cottrell raises a different objection to specific sovereignty to the effect that the decree is actually conditional rather than unconditional. It is conditional because God foresees what we will do, and then plans his response to our actions. In the earlier chapter on the decree, we saw the answer to this. Scripture teaches that God's decisions are based on his will alone. Passages that say God decided on the basis of his foreknowledge do not mean that God's decree is conditioned by what he foresees us doing. Rather, the biblical terms for foreknowledge in the passages in question mean foreordination, not prescience. Hence, those passages do not teach a conditional decree but underscore the unconditionality of God's decree. We also noted a sense in which the decree is conditional, namely, it contains means to accomplishing various ends. But since both means and ends are unconditionally decreed on the basis of God's will alone, the decree is still unconditional as to its origin.

THE GOODNESS OF GOD.   Jerry Walls's argument from the goodness of God must also be addressed. Walls says that Arminian views ultimately rest on God's goodness, not on libertarian free will. The key issue is what a good God would do in relation to his creatures. God desires his creatures' happiness, so he would do whatever he could to enhance that. Sending people to hell for eternity will not enhance their happiness, so a good God would avoid that if he could. But he has not saved everyone, so we must ask why. Walls thinks the only sensible answer is that God gave those creatures libertarian free will, and if God is to maintain the integrity of that freedom, he cannot override it to force them to be saved. So people go to hell, despite God's goodness, because they choose it and God cannot stop them from doing so without removing their freedom.

In contrast, determinists, including Calvinists, allow whoever or whatever is in charge to get their way. Compatibilists even say that God can causally determine us to do freely what he chooses for us to do. If so, why wouldn't a good God just decree salvation for all? If Calvinists say God can do this but has not, then it seems that the Calvinist God is not good after all.

In reply, I won't quibble over whether a good God desires, let alone actualizes, his creatures' happiness. Let us grant that for the sake of argument. The key issue is whether God can save everyone if he so chooses. If God can save all without forfeiting anything else valuable that he has put in our world, then he must. Walls and other free will theists claim that God does not save all because he cannot. It isn't that God cannot *simpliciter,* if saving people is all he wants to do with our world. Rather, he cannot if he also wants to maintain the integrity of the libertarian freedom he gave us.

What about Calvinistic systems? Again, I agree that a good God must save all people if he can. Walls believes that since Calvinists such as myself believe humans are compatibilistically free, God can save us all without violating our free will, so why hasn't he done so? The answer is again that he cannot. It isn't that God cannot *simpliciter,* if saving compatibilistically free people is all he wants to do with our world. But God may have other goals for his creatures and creation (goals that are values of the first order) that cannot be achieved if he decrees to save everyone, even though everyone has compatibilistic free will. What could those other goals and values be that would justify not saving all of humanity? The answer will be offered when addressing the problem of evil. In fact, the challenge Walls raises is really the problem of evil, though his focus is the specific evil of hell. Each theology faces the question of why an omnipotent God would allow evil, including hell, if he can avoid it. Walls, following the usual Arminian approach, offers the free will defense. Elsewhere I have offered a defense for my own Calvinistic theology, and in the chapter on the problem of evil I will repeat it.

DETERMINISM AND MORAL RESPONSIBILITY.   There is another objection that involves moral responsibility which I can discuss now. Critics complain that deterministic systems destroy moral responsibility. If everything is causally determined and no one can do other than what they do, how can they be morally accountable for their actions? Yet Scripture affirms that humans are morally culpable for their actions, and Calvinistic systems which incorporate some form of determinism agree that we are morally accountable. Some critics of specific sovereignty may even object to the idea that compatibilistically free humans are morally accountable for their free actions. If God decreed their acts, and those deeds are causally determined, even if they are free (compatibilistically), it is hard to see them as morally culpable since the agent could not do otherwise.

In Romans 9 there is biblical precedent for this objection when Paul extensively discusses God's sovereign choice of what occurs. Paul teaches that God's choice of Jacob over Esau was totally a matter of divine mercy, not election on the basis of human merit, and then asks if this is unjust (v. 14). He denies emphatically that it is (*mē genoito*, Paul says). Then (v. 16) Paul adds that God's choice of us does not depend on us but rather on God's mercy. The case of Pharaoh's hardening (v. 17) illustrates the point that God hardens whom he wants and gives mercy to whomever he wants (v. 18). In verse 19 Paul raises the question of an imagined critic: "You will say to me then, 'Why does He still find fault? For who resists His will?'"

This is a very significant objection, which raises several problems. Two are intellectual and a third is attitudinal. The most obvious intellectual problem is how humans (even people like Pharaoh) can be guilty before God when they do what displeases him, since he has decreed that they will do it. This is really the same objection general sovereignty advocates pose against specific sovereignty models of providence. It also suggests another intellectual question. If God decrees all things, then we could also ask why *he* is not guilty for what we do. Isn't God (by the decree) the cause of whatever happens? If so, how can he be causally responsible for something and not also morally accountable?

The imagined objection also evidences an attitudinal problem. It sounds like an attempt to justify man and to complain about God's justice in holding us guilty for doing the evil he foreordained. Even more, the objection suggests that God (or at least his defenders) owes us an explanation; otherwise God seems to be unjust in holding us culpable for our actions.

The most obvious of the three problems is the first intellectual issue about human responsibility, for that is explicit in the text. We expect Paul at least to answer that question, though we would also like his reply to the other intellectual problem as well. In verses 20-21 Paul addresses neither intellectual question, but responds to the attitude behind these questions. He replies that, as creator, God has a right to do whatever he pleases, and his creatures have no right to put him on trial and demand that he explain his actions. Accusing God of wrongdoing may seem appropriate in light of Paul's teaching in Romans 9, but Paul says such accusation is totally out of order.

Though Paul does not resolve the intellectual questions, he doesn't say that they are unanswerable. In fact, these questions do have answers. As to the question about human responsibility for divinely decreed actions, as a compatibilist, I have an answer. The reason we are guilty of such deeds is that we do them freely, i.e., nothing constrains us to do them.[13] Though some think the decree causes the deeds to occur, we have already shown that this is not so, because the decree is not an agent nor does it exercise causal powers. It is the blueprint for what happens, but it is agents, divine and human, who cause the acts that occur, not the decree. As explained in presenting my compatibilist specific sovereignty model, God's causal activity is necessary to enable us to do moral good. We alone can do morally neutral or evil deeds without any help from God. While God decrees the circumstances in which we let ourselves become tempted and fall into sin, he neither tempts us nor enables or empowers us to do evil, nor does the decree. We do these acts in concert with our desires, and hence do them freely (in the compatibilist sense), and what one does freely is something for which one is culpable.

What about God's moral responsibility for decreeing evil? Isn't he guilty for doing so? What we must see is that this is really the problem of evil in a slightly different form. The problem of evil asks why an all-powerful, all-loving God would create a world with evil in it. From what we have seen, we can say that God would not *create* a world he had not first decided/decreed to make. So the question becomes why an all-powerful, all-loving God would decree to make a world with evil in it. If he does decree and make it, why isn't he guilty for the evil in it? This is the problem of evil posed at the level of God's decree rather than at the level of a created world that contains evil. Thus, however we defend God for making a world with evil in it, that answer also explains why God is not guilty for decreeing such a world when he didn't have to. In the chapter on the problem of evil, we will answer these questions. My point now is that these are not intractable problems as critics of specific sovereignty suggest.

DIVINE ATTRIBUTES AND DIVINE CONTROL.   The next argument is one that open view advocates base on their understanding of the divine attributes. Their revision of divine attributes such as immutability and eternity and their rejection of attributes such as impassibility fit their picture of a relational God. As I argued in the chapters on the divine attributes, I believe these attributes should be nuanced differently than traditional theism does. My understanding of these attributes is not the same as that of the open view, but I am sympathetic to their understanding, and agree that many of God's non-moral attributes need revision. When we do, the resultant portrait of God is of a king who cares.

What is greatly troublesome, however, is the impression given by open view proponents that the revised divine attributes are an *argument* or *evidence* for the open view's model of providence. This is just wrong. I have also offered reasons for rejecting divine simplicity and impassibility, I have agreed that God is temporally eternal, and my nuancing of immutability differs significantly from the classical conception. But none of that means I must hold a *general sovereignty* model of providence and cannot with logical consistency be a soft determinist of the sort described in this and the previous chapter.

Those divine attributes don't impact our understanding of whether humans have libertarian free will, compatibilistic free will, or no freedom at all. Nor do they tell us whether God decrees all things, some things, or nothing. There just is not any logical entailment between this understanding of the divine attributes and any position on human freedom and divine sovereignty. That this is so is also evident in that holding the classical conception of the divine attributes does not require a deterministic position on divine sovereignty and human freedom. To convince oneself of this, one needs only to consult many standard Arminian theologies which adopt a classical conception of the divine attributes (some even hold that God foreknows the future), and wed it to a general sovereignty model of providence with libertarian free will.

To be fair, I must add that open view advocates are not always clear about whether their espousal of these nuanced divine attributes is intended as an argument for their model of providence, or whether it is just part of their overall argument for a God who is more relational than the classical God. Still, even if open view proponents don't intend their picture of the divine attributes as an *argument* for their model of providence, readers may think of it as such, and if it is, it is a badly mistaken argument.

DETERMINISM AND EVANGELISM AND PRAYER. Another objection often raised against specific sovereignty centers on evangelism and petitionary prayer. As to the former, it is said that if God has already unconditionally decided who will be saved and who won't, he will surely work these matters out without our help. Hence, there is no reason to witness to nonbelievers unless we already know that they are elect, and even if they are, our witness may still be useless, since God has already planned to save them and will, regardless of what we do. Calvinism, then, seems to cut the nerve of evangelism. But how can this be right, since Jesus commands us to preach the gospel to all? Why would he say this if he knows that only some will be saved and has already decided who that will be? Commands to witness show that we must witness, and that our witness matters.

Petitionary prayer also seems useless. After all, if God has already decided what will happen and if his will is immutable, our prayers cannot change anything. We kid ourselves if we think our prayers matter. However, Scripture commands us to pray, and teaches that it makes a difference when we pray. God is depicted as being moved to act, sometimes even to do things he apparently wasn't planning to do. Think of Moses' intercession for Israel (Exodus 32–34); that made a great difference. Abraham pleaded with God to spare Sodom and Gomorrah, and though God did not spare them, he never told Abraham to stop praying because prayer makes no difference. Nor did Abraham think this was a fruitless exercise. Apparently, God can be "put upon" by our prayers, and does respond when we pray.[14]

These objections show that one's model of providence has significant practical implications. Though there are answers to each of these matters respectively, some responses apply to both evangelism and prayer, and I shall begin with those. With respect to God's decree, we have seen repeatedly that if God decrees everything, he decrees not only his goals but also the means to those ends. If God decrees that someone will be saved, that must happen some way. God could strike someone from on high with salvation, but no evidence shows that God has saved anyone that way. Alternately, God could do to everyone what he did to Paul on the road to Damascus. He could confront each of us and challenge us to respond to him. Most people, however, don't accept Christ in this way either. Most come to Christ after hearing the gospel message (in some cases, we heard it from more than one person), or upon reading the Bible or some religious writing that explains salvation. Some come to Christ through a combination of these means. Regardless of how we come to accept Christ, there are means to that end, and God has decreed both the means and the ends. For all we know, our testimony is the decreed means to bringing someone to Christ. Perhaps not, but we don't know that, so we must witness.

Similarly, whatever God does, he can do apart from our prayers. But God decrees means to ends, and he may have ordained that in answer to our prayers he will do a particular work in our life. Perhaps not, but we don't know that either, so we need to pray. It is foolish not to communicate with your creator and God, but God may also have ordained that he would be moved to act as a result of our prayer.

Some may reply that this is fine if God has decreed our witness and prayers as means to someone's salvation or some other event in their life. But I have granted that God may not have ordained that, so in those cases, are not prayer and witnessing irrelevant, since they don't accomplish the goal of either our witness or our petition? Such questions are understandable, but misguided. For one thing, just because our witness doesn't result in someone's conversion now does not mean God won't use it later to bring that sinner to himself. Likewise, a prayer that seems unanswered may get a positive response, at a time and in a way we did not anticipate.

Such objections are also misguided because they assume that our witness or prayer must achieve the goal we intend or it accomplishes nothing. This is clearly wrong. With the same action, we often intend to accomplish a number of things.[15] Similarly, with one and the same action or event God may have chosen to accomplish several things. Just because someone doesn't accept Christ now or ever in response to our witness it does not mean our witness didn't accomplish *God's* goals in our life. While we intended our witness to bring someone to Christ, perhaps God planned it just to strengthen our faith and boldness for him and to cause us to rely upon him to fight the spiritual warfare. Perhaps God wants us to witness because he knows that through the experience we will see more clearly what is most important in life. And it is surely possible to reach all these goals (and more), even if the one who hears our witness doesn't turn to Christ. Moreover, if someone does come to Christ as a result of our witness, that doesn't prove that God didn't intend our witnessing to accomplish these other goals as well. God commands us to witness. That the results are not what *we* intended doesn't mean that God's goals are not met.

The same point applies to prayer. When we pray, we hope to meet one objective, but God may intend our prayer to keep us looking to him and trusting him for our needs. It may just be his way of getting us to communicate with him rather than ignoring him, or his way to help us stay in fellowship with him. Even if he grants our petition, praying may also accomplish these other ends as well. Just because the results are not exactly what *we* intended by praying, that doesn't mean God's goals were not achieved.

There is a further point about witnessing, and a point or two about prayer. As to witnessing, because specific sovereignty guarantees that there are elect and that there are means to bring them to Christ, believers should be even more eager to witness. Calvinism, rather than stifling witnessing, encourages it for these reasons. In fact, Calvinists may have even greater motivation to witness than do those who believe in libertarian free will. Since God cannot bring it about that any one freely (in a libertarian sense) accepts him, it is possible that no one will accept Christ. So far, that hasn't been so, but there are no guarantees that there will ever be another convert. Not even God can guarantee any converts so long as libertarian freedom is unchecked. Christians who realize this might be very discouraged at the thought that they might witness relentlessly with no converts, and they might just give up. On a Calvinistic understanding, however, there is reason to witness. Our witness may be the means to someone's salvation, and if not, God can still use our testimony in our life to perform valuable things. Beyond that, believing that there are elect who haven't yet been saved, we can be enthusiastic about the enterprise of missions. Even if our witness is not the means to others coming to Christ, it is dubious that no missionary efforts will bear fruit. But what if the full number of elect has already been filled? That is possible, but unlikely since biblical prophecy of the tribulation during the end time, for example, shows that some people living then will turn to Christ. Since there is no evidence that we are now living in the tribulation period, there is no reason to think the number of the elect is complete. Moreover, it is reasonable to think that between today and the tribulation others will be saved. So there is ample reason to witness and to do so with much enthusiasm and expectancy.

In turning to petitionary prayer, I believe libertarian free will creates tremendous problems. Consider libertarian free will and petitionary prayer from two standpoints: petitions about ourselves and intercession for or relating to others. I have already explained why, on a deterministic model like mine, prayer makes abundant sense. Now I want to explain why with libertarian free will many prayers make no sense. Certainly, prayers that ask God to do something that in no way involves human free will don't run aground on libertarian free will. For example, if we have a terrible disease that isn't connected to human freedom, nothing is wrong with asking God to remove the disease.

But now consider petitions about ourselves that do involve our free will.

Suppose we ask the Lord to help us be more faithful in Bible reading, prayer, and witnessing. Or suppose we pray that the Lord will help us treat our family or neighbor better. I maintain that if libertarian free will obtains in our world, these are to a large degree absurd requests. For what are we asking God to do? In order for me to be more faithful in Bible reading, prayer, and witnessing, won't I have to decide to do these things? But if I have libertarian free will and am allowed to exercise it, how can God fulfill my request? If he doesn't override my libertarian freedom, he cannot *guarantee* the fulfillment of my request. So what am I asking him to do? Override my freedom? Make it the case that I freely decide to do these things? But here libertarians tell us that, if God brings it about that we do anything, we don't do it freely. It seems that God cannot be certain to grant my request unless he overrides my freedom, but why would God want me to engage in these spiritual exercises because I'm forced to do so (according to libertarian free will, I would be forced, but God wants my love and devotion freely!)? Shouldn't I, then, petition *myself* in an attempt to convince myself to do these things? After all, only I can *freely* effect what *I* choose to do, given libertarian free will. But if I did petition myself, wouldn't that usually mean I had already decided to do these things, and if so, the petition becomes unnecessary? I submit, then, that unless I really want God to override my freedom, what I ask him in these cases is absurd. If he doesn't tamper with my libertarian free will, he can't do what I ask; only I can, but petitioning myself engages me in the further absurdities mentioned.

As to intercessory prayer for others, the problems multiply further. If I plead with God to remove my friend's illness, that is not absurd, for God can answer that prayer without negating anyone's freedom. But what about the request that God change the attitudes and actions of my friend's tyrannical boss? What about petitions that ask God to move those processing applications for graduate school to accept my friend? Or what about prayers that ask God to keep my enemies at work from bothering me? And what about pleading with God to save a dear relative or friend? In all of these cases, what am I asking God to do, if libertarian free will obtains? I am either asking God to override others' freedom, or I am asking him to move them to do something *freely* in spite of the fact that my belief in libertarian free will means that I believe God *cannot get anybody to do anything* freely. If I truly value libertarian free will as much as libertarians say they do, why would I ask God to override it just because of my petition? Most libertarians would not see intercessory prayers as asking God to override someone else's free will, anyway, but then, given libertarian free will, what is the point of the petition unless it is to plead that God will do something that in fact negates someone's freedom? Libertarians may be asking God to try to persuade their friends, but I repeat that God can only *guarantee* their persuasion by causal determinism, and that abridges libertarian free will.

On the other hand, if I am not asking God to override someone else's freedom, then I'm asking him to do something which I believe he cannot do (make it the case that someone else does something freely). I may ask him to try to persuade the person, but I know that without God overriding their freedom, he cannot guarantee that they will change. In fact, since at the moment of free decision making nothing decisively inclines their will, regardless of what God or anyone else does or says, the matter may be hopeless. In light of such problems with interceding with God to change someone's incompatibilistically free actions or attitudes, there is good reason for anyone committed to libertarian free will who understands the implications of the position to think twice before offering intercessory prayers of the kind mentioned. In fact, prayer to change either our or others' actions seems problematic.

FURTHER BIBLICAL PASSAGES ABOUT DIVINE CONTROL. One further line of argument from the general sovereignty camp must be addressed: their handling of passages such as Romans 9, Acts 2, and passages in Proverbs. I begin with John Sanders's handling of Proverbs. He claims that the proverbs should be seen as guidelines for godly living, not timeless principles that always hold true. This is certainly a false dichotomy, for why can't a guideline for godly living be timelessly true? So long as human nature is what it is, these teachings are true, and they have implications for how we should live.

There is a more fundamental error in Sanders's coverage of proverbs such as 16:9 and 21:1. Neither verse gives a command for living; rather they tell us how things are. Prov 16:9 says a man plans his way, but God directs the path. Where is the command or guideline for living? Prov 21:1 says that the king's heart is in God's hands and that he turns it however he wants. Where again is the guideline for living? These are statements of fact, and both verses speak of God's actions in general, not just in one or two cases.

Sanders might answer that though these passages describe God's relation to man, the reader should infer some guidelines for living. If God directs our path, we shouldn't make plans without considering God. If God controls the king's decisions so that he does what God wants, the king should submit to God. These guidelines for living are *implications* of the general principles the passages teach, and they are probably implications the Holy Spirit wants us to draw out. But it is principles the writer states, not their implications. Finally, Sanders says that the verses teach that God directs his people's steps (16:9) and guides the king of Israel (21:1) *when they seek God's wisdom,* but such interpretations are cases of eisegesis. Neither verse says anything about seeking God's wisdom. Seeking it would be a wise move, and we might advise others to do so in light of what the verses actually teach, but it is not what the verses teach.

Handling these proverbs as Sanders does makes them say more than they intend, and obscures what they actually say. Would Sanders use the same methodology on the proverb about the Lord deciding the outcome of the lot cast into the lap (Prov 16:33)? Using Sanders's strategy, this verse must be understood as offering counsel for godly living. But what could that be? That before you play dice, you should ask for God's help to win? Or that you shouldn't hesitate to cast lots, even for money, because God is in charge of the outcome? Such understandings of this verse would be ludicrous, but they seem likely if we treat this verse like other proverbs which Sanders says are advice for godly living.

The truth is that these verses offer examples of things God controls. He is sovereign over kings and what they do, but also sovereign over our plans and over even seemingly incidental things like the casting of lots. What about Sanders's handling of Isa 29:15-16; 45:9-13; and Jer 18:1-10, passages about the potter and the clay? Many things Sanders says are correct. Isaiah 29 speaks of judgment on Israel, and Isaiah 45 speaks of God using Cyrus to bless his people. As to the former, Sanders is correct that God's right to do what he wants is being challenged. But after announcing judgment on the wicked, God chides those who think they can hide their plans from God and escape his notice. God says this cannot happen, for he is not just another human being (their equal). He is their maker, the potter, and they are the clay. He knows everything about them, so they can't hide. It is certainly true that this passage doesn't apply this notion specifically to God's decree and control of all things. It does, however, remind readers that humans are not equal to God, and they cannot hide their plans from him; and the language is universal in nature, i.e., this isn't just a point God makes about Israel.

Though Isaiah 29 is not in its context used to teach God's control over whatever happens, Isaiah 45 is more in line with that notion. In verses 1-8, the Lord predicts the success of Cyrus, and forecasts that he will use Cyrus to bless and restore Israel. God adds that he will do this so that men will know that he is the Lord, the mighty God. God knows that it might seem strange to use a pagan king to serve his purposes for Israel, so he adds verses 9-10: lest anyone think God has no right to use Cyrus in this way, let them remember that God is the potter and we are the clay. He has the right to use any of us however he wants. He may astound us by accomplishing his goals through unexpected means, but that should only underscore for us that he is God and is sovereign over all things.

As to Jeremiah 18, the Lord is angry with Israel and wants to teach her a lesson. Israel may think that because she is God's chosen people, he will bless her no matter what. God tells Jeremiah to go to the potter's shop, because God wants to use what happens there to teach his people a lesson. Jeremiah goes and sees the potter making a vessel, but it becomes spoiled, and he refashions it into another vessel that pleases him. God says that just as the potter makes the clay into whatever he wants, even reshaping it if it is spoiled, God can do whatever he wants with his people. He is entitled to speak blessing to them, and then discard them if they turn from him. He also has the right to speak judgment, but then bless them if they repent. Sanders says this means that God has a right not to fulfill a prophecy, if the people involved do not comply. But where in Jeremiah 18 does God make such a comment? God does instruct (v. 11) Jeremiah to tell Israel that he is devising judgment for them and will carry it out unless they turn from their evil ways. This is a genuine example of God threatening judgment. It also shows that those who speak of conditional prophecies (if this is a prophecy at all) can find some passages that fit that category. What we must see here, however, is how God's object lesson of the potter and the clay fits this conditional threat of judgment. Just as the potter can do whatever he wants with the clay, so God can do whatever he wants with Israel. He can set up a situation wherein he will do one thing if they don't turn from their ways, and another if they do.

Does this passage teach as Sanders suggests that God has a right to change his plans for his people? Can God forego fulfilling a prophecy if his people repent? The very way Sanders states these points shows his presuppositions. God changing his plans is for Sanders a real case of God not having entirely decided what he would do and being open to change in response to his people. In keeping with the open view's claim that God doesn't know our future free actions, this means that God may wind up doing things very different from his original plans. This doesn't mean for Sanders that God would change his decree, for open view proponents don't believe there is a decree. On the other hand, for a determinist who believes in a decree, God has all contingencies accounted for already in what he decreed. He really does something different from what was announced, but not different from what he decreed. It appears that God changed his plans in the sense Sanders suggests, but a determinist would likely say this is phenomenological language, describing how God's actions appear to us. Of course, what I have just said betrays determinist presuppositions, so which interpretation about God changing his plans correctly understands this passage? I don't think we can choose from just Jeremiah 18 in favor of either option, because the passage is not a metaphysical treatise about the meaning of immutability, etc.

Hence, neither position is proved *from this passage alone*. Still, the passage does teach the lesson of the potter and the clay. God is supreme and has the right to do whatever he wants with his creatures. That truth can fit consistently either a general or a specific sovereignty model of providence, but seems better suited to the latter. I agree with Sanders, however, that this passage doesn't teach God's pancausality of everything; that truth appears in other passages. But as sovereign, God has a right to do whatever he wants, including act in ways contrary to what he threatens. Nothing in this passage, however, answers whether the language is phenomenological or whether it relates what actually happens from God's perspective.

As to Sanders's claim that the passage teaches that God can forego fulfilling a prophecy of doom if people repent, this simply confuses the issue. The passage clearly says that God will judge, but then he pleads with them to repent. Thus, the whole verse must be seen as a conditional statement, not a flat promise of judgment regardless of what happens. But then, God is not foregoing fulfilling any prophecy if people repent and he doesn't bring judgment. Sanders's view makes it sound as though God promised judgment unconditionally but the people could do something to get him to overturn that unconditional promise. This is not so, however, because the warning of what

God plans to do *includes a condition*. When the verse is taken as a whole, it says there will be judgment unless they repent. Given that statement, there is no way the prophecy can fail to be fulfilled because of what it promises. It promises judgment if Israel does not repent, and no judgment if she does. This threat includes a condition that allows Israel either to repent or to reject God's offer of forgiveness, and allows God either to judge or to forego judgment. Israel will either repent or not. If she does the former, God is implicitly promising to forego judgment (it is unthinkable that if she repents God will still bring calamity). If she doesn't repent, he promises to judge. In either case the prophecy will be fulfilled.

In sum, I can agree with Sanders that two of the passages about the potter and clay do not require God to decree and cause all things. The third seems more likely to teach that, and all three certainly say more than Sanders allows regarding God's power and control. In addition, the passages do not prove that God foregoes fulfilling a prophecy in certain circumstances. What is crucial, however, is how the apostle Paul uses these passages in Romans 9. Those who think an OT passage must be used in the NT in exactly the same sense as in the OT should examine more carefully the biblical passages involved and should read treatises about how the NT uses the OT.[16] In Romans 9, Paul clearly uses these passages to teach God's sovereign control over everything and his right to hold us morally accountable for doing what he has decreed (9:19-22).

This brings us to several key NT passages, starting with Sanders's handling of Romans 9. Sanders correctly sees Romans 9 as part of a larger section (9–11) about Israel's place before God since she rejected her Messiah. He is also right that God intends to save both Gentiles and Jews, though it is dubious that 9:6-16 makes this point (it is clearer in chapter 11). Still, there are many problems with his handling of Romans 9. For one thing, Sanders seems to think that the chapter's talk of election is about election to service, not to salvation. However, as commentators note, the chapter actually teaches a two-fold election. The first is election to privilege, spoken of in verses 1-6. Israel as a whole is God's chosen people, but she was chosen to receive the privileges mentioned in verses 1-6.

A second election goes beyond election to privilege and service. Paul notes that election to privilege doesn't mean that one automatically has a proper relation to God. Verses 6-7 say that not all are Israel who are descended from Israel and not all are God's children because they descend from Abraham. What could this possibly mean—being of Israel but not Israel, and being a child of Abraham but not one? Paul helps us understand in two places. In Romans 4 Paul teaches that people have a right relation to God by faith, even as Abraham did. The whole chapter clarifies what it means to be a spiritual descendent of Abraham. It has nothing to do with outward works such as circumcision, but everything to do with one's faith. Paul's point, then, in chapter 9 (if it agrees with chapter 4) is that just because Israel was elected to privilege, that doesn't save her spiritually.

The context of Romans 9 also helps us understand what Paul means, for

Paul teaches that God, having elected Israel to privilege, made further distinctions within Israel. He chose Isaac as the son of promise over Ishmael, and Jacob over Esau. Now if these choices are only election for service, what Paul says is very odd. Ishmael (rejected in favor of Isaac) is called a child of the flesh (v. 8), and we are told that God hated Esau (v. 13). Being of the flesh in Scripture is not a positive thing; it typically refers to being unregenerate. Being hated by God isn't positive either. But if God's choice of Isaac and Jacob over Ishmael and Esau is purely a matter of service, why is God so negative to those not chosen for service? God also didn't choose the Gentiles for this service, but nowhere does God say he hates them or thinks they are unspiritual because he didn't select them for service.

The impression that this second election is more than just to service is heightened when Paul speaks of God's handling of Pharaoh. The choice to harden Pharaoh's heart is seen as parallel to the positive choice of Isaac and Jacob. Indeed, all three serve God's purposes in one way or another, but there is more. Hardening Pharaoh's heart clearly seals his spiritual damnation before God. And Paul sums up all of these illustrations (v. 18) by saying that God has mercy on whom he wills and hardens whom he wills. It all depends ultimately on God. Surely, Pharaoh's eternal fate and the fact that Isaac and Jacob not only served God but also had a positive spiritual relation to him make it likely that this second election is election to salvation, not just to service. Besides, in light of God's intentions for Isaac, Jacob, and their descendents not only to bear the promised seed but also to bring the gospel to the Gentiles, they must be saved.

Next we turn to Sanders's treatment of Pharaoh's hardening. Sanders says that God hardened Pharaoh's heart hoping that this would bring him to his senses and he would repent. However, this is never said either in Exodus or in Romans 9. Moreover, hardening Pharaoh with this intent doesn't make sense. People who go deeper into sin and rebellion against God don't normally as a result become more open to the gospel. They become more spiritually blind, so if this is God's way of bringing Pharaoh around, it is quite strange. Beyond that, Sanders ignores what Paul claims is the reason for Pharaoh's hardening. Paul writes (v. 17), "For the Scripture says to Pharaoh, 'For this very purpose I raised you up, to demonstrate My power in you, and that My name might be proclaimed throughout the whole earth.'" What does this mean? Exactly what I said when dealing with creation, namely, that the plagues upon Egypt were all judgments against their gods, which gave Yahweh the opportunity to show his power and superiority over all gods. Hence, it is dubious that God really intended Pharaoh to repent.

It is also crucial to note that Rom 9:17 quotes Exod 9:16. After the plague of boils, God told Moses to go to Pharaoh and tell him that henceforth the plagues would fall on Pharaoh's very person and that of his people. Moses was to say that these kinds of plagues would have come sooner, but if they had, Pharaoh and the Egyptians would have died; and if Pharaoh had already died from the plagues, that would not have given God the opportunity to show his power in the way he wanted. The point is clear: God didn't keep Pharaoh alive and harden his heart so that he would get the message and repent. The reason Paul offers is exactly the reason God gave Moses to tell Pharaoh. Telling Pharaoh that God allowed him to live so that he could mete out more judgment on him and his people so that Yahweh's name would be proclaimed in all the earth is hardly a call to repentance!

All of this supports claims that God has absolute control over both the elect and the reprobate. He has mercy on whom he wills, and hardens whom he wills (Rom 9:18). Mercy is not extended in virtue of some foreseen faith or merit, for as with God's choice of Jacob over Esau, the decision was not made on merit since it was made before they were born or had done anything (v. 11). There is, however, one other noteworthy point about Sanders's treatment. Nowhere in Sanders's book (according to his Scripture index) nor in his lengthy treatment of Romans 9–11 does he mention Rom 9:17-18. These crucial verses reveal God's intent with Pharaoh and then offer (v. 18) a summary statement about God's mercy and judgment. Even more revealing is that nowhere in his lengthy treatment of Romans 9 does Sanders discuss verse 19.[17] Instead, he skips from verse 16 to verses 20-21 about the potter and the clay, and claims these verses make no other point than that made in the OT contexts where they first appear.

This is not only improper exegesis, but also a fatal error. Verses 20-22 respond to the teaching in verses 6-18, and specifically to the objection raised in verse 19. Hence, what Paul means by citing the passages about the potter and the clay must be seen in the context of the preceding discussion and the verses that follow 20-22. But why does Sanders ignore the question that elicits the answer? Could it be because of the implications of that question and the verses that immediately precede it (vv. 17-18)? Paul has just said that whatever happens, good or bad, ultimately depends on God. That elicits the question of verse 19. If God has determined everything we will do, including Pharaoh's stubbornness and our own sin, why does he get angry with us for doing what he foreordained? What is the point of the question? It grants what Paul has been teaching, namely, that God controls all things, and then it asks a very logical question. If God decided apart from our merits or demerits (as when he chose Jacob over Esau) everything that will happen, why would he hold us guilty for doing what he chose?

Sanders and others committed to general sovereignty may like this verse because it raises the same question for Calvinistic systems that they do, but they shouldn't like it, because it does grant God control over everything. And they shouldn't like it in light of Paul's reply. If what Paul has been teaching in chapter 9 does not mean that God controls all things, this would have been a perfect time to say so. In reply to the question (v. 19), Paul could easily have said, "I must have misled you; I never said that God decrees or chooses for us to do evil deeds. I can see how you would wonder how it could be fair to hold us guilty for what God decided we would do. But, I'm not saying that

God decides everything that happens." But Paul says nothing of the sort. Paul responds to the attitude portrayed by the question, but his response does nothing to undercut the basic idea behind the question, namely, that God decrees all things, even evil. Paul responds that, if we don't like it that we are held accountable for doing the evil God decreed, we don't have a right to pick a fight with God about this, accuse him of wrongdoing, or put him on trial and demand that he explain how this can be fair.

Much more could be said about Romans 9, but I only add that this also addresses Cottrell's claim that the passage speaks only about election to service. Moreover, it is amazing that he thinks the passage teaches conditional election based on a person's faith. Again, the error is not understanding that an unconditional decree has means to ends. The means or conditions to someone's salvation include their believing, but no Calvinist denies that. Calvinists merely say that the means and ends have been decreed unconditionally. It is also revealing that Cottrell's treatment at this point relies on Rom 9:32, verses in chapter 10, and a few verses in chapter 11. He simply ignores the point made in 9:6-19—that God's choices were not made on the basis of anything the people involved did! Moreover, it should not surprise us that chapter 10 talks about belief and unbelief, for this is also part of Paul's point. Though God elected all Israel to privilege, and specific Jews to service and salvation, chapter 10 shows that Israelites who rejected Christ willingly did so; hence, they are justly accounted guilty.

Let us turn next to Sanders's handling of 1 Pet 1:20; Eph 1:4; and Acts 2:23. Sanders contends that comments about God foreordaining something before the world's foundation (1 Pet 1: 20 and Acts 2:23) simply means that God planned for Christ to become incarnate as part of his general plans, and God foresaw that some would be angry enough with Jesus to kill him. That interpretation is not only contrary to the text but also contradicts Sanders's own position. Sanders, along with other open view proponents, claims that God has present knowledge, i.e., exhaustive knowledge of the past and present, but no knowledge of our future free (in a libertarian sense) actions. With libertarian free will, no one can predict, not even us, what we will do. Even if circumstances seem to dictate one course of action, we can always do otherwise. Moreover, advocates of present knowledge typically deny that God has middle knowledge, knowledge of what we would do if placed in a certain situation.

Upon reflection, it becomes evident that such views raise major problems for Sanders's interpretation of these passages. For one thing, if God doesn't know our future actions, why is he making plans *before the foundation of the world* (as these verses say) to correct mistakes he cannot have foreseen we would make? Moreover, why would he plan for Christ to become incarnate? Given libertarian free will, it is possible that no one would ever sin, so Christ's incarnation to die for our sin would be unnecessary. Granted, the incarnation would have served many positive ends even if it were unnecessary for our salvation, but Scripture clearly teaches that the major purpose of the incarnation was to work out our salvation. Given libertarian free will, *before the foundation of the world* God could not have known that this would be necessary. Having only present knowledge and no middle knowledge, God couldn't even plan for Christ to be Savior in all the possible worlds that would need a savior. Without middle knowledge, God wouldn't know that a savior would be needed under any circumstances. Sanders also understands the Acts 2 passage to mean that God foresaw that someone would be angry enough at Christ to put him to death. But again, if God only has present knowledge, he could not foresee this, and if humans have libertarian free will, it is possible that no one would get angry enough to kill Christ. As open view advocates often say, history involves the unexpected and surprises, even for God. But then, what is God doing making plans before the foundation of the world as though he knows what will happen? Clearly something is amiss, and it isn't what Peter wrote and said (Acts 2) or what Paul said!

Sanders's handling of Eph 1:4 is even further afield from the text. I agree that the verse speaks of corporate election, but after that I part company with his interpretation. He says that we must understand what this election means; it doesn't mean God's choice of people but of a course of action and of conditions by which people will be counted as in Christ. Presumably, this means that God decided that anyone who would believe in Christ would be saved— that's God's method of salvation. Indeed, it is God's method of salvation, but that is not what Eph 1:4 says God chose. What he chose was a set of people. Indeed, he chose them, verse 4 says, to be holy and blameless, but Paul and the rest of the NT are very clear that one is not sanctified (holy and blameless) unless first justified, and justification comes to those who are foreordained and predestined (Rom 8:29-30). Moreover, note Paul's further words in Eph 1:5 about these people God chose. He writes, "He predestined us to adoption as sons through Jesus Christ to Himself, according to the kind intention of His will." Clearly, this doesn't speak of God's choosing a method of salvation, but rather of people to be saved!

As a compatibilist, I see verses such as the Proverbs passages and Acts 2:23 as fitting perfectly with compatibilism, for they show both God's and man's activity in the same action. Moreover, from the perspective of specific sovereignty, these passages make abundant sense as they affirm God's control but also show that his sovereign decree doesn't mean we should be idle or that we are not responsible for our actions. Moreover, passages such as Phil 2:12-13 make little sense if libertarian free will is correct, but make abundant sense if compatibilism is correct. To say that we are to work out our salvation because God works in us to will and to do of his good pleasure means one of two things: 1) God's activity in us, given libertarian free will, means that we don't *freely* progress in sanctification; or 2) on a compatibilist reading, God is sovereignly in control, and at the same time we act freely because we do what we wish to do. Libertarians cannot afford for 1) to be correct, and 2) fits compatibilism.

There are other biblical and theological arguments for a compatibilist specific sovereignty conception of providence, but this section is already long enough.[18] In the next section I turn to philosophical arguments favoring this model of providence.

PHILOSOPHICAL CONSIDERATIONS

In addition to biblical and theological arguments for a soft deterministic model of providence, there are many philosophical supports. Some answer indeterminist objections while others provide positive evidence for soft determinism.

Controlling Events, But Not Actions

Some intent on maintaining libertarian free will, or simply unconvinced that compatibilistic freedom works as described earlier, may ask why God cannot leave human actions indeterminate and determine only various events that don't involve human agency. That would grant God enough control (without giving him total control) over what happens in our world to ensure that his general ends will be met. In an article written some time ago,[19] I considered this proposal and rejected it. I still reject it for the same reasons. If actions and events in our world were unconnected to other actions and events, the proposal might work. But a possible world, including the one God actualized, is an interconnected world. That doesn't mean that every event is somehow tied to some human action, but that is not necessary for me to make my point. Some actions will depend on the occurrence of certain events and vice versa, and if the actions must be free in a libertarian sense, there is a problem for the proposal that God control and foreordain events but not actions.

Consider the following situation as an illustration. Jane lives in Chicago and is looking forward to her summer vacation in Europe. After checking her work schedule and consulting with a travel agent, she sees that there are three basic options of when to leave. She can leave on a Monday (June 5), or on Tuesday, June 6, on either a morning or an early evening flight. The decision is up to her, and God hasn't foreordained which flight she will take. In fact, it is possible that something might cause her to cancel the trip, but let's assume that it is very likely she will take the trip. Now, God has foreordained three separate *events*. One is that the June 6 Tuesday morning flight, several hours after departure, through no human error or action will suddenly explode, killing all passengers aboard. The second is that on Wednesday, June 7 in Paris (Jane's plans are to fly to Paris for a day and then travel the next day to southern France) it will be rainy with thunderstorms and lightning, but toward evening there will be a beautiful rainbow over the city that anyone in Paris could see. The third event God foreordains is that Jane will be struck and killed by lightening in Paris on Wednesday afternoon, June 7, during the thunderstorm. These events don't occur because of any human actions that cause them, so on the general sovereignty model of providence we are considering, God's foreordaining these events but none of Jane's actions should fit.

Prior to her trip Jane, of course, knows nothing about these three events. She only knows that her options are to leave Monday evening, Tuesday morning, or Tuesday evening. Now clearly there are problems ahead for Jane, but also problems for God's sovereign control. Suppose Jane decides to take the Monday flight and arrives in Paris on Tuesday. She has a great day, but hearing weather reports that there will likely be foul weather on Wednesday, she leaves Paris early Wednesday morning. In this case God's decree about lightning striking her dead cannot be fulfilled. There will still be a thunderstorm and lightning on June 7 in Paris, but Jane's actions will have undone what the Lord supposedly could decree and control.

Or suppose that when Jane awakens on Wednesday it is already raining hard, and weather reports suggest that a very bad storm is heading in the direction she will be traveling. Hearing this news, and very tired anyway from jet lag, Jane stays in her hotel room for the morning and, after lunch in the hotel restaurant, she goes back to her room, lies down, and falls asleep. She sleeps through the whole afternoon, and finally awakes around 6 P.M. It is sunny outside and the storm is over, and as she looks out the window she sees a beautiful rainbow over the city. Again, Jane is safe, because her actions thwarted the event God decreed.

Suppose instead that Jane leaves Chicago on Tuesday morning, June 6. As it happens, Jane gets on the plane God decreed to explode, but he also decreed that Jane would be struck by lightening Wednesday afternoon in Paris. Jane's free decision has thwarted God's plan again, for she cannot die both in Paris and in the sky over the Atlantic. Sadly, Jane took the flight and died in the explosion. Her friends think that she would still be alive if only she had taken a different flight. Little do they know God's plans about the lightening bolt, but in any case God cannot fulfill his decree.

Consider now Jane's third option, leaving on Tuesday evening. Jane takes this flight, a bit rattled by news of the explosion of the earlier flight, but still determined to go on vacation. Jane's flight is safe and smooth, arriving on Wednesday morning in Paris, but it is raining in Paris, so the flight arrives a bit later than expected, and more rain is forecast for the rest of the day. Jane goes through customs, and figures she just ought to get to her hotel and relax. She arrives, eats lunch, and lies down to get off her feet for a few moments before doing some sight-seeing. However, she is exhausted and falls into a sound sleep. About 9 P.M. that evening she awakens and feels somewhat refreshed, but looks at the clock and realizes she has slept away the afternoon and early evening. Worse yet, she wonders if she'll get any more sleep that evening. But there is good news for Jane. Though she doesn't know it, she missed seeing a beautiful rainbow over the city around 6 P.M., but she also missed being struck by lightning Wednesday afternoon. God's plans have been thwarted again.

Jane will actually die someday in a tornado God has decreed to go through suburban Chicago and destroy her home. Of course, when God planned that event, he didn't figure it would kill Jane, because he had already planned her death in Paris by lightning.

There is, of course, at least one way God's decree can be fulfilled. Jane takes the flight Tuesday evening and arrives Wednesday morning. Having heard that the best way to start getting over jet lag is not to go to sleep until evening in Paris, Jane decides to go sight-seeing on Wednesday afternoon. It's raining, and she knows it's supposed to continue raining, but thinks it probably won't be too bad. Sadly, she is mistaken and is struck by lightening on Wednesday afternoon. Jane did everything freely (in a libertarian sense), but God's decreed event was also accomplished.

What should we learn from all of this? General sovereignty proponents who think God can sovereignly control events without controlling our actions should not be encouraged. Though in the last scenario things work out fine for God's planned event and Jane's free choices, in all the other cases mentioned, Jane's libertarian freedom, which God cannot control, foils God's planned event. And surely there must be many decisions each of us make every day that are capable of generating such scenarios where God's planned event and its consequences cannot occur because our free choice thwarts God's plan. Hence, this attempt to modify God's total control of everything to control only of *events*, so that libertarian freedom is maintained, will not succeed.

What Kind of Determinism?

Before going any further, I must underscore the kind of determinism I espouse. Many forms of determinism in my judgment are unacceptable as accounts of human action. Determinism in the physical sciences (often called LaPlaceian determinism) claims that there are laws of nature such that those laws plus the state of the world at any given moment causally determine what will happen next.

It is easy to think that this is the sort of determinism in mind when discussing human action. In fact some even seem to suggest that although humans are animate and have a will, physical processes still impinge upon them, so there should be some laws of human behavior which (if we knew them) would make human actions as predictable and regular as the occurrences of nature.[20]

In chapter 13, we noted Lionel Keener's analysis of different types of causation. Among the various types, there is a distinction between natural causation (which obtains in the natural order and physical sciences) and causation in the social sciences (including things like human behavior). If the kind of determinism I espouse were akin to what Keener labels natural causation, then I am inclined to agree with Keener that such determinism is incompatible with free will in any sense. However, that position would likely be a form of either fatalism or hard determinism, and I have argued that one should not adopt either of those positions in any form. They don't square with Scripture, and once we understand that human action involves the volitions of animate agents, not the reactions of inanimate objects and processes, we see further reason to reject any fatalistic or hard deterministic account of human action based on determinism in the natural sciences.[21]

What I espouse echoes points made clearly and forcefully by Edward Sankowski and Adolf Grünbaum. As they explain, there are not only different concepts of freedom but also different notions of determinism and causation. Some of the latter notions involve compulsion, but compulsion *per se* is not equivalent to causation.[22] I stress this point for several reasons. One is that determinists need to understand the kind of determinism they hold, lest when they wed it to theological concepts they wind up holding views that roughly match many caricatures of Calvinism. This is also important because it helps us evaluate arguments against determinism in general and against specific sovereignty models of providence. Critics often assume that specific sovereignty proponents hold LaPlaceian determinism, and that since that sort of determinism excludes freedom and requires that our actions result ultimately from factors beyond our control that existed well before we were born, specific sovereignty must be wrong. No one seriously believes, for example, that the state of the world a hundred years before our birth causally determined our present actions.[23]

As to my own specific sovereignty model of providence, by now readers should know that it rejects LaPlaceian determinism and natural causation as operative on human behavior. Rather, I invoke the kind of causation that Keener says obtains in the social sciences. According to that kind of causation, it is dubious that there are any laws of human behavior that let us predict what an agent will do, or that determine in advance what she will choose. All that my model of providence requires is that in any situation where an agent makes a decision there are antecedent conditions of various sorts (including the person's character, his preferences, events that have already occurred and brought him to the point of decision, and his knowledge of the various arguments and reasons in favor of the available options) which conjointly are sufficient to incline the person decisively to choose one option rather than the others. My model doesn't require that there be laws of nature and physical (or any other kind of) processes that rigidly guarantee what an agent will choose with machine-like precision, and I don't espouse that. Moreover, since my model is one of *theological* determinism, I believe that God acts in our world, and that his deeds, commands, etc., may also be part of the complex sufficient condition that moves a person to choose one option over another. This is especially so when someone chooses what is morally good.

The preceding paragraphs clarify my position, but they also answer many general sovereignty complaints about specific sovereignty models of providence. That is, many critics of specific sovereignty assume that its proponents hold LaPlaceian determinism. Since my position is different, it is untouched by objections based on the idea that such determinism governs human action. There are also many positive arguments for a position like mine.

Choosing an Action

A first positive argument for my model of providence is about how an agent comes to choose a given action. Jonathan Edwards cogently argues the point in his *Freedom of the Will*. One of Edwards's fundamental theses is that the will chooses according to the dictates of the understanding, or, put differently, the will chooses according to the strongest motive or in accord with what seems the greatest good.[24] Edwards argues that if there were not some factor or factors in the situation which, as the agent deliberates, "tips the balances" decisively in favor of one option, the agent would not choose. The idea that the will chooses out of a state of indifference makes no sense. If a person were not partial enough to any option to move him to choose it, he simply would not choose.

This must not be misunderstood. Edwards is not arguing for some sort of natural causality or necessity. Nor would he deny that the causes of free actions are agents themselves. His point addresses why the agent chose one option instead of another. Proponents of libertarian freedom frequently reply that the agent just chooses. By this they mean that nothing was a sufficient cause for the agent to choose and act other than the agent himself. In keeping with the spirit of Edwards's point, the determinist will reply that this really doesn't explain what moves the agent to act, but just reasserts the indeterminist position. If we accept the indeterminist's claim that nothing decisively moved the agent to act, then there is no reason to think the agent would act at all. Granted, there are choices all of us make with little preference. Perhaps after taking a shower we choose whether to dry off with a red or a green towel. If both are clean and both are available and if we don't prefer one color over the other, the indeterminist says that when we choose one, there is no sufficient reason or condition that moved us to choose it and not the other. Following Edwards, the determinist answers that if this is so, the agent wouldn't choose either one. Of course, the agent's choosing doesn't require a long deliberative process with arguments and evidences marshaled for each option. The reason for deciding may be rather trivial (e.g., yesterday we used a green towel, so for variety we choose the red one today), but something moved us to choose one over the other. If nothing, not even something trivial, tipped the scales in favor of one option over the other, then we would not choose.

This line of argument has always seemed cogent to me and a problem for an indeterminist account of free will. It refers to intentional actions, not unintentional or reflex actions. Indeed, reflex actions typically don't require the one doing them to make a choice. I also agree that we sometimes choose to do one thing and yet something entirely unexpected and unintentional occurs; for example, we intend to drive our car safely through an intersection, but by pushing the accelerator we wind up hitting another car that is also going through the intersection. With either reflex or unintentional acts, we cannot say that the result was something intended or that there were causal factors that convinced us to do what unintentionally happened. Edwards's and my point relates to intentional actions. Another misunderstanding must also be avoided. I am not saying that every causally determined act is free in the soft determinist sense. Sometimes causes do constrain the agent, and in those cases the agent does not act freely. My claim is that this is not so for all causally determined acts. And I contend that unless acts are causally determined (by non-constraining or constraining causes), there is no reason to think the agent would have done them, and no explanation of why the agent picked the act chosen, other than to say the agent just chose (and that is no explanation).

Are Reasons Causes?

From the previous argument stems another issue and a further argument for my position. Previously, I talked about acting from reasons or the strongest motives. This raises the question of whether reasons can be causes. This is debated by philosophers, but a starting point is clarifying what sort of causes reasons might be. As some argue, it is hard to imagine reasons serving as physical or natural causes.[25] I agree, but as already noted, I am not talking about physical causation or determinism in the natural world. The kind of causation I propose allows reasons to be causes. It does so in that the agent, upon considering various arguments, reasons, and evidences finds himself or herself persuaded to adopt a particular point of view or do a particular deed. Of course, the movement of the agent's physical body brings the action about, but that physical movement stems from mental states such as intentions and choices that arise from deliberating on how best to accomplish one's act, and those mental states arise as a result of considering various reasons for and against holding a belief or doing a given action.

Indeterminists might respond in one of several ways. They might say that since an act done for a reason is causally determined (the reason[s] being a large part of the sufficient condition), no free act is connected to any reason(s) sufficient to incline the agent decisively in one direction or the other. To that answer I would respond (as does Edwards) that if a voluntary act is not done for a decisive reason or motive, there is no reason to think the agent would act at all.

A second possible indeterminist reply is that people do act for a reason, but that just means that the act is contra-causally produced. As Patricia Churchland argues, if the opponent of determinism argued this, "that is begging the question. He needs to *show* that acting for a reason *is* uncaused behaviour, and if his anti-deterministic conviction is so strong that he relates 'acting for a reason' to 'contra-causally produced' analytically, this only tells us something about the strength of his conviction, and nothing

about how reasoned behaviour *is in fact* produced."[26] If the indeterminist means that acting for a reason is not an example of natural or physical
causation, that is agreed. What must be shown is that it is not any kind
of deterministic causation. Defining it as such only begs the question, as
Churchland explains.

There is another way indeterminists might answer this argument, and it
is suggested by those described above as causal indeterminists. According
to their views, reasons would serve or function as causes, but that wouldn't
involve any form of determinism. Their argument is that though at the time of
decision making there is a causal connection between the agent's mental states
and the action, prior to making the decision nothing dictates which reasons
the agent will deem most significant. Hence, choosing an alternate course of
action is a real possibility because a case can be made from the reasons for
more than one option, and nothing prior to the agent's deciding dictates which
case will be deemed most compelling. As to why the agent chose a particular
option, no iron-clad behavioral laws would cover what happened. The most
we could do is point to relevant statistical/probabilistic laws, i.e., "laws" that
say an agent (or a group of agents) when confronted with those reasons in
such circumstances typically takes alternative two, for example, not option
one or three.[27] Such a view is not very far from the compatibilistic picture I
am painting, but whether or not it is equivalent to compatibilism, the basic
point I would make is that it grants precisely what I am arguing, namely, that
reasons can serve as causes in that they are part of the sufficient condition for
one act as opposed to other alternatives.

The Agent Could Have Done Otherwise

Another line of indeterminist objection to any form of determinism is sufficiently strong and widely enough held that determinists have felt it necessary
to respond. I think some of their answers do not adequately blunt the force
of the indeterminist's objections, whereas others do. The argument is that in
order for an act to be free, we must be able to say that the agent could have
done otherwise than she did. If this is a crucial criterion for a free act, then
no causally determined act could be free, since determinists typically say
that, given prevailing conditions, the agent could not have done otherwise.
But this matter goes beyond the mere freedom of an act to moral responsibility for the act. Again, it is widely held that no one can be held morally
responsible for what they do, if they could not have done otherwise. If they
could do otherwise but did not, then we feel assured that they did what they
really intended and wanted, and hence they should be held responsible for
it. If they could not do otherwise, then they may be mere victims of forces
they are powerless to overcome, and that is why they acted as they did. In
that case, we wouldn't deem them morally praiseworthy or blameworthy.
Indeterminists clearly believe that an agent acts freely and is morally respon-

sible for the deed only if he can do otherwise. Many determinists agree, and because they do, they think their form of determinism removes freedom and moral responsibility.

Though we might challenge the claim that for an act to be free the agent must be able to do otherwise, I'm not sure about the success of such a challenge. Moreover, many determinists, including some soft determinists, believe that even if being able to do otherwise is a criterion of freedom, there are many senses in which a determinist can say that the agent could do otherwise. Determinists have offered three basic strategies for showing their position compatible with the agent doing otherwise. I believe the first doesn't work, but the second and third do succeed in meeting indeterminist objections.

At least since J. L. Austin's article "Ifs and Cans," many have held that a claim about what an agent can or could do is really a disguised conditional statement. And when one properly understands the conditional statement, one sees that it is compatible with determinism. Much ink has been spilled on this subject by proponents and critics of this argument.[28] Though many have tried to write such a conditional analysis in a way that is both true and consistent with determinism, it is dubious that any of these attempts succeed. Let me offer examples of attempts to construe "could have" claims conditionally. Peter van Inwagen's handling of this issue is especially compelling. Van Inwagen offers various formulations of the conditional and shows how they err. As he notes, one version says that what the proposition

> Smith could have saved the drowning child

"really means" is

> If Smith had chosen to save the drowning child, Smith would have saved the drowning child.

While this seems to make abundant sense (determinists could agree with this analysis and maintain that even with determinism, the agent could do otherwise), upon further analysis it is deficient. Suppose that Smith doesn't know how to swim or that he does but has a pathological fear of water. In the former case, he could choose to save the drowning child but still could not do so because of not knowing how to swim. In the second case, if he could bring himself to choose to rescue the child, since he knows how to swim he could pull it off, but it is dubious that he could bring himself to make that choice. All of this shows that while it may be possible to render some ascriptions of ability in conditional forms, this isn't so for many. Hence, it just is not true that ascriptions of ability can always be rendered in some conditional form consistent with determinism.[29]

As van Inwagen says, some "could" statements, if rendered as conditionals, very clearly would not be true. We wouldn't have to think about them long at all to see that the conditional is not a proper way of rendering the "could" claim. For example, consider that "Napoleon could have won at Waterloo" really means "If Napoleon had chosen to win at Waterloo, Napoleon would have won at Waterloo." This is clearly false, and one need not be a philosopher to see that.[30]

There have been other attempts to render "could have" claims as conditionals, and van Inwagen details them and convincingly explains why they fail.[31] There may be some unobjectionable way to construe such statements conditionally, but I think the determinist should go in another direction. That brings me to a second determinist response to this issue. This answer says that before we can decide whether a determinist can say that an agent could do otherwise, we must understand what being able to do otherwise means. The preceding determinist response agreed, but this response doesn't look to a conditional analysis of "could" statements. Rather it says that "can" and "could" are ambiguous terms, and claims about what the agent could have done can be understood in various ways. The determinist argues that most senses of "the agent could have done otherwise" are true for a determinist account of human action. Elsewhere I have offered this argument, but it is worth repeating.

In constructing this argument, the work of John Canfield, Winston Nesbitt, and Stewart Candlish is especially helpful,[32] and my argument is adapted from what they say. There are various senses in which "can" and "could" may be used, and most are senses in which a soft determinist could say that the agent could do otherwise. Hence, if being able to do otherwise is a criterion for free action, compatibilistically done actions are free. Let me sketch the various senses of "can."

An initial sense of "can" is the *ability* sense. To say that someone can do otherwise means he has the ability or the power to do so. This refers both to ability to choose and ability to do. For example, if someone chooses not to go to the golf course for a round of golf on a given afternoon, he still has the ability to do so. He could drive or walk to the country club, he is able to swing the clubs, and he knows the rules and procedures of the game. So whatever is required for getting to the golf course and playing golf is within his power or ability, even if he does none of it. On the other hand, someone paralyzed from the waist down may choose to walk a mile, but he doesn't have the ability to carry out that choice.

A second sense of "can" is the *opportunity* sense. "Can" in this sense involves more than just physical or mental abilities. One must be in circumstances that allow him to do the act. Take the golfer again. Suppose everything about him is the same as described above, but he is in prison for committing a crime. Moreover, suppose that he is locked up in solitary confinement. Under those circumstances, he has the ability to play a round of golf, but he doesn't have the opportunity. Of course, a person may also have the opportunity and ability to do something, but refrain. Still, in the opportunity sense of "can" it would be correct to say he could do otherwise.

Third, there is what John Canfield calls a *rule consistent* sense of "can." Here what one proposes to do (or what one could do but doesn't) is consistent with all known rules. For example, in a game of chess, one player cannot take the other player's king without first putting it in "check." That is, the rules of the game don't allow a player to capture an opponent's king without first putting it in danger of being taken on the next move. On the other hand, a driving instructor may tell a student "you can go 35 miles per hour on this street." This means more than that the student has ability and opportunity to drive. The teacher also means that the speed laws allow him to drive this fast. Saying that he couldn't drive 55 miles per hour in a 35 mile per hour zone means that it would be inconsistent with the rules to do so, though of course he has ability and perhaps opportunity to break the law.

Fourth, Canfield also delineates an *ill-consequence free* sense of can. In this sense, being able to do something means that one can do it without any harmful consequences. Not being able to do it means that doing it would have bad consequences. For example, it is very unlikely that in this sense I *can* jump off the roof of a ten story building. There is no rule against it, I have the ability to do so, and I may even have the opportunity to do it, but if I did it, it is dubious that I could avoid some very devastating consequences.[33]

We can also use "can" or "could" in other senses. One of them I would call the *authority* sense of can. In this case, the person who can do something has the authority to do it, regardless of whether that authority is used or not. As an example, we might say that "though Hitler ordered the genocide of Jews during World War II, he could have stopped the killing at any time. No one else could have, but he could have." The point is that only someone in a position of authority has the right to order or stop such a thing. Others may have the ability and opportunity to carry out the order, but they cannot do so until someone in authority commands a particular action.

A sixth sense of "can" understands it to mean "reasonable." That is, to say that someone can do something means that there are good reasons for it, the person knows those reasons, and in light of them does the act. What she does is exactly what we would expect, since we know her to be a person who can be persuaded by reason. On the other hand, when someone says that another person cannot do a particular action, they may mean only that it would be unreasonable to do so since all the arguments are in favor of foregoing it. We might tell someone with family responsibilities and a limited income, "you can't take the paycheck you just received and squander it at the racetrack." Now, he certainly has the ability to do so, and the opportunity to go to the racetrack is there. Moreover, doing it would break no rule. There would be ill consequences if he did it (so this might be our meaning), but our basic point may be that it would be an irrational and irresponsible thing to do; all arguments are against it. Before leaving this sense of "can," I note that many times when a soft determinist like myself says, "given the prevailing conditions, the agent couldn't have done otherwise," this doesn't deny the agent's ability or opportunity to do otherwise but only means that it would be unreasonable for him to do so.

A seventh sense of "can" or "could" is the *conditional* sense mentioned above. This must not be misunderstood. I am not saying that all the evidence presented against conditional analysis of "can" and "could" statements should be ignored. I agree with those objections. However, while the objections show that this is an unacceptable way to understand *all* "can" statements, that doesn't mean a conditional analysis is never what we mean when we say "can" or "could." For example, if I say to someone, "you could have gone to the movies tonight," I may mean nothing more than that of all the options before him for this evening's activities, he could have done this if he had wanted, desired, chosen to do it. Of course, this presupposes that he has the ability and opportunity to do it, as well as reason to do it, etc., but still the basic point may be that if he had chosen, he could have done it. Undoubtedly, some "can" statements can be interpreted this way, even if most cannot be.

Finally, there is what we may call the *contra-causal* or *libertarian* sense of "can." To say that someone could have done otherwise in this sense means that though there were various causal factors playing on one's will at the time of decision making, none of those factors individually nor all of them conjointly were sufficient to incline the person's will decisively one way or the other. Thus, though causes may have pointed to one choice, the agent still could just as easily have done the other. If someone could not have done otherwise in this sense, that would mean that causal conditions were strong enough to determine the choice one way or another. In that case, libertarians, by saying that the agent could not do otherwise, mean that what was done was not done freely.

In considering these eight senses of "can" and "could," one should see that both a soft determinist like myself and an indeterminist can hold that an agent could have or could not have done a particular action in all of the first seven senses of "can." That is, when the agent has ability, opportunity, reason to act, etc., from an indeterminist perspective, the same is true from a soft determinist point of view. Likewise, whenever an agent does not have the ability, opportunity, reason to act, etc., from an indeterminist perspective, the same is true for soft determinism. Therefore, if an action counts as free only if the agent could have done otherwise, then in the first seven senses of "could have" the soft determinist has just as much right to claim that the agent could have done otherwise as does the indeterminist. And this means that soft determinism counts as freedom just as much as does libertarian freedom.

The one area of disagreement between the soft determinist and indeterminist relates to the eighth sense. No one can, consistent with determinism, hold that an agent can do otherwise in that sense, for to do so adopts libertarian free will, which contradicts compatibilistic free will. But is this failure on the part of compatibilism a critical problem? Not at all, and we should see this once we recognize that it is the eighth sense about which both determinists and indeterminists argue. This is so because the eighth sense incorporates the indeterminist's definition of free will, and that is something a soft determinist will not allow. If the indeterminist says that unless one says that the agent could have done otherwise in this eighth sense, one's position is not "real" or "genuine" freedom, this is nothing more than question begging by demanding that an indeterminist definition of freedom is correct without proving it so. Soft determinists would deny that anyone can do otherwise in this eighth (contra-causal) sense of "can," for to admit that there are such actions undercuts soft determinism.

The net result of the preceding is that, if both sides avoid question begging (i.e., neither demands a sense of "can" that presupposes their definition of free will), then the soft determinist has just as much right as the indeterminist to say that, on his account of human action, the agent can do otherwise in the first seven senses. No questions are begged by the first seven senses of "can" and "could." But if being able to do otherwise is crucial for freedom, then soft determinism of the sort I espouse meets this criterion and qualifies as genuine free action. Demanding that soft determinism is also compatible with "could" in the contra-causal sense is question begging.

There is a third line of argument that answers the objection to determinism that the agent must be able to do otherwise for an act to be free. It relates to whether one must be able to do otherwise to be morally accountable. Since indeterminists believe that any form of determinism makes it impossible for an agent to do other than he does, indeterminists are also convinced that if determinism is true, no one is ever responsible for his or her acts, since moral responsibility depends on acting freely. However, it is just this principle that the agent must be able to do otherwise to be morally responsible, that has come under attack in recent years.

In an extremely influential article, Harry Frankfurt challenges this principle, which is often labeled the principle of alternate possibilities.[34] Frankfurt presents examples of cases wherein an action is not only causally determined, but regardless of what the agent does, the same outcome will occur. Nonetheless, Frankfurt argues that in such situations it makes no sense to claim that the agent isn't morally responsible for his action. Though this sounds strange, there are many illustrations of what are known as Frankfurt counterexamples. Let me offer two.

First, consider a situation in which Peter is carried, while asleep, into a room where Paul is also sleeping. Peter is locked in the room, and can't leave the room when he awakes unless someone else unlocks the door. Peter eventually awakens and is pleased to see Paul there, because he dislikes and enjoys annoying Paul. Instead of leaving the room, he waits for Paul to wake up, knowing that Paul will be annoyed when he sees Peter. Eventually Paul does awaken, and is furious when he sees Peter. Now in this case Peter could not have left the room even if he had wanted to do so, but does that mean he is not responsible for annoying Paul? It is dubious that we would deny such responsibility, but this shows that even when alternate possibilities are not open to someone, he can still be morally responsible for his actions. Hence, the principle that one is not morally accountable unless one could do otherwise, if true at all, is not universally true.[35]

David Hunt offers a second example:

> Jones murders Smith, and does so under conditions which are as favorable as possible to Jones's freedom and responsibility, given the following peculiarity. There is a third party, Black, who wishes Jones to murder Smith, and who possesses a mechanism capable of monitoring and controlling a person's thoughts. Thinking that Jones might well do what he wishes him to do anyway, but unwilling to be disappointed in this expectation, Black programs the mechanism to monitor Jones's thoughts for evidence for his intentions with respect to murdering Smith, and to manipulate those thoughts to ensure the murder of Smith should it appear that Jones is not going to acquire the requisite intention in any other way. As it happens, the mechanism does not have to intervene in the course of events, because Jones goes ahead and murders Smith on his own.[36]

In a case like this, Frankfurt thought two basic things were true. One is that Jones was unable to forego killing Smith, given Black's mechanism for controlling Jones's thoughts when necessary. But on the other hand, it is also abundantly clear that Jones is still morally accountable for killing Smith. Just because he really could not have done otherwise, that doesn't mean Jones is free of moral blame in this case.[37] As Randolph Clarke says of these sorts of examples, "She could not have done otherwise; but since what makes it the case that she could not have done otherwise does not causally affect her at all, she may still be responsible for what she does."[38]

We must clarify what these kinds of cases do and do not show. The main thing they show is that there are cases wherein an agent could not have done otherwise and yet should be assessed moral blame or praise. Hence, the rule that the agent must be able to do otherwise to be morally responsible is not exceptionless. However, this doesn't mean that every case is an exceptional case. In many cases when the agent could not do otherwise, it wouldn't make sense to assess her moral blame. Think of the case where a bank robber forces the clerk to hand over the money in the safe. The teller surely has the ability to do otherwise, but couldn't fail to hand over the money in that it would be unreasonable for her to refuse in this situation. In this kind of situation, the act was not free, but that is so not just because there were no other genuine options she dared to take, but also because she was forced to do something contrary to her wishes.

This last point, however, holds the key as to why, with Frankfurt counterexamples, the agent is morally accountable, even though the agent could not do otherwise. The reason is that, in the cases of Paul and Peter and Jones and Smith, Peter stays in the room because he wants to annoy Paul and Jones kills Smith because he wants to (and those wants are not manipulated by Black).

Now, an indeterminist might well say that Peter and Jones are not really free in part because they couldn't do otherwise and also because their acts were causally determined by their desires and whatever other factors led them to act. On the other hand, a soft determinist would say that since the unknown forces external to Peter and Jones didn't enter into what they decided and did, and since they acted according to their desires, they acted freely, even though if they had tried to act differently they would have been blocked from doing so. And when one acts freely in this compatibilist sense, one is morally responsible. It is only indeterminists who conclude that not being able to do otherwise always removes freedom and moral responsibility. Frankfurt-type situations, however, suggest that indeterminists are wrong on this point.

In Frankfurt-type cases, then, being unable to do otherwise (because something makes the outcome inevitable) does not remove grounds for assessing moral blame or praise. In such cases, blame or praise is properly assessed because the agent does what she wants or desires to do, despite the fact that she could do nothing else. This fits what soft determinists like myself advocate, namely, that freedom and moral accountability depend on whether the agent acts according to her wishes. Indeterminists might say that her act was not free in a libertarian sense but it was morally accountable. Indeed, that is an odd position, but so much the worse for indeterminism.

Of course, this doesn't mean that every time someone cannot do otherwise we have a Frankfurt-type case. Moreover, when an agent cannot do otherwise because it would be unwise to do so, or because there is no opportunity, etc., to do so, invariably she also does whatever she does contrary to her desires. In those cases, neither determinists nor indeterminists would say she acted freely, and neither would hold her morally responsible.

This whole discussion of an agent's ability to do otherwise shows that the issue is far more complex than one might think, and it isn't at all clear that the picture is damaging to a soft determinist position such as mine. In fact, Daniel Dennett has recently argued that even if someone could not do otherwise, that is unimportant to whether they are free or morally responsible. He argues this for a number of reasons, but let me offer just two. Dennett hopes that it would be impossible to get him to torture an innocent person by offering him $1,000 to do so. Of course, if an evil alien was about to destroy the world unless Dennett tortured that person, that might make a difference, but Dennett thinks this counter situation is sufficiently different from being offered $1,000 in a normal situation to torture an innocent person that this nuance proves nothing about what he would do in the normal situation. Dennett relates this to moral responsibility in such a case as follows:

> Those who hold the CDO [could have done otherwise—my insertion] principle dear are always insisting that we should look at whether one could have done otherwise in *exactly* the same circumstances. I claim something stronger; I claim that I could not do otherwise even in any

roughly similar case. I would *never* agree to torture an innocent person for a thousand dollars. It would make no difference, I claim, what tone of voice the briber used, or whether I was tired and hungry, or whether the proposed victim was well illuminated or partially concealed in shadow. I am, I hope, immune to all such efforts.

Now why would anyone's intuitions suggest that, if I am right, then if and when I ever have occasion to refuse such an offer, my refusal would not count as a responsible act?[39]

All of this fits what Dennett argues in his book *Elbow Room* and what Susan Wolf argues in her *Freedom Within Reason*. They describe cases wherein an agent is of such good moral character and sees so clearly what is right and why that the person couldn't bring himself to do anything but what is right. That the agent in such cases could not do otherwise wouldn't cause us to say that the agent was not praiseworthy (in an opposite case where a person acts out of a genuinely evil character, we wouldn't fail to assess blame). But, then, this shows that "being able to do otherwise" cannot be a requirement in every case for being morally accountable.[40]

Dennett offers a second reason why it really shouldn't matter for moral accountability whether an agent could do otherwise. Some think there must be laws of nature and states of affairs that determine what happens in our physical brains, if determinism is true. They also believe that this tells us whether we could do otherwise. Dennett explains why this would be disastrous for determining moral accountability:

> If our responsibility really did hinge, as this major philosophical tradition insists, on the question of whether we ever could do otherwise than we in fact do *in exactly those circumstances,* we would be faced with a most peculiar problem of ignorance: it would be unlikely in the extreme, given what now seems to be the case in physics, that anyone would ever know whether anyone has ever been responsible. For today's orthodoxy is that indeterminism reigns at the subatomic level of quantum mechanics; so, in the absence of any general and accepted argument for universal determinism, it is possible for all we know that our decisions and actions truly are the magnified, macroscopic effects of quantum-level indeterminacies occurring in our brains. But it is also possible for all we know that, even though indeterminism reigns in our brains at the subatomic quantum-mechanical level, our macroscopic decisions and acts are all themselves determined; the quantum effects could just as well be self-canceling, not amplified (as if by organic Geiger counters in the neurons). And it is extremely unlikely, given the complexity of the brain at even the molecular level . . . , that we could ever develop good evidence that any particular act was such a large-scale effect of a critical subatomic indeterminacy. So if someone's responsibility for an act did hinge on whether, at the moment of decision, that decision was (already) determined by a prior state of the world, then barring a triumphant return of universal determinism in microphysics (which would rule out all responsibility on this view),

the odds are heavy that we will never have *any* reason to believe of any particular act that it was or was not responsible. The critical difference would be utterly inscrutable from every macroscopic vantage point and practically inscrutable from the most sophisticated microphysical vantage point imaginable.[41]

That is, if we must know whether the agent could have done otherwise in the sense of the relation of mental states to brain states (and the physical laws and processes involved therein), we would be hopeless to assign any moral praise or blame for any act. For Dennett that shows that really knowing if the agent was physically determined in this way is not possible, and hence knowing whether the agent could have done otherwise really does not matter. For those who hold that mind is immaterial and that it isn't clear how the physical states of our brains effect mental phenomena, it becomes even harder to know, given current knowledge about these things, if the agent really could have done otherwise. But, as Dennett argues, it would be ludicrous, lacking the sort of information mentioned, to forego on that ground ascribing moral responsibility to actions.

In sum, I have spent many pages discussing being able to do otherwise, because it is a major complaint that indeterminists raise against determinism in any form. My contention is that a proper and full understanding of all the issues involved is totally consistent with anything the soft determinist would say about human freedom and about moral responsibility. The further point in light of Frankfurt-type cases and the issues raised by Dennett and Wolf is that there are many cases wherein whether the agent could do otherwise (and whether we know this) in some sense is irrelevant to ascribing moral culpability to him. Regardless of whether one thinks the act is indeterminate or causally determined but unconstrained, the act can be free and morally accountable.

Libertarian Freedom and the Ontological Argument

Wesley Morriston offers a further philosophical argument for compatibilism. Morriston notes the great importance of Alvin Plantinga's work in philosophy of religion and in philosophical theology. Plantinga's earlier work contained a defense of the ontological argument and a very sophisticated version of the free will defense in answer to the problem of evil. The free will defense rests on libertarian free will, and Morriston believes that when libertarian freedom is joined to what Plantinga says about the ontological argument, a contradiction is generated. I believe Morriston's argument is cogent and is a strong argument against libertarian free will.

As Morriston notes, Plantinga calls libertarian free will "significant freedom." It involves the agent being free to perform or refrain from an action because no antecedent conditions and/or causal laws determine what the agent will do. As to moral issues, this freedom gives us ability to choose either good or evil, and without such freedom we could not realize moral goodness in our lives. Though this freedom allows the possibility of moral evil, it also makes possible moral goodness in our lives.[42]

All of this is standard libertarian fare, but Morriston next moves to Plantinga's handling of the ontological argument. The key issue is Plantinga's account of maximal greatness and maximal excellence. Plantinga defines these concepts as follows:

> (27) A Being has maximal greatness in a given world only if it has maximal excellence in every world.
> (28) A being has maximal excellence in a given world only if it has omniscience, omnipotence, and moral perfection in that world.[43]

Given these definitions, suppose that God exists and possesses maximal greatness. If (27) and (28) are taken together, then God is morally perfect in every possible world. But moral perfection is incompatible with any wrongdoing, so in no possible world does God do evil. This is also standard Christian doctrine, and Christians would add that God's absolute holiness requires more than that he can do evil but always refrains. Rather, it mandates that it is impossible for God, in virtue of his nature, to sin. But then this means that his nature determines that in moral matters he has only one option; he must always choose the good.[44]

Though the comments about freedom are standard libertarian fare and the remarks about divine moral perfection are standard fare for many religious traditions, including Christianity, when the two are joined, a fascinating problem arises for the libertarian. The problem is that if an agent must be capable of doing or refraining from an act in order to be significantly free, then in regard to his own moral choices and deeds, a morally perfect God cannot be significantly free. As a result, he cannot actually be morally good, although he might be the exemplar of other types of goodness. With libertarian free will, someone who can only do good is not a moral paragon, nor is someone who cannot do anything but evil a moral reprobate. Such agents are not significantly free (in the libertarian sense), so they cannot be moral agents, and hence, we can neither praise nor blame them. As Morriston sums up the problem,

> The problem, in short, is that the presuppositions of the free will defense entail that moral goodness cannot be an essential property of any person, whereas the premises of the ontological argument entail that moral goodness is an essential property of at least one person, *viz.* God. So, either God is "significantly free" but then cannot be essentially morally good, for that would make doing evil impossible, and if doing evil were impossible, that would rule out libertarian free will. Or God is essentially morally good, as the ontological argument requires, but then he could not be significantly free in the libertarian sense required by proponents of libertarian freedom. And, that would surely be odd, in that God's human creatures are significantly free, but he is not![45]

It seems abundantly clear that any evangelical Christian theist would demand that God is morally perfect and essentially so. But Christians would also demand that their God is free. With libertarian free will, however, it seems that God cannot be both. I believe this is a significant problem for anyone committed to libertarian free will and any theological system that incorporates it. On the other hand, there is no problem for a soft deterministic system like mine. For God can be essentially morally good and still be free in the compatibilist sense. That is, God's actions are determined in large part by his nature. Thus, in moral decisions, he cannot do anything other than what is morally right; his nature both demands and determines that this is so. But, with compatibilism, this in no way eliminates divine freedom. Since his acts always stem from his character, it would be hard to argue that he ever acts under constraint, i.e., against his wishes. When confronted with a moral choice, it is hard to imagine that he chooses contrary to his desires or wishes. Even his choice to actualize a possible world (ours) with evil in it is not a choice he had to make or was forced to make against his wishes to create.[46] How the evil in that world squares with a God who doesn't desire it and apparently has power to remove it will be treated in the chapter on the problem of evil. But none of that means that when it came to choosing to create or not, and choosing which world to create, he wound up creating a world he didn't wish to create. Thus, according to compatibilism, *God's* actions in moral matters are free, even though his moral perfection guarantees that he could only choose the good. A specific sovereignty model of providence like mine can solve this problem, whereas it is a major problem for advocates of libertarian free will.

Other Indeterminist Objections

Let me respond now to several philosophical arguments for libertarian freedom. The first is the consequence argument, and initially I note that its notion of causation and determinism invokes covering laws and the complete state of the universe at the time an act or event occurs. As we have seen, this sort of causation and determinism is appropriate if the topic is determinism in the natural or physical sciences. However, when it comes to social sciences that deal with human actions, it is not clear that any such laws covering human behavior exist. Moreover, if there are such laws, they are probably nothing more than statistical or probabilistic laws which state what human beings generally do in such situations. Obviously, if there are no laws of behavior, or only statistical laws, that falsifies the consequence argument in relation to human behavior.

Moreover, that the causation and determinism involved in the consequence argument is natural or physical determinism and causation is also seen in the argument's claims about a complete description of the state of affairs in the world. The argument seems to assume that the state of affairs must be identical to or indistinguishably different from other such states of affairs, for if not and if there are not some constantly applicable causal laws that cover such cases, how could we surmise that just this combination of laws and circumstances would produce the expected result? In the natural realm, we can speak about repeatable and identical situations and what, according to applicable laws, would happen in such circumstances. So the argument seems to assume that what is true about a physical state of affairs is also true of human behavior. But given the complexity of human nature (and differences in personalities), how could we ever be certain that any two situations are identical? Even if it is the same person in both situations, people change over time, and they even learn from past experiences. So it is dubious that the state of the world would be identical with respect to human behavior from time to time, and if that is so, how can we sensibly talk about laws that guarantee the same result every time? We cannot, but I note further that this doesn't mean that whatever an agent does in any situation isn't causally determined. It only means that the kind of guarantees the argument requires rest on a type of determinism that doesn't apply to human actions. Hence, though the argument may be sound in regard to physical and natural causation, it is dubious in regard to human action.

A second problem with the argument stems from my analysis of the different senses of "can." The argument asserts that the judge cannot raise his hand if determinism is true, but what does "can" mean? Surely, the judge has the ability to raise his hand. He also has the opportunity to do so and in a way that would make a difference in the life of the accused. Moreover, there will be no ill consequences to himself if he raises his hand, he has the authority to do so, and no rule forbids him from raising his hand. Van Inwagen says that the judge decided after calmly and rationally considering the evidence. This fits another sense of "can." Van Inwagen doesn't say whether the case is strong against the criminal so that it would be unreasonable to let him go, or whether it is weak so that it would be unreasonable to execute him. This is to be expected, since reasons and arguments don't matter much to the form of determinism van Inwagen treats. However, human behavior is not governed by that kind of determinism, so reasons and arguments do matter. If the case is very strong in one direction or the other, the judge might not be able to do the opposite in the sense that it would be unreasonable to do so, but that is far different from saying that the judge couldn't raise his hand because of things that happened well before he was born. If the case is rather inconclusive, the judge could raise his hand in that it would be reasonable to do so. All of this shows that on a careful analysis of what it might mean to say that the judge couldn't raise his hand, the soft determinist can rebut van Inwagen's argument. It may create problems for strong forms of determinism, but it isn't telling against soft determinism.[47]

Can a compatibilist answer the indeterminist argument about deliberating about the inevitable? I believe so. Again the argument presupposes the strict determinism of the natural sciences which van Inwagen wants to apply to human behavior, but this is problematic, for human behavior is nowhere near as predictable as are natural processes. On my soft determinist model, God foreordained everything I do, and when I do any act, there will be conditions causally sufficient to move me to do it. But since I don't know in advance what God decreed about my actions, in most cases, though a given act is predetermined before the foundation of the world and will be causally determined, there is no inconsistency in my deliberating about what to do. For all I know, God may have foreordained that I go through this deliberative process, because without it I would have no clue about what to do. So, on my soft determinist model, there is no reason to think that I cannot or should not deliberate about whether to do a given deed.

There is yet a further reply. Even if we grant van Inwagen's argument, the type of determinism he has in mind, Bruce Waller argues that it still makes sense to deliberate over the inevitable. As Waller says, part of the problem with van Inwagen's argument is that the case he offers is too simple and the answer too obvious. Van Inwagen imagines someone in a room with two doors who believes that one door is unlocked and the other is locked and impassable. The person in the room doesn't know which one is locked. This is too simple, because one option is literally and obviously barred. Waller says that deliberation is removed by the salience, not the inevitability of the conclusion. Similarly, one cannot deliberate about whether to walk or fly to the corner, but one could deliberate about walking or driving, even if one thought the eventual choice would be inevitable.[48] Waller says that the possibility of deliberating over an inevitable result can be shown to make sense if we imagine a more complicated case, such as a situation where someone tries to decide what horse to bet on in a steeplechase. Waller explains:

> I am a determinist, and I believe that my ultimate choice is completely and uniquely determined (by my learning history, my past patterns of reinforcement, the current influences on me): my bet will be the causal result of those determining factors, and I could not choose other than I shall choose. Will I now find it impossible to deliberate about a number of options, since I believe that only one is really possible? Certainly not. For I must still carry out the determined deliberation process in order to arrive at my betting choice; just as I must still trudge to the betting window, even if I believe that it is determined that I shall arrive at that window. I recognize that my deliberation process—involving my beliefs, memories, hopes, changing knowledge of odds and jockeys and weather conditions—is an essential part of my choosing among various horses. Even though that deliberation process is completely determined it will be no less a process of genuine deliberation and no less important in selecting a fancy (it will still play a causal role in determining my wager). Without that deliberation process (if I instead bet on an appealing name, or my reasoning process were addled by drugs) the final selection would probably be quite different. It is determined *that* I shall deliberate, *how* I shall deliberate, and what the

result of my deliberation will be; but why should any of that preclude deliberation or lessen its importance?[49]

This seems correct for several reasons. For one thing, there are many horses in the race and it would be possible to pick any of them. Unlike the room with one barred door, there is no reason why, if one chooses any horse in the race, one couldn't actually bet on it. Knowing that, it is genuinely possible to deliberate about which one to choose. Beyond that, I believe Waller is right because all of the factors that will determine a decision and how they will interact to do so are unknown to the person at the time he decides about his bet. If he knew all those factors and knew the inevitable result, there would be little need to deliberate, but he doesn't know these things, so it makes sense to deliberate. Waller argues that even if the result is foreknown because some machine calculates all the variables and tells us what we will do, it still makes sense to deliberate even if only because the machine's calculation and prediction may surprise us. We thought the best option was a different horse, and so we think everything through to see how it confirms the prediction.[50] Of course, in the horse race, as with most of our actions, we don't have a prediction prior to our choosing. So even though our act is causally determined, it still makes sense for us to deliberate.

In light of all these philosophical considerations, I conclude that it is not only possible that a compatibilist specific sovereignty model of providence is true, but also quite plausible to think so. When coupled with the biblical and theological arguments also presented, I believe it is the best model for explaining God's providential control over our world. There is, however, more to the story than this, for there are two more topics yet to consider in the next two chapters.

FIFTEEN

THE ISSUE OF FREEDOM AND FOREKNOWLEDGE

At various points in this book I have said that there is a problem in relating free will to divine foreknowledge. We must now consider this topic. There are actually two different problems connected with biblical teaching on divine foreknowledge. In chapter 11, I explained that many scholars understand biblical terms for foreknowledge to refer only to God's intellectual awareness of the future before it happens. However, biblical terms for foreknowledge often refer to foreordination, not prescience. I argued that many passages which general sovereignty advocates believe teach that God decrees the future on the basis of what he foresees really don't teach that at all. Instead, they teach that God has foreordained the future. So an initial problem surrounding divine foreknowledge relates to what the biblical term means. Of course, even if foreknowledge means foreordination in many passages, there is still a question about how things that are foreordained can be free. In chapter 14, I defended a soft deterministic model of divine providence, and I showed how God's foreordaining everything could fit with human free will. Of course, the kind of freedom involved in that explanation is compatibilistic free will.

The question for this chapter is whether divine foreknowledge of our future actions harmonizes with libertarian free will. Throughout the centuries biblical scholars, theologians, and philosophers have concluded that Scripture teaches that God knows the future. This conviction comes partly from passages which suggest that God's knowledge is unlimited, but also from passages in which God predicts future events. Though many of these prophecies are about Christ's second advent and haven't yet been fulfilled, many are about his first advent, and have been fulfilled. So there is ample biblical reason to conclude that God knows the future. On the other hand, there is an equally settled opinion that human beings have free will. Philosophers, theologians, and biblical exegetes have wondered how humans could be free to do whatever they choose, if God already knows what they will do. It seems that if God knows what we will do in the future, there is no option to do something other than what God foresees.

Of course, one way to reconcile human freedom and divine foreknowledge is to reject one or the other, but most evangelical Christians haven't found that resolution satisfactory. If one were forced to choose between the two, it would be almost impossible to do so. If God doesn't foreknow the future, how can we explain all the Scriptures in which he predicts future events? On the other hand, if we give up human free will, all the biblical evidence for free will must be discounted. And if humans don't have free will, it seems immensely unjust for God to hold them morally accountable for what they do.

In light of such considerations, theologians and philosophers have tried to solve the problem of divine foreknowledge and human freedom in ways which maintain both concepts. In this chapter, I want to present the various resolutions offered and evaluate them. If this problem can be solved, can it be solved by both a general sovereignty and a specific sovereignty approach to providence? If so, then the issue of freedom and foreknowledge should make little difference to which model of providence one chooses. However, if one model can solve this problem and others cannot, that would be a significant argument for the model that can solve the problem, and a major objection to those that cannot.

CLARIFYING THE PROBLEM

Before examining various resolutions, I must clarify what is at stake in this problem. I note first that we find the terms "compatibilism" and "incompatibilism" in this discussion. We have seen these terms before, but in prior discussions they referred to different notions of free human action. In the discussions of freedom and foreknowledge, the terms appear again, but they are used in a different sense. Someone who is a compatibilist on the matter of freedom and foreknowledge believes that divine foreknowledge is compatible with human free will (typically, the kind of freedom in view is libertarian). On the other hand, someone who does not think divine foreknowledge is compatible with human freedom is an incompatibilist. Those who hold a compatibilistic notion of free will believe their view of freedom is compatible with divine foreknowledge, and they charge that divine foreknowledge is incompatible with libertarian free will.

Those who hold libertarian free will are divided on whether that freedom is compatible with divine foreknowledge. Libertarians have offered various proposals to harmonize free will and divine foreknowledge, but some believe they are incompatible. In a very influential and significant article titled "Divine Foreknowledge and Alternative Conceptions of Human Freedom,"[1] William

Alston argued that those who hold a compatibilist line on the freedom/fore-knowledge issue actually espouse a different concept of human freedom than libertarianism. In fact, they have adopted a view of freedom that places them in the determinist camp. I contend that many resolutions to the freedom/foreknowledge problem offered by proponents of libertarian free will are guilty of the error Alston mentions, and hence their proposed resolution doesn't render a system with libertarian freedom internally consistent. But more on that as we proceed.[2]

Second, we must understand how divine foreknowledge is supposedly incompatible with human freedom. Many think the problem is that God's foreknowledge of our actions *causes* those deeds. If so, then the acts must be causally determined by something other than the agent who does them, and hence they cannot be free in a libertarian sense. Of course, if this is what the issue is all about, then, as many compatibilists on freedom and foreknowledge point out, there is no reason to think God's knowledge is causative. After all, if I know that next week a meeting is scheduled and I know that I'll be there unless providentially hindered, that doesn't mean my knowledge caused the meeting or caused my presence at it. If my knowledge doesn't cause what happens, why should we assume that it is any different in God's case?

Neither indeterminists nor determinists claim that divine foreknowledge *causes* free human actions or anything else that occurs. Instead, the point is an epistemological one. Knowledge has traditionally been understood as a stronger notion than mere belief. Belief is an opinion that something is true, and the opinion may be supported by evidence, but the belief could be wrong. On the other hand, philosophers contend that the claim to know means that one has grounds that justify holding that belief and that what one claims to know is in fact true.[3] Of course, while this distinction between knowledge and belief makes sense in relation to us, in God's case it isn't clear that it does. Since God is omniscient and infallibly knows everything there is to know, if God believes something, he could not be mistaken. But now the nature of the freedom/foreknowledge problem becomes clearer. If God's beliefs about my future actions are correct, i.e., if he knows what I will do, how can I do anything other than what he knows I will do? It isn't that as I make my decisions, I am aware of what God knows about my decision and subsequent action. God could divulge such information to us, but in most cases he hasn't. But the mere fact that there is something I will do and God knows what it is before I do it (he knew it before the foundation of the world) seems to mean that I only really have one genuine option. However, with libertarian free will, the various options confronting the agent must all be "live" options, for the agent can always do otherwise than she does. According to libertarians, "can" here must be a contra-causal "can" in order to uphold libertarian freedom. But with God infallibly knowing the future deeds of his creatures, it seems impossible for them to be free in this sense.

While this problem has occupied philosophers' and theologians' attention for many centuries, in contemporary discussions it has seemingly taken on a new life. The impetus for this stems largely from a very influential article by

Nelson Pike titled "Divine Omniscience and Voluntary Action." Pike revised the essay and included it in his book *God and Timelessness*. The issue raised by the argument is the freedom/foreknowledge problem, and it has come to be known as the argument for theological fatalism.[4] In Pike's formal presentation, the argument has many steps, and to clarify the problem exactly, I offer his construction of the argument in *God and Timelessness*:

(1)　'Yahweh is omniscient and Yahweh exists at T1' entails 'If Jones does A at T2, then Yahweh believes at T1 that Jones does A at T2'.

(2)　If Yahweh is (essentially) omniscient, then 'Yahweh believes P' entails 'P'.

(3)　It is not within one's power at a given time so to act that both 'P' and 'not-P' are true.

(4)　It is not within one's power at a given time so to act that something believed by an individual at a time prior to the given time was not believed by that individual at the prior time.

(5)　It is not within one's power at a given time so to act that an individual existing at a time prior to the given time did not exist at the prior time.

(6)　If Yahweh believes at T1 that Jones does A at T2, then if it is within Jones's power at T2 to refrain from doing A then either: (1) It was within Jones's power at T2 so to act that Yahweh believed P at T1 and 'P' is false; or (2) it was within Jones's power at T2 so to act that Yahweh did not believe as He did believe at T2; or (3) it was within Jones's power at T2 so to act that Yahweh did not exist at T1.

(7)　If Yahweh is (essentially) omniscient, then the first alternative in the consequent of line 6 is false (from lines 2 and 3).

(8)　The second alternative in the consequent of line 6 is false (from line 4).

(9)　The third alternative in the consequent of line 6 is false (from line 5).

(10)　Therefore: If Yahweh is (essentially) omniscient and believes at T1 that Jones does A at T1 [*sic*], then it was not within Jones's power at T2 to refrain from doing A (from lines 6 and 7-9).

(11)　Therefore: If Yahweh is (essentially) omniscient and exists at T1, then if Jones does A at T2, it was not within Jones's power at T2 to refrain from doing A (from lines 10 and 1).[5]

(In Pike's tenth step, the second occurrence of 'T1' should read 'T2'.)

In response, Pike imagines an objector claiming that this isn't necessarily true, for when we foreknow someone's actions, that does not remove their power to do otherwise. Suppose I really know that a friend will leave on vacation tomorrow. If I really know this, I could not be mistaken. If my friend doesn't depart tomorrow, then I only believed it, but was mistaken. But if I really know it, it seems that he cannot do otherwise; otherwise, he could make my true belief false, and that is contradictory. Pike responds that my knowing that a friend will leave on vacation tomorrow means only that he will leave, not that he *must*. If I currently believe that he will leave tomorrow and he doesn't, then my belief would have been false. So my friend doesn't have it in his power to make a true belief of mine false, but he does have power (a power that goes unused) to do something such that my belief *would have been* false. However, Pike argues, this doesn't remove the problem of theological fatalism, for God's beliefs are not like ours. God knows infallibly, so his beliefs could not have been false. Hence, there is no power that anyone has which, if they used it to keep my friend from leaving tomorrow, would have made God's beliefs false. While my beliefs about my neighbor could be mistaken, God's cannot be. Thus, the argument from theological fatalism seems to remain intact.[6]

Various philosophers have replied that this argument contains an implicit argument that is guilty of a logical fallacy. As William Lane Craig explains it, the argument runs as follows:

> Necessarily if God foreknows x, then x will happen.
>
> God foreknows x.
>
> Therefore, x will necessarily happen.[7]

Craig explains the error as follows:

> But such reasoning is universally recognized to be logically fallacious. It is like reasoning:
>
> > Necessarily, if Jones is a bachelor, Jones is unmarried.
> >
> > Jones is a bachelor.
> >
> > Therefore, Jones is necessarily unmarried.
>
> But Jones is not *necessarily* unmarried. He just *is* unmarried. He is perfectly free to be married; no necessity compels him to be unmarried. The valid form of the argument would thus read:
>
> > Necessarily, if Jones is a bachelor, Jones is unmarried.
> >
> > Jones is a bachelor.
> >
> > Therefore, Jones is unmarried.
>
> This form of the argument does not preclude that Jones has it in his power to be married. If he were married, then he would not be a bachelor. From the fact that he is a bachelor, we know with absolute

certainty that he is unmarried. But he is not necessarily unmarried; that
is, it is not impossible for him to be married.[8]

Now it is true that the argument in the first form Craig offers is guilty of
what is called a modal fallacy (the one Craig points out), but this doesn't
answer the dilemma of freedom and foreknowledge altogether. For even
granting that someone *will* do what God foreknows, rather than that they
must do so, the problem raised by Pike's argument still remains. How can
God infallibly know this information about our future actions and yet it still
be within our power to refrain from them?

Finally, the argument for theological fatalism accuses theological systems
which hold to divine foreknowledge of future human actions of contradicting
another belief they hold, namely, that humans act freely. Since the charge of
contradiction means that there is no possible way to fit these ideas together
without contradiction, the way to answer that accusation is to show a possible
way for divine foreknowledge and human freedom both to be true without
contradiction. Hence, the first question for any proposed resolution of this
problem is whether it removes the alleged contradiction. But, we must do
more than this, for it is surely possible to incorporate notions in one's explanation that are utterly outrageous but which, if adopted, would render one's
system internally consistent. Hence, after discerning whether a resolution to
this problem is logically consistent, we must further ask whether there are
grounds for believing the story true that the theologian tells. Of course, if the
offered resolution to the freedom/foreknowledge dilemma does not remove
the logical inconsistency, answers to this second question are beside the point.

DETERMINIST RESPONSES TO THE
FREEDOM/FOREKNOWLEDGE PROBLEM

For theological determinists, the freedom/foreknowledge issue is not a significant problem. This is not to say that every specific sovereignty position
upholds both, but only that each deterministic system can handle this issue in
a way consistent with the basic notions of the system. Hard deterministic and
fatalistic notions of determinism rule out free will in any sense. Such systems
have no problem upholding divine foreknowledge of everything that occurs.
In fact, since many of these harder forms of theological determinism claim that
God decreed everything that occurs, it is only natural that he would know the
whole course of history in advance. What he knows about the future logically
comes after his decree, so it is hard to imagine him not knowing in advance
everything that will happen.

Specific sovereignty systems committed to a form of hard determinism,
then, uphold divine foreknowledge at the expense of human freedom. Since
rejecting free will in any sense is consistent with the broader picture these sys-

tems offer, denying free will as inconsistent with divine foreknowledge doesn't render such systems internally inconsistent. So if these deterministic systems are objectionable, it won't be because of their inability to solve the freedom/ foreknowledge problem. Rather, they will be objectionable because of their form of determinism and/or their rejection altogether of free will.

As to soft deterministic systems such as mine, the freedom/foreknowledge question is resolvable. Given the belief that God decrees all things solely on the basis of his desires, it is only natural to hold that God has exhaustive knowledge in advance of everything that ever occurs. Of course, that knowledge in no way causes anything to happen; it merely guarantees that what God knows will in fact happen. But does his knowledge of what his creatures will do rule out freedom in the way the problem of freedom and foreknowledge suggests? Not at all, given compatibilistic free will. On that view of freedom, human actions, though causally determined, are still free if they are done in accord with the agent's wishes. In decreeing and knowing all things, God certainly has decreed not only what we will do but also the factors that will lead us to act. And he knows in which cases the causes will constrain our action and in which they won't. In cases where causes do not constrain our deeds, God's knowledge of those causes and of our resultant act in no way constrains us as we act. In fact, even when causal conditions do constrain our will, it is the conditions that constrain us, not God's knowledge that does so. Hence, exhaustive divine foreknowledge of everything that will ever occur is entirely consistent with the story the compatibilist on free will tells. God foresees because he decrees. He decrees actions and events and means to both; hence, he foresees causes in each case that will bring about the act or event. Moreover, having decreed all things, he also knows what he will do himself at various points in history. Knowing that information puts him in a perfect position to intervene at just the right time in whatever way he has chosen (as exemplified in the decree).

So the soft determinist can uphold both divine foreknowledge and human freedom so long as the freedom is compatibilistic free will. Still, a logically consistent story may be false as a whole, but in this case I contend that it is not false. The argumentation for specific sovereignty offered in the preceding chapter is why I say this. The fact that compatibilistic free will fits consistently with a belief in divine foreknowledge of our actions is further support (though not conclusive proof) for my model of divine providence.

INDETERMINIST RESPONSES TO THE FREEDOM/FOREKNOWLEDGE PROBLEM

The problem of freedom and foreknowledge is especially acute for systems committed to libertarian free will. Since general sovereignty models of providence incorporate that notion of free will, proponents of those systems must answer this problem adequately. Advocates of libertarian free will are acutely aware of this, and have at various times during the history of this debate offered different answers. Over the last thirty to forty years, there have been defenders of each of the resolutions proposed at one time or another during the history of this debate. Hence, in contemporary philosophy and theology this is a very live debate.

Specifically, indeterminists have proposed five major answers to this problem. In what follows I shall present and assess each. The five are: the Boethian solution, simple foreknowledge, middle knowledge or the Molinist solution, the Ockhamist solution, and present knowledge.

The Boethian Resolution

In discussing divine eternity, we saw that Boethius proposed atemporal eternity as the way to resolve the problem of freedom and foreknowledge. According to this approach, God is outside of time, so temporal distinctions between past, present, and future do not apply to him. Moreover, it is not correct even to say that he is simultaneous to all times, for simultaneity is itself a temporal notion. Nonetheless, he sees all of time at once; it is all there before him just as a whole parade is entirely in view of someone standing atop a mountain near the parade route. Things that are past, present, or future from our perspective, are all within God's view. This allows God to know what is future to us, but since all of this is present from his perspective, Boethius thought there really is no problem of *fore*knowledge and freedom. The future is still open from our perspective. This is so, in part at least, because what God knows doesn't cause anything to happen. Moreover, since we don't know what he knows about our future, we cannot be driven by that information when we make our choices in the future.[9]

In evaluating this resolution, we must ask two questions. Does it render a theological system with libertarian free will internally consistent? Is there any reason to think that what it says about God and how he knows our future is true? As to the latter issue, I can address it briefly, because I already devoted a chapter to the topic. As argued in chapter 9, I believe a much stronger case can be made for a temporal God than an atemporal one. So, even if the Boethian solution to the problem of freedom and foreknowledge renders an indeterminist's system logically consistent, there are plenty of grounds for rejecting it, because it incorporates an intellectual commitment to divine atemporal eternity, which I believe is suspect.

Let us consider, however, whether this proposal even solves the problem it was intended to answer. On the positive side, this approach does allow God to know our future. Hence, it upholds the foreknowledge side of the question. On the other hand, the solution runs into trouble with libertarian free will. Though the solution is ingenious, it is unconvincing. Even though God sees all these things as present, he sees things that from our perspective are still future. Even if he doesn't know exactly where *we* are *temporally now* in that stream of events and actions, he still knows things which *from our perspective* are *future*. So, with the Boethian solution we are back to the same problem. How can the things God sees be avoided, and how is it within our power to do otherwise than what God knows? Libertarian free will seems to be sacrificed in favor of divine foreknowledge. Hence, this solution does not render internally consistent belief in libertarian freedom and divine foreknowledge of our future free acts, since it seems to negate the former.[10]

Simple Foreknowledge

A second libertarian solution to this problem invokes what is called simple foreknowledge. According to this view, God exhaustively knows everything that will ever happen in our world once he decides to create a world at all. Thus, he knows every act his creatures will do. He simply sees them doing these acts freely (in a libertarian sense) once he decides to create a world. How does God know this? He knows by means of a direct apprehension of the future. He doesn't infer it from antecedent conditions at each point in time; he just directly and clearly sees what will occur.[11]

Simple foreknowledge can be thought of along the lines of ordinary perception of an object. The difference here, of course, is that the "object" is a future which doesn't yet exist. Nevertheless, advocates of this view hold that God can see what will occur, much as someone might claim to see something when looking at a crystal ball or through a telescope.[12] As Hasker explains, we must understand that such knowledge is not knowledge of propositions about what will occur, but rather knowledge (we might even call it prevision) of events and acts that will actually occur.[13]

Now it is important not to confuse this with middle knowledge, the next resolution to be considered. According to middle knowledge, God knows all possible worlds, and in doing so, he knows what would happen in every possible world, if he were to put someone in a given situation. Armed with such knowledge, God makes a decision about which outcome he prefers, and then chooses to actualize the possible world that contains the situations and following outcomes he wants. In contrast, simple foreknowledge holds that God just decides whether he will create a world or not, and having decided to create, he does and then sees directly what will happen in that world. He does not first see every possible world and then choose one of them. Since simple foreknowledge advocates hold that God doesn't know exactly what sort of world he will get until he creates, David Basinger argues that a God with simple foreknowledge is somewhat of a gambler. The initial gamble is whether to risk creating at all. Basinger suggests that before God creates he might think through how he might respond in the various situations that could arise in this world. For example, God might say to himself, "If after I create this world I see that there will exist in it Joe and Sue who will fall in love and marry, but the outcome will be sad because a year later Joe will run off with another woman; in that case I'll try to encourage Sue not to marry Joe in the first place. On the other hand, if I see that they will fall in love and have a long, happy life together, I will encourage Sue to accept Joe's marriage proposal when it is offered."[14] Though Basinger raises this possibility, simple foreknowledge proponents normally say that God first creates, then sees what will happen, and then decides how to respond and react.

Although appeal to simple foreknowledge might be used to solve the freedom/foreknowledge problem, in contemporary discussions that hasn't been the primary concern with simple foreknowledge. Rather, the key issue has been whether a God who possesses simple foreknowledge would be able (and how he would be able) to put that knowledge to practical use in his providential control of the world. I think we can evaluate simple foreknowledge in relation to both issues. I begin, however, where contemporary discussions do, i.e., with the practical value and use of such knowledge if God has it. If the doctrine runs into incoherence here, as many argue, then there is little need to ask whether this incoherent doctrine could save the day for indeterminists on the freedom/foreknowledge issue.

Three basic questions have been raised about the practical use of simple foreknowledge (if God should have it), though the second and third questions are very similar. Before raising any of them, however, we must note what simple foreknowledge includes. According to this concept, God knows everything that will ever occur, including his own future actions, simply by directly apprehending it. If something will happen that he does not foresee, then he doesn't have simple foreknowledge of everything, but only of some things. But, given divine omniscience and the interconnection of events and acts, including how various acts of a given set of agents will impact others in that set, it is hard to see how God could actually see the future without seeing all of it.

With this clarification, we are ready for objections to simple foreknowledge as serving any positive advantage to God. The first is called the "Doxastic Problem." Simple foreknowledge portrays God as making his decisions about what to do in our world after viewing the future. That future, of course, includes his own future decisions. Tomis Kapitan explains the problem by offering what he calls the doxastic principle:

> It is impossible for a rational, self-reflective agent to consciously entertain the belief that he/she will perform an action A while, at the same time, deliberating about whether to perform A.[15]

In order to be able to deliberate about a decision, doing the act or refraining from it must be genuine options for the one deliberating. But if God already knows via simple foreknowledge that he will perform a given action, it is impossible for him to do anything other than what he foresees. If he can genuinely deliberate and make a different choice than the one he foreknows he will make, then he doesn't have simple foreknowledge of that matter after all. Since simple foreknowledge says God just sees all actions, including his own, in advance, there can be no deliberating about whether to do or refrain from any of them. If God cannot deliberate and choose in light of what he knows about the future, this information cannot help him plan responses to what he sees.[16]

David Hunt calls a second objection to the practical use of any simple foreknowledge God would possess the metaphysical problem. This can perhaps best be explained by an example. Imagine that God through simple foreknowledge knows that a person (call him Osmo, as in the example Hunt takes from Richard Taylor) will find a winning lottery ticket worth millions. He will find it at the intersection of 7th and Elm Streets on May 8. For whatever reason, God has someone record all the events of Osmo's life in a book, and somehow Osmo finds this book. Osmo reads about his impending good fortune, and gets very excited. He also sees that, for this to happen, he must walk by 7th and Elm on the appointed day. This seems a bit odd to Osmo, because while he normally walks to work, he has never taken this route before. Nonetheless, armed with this information, Osmo decides to walk by 7th and Elm on May 8, and finds the winning lottery ticket.

All of this means that Osmo's belief that if he walks the appointed route he will find the ticket, and the very decision to walk by 7th and Elm, both depend on his knowledge (thanks to God's simple foreknowledge) that he will find the ticket. So the decision to go the appointed route depends on his belief, and the discovery of the ticket depends on his decision. Moreover, the belief depends on his knowledge that he will discover the ticket. If he doesn't have that belief and make that decision, he won't get the lottery ticket. But unless he believes already that he will get the lottery ticket, he won't believe there is a reason to go by 7th and Elm, nor will he decide to do so. Hunt explains the apparent problem as follows:

> It looks like Osmo's discovery of the ticket involves a circle of dependence in which his foreknowledge helps bring about the very future that he foreknows. But the assumption that such a metaphysical "loop" is possible might well be incoherent. The principle at stake—call it the 'Metaphysical Principle'—can be stated as follows:
>
> (MP) It is impossible that a decision depend on a belief which depends on a future event which depends on the original decision.
>
> I shall call the conflict between the Metaphysical Principle and the providential use of foreknowledge the 'Metaphysical Problem.'[17]

Now if Osmo has the metaphysical problem, then there must also be a similar metaphysical problem for a God possessing simple foreknowledge. For, foreknowing all that will occur, how could he then decide to make a decision that he foresees he already has decided to make, in that it leads to certain ends he also foresees? In my judgment, this is a major problem for simple foreknowledge, and implicit in it also is the doxastic problem, for if Osmo foresees that he will win the lottery, he will also foresee some of the means to that end, namely, believing that if he goes by 7th and Elm on May 8 he will find the lottery ticket. But, then, he cannot really decide, after foreseeing all of this, to go the appointed route, for he will already have foreseen that he would make that decision.

William Hasker has raised an objection that plays on many of the same themes as the metaphysical problem. He contends that if God has simple foreknowledge, it is utterly useless to his providential control of anything. Simple foreknowledge gives God complete knowledge of actual events and actions that will occur, but then it includes all the causal antecedents to those events and actions. If all of this is foreknown, however, and God doesn't like what will happen, he cannot intervene to change anything he knows will happen, for doing so would bring a different future, but there cannot be a different future from the one he foresees. On the other hand, if God likes what he foresees, but it is to come about by factors other than his intervention, he can't intervene to try to guarantee the result, for doing so might change the result, which is impossible since the result is already certain. Moreover, even if his action would not change the result, he still cannot do anything he didn't already foresee himself doing. Hence, whether or not God likes what he sees via simple foreknowledge, he can't use the information to do anything he would not already do.[18]

Hasker adds (I believe correctly) that the uselessness of simple foreknowledge to providence would accrue with either libertarian free will or determinism, for it depends on neither. It depends on the fact that one can't change what one infallibly sees will happen, nor can one change means to that end when one already foresees what the means will be.[19] Of course, this isn't a problem for a determinist such as myself who believes that God foreknows on the basis of what he foreordains.[20]

What should we conclude about simple foreknowledge? As to the usefulness of simple foreknowledge for divine providential control, I think the doxastic and metaphysical problems, plus the problems raised by Hasker, cast serious doubts about whether simple foreknowledge would help a God with such foreknowledge to control the world. Hence, even if it solves the problem of freedom and foreknowledge for systems committed to libertarian free will, it still seems inconsistent with those same systems' claims about God's providential dealings in our world to accomplish his general goals. If God via simple foreknowledge does not already foresee those general goals being achieved, simple foreknowledge won't help him to reach them.

What about simple foreknowledge as a solution to the freedom/foreknowledge problem? We must ask this question from the standpoints of logical consistency and factual adequacy. If God has simple foreknowledge of everything that will occur, this surely upholds the foreknowledge end of the equation, but we run into problems on the freedom side of things. For this solution to be internally consistent we must grant that God foreknows the free (in a libertarian sense) deeds of his creatures; he knows them all plus all deeds that are not free in this sense. But we must first ask, in virtue of *what* does he see these free actions? If he foresees them in virtue of seeing the antecedent causal conditions that bring them about, that is determinism, not libertarian free will. If he supposedly just infallibly sees people freely (in a libertarian sense) making such choices, this is no answer at all, for if these people are free in the libertarian sense, they must be able both to do the acts and to refrain, but how can they refrain from doing what God infallibly sees they will do? To say that God just sees them doing these actions freely doesn't explain how it could be so; it just reasserts that freedom (libertarian) and foreknowledge do after all fit together consistently with one another. However, simple foreknowledge was intended to explain how that can be so. Asserting that it is so without explaining how it could be so won't do.

In light of these considerations I believe that, while simple foreknowledge upholds divine foreknowledge, it doesn't explain how that fits with libertarian free will. Does this mean that God does not possess simple foreknowledge? The question is confused, for simple foreknowledge was invoked to mesh with libertarian free will, and we still have no explanation of how that can be so. So if the question is whether God has simple foreknowledge of our free (in a libertarian sense) actions, I respond that the question as posed is incoherent, for God's foreknowing infallibly that certain acts will be done with libertarian free will is incoherent. Do I as a determinist think God has simple foreknowledge of compatibilistically free human actions? I believe God infallibly knows every free (compatibilistically) action we will perform, but I think God has more than simple foreknowledge, as will become evident in the next sections.

Middle Knowledge

Stemming from Luis de Molina, another approach to this problem appeals to what is called middle knowledge. This resolution has received much attention in contemporary discussions, not only as a way to handle the freedom/foreknowledge question, but also because of the use made of it by Alvin Plantinga's free will defense in reply to the problem of evil.

Before we can evaluate this proposal, we must understand it. One of its ablest contemporary defenders is William Lane Craig. Craig explains that Molina distinguished three logical moments in God's knowledge (something could be logically prior without being temporally prior to something else). The first logical moment of God's knowledge is his knowledge of all necessary truths such as the laws of logic. This knowledge also includes knowledge of all possibilities, including possible persons God could create, possible situations they could be placed in, and all their possible actions. True statements of this sort are true in virtue of God's nature, i.e., he knows them to be true by his very nature. Hence, this type of knowledge is called God's *natural knowledge*.[21]

God knows more, however, than just everything possible. Prior to creating, he decided to create one of the many possible worlds. He did not have to create, and having decided to create, he could have chosen another possible world than the one he chose. Hence, God's choice and creation were free. Of course, having decided to create, God has exhaustive foreknowledge of everything that will occur. Because his decision to create a particular world was a free decision, the knowledge that stems from it is called God's *free knowledge*. It is his complete knowledge of the actual world, and it represents the third logical moment of God's knowledge.[22]

In between God's natural knowledge and free knowledge is a second logical moment in God's knowledge. By his natural knowledge, God knows everything that could happen to every possible existent. By God's middle knowledge, he knows even more than pure possibilities, for according to his middle knowledge he knows what any possible creature *would* in fact do in any given situation. Moreover, God knows this information for every creature in every possible world. The Molinist adds, however, that while God knows what everyone would do in any situation, what they would do would be done freely in the libertarian sense. So God by means of middle knowledge knows what everyone would freely do in any given situation. Craig is helpful in distinguishing natural and middle knowledge when he writes about Peter's denial of Christ:

> By his natural knowledge God knew in the first moment all the possible things that Peter *could* do if placed in such circumstances. But now in this second moment he knows what Peter would in fact freely choose to do under such circumstances. This is not because Peter would be causally determined by the circumstances to act in this way. No, Peter is entirely free, and under the same circumstances he could choose to act in another way. But God knows which way Peter *would* freely choose.[23]

So God's middle knowledge is his knowledge of what a person would freely do, if placed in any circumstance. How does middle knowledge differ from simple foreknowledge? We might say that simple foreknowledge is equivalent to what Molinists call God's free knowledge—in other words, what God knows with simple foreknowledge are the contents of the actual world once he freely decides to create it. Simple foreknowledge in particular requires that the actual world which God knows, to use Nelson Pike's terminology, "has distinct being" that is "outside" of God. In the case of middle knowledge, God knows more. He knows not only everything actual, but also every possible world and what every free creature would do freely in any and every situation where they exist. Such knowledge does not depend on this information (again to use Pike's terminology) being "outside of" or "distinct from" God. In fact, it cannot be "outside" of him unless he creates it, but at the logical moment of middle knowledge God has not created or even necessarily decided to create any world at all.[24]

Proponents of middle knowledge claim that one of its great advantages is that a God possessing it would have tremendous help in planning his providential control of our world. Prior to deciding to create, God could survey all possible worlds and choose just that one in which things would turn out in a way pleasing to him. God need not plan providential intervention, so to speak, in the dark. Nor do the problems with simple foreknowledge about providential control arise, for with simple foreknowledge God sees what will happen after the world in which it will occur is actual. By then it is too late to do something other than what he foresees himself doing. But with the Molinist scheme, as God considers all possible worlds via his middle knowledge, nothing has been actualized, so it appears that God can still decide how to intervene providentially. He surveys each possible world and sees what kind of intervention would be appropriate, and then picks a world to actualize. He doesn't later consider how he might intervene in the midst of what is happening, for he already deliberated about this when consulting his middle knowledge. Even though God's knowledge of a possible world includes everything in it, including his own deeds, until he chooses to actualize a specific possible world, God is locked into nothing.

According to God's middle knowledge, he knows many propositions of the following form:

If agent x were to be in situation S, then x would freely do action A.

Statements of this sort are conditional statements. Moreover, each of these statements that obtains in a world God didn't choose to actualize is contrary to the facts of the actual world; hence, these propositions are called *counterfactual conditionals*. Since they also tell us what an agent would do *freely*, they are often referred to as *counterfactuals of freedom*. In having middle knowledge, God knows all counterfactuals of freedom that are true of every possible world. Of course, for some possible worlds that were not created there are no counterfactuals of freedom (in the libertarian sense), for in those worlds God's creatures don't have libertarian free will.[25]

How does middle knowledge solve the freedom/foreknowledge problem? By God's natural knowledge, he knows all possibilities, and somewhere in those possibilities is the future that will be actual.[26] But God knows more than this. God knows what we would freely do in every situation in which we might find ourselves. Somewhere in those conditionals is the set which describes the future that actually will occur once God decides to create a particular possible world. But God knows even more than this, for after surveying all possible worlds with humans with libertarian free will, God chooses to actualize one of them. As a result of his choice, God knows the future of our actual world; he also knows which conditionals turn out to be counterfactuals of freedom.

So, with Molinism, God really knows the future. He knows not only what possibly could occur; he also knows what will occur. In addition, he knows what would have occurred freely if he had placed his creatures in situations that obtain in other unactualized worlds. Since God's middle knowledge is knowledge of what his creatures would do freely (in a libertarian sense) in any circumstance, choosing one of those possible worlds will actualize a world in which humans do whatever they do with libertarian free will. So it appears that Molinism upholds both divine foreknowledge and human freedom.

Despite the apparent plausibility of this solution, many philosophers remain unconvinced. An initial problem stems from applying the law of excluded middle to counterfactual conditionals. According to this law, a sentence is either true or false. Some philosophers, however, argue that counterfactual conditionals cannot be either true or false (truth and falsity are typically understood in terms of correspondence to states of affairs). The claim 'snow is white' is true just in case in the real world snow is white. But counterfactuals do not now correspond to any actual state of affairs in our world, and since these conditionals are counterfactual, it is hard to see that they ever would or would not correspond to any actual state of affairs since states of affairs and possible worlds relevant to their truth or falsity will never obtain.

Richard Otte is undaunted by this problem, for there is a similar question concerning claims about the future of our actual world. Future states of affairs of the world in which we live do not obtain now, but that doesn't mean that propositions about them are false. Propositions about the future can be true in a correspondence sense, and if they are true, we will know this once we get to the future. So, if a proposition about the future can be true, though it corresponds to a currently nonexistent state of affairs, why can't a counterfactual conditional be true even if it also corresponds to a state of affairs which does not now exist? Otte contends that such a counterfactual is true in virtue of its corresponding to a state of affairs which would be true if a different possible world obtained.[27] However, since a different possible world won't ever obtain, since *we* don't have middle knowledge of all possible worlds, and since God hasn't told us the contents of his middle knowledge, we apparently will never be in a position to verify or falsify any counterfactual conditional. This is not so, however, with simple statements about the future, for someone will be in a position to verify or falsify them, so Otte's analogy seems deficient.

Considerations like these lead many philosophers to argue that counterfactual conditionals are neither true nor false. Hence, the idea of middle knowledge is incoherent. Other philosophers are even more negative, for they think we can know that these counterfactuals are false. Of course, if this is so but counterfactuals of freedom form much of the content of many possible worlds and are themselves the content of middle knowledge, then God doesn't have middle knowledge, and it is dubious as to what he knows about any number of possible worlds. In assessing these objections about the truth of these counterfactuals, Basinger writes:

Everyone agrees that if hypothetical conditions of freedom *were* true, God would have knowledge of them. But some philosophers deny or at least doubt, in the words of Robert Adams, that such conditionals 'ever were or ever will be true'. Some, such as Adams and Bruce Reichenbach, hold this view because they do not see any comprehensible grounds on which such propositions can be true. Others, for example, William Hasker, go even further, claiming that the concept of a true counterfactual of freedom is self-contradictory.[28]

What shall we say about these things? Does God have middle knowledge? If he does, does it help him in providentially dealing with the world? And for our purposes, most importantly, does this proposal solve the freedom/foreknowledge problem? Let me begin by responding to the second question first. I think it unquestionable that if God has middle knowledge, if humans have libertarian free will, and if God's decree (assuming he makes one) is based on his foreknowledge, then middle knowledge should give him considerable help in determining which possible world to create. He can see what he and his creatures would do in any possible world, and hence he can see in which world his providential involvement best accomplishes his goals.

But does God have middle knowledge? It seems that the answer need not ultimately rest on one's decision about whether counterfactuals of freedom are true, false, or neither. Rather, another consideration helps us answer this question and the question about whether this resolution solves the freedom/foreknowledge problem. On the proposal we are considering, humans have libertarian free will, but if libertarian free will obtains in possible worlds that God sees via middle knowledge, how can he *know* what *would* happen if a person were placed in any situation and has libertarian freedom to decide what to do? Would he know this by seeing all the antecedent conditions which bring about the agent's choices? If so, such bringing about in virtue of antecedent conditions invokes determinism, but then the agent does not choose freely (in the libertarian sense). Well, then, perhaps God just sees with direct vision people freely acting in every possible world. But this falls prey to the same objection, an objection also raised against simple foreknowledge. If an act is not causally determined, there simply is no guarantee about what an agent would do if placed in a situation. There is no more to see than world history leading up to the situation, and then the agent in the situation. Moreover, if God actually chooses one of these possible worlds, the agent will do what God has chosen in choosing that possible world. But if the agent will do what God foresees, how can he do it freely in the libertarian sense?

What I am suggesting is that for the middle knowledge solution to leave libertarian free will intact, it seems that the only possible worlds God can know via middle knowledge are ones wherein humans do not have libertarian freedom. In possible worlds where humans have libertarian freedom, it seems difficult to know exactly what they would do freely in various situations, for seeing exactly what they would do seems to mean that doing otherwise is not a genuine option. But then, if God really sees what they would do, some form of determinism seems to be required. So, if libertarian freedom is left intact, it appears that God cannot know the future, unless he knows it as a pure set of possibilities. On the other hand, if he really does know all possible worlds, how then is there room for libertarian free will?[29]

As a result, I don't find the appeal to middle knowledge an adequate resolution to the problem of freedom and foreknowledge. Moreover, I don't believe God has middle knowledge, if middle knowledge includes knowledge of what humans would freely do in the libertarian sense. On the other hand, if one holds some form of determinism as I do, there is no reason to deny that God has middle knowledge of what humans would do (compatibilistically) freely. The only question is whether the conditionals would be true or false. Given God's knowledge of all possible worlds, I think God does know which conditionals would be true of each possible world. He could know them because he would see in every case the causal antecedents that would bring about the actions of which the conditionals speak. So, while I doubt that an indeterminist could consistently hold that God has middle knowledge, I see no reason for a determinist to deny this. Unfortunately for the libertarian, incorporating middle knowledge into a *deterministic* system offers no help to the *libertarian* in solving the problem of freedom and foreknowledge.

The Ockhamist Resolution

A fourth libertarian approach to the problem of freedom and foreknowledge stems from William of Ockham. It is a more complex solution than others and raises interesting questions about issues such as backward causation. Thomas Morris's general description of this approach is a helpful place to begin:

> Suppose God has always believed that in exactly five minutes my right index finger will lightly scratch the tip of my nose. God is necessarily omniscient and so, as a believer, he is absolutely infallible. He cannot be wrong. Does it follow that no one is in a position to prevent it from being the case that, nearly five minutes hence, my finger will scratch my nose? Does it follow, in particular, that I am not free with respect to scratching? No, the Ockhamists insist, all that follows is that I *shall* scratch, not that I *must*, or that I lack the power to refrain from scratching. I can prevent the event in question. I can refrain from scratching. This option is open to me. I shall not take it, as a matter of fact, but the alternative is there. And, the Ockhamists add, if I did refrain from scratching, I would not prove God wrong. For if I were to exercise this option and leave the tip of my nose alone, God would have held a belief different from the one he in fact holds—he always would have believed that I would, at the appointed time, have done something else with my right index finger rather than scratching my nose. So the Ockhamists hold that for this event *x*, I am in a position to prevent *x*, but as a matter of fact will freely perform *x* instead.[30]

This may sound confusing, so let me explain. I begin with two important definitions. The first is Ockham's notion of accidental necessity and the second is his distinction between hard and soft facts. According to Ockham, the past is necessary in a sense he calls accidental necessity:

> I claim that every necessary proposition is *per se* in either the first mode or the second mode. This is obvious, since I am talking about all propositions that are necessary *simpliciter*. I add this because of propositions that are necessary *per accidens,* as is the case with many past tense propositions. They are necessary, because it was contingent that they be necessary, and because they were not always necessary.[31]

Something that is accidentally necessary did not have to occur, but once it happened, it cannot be changed. This can be true as well of any proposition, regardless of whether it is about past, present, or future. For example, no future action or event must occur, and hence, no proposition about the future specifies what must occur. An agent can still do other than what the future tensed proposition states. At some future date, if the agent does what is predicted, the deed becomes accidentally necessary, i.e., once the act occurs, no one can change it, but that doesn't mean it had to be done.[32]

Ockham also distinguished hard and soft facts. In contemporary discussions, there is much debate over how to define hard and soft facts and over which types of sentences qualify as hard or soft facts. The intricacies of this debate can be followed in the relevant literature,[33] but need not detain us so long as we understand the basic notion of a hard and a soft fact. A proposition that is a hard fact is a genuine fact about the past. That is, what the proposition asserts has occurred and is completely finished. Moreover, a hard fact is exclusively about a past finished event, and hence is indifferent to whatever happens in the present or future. If world history ended right now, that would not falsify a proposition that states a hard fact.[34] On the other hand, a soft fact mixes past and future, past and present, or present and future (future from our present perspective); its truth or falsity is not future-indifferent. Examples illustrate the distinction. The proposition "Frank is a high school student the whole month of October, 1999," if true, is not a hard fact as long as Frank is in high school and it is still October, 1999. If Frank drops out of school during October, 1999, that would falsify the claim. So, the proposition in question qualifies as a soft fact before the end of October, 1999. On the other hand, once October, 1999 ends and Frank has not withdrawn from school during that month, a corresponding proposition "Frank was a high school student in October, 1999" will not only be true, but accidentally necessary and a hard fact.

Consider another proposition: "Frank was a junior high school student in May, 1997." Assuming that the proposition is true, then since we are past May, 1997, the proposition is a hard fact and is accidentally necessary. Consider one more proposition: "Frank correctly believed in June, 1998 that he would graduate from high school in June, 2003." Since Frank really believed this in

June, 1998, and since June, 1998 is now past, one might think this proposition is a hard fact. However, since 2003 is not yet here, we do not yet know if the belief is correct, so the proposition is now (in 2000) a soft fact. Moreover, though hard facts about the past are accidentally necessary, soft facts are not necessary at all, so this one isn't either. Of course, all of this means that Frank can still do something so that he won't graduate in June, 2003, and so that his belief will have been wrong. In fact, he might do something so that he will never graduate from high school. Graduation in June, 2003, is not necessary and unavoidable, though he and his parents might wish otherwise.[35]

Let us apply this to God's foreknowledge and human freedom. God, unlike Frank, could not be mistaken in his beliefs, so if he really believes something, it must be true. Still, *propositions* about God's past beliefs about our future (from our current perspective) are soft facts. If God *fore*knows the future, then we can construct a tensed proposition about his knowledge as follows: "God believed (believes, or will believe)[36] at time T_1 that x will do A at time T_2." No matter how one tenses the verb "believe," the proposition expresses a soft fact, not a hard fact. It is not now accidentally necessary, though after T_2 it will be, assuming that it occurs.

To make matters more specific, consider the following proposition: "God believed in 1980 that I shall mow my lawn in June, 2003." If God foreknows the future, then it must be possible that this proposition is true, but this proposition is now a soft fact, because as I write this, it is 2000, so the proposition says something about the future. Should I mow my lawn in June, 2003, the proposition will be both true and accidentally necessary after that. Of course, it is not necessary (in the sense that it has to happen and is unavoidable) that when June, 2003 comes, I'll mow my lawn. I am free to do it or to refrain from doing it. The freedom side of the freedom/foreknowledge dilemma is upheld.

Consider two more propositions: 1) "In 1950 God believed that John Kennedy would be assassinated in November, 1963"; 2) "In 1950 God believed that I would be writing this sentence thirty-six years and four months after the assassination of John Kennedy." Prior to November 22, 1963, proposition 1) was a soft fact. Thereafter, it is a hard fact and accidentally necessary. As to the second proposition, since I completed writing that proposition in March 2000, the proposition is true, accidentally necessary, and a hard fact. Prior to my writing it, despite its reference to a past historical event (Kennedy's assassination), it was a soft fact. That the second proposition is now a hard fact doesn't mean that I had to be writing these sentences in March, 2000. I could have been on vacation for all of that month and away from my writing entirely. In that case, the proposition would be false. This just shows that prior to March, 2000, it was a soft fact, and it was within my power to work on this chapter in March, 2000, or to refrain from doing so.

What I have just written may be very disturbing. Does it mean that it was within my power to falsify one of God's beliefs? Or does it mean that I could have brought it about that God believed something other than what he actually believed in 1950? If God is omniscient and believed something about my future, how can it be only a soft fact that God believed? Doesn't that suggest that he could have held a wrong belief? Remember also the propositions about my mowing the lawn in 2003. Do I have the power to falsify what God has believed about this since at least 1980? Or could I now do something that would cause God to have a different belief about my lawn mowing than he does? Such questions are disturbing for many reasons, not least of which is that they invoke Pike's argument for theological fatalism (in particular, premise 6). That argument says that for me to do something God does not foreknow, I would either have power to falsify one of God's beliefs, power to make it the case that God held a different view than he did, or power to show that the being we know as God who is omniscient and has infallible knowledge of the future does not exist. Pike's argument claims that, since none of these three things is within my power, I cannot do something other than what God foreknows; hence, theological fatalism seems true. Are we now saying that Pike's argument can be rejected because we really can do one or more of those three things that he said were impossible? If so, then, it seems that right now we can exercise causal power over the past; we can even exercise causal power over God's past!

These questions bring us to the crux of the Ockhamist strategy. The Ockhamist answers questions about changing God's past beliefs, etc., negatively, and explains that, for example, if I had not been writing this chapter in March, 2000, and if I will not mow the lawn in June, 2003, God never would have believed that I would. Since, as omniscient, God's beliefs cannot be wrong, he would have believed (in the past) and now believes (in the present) something different about my future. What God believed in the past about my lawn mowing in June, 2003 *we* won't know until we get to the future. At that time, we can speak accurately about what God believed in the past about our future. If I do mow my lawn, then I'll know that I was correct in thinking that in 1980 God believed I would mow my lawn in June, 2003. If I don't mow it then, I'll know that in 1980 God believed differently about my lawn mowing in June, 2003.

Someone may ask, "If God believes about the future only what actually will happen, doesn't his belief necessitate its occurrence?" The answer is no, because on the one hand, God's beliefs have no causal power to make an event or act happen (determinists also agree with this). Moreover, given Ockham's claims, any such proposition about the future will be a soft fact and hence cannot before the future be even accidentally necessary. Furthermore, I do not yet know the truth or falsity of the proposition about God's belief about my mowing, so even though I can write the proposition, that hardly guarantees that the proposition will causally *determine* me to mow my lawn. The proposition, if I think it true, may influence what I do in June, 2003, but it guarantees nothing about what I shall do. I can still decide to do otherwise. In fact, I might be paralyzed, dead, or just out of town during all of June, 2003, so that I could not mow the lawn. Hence, it is not necessary that I mow my lawn in June, 2003.

It is crucial to understand that the Ockhamist strategy does *not* say that God does not know what the future really will be. It says that since *we* don't know, we don't know exactly what *he* knows about the future. Hence, we can write any number of propositions about God's knowledge of the future only to find out later that most or even all of them are wrong. Our errors don't mean God didn't know the truth. We just won't know what he actually believed until we see it happen (unless he reveals beforehand what will happen). Of course, since God's knowledge does not cause actions, and since we cannot be causally determined by what God knows about the future, because we don't yet know what he knows about it, we seem to be *free* (in a libertarian sense) to do other than what God knows we shall do, even though he knows we will not do otherwise.

Still, questions remain. It seems that we have some causal power over God's past beliefs, and if so, then there appears to be such a thing as backward causation. In contemporary literature there have been rather interesting discussions of such topics. Several key points will help on this issue. William Craig is very helpful on backward causation. As he notes, whether one believes there can be such a thing depends a lot on whether one holds the A-theory or the B-theory of time. If one holds the B-theory, there is a certain subjectivity to time, i.e., it is dubious whether there really is temporal succession or only the psychological perception of it. Moreover, given relativity theory, something present from our reference frame might be past from that of someone elsewhere in the universe. Remember from our discussion of atemporal eternity the example of lightning hitting the train. In light of these considerations, if one holds a B-theory of time, it might well be possible that something I do now (in my temporal reference frame) could affect something that is past from my temporal perspective but is still present from someone else's reference frame. If so, that seems to be a case of backward causation.[37]

On the other hand, if we hold the A-theory of time, it makes little sense to say that something I can do today or tomorrow would cause an effect some time prior to today. I think temporal succession is real, so I hold the A-theory of time. This may seem to end the issue, but it doesn't. In spite of everything said about backward causation, it still seems that what God believed at some time before the present about what I will do in June, 2003 is somehow dependent on what I do when that time comes. And if God's past beliefs depend on my future actions, doesn't that mean that somehow I have power (i.e., causal power) over God's past beliefs? Contrary to premise 6 and 8 of the argument for theological fatalism, I do have causal power over God's past beliefs.

Though one might conclude this, most philosophers disagree, because they distinguish two sorts of powers one might have. On the one hand, someone might have *causal* power over someone or something. In that case causal power should be construed along the lines of efficient causation (the sort of causality I have argued for in regard to human actions, not the causation involved in the natural sciences). But there is a second kind of power one might have, namely, *counterfactual* power. Counterfactual power is not power to bring it about that something is the case. Hence, counterfactual power over the past is not power to change what has already happened. Rather, counterfactual power is power to do something which would, if we did it, mean that something else that didn't occur would have occurred. Notice all the "woulds"; that means the sentences are in the subjunctive mood and are contrary to fact. They relate not what has happened or will happen, but what would happen in some situation if something else occurred.

The crucial point as this relates to God's past beliefs is that none of us has causal power over what God believed in the past (or over anything else that happened). His beliefs are not *causally* dependent on what we will do, but they are *counterfactually* dependent on what we would do, and this means that we have counterfactual power over God's past beliefs.[38] But counterfactual power over God's past beliefs means that we have it now within our power to do something which would mean, if we were to do it, that God would have held a different belief about our future than he in fact holds. As Plantinga explains, such power is entirely innocuous to divine foreknowledge, and in no way damages human freedom.[39] In addition, Craig argues that such counterfactual power means that premise 6 of Pike's argument for theological fatalism needs a fourth option. Even if God believed that Jones would mow his lawn, Jones can refrain from so doing, but not in any of the first three respects Pike mentions. He could do so as follows: "Jones has the power to act in a different way, and if he *were* to act in that way, God *would have* believed differently."[40] With this amendment, the conclusion of the fatalistic argument does not follow. Of course, the added option is that Jones has counterfactual power over God's past beliefs. Hasker is dubious about this distinction between causal and counterfactual power over the past. In his "Foreknowledge and Necessity" he argues that counterfactual power over the past actually collapses into power to bring about the past. Hence, if "we are to have the power to act in ways other than those in which God has always believed we would act, we must also have the power to bring it about that God has not believed the things which in fact he always has believed."[41]

In my judgment, we don't have to side with Hasker as opposed to Plantinga, Craig, etc., in order to assess the Ockhamist strategy.[42] Suffice it to say that if one opts for counterfactual power over the past, this apparently refutes the argument for theological fatalism. But we can still ask what kind of power counterfactual power is. Is it a power that anyone realistically could use? In what circumstances that are likely to obtain in our world would it be usable? My point is reminiscent of Pike's point about middle knowledge and our ability to do other than what God knows we will do in this world. If we are really to have power over what God believed in the past, then we must be able to do something to bring about God's having a different belief than he had. But we agree that this is absurd. So where does this leave us? It leaves us either with a commitment to being able to bring it about that God has a different belief about our future than he does have (which is absurd); or with a commitment that we have counterfactual power over God's past beliefs though we never exercise it; or with a belief that we simply must do what God foresees us doing all along (in this case, we cannot do other than God foresees, so the problem of libertarian free will and foreknowledge is not resolved).

One question remains for the Ockhamist strategy. According to this approach, we don't know what God knows about our future (unless he tells us), but God knows our future. Given libertarian free will, how does God know it? One passage in Ockham's writings addresses this matter. It isn't entirely clear, but it is about as close as he comes to explaining how God knows the future. He writes:

> Despite [the impossibility of expressing it clearly], the following way [of knowing future contingents] can be ascribed [to God]. Just as the [human] intellect on the basis of one and the same [intuitive] cognition of certain non-complexes can have evident cognition of contradictory contingent propositions such as 'A exists,' 'A does not exist,' in the same way it can be granted that the divine essence is intuitive cognition that is so perfect, so clear, that it is evident cognition of all things past and future, so that it knows which part of a contradiction [involving such things] is true and which part false.[43]

Does this mean God knows the future in a way similar to the way we know the truth of propositions such as "all bachelors are unmarried men"? That would be odd, since events of world history are factual matters, not analytic truths. Ockham is more likely speaking by way of analogy. Just as we intuitively understand whether analytic propositions are true or false, so God intuitively understands the course of world history. This doesn't mean that history is an analytic proposition. Rather, Ockham's point is about God's method of knowing. He doesn't need to use a process of inferential reasoning, tracing antecedent causal conditions to their results; he just knows what will occur.

How does the Ockhamist approach fare in handling the freedom/fore-knowledge problem? With this view, God really knows the future, and since we don't know what God knows about our actions, our choices cannot be causally affected by God's knowledge. We make our decisions believing that we can equally do or refrain from a given action. So this approach seems to uphold libertarian free will. All sides agree that God's foreknowledge doesn't cause us to do anything. So the Ockhamist strategy seems to handle this problem in an internally consistent way.

Despite this consistency, one still wonders how God just intuitively knows the future, when actions are not causally connected (given libertarian free will) to causally sufficient antecedent conditions. That is, on what basis can God know that one act follows another or follows some event? Ockham says God knows intuitively, but he doesn't explain how that can be so when there are no sufficient antecedent conditions connecting any two acts or any event and a subsequent action (if there were, that would be determinism). Since the act is not causally determined, more than one option is open to us, so until we decide, it seems that there is nothing for God to see. Indeed, as the Ockhamist suggests, we sense that we could do otherwise. However, if God really knows what we will do, we won't be able to do otherwise. If one tries to rescue the position by claiming that at least we have counterfactual power over God's past beliefs, I can grant that. However, since I see no way that we could use it, I don't see how this rescues libertarian free will. The only ways that seem possible for us to do other than what God actually knows are that we do have power to bring it about that God's belief was false, or that he held a different belief, or that we do have libertarian free will in regard to our current and future decisions because God doesn't know the future. The first option (our having causal power over God's past beliefs) is absurd, the second still limits us to what God foreknows we will do, and the final option is not Ockhamism.

In sum, if one grants the basic assumptions of the Ockhamist approach, this strategy does yield an internally consistent theology with respect to the freedom/foreknowledge problem. However, if humans have libertarian free will, it is hard to see how their future free acts can be foreseen by anyone. So, upon closer inspection we can say that while this approach may yield an internally consistent position, there is good reason to think that it is wrong as a whole, because it doesn't adequately explain how God can intuitively (or otherwise) see incompatibilistically free actions. As with the previous strategies, it seems that to rescue libertarian free will, one must at some point restrict God's foreknowledge in part or in toto. The next option affirms just that.

Present Knowledge

The options considered so far all uphold divine foreknowledge, but they seem to create problems with libertarian free will. A final indeterminist answer to this problem opts for sacrificing divine foreknowledge and retaining libertarian free will. This is not a new approach to the problem, for historically many indeterminists have held it. What is novel in our day is the open view's claim that this view not only is correct on philosophical grounds but also is biblically and theologically defensible. According to this solution, God is omniscient; omniscience, however, means God knows everything there is to know, and the future just is not something that can be known. This means that God has present knowledge but no foreknowledge. Present knowledge is exhaustive knowledge of the past and the present, including awareness of all of our personalities and preferences. From that knowledge God can predict some things we will do, but he cannot be certain that we will do them. Of course, the more distant future is beyond his knowledge. We shall first examine an example of this position within contemporary secular philosophy, and then turn to the open view.

In espousing this position, Joseph Runzo argues that if proponents of libertarian free will think God knows the future, they must explain how he could know it. Runzo considers and refutes various alternatives, and ultimately concludes that God cannot know the future.[44] A major point in Runzo's argument is the definition of knowledge. Knowledge is typically defined as justified true belief. This means God cannot *know* something (nor can anyone else) unless it is true. But *before an event or action occurs,* a proposition about it is neither true nor false. At time T_1 any proposition of the form "x will do A at T_2" is neither true nor false, and if that is so, God cannot *know* it ahead of time. In fact, Runzo says, God might not even believe it ahead of time. On what grounds would he be inclined to believe it? He might believe it or know it, because he knows everything now and knows how each thing will logically or even causally entail something later. But this cannot be so for an indeterminist, for if God knows the logical and/or causal antecedents of an act, the act is not incompatibilistically free.[45] In discussing middle knowledge, we saw a similar line of argument against the truth or falsity of counterfactuals of freedom. Now we see that argument raised against God knowing the future of the actual world.

Does this answer solve the problem? This answer does resolve the apparent contradiction between divine omniscience and libertarian freedom, and this position has another advantage. As Runzo explains, adopting this approach rebuts the complaint that God could have and should have created a better world than ours. It does so, because the objection assumes that God knows of a better world, but if libertarian free will obtains in our world, and if sentences about the future cannot be true or false in the present, there is no way for God to know of a better world. If he cannot know of a better world, he cannot be expected to produce it. Runzo makes the point as follows:

> Imagine the actual moment, T_o, at which God decides to instantiate a created world. Which world would He create? Presumably a world containing as little moral evil as possible. But which world is that? For any morally responsible agent which God creates, He could not foreknow how much evil—or good—that *actual* moral agent would produce. Moreover, given human free will acts of reproduction, God could not even foreknow how many human moral agents there would be—each agent acting for evil and/or good. And finally, God could not even have a sure foreknowledge that if He creates certain conditions, then *some* human agents or others will commit evil acts, even though the identity of the actual malefactors is dependent on the free, interpersonal relations among the human agents. For if every particular moral act of every human agent is indeed a freely-committed act, then it must be causally possible—however improbable—that no human agent ever in fact commits an immoral act. Therefore, at T_o, for any possible world W containing free moral agents, which God instantiates, He could not foreknow the eventual incidence of morally evil versus morally good actions in W.[46]

If this is right, no one can complain that God should have created a better world than ours. How can he be required to do something he doesn't know how to do?

Indeed, there are many advantages to this resolution to the problem of freedom and foreknowledge, but of course anyone who adopts it must give up the idea that God knows the future. Though some theists would see this as problematic, proponents of the open view of God see no problem. A God who doesn't know what his free creatures will do can be much more open and responsive to them as they confront whatever happens. Such a God is less controlling both because he has not planned everything in advance and also because he learns about the future as it occurs, as we do, and then works with us to make the best of each situation.

In addition to these positive theological implications of a God with present knowledge, advocates of the open view believe that Scripture supports their contention that God does not know our future free actions. Scripture portrays God as learning things along the way, as surprised or disappointed about what happens, as regretful of what has happened, and as open to changing his mind about his plans. For example, only after Abraham passes the ultimate test of faith (Genesis 22) does God says "Now I know that you fear God." Gen 6:5-6 says God saw the wickedness of people before the flood and regretted that he had made them. This shows God's disappointment over what happened, and it would have been difficult for him to react this way if he had always known what would occur. We also cited Moses pleading with God to spare his people when God was about to destroy them (Exodus 32–34). Moses convinced God and changed his mind, so it hardly seems that God had irrevocably decided what would happen and knew exactly what he would do in the situation. Rather, God was angry but was not claiming with exact certainty that Israel would be destroyed. He was still open to things turning out otherwise.[47] Pinnock notes that there are Scriptures in which the Lord says "Perhaps they will understand" or "It may be that they will listen." These are not the words of someone who knows exhaustively what people will do; they are statements of someone who doesn't know.[48]

In addition to such OT evidence, there is further evidence in the Gospels. Of particular note is Sanders's handling of Jesus' prediction that Judas would betray him. At the Last Supper, Jesus predicted that one of his disciples would betray him. On the surface, this sounds like a straight prediction of something future, but when we dig deeper we find otherwise. Judas was on friendly terms with Jesus, and he was convinced after talking with Jesus that an opportunity to meet the high priest and those in authority in the Temple should be arranged. After all, Jesus' teaching in Matt 18:15-20 says that when two people have a grievance with one another, they should get together, talk it out and try to resolve it. When Jesus told Judas to carry out his mission quickly (John 13:27), this need not be understood as meaning anything more than that he should go ahead and arrange the meeting. Sanders says this interpretation comes from William Klassen, but we need not follow it to rule out a prediction of Jesus' betrayal, for there is another understanding of this passage that rules out that prediction.[49]

Sanders suggests that Jesus and Judas likely had many discussions, since

Judas was a disciple and was treasurer. Among the topics they discussed would have been the role of the Messiah. Perhaps Judas expected a more nationalistic Messiah, and if so, Jesus would try to change Judas's thinking. Apparently, Jesus hadn't been very successful in doing so, but he didn't give up on Judas. At the Passover meal Judas seems to be put in a place of honor at the table (John 13:26). When Jesus dips the bread into the bowl and gives it to Judas, this is a sign of friendship, and need not be seen as anything more. As to how this turns out, Sanders explains:

> One can envision Jesus looking Judas in the eye, probing him, bringing him to a point of decision. After this moment Jesus says, "Do quickly what you are going to do" (John 13:27). Jesus here pushes Judas to show his cards, to make up his mind regarding what sort of messiah he desires Jesus to be. A risk is involved here, since there is no guarantee which way Judas will decide. Judas does "lay down his cards" and takes steps that he believes will force Jesus to show his hand. Judas gambles on his hunch that being confronted by the authorities will force Jesus to take on the role of political liberator and thus become a "genuine" messiah. None of this was predetermined. Genuine options face both Jesus and Judas. The actual course of divine providence works itself out through and in response to these specific human choices. Jesus sought to change Judas's mind but apparently without success. Judas leaves the group and goes to the high priest.[50]

From this we see that Jesus' statements about what Judas would do are not a prediction but an attempt to confront him and challenge him to change. Moreover, according to this quote, even Jesus apparently hadn't yet decided whether to take the role of political liberator or not. Sanders then tells us that, while Jesus' prayer in the Garden about this cup passing from him is often seen as a prayer of submission to God's will, that interpretation overlooks the fact that Jesus presented his petition three times and asked not for strength to go through with the crucifixion but for an alternate route. Hence, the petition "let this cup pass from me" is not empty rhetoric, "but a serious effort to determine the will of God. Jesus wrestles with God's will because he does not believe that everything must happen according to a predetermined plan."[51] Sanders doesn't offer these passages and interpretations to suggest merely that there is no divine preset plan. Rather, he considers Jesus to be the Son of God, so these interpretations are to Sanders further evidence that the future isn't set and that God doesn't know the future.

Passages like these lead proponents of the open view to believe that God does not know our future free actions. But all open view advocates recognize that their position seems to fly in the face of biblical prophecies about events future to the time of the writer. Since the authors are writing under divine inspiration, they pen God's Word, but then it is God making these predictions. If so, however, how can God make such predictions without actually knowing what will occur? Doesn't predictive prophecy show that God knows the future? Defenders of the open view think not, but they recognize that they have some explaining to do.

The common response from this camp is that all prophecies fit into three categories. Once we understand those categories, we see that there is nothing inconsistent with claiming that God doesn't foreknow our future free actions. First, some prophecies "may express God's intention to do something in the future irrespective of creaturely decision. If God's will is the only condition required for something to happen, if human cooperation is not involved, then God can unilaterally guarantee its fulfillment, and he can announce it ahead of time."[52] Rice doesn't offer us an example of such a prophecy, but merely quotes Isa 46:10-11 where God says he will do all that he pleases and will bring about his plans. Sanders says the same thing.[53]

A second category of prophecies stems from God's exhaustive knowledge of the past and present, including knowledge of our character. In light of this information, including existing trends and tendencies, God announces what will happen. Rice states this in stronger terms than does Sanders. Rice calls these prophecies "God's knowledge that something will happen because the necessary conditions for it have been fulfilled and nothing could conceivably prevent it."[54] He offers as an example God's predicting to Moses what Pharaoh would do in response to pleas to let Israel go. Sanders is a bit more cautious at this point, recognizing the implications of libertarian free will. He says about these predictions that "given the depth and breadth of God's knowledge of the present situation, God forecasts what he *thinks* [italics mine] will happen. In this regard God is the consummate social scientist predicting what will happen. God's ability to predict the future in this way is far more accurate than any human forecaster's, however, since God has exhaustive access to all past and present knowledge."[55] We might, then, call these prophecies very highly "educated guesses" about the future, for that seems the most they can be, given libertarian free will. If this past and present information "guarantees" the prophecy to be correct, then wouldn't the factors known in such past and present knowledge causally determine what the agent does? But since such determinism rules out libertarian free will, these prophecies cannot be guarantees.

There is a third category of prophecies. A prophecy may be conditional. That is, it may express what God intends to do if something occurs or unless something occurs. Examples of such prophecies are cases of apparently failed predictions such as Jonah's preaching of destruction to Nineveh and God's prediction to David in 1 Sam 23:9-13. In addition, we are told that Jer 18:7-11 states the principle that God can give a prophecy that won't come true if a certain condition is met, and then verse 11 serves as an example of such in regard to Israel.[56]

What should we say to these things? Denying God's knowledge of the future successfully removes the tension between divine foreknowledge and libertarian free will. Of course it doesn't explain away the apparent contradiction but grants it and then chooses one of the two conflicting concepts. General sovereignty models of providence based on libertarian free will can breathe easily if they adopt presentism. On the other hand, if such models incorporate divine foreknowledge, they cannot hold presentism. The open view is consistent with libertarian free will and this handling of divine foreknowledge.

Of course, I have maintained that logical consistency is not the only issue. It is thoroughly possible to tell a story without contradicting oneself, even though the story doesn't correspond to our world. Granting that presentism solves the apparent contradiction between freedom and foreknowledge, we still want to know whether it squares with the facts. Despite presentism's claims to fit biblical and theological data, I disagree. In what follows, I want to present the most serious objections to rejecting divine foreknowledge as the open view does.

First, let us examine some of the passages which supposedly show that God doesn't know the future. Take the Genesis 6 passage, where God expresses his displeasure and regret at having made human beings. We are told this passage shows not only that God has and expresses emotions but also that God's plans were frustrated. He must not have foreseen what would happen, and now that it has happened, he is sorry he created the human race. But does any verse in Genesis 6 say that God didn't know this would happen? Of course not. Nor do any of the verses say he did know it would happen. That means that using this passage to show that God either did or did not know what would happen is to draw an inference from the passage. But inferential reasoning is always very slippery, especially when the thing we want to infer isn't hinted at or rejected in the data we have. One could infer from the passage that God didn't know this would happen, but another inference is equally possible. In light of other passages that say God knows all things (see my discussion on omniscience in chapter 7), one might infer that since this event was foreknown by God, verse 6 expresses God's reaction upon seeing how sinful his creatures are. He knows it not only as propositional knowledge from all eternity but also now as an item of experiential knowledge. As I have argued, divine omniscience doesn't require God to have experiential knowledge of everything, nor does it preclude his gaining experiential knowledge of things known intellectually beforehand. So we need not go so far as to say that God really doesn't feel the emotions mentioned in these verses. My point is that feeling these emotions at that point in time need not mean anything more than that God felt this way upon experiencing what he always knew would happen.

What about Gen 22:12 where God says that he now knows that Abraham fears him? Doesn't that mean God learned something intellectually that he did not previously know? Indeed, someone unaware of biblical teaching on divine omniscience might conclude this. If God already knows this, in what sense is it a test from God's perspective? We must see, however, that despite the seeming plausibility of this interpretation, it isn't the only way to understand the verse. First, the chapter begins by saying that God tested Abraham. Heb 11:17, the NT commentary on this event, says that when Abraham was tested, by faith he offered up Isaac. Thus, what happens in Genesis 22 is said to be a test of Abraham, not a test of God or of his knowledge.

Second, this is not God's first test of Abraham, though it certainly is the most difficult one. God has already seen Abraham pass a number of tests of faith, beginning with his response to leave Ur and follow God. So whatever Gen 22:12 means, it cannot mean that God never had any idea of how Abraham felt about him before. Third, if God knew by past experience that Abraham trusted and revered him, in the Genesis 22 incident what does God learn that he didn't previously know (assuming we should understand verse 12 literally, not anthropomorphically)? The best answer seems to be that God, by putting Abraham through the most trying of experiences, experientially comes to see the fullness of Abraham's devotion. God always knew this intellectually, and having dealt with Abraham before, he has experienced it to some extent. God's experience of Abraham's fullest devotion now matches what he has always known intellectually.

In light of the first two arguments, I believe the explanation offered in my third response is the best way to understand the passage. There is a further reason for thinking so. Proponents of the open view often note that once this incident ends and God sees how Abraham feels, God reaffirms the covenant with him (see the end of Genesis 22). Hence, apparently God's covenant relationship with Abraham was in doubt, or so it seems. What this fails to recognize and what this entire open view interpretation of Gen 22:12 seems to ignore, however, is the events recorded in Genesis 15 and 17. In chapter 15, God ratifies his covenant with Abraham. He does so by unilaterally passing through the bones and meat of the animal of sacrifice. OT scholars agree that in that culture and time this activity was a unilateral and unconditional way to make a covenant. That is, even if the one with whom the covenant is made makes no promise, what God did in Genesis 15 meant that he unconditionally committed himself to fulfill the covenant.[57] In addition, in Genesis 17 God reconfirmed his covenant with Abraham and instituted circumcision as the sign of the covenant.

What does ratifying the covenant show about our issue? It shows the improbability that God would make an unconditional commitment to Abraham in Genesis 15, reconfirm it in Genesis 17, but still would not know intellectually in Genesis 22 whether Abraham would defect. To make this commitment means that God knows Abraham is his man. If he doesn't really know that, then it is foolish for God to swear unilaterally to fulfill promises to someone who (for all God knows on the open view) may apostatize and turn out to be a reprobate. No, God's actions in Genesis 15 and 17 don't make sense if in Genesis 22 he doesn't yet really know intellectually that Abraham is his man and that Abraham will pass the test. Hence, without treating 22:12 as entirely anthropomorphic, I contend that my interpretation is the best. It upholds both God's foreknowledge of what Abraham would do and is entirely consistent with what God did in Genesis 15 and 17.

As to Sanders's handling of Christ's betrayal and his prayers in the Garden, it gets high marks for creativity but surely falters on even a cursory reading of the relevant texts. Sanders doesn't rest the open view entirely on this particular interpretation, and one surely shouldn't do so. The text in Matthew 26/Mark 14/Luke 22 simply does not match Sanders's handling of Christ's betrayal. The first point it ignores appears in Luke 22:3-4, which says that Satan entered Judas, who then went and discussed with the chief priests and officers how he might betray Jesus. This is no meeting with the chief priests in hopes that Judas can get them and Jesus to sit down, talk, and come to a mutual understanding. The only bargain Satan wants is one that will destroy Jesus.

We move next to the upper room. Sanders says that Jesus' offer of bread to Judas after dipping it in the bowl is a sign of friendship, for he hopes to change Judas's mind about what sort of Messiah he should be. This interpretation does not square with the text. In John 13:21 Jesus says that one of the disciples will betray him. The disciples are troubled and Peter asks who will do it (vv. 22-25). In verse 26a Jesus says, "That is the one for whom I shall dip the morsel and give it to him." And then we read (v. 26b), "So when He had dipped the morsel, He took and gave it to Judas." This is no sign of friendship. The Synoptics show Jesus predicting that the one who dips with him will betray him (Matt 26:21-23; Mark 14:20; Luke 22:21), but John says that Jesus and Judas dipped together. In Matt 26:25 Judas asks Jesus point-blank if he will betray Jesus. Jesus affirms that it is so.

What about Sanders's handling of Gethsemane? This is exceptionally problematic. Sanders says Jesus' petition wrestles with God's will because Jesus doesn't think everything must happen according to a predetermined plan; this is Jesus' attempt to determine God's will for him. But this ignores first the fact that Jesus himself is God. This attempt to pit members of the Godhead against one another is similar to an old ploy used to explain soteriological doctrines such as propitiation; now Sanders uses it to support lack of divine foreknowledge. This will not do; Jesus is fully God and fully man. As God, he already knows and has agreed to the plan. If Jesus foregoes the cross, what happens to the plan of salvation revealed throughout the OT and through Christ's life? If he foregoes the cross, the major reason for the incarnation is overturned. No, the petition cannot mean that Christ doesn't know the plan, or that he thinks maybe he can get the Father (plus his own divine nature) to let him off the hook. It is best understood as the anguish of a real human being facing a tortuous death. It is a natural human emotion to want to avoid a horrible experience, especially if we don't absolutely have to go through it but have chosen to do so for the sake of others. But that doesn't mean the plans are not set, nor that Jesus thinks there might be some other way to purchase our salvation. A final problem with this understanding of Gethsemane is that it contradicts what Sanders and other general sovereignty proponents say about God's plans for our world. Though he doesn't have minute plans for everything, God is said to have general goals he wants to accomplish. Among them are calling out a people for a special relationship with them. But this means providing salvation for them, as Sanders grants. But if the crucifixion of

Christ is not set and may possibly be overturned in the way Sanders intimates, then God's most general plans are in deep trouble. If anything must be set in advance, it must be these events. Without Christ's crucifixion and resurrection God's most general plans for establishing a relationship with his people cannot be carried out. For those who might reply that this is not an attempt to cancel salvation altogether, but only to postpone the death until another day, I reply that Jesus' petition in the Garden cannot be seen either as just a request to die on a different day (to put this off a bit until he feels more like it) or as a request that suggests salvation could be done another way. Jesus knows the plans are set and that no other alternatives are open. His petition means that, in his humanity, he wishes he could forego this terrible experience. Even knowing that he will rise three days after he dies doesn't mean the nails in his hands and feet won't hurt. This will be torture, and Jesus knows it. His petition expresses a very human emotion, but the petition also shows his submission to what is planned and must be done (Luke 22:42—"nevertheless" [KJV]).

Turning to the open view's handling of biblical prophecy, there are tremendous problems. I don't deny that some prophecies fit some of the categories proposed. Though open view advocates offer few biblical examples of the three forms, we can fill in some gaps. As to the first category that speaks of things that don't involve human decisions, things God can do unilaterally, one thinks of prophecies about destroying the current heavens and earth and making a new heaven and earth. Likewise, Scripture speaks of God resurrecting the dead, some to stand in judgment at the Great White Throne Judgment and to be cast into the lake of fire, and others to eternal bliss in God's presence. But we need not go to the future to see that this sort of prediction can occur. In Genesis 6, God sees the wickedness of mankind and tells Noah to build an ark, because God is going to send the great flood. Sending the flood requires no help from anyone.

As to the second group of prophecies, it is harder to affirm the open view proposal, because now the prediction's fulfillment rests largely on the shoulders of God's human creatures. Since those creatures have libertarian free will, one cannot guarantee how they will act. Rice offers as an example of this kind of prophecy God's prediction of how Pharaoh would respond to Moses' pleas. Rice claims that God knows Pharaoh's character and past so well that he can accurately predict what will occur. Necessary conditions are so set that nothing could prevent it. But if necessary conditions are such that nothing could prevent it, then Pharaoh's acts are not free in the libertarian sense. If his reaction is truly free in that sense, then talk about necessary conditions and unpreventability is nonsense. Sanders recognizes this and speaks instead of what God thinks Pharaoh will do. God is portrayed as the master psychologist and social scientist with all the data. But of course, on the open view, one piece of data God cannot know is exactly what a given person will do when actually in the situation, for libertarian free will precludes God from knowing. Maybe God will be "lucky" and Pharaoh will confirm his prediction, but maybe not.

Hence, even if we grant that there are such prophecies as the second category describes, there is no guarantee that those predictions will be fulfilled, since they involve the acts of agents with libertarian free will. With this kind of prediction, God really runs the risk of being a false prophet. Still, God makes such predictions in words that suggest he has no doubts about them being fulfilled. How can this be? Shouldn't God say, "My guess or hunch is that Pharaoh will . . ." or "In light of Pharaoh's past track record, I think he will probably do . . ."? There simply isn't room for God to have such confidence as these predictions propose if God's creatures have libertarian free will.[58]

What about the third category, conditional prophecies? Here we can grant that there are such prophecies. Prediction of Nineveh's destruction is one, and I grant that Jer 18:7-11 contains another. Since such prophecies state what God will do under various conditions, they seem to leave the future open. What is not entirely clear is whether such prophecies leave room for libertarian free will of the people involved. If God threatens to destroy your city unless you repent and you do repent because of the threat, it is hard to see how the repentance avoids qualifying as being causally determined. Some would even say that it was not only causally determined but also constrained, and thus not even free in a compatibilistic sense. But for the libertarian, if the threat causes the people to repent, then the repentance cannot be free (whether or not it is constrained). Are all conditional prophecies of this sort? It seems that since these prophecies give the recipients options, and since their subsequent actions are motivated by the particulars of the prophecy, it would be hard to say that their acts in response to the prophecy are not causally determined. This need not be understood as hard determinism; any form of determinism will do to make my point. And that point is that it appears that there are conditional prophecies, but it is likely that the particulars of many of these prophecies remove libertarian free will. So, are the proponents of the open view saying that fulfillment of the human part of a conditional prophecy is never done freely? Would these cases be some of the instances (which libertarians admit occur) where humans do not act freely? Perhaps so, but this may be an unwelcome conclusion for defenders of the open view.

But let us be charitable and grant the open view that there are prophecies that fit in each of the three categories they propose, and forget for a moment the problems some of those categories raise for libertarian free will. Still, there is a major objection to this handling of biblical prophecy. The problem is that there are just too many prophecies that fall into none of these categories. Several examples demonstrate the problem. First, think of the prophecy of the ram and he-goat in Daniel 8. In verses 20-21 Daniel is told that the ram represents Medo-Persia and the he-goat Greece. The prophecy predicts the transition of power from the former to the latter. Now, this is not a prophecy that fits the first category, for while God is involved in the change of empires, this prophecy also involves the rulers of the Medes and Persians and the ruler of Greece, and their armies. If all of these people have libertarian free will, how can God be so sure about this transition of power to Greece? Maybe another country will come along and destroy the Medo-Persian empire and Greece will come along later. That would falsify this prophecy.

Is this a prophecy of the second kind? Not at all! This prophecy is given to Daniel at the time of the Babylonian empire. Now it might be possible to see that the Medes and Persians will come to power, and even to suspect that they will conquer Babylon. But this prophecy also involves the transition to Greece. That's just too far off from Daniel's time. This is not like God telling Moses what Pharaoh will do within the next few days. Well, then, maybe this is a prophecy of the third sort, a conditional prophecy of what God will do, depending on what humans do? Again, this doesn't work, for the fulfillment of the prophecy doesn't depend on reactions to what God does, but rather on reactions of the Grecian kingdom to the Medo-Persian empire. Moreover, the prediction tells us the exact outcome. It doesn't say that if Medo-Persia does one thing, they will win, and if another, Greece will win.

So this prophecy fits none of the categories, and its fulfillment is too far off temporally from when it is given to be just a lucky guess. Consider another example, this time from the end of the age. Zechariah 12 moves to the consummation of God's program with his ancient people Israel. I have chosen this example in part because Zechariah is post-exilic. Hence, objections that this was fulfilled somehow during the Babylonian exile and restoration from it (a short time after the prophecy was given) are precluded. The prophecy opens by saying that Israel will be surrounded by all the nations of the world in an attempt to blot her out (12:2-3). In spite of this confederacy set against her, God will intervene to deliver her (vv. 2-9, esp. 4-9) . On the one hand, God will empower the people of Israel to fight as never before (vv. 6-8). On the other hand, God will overpower and confuse the confederacy (v. 4). Verse 10 predicts that in the midst of all of this, God will pour out his Spirit on Israel, and they will look upon him whom they have pierced and mourn for him. Many Bible commentators agree that this is what Jesus speaks of in Matt 24:29-31. Hence, they understand this passage to speak of Christ's second advent and of Israel's turning to Christ as the Holy Spirit is poured out on them and they see him whom they have pierced.

Does this prophecy fit any of the three categories proposed by the open view? It cannot fit the first, because it doesn't involve God only acting unilaterally. The nations must decide to attack Jerusalem, and later when Christ returns, they must decide to fight him (see also Zechariah 14). In addition, for 12:10ff. to be true, Israel must accept Christ. Given libertarian free will, there can be no such guarantees, but my main point now is that this is not a prophecy of the first sort.

As to the second kind, the fulfillment is much too far off from Zechariah's day to qualify. If one counters that maybe God makes this prediction in light of his thorough knowledge of the character of the people of that day, that won't work. God has exhaustive knowledge of past and present according to presentism, but not of people and events as far off as those of Zechariah 12–14. God cannot even know for sure who will be born and be alive at that time, for people are born through natural reproduction, and to engage in such is a decision humans will have to make with libertarian freedom. Until they do, God cannot know exactly who will get pregnant and when or who exactly will be born. So, given presentism, God could not know the character now of people who will be living in the distant future, because he cannot know who will be alive at all.

Is this a conditional prophecy of the third type? Not at all. The decision of the nations to surround Israel is not a conditional claim about what *God* will do. Moreover, while it is true that Israel will repent upon seeing their Messiah (12:10), God is not saying that Christ will come if they will repent. Nor is he saying that Christ won't come if they don't repent. God is saying that Christ will most definitely come, the Holy Spirit will certainly be poured out on them, and they will respond by turning to Christ. This prophecy doesn't predict what God alone will do if or unless people respond a certain way.

I could continue with many other examples, but the point is clear enough. There are many biblical prophecies that cannot be accounted for under the open view's proposal, and those prophecies demand that God know things far into the future. Presentism's handling of biblical prophecy is inadequate.

Two other points need treatment before leaving this discussion of presentism. The first deals with my handling of passages that seem to teach that God learns something he did not know. Typically, these passages are considered anthropomorphic. Though I don't handle all such passages this way, I agree that some are best understood that way. This invariably moves open view proponents to complain about arbitrarily picking and choosing which passages are to be taken literally. Those who say open view proponents are arbitrary in considering these passages literal and other passages about divine omniscience as metaphorical are equally guilty of doing the same thing in reverse.[59]

Is this complaint correct? Are we just left to choose our own passages as primary and others as anthropomorphic, metaphorical, and secondary on the basis of our presuppositions? If so, open view defenders have as much right to emphasize their passages as their opponents do to emphasize their own passages. Thankfully, we are not left at an impasse. I have already addressed this point about primary and secondary passages, so I need not rehearse it all again. Suffice it to say that the primary passages are those that directly tell us what and how much God knows, not narrative passages where God is described as doing one thing or another. The latter passages can't be ignored, but the primary passages must be the ones that directly offer teaching that explains the concept or tells us what the concept is. Hence, it is quite an inferential stretch to move from a divine statement such as "Perhaps they will do so and so" to the conceptual understanding of divine omniscience presentism proposes. It is an even greater stretch to hold that those passages *teach* that notion. The truth is that those passages just record what God said on given occasions. How we should understand such statements must be decided in light of passages that directly tell how much and what kind of knowledge God has.

Finally, presentism is objectionable because of the implications of God not knowing the future. Let me sketch a few. Since God cannot know prior to creating the world with humans who have libertarian freedom whether any of them will freely do evil, prior to creation God cannot know that it will be necessary to save anyone from sin. Hence, before creating he cannot plan to have Christ die on Calvary and rise from the dead for the forgiveness of our sins. Proponents of presentism might reply that this doesn't matter, since once humans are created and sin, God can then plan Christ's incarnation, death, and resurrection. However, this answer still leaves the problem that Scripture clearly teaches that Christ's death was foreordained before the foundation of the world.

Some might answer that before the foundation of the world could be just a few minutes before God creates. Hence, since it wasn't long until Adam and Eve would arrive, God could infer from their character that they would sin, and then before the foundation of the world plan salvation. The problem with this, however, is that Adam and Eve as created were sinlessly perfect. Moreover, it isn't likely that their very first actions upon being created would be to sin. So, if before God creates, he makes any guess about their likely actions, there is every indication that he would expect them to remain holy and not to need saving. Even Sanders grants that when Adam and Eve were first created, falling into sin was unthinkable, given how much God blessed them and put them in an ideal situation.[60] So, even if we grant that Christ was foreordained as Savior even just a few minutes before creation (hence before the foundation of the world, as Scripture says), even at that point there is no reason for God to plan salvation, given his then present knowledge and human libertarian free will.

Once Adam and Eve are created and fall, then God can plan salvation, but there are still problems with planning the incarnation. Genesis records promises God made to Abraham about being a great nation and about all peoples ultimately being blessed through Abraham's seed. Bible expositors agree that the ultimate seed who fulfills this promise is Jesus Christ. Likewise, God promises David that the Messiah will come from his lineage. Hence, God promises a Jewish Messiah ultimately from the house of David. This has obvious implications for the incarnation. It means the God-man must be of Jewish descent and from the lineage of David. But if presentism and libertarian free will are correct, God has no business making such promises to Abraham or David. After all, how does God know that Abraham's descendents won't be destroyed by hostile armies? How does he know this far in advance that there will be any of Abraham's biological descendents around when it comes time for the incarnation?

Well, God gets lucky and the nation thrives, but God didn't know that would happen, so he shouldn't have made such promises. The nation does survive, though, and under David, God makes the promise (2 Sam 7:13-16) about never lacking a man to sit on David's throne. Again, God has no right to make such a promise. Just because Israel is doing well under David is no proof that the nation will survive up to the time of the incarnation. As matters of historical fact, both northern and southern kingdom go into exile several hundred years after David's time; at David's point in history, God would not foresee that either (given presentism), but he would know that a total destruction of the nation and its people *could* happen. So he shouldn't make such long-range promises to David, especially when he doesn't intend to fulfill them very soon.

Again, however, God gets lucky and the nation survives to the time when God is ready for the incarnation. Prior to this time, however, how does God know there will be a Jewish girl willing to serve as the virgin with child, and how does he know that she will be of David's lineage? There is no way he can know that, given presentism and libertarian free will. It is possible that no Jewish girl would agree to what the angel tells Mary, so God would have to go to a Gentile girl, postpone the incarnation, or call the whole thing off. God again gets lucky and Mary complies, but he still had no business counting on things happening this way and making the sort of promises he did to Abraham and David.

This is what I mean when I say that if God really only has present knowledge and we have libertarian freedom, it seems inconceivable that he can plan the incarnation very far in advance. But now who would read the promises of the Messiah and prophecies about his place and manner of birth (Isa 7:14; Mic 5:2) and think God is just offering his wishful plans, or worse yet, is just planning things as he goes? Open view proponents tell us to take Scripture at face value, but what is the face value of OT prophecies about the coming of Christ if not something that refutes presentism? And what does Scripture mean at face value when it says that Christ was foreordained as the lamb before the foundation of the world? The most natural understanding is that God made promises and predictions to Abraham, David, and Israel long before they were fulfilled, and he did so because he knew what would happen and he can guarantee what he promises, even though many promises and prophecies require co-operation from his human creatures. Presentism's proposal is in trouble when applied to such prophecies.

A further implication of presentism was alluded to in what was just said and in my coverage of prophecy. With presentism and libertarian free will, God cannot guarantee fulfillment of any prophecy involving future free choices of his creatures. Think of prophecies about the Antichrist at the end time. Scripture doesn't tell us who that person will be, but that there will be such a person is prophesied in many biblical passages. Since Christ hasn't returned and set up his kingdom after defeating the Antichrist, these prophecies about the Antichrist seem so far to be unfulfilled. Despite many centuries of god-defying political tyrants, no one has yet fulfilled that role. Moreover, there is no guarantee that anyone ever will, if presentism and libertarian free will are true. To fill that role, someone must decide to do so, but given libertarian free will, everyone could choose other than to be the Antichrist. God cannot make anyone (incompatibilistically) freely fill that role. But if no one does, then God cannot fulfill prophecies about the Antichrist. In addition, since prophecies of the end time involve Christ destroying Antichrist and his armies upon Christ's return, God can't even guarantee that what he plans for Christ to do unilaterally will occur. God must put Christ's return on hold until he gets someone to fill the role of Antichrist, but given libertarian free will, perhaps no one will ever fill that role. This will have to be an unusually evil person, for think of how evil Hitler was, but even he didn't do what is predicted of the Antichrist. How could God predict, then, so long ago, that there would be such a horrible person as the Antichrist, if libertarian free will is true? Even if someone steps in to play that role in the future, God still cannot guarantee fulfillment of those prophecies. What if somewhere in his career the Antichrist decides to accept Jesus as his Savior? Given libertarian free will, that must be at least as possible as the option that the Antichrist will carry on his anti-God campaign.

Considerations like these lead to the conclusion that God has no right making any prophecies about the end time that involve the free acts of human beings, but many prophecies are of that nature. Two other implications of presentism and libertarian free will should be mentioned. First, if, as open view defenders hold, God's knowledge increases as he lives from day to day, then in light of the new things God is learning, it is quite possible that he will give us further revelation. That is, perhaps more Scripture is forthcoming to relate new decisions God is making in light of the many things he is learning. In fact, God may just decide to change some of his rules about daily living now that he sees the nature of contemporary society and its demands. After all, God has cancelled instructions before; we no longer need to bother with the OT sacrificial system, and many OT case laws no longer apply. With God's knowledge growing and no further Scripture having been given since the end of the NT era, God may just be bursting with new things to tell us. Of course, for hundreds of years it has been the consensus of Christians that the canon of Scripture is closed. Such beliefs are predicated at least in part on the idea that God at any time knows intellectually whatever he will know at any other time about the basic nature of reality, his relationship to the world, etc. Hence, it is reasonable to think that if there hasn't been more Scripture since the era of the early church, that is because God has finished revealing what is to be inscripturated.

In contrast, presentism's ever-learning God cannot possibly know everything he will know in his future, so something he will learn could stir him to give us more Scripture. If so, how can we be sure that when some lunatic walks into a McDonald's restaurant or into a school and starts shooting at everyone he sees, because he says God told him to do this—how can we be sure he's not right? God has issued strange commands like this before. Genesis 22 looked like a case of God changing his rules to fit the situation. How are we to know that this isn't happening again? Couldn't such a person say that, just as God told Israel

774 □ No One Like Him

to wipe out the Canaanites, now God has learned of another evil society; he doesn't know whether they will contaminate God's people (who can know such things with only present knowledge of creatures with libertarian freedom?) with their paganism, but he fears they might, so God instructed this person and his friends to destroy these people? Could we be certain this isn't true?

This must not be misunderstood. I am not saying these things will happen or are inevitable, but only that with presentism and human libertarian free will, it isn't impossible that someone should do such things, tell such a story, and be right! This, of course, isn't conclusive proof that presentism is wrong (arguments above offer such evidence), but when a view has such potential implications, it should lead us to wonder very seriously about its truth. And, we must not confuse the issue by saying that, well, deterministic systems have a lot of implications that seem undesirable, so they are no better. This type of retort commits the logical fallacy known as *tu quoque* ("you too"). Determinists must address those problems, but presentism can't win the debate by telling its opponents that they have problems too!

Finally, presentism has seriously negative implications for God's providential guidance of his children, and that has great practical implications for believers who petition God, seek his leading, and trust his judgment. If we ask God for something that breaks none of his moral rules, he just might give it to us. But if he has only present knowledge, he cannot know whether what he gives will ultimately be in our best interests. Why, then, should one ask God's guidance for decisions such as whom to marry, where to work, how many children to have? God really doesn't know how any of these decisions will turn out in the long run. Surely, he knows more about the present than I do, and so, for example, in terms of whom I should marry, he knows more about a prospective mate for me than I do; but he doesn't know how this will work out fifteen years to twenty years down the road. So if I consult him on this matter, I should lower my expectations about how good his advice will prove to be later on. Advocates of the open view try to reassure us that even if things go poorly, God is tremendously resourceful and can come up with something at that time. But there can be no guarantees. If I marry a women who fifteen years later starts an affair with some other man or woman, given my wife's libertarian free will and that of her lover's, there may be nothing God can do to rescue the situation, if he leaves their freedom intact. Advocates of presentism say that God can on some occasions override our freedom, but even if we grant that, think of how many stories there are like the one I just told! Will God override freedom in every case of someone being wronged in this way? Remember, overriding someone's freedom to get them to change is not necessarily a one-incident, one-day affair. No, this will take much more effort on God's part (and abridgement of our freedom) to correct the injustice and evil.

Considerations like these lead one to say that seeking counsel from such a God is little better than consulting a good friend who knows you well. How can a God with the limited capacities described be at all religiously adequate?

On the other hand, if God knows all things, controls all things, has a specific plan for my life, and not only sees how everything in my life will fit that plan but also has power to bring about what he has ordained for me, that is a God whose counsel is worth seeking. That is a God who can be trusted as knowing what he is doing, rather than trusting a God who doesn't know what the future holds and constructs his plans along the way as he sees what happens and hopes for the best. All of this means that to buy into presentism and the open view more generally is not just to buy a *God* who takes risks; it is also to hold beliefs that mean *we* must be risk takers, *even in our dealings with God*. There are already enough uncertainties and risks in this life (some of us have already had more than our share of unpleasant surprises) without adding to the risks and further potentially negative surprises by trusting in a God who doesn't know exactly what will happen and is a risk taker himself!

CONCLUSION

In light of this discussion of the libertarian freedom/divine foreknowledge issue, I conclude that the position which most clearly removes the apparent contradiction between the two is presentism. However, this view should be rejected as contrary to Scripture and evangelical theology. Those who hold it anyway should not only consult the biblical data carefully but also consider very seriously the implications (conceptual and practical) of holding the view. As to the other libertarian proposals to solve the freedom/foreknowledge dilemma, we have also seen their deficiencies.

In my judgment, a specific sovereignty position of the sort espoused in this book handles best the issue of freedom and foreknowledge. Moreover, the inability of libertarian positions to answer the freedom/foreknowledge problem acceptably by upholding both concepts and squaring with biblical and theological teaching serves as a further evidence *against* general sovereignty models of providence and *for* specific sovereignty models such as mine.

In sum, I affirm that the specific sovereignty model proposed best handles issues covered so far, but there is still a major question that must be addressed to confirm this assessment. If my soft deterministic position cannot solve the problem of evil, there is significant reason to reject it. To the problem of God's relation to evil, then, we must turn in the next chapter.

DIVINE PROVIDENCE AND EVIL

The traditional problem of evil is both an intellectual and a personal challenge to Christians. For centuries atheists have maintained that the problem cannot be resolved and that this is a fatal blow to the credibility of religions such as Christianity. In addition, many Christians who are fully committed to their God and religion find their faith severely rattled when they undergo horrendous afflictions.

As we have seen in previous chapters, process theism and the open view of God are convinced that their theologies successfully handle the problem of evil, whereas this problem is said to be the Achilles heel of classical theism in general and of specific sovereignty models of providence in particular. I have argued that the best case biblically, theologically, and philosophically can be made for a specific sovereignty model such as mine. However, I agree that to confirm that judgment my system must be able to solve the problem of evil.

INTRODUCING THE PROBLEM

The problem of evil traditionally has been understood to center on the alleged inconsistency of three propositions deemed central to theism. Those propositions are: 1) God is all-loving, 2) God is all-powerful, and 3) evil exists in our world. Critics claim that these three propositions as a set are self-contradictory. Hence, if any two are true, the third appears to be false. For example, if God really cares about us enough to remove the evil in our world, but evil still exists, then he must not have enough power to get rid of it.[1]

Philosophers and theologians have assumed that this formulation of the problem confronts all theistic systems alike. However, I have argued elsewhere in great detail that the traditional formulation of the problem is too simplistic.[2] There is not just one problem of evil, but rather many different problems. I can best demonstrate this by enumerating the various problems.

First, we can distinguish the religious problem of evil from the philosophical/theological problem of evil. The religious problem stems from some pain and suffering that someone is actually experiencing. As a result of this affliction, the sufferer's relation to God is disrupted; the suffering precipitates a religious crisis. The afflicted wonders why God allows this to happen to her and why now. Because God does not remove the pain and suffering, the sufferer wonders if it is still possible to love, worship, and serve the God who has allowed this to happen and who won't remove it.

In contrast, the philosophical/theological problem is much more abstract. It is not about particular evils, but evil in general. One doesn't have to be suffering to ask this question. This is the intellectual question that asks why there should be any evil at all in a world with an omnipotent, all-loving God. It is this problem that has been addressed most frequently over the centuries.

Second, we can distinguish between the problem of moral evil and the problem of natural evil. The former is actually the same as the philosophical/theological problem. Moral evil is sin, the evil things God's creatures do, and this problem asks why an all-loving, omnipotent God would allow us to sin. Natural evil, on the other hand, is evil that results from natural processes going awry. It includes earthquakes, floods, famines, volcanic eruptions, forest fires, genetic defects, and the like. While some of these evils can be started by humans (and made worse by how we handle them), the natural evils in question don't result from human sin. Here one wonders why an all-powerful, all-benevolent God would not eliminate such evils.

Third, there are also problems about the degree or amount, and the intensity, and the apparent gratuitousness (purposelessness) of many evils. Some might say that they can see why God might allow some evil, but they cannot understand why there is so much evil in our world. Whatever God wants to accomplish could surely be done with less. This is the problem of the amount of evil, and one variation of it points to someone who is a serial killer and kills eight people. Even if God needs to allow this killer freedom to do as he pleases in order to develop and clarify his moral character, certainly all of that is accomplished by the third or fourth victim. Why would God allow this person to kill further?

The problem of the intensity of evil is not about how much evil there is but about why some evils are so evil. For example, someone not only has terminal cancer, but it is excruciatingly painful to the point that no medication gives even brief relief from pain. The critic of theism may grant that God has a purpose in allowing this person to have cancer, but the critic wonders what is accomplished by God's inability or unwillingness to staunch the pain even minimally.

Then there is the problem of the apparent purposelessness of some evils. Here the critic grants that God may have a reason for allowing many of the evils that happen. In fact, many theists and atheists alike believe that if an evil serves some positive purpose in our world, that purpose might well justify God's refusal to remove it. However, there are just some evils, the critic complains, for which there seem to be no possible use, and God surely could have and should have avoided them. One of the more frequently used examples of such evil is the example of a helpless fawn caught in a forest fire started by a bolt of lightning. No one owns the forest or the fawn, so what happens isn't used to punish anyone or to teach a lesson. Moreover, the pain and death of the fawn in no way teaches the fawn's "parents" or "family" a lesson. So, why would a good and omnipotent God allow such suffering?

This last problem suggests another, the problem of animal pain and suffering in general. In the natural world, animals undergo much pain and suffering. In many of those cases, the suffering cannot be recompense to anyone or anything for evil they have committed. Nor does it teach anyone, least of all the animals involved, any moral or spiritual lesson. So why is this necessary, and why doesn't an all-loving and all-powerful God remove it? In the chapter on creation, I noted that the problem of animal suffering is especially troublesome if one postulates eons of time for animals to be on earth, live, and die before the creation of human beings. What possible ends could that serve? Even if we grant that what happens to animals somehow teaches moral and spiritual lessons to humans, wouldn't a good God have created animals much later in time (or humans sooner) so that there would actually be humans to learn whatever lessons God wants them to learn from animal suffering?

In addition to these problems of evil, philosophical discussions of the problem of evil over the last fifteen to twenty years have introduced another distinction that increases the number of problems of evil. The intellectual problems (specifically, those other than the religious problem) may be posed in either a logical or an evidential form. Traditionally, the problem has only been raised in what is now called its logical form. This form of the problem asserts that theistic systems are logically self-contradictory; that is, there is no way that the three above-mentioned propositions central to theism can all be true.

Largely because of the massive and monumental work of Alvin Plantinga in articulating and defending the free will defense, many theists and atheists alike have conceded that there is a way that the three propositions could all be true. But theism still is not off the hook, for even if evil's existence doesn't generate a contradiction in theistic systems, it is still strong evidence against the likelihood that theism is true. This is the evidential form of the problem of evil, which is also called the inductive or probabilistic problem of evil. Here the charge is not that theism contradicts itself but rather that the very facts of evil that all can see are strong evidence against the probability that there is a God.

This distinction between the logical and evidential forms of the problem of evil means that all of the intellectual problems (the problems of moral evil, natural evil, the amount of evil, the intensity of evil, the apparent gratuitousness of some evils, and animal suffering) may be posed in either the logical or the evidential form. But there is another sense in which there is not just one problem of evil: the philosophical/theological problem of evil is not just one problem. Rather, there are as many of these problems as there are theistic systems committed to God as omnipotent (in some sense of 'omnipotent'), God as all-loving (in some sense of 'all-loving'), and evil's existence (in some sense of 'evil'). This may sound odd, for example, to Christians who tend to think there is one Christian theology and no more. On the contrary, even evangelical and conservative Christians don't all mean the same thing by omnipotence, benevolence, and evil. Hence, as we have seen, there are various forms of Arminian theology and various forms of Calvinistic theology. We have also seen further variations of Christian theism in the open view and process theism, theologies that claim to be Christian but go beyond the boundaries of evangelical theology. So my point here is not that each religion has its own philosophical/theological problem of evil, but rather that there are variations of Christian theism, and each confronts problems of evil specifically germane to its form of theism.

There are important implications of the fact that there are many problems of evil. For theists, the point is to be sure to identify the specific problem the critic, sufferer, or whoever, is raising before offering a solution. Otherwise, we may offer answers to questions that aren't being asked. For atheists, the implication is that it is illegitimate to complain that a given theistic defense is inadequate because it doesn't cover all evils and all problems of evil. No defense does, nor is that its intent. But just because a defense doesn't solve all problems of evil, that doesn't mean it solves none. Thinking a given defense must solve all problems of evil erroneously assumes that there is only one problem of evil, when there are actually many distinct problems.

There is a further "ground rule" for the logical form of the problem of evil. The logical form of the problem accuses theistic systems committed to divine omnipotence and benevolence and the existence of evil of being internally inconsistent. Hence, the theist's own system contradicts itself. If this is true of a given theology, it collapses.

In light of this point, theists must be careful not to incorporate in their theology contradictory accounts of God, evil, and human free will. As for atheists, the implication is that they may not legitimately attribute their own views to theists and then tell theists that their theology is *internally* inconsistent. Unless the theist holds the views in question, there may be a contradiction in the views under discussion, but it isn't *internal* to the theist's system.

Since the logical problem of evil is about contradiction, we must clarify what the charge of contradiction means. To say that two propositions contradict each other means that they affirm and deny at the same time the same thing. It doesn't mean there may be a way to reconcile the propositions but we don't know it yet. It doesn't even mean God knows how to reconcile the propositions but we don't. It means there is no *possible* way the propositions can both be true. Since this is the charge, the answer need only show a possible way to fit them together consistently. Hopefully, theists will propose plausible explanations of how their doctrines harmonize, but the only requirement is that the explanation is possible.[3]

Strategy of Defenses and Theodicies

In light of these ground rules, how should theists in general and Calvinists like myself in particular respond to the charge of contradiction in their system?[4] Elsewhere I have detailed the basic strategy that theistic defenses normally take, and it would help to articulate it here. This four part strategy doesn't apply to the religious problem of evil, but seems implicit in handling the logical and evidential forms of the problem of evil for Christian theologies other than theonomy.[5]

The theologian begins by defining divine omnipotence as requiring God to do what is logically possible. Thus, he cannot actualize a world with contradictory states of affairs. If the theist holds a view of divine omnipotence which allows God to actualize contradictory states of affairs, then the theist's theology which describes the world may in fact contain a contradiction as it accurately reflects the world around us. So, in order for theists to show that their system does not contain a contradiction, it would be best to hold a notion of divine omnipotence which doesn't allow God to actualize contradictions.

The second step of this strategy argues that, in creating a world, God had to choose between actualizing one of two good things. The two goods are mutually contradictory, so God couldn't do both, because the theist's definition of omnipotence won't allow God to actualize a contradiction. Regardless of the particular theology, one of the two options is removing evil. Depending on the theology, the other option is some other valuable thing God could do in creating a world. For Leibniz, it is creating the best of all possible worlds. The free will defender says God's second option was to create a world with incompatibilistically free creatures. John Hick (*Evil and the God of Love*)[6] holds that the second option was to create a world where souls are built. For my theology, the second option is creating a world with non-glorified human beings.

Once the theist presents these two options, he argues that God cannot do both conjointly. If he removes evil, he cannot also create the best of all possible worlds. If he gives us libertarian free will, he cannot remove evil. Hick claims that to build souls there must be evil, so God cannot both build souls and remove evil. My defense says that if he removes evil, he cannot also create non-glorified human beings and let them function as they were intended to function. In each case, one option logically excludes the other. Since the theist's concept of divine omnipotence doesn't allow God to actualize contradictions, God cannot both remove evil and include the other valuable thing in our world.

The third step in the strategy of defense and theodicy-making invokes a commonly held ethical principle. That principle says that no one can be held morally accountable for failing to do what they could not do or for doing what they could not fail to do. In other words, no one is morally accountable unless they act freely. But with all of the theologies in questions, God is not free both to remove evil and to accomplish the other positive goal in our world. Hence, he is not guilty for failing to do both. For example, God can either remove evil or give us free will. If he removes evil, he isn't guilty for failing to give us free will. If he gives us free will, he isn't guilty for failing to remove evil. He cannot do both conjointly, so he isn't guilty for failing to do both.

Someone might agree that God is not guilty for failing to do both options but still wonder why God chose the one he did, rather than removing evil. If God chose something evil or at least a lesser good than removing evil, then it still seems that God did something wrong. This brings us to the final step in the strategy. The theist agrees that if God had chosen to remove evil, he would have done something very good. However, the theist argues that the option God chose is a value of such magnitude that it is at least as valuable as removing evil. It either counterbalances or overbalances the evil present in our world. Hence, in choosing this option instead of removing evil, God has done nothing wrong.

In sum, the basic strategy of theodicy and defense-making is to argue that God is a good God, despite the evil in our world, because he cannot remove it. He cannot do so because even an omnipotent God cannot actualize a contradiction. God could either remove evil or do something else of value with our world, but not both conjointly, because the two contradict one another. Since he cannot do both, he isn't guilty for failing to do both. Moreover, what he did choose put a value of the highest order into our world. God has fulfilled his moral obligation; he is a good God.

Two Modified Rationalist Defenses

Given this strategy, how would a Christian theist solve the problem of evil? Here we must remember that we must first specify which problem is in view and also articulate the essentials of the theology under consideration. Since the most typically discussed problem is the theological/philosophical problem (the problem of moral evil) in its logical form, that will be my focus. Those interested in the other problems and the evidential form of the problems can consult my *The Many Faces of Evil*.[7]

In chapter 2 of this book, I described three Christian forms of theism: theonomy, Leibnizian rationalism, and modified rationalism. The two theologies I want to discuss in more detail are both forms of modified rationalism, so I shall here only recount the metaphysics and ethics of that broad form of theism.[8] I am concerned now with only two modified rationalist answers to the problem of moral evil, because they represent ways that an Arminian (traditional or otherwise) and a Calvinist can solve this problem of logical consistency.

Modified rationalism is a metaphysical system that holds that God is not required to create anything, for his own existence is the highest good. However, creating a world is a fitting thing for him to do, but not the only fitting thing he can do. There is an infinite number of finite, contingent possible worlds that God could create. Some are intrinsically evil, so God had better not create any of them, but at least more than one is a good possible world. There is no best possible world. God is free either to create one of the good possible worlds or not to create at all. In the modified rationalist's universe, some things are known by reason alone, whereas other things can only be known through divine revelation.

Modified rationalist theologies incorporate one of two broad accounts of ethics: consequentialism and non-consequentialism. Consequentialist ethical theories hold that what makes an action morally right is its consequences. Whatever deeds produce a desired non-moral value (such as increasing pleasure and removing pain) are both morally good and obligatory to do. In contrast, non-consequentialist theories contend that whatever makes an act morally right or wrong is something other than its consequences. An act may be right and obligatory because duty demands it or God prescribes it, for example, but what makes it morally right is something besides its results.

Consequentialism and non-consequentialism apply to the problem of evil in very specific ways. According to consequentialist ethics, the world as created from God's hand contains evil in it, but that results in no moral stain on God because God will ultimately use this evil to maximize good. Clearly, with this account of ethics, God has acted morally despite the evil in our world if God uses that evil to produce some counterbalancing or overbalancing good. In contrast, non-consequentialist systems say that the world as created from God's hand contains no evil in it. Evil is introduced into the world by the activities of God's creatures. On this account of ethics, God has acted morally despite the evil in our world, if the world as created contained no evil, and if he placed in it some value of the first order. Then, even though God's creatures do evil, God in creating our world did nothing wrong.

In light of this account of metaphysics and ethics, how would a problem of evil arise for a modified rationalist theology? The problem can be stated in the form of the following question: is our world one of those good (in the sense the modified rationalist uses 'good') possible worlds that the modified rationalist contends that God could have created? In addressing this question, modified rationalist theologians will point to some valuable feature of our world and claim that it makes our world one of those good worlds. Note that the modified rationalist's God is not required to create the best of all possible worlds, for the modified rationalist doesn't believe there is such a thing. Nor must this God create a good world which is better than other good worlds he might have created. The modified rationalist maintains that there are good and evil possible worlds. God's moral obligation is to create one of the good ones. So long as modified rationalists can explain why our world is a good world, despite the moral evil in it, then their God is not guilty of failing on his moral obligation.

The Free Will Defense

Is our world one of those good possible worlds? Many Christian theists have held that it is because it contains human beings with free will, a value deemed to be of the first order. In fact, even many Calvinists have appealed to the free will defense in answer to the problem of evil. Unfortunately, making such an appeal generates a contradiction in the Calvinist's theology. The reason is, as we shall see, that the free will defense presupposes incompatibilistic free will. However, as I have argued in the preceding chapters, Calvinists are determinists. Those who believe humans have free will hold compatibilism and reject libertarian free will. Hence, Calvinists should look elsewhere to solve their problem of evil.[9]

Though soft determinists such as myself cannot use the free will defense to solve their problem of moral evil, it is still worthwhile to examine this defense. After all, the Calvinist is concerned not only to convince Christians committed to libertarian free will, but also to show nonbelievers that Christian theology is not self-contradictory on these issues. In fact, it isn't only Calvinists who must and can solve their problem of evil, but Arminians as well. Since various forms of free will theism (traditional Arminianism, open view of God, etc.) hold libertarian free will, the free will defense is their typical answer to the problem of moral evil in its logical form. So it is worth our while to see that these Christian theologians can solve this problem.

The free will defense presupposes a modified rationalist metaphysic. Moreover, it is fundamentally non-consequentialist in its ethics; hence, it claims that the world as created by God is good, but moral evil is introduced into the world by the actions of God's creatures, humans in particular.[10] Augustine is one of the free will defense's earliest proponents, and we can see in his work the essentials of this defense.

Augustine begins *On the Free Choice of the Will* by asking whether God is the cause of evil, and he answers that God is not. Instead, each of us causes the evil we willfully commit.[11] In the rest of Book I, Augustine discusses God's nature, and then turns to a lengthy consideration of the various kinds of evils (how they arise and how they relate to the will). As to how evils arise, Augustine says the problem stems from our desires. Desires in themselves need not be problematic, but we get into trouble when we desire temporal things rather than eternal things, and when we do so excessively.[12] Once excessive desires are present in us, we will in accord with them and bring evil into the world.

Toward the end of Book I Augustine asks why God gave us free will, if he knew we could and would abuse it.[13] Augustine begins Book II with his basic answer, and in the rest of Books II and III fills in further details. He delineates three types of goods as follows:

> Therefore the virtues, by which men live rightly are great goods, while all kinds of physical beauties [*species*], without which no one can live rightly, are the intermediate goods [*media bona*] between these two. No one uses the virtues for evil. However, the other goods, the lowest and the intermediate ones, can be used not only for good, but also for evil.[14]

According to Augustine, all three kinds of goods come from God, and free will is an intermediate good, because it can be used to produce either good or evil.[15]

Since free will is an intermediate good that can be used for evil, should God have given it to us? Augustine answers that God was right in giving it, because we can use it to do good. If we abuse our free will, that is not God's fault, and the possibility of abusing free will is worth it in view of the possibility of using free will to do good.[16]

Another question still remains, however. Isn't God still responsible for the evil we do with free will, because he must have foreknown that we would use our freedom to do evil? In Book III Augustine emphatically argues that God's foreknowledge of our sins doesn't make them necessary. Moreover, we are responsible for our sin because we could have done otherwise; our decision to sin is voluntary.[17] In addition, free will defenders add that God also knew that though we would use this freedom to do evil, many would use it to do good and to love him. God reasoned that it was worth putting up with the possibility and actuality of us using freedom to do evil, because he preferred to have creatures who love and obey him because they want to rather than because they are forced to do so.

So free will is a value of the first order that shows that ours is one of those good possible worlds God could have created. But he cannot both give us free will and guarantee that there will be no moral evil in our world. Sadly, we have used our freedom to sin, but ours is still a good world, and many use their freedom to do good as well.

On the contemporary scene, no one has defended the free will defense as vigorously and ably as Alvin Plantinga. But it has also had its detractors, and it would be worth noting one of the major objections raised against the defense. I maintain that the complaint is misguided, but hearing it and seeing how it is problematic is very instructive. I summarize the main thrust of the objection that J. L. Mackie has raised against the free will defense. We may call it Mackie's "good choosing argument."[18] Mackie writes:

> I should ask this: if God has made men such that in their free choices they sometimes prefer what is good and sometimes what is evil, why

could he not have made men such that they *always freely choose the good?* If there is no logical impossibility in a man's freely choosing the good on one, or on several occasions, there cannot be a logical impossibility in his freely choosing the good on every occasion. God was not, then, faced with a choice between making innocent automata and making beings who, in acting freely, would sometimes go wrong: there was open to him the obviously better possibility of *making beings who would act freely but always go right.* Clearly, his failure to avail himself of this possibility is inconsistent with his being both omnipotent and wholly good.[19] (Italics mine)

Mackie's objection sounds cogent in part, because free will means that a person can do either good or evil. If so, on one occasion a person might use his freedom to do good. Moreover, it is at least possible that someone would use his freedom on every occasion to do good. If it isn't impossible for us to do good on every occasion, and if God is omnipotent, why can't he make it the case that we always freely do what is right? In essence, Mackie rejects the underlying assumption of the free will defense, namely, that if God creates a world with free creatures, he cannot at the same time create a world with no moral evil. Mackie argues that God can do both, and hence, the free will defense fails.

Alvin Plantinga and hosts of other free will defenders have responded as we might expect. What Mackie proposes may sound cogent, but it is not, for a very simple reason. If God makes it the case or brings it about that we do anything, then we don't do it *freely!* Hence, God cannot guarantee that there will be no moral evil and give us free will at the same time.[20]

As one reflects on this response, it certainly seems to make sense; in essence, isn't it implying that Mackie has a misunderstanding about the very meaning of free will? That seems to be the underlying message of this rejoinder. However, how likely is it that Mackie doesn't know how to define free will? Not very likely, but then what is going on in this interchange between the free will defender and its critic? The answer is that we have before us two different concepts of free will. Given libertarian free will, it is impossible for God to guarantee ("make it the case" or "bring it about") that anyone will do anything freely, for guarantees invoke causal determinism, but libertarian free will cannot coexist with causal determinism. On the other hand, if one defines free will as do compatibilists/soft determinists, then what Mackie proposes makes abundant sense. So it seems clear that the free will defense and this objection rest on competing notions of human freedom.

What does this mean, however, for whether the free will defense solves the problem of moral evil for its theology? When we remember the "ground rules" of the logical form of the problem of evil (and that is the form under discussion now), we see that Mackie's objection is misguided. The logical problem of evil accuses theists of contradicting *themselves,* and that just means that to succeed in destroying the theist's system, the critic must show that positions the theist in question actually holds contradict other views that same theist holds. Now, it is clear that Mackie holds compatibilistic free will, but what free will defender holds that same notion? It is dubious that any do. But then, Mackie is generating a problem in the free will defender's system by attributing to it compatibilism, and of course, any free will defender who incorporates compatibilism in his system contradicts himself. Since free will defenders hold libertarian free will, not compatibilism, Mackie has not shown that the free will defense doesn't solve the logical problem of moral evil for theologies holding libertarian freedom. In short, his objection does not demonstrate that God could both give humans *libertarian* free will *and* guarantee at the same time that our world will be rid of moral evil. The free will defense does render free will theologies internally consistent on this matter. Traditional Arminians and open view theists use the free will defense to solve this problem, and they succeed.

As a Calvinist, I welcome this result, for it shows that atheists who claim that no theist can solve the problem of evil are wrong. Nonetheless, I have argued in chapters 11 and 13–15 that there are good reasons for rejecting libertarian free will and the general sovereignty theologies that incorporate it. Hence, while I agree that the free will defense renders these theologies internally consistent, I think these theologies as a whole are deficient. My objections, however, in no way show that the free will defender doesn't succeed in resolving this particular problem of alleged internal inconsistency.

There is a price to pay for rejecting free will theologies with their libertarian freedom in favor of soft determinism. The price is that what Mackie proposes seems totally possible with compatibilism. That is, with compatibilism, it appears that God can make it the case that we always freely (compatibilistically) do what is right. But then, why hasn't he done so? My answer cannot be an appeal to the free will defense, for that assumes a different notion of freedom than I hold. Instead, I must offer an answer that incorporates compatibilism and still explains why God cannot remove moral evil at the same time. If our world does not include some other valuable item which makes it impossible for God at the same time to remove moral evil, then our world is not after all a good possible world. To my defense of why this is a good world, despite the evil in it, I now turn.

Integrity of Humans Defense

My soft determinist Calvinist theology also presupposes a modified rationalist metaphysic. As to ethics, I am a nonconsequentialist. In particular, I hold a modified divine command theory. That is, I believe moral norms are prescribed by God, but I don't believe God prescribes arbitrarily. Instead, his precepts reflect his character.[21]

My defense against the logical problem of moral evil has three stages.[22] I ask first what sort of beings God intended to create when he made human beings. Here I refer to the basic abilities and capacities God gave us as human beings. At a minimum, I believe he intended to make creatures with ability to reason (that ability varies for each person), beings with emotions, beings with wills that are compatibilistically free (although freedom is not the emphasis of my defense), beings with desires, beings with intentions (formed on the basis of desires), and beings with the capacity for bodily movement. Moreover, he intended us to use these capacities to live and function in a world suited to beings like us. Hence, he created our world, which is run according to natural laws, and he evidently didn't intend to annihilate creation once he made it.

In addition, God did not want each of us to be identical in respect to these capacities. For example, some might have certain desires to the same degree other humans do, but in no two people would all these qualities of human nature be conjoined so as to obliterate individuality. In other words, character traits would not be so similar in any two people that they would be stereotypes of one another. Finally, God intended to make beings who are finite both metaphysically and morally (as to the moral aspect, our finitude doesn't necessitate doing evil, but only that we don't have God's infinite moral perfection). In sum, God intended to create non-glorified human beings, not subhuman or superhuman beings or even gods.

I do not believe that any of these qualities were lost by the race's fall into sin. Of course, I believe that sin has affected us and our world, but my point is that it did not result in the removal of desires, intentions, free will, bodily movement, and the like. Because of our fall into sin, these capacities don't function as well as they would have without sin, but that doesn't mean we no longer have them. Likewise, the fall didn't overturn the basic laws of nature and physics according to which our world runs. The fundamental features of humanity and of our world are still as God created them.

How do I know that this is what God intended? I know it by looking at the kind of beings he created when he formed us, and by noting also that the world in which we live is suited to our capacities. Someone may reply that this same line of reasoning could be used to say that God also intended to create moral evil, because we have it, but that is not so. Moral evil is not something God created when he made other things. It is not a substance at all. God created substances, including the world and the people in it. God intended that we could act, for he made us able to act. But he neither made our actions nor does he perform them. Hence, we cannot say that God intended there to be moral evil because we have it in our world. God intended to create and did create agents who can act; he did not make their acts (good or evil).

How do we know by looking at what God did that he really intended to do it? Don't others at times act without fully understanding their own intentions? It is true that humans don't always know what they intend to do, but that cannot be true of an omniscient being's awareness of his intentions. By seeing what God did, we can be sure we know what he really intended to do.

If humans are the kind of creatures I have described, how do they come to do moral evil (sin)? This brings me to the second stage of my defense, a consideration of the ultimate source of evil deeds. My answer is not free will, although I agree that free exercise of will is instrumental in bringing about moral evil. However, as a compatibilist, I dare not use the free will defense.

In accord with Jas 1:13-15, I hold that morally evil deeds stem from human desires. Desires in and of themselves are not evil nor do they perform the evil. James says, however, that desires (*epithumia* is the word for desire, and it can refer to any desire) are carried away (*exelkomenos*) and enticed (*deleazomenos*) to the point where sin is actually committed (conceived).[23] Many moral philosophers would agree that the point of "conception" is when a person wills to do the act if she could. Once that decision is made, it remains only for her to translate that choice into overt public action.[24]

Morally evil acts, then, ultimately stem from our desires. Desires in themselves are not evil, but when they are aroused so as to lead us to disobey God's prescribed moral norms, then we have sinned. Desires are not the only culprit, however, for will, reason, and emotion, for example, also enter into the process, but James says temptation and sinful deeds start with our desires.

If humans are the sort of creatures described, and if moral evil arises as I have suggested, what would God have to do to get rid of moral evil? This brings me to the final stage of my defense. If removing evil is God's only goal, he certainly can accomplish it. However, my view of divine omnipotence does not allow God to actualize contradictions, so if I can show that by removing evil God would contradict some other goal(s) he wants to accomplish, then I will have shown why God cannot remove evil. Of course, if he *cannot* create a utopia without producing further and greater problems, he is not required to do so.

It is my contention that if God did what is necessary to rid our world of moral evil, he would either contradict his intentions to create human beings and the world as he has; cause us to wonder if he has one or more of the attributes ascribed to him; and/or do something we would not expect or desire him to do, because it would produce greater evil than there already is. To see this, let us look at how God might get rid of moral evil.

Some may think that all God needs to do to remove moral evil is just arrange affairs so that his compatibilistically free creatures are causally determined to have desires only for the good and to choose only good without being constrained at all. For each of us, God should know what it would take, and he should be powerful enough to do it.

However, this is not as simple as it sounds. If people are naturally inclined to do what God wants, God may need to do very little rearranging of our world to accomplish this goal. If people are stubborn and resist his will, it may take a great deal more maneuvering than we think. God would have to do this for everyone every time we resist his will. Moreover, changes in circumstances for one of us would affect circumstances for others, for we don't live in isolation. But what might be needed to get us to do good might disrupt others' lives, constrain them to do something that serves God's purposes in regard to us, and perhaps even turn them toward doing evil.

Consider, for example, what God might have to do to move even one person to choose good freely. To convince that person to do right would probably require rearrangements in other people's lives, changes that would require them to do things they don't want to do. If God wants those other people to do what he wants unconstrainedly, he may need to rearrange even other people's lives. To get that third group of people to do what he wants unconstrainedly may require yet more people to do something they don't want to do. I could continue, but the picture is clear. To uphold everyone's freedom may be much more difficult than we suppose. It is more likely that the free will of some will be abridged as a result of God's attempts to convince certain people to do good.

There is further reason to believe it may be harder for God to get us to do right than we think. God didn't create us with an inclination toward sin, but even Adam in ideal surroundings and circumstances sinned. According to Scripture, the race inherited from Adam a sin nature that disposes us toward evil. In light of that sin nature, it isn't at all clear that a minimal rearranging of events, actions, and circumstances would achieve the goal of getting us to do good without constraining us. It might turn out that God would have to constrain many people to do things he needed done in order to organize circumstances to convince a few of us to do the right thing without constraining us. Of course, that would contradict compatibilistic free will for many of us, and would likely do so more frequently than we might imagine. Moreover, one begins to wonder how wise this God is if he must do all of this just to bring it about that his human creatures do good. Why not at the outset just make a different creature who couldn't do evil? But of course, that would contradict God's decision to make humans, not subhumans or superhumans.

There is a further problem with getting rid of evil this way. This method also assumes that if God rearranged the world, all of us would draw the right conclusion from our circumstances and do right. Our desires, intentions, emotions, and will would all fall into place as they should without abridging freedom at all. This is most dubious, given our finite minds and wills as well as the sin nature within us that inclines us toward evil. Hence, it is not clear that we can coherently conceive all the changes God would have to make to ensure that we got the right message and acted morally.

Perhaps there is a simpler, more direct way for God to get rid of evil. Although we might wonder what other avenue is open to God, there are at least eight other ways God might get rid of evil. However, none of them would be acceptable. First, he could remove moral evil by doing away with mankind. Not only is this a drastic solution all of us would deem unacceptable, but it would also contradict his intent to create humans who live and function in the world he made.

A second way to remove moral evil is for God to eliminate all objects of desire. Without objects of desire, it is hard to see how our desires could be led astray to do moral evil. However, to eradicate all objects of desire God would have to destroy the whole world and everything in it, including human bodies. Minds alone would remain, unless minds could be objects of desire that might lead someone astray.

Objections to this option are obvious. Its implications for human life and well-being make it unacceptable. Moreover, the God I have described would have to reject it, because adopting it would contradict his intentions to create humans and put them in a world which he didn't plan to annihilate once he created it.

Since sin ultimately stems from desires, a third way for God to rid the world of moral evil would be to remove human desires. Problems with this solution again are obvious. God intended to create creatures who have desires, but if he removes all human desires, that contradicts his plans about the creature he wanted to create. Moreover, removing desires would also remove the ultimate basis of action, so that people would not act, and that would contradict God's decision to create beings who perform the various actions necessary to remain alive. Of course, if that happened, the ultimate demise of the race would result. Surely, that would be less desirable than our world is now.

A fourth possibility seems to be one of the more likely things God could do. He could allow us to have desires but never let them be aroused to the point where we do moral evil (perhaps not even to the point where we would form intentions to do evil). Now, since any desire can lead to evil, this means that we would retain all our desires but God would eliminate or neutralize them once they approach or reach a degree of arousal that would result in intending or willing an act of moral evil. If God chose this option, he could accomplish it in one of two ways. He could make us with the capacity for our desires to run rampant, but then perform a miracle to stop them whenever they start to do so. Or he could make us so that our desires would only be aroused to a certain degree, a degree that would never be or lead to evil. I shall address the former option when I discuss more generally God removing evil by perform-ing a miracle. The latter option concerns me now.

As for that option, there are several problems. For one thing, it contradicts God's intent to create people who are not stereotypes of one another. I do not mean that people would always desire the same things. Rather, whenever someone's desires were allured to something forbidden, those desires could be enticed only up to a point, a point that wouldn't be or lead to evil. What would be true of one person would be true of all. This might appear to leave much room for individuality, but not necessarily. Any desire can lead to evil, and God knows when a given desire, if pursued, would do so. In every such case, we would need to be preprogrammed to squelch the desire before it went too far. That would seem to make us stereotypes of one another more often than we might think.

There is another problem with God making us this way. Imagine what life would be like. Whenever a desire would start to run amuck, we would have to stop having the desire (or at least not follow it), change desires, and begin a new course of action. The picture that comes to mind is one where our daily routines are constantly interrupted (if not stopped altogether) and new courses of action are implemented only to be interrupted and new ones implemented and interrupted *ad infinitum*. Life as we know it would probably come to a standstill. The world envisioned would be a different world (perhaps radically different), but not necessarily better or even as good as our world. Moreover, it would seemingly contradict God's intent to create us so as to function in this world.

Perhaps the greatest objection to this fourth option is that to make us this way God would have to make us superhuman both morally and intellectually. We wouldn't have to be divine or angelic, but we would have to be much different morally and intellectually than we now are. In order to make us so that our desires wouldn't get out of hand, God would have to make us willing to squelch them whenever they would lead to evil (a hard enough thing to do). To do this we would also need to *know* when desires would lead to evil, so that we could stop them from being overly enticed. Whatever God would have to do to make us this way, it seems it would involve making us more than human. If so, God would contradict his decision to make human beings, not superhuman beings.

Fifth, God could allow all desires and allow us to form intentions for actions based on those desires unless the intentions would lead to evil. God could remove these intentions in either of the ways mentioned for handling evil-producing desires (by miracles or by making us so we would never develop intentions that lead to evil). However, removing evil by handling intentions this way faces the same problems raised in regard to desires.

Sixth, God might remove moral evil by erasing any willing that would produce evil. We could will good things freely (compatibilistically), but whenever we might will evil, the willing would be eliminated. God could do this either by miraculous intervention (to be discussed later) or by making us so that we would never will evil. However, removing evil this way faces the same kinds of objections that confront the desire and intention options.

Seventh, God could eliminate the public expression of moral evil by stopping our bodily movement whenever we try to carry out evil. He could do this either by miracle or by making us so as to stop bodily movement when it would lead to evil. Bodily movement would probably be interrupted and stopped quite often. However, this option faces the same kinds of objections the desire, intention, and will options face.

If all of these ways are problematic, perhaps God could still rid the world of moral evil by miraculous intervention at any of the various mental and physical phases of action. Several problems, however, beset this method of removing moral evil. First, if God did this, it would greatly change life as we know it. At any moment, God would miraculously stop desires, intentions, willing, or bodily movement if he knew they would lead to evil. Since we would not always know when our actions would lead to evil,[25] we often wouldn't know when to expect God to interfere. We might become too afraid to do, try, or even think anything, realizing that at any moment, our movements or thoughts could be eliminated. Under those circumstances, life as we know it might come to a standstill, and that would contradict God's desire to create people who live and function in this world. Moreover, it is not at all clear that a world in which there is a constant threat of removing our thoughts, willing, or bodily movements would be a better world or even as good a world as the one we have.

Second, it is one thing to speak of God miraculously intervening to eradicate desires, intentions, willing, or bodily movements that lead to evil. It is another to specify exactly what that means. As for bodily movement, God would probably have to paralyze a person as long as necessary (perhaps indefinitely) to stop bodily movements that would carry out an evil act. Of course, stopping bodily movement this way even momentarily would alter the nature of life altogether. Every few moments, series of people would be paralyzed while trying to carry out an action. Once they agree to change their actions, they would begin to move again, while yet other people would be paralyzed. It isn't clear that this would be a better world than ours, and it would apparently contradict God's intention to make creatures who can live and function in this world.

In addition, it is difficult to imagine what miracle God would have to do to remove a desire, intention, or act of willing that would lead to evil. It hardly makes sense to talk about paralysis of intention, desire, or will. God would probably have to knock us unconscious or cause us to lose our memory for as long and as often as needed in order to remove evil-producing thoughts. The picture one gets is of a world of people who fall in and out of consciousness and undergo periodic spells of amnesia. Wouldn't that virtually bring life to a standstill and thereby be inconsistent with God's intention to make us so that we can live and function in this world?

Up to this point in my defense, I have been discussing evil that is voluntarily produced. If a world where God removes those sorts of actions is problematic, then there is even more reason for concern when one realizes that involuntary and reflex actions can also produce evil. If it would be disruptive to normal life to remove our evil-intentioned acts, it would be even more disruptive to remove our good-intentioned actions and reflex actions that produce evil. Regardless of someone's intentions, God would know when an act would bring evil to someone else. In order to rid our world of evil, God would have to remove those actions as well.[26] If life would likely come to a standstill if we knew evil-intentioned acts would be interrupted, think of how much more paralyzing it would be to know that *any* action could be stopped![27]

A final objection to removing evil miraculously is that it would give reason to question God's wisdom. If God goes to all the trouble to make human beings as he has, but then must perform these miracles to counteract them when they express that humanness in ways that would produce evil, there is reason to ask about God's wisdom in making us as he did. Of course, had God made us differently so that he would not have to remove evil by miracles, that would contradict his desire to make the sort of beings he has made. So either God must perform miracles and thereby raise questions about his wisdom, or he must change our nature as human beings, something that would contradict his goal of making humans, not superhumans or subhumans.

This discussion about what God would have to do to remove moral evil shows that God *cannot* remove it without contradicting his desires to make the kind of creature and world he has made (causing us to doubt the accuracy of ascribing to him attributes such as wisdom) or making a world we wouldn't want and would consider more evil than our present world. Someone may suggest that God could avoid all these problems if he made different creatures than human beings. In other words, why not make creatures without desires, intentions, will, and/or bodily movement?

God could do this, and if he did, it would likely remove moral evil, but it would also remove human beings as we know them. It is hard to know what to call the resultant creature, since it would neither move nor think—even "robot" seems too complimentary. Anyone who thinks there is any worth in being human would find this unacceptable.

Someone else might object that God should not make us subhuman, but moral evil could be avoided if he made us superhuman. I agree that God could do this, but I contend that humans as we know them are a value of the first order. Scripture says humans are created in God's image (Gen. 1:26-27); it never says this of angels, animals, or any other creature. Moreover, when God completed his creative work, he saw that all of it, including human beings, was very good (Gen. 1:31). Ps 8:5-8 speaks of God crowning us with glory and honor and giving us dominion over the other parts of his creation. In light of this evaluation by God, who are we to say that humans as created by God are not valuable? As a modified rationalist all I need to show is that our world is one of those good possible worlds God could have created. Clearly, a world with human beings in it is a good world.

Another objection confronts not only my theology but also many other evangelical Christian systems. Theists, including myself, often say our world is a good world because of some feature in it, but we also believe in a future state (call it the kingdom of God or the eternal state) in which there will be no evil. It is agreed that, morally speaking, this will be a better world than our present world. Since God not only can create this better world but also will someday, why didn't he do it in the first place? Since it will be a better world and God could have created it, the fact that he didn't suggests to some that something is wrong with him.

I respond initially that this objection demonstrates no internal inconsistency in my theology or in any other evangelical Christian system. Critics of theism might reject all evangelical theologies on this ground, but that wouldn't be a rejection on grounds of inability to solve a logical problem of evil, a problem of *internal* inconsistency.

More directly to the point, this is a significant objection, but it contains a confusion. The confusion centers around what a modified rationalist theology is required to do to solve its logical problem of evil. Modified rationalists don't claim that there is a best world, but they do claim that there is more than one good possible world. Moreover, modified rationalism does not demand that God create the best world or even a better world than some other good world. It only requires God to create a good possible world. The task for a modified rationalist, then, is to look at the world God *did* create and explain why it is good in spite of the evil in it.

Since this is the requirement, neither I nor any other modified rationalist needs to show that our world is the best or even better than some other good world God might have created. We need only to show that ours is one of those good worlds God could have created. I have done that by pointing to human beings, and arguing that God cannot both create them and remove evil. Hence, I have solved my theology's logical problem of moral evil.[28]

Can God remove moral evil from our world? I believe he can, if he creates different creatures than human beings. He also can if he creates humans and then removes evil in any of the ways imagined. But we have seen the problems that arise if God takes any of those options.

Has God done something wrong in creating human beings? Not at all, when we consider the great value human beings have and the great worth God places upon us. As an empirical fact, we can say that moral evil has come as a concomitant of a world populated with human beings. Still, it is one of those good possible worlds God could have created. God is a good God; our world with human beings demonstrates his goodness. This defense against moral evil renders my theology internally consistent, and hence solves its logical problem of evil.

Though showing internal consistency is all that is required of my theology in order to solve its logical problem of evil, we still want to know whether there is any reason to believe this theology as a whole with its various intellectual commitments about God, evil, and human freedom. This is an appropriate question to pose not only for my theology but also for any other theology. In the pages of this book, I have set forth the biblical, theological, and philosophical arguments for my theological system. I have argued that there is both good reason to believe that it accurately reflects Scripture and good reason to reject other conceptions of God and his relation to our world. This, of course, does not mean that there will be universal agreement with my assessments. However, it explains the reasons why I believe the theology and defense against the problem of moral evil in its logical form which I have presented in this book not only results in a logically consistent theology but also articulates a plausible conception of God.

Conclusion

Both a Calvinistic and an Arminian theology can solve their problem of moral evil in its logical form. There are other problems of evil, and other theists and I have addressed them elsewhere.[29] Some may still reject Calvinism altogether, because they believe it has an inadequate account of God, man, sin, or salvation. In earlier chapters, I have explained why Calvinism is not inadequate in its views on God. Other volumes in this series make (or will make) the case for Calvinism's position on the other doctrines mentioned. However, from what I have shown in this chapter, one cannot legitimately reject a Calvinistic system like mine on the ground that it cannot solve its problem of moral evil in its logical form. If one understands the ground rules of this problem, one sees that the preceding discussion handles those problems successfully.

CONCLUSION

"No One Like Me"

One of the catch-phrases of our day is "user-friendly." We want our appliances and computers to be "user-friendly." Our "how-to" manuals must also have this quality. And we demand the same of our institutions such as governments, universities, and corporations. In the pages of this book, we have studied the various conceptions of God in contemporary thought and religious practice. It is clear that people in our time are also demanding a "user-friendly" God.

On the one hand, this is encouraging, for it says that people want to have a genuine relationship with their God. An aloof, unrelated, and unresponsive God is simply inadequate for the needs of contemporary society. We want a God who matters in our personal life, and a God to whom we sense that we matter. On the other hand, the problem with conceptions of God as only "user-friendly" is that we sense that our contemporaries are clamoring for a God who is little more than a cosmic bellhop, always at the ready to cater to our every wish and whim. God must be responsive to us, but he dare not have or exercise much power and authority over us. We are happy for a God who cares, but our contemporaries reject a God who is king.

The problem, however, is that the options are presented as an either/or. Either we must worship the absolute monarch of classical theism who is unresponsive and absolutely transcendent, or we must embrace the relational, caring, gentle persuader God of process theism and other contemporary theologies. In the pages of this book I have argued that the most biblically and theologically accurate and the most religiously adequate conception of God depicts him as "both/and"; he is the king who cares. But let us review exactly what this means and how we arrived at this portrait.

The classical conception of God has been under great attack during the last century. This God is thought by many to be no more than the God of the philosophers who sits alone in his heaven, removed from time, change, and emotion. He always gets his way and shares his power with no one. In the opinion of many, it is hard to think of such a God as a Father who cares for his human creatures. If there is any relation to him at all, it seems that it can be none other than as our judge. We sense that we experience at one time or another his wrath, but it is hard to think of him as a loving God.

In this book, I have argued that we need to reconstruct and revise our conception of the classical God, and in part 2, I detailed many of the changes. I suggested that we are biblically required to maintain divine immutability, but not the absolute immutability of the classical tradition. God must still be unchanging in his being, attributes, will, purposes, and ethical norms. But he can change relationally and he can interact with his creatures. This also means that divine impassibility must be rejected. I have also argued that the best conclusion about divine eternity is that it is temporal, not atemporal. God as temporal knows exactly what time it is in human history, and he can enter into our world to act and to react to us.

Undoubtedly, process and open view theists will applaud these modifications to the concept of God, even if they don't entirely agree with my nuancing of these and other divine attributes. Those who favor a more relational God than the God of classical theism may remind us that as we conceive of God we must remember how he has shown himself to us in the person of Jesus Christ, the incarnate God-man. Though Christ is fully God, we remember that he humbled himself. He took up the basin and the towel to wash the feet of his disciples and encouraged us likewise to serve one another. But Christ's humiliation went even further; he died on a cruel cross to serve us and our salvation. Indeed, this is a portrait of a "user-friendly" God if there ever was one.

While we can applaud this portrait of a relational, caring God who is ready to roll up his sleeves, take the basin and the towel, and serve his creatures, that does not mean that the God of Scripture is the God of process theism. The God of the Bible is pure Spirit; he has no consequent physical pole, and his immaterial nature is not the process primordial nature as the "realm of the possibilities" or even as the ordering of that realm. Even more, the God of Scripture is not the impotent God of process theism, a God who deeply sympathizes with our pains and suffers them along with us but is helpless to do anything to remove them. This God is a victim of the evil in our world even as we are. It is hard to see why process theists believe that this makes their God attractive. Moreover, this God may or may not really know what is best for us, but he can only attempt to persuade us to see things as he does and to follow his highest aims for us; there is no guarantee that he will succeed in convincing us to follow his wish.

Nor is the caring God of Scripture the open view's gambler God who goes into the darkness of the unknown future in ignorance of what it holds and with only general goals that may be frustrated by his creatures' free actions. In Isa 46:9-11 Yahweh compares himself to the gods of the Babylonians. He says that there is no God like him, but he goes on to explain what is so different about himself in comparison to their gods. What God revealed about himself we would do well to take very seriously as we evaluate the open view's vision of God. God says, "I am God, and there is no one like Me, declaring the end from the beginning and from ancient times things which have not been done, saying 'My purpose will be established, and I will accomplish all My good pleasure'; calling a bird of prey from the east, the man of My purpose from a far country. Truly I have spoken; truly I will bring it to pass. I have planned it, surely I will do it." This is no gambler God who restricts the use of his power to cater to the whims of our freedom!

The picture that emerges, then, is of a God who is both the God of the basin and towel and the mighty King of Kings and Lord of Lords. He has planned all of history for his glory and our benefit. He does not sit impotently in heaven waiting for us to act in order to plan his next move. God and we are not somehow equal players in a cosmic game of chess. At various points in Scripture (e.g., Isaiah 6; Revelation 4), the curtain of heaven is drawn back so that we get a glimpse of what is happening. The picture is one of a majestic, awesome, omnipotent king upon his throne surrounded by the angelic hosts and the saved of all ages bowing in humble adoration and worship. We need to take such pictures seriously! We also need to reflect upon God's answer to Job (Job 38–41) and even upon the glory Christ's disciples saw when they viewed him on the Mount of Transfiguration. This is no impotent God; he is the king of the universe!

Some will complain that granting God such power inevitably leads to tyranny. Love and authority cannot be harmonized in one and the same person. After all, was it not Lord Acton who remarked that "power tends to corrupt, absolute power corrupts absolutely"? What Lord Acton said can and often does happen when power is given to human beings. But God is no man that he should abuse the power that is rightly his. The same God who is faithful to keep his promises is also faithful to act in concert with his holy and just character. There is no need to fear power in the hands of the king who cares!

Others may object that a God who has planned everything in advance must be very bored with history. Since he already has planned and knows what will happen, why even bother playing out the script? Only when there is uncertainty because things are not set in advance can our history be of any real interest to God. But this is surely not so. Why would God want to go through history with us as it unfolds when he already knows everything he and we will do? For the same reason that the person who meticulously plans every detail of a business meeting or a worship service still wants to attend. For the same reason that someone who knows all the lines of every actor in a play still wants to experience the live performance. Knowing intellectually the blueprint for what will happen cannot take the place of experiencing the actual occurring of everything that is planned. As we saw in nuancing the divine attribute of omniscience, there is a difference between propositional knowledge and experiential knowledge. God's knowing propositionally everything that will occur because he has foreordained it cannot take the place of experiencing history's flow as it passes. Knowing that I will seek his help in time of trial and that he will respond cannot take the place of actually hearing me pray and then responding to my need. No, the "doing" of history is not boring for the king who has planned each moment of it.

Throughout this book I have argued that if we understand God's nature in a way that makes him a relational, caring God, we are not automatically locked into the process or open view's account of the amount of control God has in our world. Nor if God is king must he also be aloof, impassive, and unrelated. The proper depiction of God is not as *either* the caring God of the "basin and towel" *or* the absolute monarch God. It is both; it is the king who cares!

What I have been urging is that we allow ourselves to see the full biblical portrait of our God. When we do we find a God who is the caring king. Let this picture be seen in all of its grandeur and majesty! Let God be God as he presents himself in the pages of his Word. Only when we let God be himself can we even hope to begin to allow ourselves to be what God intended us to be. Let God be God! There is no one like him!

CHAPTER 1

1. Bruce Demarest, *The Cross and Salvation: The Doctrine of Salvation*, Foundations of Evangelical Theology (Wheaton, Ill.: Crossway, 1997).

CHAPTER 2

1. Quoted in John Dietrich, "Thoughts on God," *Relig Hum* 23 (Summer 1989): 110.
2. Anselm, "Proslogium" and "Monologium," in *St. Anselm: Basic Writings*, trans. S. N. Deane (La Salle, Ill.: Open Court, 1968).
3. Paul Tillich, *Systematic Theology*, vol. 1 (Chicago: University of Chicago Press, 1971), p. 211.
4. John Hick, *An Interpretation of Religion* (New Haven, Conn.: Yale University Press, 1989), pp. 241-243. Cited and discussed in Harold Netland, *Dissonant Voices* (Grand Rapids, Mich.: Eerdmans, 1991), pp. 205-206.
5. Tillich, *Systematic Theology*, p. 212.
6. See Netland's description of these religious traditions' conceptions of ultimate reality in *Dissonant Voices*, chapters 2–3.
7. Here I note that not all theologians use these terms synonymously. As the discussion progresses, I'll point out differences where appropriate. However, for the most part I shall use terms such as "model," "metaphor," "image," and "motif" to refer to ways of understanding or conceptualizing God's role and relationships in our universe.
8. D. Z. Phillips, "Philosophy, Theology and the Reality of God," in William Rowe and William Wainwright, eds., *Philosophy of Religion: Selected Readings* (New York: Harcourt Brace, 3d ed., 1998), p. 300.
9. Ludwig Feuerbach, *The Essence of Christianity*, trans. George Eliot (New York: Harper Torchbooks, 1957), pp. 12-13.
10. Ibid., p. 13.
11. Ibid., p. 25. See also Eugen Schoenfeld, "Images of God and Man: An Exploratory Study," *Review of Religious Research* 28 (March 1987); and Richard B. Miller, "The Reference of 'God'," *Faith Phil* 3 (January 1986): 8-9 for further discussions of Feuerbach's thesis.
12. Alasdair MacIntyre, "Freud, Sigmund," in *Encyclopedia of Philosophy*, vol. 3, Paul Edwards, ed. (New York: Macmillan, 1972): 251.
13. Miller, "Reference of 'God'," p. 9.
14. MacIntyre, "Freud, Sigmund," p. 251. For a detailed study of the impact of Freud's thinking on theology and theological responses to Freud, see Peter Homas, *Theology after Freud* (Indianapolis: Bobbs-Merrill, 1970). For a thorough analysis of Freud's thought, see Paul Ricoeur, *Freud and Philosophy: An Essay on Interpretation*, trans. Denis Savage (New Haven, Conn.: Yale University Press, 1970). For a more contemporary example of a thinker who sees God as a mental projection see Don Cupitt's *The Sea of Faith* (New York: Cambridge University Press, 1988).
15. See Helmut Hoping's helpful discussion on the difference between Being and God in Heidegger's thinking: Helmut Hoping, "Understanding the Difference of Being: On the Relationship Between Metaphysics and Theology," *The Thomist* 59 (1995): 208-214. See also Marjorie Greene's helpful article on Heidegger in "Heidegger, Martin," *Encyclopedia of Philosophy*, vol. 3, Paul Edwards, ed. (New York: Macmillan, 1972).
16. Tillich, *Systematic Theology*, pp. 234-236.
17. Ibid., pp. 186-189.
18. Ibid., p. 237.
19. Ibid., p. 239.
20. John Macquarrie, *Principles of Christian Theology* (New York: Scribners, 1966), pp. 98-102.

21. John Macquarrie, *Studies in Christian Existentialism* (Philadelphia: Westminster, 1965), pp. 89, 225; see also Macquarrie, *Principles of Christian Theology,* pp. 87, 99, 103-106, 110, 132, 183, 186, 194.

22. Tim Bradshaw, "Macquarrie's Doctrine of God," *Tyndale Bul* 44 (1993): 10.

23. O. C. Thomas, "Being and Some Theologians," *Harvard Theological Review* 70 (1977): 149. Thomas quotes Macquarrie, *Principles of Christian Theology,* p. 106.

24. For those interested in pursuing Macquarrie's views further, see his *God and Secularity* (London: Lutterworth Press, 1968); *Twentieth Century Religious Thought* (London: SCM, 1981); *In Search of Deity* (London: SCM, 1984); and *Thinking about God* (London: SCM, 1975). The articles by Bradshaw and Thomas are helpful secondary literature on Macquarrie's views.

25. Kees W. Bolle, "Animism and Animatism," in Mircea Eliade, ed., *The Encyclopedia of Religion,* vol. 1, (New York: Macmillan, 1987), p. 298.

26. I am indebted to Harold Netland (personal conversation) for this point about animism's relation to Japanese culture, etc.

27. Netland, *Dissonant Voices,* p. 42.

28. Ibid., p. 49.

29. Ibid., pp. 47-49.

30. Ibid., p. 48.

31. Ibid., p.101.

32. Ibid., p. 100. See also pp. 100-103 for further discussion of the Shinto *kami.*

33. Jean Hyppolite, *Genesis and Structure of Hegel's Phenomenology of Spirit* (Evanston, Ill.: Northwestern University Press, 1974), p. 324.

34. See Hans-Georg Gadamer, *Hegel's Dialectic* (New Haven, Conn.: Yale University Press, 1976), p. 107 for the relation of Spirit and Dialectic in Hegel.

35. Netland, *Dissonant Voices,* pp. 200-206. For elaboration of these views see John Hick, *God Has Many Names* (Philadelphia: Westminster, 1982); (ed.) *Truth and Dialogue in World Religions: Conflicting Truth-Claims* (Philadelphia: Westminster, 1974); and *An Interpretation of Religion.*

36. John Hick, *An Interpretation of Religion,* pp. 241-243, as cited in Netland, *Dissonant Voices,* p. 205. Gordon Kaufman is another contemporary theologian who has argued that God is an immaterial being, although he claims there isn't much more we can say about God in himself. See Kaufman's *The Theological Imagination: Constructing the Concept of God* (Philadelphia: Westminster, 1981). Kaufman distinguishes the word "God" and the reality *God* (p. 21). Relying on Kant, Kaufman explains that the reality *God* is not something we can know by inspection; we depend instead on the "the image of God" ("God") that our mind puts together (p. 21). Whereas in his earlier work he claimed that theological construction is a combination of the imagination working with divine revelation, in this book Kaufman argues that the concept of God is purely a product of imaginative construction. In fact, Kaufman believes this has always been so, but contends that theologians should recognize this and continue the task of constructing the concept of God with their eyes wide open to what they are doing. Though this sounds like God is nothing more than a concept, we must remember Kaufman's distinction between "God" and *God.* There is for him evidently an extra-mental reality that is God, though we are only in a position to construct imaginatively our notions of what that God is. See a helpful review and interaction with Kaufman by Garrett Green in *Relig Stud Rev* 9 (July 1983): 219-222; and another by Douglas F. Ottati, pp. 222-227 in the same journal.

37. For an interesting interchange over Jantzen's and Gaskin's views, see Charles Taliaferro, "The Incorporeality of God," *Mod Theol* 3 (1987); and Grace Jantzen, "Reply to Taliaferro," *Mod Theol* 3 (1987).

38. See Douglas Groothuis, *Unmasking the New Age* (Downers Grove, Ill.: InterVarsity, 1986), p. 18.

39. For further discussion of pantheism in its various forms see Colin Gunton, "Transcendence, Metaphor, and the Knowability of God," *JTS* 31 (October 1980): 505-507; and Douglas Hedley, "Pantheism, Trinitarian Theism and the Idea of Unity: Reflections on the Christian Concept of God," *Relig Stud* 32 (1996).

40. For a description of Ramanuja's views and endorsement of some of his ideas as helpful to Christian theism see Ninian Smart, "God's Body," *Union Seminary Quarterly Review* 37 (Fall/Winter 1981–1982).

41. Sallie McFague, *Models of God: Theology for an Ecological, Nuclear Age* (Philadelphia: Fortress, 1987), pp. xii, 61, 97.

42. Sallie McFague, "Response," *Religion & Intellectual Life* 5 (Spring 1988): 40. This response was given to other papers in a symposium published in the same issue of *Religion & Intellectual Life* as follows: Mary Jo Weaver, "A Discussion of Sallie McFague's *Models of God: Theology for an Ecological, Nuclear Age:* Introduction"; Gordon D. Kaufman, "*Models of God:* Is Metaphor Enough?"; Rosemary R. Ruether, "*Models of God:* Exploding the Foundations"; David Tracy, "*Models of God:* Three Observations"; and James Hart, "*Models of God:* Evangel-Logic."

43. Graham Ward, "Introduction, or, A Guide to Theological Thinking in Cyberspace," in Graham Ward, ed., *The Postmodern God: A Theological Reader* (Malden, Mass.: Blackwell Publishers, 1997), pp. xxviii-xxx.

44. Jean-Luc Marion, *God without Being* (Chicago: University of Chicago Press, 1991), p. xxiii.

45. Ibid., pp. xxi-xxiv.

46. Ian T. Ramsey, *Models and Mystery* (London: Oxford University Press, 1964), pp. 15-17. Ramsey's taxonomy is adopted and elaborated in Ruth Ann Haunz, "Development of Some Models of God and Suggested Relationships to James Fowler's Stages of Faith Development," *Religious Education* 73 (November–December 1978). Haunz uses "model" in the sense that I use "image," "motif" and "metaphor."

47. McFague, *Models of God*, chapter 5.

48. See Haunz, "Development of Some Models of God," pp. 643-645 for the general outline of these three main categories of images of God. I have adopted that scheme and expanded and elaborated it.

49. See Millard Erickson's helpful discussion of divine immanence in his *Christian Theology*, vol. 1 (Grand Rapids, Mich.: Baker, 1983), pp. 302-312.

50. Ibid., pp. 312-313. On pages 313-319 Erickson describes a series of systems that heavily stress divine transcendence.

51. In a comment on an earlier draft of this chapter, Kevin Vanhoozer writes that "many Barth scholars now deny that his mature thought is 'neo-orthodox.' It's pretty clear that Barth broke with others (e.g., Brunner, Gogarten) who are more appropriate bearers of this label. The serious point behind the nomenclature is that Barth moves away from paradox (but not dialectic) towards analogy: the analogy of faith."

52. Karl Barth, *Church Dogmatics*, vol. 1, part 1 (Edinburgh: T. & T. Clark, 1960), pp. 368-372. See also Søren Kierkegaard, *Philosophical Fragments* and *Concluding Unscientific Postscript* for similar views on Christ as the Absolute Paradox and as revealing God to us in the moment of encounter.

53. The models I shall present aren't the only possible ones, but they are the main ones most imping-ing upon evangelical thinking and attention in our day. For example, in a personal note Kevin Vanhoozer writes that "just as the 'openness' view qualifies the classical view, I think there is a 'Trinitarian panentheism' view that seeks to qualify the process view. . . . There may also be a 'postmodern' model that seeks to conceive the God/world relation other than with the category of being." As to this last point, we have already noted it as a fourth category in the taxonomy pre-sented to answer questions about God's reality.

54. John Sanders, "Historical Considerations," in Clark Pinnock, Richard Rice, John Sanders, William Hasker, and David Basinger, *The Openness of God* (Downers Grove, Ill.: InterVarsity, 1994), p. 69ff. For further elaboration of the various Greek influences and subsequent developments in Christian theology, see the remainder of Sanders's chapter. See also Georg Picht, "The God of the Philosophers," *Journal of the American Academy of Religion* 48 (1980): 72-78; Henry Jansen, "Moltmann's View of God's (Im)mutability: The God of the Philosophers and the God of the Bible," *Neue Zeitschrift für Systematische Theologie und Religionsphilosophie* 36 (1994); and William J. Hill, "The Historicity of God," *Theol Stud* 45 (1984).

55. Of course, infinity can be predicated of some attributes but doesn't seem to be applicable to others. For example, it applies to eternity, but not to aseity or simplicity.

56. Ronald Nash, *The Concept of God* (Grand Rapids, Mich.: Zondervan, 1983), pp. 19-22.

57. William Alston, "Hartshorne and Aquinas: A Via Media," in William P. Alston, *Divine Nature and Human Language: Essays in Philosophical Theology* (Ithaca, N.Y.: Cornell University Press, 1989).

58. Ibid., p. 123.

59. Ibid., p. 124.

60. Nash, *Concept of God*, p. 20.

61. Ibid., pp. 21-22; and Alston, "Hartshorne and Aquinas," p. 123.

62. Anselm, "Proslogium," chapter 8, pp. 13-14. Charles Hartshorne, *The Divine Relativity* (New Haven, Conn.: Yale University Press, 1948), p. 54, quotes this passage from Anselm.

63. Nash, *Concept of God*, p. 21. Of course, there is a major question as to which language about God is anthropomorphic and which is literal. I plan to take up this issue when discussing the being and attributes of God (part 2 of the book) and his providential control over the world (part 3).

64. Leibniz argued that God had to create a world and that it had to be the best. But this surely hasn't been the predominant opinion within the Christian tradition.

65. Alston, "Hartshorne and Aquinas," p. 123.

66. Ibid., p. 124.

67. Ibid., p. 123.

68. See William Hill, "Historicity of God," pp. 325-327, for an interesting discussion of the process God's temporal eternity.

69. Alston, "Hartshorne and Aquinas," p. 123.

70. See Haunz ("Development of Some Models of God"); and McFague (*Models of God*) for feminist views that are positively disposed toward the process God. See also David Griffin's revisionary postmodernism in David Griffin, William Beardslee, and Joe Holland, *Varieties of Postmodern Theology* (Albany, N.Y.: State University of New York Press, 1989) for another example of Whitehead's process theism put to contemporary use.

71. Clark Pinnock, Richard Rice, John Sanders, William Hasker, and David Basinger, "Preface," in Pinnock, et al., *Openness of God*, p. 9.

72. Ibid., pp. 8-9.

73. Richard Rice, "Biblical Support for a New Perspective," in ibid., p. 15.

74. Ibid.

75. Ibid., p. 23.

76. Ibid., pp. 27-33.

77. Ibid., p. 45.

78. Ibid., pp. 22-25.

79. Ibid., pp. 40-42.

80. Ibid., pp. 43-45.

81. William Hasker, "A Philosophical Perspective" in ibid., pp. 136-137.

82. David Basinger, "Practical Implications," in ibid., pp. 159, 170.

83. This is, for example, the conclusion John Sanders draws after his lengthy survey of OT materials which he believes support the open view of God. See John Sanders, *The God Who Risks* (Downers Grove, Ill.: InterVarsity, 1998), pp. 88-89.

84. See, for example, David Basinger, "Can an Evangelical Christian Justifiably Deny God's Exhaustive Knowledge of the Future?" *CSR* 25 (December 1995): 133-134.

85. Sanders, *God Who Risks*, pp. 230-235.

86. Rice, "Biblical Support for a New Perspective," p. 51.

87. Ibid.

88. Ibid.

89. Ibid.

90. Basinger, "Practical Implications," pp. 156-162.

91. Hasker, "Philosophical Perspective," p. 152. This position will immediately be recognized as the free will defense.

92. Ibid., pp. 140 and 152.

93. For another model that attempts to steer a mediating course between the two extremes, see William Alston's proposal in his "Aquinas and Hartshorne: A Via Media." Alston also holds libertarian free will, but does not go the exact route of the open view.

94. For a more complete discussion of theonomy, Leibnizian rationalism, and modified rationalism and their relation to the problem of evil, see my *The Many Faces of Evil* (Grand Rapids, Mich.: Zondervan, 1994), chapters 1-4. See also the last chapter of this book.

95. For some interesting discussion of this issue, see Richard B. Miller, "Reference of 'God'"; and Ronald Marshall, "In Between Ayer and Adler: God in Contemporary Philosophy," *Word & World* 2 (1982): 72-73.

96. See the symposium titled "Theology and Falsification," in Anthony Flew and Alasdair McIntyre, eds., *New Essays in Philosophical Theology* (New York: Macmillan, 1973). Also the work of the logical positivists gives further perspectives on this topic. See also the later philosophy of Wittgenstein, especially his *Lectures and Conversations on Aesthetics, Psychology and Religious Belief* (Berkeley: University of California Press, 1966). Noteworthy as well is R. B. Braithwaite's, "An Empiricist's View of the Nature of Religious Belief," in Basil Mitchell, ed., *The Philosophy of Religion* (Oxford: Oxford University Press, 1971); D. Z. Phillips, "The Friends of Cleanthes," *Mod Theol* 1 (January 1985); and "The Friends of Cleanthes: A Correction," *Mod Theol* 3 (1987).

97. Baruch Brody, "Part Introduction and Bibliographical Notes" (on God's Attributes) in Baruch Brody, ed., *Readings in the Philosophy of Religion: An Analytic Approach* (2d ed.) (Englewood Cliffs, N.J.: Prentice-Hall, 1992), p. 330.

98. William Alston, "Can We Speak Literally of God?" in Axel D. Steuer and James McClendon, Jr., eds., *Is God God?* (Nashville: Abingdon, 1981), p. 147, as cited in Michael P. Levine, "Can We Speak Literally of God?" *Relig Stud* 21 (1985): 54.

99. Alston writes, "It is rather a question of whether any such truth-claim can succeed. . . . what is being denied is that any predicate term, used literally, can be *truly applied* to God, or, as we might say, that any predicate is *literally true* of God." Alston, "Can We Speak Literally of God?" p. 147, quoted in Levine, "Can We Speak Literally of God?" p. 53.

100. John Whittaker, "Literal and Figurative Language of God," *Relig Stud* 17 (1981): 39. See also Levine, "Can We Speak Literally of God?" pp. 56-57.

101. Netland, *Dissonant Voices*, pp. 133-137.

102. Ibid., pp. 138-141.

103. Ibid., p. 138.

104. Ibid. See also Michael Durrant, "The Meaning of 'God'—I," in Martin Warner, ed. *Religion and Philosophy*, Royal Institute of Philosophy Supplement 31 (Cambridge: Cambridge University Press, 1992), pp. 74-75 for a further critique of the ineffability thesis which also argues that it is self-defeating.

105. See Maimonides, "Negative Predication," in Brody, ed., *Readings in the Philosophy of Religion,* p. 338.
106. A. H. Armstrong, "On Not Knowing Too Much about God," in Godfrey Vesey, *The Philosophy in Christianity* (Cambridge: Cambridge University Press, 1989), pp. 134-140.
107. See, for example, Wentzel van Huysteen, *Theology and the Justification of Faith* (Grand Rapids, Mich.: Eerdmans, 1989); and Sallie McFague, *Models of God.* Also the symposium on McFague's book in *Religion & Intellectual Life 5* (Spring 1988) seems to agree with this assessment. See also Elizabeth Johnson, *She Who Is: The Mystery of God in Feminist Theological Discourse* (New York: Crossroad, 1993).
108. I have made this point in some detail in a review of van Huysteen's book. See John Feinberg, "Rationality, Objectivity, and Doing Theology: Review and Critique of Wentzel van Huysteen's *Theology and the Justification of Faith,*" *Trin J* 10NS (Fall 1989): 161-184. See also John H. Whittaker, "Literal and Figurative Language of God," pp. 39-40; and William P. Alston, "Being-Itself and Talk about God," *Center Journal* 3 (Summer 1984) who also make this point very convincingly.
109. Thomas Aquinas, "Analogical Predication," in Baruch Brody, ed., *Readings in the Philosophy of Religion,* p. 345.
110. Ibid., p. 346.
111. Ibid.
112. William Alston, "Functionalism and Theological Language," in Brody, ed., *Readings in the Philosophy of Religion.* See also Alston's other helpful articles on theological language in his *Divine Nature and Human Language: Essays in Philosophical Theology* (Ithaca, N.Y.: Cornell University Press, 1989), chapters 1–2, 4-5.
113. Alston, "Functionalism and Theological Language," p. 348.
114. Ibid., p. 349.
115. Ibid.
116. Ibid.
117. Ibid., p. 350.
118. Ibid., p. 353 (see also p. 350).
119. Ibid., p. 351.
120. Ibid., p. 354.
121. Ibid., p. 355.
122. Ibid., p. 361.

C H A P T E R   3

1. Anyone unconvinced of this in regard to historic evangelical Christian theology needs only to read Diogenes Allen's *Philosophy for Understanding Theology* (Atlanta: John Knox, 1985) to disabuse himself of that notion.
2. William Beardslee, "Christ in the Postmodern Age: Reflections Inspired by Jean-François Lyotard," in David Griffin, William Beardslee, and Joe Holland, *Varieties of Postmodern Theology* (Albany, N.Y.: State University of New York Press, 1989), p. 63.
3. Jürgen Habermas, "Modernity—an Incomplete Project," in Hal Foster, *Postmodern Culture* (London and Sydney: Pluto, 1985), p. 9.
4. Langdon Gilkey, *Naming the Whirlwind: The Renewal of God-Language* (Indianapolis: Bobbs-Merrill, 1969), pp. 32-34, 40, 48, 53, 57-58.
5. Nancey Murphy and James W. McClendon, Jr., "Distinguishing Modern and Postmodern Theologies," *Mod Theol 5* (April 1989): 192-199. See also Nancey Murphy, "Philosophical Resources for Postmodern Evangelical Theology," *CSR* 26 (Winter 1996).
6. Charles Davis, "Our Modern Identity: The Formation of the Self," *Mod Theol* 6 (January 1990): 165.
7. Immanuel Kant, *Critique of Pure Reason,* trans. Norman Kemp Smith (New York: St. Martin's, 1965), pp. 257-275.
8. Ibid., p. 41.
9. See Alvin Plantinga, "Reason and Belief in God," in Alvin Plantinga and Nicholas Wolterstorff, eds., *Faith and Rationality* (Notre Dame, Ind.: University of Notre Dame Press, 1984), pp. 24-34. See also Kelly James Clark, *Return to Reason* (Grand Rapids, Mich.: Eerdmans, 1990), p. 5.
10. See Plantinga, "Reason and Belief in God," pp. 55-59; and Clark, *Return to Reason,* pp. 134-135.
11. David Griffin, "Postmodern Theology as Liberation Theology: A Response to Harvey Cox," in Griffin, Beardslee, and Holland, *Varieties of Postmodern Theology,* p. 85.
12. Metaphysics traditionally includes topics such as God, freedom, and immortality, but none of these is an object of sense, so according to Kant's classification, they would all be noumena and hence not objects of knowledge.
13. Murphy and McClendon, "Distinguishing Modern and Postmodern Theologies," p. 193. See also A. J. Ayer, *Language, Truth and Logic* (New York: Dover, Prentice-Hall, 1964), chapters 1 and 6.

14. See Ludwig Wittgenstein, *Tractatus Logico-Philosophicus* (London: Routledge & Kegan Paul, 1971), 5.6, p. 149; 7, p. 189; and 6.522, p. 187.

15. For some, a proposition is the thing a sentence is about. Hence, in this ontology there exists between language and the world the proposition which links the two. Even if a sentence isn't an assertion, it is still about some propositional idea, and it is possible to see what the sentence says about the proposition and to see whether the proposition matches things in our world.

16. Murphy and McClendon ("Distinguishing Modern and Postmodern Theologies," p. 194) call such theories expressivist or emotivist. See their whole discussion (pp. 193-196) of the various theories of language used by moderns. See also Murphy, "Philosophical Resources for Postmodern Evangelical Theology," pp. 188-190.

17. See, for example, R. B. Braithwaite, "An Empiricist's View of the Nature of Religious Belief," in Basil Mitchell, ed., *The Philosophy of Religion* (Oxford: Oxford University Press, 1971), pp. 79-80.

18. Griffin, "Postmodern Theology as Liberation Theology," pp. 85-86.

19. Ibid.

20. Ibid.

21. Joe Holland, "The Postmodern Paradigm and Contemporary Catholicism," in Griffin, Beardslee, and Holland, *Varieties of Postmodern Theology*, p. 15 and also p. 12. See also William Edgar, "No News Is Good News: Modernity, The Postmodern, and Apologetics," *WTJ* 57 (1995): 364.

22. David Tracy, "Theology and the Many Faces of Postmodernity," *Theol Today* 51 (April 1994): 104.

23. Murphy, "Philosophical Resources for Postmodern Evangelical Theology," p. 190.

24. Holland, "Postmodern Paradigm," p. 11.

25. Tracy, "Theology and the Many Faces of Postmodernity," p. 105.

26. Holland, "Postmodern Paradigm," p. 10.

27. Tracy, "Theology and the Many Faces of Postmodernity," p. 105.

28. See, for example, Michael Denton, *Evolution: A Theory in Crisis* (Bethesda, Md.: Adler & Adler, 1985); and Phillip Johnson, *Darwin on Trial* (Downers Grove, Ill.: InterVarsity, 1991).

29. Holland, "Postmodern Paradigm," p. 12.

30. Griffin, "Postmodern Theology as Liberation Theology," p. 86.

31. See, for example, the helpful discussion of postmodern themes in art, architecture, literature, and more broadly in popular culture in Todd Gitlin, "The Postmodern Predicament," *The Wilson Quarterly* 13 (Summer 1989).

32. David Griffin, "Introduction to SUNY Series in Constructive Postmodern Thought," in Griffin, Beardslee, and Holland, *Varieties of Postmodern Theology*, p. xii.

33. Clive Marsh, "Postmodernism: What Is It, and Does It Matter?" *Epworth Review* 21 (1994): 44-45. Marsh finds very helpful a summary by James Miller in Miller's, "The Emerging Postmodern World," in F. B. Burnham, ed., *Postmodern Theology* (San Francisco: Harper, 1989).

34. For a very helpful overview of postmodernism and the postmodern God, see Graham Ward, "Introduction, or, A Guide to Theological Thinking in Cyberspace," in Graham Ward, ed., *The Postmodern God* (Malden, Mass.: Blackwell, 1997).

35. Michel Foucault, *The Order of Things: An Archaeology of the Human Sciences* (New York: Vintage, 1973), p. xxiii.

36. Davis, "Our Modern Identity," p. 164. For further confirmation of this interpretation of Foucault, see James M. Byrne, "Foucault on Continuity: The Postmodern Challenge to Tradition," *Faith Phil* 9 (July 1992): 335-336.

37. In an interesting article, Wentzel van Huysteen asks whether postmoderns are postfoundationalists. The gist of the article is that postmoderns should be postfoundationalists, but that doesn't mean they all are. Van Huysteen offers some examples of theologians who claim to be postmodern but still hold onto some form of foundationalism. See J. Wentzel van Huysteen, "Is the Postmodernist Always a Postfoundationalist? Nancey Murphy's Lakatosian Model for Theology," in J. Wentzel van Huysteen, *Essays in Postfoundationalist Theology* (Grand Rapids, Mich.: Eerdmans, 1997).

38. Thomas Kuhn, *The Structure of Scientific Revolutions*, 2d ed. (Chicago: University of Chicago Press, 1970). See chapter 3-4 and especially chapter 5 where Kuhn discusses the role of scientific paradigms in the work of the scientist.

39. Ibid., chapters 7–10.

40. How well I remember, during doctoral studies in philosophy at the University of Chicago in the early 1970s, sitting in classes and hearing professors critique Kuhn's work, pointing out its many flaws. Hearing such clear-cut objections, one takes it for granted that others will see the same problems and reject it. Much to my surprise and consternation, however, within a decade of finishing my doctoral work I could tell that this view was deemed "orthodox" by a large segment of the philosophical community.

41. Richard Rorty, *Philosophy and the Mirror of Nature* (Princeton: Princeton University Press, 1979), p. 12.

42. W. V. O. Quine, "Two Dogmas of Empiricism," cited in Murphy and McClendon, "Distinguishing Modern and Postmodern Theologies," p. 200. This essay is anthologized in W. V. O. Quine, *From a Logical Point of View: Logico-Philosophical Essays* (New York: Harper Torchbooks, 1963).

43. See my article on theories of truth for further explanation of these various theories of truth: "Truth: Relationship of Theories of Truth to Hermeneutics," in Earl Radmacher and Robert Preus, eds., *Hermeneutics, Inerrancy, and The Bible* (Grand Rapids, Mich.: Zondervan, 1984).

44. See the interesting discussion of truth between Richard Rorty, Alvin Plantinga, and Nicholas Wolterstorff. In *Philosophy and the Mirror of Nature* Rorty, in rejecting foundationalism and the correspondence notion of truth, said in defining truth that "truth is what your peers will let you get away with." Plantinga takes him to task for this. Rorty replies, "I do not think that you can define 'truth,' either as what your peers will let you get away with, or as correspondence with the intrinsic nature of reality, or as anything else. 'True,' like the word 'good,' is a primitive predicate, a transcendental term which does not lend itself to definition." See page 180 in Stephen Louthan, "On Religion—A Discussion with Richard Rorty, Alvin Plantinga, and Nicholas Wolterstorff," *CSR* 26 (Winter 1996). This certainly is of little help, but also suggests why the door is so open to pragmatism, and Plantinga continues to chide Rorty, in light of his retraction, for saying that "truth is what your peers will let you get away with" (p. 180).

45. Lyotard as cited in Edgar, "No News is Good News," pp. 373-374. Huston Smith argues that among postmoderns there are three versions of how to view narratives. What he calls *minimal* postmodernism claims that today no accepted worldview exists. *Mainline* postmodernism argues that we will never again have such an authoritative meta-narrative, for now that we understand how the mind works, we recognize the impossibility of an accurate universal worldview. Finally, *hardcore* postmodernism not only agrees with the mainline position but adds that it is "good riddance" that worldviews are gone, for they absolutize and in doing so oppress and marginalize minorities who don't fit the predominant structures the worldview puts in place. In contrast, Smith argues that worldviews are something we need, it is possible to form valid ones, and valid worldviews already exist in the world's great enduring religious traditions. See Huston Smith, "The Religious Significance of Postmodernism: A Rejoinder," *Faith Phil* 12 (July 1995).

46. Diogenes Allen, "Christianity and the Creed of Postmodernism," *CSR* 23 (1993): 118-119.

47. Ibid., p. 119.

48. Ludwig Wittgenstein, *Philosophical Investigations* (New York: Macmillan, 1968), sec. 43, p. 20e.

49. Ibid., sec. 23, pp. 11e-12e.

50. For further helpful discussions of postmodern epistemology see Allen, "Christianity and the Creed of Postmodernism"; Gary Percesepe, "The Unbearable Lightness of Being Postmodern," *CSR* 20 (September 1990); and Kevin Vanhoozer and Andrew Kirk, eds. *To Stake a Claim: Mission and the Western Crisis of Knowledge* (Maryknoll, N.Y.: Orbis, 1999). For an excellent and extensive handling of the hermeneutical issues associated with postmodernism, especially in relation to interpreting literary texts, including Scripture, see Kevin J. Vanhoozer's, *Is There a Meaning in the Text?* (Grand Rapids, Mich.: Zondervan, 1998).

51. Murphy, "Philosophical Resources for Postmodern Evangelical Theology," p. 193.

52. See Clive Marsh's helpful discussion of evolution and relativity in postmodern thinking, and their relation to postmodern theologies in "Postmodernism: What Is It, and Does It Matter?" pp. 45-49.

53. See, for example, John W. Montgomery to this effect in making his case for the miraculous (John W. Montgomery, *Where Is History Going?* [Minneapolis: Bethany Fellowship, 1969], p. 71).

54. David Griffin, "Postmodern Theology and A/Theology: A Response to Mark C. Taylor," in Griffin, Beardslee, and Holland, *Varieties of Postmodern Theology,* p. 45ff.

55. Ronald J. Allen, "As the Wordviews Turn: Six Key Issues for Preaching in a Postmodern Ethos," *Encounter* 57 (Winter 1996): 33.

56. See Emil Fackenheim's excellent discussion of the relation of religion to Hegel's philosophy in his *The Religious Dimension in Hegel's Thought* (Boston: Beacon, 1967), chapter 5.

57. G. W. F. Hegel, *The Phenomenology of Spirit* (New York: Harper & Row, 1967), pp. 251-267.

58. Fackenheim, *The Religious Dimension in Hegel's Thought,* pp. 120-149. Fackenheim cites various passages in Hegel's *Philosophy of Religion* and other works.

59. Interested readers may also want to investigate Hegel's concept of the Trinity. He held what he called a double-Trinity. See Fackenheim, *The Religious Dimension in Hegel's Thought,* pp. 149-159 for explanation of this notion.

60. Richard R. Niebuhr, "Schleiermacher, Friedrich Daniel Ernst," *Encyclopedia of Philosophy* vol. 7 (New York: Macmillan, 1972), p. 318.

61. Ibid.

62. Ibid.

63. Ibid. For a further discussion of Schleiermacher's theology see Eugene F. Klug, "The Roots of Theological Liberalism," *Concordia Theological Quarterly* 44 (1980): 220-221.

64. Gilkey, *Naming the Whirlwind,* pp. 74-75.

65. Ibid., p. 75.

66. Ibid.

67. Ibid.
68. Ibid., p. 76.
69. Ibid., pp. 76-77. For further helpful discussions on liberal theology see Eugene Klug, "Roots of Theological Liberalism"; Gerald Parsons, "Reforming the Tradition: A Forgotten Dimension of Liberal Protestantism," *Religion* 13 (1983): 257-271; Curtis W. Reese, "The Content of Religious Liberalism," *Relig Hum* 25 (Summer 1991): 140-144; and Bernard Ramm, "The Fortunes of Theology from Schleiermacher to Barth and Bultmann," in Stan Gundry and Alan Johnson, eds. *Tensions in Contemporary Theology* (Chicago: Moody, 1976), especially pages 31-32 on liberal theology's doctrine of God.
70. Tolerance and respect for all people and all viewpoints is also a hallmark of postmodernity, but for somewhat different reasons. The emphasis on individual freedom is part of the point, but a major reason for postmodern tolerance is the belief that no one has the grand narrative which tells all of us who is right and who is wrong. Since we all are products of our time and culture and aren't in a position to know absolute truth, and since the world has become more crowded and peoples and cultures have much closer contact with one another than in earlier centuries, if we are to avoid constant wars over beliefs that would fragment societies, tolerance of all views is the only sane option.
71. Søren Kierkegaard, *Philosophical Fragments* (Princeton: Princeton University Press, 1971), chapter 1.
72. Søren Kierkegaard, *Concluding Unscientific Postscript* (Princeton: Princeton University Press, 1971), pp. 86-88.
73. Kierkegaard, *Fragments*, pp. 16-22.
74. Søren Kierkegaard, *Fear and Trembling* (Princeton: Princeton University Press, 1970), pp. 46-57.
75. Kierkegaard, *Postscript*, chapter 1, especially secs. 1 and 3.
76. Ramm, "Fortunes of Theology," p. 36.
77. Karl Barth, *Church Dogmatics*, vol. 1, part 1 (Edinburgh: T. & T. Clark, 1960), pp. 98-137.
78. Ibid., p. 368.
79. Ibid., p. 363.
80. Ibid., p. 369.
81. Ibid.
82. I am indebted to Kevin Vanhoozer for these distinctions between Barth's earlier and later thought.
83. Paul Tillich, *Systematic Theology*, vol. 1 (Chicago: University of Chicago Press, 1971), pp. 62-64.
84. Ibid., p. 163.
85. Ibid., p. 211ff.
86. Ibid., pp. 235-239.
87. Paul Tillich, *Systematic Theology*, vol. 2, pp. 118-119.
88. Ibid., pp. 118-135.
89. Moritz Schlick, "Meaning and Verification," in H. Feigel and W. Sellars, eds., *Readings in Philosophical Analysis* (New York: Appleton-Century-Crofts, 1949), p. 148.
90. Friedrich Nietzsche, *The Gay Science* (New York: Vintage, 1974), book 3, sec. 125, p. 180.
91. William Hamilton and Thomas J. J. Altizer, *Radical Theology and the Death of God* (Indianapolis: Bobbs-Merrill, 1966), pp. 24-25.
92. Thomas J. J. Altizer, *The Gospel of Christian Atheism* (Philadelphia: Westminster, 1966), p. 15.
93. Ibid., p. 16.
94. Ibid., pp. 16-17.
95. Altizer quotes Nietzsche's *The Antichrist* to make his point (ibid., pp 21-22).
96. Ibid., pp. 40-41.
97. Ibid., pp. 43-44.
98. For example, p. 51, 52 (middle), 67, 68-69.
99. See p. 67, first full paragraph. See also pp. 68 (last paragraph)-69.
100. See pp. 71-72.
101. Ibid., pp. 73-74.
102. Ibid., pp. 103 (bottom)-104.
103. George Lindbeck, *The Nature of Doctrine: Religion and Theology in a Postliberal Age* (Philadelphia: Westminster, 1984), p. 16.
104. Ibid., pp. 17-18.
105. Ibid., p. 33.
106. Ibid., pp. 47-48.
107. Ibid., p. 64.
108. Ibid., p. 65.
109. Ibid.
110. Ibid., p. 67.
111. Ibid., p. 51.

112. For further discussion of Lindbeck's book see Murphy, "Philosophical Resources for Postmodern Evangelical Theology," pp. 197-199; Murphy and McClendon, "Distinguishing Modern and Postmodern Theologies," pp. 205-207; and Bradford E. Hinze's and George P. Schner's separate reviews of Lindbeck's book in *Relig Stud Rev* 21 (October 1995): 299-304 and 304-310 respectively.

113. Jürgen Moltmann, *Theology of Hope* (New York: Harper & Row, 1975), pp. 25-26.

114. Ibid., p. 143.

115. Carl Braaten, *The Future of God* (New York: Harper & Row, 1969), p. 69.

116. Ibid., p. 73. See also pp. 66-71 on Jesus and the power of the future. See also Moltmann, *Theology of Hope*, p. 194, for a similar interpretation of the resurrection's significance.

117. Moltmann, *Theology of Hope*, p. 21. See also pages 327-330.

118. Ibid., p. 335.

119. Harvey Cox as cited in David Griffin, "Postmodern Theology as Liberation Theology," pp. 83-84.

120. For an excellent description of and discussion of People's Theology, see Peter Beyerhaus, *God's Kingdom and the Utopian Error* (Wheaton, Ill.: Crossway, 1992), chapter 6.

121. Gustavo Gutiérrez, *A Theology of Liberation* (Maryknoll, N.Y.: Orbis, 1973).

122. Ibid., pp. 1-11.

123. Ibid., pp. 33-37.

124. Ibid., p. 195.

125. Ibid., pp. 197-202.

126. Ralph Moel, "North American Responses to Liberation Theology," *Currents in Theology and Mission* 7 (1980): 224. A small sampling of other works on liberation theology includes Juan Luis Segundo, *The Liberation of Theology* (Maryknoll, N.Y.: Orbis, 1976); J. Andrew Kirk, *Liberation Theology: An Evangelical View From the Third World* (Atlanta: John Knox, 1979); David R. Griffin, "North Atlantic and Latin American Liberation Theologians," *Encounter* 40 (1979); and Tom Hanks, "Liberation Theology after 25 Years: Passe or Mainstream?" *Anvil* 10 (1993).

127. Mary Catherine Hilkert, "Feminist Theology: A Review of Literature," *Theol Stud* 56 (1995): 328.

128. See, for example, Anne Carr's helpful attempts to demonstrate that it is possible to stay within Christianity and be a feminist by reforming the tradition. Anne Carr, "Is a Christian Feminist Theology Possible?" *Theol Stud* 43 (June 1982).

129. See Elizabeth A. Johnson, *She Who Is: The Mystery of God in Feminist Theological Discourse* (New York: Crossroad, 1993), p. 10ff. for the distinction between the two kinds of feminist theologies, and her identification of her own theology as reformist.

130. It might be helpful to list some of the many books and articles that elaborate feminist theology in one form or another. One of the more important books is Elisabeth Schüssler Fiorenza's *In Memory of Her: A Feminist Theological Reconstruction of Christian Origins* (New York: Crossroad, 1992). See also Sallie McFague, *Models of God: Theology for an Ecological, Nuclear Age* (Philadelphia: Fortress, 1987); and the symposium on her book in *Religion & Intellectual Life* 5 (Spring 1988) by Gordon Kaufman, Rosemary Ruether, David Tracy, James G. Hart, and McFague.

    For general overviews of feminist theology in its various forms see Rosemary Radford Ruether, "The Feminist Critique in Religious Studies," *Soundings* 64 (1981); Deane W. Ferm, "Feminist Theology in America," *SJT* 34 (1981); Betty Talbert-Wettler, "Secular Feminist Religious Metaphor and Christianity," *JETS* 38 (March 1995); Letha D. Scanzoni, "Reflections on Two Decades of Christian Feminism," *Daughters of Sarah* 20 (Fall 1994); and Carolyn Sharp, "The Emergence of Francophone Feminist Theology," *Studies in Religion* 25 (1996).

    For a work discussing feminist theology in light of the threefold taxonomy of religions set forth in George Lindbeck's *The Nature of Doctrine*, see Linell E. Cady, "Theories of Religion in Feminist Theologies," *American Journal of Theology & Philosophy* 13 (September 1992).

    For literature discussing feminist theology in relation to process theology, see Nancy Frankenberry, "Classical Theism, Panentheism, and Pantheism: On the Relation Between God Construction and Gender Construction," *Zygon* 28 (March 1993); Timothy Liau, "Biblical Concept of God in Light of Feminist and Process Critiques," *Taiwan Journal of Theology* 14 (March 1992); and a set of articles in one edition of *Process Studies* concentrating on a blending of feminist and process themes and issues as follows: Nancy R. Howell, "Feminism and Process Thought"; Kathlyn A. Breazeale, "Don't Blame It on the Seeds: Toward a Feminist Process Understanding of Anthropology, Sin, and Sexuality"; Ann Pederson, "Forensic Justification: A Process Feminist Critique and Construction"; and Heather Ann Ackley Bean, "Eating God: Beyond a Cannibalizing Christology"; all of these appeared in *Process Stud* 22 (Summer 1993). See also a special edition of the journal *Pacifica* 10 (June 1997), the overall theme of which is "Feminist Theology: The Next Stage," ed. Dorothy Lee and Muriel Porter. Articles include Dorothy Lee, "Abiding in the Fourth Gospel: A Case-Study in Feminist Biblical Theology"; Patricia Moss, "Unravelling the Threads: The Origins of Women's Asceticism in the Earliest Christian Communities"; Elaine Wainwright, "'But Who Do You Say That I Am?' An Australian Feminist Response"; Graeme Garrett, "Rule 4? Gender Difference and the Nature of Doctrine"; Denis Edwards, "Evolution and the God of Mutual Friendship"; Maryanne Confoy, "The Procrustean Bed of Women's Spirituality: Reclaiming Women's Sexuality as an Integral Aspect of Christian Spirituality"; and Elisabeth S. Fiorenza, "Struggle is a Name for Hope: A Critical Feminist Interpretation for Liberation."

For more on whether feminism can fit with Christianity, see Rosemary Ruether's critique of Daphne Hampson's proposal that it cannot: Rosemary Ruether, "Is Feminism the End of Christianity? A Critique of Daphne Hampson's *Theology and Feminism*," *SJT* 43 (1990). For reviews of Elizabeth Johnson's *She Who Is*, see Harold Wells, "Review Article: *She Who Is: The Mystery of God in Feminist Theological Discourse*," *Touchstone* 13 (January, 1995); and two reviews by Mary Aquin O'Neill and Mary McClintock Fulkerson, respectively. Those appeared in *Relig Stud Rev* 21 (January 1995). This is but a small sampling of contemporary literature in feminist theology.

131. Johnson, *She Who Is*, p. 5.
132. Ibid., p. 6.
133. Ibid., p. 7.
134. Ibid., p. 18.
135. Ibid., p. 21.
136. On pages 23-24 Johnson defines these terms, and in the following pages offers illustrations of how Christianity is guilty of such things and has negatively affected women socially, politically, ecclesiastically, and theologically.
137. Johnson, *She Who Is*, p. 25.
138. Ibid., p. 33.
139. Ibid., pp. 47-48.
140. Ibid., pp. 47-49.
141. Ibid., p. 49.
142. Ibid., p. 50.
143. Ibid., pp. 54-55.
144. Ibid., p. 77.
145. See Elisabeth S. Fiorenza, *In Memory of Her*, chapter 1 for a discussion of feminist hermeneutics.
146. Johnson, *She Who Is*, pp. 86-87.
147. Ibid., pp. 94-97.
148. See ibid., pp. 100 and 101 for Johnson's discussion of biblical talk of God in terms of language of female mothering.
149. Ibid., pp. 133-148.
150. Ibid., p. 150.
151. Ibid., pp. 157-158.
152. Ibid., pp. 161-166.
153. Ibid., pp. 170-185. See her comments especially on pp. 185-186 about what the maternal metaphor adds to our understanding of God.
154. Ibid., chapters 10–12.
155. Douglas Groothuis, *Unmasking the New Age* (Downers Grove, Ill.: InterVarsity, 1986), p. 19.
156. Ibid., p. 20.
157. Ibid., p. 21. See further quotes from New Age thinkers to this effect as well, cited by Groothuis on pp. 21-22.
158. Ibid., p. 25. See pp. 22-25 for summary and discussion of these various methods.
159. Ibid., pp. 28-29. For a detailed explanation of the New Age understandings of Jesus, see Groothuis's *Revealing the New Age Jesus* (Downers Grove, Ill.: InterVarsity, 1990).
160. Quoted in ibid., p. 29.
161. Ibid.
162. See ibid., pp. 132-155 for a description and discussion of these various forms of New Age spirituality.
163. Alfred N. Whitehead, *Process and Reality* (New York: Macmillan, 1929).
164. See the interesting articles (cited in note 130 above) in the symposium in *Pacifica* 10 (June 1997). In these articles various feminist theologians creatively set forth their version of different areas of Christian theology, which blends their own feminism with process doctrines.
165. See Joe Holland's discussions of Pope John Paul II's theology in "The Cultural Vision of Pope John Paul II: Toward a Conservative/Liberal Postmodern Dialogue" in Griffin, Beardslee, and Holland, *Varieties of Postmodern Theology*.
166. See John Caputo, ed., *Deconstruction in a Nutshell: A Conversation with Jacques Derrida* (New York: Fordham University Press, 1997). This book is very helpful in clearing up various misunderstandings of Derrida. One of its most helpful aspects is its inclusion of a conversation with Derrida and several professors at Villanova University, and then a lengthy commentary by Caputo on the conversation and on Derrida's views. Caputo tells us that before submitting the final manuscript for publication he showed it to Derrida, and Derrida approved of its contents. See also John Caputo, "The Good News about Alterity: Derrida and Theology," *Faith Phil* 10 (October 1993).
167. Griffin, "Postmodern Theology and A/Theology," p. 31.

168. Ibid., p. 32.
169. Ibid., pp. 32-33.
170. Ibid., p. 33.
171. Ibid.
172. Ibid., p. 34.
173. Ibid.
174. Ibid.
175. Ibid. As Graham Ward says ("Guide to Theological Thinking in Cyberspace," p. xliii), there are two ways to respond to the postmodern situation. One is the primrose path of nihilism which leads to various forms of self-indulgence. The other is the response of faith. But, given the postmodern critique of truth and knowledge, it is hard to see the path of faith as very attractive.
176. Griffin, "Postmodern Theology and A/Theology," pp. 41-42.
177. Ibid., pp. 42-43.
178. Ibid., p. 45.
179. Ibid., pp. 48-49. Griffin further explains how such a God allows us to escape moral relativism (pp. 49-50). Moreover, this God allows us to speak about "the truth" of things (p. 50), but this God does not know the truth about the future, nor can we (p. 50). Finally, Griffin discusses a meaning and purpose to history, but it is not one that includes supernaturalistic theism's commitment to a center of history or an eschatological destiny. For Griffin's understanding of the meaning and purpose of history, see p. 51.
180. For excellent discussions of and critique of Hick's views see Harold Netland, *Dissonant Voices* (Grand Rapids, Mich.: Eerdmans, 1991), chapter 6; and Robert McKim, "Could God Have More Than One Nature?" *Faith Phil* 5 (October 1988).

C H A P T E R   4

1. Portions of this chapter appeared as an article by the author, "Process Theology," in *The Evangelical Review of Theology* 14, no. 4 (October 1990): 291-334. Used by permission.
2. For examples of contemporary attempts either to wed process theology with another contemporary theology or at least to show its similarities and affinities with other contemporary conceptions of God, see: Michael Vertin, "Is God in Process?" in Timothy Fallon and Philip Riley, eds., *Religion and Culture: Essays in Honor of Bernard Lonergan, S. J.* (Albany, N.Y.: State University of New York Press, 1987); June O'Connor, "Process Theology and Liberation Theology: Theological and Ethical Reflections," *Horizons* 7 (1980); William Dean, "Deconstruction and Process Theology," *J Relig* 64 (1984); John B. Cobb, Jr., "Two Types of Postmodernism: Deconstruction and Process," *Theol Today* 47 (July 1990); Timothy Liau, "Biblical Concept of God in Light of Feminist and Process Critiques," *Taiwan Journal of Theology* 14 (March 1992). See also the following articles in a special issue of *Process Stud* 22 (Summer 1993) devoted to Feminism and Process Thought: Nancy R. Howell, "Feminism and Process Thought"; Kathlyn A. Breazeale, "Don't Blame It on the Seeds: Toward a Feminist Process Understanding of Anthropology, Sin, and Sexuality"; Ann Pederson, "Forensic Justification: A Process Feminist Critique and Construction"; and Heather Ann Ackley Bean, "Eating God: Beyond a Cannibalizing Christology." See also Nancy Frankenberry, "Classical Theism, Panentheism, and Pantheism: On the Relation Between God Construction and Gender Construction," *Zygon* 28 (March 1993).
3. For an interesting discussion of some of the ways evangelicals have tried to accommodate themselves to process theology see Randall Basinger, "Evangelicals and Process Theism: Seeking a Middle Ground," *CSR* 15 (December 1986). Of course, since Basinger wrote this article, he and others who have promoted the open view of God have made further overtures to process thinking without entirely capitulating to it. Suffice it to say that, from many evangelical quarters, attempts at rapprochement continue.
4. Alfred N. Whitehead, *Religion in the Making* (New York: Macmillan, 1926), p. 50.
5. As Lewis Ford explains, originally Whitehead didn't intend to include the notion of God in his system, but found it necessary to shore up his metaphysical scheme. Ford further argues that once Whitehead decided to include God, he didn't immediately conceive of God in personal terms. Nonetheless, during Whitehead's composition of *Process and Reality,* he came to the conclusion that it was necessary to conceive of God as personal, and so introduced that idea. For an explanation of the process leading Whitehead to these views see Lewis S. Ford, "When Did Whitehead Conceive God to Be Personal?" *Anglican Theological Review* 72 (1990).
6. Norman Pittenger, "Understanding the World and the Faith," *Theology* 90 (1987): 179-180. Bernard Loomer ("Process Theology: Origins, Strengths, Weaknesses," *Process Stud* 16 [Winter 1987], p. 245) claims that though others have attributed the origin of the term to him, if he did originate it, he is not pleased with it. He prefers the designation "process/relational thought."
7. Loomer, "Process Theology," pp. 248-249.
8. Victor Lowe, "Whitehead's Metaphysical System," in Delwin Brown, Ralph James, Jr., and Gene Reeves, eds., *Process Philosophy and Christian Thought* (Indianapolis: Bobbs-Merrill, 1971), pp. 24-25, suggests that ultimately the influence of John Dewey with his emphasis on empiricism and

pragmatism was greater on Wieman than that of Whitehead. It is safe to say that the empirical approach to process thought has been more inclined in this pragmatic direction. For an excellent detailed discussion of the origin of process theology and the different directions of the empirical and rationalist strands within it, see Bernard Meland's discussion of the empirical tradition of theology at the University of Chicago in Bernard Meland, "Introduction: The Empirical Tradition in Theology at Chicago," in Bernard Meland, ed., *The Future of Empirical Theology* (Chicago: University of Chicago Press, 1969).

9. Ivor Leclerc, "The Problem of God in Whitehead's System," *Process Stud* 14 (Winter 1985): 303.

10. Ibid., p. 302.

11. Ibid., p. 301.

12. Alfred N. Whitehead, *Science and the Modern World* (New York: Macmillan, 1925), pp. 144-145.

13. Ibid., p. 147.

14. Leclerc, "Problem of God in Whitehead's System," p. 303. See Whitehead, *Science and the Modern World*, p. 151: "We must start with the event as the ultimate unit of natural occurrence." This follows his discussion on pages 147-150 of energy.

15. Leclerc, "Problem of God in Whitehead's System," p. 303. The implications of the last portion of the quote will become clear when we explore process metaphysics.

16. Whitehead, *Science and the Modern World*, pp. 171-172.

17. Ibid., p. 187.

18. Ibid., p. 196.

19. Ibid., p. 147.

20. George R. Lucas, Jr., "Evolutionist Theories and Whitehead's Philosophy," *Process Stud* 14 (Winter 1985). On pages 287-288 Lucas differentiates an evolutionary theory and an evolutionary cosmology.

21. Even Lucas admits (p. 297) that while "there is little explicit influence from the field of biology, from biological evolution, or from evolutionist theories generally," all of them are "unsystematically presupposed."

22. Schubert Ogden, "Toward a New Theism," in Brown, James, and Reeves, eds., *Process Philosophy and Christian Thought*, pp. 177-178.

23. Alfred N. Whitehead, *Process and Reality* (New York: Macmillan, 1929), pp. 519-521. As cited in Claude Stewart, "Process Theology: An Alternative Model for Christian Thinking," *Perspect Rel S* 9 (1982).

24. Stewart, "Process Theology," p. 118. Stewart cites Cobb and Griffin's *Process Theology: An Introductory Exposition* (Philadelphia: Westminster, 1976), pp. 8-10, and suggests to compare this with John B. Cobb, Jr., *God and the World* (Philadelphia: Westminster, 1969), chapter 1.

25. Ogden, "Toward a New Theism," p. 179.

26. Ibid., pp. 179-180.

27. James W. Felt, "Whitehead's Misconception of 'Substance' in Aristotle," *Process Stud* 14 (Winter 1985). Felt shows that when the passages from Aristotle that process thinkers most complain about are taken in their context, they don't mean what Whitehead understood them to mean. Moreover, Felt offers a series of other citations from Aristotle that show he believed substances were capable of relating to other substances and changing.

28. Moreover, as Hartshorne argues, to say that God is love and to speak of him as Lord (which suggests that he can express emotions and enter into relationships) and then to speak of him as absolute, immutable, and impassive is to contradict oneself. Charles Hartshorne, *The Divine Relativity* (New Haven, Conn.: Yale University Press, 1948), p. 26. It is these attributes of pure actuality, immutability, impassivity, aseity, immateriality which, as Schubert Ogden notes, "all entail an unqualified negation of real internal relationship to anything beyond his own wholly absolute being" (Ogden, "The Reality of God," *The Reality of God and Other Essays* [New York: Harper & Row, 1966], pp. 48-49).

29. Hartshorne, *Divine Relativity*, p. 43.

30. Ogden, "Reality of God," p. 51.

31. Hartshorne, *Divine Relativity*, p. 58.

32. Ibid.

33. Eugene Peters, "Theology, Classical and Neo-Classical," *Encounter* 44 (Winter 1983): 8-9.

34. Hartshorne, *Divine Relativity*, p. 1.

35. Peters, "Theology, Classical and Neo-Classical," p. 10.

36. Leclerc, "Problem of God in Whitehead's System," p. 304.

37. Ibid., pp. 305-306.

38. Ibid., p. 314. Other influences from Plato and Aristotle could be traced, but suffice it to say that Plato's *Timaeus* was especially significant for Whitehead, and his acquaintance with Plato was in greater depth than was his familiarity with Aristotle. Indeed, some have argued that Whitehead probably misunderstood the "process character" of Aristotle's natural philosophy as set forth in his *Physics* (see Ernest Wolf-Gazo, "Editor's Preface: Whitehead within the Context of the History of Philosophy," *Process Stud* 14 [Winter 1985]: 217-218). In fact, when one considers that Thomism

is so heavily indebted to Aristotelianism and yet process thinkers generally are negative toward Thomistic theism, one begins to wonder if Whitehead and others properly understand Aristotle or Thomas's use of him.

39. Wolf-Gazo, "Editor's Preface: Whitehead within the Context of the History of Philosophy," pp. 220-222, for example. For further adaptations of Locke to Whitehead's system see Ernest Wolf-Gazo, "Whitehead and Locke's Concept of 'Power'," *Process Stud* 14 (Winter 1985).

40. Whitehead, *Science and the Modern World,* p. 103 referring to Berkeley.

41. Ibid., pp. 101-102.

42. Ibid., p. 101. See also Wolf-Gazo's explanation of the relation of Berkeley's theory of perception to Whitehead's theory of prehension. He writes (pp. 222-223) in reference to the passage from Whitehead cited in the text: "This passage, applied to the Berkeleyan situation, means that the 'prehending' here and now is a mode of grasping the unity of the things perceived. The objective reality is constituted through the relations between the two locations which relate to two entities. Whitehead emphasizes not merely the entities perceived, but the realization of the entities manifested through the unity of the act of prehension. Berkeley's conception of mind is thus translated into a Whiteheadian 'process of prehensive unification'." Others have traced the relation of Whitehead to such thinkers as Coleridge and Wordsworth (through their relation to Kant) and Schelling. In particular, Braeckman shows the correlation between Whitehead's concept of creativity and imagination and the philosophy of Schelling. Likewise, Whitehead's interest in the Romantic writers (like Wordsworth) indicates not only interest in their underlying philosophy but also suggests Whitehead's concern for the aesthetic. See Antoon Braeckman, "Whitehead and German Idealism: A Poetic Heritage," *Process Stud* 14 (Winter 1985).

43. See, for example, Ogden's discussion of the import of logical positivism on theological discussions and how process thinkers have taken it seriously: "Reality of God," pp. 25-27.

44. Ogden, "Reality of God," pp. 44-56.

45. As Norman Pittenger says ("Redemption: A 'Process Theology' Interpretation," *Theology* 88 [1985]: 451-452), the church must recognize in fulfilling its mission that Jesus in no sense is an exclusive savior. He is the classic example of God's love, but that is only to say he isn't the only example. There is no finality to Christ. If one fears that this will wind up as universalism, those fears are realized. Pittenger cites Ogden approvingly when Ogden writes: "The phrase 'only in Jesus Christ' must be taken to tell us not that God acts to redeem in the history of Jesus and in no other history, but that the only God who redeems any history—*although he in fact redeems every history*—is the God whose redemptive action is decisively re-presented in the word that Jesus speaks and is" (Ogden, "Reality of God," p. 172 as cited in Pittenger, p. 452).

46. For excellent sketches of the main theological and religious trends of the twentieth century see Langdon Gilkey, *Naming the Whirlwind* (Indianapolis: Bobbs-Merrill, 1969), chapter 1; and Ogden, "Reality of God." See also Loomer's description ("Process Theology") and Meland's descriptions (*Future of Empirical Theology*) of the influences and trends leading to process theology, as well as Pittenger's "Understanding the World and the Faith." For an excellent discussion of the history of process theology in the twentieth century in its various phases, see Gene Reeves and Delwin Brown, "The Development of Process Theology," in Brown, James, and Reeves, eds., *Process Philosophy and Christian Thought.*

47. Whitehead, *Process and Reality,* p. 27.

48. Ibid., p. 33.

49. Ibid., pp. 34-36.

50. Ibid., pp. 34-35.

51. Lowe, "Whitehead's Metaphysical System," p. 4.

52. Daniel Day Williams, "How Does God Act?" *Process and Divinity* (La Salle, Ill.: Open Court, 1964), p. 166.

53. Whitehead, *Process and Reality,* p. 353 as quoted in Williams, p. 166.

54. Lowe, "Whitehead's Metaphysical System," p. 6. See also page 7 for Lowe's further characterization of the nature of a prehension.

55. Whitehead, *Process and Reality,* p. 35.

56. Ibid., pp. 32, 34.

57. Ibid., p. 392.

58. Lowe, "Whitehead's Metaphysical System," p. 6.

59. Whitehead, *Process and Reality,* p. 33.

60. William C. Tremmel, "Comments on God, Neo-Naturalism and A. N. Whitehead's Philosophy," *Iliff Review* 45 (Spring 1988): 28.

61. Whitehead, *Process and Reality,* p. 134.

62. Ibid., p. 37.

63. Ibid., pp. 36-37.

64. John Hayward, "Process Thought and Liberal Religion," *American Journal of Theology and Philosophy* 6 (May and September 1985): 118.

65. Pittenger, "Understanding the World and the Faith," p. 182. See also Hartshorne's detailed explanation of the problems with a philosophy of substance in "The Development of Process Philosophy," in Ewert H. Cousins, ed., *Process Theology* (New York: Newman Press, 1971).
66. Hartshorne, "Development of Process Philosophy," pp. 49-50.
67. Ibid., pp. 61-62.
68. See Bowman Clarke, "Process, Time, and God," *Process Stud* 13 (1983): 249-250; and Robert C. Neville, *Creativity and God: A Challenge to Process Theology* (New York: Seabury, 1980), p. 21.
69. Tremmel, "Comments on God," p. 26.
70. Whitehead, *Process and Reality*, p. 28.
71. Ibid., p. 521.
72. John B. Cobb, Jr., "A Whiteheadian Doctrine of God," in Brown, James, and Reeves, eds., *Process Philosophy and Christian Thought*, p. 230.
73. Williams, "How Does God Act?" p. 171.
74. See, for example, Williams's description of God's primordial nature as the "envisagement of the realm of possibility" and the order which characterizes the world so that it can be one determinate world and yet that primordial nature is something actual, for "there is a definite *structure* [italics mine] of possibility which characterizes every existing reality" (Williams, *Process and Divinity*, 171). See also Bernard Loomer, "Christian Faith and Process Philosophy," in Brown, James, and Reeves, eds., *Process Philosophy and Christian Thought*, pp. 83-84, who says: "the primordial nature of God is the conceptual ordering of all eternal objects and possibilities such that a graded scale of relevance is established between each possibility and each actual entity. Because of this unchanging order in the world, each possibility has a different relevance or significance for each actuality. This ordering of all possibilities constitutes the abstract and not the concrete nature of God. This is Whitehead's 'principle of concretion'."
75. Cobb, "Whiteheadian Doctrine of God," p. 230.
76. Whitehead, *Process and Reality*, p. 521.
77. Ibid., p. 46.
78. Whitehead speaks of *physical prehensions, conceptual prehensions,* and *hybrid prehensions.* Whitehead explains that while a physical feeling is the feeling of another actual entity, if that actuality is objectified by its conceptual feelings, "the physical feeling of the subject in question is termed 'hybrid'." On the other hand, when the actual entity which is the datum for prehension is objectified by one of its own physical feelings, the prehension of the datum is called a *pure physical feeling.* See Whitehead, *Process and Reality*, pp. 35, 343, and 375-376.
79. Cf. Pittenger, "Understanding the World and the Faith," p. 184 as exemplary of this notion.
80. Cobb, "Whiteheadian Doctrine of God," p. 223.
81. In a very interesting article, Colin Grant explains how Charles Hartshorne's dipolar theism was a reaction to both classical theism and logical positivism. On the one hand, Hartshorne agreed with classical theology about the absoluteness of God, though classical theology didn't see that this absoluteness is an abstraction. By retaining divine absoluteness, Hartshorne was able to offer a reformulation and defense of Anselm's ontological argument. On the other hand, in concert with the demands of positivism, the consequent nature of God, his physical pole is able to satisfy positivist demands. Grant also explains how the derivation of Hartshorne's views in these ways differs from how Whitehead came to his notion of God. See Colin Grant, "The Theological Significance of Hartshorne's Response to Positivism," *Relig Stud* 21 (1985).
82. Cobb, "Whiteheadian Doctrine of God," pp. 216-217.
83. Lewis Ford, "The Divine Activity of the Future," *Process Stud* 11 (Fall 1981): 169. See also Robert C. Neville, *Creativity and God,* for a fuller explanation of the same difficulty from the perspective of God's inability to know anything in its subjective immediacy as it is becoming. He raises the problem initially in chapter 1, but repeatedly discusses it throughout the book.
84. Ford, "Divine Activity of the Future," pp. 169-170. See Hartshorne, *Divine Relativity*, pp. 22-29 for his discussion of God and reality as social. For Hartshorne this not only means that God and other realities are an aggregate of actual occasions, but the social aspect of being means that God is related to all things. For further discussion of Hartshorne's proposal and a different solution, see Ford, " The Divine Activity of the Future," p. 172; and Lewis S. Ford, "God as the Subjectivity of the Future," *Encounter* 41 (1980). For further discussion of Ford's views see Theodore Vitali, "Lewis S. Ford's Revision of Whitehead: God as the Future of All Occasions," *Encounter* 44 (Winter 1983).
85. Hartshorne, *Divine Relativity*, pp. vii-viii.
86. Ibid., p. vii and throughout the work.
87. Ibid., p. viii. See a somewhat similar definition of "personal" in David R. Mason, "Reflections on 'Prayer' from a Process Perspective," *Encounter* 45 (Autumn 1984): 349.
88. Hartshorne, *Divine Relativity*, pp. 45-46.
89. Ibid., p. 46. For further discussions of the question of divine immutability in traditional and process theism see Barry Whitney, "Divine Immutability in Process Philosophy and Contemporary Thomism," *Horizons* 7 (1980): 50-68; W. Norris Clarke, "Christian Theism and Whiteheadian

Process Philosophy: Are They Compatible?" in Ronald Nash, ed., *Process Theology* (Grand Rapids, Mich.: Baker, 1987), pp. 234-242; and Thomas V. Morris, "God and the World," in Nash, ed., *Process Theology*, pp. 286-294.

90. Hartshorne, *Divine Relativity*, pp. 42-59. See also Ogden, "Reality of God," pp. 44-70 passim.
91. Whitehead, *Process and Reality*, p. 532.
92. Hartshorne, *Divine Relativity*, p. 133.
93. Stewart, "Process Theology," p. 121.
94. Charles Hartshorne, "The Dipolar Conception of Deity," *Review of Metaphysics* 21 (1967): 274.
95. Williams, "How Does God Act?" p. 170.
96. David Griffin, *God, Power and Evil: A Process Theodicy* (Philadelphia: Westminster, 1976), p. 270, as cited in David Basinger and Randall Basinger, "Divine Omnipotence: Plantinga vs. Griffin," *Process Stud* 11 (Spring 1981): 13.
97. Griffin, *God, Power and Evil*, p. 269ff.
98. Basinger and Basinger, "Divine Omnipotence," p. 16. Otherwise, the position of process theologians on the notion of human free will in relation to God's power is not substantially different from that of traditional Arminian indeterminists.
99. Williams, "How Does God Act?" p. 171.
100. Ibid., p. 176.
101. Arthur Holmes, "Why God Cannot Act," in Nash, ed., *Process Theology*. This is Holmes's helpful explanation of Williams's comments on p. 176ff. in "How Does God Act?"
102. Morris, "God and the World," pp. 300-304.
103. Williams, "How Does God Act?" p. 180. For further discussion of divine action in process thought see the following: Randolph Crump Miller, "Process, Evil and God," *American Journal of Theology and Philosophy* 1 (1980): 63-68; and Sharyn Dowd, "Is Whitehead's God the 'God Who Acts'?" *Perspect Rel S* 9 (1982).
104. William Power, "The Doctrine of the Trinity and Whitehead's Metaphysics," *Encounter* 45 (Autumn 1984): 293.
105. Cobb, "Whiteheadian Doctrine of God," p. 236.
106. Whitehead, *Process and Reality*, p. 529. See also Tremmel, "Comments on God," p. 30.
107. Lewis Ford, "Divine Persuasion and the Triumph of Good," in Brown, James and Reeves, eds., *Process Philosophy and Christian Thought*, p. 290. For an excellent discussion of the question of coercion as it relates to process thinking in general, see David Basinger, "Human Coercion: A Fly in the Process Ointment?" *Process Stud* 15 (Fall 1986).
108. John B. Cobb, Jr., *God and the World*, p. 138.
109. Whitehead, *Process and Reality*, pp. 343-344. See also Joseph A. Bracken, "Process Philosophy and Trinitarian Theology—II," *Process Stud* 11 (Summer 1981): 85-86.
110. Cobb, "Whiteheadian Doctrine of God," p. 236.
111. Whitehead, *Process and Reality*, p. 31.
112. Ibid.
113. Cobb, "Whiteheadian Doctrine of God," p. 237.
114. Ibid., pp. 237-241.
115. Ibid., pp. 241ff. For a thorough handling of the whole issue of God and creativity see Neville's *Creativity and God*. Neville presents a variety of problems with the process conception of God and repeatedly argues that what is needed is a stronger notion of God as creator.
116. Whitehead, *Process and Reality*, p. 517.
117. Michael Peterson, "God and Evil," in Nash, ed., *Process Theology*, pp. 131-133.
118. See Jeffrey Rada, "Problems with Process Theology," *Restoration Quarterly* 29 (1987): 32; Power, "Doctrine of the Trinity," p. 294; Basinger and Basinger, "Divine Omnipotence"; and Peterson, "God and Evil."
119. Ogden, "Reality of God," pp. 64-65.
120. For further discussion of God and evil in process theology, see Randolph Crump Miller's "Process, Evil and God"; and Nancy Frankenberry, "Some Problems in Process Theodicy," *Relig Stud* 17 (June 1981).
121. Ogden, "Reality of God," p. 61.
122. Ibid., pp. 61-62.
123. Hartshorne, *Divine Relativity*, p. 89.
124. Ibid., p. 90, but the overall discussion is reflective of his discussion on pages 88-92.
125. For a fuller discussion of the process conception of the Trinity, see Power, "The Doctrine of the Trinity"; Bracken, "Process Philosophy and Trinitarian Theology—II"; and Bruce Demarest, "The Process Reduction of Jesus and the Trinity," in Nash, ed., *Process Theology*.
126. Reeves and Brown, "Development of Process Theology," p. 63.
127. Peter Hamilton, *The Living God* (London: Hodder and Stoughton, 1967).

128. Peter Hamilton, "Some Proposals for a Modern Christology," in Brown, James, and Reeves, eds., *Process Philosophy and Christian Thought*, p. 379. On p. 380 he says with respect to Christ's resurrection (which he calls God's representation to us of the finite sequence of events known as Christ's life) that "this sequence lives on in God, continually re-created afresh in God's living memory and re-presented to Christ's followers as they turn to god in prayer and sacrament. But it is the sequence as a whole that is re-presented; *no new subjective experiences are added* [italics mine]—or if they are, that is another story."

129. Tremmel, "Comments on God," pp. 34-35. See also Hamilton, "Some Proposals," pp. 378-379; and Reeves and Brown, "Development of Process Theology" (pp. 62-63) who on page 63, quoting from Whitehead (*Process and Reality*, p. 532), say, "since God's consequent nature 'passes back into the temporal world and qualifies this world,' our lives being elements in God, also 'reach back to influence the world' even apart from our direct social immortality." For process notions of Christology, see Hamilton, "Some Proposals,"; John B. Cobb, Jr., "A Whiteheadian Christology," in Brown, James, and Reeves, eds., *Process Philosophy and Christian Thought;* David Griffin, *A Process Christology* (Philadelphia: Westminster, 1973); and my own "Process Theology," *The Evangelical Review of Theology* 14 (October 1990): 320-324. For elaboration of other process concepts, see the following: Roger Ellis, "From Hegel to Whitehead," *J Relig* 61 (1981); Philip E. Devenish, "Divinity and Dipolarity: Thomas Erskine and Charles Hartshorne on What Makes God 'God'," *J Relig* 62 (October 1982); Joseph A. Bracken, "The Two Process Theologies: A Reappraisal," *Theol Stud* 46 (1985); Santiago Sia, "Charles Hartshorne on Describing God," *Mod Theol* 3 (1987); Nancy Frankenberry, "The Emergent Paradigm and Divine Causation," *Process Stud* 13 (Fall 1983); John B. Cobb, Jr., "The Presence of the Past and the Eucharist," *Process Stud* 13 (Fall 1983); and David Basinger, *Divine Power in Process Theism* (Albany, N.Y.: State University of New York Press, 1988).

130. See David Burrell, "Does Process Theology Rest on a Mistake?" *Theol Stud* 43 (1982) for an analysis of the ways in which process theology claims to be superior but is not. As Burrell shows, process thinkers argue for the need of a new theism because of inadequacies with the old, but what they offer is hard to see as an improvement, let alone adequate in itself.

131. Neville, *Creativity and God*, pp. 15, 17, 19-20.

132. See Ford, "Divine Activity of the Future," pp. 170-171, for difficulties in the social conception of God. See also Neville, *Creativity and God*, chapter 1, for further problems with the social conception in general.

133. See, for example, William Lane Craig, "Divine Foreknowledge and Future Contingency," in Nash, ed., *Process Theology;* and his "Process Theology's Denial of Divine Foreknowledge," *Process Stud* 16 (1987).

134. Royce Gruenler, "Reflections on the School of Process Theism," *TSF Bulletin* 7 (1984): 8.

135. Neville, *Creativity and God*, p. 11.

136. David Basinger, "Human Coercion," pp. 164-165. The argument is Basinger's and he has laid it out in great detail.

137. See my *Many Faces of Evil* for examples of what theists typically say. They argue that God has the power to get rid of evil but doesn't because there is a morally sufficient reason for not doing so. Hence, he is not guilty for not removing evil. See also Michael Peterson in Nash, ed., *Process Theology*. Among his other objections to process theism, Peterson correctly complains that it doesn't take seriously enough the moral dimension of evil in the world, i.e., its account of sin and evil is inadequate.

138. Burrell isn't convinced that they have even understood Aquinas on this matter (as well as others), and he explains why. See Burrell, "Does Process Theology Rest on a Mistake?" p. 127.

139. See Ronald Nash, "Process Theology and Classical Theism," in Nash, ed., *Process Theology,* on process theologians presenting only two options and the options as caricaturing orthodoxy.

140. Neville, *Creativity and God*, chapter 3, sets forth this problem. Also see Cobb, "Whiteheadian Doctrine of God," pp. 235-243.

141. See William Alston, "Hartshorne and Aquinas: A Via Media," in William P. Alston, *Divine Nature and Human Language: Essays in Philosophical Theology* (Ithaca, N.Y.: Cornell University Press, 1989). In the first group are absoluteness/relativity; pure actuality/potentiality; total necessity/ necessity and contingency; and absolute simplicity/complexity. The second group includes divine creation *ex nihilio*/God and world exist necessarily, though details are contingent; omnipotence/ limited power; incorporeality/corporeality; atemporality/temporality; immutability/mutability; and absolute perfection/relative perfection. For those interested in the details, see Alston's article. My appeal to Alston is to make the more general point I am presenting in the text.

142. Alston, "Hartshorne and Aquinas," pp. 121-124. In the remainder of the essay Alston offers his account of God which weds Hartshornean and Thomistic concepts together, and makes his case that attributes in one group don't logically necessitate adopting attributes in the second group.

143. For further critiques of various aspects of process theology see the following: Nancy Frankenberry, "Some Problems in Process Theodicy"; W. Norris Clarke, "Charles Hartshorne's Philosophy of God: A Thomistic Critique," in Santiago Sia, ed., *Charles Hartshorne's Concept of God: Philosophical and Theological Responses* (Boston: Kluwer, 1990); Michael L. Peterson, "Orthodox

Christianity, Wesleyanism, and Process Theology," *Wesleyan Theological Journal* 15 (1980); and Warren McWilliams, "Daniel Day Williams' Vulnerable and Invulnerable God," *Encounter* 44 (Winter 1983).

C H A P T E R   5

1. Here one is reminded of God's inquisition of Job in Job 38–41. God asks Job if he can make any number of things that deal with the created world. The things mentioned, however, are things which no one but a supreme being could possibly do. God uses this to show Job that he is all-powerful, in order to teach Job that it is foolish to question whether God is in control of his situation or knows how to overcome his circumstances. The point is certainly not to argue for God's existence, but I think these chapters can be put to use in making a case for God's existence. All of the things God mentions are things no mere mortal could do; in fact, it is hard to imagine even a very special human doing them. But, since these things exist, there must be a God.

2. See René Descartes, "Third Meditation: Concerning God: That He Exists," in "Meditations on First Philosophy," in Elizabeth Anscombe and Peter Geach, eds., *Descartes: Philosophical Writings* (London: Thomas Nelson, 1966).

3. J. L. Mackie, "Evil and Omnipotence," in Basil Mitchell, ed., *Philosophy of Religion* (London: Oxford, 1971), p. 93.

4. See Alvin Plantinga, "Reason and Belief in God," in Alvin Plantinga and Nicholas Wolterstorff, eds., *Faith and Rationality* (Notre Dame, Ind.: University of Notre Dame Press, 1983).

5. René Descartes in his *Meditations* (1641) gives the second major emphasis to the first form of the ontological argument. His formulation, though slightly different from the first form of Anselm's argument, really captures the basic elements of Anselm's position. As John Hick notes, Descartes' primary contribution to the argument was to highlight the hitherto unstated assumption in Anselm's argument that existence is an attribute or predicate. Descartes' basic point is that if one conceives properly of the notion of God, one must conceive of God as existing. Just as it is impossible to think properly of a mountain without also realizing that its existence entails a valley, and just as it is impossible to think of a triangle without thinking of it as having three angles, so it is impossible to think of God without thinking of him as having existence. It is part of the essence of a mountain that it is accompanied by a valley, and of the triangle that it consists of three angles. Likewise, it is part of the very essence of God that he has the quality of existence. In each of the three cases mentioned (mountain, triangle, God) some attribute is taken to be essential to its very nature. In God's case, that attribute is existence.

6. A second way of making Gaunilo's objection says that the definition of God as the GCB is just that, a definition, but one cannot move from a mere definition to the existence of the thing defined. As J. L. Mackie says, the problem with any ontological argument is that it fails to recognize "the impossibility of establishing some concrete reality on the basis of a mere definition or concept, even with the help of the minor empirical fact that someone, such as the fool actually has the concept." J. L. Mackie, *The Miracle of Theism* (Oxford: Clarendon, 1982), p. 52.

7. Mackie argues that this objection raises a dilemma for the theist. If Kant is right, the ontological argument won't work. If Kant is wrong and "God exists" is analytic, then the conclusion has been assumed already by the mere use of the term "God," and that begs the question. So whether Kant is right or wrong, the argument does not work. Mackie, *Miracle of Theism*, p. 44.

8. See, for example, Charles Hartshorne, *The Logic of Perfection* (LaSalle, Ill.: Open Court, 1962); and Alvin Plantinga, *God and Other Minds* (Ithaca, N.Y.: Cornell University Press, 1967).

9. Here I must also mention William Lane Craig's defense of what is known as the *kalaam* cosmological argument. See William Lane Craig, *The Kalaam Cosmological Argument* (New York: Barnes and Noble, 1979).

10. Thomas Aquinas, *Summa Theologiae*, vol. 1 (Garden City, N.Y.: Image, 1969), IA, 2, 3, p. 68.

11. J. L. Mackie (*Miracle of Theism*, pp. 88-89) raises three objections which he thinks at least suggest that the contingency argument is not entirely airtight.

12. See Rowe's discussion of the principle of sufficient reason in William Rowe, *The Cosmological Argument* (Princeton: Princeton University Press, 1975), chapter 2 and pp. 146-151. Rowe offers an objection to the principle of sufficient reason which he thinks destroys it in any form. Rowe asks us to consider the state of affairs expressed by the proposition "there are contingent states of affairs." It is clearly contingent that there are contingent states of affairs; hence, according to the principle of sufficient reason, there must be some state of affairs that is the sufficient reason for there being contingent states of affairs. Suppose that God's existence is the state of affairs that explains the existence of contingent states of affairs. His existence must be necessary, not contingent, if it is to serve as a sufficient reason for there being states of affairs. But then we must also ask whether the proposition "God caused there to be contingent states of affairs" is contingent or necessary. If it is contingent, it cannot be a sufficient reason for there being contingent states of affairs; we must look further for a reason which is not contingent. So, God's causing there to be contingent states of affairs must itself be a necessary state of affairs. However, as Rowe notes, this simply means that it is necessary that there are contingent states of affairs. But at the outset we claimed that it is contingent that there are contingent states of affairs. Thus, we have, in fact, no sufficient explanation for

the fact that there are contingent states of affairs, if the principle of sufficient reason is correct. All of this suggests that the principle of sufficient reason is false.

13. Richard Swinburne, *The Existence of God* (New York: Oxford University Press, 1991).

14. Richard Taylor, *Metaphysics* (Englewood Cliffs, N.J.: Prentice-Hall, 1992).

15. See, for example, J. P. Moreland and John Mark Reynolds, "Introduction," in Moreland and Reynolds, eds., *Three Views on Creation and Evolution* (Grand Rapids, Mich.: Zondervan, 1999), pp. 34-35. See also Michael Behe, *Darwin's Black Box* (New York: Free Press, 1996); William Dembski, ed., *Mere Creation* (Downers Grove, Ill.: InterVarsity, 1998); Michael Denton, *Evolution: A Theory in Crisis* (Bethesda, Md.: Adler and Adler, 1986); and Phillip Johnson, *Darwin on Trial* (Downers Grove, Ill.: InterVarsity, 1991).

16. David Hume, *Dialogues Concerning Natural Religion* (Garden City, N.Y.: Doubleday, 1974).

17. For an explanation of the nature of a cumulative case argument see Basil Mitchell, *The Justification of Religious Belief* (New York: Oxford University Press, 1981). Mitchell argues that there are many complex beliefs for which we make a cumulative case. He offers as examples complex scientific theories, explanations of some historical event, and even a given interpretation of a problem passage in a piece of literature. Similarly, he explains that we can and should use a cumulative case approach to the justification of religious beliefs.

18. In contrast to the idea that one is truly free and able to make life meaningful once the notion of God is discarded, see the excellent treatment of the futility of life without God in William Lane Craig, *Reasonable Faith* (Wheaton, Ill.: Crossway, 1994), chapter 2.

19. Thomas V. Morris, *Our Idea of God* (Downers Grove, Ill.: InterVarsity, 1991), pp. 31-34.

20. Thiessen writes, "The terms 'essence' and 'substance' are practically synonymous when used of God. They may be defined as that which underlies all outward manifestation; the reality itself, whether material or immaterial; the substratum of anything; that in which the qualities or attributes inhere." Henry C. Thiessen, *Lectures in Systematic Theology,* revised by Vernon D. Doerksen (Grand Rapids, Mich.: Eerdmans, 1979), p. 75. See also Charles Hodge, *Systematic Theology,* vol. 1 (London: James Clarke, 1960), p. 367.

21. Moises Silva, *Philippians,* The Wycliffe Exegetical Commentary (Chicago: Moody, 1988), pp.113-114.

22. Ibid., p. 115.

23. See, for example, O. C. Thomas's helpful exposition of nearly a dozen thinkers who think of God as being-itself in one way or another. O. C. Thomas, "Being and Some Theologians," *Harvard Theological Review* 70 (1977). See also Tim Bradshaw's helpful discussion of John Macquarrie's views of God as being-itself. "Macquarrie's Doctrine of God," *Tyndale Bul* 44 (1993).

24. Thomas, "Being and Some Theologians," p. 145.

25. Ibid., p. 147.

26. Morris, *Our Idea of God,* pp. 28-35.

27. Ibid., p. 35.

28. Ibid.

29. Ibid., p. 37. Morris, of course, is not saying that either being a bachelor or being married is a greatness-making property. He simply uses these as examples of properties that are not compossible in one being.

30. Ibid., pp. 40-45.

31. For further discussion of God as a necessary being, including responses to arguments philosophers have raised against this notion, see Morris, *Our Idea of God,* pp. 106-113; and Robert M. Adams, "Divine Necessity," in Thomas V. Morris, ed., *The Concept of God,* Oxford Readings in Philosophy (Oxford: Oxford University Press, 1987), chapter 2.

32. Trichotomists with respect to human nature claim that humans have two immaterial parts, a soul and a spirit, along with a material body. However, the disagreement between dichotomists and trichotomists is a subject for the volume on the doctrine of man.

33. There are some rather interesting discussions in contemporary philosophical literature about whether or not God is a body or has one. Such views stem somewhat from process views of God, but process theists are not the only ones who discuss this issue. See Grace Jantzen, *God's World, God's Body* (Philadelphia: Westminster, 1984); and J. C. A. Gaskin, *The Quest for Eternity* (Harmondsworth, Middlesex, England: Penguin, 1984). Both argue that God is not incorporeal. See interaction with these views in Charles Taliaferro, "The Incorporeality of God," *Mod Theol* 3 (1987); and Grace Jantzen, "Reply to Taliaferro," *Mod Theol* 3 (1987); In addition see Ninian Smart, "God's Body," *Union Seminary Quarterly Review* 37 (Fall/Winter 1981–1982). Smart discusses Indian thinker Ramanuja's views of the world as God's body. Smart compares this with Christian thinking and suggests ways to wed Ramanuja's ideas with Christian theology. Smart believes there would be advantages for Christian thinking about God by adopting such views. For an interesting discussion of the philosophical arguments surrounding the question of God having a body, see especially William J. Wainwright, "God's Body," in Thomas V. Morris, ed., *The Concept of God,* Oxford Readings in Philosophy (Oxford: Oxford University Press, 1987). Wainwright discusses whether God is a body, whether (if not a body) God has a body, and finally whether our

world itself is God's body. Of related interest is P. J. Sherry's "Are Spirits Bodiless Persons?" *Neue Zeitschrift für Systematische Theologie und Religionsphilosophie* 24 (1982).

34. In contrast, see P. J. Sherry's somewhat misguided handling of John 4:24. He notes correctly that there is no article with pneuma, so the phrase could just as easily be translated "God is spirit" as "God is a spirit." The result for Sherry is that we cannot take the verse as stating that God is literally ontologically an immaterial being. Rather, he says, following Origen, we should see this verse as parallel to passages such as 1 John 1:5 ("God is light") and Deut 4:24 ("God is a consuming fire"). From this Origen argues that spirit is to be understood figuratively. However, Sherry further says that for Origen this meant that God is incorporeal, an intelligent being, and that God fills us with new life. (See P. J. Sherry, "Are Spirits Bodiless Persons?" p. 43.) At least the first part of this (incorporeal) does not sound figurative, so it is hard to see why that claim is made. In addition, when a noun without an article is used in the predicate position in Greek it typically refers to the quality of the thing designated by the noun. Hence, John is saying that God is of the quality of spirit or qualitatively spirit, but this is just a roundabout way of saying that he is an immaterial being, a spirit.

35. Gedaliahu Stroumsa, "The Incorporeality of God," *Religion* 13 (1983): 346.

36. See the remainder of Stroumsa's article.

37. Douglas J. Moo, *Romans 1–8,* The Wycliffe Exegetical Commentary (Chicago: Moody, 1991), p. 100.

38. An example of a theologian who argues this point is John Gill in his *Complete Body of Doctrinal and Practical Divinity,* vol. 1 (1839; reprint, Grand Rapids, Mich.: Baker, 1978), p. 48. This sort of reasoning also seems implicit in Lewis and Demarest's comment as follows: "As spirit, furthermore, God is *living and active*" (Gordon R. Lewis and Bruce A. Demarest, *Integrative Theology* vol. 1 [Grand Rapids, Mich.: Zondervan, 1987], p. 197).

39. Gill, *Complete Body,* vol. 1, pp. 48-49.

40. An example of a very important work which shows the complexity of the issue is P. F. Strawson's *Individuals: An Essay in Descriptive Metaphysics* (Garden City, N.Y.: Doubleday, 1963).

41. In particular, since many laws in various countries are written to protect the rights of persons, it is crucial to determine what constitutes personhood. In the United States this issue is a major consideration in attempting to determine the morality of the practice of abortion and euthanasia of people in a terminal condition who cannot interact with their environment.

42. Lewis S. Chafer, *Systematic Theology,* vol. 1 (Dallas: Dallas Seminary Press, 1947), p. 180ff.

43. Keith Ward, "Is God a Person?" in Gijsbert van den Brink, et al., eds., *Christian Faith and Philosophical Theology* (Kampen, Netherlands: Kok Pharos, 1992), p. 263.

44. Ibid., pp. 262-263.

45. Stanley Grenz, *Theology for the Community of God* (Nashville: Broadman & Holman, 1994), p. 110.

46. Ibid., pp. 110-111.

47. As in the case of Herman Bavinck, *The Doctrine of God* (Grand Rapids, Mich.: Baker, 1977), pp. 124-125.

48. As in William G. T. Shedd, *Dogmatic Theology,* vol. 1 (Grand Rapids, Mich.: Zondervan, 1969), p. 194.

49. Alister McGrath, *Christian Theology: An Introduction* (Oxford: Basil Blackwell, 1997), pp. 243-244.

50. See my "Truth: Relationship of Theories of Truth to Hermeneutics," in Earl Radmacher and Robert Preus, eds., *Hermeneutics, Inerrancy, and the Bible* (Grand Rapids, Mich.: Zondervan, 1984), p. 4, for an explanation of the distinction.

51. McGrath, *Christian Theology,* p. 244.

52. See John and Paul Feinberg, *Ethics for a Brave New World* (Wheaton, Ill.: Crossway, 1993), chapters 1–4, for bases of personhood in the unborn and terminally ill.

53. See, for example, Shedd's lengthy discussion (pp. 178-194) of these qualities of cognition and their application to God.

54. See, for example, Amy Pauw-Plantinga, "Personhood, Divine and Human," *Perspectives* 8 (February 1993).

CHAPTER 6

1. Alvin Plantinga seems to refer to these attributes using this convention in *Does God Have a Nature?* (Milwaukee: Marquette University Press, 1980). On the other hand, as Millard Erickson notes (*Christian Theology* [Grand Rapids, Mich.: Baker, 1983], I:265), many theologians reserve the term *property* for "the distinctive characteristics of the various persons of the Trinity. Properties are functions (general), activities (more specific), or acts (most specific) of the individual members of the Godhead."

2. Herman Bavinck, *The Doctrine of God,* trans. William Hendricksen, (Grand Rapids, Mich.: Baker, 1977 paperback edition), pp. 132-134.

3. A. H. Strong, *Systematic Theology* (Valley Forge, Pa.: Judson, 1969), p. 248.

4. Louis Berkhof, *Systematic Theology* (Grand Rapids, Mich.: Eerdmans, 1968), p. 55.
5. James Barr, *Biblical Words for Time*, 2d ed. (London: SCM Press LTD, 1969). Barr not only explains the problems but also illustrates them in the works of scholars such as Cullmann (*Christ and Time*); Marsh (*The Fulness of Time*); J. A. T. Robinson (*In the End, God*); and C. von Orelli (*Die hebraischen Synonyma der Zeit und Ewigkeit gnetisch und sprachvergleichend dargestellt*).
6. As argued elsewhere, words have meaning that relates to states of affairs in the world only within the context of a sentence. See my article "Truth: Relationship of Theories of Truth to Hermeneutics," in Earl D. Radmacher and Robert D. Preus, eds. *Hermeneutics, Inerrancy and the Bible* (Grand Rapids, Mich.: Zondervan, 1984), where I make this point and cite many philosophers of language who agree.
7. Barr, *Biblical Words for Time*, p. 161. See also pp. 110-115.
8. Ibid., p. 56.
9. Ibid., p. 54. See also pp. 55-57ff. for reasons why it is problematic to talk of notions such as the 'kairos concept'.
10. This is the message one gets in Clark Pinnock, et al., *The Openness of God* (Downers Grove, Ill.: InterVarsity, 1994); and John Sanders, *The God Who Risks* (Downers Grove, Ill.: InterVarsity, 1998).
11. Robert F. Brown, "Divine Omniscience, Immutability, Aseity and Human Free Will," *Relig Stud* 27 (1991): 285.
12. Ibid., p. 288.
13. Ibid., *passim*. Brown also notes that if one holds theological determinism, these problems dissolve, for God's knowledge of all that will happen depends entirely on his will, so whatever God is going to do and be in relation to the world depends on his choices, not ours. The comment about theological determinism avoiding this problem appears in a footnote on page 287. The basic point about indeterminism, however, is made throughout the article repeatedly.
14. Two other verses (Exod 3:14; 6:3) are sometimes cited as teaching self-existence. In 3:14 God reveals himself as "I AM THAT I AM," and in 6:3, he says that though he appeared to Abraham, Isaac, and Jacob, he didn't reveal his name Yahweh to them. Because Yahweh comes from a Hebrew root meaning "to be" and because 3:14 is taken to mean that it is God's nature to be, some theologians conclude that these verses imply self-existence.
15. Stephen T. Davis, "Why God Must Be Unlimited," in Linda Tessier, ed., *Concepts of the Ultimate* (London: Macmillan, 1989), p. 4.
16. Ibid., pp. 4-5.
17. Ibid. p. 5.
18. Jill LeBlanc, "Infinity in Theology and Mathematics," *Relig Stud* 29 (1993): 52.
19. Ibid., p. 53.
20. Ibid., pp. 54-58.
21. Franz Delitzsch, *Biblical Commentary on the Psalms*, vol. 3 (Grand Rapids, Mich.: Eerdmans, 1968), p. 389.
22. Charles Hodge, *Systematic Theology*, vol. 1 (London: James Clarke, 1960 ed.), p. 383.
23. See, for example, Berkhof, *Systematic Theology*, pp. 60-66; and Strong, *Systematic Theology*, pp. 278-280.
24. The general idea of understanding omnipresence in terms of God being present and absent in various distinct respects was suggested to me by a student paper by Samuel Dawson for a doctoral seminar I taught at Trinity Evangelical Divinity School. However, the elaboration of this idea in the upcoming sections is my own.
25. Here my point is not to introduce a lengthy discussion of OT and NT salvation. Rather, my point is that even though God was and is present ethically to both OT and NT saints, there seems to be a further dimension of that ethical presence in the NT, indicated by the indwelling of the Holy Spirit.
26. Strong, *Systematic Theology*, p. 280.
27. Boethius, "The Consolation of Philosophy," in *Boethius: The Theological Tractates*, trans. S. J. Tester, Loeb Classical Library (Cambridge, Mass.: Harvard University Press, 1990 printing), book 5, prose 6, p. 423.
28. Nelson Pike, *God and Timelessness* (New York: Schocken, 1970), p. 7.
29. Thomas V. Morris, *Our Idea of God* (Downers Grove, Ill.: InterVarsity, 1991), p. 120. For further discussion of whether a sempiternal being can be a necessary being, see William Kneale, "Time and Eternity in Theology," *Proceedings of the Aristotelian Society* 61 (1960–1961): 101-107.
30. Morris, *Our Idea of God*, p. 120.
31. *TWOT* 2:672-673, 785.
32. Ibid., p. 645.
33. Ibid., p. 785.
34. Barr, *Biblical Words for Time*, pp. 67-82. I don't intend to rehearse Barr's evidence, because that goes beyond the point of this discussion, and because I believe he convincingly makes his case. Interested readers should consult his discussion.

35. See Robert Badenas, *Christ the End of the Law* (Sheffield, England: JSOT Press, 1985) for a careful study of *telos* and how it relates specifically to Rom 10:4. Badenas's book and Rom 10:4 are not about God's eternity, but the book illustrates my point about the possible meaning of *telos*.

36. Stephen Charnock, *The Existence and Attributes of God* (reprint, Minneapolis: Klock & Klock, 1977), pp. 69-71, 74.

37. Ibid., pp. 71-72, 75.

38. Ibid., pp. 79-80.

39. Charnock also adds (ibid., p. 81) that divine eternity means God is timeless, and it entails immutability (in this case a rather strong notion of immutability). Since all of these issues are involved in the debate over atemporal vs. temporal eternity, I shall save my discussion of them for my treatment of divine eternity later in the book.

40. For a sympathetic exposition and explanation of both divine immutability and impassibility as held by Thomas Aquinas, see Gerald Hanratty, "Divine Immutability and Impassibility Revisited," in Fran O'Rourke, ed., *At the Heart of the Real* (Dublin: Irish Academic Press, 1992), pp. 148-162. For an interesting explanation of how the doctrine of divine immutability shaped much of the theology of the reformer John Knox, see Richard Kyle, "The Divine Attributes in John Knox's Concept of God," *WTJ* 48 (1986): 164ff.

41. See, for example, Nicholas Wolterstorff, "God Everlasting," in *God and the Good*, Clifton Orlebeke and Lewis Smedes, eds. (Grand Rapids, Mich.: Eerdmans, 1975); and Thomas V. Morris, "Properties, Modalities, and God," *Phil Rev* 93 (January 1984): 42ff.

42. The KJV uses the term in some places (e.g., Heb 6:17) but the word is not in the original.

43. Richard Swinburne, *The Coherence of Theism* (Oxford: Clarendon, 1986), p. 212.

44. William Mann, "Simplicity and Immutability in God," in Thomas V. Morris, ed., *The Concept of God* (Oxford: Oxford University Press, 1987), p. 254, cites the strongest and most influential statements of this strong sense of immutability as follows: St. Augustine, *De Trinitate*, v, 2, 3; xv, t, 7-8; Anselm, *Monologion*, 25; Thomas Aquinas, *Summa Theologiae*, pt. I, q. 9.

45. Paul Helm, *Eternal God* (Oxford: Clarendon, 1988), pp. 85-86.

46. See my "Salvation in the Old Testament," *Tradition and Testament*, John S. Feinberg and Paul D. Feinberg, eds. (Chicago: Moody, 1981).

47. Peter Geach, *God and the Soul* (New York: Schocken, 1969), p. 71.

48. Swinburne, *Coherence of Theism*, p. 164.

49. Hector-Neri Castañeda, "Omniscience and Indexical Reference," *J Phil* 64 (April 13, 1967): 203.

50. For further explication of how this can be so in the sense that Scripture teaches it, and how the picture of Christ it gives is logically consistent, see my "The Incarnation of Jesus Christ," in *In Defense of Miracles*, Gary Habermas and Doug Geivett, eds. (Downers Grove, Ill.: InterVarsity, 1997).

51. See chapter 1 of John S. Feinberg and Paul D. Feinberg, *Ethics for a Brave New World* (Wheaton, Ill.: Crossway, 1993), in which I explain various systems of Christian ethics and argue in favor of a modified divine command theory of ethics. See also my chapter on theonomy in *The Many Faces of Evil* (Grand Rapids, Mich.: Zondervan, 1994) for a clearer and fuller exposition of the metaphysic and ethic of that system.

52. I should add that some OT laws are applications of more fundamental ethical laws, and they relate to a specific situation. For example, the rule to build a railing around one's roof is an application of the more fundamental ethical norm to love one's neighbor, but it applies to a time when houses had flat roofs and people spent time on them. The rule to love one's neighbor might appropriately be applied today by making sure that a passenger in one's car puts on his or her seat belt. These are changes in application of a more foundational rule, but God's ethical rules have not changed. For more on this see *Ethics for a Brave New World*, chapter 1.

53. If God is timeless, indexical propositions do not jeopardize his immutability, because his knowledge of them cannot change since as atemporal he cannot know the truth of any of them. This may seem to compromise divine omniscience, but the atemporalist can respond that failure to know indexicals does not endanger divine omniscience since divine omniscience means one knows all that can be known, and indexical propositions are unknowable for an atemporal being. In chapter 9, on God, time, and eternity, we will discuss the cogency of such claims.

54. Of course, if God is outside of time, that is another story. As we shall see in chapter 9, this is one of the issues that figures in the argumentation over whether God is temporal or atemporal.

55. See O. T. Allis, *Prophecy and the Church* (Nutley, N.J.: Presbyterian & Reformed, 1977), p. 32, for this understanding of the Jonah passage. Though I disagree that this verse proves that the Abrahamic Covenant is really conditional (the use to which Allis puts this interpretation), it seems correct that there must have been an implicit condition that God intended in Jonah's message, even if Jonah was not aware of it.

56. There is one qualification to this point. For libertarians (such as proponents of the open view of God) who don't believe God knows the future and believe that he may present conditional options but must wait until we act to decide what he will do, there may be a compromise with immutability of purposes or will (decree). But most evangelical incompatibilists have maintained that God does know the future in some way; hence, there need not be any change in purposes and choices on his part, for he already knows what we will do and has long ago decided how to respond.

CHAPTER   7

1. Peter T. Geach, *Providence and Evil* (Cambridge: Cambridge University Press, 1977), pp. 4-5.

2. Other passages that mention in one way or another God's power are Gen 23:6; Exod 9:16; Num 14:17; Deut 11:2; Josh 4:24; Neh 9:32; Job 5:17; 6:4, 14; 8:3; 22:25-26; 23:6, 16; 24:1, 22; 26:14; 27:2, 10, 11, 13; 32:8; 33:4; 34:10, 12; 35:13; 36:22; Ps 59:11; 63:2; 68:14, 35; 106:8; 110:3; Isa 30:29; 43:16; 60:16; Jer 32:19; Ezek 20:33-34; Dan 4:3; Hos 13:14; Zeph 3:17; Matt 22:29; Mark 12:24; Luke 1:49; Acts 1:7; Rom 1:4; 15:13, 19; 16:25; 1 Cor 2:5; 4:20; 5:4; 2 Cor 4:7; 6:7; 10:4; Eph 3:20; 2 Tim 1:8; 1 Pet 5:6; 2 Pet 1:16; Rev 11:17; 12:10; 15:3, 8; 16:7; 19:1, 6.

3. Though it is debated, there is evidence that René Descartes held that God could actualize a logically contradictory state of affairs. For further discussion of Descartes' position see Harry G. Frankfurt, "The Logic of Omnipotence," *Phil Rev* 72 (1963); D. Goldstick, "Could God Make a Contradiction True?" *Relig Stud* 26 (1990); David E. Schrader, "Frankfurt and Descartes: God and Logical Truth," *Sophia* 25 (April 1986); and Alvin Plantinga, *Does God Have a Nature?* (Milwaukee: Marquette University Press, 1980).

4. Heiko A. Oberman, *The Harvest of Medieval Theology* (Grand Rapids, Mich.: Eerdmans, 1967), p. 37. See also Leff's explanation of the two powers in Gordon Leff, *Medieval Thought* (Baltimore: Penguin, 1970), p. 288.

5. William of Ockham, *"Sententiarum IV," Opera Plurima,* 4:1494-1496 (London: Gregg Press, 1962), q. 8-9, E-F.

6. For evidence that even into the fifteenth century on the eve of the Reformation there were theonomists who believed these and other doctrines that granted God the ability to do any number of seemingly impossible things, see L. A. Kennedy, "The Fifteenth Century and Divine Absolute Power," *Vivarium* 27 (1989): 125-152.

7. This point has been argued by such thinkers as Hendrikus Berkhof, *Christian Faith: An Introduction to the Study of the Faith* (Grand Rapids, Mich.: Eerdmans, 1986), pp. 157-160; Grace M. Jantzen, "Human Autonomy in the Body of God," in Alastair Kee and Eugene T. Long, eds., *Being and Truth: Essays in Honour of John Macquarrie* (London: 1986), p. 195; and Simone Weil, *Gateway to God* (London: Fontana, 1974), p. 80.

8. Marcel Sarot, "Omnipotence and Self-limitation," in Gijsbert van den Brink, et al., eds., *Christian Faith and Philosophical Theology* (Kampen, Netherlands: Kok Pharos, 1992), p. 177.

9. For further discussion on the limitation and self-limitation of God's power, see Sarot, "Omnipotence and Self-limitation"; D. J. Louw, "Omnipotence (Force) or Vulnerability (Defencelessness)?" *Scriptura* 28 (1989): 41-58 (esp. 50-56); and Nicholas Gier, "Three Types of Divine Power," *Process Stud* 20 (Winter 1991): 221-232. For an interesting and helpful study of belief within the Jewish tradition in a God who is finite in knowledge and power, see Gilbert S. Rosenthal, "Omnipotence, Omniscience and a Finite God," *Judaism* 39 (Winter 1990): 55-72.

10. For a discussion of my problems with theonomy, see, for example, John S. Feinberg and Paul D. Feinberg, *Ethics for a Brave New World* (Wheaton, Ill.: Crossway, 1993), chapter 1; and my *The Many Faces of Evil* (Grand Rapids, Mich.: Zondervan, 1994), chapter 2, as well my discussion of theonomy elsewhere in this book.

11. Anthony Kenny, *The God of the Philosophers* (Oxford: Clarendon, 1979), p. 91.

12. Ibid., pp. 91-92.

13. Ibid., p. 92.

14. Thomas Aquinas, *Summa Theologiae,* part Ia, 25, 3.

15. Kenny, *God of the Philosophers,* p. 93.

16. Alvin Plantinga, *God and Other Minds* (Ithaca, N.Y.: Cornell University Press, 1967), p. 169.

17. Ibid., pp. 169-170.

18. Ibid., p. 170.

19. Ibid. See also Kenny, *God of the Philosophers,* p. 95.

20. Ibid.

21. Ibid.

22. Richard Swinburne, *The Coherence of Theism* (Oxford: Clarendon, 1977), pp. 154-158.

23. Kenny, *God of the Philosophers,* p. 96.

24. Ibid.

25. Ibid., pp. 96-97.

26. Ibid., p. 97.

27. Ibid., p. 98.

28. Ibid.

29. Philip E. Devenish, "Omnipotence, Creation, Perfection: Kenny and Aquinas on the Power and Action of God," *Mod Theol* 1 (1985): 108-109.

30. Ibid.

31. For a different definition of omnipotence along with an excellent discussion of the set of issues surrounding divine omnipotence, see Thomas P. Flint and Alfred J. Freddoso, "Maximal Power," in Thomas V. Morris, ed., *The Concept of God* (Oxford: Oxford University Press, 1987), pp.

134-167; originally printed in Alfred J. Freddoso, ed., *The Existence and Nature of God* (Notre Dame, Ind.: University of Notre Dame Press, 1983). Flint and Freddoso offer five conditions of philosophical adequacy which they believe an account of maximal power must meet. They explain why one or another account doesn't meet one or more of these conditions. They then offer an account which they think meets all five conditions and solves various problems with omnipotence. In contrast to Kenny, they define omnipotence in terms of states of affairs an omnipotent being can create, whereas Kenny focuses on powers an omnipotent being can logically possess. Kenny's definition seems simpler and more straightforward, but it also captures the main concerns of Flint and Freddoso without some of the complexity of their conditions of adequacy.

32. Yeager Hudson, "Omnipotence: Must God Be Infinite?" in W. Creighton Peden and Larry E. Axel, eds. *God, Values, and Empiricism: Issues in Philosophical Theology* (Macon, Ga.: Mercer University Press, 1989), p. 93.

33. In addition, this seems the best way to handle puzzles such as the paradox of the stone and J. L. Mackie's paradox of omnipotence. As to the former, George Mavrodes argues that the answer comes once we see that the notion of a stone so heavy that an omnipotent being could not lift it is self-contradictory. Since logical contradictions specify no power for doing any doable act, the paradox dissolves, and in no way damages omnipotence. I believe this is also the best way to answer Mackie's paradox of omnipotence. See George I. Mavrodes, "Some Puzzles Concerning Omnipotence," in Baruch A. Brody, ed., *Readings in the Philosophy of Religion: An Analytic Approach*, 2d ed. (Englewood Cliffs, N.J.: Prentice-Hall, 1974), p. 411. For further discussion of the paradox of the stone from a different perspective, see Alfred R. Mele and M. P. Smith, "The New Paradox of the Stone," *Faith Phil* 5 (July 1988). For Mackie's paradox, see J. L. Mackie, "Evil and Omnipotence," *Mind* 64 (1955): 210.

34. See my chapter "God Ordains All Things," in David Basinger and Randall Basinger, eds., *Predestination and Free Will* (Downers Grove, Ill.: InterVarsity, 1986).

35. Thomas V. Morris, *Our Idea of God* (Downers Grove, Ill.: InterVarsity, 1991), pp. 69-73. See also my article in Basinger and Basinger for other senses of "can."

36. Thomas V. Morris, "Perfection and Power," *Phil Rel* 20 (1986): 166-167.

37. Ibid., p. 167.

38. For further discussion and support of the notion that God can have various powers which he would never use because of his moral attributes, see the provocative and helpful paper by Thomas B. Talbott, "On the Divine Nature and the Nature of Divine Freedom," *Faith Phil* 5 (January 1988): 3-24, especially secs. i-iii.

39. See my *Many Faces of Evil,* chapters 2–3.

40. Anne Minas, "God and Forgiveness," *Phil Quart* 25 (1975): 138-150.

41. For further discussion of and responses to the claim that God cannot forgive, see Margaret Paton, "Can God Forgive?" *Mod Theol* 4 (1988): 225-233.

42. The position just described is that articulated by openness of God proponents. See, for example, John Sanders on God's sovereign control in *The God Who Risks* (Downers Grove, Ill.: InterVarsity, 1998).

43. The views just discussed might also be held by openness of God defenders, but it is certainly a position many traditional Arminians have taken.

44. The biblical words for will (and thus, divine will) are *ḥapēṣ, ṣēbû,* and *raṣôn* in Hebrew, and *boulē* and *thelēma* in Greek.

45. Scripture also teaches that Christ, the second member of the Trinity, knows various things that only God could know. John frequently talks of Christ's knowledge, and the point is often more than mere intellectual awareness; Christ knows by personal relationship (see John 7:29; 8:55; 10:14, 15, 27). Jesus also knew various facts about people (John 5:42; 8:37; 13:18). Jesus also clearly knew his mission and knew various spiritual truths (John 5:32; 8:14; 11:22; 12:50). Finally, in Revelation 1–3, we have Christ's messages to the seven churches. Repeatedly he shows that he knows what is happening (good and bad) in each church: Ephesus (Rev 2:2); Smyrna (2:9); Pergamos (2:13); see also 2:19; 3:1, 8, 15.

46. Kenny, *God of the Philosophers,* p. 91 (emphasis mine).

47. Ibid., pp. 29-32.

48. David Blumenfield, "On the Compossibility of the Divine Attributes," in Morris, ed., *Concept of God,* pp. 206-207.

49. Kenny, *God of the Philosophers,* p. 31.

50. Ibid., pp. 31-32.

51. Ibid., p. 34.

52. Ibid.

53. For further discussion of these two responses and the whole issue of omniscience and knowing by experience, see Marcel Sarot, "Omniscience and Experience," *Phil Rel* 30 (1991): 89-102.

54. Bruce Reichenbach, "Omniscience and Deliberation," *Int J Phil Relig* 16 (1984): 227.

55. Tomis Kapitan raises a similar issue in terms of intentional agency rather than deliberation. Kapitan claims that to act intentionally what one does "is connected, at least causally, to one's being settled

upon undertaking a particular course of action" (p. 107). But, if God is omniscient, it is impossible for him to be unsure of what he will do, for he already knows everything, and thus, knows in advance any action that he will do. Hence, it seems impossible for him to qualify as an intentional agent. The type of responses I shall offer to the deliberation issue also apply here. For Kapitan's views and interaction with them see "Agency and Omniscience," *Relig Stud* 27 (1991): 105-120 from which the quote in this footnote comes. See also a response to Kapitan and his counter-response in David P. Hunt, "Omniprescient Agency," *Relig Stud* 28 (1992): 351-369 and Tomis Kapitan, "The Incompatibility of Omniscience and Intentional Action: A Reply to David P. Hunt," *Relig Stud* 30 (1994): 55-66.

56. Reichenbach, "Omniscience and Deliberation," pp. 230-232. For a brief response to Reichenbach on the whole complex of issues he raises in his paper, see David Basinger, "Omniscience and Deliberation: A Response to Reichenbach," *Phil Rel* 20 (1986): 169-172.

57. Here I should add that though the language used makes it sound as if God is in time, at this point in the book I am not making a decision about that one way or another. Both atemporalists and temporalists holding to omniscience must address this question of whether God always knew that he would create and which world he would create, or whether God made a decision about such matters. The issue I'm raising confronts theism, regardless of how one handles the temporalism/atemporalism question, and my basic responses are usable by either a temporalist or an atemporalist.

58. A further issue of interest concerns omniscience and privacy. For details see Margaret Falls-Corbitt and F. Michael McLain, "God and Privacy," *Faith Phil* 9 (July 1992): 370-371.

59. For further stimulating discussions of divine omniscience, see Jonathan L. Kvanvig, "Unknowable Truths and the Doctrine of Omniscience," *Journal of the American Academy of Religion* 57 (Fall 1989): 485-507; Kvanvig, "The Analogy Argument for a Limited Account of Omniscience," *International Philosophical Quarterly* 29 (June 1989): 129-137; and William E. Mann, "Epistemology Supernaturalized," *Faith Phil* 2 (October 1985): 436-456.

60. Charles Taliaferro, "Divine Cognitive Power," *Int J Phil Relig* 18 (1985): 133-134.

61. Ibid., pp. 134-136.

62. Alston considers whether God's knowledge is propositional or non-propositional, and interested readers may consult his discussion. On either supposition, however, Alston argues that God acquires knowledge intuitively, and that is the significant point for our discussion. See William P. Alston, "Does God Have Beliefs?" *Relig Stud* 22 (1986).

63. Ibid., pp. 294-295.

64. Ibid., pp. 297-298. For further amplification of Alston's view and his application of this discussion to the question of whether God has beliefs, see the remainder of his article. For a response to Alston which agrees with much of what he says but offers a slight modification see William Hasker, "Yes, God Has Beliefs!" *Relig Stud* 24 (1988): 385-394.

65. Of course this will not necessarily solve all problems, for we must recognize that each member of the Trinity shares the same divine essence and divine mind. Still, Scripture portrays each as somehow individuating that divine mind to their particular subsistence without also multiplying divine essences. We are clearly in the presence of mystery at this point, but if somehow (as seems required to avoid unitarianism) there are three distinct subsistences, then it makes sense to talk of conversation, etc., within the Godhead.

66. Louis Berkhof, *Systematic Theology* (Grand Rapids, Mich.: Eerdmans, 1968), p. 69.

67. Biblical authors also speak of Christ's wisdom. See, for example, Isa 11:2; Matt 13:54; Mark 6:2; Luke 2:40, 52; and Col 2:3).

68. *TWOT* 1:30.

69. William E. Mann, "Simplicity and Immutability in God," in Morris, ed., *Concept of God*, p. 255.

70. Eleonore Stump and Norman Kretzmann, "Absolute Simplicity," *Faith Phil* 2 (October 1985): 354-355. See also Herman Bavinck, *The Doctrine of God* (Grand Rapids, Mich.: Baker, 1977), pp. 168, 170.

71. Mann, "Simplicity and Immutability in God," p. 255.

72. As to why the doctrine was frequently held during the Middle Ages and didn't seem as odd to medievals as it does to us, Nicholas Wolterstorff argues that the basic reason is that they were working from a different ontology than we are: a constituent ontology rather than a relational one. For a full development of this point, see Nicholas Wolterstorff, "Divine Simplicity," in Kelly J. Clark, ed., *Our Knowledge of God: Essays on Natural and Philosophical Theology* (Boston: Kluwer, 1992), p. 140ff.

73. Anselm, "Monologium," chapter 1 in *St. Anselm: Basic Writings*, trans. S. N. Deane (La Salle, Ill.: Open Court, 1968), p. 40.

74. Ibid., chapter 16, p. 65.

75. The relation between simplicity and eternity will be discussed in dealing with arguments for divine atemporal eternity. For our purposes now, I have only described the portion of Anselm's argument relevant to aseity.

76. L. Berkhof, *Systematic Theology*, p. 62.

77. Bavinck, *Doctrine of God*, p. 168.

78. Morris, *Our Idea of God,* p. 114.
79. Thomas V. Morris, "On God and Mann: A View of Divine Simplicity," *Relig Stud* 21 (1985): 300.
80. Alvin Plantinga, *Does God Have a Nature?* (Milwaukee: Marquette University Press, 1980), p. 47.
81. Ibid.
82. Ibid., pp. 51-52.
83. Ibid., pp. 52-53.
84. Brian Leftow, "The Roots of Eternity," *Relig Stud* 24 (1988): 198-199, says that such attributes aren't really to the point, because "a simple being is identical only with its real or intrinsic attributes, for only having a distinct real, intrinsic attribute would entail involving real, intrinsic complexity" (p. 199). However, Plantinga uses the term 'property' in the broad sense in which it is used in contemporary discussions. Moreover, it also seems that the point of dependence on one's attributes (intrinsic or extrinsic) is still the point that generates the urge to hold simplicity. Hence, it is appropriate for Plantinga to raise these sorts of attributes. Finally, it is indeed debatable that the doctrine of divine simplicity is only about intrinsic attributes. As Morris shows, it is about, in part, property identity, regardless of what sort of properties we are talking about. And if one holds simplicity and says it relates only to intrinsic properties but also admits that God has these extrinsic properties, one must still say something about how those extrinsic properties relate to his being. Are they identical with it or not? If identical, then Leftow's point about intrinsic/exstrinsic properties is beside the point, for all God's properties become intrinsic. If the "extrinsic" ones are not identical with God's being but do relate to him, then what becomes of the notion of simplicity?
85. I am basing this discussion on Plantinga's argumentation in *Does God Have a Nature?* (pp. 40-44). For an interesting discussion of another problem involving divine simplicity, see William Hasker, "Simplicity and Freedom: A Response to Stump and Kretzmann," *Faith Phil* 3 (April 1986).
86. William E. Mann, "Divine Simplicity," *Relig Stud* 18 (1981): 451-71. See also William E. Mann, "Simplicity and Properties: A Reply to Morris," *Relig Stud* 22 (September/December 1986): 344.
87. Morris, "On God and Mann," p. 301.
88. Mann, "Simplicity and Properties," p. 344.
89. Ibid., pp. 343-344, citing his views in "Divine Simplicity," pp. 465-467.
90. Leftow, "Roots of Eternity," p. 195.
91. Morris, "On God and Mann," p. 302.
92. Mann, "Simplicity and Properties," p. 352.
93. Ibid.
94. Wolterstorff, "Divine Simplicity," p. 139.
95. Ibid.
96. Mann, "Simplicity and Properties," p. 352.
97. In addition, William Vallicella offers another argument against this view. For details see William Vallicella, "Divine Simplicity: A New Defense," *Faith Phil* 9 (October 1992): 511.
98. Morris, *Our Idea of God,* p. 116.
99. Hence, a theonomist can uphold divine aseity as self-reliance in the sense that God doesn't depend on properties or his nature for his attributes by holding simplicity. Another way a theonomist might support divine aseity is to grant that God does have a nature which depends on properties that are independent of himself, but that God is the one who created the properties and controls them, so his self-reliance is still entirely intact. Whether such a proposal is even logically coherent is a matter I shall leave for the reader's consideration, but even if it is not, the theonomist may hold a form of theonomy that allows God to do the logically contradictory, so a logically inconsistent position would not seem to damage this form of theonomy.
100. If I understand him correctly, this is fundamentally Plantinga's position. See Plantinga, *Does God Have a Nature?* pp. 126-146.

C H A P T E R   8

1. *TWOT* 2:786-787.
2. Ibid. 2:787.
3. *TWOT* 1:305-307.
4. For further discussion of the various uses of these terms in the OT see *TWOT* 2:752-755.
5. For elaboration of this and other uses of these terms, see *TDNT* 2.
6. *TWOT* 1:14.
7. Ibid. 1:332.
8. Ibid. 1:302.
9. Ibid. 1:303.
10. Hans Conzelmann, "Charis," in *TDNT* 9:391-396.
11. Konrad Weiss, "Chrestos," in *TDNT* 9:487.
12. *TWOT* 2:842.
13. Ibid. 2:843.

14. Ibid. 2:302.
15. Rudolf Bultmann, "Eleos," in *TDNT* 2:477-485.
16. *TWOT* 1:72.
17. See J. Horst, "Makrothumia," in *TDNT* 4:379-387, for NT usage.
18. Franz Delitzsch, *Biblical Commentary on the Psalms*, vol. 3 (Grand Rapids, Mich.: Eerdmans, 1968 ed.), p. 15.
19. *TWOT* 1:346.
20. Ibid. 2:859-860. In the English translation this verse is Ps 40:7.
21. Konrad Weiss, "Chrestotes," in *TDNT* 9:491.
22. Ethelbert Stauffer, "Agapao," in *TDNT* 1:51-53.
23. John S. Feinberg, "Truth: Relation of Theories of Truth to Hermeneutics," in Earl Radmacher and Robert Preus, eds., *Hermeneutics, Inerrancy, and the Bible* (Grand Rapids, Mich.: Zondervan, 1984).
24. See chapter 1 of John S. Feinberg and Paul D. Feinberg, *Ethics for a Brave New World* (Wheaton, Ill.: Crossway, 1993).

C H A P T E R   9

1. Stephen Charnock, *The Existence and Attributes of God* (reprint, Minneapolis: Klock & Klock, 1977), p. 72.
2. Nelson Pike, *God and Timelessness* (New York: Schocken, 1970), p. 7.
3. Ibid.
4. Ibid., p. 8. If this is the sense of timelessness involved, how should we conceive it? Hasker considers God's timelessness along the lines of the timelessness of mathematical objects and explains the problems in thinking of God's timelessness along these lines. See William Hasker, "Concerning the Intelligibility of 'God is Timeless'," *New Scholasticism* 57 (Spring 1983): 173-174.
5. Boethius, "The Consolation of Philosophy," in *Boethius: The Theological Tractates*, Loeb Classical Library (reprint, Cambridge, Mass.: Harvard University Press, 1990), book 5, prose 6, p. 423.
6. Eleonore Stump and Norman Kretzmann, "Eternity," in Thomas V. Morris, ed., *The Concept of God* (Oxford: Oxford University Press, 1987), pp. 222-224. Paul Fitzgerald ("Stump and Kretzmann on Time and Eternity," *J Phil* 84 [1985]) cites these four items from Stump and Kretzmann, but thinks that two other elements are required by the definition: 1) all events are what Stump and Kretzmann label ET-simultaneous with every eternal entity or event, and 2) each eternal feature of an eternal entity is somehow simultaneous with every other feature (pp. 261-262). Later in this chapter I shall explain and evaluate ET-simultaneity.
7. Stump and Kretzmann, "Eternity," p. 225.
8. Ibid.
9. Ibid., p. 237.
10. Ibid., p. 238.
11. Eleonore Stump and Norman Kretzmann, "Atemporal Duration," in *J Phil* 84 (1987): 218-219.
12. Stump and Kretzmann, "Eternity," pp. 238-239.
13. Thomas V. Morris, *Our Idea of God* (Downers Grove, Ill.: InterVarsity, 1991), p. 120. For further discussion of whether a sempiternal being can be a necessary being, see William Kneale, "Time and Eternity in Theology," *Proceedings of the Aristotelian Society* 61 (1960-61): 101-107.
14. Paul Helm, *Eternal God* (Oxford: Clarendon, 1988), p. 5.
15. James Barr (*Biblical Words for Time*, 2d ed. [London: SCM Press LTD, 1969], p. 138) concurs when he writes that we find a "very serious shortage within the Bible of the kind of *actual statement* about 'time' or 'eternity' which could form a sufficient basis for a Christian philosophical-theological view of time."
16. Helm, *Eternal God*, p. 11.
17. For details see William Kneale, "Time and Eternity in Theology," p. 87. See also Stump and Kretzmann, "Eternity." The famous passage on eternity from Plato is taken from the *Timaeus*, 38B5.
18. Augustine, *De Civitate Dei*, XI, 21. This point is made in Kneale, "Time and Eternity in Theology," p. 94.
19. Augustine, *Confessions* (Baltimore: Penguin, 1964), XI, 10, p. 261.
20. Ibid., XI, 11, pp. 261-262.
21. Ibid., XI, 13, p. 263.
22. Ibid.
23. Pike, *God and Timelessness*, pp. 8-9.
24. Boethius, "The Consolation of Philosophy," book 5, prose 6, pp. 115-118 *passim*.
25. Anselm, "Proslogium," chapter 19, p. 25, in *St. Anselm: Basic Writings*, trans. S. N. Deane (La Salle, Ill.: Open Court, 1968). See also Anselm, "Monologium," chapter 22, p. 81 in *St. Anselm: Basic Writings* for a similar statement.

26. Pike, *God and Timelessness*, p. 9.
27. Anselm, "Proslogium," chapter 5, p. 11.
28. Ibid., chapter 11, p. 19.
29. Anselm, "Monologium," chapter 3, p. 42, and chapter 4, p. 44.
30. He writes, "Since, then, it is true of whatever else there is, that, if it is taken independently, *to be it* is better than *not to be it*; as it is impious to suppose that the substance of the supreme Nature is anything, than which what is not it is in any way better, it must be true that this substance is whatever is, in general, better than what is not it." "Monologium," chapter 15, pp. 63-64.
31. Ibid., chapter 21, pp. 76-77.
32. Thomas Aquinas, *Summa Theologiae*, ed. Thomas Gilby (Garden City, N.Y.: Image, 1969), 1A, Q 10, 1, pp. 144 and 145.
33. Pike, *God and Timelessness*, p. 10.
34. Aquinas, *Summa Theologiae*, 1A, Q 10, 2, p. 146.
35. Ibid., 1A, Q 2, Article 3, p. 71.
36. Ibid., p. 70.
37. For several other ways to derive atemporal eternity by logical connection from other views about God, see Stephen Charnock, *Existence and Attributes of God*, p. 81; Morris, *Our Idea of God*, pp. 129-130. Pike's argument for this is contained in *God and Timelessness*, pp. 135-165. See also Helm, *Eternal God*, pp. 16-22 for a response to Pike.
38. Anselm, "Monologium," chapter 1, p. 40.
39. Ibid., chapter 16, p. 65.
40. Alvin Plantinga's *Does God Have a Nature?* (Milwaukee: Marquette University Press, 1980) is extremely helpful in clarifying the move from aseity to simplicity. See his explanation on pages 32-33. See also his pp. 30-31 citing Aquinas, *Summa Theologiae*, IA 3, 4, and *Summa Contra Gentiles* I, 38.
41. As confirmation of this interpretation, see what Anselm says in chapter 17 of the "Monologium" (pp. 66-67): "Is it to be inferred, then, that if the supreme Nature is so many good, it will therefore be compounded of more goods than one? Or is it true, rather, that there are not more goods than one, but a single good described by many names? For, everything which is composite requires for its subsistence the things of which it is compounded, and, indeed, owes to them the fact of its existence, because, whatever it is, it is through these things; and they are not what they are through it, and therefore it is not at all supreme. If, then, that Nature is compounded of more goods than one, all these facts that are true of every composite must be applicable to it. . . . Since, then, that Nature is by no means composite, and yet is by all means those so many goods, necessarily all these are not more than one, but are one. Any one of them is, therefore, the same as all, whether taken all at once or separately. Therefore, just as whatever is attributed to the essence of the supreme Substance is one; so this substance is whatever it is essentially in one way, and by virtue of one consideration."
42. Helm, *Eternal God*, chapter 5, argues in some detail that immutability does entail timelessness. He notes different senses of immutability and shows how they relate to timelessness.
43. William E. Mann, "Simplicity and Immutability in God," in Morris, ed., *Concept of God*, p. 255.
44. Ibid., pp. 256-257. Mann uses DDI to refer to the doctrine of divine immutability.
45. Pike explains the argument in a more detailed fashion (*God and Timelessness*, p. 43). See also Helm's explanation of the connection between immutability and timelessness in Helm, *Eternal God*, pp. 16-22. Helm's emphasis tends to focus on why a timeless God must be immutable, rather than on the other way around, but both entailments are discussed. See also Charnock, *Existence and Attributes of God*, p. 81; and Morris, *Our Idea of God*, p. 127, for further explanations of the connection between these attributes.
46. Morris, *Our Idea of God*, p. 125.
47. Ibid.
48. Ibid., pp. 125-126.
49. Helm, *Eternal God*, p. 38. See also Morris, *Our Idea of God*, p. 126.
50. Morris, *Our Idea of God*, p. 126.
51. Helm, *Eternal God*, p. 38.
52. Ibid., pp. 38-39.
53. Morris, *Our Idea of God*, p. 124. See also William P. Alston, "Hartshorne and Aquinas: A Via Media," in William P. Alston, ed., *Divine Nature and Human Language: Essays in Philosophical Theology* (Ithaca, N.Y.: Cornell University Press, 1989), p. 133. Alston concludes that in light of this problem, the only real alternative for the temporalist is to adopt Hartshorne's view that God and the world are equally basic metaphysically. God's creative activities then would be limited to bringing it about that the world agrees with his aims. Creation *ex nihilo* would be ruled out.
54. Augustine, *Confessions*, XI, 12, p. 262.
55. Morris offers two replies in behalf of temporalists, but neither is particularly convincing. See Morris, *Our Idea of God*, p. 124.
56. Brian Leftow, *Time and Eternity* (Ithaca, N.Y.: Cornell University Press, 1991), p. 281.

57. See Leftow, p. 281, for some objections to the premises.
58. Ibid., p. 282.
59. William Hasker, *God, Time and Knowledge* (Ithaca, N.Y.: Cornell University Press, 1989), p. 179.
60. Stump and Kretzmann, "Eternity," p. 237.
61. Hasker, *God, Time and Knowledge*, p. 183. Hasker raises this argument initially on pp. 179-180.
62. Friedrich Schleiermacher, *The Christian Faith* (Edinburgh: Clark, 1956), numbered paragraph 53, sec. I, pp. 206-208.
63. Pike, *God and Timelessness*, p. 6, citing Schleiermacher, numbered paragraph 53, sec. 2, p. 209.
64. See Helm, *Eternal God*, pp. 41-55. For further discussion of the relation of space and time and the use of that relation to argue for God as atemporal, see Brian Leftow, *Time and Eternity*, chapter 3.
65. Robert Coburn, "Professor Malcolm on God," *Austl J Phil* 40-41 (1962–1963): 155.
66. R. L. Sturch, "The Problem of Divine Eternity," *Relig Stud* 10 (1974): 489-490. Richard Gale discusses two activities said to be impossible for a timeless being, intentional actions and interaction with other beings. See Richard M. Gale, "Omniscience-Immutability Arguments," *Amer Phil Quart* 23 (October 1986): 333.
67. Sturch, "Problem of Divine Eternity," p. 490.
68. Pike (*God and Timelessness*, pp. 122-123) explains why a timeless being couldn't do many of these activities. Reflecting and deliberating take time, so they require temporal extension. Anticipating, remembering, and intending require temporal location. Atemporal beings have neither temporal extension nor location.
69. Sturch, "Problem of Divine Eternity," p. 490.
70. Ibid. For further discussion of how a timeless being could intend an action, see Brian Leftow, *Time and Eternity*, pp. 295-297.
71. His answer is a pared down sense of "affect." See Sturch, "Problem of Divine Eternity," p. 491.
72. Ibid.
73. Here I note that this particular problem confronts the theist in the form I raise it just in case he is an indeterminist. Sturch surely is and offers his explanation of Ahab and Naboth's vineyard accordingly. For an atemporalist who is a determinist, this isn't so difficult a problem, for the determinist can say that God, in determining all things, decided all at once what will happen and how he will react to whatever occurs. The only problem, then, for the determinist is whether it makes sense to say that a God who has decided all things in one timeless act is truly able to bring about the things in our world that he has planned. But that difficulty at least focuses on the temporal/atemporal debate over eternity without complicating it by tacking on the complications that arise when one holds libertarian free will.
74. Paul Helm has addressed several of these activities as an atemporalist might. Representative of his treatment is his handling of remembering. See Helm, *Eternal God*, pp. 59-61.
75. Mann, "Simplicity and Immutability in God," p. 257.
76. Ibid.
77. Ibid., p. 260.
78. Ibid., p. 259.
79. Ibid., p. 258.
80. Stump and Kretzmann, "Eternity," p. 240.
81. Pike, *God and Timelessness*, p. 118, sees the problem of temporal location (not so much temporal duration) as the inconsistency with timelessness. See also Richard Swinburne, *The Coherence of Theism* (Oxford: Clarendon, 1986), pp. 220-221. It also seems that if God acts in time, his actions partake of the nature of time, and many acts in time take time to do (i.e., they have a beginning, middle, and end—there is temporal succession in them). Hence, if God does such actions, there is a change in God's states which is impossible for an immutable and atemporal being.
82. Pike, *God and Timelessness*, pp. 104-105. See also Helm, *Eternal God*, pp. 67-68 for an exposition of this argument as found in Pike.
83. Stump and Kretzmann, "Eternity," p. 241.
84. Ibid.
85. Helm offers two arguments to show the error in this line of reasoning (Helm, *Eternal God*, p. 70).
86. Helm (*Eternal God*, pp. 70-71) offers this answer, but it is fairly standard fare for Calvinists.
87. Nicholas Wolterstorff, "God Everlasting," in *God and the Good*, Clifton Orlebeke and Lewis Smedes, eds. (Grand Rapids, Mich.: Eerdmans, 1975), pp. 195-196.
88. For presentations of this line of argument, see Wolterstorff, "God Everlasting," pp. 197ff.; Hasker, "Concerning the Intelligibility of 'God Is Timeless'," p. 182ff.; and Morris, *Our Idea of God*, pp. 132-133.
89. For this basic line of argument see Wolterstorff, "God Everlasting," pp. 181-182,192-194. See also Morris, *Our Idea of God*, pp. 134-135.
90. Morris, *Our Idea of God*, pp. 134-135.
91. Wolterstorff, "God Everlasting," p. 194.
92. Ibid., pp. 194-195.

93. Ibid., pp. 195-196.

94. Ibid., p. 196.

95. Anthony Kenny, *Aquinas: A Collection of Critical Essays* (London, 1969), p. 264, as cited in Anthony Kenny, *The God of the Philosophers* (Oxford: Clarendon, 1979), pp. 38-39. Swinburne (*Coherence of Theism*, pp. 220-221) offers a differently stated version of the same problem.

96. Other resolutions have been offered as well. William Hasker, a temporalist, offers one in behalf of atemporalists and then critiques it. See Hasker, *God, Time, and Knowledge*, pp. 162-184. A third proposal has been advanced by Brian Leftow. See Brian Leftow, "Eternity and Simultaneity," *Faith Phil* 8 (April 1991): 149-164; and Leftow's *Time and Eternity*. See also Helm, *Eternal God*, p. 27.

97. Stump and Kretzmann, "Eternity," p. 225.

98. Ibid., p. 226.

99. Ibid., p. 227.

100. Ibid., p. 228. The last sentence of the quote is from Wesley Salmon, *Space, Time, and Motion* (Minneapolis: University of Minnesota Press, 1980), p. 76.

101. Stump and Kretzmann, "Eternity," p. 229.

102. Ibid., p. 230.

103. Ibid., pp. 230-231.

104. Stump and Kretzmann, "Eternity, Awareness, and Action," *Faith Phil* 9 (October 1992): 475.

105. Stump and Kretzmann, "Eternity," p. 231.

106. Ibid., pp. 232-236. Stump and Kretzmann offer their example in terms of Nixon. Since Nixon wasn't dead at the time they wrote but is dead as I now write, I am updating the example.

107. Ibid., pp. 239-243.

108. Others have also raised problems with Stump and Kretzmann's understanding of atemporal eternity, but since they don't touch the core of the debate over ET-simultaneity, they need not detain us. For example, Paul Fitzgerald complains that atemporal eternity seems to require timeless duration, whereas Stump and Kretzmann's handling of Boethius's definition seems to make the eternal now more like a point than a duration. For details of this objection and replies to it, see Paul Fitzgerald, "Stump and Kretzmann on Time and Eternity," *J Phil* 82 (1985); Eleonore Stump and Norman Kretzmann, "Comments and Criticism: Atemporal Duration: A Reply to Fitzgerald" *J Phil* 84 (1987); and Eleonore Stump and Norman Kretzmann, "Eternity, Awareness, and Action," *Faith Phil* 9 (October 1992): 464-467.

109. Delmas Lewis, "Eternity Again: A Reply to Stump and Kretzmann," *Int J Phil Relig* 15 (1984): 74-75.

110. Brian Leftow, "The Roots of Eternity," *Relig Stud* 24 (1988): 211ff. raises the same objection.

111. Lewis, "Eternity Again," p. 75.

112. See Lewis's explanation of the problem (ibid.).

113. One objection raises problems with ET-simultaneity when it is joined with divine simplicity, an attribute atemporalists typically predicate of God. See Brian Leftow, "Roots of Eternity," pp. 207-208.

114. Leftow, "Roots of Eternity," p. 207.

115. Eleonore Stump and Norman Kretzmann, "Eternity, Awareness, and Action," pp. 477-478.

116. Ibid., p. 478.

117. Hasker raises the same objection on p. 169 of *God, Time, and Knowledge*, though his point is more about awareness than about causal interaction.

118. Stump and Kretzmann, "Eternity, Awareness, and Action," pp. 475-476.

119. Ibid., p. 476.

120. Ibid.

121. Even Paul Helm, an atemporalist, agrees and offers many of the same objections others have against ET-simultaneity. See Helm, *Eternal God*, pp. 32-36.

122. For those who want to pursue further the issue of freedom and foreknowledge, let me suggest some contemporary literature that discusses it from one vantage point or another. In my handling of divine sovereignty, human freedom, and divine foreknowledge, of course, there will be fuller coverage. Marilyn Adams, "Is the Existence of God a 'Hard' Fact?" *Phil Rev* 75 (1966); Robert Adams, "Middle Knowledge and the Problem of Evil," *Amer Phil Quart* 14 (1977); William Lane Craig, *The Only Wise God* (Grand Rapids, Mich.: Baker, 1987); John M. Fischer, "Freedom and Foreknowledge," *Phil Rev* 92 (January 1983); Alfred J. Freddoso, "Accidental Necessity and Logical Determinism," *J Phil* 80 (May 1983); Paul Helm, *Eternal God*, pp. 95-170; Anthony Kenny, *God of the Philosophers*, chapter 5; Brian Leftow, "Eternity and Simultaneity," *Faith Phil* 8 (April 1991): 148-151, 172-175; Brian Leftow, *Time and Eternity*, chapter 11; Brian Leftow, "Timelessness and Foreknowledge," *Phil Stud* 63 (1991); William Mann, "Simplicity and Immutability in God," pp. 262-264; Thomas V. Morris, *Our Idea of God*, p. 129; Nelson Pike, "Divine Omniscience and Voluntary Action," in Steven M. Cahn, ed. *Phil Rel* (New York: Harper & Row, 1970); Nelson Pike, *God and Timelessness*, pp. 53-86, 174-175; Alvin Plantinga, "On Ockham's Way Out," *Faith Phil* 3 (July 1986); and Bruce Reichenbach, "Omniscience and Deliberation," *Int J Phil Relig* 16 (1984).

123. Those interested in pursuing this issue should consult William Hasker, "Concerning the Intelligibility of 'God Is Timeless'."

124. Robert Coburn, "Professor Malcolm on God," pp. 155-156, cited in Pike, *God and Timelessness*, pp. 88-89. See also Prior's much quoted statement in Arthur Prior, "The Formalities of Omniscience," *Philosophy* 37 (1962) as quoted in Kenny, *God of the Philosophers*, p. 39.

125. Norman Kretzmann, "Omniscience and Immutability," in Steven Cahn, ed. *Phil Rel* (New York: Harper & Row, 1970), p. 95.

126. Ibid., pp. 89-90.

127. Richard Gale points out that there is actually a form of the argument that confronts temporalists as well. In its omnitemporal version, however, the argument simply says that though God remains omniscient by knowing each moment what is happening, for God to change his knowledge in the way necessitated by a being in time is to compromise his immutability. See Richard M. Gale, "Omniscience-Immutability Arguments," *Amer Phil Quart* 23 (October 1986): 319. Now, this is true, of course, if one thinks of immutability in the strong sense that allows God to undergo no change whatsoever. If, however, we understand immutability as I have nuanced it, there is no argument to make against divine immutability on the basis of God's knowledge of what is happening now.

128. Leftow, *Time and Eternity*, pp. 321-334.

129. Ibid., pp. 321-322.

130. Ibid., p. 323.

131. Ibid., p. 325.

132. Ibid., p. 334.

133. My point about being careful not to beg the question on this issue is similar to a point Stump and Kretzmann make in "Eternity," pp. 250-251. In commenting on the argument in Kretzmann's "Omniscience and Eternity," they note that premise (3) may be read in several ways, including (3)(a) "A being that knows everything always knows in the temporal present what time it is in the temporal present." As Stump and Kretzmann argue, the problem with this interpretation of premise (3) is that it begs the question. While (3)(a) is obviously the intended sense of the premise, according to Stump and Kretzmann, the problem is that "(3)(a) is true just in case only a temporal entity can be omniscient, since an omniscient atemporal entity cannot be said to know in the temporal present, and it begs the question at issue to assume that no atemporal entity can be omniscient" (p. 250). This in general is my point. Before we say that God cannot be omniscient unless he knows the truth of temporal indexicals, we must decide whether God really must know such things. If he is atemporal, he must not. If he is temporal, he must. Since we are trying to decide whether he is temporal or atemporal, we cannot assume that the temporalist has already won that debate so that God must know these indexicals. To do so begs the question, and it is also question begging to assume that atemporalism is correct and thus, God can be omniscient without knowing temporal indexicals. In addition, I note that Leftow's treatment of this problem is atypical of atemporalists. Atemporalists usually think this is something an omniscient being should know, and hence, they try to explain how God does know the truth of these propositions, despite being atemporal.

134. Gale, "Omniscience-Immutability Arguments," p. 319.

135. Hector-Neri Castañeda, "Omniscience and Indexical Reference," *J Phil* 64 (1967): 203.

136. Ibid., p. 204.

137. Ibid. In this case X is the name of the being Kretzmann is talking about.

138. Ibid., p. 205.

139. Ibid., pp. 205-206.

140. Ibid., pp. 206-207.

141. Ibid., p. 207.

142. Ibid., p. 208.

143. In a similar way, Nelson Pike (*God and Timelessness*, chapter 5) seems to think this sort of answer is acceptable to uphold atemporal eternity. After setting forth a defense of atemporalism on this point, a defense that amounts to similar notions as those found in Castañeda, Pike concludes (p. 95): "Prior, Coburn, and Kretzmann claim to have identified a range of facts that a timeless individual could not know. But this claim has not been established. So far as I can determine, all that has been established is that there are certain *forms of words* that a timeless individual could not use when formulating or reporting his knowledge."

144. Peter Geach, *Providence and Evil* (Cambridge: Cambridge University Press, 1977), p. 40.

145. Ibid.

146. Gale, "Omniscience-Immutability Arguments," p. 321.

147. Ibid.

148. Ibid.

149. Ibid., p. 319.

150. Ibid., p. 322.

151. For further problems with a Castañeda-type response to this problem, see Gale's arguments in "Omniscience-Immutability Arguments," pp. 330-331. In addition, Paul Helm offers a further

response to the issue of divine omniscience and temporal indexicals. Space doesn't permit treating it here, though I do so in a forthcoming work on God, time, and eternity. For those interested in Helm's resolution, see his *Eternal God,* pp. 42-48. Finally, there is a further recent attempt to resolve this dilemma that comes from Thomas Sullivan and appeals to ideas in Aquinas. See Thomas D. Sullivan, "Omniscience, Immutability, and the Divine Mode of Knowing," *Faith Phil* 8 (January 1991).

152. By fellowship I mean a sharing or relating of one's thoughts, feelings, experiences with another who does the same with you. Typically, it involves relating things that the other person doesn't know or isn't thinking about, so that both may think about the same thing and interact with one another as they think about it.

153. A final reason for questioning whether atemporal duration makes sense is that it is not clear that all atemporalists mean by timelessness as timeless *duration*. Stump and Kretzmann have interpreted Boethius's definition of eternity that way (and argued that other theists in the classical Christian tradition have held a similar view), but there is reason to wonder. In a recent article, Katherin Rogers has argued persuasively that many classical theists such as Boethius didn't mean that timelessness should be understood as atemporal duration. See Katherin A. Rogers, "Eternity Has No Duration," *Relig Stud* 30 (1994).

154. In response to why God waited to create until he did, both temporalists and atemporalists should answer that, like other questions about God and his actions, the answer is hidden in God's mind. We don't have to know God's reasoning behind his timing. That we don't know God's reasoning for creating when he did doesn't seem a cogent complaint against either an atemporal or a temporal notion of divine eternity.

155. See, for example, on freedom and sovereignty, my article "God Ordains All Things," in Randall Basinger and David Basinger, eds., *Predestination and Free Will* (Downers Grove, Ill.: InterVarsity, 1986); and my article "God, Freedom, and Evil in Calvinist Thinking," in Thomas Schreiner and Bruce Ware, eds. *The Grace of God, the Bondage of the Will,* vol. 2 (Grand Rapids, Mich.: Baker, 1995). For handling of the problem of evil as a determinist, see my *The Many Faces of Evil* (Grand Rapids, Mich.: Zondervan, 1994).

156. See, again, my Basinger and Basinger article; and chapter 4 of *The Many Faces of Evil.*

157. Alfred N. Whitehead, *Process and Reality* (New York: Macmillan, 1929), p. 529. See also William C. Tremmel, "Comments on God, Neo-Naturalism and A. N. Whitehead's Philosophy," *Iliff Review* 45 (Spring 1988): 30.

158. Thomas V. Morris, "God and the World," in Ronald Nash, ed., *Process Theology* (Grand Rapids, Mich.: Baker, 1987), pp. 300-304.

159. See Jeffrey Rada, "Problems with Process Theology," *Restoration Quarterly* 29 (1987): 32; William Power, "The Doctrine of the Trinity and Whitehead's Metaphysics," *Encounter* 45 (Autumn 1984): 294, D. & R. Basinger, "Divine Omnipotence: Plantinga vs. Griffin," *Process Stud* 11 (Spring 1981); and Michael Peterson, "God and Evil in Process Theology," in Ronald Nash, ed., *Process Theology.*

160. Schubert Ogden, *The Reality of God and Other Essays* (New York: Harper & Row, 1963), pp. 64-65.

161. See my *Many Faces of Evil,* chapters 6–7, as an example of how a Calvinist such as myself might handle the logical problems of moral and natural evil.

CHAPTER 10

1. For this formal expression of the seven propositions, see Richard Cartwright, "On the Logical Problem of the Trinity," in Richard Cartwright, *Philosophical Essays* (Cambridge, Mass.: MIT Press, 1987), p. 188. This is cited in Edward C. Feser, "Swinburne's Tritheism," *Int J Phil Relig* 42 (1997): 175; and John Zeis, "A Trinity on a Trinity on a Trinity," *Sophia* 32 (1993): 45.

2. There are many contemporary treatments of the doctrine of the Trinity. The following is only suggestive of what is available. For feminist handlings of the Trinity, see Elizabeth A. Johnson, *She Who Is* (New York: Crossroad, 1993), chapter 10; Marjorie Suchocki, "The Unmale God: Reconsidering the Trinity," *Quarterly Review* 3 (Spring 1983); Rebecca Oxford-Carpenter, "Gender and the Trinity," *Theol Today* 41 (April 1984); and Gail Ramshaw-Schmidt, "Naming the Trinity: Orthodoxy and Inclusivity," *Worship* 60 (1986). For discussion of process notions of the Trinity, see Joseph A. Bracken, "Process Philosophy and Trinitarian Theology-II," *Process Stud* 15 (1981-1982); R. J. Pendergast, "A Thomistic-Process Theory of the Trinity," *Science et Esprit* 42 (1990); Bruce A. Demarest, "The Process Reduction of Jesus and the Trinity," in Ronald Nash, ed., *Process Theology* (Grand Rapids, Mich.: Baker, 1987); and Thomas V. Morris, "God and the World," in Ronald Nash, ed., *Process Theology.* For other contemporary handlings of the doctrine of the Trinity, see G. W. H. Lampe, *God as Spirit* (Oxford: Clarendon, 1977); and the article on Lampe's views by Christopher B. Kaiser, "The Prospects for a Thoroughgoing Model of 'God as Spirit'," *Reformed Review* 32 (1978–1979). See also Thomas D. Parker, "The Political Meaning of the Doctrine of the Trinity: Some Theses," *J Relig* 60 (1980); Geevarghese Mar Osthathios, "The Holy Trinity and the Kingdom," *The Indian Journal of Theology* 31 (1982); John J. O'Donnell, "The Doctrine of the Trinity in Recent German Theology," *The Heythrop Journal* 23 (April

1982); Tadd Dunne, "Notes: Trinity and History," *Theol Stud* 45 (1984); Carl E. Braaten, "The Question of God and the Trinity," in Walter Freitag, ed., *Festschrift: A Tribute to Dr. William Hordern* (Saskatoon: University of Saskatchewan, 1985); Mercy A. Oduyoye, "The Doctrine of the Trinity—Is It Relevant for Contemporary Christian Theology?" in Robert Scharlemann, ed., *Naming God* (New York: Paragon House, 1985); Jürgen Moltmann, "The Unity of the Triune God," *St. Vladimir's Theological Quarterly* 28 (1984), with responses by John B. Cobb, Jr., Susan B. Thistlethwaite, and Fr. John Meyendorff; Jürgen Moltmann, "The Inviting Unity of the Triune God," in Claude Geffre and Jean-Pierre Jossua, eds., *Monotheism* (Edinburgh: T & T Clark, 1985); Eric C. Rust, "The Dynamic Nature of the Triune God," *Perspect Rel S* 14 (Winter 1987); Robert W. Jenson, "The Logic of the Doctrine of the Trinity," *Dialog* 26 (1987); Wolfhart Pannenberg, "Problems of a Trinitarian Doctrine of God," *Dialog* 26 (1987); Paul R. Hinlicky, "Theocentrism," *Dialog* 26 (1987); Nicholas Lash, "Considering the Trinity," *Mod Theol* 2 (April 1986); Rowan Williams, "Trinity and Revelation," *Mod Theol* 2 (April 1986); John Milbank, "The Second Difference: For a Trinitarianism without Reserve," *Mod Theol* 2 (April 1986); Geoffrey Wainwright, "The Doctrine of the Trinity: Where the Church Stands or Falls," *Interpretation* 45 (April 1991); Harold Wells, "The Trinity and the Good News (parts I and II)," *Touchstone* 8 (May, September 1990); Randall E. Otto, "The *Imago Dei* as *Familitas*," *JETS* 35 (December 1992); Philip Cary, "On Behalf of Classical Trinitarianism: A Critique of Rahner on the Trinity," *The Thomist* 56 (1992); and Edward C. Feser, "Swinburne's Tritheism," *Int J Phil Relig* 42 (1997). Of special influence and interest are the following: Robert W. Jenson, *The Triune Identity* (Philadelphia: Fortress, 1982); Eberhard Jungel, *The Doctrine of the Trinity: God's Being Is in Becoming* (Grand Rapids, Mich.: Eerdmans, 1976); Bernard Lonergan, *De Deo trino: Pars Analytica* (Rome: Gregorian University, 1964); Jürgen Moltmann, *Trinity and the Kingdom* (New York: Harper & Row, 1981); Wolfhart Pannenberg, "Die Subjektivitat Gottes und die Trinitatslehre," in his *Grundfragen systematischer Theologie* 2 (Gottingen: Vandenhoeck & Ruprecht, 1980); Karl Rahner, *The Trinity* (London: Burns & Oates, 1970); and Karl Barth's extensive treatment of the doctrine in his *Church Dogmatics,* vol. 1, part 1 (reprint, Edinburgh: T & T Clark, 1960).

3. Wolfhart Pannenberg, "The Christian Vision of God: The New Discussion on the Trinitarian Doctrine," *Trinity Seminary Review* 13 (1991): 53-54.

4. *TWOT* 1:30.

5. A. H. Strong, *Systematic Theology* (Valley Forge, Pa.: Judson, 1907), pp. 318-319, seems to think this is the meaning of the plural form.

6. See Millard Erickson's discussion of this issue in his *Christian Theology* (Grand Rapids, Mich.: Baker, 1983), vol. 1, p. 328. Erickson discusses several who understand '*ĕlōhîm* as indicating plurality (especially plurality of majesty), and several who reject that view. In this volume, he does not himself take one position or the other.

7. Franz Delitzsch, *Biblical Commentary on the Prophecies of Isaiah,* vol. 1 (reprint, Grand Rapids, Mich.: Eerdmans, 1967), p.198; and George B. Gray, *A Critical and Exegetical Commentary on the Book of Isaiah,* vol. 1, ICC (Edinburgh: T & T Clark, 1949), p. 109.

8. John Calvin, *Commentary on the Book of the Prophet Isaiah,* vol. 1 (reprint, Grand Rapids, Mich.: Eerdmans, 1948), p. 213.

9. Geoffrey Grogan, *Isaiah,* vol. 6 of The Expositor's Bible Commentary, ed. Frank Gaebelein (Grand Rapids, Mich.: Zondervan, 1986), p. 57.

10. Probably the closest we come to it is the blessing of God as the Lord God of Israel, our father, found in 1 Chron 29:10. While some modern translations suggest that "our father" refers to Israel, the Hebrew allows it to refer to either Israel or God.

    Some have also seen various references in OT wisdom literature to wisdom as pointing to a member of the Godhead. In particular, Proverbs 8 personifies wisdom, and some have argued that this is ultimately a reference to Christ (see Prov 8:1, 22, 30, 31). For an interesting presentation of this position see Wayne Grudem, *Systematic Theology* (Grand Rapids, Mich.: Zondervan, 1994), pp. 229-230.

11. Hermann Kleinknecht, "The Greek Use of *eikon,*" in *TDNT* 2:389.

12. F. F. Bruce, *Commentary on the Epistle to the Hebrews* (Grand Rapids, Mich.: Eerdmans, 1972), p. 5.

13. Ibid., p. 6. See also B. F. Westcott's confirmation of these interpretations in B. F. Westcott, *The Epistle to the Hebrews* (reprint, Grand Rapids, Mich.: Eerdmans, 1967), pp. 10-14.

14. For a thorough explanation and illustration of this grammatical point see David B. Wallace, *Greek Grammar Beyond the Basics* (Grand Rapids, Mich.: Zondervan, 1996), pp. 256-270. Wallace shows the relation of this point to what is often called Colwell's rule, both explaining and correcting errors that Colwell and others have made on this point. (A word of thanks is due to Robert Yarbrough for bringing this material to my attention.) For further explanation of the exegetical grounds for thinking that John is predicating deity of Christ, see Grudem, *Systematic Theology,* p. 234, fn 12.

15. In constructing my discussion of the biblical data relating to the Trinity, I found helpful the following works: J. O. Buswell, *A Systematic Theology of the Christian Religion* (Grand Rapids, Mich.: Zondervan, 1972), pp. 103-106, 113-123; Charles Hodge, *Systematic Theology,* vol. 1 (London: James Clarke, 1960), pp. 443-448; W. G. T. Shedd, *Dogmatic Theology,* vol. 1 (Grand

Rapids, Mich.: Zondervan, 1969), pp. 258-266, 312-331; Herman Bavinck, *The Doctrine of God* (Grand Rapids, Mich.: Baker, 1977), pp. 255-274; Bruce Demarest and Gordon Lewis, *Integrative Theology*, vol. 1 (Grand Rapids, Mich.: Zondervan, 1987), pp. 257-270; Henry Thiessen, *Lectures in Systematic Theology* (Grand Rapids, Mich.: Eerdmans, 1983), pp. 90-98; Erickson, *Christian Theology*, pp. 322-332; Grudem, *Systematic Theology*, pp. 226-239; Louis Berkhof, *Systematic Theology* (Grand Rapids, Mich.: Eerdmans, 1968), pp. 85-86, 90-92; Strong, *Systematic Theology*, pp. 304-326; Eugene Merrill and Alan J. Hauser, "Is the Doctrine of the Trinity Implied in the Genesis Creation Account?" in Ronald Youngblood, ed., *The Genesis Debate: Persistent Questions about Creation and the Flood* (Grand Rapids, Mich.: Baker, 1990); Wolfhart Pannenberg, "The Christian Vision of God: the New Discussion on the Trinitarian Doctrine," *Trinity Seminary Review* 13 (1991); Colin Brown, "Trinity and Incarnation: In Search of Contemporary Orthodoxy," *Ex Auditu* 7 (1991); and Randall E. Otto, "The *Imago Dei* as *Familitas*," *JETS* 35 (December 1992).

16. Roger Haight, "The Point of Trinitarian Theology," *Toronto Journal of Theology* 4 (Fall 1988): 194.
17. Hodge, *Systematic Theology*, p. 450.
18. Ibid., p. 451.
19. For a development of the case for this view, see William R. Schoedel, "A Neglected Motive for Trinitarianism," *JTS* 31 (October 1980). Schoedel makes special reference to the works of Athenagoras, but also invokes other early fathers.
20. Hippolytus is also noteworthy, but as Kelly shows, his views are similar to Tertullian's, and Tertullian's expression of these views seemed to have more of a lasting impact. See J. N. D. Kelly, *Early Christian Doctrines* (New York: Harper & Row, 1978), p. 110.
21. Ibid., pp. 104-105.
22. Ibid., p. 110.
23. Ibid., p. 113, citing Tertullian.
24. Ibid., citing Tertullian.
25. Ibid., pp. 113-114.
26. Ibid., p. 115. See also Alister McGrath, *Christian Theology: An Introduction* (Cambridge, Mass.: Basil Blackwell, 1997), pp. 294-295, for a discussion of these terms.
27. Kelly, *Early Christian Doctrines*, pp. 117-118.
28. Erickson, *Christian Theology*, p. 334.
29. Kelly, *Early Christian Doctrines*, pp. 119-123; Erickson, *Christian Theology*, pp. 334-335.
30. Kelly, *Early Christian Doctrines*, p. 129.
31. Ibid.
32. Ibid.
33. Atanasije Jevtich, "Between the 'Nicaeans' and the 'Easterners': The 'Catholic' Confession of Saint Basil," *St. Vladimir's Theological Quarterly* 24 (1980): 248.
34. Ibid., pp. 235-245.
35. R. D. Williams, "The Logic of Arianism," *JTS* 34 (April 1983): 57-58.
36. Ibid., p. 58.
37. Sage Library (CD), "The Nicene Creed," p. 55.
38. Jevtich, "Between," p. 238.
39. Of interest here is Jevtich's quote from Athanasius's *Letter concerning the Synods of Ariminum and Seleucia* (41, 1-2), which was written in 359. Athanasius's letter says, "Toward those who accept everything that is written in Nicaea but hesitate only at the expression *to homoousion*, we should not act as enemies. Because we speak with them not as with Arians, nor as with those who oppose the fathers, but rather as with brothers who think as we do, except that they doubt the word *homoousios*. By confessing that the Son is from the essence of the Father and not from some other hypostasis, and that the Son is not a creature, but that He is the true Son by nature (*gennema*), and that, as the Logos and Wisdom, He is coeternal with the Father, they are not far from accepting the word *homoousios*. Such was exactly Basil of Ancyra who wrote about the faith." Quoted in Jevtich, pp. 243-244, fn 24.
40. Sage Library (CD), "Creed of the Council of Constantinople," p. 441.
41. *Epistula Constantinopolitani concilii ad papam Damasum et occidentales episcopos, Conciliorum Oecumenicorum Decreta* (Freiburg, Germany: Herder, 1962), p. 28; *Nicene and Post-Nicene Fathers* Series 2, 14:189. Quoted in Daniel F. Stramara, Jr., "Introduction" to "Gregory of Nyssa, *Ad Graecos* 'How It Is That We Say There Are Three Persons in the Divinity But Do Not Say There Are Three Gods' (To the Greeks: Concerning the Commonality of Concepts)," *The Greek Orthodox Theological Review* 41 (1996): 375.
42. See the interesting discussion of the relation of the Nicene to the Constantinopolitan Creed and the significance of the doctrine formulated therein, in J. N. D. Kelly, "The Nicene Creed: A Turning Point," *SJT* 36 (1983).
43. Jevtich, "Between," pp. 246-247; Cornelius Plantinga, Jr., "Gregory of Nyssa and the Social Analogy of the Trinity," *The Thomist* 50 (July 1986): 330.
44. Jevtich, "Between," p. 247.

45. Plantinga, "Gregory of Nyssa," pp. 330-331.
46. For further elaboration of Cappadocian Trinitarianism, see Stramara's translation of Gregory of Nyssa's *Ad Graecos*. See also Plantinga, "Gregory of Nyssa," pp. 328-338; McGrath, *Christian Theology,* pp. 302-304; and Erickson, *Christian Theology,* pp. 335-337.
47. McGrath, *Christian Theology,* p. 314. See his complete discussion of this controversy on pp. 312-316.
48. For a most thorough analysis and explanation of the history and theology of the *filioque* controversy, see Gerald Bray, "The *Filioque* Clause in History and Theology," *Tyndale Bul* 34 (1983): 91-144.
49. McGrath, *Christian Theology,* pp. 306-307.
50. Ibid., pp. 304-305, 314-315. For further helpful analyses of Augustine's teaching on the Trinity, see George Rudebusch, "Aristotelian Predication, Augustine, and the Trinity," *The Thomist* 53 (1989); and Sarah Lancaster, "Three-Personed Substance: The Relational Essence of the Triune God in Augustine's *De Trinitate,*" *The Thomist* 60 (1996).
51. Grudem, *Systematic Theology,* pp. 229-230.
52. Buswell, *Systematic Theology,* p. 107.
53. Ibid., pp. 108-109.
54. Ibid., p. 111.
55. Grudem, footnote 24 to page 244 of *Systematic Theology.* For some reason the publishers omitted this footnote, but Dr. Grudem graciously shared it with me.
56. Ibid.
57. Buswell, *Systematic Theology,* pp. 109-110.
58. Timothy W. Bartel, "The Plight of the Relative Trinitarian," *Relig Stud* 24 (1988): 130.
59. Ibid.
60. Ibid., pp. 130-131.
61. Ibid., p. 144.
62. Ibid.
63. Ibid., pp. 149-152. In contemporary literature on the Trinity, there is a lot of reference to a "social view" of the Trinity. It isn't clear whether this means that the Trinity should be thought of as a "society of persons," all of whom share one essence, or whether this view actually espouses some form of tritheism. Several have argued that for Richard Swinburne, it is the latter. Bartel seems to espouse the latter as well. On the other hand, historically, it seems to be the former (see Plantinga on Gregory of Nyssa). Because of this ambiguity I have avoided reference to a "social" view of the Trinity in my formulation of the doctrine.
64. For further discussion of the logic of the doctrine of the Trinity, see Lawrence B. Porter, "On Keeping 'Persons' in the Trinity: A Linguistic Approach to Trinitarian Thought," *Theol Stud* 41 (1980); John King-Farlow, "Is the Concept of the Trinity Obviously Absurd?" *Sophia* 22 (October 1983); Leroy T. Howe, "Ontology, Belief, and the Doctrine of the Trinity," *Sophia* 20 (April 1981); C. Stephen Layman, "Tritheism and the Trinity," *Faith Phil* 5 (July 1988); James Cain, "The Doctrine of the Trinity and the Logic of Relative Identity," *Relig Stud* 25 (1989); T. W. Bartel, "Could There Be More Than One Almighty?" *Relig Stud* 29 (1993); T. W. Bartel, "Could There Be More Than One Lord?" *Faith Phil* 11 (July 1994); Keith E. Yandell, "The Most Brutal and Inexcusable Error in Counting?: Trinity and Consistency," *Relig Stud* 30 (1994); Charles J. Kelly, "Classical Theism and the Doctrine of the Trinity," *Relig Stud* 30 (1994); Edward C. Feser, "Swinburne's Tritheism," *Int J Phil Relig* 42 (1997); Peter van Inwagen, "And Yet They Are Not Three Gods But One God," in Thomas V. Morris, ed., *Philosophy and the Christian Faith* (Notre Dame, Ind.: University of Notre Dame Press, 1988); A. P. Martinich, "Identity and Trinity," *J Relig* 58 (1978); P. T. Geach, "Aquinas," in G. E. M. Anscombe and P. T. Geach, *Three Philosophers* (Ithaca, N.Y.: Cornell University Press, 1961); P. T. Geach, *Reference and Generality* (Ithaca, N.Y.: Cornell University Press, 1962); P. T. Geach, *Logic Matters* (Berkeley: University of California Press, 1972); W. L. Power, "Symbolic Logic and the Doctrine of the Trinity," *Illif Review* 32 (1975); Richard Cartwright, "On the Logical Problem of the Trinity," *Philosophical Essays* (Cambridge, Mass.: MIT Press, 1987); David Wiggins, *Sameness and Substance* (Cambridge, Mass.: Harvard University Press, 1980); and John Zeis, "A Trinity on a Trinity on a Trinity," *Sophia* 32 (1993).
65. John Macnamara, Marie La Palme Reyes, and Gonzalo E. Reyes, "Logic and the Trinity," *Faith Phil* 11 (January 1994): 7.
66. All of this is my adaptation of ibid., p. 7.
67. Ibid., p. 8.
68. Ibid., pp. 8-9.
69. Ibid., p. 9.
70. Ibid., p. 10.

CHAPTER 11

1. *Westminster Shorter Catechism,* as cited in Louis Berkhof, *Systematic Theology* (Grand Rapids, Mich.: Eerdmans, 1968), p. 102.

2. Millard Erickson, *Christian Theology* (Grand Rapids, Mich.: Baker, 1983), pp. 345-346. Erickson prefers the term "plan" because "it stresses the unity of God's intention together with the resultant consistency and coherence of his actions. Second, it emphasizes what God does, that is, what he wills, rather than what man must do or what happens to man as a consequence of God's will. Third, it emphasizes the intelligent dimension of God's decisions. They are not arbitrary or haphazard" (p. 346).

3. Berkhof, *Systematic Theology*, p. 101; Erickson, *Christian Theology*, p. 347.

4. Erickson, *Christian Theology*, p. 347; Berkhof, *Systematic Theology*, pp. 101-102.

5. John Calvin, *The Institutes of the Christian Religion*, vol. 20 of The Library of Christian Classics, ed. John T. McNeill (Philadelphia: Westminster, 1954), pp. 228-229 [I, xviii, 1].

6. Bruce Demarest and Gordon Lewis, *Integrative Theology*, vol. 1 (Grand Rapids, Mich.: Zondervan, 1987), pp. 295-296. They also note that though Calvin himself doesn't state a specific position, they understand his view to be closest to supralapsarianism.

7. Augustine, as cited in ibid., p. 298.

8. Aquinas, as cited in ibid., p. 299.

9. Here I am thinking, as an example, of William Lane Craig as exemplified in his *The Only Wise God* (Grand Rapids, Mich.: Baker, 1987). Craig is clearly committed to libertarian free will and middle knowledge as the solution to the freedom/foreknowledge problem. Moreover, in other publications it is clear that he has rejected at least some of the classical notion of God's attributes—most notably atemporality. Whether Craig believes in a decree of God isn't easy to tell, but with what he says about God's foreknowledge of the future via middle knowledge, there is no reason to deny an account of the decree such as I am describing in the text.

10. John Sanders, *The God Who Risks* (Downers Grove, Ill.: InterVarsity, 1998), chapter 1.

11. Richard Rice, "Biblical Support for a New Perspective," in Clark Pinnock, et al., *The Openness of God* (Downers Grove, Ill.: InterVarsity, 1994), pp. 15-16.

12. Sanders, *God Who Risks*, p. 214.

13. Clark Pinnock, "Systematic Theology," in Pinnock, et al., *Openness of God*, p. 115.

14. Sanders, *God Who Risks*, p. 234.

15. Ibid., p. 235.

16. Ibid., pp. 228-229.

17. See ibid., pp. 228-230, and Sanders's handling of OT and NT data in chapters 3 and 4 of the same book.

18. William Hasker, "A Philosophical Perspective," in Pinnock, et al., *Openness of God*, p. 136.

19. See Sanders's sections on omniscience and foreknowledge in *The God Who Risks*. See, for example, pp. 198-199 on present knowledge or presentism.

20. See Sanders, *God Who Risks*, chapter 4, on NT materials in which he handles Christ's crucifixion, etc.

21. For further discussion of this point, see Charles Hodge, *Systematic Theology*, vol. 1 (London: James Clark & Co., 1960), pp. 535-537; and Erickson, *Christian Theology*, p. 352.

22. See Wayne Grudem, *Systematic Theology* (Grand Rapids, Mich.: Zondervan, 1994), pp. 322-327, for further presentation of passages that describe evil human actions that God ordained and used for his purposes.

23. See Erickson, *Christian Theology*, pp. 351-352, for the elaboration of Paul's use of Isaiah's point.

24. See C. E. B. Cranfield, *A Critical and Exegetical Commentary on the Epistle to the Romans*, vol. 2, ICC (Edinburgh: T. & T. Clark, 1979) on the issues at stake in Romans 9–11.

25. Demarest and Lewis, *Integrative Theology*, vol. 1, pp. 295-297.

26. Berkhof, *Systematic Theology*, p. 118.

27. Demarest and Lewis repeatedly cast the debate between infra- and supralapsarians as involving the question of whether the decree of reprobation and decree of sin are permissive as foreknown by God or positive. Indeed, this may be debated among various Calvinists, but it isn't the primary point of the *order* of the decrees issue. The debate to which Demarest and Lewis refer concerns more the debate 1) about the basis of the decree (foreknowledge as prescience or not), 2) how, if God positively decrees evil, he escapes responsibility as the author of sin, and 3) whether there is a double decree, a positive decree to save certain individuals and a positive decree to reprobate all others. See Demarest and Lewis, *Integrative Theology*, vol. 1, pp. 295-299, 319-322.

28. See, for example, Berkhof's discussion of arguments pro and con for supra- and infralapsarianism in *Systematic Theology*, pp. 120-125.

CHAPTER 1 2

1. Matthew Arnold, *"In Utrumque Paratus,"* in Jerome Buckley and George Woods, eds., *Poetry of the Victorian Era*, 3d ed. (Chicago: Scott, Foresman and Co., 1965), p. 439.

2. Matthew Arnold, "Dover Beach," in Buckley and Woods, *Poetry of the Victorian Era*, p. 499.

3. In Thomas Hardy, another great Victorian writer, we find a much more pessimistic tone. For Hardy, the scientists are right, and as a result there is no God. Many might find this liberating,

but Hardy's pessimism is all-pervasive. According to his poem "Hap" (published first in 1866), the worst possible scenario faces us. Our world is run solely by chance, and chance is entirely indifferent to our plight.

4. See Robert Jastrow's discussion of Einstein and the series of scientific discoveries that led to the conclusion among scientists, including Einstein, that some sort of Big Bang must have occurred. Robert Jastrow, "Science and the Creation," *Word and World* 4 (Fall 1984): 346-348.

5. Robert Jastrow, *God and the Astronomers* (New York: Norton, 1978), p. 116.

6. Colin Gunton, *The Triune Creator: A Historical and Systematic Study* (Grand Rapids, Mich.: Eerdmans, 1998), p. 37.

7. Ibid., p. 39.

8. A. H. Strong, *Systematic Theology* (Valley Forge, Pa: Judson, 1907), pp. 378-381. See also Louis Berkhof, *Systematic Theology* (Grand Rapids, Mich.: Eerdmans, 1968), p. 138.

9. Strong, *Systematic Theology,* pp. 381-382.

10. Ibid., p. 383; Berkhof, *Systematic Theology,* p. 138; and Bruce Demarest and Gordon Lewis, *Integrative Theology,* vol. 2 (Grand Rapids, Mich.: Zondervan, 1990), p. 18.

11. Gunton, *Triune Creator,* pp. 33-34.

12. Ibid., p. 34, citing Plotinus 3.8.8-9.

13. Ibid.

14. I leave to the reader to work out the correlations between these ideas and a trichotomous understanding of human nature. Trichotomists grant that both soul and spirit are immaterial, but because they claim that they are two separate substances (thus, two distinct parts of human nature), there must be some way to distinguish one from the other.

15. Gunton, *Triune Creator,* pp. 34-35.

16. Ibid., p. 35.

17. Demarest and Lewis, *Integrative Theology,* vol. 2, p. 18. For a further historical study of an emanation theory, see Barry S. Kogan, "Averroes and the Theory of Emanation," *Mediaeval Studies* 43 (1981).

18. Richard Dawkins, *The Blind Watchmaker* (London and New York: W. W. Norton, 1986), pp. 6 and 7. Cited in Alvin Plantinga, "When Faith and Reason Clash: Evolution and the Bible," *CSR* 21 (September 1991): 17.

19. See Jastrow, "Science and the Creation," for details of discoveries in astronomy, etc., that led to such conclusions.

20. Robert J. Deltete, "Hawking on God and Creation," *Zygon* 28 (December 1993): 488, citing S. W. Hawking, "Quantum Cosmology," in B. S. DeWitt and R. Sosa, eds., *Relativity, Groups, and Typology II* (Amsterdam: North Holland, 1984a), p. 337, and S. W. Hawking, *A Brief History of Time* (New York: Bantam, 1988), pp. 50-51, 133, 139, 148.

21. Deltete, "Hawking on God and Creation," pp. 488-489. See Hawking's explanation of this in various works as quoted and cited in Deltete, pp. 489 and 490. Hawking, *Brief History of Time,* pp. 44, 50-51, 61, 115-16, 135-136, 140-141, 173; "The Edge of Spacetime," *American Scientist* 72 (1984b): 358; and "The Edge of Spacetime," *New Scientist* 103 (1984c): 13-14.

22. See the remainder of Deltete's article for objections to this theory.

23. Strong, *Systematic Theology,* p. 392, took this position. Cited in Demarest and Lewis, *Integrative Theology,* vol. 2, p. 20. See their further discussion of other varieties of theistic evolution. See also Arthur Peacock, "Science and God the Creator," *Zygon* 28 (December 1993); and John C. Polkinghorne, "Creation and the Structure of the Physical World," *Theol Today* 44 (April 1987). These authors clearly invoke God's activity while there seems to be an underlying belief that evolution explains how God went about producing our world.

24. Howard Van Till, "The Fully Gifted Creation," in J. P. Moreland and John Mark Reynolds, eds., *Three Views on Creation and Evolution* (Grand Rapids, Mich.: Zondervan, 1999), pp. 163-169.

25. Ibid., p. 184.

26. Ibid., pp. 185-186.

27. Ibid., p. 203.

28. Ibid, passim.

29. Origen, *On First Principles,* III.5.3. Cited and discussed in Demarest and Lewis, *Integrative Theology,* vol. 2, p. 18.

30. Eleonore Stump and Norman Kretzmann, "Eternity," in Thomas V. Morris, ed. *The Concept of God* (Oxford: Oxford University Press, 1987), p. 241.

31. Gunton, *Triune Creator,* p. 48.

32. Ibid., pp. 48-49.

33. Ibid., p. 49. The last line is from Plotinus's *Enneads,* 3.2.3.

34. Augustine, *City of God,* XI. 6; cited in Gunton's discussion of Augustine in *Triune Creator,* p. 82.

35. See Gunton, *Triune Creator,* p. 77, for a discussion of Augustine's views on the days of creation.

36. For further discussion and elaboration of this point, see Strong, *Systematic Theology,* pp. 372-373.

37. For further discussion of the doctrine of creation *ex nihilo* from various perspectives, see Paul Copan, "Is *Creatio Ex Nihilo* a Post-Biblical Invention? An Examination of Gerhard May's Proposal," *Trin J* 17NS (1996); George S. Hendry, "Nothing," *Theol Today* 39 (1982–1983); Ted Peters, "Cosmos and Creation," *Word and World* 4 (Fall 1984): 385-390; and Thomas V. Morris, "Creation *Ex Nihilo*: Some Considerations," *Int J Phil Relig* 14 (1983). Though creation *ex nihilo* is warranted by biblical teaching, that doesn't mean that it was widely held in the Jewish tradition, at the time of Christ, or in the early years of Christianity. For discussions of this matter see the following: Frances Young, "'Creatio Ex Nihilo': A Context for the Emergence of the Christian Doctrine of Creation," *SJT* 44 (1991); Jonathan Goldstein, "The Origins of the Doctrine of Creation *Ex Nihilo*," *Journal of Jewish Studies* 35 (Autumn 1984); Alexander P. D. Mourelatos, "Pre-Socratic Origins of the Principle That There Are No Origins From Nothing," *J Phil* 78 (November 1981); Gerhard May, *Schopfung aus dem Nichts, Arbeiten zür Kierchengeschichte*, no. 48 (1978); and Ian Barbour, *Issues in Science and Religion* (New York: Harper & Row, 1971). For a further discussion of the doctrine of creation in church history (especially in early theologians like Irenaeus and Augustine), see Gunton, *Triune Creator*, pp. 52-86.

38. Berkhof, *Systematic Theology*, p. 132.

39. Ron Allen, "Procksch: Creation as a Wonder," unpublished paper on *bārā'*, Western Baptist Seminary, pp. 2-5.

40. Berkhof, *Systematic Theology*, p. 132.

41. Ibid.

42. Allen, "Procksch: Creation as a Wonder," p. 8.

43. Millard Erickson, *Christian Theology*, vol. 1 (Grand Rapids, Mich.: Baker, 1983), p. 368. See also Allen, "Procksch: Creation as a Wonder," pp. 10-11, citing Werner Foerster, "Ktizo," in *TDNT* 3:1008.

44. That seems to be the sense of 2 Macc 7:28, but the phrase doesn't occur in Scripture.

45. Wayne Grudem, *Systematic Theology* (Grand Rapids, Mich.: Zondervan, 1994), p. 263.

46. See Jon Levenson, *Creation and the Persistence of Evil: The Jewish Drama of Divine Omnipotence* (Princeton: Princeton University Press, 1988), chapters 1–2 especially, but these themes are developed throughout the book.

47. Erickson, *Christian Theology*, pp. 368-369.

48. Grudem, *Systematic Theology*, p. 263. See also Copan, "Is *Creatio Ex Nihilo* a Post-Biblical Invention?" p. 90.

49. Levenson, *Creation and the Persistence of Evil*, pp. 17-20.

50. Here again Levenson sees this as consistent with the divine mastery over chaos theme. Despite Yahweh's initial victory over chaos which resulted in creation (an ordering of the world), from time to time the battle erupts again. Eschatologically, chaos will again break out in revolt against the supremacy of Yahweh, and he will again have to reassert his right as sovereign, not only by defeating the forces of evil but also by creating a new heaven and earth. Thus, themes present in original creation narratives are recapitulated eschatologically. See ibid., chapter 3.

51. B. F. Westcott, *The Epistle to the Hebrews* (reprint, Grand Rapids, Mich.: Eerdmans, 1967), p. 48.

52. We could also add Paul's teaching (Rom 5:12-14) that through Adam's sin death came to all. If Paul doesn't really think Adam's sin is a historical fact (or even that there was a first man named Adam), and if it isn't, the doctrine of the imputation of Adam's sin is fabricated on a fairy tale.

53. See, for example, Westermann's commentary on this as described in R. E. Clements, "Claus Westermann on Creation in Genesis," *Southwestern Journal of Theology* 40 (Spring 1990): 20.

54. Henri Blocher, *In the Beginning,* trans. David G. Preston (Downers Grove, Ill.: InterVarsity, 1984), p. 31.

55. Rosemary Nixon, "Images of the Creator in Genesis 1 and 2," *Theology* 97 (May/June 1994): 188-191.

56. Ibid., p. 193.

57. Ibid., pp. 193-194.

58. J. Oliver Buswell, *A Systematic Theology of the Christian Religion* (Grand Rapids, Mich.: Zondervan,1972), pp. 157-158.

59. See for example, Blocher, *In the Beginning*, p. 30; and the detailed case for this position presented in Stephen Kempf, "Introducing the Garden of Eden: The Structure and Function of Genesis 2:4b-7," *Journal of Translation and Textlinguistics* 7 (1996).

60. See U. Cassuto, *A Commentary on the Book of Genesis*, part 1 (Jerusalem: The Magnes Press, 1989), pp. 96-99, for the details of this proposal plus a vigorous refutation of this fragmentation of the parts of the verse.

61. Ibid., p. 99.

62. See Clements, "Claus Westermann on Creation in Genesis," pp. 18-19, 23, on both similarities and differences.

63. Cassuto, *Commentary on the Book of Genesis*, part 1, pp. 7-8. See also Levenson, especially chapter 6 where he most clearly articulates his explanation of the relation of the seven days of creation to other motifs, etc., in Ancient Near Eastern literature.

64. Bruce K. Waltke, "The Literary Genre of Genesis, Chapter One," *Crux* 27 (December 1991): 3.

65. Waltke (ibid., p. 5) says that this view has been typical ever since the time of Herder (around A.D. 1750).

66. Many writers note this symmetrical arrangement of the creative days. See, for example, Blocher, *In the Beginning*, pp. 27-29, 51-55; Meredith Kline, "Space and Time in the Genesis Cosmogony," *Perspectives on Science and Christian Faith* 48 (March 1996): 6-10; Grudem, *Systematic Theology*, pp. 300-301, Waltke, "Literary Genre of Genesis, Chapter One," p. 5, as examples. For detailed explanation of the contents of each day of creation, see Buswell's description (*Systematic Theology*, pp. 151-156) and that of Demarest and Lewis, *Integrative Theology*, vol. 2, pp. 26-30.

67. Conrad Hyers, "Biblical Literalism: Constricting the Cosmic Dance," in *Is God a Creationist? The Religious Case Against Creation-Science*, ed. Roland M. Frye (New York: Charles Scribner's Sons, 1983), p. 101, quoted in Waltke, "Literary Genre of Genesis, Chapter One," p. 3. See also Clements, "Claus Westermann on Creation in Genesis," p. 22. As already noted, Levenson sees differences between the biblical account of creation and those of Ancient Near Eastern literature, but he sees more parallels than many do. Yahweh is supreme, but he isn't without opposition, even in the Genesis 1–2 narratives.

68. Clements, "Claus Westermann on Creation in Genesis," p. 22.

69. See, for example, Blocher (*In the Beginning*, chapter 2, especially pp. 52-59), who rightly notes this theme but then seems to overemphasize it by claiming that the whole structure of the first two chapters of Genesis is constructed ultimately to lead to the point of the Sabbath, a point greatly emphasized in the Decalogue.

70. For a detailed description of the different sets of ideas and the numerically parallel sets of ideas, see Cassuto, *Commentary on the Book of Genesis,* part 1 pp. 12-15.

71. Various writers argue that there appear to be contradictions between the two accounts. Even scholars committed to inspiration and inerrancy have serious doubts about whether a straightforward historical reading of both chapters can avoid creating conflicts between the two. See, for example, Waltke's concerns, ("Literary Genre of Genesis, Chapter One," p. 7).

72. Buswell, *Systematic Theology*, p. 140.

73. Ibid., p. 141.

74. George J. Brooke, "Creation in the Biblical Tradition," *Zygon* 22 (June 1987): 233. Brooke reflects the thought of John Rogerson's *Myth in the Old Testament Interpretation* (1976); and a subsequent article by Rogerson, "Slippery Words: V. Myth," *Expository Times* 90 (1978): 10-14. See also Mark Brett's discussion of this option in "Motives and Intentions in Genesis 1," *JTS* 42 (April 1991): 13.

75. Claus Westermann, *Genesis 1–11: A Commentary* (Minneapolis: Augsburg, 1984), pp. 26-41. Described in Brooke, "Creation in the Biblical Tradition," p. 233.

76. Brooke, "Creation in the Biblical Tradition," p. 234.

77. George Coats, *Genesis with an Introduction to Narrative Literature* (Grand Rapids, Mich.: Eerdmans, 1983), p. 47. Cited in Brooke, "Creation in the Biblical Tradition," p. 234.

78. Mark G. Brett, "Motives and Intentions in Genesis 1," *JTS* 42 (April 1991): 14.

79. Ibid.

80. Waltke, "Literary Genre of Genesis, Chapter One," p. 8-9.

81. Ibid., p. 9.

82. Ibid., pp. 6-7.

83. Blocher, *In the Beginning*, p. 34. See also p. 32 for his comments on the chapters as narrative and p. 34 for his rejection of them as reflecting revelation of God handed down from one century to the next, even possibly going back to Adam and then recorded by Moses. Likewise, Blocher doesn't think the genre records visions as does the book of Revelation.

84. Ibid., p. 36.

85. Ibid., pp. 49-59, on literary framework; and pp. 98-99.

86. Here I am reacting against the *modus operandi* of interpreters like Henry Morris who see this as straightforward history (we might also say "science") which is open to verification by marshalling empirical facts through scientific investigations. See Morris's commentary on Genesis (*The Genesis Record* [Grand Rapids, Mich.: Baker, 1976]) and also his and others' projects to prove creation science. We must be careful not to impose upon the text modern debates between creationists and evolutionists about origins, when biblical writers could not have had that in mind.

87. Demarest and Lewis, *Integrative Theology*, vol. 2, p. 24; Erickson, *Christian Theology*, p. 381; Henry Thiessen, *Lectures in Systematic Theology*, revised by Vernon Doerksen (Grand Rapids, Mich.: Eerdmans, 1983), p. 114.

88. Thiessen describes this view in general terms (*Lectures in Systematic Theology*, p. 114).

89. Blocher, *In the Beginning*, p. 41.

90. See various descriptions of the gap theory in Demarest and Lewis, *Integrative Theology*, vol. 2, p. 23; Erickson, *Christian Theology*, p. 380; Blocher, *In the Beginning*, p. 41; and Grudem, *Systematic Theology*, p. 287.

91. Demarest and Lewis, *Integrative Theology*, vol. 2, p. 23.

92. *TWOT* 1:213 counts 3,540 times in biblical Hebrew, all in the Qal stem except for 21 uses in the Niphal.
93. Grudem, *Systematic Theology,* p. 288.
94. Ibid., p. 291, citing several works as source.
95. Phillip Johnson, *Darwin on Trial* (Downers Grove, Ill.: InterVarsity, 1991), pp. 20-23.
96. Ibid., pp. 17-18.
97. Ibid. The comment by Darwin is quoted in ibid., p. 36.
98. See chapter in ibid. on the fossil record.
99. Ibid. (see p. 51).
100. Ibid., p. 54.
101. G. G. Simpson, *The Meaning of Evolution* (New Haven, Conn.: Yale University Press, 1964), p. 137.
102. J. P. Moreland and John Mark Reynolds, "Introduction," in Moreland and Reynolds, eds., *Three Views on Creation and Evolution,* pp. 34-35. See also Michael Behe, *Darwin's Black Box* (New York: Free Press, 1996); William Dembski, ed. *Mere Creation* (Downers Grove, Ill.: InterVarsity, 1998); Michael Denton, *Evolution: A Theory in Crisis* (Bethesda, Md.: Adler and Adler, 1986); and Johnson, *Darwin on Trial.* In addition, there is a great deal of literature on creation and evolution in the journals. Some of it is very favorable to evolution, while other articles are more favorable to creationism. And then, there is a lot of literature that discusses the relation of the scriptural account of creation with the findings of science. See, for example, the following in favor of evolution: Adolf Grünbaum, "Creation as a Pseudo-Explanation in Current Physical Cosmology," *Erkenntnis* 35 (1991); Sol Tax, "Creation and Evolution," *Free Inquiry* 2 (Summer 1982); Arthur N. Strahler, "The Creationist Theory of Abrupt Appearances: A Critique," *Free Inquiry* 11 (Summer 1991); Jastrow, "Science and the Creation"; Jack D. Maser and Gordon G. Gallup, Jr., "Theism as a By-Product of Natural Selection," *J Relig* 70 (October 1990); Deltete; "Hawking on God and Creation"; Rudolf B. Brun, "Integrating Evolution: A Contribution to the Christian Doctrine of Creation," *Zygon* 29 (September 1994); Ernan McMullin, "Evolution and Special Creation," *Zygon* 28 (September 1993); Delos McKown, "Scientific Creationism: The Modern Mythmakers' Magic," *Relig Hum* 16 (1982); and A. J. Matill, Jr., "Three Cheers for the Creationists! For the Services They Are Rendering to the Cause of Rational Religion," *Free Inquiry* 2 (Spring 1982). More favorable to creationism are the following: Paul Elbert, "Biblical Creation and Science: A Review Article," *JETS* 39 (June 1996); Polkinghorne, "Creation and the Structure of the Physical World"; Peacocke, "Science and God the Creator"; and William Lane Craig, "Theism and Big Bang Cosmology," *Austl J Phil* 69 (December 1991). For works more generally discussing the interface of science and creationism, see the following: Ted Peters, "Cosmos and Creation," *Word and World* 4 (Fall 1984); Davis A. Young, "Nineteenth Century Christian Geologists and the Doctrine of Scripture," *CSR* 11 (March 1982); Bernard Lovell, "Creation," *Theology* 83 (1980); Wolfhart Pannenberg, "The Doctrine of Creation and Modern Science," *Zygon* 23 (March 1988); Dennis Ormseth, "Darwin's Theory and Christian Orthodoxy," *Word and World* 4 (Fall 1984); Richard W. Berry, "The Beginning," *Theol Today* 39 (1982–1983); Friedemann Hebart, "Creation, Creationism, and Science," *Lutheran Theological Journal* 15 (1981); Frederic B. Burnham, "Maker of Heaven and Earth: A Perspective of Contemporary Science," *Horizons in Biblical Theology* 12 (December 1990); Garret Green, "Myth, History, and Imagination: The Creation Narratives in Bible and Theology," *Horizons in Biblical Theology* 12 (December 1990); Lenn E. Goodman and Madeleine J. Goodman, "Creation and Evolution: Another Round in an Ancient Struggle," *Zygon* 18 (March 1983); Karl Giberson, "The Anthropic Principle: A Postmodern Creation Myth?" *Journal of Interdisciplinary Studies* 9 (1997); and a symposium on creation/evolution and faith in *CSR* 21 (September 1991) with articles by Alvin Plantinga, Howard J. Van Till, Pattle Pun, Ernan McMullin, and a final response by Alvin Plantinga to Van Till and McMullin.
103. Dick Fischer, "The Days of Creation: Hours or Eons?" *Perspectives on Science and Christian Faith* 42 (March 1990): 15-16, citing a then unpublished work by Hugh Ross titled *Biblical Evidence for Long Creation Days.*
104. As noted, there are even varieties of progressive creationism. One noteworthy variant is proposed by Newman and Eckelmann. The days of Genesis 1–2 are literal twenty-four-hour solar days on which God performed the creative acts Scripture mentions. However, after each day there was a lengthy geological epoch that came before the next day and its miraculous intervention. For details see Robert C. Newman, "Progressive Creationism," in Moreland and Reynolds, eds., *Three Views on Creation and Evolution,* pp. 106, 107; and Robert C. Newman and Herman J. Eckelmann, Jr., *Genesis One and the Origin of the Earth* (Grand Rapids, Mich.: Baker, 1981). See also Demarest and Lewis's helpful description of this and other variants of the day-age view (*Integrative Theology,* vol. 2, pp. 24-26).
105. See this line of argument as presented in Demarest and Lewis, *Integrative Theology,* vol. 2, pp. 43-44; Grudem, *Systematic Theology,* pp. 293-294; Berkhof, *Systematic Theology,* p. 153; and Thiessen, *Lectures in Systematic Theology,* p. 114.
106. Gleason L. Archer, *Encyclopedia of Bible Difficulties* (Grand Rapids, Mich.: Zondervan, 1982), p. 61. The point is cited and argued in Dick Fischer, "Days of Creation: Hours or Eons?" 18, among others.

107. Grudem, *Systematic Theology*, p. 297. See also Buswell, *Systematic Theology*, p. 145; Berkhof, *Systematic Theology*, p. 153; Demarest and Lewis, *Integrative Theology*, vol. 2, p. 29; and Blocher's citation (*In the Beginning*, p. 44) of this argument in Derek Kidner's commentary on Genesis.

108. Archer, *Encyclopedia of Bible Difficulties*, p. 68.

109. See this argument, for example, in Fischer, "Days of Creation: Hours or Eons?" pp. 19-20; Grudem, *Systematic Theology*, p. 294; and C. John Collins, "How Old Is the Earth? Anthropomorphic Days in Genesis 1:1–2:3," *Presbyterion* 20 (1994): 118-119.

110. Grudem, *Systematic Theology*, p. 294; Berkhof, *Systematic Theology*, p. 153; Buswell, *Systematic Theology*, pp. 145-146; and Collins, "How Old Is the Earth?" p.119.

111. See for example, Collins's ("How Old Is the Earth?" pp. 115-116) discussion of this issue and his reference to the work of W. H. Green on genealogies.

112. Demarest and Lewis, *Integrative Theology*, vol. 2, p. 44.

113. Grudem, *Systematic Theology*, pp. 292-293.

114. Robert C. Newman and Herman J. Eckelmann, *Genesis One and the Origin of the Earth* (Downers Grove, Ill.: InterVarsity, 1977); Hugh Ross, *Genesis One: A Scientific Perspective;* Davis Young, *Creation and the Flood* (Grand Rapids, Mich.: Baker, 1977).

115. Newman, "Progressive Creationism," p. 109. See also Collins, "How Old Is the Earth?" p. 112.

116. See Collins's appendix ("How Old Is the Earth?") for details on this.

117. Demarest and Lewis, *Integrative Theology*, vol. 2, p. 23, citing Richard Bube and Newman and Eckelmann's noting of this matter.

118. See, for example, Donald B. DeYoung and John C. Whitcomb, "The Origin of the Universe," *Grace Theological Journal* 1 (Fall 1980), as an example of a piece which argues from science against concordist attempts to fit Genesis with an old earth.

119. Berkhof, *Systematic Theology*, pp. 154-155; and Thiessen, *Lectures in Systematic Theology*, p. 115.

120. Waltke, "Literary Genre of Genesis, Chapter One," p. 10, fn 30. See also Collins, "How Old Is the Earth?" p. 110 for the same basic point stated somewhat differently.

121. Terence E. Fretheim, "Were the Days of Creation Twenty-Four Hours Long? Yes," in Ronald Youngblood, ed., *The Genesis Debate: Persistent Questions about Creation and the Flood* (Grand Rapids, Mich.: Baker, 1990), p. 18. See also Thiessen, *Lectures in Systematic Theology*, p. 115.

122. Berkhof, *Systematic Theology*, p. 154. See also Fretheim, "Were the Days of Creation Twenty-Four Hours Long? Yes," p. 19.

123. Berkhof, *Systematic Theology*, p. 155.

124. Fretheim, "Were the Days of Creation Twenty-Four Hours Long? Yes," pp. 19-20.

125. Buswell, *Systematic Theology*, pp. 144-147.

126. See Grudem, *Systematic Theology*, p. 294, fn 54, for this option. Grudem presents these options but thinks neither is very likely.

127. See ibid., p. 305, for this line of argument.

128. See Cassuto, *Commentary on the Book of Genesis*, part 1 for more information.

129. Blocher, *In the Beginning*, p. 50.

130. As an example of a thinker who explains why Genesis 1 is not a chronological sequence, one might consult David Sterchi's article, "Does Genesis 1 Provide a Chronological Sequence?" *JETS* 39 (December 1996).

131. Blocher, *In the Beginning*, p. 51; Grudem, *Systematic Theology*, p. 301.

132. Kline, "Space and Time in the Genesis Cosmogony," p. 2.

133. Ibid., p. 7.

134. Ibid., p. 8.

135. Ibid., pp. 8-9.

136. Ibid., p. 13.

137. Blocher, *In the Beginning*, p. 56. See also Kline, "Space and Time in the Genesis Cosmogony," pp. 12-14; and Meredith G. Kline, "Because It Had Not Rained," *WTJ* 20 (1958): 146-157, wherein Kline first argued this point in print.

138. See the various essays in Moreland and Reynolds, eds., *Three Views on Creation and Evolution*. My main concern is to draw attention to Van Till's lengthy article on what he likes to call the fully gifted creation. Note how his assessment of the fossil record differs from that of the other two essayists in the volume.

139. Collins, "How Old Is the Earth?" p. 110.

140. See Paul H. Seely, "The First Four Days of Genesis in Concordist Theory and in Biblical Context," *Perspectives on Science and Christian Faith* 49 (June 1997): 85-95.

141. For example, consider "getting to the lighthouse" in Virginia Woolf's *To the Lighthouse*. This is a symbolic novel, and commentators agree that the lighthouse and getting to it is a symbol, but it doesn't symbolize actually traveling to a literal lighthouse. Another example might be the whale Moby Dick in the novel *Moby Dick*.

142. Blocher, *In the Beginning*, p. 45.

143. Ibid., pp. 98-99.

144. An example is the time between Jesus' death and resurrection. He predicted three days and three nights; he predicted that he would rise on the third day. If we demand exact precision, the resurrection would have to occur at least some seventy-two hours after he died or was buried, but of course, he arose sooner than that. Still, he was dead for parts of three days, and so he kept his promise to rise in three days, despite the fact that it happened less than seventy-two hours after he died.

145. Cassuto, *Commentary on the Book of Genesis*, part 1, p. 101.

146. Ibid., p. 102.

147. Ibid., pp. 102-103. For an explanation of why the Genesis 2 account of the creation of animals after the creation of Adam doesn't contradict the chapter 1 account of the creation of animals before Adam, see pp. 126-129.

148. See, for example, Cranfield's discussion of Romans 5 and 8 in C. E. B. Cranfield, *A Critical and Exegetical Commentary on the Epistle to the Romans*, vol. 1, ICC (Edinburgh: T & T Clark, 1975).

CHAPTER 13

1. Peter van Inwagen, *An Essay on Free Will* (Oxford: Clarendon, 1983), pp. 2-3.

2. Edward Sankowski, "Some Problems about Determinism and Freedom," *Amer Phil Quart* 17 (October 1980): 293.

3. Francis A. Gangemi, "Indeterminacy and Human Freedom," *Relig Hum* 10 (1976): 55.

4. Edward Walter and Arthur Minton, "Soft Determinism, Freedom, and Rationality," *Personalist* 56 (1975): 368, and the whole discussion on pp. 368-369.

5. See the rest of Gangemi's article ("Indeterminacy") for a variety of reasons as to why the Heisenberg Principle doesn't help us in attempts to explain human actions.

6. Alvin Plantinga, *The Nature of Necessity* (Oxford: Oxford University Press, 1978), pp. 170-171.

7. Peter van Inwagen complains that the phrase contra-causal free will is misleading, but that is because it might be understood to mean that the person goes outside of natural laws and performs a miracle. Other senses of the phrase must be rejected as well, and van Inwagen is correct in doing so, but so long as one offers the definition mentioned in my text, (and many proponents of the view say something similar to my definition), there is no need to fear using this terminology. See van Inwagen, *Essay on Free Will*, pp. 14-15.

8. Walter and Minton ("Soft Determinism," p. 364) make a distinction between indeterminism and libertarianism. "The former claims that there are contra-causal acts; the latter adds that contra-causal acts by human beings are determined by a 'self.'" However, I think these are refinements that need not bother us here, so I won't be concerned about these distinctions.

9. Van Inwagen, *Essay on Free Will*, pp. 3-5. In these pages van Inwagen explains what would have to be true in order for universal causation to logically entail causal determinism. As he shows, the fact that every action is caused does not automatically entail that determinism is true.

10. A rare position that attempts to disconnect the agent causally from his act is Carl Ginet's version of what is sometimes called "simple indeterminism," the general position that free agency doesn't require any sort of causal connection between agents and their free actions. See Carl Ginet, "The Conditional Analysis of Freedom," in Peter van Inwagen, ed., *Time and Cause* (Dordrecht: D. Reidel, 1980), pp. 171-186. See also his *On Action* (Cambridge: Cambridge University Press, 1990). Ginet's views are explained and discussed in a portion of Timothy O'Connor's very helpful article, "Indeterminism and Free Agency: Three Recent Views," *Phil Phenomenol Res* 53 (September 1993).

11. This pertains to intentional actions, but in a certain sense also applies to unintentional ones. In cases of unintentional acts, the agent did intentionally act, and that act was instrumental in bringing about whatever resulted, even if she did not intend the result that occurred. For example, a woman chooses to drive her car and does so, but she didn't choose to hit another car as a result of her driving. The result was unintended, but her action was part of the cause of the accident. As to reflex actions, it is harder to say whether the agent can be said to have caused them in any meaningful sense of "cause." Certainly, if someone bumps into us and we by reflex move an arm or leg, the result of our arm or leg moving may cause someone else to be struck by our foot or hand. So the action of striking someone else in this case is caused, but since the person so moving intended no action whatsoever, it isn't clear that we should say that person caused the striking of another or that they struck the other person. Despite such technicalities, the basic point remains. Every action and event may well have a cause, and in the case of many of them, libertarians would say that the agent is the cause.

12. See, for example, Norman Geisler, "God Knows All Things," in David Basinger and Randall Basinger, eds., *Predestination and Free Will* (Downers Grove, Ill.: InterVarsity, 1986), who proposes that the way to resolve the debate between Calvinists and Arminians and to synthesize the matters of predestination and free will is to appeal to actions as self-determined.

13. See Thomas Talbott, "Indeterminism and Chance Occurrences," *Personalist* 60 (1979): 254; and Tom Settle, "How Determinism Refutes Compatibilism," *Relig Stud* 29 (1993): 353.

14. Talbott, "Indeterminism," p. 254. Though this terminology is rarely used today, writers in past centuries sometimes spoke of the will choosing out of a position of equipoise of equilibrium. In other words, the will is not decisively inclined in one direction or another. There are causal factors that

may push it one way, and others that pull it another way, and all of those factors may play a part in the agent's thinking at the moment of choice. But despite such factors, the will at the moment of choosing is equally poised to choose any of the available options, and does choose out of a state of equilibrium or rest.

15. Robert Nozick, *Philosophical Explanations* (Cambridge, Mass.: Harvard University Press, 1981); and Robert Kane, *Free Will and Values* (Buffalo, N.Y.: State University of New York Press, 1985); and "Two Kinds of Incompatibilism," *Phil Phenomenol Res* 50 (December 1989): 219-254. See also such an agent causal view in William Rowe's work on Thomas Reid (Reid's work is a modern source of such a view) *Thomas Reid on Freedom and Morality* (Ithaca, N.Y.: Cornell University Press, 1991); Michael Zimmerman, *An Essay on Human Action* (New York: Peter Lang, 1984); Alan Donagan, *Choice* (London: Routledge and Kegan Paul, 1987); and Richard Taylor, *Metaphysics* (Englewood Cliffs, N.J.: Prentice-Hall, 1992).

16. O'Connor, "Indeterminism," pp. 500-501. O'Connor gives a very helpful discussion and evaluation of the theories of Carl Ginet, Robert Nozick, and Robert Kane, all of whom he labels causal indeterminists.

17. In an interesting article, Mark Pestana distinguishes six kinds of will acts (wishing, intending, consenting, choosing, using, and enjoying), and then shows how the theory of action held by Thomas Aquinas differs in its understanding of these and other items from Duns Scotus's theory of action. See Mark Pestana, "The Three Species of Freedom and the Six Species of Will Acts," *The Modern Schoolman* 74 (November 1996): 19-29.

18. Richard Taylor, "Determinism," in Paul Edwards, ed., *Encyclopedia of Philosophy*, vol. 2 (New York: Macmillan, 1972), p. 359.

19. Kadri Vihvelin, "Freedom, Causation, and Counterfactuals," *Phil Stud* 64 (1991): 161.

20. Bertrand Russell, "On the Notion of Cause" in *Our Knowledge of the External World* (London, 1914), p. 221. Cited in Philippa Foot, "Free Will as Involving Determinism," in Bernard Berofsky, ed., *Free Will and Determinism* (New York: Harper & Row, 1966), p. 97; and Sankowski, "Some Problems," p. 292.

21. Laurence A. BonJour, "Determinism, Libertarianism, and Agent Causation," *Southern J Phil* 14 (1976): 145. For a more formal definition of determinism, see John V. Canfield, "The Compatibility of Free Will and Determinism," *Phil Rev* 71 (1962): 354.

22. See Randolph Clarke's discussion of recent literature on this and other issues related to the freedom and determinism question in "Freedom and Determinism," *Philosophical Books* 36 (January 1995). Specific reference to the question of whether LaPlaceian determinism obtains in our world and how contemporary science evaluates the issue is found on pages 11-12.

23. For elaboration of this sort of determinism see, for example, Adolf Grünbaum, *Modern Science and Zeno's Paradoxes* (London: Allen & Unwin, 1967). See also his passing reference to this in "Free Will and Laws of Human Behavior," *Amer Phil Quart* 8 (October 1971): 303.

24. Grünbaum, "Free Will and Laws," p. 302. This sort of fatalism is what van Inwagen refers to as strong inevitability, and events or actions that are strongly inevitable would occur no matter what we would do. Van Inwagen, *Essay on Free Will*, p. 25ff.

25. Grünbaum, "Free Will and Laws," p. 302, is the source for these illustrations. Van Inwagen, *Essay on Free Will*, pp. 23-28 passim.

26. Grünbaum, "Free Will and Laws," p. 302.

27. Van Inwagen, *Essay on Free Will*, pp. 25-26.

28. See Grünbaum, "Free Will and Laws," p. 303, explaining this form of fatalism that he takes from Gilbert Ryle's book *Dilemmas* (Cambridge: Cambridge University Press, 1956). See also van Inwagen, *Essay on Free Will*, p. 29f., for this sort of fatalism, and van Inwagen argues that the fatalist of this sort is neither a strong nor a weak inevitabilist in the senses in which he uses those terms.

29. For a thoroughgoing treatment of the broad concept of necessity, see Alvin Plantinga's *Nature of Necessity*.

30. Grünbaum, "Free Will and Laws," pp. 303-304. As Andrew Ward explains, "In crude outline, the compatibilist holds that, given the agent understands the morality of the situation confronting him, his behaviour is morally free to the extent to which he is not constrained from acting on his own decisions. But the mere fact that all his desires, and so (on this view) all his decisions, are the causal consequence of the agent's naturally formed character, in conjunction with surrounding circumstances, constitutes by itself no constraint or limitation on his moral freedom." Andrew Ward, "Talking Sense about Freedom," *Phil Phenomenol Res* 50 (June 1990): 732.

31. For a discussion of these different senses of "free will," etc., in Calvin, see E. Doumergue, *La Pensee Religieuse de Calvin*, vol. 4 of *Jean Calvin: Les Hommes et Les Choses de Son Temps* (Lausanne: Georges Bridel & Cie Editeurs, 1910), pp. 168-170.

32. Lionel Kenner, "Causality, Determinism, and Freedom of the Will," *Philosophy* 39 (1964): 234-235.

33. A. J. Ayer, "Freedom and Necessity," in *Philosophical Essays*, pp. 281-282; cited in Kenner, "Causality," p. 236.

34. Kenner makes this point nicely in "Causality," p. 238.

35. Louis Berkhof, *Systematic Theology* (Grand Rapids, Mich.: Eerdmans, 1968), p. 165.

36. Paul Helm, *The Providence of God* (Downers Grove, Ill.: InterVarsity, 1994), p. 18.

37. Brian L. Hebblethwaite, "Providence and Divine Action," *Relig Stud* 14 (June 1978): 224.

38. Randall Basinger and David Basinger, "Introduction," in Basinger and Basinger, eds., *Predestination and Free Will* (Downers Grove, Ill.: InterVarsity, 1986), p. 13.

39. John Sanders, *The God Who Risks* (Downers Grove, Ill.: InterVarsity, 1998), p. 213.

40. Basinger and Basinger, "Introduction," p. 13.

41. Sanders, *God Who Risks*, pp. 213-214.

42. See, for example, Sanders's description of specific sovereignty and his comparison of it to general sovereignty, in ibid., pp. 211-217. See also Jack Cottrell, "The Nature of the Divine Sovereignty," in Clark Pinnock, ed., *The Grace of God, the Will of Man* (Grand Rapids, Mich.: Zondervan, 1989), passim.

43. See my "The Incarnation of Jesus," in Gary Habermas and Douglas Geivett, eds., *In Defense of Miracles* (Downers Grove, Ill.: InterVarsity, 1997).

44. See Sanders, *God Who Risks*, pp. 170 and 228-235, where he says that God accomplishes general goals, but not always in the way he had anticipated.

45. David Basinger, "Can an Evangelical Christian Justifiably Deny God's Exhaustive Knowledge of the Future?" *CSR* 25 (December 1995): 138, says, "On the other hand, *if God can unilaterally intervene in earthly affairs,* then God can in principle ensure that certain ends will come about—specifically, that good will ultimately triumph over evil in some contexts—*whether he has exhaustive knowledge of the future or not.* Accordingly, since proponents of PK do not (need not) deny that God can unilaterally intervene in earthly affairs—that God can, for instance, override or withdraw freedom of choice—it is simply not true that a God with PK cannot ensure the future in a meaningful sense."

46. Sanders, *God Who Risks*, pp. 63-66.

47. I should note as well that, even though I reject the classical understanding of many of these attributes, a reading of my discussion of the divine attributes shows that my nuancing of these attributes differs from that of the open view. For example, I wouldn't say that the Exodus 32–34 incident is a genuine case where God actually changed his plans and purposes. From my perspective everything that happened was planned by God; he foreordained that the means to his sparing Israel would be Moses' intercessory prayer. If this means that the language of Exodus 32–34 is anthropomorphic, so be it. More on this later.

48. Probably as close a match as any to the position being described in the text is found in Loraine Boettner's *The Reformed Doctrine of Predestination* (Grand Rapids, Mich.: Eerdmans, 1951).

49. From the preceding, we note that both specific and general sovereignty models of divine providence have a paradox form. The difference between the two paradox positions, however, is very clear. In paradox indeterminism, the tension is between divine sovereignty and libertarian free will. With paradox determinism, the tension is between a view of divine sovereignty that removes human freedom but still holds that humans are morally responsible for their actions, anyway.

50. Some wonder if the divine control envisioned extends to the atomic and sub-atomic levels of reality. If that is needed to guarantee that larger physical bodies (of which those atoms are a part) function so as to contribute to the occurrence of events and actions God has decreed, then God's control extends to that level. On the other hand, if God can get each object and person to fulfill his decreed ends without controlling things at the sub-atomic and atomic level, that is fine. How the atomic structure of an entity relates to the functioning of the larger bodies is an issue that science continues to investigate. Whatever answer science ultimately offers, it can fit this model of sovereignty. Theologians of both specific and general sovereignty can and do agree that God sustains everything in being even down to the sub-atomic levels of existence. Exactly how that sustaining power impacts what entities will do from moment to moment is unclear, but *prima facie* it need not either mandate or preclude God's control over what persons and objects do.

51. George Mavrodes, "Is There Anything Which God Does Not Do?" *CSR* 16 (July 1987): 384.

52. Ibid., 391.

53. I take seriously those passages which teach that in our own power, we can't do anything that pleases God (see, e.g., Rom 3:10-12; Ps 14:1-3; 53:1-4). Hence, if we are to do something good in his eyes, we must be empowered and enabled by him to do so.

54. Sanders, *God Who Risks*, pp. 45-47, claims that the case of Adam and Eve is a prime example of people having freedom of choice. God blesses them greatly so it is implausible that they would disobey him; nonetheless, the implausible happened through free will. All of this shows that there is genuine freedom and that God takes risks in creating the sort of creatures he made by giving them this freedom.

55. Geisler, "God Knows All Things," pp. 64-65; and Bruce Reichenbach, "God Limits His Power," in Basinger and Basinger, eds., *Predestination and Free Will*, p. 104.

56. Richard Ruble, "Determinism vs. Free Will," *Journal of the American Scientific Affiliation* 28 (June 1976): 73.

57. Richard Rice, "Biblical Support for a New Perspective," in Clark Pinnock, et al., *The Openness of God* (Downers Grove, Ill.: InterVarsity, 1994), pp. 54-55; see also Reichenbach, "God Limits His Power," pp. 117-118.

58. Geisler, "God Knows All Things," p. 65.

59. Clark Pinnock, "God Limits His Knowledge," in Basinger and Basinger, eds., *Predestination and Free Will,* p. 149.

60. Ibid.

61. Sanders, *God Who Risks,* p. 222. See also p. 223 for further discussion of the case of Adam and Eve.

62. Cottrell, "Nature of the Divine Sovereignty," p. 103.

63. Ibid., p. 102. See p. 103 for unconditionality as the problem with this being genuine freedom or meaningful freedom.

64. Ibid., pp. 103-104.

65. Pinnock, "God Limits His Knowledge," p. 146. Pinnock says that this ultimately stems from divine omnipotence, properly understood. Omnipotence is not "the power to determine everything but rather . . . the power that enables God to deal with any situation that arises" (Clark Pinnock, "Systematic Theology," in Pinnock, et al., *Openness of God,* p. 114).

66. Rice, "Biblical Support," p. 38. See his more general discussion of this point on pp. 36-38.

67. Sanders, *God Who Risks,* pp. 233-235.

68. Ibid., p. 234. From a more philosophical perspective, see David Basinger's argument that God has only limited control of ultimate ends that occur ("Human Freedom and Divine Providence: Some New Thoughts on an Old Problem," *Relig Stud* 15 [1979]: 498-509).

69. Pinnock, "God Limits His Knowledge," p. 151.

70. Sanders, *God Who Risks,* p. 225.

71. Cottrell, "Nature of the Divine Sovereignty," p. 108.

72. Marcel Sarot, "Omnipotence and Self-limitation," in Gijsbert van den Brink, et al., eds., *Christian Faith and Philosophical Theology* (Kampen, Netherlands: Kok Pharos, 1992), p. 177.

73. Cottrell, "Nature of the Divine Sovereignty," pp. 108-109. See also Sanders, *God Who Risks,* p. 225. See also Sarot, "Omnipotence," p. 182. Sarot distinguishes self-limitation from self-restraint. The former means to give up entirely, whereas the latter means to hold onto something but restrain oneself from using it. Sarot thinks it is problematic to say that God limits his own omnipotence, for then he would no longer be omnipotent. Rather, he holds on to his power, but simply refrains from using it (pp. 182-183). As Cottrell explains ("Nature of the Divine Sovereignty," p. 110), "A sovereign God is a God who is free to limit himself with regard to his works, a God who is free to decide *not* to determine if he so chooses, a God who is free to bestow the gift of relative independence on his creatures. Such freedom does not diminish God's sovereignty; it magnifies it."

74. Cottrell, "Nature of the Divine Sovereignty," p. 107.

75. Jerry Walls makes this point in the article "The Free Will Defense, Calvinism, Wesley, and the Goodness of God," *CSR* 13 (September 1983): 24-31.

76. David Basinger argues this as pointedly as anyone. See his "Human Freedom and Divine Providence," pp. 492-493.

77. As we shall see in the chapter on the problem of evil, what I have just presented in this paragraph is really the Free Will Defense. We will discuss it there in greater detail. For now, it is sufficient to note that the general sovereignty advocate simply presents this line of argument as an alternative to the apparently logically inconsistent story the determinist tells. For these points see David Basinger, "Practical Implications," in Pinnock, et al., *Openness of God,* pp. 170ff.; and Sanders, *God Who Risks,* pp. 92-94 (about the slaughter of innocent children when Herod sought to kill the baby Jesus).

78. Walls, "Free Will Defense," pp. 29-30.

79. Geisler, "God Knows All Things," p. 69.

80. Here, there are many sources where the divine attributes are redefined as part of the overall case for the open view of God and a more general notion of God's providential control. See Reichenbach, "God Limits His Power," pp. 114-115; Pinnock, "God Limits His Knowledge," pp. 152-157; Rice, "Biblical Support," pp. 18-33, 38-46; and Sanders, *God Who Risks,* pp. 66-75, 173-194 as examples of this understanding of the divine attributes and of this sort of argument proposed from that understanding.

81. Sanders, *God Who Risks,* pp. 82-83.

82. Ibid., p. 84.

83. Ibid., p. 86.

84. Ibid., p. 102. For handling of 1 Pet 1:20, see p. 101.

85. Ibid., pp. 103-104.

86. Ibid., pp. 120-123, for the full handling of these verses by Sanders.

87. Cottrell, "Nature of the Divine Sovereignty," p. 114.

88. Ibid.

89. Ibid.

90. Bernard Berofsky, "Three Conceptions of Freedom," *J Phil* 67 (1970): 209-210.

91. Alvin Plantinga, *God, Freedom, and Evil* (New York: Harper & Row, 1974), p. 29.

92. Axel Steuer makes this very sort of point in regard to God's control and our control of our own actions. He writes, "In brief, human beings cannot both have freedom or self-control and yet remain absolutely under God's control unless one maintains the identity of God and finite persons." To the extent that God's control limits our control of our actions, our freedom is limited. Axel Steuer, "The Freedom of God and Human Freedom," *SJT* 36 (1983): 172-173.

93. Patrick Francken, "Incompatibilism, Nondeterministic Causation, and the Real Problem of Free Will," *Journal of Philosophical Research* 18 (1993): 42-43.

94. Steuer, "Freedom of God," p. 164.

95. Michael Zimmerman, "Moral Responsibility, Freedom, and Alternate Possibilities," *Pacific Philosophical Quarterly* 63 (July 1982): 244, makes this point, and when we turn to arguments for a soft deterministic approach, we shall see that compatibilists typically respond to incompatibilists that there are significant senses in which an agent could do otherwise, even given compatibilism. Hence, if being able to do otherwise is a requirement for freedom, compatibilistically made choices must be free.

96. Ibid., pp. 244-245.

97. See, for example, Wolf's adumbration of how such a line of argument might go in response to compatibilist interpretations of "could have done otherwise." Susan Wolf, "Asymmetrical Freedom," *J Phil* 77 (1980): 154.

98. Steuer, "Freedom of God," pp. 164-165; and Robert Young, "Compatibilism and Freedom," *Mind* 83 (1974): 36-37.

99. Wolf, "Asymmetrical Freedom," p. 154.

100. A. C. MacIntyre, "Determinism," *Mind* 66 (1957): 33.

101. Richard Taylor, "'I Can'," *Phil Rev* 69 (1960): 88-89; Max Hocutt, "Freedom and Capacity," *Review of Metaphysics* 29 (1975): 258.

102. Van Inwagen, *Essay on Free Will*, p. 56.

103. For a fuller elaboration of this whole argument, premise by premise, see van Inwagen, *Essay on Free Will*, pp. 71-78. For further discussion of the argument see John Martin Fischer, "Van Inwagen on Free Will," *Phil Quart* 36 (April 1986). For an earlier version of this line of argument, see Peter van Inwagen, "The Incompatibility of Free Will and Determinism," *Phil Stud* 27 (1975). For further explanation and discussion of this sort of argument, see James W. Lamb, "On a Proof of Incompatibilism," *Phil Rev* 86 (January 1977).

104. Charles Fethe, "Rationality and Responsibility," *Personalist* 53 (1972): 195.

105. See Thomas Talbott's explanation and elaboration of this point in Talbott, "Indeterminism," p. 259.

106. Winston Nesbitt and Stewart Candlish, "On Not Being Able to Do Otherwise," *Mind* 82 (July 1973): 321.

107. Paul Gomberg goes even further, for he knows that an act may stem from the agent's character, beliefs, etc., but if those things don't arise from something else about the agent but rather from something the agent doesn't control, then we still cannot ascribe moral responsibility to the agent. Such considerations have led many libertarians to argue for a view of agent causation according to which not only do agents cause their acts, but they also cause or control whatever moves them to act. See Paul Gomberg, "Free Will as Ultimate Responsibility," *Amer Phil Quart* 15 (July 1978): 206-207. For further interesting discussions of this issue, see the whole of Gomberg's article; Edward Sankowski's "Some Problems about Determinism and Freedom"; and a very stimulating article on this topic by William Rowe titled "Causing and Being Responsible for What Is Inevitable," *Amer Phil Quart* 26 (April 1989).

108. Talbott, "Indeterminism," p. 254.

109. This is my adaptation and application of a basic set of points Talbott makes on pp. 254-255 in interacting with Moritz Schlick's argument that an action must be either causally determined, or totally uncaused.

110. Talbott, "Indeterminism," p. 256ff.

111. Here those causally sufficient conditions would likely include many things true of the world at that moment (but wouldn't have to include the whole history of the world up to that point in time), and might even include some laws of nature that have produced events that are factors in the agent's decision-making process. For all we know, there might even be certain laws that cover how humans (or this particular human) will act in a given circumstance, even though we wouldn't be in a position to state what such laws are. Moreover, if physical brain states are at all causally decisive for mental states, then there are likely physical laws that explain why the brain (and derivatively, the mind) is in a particular state at any given moment, a state that would have significant effects upon what the agent chooses on a particular occasion.

112. Steuer, "Freedom of God," pp. 168-169.

113. In my description of the different positions on this issue (definitional part of this chapter), I noted the position of causal indeterminism. That is the view that an action is caused by the agent in light

of a particular portion of his beliefs, but nothing prior to the agent's choice and action made it inevitable that he would focus on the reasons and arguments he did or that he would weigh them as more significant than others. This is now the sort of position I am dealing with in the text.

114. Patrick Francken, "Incompatibilism," p. 49, citing Fred Dretske and Aaron Snyder, "Causal Irregularity," *Philosophy of Science* 39 (1972): 69-71.

115. Libertarians want to make the further point that just because an act is caused (though undetermined), that doesn't make it free in their sense of freedom. If something other than the agent caused an action, that wouldn't help the libertarian's case. Hence, contemporary libertarians hold agent causation, but there are variations of agent causation. For discussion of agent causation theories and their relation not only to this issue but to the libertarian case for freedom more generally, see Susan L. Anderson, "The Libertarian Conception of Freedom," *International Philosophical Quarterly* 21 (1981): 396ff.; Andrew Ward, "Talking Sense about Freedom," pp. 733-735; BonJour, "Determinism," pp. 148-153. Especially helpful is Robert Kane's "Two Kinds of Incompatibilism," *Phil Phenomenol Res* 50 (December 1989), in which Kane discusses various agent causation theories and teleological intelligibility theories, both of which are different theories an incompatibilist might hold in rounding out his theory of action. These are not simply two different ways of trying to answer the charge that incompatibilism is randomness; rather they are separate approaches to offering an intelligible account for the entirety of what libertarian free will claims. See Kane for the details.

116. Van Inwagen, *Essay on Free Will*, p. 154.

117. Ibid., pp. 114-126, for his rejection of "could" claims as conditional statements.

118. Ibid., pp. 153-161. For discussion of this argument and the broader issue of deliberating about something that is determined, see Bruce N. Waller, "Deliberating about the Inevitable," *Analysis* 45 (January 1985). A further argument relates to soft determinism and focuses on mind control. See David Blumenfield, "Freedom and Mind Control," *Amer Phil Quart* 25 (July 1988). Aaron Snyder offers a final argument that determinism is actually self-refuting. See A. Aaron Snyder, "The Paradox of Determinism," *Amer Phil Quart* 9 (October 1972).

CHAPTER 14

1. See my "God Ordains All Things," in David Basinger and Randall Basinger, eds., *Predestination and Free Will* (Downers Grove, Ill.: InterVarsity, 1986), pp. 19-43; and "God, Freedom, and Evil in Calvinist Thinking," in Tom Schreiner and Bruce Ware, eds., *The Grace of God, the Bondage of the Will*, vol. 2. (Grand Rapids, Mich.: Baker,1995), pp. 459-483.

2. Bruce Reichenbach, "God Limits His Power," in Basinger and Basinger, eds. *Predestination and Free Will*, rightly states that Scripture doesn't discuss freedom *per se*, though it challenges us to make many choices, and it does speak of the relation of freedom to the law and sin (p. 104). This is surely correct, but it underscores the point I am making; Scripture doesn't offer a precise definition of what it means by freedom. Hence, by noting that Scripture teaches freedom and moral responsibility, we have eliminated certain deterministic positions, but not all.

3. B. F. Westcott, *Saint Paul's Epistle to the Ephesians* (reprint, Minneapolis: Klock & Klock, 1978), p. 15. See also T. K. Abbott, *A Critical and Exegetical Commentary on the Epistles to the Ephesians and to the Colossians*, ICC (Edinburgh: T. & T. Clark, n.d.), p. 20; and John Eadie, *A Commentary on the Greek Text of the Epistle of Paul to the Ephesians* (Grand Rapids, Mich.: Baker, 1979), p. 60.

4. Bruce Reichenbach, "Bruce Reichenbach's Response," in Basinger and Basinger, eds., *Predestination and Free Will*, pp. 52-53.

5. Jack Cottrell, "The Nature of Divine Sovereignty," in Clark Pinnock, ed., *The Grace of God, the Will of Man* (Grand Rapids, Mich.: Zondervan, 1989), pp. 115-116.

6. See my "God Ordains All Things," pp. 31-32.

7. See John Sanders, *The God Who Risks* (Downers Grove, Ill.: InterVarsity, 1998), chapter 1 and pp. 67-70; see also Richard Rice, "Biblical Support for a New Perspective," Clark Pinnock, et al., *The Openness of God* (Downers Grove, Ill.: InterVarsity, 1994), pp. 22-25.

8. David Basinger, "Can an Evangelical Christian Justifiably Deny God's Exhaustive Knowledge of the Future?" *CSR* 25 (December 1995): 144.

9. Rice, "Biblical Support," pp. 54-55.

10. John Calvin, *Institutes of the Christian Religion,* vol. 20 of The Library of Christian Classics, ed. John T. McNeill and Ford L. Battles (Philadelphia: Westminster, 1954), pp. 228-229 [I, xviii, 1]. Cf. Institutes, 956 [III, xxiii, 8]; and Etienne, De Peyer, "Calvin's Doctrine of Divine Providence," *The Evangelical Quarterly* 10 (January 15, 1938): 42.

11. In addition, God's decree includes natural good and natural evil. Some events that occur will promote our health and physical and material well-being, whereas others such as fires, earthquakes, floods, and diseases normally are detrimental to human well-being. Since many of these occurrences are not tied to human actions as their cause, I am omitting them from my definition of perfect will and undesired will and using those categories only to refer to actions of God's moral creatures. Nonetheless, all such events are part of God's decree; those which produce natural good may also

fall under the category of God's perfect will, whereas those which produce natural evil may fit the category of God's undesired will.

12. Historically, various camps within the Christian tradition have also distinguished God's absolute and conditional will or his antecedent and consequent will. However, these terms are used to mean different things by those who use them. Moreover, I don't see that they add anything that we must know in order to understand what Scripture says about God's sovereign will. Hence, I have omitted them from discussion. For those who want to pursue these concepts and their various meanings, see Charles Hodge, *Systematic Theology*, vol. 1 (London: James Clark & Co., 1960), pp. 402-406; Herman Bavinck, *The Doctrine of God* (Grand Rapids, Mich.: Baker, 1977), pp. 237-238; and Louis Berkhof, *Systematic Theology* (Grand Rapids, Mich.: Eerdmans, 1968), pp. 77-78.

13. I should add that there is a problem here for hard determinist and fatalist positions on this issue. These views claim that we don't have free will in any sense. If so, then it does seem unjust to hold humans responsible for their evil deeds, since they didn't do them freely. Likewise, I find the paradox determinism position unacceptable, for it claims that we are morally accountable, despite the fact that our actions are not free. If God really holds us guilty under such conditions, I do not see how that can be just. Paul's imagined objector does have reason to complain!

14. Here see Sanders's discussion of Moses' pleading for his people (Exodus 32–34), *God Who Risks*, pp. 63-66, and of Abraham pleading for Sodom and Gomorrah (Genesis 18), p. 53. See also Rice's handling of these passages ("Biblical Support," pp. 27-30).

15. For example, if one is playing baseball and it's the bottom of the ninth inning in the championship game with the score tied and bases are loaded with two outs, the batter wants to get a base hit. With that one act he wants to accomplish several things: knock in the winning run, raise his total of RBIs, win the championship, raise the pitcher's ERA, and raise his own batting average.

16. See Walter C. Kaiser, Jr., *The Uses of the Old Testament in the New* (Chicago: Moody, 1985); and S. Lewis Johnson, Jr., *The Old Testament in the New* (Grand Rapids, Mich.: Zondervan, 1980).

17. In fact, this verse is mentioned only once in the whole book, but it comes in a paragraph where Sanders is reporting Augustine's views and says that Augustine claims that no one resists God's will. Sanders puts the verse (Rom 9:19) in parenthesis after the phrase "no one resists God's will," which claim Sanders says is what Augustine claimed. See Sanders, *God Who Risks*, p. 217 for this reference to the verse in question.

18. One concerns the verbal, plenary inspiration of Scripture. The Bible teaches that it is all God's word (2 Tim 3:16), but it is also the product of human authorship. Second Peter 1:21 shows that both God and the human writers at work in producing Scripture. God bore the writers along so that what they penned was his word. The term "carried along" is the Greek word *pheromenoi*. It conveys the idea of being taken up by the bearer and carried to his intended goal. Commentators liken the idea to that of wind in the sails of a boat carrying the boat along. It teaches close superintendence of the biblical authors. Because of the continual involvement of God's activity in inspiration, evangelicals have traditionally held that a book so produced must also be inerrant. David Basinger astutely sees the implications of this for libertarian free will, and argues that given libertarian free will, God can only guarantee inerrancy by dictating Scripture so as to remove any human freedom and creativity in the writing of Scripture. Since Basinger wisely rejects the dictation theory of inspiration, he asks about other options. Given libertarian free will, he grants that if human writers really were involved as more than passive secretaries taking dictation, there could be no guarantee of inerrancy. If God doesn't override their freedom, he cannot guarantee that they will escape error. Of course, on a compatibilist reading of free will, God can do exactly what the texts cited say he does without turning biblical writers into passive secretaries. Since God can decisively incline their wills without constraint to write what he wants, we have reason to think a book so produced is really God's word and inerrant. Thus, if one understands properly the biblical doctrine of the inspiration of Scripture, one sees that it is unlikely that this could happen unless the writers have some kind of compatibilistic freedom. For a discussion of this issue as it relates to freedom and other issues in the doctrine of God, see Stephen J. Wellum, "An Investigation of the Interrelationship Between the Doctrines of Divine Action, Sovereignty, Omniscience, and Scripture for Contemporary Debates on Biblical Authority," unpublished Ph.D. dissertation, Trinity Evangelical Divinity School.

19. What I shall say in the following paragraphs is an elaboration of a point made briefly in an article of mine titled "And the Atheist Shall Lie Down with the Calvinist: Atheism, Calvinism, and the Free Will Defense," *Trin J* 1NS (Fall 1980): 150.

20. This position is especially powerful for those who believe that mind is material, for then ultimately all mental concepts, including will and willing, are reducible to physical things and the processes and laws that govern them. But what if mind is not material? Are there then such natural laws that govern behavior, and are human minds and wills such that we can speak about what they will choose and do with the kind of inevitability and certainty we find in the natural order? As Andrew Ward explains, there is much empirical evidence from modern science (specifically in neurophysiology) that "increasingly strongly favours a physical base in the brain for *all* our mental states, including reasoning. More particularly, character traits and intellectual abilities are equated with brain structures rather than with non-material properties of an independently existing substance, the mind; and conscious experiences themselves are taken to be emergent properties or side-effects of brain events" (Ward, "Talking Sense about Freedom," *Phil Phenomenol Res* 50 (June 1990): 735).

But as Ward explains, even if this is true, "it is impossible for our notion of moral freedom to be understood on any basis other than (roughly) absence of constraint on the expression of a naturally formed character" (p. 739). In other words, Ward's point is that even if one is a materialist with respect to mind, that still wouldn't mean that it is meaningless to speak of freedom of the person. Such determinism as would be true could still leave room for free will. If even with a materialist view of mind it is possible to speak meaningfully of free human action, it seems even more so that this is true for those like myself who believe that mind is immaterial.

21. I should add that a fatalism or hard determinism based on other types of causation than physical or natural causation should also be rejected and would be rejected by a soft determinist such as myself.

22. Edward Sankowski, "Some Problems about Determinism and Freedom," *Amer Phil Quart* 17 (October 1980); and Adolf Grünbaum, "Free Will and Laws of Human Behavior," *Amer Phil Quart* 8 (October 1971).

23. Here think of van Inwagen's consequence argument. One can be seduced by such arguments into thinking that specific sovereignty models, as deterministic, presuppose the sort of determinism rigorously attacked by van Inwagen's argument, and hence cannot be true. If a specific sovereignty model did incorporate the kind of determinism the consequence argument attacks, that form of specific sovereignty should be rejected. But any form not committed to such a notion of causality and determinism need not feel threatened.

24. Jonathan Edwards, "A Careful and Strict Inquiry into the Prevailing Notions of the Freedom of the Will," *The Works of Jonathan Edwards,* vol. 1 (Edinburgh: Banner of Truth Trust, n.d.).

25. See, for example, A. Aaron Snyder, "The Paradox of Determinism," *Amer Phil Quart* 9 (October 1972): 354-355, on reasons not sufficing as physical causes.

26. Patricia S. Churchland, "Is Determinism Self-Refuting?" *Mind* 90 (1981): 100.

27. See Timothy O'Connor, "Indeterminism and Free Agency: Three Recent Views," *Phil Phenomenol Res* 53 (September 1993): 508-511, and then the samples of such theories he discusses on pages 511-525. See also Randolph Clarke's discussion of this sort of theory in "Recent Work: Freedom and Determinism," *Philosophical Books* 36 (January 1995): 12-14.

28. See J. L. Austin, "Ifs and Cans," in Austin, *Philosophical Papers* (Oxford: Oxford University Press, 1961); Richard Taylor, "I Can," *Phil Rev* 69 (1960); Keith Lehrer, "'Can' in Theory and Practise: A Possible Worlds Analysis," in M. Brand and D. Walton, eds., *Action and Theory: Proceedings of the Winnipeg Conference* (Dordrecht, 1976); Terence Horgan, "Lehrer on 'Could'-Statements," *Phil Stud* 32 (1977); Winston Nesbitt and Stewart Candlish, "On Not Being Able to Do Otherwise," *Mind* 82 (July 1973); and "Determinism and the Ability to Do Otherwise," *Mind* 87 (1978); and Susan Wolf, "Asymmetrical Freedom," *J Phil* 77 (1980).

29. See Peter van Inwagen, *An Essay on Free Will* (Oxford: Clarendon, 1983), pp. 114-116, for this basic line of argument based on examples like those I've mentioned.

30. Ibid., p. 115. Van Inwagen further explains that sometimes the conditional analysis of "could have" claims vary in the "if" clause. That clause may read "If Smith had chosen," but it might also read "had willed," "had decided," "had wanted," or "had tried." But as Susan Wolf argues, in all of these cases it still would make sense to ask "but could Smith have chosen, willed, decided, wanted, tried?" That should show that conditional analyses of "could have" claims are not complete ascriptions of power, and it should also convince us that they are not likely equivalent to plain "could have" statements.

31. See ibid., pp. 114-126, for a thorough discussion of these options for conditional analyses.

32. See John Canfield, "The Compatibility of Free Will and Determinism," *Phil Rev* 71 (1962); and Nesbitt and Candlish's "On Not Being Able to Do Otherwise" and "Determinism and the Ability to do Otherwise."

33. Canfield, "Compatibility," p. 356-359, outlines these first four senses.

34. Harry G. Frankfurt, "Alternate Possibilities and Moral Responsibility," *J Phil* 66 (1969).

35. This example is taken from Michael Zimmerman, "Moral Responsibility, Freedom, and Alternate Possibilities," *Pacific Philosophical Quarterly* 63 (July 1982): 243.

36. David P. Hunt, "Frankfurt Counterexamples: Some Comments on the Widerker-Fischer Debate," *Faith Phil* 13 (July 1996): 395.

37. Ibid., pp. 395-396. For further discussion and elaboration of the issues raised by these sorts of examples, see William Rowe, "Causing and Being Responsible for What Is Inevitable," *Amer Phil Quart* 26 (April 1989).

38. Clarke, "Recent Work," pp. 14-15.

39. Daniel Dennett, "I Could Not Have Done Otherwise—So What?" *J Phil* 81 (1984): 556.

40. Clarke ("Recent Work") describes this point on p. 15. He also notes that van Inwagen, "When Is the Will Free?" *Philosophical Perspectives* 3 (1989), still attempts to link ability and responsibility: "when such an agent acts without the ability to do otherwise, she is responsible for her action only if it results (by way of her character) from certain of her earlier actions which she *did* perform with the ability to do otherwise. If an agent never has that ability in her life, she is not a morally responsible agent" (p. 15). Here again, it becomes very important to see what the ability sense of "can" means. If it must be interpreted as contra-causal ability to do otherwise, van Inwagen's requirement begs the question in favor of incompatibilism. If, on the other hand, ability means what I have suggested

it means (and both compatibilists and incompatibilists do talk of ability in this sense), then a compatibilist could agree with van Inwagen's requirement since it is unlikely that it would not be true of everyone. On the other hand, one might still reject it as arbitrary; i.e., why should this requirement overturn responsibilities in cases Dennett and Wolff describe where it would seem ad hoc (in virtue of one's commitment to incompatibilism) to deny such persons moral responsibility?

41. Dennett, "I Could Not Have Done Otherwise—So What?" pp. 557-558.
42. See Wesley Morriston, "Is God 'Significantly Free'?" *Faith Phil* 2 (July 1985): 257; and Alvin Plantinga, *God, Freedom, and Evil* (New York: Harper & Row, 1974).
43. Plantinga, *God, Freedom, and Evil*, p. 108; Morriston, "Is God 'Significantly Free'?" 258.
44. Morriston, ibid.
45. Ibid., pp. 258-259. Morriston offers two ways an indeterminist might respond, but finds that in either case one of the two divine attributes must be ceded—the libertarian grants either that God is not significantly free or that he is not essentially morally good. See pp. 259-264.
46. Here we must distinguish between God creating a world with agents who can do evil, and God himself doing evil. God's creatures do the evil, and he wishes they would not. On the other hand, God doesn't do their evil acts, and creating a world (even with evil in it) is a morally good deed on God's part so long as he creates a morally good world. A possible world as a whole can be morally good even if it contains morally evil creaturely deeds. More on this in the chapter on the problem of evil.
47. For further discussion and objections to the consequence argument, see John M. Fischer, "Van Inwagen on Free Will," *Phil Quart* 36 (April 1986). Fischer focuses especially on premise 6 as the problem and argues that the key is the meaning of the phrase 'S can render P false'. The meaning of this is nowhere near as clear as it might seem, and when one looks more closely at possible ways to understand it, it isn't clear that van Inwagen's defense of premise 6 is convincing.
48. Bruce N. Waller, "Deliberating about the Inevitable," *Analysis* 45 (January 1985): 49.
49. Ibid., pp. 49-50.
50. Ibid., p. 50.

CHAPTER 15

1. William Alston, "Divine Foreknowledge and Alternative Conceptions of Human Freedom," *Int J Phil Relig* 18 (1985). See also William Hasker, *God, Time and Knowledge* (Ithaca, N.Y.: Cornell University Press, 1989), pp. 96-143, who argues the same position.
2. The relation of incompatibilism to foreknowledge of future contingent actions is an important issue in itself. However, it also has significant implications for the free will defense. According to the free will defense, God is not guilty of the moral evil in the world, for it happens as a result of the free and independent actions of human beings. But as Joseph Runzo explains: "But as Augustine saw, the success of the free will defense is logically dependent on the solution to another difficulty: viz., if an omniscient God foreknows what I shall do—and surely, it seems, He must—then I cannot act other than I do and, consequently, I do not act freely. Hence, the insistence that God is omniscient seems logically incompatible with the free will defense against the problem of evil." See Joseph Runzo, "Omniscience and Freedom for Evil," *Int J Phil Relig* 12 (1981): 131. For a further expression of this problem see Frederick W. Kroon, "Plantinga on God, Freedom, and Evil," *Int J Phil Relig* 12 (1981): 90.
3. The definition of knowledge here is justified true belief. Like many notions in philosophy, this definition has come under considerable attack in contemporary epistemology, but I need not enter into that debate. My point is just that the claim to know something has traditionally been taken as a stronger claim than the mere claim to believe it. If someone claimed to know something that was false, a philosopher would say that the person didn't really know it; they only believed it and they were mistaken in so doing.
4. This should not be confused with the notions of fatalism described earlier in chapter 13. As we proceed, we shall see why this argument is taken to uphold a position labeled as fatalism.
5. Nelson Pike, *God and Timelessness* (New York: Schocken, 1970), pp. 59-60. See also other descriptions of this argument in William Lane Craig, *The Only Wise God* (Grand Rapids, Mich.: Baker, 1987), chapter 3.
6. This is my reconstruction from Craig's description on pp. 53-54 of *Only Wise God*.
7. Craig, *Only Wise God*, p. 72.
8. Ibid.
9. See Thomas V. Morris, *Our Idea of God* (Downers Grove, Ill.: InterVarsity, 1991), pp. 97-99, for a lengthier explanation of and interaction with this view. See also Norman Geisler's essay "God Knows All Things," in David Basinger and Randall Basinger, eds., *Predestination and Free Will* (Downers Grove, Ill.: InterVarsity, 1986), for an example of someone who resolves the problem of freedom and foreknowledge this way.
10. For further discussion of this solution from both positive and negative perspectives, see Eleonore Stump and Norman Kretzmann, "Eternity," *J Phil* 78 (1981); David Widerker, "A Problem for the Eternity Solution," *Phil Rel* 29 (1991); Eleonore Stump and Norman Kretzmann, "Prophecy,

Past Truth, and Eternity," *Philosophical Perspectives* 5 (1991); and David Widerker, "Providence, Eternity, and Human Freedom: A Reply to Stump and Kretzmann," *Faith Phil* 11 (April 1994).

11. David P. Hunt, "Divine Providence and Simple Foreknowledge," *Faith Phil* 10 (July 1993): 398.

12. Hasker, *God, Time and Knowledge*, p. 56.

13. Ibid., p. 59.

14. This is an adaptation of an option Basinger proposes in his discussion of Hunt's attempt to support simple foreknowledge. See David Basinger, "Simple Foreknowledge and Providential Control: A Response to Hunt," *Faith Phil* 10 (July 1993): 423ff.

15. Tomis Kapitan, "Providence, Foreknowledge, and Decision Procedures," *Faith Phil* 10 (July 1993): 416. Kapitan offers an earlier version of the doxastic principle, but settles on the revised version mentioned in my text as more defensible.

16. See the rest of Kapitan's article for elaboration of this point. Hunt attempts a response to Kapitan's argument, but it doesn't seem particularly convincing. See David P. Hunt, "Prescience and Providence: A Reply to My Critics," *Faith Phil* 10 (July 1993): 428-431.

17. Hunt, "Divine Providence and Simple Foreknowledge," p. 398. See also the preceding pages for development of this illustration.

18. Hasker, *God, Time*, pp. 58-62. Hasker offers two illustrations of this point: an imagined future marriage of Susan and Kenneth; and the encirclement of the Allied armies in World War II by the Germans at Dunkirk in 1940. Anything God would know in advance about either of those events by means of simple foreknowledge wouldn't make it possible for him to help either side by enhancing weather conditions, for example, for if God does not see himself doing this already, he couldn't decide to do it and change a future he has already foreseen as occurring.

19. Ibid., pp. 62-63.

20. David Hunt believes that he can answer this, but I believe his suggestion is incoherent. For further discussion of this argument see Hunt, "Divine Providence and Simple Foreknowledge," pp. 404-405. See also Basinger's response to Hunt, "Simple Foreknowledge and Providential Control: A Response to Hunt"; and Hunt's rejoinder in "Prescience and Providence: A Reply to My Critics."

21. Craig, *Only Wise God*, p. 129.

22. Ibid., p. 129-130.

23. Ibid., p. 130. See also Thomas Morris's (*Idea of God*, p. 95) more cryptic explanation of these three moments in God's knowledge. See also Nelson Pike, "A Latter-Day Look at the Foreknowledge Problem," *Phil Rel* 33 (1993): 150-151.

24. Pike, "Latter-Day Look," p. 151.

25. From this claim, one can begin to see how God, while contemplating the various possible worlds, would begin to narrow down the options that are genuine ones for the world he will create. If he decides to create a world in which his human creatures have libertarian free will, that will automatically narrow his focus to only those worlds with creatures who have libertarian freedom. God will then survey those worlds, noticing what would occur to such creatures in all possible circumstances.

26. Some have expressed the notion of middle knowledge as meaning that God knows that if x were to occur, y *could* follow. Of course, if this is what middle knowledge means, then God has only knowledge of pure possibilities. But we have seen that the Molinist resolution grants God much more. The more typical formulation says that if x were to occur, y *would* follow.

27. Richard Otte, "A Defense of Middle Knowledge," *Phil Rel* 21 (1987). See also David Hunt's discussion of Otte's defense in "Middle Knowledge: The 'Foreknowledge Defense'," *Phil Rel* 28 (1990). See also William Lane Craig's argument along the same lines as Otte in Craig's *Only Wise God*, pp. 139-140.

28. David Basinger, "Middle Knowledge and Classical Christian Thought," *Relig Stud* 22 (1985): 413. For further discussion of this issue, see Robert M. Adams, "Middle Knowledge and the Problem of Evil," *Amer Phil Quart* 14 (April 1977); Bruce Reichenbach, "The Deductive Argument from Evil," *Sophia* 20 (1981): 35-36; William Hasker, "A Refutation of Middle Knowledge," *Nous* 20 (1986): 545-557; and Hasker, *God, Time and Knowledge*, chapter 2. In contrast, see in addition to Otte's article, William Lane Craig, "Hasker on Divine Knowledge," *Phil Stud* 67 (1992).

29. Nelson Pike has made a similar point, i.e., a point that questions whether Molinism leaves libertarian freedom intact. See Pike's powerful explanation of the problem on pp. 152-153 in "Latter-Day Look."

30. Morris, *Idea of God*, p. 94.

31. William of Ockham, *Ordinatio*, I, Prologue, q. 6.

32. Not even all determinists would say the action in question was the only one that might have occurred. Even strong determinists would say that, given antecedent causal conditions at time *t*, x must occur, but before any possible world is chosen, nothing dictates that the world as we will know it at *t* must be actualized. Only on a fatalistic view is there only one world that could be chosen. Hence, the notion of accidental necessity rules out fatalism, but it does not necessarily rule out all forms of determinism. Moreover, it fits with both incompatibilism and compatibilism.

33. See, for example, the following literature that treats this issue: Marilyn Adams, "Is the Existence of God a 'Hard' Fact?" *Phil Rev* 76 (October 1967): 492-503; John M. Fischer, "Freedom and Foreknowledge," *Phil Rev* 92 (January 1983); E. M. Zemach and D. Widerker, "Facts, Freedom and Foreknowledge," *Relig Stud* 23 (1987); John M. Fischer, "Hard-Type Soft Facts," *Phil Rev* 95 (1986); William Lane Craig, "'Nice Soft Facts': Fischer on Foreknowledge," *Relig Stud* 25 (1989); John M. Fischer, "Soft Facts and Harsh Realities: Reply to William Craig," *Relig Stud* 27 (1991).

34. See William Hasker, "Foreknowledge and Necessity," *Faith Phil* 2 (April 1985): 134-137.

35. In my exposition of the differences between soft and hard facts, I am relying primarily on Alvin Plantinga's description and explanation of the concepts in his "On Ockham's Way Out," *Faith Phil* 3 (July 1986): 245-248. See also Alston, "Human Foreknowledge and Alternative Conceptions of Human Freedom," pp. 21-22.

36. Here my choice of "believes" rather than "knows" is not significant. Since God is omniscient, if he really believes something, then it is true. Hence, once we know what he really believed, believes, or will believe, we know that he knows it as well.

37. Craig, *Only Wise God*, chapters 6–7.

38. Pike, "Latter-Day Look," p. 142.

39. See Plantinga, *God, Freedom and Evil* (New York: Harper & Row, 1974), pp. 70-71; and his "On Ockham's Way Out," p. 26ff. See also Hasker's discussion of this in "Foreknowledge and Necessity," pp. 137-144.

40. Craig, *Only Wise God*, p. 70.

41. Hasker, "Foreknowledge and Necessity," p. 144.

42. I have been greatly helped in my understanding of these issues by a series of discussions. The reader may wish to pursue this matter further, so I present the following list of items that I found especially helpful: William Hasker, "Foreknowledge and Necessity;" Thomas Talbott, "On Divine Foreknowledge and Bringing about the Past," *Phil Phenomenol Res* 46 (March 1986); Alvin Plantinga, "On Ockham's Way Out"; William Lane Craig, *Only Wise God;* William Hasker, "The Hardness of the Past: A Reply to Reichenbach," *Faith Phil* 4 (July 1987); David Widerker, "Troubles with Ockhamism," *J Phil* 87 (September 1990); Thomas P. Flint, "In Defence of Theological Compatibilism," *Faith Phil* 8 (April 1991); Nelson Pike, "Latter-Day Look"; and David Widerker, "Contra Snapshot Ockhamism," *Int J Phil Relig* 39 (1996).

43. William of Ockham, *Predestination, God's Foreknowledge, and Future Contingents,* trans. Marilyn McCord Adams and Norman Kretzmann (New York: Appleton-Century-Crofts, 1969), p. 50. The passage quoted is in the discussion of question I, assumption 6. See also Adams and Kretzmann's helpful introduction to the volume.

44. Runzo, "Omniscience and Freedom for Evil," pp. 133-139.

45. Ibid., pp. 139-141.

46. Ibid., p. 144.

47. Clark Pinnock, "Systematic Theology," in Clark Pinnock, et al., *The Openness of God* (Downers Grove, Ill.: InterVarsity, 1994), pp. 121-122. See also John Sanders, *The God Who Risks* (Downers Grove, Ill.: InterVarsity, 1998), pp. 63-66.

48. Pinnock, "Systematic Theology," p. 122.

49. Sanders, *God Who Risks*, pp. 98-99.

50. Ibid., p. 99.

51. Ibid., p. 100.

52. Richard Rice, "Biblical Support for a New Perspective," in Pinnock, et al., *Openness of God,* p. 51.

53. Sanders, *God Who Risks*, pp. 130-131.

54. Rice, "Biblical Support," p. 51.

55. Sanders, *God Who Risks*, p. 131.

56. Rice, "Biblical Support," pp. 51-52. Sanders, *God Who Risks,* p. 131. This tripartite handling of biblical prophecies is standard fare for the open view. One finds it not only in Rice and Sanders, but also in David Basinger, "Can an Evangelical Christian Justifiably Deny God's Exhaustive Knowledge of the Future?" *CSR* 25 (December 1995): 141; and in William Hasker, "The Openness of God," *CSR* 28 (Fall 1998): 118.

57. O. Palmer Robertson, *The Christ of the Covenants* (Grand Rapids, Mich.: Baker, 1980), pp. 7-11 and 128-131.

58. A defender of the open view might say that the case of Pharaoh is one where God is so dogmatic because he will see to it that Pharaoh does what God predicts. Thus, in this case Pharaoh won't act freely and that's why God speaks with such certainty. Quite possible, but remember, this example was chosen by open view defenders themselves, not by me. It was meant to illustrate how God could make very accurate predictions that involve people with libertarian free will. Hence, to say that maybe Pharaoh will be causally determined to act as God predicts spoils the illustration the open view itself offered.

59. See Basinger's complaint (p. 144) to this effect in "Can an Evangelical Christian Justifiably Deny?"

60. See Sanders's handling of OT material in chapter 3 of *The God Who Risks.*

CHAPTER 16

1. See David Hume, *Dialogues Concerning Natural Religion*, part X, in *The Empiricists* (Garden City, N.Y.: Doubleday, 1974), p. 490; and J. L. Mackie, "Evil and Omnipotence," in Basil Mitchell, ed. *Philosophy of Religion* (Oxford: Oxford University Press, 1971), p. 92, for examples of this traditional formulation of the problem.

2. John S. Feinberg, *The Many Faces of Evil* (Grand Rapids, Mich.: Zondervan, 1994).

3. As Alvin Plantinga explains, "Clearly it need be neither true, nor probable, nor plausible, nor believed by most theists, nor anything else of that sort. . . . The fact that a particular proffered *r* is implausible, or not congenial to 'modern man,' or a poor explanation of *q*, or whatever, is utterly beside the point" (Alvin Plantinga, "Reply to the Basingers on Divine Omnipotence," *Process Stud* 11 [Spring 1981]:26-27).

4. Here I use the term *defense* as opposed to *theodicy*. In contemporary discussions philosophers distinguish between offering a possible reason for God allowing evil and explaining the actual reason for God doing so. The former explanation is referred to as a defense, while the latter is called a theodicy. Given the charge of contradiction, it should be clear that all theists need to do is offer a possible explanation (defense) of how evil fits with the existence of an omnipotent, all-loving God. A case can be made that my defense offers God's actual reason for allowing evil, but for purposes of solving the logical problem of evil, it isn't necessary to prove that one has specified God's actual reason for allowing evil. Hence, I offer my explanation as a defense rather than a theodicy.

5. It may be possible to show that this strategy is implicit in defenses of theonomy. However, because that theology so heavily emphasizes God's power to do whatever he wants (even act arbitrarily in some cases), different approaches to solving theonomy's problem of evil are possible. For example, the theonomist's God might reveal that categories of good and evil apply to us but not to God. Hence, typical strategies theists use to show that God is good, despite the evil in our world, do not necessarily apply to theonomy.

6. John Hick, *Evil and the God of Love* (New York: Harper, 1966).

7. See note 2, above.

8. For a description of theonomy and Leibnizian Rationalism plus their problems of evil and answers to those problems, see chapters 2–3 of my *Many Faces of Evil*.

9. For detailed proof that the free will defense rests on incompatibilism and that this contradicts compatibilism, see my *Many Faces of Evil* (chapter 4); and my article "And the Atheist Shall Lie Down with the Calvinist: Atheism, Calvinism, and the Free Will Defense," *Trin J* 1NS (1980): 142-52.

10. I must note here that Arminians committed to consequentialist ethics cannot use this defense. Instead, they might well turn to the soul-building theodicy. That defense incorporates consequentialist ethics, and at least as John Hick presents it, it also espouses libertarian free will.

11. Augustine, *On the Free Choice of the Will*, trans. Anna Benjamin and L. H. Hackstaff (New York: Bobbs-Merrill, 1964), I, 1, p. 3.

12. Ibid., book I, 3, pp. 6-8; ibid., book I, 15, pp. 29-33.

13. Ibid., book I, 16, p. 34.

14. Ibid., book II, 19, pp. 80-81.

15. Ibid., p. 81.

16. Ibid., book II, 1, p. 36; and book II, 18, p. 79.

17. Ibid., book III, 3, pp. 90-93.

18. Bennett refers to Mackie's argument this way in Philip W. Bennett, "Evil, God, and the Free Will Defense," *Austl J Phil* 51 (May 1973): 39-50.

19. Mackie, "Evil and Omnipotence," pp. 100-101.

20. Those familiar with Plantinga's defense of the free will defense immediately recognize that it is much more complicated and sophisticated than this brief summary of one of its key points. For details of Plantinga's presentation see his *God, Freedom, and Evil* (New York: Harper & Row, 1974).

21. For explanation of this and other ethical theories, see John S. Feinberg and Paul D. Feinberg, *Ethics for a Brave New World* (Wheaton, Ill.: Crossway, 1993), chapter 1.

22. Here I note that I am addressing the philosophical/theological problem of evil, which is really the problem of moral evil. This is not peculiar to my system, for most defenses address that problem. Unfortunately, many theists and atheists don't see that there are other problems of evil that must also be addressed, and that a defense against moral evil doesn't answer all problems of evil, nor need it do so.

23. Joseph B. Mayor, *The Epistle of St. James*, in The Classic Commentary Library (Grand Rapids, Mich.: Zondervan, 1954), pp. 54-55.

24. This interpretation of the point of sin's conception certainly squares with the tenor of Jesus' teachings, when he claimed that sin is committed in a person's thoughts first and made public later. Think, for example, of Matt 5:27-28, where Jesus teaches that if a man desires a woman in his heart, he has already committed adultery with her before doing any overt act.

25. In this case, people wouldn't have to be able to have such knowledge, since God would take care of any possible problems by means of miracles.

26. My point here is similar to Dilley's response to Steven Boer's proposal (see chapter 4 of my *Many Faces of Evil*). See Steven E. Boër, "The Irrelevance of the Free Will Defence," *Analysis* 38 (1977); and Frank B. Dilley, "Is the Free Will Defence Irrelevant?" *Relig Stud* 18 (1982). For God to get rid of evil in any of the ways imagined would produce a world far more different from ours than we might imagine.

27. This must not be misunderstood. Were I a consequentialist, the decision about which actions are evil would depend on the consequences of those actions. But even here, I might intend to do an act whose consequences would be beneficial to others, and yet there might be unforeseen consequences that turn out otherwise. In this case, the evil is unintentional, but it is still real. God would have to stop those acts, too. Moreover, reflex actions which are preceded by neither good nor evil intentions but lead to evil consequences would have to be stopped. As a non-consequentialist, I determine rightness or wrongness of an act otherwise than by consequences. The point about involuntary and reflex actions, however, still applies. I may intend to do and perform an act which obeys God's command. Even so, there may be unforeseen results that are negative toward the well-being of others. Even though I am not guilty of evil, the evil that befalls others unintentionally is still real. Hence, God would have to stop my good-intentioned act in that case. Likewise, reflex actions which attach to neither good nor evil intentions but produce evil for others would have to be stopped.

28. I agree that this other world would be better morally, because there would be no moral evil in it. But God cannot make that world and also make the non-glorified human beings he has. Was God wrong in making non-glorified humans? Only if making such creatures is evil in itself, and it isn't. Is God obligated to create this other world, anyway? According to modified rationalism, God is free either to create or not to create at all. If he creates, he is free to create any good possible world available. He isn't obligated to forego our world in favor of the eternal state, so long as our world is a good world. I have shown why ours is a good world.

29. See my *Many Faces of Evil* as well as the vast amount of literature on this topic in books and philosophical and theological journals.

relativity theory, 104-106, 109, 149, 152-
153, 175, 388, 756
general theory of relativity, 545
special theory of relativity, 409
Renaissance, 93
Reyes, Gonzalo E., 496-498, 836
Reyes, Maria La Palme, 496-498, 836
Reynolds, John Mark, 609, 820, 838, 841,
842
Rice, Richard, 69-72, 659, 691-694, 763,
767, 805, 806, 837, 846, 848, 849, 853
Ridderbos, N. H., 603
Ritschl, Albrecht, 112-113, 115
Rogerson, John, 574-575, 840
Rorty, Richard, 98-99, 809
Ross, Hugh, 596, 841, 842
Roszak, Theodore, 139
Rowe, William, 190-192, 194, 803, 819-820,
844, 847, 850
Ruether, Rosemary Radford, 132, 804,
811-812
Runzo, Joseph, 759-760, 851, 853
Russell, Bertrand, 150, 190, 193-194, 268,
632, 844

Sabellius, 475, 482
sanctification, 222, 297, 357, 369, 516, 517,
713
Sanders, John, 63, 508-510, 644, 648, 658-
659, 664-666, 668, 690-692, 706-713,
761-763, 765-767, 771, 805, 806, 822,
825, 837, 845, 846, 847, 848, 849, 853,
854
Sankowski, Edward, 627, 717, 843, 844,
847, 850
Schaeffer, Francis A., xvii
Schleiermacher, Friedrich, 112-115, 117, 125,
394, 400, 438, 809, 810, 830
Schoedel, William, 472, 835
scientific creationism, 598
Seely, Paul, 612, 842
Shedd, W. G. T., 592, 821, 835
Shintoism, 40, 47, 50, 59, 804
Silva, Moises, 206, 820
Simpson, George Gaylord, 591, 609, 841
simultaneity, 175, 402-403, 406-410, 413-
414, 416-417, 431, 742
E, 408, 410
ET, 403, 408-411, 413-417, 831
RT, 409
T, 408
skepticism, 84, 98, 144, 204, 581
Snyder, Aaron, 674-675, 848, 850
Socinianism, 327
sovereignty, divine, see God: as sovereign
Spinoza, 48
Steuer, Axel, 674, 806, 847, 848

Stewart, Claude, 153, 165, 722, 814, 817,
847, 850
Stoicism, 63, 215, 472
Stramara, Daniel F., Jr., 481, 835-836
Strong, A. H., 236, 252, 822, 834, 835, 838,
839
Stroumsa, Gedaliahu, 215, 821
Stump, Eleonore, 325, 376-378, 380, 393,
400-401, 403, 408-416, 428, 826, 827,
828, 830, 831, 832, 833, 838, 852
Sturch, R. L., 396-398, 830
sublapsarianism, 511
subsistence, 477, 487, 494-495, 826, 829
sufficient reason, principle of, 74, 192-195,
819-820, see also *cosmological argument
for the existence of God*
supralapsarianism, 505, 837
Swinburne, Richard, 190-191, 195-196, 203,
267, 269, 286-287, 310, 820, 823, 824,
830, 831, 833, 834, 836
systematic theology, xxi-xxiii, xxvi, 136, 171,
237, 406, 579, 816

Talbott, Thomas, 673-674, 825, 844, 847,
853
Taliaferro, Charles, 315-317, 804, 820, 826
Taoism, 140
Taylor, Mark, 143-145, 809
Taylor, Richard, 190, 196, 745, 820, 844,
847, 850
teleological argument for the existence of
God, 184, 196-200, 203-204
temptation, 322, 377, 445, 567, 571, 654-
655, 789
Tennant, F. R., 196
Tertullian, 226-227, 473-474, 476, 835
Theodosius, 481-482
Theodotus, 475
Theology of Hope, 105, 128-130, 811
theonomy (voluntarism), 73-75, 270, 284-
285, 292, 337, 781-782, 806, 823-824,
827, 854
Thomas Aquinas, 31, 54, 60, 62-64, 77-78,
85, 134, 155, 190-192, 264, 267, 276,
285, 308, 331-332, 376, 380, 383-384,
405, 432-433, 505, 592, 805, 806, 807,
818, 819, 823, 824, 825, 829, 831, 833,
836, 837, 844
Thomas, O. C., 45, 208, 804, 820
Thomson, James, 92
Tillich, Paul, 39-40, 43-45, 54, 59, 77, 120-
121, 128, 157, 208, 803, 810
time, theories of
A-proposition, 421-422, 425-427
B-proposition, 421, 425
Tracy, David, 91, 93-94, 143, 804, 808, 811
Tremmel, William C., 161, 170, 815, 816,
817, 818, 833